Contents

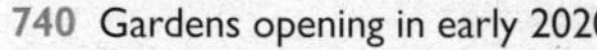

The National Garden Scheme

A company limited by guarantee. Registered in England & Wales. Charity No. 1112664. Company No. 5631421

Registered & Head Office: Hatchlands Park, East Clandon, Guildford, Surrey, GU4 7RT.
01483 211535 www.ngs.org.uk

Published by Constable, an imprint of Little, Brown Book Group, Carmelite House, 50 Victoria Embankment, London EC4Y 0DZ. An Hachette UK Company www.hachette.co.uk www.littlebrown.co.uk

CLARENCE HOUSE

I greatly enjoyed meeting a large number of my charities at a Garden Party at Buckingham Palace last year and was struck by the enormous contribution they make in so many different ways.

For instance, the National Garden Scheme plays a particularly remarkable role in supporting nursing. The generosity and hard work of the volunteers, garden owners and visitors raises millions of pounds every year, which I know makes a huge difference to the wonderful work of the nursing charities.

As well as raising much-needed funds, the scheme also gives enormous pleasure to all those of us who love to visit gardens, both great and small, grand and simple, in town and country. In doing so, we gain not only some peace and time for reflection in places of calm and beauty – and possibly a very nice cup of tea as well – but an opportunity to harvest ideas for our own gardens.

So it is with enormous concern that I have been trying over recent years to raise awareness about the ways in which our gardens and countryside are increasingly under threat from a spate of alarming tree and plant diseases, as well as destructive insects, inadvertently imported from around the world and exacerbated by accelerating climate change. The urgent need for biosecurity to protect plant health is now well understood by the relevant government bodies, and by the Royal Horticultural Society and other garden institutions, but individual gardeners also have a crucial part to play. So I want to take this opportunity to urge you all to ask questions about the provenance of imported plants and buy only from reputable sources that operate a proper quarantine policy.

This may all seem somewhat dramatic, but I fear the threats are all too real. Even our iconic English Oaks, which frame so many of our grand gardens and grace the wider landscape, are under threat from the mysterious, but devastating Acute Oak Decline. If this greatly concerns you, as it does me, you may be interested in "Action Oak," the campaign to find solutions to this threat…

As we embark on the 2019 season of garden visiting and fundraising, I can only once again express an admiration for the National Garden Scheme, the work of the volunteers, the enjoyment it brings to so many people and the remarkable support it provides to our hard-pressed nurses.

Charles

Right: Martin McMillan addressing the 2018 Hospice UK Conference

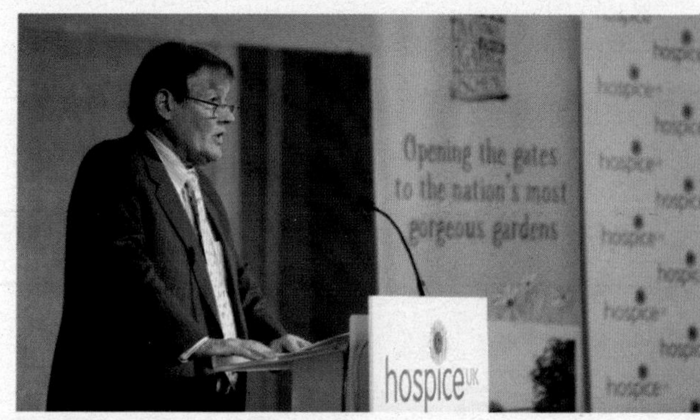

Who's who

Chairman's message

Our biggest challenge is getting across to people the remarkable impact that the National Garden Scheme has with its annual donations to nursing charities. Having been established more than 90 years ago to raise money for district nursing we are still giving very substantial sums to nursing charities from the money raised at our gardens. In 2018 it was a record £3.1 million, this year will be about the same.

Fortunately there is constant visible evidence to demonstrate to people the enormous good that our money generates. As an example I am very proud that, following the opening in 2017 of the magnificent NGS Macmillan unit for cancer patients in Chesterfield, Derbyshire, in 2019 we will open another NGS Macmillan unit at Y Bwthyn in South Wales, which has been similarly funded by the National Garden Scheme and Macmillan. These units will make life-changing differences to cancer patients in those regions.

September 2018 saw the opening at the National Spinal Injuries Centre, Stoke Mandeville, of a new Horatio's Garden for which the National Garden Scheme was the largest single funder. It is the latest garden to be created by this remarkable charity. Also in 2018 we gave donations for new gardens at two Maggie's centres and gardens created by Leonard Cheshire for the enjoyment of people with a wide range of disabilities.

But in these tough – and uncertain – economic times, for a number of our beneficiaries our annual donations are fundamental to their successful survival, enabling them to carry on their great work for the benefit of many thousands of people all over England and Wales. So if, as I hope, your *Garden Visitors Handbook* inspires you to visit some gardens, do remember that you will directly help our charitable work. It will also introduce you to our garden owners who are so generous in their support of the National Garden Scheme.

Martin McMillan, OBE

Some tips on using your Handbook

This book lists all the gardens opening for the National Garden Scheme between January 2019 and early 2020. It is divided up into county sections, each including a map, calendar of opening dates and details of each garden, listed alphabetically.

Symbols explained

NEW Gardens opening for the first time this year or re-opening after a long break.

◆ Garden also opens on non-National Garden Scheme days. (Gardens which carry this symbol contribute to the National Garden Scheme either by opening on a specific day(s) and/or by giving a guaranteed contribution.)

Wheelchair access to at least the main features of the garden.

Dogs on short leads welcome.

Plants usually for sale.

NPC Plant Heritage National Plant Collection.

Gardens that offer accommodation.

Refreshments are available, normally at a charge.

D Garden designed by a Fellow, Member, Pre-registered Member, or Student of The Society of Garden Designers.

Garden accessible to coaches. Coach sizes vary so please contact garden owner or County Organiser in advance to check details.

Group Visits Group Organisers may contact the County Organiser or a garden owner direct to organise a group visit to a particular county or garden. Otherwise contact our Visitor Development Manager, Linda Shelton, on 01483 213919 or linda@ngs.org.uk.

Children must be accompanied by an adult.

Photography is at the discretion of the garden owner; please check first. Photographs must not be used for sale or reproduction without prior permission of the owner.

Donation To indicates that a proportion of the money collected will be given to the nominated charity.

Toilet facilities are not always available at gardens.

If you cannot find the information you require from a garden or County Organiser, call the National Garden Scheme office on 01483 211535.

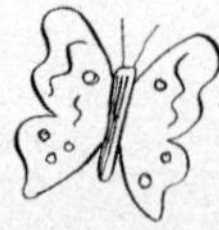

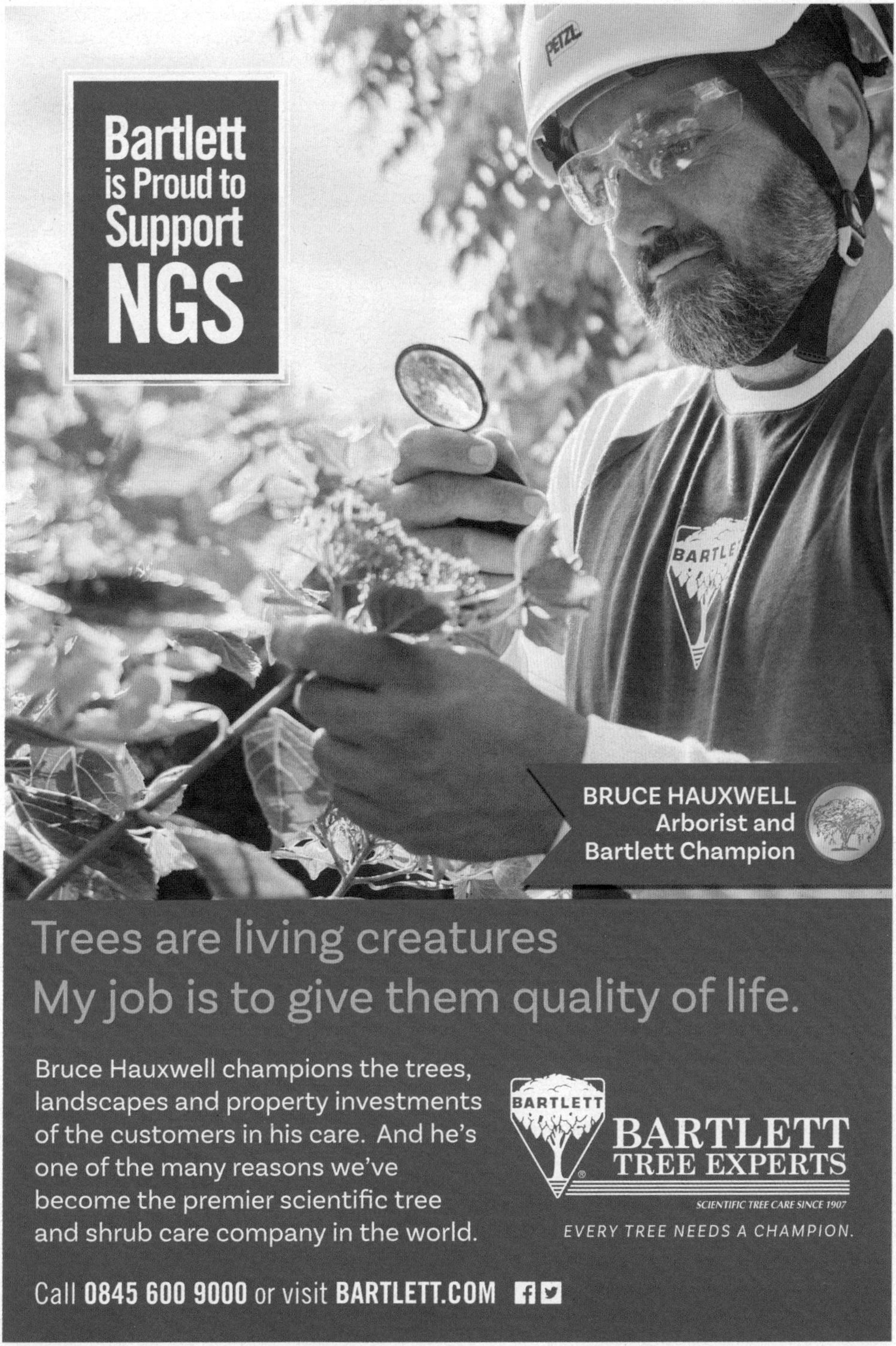
Bartlett
is Proud to
Support
NGS
BRUCE HAUXWELL
Arborist and
Bartlett Champion
Trees are living creatures
My job is to give them quality of life.
Bruce Hauxwell champions the trees, landscapes and property investments of the customers in his care. And he's one of the many reasons we've become the premier scientific tree and shrub care company in the world.
BARTLETT
BARTLETT
TREE EXPERTS
SCIENTIFIC TREE CARE SINCE 1907
EVERY TREE NEEDS A CHAMPION.
Call 0845 600 9000 or visit BARTLETT.COM

Where the money goes: supporting our beneficiaries

George Plumptre, Chief Executive of the National Garden Scheme, highlights the importance of the charity's annual donations

Currently more than 80% of all the money raised at our gardens is donated annually to our nursing and health beneficiary charities. This meant that in 2018 we were able to donate a record £3.1 million – all raised at our gardens in 2017.

For everyone involved in the National Garden Scheme: our garden owners who commit so much hard work to opening their gardens; our volunteers who support them; and our visitors from whom the money originates, giving away such a substantial proportion of the funds raised is hugely important. It also helps us to really make a difference with each of our beneficiary charities, whether it is funding specific projects or, as Martin McMillan points out in his *Chairman's Message* on page 3, in today's challenging economic landscape ensuring some of our beneficiaries are able to carry out their key activities by providing a substantial contribution to their core operations.

During the last year we have funded a wide range of projects, all of which will make a substantial difference to the people supported by the individual beneficiaries. Perhaps most spectacular is the new NGS Macmillan specialist palliative care unit being built at Y Bwthyn in South Wales which will open later this year, to which the National Garden Scheme has committed £2.5 million to make possible a transformation of cancer care in the region.

Another opening took place in September 2018 at the world-famous National Spinal Injuries Centre at Stoke Mandeville in Buckinghamshire, the third Horatio's Garden, of which the National Garden Scheme was the largest single funder.

Below: The opening of Horatio's Garden, Stoke Mandeville in 2018: Joe Swift, the garden's designer and ex-President of the National Garden Scheme; Jacqui Martin-Lof, head gardener; Mary Berry, President of the National Garden Scheme; Olivia Chapple, founder and chairman of Horatio's Garden; The Countess of Radnor, Patron of Horatio's Garden. *Photo: Horatio's Garden*

Quite different, but equally important, is the leadership programme for community nurses which was launched in 2018 by our founding beneficiary the Queen's Nursing Institute. The first group of nurses have now completed the programme and it is envisaged that they and future candidates will be able to fill senior positions in the nursing profession where currently nurses from a community background are rare.

For Marie Curie, some of our annual donation now goes to fund a similar bursary scheme for their nurses and other professionals (like Claire pictured below), enabling them to complete a variety of courses and other qualifications that help them to progress in their careers and – critically – not leave the profession.

And the photograph of our Chairman, Martin McMillan, on page 3, was taken at the 2018 Hospice UK Awards which are funded out of our annual donations to Hospice UK. These are just a few highlights from our recent annual donation and on page 10 you can read about some of our new beneficiaries for 2019.

Right: Claire Collins, a bereavement counsellor for Marie Curie, who has received a bursary funded by the National Garden Scheme

Your visits to our gardens help change lives

In 2018, the National Garden Scheme donated a record £3.1 million to nursing and health charities.

Macmillan Cancer Support	Marie Curie	Hospice UK
£500,000	£500,000	£500,000
Carers Trust	**Queen's Nursing Institute**	**Parkinson's UK**
£400,000	£250,000	£185,000
Perennial	**MS Society**	**Other donations**
£130,000	£145,000	£490,000

Thank you

To find out more about all our donations visit ngs.org.uk/beneficiaries

Supporting mental health and children

In 2019 for the first time the National Garden Scheme will add a mental health charity to its group of beneficiaries as MIND, the leading mental health charity in England and Wales, becomes our new guest charity.

The King's Fund report: *Gardens and Health: Implications for Policy and Practice*, that was commissioned by the National Garden Scheme and published in 2016 noted; 'The mental health benefits of gardening are broad and diverse. Studies have shown reductions in depression and anxiety, improved social functioning and wider effects, including opportunities for vocational development.'

Annual donations from the National Garden Scheme will help fund MIND's pioneering peer support programme. However and wherever it happens, mental health peer support involves people in similar situations talking, sharing experiences and being there for each other. And while that might sound simple, the impact can be life changing.

Co-created and led by and for people with mental health problems, the format of peer support activities varies from group to group so everyone can find a type of support that suits them. Many peer support activities take place in outdoor spaces and in nature, including gardening. Spending time in nature can be a transformative experience for people with mental health problems and has been proven to help with anxiety and depression.

Together the two charities will drive the agenda on gardens, nature and mental health, so that as many people as possible can benefit, as MIND's Chief Executive, Paul Farmer, suggests:

> *"We are delighted to be working with the National Garden Scheme this year. At MIND, we know the close connection between gardens, gardening and our mental health. Many people tell us that their time in the garden can make all the difference when they are struggling or at a low ebb. The connection with nature, the sense of purpose, as well as physical endeavour can all help contribute to positive mental health. We're looking forward to a productive time in 2019."*

In 2019 our gardens and health donations are focusing on children, with support for two remarkable charities, KIDS and Treloar's. KIDS provides a wide range of support services to disabled children, young people and their families. Sadly the opportunity to explore nature, play on a swing or build a den is often a rare experience for children who have a disability. The right to have a childhood is often taken away and the impact this can have on not only the disabled child, but also the parents and siblings, is devastating.

Left: A gardening project organised by MIND as part of their peer support group

Opposite, above: Youngsters getting an early introduction to the fun of gardening from KIDS (left) and Treloar's (right)

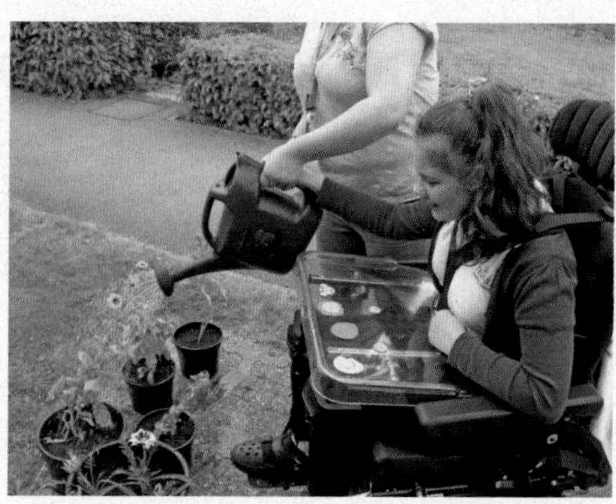

KIDS work focuses on children with disadvantaged backgrounds and from areas of deprivation, where access to any green space can be non-existent or severely limited, as acknowledged in a 2013 report by the National Children's Bureau; 'Children in deprived areas are nine times less likely to have access to green space and places to play.'

The National Garden Scheme's donation will enable KIDS to build two or three gardens which are fully inclusive and provide a range of sensory, play, quiet areas, planting and flowering areas and opportunities to socialise. Two of the projects are based in the Midlands, in Sutton Coldfield and Lye, areas of high deprivation and the third is based in the south of Basingstoke.

In her letter accompanying KIDS application to the National Garden Scheme, their Chief Executive, Caroline Stevens wrote:

> *"During your visit you observed first-hand the transformative impact that gardens and outside spaces can have on our children who are some of the most disadvantaged in the country. As you saw some of our children can be difficult to reach and interact with however being outside and connecting with nature frees them from their day-to-day constraints and enables them to be children again in a safe and supportive environment."*

Treloar's in Hampshire is the UK's leading centre for severely disabled children and young people. The students who come from all over the country are contending with the most complex physical disabilities. Unfortunately with these disabilities come further conditions such as learning difficulties, visual impairment, no verbal communication, lack of social awareness, mental health issues and life-limiting conditions.

There has long been a tradition of horticultural activities at Treloar's which has been supported over many years by their patron and near-neighbour, Alan Titchmarsh who says, "The accomplishments of Treloar's are so worthwhile and so enriching for all those involved. I'm a great supporter of their work and marvel at what they can achieve". The horticultural activities have been built up around recognition that gardens and external landscapes can offer a wide range of opportunities to nurture both student's educational and social development together with addressing their physical, emotional and intellectual needs.

The National Garden Scheme's donation will make a major contribution to the funding of an ambitious new horticulture and outdoor learning centre that will replace the current ageing horticultural facility. The new centre will provide the young people who attend Treloar's the chance to get involved in learning more about horticulture and the environment around them.

Launching our legacy programme

Over the last few years the National Garden Scheme has been incredibly fortunate to have been the recipient of a number of very generous gifts from long-term supporters.

It has become clear to us that people who love visiting our exceptional gardens throughout their life actively want the opportunity to pass that love onto future generations though a gift in their will to the National Garden Scheme.

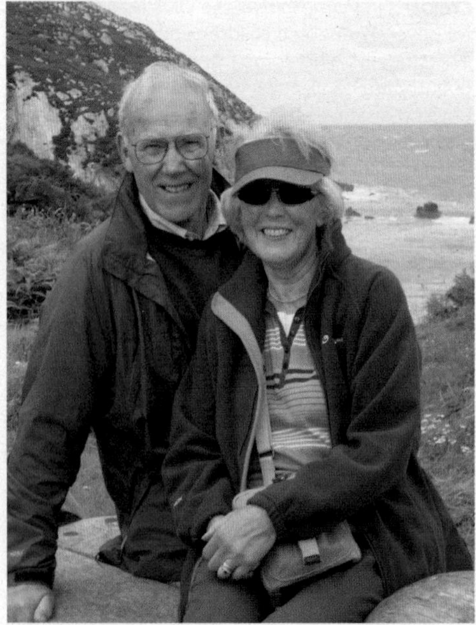

"Both my sister and brother-in-law were avid supporters of your work and for many years ran their own garden nursery cultivating rare plants in Derbyshire. They loved nothing more than to visit National Garden Scheme open gardens and it was their express wish that a gift in their will should be made to your organisation in order to help your work for the benefit of others in the future."

National Garden Scheme supporters

Every gift we receive, however large or small, makes an enormous difference – ensuring that we can continue making the wonderful variety of our gardens available to more visitors, enabling them to find solace, health and happiness – as well as horticultural inspiration.

The National Garden Scheme isn't just about opening beautiful gardens for charity – we are passionate about the physical and mental health benefits of garden too. We fund projects which promote gardens and gardening as therapy and in 2017 we launched our annual Gardens and Health Week to raise awareness of the topic. We also fund community gardening projects all over England and Wales.

If you are amending a current will with a simple codicil, or writing a will for the first time, and would like to find out more about leaving a charitable gift you can request our booklet, call us or view our information online at ngs.org.uk/giftinwill

Why I'm leaving a gift in my will:

"I love visiting beautiful National Garden Scheme gardens, and I have also been a volunteer for many years which has been immensely rewarding. The National Garden Scheme provides such valuable funding to nursing and health charities and I hope my modest legacy will help them continue for many years to come."

Graham, National Garden Scheme volunteer and visitor

The Nation's Favourite Gardens

In 2019 the National Garden Scheme is teaming up with *The English Garden* magazine, generously supported by Viking Cruises, to find the Nation's Favourite Gardens. Nowhere in the world can you find such a rich array of gardens that all open their gates to visitors in order to raise money for charity.

We are very proud that our portfolio of more than 3,500 gardens showcases such an amazing variety, from spectacular country gardens with burgeoning borders to tiny urban plots designed with extraordinary skill; and including gardens that open together as a group, the gardens of hospices and primary schools, allotments, seaside and hillside gardens and even gardens on a group of barges on the River Thames.

And we know that many of our visitors have their favourites. Places they especially admire or love, where they have had memorable moments or happy experiences. In many cases these are gardens they return to every year, so that the garden becomes like an old friend, always there but often offering something new and exciting.

Now we want to hear about those favourites and to find out which are the most popular. First, we will ask people to nominate gardens, giving their reasons for their nomination. Next a panel of judges will choose a shortlist, with gardens in each of the six National Garden Scheme regions: Wales and the Marches, North, Midlands, East, South East and South West. Then the public will be asked to vote on the short list to produce the winners – one for each region and one overall winner.

The competition will be launched in the April issue of *The English Garden* (on sale 27 February) and on the National Garden Scheme website and all details will continue to be promoted and explained through the summer from nominations to voting on the short list and the final results to be announced in the autumn.

We hope you will want to take part and we know that the competition will produce fascinating stories of brilliant gardens created by their talented owners. Paul Dobson, Chairman of Chelsea Magazine Company which publishes *The English Garden* says:

> *"We are delighted to be working with the National Garden Scheme to find the nation's favourite gardens to visit. While the competition is meant to be light-hearted, the Scheme does very valuable work raising money for nursing and health charities, and we're so pleased we'll be able to reward the hard-working gardeners who do so much to help these worthwhile causes."*

As part of the competition *The English Garden* is very generously making a donation to the National Garden Scheme.

The gardens range from intimate, modern urban spaces like 5 Blackthorn Avenue, London (left) to expansive, historic country house gardens like Goodnestone Park, Kent (above)

Music in the garden

'Music in the garden' is the theme for a spectacular garden party that will be held in aid of the National Garden Scheme on 21st June at Hazelby House, Hampshire, by kind permission of Hazelby's owners Patrick and Gabrielle Hungerford.

Seven hundred guests will enjoy exclusive access to the 14-acre garden, which has views out to the wonderful countryside of the North Wessex Downs Area of Outstanding Natural Beauty, serenaded by soul singer Natasha Watts and the East Woodhay Silver Band. Another highlight of the event will be a live auction, conducted by veteran auctioneer Nick Bonham, for which exclusive lots include a private visit to the garden of world-renowned designer Tom Stuart-Smith and a box at the Royal Albert Hall for the Last Night of the Proms, as well as a silent auction with a further mouth-watering selection of lots.

The Hazelby garden is one of the most distinguished in the region, not least because it was originally created by the designer Martin Lane Fox who lived here in the 1980s and 1990s. He created the classically formal structure and planting which the Hungerfords have built upon and expanded in exhilarating style, opening the garden up to a new lake and adding a range of superb ornaments including works by David Harber and William Pye.

Savills are generously supporting the event as lead sponsor and other sponsors include NFU Mutual and Waverton. It promises to be a memorable way to spend the Summer Solstice and to support the National Garden Scheme. For more information and to book tickets, go to www.ngs.org.uk/hazelby.

BEDFORDSHIRE

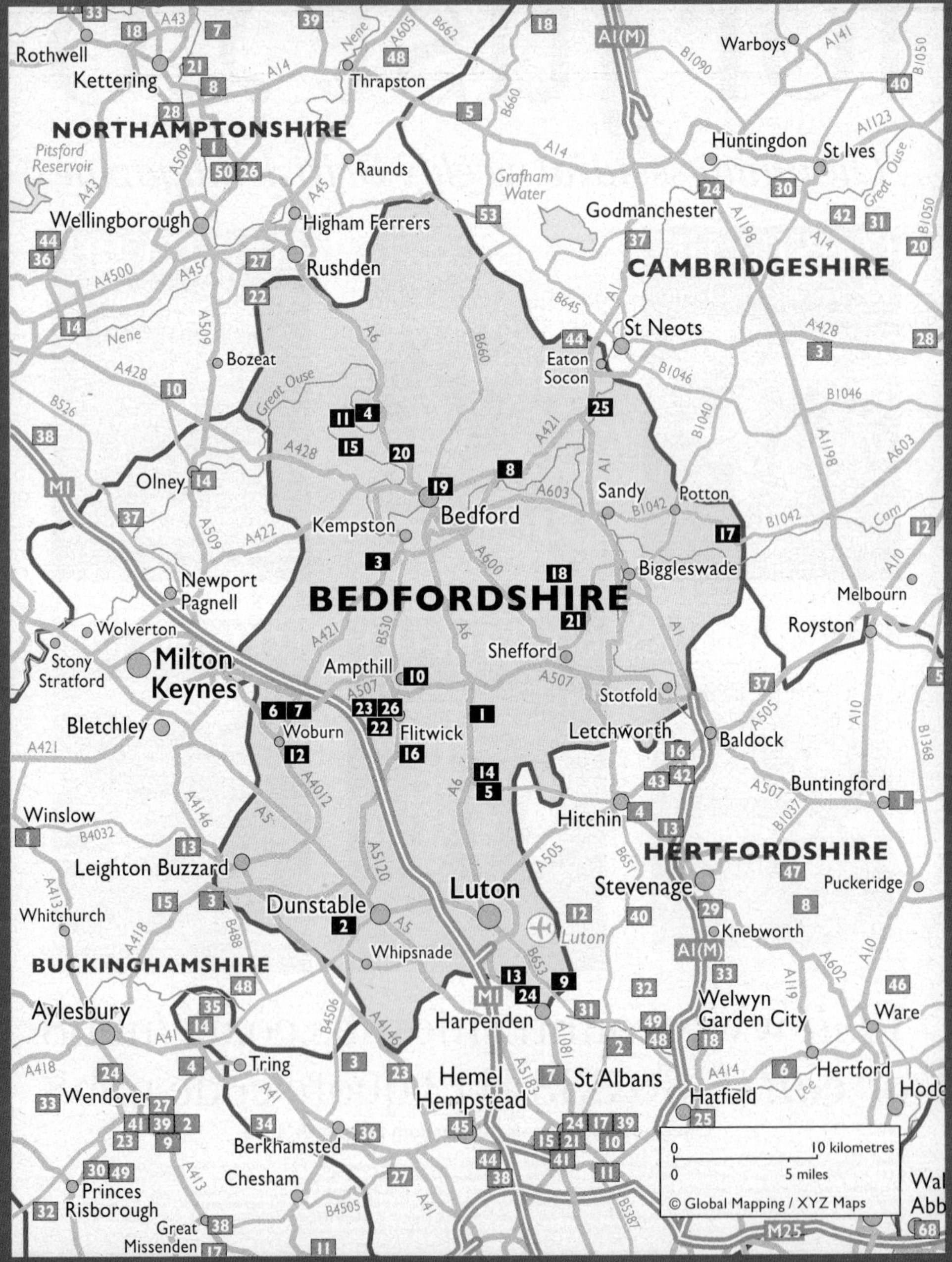

The Birthplace of John Bunyan, it is little wonder the county of Bedfordshire inspired the author of Pilgrim's Progress.

Running North to South through scenic countryside, a number of National Garden Scheme gardens lie along the John Bunyan Trail, from Stevington and Clapham, through Bedford, Ampthill, Steppingley to Westoning and Barton-le-Clay.

Bedfordshire also boasts a trio of 18th century gardens designed by Capability Brown, two of which open for the National Garden Scheme. First, Southill Park, an imposing country house with rolling lawns, flanked by belts, lakes and a Tuscan temple. It is also a founding garden which first opened its gates toNational Garden Scheme visitors in 1927. Second, Luton Hoo, where, wrote Samuel Johnson, "magnificence is not sacrificed to convenience, nor convenience to magnificence".

Once celebrated for its market gardens, many of the county's garden owners are as enthusiastic about their edibles as they are of their flowers. From the historic to the contemporary and from the village to the town, a warm welcome awaits you at a National Garden Scheme open garden in Bedfordshire. Join us for a truly British experience of garden, tea and well-being.

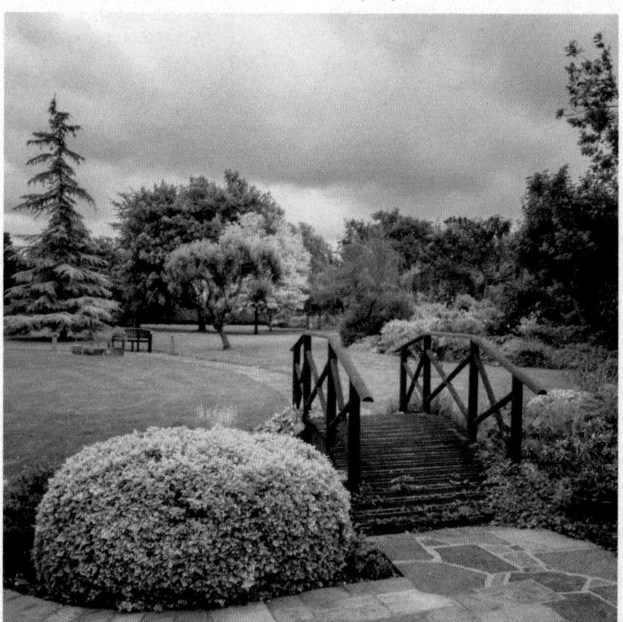

Volunteers

County Organiser
Indi Jackson
01525 713798
indi.jackson1@gmail.com

County Treasurer
Colin Davies
01525 712721
colin1davies1@gmail.com

Press
Ann Davies
01525 712721
ann@no1colin.plus.com

Facebook
Jolene Lynch
077791 58593
jolene_akehurst@hotmail.com

Booklet Co-ordinator
Indi Jackson
(as above)

Photography & Twitter
Venetia Barrington
07767 668027
venetiajanesgarden@gmail.com

Talks
Victoria Diggle
01767 627247
victoria@diggledesign.com

Kate Gardner
07725 307803
kgardner287@gmail.com

Assistant County Organisers
Geoff & Davina Barrett
geoffanddean@gmail.com

Ann Davies
(as above)

Brenda Hands
brenda.hands@outlook.com

Left: Gifla House

OPENING DATES

All entries subject to change. For latest information check **www.ngs.org.uk**

Map locator numbers are shown to the right of each garden name.

February

Snowdrop Festival

Sunday 3rd

The Folly 4

The Knoll 11

Saturday 23rd

The Folly 4

The Knoll 11

Sunday 24th

The Folly 4

◆ King's Arms Garden 10

The Knoll 11

April

Sunday 7th

The Old Rectory, Westoning 16

Sunday 28th

Townsend Farmhouse 23

West Oak 26

May

Sunday 5th

Secret Garden 20

Monday 6th

◆ The Manor House, Stevington 15

Saturday 11th

NEW 88 Castlehill Road 2

Sunday 12th

The Old Rectory, Wrestlingworth 17

Sunday 26th

The Old Rectory, Wrestlingworth 17

Steppingley Village Gardens 22

Monday 27th

Steppingley Village Gardens 22

June

Saturday 1st

22 Elmsdale Road 3

Sunday 2nd

22 Elmsdale Road 3

Southill Park 21

Saturday 8th

NEW 88 Castlehill Road 2

Howbury Hall Garden 8

NEW 40 Leighton Street 12

Sunday 9th

Old Warden Village Gardens 18

Sunday 16th

Gifla House 5

The Hyde Walled Garden 9

The Manor House, Barton-le-Clay 14

Sunday 30th

10 Alder Wynd 1

The Hyde Walled Garden 9

July

Saturday 6th

22 Elmsdale Road 3

NEW Glade House 6

NEW Hollydale, Woburn Lane 7

Sunday 7th

22 Elmsdale Road 3

NEW Glade House 6

NEW Hollydale, Woburn Lane 7

Saturday 20th

Walnut Cottage 24

Sunday 21st

Luton Hoo Hotel Golf & Spa 13

Walnut Cottage 25

August

Saturday 3rd

1a St Augustine's Road 19

◆ The Walled Garden 24

September

Saturday 14th

NEW 40 Leighton Street 12

October

Saturday 26th

Townsend Farmhouse

Sunday 27th

◆ King's Arms Garden 10

By Arrangement

Arrange a personalised garden visit with your club, or group of friends, on a date to suit you. See individual garden entries for full details.

10 Alder Wynd 1

22 Elmsdale Road 3

The Old Rectory, Wrestlingworth 17

1a St Augustine's Road 19

Secret Garden 20

Walnut Cottage 25

Secret Garden

THE GARDENS

1 10 ALDER WYND

Silsoe, Bedford, MK45 4GQ. David & Frances Hampson, 01525 861356, mail@davidhampson.com. *From Barton Rd, turn into the estate on Obelisk Way. At end of Obelisk Way turn R at school, then 1st L into Alder Wynd & bear R. 10 Alder Wynd is the 1st house on R.* **Sun 30 June (2-5). Adm £4, chd free. Light refreshments. Visits also by arrangement for groups of up to 20.**

Runners up in the 2017 Gardeners World Competition, 'Small Garden Category'. The garden demonstrates what can be achieved in a relatively small space, 10m x 11m. Created from scratch in the Autumn of 2014, the garden is roughly courtyard in style and formed from a series of raised beds and oak structures. Lush plantings of banana, tree ferns, hostas, bamboos and colourful herbaceous perennials. This small area has a wide selection of plants, tetrapanax, roses, wisteria, clematis, a variety of grasses and traditional perennials. A water feature provides a subtle background noise. The pathways are narrow and made of slate chippings, there are two shallow steps to the decked area.

2 NEW 88 CASTLEHILL ROAD

Totternhoe, LU6 1QG. Chris & Carole Jell. *Middle End. Turn R off B489 Aston Clinton rd. Fronting main rd approx ½m through village. Garden is in the center of the village.* **Sat 11 May, Sat 8 June (2-6). Adm £5, chd free. Home-made teas.**

Diverse planting managed in a natural and artistic way, creating a feel of peace and beauty and a wildlife haven. Roses, clematis, shrubs, trees and perennials are arranged in glorious disarray with a gentle plea for chaos. Sloping on limestone and clay, created and evolved by the owners over 40 years, this garden enjoys its own micro climate. Views of Chiltern Hills from the top. No access for wheelchairs.

3 22 ELMSDALE ROAD

Wootton, Bedford, MK43 9JN. Roy & Dianne Richards, 07733 222495, roy.richards60@ntlworld.com. *4m from J13 M1. Join old A421 towards Bedford, follow signs to Wootton. Turn R at The Cock PH follow Rd to Elmsdale Rd.* **Sat 1, Sun 2 June, Sat 6, Sun 7 July (12-5). Adm £4, chd free. Home-made teas. Visits also by arrangement Mar to Oct for groups of 10+. Tea coffee and home made cakes can be served.**

Topiary garden greets visitors before they enter a genuine Japanese Feng Shui garden including bonsai. Every plant is strictly Japanese, large Koi pond and lily pond and Japanese Tea House. The garden was created from scratch by the owners about 20 years ago and has many interesting features. Japanese lanterns and a large collection of Japanese plants and bonsai. From China the Kneeling Archer terracotta soldier, Koi pond and lily pond. Partial wheelchair access. The Garden is on 2 levels and has gravel type paths but some of the garden can be viewed from the lower level.

4 THE FOLLY

High Street, Pavenham, Bedford, MK43 7PE. Mr & Mrs J Kirby. *Approx 6m N of Bedford off the A6 towards Kettering signed Oakley & Pavenham. Enter Pavenham. Garden is 3rd house on L past the 30 MPH sign.* **Sun 3, Sat 23, Sun 24 Feb (1-4). Combined adm with The Knoll £5, chd free.**

Medium sized cottage garden with an extensive collection of snowdrops, hellebores and other spring bulbs. Small parterre, pergola and pond. Light refreshments at the Knoll. Gravel drive and narrow twisting paths so wheelchair access difficult.

5 GIFLA HOUSE

Manor Road, Barton-Le-Clay, Bedford, MK45 4NR. Jim & Rosemary Bottoms. *The house is next door to the Manor House on the very sharp bend of Manor Rd on L. The entrance is via a gate at the side of the garden adjacent to the parking behind the Manor House.* **Sun 16 June (2-5). Combined adm with The Manor House, Barton-le-Clay £5, chd free. Light refreshments.**

When we first moved to the house (some 20+ years ago) the garden was essentially a field with a couple of trees in it. Over the years we have had the entire space carefully and sympathetically landscaped. Now there are beautiful decorative bridges over the natural river, many different shrubs in the flower beds, crazy paved pathways and patios which add to the character of this fantastic garden.

6 NEW GLADE HOUSE

Spinney Lane, Aspley Guise, Milton Keynes, MK17 8JT. Alex Ballance & Lindsay Walker. *1½m from M1 J13 head for Husborne Crawley. Follow rd to Aspley Guise square, turn L up Woburn Lane, L into Spinney Lane, R into car park. Garden 150m along Spinney Lane. 2 blue badge spaces at garden. Please park at Aspley Guise Village Hall.* **Sat 6, Sun 7 July (2-5). Combined adm with Hollydale £5, chd free. Home-made teas.**

A colourful, multi-level garden of about half an acre, divided into different areas by perennial and shrub borders and banks, plus a sunny terrace, fish pond and woodland areas planted with shade loving plants. There are over 400 varieties of herbaceous perennials, shrubs and herbs, many of them unusual, plus several seating areas from which you can enjoy different vistas within the garden. Due to the slope, only the brick terrace by the house is wheelchair accessible - please note that it is accessed via 12m of gravel path.

We help ordinary people open the gates to their extraordinary private gardens to raise impressive amounts of money through admissions, teas and slices of cake!

7 NEW HOLLYDALE, WOBURN LANE

Woburn Lane, Aspley Guise, MK17 8JH. Mrs Gill Cockle. *2m from J13 M1. Head for Husborne Crawley. Follow rd to Apsley Guise square, turn L to Woburn Lane.* **Sat 6, Sun 7 July (2-5). Combined adm with Glade House £5, chd free. Home-made teas at Glade House.**
Set in ⅓ acre on three levels around Grade II Listed Georgian house, this classically styled garden is a series of rooms - flowers gardens, leisure area for entertaining, vegetable garden, herb garden, fruit tree orchard and chicken pen. There are some steep steps but lots of seating around the garden. The large front garden with specimen shrubs and flower borders is wheelchair accessible. During your visit to our garden, you can try tasting some of our prize winning local honey. If you enjoy it, our honey is available to buy and for every jar sold, we donate £1 to the NGS charities. Wheelchair access to front garden only.

8 HOWBURY HALL GARDEN

Howbury Hall Estate, Renhold, Bedford, MK41 0JB. Julian Polhill & Lucy Copeman. *2m E of Bedford. Off A421 A1 - M1 link. Leave A421 at the A428/Gt Barford exit, take A428 to Bedford. Entrance to house & gardens ½m on R. Parking in field. Short walk to garden.* **Sat 8 June (2-5). Adm £5, chd free. Home-made teas.**
A late Victorian garden designed with mature trees, sweeping lawns and herbaceous borders. The large walled garden is a working garden, where one half is dedicated to growing a large variety of vegetables whilst the other is run as a cut flower business. In the woodland area, walking towards the large pond, the outside of a disused ice house can be seen.

9 THE HYDE WALLED GARDEN

East Hyde, Luton, LU2 9PS. D J J Hambro Will Trust. *2m S of Luton. M1 exit/10a Exit to A1061 towards Harpenden take 2nd on L signed East Hyde. From A1 exit J4 follow A3057 N to r'about 1st L to B653 follow rd to Wheathampstead/Luton to East Hyde.* **Sun 16, Sun 30 June (2-5). Adm £5, chd free. Home-made teas.**
Walled garden adjoins the grounds of The Hyde (not open). Extends to approx 1 acre and features rose garden, seasonal beds and herbaceous borders, imaginatively interspersed with hidden areas of formal lawn. An interesting group of Victorian greenhouses, coldframes and cucumber house are serviced from the potting shed in the adjoining vegetable garden. Gravel paths.

10 ◆ KING'S ARMS GARDEN

Brinsmade Road, Ampthill, MK45 2PP. Ampthill Town Council, 01525 755648, bryden.k@outlook.com. *8m S of Bedford. Free parking in town centre. Entrance opp Old Market Place, down King's Arms Yard.* **For NGS: Sun 24 Feb; Sun 27 Oct (2.30-4.30). Adm £3, chd free.** For other opening times and information, please phone or email.
Small woodland garden of about 1½ acres created by plantsman the late William Nourish. Trees, shrubs, bulbs and many interesting collections throughout the yr. Maintained since 1987 by 'The Friends of the Garden' on behalf of Ampthill Town Council. See us on Facebook Kings Arms Garden. Wheelchair access to most of the garden.

11 THE KNOLL

High Street, Pavenham, Bedford, MK43 7PD. Mr & Mrs Terry & Debby Horsman. *Approx 6m N of Bedford just off A6. From A6 take 2nd L signed Oakley & Pavenham. Follow directions for Pavenham. Garden is on the L, 300 metres inside the 30mph zone.* **Sun 3, Sat 23, Sun 24 Feb (1-4). Combined adm with The Folly £5, chd free. Home-made teas**
Cottage garden, ⅓ acre with a large collection of many varieties of snowdrops. Hellebores, spring bulbs and other colour. Pergolas, wildlife pond, kitchen garden and raised bed. Woodland area and island beds. Light refreshments at the Knoll. There is a gravel drive but most parts of the garden can be accessed by wheelchair with care. This is difficult after heavy rain.

12 NEW 40 LEIGHTON STREET

Woburn, MK17 9PH. Mrs Rita Chidley. *On main road leaving Woburn towards Leighton Buzzard. 500yds from centre of village L side of road. Last cottage in a row of 6.* **Sat 8 June, Sat 14 Sept (2-5). Adm £5, chd free. Home-made teas.**
Large cottage style garden in three parts. There are several 'rooms' with interesting features to explore and many quiet seating areas. In June there is an abundance of roses in bloom with many clematis and honeysuckles. September brings a change of colour for late summer and autumn with dahlias, fuchsias and grasses. Limited wheelchair access.

13 LUTON HOO HOTEL GOLF & SPA

The Mansion House, Luton Hoo, Luton, LU1 3TQ. Luton Hoo Hotel Golf & Spa, www.lutonhoo.co.uk. *Approx 1m from J10 M1, take London Rd A1081 signed Harpenden for approx ½m - entrance on L for Luton Hoo Hotel Golf & Spa.* **Sun 21 July (11-4). Adm £5, chd free. Light refreshments. Visitors wishing to have lunch/formal afternoon tea at the hotel must book in advance directly with the hotel.**
The gardens and parkland designed by Capability Brown are of national historic significance and lie in a conservation area. Main features - lakes, woodland and pleasure grounds, Victorian grass tennis court and late C19 sunken rockery. Italianate garden with herbaceous borders and topiary garden. Gravel paths.

14 THE MANOR HOUSE, BARTON-LE-CLAY

87 Manor Road, Barton-le-Clay, MK45 4NR. Mrs Veronica Pilcher. *Off A6 between Bedford & Luton. Take old A6 (Bedford Rd) through Barton-le-Clay Village (not the by-pass) & Manor Rd is off Bedford Rd. Parking in paddock.* **Sun 16 June (2-5). Combined adm with Gifla**

House £5, chd free. Home-made teas.
The garden was beautifully landscaped during the 1930s and much interest is created by picturesque stream which incorporates a series of waterfalls and ponds. Colourful streamside planting incl an abundance of arum lilies. Sunken garden with lily pond and a magnificent wisteria thrives at the rear of the house. Children under supervision as there is a water hazard. Partial wheelchair access, 2ft wide bridges.

♿ 🐕 ✿ ☕

15 ◆ THE MANOR HOUSE, STEVINGTON

Church Road, Stevington, Bedford, MK43 7QB. Kathy Brown, www.kathybrownsgarden.com. *5m NW of Bedford. Off A428 through Bromham.* **For NGS: Mon 6 May (1-5). Adm £6, chd free. Home-made teas in Church Rooms next to car park.** For other opening times and information, please visit garden website.
The Manor House Garden has many different rooms and views to enjoy. Bulb displays feature in borders, grasslands and containers. White stemmed birches have under plantings of white tree peonies, snakeshead fritillaria and aquilegia. Ornamental cherries, orchard trees and lilacs will be in bloom with camassias below. Bees feast on Alliums beneath the wisteria arches and Allium siculum feature in the cottage garden. Kathy plans an edible flower workshop mid afternoon. Teas in aid of Sue Ryder. Partial wheelchair access. Disabled WC.

♿ 🐕 ☕

16 THE OLD RECTORY, WESTONING

Church Road, Westoning, MK45 5JW. Ann & Colin Davies. *2m S of Flitwick. Off A5120, 2m N of M1 J12. ¼m up Church Rd, next to church.* **Sun 7 Apr (2-5.30). Adm £5, chd free. Delicious cream teas and other refreshments in C14 church next door.**
Ancient box and yew hedges surround the colour co-ordinated beds of this two acre garden. Spring is greeted by hellebores and daffodils with magnolias blooming in profusion. Hyacinths perfume the air with snake's head fritillaries adorning the meadow. Catkins hang from hazels with primroses lighting the darker corners. Come and enjoy the the sights and and smells of a traditional English garden. Wheelchair access generally good.

♿ ✿ ☕

Walnut Cottage

17 THE OLD RECTORY, WRESTLINGWORTH

Church Lane, Wrestlingworth, Sandy, SG19 2EU. Mrs Josephine Hoy, 01767 631204, hoyjosephine@hotmail.co.uk. *5m E of Sandy, 5m NE of Biggleswade. Wrestlingworth is situated on B1042. 5m from Sandy & 6m from Biggleswade. The Old Rectory is at the top of Church Lane, which is well signed, behind the church.* **Sun 12, Sun 26 May (2-5.30). Adm £6, chd free. Home-made teas. Visits also by arrangement Apr & May for groups of 10 to 30 (sorry no refreshments).**
4 acre garden full of colour and interest. The owner has a free style of gardening sensitive to wildlife. Beds overflowing with tulips, alliums, bearded iris, peonies, poppies, geraniums and much more. Beautiful mature trees and many more planted in the last 30 years. Incl a large selection of betulas. Gravel gardens, box hedging, woodland garden and wild flower meadows. Wheelchair access maybe limited on grass paths.

♿ ✿ ☕

GROUP OPENING

18 OLD WARDEN VILLAGE GARDENS

Old Warden, Biggleswade, SG18 9HB. *3m W of Biggleswade. Parking in the village hall car park opposite the Hare & Hounds pub, or on the cricket field at the eastern end of the village, near St Leonard's Church.* **Sun 9 June (2-5). Combined adm £6, chd free. Home-made teas in the Village Hall.**

NEW **MAIN LODGE**
Luke Quenby.

ORCHARD GRANGE
Robert & Victoria Diggle.

28 THE VILLAGE
Bob Parr.

30 THE VILLAGE
Shirley Benjamin.

31 THE VILLAGE
Mike & Penny Prior.

Old Warden, with its picturesque cottages, medieval church, neat holly hedges and charming pub, is one of the prettiest villages in Bedfordshire. Many of the houses were built by the 3rd Lord Ongley in the early C19 in the cottage-ornée style. Further attractive buildings were added by the Shuttleworth family. The largest garden in the group is that at Orchard Grange, which has a walled kitchen garden, formal areas, and a wild flower orchard. Numbers 28, 30 and 31 are all established gardens with year-round interest. There are plenty of seats from which to enjoy the striped lawns, cottage-garden planting and colourful containers. Main Lodge, a fine gatehouse that stands at the entrance to Old Warden Park, has a productive garden with perennial and wildflower areas and other surprises. Teas in aid of St Leonard's, Old Warden. Most gardens are accessible to wheelchairs but there are some steps, banks and gravel paths.

The Old Rectory, Wrestlingworth

19 1A ST AUGUSTINE'S ROAD

Bedford, MK40 2NB. Chris Bamforth Damp, 01234 353730/01234 353465. *St Augustine's Rd is on L off Kimbolton Rd as you leave the centre of Bedford.* **Sat 3 Aug (12-4.30). Adm £3.50, chd free. Home-made teas. Visits also by arrangement June to Sept for groups of 10 to 30.**

A colourful town garden with herbaceous borders, climbers, a green house and pond. Planted in cottage garden style with traditional flowers, the borders overflow with late summer annuals and perennials including salvias and rudbeckia. The pretty terrace next to the house is lined with ferns and hostas. The owners also make homemade chutneys and preserves which can be purchased on the day. The garden is wheelchair accessible.

20 SECRET GARDEN

4 George Street, Clapham, Bedford, MK41 6AZ. Graham Bolton, 07746 864247, bolton_graham@hotmail.com. *3m N of Bedford (not the bypass). Clapham Village High St. R into Mount Pleasant Rd then L into George St. 1st white Bungalow on R.* **Sun 5 May (12.30-5.30). Adm £3.50, chd free. Light refreshments. Visits also by arrangement Apr & May for groups of 10 to 20.**

Profiled in the RHS The Garden, alpine lovers can see a wide collection of alpines in two small scree gardens, front and back of bungalow plus pans. Planting also incl dwarf salix, rhododendrons, daphnes, acers, conifers, pines, hellebores and epimediums. Two small borders of herbaceous salvias, lavenders and potentillas. Alpine greenhouse with rare varieties and cold frames with plants for sale. Partial wheelchair access. No access at the rear of property due to narrow gravel paths but garden can be viewed from the patio.

21 SOUTHILL PARK

Southill, Nr Biggleswade, SG18 9LL. Mr & Mrs Charles Whitbread. *3m W of Biggleswade. In the village of Southill. 3m from A1 junction at Biggleswade.* **Sun 2 June**

(2-5). Adm £5, chd free. Cream teas.
Southill Park is one of the founder NGS gardens which first opened its gates to visitors in 1927. A large garden with mature trees and flowering shrubs, herbaceous borders, a formal rose garden, sunken garden, ponds and kitchen garden. It is on the south side of the 1795 Palladian house. The parkland was designed by Lancelot 'Capability' Brown. A large conservatory houses the tropical collection.

GROUP OPENING

22 STEPPINGLEY VILLAGE GARDENS

Steppingley, Bedford, MK45 5AT. *Follow signs to Steppingley, pick up yellow signs from village centre.* **Sun 26, Mon 27 May (2-5). Combined adm £6, chd free. Home-made teas at Townsend Farmhouse.**

MIDDLE BARN
Bruce & Pauline Henninger.

TOP BARN
Tim & Nicky Kemp.

TOWNSEND FARMHOUSE
Hugh & Indi Jackson.
(See separate entry)

WEST OAK
John & Sally Eilbeck.
(See separate entry)

Steppingley is a picturesque Bedfordshire village on the Greensand ridge, close to Ampthill, Flitwick and Woburn. Although a few older buildings survive, most of Steppingley was built by 7th Duke of Bedford between 1840 and 1872. Four gardens in the village offer an interesting mix of planting styles and design to include pretty court yards, cottage garden style perennial borders, ponds, a well, glass houses, an orchard, vegetable gardens, a herb garden, wild life havens and country views. Live stock include chickens, ducks and fish. Long gravel paths may be difficult for wheelchairs.

23 TOWNSEND FARMHOUSE

Rectory Road, Steppingley, Bedford, MK45 5AT. Hugh & Indi Jackson. *In Steppingley Village. Follow directions to Steppingley village and pick up yellow signs from village centre.* **Sun 28 Apr (2-5). Combined adm with West Oak £5, chd free. Home-made teas. Evening opening Sat 26 Oct (5.30-8). Light refreshments. Adm £5, chd free. Opening with Steppingley Village Gardens Sun 26, Mon 27 May.**
Tree lined driveway with young specimens and mature broad leaves rising above swathes of spring bulbs, narcissi, fritillaria, tulips, hyacinths and more. Planted for year round interest, the cottage-garden style herbaceous borders are filled with early perennials, bearded iris and alliums. Pretty cobbled courtyard with a glass house and a Victorian well 30 metres deep, viewed through a glass top. This garden is also open for Diwali on Saturday 26 October 5.30 pm - 8 pm. Join us for an evening of diya lamps, flower rangoli, sweetmeats and punch. Long gravelled driveway may be difficult for wheelchairs. Saturday 26 October is a Diwali themed evening with lanterns, diya lamps and flower rangoli; bring a torch.

24 ◆ THE WALLED GARDEN

Luton, LU1 4LF. Luton Hoo Estate, www.lutonhooestate.co.uk. *Take A1081. Turn at West Hyde Road (signed for Newmill End). After approx 100 metres turn L through black gates. Follow red signs to Walled Garden.* **For NGS: Sat 3 Aug (9.30-12.30). Adm £5, chd free. Light refreshments.**
For other opening times and information, please phone, email or visit garden website.
The 5 acre Luton Hoo Estate Walled Garden was designed by Capability Brown and established by the notorious Lord Bute in the late 1760s. The Walled Garden now offers a unique opportunity to see conservation and restoration combined with outstanding volunteer involvement in action. The garden continues to be restored, repaired and reimagined for the enjoyment of all. Volunteer garden and local history experts on hand to explain and expand on what you see. An amazing cactus collection and original restored prop houses. Exhibition of Victorian tools. Walled Garden Shop with ever changing seasonal produce, including our outstanding Estate honey. Disabled parking next to Walled Garden Entrance. A hard path goes through and around the garden.

25 WALNUT COTTAGE

8 Great North Road, Chawston, MK44 3BD. D G Parker, 07784 792975, dave.parkergnr@gmail.com. *2m S of St Neots. Between Wyboston & Blackcat r'about on S-bound lane of A1. Turn off at McDonalds, at end of filling station forecourt turn L. Off rd parking.* **Sat 20, Sun 21 July (2-6). Adm £4.50, chd free. Home-made teas. Visits also by arrangement Mar to Sept for groups of 10+. Refreshments on request.**
Once a land settlement. 4 acre smallholding. 1 acre cottage garden. Over 2000 species give year round interest. Bulbs, herbaceous, water, bog plants, ferns, grasses, shrubs, trees and coppiced paulownias. Rare, exotic and unusual plants abound. Large pond and level grass paths.

26 WEST OAK

50 Rectory Road, Steppingley, Bedford, MK45 5AT. John & Sally Eilbeck. *Steppingley Village. Follow signs to Steppingley from A507 r'about between Ampthill & Flitwick, pick up yellow signs from centre of village.* **Sun 28 Apr (2-5). Combined adm with Townsend Farmhouse £5, chd free. Home-made teas at Townsend Farmhouse. Opening with Steppingley Village Gardens Sun 26, Mon 27 May.**
An informal garden of approx ¾ acre with open countryside on two sides. It consists of lawns and shrubs with perennial planting including some mature trees.There is a herb garden, greenhouse, vegetable gardens with soft fruit, and small orchard with chickens. The garden has been developed over nearly 30 years by the present owners from a completely bare plot. The garden is approached across a gravel drive and there are some steps.

OPENING DATES

All entries subject to change. For latest information check **www.ngs.org.uk**

Map locator numbers are shown to the right of each garden name.

February

Snowdrop Festival

Thursday 7th
◆ Welford Park 32

March

Saturday 9th
Stubbings House 30

Sunday 10th
Stubbings House 30

April

Wednesday 10th
Rooksnest 25

Sunday 14th
The Old Rectory, Farnborough 18

Sunday 28th
Odney Club 17
Rookwood Farm House 26

May

Sunday 5th
Rookwood Farm House 26

Sunday 12th
Sandleford Place 28

Tuesday 14th
◆ Frogmore House Garden 9

Sunday 19th
The Old Rectory, Farnborough 18

Saturday 25th
Stubbings House 30

Sunday 26th
Stubbings House 30

Monday 27th
Stubbings House 30

June

Sunday 2nd
Farley Hill Place Gardens 7
Stockcross House 29

Saturday 8th
Eton College Gardens 5

Sunday 9th
Chieveley Manor 2

Wednesday 12th
Rooksnest 25

Friday 14th
St Timothee 27

Saturday 15th
St Timothee 27

Sunday 16th
Kirby House 14
The Old Rectory Inkpen 19

Sunday 23rd
Sandleford Place 28

Wednesday 26th
The Old Rectory, Farnborough 18

Sunday 30th
Pyt House 24
Willow Tree Cottage 33

July

Sunday 7th
Lower Lovetts Farm 15
Swallowfield Village Gardens 31

Sunday 14th
NEW The Old Rectory, Lower Basildon 20

August

Sunday 4th
King's Copse House 13

Monday 26th
Rookwood Farm House 26

By Arrangement

Arrange a personalised garden visit with your club, or group of friends, on a date to suit you. See individual garden entries for full details.

NEW Boxford House 1
Compton Elms 3
NEW Fairing 6
Farley Hill Place Gardens 7
Handpost 10
NEW Highacre 11
Old Waterfield 21
The Priory 22
NEW Priory House 23
Rooksnest 25
Rookwood Farm House 26
St Timothee 27
Sandleford Place 28
Stubbings House 30

Chieveley Manor

THE GARDENS

Lower Lovetts Farm

1 NEW BOXFORD HOUSE

Boxford, Newbury, RG20 8DP. 07765 674863, dragonflygardens@btinternet.com. *4m NW of Newbury. Directions will be provided on booking.* **Visits by arrangement Feb to Nov for groups of 20+. Guided tour, tea, coffee & biscuits included. Adm £10, chd free.**

Beautiful large family garden extensively developed over the past 7 yrs. Emphasis on roses and scent throughout the 5 acre main garden. Old and new orchards, laburnum tunnel, formal and colourful herbaceous borders. Handsome formal terraces, pond, water features and garden woodland areas. Inviting cottage garden and productive vegetable gardens. Partial wheelchair access, gravel paths and sloping lawns.

2 CHIEVELEY MANOR

Chieveley, Nr Newbury, RG20 8UT. Mr & Mrs CJ Spence. *5m N of Newbury. From M4 J13, follow signs for A34 N & immed keep L on to slip road for Chieveley. At T-junction turn L into village, after ½m turn L into Manor Lane.* **Sun 9 June (2-5). Adm £5, chd free. Cream teas.** Donation to St Mary's Church, Chieveley.

Large garden surrounding listed house (not open) in the heart of Chieveley village. Attractive setting with fine views over stud farm. Walled garden containing lovely borders, shrubs and rose garden, evolving every year. Box parterre filled with alliums, white geraniums and lavender. Many viticella clematis growing through shrubs.

3 COMPTON ELMS

Marlow Road, Pinkneys Green, Maidenhead, SL6 6NR. Alison Kellett, kellettaj@gmail.com. *Situated at the end of a gravel road located opp & in between the Arbour & Golden Ball Pubs on the A308.* **Visits by arrangement Feb to Apr for groups of 10 to 30. Tea, coffee & biscuits included. Adm £8, chd free.**

A delightful spring garden set in a sunken woodland, lovingly recovered from clay pit workings. The atmospheric garden is filled with snowdrops, primroses, hellebores and fritillaria, interspersed with anemone and narcissi under a canopy of ash and beech.

4 ◆ ENGLEFIELD HOUSE GARDEN

Englefield, Theale, Reading, RG7 5EN. Mr & Mrs Richard Benyon, 01189 302221, peter.carson@englefield.co.uk, www.englefieldestate.co.uk. *6m W of Reading. M4 J12. Take A4 towards Theale. 2nd r'about take A340 to Pangbourne. After ⅙m entrance on the L.* **For opening times and information, please phone, email or visit garden website.**

The 12 acre garden descends dramatically from the hill above the historic house through woodland where mature native trees mix with Victorian conifers. Drifts of spring and summer planting are followed by striking autumn colour. Stone balustrades enclose the lower terrace, with wide lawns, roses, mixed borders and topiary. Open every Monday from Apr-Sept (10am-6pm) and Oct-Mar (10am-4pm). Please check Englefield website for any changes before travelling. Wheelchair access to some parts of the gardens.

5 ETON COLLEGE GARDENS

Eton, Nr Windsor, SL4 6DB. Eton College. *½m N of Windsor. Parking signed off B3022, Slough Rd. Walk from car park across playing fields to entry. Follow signs for tickets & maps which are sold at gazebo near entrance.* **Sat 8 June (2-5). Adm £6, chd free. Home-made teas in the Fellows garden.**

A rare chance to visit a group of central College gardens surrounded by historic school buildings, including Luxmoore's garden on a small island in the Thames reached across two attractive bridges. Also an opportunity to explore the fascinating Eton College Natural History Museum and the Museum of Eton Life and a small group of other private gardens. Plant Sale. We are sorry but the gardens are not suitable for wheelchairs due to gravel, steps and uneven ground.

6 NEW **FAIRING**

Coronation Road, Littlewick Green, Maidenhead, SL6 3RA. Mr & Mrs M P Maine, 01628 822008. *Littlewick Green is N of White Waltham & S of Hurley, nr Maidenhead. Fairing is on Coronation Rd, on the R, 5 houses past the The Cricketers, between a tall conifer & a telegraph pole.* **Visits by arrangement in Apr for groups of up to 30. Adm £5, chd free. Light refreshments.**

Many gardeners imagine that having a wildlife garden means giving into an unruly, scruffy space, yet nothing could be further from the truth. A particular delight in the spring, this 1½ acre garden incl an orchard of 15 apple trees and 8 small ponds, with wide ranging views over farmland. Some gravel paths.

7 **FARLEY HILL PLACE GARDENS**

Church Road, Farley Hill, Reading, RG7 1TZ. Tony & Margaret Finch, 01189 762544, tony.finch7@btinternet.com. *From M4 J11, take A33 S to Basingstoke. At T-lights turn L for Spencers Wood, B3349. Go 2m turn L, through Swallowfield towards Farley Hill. Garden ½m on R.* **Sun 2 June (2-5). Adm £5, chd free. Home-made teas. Visits also by arrangement May to July for groups of 10+. Please mention NGS.**

A 4 acre, C18 cottage garden. 1½ acre walled garden with yr-round interest and colour. Well stocked herbaceous borders, large productive vegetable areas with herb garden, dahlia and cutting flower beds. Enjoy wandering around the garden, with spontaneous singing from a Barber's Shop Quartet. Victorian glasshouse recently renovated and small nursery. Plants, lovely cut flowers and produce for sale. Partial wheelchair access.

8 **FOLLY FARM**

Sulhamstead Hill, Sulhamstead, RG7 4DG. *7m SW of Reading. From A4 between Reading & Newbury (2m W of M4 J12) take road marked Sulhamstead at The Spring Inn. Restricted car parking.* **Visits by arrangement on Thur 2 May for groups up to 12 max. Adm £25. Home-made teas. Pre-booking essential, please visit www.ngs.org.uk/events for information & booking.**

Gardens laid out in 1912 by Sir Edwin Lutyens and Gertrude Jekyll. Garden designs evolved during culmination of their partnership and considered one of their most complex. Extensively restored and replanted by current owners assisted by Dan Pearson. Recently reopened for private small group visits which include approx 1½ hour guided tour and tea and home-made pastries. Very limited availability. Please note paths are uneven and there are many sets of steps between areas of the garden. Sorry no children or dogs.

9 ◆ **FROGMORE HOUSE GARDEN**

Windsor, SL4 1LB. Her Majesty The Queen. *1m SE of Windsor. Entrance via Park St gate into Long Walk.* **For NGS: Tue 14 May (10-5.30). Adm to be confirmed. Pre-booking recommended. For advance tickets go to www.ngs.org.uk/events. Light refreshments & picnics welcome.**

The private royal garden at Frogmore House on the Crown Estate at Windsor. This landscaped garden set in 30 acres with notable trees, lawns, flowering shrubs and C18 lake, is rich in history. It is largely the creation of Queen Charlotte, who in the 1790s introduced over 4,000 trees and shrubs to create a model picturesque landscape. The historic plantings, incl tulip trees and redwoods, along with Queen Victoria's Tea House, remain key features of the garden today. Please

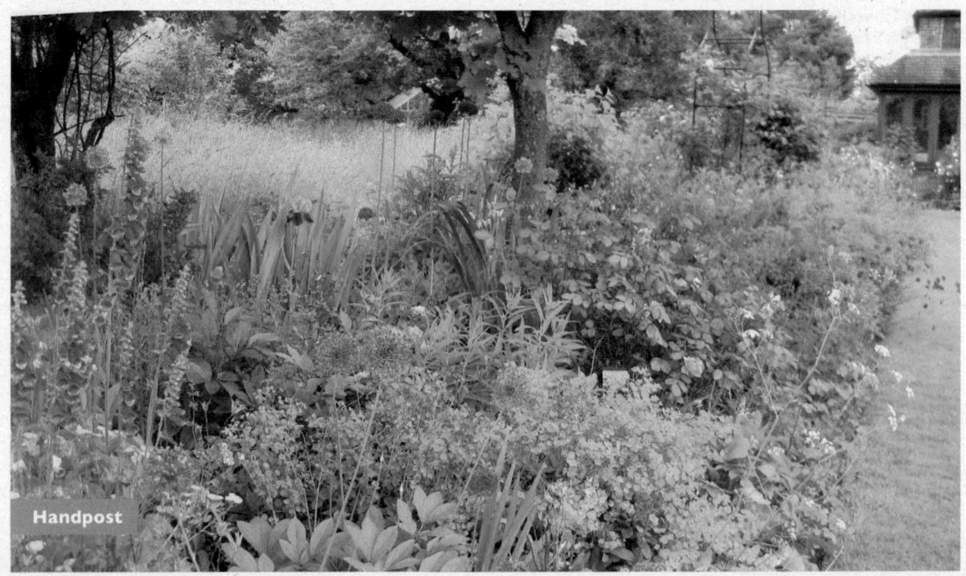

Handpost

note the Royal Mausoleum is closed due to long term restoration. To book optional garden history tours (approx 45 mins) with limited availability, go to 'Events' page at www.ngs.org.uk. Tickets for garden and to visit the house are also available on the day by cash payment only. Last entry 4pm. Please note that Windsor traffic may be halted at 11am for Guard change.

10 HANDPOST

Basingstoke Road, Swallowfield, Reading, RG7 1PU. Faith Ramsay, faith@mycountrygarden.co.uk, www.mycountrygarden.co.uk. *From M4 J11, take A33 S. At 1st T-lights turn L on B3349 Basingstoke Rd. Follow road for 2¾m, garden on L.* **Visits by arrangement May to Sept for groups of 10+. Adm £6, chd free. Home-made teas.**

4 acre designer's garden with many areas of interest. Features incl two lovely long herbaceous borders attractively and densely planted in six colour sections, a formal rose garden, an old orchard with a grass meadow, pretty pond and peaceful wooded area. Large variety of plants, trees and a productive fruit and vegetable patch. Some gravel areas but largely accessible.

11 NEW HIGHACRE

Henwick Manor Farm, Henwick, Thatcham, RG18 9HR. Rhona Tucker, 07769 973950, rtuck2008@hotmail.co.uk. *3m E of Newbury, 14m W of Reading. Do not use postcode for SatNav as this will give wrong access info. From Tull Way, Thatcham follow NGS signs.* **Visits by arrangement Apr & May for groups of up to 20. Adm £5, chd free. Home-made teas.**

A ¾ acre tiered garden with sloping lawns, mainly herbaceous beds and spring bulbs. Paddock area with several trees and wild flowers. Woodland area with wildlife pond and water feature. Greenhouse and conservatory. Views over farmland and surrounding area. The garden has been designed to provide flowers all year for flower arranging. Very much a gardener's garden. No wheelchair access.

We open the gates to the nation's best gardens, offering a relaxing, memorable and affordable day out. A perfect experience to share with friends and family.

13 KING'S COPSE HOUSE

Bradfield Gate, Nr Reading, RG7 6JR. Mr & Mrs J Wyatt. *Approx 12m W of Reading. M4 J12, A4 to Theale. At 2nd r'about take 3rd exit A340 towards Pangbourne, then soon 1st L. After 1¼m turn L to Bradfield Southend. In village turn R on Hungerford Lane, after ½m L on Cock Lane.* **Sun 4 Aug (2-5). Adm £5, chd free. Home-made teas.**

A beautiful and formal landscaped garden set in 4 acres, recently renovated to a high standard to incorporate some original and rare specimens together with new plantings. Orchard, large fish pond, secret rose garden, herbaceous borders, cut flower garden and spectacular views over the Pang Valley. Walks through 40 acre SSSI ancient woodland. WWII Air Raid Shelter.

14 KIRBY HOUSE

Upper Green, Inkpen, RG17 9ED. Mrs K Astor. *5m SE of Hungerford. A4 to Kintbury. At Xrds by Corner Stores turn L, take Inkpen Rd & follow into Inkpen. Pass common on L. Just past Crown & Garter Pub, turn L (to Combe & Faccombe), at T-junction turn L, house on R.* **Sun 16 June (2-5). Adm £5, chd free. Combined adm with The Old Rectory Inkpen £8, chd free.**

7 acres in beautiful setting with views of South Berkshire Downs and historical Combe Gibbet, across lawn with ha-ha and parkland. C18 Queen Anne House (not open). Formal borders, lily pond garden and terraces laid out by Harold Peto. Reflecting pond with fountain, lake, walled garden and contemporary sculptures. Some uneven paths. Teas at The Old Rectory Inkpen.

15 LOWER LOVETTS FARM

Knowl Hill Common, Knowl Hill, RG10 9YE. Mr Richard Sandford, www.lowerlovettsfarm.com. *5m W of Maidenhead on the A4 road toward Reading. Off A4 at Knowl Hill into Knowl Hill Common. Past pub and across common to T-junction. Turn L down dead end lane.* **Sun 7 July (12-5). Adm £5, chd free. Cream teas.**

A fascinating large modern organic kitchen garden (60 metre x 30 metre). Wide variety of vegetables and fruit grown for home consumption and nutritional value. Flowers grown for eating or herbal teas. Produce is also dried or bottled for yr-round use. Lots of interesting growing techniques and tips. See garden website for more information.

16 MALVERLEYS

Fullers Lane, East End, Newbury, RG20 0AA. *A34 S of Newbury, exit signed for Highclere. Follow A343 for ½m, turn R to Woolton Hill. Pass school & turn L to East End. After 1m R at village green, then after 100 metres, R onto Fullers Lane.* **Wed 5 June, Wed 21 Aug (11-5). Adm £12, chd free. Pre-booking essential, please visit www.ngs.org.uk/events for information & booking. Tea, cake & tours at 11am, 1.30pm or 3pm with the Garden Team included. Ticket availability is limited, so please book early to avoid disappointment.**

10 acres of dynamic gardens which have been developed over the last 7 yrs to include magnificent mixed borders and a series of contrasting yew hedged rooms, hosting flame borders, a cool garden, a pond garden and new stumpery. A vegetable garden with striking fruit cages sit within a walled garden, also encompassing a white garden. Meadows open out to views over the parkland. Due to steps and uneven paths, the garden is not suitable for wheelchairs.

17 ODNEY CLUB

Odney Lane, Cookham, SL6 9SR. John Lewis Partnership. *3m N of Maidenhead. Off A4094 S of Cookham Bridge. Signs to car park in grounds.* **Sun 28 Apr (2-6). Adm £5, chd free. Light refreshments.**

This 120 acre site is beside the Thames with lovely riverside walks. A favourite with Stanley Spencer who featured our magnolia in his work. Lovely wisteria, specimen trees, side gardens, spring bedding and ornamental lake. The John Lewis Partnership Heritage Centre will be open, showcasing the textile archive and items illustrating the history of John Lewis and Waitrose. Light refreshments in the Sir Bernard Miller Centre served 2pm-5pm (Guide dogs only). Some gravel paths. Dogs on leads please.

18 THE OLD RECTORY, FARNBOROUGH

Nr Wantage, Oxon, OX12 8NX. Mr & Mrs Michael Todhunter, 01488 638298. *4m SE of Wantage. Take B4494 Wantage-Newbury road, after 4m turn E at sign for Farnborough. Approx 1m to village, Old Rectory on L.* **Sun 14 Apr, Sun 19 May (2-5); Wed 26 June (11-4). Adm £5, chd free. Home-made teas.** Donation to Farnborough PCC.

In a series of immaculately tended garden rooms, incl herbaceous borders, arboretum, secret garden, roses, vegetables and bog garden, there is an explosion of rare and interesting plants, beautifully combined for colour and texture. With stunning views across the countryside, it is the perfect setting for the 1749 rectory (not open), once home of John Betjeman, in memory of whom John Piper created a window in the local church. Plants and preserves for sale. Some steep slopes and gravel paths.

Farley Hill Place Gardens

19 THE OLD RECTORY INKPEN

Lower Green, Inkpen, RG17 9DS. Mrs C McKeon. *4m SE of Hungerford. From centre of Kintbury at the Xrds, take Inkpen Rd. After ½m turn R, then go approx 3m (passing Crown & Garter Pub, then Inkpen Village Hall on L). Nr St Michaels Church, follow car park signs.* **Sun 16 June (2-5). Adm £5, chd free. Home-made teas at adjacent St Michael's Church. Combined adm with Kirby House £8, child free.**

On a gentle hillside with lovely countryside views, the Old Rectory offers a peaceful setting for this pretty 2 acre garden. Enjoy strolling through the formal and walled gardens, herbaceous borders, pleached lime walk and wild flower meadow (some slopes).

20 NEW THE OLD RECTORY, LOWER BASILDON

Lower Basildon, Reading, RG8 9NH. Charlie & Alison Laing. *2m NW of Pangbourne on A329. Into Lower Basildon, 200yds past petrol station, turn R down lane to church & follow signs to field parking.* **Sun 14 July (2-6). Adm £4.50, chd free. Home-made teas at adjacent St Bartholomew's Church.**

Recently remodelled 2 acre garden based around mature trees (notably cedar, magnolia and mulberry) with a pond and crinkle crankle wall. New plantings include fruit trees, white border, rose and peony beds, herbaceous long border and substantial kitchen garden. In AONB the garden also benefits from proximity to listed church (site of memorial to Jethro Tull) and Thames river walks. Garden is level but grass is uneven, some gravel paths.

21 OLD WATERFIELD

Winkfield Road, Ascot, SL5 7LJ. Hugh & Catherine Stevenson, catherine.stevenson@oldwaterfield.com. *6m SW of Windsor to E of Ascot Racecourse. On E side of A330 midway between A329 & A332.* **Visits by arrangement Apr to Oct for groups of 10 to 25. Adm £4.50, chd free. Light refreshments.**

Set in 4 acres between Ascot Heath and Windsor Great Park, the original cottage garden has been developed and extended over the past few years. Herbaceous borders, meadow with specimen trees, large productive vegetable garden, orchard and mixed hedging.

22 THE PRIORY

Beech Hill, RG7 2BJ. Mr & Mrs C Carter, 01189 883146. *5m S of Reading. M4 J11, A33 S to Basingstoke. At T-lights, L to Spencers Wood. After 1½m turn R for Beech Hill. After approx 1½m, L into Wood Lane, R down Priory Drive.* **Visits by arrangement June to Aug for groups of 10 to 20. Tea & cake by prior request. Adm £6, chd free.**

Extensive gardens in grounds of former C12 French Priory (not open), rebuilt 1648. The mature gardens are in a very attractive setting beside the River Loddon. Large formal walled garden with espalier fruit trees, lawns, mixed and replanted herbaceous borders, vegetables and roses. Woodland, fine trees, lake and Italian style water garden. A lovely garden for group visits.

23 NEW PRIORY HOUSE

Priory Road, Sunningdale, Ascot, SL5 9RQ. Mrs J Leigh, 07973 746979, rio4jen@gmail.com. *Approx 4½m SE of Ascot. Take turning opp Waitrose, Ridgemount Rd. Turn 1st L into Priory Rd. Priory House located at end of road. Parking for 15 cars.* **Visits by arrangement Apr to Sept for groups of 10 to 30. Adm £10, chd free. Tea & cake included.**

3 acre garden designed in 1930s by Percy Cane with yr-round interest, colour and fragrance. Ornamental pond, large lawn with shrub borders, yew hedges and rare trees. Lavish borders, vegetable garden, rose garden, rhododendrons, azaleas, daphne, gunnera and Lysichiton americanus by stream. Mature camellias, magnolias, fine shrubs and conifers. A truly exuberant and fragrant, rather than manicured garden. Not suitable for wheelchairs.

24 PYT HOUSE

Ashampstead, RG8 8RA. Edward & Sarah Ross. *4m W of Pangbourne. From Yattendon, head towards Reading. Road forks L into a beech wood towards Ashampstead. Keep L & join lower road. ½m turn L after long fence before houses.* **Sun 30 June (2-5). Combined adm with Willow Tree Cottage £5, chd free. Home-made teas in the barn.**

A 4 acre garden planted over the last 10 yrs, around C18 house (not open). Mature trees, yew, hornbeam and beech hedges, pleached limes, modern perennial borders, iris beds, pond, orchard and vegetable garden. Broadly organic, a haven for bees and butterflies, and we also have chickens.

25 ROOKSNEST

Ermin Street, Lambourn Woodlands, RG17 7SB. garden@rooksnest.net. *2m S of Lambourn on B4000. From M4 J14, take A338 Wantage Rd, turn 1st L onto B4000 (Ermin St). Rooksnest signed after 3m.* **Wed 10 Apr, Wed 12 June (11-4). Adm £5, chd free. Last entry 3.30pm. Visits also by arrangement Apr to June for groups of 20+.**

Approx 10 acre exceptionally fine traditional English garden. Rose garden (redesigned 2017), herbaceous garden, pond garden, herb garden, fruit, vegetable and cutting garden, and glasshouses. Many specimen trees and fine shrubs, orchard and terraces. Garden mostly designed by Arabella Lennox-Boyd. Most areas have step-free access, although surface consists of gravel and mowed grass. Plant sale on open days.

Your visits help change lives – since 1927, we've donated £55 million to nursing and caring charities

26 ROOKWOOD FARM HOUSE

Stockcross, Newbury, RG20 8JX. The Hon Rupert & Charlotte Digby, 01488 608676, charlotte@rookwoodhouse.co.uk, www.rookwoodhouse.co.uk. *3m W of Newbury. M4 J13, A34(S). After 3m exit for A4(W) to Hungerford. At 2nd r'about take B4000 towards Stockcross, after approx ¾m turn R into Rookwood.* **Sun 28 Apr, Sun 5 May, Mon 26 Aug (11-5). Adm £5, chd free. Home-made teas. Visits also by arrangement Apr to Oct for groups of 10+.**

This exciting valley garden, a work in progress, has elements all visitors can enjoy. A rose covered pergola, fabulous tulips, giant alliums, and a recently developed 'jungle garden' with banana plants and canas. A kitchen garden features a parterre of raised beds, which along with a bog garden and colour themed herbaceous planting, all make Rookwood well worth a visit. Gravel paths, some steep slopes.

27 ST TIMOTHEE

Darlings Lane, Maidenhead, SL6 6PA. Sarah & Sal Pajwani, 07976 892667, pajwanisarah@gmail.com. *1m N of Maidenhead. M4 J8/9 to A404M. 3rd exit onto A4 to Maidenhead. L at 1st r'about to A4130 Henley Rd. After ½m turn R onto Pinkneys Drive. At Pinkneys Arms Pub, turn L into Lee Lane, follow NGS signs.* **Fri 14 June (11-4); Sat 15 June (2-5). Adm £4.50, chd free. Home-made teas. 'Talk & Walk' event Wed 14 Aug (10.30-12.30). Adm £15, chd free. Pre-booking essential, please visit www.ngs.org.uk/events for information & bookings. Visits also by arrangement May to Aug for groups of 10+.**

Colour themed borders planted for yr-round interest with a wide range of attractive grasses and perennials. Includes a box parterre, wildlife pond, rose terrace, wild areas and mature trees, all set within the 2 acre plot of a 1930s house. 'Talk & Walk' event - Join us on 14 Aug 'Successional Planting' from 10.30am-12.30pm. Due to limited numbers, pre-booking essential. Adm £15, including talk (indoors) and tea and cake.

28 SANDLEFORD PLACE

Newtown, Newbury, RG20 9AY. Mel Gatward, 01635 40726, melgatward@btinternet.com. *House is on A339. 1½m S of Newbury on NW side of Swan r'about at Newtown. Please slow down on approach. Turn L into parking via field gate 50yds beyond entrance.* **Sun 12 May, Sun 23 June (2-6). Adm £5, chd free. Home-made teas. Visits also by arrangement Apr to Oct for groups of 10+. For group bookings more than a month in advance pre-payment requested.**

A plantswoman's 4 acres, more exuberant than manicured with River Enborne flowing through. Various areas of shrub and mixed borders create a romantic, naturalistic effect. Wonderful old walled garden. Long herbaceous border flanks wild flower meadow. Yr-round interest from early carpets of snowdrops and daffodils, crocus covered lawn, to autumn berries and leaf colour. A garden for all seasons. Wheelchair access to most areas. Guide dogs only.

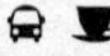

29 STOCKCROSS HOUSE

Church Road, Stockcross, Newbury, RG20 8LP. Susan & Edward Vandyk. *3m W of Newbury. M4 J13, A34(S). After 3m exit A4(W) to Hungerford. At 2nd r'about take B4000, 1m to Stockcross, 2nd L into Church Rd.* **Sun 2 June (11-5). Adm £5, chd free. Home-made teas.**

A delightful 2 acre garden set around a Grade II listed former rectory (not open), with an emphasis on naturalistic planting. Romantic wisteria and clematis covered pergola, reflecting pond with folly, rich variety of roses, vegetable and cutting garden. Orangery with vines. Pond with cascade and small stumpery with ferns. Sculptural elements by local artists. Partial wheelchair access with some gravelled areas.

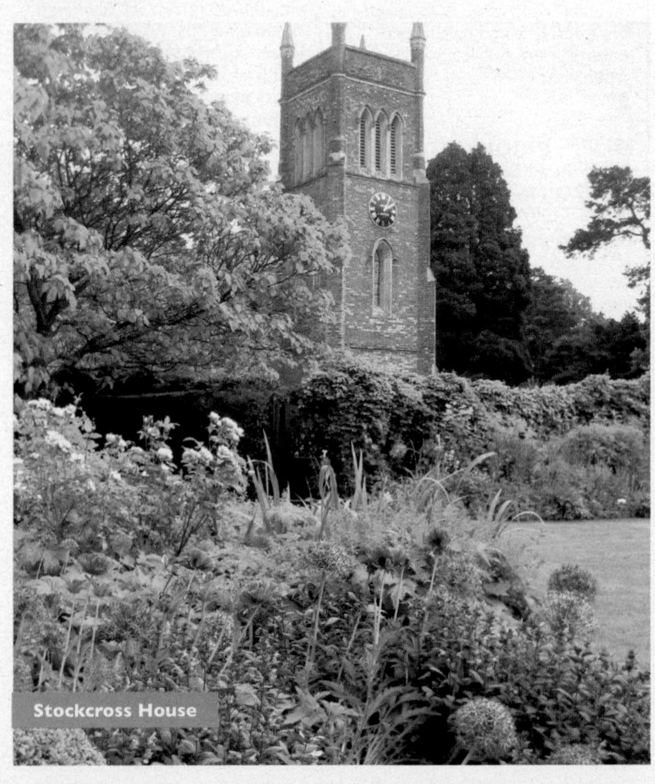

Stockcross House

30 STUBBINGS HOUSE

Stubbings Lane, Henley Road, Maidenhead, SL6 6QL. Mr & Mrs D Good, 01628 825454, info@stubbingsgroup.com, www.stubbingsnursery.co.uk. *2m W of Maidenhead. From A4130 Henley Rd follow signed private access road near Stubbings Church (on the opp side of the road). See website for further directions.* **Sat 9, Sun 10 Mar, Sat 25, Sun 26, Mon 27 May (10-3). Adm £3.50, chd free. Visits also by arrangement Mar to June for groups of 10 to 20.**

Parkland garden accessed via adjacent retail nursery. Set around C18 house (not open), home to Queen Wilhelmina of Netherlands in WW2. Large lawn with ha-ha and woodland walks. Notable trees incl historic cedars and araucaria. March brings an abundance of daffodils and in May a 60 metre wall of wisteria. Attractions incl a C18 icehouse and access to adjacent NT woodland. A level site with firm gravel paths for wheelchair access.

GROUP OPENING

31 SWALLOWFIELD VILLAGE GARDENS

The Street, Swallowfield, RG7 1QY. *5m S of Reading. From M4 J11 take A33 S. At 1st T-lights turn L on B3349 signed Swallowfield. In the village follow signs for parking. Purchase tickets & map in Swallowfield Medical Practice car park, opp Crown Pub.* **Sun 7 July (2-6). Combined adm £6, chd free. Home-made teas at Brambles.**

5 BEEHIVE COTTAGES
Ray Tormey.

BRAMBLES
Sarah & Martyn Dadds.

BROOKSIDE NURSERY
David Maskell.

GREENWINGS
Liz & Ray Jones.

LAMBS FARMHOUSE
Eva Koskuba.

LODDON LOWER FARM
Mr & Mrs J Bayliss.

WESSEX HOUSE
Val Payne.

This year Swallowfield is offering 7 gardens to visit and a few more gardens may open on the day. A number are in the village itself, others are nearby, so there is a mix of walking to some, with those in different directions needing a car or bicycle to reach them comfortably. Whilst each provides its own character and interest, they all nestle in countryside by the Whitewater, Blackwater and Loddon rivers with an abundance of wildlife and lovely views. The garden owners, many of whom are members of the local Horticultural Society, are always happy to chat and share their enthusiasm and experience. Plants for sale. Most gardens have wheelchair access, some have slopes.

32 ◆ WELFORD PARK

Welford, Newbury, RG20 8HU. Mrs J H Puxley, 01488 608691, snowdrops@welfordpark.co.uk, www.welfordpark.co.uk. *6m NW of Newbury. M4 J13, A34(S). After 3m exit for A4(W) to Hungerford. At 2nd r'about take B4000, after 4m turn R signed Welford. Entrance on Newbury-Lambourn road.* **For NGS: Thur 7 Feb (11-4). Adm £8, chd £4. Light refreshments.** **For other opening times and information, please phone, email or visit garden website.**

One of the finest natural snowdrop woodlands in the country, approx 4 acres, along with a wonderful display of hellebores throughout the garden and winter flowering shrubs. This is an NGS 1927 pioneer garden on the River Lambourn set around Queen Anne House (not open). Also the stunning setting for Great British Bake Off 2014 - 2018. Dogs welcome on leads. Coach parties please book in advance.

33 WILLOW TREE COTTAGE

Ashampstead, RG8 8RA. Katy & David Weston. *4m W of Pangbourne. From Yattendon, head towards Reading. Road forks L into beech wood to Ashampstead. Keep L & join lower road. ½m turn L after long fence just before houses.* **Sun 30 June (2-5). Combined adm with Pyt House £5, chd free. Home-made teas at Pyt House.**

Small pretty cottage garden surrounding the house (not open) that was originally built for the gardener of Pyt House. Substantially redesigned and replanted in recent yrs. Perennial borders, vegetable garden, pond with ducks and chickens. Most of the garden is accessible by wheelchair.

OPENING DATES

All entries subject to change. For latest information check **www.ngs.org.uk**

Map locator numbers are shown to the right of each garden name.

March

Sunday 24th
Wind in the Willows 52

Sunday 31st
Chesham Bois House 11

April

Sunday 21st
Overstroud Cottage 38

Monday 22nd
Aston Clinton Gardens 4

Sunday 28th
◆ Chenies Manor Gardens 10
Long Crendon Gardens 29

May

Sunday 5th
◆ Nether Winchendon House 35

Monday 6th
◆ Ascott 3
Turn End 46

Sunday 12th
The Plough 41

Tuesday 14th
Red Kites 42

Saturday 18th
Iver Environmental Centre 25

Sunday 19th
Hills House 22
Overstroud Cottage 38
Tythrop Park 47

Sunday 26th
Abbots House 1
Fressingwood 17
◆ Nether Winchendon House 35

Monday 27th
The Claydons 12
Glebe Farm 18
The Plough 41

June

Sunday 2nd
Cublington Gardens 15

Saturday 8th
◆ Cowper & Newton Museum Gardens 14

Sunday 9th
◆ Cowper & Newton Museum Gardens 14
Long Crendon Gardens 29
Overstroud Cottage 38
The White House 50

Saturday 15th
Iver Environmental Centre 25

Sunday 16th
Burrow Farm 8
Close Cottage 13
Hillesden House 21
Old Park Barn 37

Saturday 22nd
Acer Corner 2
11 The Paddocks 39

Sunday 23rd
Acer Corner 2
Aston Clinton Gardens 4
The Manor House 32
11 The Paddocks 39

Thursday 27th
NEW Bowers Farm 6

Saturday 29th
Little Missenden Gardens 28

Sunday 30th
Burrow Farm 8
Higher Denham Gardens 20
Little Missenden Gardens 28
Westend House 48

July

Saturday 6th
11 The Paddocks 39

Sunday 7th
Lowthorpe House 30
11 The Paddocks 39
The White House, Askett 49

Tuesday 16th
Red Kites 42

Saturday 20th
NEW St Michaels Convent 44

Saturday 27th
Iver Environmental Centre 25

August

Wednesday 7th
Danesfield House 16

Sunday 25th
◆ Nether Winchendon House 35

Monday 26th
◆ Ascott 3

September

Tuesday 3rd
◆ Chenies Manor Gardens 10

Friday 6th
NEW Lindengate 27

Sunday 8th
NEW Horatio's Garden 24
NEW Lindengate 27

Sunday 22nd
The Plough 41

October

Sunday 13th
◆ Stoke Poges Memorial Gardens 45

Saturday 19th
Acer Corner 2

Sunday 20th
Acer Corner 2

By Arrangement

Arrange a personalised garden visit with your club, or group of friends, on a date to suit you. See individual garden entries for full details.

Abbots House 1
Acer Corner 2
Beech House 5
18 Brownswood Road 7
Burrow Farm 8
Cedar House 9
Chesham Bois House 11
Close Cottage 13
Glebe Farm 18
Hall Barn 19
Hillesden House 21
Homelands 23
Kingsbridge Farm 26
Larkspur House, Cublington Gardens 15
Magnolia House 31
Moat Farm 33
Montana 34
North Down 36
Old Park Barn 37
Overstroud Cottage 38
11 The Paddocks 39
Peterley Corner Cottage 40
Red Kites 42
The Shades 43
20 Whitepit Lane 51
Wind in the Willows 52
Woodside 53

THE GARDENS

1 ABBOTS HOUSE

10 Church Street, Winslow, MK18 3AN. Mrs Jane Rennie, 01296 712326, jane@renniemail.com. 9m N of Aylesbury. A413 into Winslow. From town centre take Horn St & R into Church St, L fork at top. Entrance 20 metres on L. Parking in town centre & adjacent streets. **Sun 26 May (12-5). Adm £4, chd free. Home-made teas. Visits also by arrangement May to July for groups of 5 to 20.**

Behind red brick walls a ¾ acre garden on 4 different levels, each with unique planting and atmosphere. Lower lawn with white wisteria arbor and pond, upper lawn with rose pergola and woodland, pool area with grasses, Victorian kitchen garden and wild meadow. Spring bulbs in wild areas and woodland is a major feature in April, remaining areas peak in June/July. Late spring bulbs, water feature and many pots. Experimental wild areas. Some sculptures. Partial wheelchair access, garden levels accessed by steps. Guide dogs and medical-aid dogs only.

2 ACER CORNER

10 Manor Road, Wendover, HP22 6HQ. Jo Naiman, 07958 319234, jo@acercorner.com, www.acercorner.com. 3m S of Aylesbury. Follow A413 into Wendover. L at clock tower r'about into Aylesbury Rd. R at next r'about into Wharf Rd, continue past schools on L, garden on R. **Sat 22, Sun 23 June, Sat 19, Sun 20 Oct (2-5). Adm £3, chd free. Home-made teas. Visits also by arrangement May to Oct for groups of up to 20.** Donation to South Bucks Jewish Community Charity.

Garden designer's garden with Japanese influence and large collection of Japanese maples. The enclosed front garden is Japanese in style. Back garden is divided into three areas; patio area recently redesigned in the Japanese style; densely planted area with many acers and roses; and the corner which includes a productive greenhouse and interesting planting.

3 ◆ ASCOTT

Ascott, Wing, Leighton Buzzard, LU7 0PP. The National Trust, 01296 688242, amy@ascottestate.co.uk, www.ascottestate.co.uk. 2m SW of Leighton Buzzard, 8m NE of Aylesbury. Via A418. Buses: 150 Aylesbury - Milton Keynes, 100 Aylesbury & Milton Keynes. **For NGS: Mon 6 May, Mon 26 Aug (1-6). Adm £6, chd £3. Light refreshments. (NT members are required to pay to enter the gardens on NGS days).** For other opening times and information, please phone, email or visit garden website.

Combining Victorian formality with early C20 natural style and recent plantings to lead it into the C21, with a recently completed garden designed by Jacques and Peter Wirtz who designed the gardens at Alnwick Castle, and also a Richard Long sculpture. Terraced lawns with specimen and ornamental trees, panoramic views to the Chilterns. Naturalised bulbs, mirror image herbaceous borders, and impressive topiary incl box and yew sundial. Ascott House is closed on NGS Days. Outdoor wheelchairs available from car park. Mobility buggy, prior booking advised.

Your visits help change lives – we've donated over £16.7 million to Macmillan Cancer Support since 1984

GROUP OPENING

4 ASTON CLINTON GARDENS

Green End Street, Aston Clinton, Aylesbury, HP22 5JE. 3m E of Aylesbury. From Aylesbury take A41 E. At large r'about, continue straight (signed Aston Clinton). Continue onto London Rd. L at The Bell Pub, parking on Green End St & side roads. **Mon 22 Apr, Sun 23 June (2-5). Combined adm £4, chd free. Home-made teas at Lantern Cottage.**

101 GREEN END STREET
Sue Lipscomb.

THE LANTERN COTTAGE
Jacki Connell.

These two cottage gardens, one well established and the other having recently undergone a radical redesign by its new owner, share a basis of seasonal interest underpinned by evergreens and perennial planting. At The Lantern Cottage, spring hellebores and an abundance of tulips give way to an early summer display of roses, peonies, bearded iris, alliums and climbers including various clematis, wisteria and akebia. A wide selection of salvias and herbaceous perennials, mostly raised from seed and cuttings. Pelargoniums provide yr-round colour in the conservatory, and the greenhouse is always full! At 101, the new owner took up residence in autumn 2015, quickly establishing raised beds for vegetable production, a number of fruit trees and a variety of soft fruits. There is also a wildlife pond, an arbour overlooking the Victorian greenhouse, plus herbaceous borders, ornamental grasses surrounding a red kite sculpture, and varied container planting. Wildlife is encouraged to visit.

5 BEECH HOUSE

Long Wood Drive, Jordans, Beaconsfield, HP9 2SS. Sue & Ray Edwards, raychessmad@hotmail.com. From A40, L to Seer Green & Jordans for approx 1m. Turn into Jordans Way on R. Long Wood Drive 1st L. From A413 turn into Chalfont St Giles. Straight ahead until L signed Jordans. 1st L Jordans Way. **Visits by arrangement Mar to Nov for groups of up to 30. Adm £4, chd free.**

2 acre plantsman's garden built up over the last 31 yrs, with a wide range of plants in a variety of habitats providing yr-round interest. Many bulbs, perennials, shrubs, roses, ferns, and trees planted for their foliage, ornamental bark and autumn colour. Two wild meadows are a popular feature. Currently undertaking exciting replanting program. Wheelchair access dependent upon weather conditions.

6 NEW BOWERS FARM

Magpie Lane, Coleshill, HP7 0LU. John & Linda Daly. 2m S of Amersham & 3m N of Beaconsfield. Magpie Lane is off A355, by Harte & Magpies Pub. **Thur 27 June (12-5.30). Adm £5, chd free. Home-made teas.**

An established 5 acre garden that has undergone significant renovation over the past 5-6 yrs with trees, perennials, annuals and bulbs; creating a variety of planting spaces including herbaceous beds, ponds, kitchen and cutting garden, new bulb meadow, small woodland and open parkland areas.

7 18 BROWNSWOOD ROAD

Beaconsfield, HP9 2NU. John & Bernadette Thompson, 07879 282191, tbernadette60@gmail.com. From New Town turn R into Ledborough Lane, L into Sandleswood Rd, 2nd R into Brownswood Rd. **Visits by arrangement May to Sept for groups of up to 30. Tuesdays only. Payment in advance for groups. Adm £4, chd free. Home-made teas & gluten free options.**

A plant filled garden designed by Barbara Hunt. A harmonious arrangement of arcs and circles introduces a rhythm that leads through the garden. Sweeping box curves, gravel beds, brick edging and lush planting. A restrained use of purples and reds dazzle against a grey and green background. There has been considerable replanning and replanting during the winter.

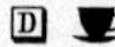

8 BURROW FARM

Hambleden, RG9 6LT. David Palmer, 01491 571256, davidvpalmer@msn.com. 1m SE of Hambleden. On A4155 between Henley & Marlow, turn N at Mill End. After 300yds, R onto Rotten Row. After ½ m Burrow Farm entrance on R. **Sun 16, Sun 30 June (11-4.30). Adm £5, chd free. Home-made teas. Visits also by arrangement May to July.**

Burrow Farm and the adjacent cottages (not open) are part Tudor and part Elizabethan, set in the Chilterns above Hambleden Valley where it meets the Thames. Views of pasture and woodlands across the ha-ha greatly enhance the setting. Special features are the parterre, arboretum and C15 barn, where home-made teas will be served.

9 CEDAR HOUSE

Bacombe Lane, Wendover, HP22 6EQ. Sarah Nicholson, 01296 622131, sarahhnicholson@btinternet.com. 5m SE Aylesbury. From Gt Missenden take A413 into Wendover. Take 1st L before row of cottages, house at top of lane. Parking for no more than 10 cars. **Visits by arrangement June to Sept for groups of 10+. No evening visits. Adm £4.50, chd free. Home-made teas.**

A plantsman's chalk garden in the Chiltern Hills with a great variety of trees, shrubs and plants. A sloping lawn leads to a natural swimming pond, with wild flowers including native orchids. A lodge greenhouse and a good collection of hardy plants in pots. Local artist sculptures can be viewed. Gently sloping lawn.

10 ◆ CHENIES MANOR GARDENS

Chenies, Rickmansworth, WD3 6ER. Boo Macleod Mathews, 07798 558150, enquiries@cheniesmanorhouse.co.uk, www.cheniesmanorhouse.co.uk. Between Little Chalfont & Chorleywood on A404. Take J18 off M25 & follow road L onto the A404 towards Amersham. **For NGS: Sun 28 Apr, Tue 3 Sept (2-5). Adm £7, chd £4. Home-made teas in the garden.** For other opening times and information, please phone, email or visit garden website.

C14/15 Manor House within award-winning gardens. Throughout the garden permanent herbaceous plantings are complemented by two distinct seasonal plantings for spring and summer. The gardens are divided into a series of compartments with various colour themes and structural forms, combining imaginative planting and beautiful plant associations. Physic garden, kitchen garden and yew maze. Tulip Festival 6th May, Dahlia Festival 26th August, Plant Fair 14th July. Wheelchair access to the tea room. Limited access to the gardens and no access to the house. Disabled WC.

11 CHESHAM BOIS HOUSE

85 Bois Lane, Chesham Bois, HP6 6DF. Julia Plaistowe, 01494 726476, julia.plaistowe@yahoo.co.uk, cheshamboishouse.co.uk. 1m N of Amersham-on-the-Hill. Follow Sycamore Rd (main shopping centre road of Amersham) which becomes Bois Lane. Do not use SatNav once in lane as you will be led astray. **Sun 31 Mar (1.30-5). Adm £4.50, chd free. Home-made teas. Visits also by arrangement Mar to Aug.**

3 acre plantswoman's garden with primroses, daffodils and hellebores in early spring. Interesting for most of the year with lovely herbaceous borders, rill with small ornamental canal, walled garden, old orchard with wildlife pond, and handsome trees of which some are topiaried. It is a peaceful oasis. Close to the garden the 800 yr old church can also be visited. Gravel in front of the house.

GROUP OPENING

12 THE CLAYDONS

East Botolph and Middle Claydon, MK18 2ND. 1½m SW Winslow. In Winslow turn R off High St, by the Bell Pub & follow NT signs towards Claydon House & The Claydons. **Mon 27 May (2-6). Combined adm £5, chd free. Home-made teas in village hall.**

CLAYDON COTTAGE
Mr & Mrs Tony Evans.

THE OLD RECTORY
Mrs Jane Meisl.

THE OLD VICARAGE
Nigel & Esther Turnbull.

4 STATION COTTAGES
Andrew & Alison Fenner.

Three small villages, originally part of the Claydon Estate with typical north Buckinghamshire cottages and two C13 churches. The Old Vicarage, a large garden on clay with mixed borders, scented garden, dell, shrub roses, vegetables and a natural clay pond. Small meadow area and planting to encourage wildlife and beehives. A free children's quiz. Access via gravel drive. Claydon Cottage has many quirky features and surprises. The Old Rectory is a large garden with a wildflower meadow, herbaceous borders, a woodland walk and cloud hedging. 4 Station Cottages is a small, perfectly formed garden sculptured out of the railway embankment. No wheelchair access at 4 Station Cottages.

13 CLOSE COTTAGE

Church Lane, Soulbury, Leighton Buzzard, LU7 0BU. Rachel Belsham & Daniel Storey, belshamstorey@btinternet.com. Approx 3m NW of Leighton Buzzard. In centre of village, next to field below church, on lane leading uphill opp The Boot Pub. Open day: parking in field opp, clearly signed. Private visits: parking on drive and up lane. **Sun 16 June (1.30-6). Adm £5, chd free. Home-made teas. Visits also by arrangement Apr to July for groups of 10+.**

The 3 acre garden at Close Cottage is 17 yrs old and encompasses a formal terraced garden, orchard and paddock. The garden is laid to lawn and planted with a wide variety of shrubs, bulbs and perennials. The orchard incl an avenue of cherry trees, various fruit trees, a wild flower meadow, woodland area, vegetable beds and a cutting garden.

14 ◆ COWPER & NEWTON MUSEUM GARDENS

Orchard Side, Market Place, Olney, MK46 4AJ. Anne Kempson, 01234 711833, www.cowperandnewtonmuseum.org.uk. 5m N of Newport Pagnell. 12m S of Wellingborough. On A509. Please park in public car park in East St. **For NGS: Sat 8, Sun 9 June (10.30-4.30). Adm £3, chd free. Home-made teas.** For other opening times and information, please phone or visit garden website.

The tranquil Flower Garden of C18 poet William Cowper, who said 'Gardening was of all employments, that in which I succeeded best', has plants introduced prior to his death in 1800, many mentioned in his writings. The Summer House Garden with Cowper's 'verse manufactory', now a Victorian Kitchen Garden, has new and heritage vegetables organically grown, also a herb border and medicinal plant bed. Features incl lacemaking demonstrations and local artists painting live art on both days. Georgian dancers on Sun. Mostly hard paths.

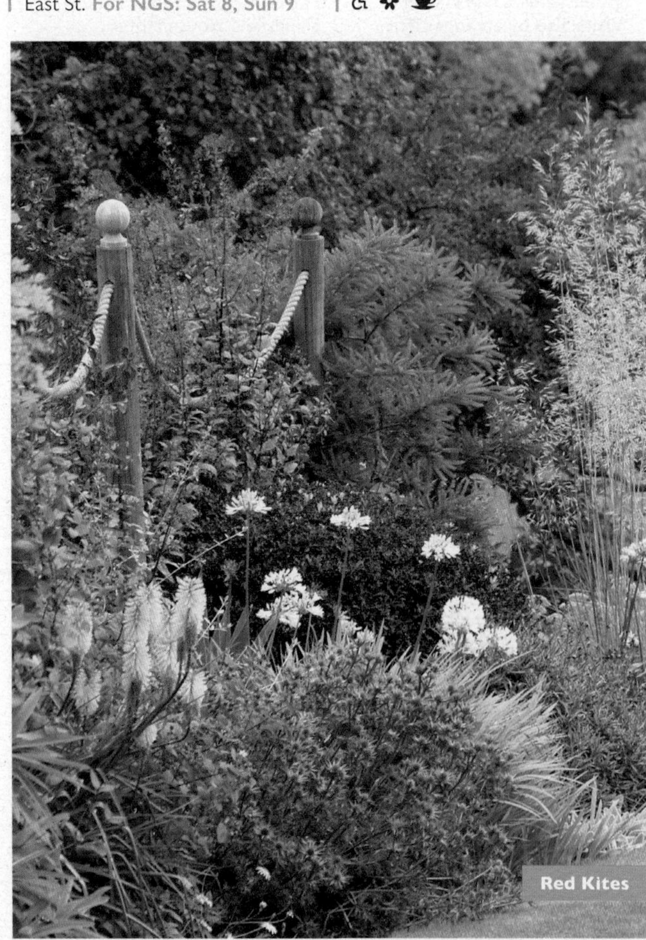

Red Kites

GROUP OPENING

15 CUBLINGTON GARDENS

Cublington, Leighton Buzzard, LU7 0LF. 5m SE Winslow, 5m NE Aylesbury. From Aylesbury take A413 Buckingham Rd. After 4m, at Whitchurch, turn R to Cublington. **Sun 2 June (2-6). Combined adm £4, chd free. Home-made teas in Biggs Pavilion, Orchard Ground.**

CHERRY COTTAGE, 3 THE WALLED GARDEN
Gwyneira Waters.

LARKSPUR HOUSE
Mr & Mrs S Jenkins, 01296 682615, gstmusketeers3@aol.com. **Visits also by arrangement June & July for groups of 10 to 20.**

OLD MANOR COTTAGE
Mr & Mrs J Packer.

1 STEWKLEY ROAD
Tom & Helen Gadsby.

A group of diverse gardens in this attractive Buckinghamshire village listed as a conservation area. Cherry Cottage is adapted for wheelchair gardening with raised beds and artificial grass. Larkspur House is a beautifully maintained modern garden with hostas and alliums being firm favourites. It has a large, newly planted orchard and wild flower meadow. 1 Stewkley Road has a strong focus on homegrown food with an idyllic organic kitchen garden, small orchard and courtyard garden. Old Manor Cottage, a garden with emphasis on recycling! Partial wheelchair access to some gardens.

♿ ☕

16 DANESFIELD HOUSE

Henley Road, Marlow, SL7 2EY. Danesfield House Hotel, 01628 891010, amoorin@danesfieldhouse.co.uk, www.danesfieldhouse.co.uk. 3m from Marlow. On the A4155 between Marlow & Henley-on-Thames. Signed on the LH-side Danesfield House Hotel & Spa. **Wed 7 Aug (10-4). Adm £4.50, chd free. Pre-booking essential for lunch & afternoon tea.**

The gardens at Danesfield were completed in 1901 by Robert Hudson, the Sunlight Soap magnate who built the house. Since the house opened as a hotel in 1991, the gardens have been admired by several thousand guests each yr. However, in 2009 it was discovered that the gardens contained outstanding examples of pulhamite in both the formal gardens and the waterfall areas. The 100 yr old topiary is also outstanding. Part of the grounds incl an Iron Age fort. Guided tours welcome on NGS open days. You may wander the grounds on your own or there will be two 1hr tours offered by our Head Gardener at 10.30am and 1.30pm for 30 max per tour. Pre-booking essential due to high demand. The gardeners will be available for questions after each tour. Gravel paths throughout the garden.

♿ 🛏 ☕

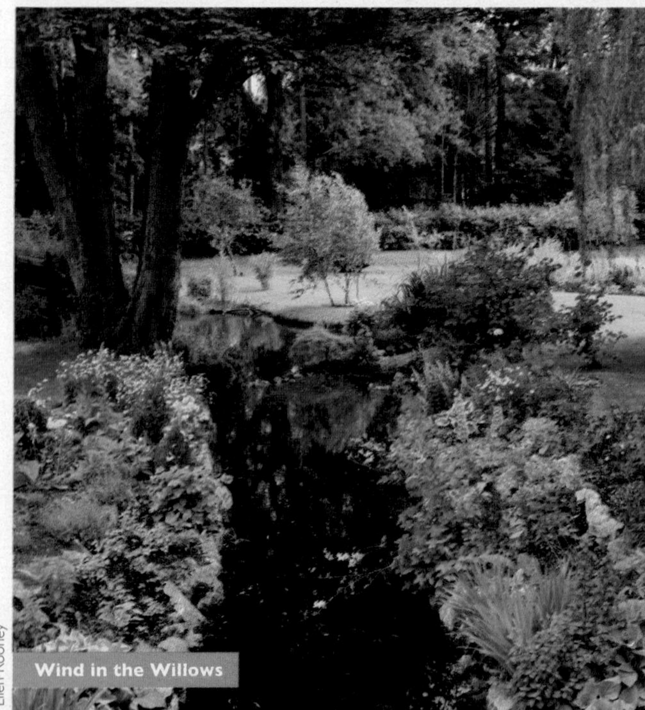
Wind in the Willows

© Ellen Rooney

17 FRESSINGWOOD

Hare Lane, Little Kingshill, Great Missenden, HP16 0EF. John & Maggie Bateson. 1m S of Gt Missenden, 4m W of Amersham. From the A413 at Chiltern Hospital, turn L signed Gt & Lt Kingshill. Take 1st L into Nags Head Lane. Turn R under railway bridge, then L into New Rd & continue to Hare Lane. **Sun 26 May (2-5.30). Adm £4, chd free. Home-made teas.**

Thoughtfully designed garden with yr-round colour and many interesting features. Shrubbery with ferns, hostas, grasses and hellebores. Small formal garden, herb garden, pergolas with roses, clematis and wisteria. Topiary and landscaped terrace. Newly developed area incorporating water with grasses. Herbaceous borders and bonsai collection. Children's quiz.

✽ ☕

18 GLEBE FARM

Lillingstone Lovell, Buckingham, MK18 5BB. Mr David Hilliard, 01280 860384, thehilliards@talk21.com, www.glebefarmbarn.co.uk. Off A413, 5m N of Buckingham &

2m S of Whittlebury. From A5 at Potterspury, turn off A5 & follow signs to Lillingstone Lovell. Mon 27 May (1-5). Adm £3.50, chd free. Cream teas. **Visits also by arrangement May to July for groups of 10 to 20.**
A large cottage garden with an exuberance of colourful planting and winding gravel paths, amongst lawns and herbaceous borders on two levels. Ponds, a wishing well, vegetable beds, a knot garden, a small walled garden and an old tractor feature. Everything combines to make a beautiful garden full of surprises.

19 HALL BARN

Windsor End, Beaconsfield, HP9 2SG. Mrs Farncombe, jenefer@farncombe01.demon.co.uk. ½m S of Beaconsfield. Lodge gate 300yds S of St Mary & All Saints' Church in Old Town centre. Please do not use SatNav. Visits by arrangement Feb to Oct. Home-made teas for groups of 10+ only. Adm £5, chd free.
Historical landscaped garden laid out between 1680-1730 for the poet Edmund Waller and his descendants. Features 300 yr old cloud formation yew hedges, formal lake and vistas ending with classical buildings and statues. Wooded walks around the grove offer respite from the heat on sunny days. One of the original NGS garden openings of 1927. Chiltern Shakespeare Company open-air performances of Midsummer Night's Dream in the garden Wed 12-Sat 22 June. Information provided. Gravel paths, but certain areas can be accessed by car for those with limited mobility.

Your visits help change lives – your generosity has supported unpaid carers through donations to Carers Trust totalling over £3.9 million since 1996

GROUP OPENING

20 HIGHER DENHAM GARDENS

Higher Denham, UB9 5EA. 6m E of Beaconsfield. Turn off A412, approx ½m N of junction with A40 into Old Rectory Lane. After 1m enter Higher Denham straight ahead. Tickets for all gardens available at the community hall, 70yds into the village. Sun 30 June (2-5.30). Combined adm £6, chd free. Home-made teas in the community hall. Donation to Higher Denham Community CIO (Garden Upkeep Fund).

9 LOWER ROAD
Mrs Patricia Davidson.

25 LOWER ROAD
Mr & Mrs Malham.

30 LOWER ROAD
Mr & Mrs Mike Macgowan.

19 MIDDLE ROAD
Sonia Harris.

5 SIDE ROAD
Jane Blythe.

WIND IN THE WILLOWS
Ron James.
(See separate entry)

At least 6 gardens will open in 2019 in the delightful Misbourne chalk stream valley. Wind in the Willows has over 350 shrubs and trees, informal woodland and wild gardens incl riverside and bog plantings and a collection of 80 hostas and 12 striped roses in 3 acres. 'Really different' was a typical visitor comment. The garden at 5 Side Road is medium sized with lawns, borders and shrubs, and many features which children will love. 9 Lower Road is a small garden backing onto the river. Recently professionally designed, it is now maturing and has new shrubs. 25 Lower Road front garden has been completely redesigned with raised beds, richly filled with plants and shrubs to create a vibrant instant garden, reminiscent of the way it is done in some TV programmes. Open first in 2018, it was greatly admired 30 Lower Road is a well-stocked garden with charm and character including a wartime underground bunker! 19 Middle Road with contrasting dry front and damper back garden is reopening this yr. In June the owner of Wind in the Willows will lead optional guided tours of the garden starting at 2.30pm and 4pm. Tours last approx 1 hour. Limited wheelchair access to some gardens.

21 HILLESDEN HOUSE

Church End, Hillesden, MK18 4DB. Mr & Mrs R M Faccenda, 01296 730451, suef@faccenda.co.uk. 3m S of Buckingham through Gawcott. Next to church in Hillesden. Sun 16 June (2-5). Adm £6, chd free. Home-made teas. **Visits also by arrangement June & July for groups of 20+.**
By superb church Cathedral in the Fields. Carp lakes, fountains and waterfalls with mature trees. Rose, alpine and herbaceous borders with 80 acres of deer park. Wild flower areas and extensive lakes developed by the owner. Lovely walks and plenty of wildlife. Also a woodland area and vegetable garden with raised beds. The orchard was created 3 yrs ago. Vines were planted last yr. All Saints Church is open and well worth a visit. No wheelchair access to lakes.

22 HILLS HOUSE

Village Road, Denham Village, UB9 5BH. Mr & Mrs B Savory. Turn off M40 J1A towards London. Turn L at T-lights, stay in middle lane, turn L at r'about & stay in RH lane. Follow sign Village Only & follow road ¼m. Turn L over bridge, next to St Mary's Church. Sun 19 May (2-5). Adm £4, chd free. Home-made teas.
A C16, 3 acre garden in Denham Village with an impressive collection of majestic specimen trees, walled garden and designated shrub borders. A large rose garden and perennial border frame a sunken buxus parterre, and annual display of baskets that flow to an orchard on long gravel paths. Walk through serene areas and woodland plantings, with a spring display of bulbs underneath mature trees. No wheelchair access to sunken parterre area. Gravel paths.

23 HOMELANDS

Springs Lane, Ellesborough, Aylesbury, HP17 0XD. Jean & Tony Young, 01296 622306, young.ellesborough@gmail.com. 6m SE of Aylesbury. On the B4010 between Wendover & Princes Risborough. Springs Lane is between village hall at Butlers Cross & the church. Narrow lane with an uneven surface. **Visits by arrangement May to Aug. Adm £4, chd free. Light refreshments.**

Secluded ¾ acre garden on difficult chalk, adjoining open countryside. Designed to be enjoyed from many seating positions. Progress from semi-formal to wild flower meadow and wildlife pond. Deep borders with all season interest, and gravel beds with exotic late summer and autumn planting.

24 NEW HORATIO'S GARDEN

National Spinal Injury Centre (NSIC), Stoke Mandeville Hospital, Mandeville Road, Stoke Mandeville, Aylesbury, HP21 8AL. Jacqui Martin-Lof, www.horatiosgarden.org.uk. The closest car park to Horatio's Garden at Stoke Mandeville Hospital is Car Park B, opp Asda. **Sun 8 Sept (2-5). Adm £5, chd free. Home-made teas in the Garden Room.**

Opened in Sept 2018, Horatio's Garden at the National Spinal Injury Centre, Stoke Mandeville Hospital is designed by Joe Swift. The fully accessible garden for patients with spinal injuries has been part funded by the NGS. The beautiful space is cleverly designed to bring the sights, sounds and scents of nature into the heart of the NHS. Everything is high quality and carefully designed to bring benefit to patients who spend months in hospital after a spinal injury. The garden features an incredible garden room designed by architect Andrew Wells. Meet the Head Gardener and volunteer team and taste our delicious tea and home-made cake! The garden is fully accessible, having been designed specifically for patients in wheelchairs or hospital beds.

D

25 IVER ENVIRONMENTAL CENTRE

Slough Road, Iver, SL0 0EB. Ruth Shelton, Iverenvironmentcentre.org. Between Slough & Uxbridge. At Black Horse r'about take Slough Rd (A4007) to Uxbridge. **Sat 18 May, Sat 15 June, Sat 27 July (10-4). Adm £4, chd free. Cream teas.**

The gardens at Iver Environment Centre are a hidden gem. A visual treat awaits you at every turn as you explore our 4½ acre site. Our winding pathways lead you through woodland, allotments, an orchard and a sensory garden. Embark on your own secret garden adventure past ponds, through willow tunnels and into our rainforest polytunnel. You can even try navigating your way through our hedge maze.
If that is not for you then why not enjoy the view on our raised decking where tea is served.

26 KINGSBRIDGE FARM

Steeple Claydon, MK18 2EJ. Mr & Mrs T Aldous, 01296 730224. 3m S of Buckingham. Halfway between Padbury & Steeple Claydon. Xrds with sign to Kingsbridge Only. **Visits by arrangement Apr to July for groups of 10+. Adm £6, chd free. Home-made teas in our cosy, converted barn.**

Stunning and exceptional 6 acre garden imaginatively created over last 30 yrs. Main lawn is enclosed by softly, curving, colour themed herbaceous borders, and many roses and shrubs interestingly planted with cleverly created landscaping features. Clipped topiary yews, pleached hornbeams lead out to the ha-ha and countryside beyond. A natural stream with bog plants and nesting kingfishers, meanders serenely through woodland gardens, with many walks. A garden always evolving, to visit again and again.

27 NEW LINDENGATE

The Old Allotment Site, Worlds End Garden Centre, Aylesbury Road, Wendover, HP22 6BD. Lindengate Charity, www.lindengate.org.uk. 4m SE of Aylesbury on A413. Turn into Worlds End Garden Centre (Wyevale), Lindengate on LH-side. **Evening opening Fri 6 Sept (6-8). Wine. Sun 8 Sept (2-5). Home-made teas. Adm £4.50, chd free.**

Lindengate's mission statement is to 'Foster an improved state of mental health and wellbeing through the healing power of nature and horticulture'. The charity's 5 acre site, has been developed into a series of wild spaces in synergy with more formalised gardens and is described as an oasis in a busy world. It successfully supports many people on their road to recovery. The garden has a sensory garden which includes a log wall, stumpery and various sensory experiences including waterball and rill.
Accessible refreshment and welfare facilities, and 60% of the site has accessible pathways.

Turn End

GROUP OPENING

28 LITTLE MISSENDEN GARDENS

Amersham, HP7 0RD. On A413 between Great Missenden & Old Amersham. **Sat 29, Sun 30 June (2-5.30). Combined adm £6, chd free. Home-made teas.**

BOURN'S MEADOW
Roger & Sandra Connor.
Open on all dates

HOLLYDYKE HOUSE
Bob & Sandra Wetherall.
Open on all dates

KINGS BARN
Mr & Mrs A Playle.
Open on all dates

LITTLE MISSENDEN CE INFANT SCHOOL
Laura Lee.
Open on Sat 29 June

MANOR FARM HOUSE
Evan Bazzard.
Open on all dates

MILL HOUSE
Terry & Eleanor Payne.
Open on all dates

MISSENDEN LODGE
Rob & Carol Kimber.
Open on all dates

NEW **ORCHARD COTTAGE**
Peter & Jeannie MacEwan.
Open on all dates

TOWN FARM COTTAGE
Mr & Mrs Tim Garnham.
Open on all dates

THE WHITE HOUSE
Mr & Mrs Harris.
Open on all dates

A variety of gardens set in this attractive Chiltern village in an area of outstanding natural beauty. You can start off at one end of the village and wander through stopping off halfway for tea at the beautiful Anglo-Saxon church built in 975. The church has recently received a lottery grant for restoration and many medieval wall paintings have been found. Tours will be given of these discoveries. The gardens reflect different style houses including several old cottages, a Mill House and a more modern house. There are herbaceous borders, shrubs, trees, old fashioned roses, hostas, topiary, koi and lily ponds, kitchen gardens, play areas for children and the River Misbourne runs through a few. Some gardens are highly colourful and others just green and peaceful. Beekeeper at Hollydyke House. Partial wheelchair access to some gardens due to gravel paths and steps.

GROUP OPENING

29 LONG CRENDON GARDENS

Long Crendon, HP18 9AN. Long Crendon village is situated on the B4011 Thame-Bicester road, 2m N of Thame. Maps showing the location of the gardens will be available at each garden & at Church House in the High St. **Sun 28 Apr, Sun 9 June (2-6). Combined adm £6, chd free. Home-made teas at Church House (Apr & June) & Lopemead Farm (June only, for NGS).**

BAKER'S CLOSE
Mr & Mrs Peter Vaines.
Open on Sun 28 Apr

BARRY'S CLOSE
Mr & Mrs Richard Salmon.
Open on Sun 28 Apr

COP CLOSE
Sandra & Tony Phipkin.
Open on Sun 9 June

25 ELM TREES
Carol & Mike Price.
Open on all dates

NEW **27 ELM TREES**
Viv Gardiner.
Open on Sun 28 Apr

NEW **LOPEMEAD FARM**
Wendy Thompson & Bryony Rixon.
Open on Sun 9 June

MANOR HOUSE
Mr & Mrs West.
Open on Sun 28 Apr

TOMPSONS FARM
Mr & Mrs T Moynihan.
Open on Sun 9 June

Five gardens will open on Sun 28 April. Baker's Close, partly walled with terraced lawns, rockery, shrubs and wild area. 1000's of daffodils, narcissi and tulips. Barry's Close, a collection of spring flowering trees, borders, pools and a water garden. 25 Elm Trees, cottage style organic garden with a large selection of spring bulbs, flowering trees and shrubs, wildlife pond and orchard area. 27 Elm Trees, new for 2019 is a medium size family garden with late flowering tulips and spring flowers grown from seed. Manor House, a large garden with views towards the Chilterns, two ornamental lakes and a large variety of spring bulbs and shrubs. Four gardens will open on Sun 9 June. Cop Close, a 1⅓ acre garden with vegetables, cutting garden and borders. 25 Elm Trees with deep borders, roses, clematis and herbaceous plants. New for 2019, Lopemead Farm with formal courtyard garden, raised beds, vegetables and flower borders. Tompsons Farm a large woodland garden with mature trees and lake. Partial wheelchair access to some gardens.

30 LOWTHORPE HOUSE

Crowbrook Road, Askett, Princes Risborough, HP27 9LS. Margaret & John Higgins. 100 metre down Crowbrook Rd (north end) on LH-side. **Sun 7 July (2-5). Combined adm with The White House, Askett £5, chd free. Home-made teas.**

The narrow hornbeam-lined drive leads to a sunny, secluded ⅔ acre garden, tucked away in the conservation area of Askett. Emphasis is on flowers in deep herbaceous borders; soft-fruit cage, tree area, fern garden and grasses. Front garden remodelled for 2019 to reflect Mediterranean style.

Your visits help change lives – we are Hospice UK's largest charitable funder donating more than £5 million to support hospices in local communities since 1996

31 MAGNOLIA HOUSE

Wooburn, HP10 0QD. Elaine & Alan Ford, 01628 525818, lanforddesigns@gmail.com. On A4094 2m SW of A40 between Bourne End & Wooburn. From Wooburn Church, direction Maidenhead, Grange Drive is on L before r'about. From Bourne End, L at 2 mini-r'abouts, then 1st R. **Visits by arrangement Feb to Aug. Combined with The Shades. Light refreshments.**

½ acre garden with mature trees incl copper beech and magnolia. Cacti, fernery, stream, ponds, greenhouses, aviaries, 10,000 snowdrops, hellebores, bluebells and over 60 hostas. Child friendly. Constantly being updated. Partial wheelchair access.

32 THE MANOR HOUSE

(Off Perry Lane), Bledlow, Nr Princes Risborough, HP27 9PB. The Lord Carrington. 9m NW of High Wycombe, 3m SW of Princes Risborough. ½m off B4009 in middle of Bledlow village. SatNav directions HP27 9PA. **Sun 23 June (2-5). Adm £6, chd free. Light refreshments.**

Paved garden, parterres, shrub borders, old roses and walled kitchen garden. Water garden with paths, bridges and walkways fed by 14 chalk springs, plus 2 acres of landscaped planting. Sculpture garden. Partial wheelchair access as there is stepped access or sloped grass to enter the gardens.

33 MOAT FARM

Water Lane, Ford, Aylesbury, HP17 8XD. Patricia Bergqvist, 01296 748560, patricia@quintadelarosa.com. Turn up Water Lane by Dinton Hermit in the middle of Ford village, after approx 200yds, turn L over cattle grid between beech hedges into Moat Farm. **Visits by arrangement Apr to Sept for groups of 5 to 20. Home-made teas.**

A country garden with herbaceous borders, roses, hostas, trees and water. A moat that flows through the garden and a blind moat through the arboretum. Small walled garden.

34 MONTANA

Shire Lane, Cholesbury, HP23 6NA. Diana Garner, 01494 758347, montana@cholesbury.net. 3m NW of Chesham. Leave A41 signed A4251 Northchurch. Follow Wigginton signs & turn R before church. Turn R after Champneys, 2nd R onto Shire Lane & Montana is ½m on L. **Visits by arrangement Mar to July. Adm £3.50, chd free. Home-made teas. Wine available for evening visits.**

The garden started being created in 1995, and is now an acre of densely planted areas leading to 3 acres of peaceful woodland with level paths and lots of seats. There are many special trees and shrubs planted in the herbaceous borders giving contrasting leaf colour and form. Montana is an unmanicured woodland country garden with bees, chickens, vegetable patch, fernery and greenhouses. It is a happy, relaxing area which visitors invariably enjoy and find interesting.

35 ◆ NETHER WINCHENDON HOUSE

Nether Winchendon, Thame, Aylesbury, HP18 0DY. Mr Robert Spencer Bernard, 01844 290101, Contactus@netherwinchendonhouse.com, www.netherwinchendonhouse.com. 6m SW of Aylesbury, 6m from Thame. Approx 4m from Thame on A418, turn 1st L to Cuddington, turn L at Xrds, downhill turn R & R again to parking by house. **For NGS: Sun 5, Sun 26 May, Sun 25 Aug (2-5.30). Adm £4, chd free. Cream teas at church on 5 May & 25 Aug only.** For other opening times and information, please phone, email or visit garden website.

Nether Winchendon House has fine and rare trees, set in a stunning landscape surrounded by parkland, with 7 acres of lawned grounds running down to the River Thame. A Founder NGS Member (1927). Enchanting and romantic Mediaeval and Tudor House, one of the most romantic of the historic houses of England and Grade I listed. Picturesque small village with an interesting church. Unfenced riverbank.

36 NORTH DOWN

Dodds Lane, Chalfont St Giles, HP8 4EL. Merida Saunders, 01494 872928. 4m SE of Amersham, 4m NE of Beaconsfield. Opp the green in centre of village, at Costa turn into UpCorner onto Silver Hill. At top of hill fork R into Dodds Lane. North Down is 7th on L. **Visits by arrangement May to Aug for groups of up to 30. Adm £4, chd free.**

A passion for gardening is evident in this plantswomans lovely ¾ acre garden which has evolved over the yrs with scenic effect in mind. Colourful and interesting throughout the yr. Large grassed areas with island beds of mixed perennials, shrubs and some unusual plants. Variety of rhododendrons, azaleas, acers and clematis. Displays of sempervivum, alpines, grasses and ferns. Small patio and water feature, greenhouse and an Italianate front patio to owner's design.

37 OLD PARK BARN

Dag Lane, Stoke Goldington, MK16 8NY. Emily & James Chua, 01908 551093, emilychua@yahoo.com. 4m N of Newport Pagnell on B526. Park on High St. A short walk up Dag Lane. Limited disabled parking near garden via Orchard Way. **Sun 16 June (2-5). Adm £4.50, chd free. Home-made teas. Visits also by arrangement in June for groups of 10+.**

We made a garden from a rough field of just under 3 acres, 21 yrs ago. Near the house a series of terraces cut into the sloping site, create the formal garden with long and cross vistas, lawns and deep borders. The aim is to provide interest throughout the yr with naturalistic planting and views borrowed from the surrounding countryside. Beyond is a wildlife pond, meadow and woodland garden. Partial wheelchair access.

38 OVERSTROUD COTTAGE

The Dell, Frith Hill, Gt Missenden, HP16 9QE. Mr & Mrs Jonathan Brooke, 01494 862701, susanmbrooke@outlook.com. ½m E Gt Missenden. Turn E off A413

at Gt Missenden onto B485 Frith Hill to Chesham Rd. White Gothic cottage set back in lay-by 100yds uphill on L. Parking on R at church. **Sun 21 Apr, Sun 19 May, Sun 9 June (2-5). Adm £4, chd free. Cream teas at parish church. Visits also by arrangement Apr to June for groups of 20 to 30.**
Artistic chalk garden on two levels. Collection of C17/C18 plants incl auriculars, hellebores, bulbs, pulmonarias, peonies, geraniums, herbs and succulents. Many antique, species and rambling roses. Potager and lily pond. Cottage was once C17 fever house for Missenden Abbey. Features incl a garden studio with painting exhibition (share of flower painting proceeds to NGS).

39 11 THE PADDOCKS

Wendover, HP22 6HE. Mr & Mrs E Rye, 01296 623870, pam.rye@talktalk.net. 5m from Aylesbury on A413. From Aylesbury turn L at mini-r'about onto Wharf Rd. From Gt Missenden turn L at the Clock Tower, then R at mini-r'about onto Wharf Rd. **Sat 22, Sun 23 June, Sat 6, Sun 7 July (2-5). Adm £3, chd free. Visits also by arrangement June & July for groups of 20 to 30.** Donation to Bonnie People in South Africa.
Small peaceful garden with mixed borders of colourful herbaceous perennials, a special show of David Austin roses and a large variety of spectacular named Blackmore and Langdon delphiniums. A tremendous variety of colour in a small area. The White Garden with a peaceful arbour, The Magic of Moonlight created for the BBC. Most of the garden can be viewed from the lawn.

40 PETERLEY CORNER COTTAGE

Perks Lane, Prestwood, Great Missenden, HP16 0JH. Dawn Philipps, 01494 862198, dawn.philipps@googlemail.com. Turn into Perks Lane from Wycombe Rd (A4128), Peterley Corner Cottage is the 3rd house on the L. **Visits by arrangement May to Aug for groups of 10 to 30. Adm £4.50, chd free. Light refreshments.**
A 3 acre mature garden, incl an acre of wild flowers and indigenous trees. Surrounded by tall hedges and a wood, the garden has evolved over the last 30 yrs. There are many specimen trees and mature roses incl a Paul's Himalaya Musk and a Kiftsgate. A large herbaceous border runs alongside the formal lawns with other borders like heathers and shrubs. The most recent addition is a potager.

41 THE PLOUGH

Chalkshire Road, Terrick, Aylesbury, HP17 0TJ. John & Sue Stewart. 2m W of Wendover. Entrance to garden & car park signed off B4009 Nash Lee Rd. 200yds E of Terrick r'about. Access to garden from field car park. **Sun 12, Mon 27 May, Sun 22 Sept (1-5). Adm £4, chd free. Home-made teas.**
Formal garden with open views to the Chiltern countryside. Designed as a series of outdoor rooms around a listed former C18 inn (not open), incl border, parterre, vegetable and fruit gardens, and a newly planted orchard. Delicious home-made teas in our barn and adjacent entrance courtyard. Jams and apple juice for sale, made with fruits from the garden.

42 RED KITES

46 Haw Lane, Bledlow Ridge, HP14 4JJ. Mag & Les Terry, 01494 481474, lesterry747@gmail.com. 4m S of Princes Risborough. Off A4010 halfway between Princes Risborough & West Wycombe. At Hearing Dogs sign in Saunderton turn into Haw Lane, then ¾ m on L up the hill. **Tue 14 May, Tue 16 July (2-5). Adm £4, chd free. Home-made teas. Visits also by arrangement May to Aug for groups of 20+.**
This much admired 1½ acre Chiltern hillside garden is planted for yr-round interest and is lovingly maintained with mixed and herbaceous borders, wild flower orchard, established pond, vegetable garden, managed woodland area and a lovely hidden garden. Many climbers used throughout the garden which changes significantly through the seasons. Sit and enjoy the superb views from the top terrace.

The White House, Little Missenden Gardens

43 THE SHADES

High Wycombe, HP10 0QD. Pauline & Maurice Kirkpatrick, 01628 522540. On A4094 2m SW of A40 between Bourne End & Wooburn. From Wooburn Church, direction Maidenhead, Grange Drive is on L before r'about. From Bourne End, L at 2 mini-r'abouts, then 1st R. **Visits by arrangement Feb to Aug. Combined with Magnolia House. Light refreshments at Magnolia House.**

The Shades drive is approached through mature trees, areas of shade loving plants, beds of shrubs, 60 various roses and herbaceous plants. The rear garden with natural well surrounded by plants, shrubs and acers. A green slate water feature and scree garden with alpine plants completes the garden. Partial wheelchair access.

44 NEW ST MICHAELS CONVENT

Vicarage Way, Gerrards Cross, SL9 8AT. Sisters of the Church. 15mins walk from Gerrards Cross station. 10mins from East Common buses. Limited parking at convent. **Sat 20 July (2-4.30). Adm by donation. Tea.**

Newly acquired garden, having been neglected for many years, is now being developed by the community as a place for quiet and reflection. Includes a walled garden which will have vegetables, a woodland dell with trees and ferns and a recently built chapel. Come at the beginning as we start and see the garden grow!

45 ◆ STOKE POGES MEMORIAL GARDENS

Church Lane, Stoke Poges, Slough, SL2 4NZ. South Bucks District Council, 01753 523744, memorial.gardens@southbucks.gov.uk, www.southbucks.gov.uk/stokepogesmemorialgardens. 1m N of Slough, 4m S of Gerrards Cross. Follow signs to Stoke Poges & from there to the Memorial Gardens. Car park opp main entrance, disabled visitor parking in the gardens. Weekend disabled access through churchyard. **For NGS: Sun 13 Oct (1.30-4.30). Adm £4.50, chd free. Home-made teas.** For other opening

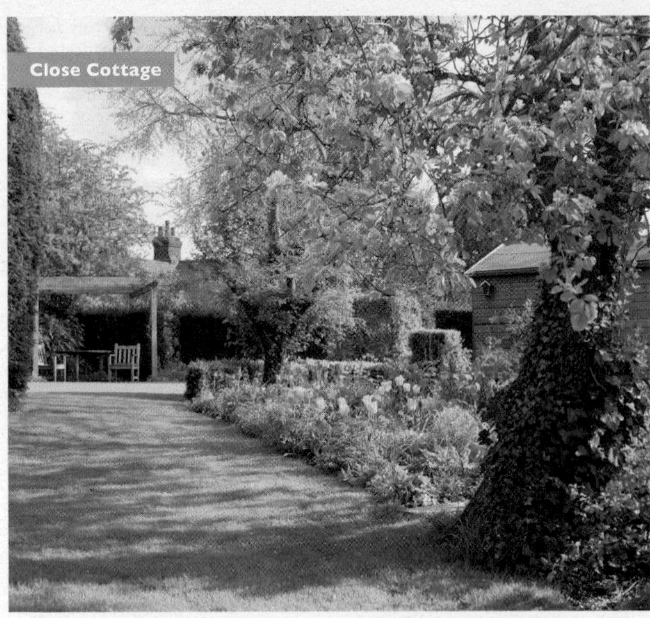

Close Cottage

times and information, please phone, email or visit garden website.

Unique 20 acre Grade I registered garden constructed 1934-9. Rock and water gardens, sunken colonnade, rose garden, 500 individual gated gardens. Lovely autumn colours around the gardens and especially in the rock garden. Guided tours every half hour. Guide dogs only.

46 TURN END

Townside, Haddenham, Aylesbury, HP17 8BG. Peter & Margaret Aldington, turnendtrustevents@gmail.com, www.turnend.org.uk. 3m NE of Thame, 5m SW of Aylesbury. Exit A418 to Haddenham. Turn at Rising Sun to Townside. Street parking, very limited. Please park in village with consideration of neighbours. Visit Turn End website for parking info. **Mon 6 May (2-5). Adm £4.50, chd free. Home-made teas.**

Intriguing series of garden rooms each with a different planting style enveloping architect's own post-war 2* listed house (not open). Dry garden, small woodland, formal box garden, sunken gardens, mixed borders around curving lawn, framed by ancient walls and mature trees. Bulbs, irises, wisteria, roses, ferns and climbers. Courtyards with pools, pergolas, secluded seating, Victorian Coach House. Open studios with displays and demonstrations by creative artists. Steps, narrow archways, stone and gravel pathways.

47 TYTHROP PARK

Kingsey, HP17 8LT. Nick & Chrissie Wheeler. 2m E of Thame, 4m NW of Princes Risborough. Via A4129, at T-junction in Kingsey turn towards Haddenham, take L turn on bend. Parking in field on L. **Sun 19 May (2-5.30). Adm £7, chd free. Light refreshments.** Donation to St Nicholas Church, Kingsey.

10 acres of garden surrounds a C17 Grade I listed manor house (not open). This large and varied garden blends traditional and contemporary styles, featuring pool borders rich in grasses with a green and white theme, walled kitchen/cutting garden with large greenhouse at its heart, box parterre, deep mixed borders, water feature, rose garden, wild flower meadow, and many old trees and shrubs.

48 WESTEND HOUSE

Cheddington, Leighton Buzzard, LU7 0RP. His Honour Judge & Mrs Richard Foster, 01296 661332, westend.house@hotmail.com, www.westendhousecheddington.co.uk. 5m N of Tring. From double mini-r'about in Cheddington take turn to Long Marston. Take 1st L & Westend House is on your R. **Sun 30 June (2-5). Adm £4, chd free. Home-made teas.**

A country garden of 2 acres restored and developed in recent yrs featuring herbaceous and shrub borders, a formal rose garden with swags, wild flower areas adjacent to the pond and in the orchard, a natural wildlife pond and stream with recently extended planting, potager with vegetables and picking flowers. Wood and metal sculptures. Rare breed sheep and hens in field next to garden. All cakes are home-made and tea is served in bone china with waitress service. Some bespoke sculptures and seasonal vegetables for sale. Wheelchair access to far side of pond restricted.

49 THE WHITE HOUSE, ASKETT

Askett, Princes Risborough, HP27 9LT. Terri Boyce. On the main road through Askett, at the junction of Letter Box Lane. Please park at Lowthorpe House, Crowbrook Rd & walk to White House (5 mins). **Sun 7 July (2-5). Combined adm with Lowthorpe House £5, chd free. Home-made teas at Lowthorpe House.**

A cottage garden surrounding a C17 thatched cottage (not open) with many flower borders, an ancient well in the small front garden, a secret garden, an evergreen border, pond, box edged herbaceous border and several peaceful seating areas.

50 THE WHITE HOUSE

Village Road, Denham Village, UB9 5BE. Mr & Mrs P G Courtenay-Luck. 3m NW of Uxbridge, 7m E of Beaconsfield. Signed from A40 or A412. Parking in village road. The White House is in centre of village. **Sun 9 June (2-5). Adm £6, chd free. Cream teas.**

Well established 6 acre formal garden in picturesque setting. Mature trees and hedges with River Misbourne meandering through lawns. Shrubberies, flower beds, rockery, rose garden and orchard. Large walled garden. Herb garden, vegetable plot and Victorian greenhouses. Gravel entrance and path to gardens.

51 20 WHITEPIT LANE

Flackwell Heath, High Wycombe, HP10 9HS. Trevor Jones, 01628 524876, trevorol4969@gmail.com. ¾m E Flackwell Heath, 4m High Wycombe. From M40 J3 (west bound exit only) take 1st L, 300yds T-junction turn R, 300yds turn L uphill to centre of Flackwell Heath, turn L ¾m, garden 75yds on R past mini-r'about. **Visits by arrangement May to Aug for groups of up to 10. Cream teas included. Adm £7, chd free.**

The front garden has a seaside type landscape with timber groynes and a rock pool. The rear garden is long and thin with colour from Apr to Oct, containing many unusual plants, with steps and bridges over two ponds. Amongst the plants are a large Banana, an Albizia, Grevillea's, Callistemon's Abutilon, Salvia's and several Alstroemeria's. The beds are filled with mixed shrubs and herbaceous plants. Many rare and unusual plants and a garden railway.

52 WIND IN THE WILLOWS

Moorhouse Farm Lane, Off Lower Road, Higher Denham, UB9 5EN. Ron James, 07740 177038, r.james@company-doc.co.uk. 6m E of Beaconsfield. Turn off A412, approx ½m N of junction with A40 into Old Rectory Lane. After 1m enter Higher Denham straight ahead. Take lane next to the community centre & Wind in the Willows is the 1st house on L. **Sun 24 Mar (2-5). Adm £5, chd free. Home-made teas in the community hall. Opening with Higher Denham Gardens on Sun 30 June. Visits also by arrangement Mar to Aug for groups of 10+.**

3 acre wildlife friendly, yr-round garden, comprising informal, woodland and wild gardens, separated by streams lined by iris, primulas and astilbe. Over 350 shrubs and trees, many variegated or uncommon, marginal and bog plantings incl a collection of 80 hostas. Stunning was the word most often used by visitors last year. 'Best private garden I have visited in 20 yrs of NGS visits' said another. Although unlikely to be seen on busy open days, 65 species of bird and 13 species of butterfly have been seen in and over the garden, which is also home to the now endangered water vole (Water Rat in the book Wind in the Willows), frogs and toads. Gravel paths and spongy lawns.

53 WOODSIDE

23 Willow Lane, Amersham, HP7 9DW. Elin & Graham Stone, 01494 261236, glsimagesuk@gmail.com. On A413, 1m SE from Old Amersham, between Barley Lane & Finch Lane. The garden is the last but one, on the RH-side. **Visits by arrangement in June for groups of up to 20. Sat 8 June, Sun 9 June (2-5) & also weekdays throughout June. Adm £3.50, chd free. Light refreshments.**

A small cottage garden, recently created on south facing slope, integrating a circular lawn, lily pond, gravel paths and steps to a curved clematis and rose pergola. Rose beds and abundant humped borders. In contrast, a secret woodland path winds past a stumpery, a shade area and wildlife hedging leading to a kitchen garden. Hidden seating areas abound. Artist's Studio.

OPENING DATES

All entries subject to change. For latest information check **www.ngs.org.uk**

Extended openings are shown at the beginning of the month.

Map locator numbers are shown to the right of each garden name.

February

Daily
Robinson College 39

Snowdrop Festival

Sunday 17th
Clover Cottage 9

Sunday 24th
Clover Cottage 9

March

Every Monday to Friday
Robinson College 39

Every Saturday and Sunday
Robinson College 39

Sunday 3rd
Clover Cottage 9

Sunday 31st
Music Maze and Garden 32

April

Every Monday to Friday to Monday 22nd
Robinson College 39

Every Saturday and Sunday to Sunday 21st
Robinson College 39

Sunday 7th
Barton Gardens 1
Kirtling Tower 26
Netherhall Manor 33

Sunday 14th
Churchill College 7
Trinity College, Fellows' Garden 47

Sunday 28th
◆ Docwra's Manor 12
Newnham Croft Primary School 34

May

Sunday 5th
Chaucer Road Gardens 6
Netherhall Manor 33

Monday 6th
Chaucer Road Gardens 6

Saturday 11th
High Bank Cottage 21

Sunday 12th
◆ Ferrar House 18
High Bank Cottage 21

Saturday 25th
Madingley Hall 28

Sunday 26th
Cambourne Gardens 3
Island Hall 24
NEW 27 Springhill Road 42
Willow Holt 50

Monday 27th
NEW 27 Springhill Road 42
Willow Holt 50

June

Every Monday to Friday from Monday 17th
Robinson College 39

Every Saturday and Sunday from Saturday 22nd
Robinson College 39

Sunday 2nd
Barton Gardens 1
Catworth, Molesworth & Brington Gardens 5
289 Dogsthorpe Road 13
Duxford Gardens 14
Highsett Cambridge 22
The Night Garden 35
Streetly End & West Wickham Gardens 45
NEW Sutton Gardens 46

Thursday 6th
Wild Rose Cottage 49

Saturday 8th
Sandpiper 40
Staploe Gardens 44

Sunday 9th
Cottage Garden 11
289 Dogsthorpe Road 13
Ely Gardens 17
Manor House, Alwalton 29
The Old Rectory
The Night Garden 35
Sandpiper 40
Staploe Gardens 44

Sunday 16th
289 Dogsthorpe Road 13
Lucy Cavendish College 27
The Night Garden 35
Stapleford Gardens 43

Saturday 22nd
45 Beaver Lodge 2

Sunday 23rd
45 Beaver Lodge 2
289 Dogsthorpe Road 13
Green End Farm 20
Madingley Hall 28

Sunday 30th
King's College Fellows' Garden and Provost's Garden 25
Kirtling Tower 26
NEW Wrights Farm 53

July

Every Monday to Friday
Robinson College 39

Every Saturday and Sunday
Robinson College 39

Saturday 6th
38 Norfolk Terrace Garden 36
Trinity Hall - Wychfield 48

Sunday 7th
Clare College Fellows' Garden 8
Green End Farm 20
38 Norfolk Terrace Garden 36
Sawston Gardens 41

Saturday 13th
Twin Tarns

Sunday 14th
Elm House 16
Twin Tarns

August

Every Monday to Friday to Friday 9th
Robinson College 39

Every Saturday and Sunday to Sunday 4th
Robinson College 39

Every Monday to Friday from Tuesday 27th
Robinson College 39

Sunday 4th
◆ Elgood's Brewery Gardens 15
Netherhall Manor 33

Sunday 11th
Netherhall Manor 33

Saturday 17th
45 Beaver Lodge 2

Sunday 18th
45 Beaver Lodge 2
Castor House 4

Saturday 31st
Robinson College 39
Wolfson College Garden 52

September

Every Monday to Friday
Robinson College 39

Every Saturday and Sunday
Robinson College 39

October

Every Monday to Friday
Robinson College 39

Every Saturday and Sunday
Robinson College 39

November

Every Monday to Friday
Robinson College 39

Every Saturday and Sunday
Robinson College 39

December

Every Monday to Friday
Robinson College 39

Every Saturday and Sunday
Robinson College 39

Friday 6th
Sandpiper 40

Saturday 7th
Sandpiper 40

Sunday 8th
Sandpiper 40

By Arrangement

Arrange a personalised garden visit with your club, or group of friends, on a date to suit you. See individual garden entries for full details.

45 Beaver Lodge 2
Chaucer Road Gardens 6
Clover Cottage 9
College Farm 10
39 Foster Road 19
Horseshoe Farm 23
5 Moat Way 31
Music Maze and Garden 32
Netherhall Manor 33
The Night Garden 35
The Old Rectory
23a Perry Road 37
Reed Cottage 38
Twin Tarns
Upwater Lodge, Chaucer Road Gardens 6
Wild Rose Cottage 49
The Windmill 51

Your visits help change lives – we are the largest single funder of the Queen's Nursing Institute

THE GARDENS

GROUP OPENING

1 BARTON GARDENS

High Street, Barton, Cambridge, CB23 7BG. *3½ m SW of Cambridge. Barton is on A603 Cambridge to Sandy Rd, ½ m for J12 M11.* **Sun 7 Apr, Sun 2 June (2-5). Combined adm £5, chd free. Home-made teas in Barton Church (April) Village Hall (June). The White Horse Inn (118 High St) serves meals.**

FARM COTTAGE
Dr R M Belbin.
Open on all dates

GLEBE HOUSE
David & Sue Rapley.
Open on Sun 2 June

114 HIGH STREET
Meta & Hugh Greenfield.
Open on all dates

11 KINGS GROVE
Mrs Judith Bowen.
Open on all dates

NEW **2 MAILES CLOSE**
Mr Patrick Coulson.
Open on Sun 2 June

31 NEW ROAD
Drs D & M Macdonald.
Open on Sun 2 June

THE SIX HOUSES
Perennial.
Open on all dates

Varied group of large and small gardens reflecting different approaches to gardening. Farm Cottage: large landscaped cottage garden with herbaceous beds and themed woodland walk. Glebe House: a 1 acre mature, partly wooded and walled garden with large (unfenced) duck pond. Italianate style courtyard garden. Landscaped secret garden with gazebo. Cedar clad Artist Studio, Paintings, prints, cards & gifts for sale by Sue Rapley Art - www.suerapley.co.uk proceeds to NGS charities. 114 High Street: small cottage garden with an unusual layout comprising several areas incl vegetables, fruit and a secret garden. 31 New Road: large, wildlife friendly cottage garden with a good show of spring flowers, mature shrubs, trees and a kitchen garden. The Six Houses: recently renovated gardens, incl winter and dry gardens, lovely spring bulbs and a small wood. 2 Mailes Close: L shaped Garden completely renovated 3 years ago with herbaceous border, veg and fruit areas. 11 Kings Grove: a garden developed from a wilderness since 1992 with a lawn, flowers and shrub area and a fruit area. The White Horse Inn (118 High Street) serves meals. Some gardens have gravel paths.

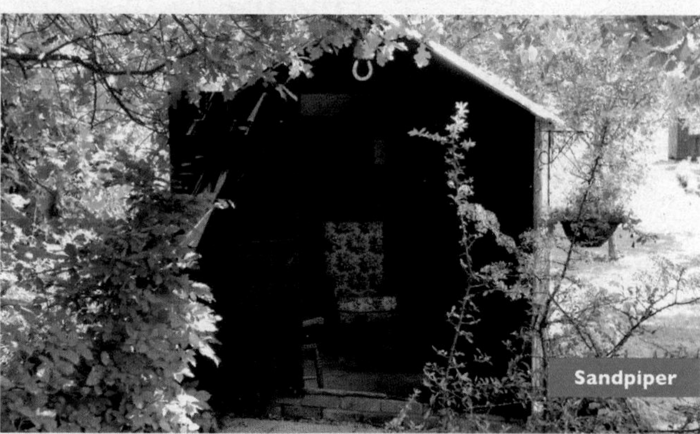
Sandpiper

2 45 BEAVER LODGE

Henson Road, March, PE15 8BA. Mr & Mrs Maria & Paul Nielsen Bom, 01354 656185, beaverbom@gmail.com. *A141 to Wisbech rd into March, turn L into Westwood Ave, follow rd leading to Henson Rd, turn R. Property opp school playground.* **Sat 22, Sun 23 June, Sat 17, Sun 18 Aug (10.30-4). Adm £3, chd free. Home-made teas.** Visits also by arrangement June to Sept for groups of up to 20.

An Oriental garden with large numbers of bonsai both large and small and different types of Acer Pagodas,oriental statues,water features and a pond with Koi carp create a peaceful and relaxing atmosphere . The garden is divided into different rooms one of which has the Mediterranean feel with Tree Ferns, Lemon trees, Bougainvilleas and a great variety of plants and water fountain.

GROUP OPENING

3 CAMBOURNE GARDENS

Great Cambourne, CB23 6AH. *8m W of Cambridge on A428. From A428: take Cambourne junction into Great Cambourne. From B1198, enter village at Lower Cambourne & drive through to Great Cambourne. Follow NGS signs via either route to start at any garden.* **Sun 26 May (11-5). Combined adm £6, chd free. Teas and cakes at 13 Fenbridge; coffee and biscotti at 43 Monkfield Lane; cold drinks at 18 Foxhollow.**

13 FENBRIDGE
Lucinda and Tony Williams.

NEW **18 FOXHOLLOW**
Babs & Bob Cox.

14 GRANARY WAY
Jackie Hutchinson.

88 GREENHAZE LANE
Darren and Irette Murray.

NEW **8 LANGATE GREEN**
Steve & Julie Friend.

5 MAYFIELD WAY
Debbie & Mike Perry.

14 MILLER WAY
Geoff Warmington.

43 MONKFIELD LANE
Tony & Penny Miles.

A unique and inspiring modern group, all created from new build in just a few years. This selection of eight, including two new for 2019, demonstrates how imagination and gardening skill can be combined in a short time to create great effects from unpromising and awkward beginnings. The grouping includes foliage gardens with collections of carnivorous pitcher plants and hostas; a suntrap garden for play, socialising and colour; gardens with ponds and many other beautiful borders showing their owners' creativity and love of growing fine plants well. New for 2019 is an inspirational garden in a tiny space featuring two areas, one a recreation of a beach complete with bar serving cold drinks. Another new this year features carefully considered borders, a wildlife pond and vegetable garden. Cambourne is one of Cambridgeshire's newest communities, and this grouping showcases the happy, vibrant place our village has become. No garden is more than 18 years old, and most are much younger.

We help ordinary people open the gates to their extraordinary private gardens to raise impressive amounts of money through admissions, teas and slices of cake!

4 CASTOR HOUSE

2, Peterborough Road, Castor, Peterborough, PE5 7AX. Ian & Claire Winfrey, www.castorhousegardens.co.uk. *4m W of Peterborough. House on main Peterborough Rd in Castor. Parking in paddock off Water Lane.* **Sun 18 Aug (2-5). Adm £6, chd free. Home-made teas.**

12 acres of gardens and woodland on a slope, terraced and redesigned 2010. Italianate spring fed ponds and stream gardens. Potager with greenhouse and exotic borders. Willow arbour and woodland garden. Peony and prunus walk. Rose and cottage gardens, 'Hot' double border, stumpery. Orchard in walled gardens. There is limited access for wheelchairs due to sloping nature of the garden.

GROUP OPENING

5 CATWORTH, MOLESWORTH & BRINGTON GARDENS

Molesworth, Huntingdon, PE28 0QD. *10m W of Huntingdon. A14 W for Molesworth & Brington exit at J16 onto B660.* **Sun 2 June (2-6). Combined adm £4, chd free. Home-made teas at Molesworth House and Yew Tree Cottage.**

32 HIGH STREET
Colin Small.

MOLESWORTH HOUSE
John Prentis.

YEW TREE COTTAGE
Christine & Don Eggleston.

Molesworth House is an old rectory garden with everything that you'd both expect and hope for, given its Victorian past. There are surprising corners to this traditional take on a happy and relaxed, yet also formal garden. Yew Tree Cottage, informal garden approx 1 acre, complements the C16 building (not open) and comprises flower beds, lawns, vegetable patch, boggy garden, copses and orchard. Plants in pots and hanging baskets. High Street, Catworth is a long narrow garden with many rare plants including ferns, herbaceous borders, woodland area and wildlife pond. Partial wheelchair access.

GROUP OPENING

6 CHAUCER ROAD GARDENS

Cambridge, CB2 7EB. 01223 361378, Jmp@pearson.co.uk. *1m S of Cambridge. Off Trumpington Rd (A1309), nr Brooklands Ave junction. Parking available at MRC Psychology Dept on Chaucer Rd.* **Sun 5, Mon 6 May (2-5). Combined adm £7, chd free. Home-made teas at Upwater Lodge.** Visits also by arrangement May & June.

11 CHAUCER ROAD
Mark & Jigs Hill.

12 CHAUCER ROAD
Mr & Mrs Bradley.

16 CHAUCER ROAD
Mrs V Albutt.

UPWATER LODGE
Mr & Mrs George Pearson, 07890 080303, jmp@pearson.co.uk.
Visits also by arrangement May & June.

11 Chaucer Road is a ¾ acre Edwardian garden that has changed rapidly over the ensuing 110 yrs. A rock garden with pond and large weeping Japanese maple dates from about 1930. 16 Chaucer Road ½ acre garden, divided by arches and hedges into separate areas, each with its own character. Front rose garden. Unusual hawthorn and late summer borders. Blackberries and apple trees. Wildlife area with new sculpture. Waterproof footwear advised. Upwater Lodge is an Edwardian academic's house with 7 acres of grounds. It has mature trees, fine lawns, old wisterias, and colourful borders. There is a small, pretty potager with A selection of fruits, and a well maintained grass tennis court. A network of paths through a wooded area lead down to a dyke, water meadows and a small flock of rare breed sheep. Enjoy a walk by the river and watch the punts go by. Buy home-made teas and sit in the garden or take them down to enjoy a lazy afternoon with ducks, geese, swans and heron on the riverbank. Cakes made with garden fruit where possible. Swings and climbing ropes. Stalls selling cards, prints and fabric crafts. Plant stall possible but please email to check. Some gravel areas and grassy paths with fairly gentle slopes.

7 CHURCHILL COLLEGE

Storey's Way, Cambridge, CB3 0DS. University of Cambridge, www.chu.cam.ac.uk/about/grounds-gardens/. *1m from M11 J13. 1m NW of Cambridge city centre. Turn into Storeys Way from Madingley Rd (A1303), or from Huntingdon Rd (A1307). Parking on site.* **Sun 14 Apr (2-5). Adm £3.50, chd free. Light refreshments in College Buttery.**

42 acre site designed in 1960s for foliage and form, to provide year round interest in peaceful and relaxing surrounds with courtyards, large open spaces and specimen trees. 10m x 5m orchid house, herbaceous plantings. Beautiful grouping of Prunus Tai Haku (great white cherry) trees forming striking canopy and drifts of naturalised bulbs in grass around the site. The planting provides a setting for the impressive collection of modern sculpture. Orchid house, Sculptures, trees, bulbs, landscape. The greenhouse is restricted in size.

8 CLARE COLLEGE FELLOWS' GARDEN

Trinity Lane, Cambridge, CB2 1TL. The Master & Fellows, www.clare.cam.ac.uk. *Central to city. From Queens Rd or city centre via Senate House Passage, Old Court & Clare Bridge.* **Sun 7 July (2-5). Adm £4.50, chd free.**

2 acres. One of the most famous gardens on the Cambridge Backs. Herbaceous borders; sunken pond garden, fine specimen trees and tropical garden. Gravel paths.

9 CLOVER COTTAGE

50 Streetly End, West Wickham, CB21 4RP. Mr Paul & Mrs Shirley Shadford, 01223 893122, shirleyshadford@live.co.uk. *3m from Linton, 3m from Haverhill & 2m from Balsham. From Horseheath turn L, from Balsham turn R, thatched cottage opposite triangle of grass next to old windmill.* **Sun 17, Sun 24 Feb, Sun 3 Mar (2-4). Adm £2.50, chd free. Light refreshments. Free hot drinks for snowdrop festival. Opening with Streetly End & West Wickham Gardens on Sun 2 June.** Visits also by arrangement in June.

In winter find a flowering cherry tree, borders of snowdrops, aconites, iris reticulata, hellebores and miniature narcissus throughout the packed small garden which has inspiring ideas on use of space. Pond and arbour, raised beds of fruit and vegetables. In summer arches of roses and clematis. Hardy geraniums, delightful borders of English roses and herbaceous plants. Snowdrops for sale in Feb & March, also plants for sale in the summer, light homemade refreshments may be purchased. NO WHEELCHAIRS, PRAMS, PUSHCHAIRS, WHEELED WALKERS OR DOG ACCESS TO THE GARDEN AT ALL.

10 COLLEGE FARM

Station Road, Haddenham, Ely, CB6 3XD. Sheila & Jeremy Waller, 07779 302777, jeremyprimavera@aol.com, www.primaveragallery.co.uk. *From Stretham & Wilburton, at Xrds in Haddenham, turn R, past the church. Exactly at the bottom of the hill, turn L down narrow drive, with a mill wheel on R of the drive.* **Visits by arrangement May & June for groups of 10+. Adm £6, chd free.**

40 acres around an intact Victorian farm. New walks, galleries and sculpture cattle yard. Further walks by ponds and through meadows. Roses, wild flowers, new water plants, foxgloves and new plantings of trees, hedges and fruit trees add colour and shape. Splendid fen views, lovely water features and ancient ridge and furrow pasture land with interesting wild flowers, original farm buildings and abundant wildlife. Amongst the farm buildings are outside galleries, and inside the house another gallery full of extraordinary paintings, art and craft. Wheelchair access is only possible around the garden near the house, but not through the gallery, farm, milking parlour and many of the walks.

11 COTTAGE GARDEN

79 Sedgwick Street, Cambridge, CB1 3AL. Rosie Wilson. *From town centre or park & ride, go down Mill Rd over railway bridge. If driving take 2nd L Cavendish Rd, then 2nd R which leads into Sedgwick St.* **Sun 9 June (2-6). Adm £3, chd free. Home-made teas.**

Long narrow and planted in the cottage garden style with over 40 roses some on arches and growing through trees. Particularly planned to encourage wildlife with small pond, mature trees and shrubs. Perennials and some unusual plants interspersed with sculptures.

12 ♦ DOCWRA'S MANOR

2 Meldreth Road, Shepreth, Royston, SG8 6PS. Mrs Faith Raven, 01763 260677, faithraven@btinternet.com, www.docwrasmanorgarden.co.uk. *8m S of Cambridge. ½m W of A10. Garden is opp the War Memorial in Shepreth. King's Cross-Cambridge train stop 5 min walk.* **For NGS: Sun 28 Apr (2-5). Adm £5, chd free. Tea.** For other opening times and information, please phone, email or visit garden website.

2½ acres of choice plants in a series of enclosed gardens. Tulips and Judas trees. Opened for the NGS for more than 40yrs. The garden is featured in great detail in a book published 2013 'The Gardens of England' edited by George Plumptre. Wheelchair access to most parts of the garden, gravel paths.

We open the gates to the nation's best gardens, offering a relaxing, memorable and affordable day out. A perfect experience to share with friends and family.

13 289 DOGSTHORPE ROAD

Peterborough, PE1 3PA. Michael & Julie Reid, www.facebook.com/AnArtistsGarden?ref=stream. *1m N of city centre. A47 Paston turn. Exit r'about South. Down Fulbridge rd to end & turn L into St Paul's Rd. Turn R at end down Dogsthorpe Rd. Garden 600 metres on R.* **Sun 2, Sun 9, Sun 16, Sun 23 June (12-6). Adm £4, chd free. Light refreshments. Light refreshments, sweet and savory. Vegan and gluten free options also.**

A peaceful urban garden designed by Fine Artist, Julie Reid. Divided into rooms using layers and texture using trees, shrubs and year round perennial planting incl ferns, bamboos and Acers. Subtle structural and sculptural additions incl water features, Japanese inspired garden and Teahouse. Social and intimate seating areas allow guests and gardeners to relax and enjoy. Open Artists Studio, Japanese garden and tea house, sculpture, water features, resident cute cat, 'Pop-up' tea shop. Home-made teas, cakes and savories available to buy, all profit to charities. Wheelchairs limited to terrace.

GROUP OPENING

14 DUXFORD GARDENS

Bustlers Cottage, 26 St Peters Street, Duxford, Cambridge, CB22 4RP. *All gardens are close to the centre of the village of Duxford, just south of the A505 between the M11 J10 & Sawston.* **Sun 2 June (2-6). Combined adm £7, chd free. Tea at United Reformed Church, Chapel Street a short walk from all the open gardens (tea and cake) and at Bustlers Cottage (for cream teas if fine). WC.**

BUSTLERS COTTAGE
John & Jenny Marks.

DUXFORD MILL
Mrs Frankie Bridgwood.

2 GREEN STREET
Mr Bruce Crockford.

NEW **16 ICKLETON ROAD**
Claire James.

6 THE BIGGEN
Mrs Bettye Reynolds.

Five gardens, one new to the NGS, of very different sizes and characters. The river Cam flows through two of them, including the Mill, which has historical associations and 11 acres of mature gardens. The garden in the Biggen has some unusual planting and leads down to the river. The garden at 2 Green Street is a charming small and colourful garden and Bustlers Cottage has an acre of traditional Cambridgeshire cottage garden including roses, herbaceous borders, vegetable garden and fruit trees. Opening for the first time, the garden at 16 Ickleton Rd is an ever-evolving, "work in progress" garden, with experimental planting that attempts to take advantage of the sunny aspect and well drained soil. A plantaholic's garden. A village scarecrow festival is planned to coincide with the opening of these five gardens, and will be an integral part of the village's offering for the NGS. Visitors to the gardens will be able to view the creative talents all around the village.

15 ♦ ELGOOD'S BREWERY GARDENS

North Brink, Wisbech, PE13 1LW. Elgood & Sons Ltd, 01945 583160, info@elgoods-brewery.co.uk, www.elgoods-brewery.co.uk. *1m W of town centre. Leave A47 towards Wisbech Centre. Cross river to North Brink. Follow river & brown signs to brewery & car park beyond.* **For NGS: Sun 4 Aug (11.30-4.30). Adm £4, chd free. Light refreshments.** For other opening times and information, please phone, email or visit garden website.

Approx 4 acres of peaceful garden featuring 250 yr old specimen trees providing a framework to lawns, lake, rockery, herb garden and maze. Wheelchair access to Visitor Centre and most areas of the garden.

16 ELM HOUSE

Main Road, Elm, Wisbech, PE14 0AB. Mrs Diana Bullard. *2½m SW of Wisbech. From A1101 take B1101, signed Elm, Friday Bridge. Elm House is ⅓m on L, well signed.* **Sun 14 July (1-5). Adm £4, chd free. Home-made teas.**

Walled garden with arboretum, many rare trees and shrubs, mixed perennials C17 house (not open). New 3 acre meadow. Children welcome.

GROUP OPENING

17 ELY GARDENS

Chapel Street, Ely, CB6 1AD. *14m N of Cambridge. Parking at Barton Rd car park, Tower Rd, (adjacent to 42 Cambridge Rd), or the Grange Council Offices. Map given at first garden visited.* **Sun 9 June (12-6). Combined adm £6, chd free. Home-made teas at 42 Cambridge Road.**

THE BISHOPS HOUSE
The Bishop of Ely.

42 CAMBRIDGE ROAD
Mr & Mrs J & C Switsur.

12 CHAPEL STREET
Ken & Linda Ellis, www.simplygardeningofely.co.uk.

NEW **5B DOWNHAM ROAD**
Mr Christopher Cain.

NEW **17B HILLS LANE**
Mr & Mrs John and Alison Eden-Eadon.

BISHOP WOODFORD HOUSE
Miss Michelle Collins.

A delightful and varied group of gardens in an historic Cathedral city: The Bishop's house adjoins Ely Cathedral and has mixed planting with a formal rose garden, wisteria and more. Jane Frost, local artist, will display and sell pieces in The Bishops garden. 20% of sales to charity 'Branching Out'. Bishop Woodford House has an informally planted garden with colour and interest - and a wide variety of plants. 12 Chapel Street, a small town garden, reflecting the owners variety of gardening interests, from alpines to herbaceous and vegetables all linked with a railway! 42 Cambridge Road is a secluded town garden with interesting herbaceous borders, roses, shrubs and trees. 17b Hills Lane is a tiny garden with no grass! Paving and raised beds show how the owners have made their garden manageable for older people, or people with limited mobility. 5b Downham Road shows how to rise to the challenge of a small interestingly shaped area. Careful planting has created a tranquil area. Wheelchair access to areas of most gardens.

♿ ✿ ☕

18 ◆ FERRAR HOUSE

Little Gidding, Huntingdon, PE28 5RJ. Mrs Susan Capp, 01832 293383, info@ferrarhouse.co.uk, www.ferrarhouse.co.uk. *Take Mill Rd from Great Gidding (turn at Fox & Hounds) then after 1m turn R down single track lane. Car Park at Ferrar House.* **For NGS: Sun 12 May (10-5). Adm £4, chd free. Home-made teas.** For other opening times and information, please phone, email or visit garden website.

A peaceful garden of a Retreat House with beautiful uninterrupted views across meadows and farm land. Adjacent to the historic Church of St John's it was here that a small religious community was formed in the C17. The poet T. S. Eliot visited in 1936 and it inspired the 4th of his Quartets named Little Gidding. Lawn and walled flower beds with a walled vegetable garden. Games on the lawn. WC accessible at Ferrar House.

♿ ✿ 🛏 ☕

Molesworth House, Catworth, Molesworth & Brington Gardens

19 39 FOSTER ROAD

Campaign Ave, Sugar Way, Peterborough, PE2 9RS. Robert Marshall & Richard Handscombe, 01733 555978, robfmarshall@btinternet.com. *1m SW of Peterborough City Centre. A605 Oundle Rd, at T-lights N into Sugar Way. Cross 1st r'bout, L at 2nd to Campaign Ave. R at next r'bout then 2nd R to Foster Rd. Continue to end. L into cul-de-sac.* **Visits by arrangement Apr to Sept for groups of up to 30. Adm £4, chd free. Light refreshments in garden pergola or indoor lounge, weather depending. £5 per head for groups, to incl home-made cake.**

Plantsman's garden in compact, new estate plot. Mixed borders; woodland/shade; 'vestibule' garden; exotics and ferns; espaliered fruit; pergola; patio; pond; parterre; many pots; octagonal greenhouse; seating and sculpture. Uncommon snowdrops, over 250 hostas, plus daphnes, acers and other choice/ unusual cultivars. Trees and hedges create enclosure and intimacy. 4 x British Shorthair cats. Compact 'town garden' conceals many design ideas to maximize planting and create intimacy - without grass to cut. See how trees (x12) and hedges can be used in a small garden. Large collection of Hostas (250+ cultivars). Rare snowdrops. Ensembles of unusual plants in pots extend season and interest. All viewings accompanied by garden owner(s). Main garden and WC accessible by wheelchair.

20 GREEN END FARM

Over Road, Longstanton, Cambridge, CB24 3DW. Sylvia Newman, www.sngardendesign.co.uk. *From A14 take the direction of Longstanton At the r'about, take the 2nd exit At the next r'about, turn L (this shows a dead end on the sign) We're a couple of hundred metres on L.* **Sun 23 June, Sun 7 July (12-4). Adm £4, chd free. Home-made teas and refreshments.**

A developing garden that's beginning to blend well with the farm. An interesting combination of new and established spaces interlinked with a design eye. An established orchard with beehives; two wildlife ponds. An outside kitchen, productive kitchen and cutting garden. Doves, chickens and sheep complete the picture!

21 HIGH BANK COTTAGE

Kirkgate, Tydd St. Giles, Wisbech, PE13 5NE. Mrs F Savill. *Heading from Wisbech, North Cambs. A1101 take turn signed Tydd St Giles. Parking at Tydd St Giles golf & country club, a few minutes walk from the garden. www.pure-leisure.co.uk/parks/tydd-st-giles/ overview/.* **Sat 11, Sun 12 May (10.30-4). Adm £4, chd £1.50. Light refreshments. Meals are available at the golf course.**

The garden is a tranquil oasis from the hurry of life. A cottage garden, mainly, but it has many mature trees and shrubs. It is separated into different areas with seating so that the views of the garden can be appreciated. There are two ponds, one of which has fish, and a river bank with areas for wildlife, and, also an allotment. Please supervise children closely. NGS discretionary ticket holders £2. There will be coffee/tea and home-made cakes and biscuits available to purchase. Also, plants and garden related craft items. There are gravelled areas, and some steps. The brick paths are uneven, and can be slippery when wet.

39 Foster Road

GROUP OPENING

22 HIGHSETT CAMBRIDGE

Cambridge, CB2 1NZ. 40, 49, 50, 53, 59, 70, 73, 82 & 85. *Centre of Cambridge. Via Station Rd, Tenison Rd, 1st L Tenison Ave, entrance ahead. SatNav CB1 2DX.* **Sun 2 June (2-5). Combined adm £6, chd free. Home-made teas at 82 & 83 Highsett.**

9 delightful town gardens within Central Cambridge. Set in large communal grounds with fine specimen trees and lawns. A haven for children and wildlife. Architect Eric Lyons planned the whole estate in the late 1950's with a mixture of flats, small houses and large town houses, the very ethos of tranquil living space for all generations. Several of the Open Gardens have been skilfully modernised by garden designers. Most paths accessible into the gardens.

23 HORSESHOE FARM

Chatteris Road, Somersham, Huntingdon, PE28 3DR. Neil & Claire Callan, 01354 693546, nccallan@yahoo.co.uk. *9m NE of St Ives, Cambs. Easy access from the A14. Situated on E side of B1050, 4m N of Somersham Village. Parking for 8 cars in the drive.* **Visits by arrangement May to July. For any number up to 20. Adm £4, chd free. Home-made teas.**

This ¾ acre plant-lovers' garden has a large pond with summer-house and decking, bog garden, alpine troughs, mixed rainbow island beds with over 30 varieties of bearded irises, water features, a small hazel woodland area, wildlife meadow, secret corners and a lookout tower for wide Fenland views and bird watching. Featured in WI Life, Amateur Gardening and Garden News.

24 ISLAND HALL

Godmanchester, PE29 2BA. Mr Christopher & Lady Linda Vane Percy, www.islandhall.com. *1m S of Huntingdon (A1). 15m NW of Cambridge (A14). In centre of Godmanchester next to free Mill Yard car park.* **Sun 26 May (11-5). Adm £4, chd free. Home-made teas in the 'Hut' on the Island set within the grounds.**

3-acre grounds. Tranquil riverside setting with mature trees. Chinese bridge over Saxon mill race to embowered island with wild flowers. Garden restored in 1983 to mid C18 formal design, with box hedging, clipped hornbeams, parterres, topiary, good vistas over borrowed landscape and C18 wrought iron and stone urns. The ornamental island has been replanted with Princeton elms (ulmus americana). Mid C18 mansion (not open).

25 KING'S COLLEGE FELLOWS' GARDEN AND PROVOST'S GARDEN

Queen's Road, Cambridge, CB2 1ST. Provost & Scholars of King's College. *In Cambridge, the Backs. Entry by gate at junction of Queen's Rd & West Rd. Parking at Lion Yard 10mins walk, or some pay & display places in West Rd & Queen's Rd.* **Sun 30 June (2-5). Adm £4, chd free. Cream teas.**

Fine example of a Victorian garden with rare specimen trees. With a small woodland walk and a kitchen/allotment garden created in 2011 and a rose pergola and herbaceous border created in 2013. Now with an exciting sub -tropical border together with a new Rond Pont entrance feature celebrating the mathematicians who studied and researched at King's over the centuries. Gravel paths.

26 KIRTLING TOWER

Newmarket Road, Kirtling, Newmarket, CB8 9PA. The Lord & Lady Fairhaven. *6m SE of Newmarket. From Newmarket head towards village of Saxon Street, through village to Kirtling, turn L at war memorial, signed to Upend, entrance is signed on the L.* **Sun 7 Apr, Sun 30 June (11-4). Adm £5, chd free. Light refreshments at the Church throughout the day. Selection of delicious hot and cold food, sandwiches, cakes, tea and coffee.**

Surrounded by a moat, formal gardens and parkland. In the spring there are swathes of daffodils, narcissi, crocus, muscari, chionodoxa and tulips. Closer to the house, vast lawn areas Secret and Cutting Gardens. In the summer the Walled Garden has superb herbaceous borders with anthemis, hemerocallis, geraniums and delphiniums. The Victorian Garden is filled with peonies. Views of surrounding countryside. A Classic car display will be in attendance. Mr Feinson and his Arcadia Recorder Group will be playing in the walled garden. Rougham Nurseries and Helens Herbaceous will supply the plants for sale. A variety of craft stalls on both dates as well as a display of Stonework from the Fairhaven Stoneyard. Many of the paths and routes around the garden are grass - they are accessible by wheelchairs, but can be hard work if wet.

27 LUCY CAVENDISH COLLEGE

Lady Margaret Road, Cambridge, CB3 0BU. Lucy Cavendish College. *1m NW of Gt St Mary. College situated on the corner of Lady Margaret Rd & Madingley Rd (A1303). Entrance off Lady Margaret Rd.* **Sun 16 June (2-5). Adm £3.50, chd free.**

The gardens of 4 late Victorian houses have been combined and developed over past 25yrs into an informal 3 acre garden. Fine mature trees shade densely planted borders. An Anglo Saxon herb garden is situated in one corner. The garden provides a rich wildlife habitat.

28 MADINGLEY HALL

Cambridge, CB23 8AQ. University of Cambridge, 01223 746222, reservations@madingleyhall.co.uk, www.madingleyhall.co.uk. *4m W of Cambridge. 1m from M11 J13.* **A 'Celebrity Gardeners' Question Time' and more. Sat 25 May (12-5). Adm £35 includes lunch. Pre-booking essential, please visit www.ngs.org.uk for information & booking. Sun 23 June (2.30-5.30). Adm £5, chd free. Tea.** Donation to St Mary Magdalene Church Restoration Fund.

C16 Hall (not open) set in 8 acres of attractive grounds landscaped by Capability Brown. Features incl landscaped walled garden with hazel walk, alpine bed, medicinal border and rose pergola. Historic meadow, topiary, mature trees and wide variety of hardy plants.

29 MANOR HOUSE, ALWALTON

Church Street, Alwalton, Peterborough, PE7 3UU. Malcolm & Jane Holmes. *Alwalton Village. Turn into centre of old village, park on street or Village Hall car park. Garden 100yds on R after Village Hall.* **Sun 9 June (1-5). Adm £5, chd free. Home-made teas.**
Walled garden surrounding C17 farmhouse, divided into rooms with tall hedges, topiary and mixed borders. Paths leading to wild garden overlooking Nene valley.

30 ◆ THE MANOR, HEMINGFORD GREY

Hemingford Grey, PE28 9BN. Mrs D S Boston, 01480 463134, diana_boston@hotmail.com, www.greenknowe.co.uk. *4m E of Huntingdon. Off A14. Entrance to garden by small gate off river towpath. Limited parking on verge halfway up drive, parking near house for disabled. Otherwise park in village.* For opening times and information, please phone, email or visit garden website.
Garden designed and planted by author Lucy Boston, surrounds 12th Century manor house on which Green Knowe books based (house open by appt). 3 acre 'cottage' garden with topiary; snowdrops, old roses, extensive collection of irises incl Dykes Medal winners and Cedric Morris varieties, herbaceous borders with mainly scented plants. Meadow with mown paths. Enclosed by river, moat and wilderness. Late May splendid show of irises followed by the old roses. Care is taken with the planting to start the year with a large variety of snowdrops and to extend the flowering season with colour through to the first frosts from unusual annuals. The garden is interesting even in winter with the topiary. Gravel paths but wheelchairs are encouraged to go on the lawns.

31 5 MOAT WAY

Swavesey, CB24 4TR. Mr & Mrs N Kyberd, 01954 200568, n.kyberd@ntlworld.com. *Off A14, 2m beyond Bar Hill. Look for School Lane/Fen Drayton Rd, at mini r'about turn into Moat Way, no.5 is approx 100 metres on L.* **Visits by arrangement June & July for groups of up to 10. Adm £4, chd free.**
Colourful garden filled with collection of trees, shrubs and perennials. Large patio area displaying many specimen foliage plants in planters, incl pines, hostas and acers.

32 MUSIC MAZE AND GARDEN

2a Nine Chimneys Lane, Balsham, CB21 4ES. Mr & Mrs Jim & Hilary Potter, 01223 891211, hppotter@btinternet.com. *In centre of Balsham just off High St. 3m E of A11, 12m S of Newmarket & 10m SE of Cambridge. Car parking in the High St or the Church car park. 2 disabled spaces in Nine Chimneys Lane.* **Sun 31 Mar (12-5). Adm £4, chd £1. Home-made teas.** Visits also by arrangement Feb to Oct for groups of 10 to 20. Min cost £60 per group, refreshments incl. Allow 2 hours.
Two acres of garden with spring bulbs, herbaceous border, raised vegetable beds, gravel garden, large duck pond, wild flower meadow, an orchard, modern sculptures and human sundial. A yew Music Maze was planted in 1993 with golden yew (Taxus elegantissima) in the shape of a treble clef, overlooked by a viewing hill. Mature and new trees. In the maze there are over 1500 trees in total. Also two paved areas form the shape of French horns which enclose an alpine garden and a mobile fountain. Refreshments (provided by Macmillan Cancer Support, Cambridge) overlooking large duck pond. Hard paths around formal garden area. Limited wheelchair access to grassland areas. Fine in dry weather with a good driver.

33 NETHERHALL MANOR

Tanners Lane, Soham, CB7 5AB. Timothy Clark, 01353 720269. *6m Ely, 6m Newmarket. Enter Soham from Newmarket, Tanners Lane 2nd R 100yds after cemetery. Enter Soham from Ely, Tanners Lane 2nd L after War Memorial.* **Sun 7 Apr, Sun 5 May, Sun 4, Sun 11 Aug (2-5). Adm £3, chd free. Home-made teas.** Visits also by arrangement Mar to Aug for groups of up to 30.
An elegant garden 'touched with antiquity'. Good Gardens Guide. An unusual garden appealing to those with historical interest in individual collections of plant groups: March-old primroses, daffodils, Victorian double flowered hyacinths & first garden hellebore hybrids. May-old English tulips, Crown Imperials. Aug-Victorian pelargonium,heliotrope,calceolaria, dahlias. Author-Margery Fish's Country Gardening & Mary McMurtrie's Country Garden Flowers. Historic Plants 1500-1900. The only bed of English tulips on display in the country. Author's books for sale. Featured on Gardeners' World twice. Flat garden with two optional steps. Lawns.

34 NEWNHAM CROFT PRIMARY SCHOOL

Chedworth Street, Cambridge, CB3 9JF. Mrs Sharon Williams, www.newnhamcroft.cambs.sch.uk. *M11 J12. Follow Barton Rd to City Centre. There is no R turn into Grantchester St at T-lights. Follow rd L to Newnham garage r'about to return to Grantchester St. Chedworth St on L.* **Sun 28 Apr (10-5). Adm £3, chd free. Home-made teas.**
Children are encouraged to take part in gardening activities carried out by our volunteers. The gardens start with a courtyard with planters and woodland path. There are two herbaceous borders and a number of flower beds. The vegetable garden provides produce for the school kitchen. In spring bulbs and tree blossom from the many variety of trees dominate this beautiful learning environment. Refreshments will be provided by the school Parent Teachers Association. Some rough ground but most areas accessible by wheelchair.

35 THE NIGHT GARDEN

37 Honeyhill, Paston, Peterborough, PE4 7DR. Andrea Connor, 07801 987905, andrea.connors@ntlworld.com. *From A47 Soke Parkway at J19. Take exit N on Topmoor Way. R at next r'about (3rd exit) to Paston Ridings, over the speed humps. Take 4th L to Honeyhill. 1st R into car park. No.37 at top L corner.* **Evening**

opening Sun 2, Sun 9, Sun 16 June (7-10). Adm £4, chd free. Light refreshments in garden, or house if weather inclement. Light refreshments incl. in entry fee, but donation appreciated. Visits also by arrangement May to Sept.

Small town garden with shrubs, roses, clematis, colourful bedding plants and Ash tree for shade, seclusion and privacy. Salvia collection for 'wellbeing'. Arches and trellis give height, water adds tranquility. At dusk the solar powered lighting gradually transforms the space into an enchanting magical world. Sit and enjoy the gradual transformation from either seating area at the ends of the garden. Night time garden lighting brings an unusual dimension, transforming the experience, hence suggested evening visiting times.

36 38 NORFOLK TERRACE GARDEN

Cambridge, CB1 2NG. John Tordoff & Maurice Reeve. *Central Cambridge. A603 East Rd turn R into St Matthews St to Norfolk St, L into Blossom St & Norfolk Terrace is at the end.* **Sat 6, Sun 7 July (11-6). Adm £3, chd free. Light refreshments.**

A small, paved courtyard garden in Moroccan style. Masses of colour in raised beds and pots, backed by oriental arches. An ornamental pool done in patterned tiles offers the soothing splash of water. The garden is included in the book 'The Secret Gardens of East Anglia'. The owners' previous, London garden, was named by BBC Gardeners' World as 'Best Small Garden in Britain'. There will also be a display of recent paintings by John Tordoff and handmade books by Maurice Reeve.

THE OLD RECTORY

312 Main Road, Parson Drove, Wisbech PE13 4LF. Helen Roberts, 01945 700415, yogahelen@talk21.com. *SW of Wisbech. From Peterborough on A47 follow signs to Parson Drove L after Thorney Toll. From Wisbech follow the B1166 through Levrington Common.*

Sun 9 June (11-4). Adm £4, chd free. Home-made teas. Visits also by arrangement May to Aug for groups of 10+. Adm incl home-made tea and cakes.

Walled Georgian cottage garden of 1 acre, opening into wild flower meadow and paddocks. Long herbaceous border, 2 ponds and unusual weeping ash tree. Terraced areas and outdoor kitchen! No hills but lovely open Fen views, bridge over wildlife dyke (Monet!) and par 3 golf hole come and have a putt!

37 23A PERRY ROAD

Buckden, St Neots, PE19 5XG. David & Valerie Bunnage, 01480 810553, d.bunnage@btinternet.com. *5m S of Huntingdon on A1. From A1 Buckden r'about take B661, Perry Rd approx 300yds on L.* **Visits by arrangement. Adm £4, chd free. Light refreshments. - Donation appreciated.**

Approx 1 acre garden consisting of many garden designs incl Japanese interlinked by gravel paths. Large selection of acers, pines, rare and unusual shrubs. Also interesting features, a quirky garden. Plantsmans garden for all seasons, small bog garden. WC. Coaches welcome.

38 REED COTTAGE

1 Rectory Farm Road, Little Wilbraham, Cambridge, CB21 5LB. Mr Robert Turner, 07972 439881, rj-turner@hotmail.co.uk. *5m S of Newmarket, 5m E of Cambridge. In centre of village on corner opp grass triangle.* **Visits by arrangement Apr to Sept for groups of 10 to 30. Adm £5, chd free. Sandwiches, tea, coffee, wine, cakes.**

A delightful traditional cottage garden with stunning borders of many mature herbaceous perennials. 5000 bulbs in spring, and full colour in summer. A garden pond adds to the enjoyment and brings wildlife benefits. A well stocked vegetable garden makes us 60% self efficient. A shaded area hosts ferns and hostas.

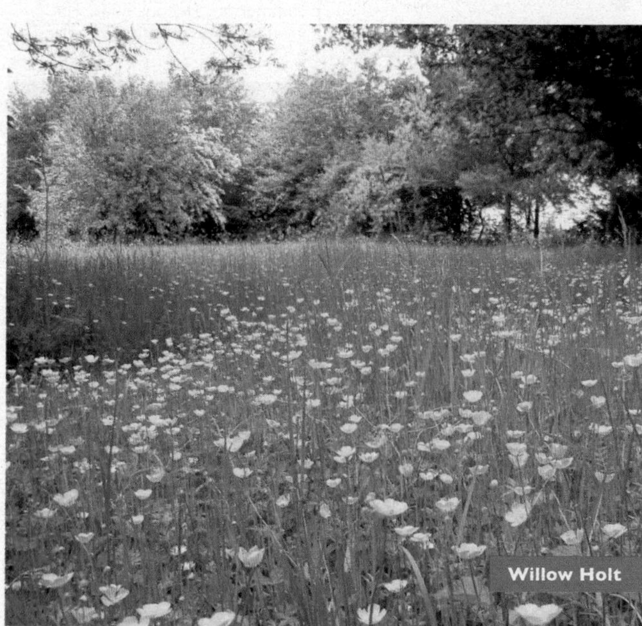

Willow Holt

Your visits help change lives – since 1927, we've donated £55 million to nursing and caring charities

39 ROBINSON COLLEGE

Grange Road, Cambridge, CB3 9AN. Warden and Fellows, www.robinson.cam.ac.uk/about-robinson/gardens/national-gardens-scheme. *Garden at main Robinson College site, report to Porters' Lodge. There is only on-street parking.* **Every Mon to Fri 1 Jan to 22 Apr (10-4). Every Sat and Sun 5 Jan to 21 Apr (2-4). Every Mon to Fri 17 June to 9 Aug (10-4). Every Sat and Sun 22 June to 4 Aug (2-4). Every Mon to Fri 27 Aug to 31 Dec (10-4). Every Sat and Sun 31 Aug to 29 Dec (2-4). Adm £4, chd free. Closed Sat 29 June and Sun 6 Oct.**

10 original Edwardian gardens are linked to central wild woodland water garden focusing on Bin Brook with small lake at heart of site. This gives a feeling of park and informal woodland, while at the same time keeping the sense of older more formal gardens beyond. Central area has a wide lawn running down to the lake framed by many mature stately trees with much of the original planting intact. More recent planting incl herbaceous borders and commemorative trees. Please report to Porters' Lodge on arrival to pay for entry and guidebook. No picnics. Children must be accompanied at all times. NB from time to time some parts, or occasionally all, of Robinson College gardens may be closed for safety reasons involving work by contractors and our maintenance staff. Please report to Porters' Lodge on arrival for information. Ask at Porters' Lodge for wheelchair access.

40 SANDPIPER

30 Colnefields, Somersham, PE28 3DL. Tim & Emma Procter, 01487 740896, emma.procter1@me.com. *4m NE of St Ives. Take B1040 from St Ives to Somersham. Drive through Somersham High St until you get to a sharp R corner (just after garage), take L turn signed Chatteris. Colnefields is 1st rd on R after 150m.* **Sat 8, Sun 9 June (12-5). Evening opening Fri 6, Sat 7, Sun 8 Dec (5-9). Adm £4, chd free. Light refreshments. Pre-booking essential (see above).**

About an acre of herbaceous borders, lawn, rose arbour, secluded seating areas, kitchen, cottage and wildlife garden. A photo opportunity around every corner. Our Winter open evening provides an enchanted evening view of a garden full of nostalgia. The inspired creative lighting demonstrates the beauty and architecture of plants and trees in winter. A real winter tonic.

GROUP OPENING

41 SAWSTON GARDENS

Sawston, Cambridge, CB22 3HY. *5m SE of Cambridge. Midway between Saffron Walden & Cambridge on A1301.* **Sun 7 July (1-5). Combined adm £5, chd free. Enjoy a cream tea at the Sweet Tea café in the High Street.**

MARY CHALLIS GARDEN
A M Challis Trust Ltd, www.challistrust.org.uk.

11 MILL LANE
Tim & Rosie Phillips.

35 MILL LANE
Doreen Butler.

3 very varied gardens in this large village in South Cambs. 11 Mill Lane has an impressive semi-circular lawn at the front, edged with roses and mixed borders, and a small orchard. The secluded sun-dappled rear garden has new hard and soft landscaping and a revamped sun deck. Mary Challis Garden is a 2-acre garden gifted to the village in 2006, maintained by volunteers to benefit wildlife and for the local community. Drifts of spring flowers are followed by colourful mixed summer herbaceous beds. The grounds also comprise woodland,

27 Springhill Road

orchard, a pond, vegetable beds, a vine house, specimen trees, sculptures, wildlife meadow and beehives. Lots to see all year round. 35 Mill Lane is a modern bungalow featuring very colourful massed annual and perennial displays packed into a small garden, set off by an immaculate lawn with running water features. A delight!

42 NEW 27 SPRINGHILL ROAD

Fen Drayton, Cambridge, CB24 4SR. Mr John Deeney. *Approx 1m from J27 on A14. Drive into Fen Drayton on Mill Rd. Where the rd bends R continue onto Oak Tree Rd. After 300m continue onto Springhill Rd. The garden is on R before the bend.* **Sun 26, Mon 27 May (10-4). Adm £4, chd free. Home-made teas.**

A new, eco-friendly garden on the site of a former Land Settlement Association smallholding. It combines a woodland/wildlife area, fruit trees, a variety of different borders with lawns, a pond and vegetable plot. All areas of garden linked by grass paths, mostly flat.

GROUP OPENING

43 STAPLEFORD GARDENS

Stapleford, Cambridge, CB22 5DG. Anthony Smith. *4m S of Cambridge on A1301. In London Rd next to Church St. Parking available on site.* **Sun 16 June (2-5.30). Combined adm £5, chd free. Home-made teas at Johnson Hall, 1 Gog Magog Way CB22 5BQ.**

NEW DOVE COTTAGE
Dr & Mrs Bryan & Carol Davies.

3A DUKES MEADOW
Jan & Lee Gruncell.

6 HAVERHILL ROAD
Mr & Mrs John & Joan King.

5 PRIAMS WAY
Tony Smith.

Contrasting gardens showing a range of size, planting and atmosphere in this village just S of Cambridge. Dove Cottage this garden was created in the 1980s and when we moved in 3 years ago was badly overgrown. Since then it has been a work in progress including removing 5 giant Leylandii, the development of a border shrubbery and creation of a small vegetable garden. 3a Dukes Meadow a beautiful tranquil south-facing established garden. Lawns, perennial plants, grasses, shrubs and trees. Pergola covered in roses. Large patio with water features. Sculptures and hanging baskets. 6 Haverhill Road is a well established and relaxing garden with grass, pergolas, flower beds, vegetable garden and soft fruit. Overlooking fields. Priam's Way has small mature borders with a wide variety of plants and shrubs.

GROUP OPENING

44 STAPLOE GARDENS

Staploe, St. Neots, PE19 5JA. *Great North Rd in western part of St Neots. At r'about just N of the Coop store, exit westwards on Duloe Rd. Follow this under the A1, through the village of Duloe & on to Staploe.* **Sat 8, Sun 9 June (1-5). Combined adm £4, chd free. Home-made teas.**

FALLING WATER HOUSE
Caroline Kent.

OLD FARM COTTAGE
Sir Graham & Lady Fry.

Old Farm Cottage: flower garden surrounding thatched house (not open), with 3 acres of orchard, grassland, woodland and a pond maintained for wildlife. Ginkgo, loquat and manuka trees grown from seed, and a wildflower meadow. Falling Water House: a mature woodland garden, partly reclaimed from farmland 10yrs ago, it is constructed around several century old trees incl three Wellingtonia. Kitchen garden potager, courtyard and herbaceous borders, planted to attract bees and wildlife, through which meandering paths have created hidden vistas. Old Farm Cottage has rough ground and one steep slope.

GROUP OPENING

45 STREETLY END & WEST WICKHAM GARDENS

West Wickham, CB21 4RP. *3m from Haverhill & 3m from Linton. Clover Cottage, Streetly End is opp grass triangle next to old windmill. 25 High Street, West Wickham CB21 4RY is near T junction.* **Sun 2 June (12-5). Combined adm £4.50, chd free. Light refreshments at Clover Cottage.**

CLOVER COTTAGE
Mr Paul & Mrs Shirley Shadford. (See separate entry)

25 HIGH STREET
Mrs Jane Scheuer.

Find at Clover Cottage, Streetly End, arches of roses, clematis and many varieties of geraniums, and raised fruit and vegetable beds. Delightful pond and borders of English roses, climbers and herbaceous plants. Ferns and shade plants under an old tree, with views over open countryside from the summer house in the sunken white garden. This small garden has an inspiring use of space. 25 High Street, West Wickham is a charming informal cottage garden to ramble, wander and relax in, with many routes through borders and pathways. Plants are allowed to self-seed and hybridise freely. Several interesting and unusual shrubs and herbaceous perennials from many continents. Regret no dogs. Regret no access for wheelchairs, prams, pushchairs, or wheeled walkers.

Your visits help change lives – we've donated over £16.7 million to Macmillan Cancer Support since 1984

GROUP OPENING

46 NEW SUTTON GARDENS

Sutton nr Ely, CB6 2QQ. *6m W of Ely. On A142 turn L at r'about on to B1381 to Earith. Parking available at The Burystead. CB6 2BB. Other gardens best reached from free car park at the Brooklands Centre. CB6 2QQ.* **Sun 2 June (2-6). Combined adm £6, chd free. Home-made teas at The Burystead.**

THE BURYSTEAD
Sarah Cleverdon & Stephen Tebboth.

NEW 61 HIGH STREET
Ms Kate Travers & Mr Jon Meggenson.

NEW 63 HIGH STREET
Ms Ruth & Mr Arthur Brown.

NEW THE OLD BAPTIST CHAPEL
Janet Porter & Steve Newton.

NEW 19 THE ROW
Alistair & Jane Huck.

A varied group of gardens in this attractive village. The Old Baptist Chapel is a new garden being created around an C18 Baptist chapel, recently converted to a family home. 61 The High Street is a tiny shaded garden with a host of features: interesting trees, herb and vegetable plots, greenhouses, and boxes for birds, bats and bugs. 63 The High Street is a sloping sunny garden in the centre of the village with spectacular views over the fens. The borders are in the 'cottage garden' style containing clematis, peonies, geraniums, iris and many other cottage garden favourites. 19 The Row is a long ¾ acre family garden, started 25 yrs ago. Decking, seating, summer house, shed with green roof, pond, sculpture, some unusual trees, shrubs, perennials, fruit and vegetables. Wildlife area with long grass. The Burystead is a ½ acre walled courtyard garden of formal design, set against a backdrop of a restored C16 thatched barn. There is also a cottage garden, sculpture and a new vegetable plot.

47 TRINITY COLLEGE, FELLOWS' GARDEN

Queens Road, Cambridge, CB3 9AQ. Master and Fellows' of Trinity College, www.trin.cam.ac.uk/about/gardens. *Short walk from city centre. At the Northampton St/Madingley Rd end of Queens Rd close to Garrett Hostel Lane.* **Sun 14 Apr (1-4). Adm £4, chd free. Home-made teas. Special dietary requirements are usually catered for.**
Interesting historic garden of about 8 acres with impressive specimen trees, mixed borders, drifts of spring bulbs and informal lawns with notable influences throughout from Fellows over the years. Across the gently flowing Bin Brook to Burrell's Field you will find some modern planting styles and plants nestled amongst the accommodation blocks in smaller intimate gardens. Members of the Gardens Department will be on hand to answer any questions and serve home-made cakes, tea and coffee. There will also be some plant sales. Wheelchair access - some gravel paths.

48 TRINITY HALL - WYCHFIELD

Storey's Way, Cambridge, CB3 0DZ. The Master & Fellows, www.trinhall.cam.ac.uk/about/gardens/. *1m NW of city centre. Turn into Storey's Way from Madingley Rd (A1303) and follow the yellow NGS signs. Limited on-road parking is available.* **Sat 6 July (11-3). Adm £4, chd free. Home-made teas.** Donation to MIND.
A beautiful large garden that complements the interesting and varied architecture. The Edwardian Wychfield House and its associated gardens contrast with the recent contemporary development located off Storey's Way. Majestic trees, roses and herbaceous perennials, shady under storey woodland planting and established lawns, work together to provide an inspiring garden. Plant sale. Tea and home-made cakes. Some gravel paths.

TWIN TARNS

6 Pinfold Lane, Somersham PE28 3EQ. Michael & Frances Robinson, 01487 843376, mikerobinson987@btinternet.com. *Easy access from the A14. 4m NE of St Ives. Turn onto Church St. Pinfold Lane is next to the church. Please park on Church Street as access is narrow and limited.* **Sat 13, Sun 14 July (1-5). Adm £4, chd free. Cream teas. Visits also by arrangement May to Sept.** One-acre wildlife garden with formal borders, kitchen garden and ponds, large rockery, mini woodland, wild flower meadow (June/July). Topiary, rose walk, greenhouses. Character oak bridge, veranda and tree-house. Adjacent to C13 village church.

49 WILD ROSE COTTAGE

Church Walk, Lode, Cambridge, CB25 9EX. Mrs Joy Martin, 01223 811132, joymartin123@outlook.com. *From A14 take the rd towards Burwell turn L in to Lode & park on L after 150 metres. Walk straight on between thatched cottages to the archway of Wild Rose Cottage.* **Evening opening Thur 6 June (6-8). Adm £7.50, chd free. inc wine. Food and drink available at the local pub, The Shed.** Visits also by arrangement Apr to Oct. £5.
A real cottage garden overflowing with plants. Gardens within gardens of abundant vegetation, roses climbing through trees, laburnum tunnel, a daffodil spiral which becomes a daisy spiral in the summer. Circular vegetable garden and wildlife pond. Described by one visitor as a garden to write poetry in! It is a truly wild and loved garden where flowers in the vegetable circle are not pulled up! Chickens ducks and dog, circular vegetable garden, wild life pond, and wild romantic garden! Lots of little path ways.

50 WILLOW HOLT

Willow Hall Lane, Thorney, PE6 0QN. Angie & Jonathan Jones. *4m E of Peterborough. From A47, between Eye & Thorney turn S into Willow Hall Lane. 1.6m on R. NOT in Thorney Village.* **Sun 26, Mon 27 May (11-5). Adm £4, chd free. Home-made teas.**

Two acres, part farmer's field part gravel pit, were combined as a building plot in 1960. In 1992 the current owners began an ongoing transformation from nettle-bed and local tip to a dream garden of mature trees, wildflower meadow, wildlife ponds, scrap metal sculptures and an impressive and varied collection of plants and shrubs. 75% accessible by wheelchair users with a good pusher.

51 THE WINDMILL

10 Cambridge Road, Impington, CB24 9NU. Pippa & Steve Temple, 07775 446443, mill.impington@ntlworld.com, www.impingtonmill.org. *2½m N of Cambridge. Off A14 at J32, B1049 to Histon, L into Cambridge Rd at T-lights, follow Cambridge Rd round to R, the Windmill is approx 400yds on L.* **Visits by arrangement Apr to Sept. Adm £5, chd free. Light refreshments by arrangement.**

A previously romantic wilderness of 1½ acres surrounding windmill, now filled with bulbs, perennial beds, pergolas, bog gardens, grass bed and herb bank. Secret paths and wild areas with thuggish roses maintain the romance. Millstone seating area in smouldering borders contrasts with the pastel colours of the remainder of the garden. Also 'Pond Life' seat, 'Tree God' and amazing compost area! The Windmill - an C18 smock on C19 tower on C17 base on C16 foundations - is being restored. Guide dogs only.

52 WOLFSON COLLEGE GARDEN

Barton Road, Cambridge, CB3 9BB. Wolfson College. *On SW side of Cambridge. From M11 J12, take A603 into Cambridge. Wolfson College is approx 2m from J12, on L.* **Sat 31 Aug (12-4). Adm £3, chd free.**

Gardens are a series of lawned courtyards forming a set of garden 'rooms', and some stunning Herbacious borders. The beds and borders contain a wide variety of plants and shrubs which provide structure, colour and interest through the year. Several courts reflect a Chinese influence in the design and planting with many rare small Acers and Chinese trees. The retention of some majestic trees from the original site helps to give an atmosphere of maturity and permanence to a garden which has developed greatly over the last 30yrs. The borders contain many ornamental grasses (of all types) and 'naturalistic plantings' combined with Exotic plants such as Bananas, Cannas, a huge variety of Salvias and late summer colour. There is also Topiary galore (Penguin, Roadrunner, Cat etc etc !). Please come and see our wonderful gardens. Phil. Head Gardener

53 NEW WRIGHTS FARM

Tilbrook Road, Kimbolton, Huntingdon, PE28 0JW. Russell & Hetty Dean. *13m SW of Huntingdon. ¼ m W of Kimbolton on the B645. Do not follow sat nav.* **Sun 30 June (2-5). Adm £5, chd free. Home-made teas.**

A new garden started in 2013, set within 4 acres. Varied borders with bee and butterfly friendly planting. Formal Walled vegetable garden with raised beds, potting shed and greenhouses. Paved entrance area with plenty of pots. Riverside paths and seating areas. Large orchard and walk through meadow. Open countryside views.

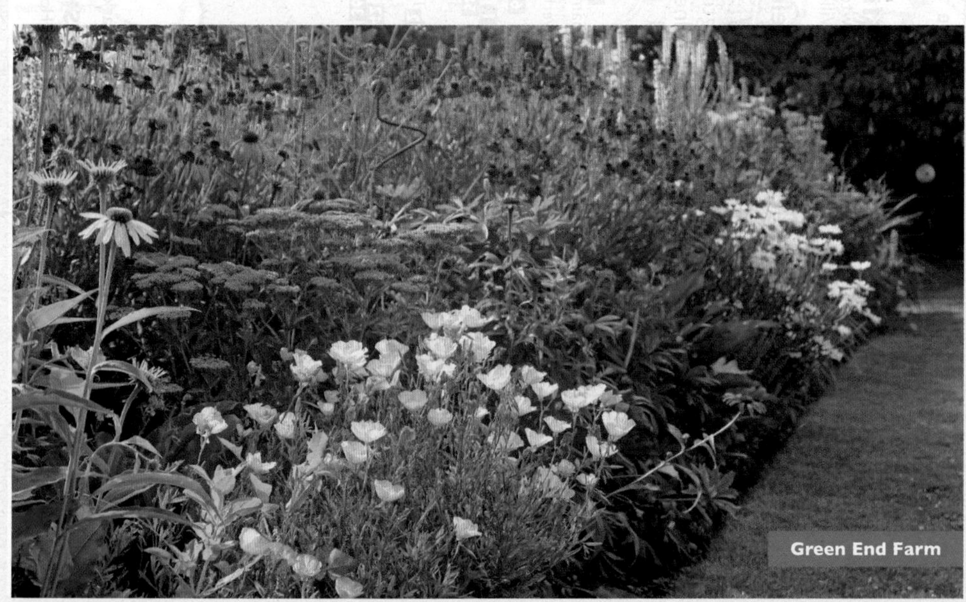

Green End Farm

OPENING DATES

All entries subject to change. For latest information check **www.ngs.org.uk**

Extended openings are shown at the beginning of the month.

Map locator numbers are shown to the right of each garden name.

February

Snowdrop Festival

By Arrangement

Rosewood 56
The Well House 69

Saturday 16th

Trafford Hall 68

Sunday 17th

West Drive Gardens 70

Sunday 24th

Bucklow Farm 16

April

Saturday 20th

Poulton Hall 54

Sunday 21st

All Fours Farm 2
Poulton Hall 54

Sunday 28th

Long Acre 36
◆ Ness Botanic Gardens 45

May

Saturday 4th

◆ Mount Pleasant 44

Sunday 5th

Manley Knoll 39
◆ Mount Pleasant 44

Monday 6th

All Fours Farm 2
Framley 24

Thursday 9th

◆ Cholmondeley Castle Gardens 20

Saturday 11th

Brooke Cottage 14
64 Carr Wood 18

Sunday 12th

◆ Abbeywood Gardens 1
Brooke Cottage 14
15 Park Crescent 51
◆ Stonyford Cottage 62
Tirley Garth Gardens 67

Wednesday 15th

Tatton Park

Saturday 18th

Inglewood 32

Sunday 19th

NEW Hall Lane Farm 26
Inglewood 32
Sandymere 58
Tattenhall Hall 65
Tirley Garth Gardens 67

Saturday 25th

Cheriton 19
10 Statham Avenue 61

Sunday 26th

Cheriton 19
73 Hill Top Avenue 29
Rowley House 57
10 Statham Avenue 61

Monday 27th

All Fours Farm 2

June

Saturday 1st

Mill House 43
◆ Peover Hall Gardens 53

Sunday 2nd

Mayfield House 42
◆ Peover Hall Gardens 53
Tirley Garth Gardens 67
Trafford Hall 68

Saturday 8th

NEW Drake Carr 22
Lane End Cottage Gardens 34
The Old Parsonage 50

Sunday 9th

NEW Drake Carr 22
Free Green Farm 25
Lane End Cottage Gardens 34
◆ Norton Priory Museum & Gardens 46
The Old Parsonage 50
Sycamore Cottage 64
West Drive Gardens 70

Wednesday 12th

Tatton Park

Saturday 15th

Ashmead 4
NEW Manor Farm 41
NEW Manor Farm 40

Sunday 16th

Ashmead 4
Bucklow Farm 16
60 Kennedy Avenue 33
Long Acre 36
NEW Manor Farm 40
15 Park Crescent 51
Winterbottom House 72

Saturday 22nd

150 Barrel Well Hill Chester 6
18 Highfield Road 28

Sunday 23rd

150 Barrel Well Hill Chester 6
61 Birtles Road 8
Bowmere Cottage 12
18 Highfield Road 28
The Homestead 31

Tuesday 25th

NEW Combermere Abbey Gardens 21

Saturday 29th

Beechwood Cottage 7
◆ Bluebell Cottage Gardens 9
10 Statham Avenue 61
NEW Wirral Hospice St John's 73

Sunday 30th

All Fours Farm 2
NEW Ashton Grange 5
Beechwood Cottage 7
◆ Bluebell Cottage Gardens 9
Bollin House 11
Burton Village Gardens 17
Hilltop 30
10 Statham Avenue 61
NEW Wirral Hospice St John's 73

July

Sunday 7th

Rowley House 57
Stretton Old Hall 63

Saturday 13th

NEW The MacIntyre New Routes Orchard and Garden 38

Saturday 27th

The Firs 23

Sunday 28th

The Firs 23
◆ Stonyford Cottage 62

August

Saturday 3rd

21 Scafell Close 59
Thorncar 66

Sunday 4th

◆ Arley Hall & Gardens 3
73 Hill Top Avenue 29
21 Scafell Close 59

Saturday 10th

Laskey Farm 35
Trafford Hall 68

Sunday 11th

◆ Abbeywood Gardens 1
Laskey Farm 35
24 Old Greasby Road 49

September

Saturday 7th

Lane End Cottage Gardens 34
◆ Mount Pleasant 44

Sunday 8th

Lane End Cottage Gardens 34
◆ Mount Pleasant 44

Sunday 15th

Briarfield 13

October

Sunday 6th

◆ The Lovell Quinta Arboretum 37

February 2020

Saturday 22nd

Briarfield 13

Sunday 23rd

Briarfield 13
Bucklow Farm 16

By Arrangement

Arrange a personalised garden visit with your club, or group of friends, on a date to suit you. See individual garden entries for full details.

THE GARDENS

1 ◆ ABBEYWOOD GARDENS

Chester Road, Delamere, Northwich, CW8 2HS. The Rowlinson Family, 01606 889477, info@abbeywoodestate.co.uk, www.abbeywoodestate.co.uk. *11m E of Chester. On the A556 facing Delamere Church.* **For NGS: Sun 12 May, Sun 11 Aug (9-5). Adm £5, chd free. Light refreshments. Restaurant in garden.** For other opening times and information, please phone, email or visit garden website.
Superb setting near Delamere Forest. Total area 45 acres incl mature woodland, new woodland and new arboretum all with connecting pathways. Approx 4½ acres of gardens surrounding large Edwardian House. Vegetable garden, exotic garden, chapel garden, pool garden, woodland garden, lawned area with beds.

2 ALL FOURS FARM

Colliers Lane, Aston by Budworth, Northwich, CW9 6NF. Mr & Mrs Evans, 01565 733286. *M6 J19, take A556 towards Northwich. Turn immed R, past The Windmill Pub. Turn R after approx 1m, follow rd, garden on L after approx 2m. We're happy to allow direct access for drop off & collection for those with limited mobility.* **Sun 21 Apr, Mon 6, Mon 27 May, Sun 30 June (10-4). Adm £5, chd free. Light refreshments.** Visits also by arrangement Apr to June for groups of 20+.
A traditional and well established country garden with a wide range of roses, hardy shrubs, bulbs, perennials and annuals. You will also find a small vegetable garden, pond and greenhouse as well as vintage machinery and original features from its days as a working farm. The garden is adjacent to the families traditional rose nursery. The majority of the garden is accessible by wheelchair.

3 ◆ ARLEY HALL & GARDENS

Northwich, CW9 6NA. Viscount Ashbrook, www.arleyhallandgardens.com. *10m from Warrington. Signed from J9 & 10 (M56) & J19 & 20 (M6) (20 min from Tatton Park, 40 min to Manchester). Please follow the brown tourist signs.* **For NGS: Sun 4 Aug (10-5). Adm £8.50, chd £3.50. All refreshments available.** For other opening times and information, please visit garden website.
Arley has been lovingly created by the same family over 550 years and is famous for its double herbaceous border, thought to be the oldest in Europe. Other outstanding features of the garden are the avenue of ilex columns, walled garden, pleached lime avenue, victorian rootree and informal Grove and Woodland Walk. A garden of great atmosphere, interest and vitality throughout the seasons.

4 ASHMEAD

2 Bramhall Way, off Gritstone Drive, Macclesfield, SK10 3SH. Peter & Penelope McDermott, 01625 434200, penelope.mcdermott@pmsurveying.plus.com. *1m W of Macclesfield. Turn onto Pavilion Way, off Victoria Rd, then immed L onto Gritstone Drive. Bramhall Way first on R.* **Sat 15, Sun 16 June (1-5). Adm £4, chd free. Home-made teas.** Visits also by arrangement Jan to June for groups of 10 to 20. No arranged openings after official opening.
⅛ acre suburban cottage garden, featuring plant packed mixed borders, rock gardens, kitchen garden, island beds, water feature, pond. The garden demonstrates how small spaces can be planted to maximum effect to create all round interest. Extensive range of plants favoured for colours, texture and scent. Pots used in a creative way to extend and enhance borders.

Your visits help change lives – your generosity has supported unpaid carers through donations to Carers Trust totalling over £3.9 million since 1996

Bucklow Farm

5 NEW ASHTON GRANGE

Grange Road, Ashton Hayes, Chester, CH3 8AE. Mr & Mrs Martin Slack, 01829 759172, kateslack1@icloud.com. *8m E of Chester. Grange Rd is a single track rd off the B5393 by the village sign at the North end of Ashton Hayes.* **Sun 30 June (2-5). Adm £6, chd free. Home-made teas.** Visits also by arrangement Apr to Oct for groups of 10 to 30.

The gardens at Ashton Grange include extensive lawns, borders, island beds, shrubberies, a large pond, an orchard and a kitchen garden all of which are set against mature woodlands. There is also a small paddock and a new wildflower meadow. The whole property extends to approximately 9 acres. Since 2015, the owners have been undertaking a restoration project which is still ongoing. Wheelchair access is possible to most parts of the garden, but woodland paths could be difficult. Limited parking for wheelchair users is available.

6 150 BARREL WELL HILL CHESTER

Boughton, Chester, CH3 5BR. Dr & Mrs John Browne, 01244 329988, john.browne@jwbcatalyst.co.uk. *On riverside ¾ m E of Chester off A5115. No parking at garden. Preferred access via Chester Boats, on the hour from the Groves, central Chester. Cost £3.50 one way. Or bus to St Pauls Church. Parking 100m at Boughton Health Centre CH2 3DP.* **Sat 22, Sun 23 June (11-5). Adm £4, chd free. Home-made teas.** Visits also by arrangement May to Sept for groups of 10 to 20.

Spectacular terraced garden with views over the R Dee to the Meadows and Clwyd Hills. Uniquely, preferred method of arrival is by leisurely river cruiser from Chester. Informal cottage style garden on historic site by the Martyrs Memorial. Lawns running down to the river, prolific shrub and flower beds, productive vegetable patch and soft and hard fruit areas, springs, stream and lily pond. River cruisers leave the centre of Chester regularly and arrangements have been made that they will drop off and pick up garden visitors on their way up river. Not suitable for wheelchairs or children under eight due to steps and unprotected drop into river.

7 BEECHWOOD COTTAGE

64 Crouchley Lane, Lymm, WA13 0AT. Ian & Amber Webb, www.beechwoodcottagegardens.com. *8m S of Altrincham. 4m from J7 or 2m J21 M6 onto A56 turn into Crouchley Ln past Lymm Rugby Club on R, 300yds on R (opp Crouchley Mews).* **Sat 29, Sun 30 June (11-5). Adm £5, chd free. Home-made teas. Undercover seating.**

2 acre garden looking out to fields. Large lawn with herbaceous borders. Cutting Garden, topiary garden and orchard. Wild flower meadow - shaded area with tree ferns, hellebores and ferns. The grandest chicken shed outside Highgrove. Some gravel paths.

8 61 BIRTLES ROAD

Macclesfield, SK10 3JG. Kate & Graham Tyson. *Close to Macclesfield Leisure Centre & Macclesfield Hospital. Follow NGS signs - B5087 Prestbury Rd onto Priory Lane, R Birtles Rd, or from Fallibroome Road, L onto Priory Lane, L Birtles Rd. Graham & Kate 07850768885 tysonfamily4@yahoo.com.* **Sun 23 June (10-4). Adm £3.50, chd free. Home-made teas.**

A South facing suburban garden created to give year round interest and colour. Well stocked herbaceous borders, Rose garden, island beds and a pond creating a habitat for frogs and newts all add to an ever changing colour palette. We look forward to greeting you! There is plenty of seating for homemade cake and afternoon tea! Gazebo provision for inclement weather! Wheelchairs will be able to access onto the patio there are steps down onto the garden.

9 ◆ BLUEBELL COTTAGE GARDENS

Lodge Lane, Dutton, WA4 4HP. Sue & Dave Beesley, 01928 713718, info@bluebellcottage.co.uk, www.bluebellcottage.co.uk. *5m NW of Northwich. From M56 (J10) take A49 to Whitchurch. After 3m turn R at T-lights towards Runcorn/ Dutton on A533. Then 1st L. Signed with brown tourism signs from A533.* **For NGS: Sat 29, Sun 30 June (10-5). Adm £5, chd free. Home-made teas.** For other opening times and information, please phone, email or visit garden website.

South facing country garden wrapped around a cottage on a quiet rural lane in the heart of Cheshire. Packed with thousands of rare and familiar hardy herbaceous perennials, shrubs and trees. Unusual plants available at adjacent nursery. The opening dates coincide with the peak of flowering in the herbaceous borders. Some gravel paths. Wheelchair access to 90% of garden. WC is not fully wheelchair accessible.

10 BOLESWORTH CASTLE

Tattenhall, CH3 9HQ. Mrs Anthony Barbour, 01829 782210, dcb@bolesworth.com. *8m S of Chester on A41. Enter by Lodge on A41.* **Visits by arrangement Apr to Oct for groups of 10+. Please note visits April, May and Oct only. Adm £5, chd free.**

The Spring garden on The Rock Walk above Castle, planted with superb collection of Rhododendrons, Camellias and specimen trees in the 90's, is undergoing restoration and development with exciting new planting. Well planted shrub/ herbaceous borders around Castle. Unusual and rare trees planted over a period of 25 years by Anthony Barbour now at their best (Autumn colour in October). Regret no wheelchair access.

Sandymere

11 BOLLIN HOUSE

Hollies Lane, Wilmslow, SK9 2BW. Angela Ferguson & Gerry Lemon, 07828 207492, fergusonang@doctors.org.uk. *From Wilmslow past Station & proceed to T-junction. Turn L onto Adlington Rd. Proceed for ½m, then turn R into Hollies Lane(just after One Oak Lane). Drive to the end of Hollies Lane and follow yellow signage. Park on Hollies L, or Browns L(other side Adlington Rd).* **Sun 30 June (10-4). Adm £4, chd free. Home-made teas, cake or scones at £4.** Visits also by arrangement May to July for groups of 10 to 30. Check parking arrangements.

There are 2 parts to the garden, a formal garden and the rarer, wild flower meadow. The garden has deep herbaceous borders, (think hollyhocks and roses), and an orchard. A new landscaped area has just been added with a central water feature. The meadow with it's annual and perennial wild flower areas (with mown pathways and benches) attracts lots of butterflies and humming insects on a sunny day. Bollin House is in an idyllic location with the garden, orchard and meadow flowing into the Bollin Valley. Here the meadow is a combination of perennial and annual wild flowers areas. Ramps to gravel lined paths to most of the garden. Some narrow paths through borders. Mown pathways in the meadow.

12 BOWMERE COTTAGE

5 Bowmere Road, Tarporley, CW6 0BS. Romy & Tom Holmes, 01829 732053, romy@bowmerecottage.co.uk. *10m E of Chester. From Tarporley High St (old A49) take Eaton Rd signed Eaton. After 100 metres take R fork into Bowmere Rd, Garden 100 metres on LH-side.* **Sun 23 June (1-5). Adm £4.50, chd free. Home-made teas.** Visits also by arrangement June & July.

A colourful and relaxing one acre country style garden around a Grade II listed house. The lawns are surrounded by well stocked herbaceous and shrub borders and rose covered pergolas. There are two plant filled courtyard gardens and a small vegetable garden. Shrub and rambling roses, clematis, hardy geraniums and a wide range of mostly hardy plants make this a very traditional English garden.

13 BRIARFIELD

The Rake, Burton, Neston, CH64 5TL. Liz Carter, 0151 336 2304, carter.burton@btinternet.com. *9m NW of Chester. Turn off A540 at Willaston-Burton Xrds T-lights & follow rd for 1m to Burton village centre.* **Sun 15 Sept (1-5). Adm £5, chd free. Home-made teas in St Nicholas Church, just along the lane. Opening with Burton Village Gardens on Sun 30 June. 2020: Sat 22, Sun 23 Feb.** Visits also by arrangement July to Sept.

Tucked under the S-facing side of Burton Wood the garden is home to many specialist and unusual plants, some available in plant sale. This 2 acre garden is on two sites, a couple of minutes along an unmade lane. Shrubs, colourful herbaceous, bulbs, alpines and water features compete for attention as you wander through four distinctly different gardens. Always changing, Liz can't resist a new plant! Rare and unusual plants sold (70% to NGS) in Neston Market most Fridays.

14 BROOKE COTTAGE

Church Road, Handforth, SK9 3LT. Barry & Melanie Davy. *1m N of Wilmslow. Centre of Handforth, behind Health Centre. Turn off Wilmslow Rd at St Chads, follow Church Rd round to R. Garden last on L. Parking in Health Centre car park.* **Sat 11, Sun 12 May (12-5). Adm £4, chd free. Home-made teas.**

Rare chance to see this plant-filled garden in Spring: Shady woodland area of ferns, azaleas, rhododendrons, camellias, magnolia, erythroniums, trilliums, arisaema and blue poppies. Patio with hostas, daylilies, small pond. Borders with grasses, perennials, euphorbia, alliums and tulips. Anthriscus, aquilegia, persicaria and astrantia create meadow effect popular with insects. Featured in RHS magazine.

15 BROOKLANDS

Smithy Lane, Mouldsworth, CH3 8AR. Barbara & Brian Russell-Moore, 01928 740413, ngsmouldsworth@aol.co.uk. *1½m N of Tarvin. 5½m S of Frodsham. Smithy Lane is off B5393 via A54 Tarvin/Kelsall rd or the A56 Frodsham/Helsby rd.* **Visits by arrangement May to Aug for groups of 10 to 30. Adm £4, chd free. Home-made teas and cakes using eggs from our own hens.**

A lovely country style, ¾ acre garden with backdrop of mature trees and shrubs. The planting is based around azaleas, rhododendrons, mixed shrub and herbaceous borders. There is a small vegetable garden, supported by a greenhouse and hens providing eggs for all the afternoon tea cakes!! Repeat visitors will notice significant changes following damage and tree loss caused by 'Storm Doris.'.

16 BUCKLOW FARM

Pinfold Lane, Plumley, Knutsford, WA16 9RP. Dawn & Peter Freeman. *2m S of Knutsford. M6 J19, A556 Chester. L at 2nd set of T-lights. In 1¼m, L at concealed Xrds. 1st R. From Knutsford A5033, L at Sudlow Lane. becomes Pinfold Lane.* **Sun 24 Feb (12.30-4). Adm £3.50, chd free. Light refreshments. Sun 16 June (2-5). Adm £4.50, chd free. Cream teas. Mulled Wine in February. Cream teas in June 2020: Sun 23 Feb.** Donation to Knutsford Scouts.

Country garden with shrubs, perennial borders, rambling roses, herb garden, vegetable patch, wildlife pond/water feature and alpines. Landscaped and planted over the last 30yrs with recorded changes. Free range hens. Carpet of snowdrops and spring bulbs. Leaf, stem and berries to show colour in autumn and winter. Featured in Cheshire Life. Cobbled yard from car park, but wheelchairs can be dropped off near gate.

GROUP OPENING

17 BURTON VILLAGE GARDENS

Burton, Neston, CH64 5SJ. *9m NW of Chester. Turn off A540 at Willaston-Burton Xrds T-lights & follow rd for 1m to Burton. Maps given to visitors. Buy your ticket at first garden.* **Sun 30 June (11-5). Combined adm £5, chd free. Home-made teas in the Sports and Social Club behind the village hall.**

BRIARFIELD
Liz Carter.
(See separate entry)

◆ BURTON MANOR WALLED GARDEN
Burton Manor Gardens Ltd, 0151 3451107, www.burtonmanorgardens.org.uk.

TRUSTWOOD
Peter & Lin Friend, lin@trustwoodbnb.uk, , www.trustwoodbnb.uk.
Visits also by arrangement May & June for groups of up to 20.

Burton is a medieval village built on sandstone overlooking the Dee estuary. Three gardens are open. Trustwood is a country wildlife garden with fruit, flowers and vegetables in raised beds at the front; at the back a more formal garden blends into the wood where the hens live. Briarfield's sheltered site, on the south side of Burton Wood (NT), is home to many specialist and unusual plants, some available in the plant sale at the house. The 1½ acre main garden invites exploration not only for its huge variety of plants but also for the imaginative use of ceramic sculptures. Period planting with a splendid vegetable garden surrounds the restored Edwardian glasshouse in Burton Manor's walled garden. Plants for sale at two gardens. Well signed free car parks. Maps available; all within easy walking distance. Briarfield is unsuitable for wheelchairs.

18 64 CARR WOOD

Hale Barns, Altrincham, WA15 0EP. Mrs John Booth & Mr David Booth. *10m S of Manchester city centre. 2m from J6 M56: Take A538 to Hale Barns. L at 'triangle' by church into Wicker Lane & L at mini r'about into Chapel Lane & 1st R into Carr Wood.* **Sat 11 May (2-6). Adm £5, chd free. Home-made teas.**

Two-thirds acre landscaped, S-facing garden overlooking Bollin Valley laid out in 1959 by Clibrans of Altrincham. Gently sloping lawn, woodland walk, seating areas and terrace, extensive mixed shrub and plant borders. Partial wheelchair access and ample parking on Carr Wood. Wheelchair access to terrace overlooking main garden.

19 CHERITON

34 Congleton Road, Alderley Edge, SK9 7AB. David & Jo Mottershead. *400yds S of Alderley Edge on R of Congleton Road. Park on rd.* **Sat 25, Sun 26 May (11-5). Adm £5, chd £2. Home-made teas. Selection of teas, coffee, wine and light foods incl cakes.**

SW-facing, 1-acre garden with views on a fine day to the Clwydian Range. Garden of mature rhododendron, magnolias and wisteria with early clematis, hellebores and a range of unusual herbaceous plants and young specimen trees. The second year of the new and previously open garden with significant and exciting changes made. Large free-standing Wisteria. Interesting planted flowing water feature with ponds. Front garden now planted as a stunning winter garden, with white barked birches underplanted with heuchera and hellebore. Wheelchair access to rear garden only via a short flight (4) of low steps. No wc facilities for wheelchair users.

Your visits help change lives – we are the largest single funder of the Queen's Nursing Institute

20 ◆ CHOLMONDELEY CASTLE GARDENS

Cholmondeley, nr Malpas, SY14 8AH. Marquess of Cholmondeley, 01829 720383, dilys@cholmondeleycastle.co.uk, www.cholmondeleycastle.com. *4m NE of Malpas Sat Nav SY14 8ET. Signed from A41 Chester-Whitchurch rd & A49 Whitchurch-Tarporley rd SAT NAV SY14 8ET.* **For NGS: Thur 9 May (11-5). Adm £8.50, chd £4. Light lunches & home-made teas in Tea Room located in the heart of the gardens.** For other opening times and information, please phone, email or visit garden website.

Over 50 acres of romantically landscaped gardens with fine views and eye-catching water features, but still manages to retain its intimacy. Beautiful mature trees form a background to spring bulbs, exotic plants in season incl magnolias, rhododendrons, azaleas and camellias and many other, particularly *Davidia Involucrata* which will be in flower in late May. Magnificent magnolias. One of the finest features of the gardens are its trees, many of which are rare and unusual and Cholmondeley Gardens is home to over 40 county champion trees. 100m long double mixed border and newly planted Rose Garden with 250 new roses. Partial wheelchair access.

21 NEW COMBERMERE ABBEY GARDENS

Combermere Abbey, Whitchurch, SY13 4AJ. Sarah Callander Beckett, www.combermereabbey.co.uk/gardens. *At the centre of the Combermere Estate. Post Code for Sat Nav SY13 4AN at the main entrance, situated on the A530/A525 between Nantwich & Whitchurch on the Cheshire/Shropshire border. Follow estate signs down 1m long drive.* **Tue 25 June (1-5). Adm £5, chd £2. Light refreshments in the Pavilion Cafe in the Walled Gardens.**

Open for the first time for the NGS, come and explore the ever evolving, restored Walled Gardens, the Pleasure Garden and Garden Wood with its stunning views across the mere. A rare chance to enter the gates of this privately-owned historic estate and explore its horticultural splendours. Large 6 acre walled garden featuring a Messenger Glasshouse; world's only Fruit Tree Maze designed by Randoll Coate; Pleasure Garden planted in C18 and woodland garden with views of 143 acre mere. Wheelchair access is available in the Walled Gardens only on compacted gravel paths and there are disabled toilets and ramps into the Pavilion cafe.

22 NEW DRAKE CARR

Mudhurst Lane, Higher Disley, SK12 2AN. Alan & Joan Morris. *8m SE of Stockport, 12m NE of Macclesfield. From A6 in Disley centre turn into Buxton Old Rd, go up hill 1m & turn R into Mudhurst Lane. After ⅓m park on lay-by or grass verge. No parking at garden. Approx 150 metre walk.* **Sat 8, Sun 9 June (11-5). Adm £4, chd free. Home-made teas. Home-made gluten-free cakes available.**

⅓ acre cottage garden in beautiful rural setting with natural stream running into large wildlife pond containing many native species. Surrounding C17 stone cottage, the garden, containing herbaceous borders, shrubs and veg plot, is on several levels divided by grassed areas, slopes and steps. This blends into boarded walk through bog garden and mature wooded area. Not suitable for wheelchairs.

23 THE FIRS

Old Chester Road, Barbridge, Nantwich, CW5 6AY. Richard & Valerie Goodyear, 07775 924929, Goodyear.Pickford@btinternet.com. *3m N of Nantwich on A51. After entering Barbridge turn R at Xrds after 100 metres. The Firs is 2nd house on L.* **Sat 27, Sun 28 July (1-5). Adm £4, chd free. Home-made teas.** Visits also by arrangement Apr to Aug for groups of 10 to 30.

Canalside garden set idyllically by a wide section of the Shropshire Union Canal with long frontage. Approx 0.4 acre of varied trees, shrubs and herbaceous beds, with some wild areas. All leading down to an observatory at the end of the garden. There is wheelchair access to most of the garden.

24 FRAMLEY

Hadlow Road, Willaston, Neston, CH64 2US. Mrs Sally Reader, 07496 015259, sllyreader@yahoo.co.uk. *½m S of Willaston village centre. From Willaston Green, proceed along Hadlow Rd, crossing the Wirral Way. Framley is the next house on R.* **Mon 6 May (10.30-4). Adm £4, chd free. Home-made teas.** Visits also by arrangement Apr to July for groups of up to 20.

This 5 acre garden holds many hidden gems. Comprising extensive mature wooded areas, underplanted with a variety of interesting and unusual woodland plants - all at their very best in spring. A selection of deep seasonal borders surround a mystical sunken garden, planted to suit its challenging conditions. Wide lawns and sandstone paths invite you to discover what lies around every corner. Please phone ahead for parking instructions for wheelchair users - access around much of the garden although the woodland paths may be challenging.

25 FREE GREEN FARM

Free Green Lane, Lower Peover, WA16 9QX. Sir Philip Haworth. *3m S of Knutsford. Near A50 between Knutsford & Holmes Chapel. Off Free Green Lane.* **Sun 9 June (1-5). Adm £5, chd free. Home-made teas.**

2-acre garden with pleached limes, herbaceous borders, ponds, parterre, garden of the senses, British woodland with fernery, quasi-jungle area with Banana. Topiary. Wildlife friendly. Assortment of trees, and ten different forms of hedging. Ponds and underplanted woodland. Wheelchair access not easy in the wood.

Your visits help change lives – we are Hospice UK's largest charitable funder donating more than £5 million to support hospices in local communities since 1996

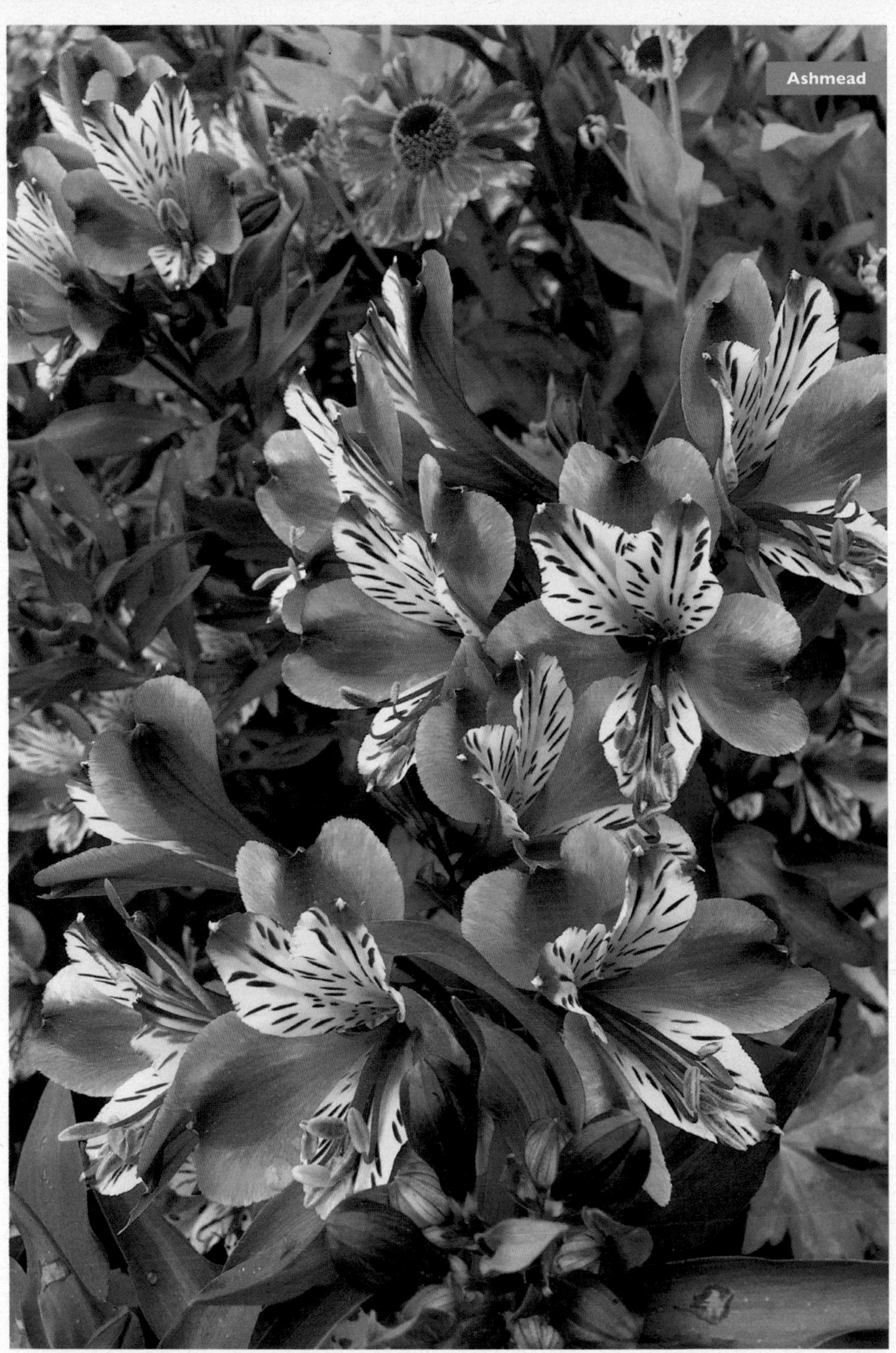
Ashmead

26 NEW HALL LANE FARM

Hall Lane, Daresbury, Warrington, WA4 4AF. Sir Michael & Lady Beverley Bibby. *1m from J11 of M56. Leave M56 at J11, head towards Warrington take 2nd R turn into Daresbury village go around sharp bend then take L into Daresbury Lane. Entrance on L after 100 yds.* **Sun 19 May (1-5). Adm £5, chd free. Tea.**

The 2 acres of private formal garden originally designed by Arabella Lennox-Boyd are arranged in a 'gardens within gardens' style to create a series of enclosed spaces each with their own character and style. The gardens also include a vegetable garden, orchard, Koi pond, surrounded by a fantastic display of primula in the spring as well as lawns and a tree house.

27 NEW HIGHER DAM HEAD FARM

Damson Lane, Mobberley, WA16 7HY. Richard & Alex Ellison, 01565 873544, alex.ellison@talk21.com. *2m N E of Knutsford. 4m W of Alderley Edge. Turn off B5085 into Mill Lane at sign for Roebuck Inn. Damson Lane runs alongside the Roebuck car park and property lies 150yds further on R.* **Visits by arrangement June to Sept for groups of 10+. Adm £5. Light refreshments. Light lunches and afternoon teas can be provided by prior arrangement.**

Two acre country garden with box lined courtyards, large terracotta pots, deep herbaceous borders, topiary, pergola, orchard, walled vegetable garden, large glass house with stoned fruit. Natural pond with oak framed summerhouse and waterside deck. Newly planted area of silver birch and grasses in modern style. Plenty of areas to sit.

28 18 HIGHFIELD ROAD

Bollington, Macclesfield, SK10 5LR. Mrs Melita Turner. *3m N of Macclesfield. A523 to Stockport. Turn R at B5090 r'about signed Bollington. Pass under viaduct. Take next R (by Library) up Hurst Lane. Turn R into Highfield Rd. Property on L. Park on wider road just past it.* **Sat 22, Sun 23 June (10-4). Adm £4, chd free. Home-made teas. Refreshments by East Cheshire Hospice.**

This small terraced garden packed with plants was designed by Melita and has evolved over the past 11yrs. This plantswoman is a plantaholic and RHS Certificate holder. An attempt has been made to combine formality through structural planting with a more casual look influenced by the style of Christopher LLoyd. Steep step on to top tier at front. Steps up to higher tiers at rear.

Combermere Abbey Gardens

29 73 HILL TOP AVENUE

Cheadle Hulme, Stockport, SK8 7HZ. Mrs Elaine Land, 0161 486 0055. *4m S of Stockport. Leave A34 (new bypass) at r'about signed Cheadle Hulme (B5094). 2nd turn L into Gillbent Rd signed Cheadle Hulme Sports Centre. At end, small r'about, R into Church Rd. Garden 2nd rd on L. From Stockport or Bramhall turn R/L into Church Rd by Church Inn. Garden 1st rd on R.* **Sun 26 May, Sun 4 Aug (2-6). Adm £3.50, chd free. Home-made teas.** Visits also by arrangement May to Aug for groups of 5+. Donation to Arthritis Research UK.

⅙ acre plantswoman's garden. Well stocked with a wide range of sun-loving herbaceous plants, shrub and climbing roses, many clematis varieties, pond and damp area, shade-loving woodland plants and some unusual trees and shrubs, in an originally designed, long narrow garden.

30 HILLTOP

Flash Lane, Prestbury, SK10 4ED. Martin & Clare Gardner, 07768 337525, hughmartingardner@gmail.com, www.yourhilltopwedding.com. *2m N of Macclesfield. A523 to Stockport. Turn R at B5090 r'about signed Bollington, after ½m turn L at Cock & Pheasant Pub into Flash Lane. At bottom of lane turn R into cul de sac. Hilltop Country House signed on R.* **Sun 30 June (1-5). Adm £5, chd free.** Visits also by arrangement June to Aug for groups of 10 to 20. Tea and cake £2.

Interesting country garden of approx 4 acres. Woodland walk, parterre, herb garden, herbaceous borders, dry stone walled terracing, lily ponds with waterfall. Wisteria clad 1693 house (not open). Mature trees, orchard, magnificent views to Pennines and to West. Partial wheelchair access, disabled WC, easy parking.

31 THE HOMESTEAD

2 Fanners Lane, High Legh, Knutsford, WA16 0RZ. Janet Bashforth, 01925 349895, janbash43@sky.com. *J20 M6/J9 M56 at Lymm interchange take A50 for Knutsford, after 1m turn R into Heath Lane then 1st R into Fanners Lane. Follow parking signs.* **Sun 23 June (11-5.30). Adm £4, chd free.** Visits also by arrangement May to Aug for groups of 10 to 20.

Nestled in the Cheshire countryside this compact gem of a garden has been created over the last 3 years by a keen gardener and plants woman. Enter past groups of Liquidamber and White Stemmed Birch, visit shaded nooks with their own distinctive planting. Past topiary nestled in grasses, enjoy the exuberant colours of the hot area. Greenhouse and a small pond. Further on there is a small pond with water lilies and Iris. Many types of roses and clematis adorn the fencing along the paths and into the trees.

32 INGLEWOOD

4 Birchmere, Heswall, CH60 6TN. Colin & Sandra Fairclough, www.inglewood-birchmere.blogspot.co.uk. *6m S of Birkenhead. From A540 Devon Doorway/Clegg Arms r'about go through Heswall. ¼m after Tesco, R into Quarry Rd East, 2nd L into Tower Rd North & L into Birchmere.* **Sat 18, Sun 19 May (1-4.30). Adm £4, chd free. Home-made teas.**

Beautiful ½ acre garden with stream, large koi pond, 'beach' with grasses, wildlife pond and bog area. Brimming with shrubs, bulbs, acers, conifers, rhododendrons, herbaceous plants and new hosta border. Interesting features including hand cart, antique mangle, wood carvings, bug hotel and Indian dog gates leading to a secret garden. Lots of seating to enjoy refreshments. Live music may be available.

Your visits help change lives – your generosity helps Marie Curie fund nurses to care for people night and day in their homes, with donations of more than £8.8 million

33 60 KENNEDY AVENUE

Macclesfield, SK10 3DE. Bill North. *5min NW of Macclesfield Town Centre. Take A537 Cumberland St, 3rd r'bout (West Park) take B5087 Prestbury Rd. Take 5th turn on L into Kennedy Ave, last house on L before Brampton Ave opp Belong Care Home.* **Sun 16 June (12.30-5). Adm £4, chd free. Home-made teas.**

Small suburban garden which featured in 2017 August edition of Amateur Gardening magazine, designed to provide Al Fresco dining and relaxed entertaining, also providing relaxing Cottage Garden tranquillity which for 2019 new planting features and 65 hanging baskets. A Bee Keeper's Garden. Unusually, front garden set out in Cottage Garden style. Seating. Teas and cakes provided by The East Cheshire Hospice. Not suitable for disabled access.

34 LANE END COTTAGE GARDENS

Old Cherry Lane, Lymm, WA13 0TA. Imogen & Richard Sawyer, 01925 752618, imogen@laneendcottagegardens.co.uk, www.laneendcottagegardens.co.uk. *1m SW of Lymm. J20 M6/J9 M56/A50 Lymm interchange. Take B5158 signed Lymm. Turn R 100 metres into Cherry Corner, turn immed R into Old Cherry Lane.* **Sat 8, Sun 9 June, Sat 7, Sun 8 Sept (10-5). Adm £4, chd free. Home-made teas.**

Formerly a nursery, this 1 acre cottage garden is densely planted for all year round colour with many unusual plant varieties. Features include deep colour themed mixed borders, scented shrub roses, ponds, herb garden, walled orchard with trained fruit, shady woodland walk, sunny formal courtyard, vegetable garden and chickens. Teas served in large greenhouse. Wheelchair accessible WC.

35 LASKEY FARM

Laskey Lane, Thelwall, Warrington, WA4 2TF. Howard & Wendy Platt, 07740 804825, wendy.platt1@gmail.com, www.laskeyfarm.com. *2m From M6/M56. From M56/M6 follow directions to Lymm. At T-junction turn L onto the A56 in Warrington direction. Turn R onto Lymm Rd. Turn R onto Laskey Lane.* **Sat 10, Sun 11 Aug (11-5). Adm £5, chd free. Home-made teas.** Visits also by arrangement June to Aug for groups of 10+.

1½ acre garden packed with late summer colour including herbaceous and rose borders, vegetable area and a maze showcasing sculptures set among grasses and prairie style planting. Interconnected pools for wildlife, fish and terrapins form an unusual water garden and there are also a greenhouse and treehouse to explore. Live music and an art exhibition will take place over the weekend. Exhibition of the work of Lymm Artists both days. Live music between 1pm and 4pm both days. Sculpures by Jo Risley. Quiz for children. Most areas of the garden may be accessed by wheelchair.

36 LONG ACRE

Wyche Lane, Bunbury, CW6 9PS. Margaret & Michael Bourne, 01829 260944, mjbourne249@tiscali.co.uk. *3½m SE of Tarporley. In Bunbury village, turn into Wyche Lane by Nags Head Pub car park, garden 400yds on L.* **Sun 28 Apr, Sun 16 June (2-5). Adm £5, chd free. Home-made teas.** Visits also by arrangement Apr to June for groups of 10+. Donation to St Boniface Church Flower Fund and Bunbury Village Hall.

Plantswoman's garden of approx 1 acre with unusual and rare plants and trees including Kentucky Coffee Tree, Scadiopitys, Kalapanax Picta and others, pool garden, exotic conservatory with bananas, anthuriums and medinilla, herbaceous, greenhouses with Clivia in Spring and Disa Orchids in Summer. Spring garden with camellias, magnolias, bulbs; roses and lilies in summer.

37 ◆ THE LOVELL QUINTA ARBORETUM

Swettenham, CW12 2LD. Tatton Garden Society, 01565 831981, admin@tattongardensociety.org.uk, www.lovellquintaarboretum.co.uk. *4m NW of Congleton. Turn off A54 N 2m W of Congleton or turn E off A535 at Twemlow Green, NE of Holmes Chapel. Follow signs to Swettenham. Park at Swettenham Arms. Do not follow Sat Nav.* **For NGS: Sun 6 Oct (1-4.30). Adm £5, chd free. Refreshments at the Swettenham Arms during licenced hours or by arrangement.** For other opening times and information, please phone, email or visit garden website.

The 28-acre arboretum has been established since 1960s and contains around 2,500 trees and shrubs, some very rare. Incl National Collections of Pinus and Fraxinus, large collection of oak, a collection of hebes and autumn flowering, fruiting and colouring trees and shrubs. A lake and way-marked walks. Autumn colour, winter walk and spring bulbs. Refreshments at the Swettenham Arms during licenced hours or by arrangement. Care required but wheelchairs can access much of the arboretum on the mown paths.

NPC

38 NEW THE MACINTYRE NEW ROUTES ORCHARD AND GARDEN

Knutsford Road, Victoria Park, Warrington, WA4 1DU. MacIntyre, www.macintyrecharity.org. *Go straight through the main drive in Victoria park, past the stadium on your R, the Orchard is located behind the Spirit Restaurant.* **Sat 13 July (11-3). Adm £4, chd free. Light refreshments.**

A unique community orchard offering wildflower areas, a pond, unusual planting, medical herbs, beautiful floral gardens and a tipi area. We sell veg and plants grown using permaculture principles.

39 MANLEY KNOLL

Manley Road, Manley, WA6 9DX. Mr & Mrs James Timpson, 07961 202327, Jt.rowlinson@gmail.com, www.manleyknoll.com. *3m N of Tarvin. On B5393, via Ashton & Mouldsworth. 3m S of Frodsham, via Alvanley.* **Sun 5 May (12-5). Adm £5, chd free. Home-made teas.** Visits also by arrangement Apr to June for groups of 10 to 30.

Arts and Crafts garden created early 1900s. Covering 6 acres, divided into different rooms encompassing parterres, clipped yew hedging, ornamental ponds and herbaceous borders. Banks of rhododendron and azaleas frame a far-reaching view of the Cheshire Plain. Also a magical quarry/folly garden with waterfall and woodland walks.

40 NEW MANOR FARM

Egerton, Malpas, SY14 8AN. Tim Dilworth & Ivor Tatlow, 01829 720261. *Close to Cholmondeley Castle gardens. From Chester A41 S, Broxton r'about L to A534, R after Sandstone pub. L at Bickerton School, garden 3rd on R. A49 opp Cholmondeley Arms to Cholmondeley Castle. Garden 3m on L.* **Sat 15, Sun 16 June (1-5.30). Adm £4, chd free. Light refreshments.**

Acre and a half of formal gardens in a country house setting. Featuring a Dutch summer house, formal canal fish ponds, apple and catmint walks surrounded by topiary hedges and herbaceous borders. Large natural pond, stunning views. 2 summer houses, secret garden, espalier fruit trees and a Nepeta walk. Box and Yew hedges. Limited access.

41 NEW MANOR FARM

Wychough, Malpas, SY14 7NQ. The Lady Daresbury. *0.7m SW of Malpas. Turn onto Mastiff Lane from B5395 Malpas to Whitchurch Rd, then 1st L signed Lower Wych. (post code takes you to just past our turning to Preston Hall - turn around!).* **Sat 15 June (2.30-5). Adm £25, chd free. Pre-booking essential, please visit www.ngs.org.uk for information & booking. Light refreshments, tea and home-made cakes.**

3 acre garden created from scratch in 2011/2012. Designed by Angela Collins who also designed garden at Bruern Abbey. Different themed 'rooms' divided by yew and hornbeam hedging. Herbaceous borders, rose walk, kitchen garden, informal pond, orchard and wild

flower meadow. Views to the Welsh and Shropshire hills. The English Garden Magazine - June 2018.

♿ ☕

42 MAYFIELD HOUSE

Moss Lane, Bunbury Heath, Tarporley, CW6 9SY. Mr & Mrs J France Hayhurst, jeanniefh@me.com. *Mayfield House is off the A49 on Tarporley/ Whitchurch rd. Moss Lane is opp the main turn into Bunbury village (School Lane). Look out for a yellow speed camera (30 mph) across the rd.* **Sun 2 June (1.30-5.30). Adm £5, chd free. Home-made teas. Visits also by arrangement May to July for groups of 10 to 30.**

A thoroughly English mature garden with a wealth of colour and variety throughout the year. A background of fine trees, defined areas bordered by mixed hedging, masses of rhododendrons, azaleas, camellias,hydrangeas and colourful shrubs. Clematis and wisteria festoon the walls in early Summer. Easy access and random seating areas. Small lake with an island and broad lawns with glades of foxgloves. Garden statuary, little lake, swimming pool, near pretty villages and very good gastro-pubs and some beautiful gardens nearby. Very wide wrought iron gates lead to the garden and it is entirely navigable.

♿ 🐕 ✿ ☕

43 MILL HOUSE

Mill Lane, Threapwood, Malpas, SY14 7PD. Alison Stevenson. *2m W of Malpas. From Malpas go past St Oswalds Church on B5069, follow rd to Threapwood post office/garage turn 2nd L onto Sarn Rd. Yellow signs will be visible from this point.* **Sat 1 June (11-4). Adm £4, chd free. Tea. Homemade tea and cake will be available.**

A large garden set in the midst of a small holding, its split into three areas; a young meadow, a large cottage garden and a vegetable patch. The majority of the plants have been grown from seeds and cuttings. The remains of an old orchard has provided a home for unusual and exotic plants. Created by a true plantsman, the late Matthew Stevenson. Gravel paths and steps.

☕

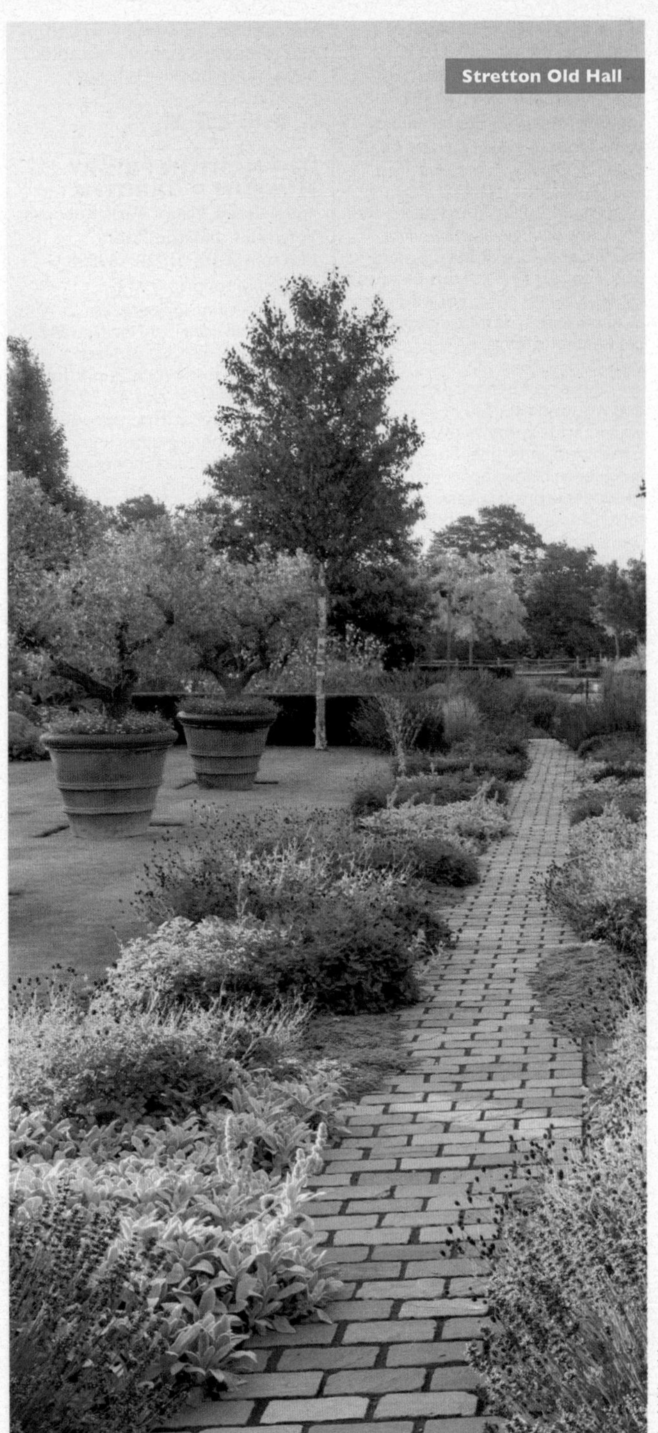

Stretton Old Hall

© Joe Wainwright

44 ◆ MOUNT PLEASANT

Yeld Lane, Kelsall, CW6 0TB. Dave Darlington & Louise Worthington, 01829 751592, louisedarlington@btinternet.com, www.mountpleasantgardens.co.uk. *8m E of Chester. Off A54 at T-lights into Kelsall. Turn into Yeld Lane opp Farmers Arms Pub, 200yds on L. Do not follow SatNav directions.* **For NGS: Sat 4, Sun 5 May, Sat 7, Sun 8 Sept (12-5). Adm £6, chd £2.50. Cream teas.** For other opening times and information, please phone, email or visit garden website.

10 acres of landscaped garden and woodland started in 1994 with impressive views over the Cheshire countryside. Steeply terraced in places. Specimen trees, rhododendrons, azaleas, conifers, mixed and herbaceous borders; 4 ponds, formal and wildlife. Vegetable garden, stumpery with tree ferns, sculptures, wild flower meadow and Japanese garden. Bog garden, tropical garden. Sculpture trail. Sculpture Exhibition. Please ring prior to visit for wheelchair access.

45 ◆ NESS BOTANIC GARDENS

Neston Road, Ness, Neston, CH64 4AY. The University of Liverpool, 0151 795 6300, nessgdns@liverpool.ac.uk, www.nessgardens.org.uk. *10m NW of Chester. Off A540. M53 J4, follow signs M56 & A5117 (signed N Wales). Turn onto A540 follow signs for Hoylake. Ness Gardens is signed locally.* **For NGS: Sun 28 Apr (10-5). Adm £7.50, chd £3.50.** For other opening times and information, please phone, email or visit garden website.

Looking out over the dramatic Dee Estuary from a lofty perch of the Wirral peninsula, Ness Botanic Gardens boasts 64 spectacular acres of landscaped and natural gardens overflowing with horticultural treasures. With a delightfully peaceful atmosphere, a wide array of events taking place, plus a cafe and gorgeous open spaces it's a great fun-filled day out for all. National Collection of Sorbus. Herbaceous borders, Rock Garden, Mediterranean Bank, Potager and conservation area. Wheelchairs are available free to hire [donations gratefully accepted] but advance booking is highly recommended.

NPC

46 ◆ NORTON PRIORY MUSEUM & GARDENS

Tudor Road, Manor Park, Runcorn, WA7 1SX. Norton Priory Museum Trust, 01928 569895, info@nortonpriory.org, www.nortonpriory.org. *2m SE of Runcorn. If using Sat-Nav try WA7 1BD & follow the brown Norton Priory signs.* **For NGS: Sun 9 June (10-4). Adm £4, chd £2.70. Light refreshments at the museum.** For other opening times and information, please phone, email or visit garden website.

Beautiful 2½-acre Georgian Walled Garden, with fruit trees, herb garden, colour borders and rose walk. Home to the National Collection of Tree Quince (Cydonia Oblonga) and surrounded by historic pear orchard and wild flower meadow. Norton Priory is also home to medieval ruins and museum. Plant Hunters Fair will be held at the garden on Sunday 9 June. Garden paths are gravel but there is level access to the whole garden site.

NPC

47 OAKFIELD VILLA

Nantwich Road, Wrenbury, Nantwich, CW5 8EL. Carolyn & Jack Kennedy, 01270 781106. *6m S of Nantwich & 6m N of Whitchurch. Garden on main rd through village next to Dairy Farm. Limited parking outside house. Parking available in Community Centre 2 minutes walk away.* **Visits by arrangement May to Aug for groups of 10 to 30. Admission £3 or £6 if also visiting Wren's Nest.**

Romantic S-facing garden of densely planted borders and creative planting in containers, incl climbing roses, clematis and hydrangeas. Divided by screens into 'rooms'. Pergola clothed in beautiful climbers provides relaxed sheltered seating area and there is a small water feature. Small front garden, mainly hydrangeas and clematis. Some gravelled areas and small lawn area.

48 THE OLD COTTAGE

44 High Street, Frodsham, WA6 7HE. John & Lesley Corfield, 07591 609311, corfield@rock44.plus.com. *DO NOT FOLLOW SATNAV - no parking at garden. On A56 close to Frodsham town centre. Follow signs from town centre to railway car park, garden signed from there (short walk). Or park in town centre and follow signs uphill N to cottage.* **Visits by arrangement June to Aug. Adm £5, chd free. Light refreshments.**

At the rear of the Grade II listed C16 cottage (not open) are ⅔ acre, organic and wildlife friendly garden featuring many aspects that support various forms of wildlife. Steps lead up to a large vegetable and herb garden, with further mixed planting in herbaceous borders. Wildlife pond and bog garden. Further areas of fruit trees and shady woodland borders. Extensive views over Mersey estuary. Numerous plants and trees found in the fossil records. Partial wheelchair access - please ring for details.

49 24 OLD GREASBY ROAD

Upton, Wirral, CH49 6LT. Lesley Whorton & Jon Price. *Approx 1m from J2A M53 (Upton Bypass). M53 J2; follow Upton sign. At r'about (J2A) straight on to Upton Bypass. At 2nd r'about, turn L by Upton Cricket Club. 24 Old Greasby Rd on L.* **Sun 11 Aug (11-4). Adm £4, chd free. Home-made teas.**

A multi-interest and surprising suburban garden. Both front and rear gardens incorporate innovative features designed for climbing and rambling roses, clematis, under-planted with cottage garden plants with a very productive kitchen garden. Unfortunately, due to narrow access and gravel paths, there is no wheelchair access.

50 THE OLD PARSONAGE

Arley Green, Northwich, CW9 6LZ. The Hon Rowland & Mrs Flower, www.arleyhallandgardens.com. *5m NNE of Northwich. 3m NNE of Great Budworth. M6 J19 & 20 & M56 J10. Follow signs to Arley Hall & Gardens. From Arley Hall notices*

to Old Parsonage which lies across park at Arley Green (approx 1m). **Sat 8, Sun 9 June (2-5.30). Adm £5, chd free. Home-made teas.**
2-acre garden in attractive and secretive rural setting in secluded part of Arley Estate, with ancient yew hedges, herbaceous and mixed borders, shrub roses, climbers, leading to woodland garden and unfenced pond with gunnera and water plants. Rhododendrons, azaleas, meconopsis, cardiocrinum, some interesting and unusual trees. Wheelchair access over mown grass, some slopes and bumps and rougher grass further away from the house.

51 15 PARK CRESCENT

Appleton, Warrington, WA4 5JJ. Linda & Mark Enderby, 07949 496 747, lmaenderby@outlook.com. *2½m S of Warrington. From M56 J10 take A49 towards Warrington for 1½m. At 2nd set of lights turn R into Lyons Lane , then 1st R into Park Crescent. No.15 is last house on R.* **Sun 12 May, Sun 16 June (12-5). Adm £4, chd free. Home-made teas. Prosecco will be available by donation.** Visits also by arrangement May to July for groups of 10 to 30.
An abundant garden containing many unusual plants, trees and a mini orchard. A cascade, ponds and planting encourage wildlife. There are also vegetable and herb plots and many roses in various forms. The garden has been split into different areas, each with their own vista drawing one through the garden. A Chinese model railway will also be on show. Look out for the Seven Dwarves on your visit!

52 PARM PLACE

High Street, Great Budworth, CW9 6HF. Peter & Jane Fairclough, 01606 891131, janefair@btinternet.com. *3m N of Northwich. Great Budworth on E side of A559 between Northwich & Warrington, 4m from J10 M56, also 4m from J19 M6. Parm Place is W of village on S side of High St.* **Visits by arrangement Mar to Aug for groups of 10 to 30. Adm £4, chd free. Tea.** Donation to Great Ormond Street Hospital.
Well-stocked ½ acre plantswoman's garden with stunning views towards S Cheshire. Curving lawns, parterre, shrubs, colour co-ordinated herbaceous borders, roses, water features, rockery, gravel bed with some grasses. Fruit and vegetable plots. In spring large collection of bulbs and flowers, camellias, hellebores and blossom.

53 ◆ PEOVER HALL GARDENS

Over Peover, Knutsford, WA16 9HW. Randle Brooks, 07443 429756, bookings@peoverhall.com, www.peoverhall.com. *4m S of Knutsford. Please do not rely on SATNAV after the A50. A50/ Holmes Chapel Rd/Whipping Stocks PH turn onto Stocks Lane. Approx 0.9m turn R onto Grotto Lane. ¼m turn r onto Goostrey Lane. Main entrance on bend.* **For NGS: Sat 1, Sun 2 June (2-5). Adm £5, chd free. Refreshments in the Park House Tea Room.** For other opening times and information, please phone, email or visit garden website.
The gardens to Peover Hall are set in 15 acres and feature five walled gardens or 'garden rooms' filled with clipped box, topiary, roses, lily pond, kitchen garden, Romanesque loggia, C19 dell and rockery, rhododendrons and pleached limes. There are Grade I listed Carolean Stables which are of significant architectural importance. Partial wheelchair access to garden.

54 POULTON HALL

Poulton Lancelyn, Bebington, CH63 9LN. The Lancelyn Green Family, www.poultonhall.co.uk. *2m S of Bebington. From M53, J4 towards Bebington; at T-lights R along Poulton Rd; house 1m on R.* **Sat 20, Sun 21 Apr (1.30-4.30). Adm £5, chd free. Home-made teas.**
3 acres; lawns fronting house, wild flower meadow. Surprise approach to walled garden, with reminders of Roger Lancelyn Green's retellings, Excalibur, Robin Hood and Jabberwocky. Scented sundial garden for the visually impaired. Memorial sculpture for Richard Lancelyn Green by Sue Sharples. Rose, nursery rhyme, witch, herb and oriental gardens and new Memories Reading room. There are often choirs or orchestral music in the garden. Level gravel paths. Separate wheelchair access (not across parking field).

Hilltop

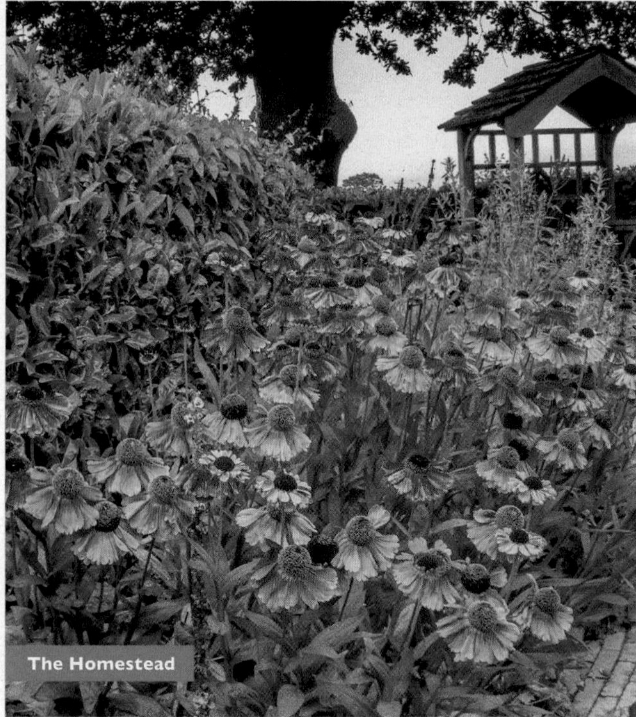
The Homestead

55 ◆ RODE HALL

Church Lane, Scholar Green, ST7 3QP. Randle & Amanda Baker Wilbraham, 01270 873237, enquiries@rodehall.co.uk, www.rodehall.co.uk. *5m SW of Congleton. Between Scholar Green (A34) & Rode Heath (A50).* For opening times and information, please phone, email or visit garden website.

Nesfield's terrace and rose garden with view over Humphry Repton's landscape is a feature of Rode, as is the woodland garden with terraced rock garden and grotto. Other attractions incl the walk to the lake with a view of Birthday Island complete with heronry, restored ice house, working two-acre walled kitchen garden and Italian garden. Fine display of snowdrops in Feb and Bluebells in May. Snowdrop Walks: 2 Feb - 3 March, 11-4, Tues - Sat (Closed Mons). Bluebell Walks: 27 Apr - 8 May daily. Summer: Weds and Bank Hol Mons until end of Sep, 11-5. Stables Tearooms offering wide variety of refreshments. Partial wheelchair access, some steep areas with gravel and woodchip paths, access to WC, kitchen garden and tearooms.

56 ROSEWOOD

Old Hall Lane, Puddington, Neston, CH64 5SP. Mr & Mrs C E J Brabin, 0151 353 1193, angela.brabin@btinternet.com. *8m N of Chester. From A540 turn down Puddington Lane, 1½m. Park by village green. Walk 30yds to Old Hall Lane, turn L through archway into garden.* **Visits by arrangement Feb to Dec. Adm £3, chd free. Tea.**

All yr garden; thousands of snowdrops in Feb, Camellias in autumn, winter and spring. Rhododendrons in April/May and unusual flowering trees from March to June. Autumn Cyclamen in quantity from Aug to Nov. Perhaps the greatest delight to owners are two large Cornus capitata, flowering in June. Bees kept in the garden. Honey sometimes available.

57 ROWLEY HOUSE

Forty Acre Lane, Kermincham, Holmes Chapel, CW4 8DX. Tim & Juliet Foden. *3m ENE from Holmes Chapel. J18 M6 to Holmes Chapel, from Holmes Chapel take A535 (Macclesfield). Take R turn at Twemlow (Swettenham) at Yellow Broom restaurant. Rowley House ½m on L.* **Sun 26 May, Sun 7 July (11-4.30). Adm £5, chd free. Home-made teas and cakes.**

Our aim is to give nature a home and create a place of beauty. There is a formal courtyard garden and informal gardens featuring rare trees, and herbaceous borders, a pond with swamp cypress and woodland walk with maples, rhododendrons, ferns and shade-loving plants. Beyond the garden there are wild flower meadows, natural ponds and a wood with ancient oaks. Also wood sculptures by Andy Burgess.

58 SANDYMERE

Middlewich Road, Cotebrook, CW6 9EH. John Timpson, 07900 567944, rme2000@aol.com. *5m N of Tarporley. On A54 approx 300yds W of T-lights at Xrds of A49/A54.* **Sun 19 May (12-5). Adm £7, chd free. Home-made teas.** Visits also by arrangement May & June for groups of 10+. Refreshments are not available.

16 landscaped acres of beautiful Cheshire countryside with terraces, walled garden, extensive woodland walks and an amazing hosta garden. Turn each corner and you find another gem with lots of different water features including a new rill built in 2014, which links the main lawn to the hostas. Partial wheelchair access.

59 21 SCAFELL CLOSE

High Lane, Stockport, SK6 8JA. Lesley & Dean Stafford, 01663 763015, lesley.stafford@live.co.uk. *High Lane is on A6 SE of Stockport towards Buxton. From A6 take Russell Ave then Kirkfell Drive. Scafell Close on R.* **Sat 3, Sun 4 Aug (1-4.30). Adm £3, chd free. Light refreshments. tea/ coffee and cakes.** Visits also by arrangement July & Aug for groups of 10+.

⅓ acre landscaped suburban garden. Colour themed annuals border the lawn featuring the Kinder Ram statue in a heather garden, passing into vegetables, soft fruits and fruit trees. Returning perennial pathway leads to the fishpond and secret terraced garden with modern water feature and patio planting. Finally visit the blue front garden. Refreshments in aid of Cancer Research UK. Partial wheelchair access.

60 68 SOUTH OAK LANE

Wilmslow, SK9 6AT. Caroline Melliar-Smith, 01625 528147, caroline.ms@btinternet.com. *¾m SW of Wilmslow. From M56 (J6) take A538 (Wilmslow) R into Buckingham Rd. From centre of Wilmslow turn R onto B5086 , 1st R into Gravel Lane, 4th R into South Oak Lane.* **Visits by arrangement June & July for groups of up to 20. Adm £5, chd free.**

With year-round colour, scent and interest, this attractive, narrow, hedged cottage garden has evolved over the years into 5 natural 'rooms'. These Hardy Plant Society members passion for plants, is reflected in the variety of shrubs, trees, flower borders and pond, creating havens for wildlife. Share this garden with its' varied history from the 1890's. Some rare and unusual hardy, herbaceous and shade loving plants and shrubs.

61 10 STATHAM AVENUE

Lymm, WA13 9NH. Mike & Gail Porter, 01925 753488, porters@mikeandgailporter.co.uk. *Approx 1m from J20 M6 /M56 interchange. From M/way follow B5158 to Lymm. Take A56 Booth's Hill Rd, left towards Warrington, turn R on to Barsbank Lane, pass under Bridgewater canal, after 50m turn R on to Statham Ave. No 10 is 100m on R.* **Sat 25, Sun 26 May (12-5). Sat 29, Sun 30 June (12-5), also open Beechwood Cottage. Adm £4.50, chd free. Light refreshments. Enjoy home made cakes or try Gail's famous meringues with fresh fruit and cream.** Visits also by arrangement May to July for groups of 10+. Group admission incl refreshments. Options can be discussed.

Peaceful, pastel shades in early summer. Beautifully structured ¼ acre south facing garden carefully terraced and planted as it rises to the Bridgewater towpath. Hazel arch opens to clay paved courtyard with peach trees. Rose pillars lead to varied herbaceous beds and quiet shaded areas bordered by fuchsias, azaleas and rhododendrons. Wide variety of plants and shrubs. Interesting garden buildings. A treasure hunt and quiz to keep the children occupied. Gail's famous Meringues to satisfy the grown ups. Short gravel driveway and some steps to access the rear garden.The rear garden is sloping.

62 ◆ STONYFORD COTTAGE

Stonyford Lane, Oakmere, CW8 2TF. Janet & Tony Overland, 01606 888970, info@stonyfordcottagegardens.co.uk, www.stonyfordcottagegardens.co.uk. *5m SW of Northwich. From Northwich take A556 towards Chester. ¾m past A49 junction turn R into Stonyford Lane. Entrance ½m on L.* **For NGS: Sun 12 May, Sun 28 July (11-4). Adm £4.50, chd free. Home-made teas. Lunches and cream teas available.**

For other opening times and information, please phone, email or visit garden website.

Set around a tranquil pool this Monet style landscape has a wealth of moisture loving plants, incl iris and candelabra primulas. Drier areas feature unusual perennials and rarer trees and shrubs. Woodland paths meander through shade and bog plantings, along boarded walks, across wild natural areas with views over the pool to the cottage gardens. Unusual plants available at the adjacent nursery. Open Tues - Sat & BH Mons Apr - Oct 10-5pm. Cottage Tea Room. Plant Nursery. Some gravel paths.

63 STRETTON OLD HALL

Stretton, Tilston, Malpas, SY14 7JA. Stephen Gore Head Gardener. *5m N of Malpas. From Chester follow A41, Broxton r'about follow signs for Stretton Water Mill, turn L at Cock o Barton. 2m on L.* **Sun 7 July (11-5). Adm £6, chd free. Home-made teas.**

5 acre Cheshire countryside garden with a planting style best described as controlled exuberance with a definite emphasis upon perennials, colour, form and scale. Divided into several discrete and individual gardens incl stunning herbaceous borders, scree garden, walled kitchen garden and glass house. Wild flower meadows, wildlife walk around the lake with breathtaking vistas in every direction. Gravel paths.

64 SYCAMORE COTTAGE

Manchester Road, Carrington, Manchester, M31 4AY. Mrs C Newton. *From M60 J8 take Carrington turn (A6144) through 2 sets of T-lights. Garden approx 1m after 2nd set of T-lights on R. From M6 J20 signed for Partington/Carrington garden approx 1m on L.* **Sun 9 June (1-5). Adm £4, chd free. Light refreshments.**

Approx ⅕ acre cottage garden split into distinct areas, arches covered with rambling roses, colourful herbaceous borders, and a woodland area planted to encourage birds and wildlife. There is a natural spring, well, and ponds. There are plenty of seating areas to sit and enjoy this very pretty garden.

65 TATTENHALL HALL

High Street, Tattenhall, CH3 9PX. Jen & Nick Benefield, Chris Evered & Jannie Hollins, 01829 770654, janniehollins@gmail.com. *8m S of Chester on A41. Turn L to Tattenhall, through village, turn R at Letters Pub, past war memorial on L through Sandstone pillared gates. Park on rd or in village car park.* **Sun 19 May (2-5.30). Adm £5, chd free. Home-made teas.** Visits also by arrangement Mar to Sept.

Plant enthusiasts' garden around Jacobean house (not open).

4½ acres, wild flower meadows, interesting trees,large pond, stream, walled garden, colour themed borders, succession planting, spinney walk with shade plants, yew terrace overlooking meadow, views to hills. Glasshouse and vegetable garden. Wildlife friendly sometimes untidy garden, interest throughout the year, continuing to develop. Limited wheelchair access because of gravel paths, cobbles and some steps.

TATTON PARK

Knutsford WA16 6QN. National Trust, leased to Cheshire East Council, 01625 374400, tatton@cheshireeast.gov.uk, www.tattonpark.org.uk. *2½m N of Knutsford. Well signed on M56 J7 & from M6 J19.* **For NGS: Wed 15 May, Wed 12 June (10-6). Adm £7, chd £5. For other opening times and information, please phone, email or visit garden website.**

Features incl orangery by Wyatt, fernery by Paxton, restored Japanese garden, Italian and rose gardens. Greek monument and African hut. Hybrid azaleas and rhododendrons; swamp cypresses, tree ferns, tall redwoods, bamboos and pines. Fully restored productive walled gardens. Wheelchair access apart from rose garden and Japanese garden.

66 THORNCAR

Windmill Lane, Appleton, Warrington, WA4 5JN. Mrs Kath Carey, 01925 267633, john.carey516@btinternet.com. *South Warrington. From M56 J10 take A49 towards Warrington for 1½m. At 2nd set of T-lights turn L into Quarry Lane, as the rd swings R it becomes Windmill Lane. Thorncar is 4th house on R.* **Sat 3 Aug (12.30-4.30). Adm £3, chd free. Light refreshments. Refreshments provided by WI.** Visits also by arrangement Mar to Sept for groups of 5 to 20.

One third acre plantwoman's suburban garden planted since 2011 within the framework of part of an older garden to provide year round interest. Having opened previously in June (peonies) and July (day lilies) now is the turn of August for hydrangeas, fuchsias and Eucryphia 'Nymansay'. Plants are chosen to require minimal watering though 2018 was very taxing and losses did occur.

67 TIRLEY GARTH GARDENS

Mallows Way, Willington, Tarporley, CW6 0RQ. Tirley Garth. *2m N of Tarporley. 2m S of Kelsall. Entrance 500yds from village of Utkinton. At N of Tarporley take Utkinton rd.* **Sun 12, Sun 19 May, Sun 2 June (1-5). Adm £5, chd free. Home-made teas.**

40-acre garden, terraced and landscaped, designed by Thomas Mawson (considered the leading exponent of garden design in early C20), it is the only Grade II* Arts and Crafts garden in Cheshire that remains complete and in excellent condition. The gardens are an important example of an early C20 garden laid out in both formal and informal styles. By early May the garden is bursting into flower with almost 3000 Rhododendron and Azalea many 100 years old. Art Exhibition by local Artists. Wheelchair access to tea rooms, but limited in areas of gardens.

68 TRAFFORD HALL

Ince Lane, Wimbolds Trafford, Chester, CH2 4JP. The National Communities Resourse Centre, 01244 300246, c.spencer@traffordhall.com, www.traffordhall.com. *5 mins from M56. M56 Jct14 take the A5117 exit to Helsby/Stanlow straight at first lights for ½m, turn L at lights along Ince Lane for approx 2m. Trafford Hall on L.* **Sat 16 Feb (11-3). Adm £4, chd free. Sun 2 June, Sat 10 Aug (11-4). Adm £5, chd free.** Visits also by arrangement for groups of 5 to 20.

Trafford Hall is the home of the National Communities Resource Centre. The grounds and gardens are managed using organic methods with sustainability in mind. They cover roughly 14 acres and include woodland, lawns, meadow, Arts and Crafts style 'sunken garden'. Kitchen garden, greenhouses, pond, apple orchard and Walter Segal eco-chalets. Accommodation available. Guide dogs only. Wheelchair access to many areas.

69 THE WELL HOUSE

Wet Lane, Tilston, Malpas, SY14 7DP. Mrs S H French-Greenslade, 01829 250332. *3m NW of Malpas. On A41, 1st R after Broxton r'about, L on Malpas Rd through Tilston. House on L.* **Visits by arrangement Feb to Sept for groups of up to 20. Pre-booked refreshments for small groups only.**

1-acre cottage garden, bridge over natural stream, spring bulbs, perennials, herbs and shrubs. Triple ponds. Adjoining ¾-acre field made into wild flower meadow; first seeding late 2003. Large bog area of kingcups and ragged robin. February for snowdrop walk. Victorian parlour and collector's items on show only. Not suitable for wheelchairs. Dogs on leads only.

GROUP OPENING

70 WEST DRIVE GARDENS

6, 9 West Drive, Gatley, Cheadle, SK8 4JJ. David & Ann Gane, Thelma Bishop & John Needham, 01614 280204, Davidjgane@btinternet.com. *4m N of Wilmslow on B5166. 4 m N of Wilmslow on B5166. From J5 (M56) drive past airport. to B5166 (Styal Rd).L to Gatley. Go over T-lights at Heald Green. West Drive is last turn on R before Gatley(approx. 1½m from T-lights).* **Sun 17 Feb (1-3). Combined adm £3, chd free. Light refreshments. Sun 9 June (11-5). Combined adm £5, chd free. Home-made teas, and WC at No 6.** Visits also by arrangement Feb to Sept for groups of up to 20.

Here are two gardens of very different character, reflecting their owner's gardening style. Although suburban , they are surrounded by mature trees and have a secluded feel. Rich variety of planting including ferns, hostas with clematis, roses, astrantia at their best. Wild life pond at no.6 and other water features. Ceramics and containers with alpines complete the picture. Home-made teas, no.6. Opening in February for displays of hellebores and snowdrops as well as well as June. Access to top of gardens giving general overview, with shallow step leading onto gravel at no.6 and several steps and narrow paths at no.9.

71 THE WHITE COTTAGE

Threapwood, Malpas, SY14 7AL. Chris & Carol Bennion, 01948 770085, chrisbennion@btinternet.com. *3m W of Malpas. From Malpas take Wrexham Road B5069 W for 3m. From Bangor on Dee take B5069 E to Threapwood. Directions for parking will be provided separately.* **Visits by arrangement Apr to June for groups of 10+. Adm £4, chd free. Home-made teas.**

Behind a long beech hedge lies an

interesting and relaxing country garden, featured in Cheshire Life, containing mature trees, shrubs, topiary, statuary and meandering herbaceous borders brimming with soft romantic planting. A formal area near the cottage is a delightful place to sit and relax. The orchard contains fruit trees, raised beds and borders. Lovely views across lush meadows. Many interesting features including a dovecote, pergola and horseshoe garden. Some steps around the cottage and a long gravel drive.

72 WINTERBOTTOM HOUSE

Winterbottom Lane, Mere, Knutsford, WA16 0QQ. Neil & Verona Stott, 01565 830464, thestotts@btinternet.com. *Half way between Mere T-lights & High Legh. Signed off A50. From A50 opp Kilton Inn turn into Hoo Green Lane, in ½m bear L down Winterbottom Lane (narrow lane - take care!). Winterbottom House at end . Follow signs for ample parking with wheelchair access.* **Sun 16 June (1-5). Adm £5, chd free. Home-made teas. Teas provided by volunteers from East Cheshire Hospice.** Visits also by arrangement Apr to Sept for groups of 10 to 30.

We have gradually started to develop more of the areas of the garden over the last 40 years. A small duck pond is now a large pool filled with many interesting koi. The trees were all planted as saplings and are now fully mature. This contrasts with the much more formal areas round the house, which includes a sunken garden with box parterre, a water feature and many interesting statuary. The area includes a period summer house, ornamental rill, large natural koi pond, with plenty of seating areas. Home made cakes and teas. Some gravel paths but no steps.

73 NEW WIRRAL HOSPICE ST JOHN'S

Mount Road, Higher Bebington, Wirral, CH63 6JE. Wirral Hospice St John's, www.wirralhospice.org. *Easy access from J4 of M53. Follow signs for Clatterbridge Hospital, enter Clatterbridge Hospital site and take 1st L at mini r'about. Free parking on site.* **Sat 29, Sun 30 June (11.30-4.30). Adm £4, chd free. Home-made teas. Pimms tent and home-made produce.**

Established garden within in the grounds of the hospice which is maintained by volunteers and patients. Interesting features include a flower framed wooden gazebo, flower beds designed by patients and supported by local Brownies, a pond, vegetable area and wild flower area. Child friendly with live entertainment, wildlife corner, competitions and stalls Access to disabled toilets, and all amenities.

74 WOOD END COTTAGE

Grange Lane, Whitegate, Northwich, CW8 2BQ. Mr & Mrs M R Everett, 01606 888236, woodendct@supanet.com. *4m SW of Northwich. Turn S off A556 (Northwich bypass) at Sandiway T-lights; after 1¾m, turn L to Whitegate village; opp school follow Grange Lane for 300yds.* **Visits by arrangement May to Aug. Adm £4, chd free. Home-made teas.**

Plantsman's ½ acre garden in attractive setting, sloping to a natural stream bordered by shade and moisture-loving plants. Background of mature trees. Well stocked herbaceous borders, trellis with roses and clematis, magnificent delphiniums, many phlox, meconopsis and choice perennials. Interesting shrubs and flowering trees. Vegetable garden.

75 WREN'S NEST

Wrenbury Heath Road, Wrenbury, Nantwich, CW5 8EQ. Sue & Dave Clarke, 01270 780704, wrenburysue@gmail.com. *12m from M6 J16. From Nantwich signs for A530 to Whitchurch, reaching Sound school turn 1st R Wrenbury Heath Rd, across the Xrds & bungalow is on L, telegraph pole right outside.* **Visits by arrangement May to Aug for groups of up to 30. Also open Oakfield Villa. Adm £3.50, chd free. Tea.**

Set in a semi-rural area, this bungalow has a Cottage Garden Style of lush planting and is 80ft x 45ft. The garden is packed with unusual and traditional perennials and shrubs incl over 100 hardy geraniums, campanulas, crocosmias, iris and alpine troughs. Plants for sale. Proceeds from this garden will be for the NGS. National collection of Hardy Geranium sylvaticum and renardii. Plant Heritage National Collection of Hardy Geraniums sylvaticum and renardii.

Manor Farm

Cornwall has some of the most beautiful natural landscapes to be found anywhere in the world.

Here, you will discover some of the country's most extraordinary gardens, a spectacular coastline, internationally famous surfing beaches, windswept moors and countless historic sites. Cornish gardens reflect this huge variety of environments particularly well.

A host of National Collections of magnolias, camellias, rhododendrons and azaleas, as well as exotic Mediterranean semitropical plants and an abundance of other plants flourish in our acid soils and mild climate.

Surrounded by the warm currents of the Gulf Stream, with our warm damp air in summer and mild moist winters, germination continues all year.

Cornwall boasts an impressive variety of beautiful gardens. These range from coastal-protected positions to exposed cliff-top sites, moorland water gardens, Japanese gardens and the world famous tropical biomes of the Eden Project.

Below: **The Lodge**

Volunteers

County Organiser
Christopher Harvey Clark
01872 530165
suffree2012@gmail.com

County Treasurer
Andrew Flint 01726 879336
flints@elizaholidays.co.uk

Publicity
Sara Gadd 07814 885141
sara@gartendesign.co.uk

Emma Skilton 07772 542143
emma24nyrorganic@gmail.com

Booklet Co-ordinator
Peter Stanley 01326 565868
stanley.m2@sky.com

Photographer
Lucie Averill 01736 711971
lucieaverill@ymail.com

Assistant County Organisers
Ginnie Clotworthy 01208 872612
ginnieclotworthy@hotmail.co.uk

Susan Edward-Collins 01208 821262
susanec007@btinternet.com

Sarah Gordon 01579 362076
sar.gordon@talktalk.net

Nutty Lim 01726 815247
christianne.gf.lim@gmail.com

Katie Nichols 01872 275786
katherinemlambert@gmail.com

Alison O'Connor 01726 882460
tregoose@tregoose.co.uk

Rachel Ruttledge 07564 256916
rachel@ruttledgegardendesigns.com

Marion Stanley 01326 565868
stanley.m2@sky.com

OPENING DATES

All entries subject to change. For latest information check **www.ngs.org.uk**

Extended openings are shown at the beginning of the month.

Map locator numbers are shown to the right of each garden name.

March

Saturday 16th
The Lodge 26

Sunday 17th
The Lodge 26
Meudon Hotel 29

Sunday 24th
◆ Trewidden Garden 54

Sunday 31st
Ken Caro 22

April

Every day
Ken Caro 22

Monday 8th
◆ Pencarrow 35

Sunday 14th
NEW Carwinnick 12

Saturday 27th
◆ Chygurno 13

Sunday 28th
Bodwannick Manor Farm 5
◆ Chygurno 13

May

Every day
Ken Caro 22

Sunday 5th
Navas Hill House 32
South Lea 45

Monday 6th
◆ Boconnoc 4
◆ Moyclare 30
Scorrier House 43
NEW South Bosent 44

Sunday 12th
NEW Alverton Cottage 1
Anvil Cottage 2
Ethnevas Cottage 17
◆ The Japanese Garden 21
Trebartha 46
NEW Tregullow 49
Windmills 56

Monday 13th
◆ The Japanese Garden 21

Saturday 18th
◆ Pinsla Garden & Nursery 39

Sunday 19th
◆ Pinsla Garden & Nursery 39

Sunday 26th
Bokelly 6
Lower Amble Gardens 28

June

Every day
Ken Caro 22

Tuesday 4th
Gardens Cottage 19

Wednesday 5th
Gardens Cottage 19

Sunday 9th
Bodwannick Manor Farm 5
NEW Caervallack 10

Sunday 16th
Arundell 3
◆ St Michael's Mount 42
South Lea 45

Tuesday 18th
◆ Trematon Castle 50

Saturday 22nd
Half Acre 20
◆ Roseland House 41

Sunday 23rd
Half Acre 20
Penheale Manor 37
◆ Roseland House 41
Trenarth 51

Friday 28th
Dye Cottage 15

Saturday 29th
Dye Cottage 15

Sunday 30th
Dye Cottage 15
NEW Trevilley 53

July

Every day
Ken Caro 22

Every Wednesday
Kestle Barton 24

Tuesday 2nd
Gardens Cottage 19

Wednesday 3rd
Gardens Cottage 19

Sunday 7th
Anvil Cottage 2
South Lea 45
Windmills 56

Sunday 14th
NEW Parkenver 34

Saturday 20th
◆ Chygurno 13

Sunday 21st
◆ Chygurno 13

Sunday 28th
Byeways 9

August

Every day
Ken Caro 22

Every Wednesday
Kestle Barton 24

Saturday 3rd
◆ Pinsla Garden & Nursery 39

Sunday 4th
Kitpurva 25
◆ Pinsla Garden & Nursery 39

Tuesday 6th
Gardens Cottage 19

Wednesday 7th
Gardens Cottage 19

Wednesday 14th
◆ Bonython Manor 7

Sunday 18th
◆ Bosvigo House 8

Sunday 25th
Crugsillick Manor 14

September

Every Wednesday
Kestle Barton 24

Tuesday 3rd
Gardens Cottage 19

Wednesday 4th
Gardens Cottage 19

Sunday 8th
Trebartha 46
NEW Tregonhayne 47

Sunday 22nd
◆ National Dahlia Collection 31

By Arrangement

Arrange a personalised garden visit with your club, or group of friends, on a date to suit you. See individual garden entries for full details.

Anvil Cottage 2
Arundell 3
Bodwannick Manor Farm 5
Carminowe Valley Garden 11
Crugsillick Manor 14
NEW Garden Cottage 18
Gardens Cottage 19
Half Acre 20
Kennall House 23
NEW New Mills Farmhouse 33
Pendower House 36
NEW Penwarne 38
South Lea 45
Tregonning 48
Trenarth 51
Trereife Park 52
Waye Cottage 55
Windmills 56

Your visits help change lives – since 1927, we've donated £55 million to nursing and caring charities

THE GARDENS

1 NEW ALVERTON COTTAGE

Alverton Road, Penzance, TR18 4TG. David & Lizzie Puddifoot. *Next door to YMCA. About 600 metres from Penlee car park travelling towards A30. Morrab Gardens are also close to car park.* **Sun 12 May (2-5). Adm £4, chd free. Home-made teas.**

Alverton Cottage is a grade 2 listed Regency house. The garden is modest in size though large for a Penzance garden, S-facing and sheltered by mature trees incl elms. Very large monkey-puzzle tree and holm oak. Laid out in 1860s, we have added a succulent area, fernery and barefoot walk. In nearby Morrab Sub-tropical Gardens the 'Friends' will also welcome visitors. Off road parking for a disabled driver but wheelchair access is limited to garden terrace.

2 ANVIL COTTAGE

South Hill, PL17 7LP. Geoff & Barbara Clemerson, 01579 362623, gcclemerson@gmail.com. *3m NW of Callington. Head N on A388 from Callington centre. After ½m L onto South Hill Rd (signed South Hill), straight on for 3m. Gardens on R just before St Sampson's Church.* **Sun 12 May, Sun 7 July (1.30-5). Combined adm with Windmills £5, chd free. Home-made teas. Gluten free refreshments.** Visits also by arrangement May and July for groups of up to 30. Donation to St Sampson's Church.

Essentially a plantsman's garden. Winding paths take you through a series of themed rooms with familiar, rare and unusual plants. Higher up, a path leads through trees to a formal rose garden, and raised viewpoint with spectacular views of Caradon Hill and Bodmin Moor. Very limited wheelchair access due to steps.

3 ARUNDELL

West Pentire, Crantock, TR8 5SE. Brenda & David Eyles, 01637 831916, david@davideyles.com. *1m W of Crantock. From A3075 take signs to Crantock. At junction in village keep straight on to West Pentire (1m). Park in field (signed) or public car parks at W Pentire.* **Sun 16 June (1-5). Adm £5, chd free. Cream teas & home-made biscuits.** Visits also by arrangement May to Aug except Fridays, for groups of up to 20.

A garden where no garden should be! - on windswept NT headland between 2 fantastic beaches. 1 acre packed with design and plant interest round old farm cottage. Front: cottage garden. Side: Mediterranean courtyard. Rear: rockery and shrubbery leading to stumpery and fernery and on to stream and pond, Cornish Corner, herbaceous borders, Beth Chatto dry garden, small pinetum and jungle garden. Wheelchair access from public car park with entrance via rear gate. 14 shallow steps in centre of garden useable with care.

4 ◆ BOCONNOC

Lostwithiel, PL22 0RG. Elizabeth Fortescue, 01208 872507, office@boconnoc.com, www.boconnoc.com. *Off A390 between Liskeard & Lostwithiel. From East Taphouse follow signs to Boconnoc. (SatNav does not work well in this area).* **For NGS: Mon 6 May (2-5). Adm £5.50, chd free. Cream teas in stable yard.** For other opening times and information, please phone, email or visit garden website.

20 acres surrounded by parkland and woods with magnificent trees, flowering shrubs and stunning views. The gardens are set amongst mature trees which provide the backcloth for exotic spring flowering shrubs, woodland plants, with newly-planted magnolias and a fine collection of hydrangeas. Bathhouse built in 1804, woodland gardens, obelisk built in 1771, house dating from Domesday, deer park, C15 church.

5 BODWANNICK MANOR FARM

Nanstallon, Bodmin, PL30 5LN. Gaia Trust, sarahmatta@btinternet.com, www.gaiatrust.org.uk/bodwannick. *From A30, take A389 signed to Lanivet and Bodmin. 1m after Lanivet turn L (signed to Nanstallon). From Bodmin, take A389 signed for A30. After 1½m turn R at Jim's hardware store.* **Sun 28 Apr, Sun 9 June (10.30-3.30). Adm by donation. Home-made teas in old farmhouse conservatory and on terrace.** Visits also by arrangement Mar to Oct for groups of up to 20.

1½-acre plantsman's garden with fern-rich rockery, water garden and new terraced garden in the making, daffodils, roses and shrubs. Remarkable for its aura of peace and tranquillity, but its air of antiquity is deceptive as it was the lifetime creation of Martin Appleton and his family. Now in the care of the Gaia Trust, it has particular features of note and yr-round interest. Wheelchair access possible to much but not all of the garden.

6 BOKELLY

St Kew, Bodmin, PL30 3DY. Toby & Henrietta Courtauld. *Follow road to Trelill from St Kew Highway, leaving Red Lion pub on L. Garden on L after approx 1m.* **Sun 26 May (1.30-5.30). Adm £5, chd free. Cream teas. Also open Lower Amble Gardens.**

The 7-acre garden surrounds a beautiful C15 barn and lichened stone outbuildings. It has been expanded and rejuvenated with new plantings to suit the varied levels and soil types, incl woodland and pond areas, herbaceous border, little orchard and vegetable plot, and cut flower beds (a particular passion of garden designer Henrietta).

7 ◆ BONYTHON MANOR

Cury Cross Lanes, Helston, TR12 7BA. Mr & Mrs Richard Nathan, 01326 240550, sbonython@gmail.com, www.bonythonmanor.co.uk. *5m S of Helston. On main A3083 Helston to Lizard Rd. Turn L at Cury Cross Lanes (Wheel Inn). Entrance 300yds on R.* **For NGS: Wed 14**

Aug (2-4.30). Adm £9, chd £2. Home-made teas. For other opening times and information, please phone, email or visit garden website.

Magnificent 20 acre colour garden incl sweeping hydrangea drive to Georgian manor (not open). Herbaceous walled garden, potager with vegetables and picking flowers; 3 lakes in valley planted with ornamental grasses, perennials and South African flowers. A 'must see' for all seasons colour.

8 ◆ BOSVIGO HOUSE

Bosvigo Lane, Truro, TR1 3NH. Wendy Perry, 01872 275774, www.bosvigo.com/. *Truro City Centre. At Highertown, nr Sainsbury r'about, turn down Dobbs Lane. After 500yds, entrance to house is on L, after sharp LH-bend.* **For NGS: Sun 18 Aug (2-6). Adm £5, chd free. Home-made teas in Servants Hall.** For other opening times and information, please phone or visit garden website.

Created by artist owner, the 2 acre garden surrounding the Georgian house has been designed to create dazzling displays of vivid colour and plant harmonies. Each garden room is designed with a different palette of colour. For the opening in August the Vean garden and walled garden will be looking their best. Very limited wheelchair access.

9 BYEWAYS

Dunheved Road, Launceston, PL15 9JE. Tony Reddicliffe. *Launceston town centre. 100yds from multi-storey car park past offices of Cornish & Devon Post into Dunheved Rd, 3rd bungalow on R.* **Sun 28 July (1-5). Adm £5, chd free. Light refreshments. Home-made teas.**

Small town garden developed over 10yrs by enthusiastic amateur gardeners. Herbaceous borders, rockery. Tropicals incl bananas, gingers and senecio. Stream and water features. Roof garden. New this year a Japanese inspired tea house and courtyard with bridge. Fig tree and Pawlonia flank area giving secluded seating. Living pergola.

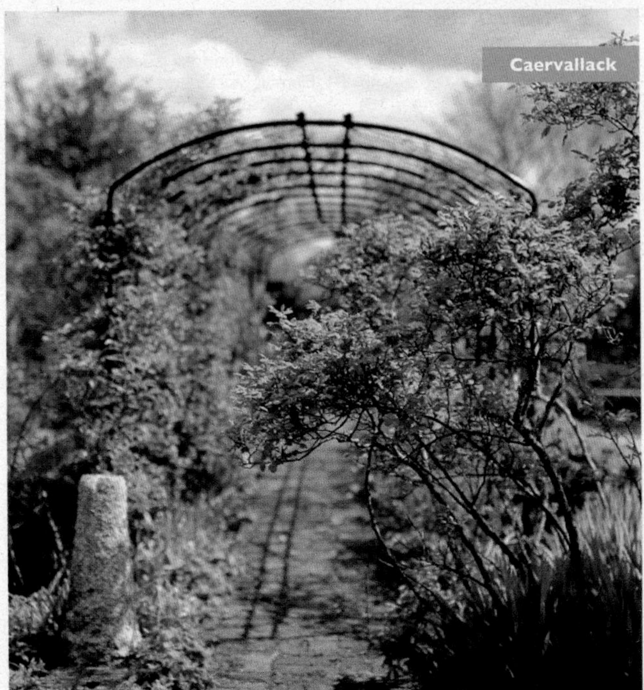

Caervallack

10 NEW CAERVALLACK

St Martin, Helston, TR12 6DF. Matt Robinson & Louise McClary, 01326 221339, mat@carvallack.f9.co.uk. *5m SE of Helston. Go through Mawgan village, over 2 bridges, past Gear Farm shop; go past turning on L, garden next farmhouse on L.* **Sun 9 June (1.30-4). Adm £5, chd free. Home-made teas.**

Romantic garden arranged into rooms, the collaboration between an artist and an architect. Colour and form of plants against architectural experiments in cob, concrete and shaped hedges. Grade II listed farmhouse and orchard. 54ft timber bridge leading to meditation studio. Roses and wisteria a speciality. 24 years in the making, last open 2010. Historic grade II farmhouse and orchard. Heroic 54ft pedestrian footbridge, 5 sided meditation studio, cast concrete pond and amphitheatre. Limited wheelchair access but if you can negotiate the opening 2 steps, some of front garden will be accessible. Brick, grass and gravel paths.

11 CARMINOWE VALLEY GARDEN

Tangies, Gunwalloe, TR12 7PU. Mr & Mrs Peter Stanley, 01326 565868, stanley.m2@sky.com, www.carminowevalleygarden.co.uk. *3m SW of Helston. A3083 Helston-Lizard rd. R opp main gate to Culdrose. 1m downhill, garden on R.* **Visits by arrangement May & June. Adm £5, chd free. Light refreshments.**

Overlooking the beautiful Carminowe Valley towards Loe Pool this abundant garden combines native oak woodland, babbling brook and large natural pond with more formal areas. Wild flowers, mown pathways, shrubberies, orchard. Enclosed cottage garden, spring colours and roses early summer provide huge contrast. Gravel paths, slopes.

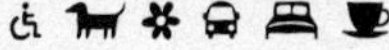

12 NEW CARWINNICK
Grampound, Truro, TR2 4RJ. Mr Bryan Coode. *Between Truro and St Austell, off A390 at Hewas Water/ Sicker. Signs displayed on A390 showing turn-off point down B3287 towards Tregony. Garden 1m on R. Access is down single track lane (one way system), so should only be approached from this direction.* **Sun 14 Apr (2-5). Adm £4.50, chd free. Home-made teas.**
Once a medieval farm, over the last 50 yrs a home to 2 families. There has been much tree planting and development of the 5 acres which has borrowed the landscapes and vistas, so the woods at Heligan to E and turbines at Gorran can both be seen. Spring garden with nearly 50 camellias, daffodils and other early shrubs and plants. Mainly semi-tropical plants around tennis court. A fine Magnolia Lanarth may be in flower if we are lucky. Level ground across gravel and lawns.

13 ◆ CHYGURNO
Lamorna, TR19 6XH. Dr & Mrs Robert Moule, 01736 732153, rmoule010@btinternet.com. *4m S of Penzance. Off B3315. Follow signs for The Lamorna Cove Hotel. Garden is at top of hill, past Hotel on L.* **For NGS: Sat 27, Sun 28 Apr, Sat 20, Sun 21 July (2-5). Adm £5, chd free.** For other opening times and information, please phone or email.
Beautiful, unique, 3 acre cliffside garden overlooking Lamorna Cove. Planting started in 1998, mainly S-hemisphere shrubs and exotics with hydrangeas, camellias and rhododendrons. Woodland area with tree ferns set against large granite outcrops. Garden terraced with steep steps and paths. Plenty of benches so you can take a rest and enjoy the wonderful views.

14 CRUGSILLICK MANOR
Ruan High Lanes, Truro, TR2 5LJ. Dr Alison Agnew & Mr Brian Yule, 01872 501972, alisonagnew@icloud.com. *On Roseland Peninsula. Turn off A390 Truro-St Austell rd onto A3078 towards St Mawes. Approx 5m after Tregony turn 1st L after Ruan High Lanes towards Veryan, garden is 200yds on R.* **Sun 25 Aug (11-5.30). Adm £5, chd free. Home-made teas. Pasties are available as well as teas, coffee, soft drinks and cakes.** Visits also by arrangement Apr to Oct for groups of 10+.
2 acre garden, substantially re-landscaped and planted, mostly over last 6yrs. To the side of the C17/C18 house, a wooded bank drops down to walled kitchen garden and hot garden. In front, sweeping yew hedges and paths define oval lawns and broad mixed borders. On a lower terrace, the focus is a large pond and the planting is predominantly exotic flowering trees and shrubs. Partial wheelchair access. Garden is on several levels connected by fairly steep sloping gravel paths.

15 DYE COTTAGE
St Neot, PL14 6NG. Sue & Brian Williams. *Opp The London Inn in centre of St Neot village. Turn off A38 to St Neot. Street parking.* **Fri 28, Sat 29 June (2-5). Light refreshments. Sun 30 June (2-5). Home-made teas. Adm £4, chd free.**
⅓ acre cottage garden, designed and completely maintained by the owners over the past 25 yrs. Many seating areas - down by the river, in courtyard garden, fire pit corner, and on rose terrace. Wisteria walk, potting shed, greenhouse, summerhouse, office (once the tree house!), fruit cage, mature borders, and roses everywhere. Regret no wheelchair access.

16 ◆ EDEN PROJECT
Bodelva, PL24 2SG. The Eden Trust, 01726 811911, www.edenproject.com. *4m E of St Austell. Brown signs from A30 & A390.* **For opening times and information, please phone or visit garden website.**
Described as 8th wonder of the world, the Eden Project is a global garden for the C21. Discover the story of plants that have changed the world and which could change your future. The Eden Project is an exciting attraction where you can explore your relationship with nature, learn new things and get inspiration about the world around you. Year-round programme of talks, events and workshops. Wheelchairs available - booking of powered wheelchairs is essential; please call 01726 818895 in advance.

17 ETHNEVAS COTTAGE
Constantine, Falmouth, TR11 5PY. Lyn Watson & Ray Chun. *6m SW of Falmouth. Nearest main rds A39, A394. Follow signs for Constantine. At lower village sign, at bottom of winding hill, turn off on private lane.*

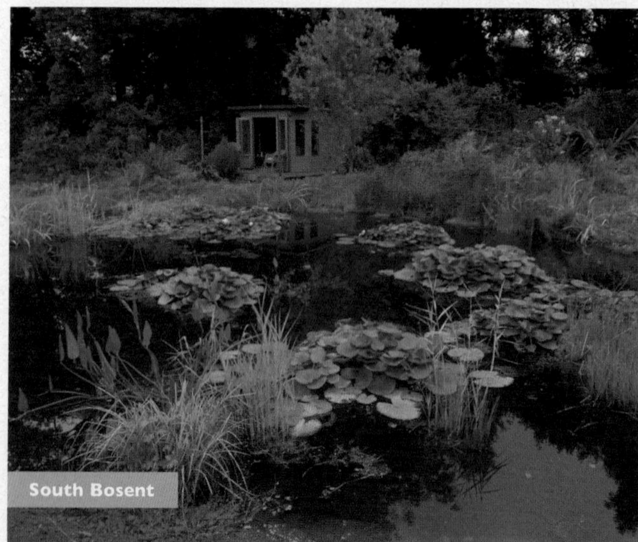
South Bosent

Garden ¾m up hill. **Sun 12 May (12-5). Adm £5, chd free. Light refreshments.**
Isolated granite cottage in 2 acres. Intimate flower and vegetable garden. Bridge over stream to large pond and primrose path through semi-wild bog area. Hillside with grass paths among native and exotic trees. Many camellias and rhododendrons. Mixed shrubs and herbaceous beds, wild flower glade, spring bulbs. A garden of discovery of hidden delights.

18 NEW GARDEN COTTAGE

Gunwalloe, Helston, TR12 7QB. Dan & Beth Tarling, 01326 241906, beth@gunwalloe.com, www.gunwalloecottages.co.uk. *Just beyond Halzephron Inn at Gunwalloe. Cream cottage with green windows.* **Visits by arrangement May to Oct for groups of up to 20. Adm £4, chd free. Cream teas.**
Coastal cottage garden. Small garden with traditional cottage flowers, vegetable garden, greenhouse and meadow with far reaching views. Instagram: seaview_gunwalloe. Featured in Country Living magazine. Gravel paths and a few steps.

19 GARDENS COTTAGE

Prideaux, St Blazey, PL24 2SS. Sue & Roger Paine, 07786 367610, sue.newton@btinternet.com. *1m from railway Xing on A390 in St Blazey. Turn into Prideaux Rd opp Gulf petrol station on A390 in St Blazey (signed Luxulyan). Proceed ½m. Turn R (signed Luxulyan Valley and Prideaux) and follow signs.* **Tues, Weds 4, 5 June; 2, 3 July; 6, 7 Aug; 3, 4 Sept (11-5). Adm £4, chd free. Home-made teas.** Visits also by arrangement June to Sept for groups of up to 30.
Newly-created garden of about 1½ acres set in tranquil location on edge of Luxulyan Valley. The vision of the owners is to create a country garden that is sympathetic to its stunning surrounding landscape, has yr-round interest with lots of colour, is productive and simply feels good to be in. Check our Facebook page for special events - @gardenscottageprideaux.

20 HALF ACRE

Mount Pleasant, Boscastle, PL35 0BJ. Carole Vincent, 01840 250263, concretecarole@btinternet.com, www.carolevincent.org. *5m N of Camelford. Park at doctors' surgery at top of village (clearly signed). Limited parking for disabled at garden.* **Sat 22, Sun 23 June (1.30-5.30). Adm £4, chd free. Home-made teas provided by Boscastle Churches.** Visits also by arrangement Mar to Sept for groups of up to 20.
Old stone cottage with 2 studios overlooking cliffs and sea, set in 1½ acres of gardens - cottage, small wood and Blue Circle garden (RHS Chelsea 2001) constructed in colour concrete. Owner has a national reputation for her sculpture in concrete, and sculptures all around occupy small spaces or command a view. Mid-June should see the flowering of the roses and echiums. Studio open. Painting exhibition. Regret no dogs.

21 ◆ THE JAPANESE GARDEN

St Mawgan, TR8 4ET. Natalie Hore & Stuart Ellison, 01637 860116, info@japanesegarden.co.uk, www.japanesegarden.co.uk. *6m E of Newquay. St Mawgan village is directly below Newquay Airport. Follow brown and white road signs on A3059 and B3276.* **For NGS: Sun 12, Mon 13 May (10-6). Adm £5, chd £2.50. Refreshments available in village 2-3 min walk from garden.** For other opening times and information, please phone, email or visit garden website.
Discover an oasis of tranquillity in a Japanese-style Cornish garden, set in approx 1 acre. Spectacular Japanese maples and azaleas, symbolic teahouse, koi pond, bamboo grove, stroll woodland, zen and moss gardens. A place created for contemplation and meditation. Adm free to gift shop, bonsai and plant areas. Featured in BBC2 Big Dreams Small Spaces. 90% wheelchair accessible. Gravel paths.

We help ordinary people open the gates to their extraordinary private gardens to raise impressive amounts of money through admissions, teas and slices of cake!

22 KEN CARO

Bicton, Liskeard, PL14 5RF. Mr & Mrs K R Willcock. *5m NE of Liskeard. From A390 to Callington turn off N at St Ive. Take Pensilva Rd, follow brown tourist signs, approx 1m off main rd. Plenty of parking. (SatNav is misleading).* **Daily Sun 31 Mar to Sat 31 Aug (10-5). Adm £5, chd £2.**
Connoisseurs' garden full of interest all yr round. Lily ponds, panoramic views, plenty of seating, picnic area, in all 10 acres. Garden started in 1970, recently rejuvenated. Woodland walk, which has one of the largest beech trees. Good collection of yellow magnolias and herbaceous plants. Large collection of hydrangeas. Partial wheelchair access.

23 KENNALL HOUSE

Ponsanooth, TR3 7HJ. Nick & Mary Wilson-Holt, kennallvale@hotmail.com. *4m NW of Falmouth. Off A393 Falmouth-Redruth rd. Turn L at Ponsanooth PO for ⅓m. Garden at end of drive marked Kennall House.* **Visits by arrangement May to Oct for groups of 10 to 30. Adm £6, chd free.**
The 12-acre garden-cum-arboretum, beautifully situated in the Kennall Valley, is an intriguing combination of typical British species and exotics, sympathetically laid out in a variety of spacious settings, incl walled garden and fast-flowing stream with ponds. Wide variety of trees incl new plantings of rare specimens. An unusual Cornish garden with yr-round interest. Limited wheelchair access.

24 KESTLE BARTON

Manaccan, Helston, TR12 6HU. Karen Townsend, info@kestlebarton.co.uk, www.kestlebarton.co.uk. *A3083 Helston - Lizard, 2m L B3293 for St Keverne. 2m L Helford, Newtown St Martin, R then L for Helford. 1m L at Xrds to Kestle Barton, R after several hundred yds, follow signs.* **Every Wed 1 July to 30 Sept (10.30-5). Adm by donation. Home-made teas.**

A delightful garden near Frenchmans Creek, on the Lizard, which is the setting for Kestle Barton Gallery; wild flower meadow, Cornish orchard with named varieties and a formal garden with prairie planting in blocks by James Alexander Sinclair. It is a riot of colour in summer and continues to delight well into late summer. Parking, honesty box tea hut, good wheel chair access. Art Gallery. Dogs on leads welcome. Large coaches cannot reach Kestle Barton.

25 KITPURVA

St. Anthony, Portscatho, Truro, TR2 5EY. Jude Lynock. *Take A3078 from Tregony to St Mawes but turn L at Trewithian to St Anthony. Kitpurva is 2.3m past Gerrans church. Also pass Trewince and Froe. Do not turn R to Bohortha.* **Sun 4 Aug (10.30-5.30). Adm £5, chd free. Cream teas and home-made biscuits.**

1920s coastal garden with some original features; extensively replanted by current owners over past 15 yrs. Agapanthus, hemerocallis, anemone, hydrangea, cordyline, trachycarpus thrive. Restoration ongoing incl paths which lead you around the garden to seating areas, borders and small pond from which to enjoy the panoramic sea and rural views. Newly planted escallonia maze with viewing areas to enjoy views from Nare Head to the Lizard. Visitors are welcome to walk the horses' track. Please note that some areas are work in progress. Most areas accessible by wheelchair.

26 THE LODGE

Fletchersbridge, Bodmin, PL30 4AN. Mr Tony Ryde. *2m E of Bodmin. From A38 at Glynn Crematorium r'about take rd towards Cardinham and continue through hamlet of Fletchersbridge. Garden first on R over river bridge.* **Sat 16, Sun 17 Mar (1-6). Adm £4, chd free. Cream teas.**

3-acre riverside garden some 20 yrs old specialising in trees and shrubs chosen for their flowers, foliage and form, embracing a Gothic lodge remodelled in 2016, once part of the Glyn estate. Early spring sees the campbellii magnolias in full glory, overlooking camellias and set in a recently extended water garden with ponds, waterfalls and sculptures framed by swathes of daffodils. Wheelchair access to gravelled areas around house and along 2 sides of garden.

27 ◆ THE LOST GARDENS OF HELIGAN

Pentewan, St Austell, PL26 6EN. Heligan Gardens Ltd, 01726 845100, info@heligan.com, www.heligan.com. *5m S of St Austell. From St Austell take B3273 signed Mevagissey, follow signs.* For opening times and information, please phone, email or visit garden website.

Lose yourself in the mysterious world of The Lost Gardens where an exotic sub-tropical jungle, atmospheric Victorian pleasure grounds, an interactive wildlife project and the finest productive gardens in Britain all await your discovery. Wheelchair access to Northern gardens. Armchair tour shows video of unreachable areas. Wheelchairs available at reception free of charge.

NPC

GROUP OPENING

28 LOWER AMBLE GARDENS

Chapel Amble, Wadebridge, PL27 6EW. *3m N of Wadebridge. Take lane signed Middle & Lower Amble opp PO. 1m to L turn by pond. Parking in field beyond farmhouse.* **Sun 26 May (2-5.30). Combined adm £5, chd free. Cream teas at Millpond Cottage. Picnic site at Lower Amble Farmhouse wood Also open Bokelly.**

In peaceful hamlet with wide valley and moorland views, developed from mill farm buildings of early 1800s, 2 very different gardens. Lower Amble Farmhouse: 1-acre garden divided into varied spaces, plus 4 acres of deciduous woodland, pond and wildflower orchard. Millpond Cottage: large 20-yr-old garden with orchard, pond, vegetable garden and mixed herbaceous borders with many roses, geraniums and interesting perennials. Disabled parking in Millpond Cottage drive or access through side gate.

29 MEUDON HOTEL

Maenporth Road, Mawnan Smith, Falmouth, TR11 5HT. Tessa Rabett, 01326 250541, wecare@meudon.co.uk, www.meudon.co.uk. *Follow signs for Mabe, then Mawnan Smith.* **Sun 17 Mar (12-5). Adm £7, chd free. Light refreshments in restaurant, 50% donated to NGS. At hotel, bar drinks, snacks, cream teas are available.**

Meudon has 9 acres of sub-tropical valley garden created by the Fox family in 1800. Wealthy Quakers and shipping agents, their Packet ships provided transport for Meudon's wonderful collection of rare and exotic trees and shrubs from around the world. Terraces, pathways, meander down to Bream Cove (private beach). Formal garden, herbaceous borders, indigenous plants, and sunken pond area. Brazilian Gunnera manicata, Japanese banana trees Musa basjoo, Wollemia pine, Dicksonia antaractica, rhodendendrons, camellias, magnolia, azaleas, Trachycarpus fortunei, Drimys winteri, Monterey cypress, bamboo, agapanthus, Cornus kousa, myrtle. Wheelchair access limited to upper terrace and ponds (although they take a little longer to get to).

30 ◆ MOYCLARE

Lodge Hill, Liskeard, PL14 4EH. Elizabeth & Philip Henslowe, 01579 343114, elizabethhenslowe@btinternet.com, www.moyclare.co.uk. *1m S of Liskeard centre. Approx 300yds S of Liskeard railway stn on St Keyne-Duloe rd (B3254).* **For NGS: Mon 6 May (11-5.30). Adm £4, chd free. Home-made teas.** For other opening times and information, please phone, email or visit garden website.

Gardened by one family for over 90yrs; mature trees, shrubs and plants (many unusual, many variegated). Once most televised Cornish garden. Now revived and rejuvenated and still a plantsman's delight, full of character. Camellia, brachyglottis and astrantia (all Moira Reid) and cytisus Moyclare Pink originated here. Meandering paths through fascinating shrubberies, herbacious borders and sunny corners. Wellstocked pond. Wildlife habitat area. Over 70 named camellias. Rare and unusual plants and ferns. Quite a lot of the garden can be enjoyed by wheelchair users.

31 ◆ NATIONAL DAHLIA COLLECTION

Varfell Farm, Long Rock, Penzance, TR20 8AQ. Greenyard Flowers, 01736 339276, louise@nationaldahliacollection.co.uk, www.nationaldahliacollection.co.uk. *3m N of Penzance. Turn off A30 near Long Rock r'about, signed Varfell.* **For NGS: Sun 22 Sept (10-4). Adm £3, chd free.** For other opening times and information, please phone, email or visit garden website.

National Dahlia Collection growing in 2 acre field of riotous colour which delights the eye. All types of dahlias are exhibited from dainty pompoms to huge decoratives amounting to 1600 named varieties bred and grown here. Displayed in ordered rows, fully labelled for identification in mail order sales. Come and see the extraordinary show. Coach parties welcome by prior arrangement. In dry conditions with some wheelchairs it is possible to move around the field or possible to view the field as a whole from road.

NPC

32 NAVAS HILL HOUSE

Bosanath Valley, Mawnan Smith, Falmouth, TR11 5LL. Aline & Richard Turner. *1½m from Trebah & Glendurgan Gdns. Head for Mawnan Smith, pass Trebah and Glendurgan Gdns then follow yellow signs. Don't follow SatNav which suggests you turn R before Mawnan Smith - congestion alert!* **Sun 5 May (2-5). Adm £5, chd free. Light refreshments. 'All you can eat' £3.50.**

8½-acre elevated valley garden with paddocks, woodland, kitchen garden and ornamental areas. The ornamental garden consists of 2 plantsman areas with specialist trees and shrubs, walled rose garden, water features and rockery. Young and established wooded areas with bluebells, camellia walks and young large leafed rhododendrons. Seating areas with views across wooded valley. Partial, limited wheelchair access, some gravel and grass paths.

33 NEW NEW MILLS FARMHOUSE

New Mills, Ladock, Truro, TR2 4NN. Jeremy & Irene Newton, 01726 883089, irene.newton@btopenworld.com. *Approx 1½m N of Ladock on B3275 in New Mills. At unsigned Xrds by converted chapel, garden is 75yds E of Xrds on R at end of weight restricted bridge.* **Visits by arrangement for groups of up to 20 from 25 May to 30 June. Adm £5, chd free.**

7-acre landscape set around farmhouse reflecting garden influences from Cornwall to New Zealand in a relaxed exuberant manner. 4 acres of meadowland, streamside willow marshland, 1 acre of young woodland. Formal area incl water features, granite-walled terraces and vistas displaying shrub roses, perennials and a range of shrubs. Mighty play area quarried out of hillside. Some flights of steps but much of garden accessible via sloping grass and gravel paths.

South Lea

34 NEW **PARKENVER**
Penventon, Redruth, TR15 3AA. Dr & Mrs David Quill Smart. *Important: To enter gardens, please use main entrance of Roman Catholic Church - about 100m to town end of our main gate (white balustrading). Leave by Exit lane.* **Sun 14 July (12.30-6). Adm £5, chd free. Light refreshments in marquee on lawn. Wine available.**
The Parkhenver Estate gardens were created in about 1850. We are in the midst of a complete restoration project to return them to their original glory. The greenhouses and walled garden have already been restored. Two fascinating woodland walks have also been found and restored. The fountain and other flower beds are in the process of restoration. Access to some gravelled areas may be difficult.

35 ◆ **PENCARROW**
Washaway, Bodmin, PL30 3AG. Molesworth-St Aubyn family, 01208 841369, info@pencarrow.co.uk, www.pencarrow.co.uk. *4m NW of Bodmin. Signed off A389 & B3266.* **For NGS: Mon 8 Apr (10-5.30). Adm £6.50, chd free. Light refreshments.** For other opening times and information, please phone, email or visit garden website.
50 acres of tranquil, family-owned Grade II* listed gardens. Superb specimen conifers, azaleas, magnolias and camellias galore. 700 varieties of rhododendron give a blaze of spring colour; blue hydrangeas line the mile-long carriage drive throughout the summer. Discover the Iron Age hill fort, lake, Italian gardens and granite rockery. Free parking, dogs welcome, café and children's play area. Gravel paths, some steep slopes.

36 **PENDOWER HOUSE**
Lanteglos-by-Fowey, PL23 1NJ. Mr Roger Lamb, 01726 870884, rl@rogerlamb.com. *Near Polruan off the B3359 towards Bodinnick. 2m from Fowey using the Bodinnick ferry. Please ask for directions when arranging to visit the garden. Do not use SatNav.* **Visits by arrangement May & June for groups of up to 20. Adm £4.50, chd free. Home-made teas. Other refreshments available by prior arrangement.**
Set in the heart of Daphne du Maurier country in its own valley this established garden surrounding a Georgian Rectory is now undergoing a revival having been wild and neglected for some years. It has formal herbaceous terraces, a cottage garden, orchard, ponds, streams and a C19 shrub garden with a fine collection of azaleas, camellias and rhododendrons plus rare mature specimen trees. House and garden available for filming and photography. Sadly difficult wheelchair access to much of this garden.

37 **PENHEALE MANOR**
Egloskerry, Launceston, PL15 8RX. Mr & Mrs James Colville. *SX26 88; 3½m NW of Launceston. Take rd from St Stephen's, Launceston, to Egloskerry. From centre of village to Penheale entrance is ½m on R.* **Sun 23 June (2-5). Adm £6, chd £2. Home-made teas.**
A rare opportunity to enjoy midsummer in the secluded peace and tranquility of the walled gardens surrounding this Jacobean manor house which was extended so distinctively by Lutyens in the 1920s. Gatehouse and courtyard pavilions frame the rose gardens, and impressive yew hedges shelter drifts of herbaceous colour, extending to the more familiar Cornish style of beautiful woodland areas beyond. Partial wheelchair access due to stony paths.

38 NEW **PENWARNE**
Mawnan Smith, Mawnan Smith, Falmouth, TR11 5PH. Mrs R Sawyer, penwarnegarden@gmail.com. *1 mile outside Mawnan Smith.* **Visits by arrangement Feb to May for groups of 5 to 20. Adm £5, chd free.**
Originally planted in the late C19, this 12 acre garden incl extensive plantings of camellias, rhododendrons and azaleas. Special features incl large magnolias and a number of fine mature trees incl copper beech, handkerchief tree and Himalayan cedar. The walled garden, believed to be the site of a medieval chapel, houses herbaceous planting, climbing roses and fruit trees.

39 ◆ **PINSLA GARDEN & NURSERY**
Cardinham, PL30 4AY. Mark & Claire Woodbine, 01208 821339, cwoodbine@btinternet.com, www.pinslagarden.net. *3½m E of Bodmin. From A30 or Bodmin take A38 towards Plymouth, 1st L to Cardinham & Fletchers Bridge, 2m on R.* **For NGS: Sat 18, Sun 19 May, Sat 3, Sun 4 Aug (9-5). Adm £3.50, chd free. Home-made teas.** For other opening times and information, please phone, email or visit garden website.
Romantic 1½-acre artist's garden set in tranquil woodland. Naturalistic cottage garden planting surrounds C18 fairytale cottage. Imaginative design, intense colour and scent, bees and butterflies. Unusual shade plants, acers and ferns. Fantastic range of plants and statues on display and for sale. Friendly advice in nursery. Wheelchair access limited as some paths are narrow and bumpy.

40 ◆ **POTAGER GARDEN**
High Cross, Constantine, Falmouth, TR11 5RF. Mr Mark Harris, 01326 341258, enquiries@potagergarden.org, www.potagergarden.org. *5m SW of Falmouth. From Falmouth, follow signs to Constantine. From Helston, drive through Constantine and continue towards Famouth.* For opening times and information, please phone, email or visit garden website.
Potager has emerged from the bramble choked wilderness of an abandoned plant nursery. With mature trees which were once nursery stock and lush herbaceous planting interspersed with fruit and vegetables Potager Garden aims to demonstrate the beauty of productive organic gardening. There are games to play, hammocks to laze in and boule and badminton to enjoy.

41 ♦ ROSELAND HOUSE

Chacewater, TR4 8QB. Mr & Mrs Pridham, 01872 560451, charlie@roselandhouse.co.uk, www.roselandhouse.co.uk. *4m W of Truro. At Truro end of main st. Park in village car park (100yds) or on surrounding rds.* **For NGS: Sat 22, Sun 23 June (1-5). Adm £4, chd free. Home-made teas.** For other opening times and information, please phone, email or visit garden website.

The 1-acre garden is a mass of rambling roses and clematis. Ponds and borders alike are filled with plants, many rarely seen in gardens. National Collection of clematis viticella cvs can be seen in garden and display tunnel, along with a huge range of other climbing plants. Some slopes.

NPC

42 ♦ ST MICHAEL'S MOUNT

Marazion, TR17 0HS. James & Mary St Levan, 01736 710507, mail@stmichaelsmount.co.uk, www.stmichaelsmount.co.uk. *2½m E of Penzance. ½m from shore at Marazion by Causeway; otherwise by motor boat.* **For NGS: Sun 16 June (10.30-5). Adm £8, chd £4.** For other opening times and information, please phone, email or visit garden website.

Infuse your senses with colour and scent in the unique sub-tropical gardens basking in the mild climate and salty breeze. Clinging to granite slopes the terraced beds tier steeply to the ocean's edge, boasting tender exotics from places such as Mexico, the Canary Islands and South Africa. Laundry lawn, mackerel bank, pill box, gun emplacement, tiered terraces, well, tortoise lawn. Walled gardens, seagull seat. The garden lawn can be accessed with wheelchairs although further exploration is limited due to steps and steepness.

43 SCORRIER HOUSE

Scorrier, Redruth, TR16 5AU. Richard & Caroline Williams, www.scorrierhouse.co.uk. *2½m E of Redruth. Signed from B3207 and Redruth Truro rd B3287.* **Mon 6 May (2-5). Adm £5, chd £5. Home-made teas.**

Scorrier House and gardens have been in the Williams family for 7 generations. The gardens are set in parkland with a new conservatory, formal garden with herbaceous borders and walled garden with camellias, magnolias and rare trees, some collected by the famous plant collector William Lobb. Unfenced swimming pool.

44 NEW SOUTH BOSENT

Liskeard, PL14 4LX. Adrienne Lloyd & Trish Wilson. *2½m W of Liskeard. From r'about at junction of A390 and A38 take turning to Dobwalls. At mini-r'about R to Duloe, after 1m at X-rds turn R. Garden on L after ¼m.* **Mon 6 May (11-5). Adm £5, chd free. Tea.**

9½ acre meadow and garden being developed by sisters Adrienne and Trish. The aim is to create an interesting garden and wildlife haven. Several themed areas, kitchen, gravel and woodland gardens, large borders, mini lake and 4 ponds, several plant collections, 1000's of bulbs, waterfall and rill on terrace. Meadow and bluebell wood trail alongside stream. Regret no disabled access to bluebell wood trail due to 79 steps.

45 SOUTH LEA

Pillaton, Saltash, PL12 6QS. Viv & Tony Laurillard, 01579 350629, tony@laurillard.eclipse.co.uk. *Pillaton, opp Weary Friar PH. 4m S of Callington. Signed from r'abouts on A388 at St Mellion and Hatt, and on A38 at Landrake. Roadside parking. Please do not park in PH car park.* **Sun 5 May, Sun 16 June, Sun 7 July (1-5). Adm £5, chd free. Home-made teas.** Visits also by arrangement May to July for groups of 10+.

In the front a path winds through interesting landscaping with a small pond. Tropical beds by front door with palms, cannas, etc. The back garden, with views over the valley, is a pretty picture in May with spring bulbs and clematis, whilst in June the herbaceous borders are a riot of colour. Lawns are separated by a fair sized fish pond and the small woodland area is enchanting in spring. Plenty of seating. Due to steps, wheelchair access is limited to front dry garden and rear terrace, from which most of garden can be viewed.

46 TREBARTHA

Trebartha, nr Launceston, PL15 7PD. The Latham Family. *6m SW of Launceston. North Hill, SW of Launceston nr junction of B3254 & B3257. No coaches.* **Sun 12 May, Sun 8 Sept (2-5). Adm £6, chd free. Home-made teas.**

Historic landscape gardens featuring ponds, streams, cascades, rocks and woodlands, incl fine trees, bluebells in spring, ornamental walled garden and private garden at Lemarne. Ongoing development of C19 American Garden. Allow at least 1 hour for a circular walk. Some steep and rough paths, which can be slippery when wet. Stout footwear advised.

47 NEW TREGONHAYNE

Tregony, Truro, TR2 5SE. Mrs Gillian Burnett. *A390 in easterly direction, then A3078 to Tregony. Pass through Tregony and after passing school on L the turning for Tregonhayne Close is on R by post box.* **Sun 8 Sept (2-5). Adm £3.50, chd free. Home-made teas.**

Extending over an acre, the garden created over 18 years is divided into 3 zones: courtyard near house, shade garden featuring a sculpture of a horse's head as the focal point and a natural garden. This ⅓ area comprises island beds featuring trees, shrubs, perennials and grasses. Of special interest is the collection of New Zealand plants. Due to steps, regret not suitable for wheelchairs.

We open the gates to the nation's best gardens, offering a relaxing, memorable and affordable day out. A perfect experience to share with friends and family.

48 TREGONNING

Carleen, Breage, Helston, TR13 9QU. Andrew & Kathryn Eaton, 01736 761840, alfeaton@aol.com, Tregonninggarden.co.uk. *1m S of Godolphin Cross. From Xrds in centre of Godolphin Cross head S towards Carleen. In ½m at fork signed Breage 1¼ turn R up narrow lane marked no through rd. After ½m parking on L opp Tregonning Farm.* **Visits by arrangement May to Aug for groups of up to 20. Guided tour with optional talk on the garden's creation. Adm £4, chd free. Home-made teas.**
Located 300ft up NE side of Tregonning Hill this small (less than 1 acre) maturing garden will hopefully inspire those thinking of making a garden from nothing more than a pond and copse of trees (in 2009). With the ever present challenge of storm force winds, garden offers yr-round interest and a self-sufficient vegetable and soft fruit paddock. Sculpted grass meadow, with panoramic views from Carn Brea to Helston. A section of the garden is designed in the form of a plant (incorporating a deck, leaf shaped beds, stream and large pond). Formal front garden, spring garden, Mediterranean patio. Carp pond/small fernery. Packed vegetable garden. Spring garden not accessible to wheelchairs. See us on Facebook - Tregonninggarden.

49 NEW TREGULLOW

Scorrier, TR16 5AY. James & Sarah Williams. *2m E of Redruth. From A30 take A3047 signed Scorrier then B3298 towards St Day. Pass Scorrier House on R. Just before Lower Tregullow sharp R-hand turn in through lodge gateway.* **Sun 12 May (12-5). Adm £5, chd free. Children over 12 £2.**
Originally created in 1820, this 20-acre garden is only open to the public this one day of the year. Lovingly restored over last 25yrs to its former glory. 47 varieties of magnolias, azaleas, rhododendrons and cornus, and springtime brings the vibrant colour of drifts of bluebell. With its historic features and unexpected vistas, this very private garden has been described by The Sunday Times as a 'truly secret' gem. Dogs on leads, plant sales. Slightly restricted disabled access.

50 ◆ TREMATON CASTLE

Castle Hill, Trematon, Saltash, PL12 4QW. Bannerman, info@bannermandesign.com, www.bannermandesign.com/trematon. *2m SW of Saltash. Lanes surrounding the castle are very narrow, please approach from Trematon and Trehan.* **For NGS: Tue 18 June (11-4.30). Adm £7, chd free. Home-made teas.** For other opening times and information, please email or visit garden website.
Property of Duchy of Cornwall since the Conquest, Trematon is a perfect miniature motte and bailey castle. On R Lynher estuary, '... one of the superb views of Cornwall .... all the more romantic for being still a private residence' (John Betjeman). Julian and Isabel Bannerman have begun to create a garden playing on its pre-Raphaelite glories, wild flowers, orchard, woodland, scented borders, seaside and exotic planting. Regrettably not suitable for wheelchair users, pea gravel throughout.

51 TRENARTH

High Cross, Constantine, Falmouth, TR11 5JN. Lucie Nottingham, 01326 340444, lmnottingham@btinternet.com, www.trenarthgardens.com. *6m SW of Falmouth. Main rd A39/A394 Truro to Helston, follow Constantine signs. High X garage turn L for Mawnan, 30yds on R down dead end lane, Trenarth is ½m at end of lane.* **Sun 23 June (2-5). Adm £5, chd free. Cream teas.** Visits also by arrangement. Good parking, tours available.
4 acres round C17 farmhouse in peaceful pastoral setting. Yr-round interest. Emphasis on tender, unusual plants, structure and form. C16 courtyard, listed garden walls, yew rooms, vegetable garden, traditional potting shed, orchard, new woodland area with childrens' interest, palm and gravel garden. Circular walk down ancient green lane via animal pond to Trenarth Bridge, returning through woods. Abundant wildlife. Bees in tree bole, lesser horseshoe bat colony, swallows, wild flowers and butterflies. Family friendly, children's play area, the Wolery, and plenty of room to run, jump and climb.

52 TREREIFE PARK

Penzance, TR20 8TJ. Mr & Mrs T Le Grice, 01736 362750, trereifepark@btconnect.com, www.trereifepark.co.uk. *2m W of Penzance on A30 on Lands End rd. Garden and house signed R through estate gates.* **Visits by arrangement Apr to Sept for groups of up to 30. Entrance fee incl teas and guided tour of house. Adm £10, chd free. Cream teas.**
Mature gardens undergoing restoration in the historic setting of Trereife Park. Established specimen camellia, rhododendron, azalea walk under mature beech trees. Modern parterre, sculptural yew hedge, S-facing walled terrace with wisteria and magnolia. New hot border with unusual Mediterranean planting. Medlar collection around events lawn and old kitchen garden awaiting restoration.

53 NEW TREVILLEY

Sennen, Penzance, TR19 7AH. Patrick Gale & Aidan Hicks. *For walkers, Trevilley lies on footpath from Trevescan to Polgigga and Nanjizal. Satnav TR19 7AH or follow A30 to far side of Sennen, past church and campsite. L fork towards Minack Theatre then L at junction in Trevescan. Trevilley up next track on R. Parking signed. If you reach a white house called Trevilley Farmhouse, you have gone too far. From Porthcurno/Lamorna along B3315, Trevilley is up turning on L just before Trevescan.* **Sun 30 June (2-5). Adm £6, chd free. Home-made teas. Pimms as well as tea and cake.**
Eccentric, romantic and constantly evolving garden, as befits the intense creativity of its owners, carved out of an expanse of concrete farmyard over 20 yrs. Incl elaborate network of decorative cobbling, pools, container garden, veg garden, shade garden, the largely subtropical mowhay garden and both owner's studios but arguably its glory is the westernmost walled rose garden in England. Plant stall. Dogs are welcome on leads and there's direct access to fields where they can let off steam.

54 ◆ TREWIDDEN GARDEN

Buryas Bridge, Penzance, TR20 8TT. Mr Alverne Bolitho - Richard Morton, Head Gardener, 01736 364275/363021, contact@trewiddengarden.co.uk, www.trewiddengarden.co.uk. *2m W of Penzance. Entry on A30 just before Buryas Bridge. SatNav TR19 6AU.* **For NGS: Sun 24 Mar (10.30-5). Adm £6.50, chd free. Light refreshments.** For other opening times and information, please phone, email or visit garden website.

Historic Victorian garden with magnolias, camellias and magnificent tree ferns planted within ancient tin workings. Tender, rare and unusual exotic plantings create a riot of colour thoughout the season. Water features, specimen trees and artefacts from Cornwall's tin industry provide a wide range of interest for all.

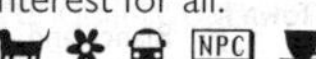

55 WAYE COTTAGE

Lerryn, nr Lostwithiel, PL22 0QQ. Malcolm & Jennifer Bell, 01208 872119, lerrynbells@gmail.com. *4m S of Lostwithiel. Parking usually available at property or village parking, garden 10min, level stroll along riverbank/ stepping stones. Open most days from 16th June - end of July, but do ring first - best after 6pm.* **Visits by arrangement June & July for groups of up to 20. Adm £4, chd free. Tea.**

An enchanting cottage garden on the footprint of an old market garden - good plants, enticing paths, secluded seats and stunning river views. New grass garden. 'Magical! The perfect place for a botanical recharge and horticultural inspiration.' Reproduced courtesy of Cornwall Life magazine. Open most days from 16 June - end of July but please ring first, best after 6 pm. Sadly the garden is too steep with too many steps for disabled access.

56 WINDMILLS

South Hill, Callington, PL17 7LP. Mr & Mrs Peter Tunnicliffe, tunnicliffesue@gmail.com. *3m NW of Callington. Head N from Callington A388, after about ½m turn L onto South Hill Rd (signed South Hill). Straight on for 3m, gardens on R just before church.* **Sun 12 May, Sun 7 July (1.30-5). Combined adm with Anvil Cottage £5, chd free. Home-made teas. Gluten free cakes available.** Visits also by arrangement May and July for groups of 10 to 20. Donation to St Sampson's Church, South Hill.

Next to medieval church and on the site of an old rectory and there are still signs in places of that long gone building. A garden full of surprises, formal paths and steps lead up from the flower beds to extensive vegetable and soft fruit area. More paths lead to a pond, past a pergola, and down into large lawns with trees and shrubs and chickens. Limited wheelchair access.

Anvil Cottage

OPENING DATES

All entries subject to change. For latest information check **www.ngs.org.uk**

Extended openings are shown at the beginning of the month.

Map locator numbers are shown to the right of each garden name.

February

Snowdrop Festival

Every Friday and Saturday from Friday 22nd
Summerdale House 42

Every day from Monday 18th
◆ Swarthmoor Hall 43

Saturday 16th
Summerdale House 42

Sunday 17th
Summerdale House 42

March

Every Friday and Saturday
Summerdale House 42

Every day to Sunday 10th
◆ Swarthmoor Hall 43

Sunday 24th
◆ Dora's Field 11
◆ High Close Estate and Arboretum 21
◆ Holehird Gardens 22
◆ Rydal Hall 38

April

Every Friday and Saturday
Summerdale House 42

Sunday 7th
Fern Bank 13

Saturday 13th
Deer Rudding 10

Thursday 25th
◆ Rydal Hall 38

May

Sunday 5th
Chapelside 5

Saturday 11th
Deer Rudding 10

Sunday 12th
Dallam Tower 9
Low Fell West 30

Saturday 18th
Hazel Cottage 20
Lower Rowell Farm & Cottage 31

Sunday 19th
Chapelside 5
Cherry Cottage 6
Hazel Cottage 20
Lower Rowell Farm & Cottage 31

Matson Ground 32
◆ Rydal Hall 38

Wednesday 22nd
Church View 7

Saturday 25th
Langholme Mill 28

Sunday 26th
Fell Yeat 12
Langholme Mill 28

Monday 27th
Langholme Mill 28
NEW The Ryebeck Hotel

Friday 31st
Summerdale House 42

June

Every Saturday
Beckside Farm 3

Every Friday and Saturday
Summerdale House 42

Saturday 1st
Galesyke 15

Sunday 2nd
Chapelside 5
Galesyke 15

Saturday 8th
Deer Rudding 10

Friday 14th
◆ Swarthmoor Hall 43

Saturday 15th
◆ Swarthmoor Hall 43

Sunday 16th
Askham Hall 2
Chapelside 5
Summerdale House 42
◆ Swarthmoor Hall 43

Thursday 20th
Haverthwaite Lodge 18
Lakeside Hotel & Rocky Bank 27

Sunday 23rd
Ivy House 26
Woodend House 48

Sunday 30th
Chapelside 5
Hazel Cottage 20
Stewart Hill Cottage 41
Ulverston Town Gardens 45

July

Every Saturday
Beckside Farm 3

Every Friday and Saturday
Summerdale House 42

Saturday 6th
Boxwood House 4

Sunday 7th
Abi and Tom's Garden Plants 1
Boxwood House 4
Fernhill Coach House 14
Hayton Village Gardens 19
Newton Rigg College Gardens 33
Yewbarrow House 49

Thursday 11th
◆ Holehird Gardens 22
Larch Cottage Nurseries 29

Sunday 14th
Chapelside 5
Holme Meadow 24
Park House 35
Sandhouse 39
Winton Park 47

Sunday 28th
Grange over Sands Hidden Gardens 17
NEW The Ryebeck Hotel

August

Every Saturday
Beckside Farm 3

Sunday 4th
Fell Yeat 12
HPB Merlewood 25
Park House 35
Yewbarrow House 49

Thursday 15th
Haverthwaite Lodge 18
Lakeside Hotel & Rocky Bank 27
Larch Cottage Nurseries 29

Sunday 18th
Grange Fell Allotments 16

Thursday 22nd
◆ Holker Hall Gardens 23

Yewbarrow House

September

Sunday 1st
Yewbarrow House 49

Saturday 7th
Beckside Farm 3

Monday 9th
◆ Sizergh Castle 40

Thursday 12th
◆ Rydal Hall 38

Thursday 19th
Larch Cottage Nurseries 29

Wednesday 25th
Church View 7

October

Sunday 20th
Low Fell West 30

Sunday 27th
NEW The Ryebeck Hotel

By Arrangement

Arrange a personalised garden visit with your club, or group of friends, on a date to suit you. See individual garden entries for full details.

Beckside Farm 3
Boxwood House 4
Chapelside 5
Cherry Cottage 6
Church View 7
Crookdake Farm 8
Deer Rudding 10
Fell Yeat 12
Fernhill Coach House 14
Grange Fell Allotments 16
Haverthwaite Lodge 18
Holme Meadow 24
Ivy House 26
Kinrara, Hayton Village Gardens 19
Lakeside Hotel & Rocky Bank 27
Langholme Mill 28
Larch Cottage Nurseries 29
Low Fell West 30
Lower Rowell Farm & Cottage 31
Newton Rigg College Gardens 33
Orchard Cottage 34
Pear Tree Cottage 36
Rose Croft 37
Stewart Hill Cottage 41
Tenter End Barn 44
West Garth Cottage, Hayton Village Gardens 19
Windy Hall 46
Woodend House 48
Yewbarrow House 49

THE GARDENS

1 ABI AND TOM'S GARDEN PLANTS

Halecat, Witherslack, Grange-Over-Sands, LA11 6RT. Abi & Tom Attwood, www.abiandtom.co.uk. *20 mins from Kendal. From A590 turn N to Witherslack. Follow brown tourist signs to Halecat. Rail Grange-over-sands 5m, Bus X6 2m, NCR 70.* **Sun 7 July (10-5). Combined adm with Fernhill Coach House £4, chd free. Home-made teas.**
The 1 acre nursery garden is a fusion of traditional horticultural values with modern approaches to the display, growing and use of plant material. Our full range of perennials can be seen growing alongside one another in themed borders be they shady damp corners or south facing hot spots. The propagating areas, stock beds and family garden, normally closed to visitors, will be open on the NGS day. More than 1,000 different herbaceous perennials are grown on the nursery, many that are excellent for wildlife. For other opening times and information please phone, e-mail or visit our website. Sloping site that has no steps but steep inclines in places.

2 ASKHAM HALL

Askham, Penrith, CA10 2PF. Countess of Lonsdale, 01931 712350, enquiries@askhamhall.co.uk, www.askhamhall.co.uk. *5m S of Penrith. Turn off A6 for Lowther & Askham.* **Sun 16 June (11-7). Adm £3, chd free. Light refreshments. Cafe serving tea, coffee, light lunches, cake. Wood-fired pizza oven. BBQ and bar in the courtyard.** Donation to Askham and Lowther Churches.
Askham Hall is a Pele Tower incorporating C14, C16 and early C18 elements in a courtyard plan. Opened in 2013 with luxury accommodation, a restaurant, spa, cafe and wedding barn. Splendid formal garden with terraces of herbaceous borders and topiary, dating back to C17. Meadow area with trees and pond, kitchen gardens and animal trails. Combined with Summer Fair.

3 BECKSIDE FARM

Little Urswick, Cumbria, nr Ulverston, LA12 0PY. Anna Thomason, 01229 869151, anna@becksidefarm.eclipse.co.uk. *On outskirts of village - good off road parking. A590 towards Barrow. S off A590 to Urswick. Go through Great Urswick & Little Urswick. Park at T-junction. Rail Ulverston 4m, NCR 70 & 700 ½m.* **Every Sat 1 June to 7 Sept (12-5). Adm £3.50, chd free. Light refreshments. Refreshments need to be pre-ordered - phone 01229 869151.** Visits also by arrangement June to Sept. Please tel in advance to advise numbers for refreshments.
Organic cottage garden with raised beds, herbaceous borders. Many unusual\new varieties of tender perennials and annuals, raised from seed and cuttings each year. Several interesting patio/seating areas. Productive greenhouse, again with unusual varieties. Ferns and summer flowering bulbs in pots. Ulverston is a pretty market town that has many tea shops and several Pubs serving food.

4 BOXWOOD HOUSE

Hartley, Kirkby Stephen, CA17 4JH. Colin & Joyce Dirom, 01768 371306, boxwoodhouse@hotmail.co.uk. *In the centre of Hartley approx, 1m from Kirkby Stephen. Exit M6 J38. Follow A685, R in Kirkby Stephen for Hartley. From A66 exit at Brough onto A685, 1st L in Kirkby St for Hartley. Kirkby Stephen Station approx. 2m. KS on Coast to Coast Walk.* **Sat 6, Sun 7 July (11-5). Adm £4, chd free. Home-made teas.** Visits also by arrangement June to Aug for groups of 10 to 30.
A peaceful natural garden. Packed herbaceous borders, shrubberies, herb, hosta and heuchera beds plus the tranquil pond are all designed to be wildlife friendly. The summer house provides one of the many seating areas around the garden overlooking a productive vegetable plot and fruit trees, whilst a meadow walk leads to a stunning view of the whole garden and the fenced off chicken area.

Askham Hall

5 CHAPELSIDE

Mungrisdale, Penrith, CA11 0XR. Tricia & Robin Acland, 01768779672. *12m W of Penrith. On A66 take minor rd N signed Mungrisdale. After 2m, sharp bends, garden on L immed after tiny church on R. Park at foot of our short drive. On C2C Reivers 71, 10 cycle routes.* **Sun 5, Sun 19 May, Sun 2, Sun 16, Sun 30 June, Sun 14 July (1-5). Adm £3.50, chd free.** Visits also by arrangement May to Sept. Refreshments for groups by arrangement.

1 acre windy garden below fell round C18 farmhouse. Open outbuildings. Fine views. Tiny stream, large pond. Alpine, herbaceous, gravel, damp and shade areas, bulbs in grass. Wide range of plants, many unusual. Relaxed planting regime. Run on organic lines. Art constructions in and out, local stone used creatively. Featured in 'Dreamscapes' by photographer Claire Takacs and in Gardens Illustrated.

6 CHERRY COTTAGE

Crosby Moor, Crosby-On-Eden, Carlisle, CA6 4QX. Mr & Mrs John & Lesley Connolly, 01228 573614, jtlaconnolly@aol.com. *Off A689 midway between Carlisle & Brampton. Take turn signed 'Wallhead'. Cherry Cottage is on the corner of junction on R. Park in the lane.* **Sun 19 May (11-5). Adm £4, chd free. Light refreshments.** Visits also by arrangement Apr to Sept for groups of 5 to 20.

Relaxed country garden surrounding an C18 cottage on an approx. ⅓ acre site. It has a wide range of habitats incl herbaceous borders, wildlife pond, bog garden, shady woodland, productive fruit and vegetable area, 2 greenhouses and summer house. Various seating areas connected by grass and gravel paths. Not suitable for wheelchairs. Refreshment proceeds to Epilepsy Action.

7 CHURCH VIEW

Bongate, Appleby-in-Westmorland, CA16 6UN. Mrs H Holmes, 017683 51397, engcougars@btinternet.com, www.sites.google.com/site/engcougars/church-view. *0.4m SE of Appleby town centre. A66 W take B6542 for 2m St Michael's*

Church on L garden opp. A66 E take B6542 & continue to Royal Oak Inn, garden next door, opp church. **Wed 22 May, Wed 25 Sept (1-4). Adm £4, chd free.** Visits also by arrangement May to Sept.
It's all about the plants! Less than ½ acre of garden but with layers of texture, colour and interest in abundance, this is a garden for plantaholics. Plant combinations are at the heart of the design. With self-contained vistas and maximum use of planting space, the garden photographs very well and has been a subject for many local and national publications and photographers over the last decade. Partial wheelchair, main garden is on a sloping site with gravel paths.

8 CROOKDAKE FARM

Aspatria, Wigton, CA7 3SH. Kirk & Alannah Rylands, 016973 20413, alannah.rylands@me.com. *3m NE of Aspatria. Between A595 & A596. From A595 take B5299 at Mealsgate signed Aspatria. After 2m turn sharp R in Watch Hill signed Crookdake. House 1m on L.* Visits by arrangement June & July for groups of 10+. Adm £4, chd free. Home-made teas.
Windswept informal farmhouse (not open) garden with a careful colour combination of interesting planting sympathetic to the landscape incl various different areas with densely planted herbaceous borders, fenced vegetable patch, wild meadow and large pond area home to moisture-loving plants, hens, ducks and moorhens.

9 DALLAM TOWER

Milnthorpe, LA7 7AG. Mr & Mrs R T Villiers-Smith. *7m S of Kendal. 7m N of Carnforth. Nr J36 off M6. A6 & B5282. Stn: Arnside, 4m; Lancaster, 15m.* **Sun 12 May (2-5). Adm £4, chd free. Cream teas.**
Dallam Tower is set in 150 acres of parkland with a large herd of Fallow deer. The gardens have extensive sunken lawns, a natural stream feeding into a limestone rock garden, a gravel woodland path with mature trees and a Yew tree walk. Wander past shrubs, topiary, roses and enjoy afternoon tea by the stunningly beautiful C19 cast iron Orangery. Limited wheelchair access Deep gravel paths.

10 DEER RUDDING

Hesket Newmarket, Wigton, CA7 8HU. Mrs Lynne Carruthers, deer.rudding@gmail.com, deerrudding.garden. *Located off the road from Millhouse to Haltcliff Bridge, not in Hesket Newmarket. From Penrith J41 of M6 take B5305 6.8m, L to Hesket Newmarket 2.2m, at Millhouse L to Haltcliffe Bridge by village hall, continue 1m, R over cattle grid.* **Sat 13 Apr, Sat 11 May, Sat 8 June (11-5). Adm £5, chd free. Light refreshments at Millhouse Village Hall.** Visits also by arrangement Apr to June for groups of 10+.
Set in the lee of the Northern Fells on the bank of the Caldew and enjoying views into the wider landscape, notably Carrock Fell. The garden surrounds a former Cumbrian farmhouse and outbuildings. Mixed shrub and perennial borders; woodland and meadow grass areas; extensive rockery and stone walls built by Cumbrian champion waller, Steve Allen of Tebay. Children's trail, free, all participating must be accompanied by an adult. Refreshments provided by Fellview Pre-School April, Friends of Fellview School May and Castle Sowerby Church June. There are a number of gates and gravel pathways.

11 ◆ DORA'S FIELD

Rydal, Ambleside, LA22 9LX. National Trust, www.nationaltrust.org.uk. *1½m N of Ambleside. Follow A591 from Ambleside to Rydal. Dora's Field is next to St Mary's Church.* **For NGS: Sun 24 Mar (11-4). Adm by donation. Also open High Close Estate and Arboretum.** For other opening times and information, please visit garden website.
Named for Dora, the daughter of the poet William Wordsworth. Wordsworth planned to build a house on the land but, after her early death, he planted the area with daffodils in her memory. Now known as Dora's field the area is renowned for its spring display of daffodils and Bluebells. 24 March; Wordsworth's Daffodil Legacy.

12 FELL YEAT

Casterton, Kirkby Lonsdale, LA6 2JW. Mrs A E Benson, 01524 271340. *1m E of Casterton Village. On the rd to Bull Pot. Leave A65 at Devils Bridge, follow A683 for 1m, take the R fork to High Casterton at golf course, straight across at two sets of Xrds, house on L, ¼m from no-through-rd sign.* **Sun 26 May, Sun 4 Aug (1-5). Adm £4, chd free. Home-made teas.** Visits also by arrangement May to Sept for groups of 10 to 30.
1 acre country garden with mixed planting, incl unusual trees, shrubs and some topiary. Small woodland garden and woodland glades. 2 ponds which encourage dragonflies. Several arbours where you can sit and relax. New paved topiary garden. Fernery, stumpery and grotto house. Old roses in mixed borders and a large collection of hydrangeas. A garden to explore. Metal sculptures in various areas. Adjoining nursery specialising in ferns, hostas, hydrangeas and many unusual plants. Mostly mown grass with one or two gravel paths.

13 FERN BANK

High House Road, St. Bees, CA27 0BZ. Chris & Charm Robson. *At the edge of the village going out towards A595. 2m from A595 down road signed St Bees unsuitable for long vehicles (or something like that), or B5345 from Whitehaven.* **Sun 7 Apr (12-5). Adm £3.50, chd free. Home-made teas.**
Located in St Bees village, this is a spring garden on different levels with natural planting. Nearest the house lawns and borders lead down to the 'secret' garden via a pergola clad with roses, wisteria and clematis. Hidden away are 5 ponds surrounded by trees and boardwalks, a haven for wildlife. In Spring this area is lit up by snowdrops, leucojum, marsh marigolds and daffodils. Poetry trail through the garden. The entrance level where teas are served is wheelchair accessible but because of the steep slopes the rest of the garden is not accessible.

14 FERNHILL COACH HOUSE

Bleacragg Road,, Witherslack, Grange-Over-Sands, LA11 6RX. Adele & Mike Walford, 015395 52102, mwandaj@btinternet.com. *Country road, ½m beyond Halecat & Abbi and Tom's nursery. From A950 turn North to Witherslack. Follow brown signs to Halecat, continue on lane for ½m. Fern Hill on L. Rail; Grange-over-sands; 5m, bus X6. 2m walk, NCR 70.* **Sun 7 July (10-5). Combined adm with Abi and Tom's Garden Plants £4, chd free. Home-made teas.** Visits also by arrangement June to Aug for groups of up to 20.

Approx one acre garden - a riot of chaotic exuberance. From a stable yard, old tip and remnants of an orchard, 8 years of hard work have resulted in a cottage garden. Mixed borders, lots of vegetables, greenhouse, polytunnel, ponds and lots of roses. Members of the South Lakes Orchard Group, we have a young orchard and northern and heritage apple trees. Witherslack Orchard Group apple juice, damson and apple juice. Numerous apple trees for sale. Wheelchair access is limited to the flower garden only. Paths are uneven and on sloping ground.

Your visits help change lives - we've donated over £16.7 million to Macmillan Cancer Support since 1984

15 GALESYKE

Wasdale, CA20 1ET. Christine & Mike McKinley. *From Gosforth, follow signs to Nether Wasdale & then to Lake, approx 5m. From Santon Bridge follow signs to Wasdale then to Lake, approx 2¼m.* **Sat 1, Sun 2 June (10.30-5). Adm £4, chd free. Cream teas.**

4 acre woodland garden with spectacular views of the Wasdale fells. The R Irt runs through the garden and both banks are landscaped, you can cross over the river via a picturesque, mini, suspension bridge. The garden has an impressive collection of rhododendrons and azaleas that light up the woodlands in springtime.

ALLOTMENTS

16 GRANGE FELL ALLOTMENTS

Fell Road, Grange-Over-Sands, LA11 6HB. Mr Bruno Gouillon, 01539 532317, brunog45@hotmail.com. *Opposite Grange Fell Golf Club. Rail 1.3 m, Bus 1m X6, NCR 70.* **Sun 18 Aug (11.30-4.30). Adm £3, chd free. Light refreshments.** Visits also by arrangement Apr to Sept for groups of up to 30.

The allotments are managed by Grange Town Council. Opened in 2010, 30 plots are now rented out and offer a wide selection of gardening styles and techniques. The majority of plots grow a mixture of vegetables, fruit trees and flowers. There are a few communal areas where local fruit tree varieties have been donated by plot holders with herbaceous borders and annuals.

GROUP OPENING

17 GRANGE OVER SANDS HIDDEN GARDENS

Grange-Over-Sands, LA11 7AF. *Off Kents Bank Rd, 3 gardens on Cart Ln then up Carter Rd for Shrublands and finally to Kilmidyke Rd for Sunbeams. Rail 1.4m; Bus X6; NCR 70.* **Sun 28 July (11.30-4.30). Combined adm £4, chd free. Light refreshments.**

21 CART LANE
Veronica Cameron.

ELDER COTTAGE
Bruno Gouillon & Andrew Fairey.

NEW **SHRUBLANDS**
Jon & Avril Trevorrow.

SUNBEAMS
Sue Lawton.

WHISTLING GEM
Joan & Peter Lawton.

5 very different gardens hidden down narrow lanes off the road south out of Grange. Off Kents Bank Road, 3 gardens on Cart Lane all back onto the railway embankment, providing shelter from the wind but also creating a frost pocket. 21 is a series of rooms designed to create an element of surprise with fruit and vegetables in raised beds. Elder cottage is an organised riot of fruit trees, vegetables, shrubby perennials and herbaceous plants. Productive and peaceful. Whistling Gem has been redesigned and replanted over the last 4 years to create a garden with colour and interest. Up the hill on Carter Road for Shrublands, a ¾ acre garden situated on a hillside overlooking Morecambe Bay. Then to Kilmidyke Road for Sunbeams, a garden managed without using pesticides that has a small pond to encourage wildlife. Lots of plants (and chickens) are packed into a small space.

18 HAVERTHWAITE LODGE

Haverthwaite, LA12 8AJ. David Snowdon, 015395 39841, sheena.taylforth@lakesidehotel.co.uk. *100yds off A590 at Haverthwaite. Turn S off A590 opp Haverthwaite railway stn. Bus 6, NCR 70.* **Thur 20 June, Thur 15 Aug (11-4). Combined adm with Lakeside Hotel & Rocky Bank £7.50, chd free. Light refreshments at Lakeside Hotel. Single adm £3.50. Refreshments - 20% discount from Lakeside Hotel Conservatory Menu on the Open Day.** Visits also by arrangement Mar to Sept for groups of 10+.

Traditional Lake District garden that has been redesigned and replanted. A wonderful display of hellebores and spring flowers. Gardens on a series of

Holker Hall Gardens

terraces leading down to the R Leven and incl: rose garden, cutting garden, dell area, rock terrace, herbaceous borders and many interesting mature shrubs. In a stunning setting the garden is surrounded by oak woodland and was once a place of C18 and C19 industry.

GROUP OPENING

19 HAYTON VILLAGE GARDENS

Hayton, Brampton, CA8 9HR. *7m E of Carlisle. Best route is from the A69. 5m E of M6 J43. ½m S of A69, 3m W of Brampton signed to Hayton. Narrow roads: Please park courteously L side only. If able, park less centrally to leave space for less able nr pub. Map also on Facebook.* **Sun 7 July (12-5). Combined adm £5, chd free. Home-made teas at Hayton Village Primary School with live music. Other refreshments usually served in a conservatory and/or garden depending on weather.** Donation to Hayton Village Primary School.

NEW **ARNWOOD**
Joanne Reeves-Brown.

NEW **ASH TREE FARM**
Mr & Mrs J Dowling.

NEW **BECK COTTAGE**
Fiona Cox.

BRACKENHOW
Johnny & Susan Tranter.

CHESTNUT COTTAGE
Mr Barry Brian.

CURLEW COTTAGE
Frances & David Scales.

HAYTON C OF E PRIMARY SCHOOL
Hayton C of E Primary School, www.hayton.cumbria.sch.uk.

KINRARA
Tim & Alison Brown, 01228 670067 (Ashton Design), tim@tjbgallery.com.
Visits also by arrangement May to Oct for groups of up to 10. Refreshments maybe possible if booked in advance.

MILLBROOK
Monica & John Carruthers.

THE PADDOCK
Phil & Louise Jones.

TOWNHEAD COTTAGE
Chris & Pam Haynes.

WEST GARTH COTTAGE
Debbie Jenkins, 01228 670430, debbiejenkins.art@gmail.com, www.westgarth-cottage-gardens.co.uk.
Visits also by arrangement Apr to Aug for groups of up to 20.

A valley of gardens of varied size and styles all within ½ m, mostly of old stone cottages. Smaller and larger cottage gardens, courtyards and containers, steep wooded slopes, lawns, exuberant borders, frogs, pools, colour and texture throughout. Home-made teas and live music at the school where the children annually create gardens within the main school garden. Gardens additional to those listed also generally open and there are views into numerous others of high standard. Facebook: Hayton Open Gardens. Two of the gardens: Westgarth Cottage and Kinrara are designed by artist/s and an architect with multiple garden design experience. Varying degrees of wheelchair access from full to none.

20 HAZEL COTTAGE

Armathwaite, CA4 9PG. Mr D Ryland & Mr J Thexton. *8m SE of Carlisle. Turn off A6 just S of High Hesket signed Armathwaite, after 2m house facing you at T-junction 1¼m walk from Armathwaite railway station.* **Sat 18, Sun 19 May, Sun 30 June (12-5). Adm £3.50, chd free. Home-made teas and featuring home made cakes.**
Flower arrangers and plantsman's garden. Extending to approx 5 acres. Includes mature herbaceous borders, pergola, ponds and planting of disused railway siding providing home to wildlife. Many variegated and unusual plants. Varied areas, planted for all seasons, S-facing, some gentle slopes. abandoned railway cutting now a woodland walk. Only partial access, small steps to WC area . Main garden planted on gentle slope.

21 ◆ HIGH CLOSE ESTATE AND ARBORETUM

Loughrigg, Ambleside, LA22 9HH. National Trust, 015394 37623, neil.winder@nationaltrust.org.uk, www.nationaltrust.org.uk/sticklebarn-and-the-langdales/features/high-close-estate. *10 min NW from Ambleside. Ambleside (A593) to Skelwith Bridge signed for High Close, turn R & head up hill until you see a white painted stone sign to 'Langdale', turn L, High Close on L.* **For NGS: Sun 24 Mar (11-4). Adm by donation. Also open Dora's Field. Small cafe in house part of the YHA.** For other opening times and information, please phone, email or visit garden website.
Originally planted in 1866 by Edward Wheatley-Balme, High Close was designed in the fashion of the day using many of the recently discovered 'exotic' conifers and evergreen shrubs coming into Britain from America. Today the garden works in partnership with the Royal Botanic Gardens Edinburgh and International Conifer Conservation Programme, preserving endangered Conifers species. Tree trail. Guided walks throughout the day.

22 ◆ HOLEHIRD GARDENS

Patterdale Road, Windermere, LA23 1NP. Lakeland Horticultural Society, 015394 46008, enquiries@holehirdgardens.org.uk, www.holehirdgardens.org.uk. *1m N of Windermere. On A592, Windermere to Patterdale rd.* **For NGS: Sun 24 Mar, Thur 11 July (10-4). Adm £5, chd free. Self-service hot drinks available.** For other opening times and information, please phone, email or visit garden website.
Run by volunteers of the Lakeland Horticultural Society to promote knowledge of gardening in Lakeland conditions. On fellside overlooking Windermere, the 12 acres provide interest year round. 4 National Collections (*astilbe*, daboecia, *polystichum*, meconopsis). Lakeland Collection of hydrangeas. Walled garden has colourful mixed borders and island beds. Alpine beds and display houses. Many interesting trees and shrubs. Wheelchair access limited to walled garden and beds accessible from drive.

23 ◆ HOLKER HALL GARDENS

Cark-in-Cartmel, Grange-over-Sands, LA11 7PL. The Cavendish Family, 015395 58328, info@holker.co.uk, www.holker.co.uk. *4m W of Grange-over-Sands. 12m W of M6 (J36) Follow brown tourist signs. Rail 1m, NCR 700 ½m.* **For NGS: Thur 22 Aug (10.30-5). NGS will receive donations for guided tours on this day not the garden adm.** For other opening times and information, please phone, email or visit garden website.
25 acres of romantic gardens, with peaceful arboretum, inspirational formal gardens, flowering meadow and Labyrinth. Summer brings voluptuous mixed borders and bedding. Discover unusually large

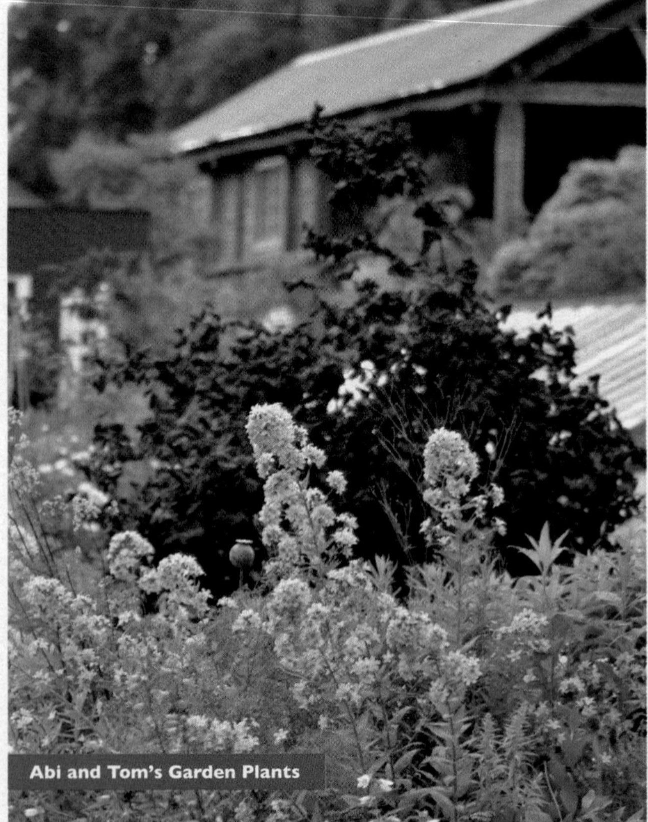
Abi and Tom's Garden Plants

rhododendrons, magnolias and azaleas, and the National Collection of Styracaceae. Discover our latest garden feature - The Pagan Grove, designed by Kim Wilkie. Guided tour of the gardens with our experienced guide. Donation to NGS required.

♿ ✽ 🚌 NPC ☕

24 HOLME MEADOW

1 Holme Meadow, Cumwhinton, Carlisle, CA4 8DR. John & Anne Mallinson, 01228 560330, jwai.mallinson@btopenworld.com. *2m S of Carlisle. From M6 J42 take B6263 to Cumwhinton, in village take 1st L then bear R at Lowther Arms, Holme Meadow is immed on R.* **Sun 14 July (11-4). Adm £3, chd free. Light refreshments.** Visits also by arrangement June to Aug for groups of 10 to 30.

Village garden developed and landscaped from scratch by owners. Incl shrubbery, perennial beds supplemented by annuals;gazebo, pergola and trellis with climbers, slate beds and water feature, ornamental copse, pond, wild flower meadow and kitchen garden. Designed, planted and maintained to be wildlife friendly.

✽ ☕

25 HPB MERLEWOOD

Windermere Road, Grange-Over-Sands, LA11 6JT. Marion St Quinton Site Manager. *Merlewood is on B5271 between Grange over Sands & Lindale. Rail 1m; Bus X6, NCR 70 (1m).* **Sun 4 Aug (10-4). Adm £5, chd free. Home-made teas.**

Extensive and varied gardens with a dramatic view to Morecambe Bay from the terrace. Newly planted formal and terraced gardens surround the house. A woodland including a nature trail for children. The wood on the limestone crags contain a variety of tree species many of which are from the original Victorian planting. The rockery is work in progress! Some areas are not accessible due to steps.

♿ ✽ ☕

26 IVY HOUSE

Cumwhitton, Brampton, CA8 9EX. Martin Johns & Ian Forrest, 01228 561851, martinjohns193@btinternet.com. *6m E of Carlisle. At the bridge at Warwick Bridge on A69 take turning to Great Corby & Cumwhitton. Through Great Corby & woodland until you reach a T-junction Turn R.* **Sun 23 June (1-5). Adm £4, chd free. Home-made teas in Cumwhitton village hall.** Visits also by arrangement Apr to Sept.

Approx 2 acres of sloping fell-side garden with meandering paths leading to a series of 'rooms': pond, fern garden, gravel garden with assorted grasses, vegetable and herb garden. Copse with meadow leading down to beck. Trees, shrubs, ferns, bamboos and herbaceous perennials planted with emphasis on variety of texture and colour. Steep slopes.

🐕 ☕

27 LAKESIDE HOTEL & ROCKY BANK

Lake Windermere, Newby Bridge, Ulverston, LA12 8AT. Mr N Talbot, 015395 39841, sheena.taylforth@lakesidehotel.co.uk, www.lakesidehotel.co.uk. *1m N of Newby Bridge. Turn N off A590 across R Leven at Newby Bridge along W side of Windermere.* **Thur 20 June, Thur 15 Aug (11-4). Combined adm with Haverthwaite Lodge £7.50, chd free. Light refreshments. Single adm to Lakeside and Rocky Bank £5. Refreshments - 20% discount from Hotel Conservatory menu on the Open Day.** Visits also by arrangement Mar to Sept for groups of 10+.

Two diverse gardens on the shores of Lake Windermere. Lakeside has been created for year round interest, packed with choice plants, incl some unusual varieties. Main garden area with herbaceous borders and foliage shrubs, scented and winter interest plants and seasonal bedding. Roof garden with lawn, espaliered local heritage apple varieties and culinary herbs. Lawn art on front lawn. Rocky Bank is a traditional garden with rock outcrops. Planted with unusual specimen alpines. Herbaceous borders, shrubs and ornamental trees. Woodland area with species rhododendrons. Working greenhouse and polytunnels. Wild flower garden and cut flower garden. Wheelchair access not available at Rocky Bank.

🚌 🛏 ☕

28 LANGHOLME MILL

Woodgate, Lowick Green, LA12 8ES. Judith & Graham Sanderson, 01229 885215, judith@themill.biz. *7m NW of Ulverston. West on A590. At Greenodd, North on A5902 towards Broughton. Langholme Mill is approx 3m along this rd on L as road divides on the hill.* **Sat 25, Sun 26, Mon 27 May (11-5). Adm £5, chd free. Home-made teas and large variety of delicious home-made cakes, tea and coffee.** Visits also by arrangement Apr to Oct for groups of up to 30.

Approx 1 acre of mature woodland garden with meandering lakeland slate paths surrounding the mill race stream which can be crossed by a variety of bridges. The garden hosts well established bamboo, rhododendrons, hostas, acers and astilbes and a large variety of country flowers. There is a surprise round every corner! A side gate entrance from the road side.

♿ 🐕 🚌 🛏 ☕

29 LARCH COTTAGE NURSERIES

Melkinthorpe, Penrith, CA10 2DR. Peter Stott, 01931 712404, plants@larchcottage.co.uk, www.larchcottage.co.uk. *From N leave M6 J40 take A6 S. From S leave M6 J39 take A6 N signed off A6.* **Thur 11 July, Thur 15 Aug, Thur 19 Sept (1-4). Adm £4, chd free.** Visits also by arrangement.

For 2 days only Larch Cottage Nurseries are opening the new lower gardens and chapel for NGS visitors. The gardens include lawns, flowing perennial borders, rare and unusual shrubs, trees, small orchard and a kitchen garden. A natural stream runs into a small lake - a haven for wildlife and birds. At the head of the lake stands a chapel, designed and built by Peter for family use only. Larch Cottage has a Japanese Dry garden, ponds and Italianesque columned garden specifically for shade plants, the Italianesque tumbled down walls are draped in greenery acting as a backdrop for the borders filled with stock plants. Newly designed and constructed lower gardens and chapel. The gardens are accessible to wheelchair users although the paths are rocky in places.

♿ ✽ ☕

30 LOW FELL WEST

Crosthwaite, Kendal, LA8 8JG. Barbie & John Handley, 015395 68297, barbie@handleyfamily.co.uk. *4½m S of Bowness. Off A5074, turn W just S of Damson Dene Hotel. Follow lane for ½m.* **Sun 12 May (2-5), Sun 20 Oct (1-4). Light refreshments. Adm £4, chd free.** Visits also by arrangement for groups of up to 30. Nearest access for coaches ½m away.

This 2 acre woodland garden in the tranquil Winster Valley has extensive views to the Pennines. The four season garden, restored since 2003, incl expanses of rock planted sympathetically with grasses, unusual trees and shrubs, climaxing for autumn colour. There are native hedges and areas of plant rich meadows. A woodland area houses a gypsy caravan and there is direct access to Cumbria Wildlife Trust's Barkbooth Reserve of Oak woodland, blue bells and open fellside. Wheelchair access to much of the garden, but some rough paths, steep slopes.

31 LOWER ROWELL FARM & COTTAGE

Milnthorpe, LA7 7LU. John & Mavis Robinson & Julie & Andy Welton, 015395 62270. *Approx 2m from Milnthorpe, 2m from Crooklands. Signed to Rowell off B6385, Milnthorpe to Crooklands Rd. Garden ½m up lane on L.* **Sat 18, Sun 19 May (1-5). Adm £3.50, chd free. Home-made teas.** Visits also by arrangement Feb to July for groups of 10+. Refreshments by arrangement.

Approx 1¼ acre garden with views to Farleton Knott and Lakeland hills. Unusual trees and shrubs, plus perennial borders; architectural pruning; retro greenhouse; polytunnel with tropical plants; cottage gravel garden and vegetable plot. Fabulous display of snowdrops in spring followed by other spring flowers, with colour most of the year. Wildlife ponds and 2 friendly pet hens.

32 MATSON GROUND

Windermere, LA23 2NH. Matson Ground Estate Co Ltd, 015394 47892, info@matsonground.co.uk. *⅔m E of Bowness. Turn N off B5284 signed Heathwaite. From E 100yds after Windermere Golf Club, from W 400yds after Windy Hall Rd. Rail 2½m; Bus 1m, 6, 599, 755, 800; NCR 6 (1m).* **Sun 19 May (1-5). Adm £4.50, chd free. Home-made teas.**

2 acres of mature, south facing gardens. A good mix of formal and informal planting including topiary features, herbaceous and shrub borders, wild flower areas, stream leading to a large pond and developing arboretum. Rose garden, rockery, topiary terrace borders, ha-ha. Productive, walled kitchen garden c 1862, a wide assortment of fruit, vegetables, cut flowers, cobnuts and herbs. Greenhouse.

33 NEWTON RIGG COLLEGE GARDENS

Newton Rigg, Penrith, CA11 0AH. Newton Rigg College, www.newtonrigg.ac.uk. *1m W of Penrith. 3m W from J40 & J41 off M6. ½m off the B5288 W of Penrith. We have The Coast to Coast cycle route (Route 7) & public pathway approx 500 metres from the garden entrance gates.* **Sun 7 July (1-4.30). Adm £4.50, chd free.** Visits also by arrangement.

Our Educational Gardens have much of horticultural interest incl herbaceous borders, ten ponds, decorative and productive organic garden, woodland walk, seasonal borders, Pictorial Meadows, Pleached Hornbeam Walkway and extensive range of ornamental trees and shrubs. Our Horticultural and Forestry staff and students will give informative tours and a variety of demonstrations.

34 ORCHARD COTTAGE

Hutton Lane, Levens, Kendal, LA8 8PB. Shirley & Chris Band, 015395 61005, chrisband67@gmail.com. *6m S of Kendal. Turn N off A590 or A6 signed Levens. From Xrds by Methodist Church, 300 metres down Hutton Lane. Park near this Xrds. Garden access via 'The Orchard'.* Visits by arrangement Mar to Oct for groups of up to 30. Adm £4, chd free.

¾ acre sloping garden in old orchard. Plantsperson's paradise. Winding paths, diverse habitats, secret vistas. All yr interest and colour. Collections of ferns (100+ varieties), hellebores (70+), grasses, cottage plants, geraniums, Acers (36) Hostas. Auricula theatres, 'imaginary' stream, bog garden. Trees support clematis, roses and honeysuckle. Wildlife friendly.

35 PARK HOUSE

Barbon, Kirkby Lonsdale, LA6 2LG. Mr & Mrs P Pattison. *2½m N of Kirkby Lonsdale. Off A683 Kirkby Lonsdale to Sedburgh rd. Follow signs into Barbon Village.* **Sun 14 July, Sun 4 Aug (10.30-4). Adm £5, chd free. Cream teas.**

Romantic Manor House (not open). Extensive vistas. Formal tranquil pond encased in yew hedging. Meadow with meandering pathways, water garden filled with bulbs and ferns. Formal lawn, gravel pathways, cottage borders with hues of soft pinks and purples, shady border, kitchen garden. An evolving garden to follow.

36 PEAR TREE COTTAGE

Dalton, Burton-in-Kendal, LA6 1NN. Linda & Alec Greening, 01524 781624, lindagreening48@gmail.com. *5m from J35 & J36 of M6. From northern end of Burton-in-Kendal (A6070) turn E into Vicarage Lane & continue approx 1m.* Visits by arrangement June & July for groups of 10+. Adm £4, chd free. Refreshments by prior arrangement.

⅓ acre cottage garden in a delightful rural setting. A peaceful and relaxing garden, harmonising with its environment and incorporating many different planting areas, from packed herbaceous borders and rambling roses, to wildlife pond, bog garden, rock garden and gravel garden. A plantsperson's delight, incl over 200 different ferns, and many other rare and unusual plants.

37 ROSE CROFT

Levens, Kendal, LA8 8PH.
Enid Fraser, 07976 977018,
enidfraser123@btinternet.com.
Approx 4m from J36. M6 J36 take A590 toward Barrow. R turn Levens, L at pub, follow rd to garden on L. From A6, into Levens, past shop, bear L, over Xrds, downhill. L turn signed 'PV Dobson'. Garden on R after Dobsons. Visits by arrangement June to Sept for groups of up to 30. Adm £4, chd free. Light refreshments. Hare and Hounds pub approx 6 min walk, 1 min drive.

Gardening on a steep slope with wildlife in mind. Naturalistic plantings, perennials and grasses pouring away from the top terrace, shrubs, rose arches and silver birches for supporting structure. August sees the peak of this colourful drama: set against the views that dominate the westerly scene beyond the summer house, past the sown wild flowers and lawn which fold into the garden-bounding stream.

NEW THE RYEBECK HOTEL

Lyth Valley Road, Bowness-on-Windermere LA23 3JP. Duncan Evans - General Manager, 015394 88195 gm@ryebeck.com. *From the A590 at Newby Bridge take A592 lakeside rd, turn R at B5360; follow it up to the T-junction, turning L, the hotel is located shortly on the L. From the A591, drive towards Bowness-on-Windermere. In Bowness, with the lake on your R, take the A5074 Kendal Rd on your L and follow it for approximately 2/3 minutes until you come to the hotel signed on your R.* Mon 27 May, Sun 28 July, Sun 27 Oct (10-4). Adm £5, chd free. Light refreshments.

Donation to Cumbria Wildlife Trust
This 5 acre garden, which was originally set out in the Edwardian period, encompasses a variety of interesting areas including, to the front, formal lawns flanked by flower beds, rockeries and specimen trees and shrubs. To the rear of the hotel are terraced borders containing year round interest and colour, with flowering perennials and shrubs. The greater garden descends into a wide vista of grass and wild flower meadows set against a glorious backdrop of Lake Windermere, and include also

Rydal Hall

a newly planted holly walk and a wild rose garden, all of which have been planted to encourage wildlife into the garden. Unfortunately, due to the presence of steps and the sloping nature of some parts of the garden, there is no wheelchair access. Dogs are welcome on a lead. No coaches, but a minibus would be acceptable with up to 24 seats.

38 ◆ RYDAL HALL

Ambleside, LA22 9LX. Diocese of Carlisle, 01539 432050, gardens@rydalhall.org, www.rydalhall.org. *2m N of Ambleside. E from A591 at Rydal signed Rydal Hall. Bus 555, 599, X8, X55; NCR 6.* **For NGS: Sun 24 Mar, Thur 25 Apr, Sun 19 May, Thur 12 Sept (9-4). Adm by donation. Light refreshments in tea shop on site.** For other opening times and information, please phone, email or visit garden website.

Forty acres of Park, Woodland and Gardens to explore. The Formal Thomas Mawson Garden has fine examples of herbaceous planting, seasonal displays and magnificent views of the Lakeland Fells. Enjoy the peaceful atmosphere created in the Quiet Garden with informal planting around the pond 'and stunning views of the waterfalls from The Grot, the UK's first viewing station.' Limited Wheelchair access, top terrace only.

39 SANDHOUSE

Burnhill, Scaleby, Carlisle, CA6 4LU. John Dalton & Ken Dodd. *5m NE Carlisle. From A6071 turn at Smithfield, follow NGS signs. From M6 J44 follow A689 Hexham, follow NGS signs.* **Sun 14 July (1-5). Adm £4, chd free.**

A cottage garden with island beds of herbaceous perennials, foliage plants suitable for the flower arranger. Hidden seating areas to surprise the visitor, and lots of nooks and crannies. John is a multiple award winner for his floral arrangements including Chelsea GOLD, his latest in 2017. Gravel paths and steps.

40 ◆ SIZERGH CASTLE

Sizergh, Kendal, LA8 8DZ. National Trust, 015395 60951, sizergh@nationaltrust.org.uk, www.nationaltrust.org.uk. *3m S of Kendal. Approach rd leaves A590 close to & S of A590/A591 interchange.* **For NGS: Mon 9 Sept (10-4). Adm £8, chd £4.** For other opening times and information, please phone, email or visit garden website.

⅔ acre limestone rock garden, largest owned by National Trust; Wild flower areas, hot wall and herbaceous borders, productive ornamental kitchen garden and fruit orchard with spring bulbs. Holders of the National Collections of Asplenium scolopendrium, Cystopteris, Dryopteris and Osmunda. Stumpery garden built 2016. National Trust members are admitted free with an opportunity to donate to the good causes the NGS supports. Non National Trust members entrance fees are donated to the NGS. Featured in The Times in their 20 best Great British gardens to visit in summer.

NPC

41 STEWART HILL COTTAGE

Hesket Newmarket, CA7 8HX. Mr & Mrs D Scott, 01768 484841, ardrannoch@hotmail.com. *7m W of Penrith. From S leave A66 at Sportsman's Inn – drive 5m Haltcliffe Bridge. Turn before Haltcliffe Bridge signed Newsham 2m garden 200yds on R.* **Sun 30 June (2.30-5.30). Adm £5, chd free. Home-made teas.** Visits also by arrangement in June. Donation to Community Action Nepal.

12yr old garden comprising mainly roses, courtyard newly designed, organic vegetable garden incl walled kitchen garden, potager, ornamental pool and croquet lawn. Wild pond and boules pitch.

42 SUMMERDALE HOUSE

Nook, Lupton, LA6 1PE. David & Gail Sheals, www.summerdalegardenplants.co.uk. *7m S of Kendal, 5m W of Kirkby Lonsdale. From J36 M6 take A65 towards Kirkby Lonsdale, at Nook take R turn Farleton. Location not signed on highway. Detailed directions available on our website.* **Sat 16, Sun 17 Feb (11-4.30). Home-made soups, bread, cakes (Feb). Every Fri and Sat 22 Feb to 27 Apr (11-4.30). Every Fri and Sat 31 May to 27 July (11-4.30). Sun 16 June (11-4.30). Home-made teas (June). Adm £4, chd free.**

1½ acre part-walled country garden set around C18 former vicarage. Several defined areas have been created by hedges, each with its own theme and linked by intricate cobbled pathways. Relaxed natural planting in a formal structure. Rural setting with fine views across to Farleton Fell. Large collections of auricula, primulas and snowdrops. Adjoining RHS Gold Medal winning nursery. Not suitable for wheelchairs, many steps.

43 ◆ SWARTHMOOR HALL

Swarthmoor Hall Lane, Ulverston, LA12 0JQ. Jane Pearson, Manager, 01229 583204, info@swarthmoorhall.co.uk, www.swarthmoorhall.co.uk. *1½m SW of Ulverston. A590 to Ulverston. Turn off to Ulverston railway stn. Follow Brown tourist signs to Hall. Rail 0.9m. NCR70 & 700 (1m).* **For NGS: Daily Mon 18 Feb to Sun 10 Mar (10.30-4.30). Fri 14, Sat 15, Sun 16 June (10.30-4.30). Adm £2, chd free. Light refreshments.** For other opening times and information, please phone, email or visit garden website.

Formal gardens and wild flower meadow. Wild purple crocus meadow in early spring: late February or early March depending on weather, earlier if mild winter later if cold and frosty. Also, good displays of snowdrops, daffodils and tulips in spring. Barn Cafe serves wonderful local food and recaptures the Hall's reputation for hospitality: delicious cakes and light lunches. Open 10.30-4.30 daily.

44 TENTER END BARN

Docker, Kendal, LA8 0DB. Mrs Hazel Terry, 01539 824447, hnterry@btinternet.com. *3m N Kendal. From Kendal take A685 Appleby rd. Then 2nd on R to Docker. At the junction bear L, take the 1st R onto a track.* Visits by

arrangement Apr to Sept. Adm £4, chd free. Light refreshments.
3 acres of cultivated and natural areas, in a secretive rural setting. A patio garden, large lawns, herbaceous borders and a small vegetable patch. Walks on the wild side around a mere and woodlands. Many birds can be seen at various feeding stations, also waterfowl on the mere. All managed by one OAP. Wheelchair access - rather uneven around the woodland paths. Could be difficult around mere in wet weather.

GROUP OPENING

45 ULVERSTON TOWN GARDENS

Ulverston, LA12 7LA. *A590 to Ulverston. 3 gardens near Booths Supermarket - a good start point. Rail Ulverston; Bus 6, 6X; NCR 70. Maps available at gardens.* **Sun 30 June (10.30-5). Combined adm £5, chd free. Light refreshments available at several of the gardens.**

HAMILTON GROVE
Helen & Martin Cooper.

11 OUBAS HILL
David & Janet Parratt.

14 OUBAS HILL
Pat & Barry Bentley.

51 DALTONGATE
Ian & Angela Hutt.

104 BIRCHWOOD DRIVE
Jane Parker.

5 gardens in a historic market town, with its canal and lighthouse monument to Sir John Barrow. Hamilton Grove garden slopes down from a large terrace to the, now dry, canal feeder via beds of annuals and perennials. There is a large collection of scented leaf pelargoniums. The two houses on Oubas Hill rise up towards the lighthouse and are busy and varied with unconventional features. Handmade pottery products at No 11 (income to NGS). 51 Daltongate is medium sized and wildlife friendly with a lovely wild flower area. 104 Birchwood makes the most of a small corner plot with roadside vegetables, formal front garden and delightful secret back garden. Regrettably none of the gardens have wheelchair access, due to slopes.

46 WINDY HALL

Crook Road, Windermere, LA23 3JA. Diane Hewitt & David Kinsman, 015394 46238, dhewitt.kinsman@gmail.com, windy-hall.co.uk. *½m S of Bowness-on-Windermere. On western end of B5284, pink house up Linthwaite House Hotel driveway. Rail 2.6m; Bus 1m, 6, 599, 755, 800; NCR 6 (1m).* Visits by arrangement Apr to Oct. Adm £5, chd free. Light refreshments. We can provide Teas and home made cake (ad lib) for any size group and Light Lunches for groups of 8+..
"Paradise". "I was bowled over by the ecologically intelligent approach you and Diane take and the exquisitely planted back garden or hill with rare species and subspecies so elegantly placed where they will flourish. It was truly superb." "The garden left a lasting impression on all. It is beautiful, exciting and charming. It nestles so comfortably in its landscape and totally belongs there.". Plant Heritage Aruncus collection. Rare Hebridean sheep, exotic waterfowl and pheasants.

47 WINTON PARK

Appleby Road, Kirkby Stephen, CA17 4PG. Mr Anthony Kilvington, www.wintonparkgardens.co.uk. *2m N of Kirkby Stephen. On A685 turn L signed Gt Musgrave/ Warcop (B6259). After approx 1m turn L as signed.* **Sun 14 July (11-5). Adm £6, chd free. Light refreshments.**
5 acre country garden bordered by the banks of the R Eden with stunning views. Many fine conifers, acers and rhododendrons, herbaceous borders, hostas, ferns, grasses, heathers and several hundred roses. Four formal ponds plus rock pool. Partial wheelchair access.

48 WOODEND HOUSE

Woodend, Egremont, CA22 2TA. Grainne & Richard Jakobson, 019468 13017, gmjakobson22@gmail.com. *2m S of Whitehaven. Take the A595 from Whitehaven towards Egremont. On leaving Bigrigg take 1st turn L. Go down hill, garden at bottom on R opp Woodend Farm.* **Sun 23 June (11-5.30). Adm £3.50, chd free. Home-made teas.** Visits also by arrangement Apr to Oct for groups of up to 20.
An interesting garden tucked away in a small hamlet. Meandering gravel paths lead around the garden with imaginative, colourful planting. Take a look around a productive, organic potager, wildlife pond, mini spring and summer meadows and a pretty summer house. Designed to be beautiful throughout the year and wildlife friendly. Plant sale, home-made teas, mini-quiz for children. Live Blues and Jazz in the garden. The gravel drive and paths are difficult for wheelchairs but more mobile visitors can access the main seating areas in the rear garden.

49 YEWBARROW HOUSE

Hampsfell Road, Grange-over-Sands, LA11 6BE. Jonathan & Margaret Denby, 015395 32469, jonathan@bestlakesbreaks.co.uk, www.yewbarrowhouse.co.uk. *¼m from town centre. Proceed along Hampsfell Rd passing a house called Yewbarrow to brow of hill then turn L onto a lane signed 'Charney Wood/Yewbarrow Wood' & sharp L again. Rail 0.7m, Bus X6, NCR 70.* **Sun 7 July, Sun 4 Aug, Sun 1 Sept (11-4). Adm £5, chd free. Light refreshments.** Visits also by arrangement May to Sept.
'More Cornwall than Cumbria' according to Country Life, a colourful 4 acre garden filled with exotic and rare plants, with dramatic views over the Morecambe Bay. Outstanding features include the Orangery; the Japanese garden with infinity pool, the Italian terraces and the restored Victorian kitchen garden. Dahlias, cannas and colourful exotica are a speciality. www.youtube.com/watch?v=v--VH2cLG18. There is limited wheelchair access owing to the number of steps.

OPENING DATES

All entries subject to change. For latest information check **www.ngs.org.uk**

Map locator numbers are shown to the right of each garden name.

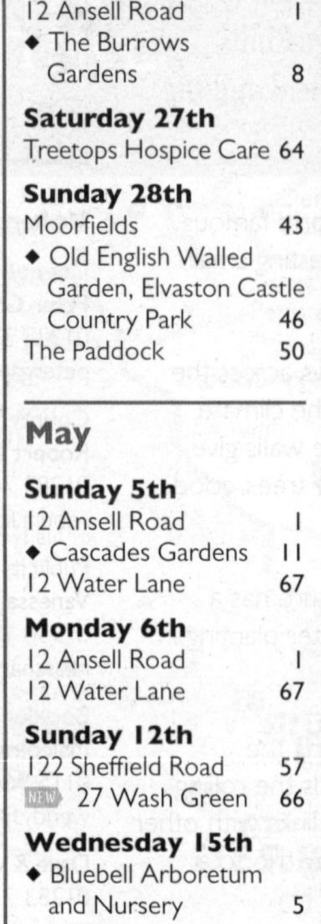

February

Snowdrop Festival

Sunday 17th
10 Chestnut Way 13

Saturday 23rd
The Dower House 19
The Old Vicarage 48

Sunday 24th
10 Chestnut Way 13
The Dower House 19
The Old Vicarage 48

March

Sunday 17th
◆ Cascades Gardens 11

April

Saturday 13th
Chevin Brae 14

Sunday 14th
334 Belper Road 4
◆ Cascades Gardens 11

Sunday 21st
12 Ansell Road 1

Monday 22nd
12 Ansell Road 1
◆ The Burrows Gardens 8

Saturday 27th
Treetops Hospice Care 64

Sunday 28th
Moorfields 43
◆ Old English Walled Garden, Elvaston Castle Country Park 46
The Paddock 50

May

Sunday 5th
12 Ansell Road 1
◆ Cascades Gardens 11
12 Water Lane 67

Monday 6th
12 Ansell Road 1
12 Water Lane 67

Sunday 12th
122 Sheffield Road 57
NEW 27 Wash Green 66

Wednesday 15th
◆ Bluebell Arboretum and Nursery 5

Thursday 16th
9 Newfield Crescent 45

Saturday 18th
◆ Melbourne Hall Gardens 41

Sunday 19th
Broomfield Hall 7
Fir Croft 21
◆ Melbourne Hall Gardens 41
NEW 15 Windmill Lane 74

Tuesday 21st
◆ Thornbridge Hall Gardens 61

Sunday 26th
12 Ansell Road 1
334 Belper Road 4
Higher Crossings 25
Tilford House 62

Monday 27th
12 Ansell Road 1
Barlborough Gardens 2
◆ The Burrows Gardens 8
Higher Crossings 25
Rectory House 53
Repton NGS Village Gardens 55
◆ Tissington Hall 63

June

Saturday 1st
The Dower House 19
The Holly Tree 31

Sunday 2nd
The Dower House 19
Fir Croft 21
Highfield House 26
The Holly Tree 31
Walton Cottage 65

Thursday 6th
NEW The Smithy 58

Sunday 9th
Hollies Farm Plant Centre 30

Wednesday 12th
◆ Bluebell Arboretum and Nursery 5

Saturday 15th
NEW Highfields House 27
Holme Grange 32
NEW Holmlea 33

Sunday 16th
◆ The Burrows Gardens 8
◆ Cascades Gardens 11
Fir Croft 21
13 Westfield Road 68

Friday 21st
330 Old Road 47

Saturday 22nd
12 Ansell Road 1
◆ Calke Abbey 10
330 Old Road 47

Sunday 23rd
12 Ansell Road 1
Hill Cottage 28
◆ Meynell Langley Trials Garden 42

Thursday 27th
10 Chestnut Way 13

Saturday 29th
Elmton Gardens 20

Sunday 30th
Elmton Gardens 20
NEW High Barn 23
High Roost 24
The Lilies 36
NEW 7 Main Street 38

July

Saturday 6th
Barlborough Gardens 2
Barton Hall 3
New Mills School 44
Otterwood 49
NEW The Smithy 58
Smithy House 59

Sunday 7th
Barlborough Gardens 2
Barton Hall 3
◆ The Burrows Gardens 8
8 Curzon Lane 17
NEW 58A Main Street 40
Moorfields 43
New Mills School 44

Monday 8th
NEW The Smithy 58

Tuesday 9th
◆ Renishaw Hall & Gardens 54

Saturday 13th
NEW 108 Macclesfield Road 37
Stanton in Peak Gardens 60

Sunday 14th
NEW 108 Macclesfield Road 37
NEW 58A Main Street 40
◆ Meynell Langley Trials Garden 42
Stanton in Peak Gardens 60
NEW 27 Wash Green 66

Wednesday 17th
◆ Bluebell Arboretum and Nursery 5

Keeper's Cottage

8 Curzon Lane

Sunday 21st
◆ Cascades Gardens 11
8 Curzon Lane 17
Hollies Farm Plant Centre 30
The Paddock 50
18 Plant Lane 52
Repton NGS Village Gardens 55

Saturday 27th
Byways 9
NEW Keeper's Cottage 34

Sunday 28th
Byways 9
NEW Keeper's Cottage 34
Wild in the Country 73

August

Saturday 3rd
9 Main Street 39

Sunday 4th
9 Main Street 39
13 Westfield Road 68
Woodend Cottage 76

Sunday 11th
8 Curzon Lane 17
Hollies Farm Plant Centre 30
◆ Old English Walled Garden, Elvaston Castle Country Park 46
18 Plant Lane 52

Wednesday 14th
◆ Bluebell Arboretum and Nursery 5
NEW 15 Windmill Lane 74

Sunday 18th
◆ Cascades Gardens 11
The Lilies 36
◆ Meynell Langley Trials Garden 42

Sunday 25th
12 Water Lane 67

Monday 26th
◆ The Burrows Gardens 8
◆ Tissington Hall 63
12 Water Lane 67

Saturday 31st
The Old Vicarage 48

September

Sunday 1st
NEW Highfields House 27
The Old Vicarage 48

Tuesday 3rd
◆ Renishaw Hall & Gardens 54

Sunday 8th
Coxbench Hall 15

Saturday 14th
◆ Calke Abbey 10

Sunday 15th
◆ Meynell Langley Trials Garden 42

Wednesday 18th
◆ Bluebell Arboretum and Nursery 5

Thursday 19th
9 Newfield Crescent 45

Sunday 22nd
Broomfield Hall 7

October

Sunday 6th
◆ Meynell Langley Trials Garden 42

By Arrangement

Arrange a personalised garden visit with your club, or group of friends, on a date to suit you. See individual garden entries for full details.

12 Ansell Road 1
Askew Cottage, Repton NGS Village Gardens 55
Barton Hall 3
334 Belper Road 4
Brick Kiln Farm 6
Byways 9
NEW 4 Chapel Walk 12
10 Chestnut Way 13
Chevin Brae 14
Coxbench Hall 15
Craigside 16
8 Curzon Lane 17
Dam Stead 18
The Dower House 19
Gamesley Fold Cottage 22
NEW High Barn 23
High Roost 24
Higher Crossings 25
Highfield House 26
Hillside 29
Holme Grange 32
9 Main Street 39
NEW 7 Main Street 38
NEW 58A Main Street 40
New Mills School 44
9 Newfield Crescent 45
The Old Vicarage 48
Otterwood 49
The Paddock 50
Park Hall 51
18 Plant Lane 52
NEW Rutland 56
Smithy House 59
Tilford House 62
NEW 27 Wash Green 66
12 Water Lane 67
13 Westfield Road 68
Westgate 69
Wharfedale 70
24 Wheeldon Avenue 71
26 Wheeldon Avenue 72
Woodend Cottage 76

THE GARDENS

1 12 ANSELL ROAD

Ecclesall, Sheffield, S11 7PE. Dave Darwent, 01142 665881, dave@poptasticdave.co.uk, www.poptasticdave.co.uk. *Approx 3m SW of City Centre. Travel to Ringinglow Rd (88 bus), then Edale Rd (opp Ecclesall C of E Primary School). 3rd R - Ansell Rd. No 12 on L ¾ way down, solar panel on roof.* **Sun 21, Mon 22 Apr, Sun 5, Mon 6, Sun 26, Mon 27 May (10.30-4.30); Sat 22, Sun 23 June (2-8). Adm £3, chd free. Light refreshments. Savoury and gluten free available.** Visits also by arrangement Apr to Sept for groups of 5 to 20.

Now in its 91st year since being created by my grandparents, this is a suburban mixed productive and flower garden retaining many original plants and features as well as the original layout. A book documenting the history of the garden has been published and is on sale to raise further funds for charity. Original rustic pergola with 90+ year old roses. Then and now pictures of the garden in 1929 and 1950's vs present. Map of landmarks up to 55m away which can be seen from garden. 7 water features. Wide variety of unique-recipe homemade cakes with take-away service available. New winter garden.

GROUP OPENING

2 BARLBOROUGH GARDENS

Chesterfield Road, Barlborough, Chesterfield, S43 4TR. Christine Sanderson, 07956 203184, christine.r.sanderson@uwclub.net, www.facebook.com/barlboroughgardens. *7m NE of Chesterfield. Off A619 midway between Chesterfield & Worksop. ½m E M1, J30. Follow signs for Barlborough then yellow NGS signs. Parking available in village.* **Mon 27 May (2-6). Combined adm £4, chd free. Sat 6, Sun 7 July (1-6). Combined adm £6, chd free. Refreshments available at 'The Hollies' on all dates listed as well as chefs canapes & cool drinks at 'Raiswells House' over the July weekend.**

GOOSE COTTAGE
Mick & Barbara Housley.
Open on Sat 6, Sun 7 July

THE HOLLIES
Vernon & Christine Sanderson, wwwfacebook.com/barlboroughgardens.
Open on all dates

LINDWAY
Thomas & Margaret Pettinger.
Open on all dates

NEW **RAISWELLS HOUSE**
Mr & Mrs Andrew and Rosie Dale.
Open on Sat 6, Sun 7 July

WOODSIDE HOUSE
Tricia & Adrian Murray-Leslie.
Open on Sat 6, Sun 7 July

Barlborough is an attractive historic village and a range of interesting buildings can be seen all around the village centre. The village is situated close to Renishaw Hall for possible combined visit. Map detailing location of all the gardens is issued with admission ticket, which can be purchased at any of the gardens listed. For more information visit our Facebook page - see details above. Local photographer, Lesley Carley will be displaying some of her work over the July weeknd opening. Digital prints will be available both as greeting cards and mounted/framed prints. Partial wheelchair access at The Hollies.

3 BARTON HALL

Church Broughton, Derby, DE65 5AN. Francine Salisbury, Bartonhall57@outlook.com. *A50 (from Stoke) take the turning for Hatton. Go through the T-lights, then take the 1st turning L for Church Broughton. Go straight on for approx 2m. Barton Blount is sign posted on the L.* **Sat 6, Sun 7 July (11-4). Adm £5, chd free. Home-made teas in the Engine Room.** Visits also by arrangement May to Sept for groups of 30+.

In the magnificent setting of Barton Blount a set of themed gardens containing wisteria archways, lavender lined pathways, rose gardens, glasshouses and a parterre garden. There is also 'Charlotte's Garden', a huge walled vegetable garden dedicated to charity. Toilets on site.

4 334 BELPER ROAD

Stanley Common, DE7 6FY. Gill & Colin Hancock, 01159 301061, gillandcolin@tiscali.co.uk, www.hamescovert.com. *7m N of Derby. 3m W of Ilkeston. On A609, ¾m from Rose & Crown Xrds (A608). Please park in field up farm drive or Working Men's Club rear car park if wet.* **Sun 14 Apr, Sun 26 May (12-4.30). Adm £4, chd free. Home-made teas. Home-made soup available in April.** Visits also by arrangement Apr to June for groups of 10+.

Beautiful country garden with many attractive features incl a laburnum tunnel, rose and wisteria domes, old workmen's hut, wild life pond and much more. Take a scenic walk through the ten acres of woodland and glades to a ½ acre lake and see thousands of cowslips in April and wild orchids in May. Plenty of seating to enjoy delicious home-made cakes. Children welcome with plenty of activities to keep them entertained. Paths round wood and lake not suitable for wheelchairs.

Your visits help change lives - your generosity has supported unpaid carers through donations to Carers Trust totalling over £3.9 million since 1996

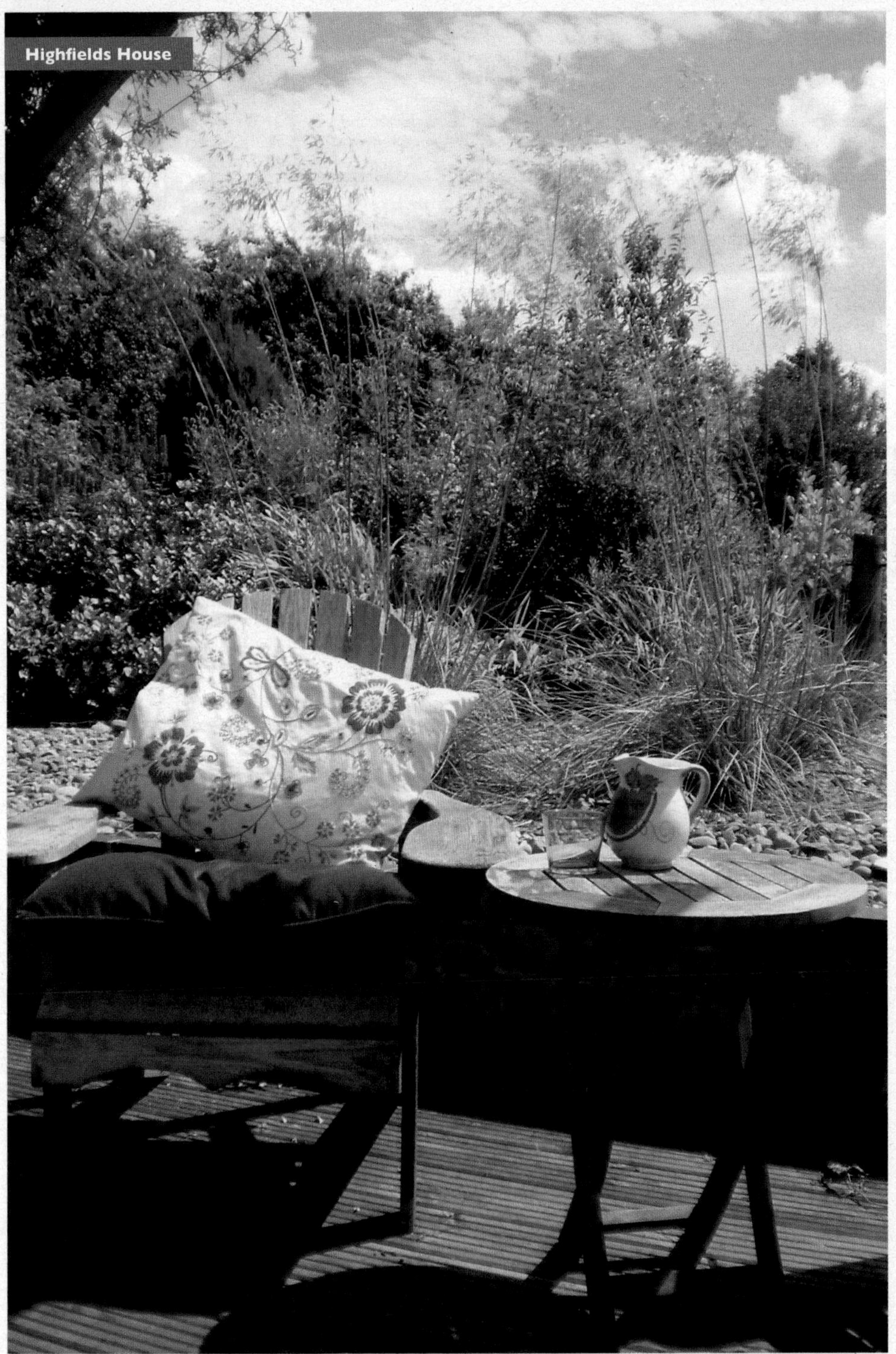

Highfields House

5 ◆ BLUEBELL ARBORETUM AND NURSERY

Annwell Lane, Smisby, Ashby de la Zouch, LE65 2TA. Robert & Suzette Vernon, 01530 413700, sales@bluebellnursery.com, www.bluebellnursery.com. *1m NW of Ashby-de-la-Zouch. Arboretum is clearly signed in Annwell Lane (follow brown signs), ¼m S, through village of Smisby off B5006, between Ticknall & Ashby-de-la-Zouch. Free parking.* **For NGS: Wed 15 May, Wed 12 June, Wed 17 July, Wed 14 Aug, Wed 18 Sept (9-5). Adm £5, chd free. Tea/coffee available on request at office.** For other opening times and information, please phone, email or visit garden website.

Beautiful 9 acre woodland garden with a large collection of rare trees and shrubs. Interest throughout the yr with spring flowers, cool leafy areas in summer and sensational autumn colour. Many information posters describing the more obscure plants. Adjacent specialist tree and shrub nursery. Please be aware this is not a wood full of bluebells, despite the name. The woodland garden is fully labelled and the staff can answer questions or talk at length about any of the trees or shrubs on display. Rare trees and shrubs. Educational signs. Woodland. Arboretum. Please wear sturdy, waterproof footwear during or after wet weather! Full wheelchair access in dry, warm weather however grass paths can become wet and inaccessible in snow or after rain.

6 BRICK KILN FARM

Hulland Ward, Ashbourne, DE6 3EJ. Mrs Jan Hutchinson, 01335 370440, robert.hutchinson123@btinternet.com. *4m E of Ashbourne (A517). 1m S of Carsington Water. From Hulland Ward take Dog Lane past church 2nd L 100yds on R. From Ashbourne A517 Bradley Corner turn L follow sign for Carsington Water 1m on L.* **Visits by arrangement May to July for groups of 10+. Adm £5, chd free. Home-made teas.** Donation to Great Dane Adoption Society.

A small country garden which wraps around an old red brick farmhouse accessed through a courtyard with original well. Irregularly shaped lawn bounded by wide herbaceous borders leading to duck pond and pet's memorial garden. Small holding. Cattle and horses grazing. Search for us on YouTube! Level garden, some uneven flagstones, gravel drive, plenty of parking.

7 BROOMFIELD HALL

Morley, Ilkeston, Ilkeston, DE7 6DN. Derby College, www.facebook.com/BroomfieldPlantCentre. *4m N of Derby. 6m S of Heanor on A608.* **Sun 19 May, Sun 22 Sept (10-4). Adm £4, chd free. Light refreshments.**

25 acres of constantly developing educational Victorian gardens/woodlands maintained by students and volunteers. Trees, shrubs, herbaceous borders as seen on Gardener's World, walled garden, themed gardens, winter garden, plant centre, rose garden, rhododendrons, tropical garden, terrace views, lawns, garden tours and much more. Most of garden is accessible to wheelchair users.

8 ◆ THE BURROWS GARDENS

Burrows Lane, Brailsford, Ashbourne, DE6 3BU. Mrs N M Dalton, 01335 360745, enquiries@burrowsgardens.com, www.burrowsgardens.com. *5m SE of Ashbourne; 5m NW of Derby. A52 from Derby: turn L opp sign for Wild Park Leisure 1m before village of Brailsford. ¼m & at grass triangle head straight over through wrought*

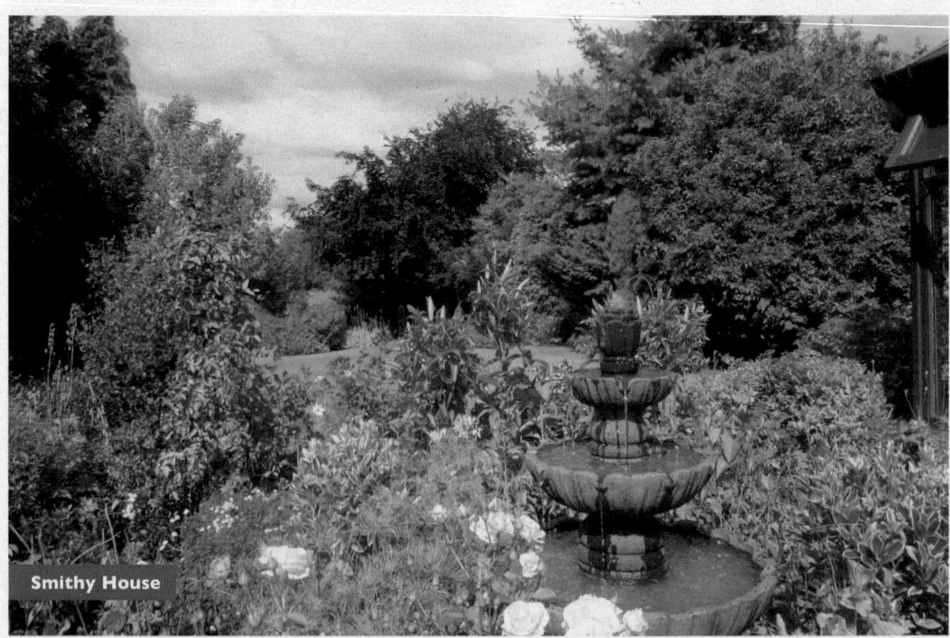

Smithy House

iron gates. **For NGS: Mon 22 Apr, Mon 27 May, Sun 16 June, Sun 7 July, Mon 26 Aug (11-4). Adm £5, chd free. Home-made teas.** For other opening times and information, please phone, email or visit garden website.
5 acres of stunning garden set in beautiful countryside where immaculate lawns show off exotic rare plants and trees, mixing with old favourites in this outstanding garden. A huge variety of styles from temple to Cornish, Italian and English, gloriously designed and displayed. This is a must see garden. Visit our website for more information. Most of garden accessible to wheelchairs.

9 BYWAYS

7A Brookfield Avenue, Brookside, Chesterfield, S40 3NX. Terry & Eileen Kelly, 01246 566376, telkel1@aol.com. *1½m W of Chesterfield. Follow A619 from Chesterfield towards Baslow. Brookfield Av is 2nd R after Brookfield Sch. Please park on Chatsworth Rd (A619).* **Sat 27, Sun 28 July (12.30-4.30). Adm £3.50, chd free. Home-made teas.** Visits also by arrangement July & Aug for groups of 10 to 30. Donation to Ashgate Hospice.
Previous winners of the Best Back Garden over 80sqm, Best Front Garden, Best Container Garden and Best Hanging Basket in Chesterfield in Bloom. Well established perennial borders incl helenium, monardas, phlox, penstenom, grasses, acers, giving a very colourful display. Rockery and many planters containing acers, hostas, fuchsias and roses. 5 seating areas.

10 ◆ CALKE ABBEY

Ticknall, DE73 7LE. National Trust, 01332 863822, calkeabbey@nationaltrust.org.uk, www.nationaltrust.org.uk/calke-abbey. *10m S of Derby. On A514 at Ticknall between Swadlincote & Melbourne. For Sat Nav use DE73 7JF.* **For NGS: Sat 22 June, Sat 14 Sept (10-5). Adm £10.70, chd £5.35. Light refreshments.** For other opening times and information, please phone, email or visit garden website.
With peeling paintwork and overgrown courtyards, Calke Abbey tells the story of the dramatic decline of a country-house estate. The large kitchen garden, impressive collection of glasshouses, garden buildings and tunnels hint at the work of past gardeners, while today the flower garden, herbaceous borders and unique auricula theatre providing stunning displays all year. Restaurant at main visitor facilities for light refreshments and locally sourced food. House is also open by timed ticket only. Electric buggy available for those with mobility problems.

11 ◆ CASCADES GARDENS

Clatterway, Bonsall, Matlock, DE4 2AH. Alan & Alesia Clements, 01629 822813, cascadesgardens@gmail.com, www.cascadesgardens.com. *5m SW of Matlock. From Cromford A6 T-lights turn towards Wirksworth. Turn R along Via Gellia, signed Buxton & Bonsall. After 1m turn R up hill towards Bonsall. Garden entrance at top of hill. Park in village car park.* **For NGS: Sun 17 Mar, Sun 14 Apr, Sun 5 May, Sun 16 June, Sun 21 July, Sun 18 Aug (12-4.30). Adm £5, chd free. Light refreshments.** For other opening times and information, please phone, email or visit garden website.
Fascinating 4 acre peaceful garden in spectacular natural surroundings with woodland, cliffs, stream, pond and ruined corn mill. Inspired by Japanese gardens, secluded garden rooms for relaxation and reflection. Beautiful views of the wide collection of unusual perennials, conifers, shrubs and trees. Nursery. View website for non-NGS openings. Plants for sale. Hellebore month in March. Mostly accessible. Gravel paths, some steep slopes.

12 NEW 4 CHAPEL WALK

Curbar, Calver, Hope Valley, S32 3YQ. Jacqueline Tame, 01433630595, Jacquelinetame@gmail.com. *Up Curbar hill find red phone box. Turn into The Hillock, turn L, & L again past Methodist church, Car Park. There are 6 bungalows, garden in RHS of alley.* **Visits by arrangement Apr to Oct for groups of up to 10. Afternoon visits preferred weekly or weekends. Adm £3.50, chd free. Home-made teas.**
My interpretation of a Japanese style garden, how you can achieve a beautiful garden in a small space, size 30ft x 30ft approx using cherry, magnolia, acer, bonsai, Zen area using blue slate, rocks for mountains. Derbyshire tufa porous limestone rock growing a bonsai tree. Fruit, figs, grapes tomatoes, olives in my Mediterranean area. Up hill is an allotment for vegetables and chickens. All on one level.

13 10 CHESTNUT WAY

Repton, DE65 6FQ. Robert & Pauline Little, 01283 702267, rlittleq@gmail.com, www.littlegarden.org.uk. *6m S of Derby. From A38/A50, S of Derby, follow signs to Willington, then Repton. In Repton turn R at r'about. Chestnut Way is ¼m up hill, on L.* **Sun 17, Sun 24 Feb (11-3). Light refreshments. Thur 27 June (12-5). Home-made teas. Adm £4, chd free. Home-made soup (Feb). Home-made teas (all dates). Opening with Repton NGS Village Gardens on Mon 27 May, Sun 21 July.** Visits also by arrangement Feb to Nov for groups of 10+ with inside seating for 30+ people if wet.
A large garden full of interesting and unusual plants designed to have colour and interest throughout the year. The felling of some large trees has given the opportunity for some unusual sculptures and fresh planting. Many benches to sit and soak up the atmosphere enjoying our renowned tea and cake. Overflowing borders and a surprise round every corner. Excellent plant stall in Spring. Special interest in viticella clematis, organic vegetables and composting. Level garden, good solid paths to main areas. Some grass/bark paths.

Your visits help change lives – we are the largest single funder of the Queen's Nursing Institute

14 CHEVIN BRAE

Milford, Belper, DE56 0QH. Dr David Moreton, 07778004374, davidmoretonchevinbrae@gmail.com. *1½m S of Belper. Coming from S on A6 turn L at Strutt Arms & cont up Chevin Rd. Park on Chevin Road. After 300 yds follow arrow to L up Morrells Lane. After 300 yds Chevin Brae on L with silver garage.* **Sat 13 Apr (1-5). Adm £3, chd free. Home-made teas.** Visits also by arrangement Mar to Oct for groups of up to 30.

A large garden, with swathes of daffodils in the orchard a spring feature. Extensive wild flower planting along edge of wood features aconites, snowdrops, wood anemones, fritillaries and dog tooth violets. Other parts of garden will have hellebores and early camelias. Tea and home-made pastries, many of which feature fruit and jam from the garden, served from the summer house in the middle of the orchard.

15 COXBENCH HALL

Alfreton Road, Coxbench, Derby, DE21 5BB. Mr Brian Ballin, 01332 880200, office@coxbench-hall.co.uk. *4m N of Derby close to A38. After passing thru Little Eaton, turn L onto Alfreton Rd for 1m, Coxbench Hall is on L next to Fox & Hounds PH between Little Eaton & Holbrook. From A38, take Kilburn turn & go towards Little Eaton.* **Sun 8 Sept (2.30-4.30). Adm £3, chd free. Home-made teas. incl diabetic and gluten free cakes.** Visits also by arrangement.

Formerly the ancestral home of the Meynell family, the gardens reflect the Georgian house standing in 4½ acres of grounds most of which is accessible and wheelchair friendly. The garden has 2 fishponds connected by a stream, a sensory garden for the sight impaired, a short woodland walk through shrubbery, rockery, raised vegetable beds, an orchard and seasonal displays in the mainly lawned areas. As a Residential Home for the Elderly, our Gardens are developed to inspire our residents from a number of sensory perspectives - different colours, textures and fragrances of plants, growing vegetables next to the C18 potting shed. There is also a veteran (500 - 800 yr old) Yew tree. Most of garden is lawned or block paved incl a block paved path around the edges of the main lawn. Regret no wheelchair access to woodland area.

16 CRAIGSIDE

Reservoir Road, Whaley Bridge, SK23 7BW. Jane & Gerard Lennox, 07939 012634, jane@lennoxonline.net, www.craigside.info. *11m SE of Stockport. 11m NNW of Buxton. Turn off A6 onto A5004 to Whaley Bridge. Turn R at train station 1st L under railway bridge onto Reservoir Rd. Park on roadside or in village. Garden ½m from village.* **Visits by arrangement June to Aug. Gluten free cakes are available, also savoury options.**

1 acre garden rising steeply from the reservoir giving magnificent views across Todbrook reservoir into Peak District. Gravel paths, stone steps with stopping places. Many mature trees incl 500+yr old oak. Spring bulbs, herbaceous borders, alpine bed, steep mature rockery many heucheras and hydrangeas. Herbs, vegetables and fruit trees. Gluten free cakes available also savoury alternatives. Refreshments also available for 4 legged visitors with a selection of home-made dog biscuits!

17 8 CURZON LANE

Alvaston, Derby, DE24 8QS. John & Marian Gray, 01332 601596, maz@curzongarden.com, www.curzongarden.com. *2m SE of Derby city centre. From city centre take A6 (London Rd) towards Alvaston. Curzon Lane on L, approx ½m before Alvaston shops.* **Sun 7, Sun 21 July, Sun 11 Aug (12-5). Adm £3, chd free. Tea.** Visits also by arrangement July & Aug for groups of 10 to 30.

Mature garden with lawns, borders packed full with perennials, shrubs and small trees, tropical planting and hot border. Ornamental and wildlife ponds, greenhouse with different varieties of tomato, cucumber, peppers and chillies. Well stocked vegetable plot. Gravel area and large patio with container planting.

18 DAM STEAD

3 Crowhole, Barlow, Dronfield, S18 7TJ. Derek & Barbara Saveall, 01142 890802, barbarasaveall@hotmail.co.uk. *Chesterfield B6051 to Barlow. Tickled Trout Pub on L. Springfield Rd on L, then R on unnamed rd. Last cottage on R.* **Visits by arrangement May to Sept. Adm £3, chd free. Light refreshments.**

Approx one acre with stream, weir, fragrant garden, rose tunnel, orchard garden and dam with an island. Long woodland path, alpine troughs, rockeries and mixed planting. A natural wildlife garden, large summerhouse with seating inside and out. 3 village well dressings and carnival over one week mid August.

19 THE DOWER HOUSE

Church Square, Melbourne, DE73 8JH. William & Griselda Kerr, 01332 864756, griseldakerr@btinternet.com. *6m S of Derby. 5m W of exit 23A M1. 4m N of exit 13 M42. When in Church Square, turn R just before going past the church - the turning is beside a board giving church service times. Gates are then 50 yds ahead.* **Sat 23, Sun 24 Feb (10-3.30). Adm £4, chd free. Light refreshments. Sat 1 June (10-5.30). Adm £4.50, chd free. Light refreshments. Sun 2 June (10-5.30). Adm £4.50, chd free.**

Beautiful view of Melbourne Pool from balustraded terrace running length of 1831 house. Garden drops steeply by paths and steps to lawn with herbaceous border and bank of flowering shrubs best in June/Sept. Interesting bog garden and other late summer beds. Rose tunnel, glade, orchard, hellebores and small woodland lovely in early spring. Herb garden, other small lawns and vegetable garden. Children can search for animals and other ornaments in the garden. Wheelchair access top half of the garden only. Shoes with a good grip are highly recommended as some slopes are steep. No parking within 50 yards.

GROUP OPENING

20 ELMTON GARDENS

Elmton, Worksop, S80 4LS. *2m from Creswell, 3m from Clowne, 5m from J30, M1. From M1 J30 take A616 to Newark. Follow approx 4m. Turn R at Elmton signpost. At junction turn R, the village centre is in ½m.* **Sat 29, Sun 30 June (1-5). Combined adm £5, chd free. Cream teas.**

ELM TREE COTTAGE
Mark and Linda Hopkinson.

ELM TREE FARM
Angie & Tim Caulton.

PEAR TREE COTTAGE
Geoff & Janet Cutts.

PINFOLD
Nikki Kirsop Barry Davies.

Elmton is a lovely little village situated on a stretch of rare Magnesian limestone in the middle of attractive, rolling farm land. It has a pub, a church and a village green. Garden opening coincides with Elmton Festival and Well Dressing celebrations. There are two exhibitions to view, both with a local theme & classic cars are on display. Other attractions incl a brass band performance at Elm Tree Farm and cream teas in the old School Room next to the church. The village green has an unimproved grassland area where quaking grass, bee orchids and harebells grow. The four very colourful but different open gardens are all surrounded by farm land and have wonderful views. They show a range of gardening styles, themed beds and all have a commitment to fruit and vegetable growing. Elmton received it's 4th silver gilt award from EMIB in 2018, and is a finalist in RHS Britain in Bloom 2018. It was judged the best small village in the East Midlands in 2018 for the fourth consecutive year. Food & drink served throughout the day at Elm Tree pub.

21 FIR CROFT

Froggatt Road, Calver, S32 3ZD. Dr S B Furness, www.alpineplantcentre.co.uk. *4m N of Bakewell. At junction of B6001 with A625 (formerly B6054), adjacent to Power Garage.* **Sun 19 May, Sun 2, Sun 16 June (2-5). Adm by donation.**

Massive scree with many varieties. Plantsman's garden; rockeries; water garden and nursery; extensive collection (over 3000 varieties) of alpines; conifers; over 800 sempervivums, 500 saxifrages and 350 primulas. Many new varieties not seen anywhere else in the UK. Huge new tufa wall planted with many rare Alpines and sempervivums.

22 GAMESLEY FOLD COTTAGE

Gamesley Fold, Glossop, SK13 6JJ. Mrs G M Carr, 01457 867856, gcarr@gamesleyfold.co.uk, www.gamesleyfold.co.uk. *2m W of Glossop. Off A626 Glossop/Marple Rd nr Charlesworth. Turn down lane directly opp St. Margaret's School, white cottage at the bottom. Car parking in the adjacent field if weather is dry.* **Visits by arrangement May to Aug. Home-made teas.**

Old fashioned cottage garden with rhododendrons, herbaceous borders with candelabra primulas, cottage garden perennial flowers and herbs also a plant nursery selling a wide variety of these plus wild flowers. Small ornamental fish pond and an orchard. Lovely views of the surrounding countryside and plenty of seats available to relax and enjoy tea and cakes. A garden planted with wildlife in mind lots of native wild flower plants on sale to visitors.

23 NEW HIGH BARN

Hognaston, Ashbourne, DE6 1PR. Stephanie Taylor & Alan Cribbens, 01335 370293, stephanietaylor@btinternet.com. *Approximately 5m NE of Ashbourne. A517 Belper to Hulland Ward then follow signs to Hognaston. Downhill (2m) to bridge then uphill through village. Opening on 1.2km beyond Red Lion. House name on wall.* **Sun 30 June (2-5). Adm £4, chd free. Light refreshments.** Visits also by arrangement May to Sept for groups of 5 to 20.

Originally to a design by Percy Thrower, the garden features a variety of contrasting spaces incl newly established rose beds; a shady area with pond, ferns, hostas and water feature; attractive trees, rhododendrons and many other shrubs and perennials. Plenty of places to sit and enjoy tea, coffee and cake with glimpses of Carsington Water. Stone steps, gravel paths and some uneven paving.

24 HIGH ROOST

27 Storthmeadow Road, Simmondley, Glossop, SK13 6UZ. Peter & Christina Harris, 01457 863888, harrispeter448@gmail.com. *¾m SW of Glossop. From Glossop A57 to M/CL at 2nd r'about, up Simmondley Ln nr top R turn. From Marple A626 to Glossop, in Chworth R up Town Ln past Hare & Hound PH 2nd L.* **Sun 30 June (12-4). Adm £3, chd free. Light refreshments.** Visits also by arrangement May to July. Donation to Donkey Sanctuary.

Garden on terraced slopes, views over fields and hills. Winding paths, archways and steps explore different garden rooms packed with plants, designed to attract wildlife. Alpine bed, gravel gardens; vegetable garden, water features, statuary, troughs and planters. A garden which needs exploring to discover its secrets tucked away in hidden corners. Craft stall, children's garden quiz and lucky dip.

25 HIGHER CROSSINGS

Crossings Road, Chapel-en-le-Frith, High Peak, SK23 9RX. Malcolm & Christine Hoskins, 01298 812970. *Turn off B5470 N from Chapel-en-le-Frith on Crossings Rd signed Whitehough/Chinley. Higher Crossings is 2nd house on R beyond 1st Xrds. Park best before crossroads on Crossings Rd or L on Eccles Rd.* **Sun 26, Mon 27 May (1.30-5). Adm £4, chd free. Light refreshments.** Visits also by arrangement for groups of 10+.

Nearly 2 acres of formal terraced country garden, sweeping lawns and magnificent Peak District views. Rhododendrons, acers, azaleas, hostas, herbaceous borders, Zen garden. Mature specimen trees and shrubs leading through a dell. Beautiful stone terrace and sitting areas. Garden gate leading into meadow.

New Mills School

26 HIGHFIELD HOUSE

Wingfield Road, Oakerthorpe, Alfreton, DE55 7AP. Paul & Ruth Peat and Janet & Brian Costall, 01773 521342, highfieldhouseopengardens@hotmail.co.uk, www.highfieldhouse.weebly.com. *Rear of Alfreton Golf Club. A615 Alfreton-Matlock Rd.* **Sun 2 June (10.30-5). Adm £3, chd free. Home-made teas.** Visits also by arrangement Feb to July for groups of 10+. £6.00 including fantastic refreshments.
Lovely country garden of approx 1 acre, incorporating a shady garden, woodland, pond, laburnum tunnel, orchard, herbaceous borders and vegetable garden. Fabulous AGA baked cakes and lunches. Groups welcome by appointment - (incl 16th -24th February for Snowdrops with afternoon tea or lunch inside by the fire). Lovely walk to Derbyshire Wildlife Trust nature reserve to see Orchids in June. Some steps, slopes and gravel areas.

27 NEW HIGHFIELDS HOUSE

Shields Lane, Roston, Ashbourne, DE6 2EF. Sarah Pennell. *6m SW of Ashbourne. A515 S from Ashbourne, after 3m turn R onto B5033. After 2m turn L and follow signposts.* **Sat 15 June, Sun 1 Sept (1-5). Adm £3, chd free. Home-made teas.**
A countryside garden with extensive views. Colourful mixed borders and alpine garden, patio, small pond, greenhouse and veg plot with fruit trees. Enjoy sitting in the summerhouse area watching the butterflies on the wildlife bank. Let the art in the garden bring a smile to your face. A warm welcome awaits you from our donkeys. Partial wheelchair access. Garden crafts. Some gravel paths.

28 HILL COTTAGE

Ashover Road, Littlemoor, Ashover nr Chesterfield, S45 0BL. Jane Tomlinson and Tim Walls. *Littlemoor. 1.8 m from Ashover village, 6.3m from Chesterfield and 6.1m from Matlock. Hill Cottage is on Ashover Rd (also known as Stubben Edge Lane). Opp the end of Eastwood Lane.* **Sun 23 June (11-5). Adm £3.50, chd free. Light refreshments.**
Hill Cottage is a lovely example of

an English country cottage garden. Whilst small, the garden has full, colourful and fragrant herbaceous borders with hostas and roses in pots along with a heart shaped lawn. A greenhouse full of chillies and scented pelargoniums and a small veg patch. Views to the horizon over a pastoral landscape. There are several steps.

29 HILLSIDE

286 Handley Road, New Whittington, Chesterfield, S43 2ET. Mr E J Lee, 01246 454960, eric.lee5@btinternet.com. *3m N of Chesterfield. Between B6056 & B0652 N of village.* **Visits by arrangement. Check refreshments when booking. Adm £3.50, chd free.**

New for 2019, there is a Japanese feature which tells the story of the Japanese Tea Garden & a tree trail with over 50 named trees and a 'walk through' facility in part of the rock garden - uphill only. Himalayan bed with about 40 species grown from wild collected seed. Streams, bog gardens, alpine house, fernery, a stumpery, a winter interest area, a salix area. An acer and bamboo section and a bark and berry section. Most of the plants are permanently labelled.

30 HOLLIES FARM PLANT CENTRE

Uppertown, Bonsall, Matlock, DE4 2AW. Robert & Linda Wells, www.holliesfarmplantcentre.co.uk. *From Cromford turn R off A5012 up The Clatterway. Keep R past Fountain Tearoom to village cross, take L up High St, then 2nd L onto Abel Lane. Garden straight ahead.* **Sun 9 June, Sun 21 July, Sun 11 Aug (11-3). Adm £3.50, chd free. Home-made teas.**

The best selection in Derbyshire with advice and personal attention from Robert and Linda Wells at their family run business. Enjoy a visit to remember in our beautiful display garden - set within glorious Peak District countryside. Huge variety of hardy perennials incl the rare and unusual. Vast selection of traditional garden favourites. Award winning hanging baskets. Ponds, herbaceous borders and glorious views. Plenty of parking available.

31 THE HOLLY TREE

21 Hackney Road, Hackney, Matlock, DE4 2PX. Carl Hodgkinson. *½m NW of Matlock, off A6. Take A6 NW past bus stn & 1st R up Dimple Rd. At T-junction, turn R & immed L, for Farley & Hackney. Take 1st L onto Hackney Rd. Continue ¾m.* **Sat 1 June (10.30-4.30). Cream teas. Sun 2 June (10.30-4.30). Home-made teas. Adm £3, chd free.**

The garden is in excess of 1½ acres and set on a steeply sloping S-facing site, sheltering behind a high retaining wall and incl a small arboretum, bog garden, herbaceous borders, pond, vegetables, fruits, apiary and chickens. Extensively terraced with many paths and steps. Spectacular views across the Derwent valley to Snitterton and Oker.

32 HOLME GRANGE

Holme Lane, Bakewell, DE45 1GF. Mrs Shirley Stubbs, 01629 814728, shirleystubbs@hotmail.co.uk. *Close to centre of Bakewell. From Bakewell town centre, follow the Baslow Rd and take the first L along Holme Lane, beside the river meadow. From Baslow turn R into Holme Lane.* **Sat 15 June (11-4). Adm £4, chd free. Home-made teas. Visits also by arrangement May to July for groups of 10 to 20.**

Holme Grange has a garden of about an acre, and offers a range of mixed borders, large lawned area and woodland offering some unusual trees, shrubs and plants. Back gate access to level gravel paths and lawned area.

33 NEW HOLMLEA

Derby Road, Ambergate, Belper, DE56 2EJ. Bill & Tracy Reid. *On the A6 between Belper and Matlock. Bungalow between BP petrol station & St Annes Church. At the end of the A610 turn R towards Belper. 200 yrds on the R. Additional parking at the Hurt Arms overflow car park.* **Sat 15 June (10.30-4). Adm £4, chd free. Light refreshments in St Anne's Church, Ambergate.**

A deceptively large garden of approx 1 acre with a formal garden incl box hedging, topiary, evergreen shrubs, perennial planting and greenhouse. The vegetable garden incl a further greenhouse, raised beds, fruit trees and bushes and is edged with mixed shrubs and trees for all yr round interest and colour. Goats, Geese, chickens and ducks all reside within the garden. The fine Victorian Church will be open for viewing. Refreshments and toilet facilities available. Partial wheelchair access. Some grass paths.

34 NEW KEEPER'S COTTAGE

Keepers Lane, Barlow, Dronfield, S18 7SX. Mike & Janice Murphy. *Between Chesterfield and Holmesfield, 11m NE from J29 M1. From Chesterfield take B6051 to Barlow. After church on L take 1st R turn on bend then keep L down single track Smeltinghouse Ln. 1st property on L.* **Sat 27, Sun 28 July (10.30-4.30). Adm £4, chd free. Home-made teas.**

This new garden has been created by the owners over the last 3 yrs on a challenging site of wild paddock and steep bramble covered woodland which had been used as a dumping ground for decades of building spoil. This new garden now features a rose covered pergola, kitchen garden, fruit trees, woodland sculptures and brookside planting. On a steep site with several steps.

35 ◆ LEA GARDENS

Lea, Matlock, DE4 5GH. Mr & Mrs J Tye, 01629 534380, www.leagarden.co.uk. *5m SE of Matlock. Off A6 & A615.* For opening times and information, please phone or visit garden website.

Rare collection of rhododendrons, azaleas, kalmias, alpines and conifers in delightful woodland setting. Gardens are sited on remains of medieval quarry and cover about 4 acres. Specialised plant nursery of rhododendrons and azaleas on site. Open daily 1 March to 31 July (9-5). Plant sales by appointment out of season. Visitors welcome throughout the yr. Coffee shop noted for home baked cakes and light refreshments. Gravel paths, steep slopes. Free access for wheelchair users.

36 THE LILIES

Griffe Grange Valley, Grangemill, Matlock, DE4 4BW. Chris & Bridget Sheppard, www.thelilies.com. *On A5012 Via Gellia Rd 4m N Cromford. 1st house on R after junction with B5023 to Middleton. From Grangemill 1st house on L after Prospect Quarry (IKO Permatrack).* **Sun 30 June, Sun 18 Aug (11.30-4.30). Adm £4, chd free. Home-made teas. Light Lunches served 11.30 to 3.00. Home-made teas all day.**

One acre garden gradually restored over the past 13yrs situated at the top of a wooded valley, surrounded by wildflower meadow and ash woodland. Area adjacent to house with seasonal planting and containers. Mixed shrubs and perennial borders many raised from seed. 3 ponds, vegetable plot, barn conversion with separate cottage style garden. Natural garden with stream developed from old mill pond. Walks in large wildflower meadow and ash woodland both SSSI's. Handspinning demonstration and natural dyeing display using materials from the garden and wool from sheep in the meadow. Locally made crafts for sale. Partial wheelchair access. Steep slope from car park, limestone chippings at entrance, some boggy areas if wet.

37 NEW 108 MACCLESFIELD ROAD

Whaley Bridge, High Peak, SK23 7DH. John Taylor & Peter Holden. *500 metres from Horwich End T-lights on B5470 towards Macclesfield. The New Mills to Macclesfield bus stops 50 metres from the house. There is on-street parking on the opposite side of the road to the house.* **Sat 13, Sun 14 July (11-5). Adm £3.50, chd free. Light refreshments.**

Taking inspiration from many an hour visiting gardens large and small we have begun our garden refurbishment; having dug over the old lawn it now forms our main herbaceous border. The garden is a collection of our favourite plants crammed into every nook and cranny. We have adopted a cottage garden style approach, with shrubs, perennials, fruit and vegetables mixing with colourful annuals. The garden is on several levels with narrow paths, and unfortunately there is no step-free access.

38 NEW 7 MAIN STREET

Walton on Trent, DE12 8LY. Sarah & Mark Smith, mark_and_sarah@live.co.uk. *1m off the A38 at the Barton/ Walton junction. Parking available at The White Swan pub. Garden 2 min walk from there.* **Sun 30 June (12-5). Adm £4, chd free. Light refreshments.** Visits also by arrangement in July for groups of 5 to 20. Thursday to Sundays only.

Delightful herbaceous borders fill this former pub garden, transformed in 5 yrs from a neglected space to a cottage garden idyll. From the courtyard, climb the steps to the large garden with hens, pond and wild flower area. Lush foliage fills the deep shade border whilst delphiniums tower over the colourful herbaceous borders. Take a moment to sit and enjoy the scents and colours of the garden. Only the Courtyard is accessible to wheelchairs as access to the main garden is via 7 steps.

39 9 MAIN STREET

Horsley Woodhouse, DE7 6AU. Ms Alison Napier, 01332 881629, ibhillib@btinternet.com. *3m SW of Heanor. 6m N of Derby. Turn off A608 Derby to Heanor Rd at Smalley, towards Belper, (A609). Garden on A609, 1m from Smalley turning.* **Sat 3, Sun 4 Aug (1.30-4.30). Adm £3.50, chd free. Cream teas.** Visits also by arrangement Apr to Sept.

⅓ acre hilltop garden overlooking lovely farmland view. Terracing, borders, lawns and pergola create space for an informal layout with planting for colour effect. Features incl large wildlife pond with water lilies, bog garden and small formal pool. Emphasis on carefully selected herbaceous perennials mixed with shrubs and old fashioned roses. Gravel garden for sun loving plants and scree garden, both developed from former drive. Wide collection of home grown plants for sale. All parts of the garden accessible to wheelchairs. Wheelchair adapted WC.

40 NEW 58A MAIN STREET

Rosliston, Swadlincote, DE12 8JW. Paul Marbrow, 01283 761011, paulmarbrow@hotmail.co.uk. *Rosliston. if exiting the M42, J11 onto the A444 to Overseal follow signs Linton then Rosliston. From A38, exit to Walton on Trent, then follow Rosliston signs.* **Sun 7, Sun 14 July (2-5). Adm £3.50, chd free. Light refreshments.** Visits also by arrangement June to Aug for groups of 5 to 30.

Large garden under construction from an open field over the last three years; although the mature trees have been there longer. The garden has developed into themed areas and is ongoing. Japanese, arid beach, bamboo grove with ferns etc. Under construction and ongoing for 2019, a large covered area for exotic and tender plants. There are also vegetable and fruit gardens. Most areas are easily accessible, although some are only for the sure of foot.

41 ◆ MELBOURNE HALL GARDENS

Church Square, Melbourne, Derby, DE73 8EN. Melbourne Gardens Charity, 01332 862502, melbhall@globalnet.co.uk, www.melbournehallgardens.com. *6m S of Derby. At Melbourne Market Place turn into Church St, go down to Church Sq. Garden entrance across visitor centre next to Melbourne Hall tea room.* **For NGS: Sat 18, Sun 19 May (1.30-5.30). Adm £6, chd free.** For other opening times and information, please phone, email or visit garden website.

A 17 acre historic garden with an abundance of rare trees and shrubs. Woodland and waterside planting with extensive herbaceous borders. Meconopsis, candelabra primulas, various Styrax and Cornus kousa. Other garden features incl Bakewells wrought iron arbour, a yew tunnel and fine C18 statuary and water features. 300yr old trees, waterside planting, feature hedges and herbaceous borders. Fine statuary and stonework. Gravel paths, uneven surface in places, some steep slopes.

42 ◆ MEYNELL LANGLEY TRIALS GARDEN

Lodge Lane (off Flagshaw Lane), Kirk Langley, Ashbourne, DE6 4NT. Robert & Karen Walker, 01332 824358, enquiries@meynell-langley-gardens.co.uk, www.meynell-langley-gardens.co.uk. *4m W of Derby, nr Kedleston Hall. Head W out of Derby on A52. At Kirk Langley turn R onto Flagshaw Lane (signed to Kedleston Hall) then R onto Lodge Lane. Follow Meynell Langley Gardens signs.* **For NGS: Sun 23 June, Sun 14 July, Sun 18 Aug, Sun 15 Sept, Sun 6 Oct (10-4). Adm £4, chd free.** For other opening times and information, please phone, email or visit garden website.

Formal ¾ acre Victorian style garden established over 25 years, displaying and trialling new and existing varieties of bedding plants, herbaceous perennials and vegetable plants grown at the adjacent nursery. Over 180 hanging baskets and floral displays. 45 varieties of apple, pear and other fruit. Summer fruit pruning demonstrations on July NGS day and apple tasting on October NGS day. Adjacent tea rooms serving lunches and refreshments daily. Level ground and firm grass.

43 MOORFIELDS

257/261 Chesterfield Road, Temple Normanton, Chesterfield, S42 5DE. Peter, Janet & Stephen Wright. *4m SE of Chesterfield. From Chesterfield take A617 for 2m, turn on to B6039 through Temple Normanton, taking R fork signed Tibshelf, B6039. Garden ¼m on R. Limited parking.* **Sun 28 Apr, Sun 7 July (1-5). Adm £3.50, chd free. Light refreshments.**

Two adjoining gardens each planted for seasonal colour. The larger one has mature, mixed island beds and borders, a gravel garden to the front, a small wild flower area, large wildlife pond, orchard and soft fruit, vegetable garden. Show of late flowering tulips. The smaller gardens of No. 257 feature herbaceous borders and shrubs. Extensive views across to mid Derbyshire.

18 Plant Lane

44 NEW MILLS SCHOOL

Church Lane, New Mills, High Peak, SK22 4NR. Mr Craig Pickering, 07833 373593, cpickering@newmillsschool.co.uk, www.newmillsschool.co.uk. *12m NNW of Buxton. From A6 take A6105 signed New Mills, Hayfield. At C of E Church turn L onto Church Lane. School on L. Parking on site.* **Sat 6 July (10-5); Sun 7 July (1-5). Adm £4, chd free. Light refreshments in School Library.** Visits also by arrangement June to Aug for groups of 10+.

Mixed herbaceous perennials/shrub borders, with mature trees and lawns and gravel border situated in the semi rural setting of the High Peak incl a Grade II listed building with 4 themed quads. The school was awarded a distinction for their first garden at Tatton RHS Flower Show 2015 and highly commended for their entry in 2017. Hot and Cold Beverages and a selection of sandwiches, cream teas and home-made cakes are available. Ramps allow wheelchair access to most of outside, flower beds and into Grade II listed building and library.

45 9 NEWFIELD CRESCENT

Dore, Sheffield, S17 3DE. Mike Jackson, 01142 366198, mandnjackson@googlemail.com. *Dore - SW Sheffield. Turn off Causeway Head Rd on Heather Lea Av. 2nd L into Newfield Crescent. Parking on roadside.* **Thur 16 May, Thur 19 Sept (2-5). Adm £4, chd free. Light refreshments.** Visits also by arrangement Apr to Oct.

Mature, wildlife friendly garden planted to provide all yr interest, particularly in Autumn and Winter. Upper terrace with alpines in troughs and bowls. Lower terrace featuring pond with cascade and connecting stream to second pond. Bog garden, rock gardens, lawn alpine bed, wilder areas, mixed borders with trees, shrubs and perennials. Featuring azaleas, rhododendrons, camellias, primulas. Wheelchair access without steps to top terrace offering full view of garden.

46 ◆ OLD ENGLISH WALLED GARDEN, ELVASTON CASTLE COUNTRY PARK

Borrowash Road, Elvaston, Derby, DE72 3EP. Derbyshire County Council, 01629 533870, www.derbyshire.gov.uk/elvaston. *4m E of Derby. Signed from A52 & A50. Car parking charge applies.* **For NGS: Sun 28 Apr, Sun 11 Aug (12-4). Adm £2.50, chd free. Light refreshments.** For other opening times and information, please phone or visit garden website.
Come and discover the beauty of the Old English walled garden at Elvaston Castle. Take in the peaceful atmosphere and enjoy the scents and colours of all the varieties of trees, shrubs and plants. Summer bedding and large herbaceous borders. After your visit to the walled garden take time to walk around the wider estate featuring romantic topiary gardens, lake, woodland and nature reserve. Estate gardeners on hand during the day. Delicious home-made cakes available.

47 330 OLD ROAD

Brampton, Chesterfield, S40 3QH. Christine Stubbs & Julia Stubbs. *Approx 1m from town centre. 50 yds from junc with Storrs Rd. 1st house next to grazing field; on-road parking available adjacent to tree-lined roadside stone wall.* **Fri 21, Sat 22 June (10.30-5). Adm £3, chd free. Home-made teas.**
Deceptive ⅓ acre plot of mature trees, landscaped lawns, orchard and cottage style planting. Unusual perennials, species groups such as astrantia, lychnis, thalictrum, heuchera and 40+ clematis. Acers, actea, hosta, ferns and acanthus lie within this interesting garden. Through a hidden gate, another smaller plot of similar planting, with delphinium, helenium, Echinacea, acers and hosta.

48 THE OLD VICARAGE

The Fields, Middleton by Wirksworth, Matlock, DE4 4NH. Jane Irwing, 01629 825010, irwingjane@gmail.com. *Garden located behind church on Main St & nr school. Travelling N on A6 from Derby turn L at Cromford, at top of hill turn R onto Porter Ln, at T-lights, turn R onto Main St. Park in Village Hall. Walk through churchyard. No parking at house.* **Sat 23, Sun 24 Feb (12-3). Light refreshments. Sat 31 Aug, Sun 1 Sept (11-5). Home-made teas. Adm £3.50, chd free.** Visits also by arrangement Mar to Sept for groups of up to 30.
Traditional front garden with lawn and mixed summer borders in gentle valley overlooking Black Rocks. To the side a courtyard garden where acid loving plants are grown in pots and, in the fernery, tender ferns. Beyond is the orchard, fruit garden, vegetable patch and greenhouse, the home of honey bees, doves and hens. Spectacular Rambling Rector rose over front of house in late June early July. Cakes, tea and coffee and cold drinks served in the garden or in fernery if wet (limited space). Path through Churchyard ends in some steps leading onto the lane and into the garden gate. Once in the garden much can be seen from the terrace.

49 OTTERWOOD

88 St Johns Road, Buxton, SK17 6TP. Ms Simone Harch & Mr Gary Mellor, simoneharch@hotmail.co.uk. *Parking on St Johns Rd & Gadley Lane.* **Sat 6 July (12-5). Adm £4, chd free. Home-made teas. Also open The Smithy. £2.50 for tea and cake.** Visits also by arrangement June & July for groups of 10+.
Opening for the second time, this is a romantic, peaceful garden featuring summer borders, kitchen garden, natural pond with viewing pontoon and a newly planted wildflower garden. A haven for wildlife, organically managed. Lovely garden terrace for tea and cake.

50 THE PADDOCK

12 Manknell Rd, Whittington Moor, Chesterfield, S41 8LZ. Mel & Wendy Taylor, 01246 451001, debijt9276@gmail.com. *2m N of Chesterfield. Whittington Moor just off A61 between Sheffield & Chesterfield. Parking available at Victoria Working Mens Club, garden signed from here.* **Sun 28 Apr, Sun 21 July (11-5). Adm £3.50, chd free. Cream teas.** Visits also by arrangement Apr to Sept.
½ acre garden incorporating small formal garden, stream and koi filled pond. Stone path over bridge, up some steps, past small copse, across the stream at the top and back down again. Past herbaceous border towards a pergola where cream teas can be enjoyed.

51 PARK HALL

Walton Back Lane, Walton, Chesterfield, S42 7LT. Kim & Margaret Staniforth, 01246 567412, kim.staniforth@btinternet.com. *2m SW of Chesterfield centre. From town on A619 L into Somersall Lane. On A632 R into Acorn Ridge. Park on field side only of Walton Back Lane.* **Visits by arrangement Apr to July for groups of 10+. Minimum group charge £50. Adm £6, chd free. Light refreshments. Donation to Bluebell Wood Childrens Hospice.**
Romantic 2 acre plantsmans garden, in a stunningly beautiful setting surrounding C17 house (not open) 4 main rooms, terraced garden, parkland area with forest trees, croquet lawn, sunken garden with arbours, pergolas, pleached hedge, topiary, statuary, roses, rhododendrons, camellias, several water features. Runner-up in Daily Telegraph Great British Gardens Competition 2018. Two steps down to gain access to garden.

52 18 PLANT LANE

Long Eaton, Old Sawley, Nottingham, NG10 3BJ. Ernie & Averil Carver, 0115 8491960. *2m SW of Long Eaton from town centre take the B6540 to Old Sawley, R at Nags Head into Wilne Rd, 400yds take R turn into Plant Lane at the Railway Inn Garden on the L 200yds.* **Sun 21 July, Sun 11 Aug (2-5). Adm £3, chd free. Home-made teas.** Visits also by arrangement July to Sept for groups of 10 to 20.
A very successful opening of the garden after being on BBC East Midlands News. A stunning garden full of colour created in just 15 months. After the removal of a great many trees and shrubs it is now a beautiful designed garden, a must see garden. Beautiful hand

made craft/screen printing hand made cards as seen on TV. Tea room with interest.

53 RECTORY HOUSE

Kedleston, Derby, DE22 5JJ. Helene Viscountess Scarsdale. *5m NW Derby. A52 from Derby turn R Kedleston sign. Drive to village turn R. Brick house standing back from rd on sharp corner.* **Mon 27 May (2-5). Adm £5, chd free. Home-made teas.**

The garden is next to Kedleston Park and is of C18 origin. Many established rare trees and shrubs also rhododendrons, azaleas and unusual roses. Large natural pond with amusing frog fountain. Primulas, gunneras, darmeras and lots of moisture loving plants. The winding paths go through trees and past wild flowers and grasses. New fernery with rare plants. An atmospheric garden. Delicious teas, soft drinks and cakes available. A sphere of Cumbrian slate built by Jo Smith, Kirkcudbrightshire. Lily fountain in tea courtyard area. Frog fountain by large pond. Uneven paths.

54 ◆ RENISHAW HALL & GARDENS

Renishaw, Sheffield, S21 3WB. Alexandra Hayward, 01246 432310, enquiries@renishaw-hall.co.uk, www.renishaw-hall.co.uk. *10m from Sheffield city centre. By car: Renishaw Hall only 3m from J30 on M1, well signed from junction r'about.* **For NGS: Tue 9 July, Tue 3 Sept (10.30-4.30). Adm £6.50, chd free.** For other opening times and information, please phone, email or visit garden website.

Renishaw Hall and Gardens boasts 7 acres of stunning gardens created by Sir George Sitwell in 1885. The Italianate gardens feature various rooms with extravagant herbaceous borders. Rose gardens, rare trees and shrubs, National Collection of Yuccas, sculptures, woodland walks and lakes create a magical and engaging garden experience. The Cafe will be open for light meals, hot and cold drinks and cakes. Wheelchair route around garden.

NPC

GROUP OPENING

55 REPTON NGS VILLAGE GARDENS

Repton, Derby, DE65 6FQ. *6m S of Derby. From A38/A50, S of Derby, follow signs to Willington, then Repton, then R at r'about towards Newton Solney to reach 10 Chestnut Way, other gardens signposted from the r'about.* **Mon 27 May, Sun 21 July (1.30-5.30). Combined adm £6, chd free. Home-made teas at 10 Chestnut Way (both dates) & Woodend Cottage (27th May in aid of St. Wystan's Church).**

ASKEW COTTAGE

DE65 6FZ. Louise Hardwick, 07970411748, louise.hardwick@hotmail.co.uk, www.hardwickgardendesign.co.uk.

Open on all dates

Visits also by arrangement May to Sept for groups of 5 to 20.

D

NEW **16 ASKEW GROVE**

Adrienne Mcstocker.

Open on all dates

10 CHESTNUT WAY

Robert & Pauline Little.

Open on all dates

(See separate entry)

22 PINFOLD CLOSE

DE65 6FR. Mr & Mrs O Jowett.

Open on all dates

REPTON ALLOTMENTS

DE65 6FX. Mr A Topping.

Open on all dates

WOODEND COTTAGE

Wendy & Stephen Longden.

Open on Mon 27 May

(See separate entry)

Repton is a thriving village dating back to Anglo Saxon times. The village gardens are all very different, ranging from the very small to very large, several of them have new features for 2019. Askew cottage is a professionally designed garden and has many structural features linked together by curving paths. 16 Askew Grove is new for 2019, it is a small "paradise" garden with a restricted colour palette of carefully selected plants. 10 Chestnut Way is a plantoholic's garden often likened to a tardis - be prepared to be surprised. 22 Pinfold Close is a small garden but is packed full with a special interest in tropical plants. Repton Allotments is a small set of allotments currently undergoing a revival with community area and attractive views across Derbyshire. Woodend Cottage is an organic garden with stunning views from the grass labyrinth. **Not all gardens are open at every opening** - check website for latest details. All gardens have plenty of seats. Some gardens have grass or gravel paths but most areas accessible.

56 NEW RUTLAND

The Green, Curbar Calver, Hope Valley, S32 3YH. Mrs Aileen Cooke, 01433 631768. *Enter Curbar village by Curbar Ln or Bar Rd, at the red telephone box, turn into The Hillock. The Green is second on the R, turn in by the Horse trough. Rutland is 4th on the L.* **Visits by arrangement June to Sept for groups of 10 to 20. Parking on the drive for a max. 5 cars. Adm £3.50, chd free.**

Small cottage garden and rockery on two levels, with borders of seasonally rotating interest , planted with traditional perennials. Wheelchair users can access the lower garden, but not the upper garden or rockery.

57 122 SHEFFIELD ROAD

Glossop, SK13 8QU. Simon Groarke. *1m from Glossop town centre. From Glossop town centre take A57 Snake Pass Sheffield. Cont on A57 3rd exit r'about cont ¾ m. House on R. Park on Shirebrook Dr. From Sheffield take A57 Glossop. After long descent, house on L.* **Sun 12 May (1.30-5). Adm £3.50, chd free. Cream teas.**

A woodland garden with an array of spring bulbs and a host of bluebells in May. Pathways meander through the garden and down to the brook. A summerhouse nestles in the trees taking a view of the woodland area. Nearer the house the garden opens up to perennial borders and lawns. There are plenty of seats to sit and enjoy the garden but please note there are several steps and uneven paths. Bluebell woodland garden with a babbling brook running through. Attractive perennial borders. Camellias, azaleas and rhododendrons are focal points.

58 NEW THE SMITHY

Church Street, Buxton, SK17 6HD. Roddie & Kate MacLean. *350 metres S of Buxton Market Place, in Higher Buxton. Located on access-only Church St, which cuts corner between B5059 & A515. Walk S from Buxton Market Place car park. Take slight R off A515, between Scriveners Bookshop & The Swan Inn.* **Thur 6 June (2-8). Sat 6 July (10-5), also open Otterwood. Mon 8 July (2-8). Adm £3, chd free.**

Architect-designed small oasis of calm in the town centre, subliminally inspired by Geoff Hamilton. Created from a sloping lawn into terraces, following the party walls of former houses on the site, demolished into themselves in 1930s - hence the garden is elevated above Church St. Herbaceous borders, wildlife pond, octagonal greenhouse, raised vegetable beds. Alliums in June; sweet peas in July. Garden with many levels; steps at entrance and around the garden.

59 SMITHY HOUSE

Mansfield Road, Heath, Chesterfield, S44 5SB. Christine & Michael Hasty, 01246850361, c.hasty@sky.com. *5m SE of Chesterfield and 1m from J29 M1. From Chesterfield take A617 for 2m, take B6039 through Temple Normanton and follow signs for Heath. From M1 take A6175 signed Clay Cross .After 400 metres turn R into Heath.* **Sat 6 July (11-5). Adm £4, chd free. Cream teas. Visits also by arrangement June to Aug for groups of 10+.**

Set among mature trees is a one acre cottage garden. A broad gravel path takes you past a formal herb garden, patio, koi pond and pergola, before sweeping lawns lead you through colour themed herbaceous borders past a large wildlife pond overlooked by a deck and summerhouse to a vegetable parterre . Seating areas allow you to enjoy colourful containers, scented rose arbour and the sound of water.

GROUP OPENING

60 STANTON IN PEAK GARDENS

Stanton-In-The-Peak, Matlock, DE4 2LR. *At the top of the hill in Stanton in Peak, on the rd to Birchover. Stanton in Peak is 5m south of Bakewell. Turn off the A6 at Rowsley, or at the B5056 & follow signs up the hill.* **Sat 13, Sun 14 July (1-5). Combined adm £4, chd free. Home-made teas at 2 Haddon View. Pop-up 'pub' serving draught local beer at Woodend.**

10 Chestnut Way

2 HADDON VIEW
Steve Tompkins.

HARE HATCH COTTAGE
Bill Chandler.

WOODEND COTTAGE
Will Chandler.

Stanton in Peak is a hillside, stone village with glorious views, and is a Conservation Area in the Peak District National Park. Three gardens are open. Steve's garden at 2 Haddon View is at the top of the village and is 1/10th acre crammed with plants. Follow the winding path up the garden with a few steps. There are cacti flowering in the greenhouse, lots of patio pots, herbaceous borders, three wildlife ponds with red, pink and white water lilies, a koi pond, rhododendrons and a summerhouse. Tea and homemade cakes served. Just down the hill is Woodend where Will has constructed charming roadside follies on a strip of raised land along the road. The hidden, rear garden has diverse planting, and an extended vegetable plot. All with breath-taking views. A pop-up 'pub' will have draught beer from a local brewery. Nearby is Hare Hatch where Bill's garden wraps around the cottage. This is carefully designed to get the best of every planting opportunity, with a little bit of everything!

---

61 ◆ THORNBRIDGE HALL GARDENS

Ashford in the Water, DE45 1NZ. Jim & Emma Harrison, 01629 640617, gardeners@thornbridgehall.co.uk, www.thornbridgehall.co.uk. *2m NW of Bakewell. From Bakewell take A6, signed Buxton. After 2m, R onto A6020. ½m turn L, signed Thornbridge Hall.* **For NGS: Tue 21 May (9-5). Adm £7, chd free. Light refreshments.** For other opening times and information, please phone, email or visit garden website.
A stunning C19, 12 acre garden, set in the heart of the Peak District overlooking rolling Derbyshire countryside. Designed to create a vision of 1000 shades of green, the garden has many distinct areas. These incl koi lake and water garden, Italian garden with statuary, grottos and temples, 100ft herbaceous border, kitchen garden, scented terrace, hot border and refurbished glasshouses. Contains statuary from Clumber Park, Sydnope Hall and Chatsworth. Tea, coffee, sandwiches and cakes available. Gravel paths, steep slopes, steps.

62 TILFORD HOUSE

Hognaston, Ashbourne, DE6 1PW. Mr & Mrs P R Gardner, 01335 372001, petergardner532@btinternet.com. *5m NE of Ashbourne. A517 Belper to Ashbourne. At Hulland Ward follow signs to Hognaston. Downhill (2m) to bridge. Roadside parking 100 metres.* **Sun 26 May (1-5). Adm £4, chd free. Home-made teas. Visits also by arrangement May to July for groups of 10+.**
A 1½ acre streamside English country garden. Woodland, wildlife areas, alpine beds and ponds lie alongside colourful seasonal planting. Fruit cage and raised beds for vegetables. New beds and borders continually under development in this plantsman's garden. Sit and relax with tea and cake whilst listening to the continuous sounds of the birds.

63 ◆ TISSINGTON HALL

Tissington, Ashbourne, DE6 1RA. Sir Richard & Lady FitzHerbert, 01335 352200, tisshall@dircon.co.uk, www.tissingtonhall.co.uk. *4m N of Ashbourne. E of A515 on Ashbourne to Buxton Rd in centre of the beautiful Estate Village of Tissington.* **For NGS: Mon 27 May, Mon 26 Aug (12-3). Adm £6, chd free. Home-made teas at Herbert's Fine English Tearooms.** For other opening times and information, please phone, email or visit garden website.
Large garden celebrating over 75yrs in the NGS, with stunning rose garden on west terrace, herbaceous borders and 5 acres of grounds. Refreshments available at the award winning Herberts Fine English Tearooms in village (Tel 01335 350501). Wheelchair access advice from ticket seller.

64 TREETOPS HOSPICE CARE

Derby Road, Risley, Derby, DE72 3SS. Treetops Hospice Care, www.treetopshospice.org.uk. *On main rd, B5010 in centre of Risley village. From J25 M1 take rd signed to Risley. Turn L at T-lights, Treetops Hospice Care on L approx ½m through village. From Borrowash direction Treetops is on R just after church.* **Sat 27 Apr (10.30-3). Adm £3, chd free. Light refreshments.**
Beginning with a modest appeal for spring bulbs, the 12 acre site of woodland and grounds now has thousands of daffodils. It has been developed over the last 10yrs taking into consideration the needs and fundraising activities of the hospice. There is a raised wheelchair walkway to enable guests to access some woodland areas, and a 20 minute circular walk on bark chipped paths and raised walkways. There is a plants and homemade preserves stall.

65 WALTON COTTAGE

Matlock Road, Walton, Chesterfield, S42 7LG. Neil & Julie Brown. *3m from Chesterfield. 6½m from Matlock. On A632 Matlock to Chesterfield main rd. From Chesterfield 1m after junction nr garage with T-lights. From Matlock 1m after B5057 junction.* **Sun 2 June (11-4). Adm £4, chd free. Home-made teas.**
A large garden that has both formal and informal areas, incl woodland, orchard, kitchen garden and sweeping lawns with views over Chesterfield.

66 NEW 27 WASH GREEN

Wirksworth, Matlock, DE4 4FD. Mr & Mrs Paul & Kathy Harvey, 01629822218, pandkharvey@btinternet.com. *⅓m E of Wirksworth centre. From Wirksworth centre, follow B5035 towards Whatstandwell. Cauldwell St leads over railway bridge to Wash Green, 200 metres up steep hill on L. Park in town or uphill from garden entry.* **Sun 12 May, Sun 14 July (1-5). Adm £3.50, chd free. Light refreshments.** Visits also by arrangement Apr to Oct for groups of up to 20.

Secluded 1 acre garden, with outstanding views over Wirksworth and the Ecclesbourne valley. Inner enclosed area has formal knot garden, pergola and lawn surrounded by mixed borders, with paved seating area. The larger part of the garden has an open sweep of grass, large borders, beds, areas of woodland and orchard. Roughly ¼ is a productive fruit and vegetable garden with polytunnel. Drop off at property entry for wheelchair access. The inner garden has flat paths with good views of whole garden.

67 12 WATER LANE

Middleton, Matlock, DE4 4LY. Hildegard Wiesehofer, 07809 883393, wiesehofer@btinternet.com. *Approx 2½m SW of Matlock. 1½m NW of Wirksworth. From Derby: at A6 & B5023 intersection take rd to Wirksworth. R to Middleton. Follow NGS signs. From Ashbourne take Matlock rd & follow signs. Park on main rd. Limited parking in Water Ln.* **Sun 5, Mon 6 May, Sun 25, Mon 26 Aug (11-5). Adm £3.50, chd free. Home-made teas.** Visits also by arrangement May to Aug for groups of 10 to 20.

Small, eclectic hillside garden on different levels, created as a series of rooms over the last 15yrs. Each room has been designed to capture the stunning views over Derbyshire and Nottinghamshire and incl a woodland walk, ponds, eastern and infinity gardens. Glorious views and short distance from High Peak Trail, Middleton Top and Engine House. Very rare specimen of a limestone vaulted ceiling, so we are told.

68 13 WESTFIELD ROAD

Swadlincote, DE11 0BG. Val & Dave Booth, 01283 221167 or 07891 436632, valerie.booth@sky.com. *5m E of Burton-on-Trent, off A511. Take A511 from Burton-on-Trent. Follow signs for Swadlincote. Turn R into Springfield Rd, take 3rd R into Westfield Rd.* **Sun 16 June, Sun 4 Aug (1-5). Adm £3.50, chd free. Home-made teas.** Visits also by arrangement June to Aug for groups of 10 to 30.

A deceptive country-style garden in Swadlincote, a real gem. The garden is on 2 levels of approx ½ acre. Packed herbaceous borders designed for colour. Shrubs, baskets and tubs. Lots of roses. Greenhouses, raised-bed vegetable area, fruit trees and 2 ponds. Free range chicken area. Plenty of seating to relax and take in the wonderful planting from 2 passionate gardeners. (WC).

69 WESTGATE

Combs Road, Combs, Chapel-en-le-Frith, High Peak, SK23 9UP. Maurice & Chris Lomas, 07854 680170, ca-lomas@sky.com. *N of Chapel-en-le-Frith off B5470. Turn L immed before Hanging Gate PH, signed Combs Village. ¾m on L by railway bridge.* **Visits by arrangement May to July for groups of 10+. Adm £3, chd free. Tea.**

Large sloping garden in quiet village with beautiful views. Features incl mixed borders and beds containing many perenials, hosta and heuchera. Large rockery. Vegetable and fruit beds. Wild flower area, grasses and fernery. Natural pond and stream with bog area. 3 formal ponds. Chicken area. Lots of places to sit and enjoy the views.

70 WHARFEDALE

34 Broadway, Duffield, Belper, DE56 4BU. Roger & Sue Roberts, 01332 841905, rogerroberts34@outlook.com, www.garden34.co.uk. *4m N of Derby. Turn onto B5023 to Wirksworth (Broadway) off A6 at T-lights midway between Belper & Derby.* **Visits by arrangement June to Aug for groups of up to 30. Individuals also welcome. Adm £3.50, chd free. Home-made teas.**

Garden design and plant enthusiast with over 500 varieties and rare specimens. Eclectic yet replicable. 12 distinct areas incl naturalistic, shrub and single colour borders. Italian walled garden. Woodland with pond and walkway. Japanese landscape with stream, moon gate and pavilion. Front cottage garden with winter shrubs and mixed planting. Stone, wire and wood sculptures. Fully labelled. Comfortable seating around the garden. 100's of plants for sale. Close to Kedleston Hall and Derwent Valley World Heritage Site.

71 24 WHEELDON AVENUE

Derby, DE22 1HN. Laura Burnett, 01332 384893, lauraburnett@outlook.com. *1m N Derby city centre. Off Kedleston Rd. Limited on street parking. Local bus stop nearby.* **Visits by arrangement June & July. Combined opening with 26 Wheeldon Avenue. Adm £5, chd free. Light refreshments at 24 Wheeldon Avenue.**

Small Victorian garden, with original walling supporting many shrubs and climbers with contrasting colour and texture. Circular lawn surrounded by herbaceous border with main colour scheme of blue, purple, black, yellow and orange tones. This leads to a new re-modelled area, mostly naturalistic, with Japanese influence and a green palette, designed to be a calming influence and peaceful to sit. Wheelchair access to side of property.

72 26 WHEELDON AVENUE

Derby, DE22 1HN. Ian Griffiths, 01332 342204, idhgriffiths@gmail.com. *1m N of Derby. 1m from city centre & approached directly off Kedleston Rd or from A6 Duffield Rd via West Bank Ave. Limited on street parking.* **Visits by arrangement June & July for groups of up to 10. Combined opening with 24 Wheeldon Ave, adm. £5, or individual opening. Adm £3, chd free. Refreshments available for £2.50 pp.**

Tiny Victorian walled garden near to city centre. Lawn and

herbaceous borders with newly expanded old rose collection, lupins, delphiniums and foxgloves. Small terrace with topiary, herb garden and lion fountain. Rose collection. Garden on one level, lawn may be soft if wet.

73 WILD IN THE COUNTRY

Hawkhill Road, Eyam, Hope Valley, S32 5QQ. Mrs Gill Bagshawe, www.wildinthecountryflowers.co.uk. *In Eyam, follow signs to public car park. Located next to Eyam Museum & opp public car park on Hawkhill Rd.* **Sun 28 July (11-4.30). Adm £2.50, chd free.**
A rectangular plot devoted totally to growing flowers and foliage for cutting. Sweet pea, rose, larkspur, cornflower, nigella, ammi. All the florist's favourites can be found here. There is a tea room, a village pub and several cafes in the village to enjoy refreshments.

74 NEW 15 WINDMILL LANE

Ashbourne, DE6 1EY. Mr & Mrs Chris and Jean Ross. *Take A515 (Buxton) from market place, at the top of the hill turn R into Windmill Lane. House is on L, 4 trees down.* **Sun 19 May, Wed 14 Aug (1-5). Adm £3, chd free.**
Small newly-established town garden with all-year interest. Using a limited palette of colours, landscaped borders are packed with shrubs, some unusual perennials and herbaceous plants, together with structures, water feature, fruit & veg areas that make use of limited space. There are several steps. Panoramic views. Limited on-street parking. Paintings by owner on display.

76 WOODEND COTTAGE

134 Main Street, Repton, DE65 6FB. Wendy & Stephen Longden, 01283 703259, wendylongden@btinternet.com. *6m S of Derby. From A38, S of Derby, follow signs to Willington, then Repton. In Repton straight on at r'about through village. Garden is 1m on R.* **Sun 4 Aug (2-5.30). Adm £3, chd free. Home-made teas. Opening with Repton NGS Village Gardens on Mon 27 May. Visits also by arrangement July & Aug for groups of 10 to 30.**
Plant lover's garden with glorious views on a sloping 2½ acre site developed organically for yr-round interest. On lower levels herbaceous borders are arranged informally and connected via lawns, thyme bed, pond and pergolas. Mixed woodland and grassed labyrinth lead naturally into fruit, vegetable and herb potager with meadows beyond. Especially colourful in July and August.
Easy and unusual perennials and grasses for sale. Why not visit St Wystan's Church Repton with its Saxon crypt, as part of your visit? Wheelchair access on lower levels only.

Barton Hall

DEVON

Lundy
Ilfracombe
Combe Martin
Lynton
Morte Point
Woolacombe
Baggy Point
Croyde
Barnstaple or Bideford Bay
Braunton
Muddiford
Barnstaple
Appledore
Westward Ho!
Northam
Bishop's Tawton
Hartland Point
Clovelly
Hartland
Bideford
Great Torrington
South Molton
Chulmleigh
Kilkhampton
Bude
Stratton
Holsworthy
Bude Bay
Winkleigh
Highampton
Hatherleigh
DE
Okehampton
Whiddon Down
Boscastle
Tintagel
Hallworthy
Launceston
Lydford
Moretonhampstead
Camelford
Port Isaac
Trevose Head
Padstow
Wadebridge
Bolventor
Colliford Lake
CORNWALL
Tavistock
Widecombe in the Moor
Dartmeet
Princetown
Gunnislake
Callington
Trenance
Bodmin
Liskeard
Yelverton
Ashburton
Buckfastleigh
Newquay
St Columb Major
Lostwithiel
Saltash
Plymouth
St Germans
St Austell
Goonhavern
Looe
Whitsand Bay
Plympton
Ivybridge
Modbury
Yealmpton
Fowey
Polperro
St Austell Bay
Probus
Truro
Mevagissey
Tregony
Rame Head
Loddiswell
Bigbury-on-Sea
Bigbury Bay
Dodman Point
Penryn
St Mawes
Salcombe
Tamar
Torridge
Taw
Tavy
Dart
Teign
Camel
Fowey

Bridgwater Bay
Lyme Bay
SOMERSET, BRISTOL AREA & S. GLOS
DORSET
VON
Taunton
Exeter
Yeovil
Bridgwater
Torquay
Weymouth
Cheddar
Wells
Shepton Mallet
Glastonbury
Street
Minehead
Porlock
Dunster
Watchet
Williton
Burnham-on-Sea
Highbridge
Wedmore
Tiverton
Cullompton
Honiton
Axminster
Chard
Crewkerne
Bridport
Dorchester
Lyme Regis
Seaton
Sidmouth
Exmouth
Dawlish
Teignmouth
Newton Abbot
Paignton
Brixham
Dartmouth
Totnes
Kingsbridge
Start Bay
Start Point
Bill of Portland
Fortuneswell
0 10 20 kilometres
0 10 miles
© Global Mapping / XYZ Maps

Volunteers

County Organisers
& Central Devon
Edward & Miranda Allhusen
01647 440296
Miranda@allhusen.co.uk

County Treasurer
Julia Tremlett
01392 832671
jandjtremlett@hotmail.com

Publicity
Brian Mackness
01626 356004
brianmackness@clara.co.uk

Cath Pettyfer
01837 89024
cathpettyfer@gmail.com

Barbara Theisen
01395 489612
theisenb@hotmail.com

Paul Vincent 01803 722227
paulvincent46@gmail.com

Booklet Co-ordinator
Edward Allhusen 01647 440296
edward@allhusen.co.uk

Assistant County Organisers

East Devon
Peter Wadeley 01297 631210
wadeley@btinternet.com

Exeter
Jenny Phillips 01392 254076
jennypips25@hotmail.co.uk

Exmoor
Anna Whinney 01598 760217
annawhinney@yahoo.co.uk

North Devon
Jo Hynes 01805 804265
hynesjo@gmail.com

North East Devon
Jill Hall 01884 38812
jill22hall@gmail.com

Plymouth
Maria Ashurst 01752 351396
maria.ashurst@sky.com

South Devon
Sally Vincent 01803 722227
sallyvincent14@gmail.com

Torbay
Gill Treweek 01626 879313
gilltreweek@hotmail.co.uk

West Devon
Alex Meads 01822 615558
ameads2015@outlook.com

Devon is a county of great contrasts in geography and climate, and therefore also in gardening.

The rugged north coast has terraces clinging precariously to hillsides so steep that the faint-hearted would never contemplate making a garden there. But here, and on the rolling hills and deep valleys of Exmoor, despite a constant battle with the elements, National Garden Scheme gardeners create remarkable results by choosing hardy plants that withstand the high winds and salty air.

In the south, in peaceful wooded estuaries and tucked into warm valleys, gardens grow bananas, palms and fruit usually associated with the Mediterranean.

Between these two terrains is a third: Dartmoor, 365 square miles of rugged moorland rising to 2000 feet, presents its own horticultural demands. Typically, here too are many National Garden Scheme gardens.

In idyllic villages scattered throughout this very large county, in gardens large and small, in single manors and in village groups within thriving communities – gardeners pursue their passion.

Below: **Hamblyn's Coombe**

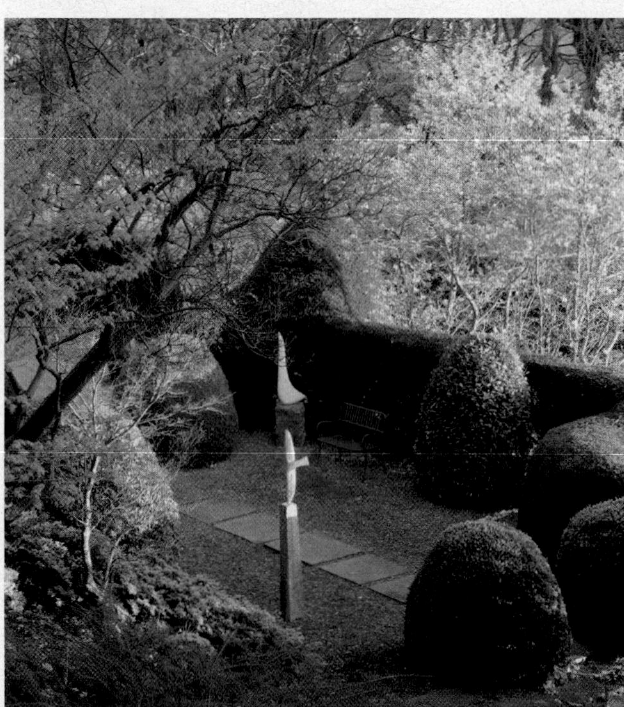

© Val Corbett

OPENING DATES

All entries subject to change. For latest information check **www.ngs.org.uk**

Extended openings are shown at the beginning of the month.

Map locator numbers are shown to the right of each garden name.

February

Every Tuesday to Friday from Tuesday 12th
High Garden 45

Snowdrop Festival

Friday 8th
Higher Cherubeer 47

Friday 15th
Higher Cherubeer 47

Saturday 16th
The Mount, Delamore 73

Sunday 17th
Bickham House 7
The Mount, Delamore 73

Saturday 23rd
Higher Cherubeer 47

March

Every Tuesday to Friday
High Garden 45

Sunday 3rd
East Worlington House 31

Sunday 10th
East Worlington House 31

Sunday 17th
Summers Place 96

Saturday 23rd
Haldon Grange 38

Sunday 24th
Haldon Grange 38

Friday 29th
◆ Holbrook Garden 50

Saturday 30th
Haldon Grange 38
◆ Holbrook Garden 50

Sunday 31st
Bickham House 7
Haldon Grange 38
Heathercombe 44
◆ Holbrook Garden 50

April

Every Tuesday to Friday
High Garden 45

Thursday 4th
◆ Holbrook Garden 50

Friday 5th
◆ Holbrook Garden 50

Saturday 6th
Coombe Meadow 23
Haldon Grange 38
◆ Holbrook Garden 50

Sunday 7th
Coombe Meadow 23
Haldon Grange 38
◆ Holbrook Garden 50
Shapcott Barton Knowstone Estate 82
Summers Place 96
Yonder Hill 108

Friday 12th
Sidbury Manor 85

Saturday 13th
Haldon Grange 38
Monkscroft 70
NEW Samlingstead 81

Sunday 14th
Bickham House 7
Haldon Grange 38
Monkscroft 70
Sidbury Manor 85
Yonder Hill 108

Wednesday 17th
Haldon Grange 38

Friday 19th
Greatcombe 37
◆ Holbrook Garden 50

Saturday 20th
Byes Reach 19
Greatcombe 37
Haldon Grange 38
◆ Holbrook Garden 50

Sunday 21st
Andrew's Corner 3
Byes Reach 19
Greatcombe 37
Haldon Grange 38
◆ Holbrook Garden 50
Kia-Ora Farm & Gardens 59
St Merryn 80
Shapcott Barton Knowstone Estate 82
Wood Barton 107
Yonder Hill 108

Monday 22nd
Byes Reach 19
Greatcombe 37
Haldon Grange 38
Kia-Ora Farm & Gardens 59
Wood Barton 107
Yonder Hill 108

Saturday 27th
Haldon Grange 38

Sunday 28th
Haldon Grange 38
Yonder Hill 108

May

Every day
The Gate House 35

Every Tuesday to Friday
High Garden 45

Friday 3rd
◆ Holbrook Garden 50

Saturday 4th
Coombe Meadow 23
Greatcombe 37
Haldon Grange 38
◆ Holbrook Garden 50
Torview 98

Sunday 5th
Andrew's Corner 3
Chevithorne Barton 22
Coombe Meadow 23
Greatcombe 37
Haldon Grange 38
◆ Holbrook Garden 50
Kia-Ora Farm & Gardens 59
Mothecombe House 72
Musbury Barton 74
Torview 98
Yonder Hill 108

Monday 6th
Andrew's Corner 3
Greatcombe 37
Haldon Grange 38
Kia-Ora Farm & Gardens 59
Musbury Barton 74
Torview 98
Yonder Hill 108

Wednesday 8th
Haldon Grange 38

Saturday 11th
East Woodlands Farmhouse 30
Haldon Grange 38
Little Dorweeke 65
Sheepwash Gardens 83

Sunday 12th
Bickham House 7
East Woodlands Farmhouse 30
NEW Fairway 32
Haldon Grange 38
Heathercombe 44
Higher Ash Farm 46
◆ Hotel Endsleigh 53
Little Dorweeke 65
Sheepwash Gardens 83
Yonder Hill 108

Friday 17th
Moretonhampstead Gardens 71

Saturday 18th
Haldon Grange 38
Kentlands 58
Kilmington (Shute Road) Gardens 60
Moretonhampstead Gardens 71
The Old Vicarage 75
Spitchwick Manor 91

Sunday 19th
NEW Fairway 32
Haldon Grange 38
Heathercombe 44
Higher Ash Farm 46
Kentlands 58
Kia-Ora Farm & Gardens 59
Kilmington (Shute Road) Gardens 60
Moretonhampstead Gardens 71
The Old Vicarage 75
St Merryn 80
Spitchwick Manor 91
Yonder Hill 108

Tuesday 21st
Heathercombe 44

Wednesday 22nd
Haldon Grange 38
Heathercombe 44

Thursday 23rd
Heathercombe 44

Friday 24th
Heathercombe 44

Saturday 25th
Bocombe Mill Cottage 9
Brendon Gardens 13
Bulland Farm 17
◆ Cadhay 21
Haldon Grange 38
Heathercombe 44
Lewis Cottage 62

Sunday 26th
Andrew's Corner 3
Bocombe Mill Cottage 9
Brendon Gardens 13
Bulland Farm 17
◆ Cadhay 21
NEW Fairway 32
Haldon Grange 38
Heathercombe 44
Kia-Ora Farm & Gardens 59
Lewis Cottage 62
Southcombe Barn 90
Yonder Hill 108

Monday 27th
Andrew's Corner 3
Bocombe Mill Cottage 9
◆ Cadhay 21
Haldon Grange 38
Kia-Ora Farm & Gardens 59
Lewis Cottage 62
Southcombe Barn 90
Yonder Hill 108

Tuesday 28th
Heathercombe 44

Wednesday 29th
Heathercombe 44

Thursday 30th
Heathercombe 44

Friday 31st
Heathercombe 44

June

Every day
The Gate House 35

Every evening from Saturday 1st to Sunday 23rd
Goren Farm 36

Every Tuesday to Friday
High Garden 45

Saturday 1st
NEW Dolton Gardens 27
Goren Farm 36
Haldon Grange 38
Heathercombe 44
Higher Orchard Cottage 49
Springfield House 92

Sunday 2nd
32 Allenstyle Drive 2
The Bridge Mill 15
Chevithorne Barton 22
NEW Dolton Gardens 27
NEW Fairway 32
Goren Farm 36
Haldon Grange 38
Hayne 43
Heathercombe 44
Higher Orchard Cottage 49
Yonder Hill 108

Saturday 8th
Abbotskerswell Gardens 1
◆ Fursdon 34
Goren Farm 36
Haldon Grange 38
Riverford Field Kitchen Garden 79
Sidmouth June Gardens 87
NEW Treetops 99

Sunday 9th
Abbotskerswell Gardens 1
Bickham House 7
◆ Docton Mill 26
◆ Fursdon 34
Goren Farm 36
Haldon Grange 38
Kia-Ora Farm & Gardens 59
Middle Well 69
Regency House 78
Sidmouth June Gardens 87
NEW Treetops 99
Yonder Hill 108

Monday 10th
Regency House 78

Tuesday 11th
Regency House 78

Wednesday 12th
Regency House 78

Friday 14th
Bramble Torre 12
◆ Holbrook Garden 50
◆ Marwood Hill Garden 68

Saturday 15th
Bramble Torre 12
Dunley House 28
Goren Farm 36
Halscombe Farm 39
Heathercombe 44
◆ Holbrook Garden 50
Sheepwash Gardens 83
Willand Old Village Gardens & Allotments 106

Sunday 16th
Bramble Torre 12
The Croft 25
Dunley House 28
Goren Farm 36
Halscombe Farm 39
Heathercombe 44
◆ Holbrook Garden 50
St Merryn 80
Sheepwash Gardens 83
Willand Old Village Gardens & Allotments 106
Yonder Hill 108

Tuesday 18th
Heathercombe 44

Wednesday 19th
Heathercombe 44

Thursday 20th
Heathercombe 44

Friday 21st
Heathercombe 44

Saturday 22nd
Bovey Tracey Gardens 10
Corscombe Gardens 24
Harbour Lights 41
Heathercombe 44
Kentisbury Gardens 57
Lewis Cottage 62
Teignmouth Gardens 97
NEW 7 West Clyst Barnyard 103

Sunday 23rd
Bovey Tracey Gardens 10
Corscombe Gardens 24
Harbour Lights 41
Heathercombe 44
Hutswell Farm 54
Kentisbury Gardens 57
Kia-Ora Farm & Gardens 59
Lewis Cottage 62
Shapcott Barton Knowstone Estate 82
Teignmouth Gardens 97
NEW 7 West Clyst Barnyard 103
Yonder Hill 108

Tuesday 25th
Heathercombe 44

Wednesday 26th
Heathercombe 44

Thursday 27th
Heathercombe 44

Friday 28th
Heathercombe 44
Idestone Barton 55

Saturday 29th
Ash Gardens 4
Heathercombe 44
Idestone Barton 55
Musbury Barton 74
Springfield House 92

Sunday 30th
Ash Gardens 4
Heathercombe 44
Musbury Barton 74
Summers Place 96
Upper Gorwell House 100
Yonder Hill 108

July

Every day
The Gate House 35

Every Tuesday to Friday
High Garden 45

Tuesday 2nd
Heathercombe 44

Wednesday 3rd
Heathercombe 44

Thursday 4th
Heathercombe 44

Friday 5th
NEW Bridge House 14
Heathercombe 44
◆ Holbrook Garden 50
Socks Orchard 88

Saturday 6th
NEW East Cornworthy Gardens 29
Heathercombe 44
◆ Holbrook Garden 50
NEW Kentisbeare House 56
NEW Samlingstead 81
Socks Orchard 88

Sunday 7th
NEW East Cornworthy Gardens 29
NEW Fairway 32
Heathercombe 44
◆ Holbrook Garden 50
◆ Hotel Endsleigh 53
NEW Kentisbeare House 56
Kia-Ora Farm & Gardens 59
Socks Orchard 88
Yonder Hill 108

Friday 12th
Shapcott Barton Knowstone Estate 82

Saturday 13th
East Woodlands Farmhouse 30
Shutelake 84

Sunday 14th
Bickham House 7
East Woodlands Farmhouse 30
NEW Fairway 32
Shapcott Barton Knowstone Estate 82
Shutelake 84
Yonder Hill 108

Saturday 20th
Hole's Meadow 52
Lewis Cottage 62
Sheepwash Gardens 83
Squirrels 93
Venn Cross Engine House 101

Sunday 21st
The Croft 25
NEW Fairway 32
Hole Farm 51
Hole's Meadow 52
Kia-Ora Farm & Gardens 59
Lewis Cottage 62
Linden Rise 63
Sheepwash Gardens 83
Squirrels 93
Venn Cross Engine House 101
Yonder Hill 108

Friday 26th
Greatcombe 37

Saturday 27th
NEW Boyton Mill 11
Greatcombe 37
Springfield House 92

Sunday 28th
NEW Boyton Mill 11
NEW Foxhole Community Garden 33
Greatcombe 37
Upper Gorwell House 100
Yonder Hill 108

Tuesday 30th
NEW Foxhole Community Garden 33

Treetops

August

Every day
The Gate House 35

Every Tuesday to Friday
High Garden 45

Sunday 4th
Chevithorne Barton 22
Kia-Ora Farm & Gardens 59
Shapcott Barton Knowstone Estate 82
Yonder Hill 108

Saturday 10th
Sheepwash Gardens 83

Sunday 11th
Bickham House 7
Sheepwash Gardens 83
Yonder Hill 108

Saturday 17th
Moretonhampstead Gardens 71
The Old Vicarage 75

Sunday 18th
The Croft 25
Kia-Ora Farm & Gardens 59
Little Ash Bungalow 64
Moretonhampstead Gardens 71
The Old Vicarage 75
Yonder Hill 108

Thursday 22nd
◆ Holbrook Garden 50

Friday 23rd
◆ Holbrook Garden 50

Saturday 24th
Brendon Gardens 13
◆ Holbrook Garden 50
Lewis Cottage 62
Sidmouth August Gardens 86
Springfield House 92
Venn Cross Engine House 101

Sunday 25th
32 Allenstyle Drive 2
Brendon Gardens 13
◆ Cadhay 21
Kia-Ora Farm & Gardens 59
Lewis Cottage 62
Sidmouth August Gardens 86
Venn Cross Engine House 101
Yonder Hill 108

Monday 26th
◆ Cadhay 21
Kia-Ora Farm & Gardens 59
Lewis Cottage 62
Sidmouth August Gardens 86
Yonder Hill 108

Friday 30th
Prospect House 77

Saturday 31st
Prospect House 77

September

Every day to Saturday 7th
The Gate House 35

Every Tuesday to Friday
High Garden 45

Sunday 1st
32 Allenstyle Drive 2
Chevithorne Barton 22
Prospect House 77
Yonder Hill 108

Thursday 5th
◆ Holbrook Garden 50

Friday 6th
◆ Holbrook Garden 50

Saturday 7th
◆ Holbrook Garden 50
Riverford Field Kitchen Garden 79

Sunday 8th
32 Allenstyle Drive 2
Bickham House 7
Hole Farm 51
Kia-Ora Farm & Gardens 59

Saturday 14th
Sheepwash Gardens 83
◆ Stone Lane Gardens 94

Sunday 15th
32 Allenstyle Drive 2
Higher Cherubeer 47
Kentlands 58
Sheepwash Gardens 83

Saturday 21st
South Wood Farm 89
◆ Stone Lane Gardens 94

Sunday 22nd
South Wood Farm 89

Saturday 28th
Brocton Cottage 16

Sunday 29th
Brocton Cottage 16
Summers Place 96

October

Every Tuesday to Friday
High Garden 45

Sunday 6th
Bickham Cottage 6

Sunday 13th
Regency House 78

Sunday 20th
Andrew's Corner 3

November

Every Tuesday to Friday
High Garden 45

February 2020

Friday 7th
Higher Cherubeer 47

Friday 14th
Higher Cherubeer 47

Sunday 16th
Bickham House 7

Saturday 22nd
Higher Cherubeer 47

By Arrangement

Arrange a personalised garden visit with your club, or group of friends, on a date to suit you. See individual garden entries for full details.

32 Allenstyle Drive 2
Andrew's Corner 3
Avenue Cottage 5
Bickham Cottage 6
Bickham House 7
Bocombe Mill Cottage 9
Breach, Kilmington (Shute Road) Gardens 60
Brendon Gardens 13
Brendon House, Brendon Gardens 13
The Bridge Mill 15
Byes Reach 19
NEW Bystock Stables 20
Chevithorne Barton 22
Coombe Meadow 23
The Croft 25
1 Deercombe Cottages, Brendon Gardens 13
The Gate House 35
Goren Farm 36
Haldon Grange 38
Hall Farm, Brendon Gardens 13
Hamblyn's Coombe 40
Harbour Lights 41
The Haven 42
Heathercombe 44
Higher Ash Farm 46
Higher Cherubeer 47
Higher Cullaford 48
Higher Orchard Cottage 49
Higher Tippacott Farm, Brendon Gardens 13
Hole's Meadow 52
Hutswell Farm 54
Kentlands 58
Lee Ford 61
Lewis Cottage 62
Linden Rise 63
Little Ash Bungalow 64
Little Webbery 66
Middle Well 69
Musselbrook Cottage Garden, Sheepwash Gardens 83
The Old Vicarage 75
Regency House 78
St Merryn 80
NEW Samlingstead 81
Shapcott Barton Knowstone Estate 82
Shutelake 84
Socks Orchard 88
South Wood Farm 89
Squirrels 93
Stonelands House 95
Summers Place 96
Sutton Mead, Moretonhampstead Gardens 71
Venn Cross Engine House 101
The Walled Garden, Lindridge 102
Whitstone Bluebells 104
Whitstone Farm 105
Wood Barton 107
Yonder Hill 108

Hotel Endsleigh

THE GARDENS

GROUP OPENING

1 ABBOTSKERSWELL GARDENS

Abbotskerswell, TQ12 5PN. *2m SW of Newton Abbot town centre. A381 Newton Abbot/Totnes rd. Sharp L turn from NA, R from Totnes. Field parking at Fairfield. Maps available at all gardens and at Church House.* **Sat 8, Sun 9 June (1-5). Combined adm £6, chd free. Home-made teas at Church House. Teas available from 2pm. Maps and tickets from 1pm.**

ABBOTSFORD
Wendy & Phil Grierson.

ABBOTSKERSWELL ALLOTMENTS
Margaret Crompton.

1 ABBOTSWELL COTTAGES
Jane Taylor.

BRIAR COTTAGE
Peggy & David Munden.

FAIRFIELD
Brian Mackness.

4 LABURNUM TERRACE
Ms Mary Down.

7 WILTON WAY
Mr & Mrs Cindy & Vernon Stunt.

10 WILTON WAY
Mrs Margaret Crompton.

16 WILTON WAY
Katy & Chris Yates.

For 2019, Abbotskerswell offers 8 gardens plus the village allotments. Ranging from very small to large they offer a wide range of planting styles and innovative landscaping. Cottage gardens, terracing, wild flower areas, a wild garden and specialist plants. Changes to some gardens from 2018. Ideas for every type and size of garden. Visitors are welcome to picnic in the field or arboretum at Fairfield. Sales of plants, garden produce, jams and chutneys and other creative crafts. Teas! Disabled access to 3 gardens.

2 32 ALLENSTYLE DRIVE

Yelland, Barnstaple, EX31 3DZ. Steve & Dawn Morgan, 01271 861433, fourhungrycats@aol.com, www.devonsubtropicalgarden.co.uk. *5m W of Barnstaple. From Barnstaple take B3233 towards Instow. Through Bickington & Fremington. L at Yelland sign into Allenstyle Rd. 1st R into Allenstyle Dr. Light blue bungalow. From Bideford go past Instow on B3233.* **Sun 2 June (11.30-5). Every Sun 25 Aug to 15 Sept (11.30-5). Adm £4, chd free. Light refreshments.** Visits also by arrangement Aug & Sept for groups of up to 30.

Wander through prairie and South African/Mediterranean inspired plantings to find the gorgeous scents, huge leaves and exotic flowers of the jungle areas and greenhouses. Our 50 x 100 ft garden focuses on ginger lilies, big leaved monsters, brugmansias, bananas and passion flowers (from the hardy to the very tender and scented), with a sneak preview and cottage garden vibe during our June opening. Wheelchair access is limited due to narrow paths and gravelled areas.

3 ANDREW'S CORNER

Skaigh Lane, Belstone, EX20 1RD. Robin & Edwina Hill, 01837 840332, edwinarobinhill@outlook.com, www.andrewscorner.garden. *3m E of Okehampton. Signed to Belstone from A30. In village turn L, signed Skaigh. Follow NGS signs. Garden approx ½m on R. Visitors may be dropped off at house, parking in nearby field.* **Sun 21 Apr, Sun 5, Mon 6, Sun 26, Mon 27 May, Sun 20 Oct (2-5). Adm £5, chd free. Home-made teas.** Visits also by arrangement Feb to Oct.

Well established, wildlife friendly, well labelled plantsman's garden in stunning high moorland setting. Variety of garden habitats incl woodland areas and pond; wide range of unusual trees, shrubs, herbaceous plants for yr-round effect with blue poppies, rhododendrons, bulbs and maples; spectacular autumn colour. Family friendly, with quiz sheet, fairy doors, playhouse, fruit, vegetables and chickens. Wheelchair access difficult when wet.

GROUP OPENING

4 ASH GARDENS

Ash, Dartmouth, TQ6 0LR. *2m SW of Dartmouth. Leave A381 Totnes to Kingsbridge rd in Halwell taking A3122 for Dartmouth. Just before Sportsmans Arms turn R At T-junction turn R then 1st L. At Xrds turn R then parking 1st L.* **Sat 29, Sun 30 June (2-5). Combined adm £5, chd free. Tea.**

BAY TREE COTTAGE
Jenny Goffe.

HIGHER ASH FARM
Mr Michael Gribbin & Mrs Jennifer Barwell.
(See separate entry)

2 delightful gardens in the tiny hamlet of Ash. The beautiful intimate little garden at Bay Tree Cottage sits in a quiet secluded valley with wonderful sunlit views across open farmland. The perfect curved lawn leads the eye to small rooms filled with surprise and clever planting. Ornamental trees punctuate the boundary and a tiny vegetable garden of raised beds overflows with produce. Higher Ash Farm has 2½ acres of established and developing garden situated around farmhouse and barn conversions. Large kitchen garden terraced into the hillside, orchard, pond, stream with bog planting and feature borders around the house offering seasonal and yr-round interest.

5 AVENUE COTTAGE

Ashprington, Totnes, TQ9 7UT. Mr Richard Pitts & Mr David Sykes, 01803 732769, richard.pitts@btinternet.com, www.avenuecottage.com. *3m SW of Totnes. A381 Totnes to Kingsbridge for 1m; L for Ashprington, into village then L by PH. Garden ¼m on R after Sharpham Estate sign.* **Visits by arrangement Mar to Oct for groups of up to 20. Adm £4, chd free. Home-made teas by arrangement.**

11 acres of mature and young trees and shrubs. Once part of an C18 landscape, the neglected garden has been cleared and replanted over the last 30 yrs. Good views of Sharpham House and R Dart. Azaleas and hydrangeas are a feature.

6 BICKHAM COTTAGE

Kenn, Exeter, EX6 7XL. Steve Eyre, 01392 833964, bickham@live.co.uk. *6m S of Exeter. 1m off A38. Leave A38 at Kennford Services, follow signs to Kenn. 1st R in village, follow lane for ¾m to end of no through rd.* **Sun 6 Oct (2-5). Adm £5, chd free.** Visits also by arrangement Sept to Nov.

Small cottage garden divided into separate areas by old stone walls and hedge banks. Front garden with mainly South African bulbs and plants. Lawn surrounded by borders with agapanthus, eucomis, crocosmia, diorama etc. Stream garden with primulas. Pond with large Koi carp. Glasshouses with National Collection of Nerine sarniensis and cultivars, 3500 pots with in excess of 450 varieties. Visitors are also welcome to wander around Bickham House gardens.

7 BICKHAM HOUSE

Kenn, Exeter, EX6 7XL. Julia Tremlett, 01392 832671, jandjtremlett@hotmail.com. *6m S of Exeter, 1m off A38. Leave A38 at Kennford Services, follow signs to Kenn, 1st R in village, follow lane for ¾m to end of no through rd.* **Suns 17 Feb; 31 Mar; 14 Apr; 12 May; 9 June; 14 July; 11 Aug; 8 Sept (2-5). Adm £5, chd free. Home-made teas. 2020: Sun 16 Feb.** Visits also by arrangement Apr to Sept.

7 acres with borders, mature trees and shrubs. Banks of snowdrops and small named collection at Bickham Cottage. Formal parterre with lily pond. Walled garden with colourful profusion of vegetables and flowers. Palm tree avenue leading to millennium summerhouse. Late summer colour with dahlias, crocosmia, agapanthus etc. Cactus and succulent greenhouse. Pelargonium collection. New gravel beds. Lake. WC, disabled access.

8 ◆ BLACKPOOL GARDENS

Dartmouth, TQ6 0RG. Sir Geoffrey Newman, 01803 771801, beach@blackpoolsands.co.uk, www.blackpoolsands.co.uk. *3m SW of Dartmouth. From Dartmouth follow brown signs to Blackpool Sands on A379. Entry tickets, parking, toilets and refreshments available at Blackpool Sands. Sorry, no dogs permitted.*

Carefully restored C19 subtropical plantsman's garden with collection of mature and newly planted tender and unusual trees, shrubs and carpet of spring flowers. Paths and steps lead gradually uphill and above the Captain's seat offering fine coastal views. Recent plantings follow the S hemisphere theme with callistemons, pittosporums, acacias and buddlejas. Gardens open 1st Apr - 30th Sept (10-4pm) weather permitting. Adm £4, chd free. Grp visits by arrangement.

9 BOCOMBE MILL COTTAGE

Bocombe, Parkham, Bideford, EX39 5PH. Mr Chris Butler & Mr David Burrows, 01237 451293, www.bocombe.co.uk. *6m E of Clovelly, 9m SW of Bideford. From A39 just outside Horns Cross village, turn to Foxdown. At Xrds follow signs for parking.* **Sat 25, Sun 26, Mon 27 May (12-5). Adm £5, chd £1. Home-made teas. Ploughmans lunches & traditional home-made cakes & cream teas.** Visits also by arrangement Apr to July for groups of 10+. Ploughmans Lunches & Cream Teas.

12 flower gardens and many unique features that punctuate an undulating landscape of 5 acres in a wooded valley. Streams, 3 bog gardens - raised walkway, 12 water features, 3 large pools. White pergola. Hillside orchard. Soft fruit and kitchen gardens. Wild meadow, a wildlife haven. Short flower garden walk or longer circular walk, boots suggested. Garden Plan incl 80+ specimen trees. All organic. Real hermit in the hermitage with adjoining shell grotto. Goats on

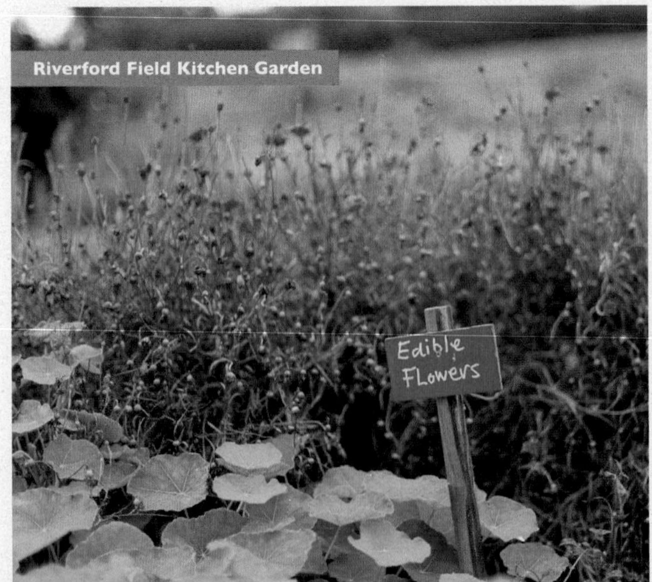

Riverford Field Kitchen Garden

hillside. Japanese pavilion. Garden kaleidoscope. New gated stone archway to hermitage walk. All organic.

GROUP OPENING

10 BOVEY TRACEY GARDENS

Bovey Tracey, TQ13 9NA. *6m N of Newton Abbot. Gateway to Dartmoor. Take A382 to Bovey Tracey. Car parking at town car parks and on some rds.* **Sat 22, Sun 23 June (1.30-5.30). Combined adm £6, chd free. Home-made teas at Gleam Tor.**

5 BRIDGE COTTAGES
TQ13 9DR. Cath Valentine.

THE BROOK
TQ13 9LL. Haytor Rd, Mrs Joy Dixon.

GLEAM TOR
TQ13 9DH. Gillian & Colin Liddy.

GREEN HEDGES
TQ13 9LZ. Alan & Linda Jackson.

2 REDWOODS
TQ13 9YG. Mrs Julia Mooney.

Bovey Tracey is a pretty cob and granite built town nestling in Dartmoor foothills. The Brook: sweeping lawns, mature trees, colourful borders, vegetables and soft fruit. Bridge Cottage: structured but quirky garden on historic pottery site; varied planting. Gleam Tor: long colourful herbaceous border, white garden, wild flower meadow, prairie planting. Green Hedges: mature garden with well established colourful borders incl shrubs, bulbs, perennials, vegetables, soft fruit. Redwoods: mature trees, unusual fernery, moorland leat. Acid loving spring and summer shrubs. Most gardens have distant views, allow dogs and sell plants. Limited wheelchair access at some gardens.

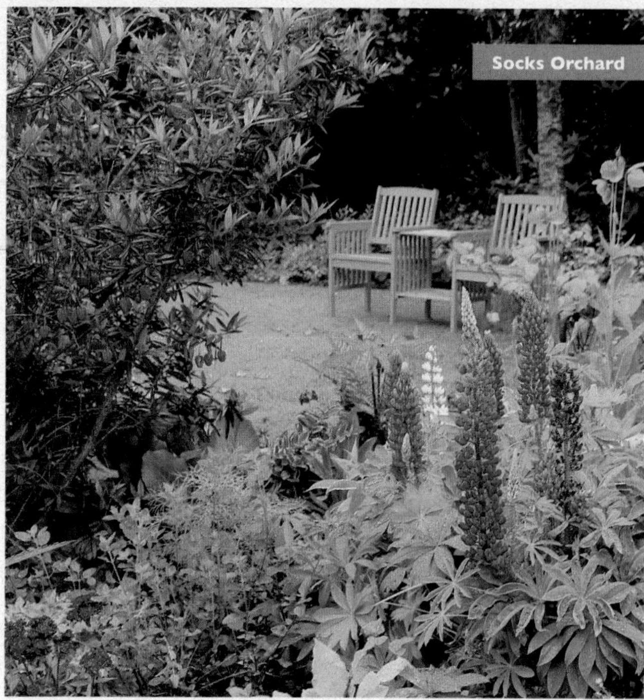
Socks Orchard

11 NEW BOYTON MILL

Boyton, Launceston, PL15 9RG. Paul & Maureen Sims, 01566 778930, paulsims@boytonmill.com, www.boytonmill.com. *On Devon/ Cornwall border. From Holsworthy take A388 S for 7m to Chapman's well turn R towards Boyton, from Launceston take A388 N for 7m turn L at Chapman's well. Turn into Boyton Mill at Boyton Bridge.* **Sat 27, Sun 28 July (10.30-5.30). Adm £3, chd free. Home-made teas. Selection of cakes, scones and biscuits, also cream teas.**
Exotic themed garden in semi-formal setting surrounding C15 water mill and picturesque miller's house. The garden is home to collections of unusual and exotic plants interspersed with formal elements. Grass theatre, acers and elevated woodland walk leading to viewing platform with views across the Tamar to Cornwall. Lengthy meadow walks along river. 800 metres of fishing in River Tamar at Boyton Mill. Partial wheelchair access from car park to lower parts of garden.

12 BRAMBLE TORRE

Dittisham, nr Dartmouth, TQ6 0HZ. Paul & Sally Vincent, www.rainingsideways.com. *¾m from Dittisham. Leave A3122 at Sportsman's Arms. Drop down into village, at Red Lion turn L to Cornworthy. Continue ¾m, garden straight ahead.* **Fri 14, Sat 15, Sun 16 June (2-6). Adm £5, chd free. Cream teas.**
Set in 20 acres of farmland, the 3 acre garden follows a rambling stream through a steep valley: lily pond, herbaceous borders, camellias, shrubs and roses dominated by huge embothrium glowing scarlet in late spring against a sometimes blue sky! A formal herb and vegetable garden runs alongside the stream while chickens scratch in an orchard of Ditsum plums and cider apples. Well behaved dogs on leads welcome. Limited wheelchair access, parts of garden very steep and uneven. Tea area with wheelchair access and excellent garden view.

GROUP OPENING

13 BRENDON GARDENS

Brendon, Lynton, EX35 6PU. 01598 741343, lalindevon@yahoo.co.uk. *1m S of A39 North Devon coast rd between Porlock and Lynton.* **Sat 25, Sun 26 May, Sat 24, Sun 25 Aug (12-5). Combined adm £5, chd free. Light refreshments. Higher Tippacott Farm serves light lunches, home-made cakes & cream teas. W.C. Brendon House serves tea & home-made cakes. WC.** Visits also by arrangement May to Sept.

BRENDON HOUSE
Pat Young & Martin Longhurst, 01598 741343.
Visits also by arrangement May to Sept.

1 DEERCOMBE COTTAGES
Valerie & Stephen Exley, 01598 741343, lalindevon@yahoo.co.uk.
Visits also by arrangement May to Sept.

HALL FARM
Karen & Nick Wall, 01598 741343.
Visits also by arrangement May to Sept.

HIGHER TIPPACOTT FARM
Angela & Malcolm Percival, 01598 741343, lalindevon@yahoo.co.uk.
Visits also by arrangement May to Sept.

Stunning part of Exmoor National Park. All gardens have views. Excellent walking along river between Brendon and Rockford and between gardens; map available online. Brendon Hse: C18 in idyllic village location. Established front garden, evolving kitchen garden, greenhouse. Emphasis on recycling and gardening in harmony with wildlife. 1 Deercombe Cottages: delightful small garden in steeply wooded valley, created using ditched stone to provide a variety of levels to display planting rich in contrasting foliage and variety of perennials. Hall Farm: C16 longhouse set in 2 acres of tranquil mature gardens, enclosed then opening out into lake area with wild area beyond. Rheas, chickens, rare-breed cattle and black bees feature. Higher Tippacott Farm: 950ft altitude on moor. Garden overlooking own idyllic valley with stream and pond. Sunny levels of planting and lawns. Bees. Organic. Plants, produce, books and bric-a-brac for sale.

14 NEW BRIDGE HOUSE

2 Church Street, Dawlish, EX7 9AU. Annette Everett. *From A379 through Dawlish follow signs to Hospital, with Hosp on L carry on to T junction, turn R, Bridge House on corner of Church St opp Swan pub.* **Fri 5 July (10.30-2). Adm £4.50, chd free. Home-made teas.**
Bridge House enjoys a quiet secluded 3 acre garden at the edge of Dawlish. The beautifully landscaped garden has wide lawns and deep colourful herbaceous borders on one side of the trout stream which runs through the grounds into Dawlish Water. An ornate bridge takes visitors to the other side where many mature trees and secluded seating areas can be found. Wheelchair access to most areas.

15 THE BRIDGE MILL

Mill Rd, Bridgerule, Holsworthy, EX22 7EL. Rosie & Alan Beat, 01288 381341, rosie@thebridgemill.org.uk, www.thebridgemill.org.uk. *In Bridgerule village on R Tamar between Bude and Holsworthy. Between the chapel by river bridge and church at top of hill. Garden is at bottom of hill opp Short and Abbott agricultural engineers. See website for detailed directions.* **Sun 2 June (11-5). Adm £4, chd free. Home-made teas. Refreshments in garden if fine or in stable if wet! Plenty of dry seating.** Visits also by arrangement May & June for groups of 20+.
One acre organic gardens around mill house and restored working water mill. Small cottage garden; herb garden with medicinal and dye plants; productive fruit and vegetable garden, and wild woodland and water garden by mill. 16 acre smallholding: lake and riverside walks, wildflower meadows, friendly livestock, woodland sculptures, local crafts. Exhibition of embroideries by Linda Chilton. The historic water mill was restored to working order in April 2012 and in 2017 was awarded a plaque by the Society for the Protection of Ancient Buildings. Mill and smallholding also open for free educational visits throughout yr to school groups. Details on website. Wheelchair access to some of gardens. WC with access for wheelchairs.

16 BROCTON COTTAGE

Pear Tree, Ashburton, Newton Abbot, TQ13 7QZ. Mrs Naomi Hindley. *¼m from A38. From A38 take Ashburton Peartree junction. Turn R towards Princetown, then 1st L towards Buckfastleigh. Park on road or at Dartmoor Lodge Hotel (lunches available). Short walk to garden entrance.* **Sat 28, Sun 29 Sept (2-5). Adm £4, chd free. Home-made teas. Lunches and refreshments also available at Dartmoor Lodge Hotel.**
1.3 acres recovered from neglect, combining established planting with newly developed areas. New orchard, woodland, ponds and productive area linked to established herbaceous borders and shrubberies. The woodland area being developed was inspired by the winter garden at Anglesea Abbey. Latest project is a new cutting garden. Views over Devon countryside. Dogs on leads only please. Gravelled drive but there is wheelchair access to patio area. Garden can be explored without using steps.

17 BULLAND FARM

Ashburton, Newton Abbot, TQ13 7NG. S & L Middleton. *1m from A38. Exit A38 at Peartree Cross near Ashburton and follow signs directing initially towards Landscove. Turning R halfway up hill, follow NGS signs. From Totnes, NGS signs will direct you from A384.* **Sat 25, Sun 26 May (11-4). Adm £5, chd free. Home-made teas.**
Once an old cider orchard that had grown wild, over the last 6 yrs it has been transformed into a

beautiful and productive garden. Set over 8 acres, it makes the most of wonderful views over rolling rural countryside. Designed with wildlife in mind it encompasses formal areas, prairie planting, boardwalk water garden, woodland trail, wildflower meadows and terraced vegetable garden. Steps and steep slopes although the central path of the garden is suitable for wheelchairs which allows great views over the countryside and garden.

18 ◆ BURROW FARM GARDENS

Dalwood, Axminster, EX13 7ET. Mary & John Benger, www.burrowfarmgardens.co.uk. *3½m W of Axminster. From A35 turn N at Taunton Xrds then follow brown signs.* **For information, please visit garden website.**

Beautiful 13 acre garden with unusual trees, shrubs and herbaceous plants. Traditional summerhouse looks towards lake and ancient oak woodland with rhododendrons and azaleas. Early spring interest and superb autumn colour. The more formal Millennium garden features a rill. Anniversary garden featuring late summer perennials and grasses. A photographer's dream. Open 1st April – 31 Oct (10 – 6). Adm £8. Café and gift shop. Various events incl spring and summer plant fair and open air theatre held at garden each yr. Visit events page on Burrow Farm Gardens website for more details.

19 BYES REACH

26 Coulsdon Rd, Sidmouth, EX10 9JP. Lynette Talbot & Peter Endersby, 01395 578081, latalbot01@gmail.com. *From Exeter on A3052 11m. R at Sidford T-lights. In ¾m turn L into Coulsdon Rd gardens, a short walk apart.* **Sat 20, Sun 21, Mon 22 Apr (1.30-5.30). Adm £4, chd free. Home-made teas. Gluten Free cakes available. Opening with Sidmouth June Gardens on Sat 8, Sun 9 June and Sidmouth August Gardens on Sat 24, Sun 25, Mon 26 Aug. Visits also by arrangement for groups of 5 to 20.**

Edible garden of ¼ acre. Potager-style, raised beds, espalier fruit archway. Garden designed for those with mobility problems. Colour-themed herbaceous borders, perennials, herbs, ferns, hostas. Pond, rill, rockeries, greenhouse, and studio. Backing onto The Byes nature reserve and R Sid, offering an opportunity for a short walk from the garden gate. Long fruit covered archway, use of recycled materials and pond and rill. Sculptured fountain. Views into Livonia Field.

20 NEW BYSTOCK STABLES

St. Johns Road, Exmouth, EX8 5EG. Susan & George Boyd, 01395 223272, geoboyd@btinternet.com. *Best accessed off B3179 from Woodbury to Budleigh Salterton, turn into St Johns Rd then 400yds down road turn R into lane alongside St Johns Lodge and Owls Cottage, Stables 100yds at end of lane.* **Visits by arrangement June & July for groups of up to 10. Adm £4, chd free. Home-made teas.**

Garden is accessed from courtyard through pergola onto paved path around lawn bordered by flowers, grasses and variety of interesting shrubs. Path leads through small shady area with various trees and ferns then via shelter onto deck that circles wildlife pond and leads to cabin. Remainder of garden is a sloping meadow and grassy bank that surrounds the property. Garden is designed with wheelchair users in mind, no steps, level courtyard area, ramps around pond, paving around garden.

21 ◆ CADHAY

Ottery St Mary, EX11 1QT. Rupert Thistlethwayte, 01404 813511, jayne@cadhay.org.uk, www.cadhay.org.uk. *1m NW of Ottery St Mary. On B3176 between Ottery St Mary and Fairmile. From E exit A30 at Iron Bridge. From W exit A30 at Patteson's Cross, follow brown signs for Cadhay.* **For NGS: Sat 25, Sun 26, Mon 27 May, Sun 25, Mon 26 Aug (2-5). Adm £4, chd £1. Our tea room serves a range of home-made cakes and cream teas. For other opening times and information, please phone, email or visit garden website.**

Tranquil 2 acre setting for Tudor manor house. 2 medieval fish ponds surrounded by rhododendrons, gunnera, hostas and flag iris. Roses, clematis, lilies and hellebores surround walled water garden. 120ft herbaceous border walk informally planted with cottage garden perennials and annuals. Walled kitchen gardens have been turned into allotments and old apple store is now tea room. Gravel paths.

22 CHEVITHORNE BARTON

Chevithorne, Tiverton, EX16 7QB. Chris McDonald (Head Gardener), 07920 038083, chris.mcdonald007@gmail.com, oaksofchevithornebarton.com. *3m NE of Tiverton. Follow yellow signs from A361, A396 or Sampford Peverell.* **Suns 5 May; 2 June; 4 Aug; 1 Sept (1.30-5.30). Adm £5, chd free. Cream teas. Home made cakes. Tea area undercover. Visits also by arrangement for groups of up to 30.**

Newly planted areas complement walled garden, summer borders and woodland of rare trees and shrubs. In spring, garden features a large collection of magnolias, camellias, and rhododendrons. Home to National Collection of Quercus (Oaks) comprising over 440 different taxa. From time to time within the gardens are a flock of Jacob sheep and rare breed woodland pigs.

NPC

We help ordinary people open the gates to their extraordinary private gardens to raise impressive amounts of money through admissions, teas and slices of cake!

23 COOMBE MEADOW

Ashburton, Newton Abbot, TQ13 7HU. Angela Patterson & Mike Walker, 07775 627237, coombemeadow2016@gmail.com. *Opp Waterleat. Enter Ashburton town centre, turn onto North St. After Victoria Inn, bear R at junction, do not cross bridge to Buckland in the Moor. Follow signs.* **Sat 6, Sun 7 Apr, Sat 4, Sun 5 May (11-4). Adm £4, chd £2. Light refreshments. Tea, coffee, sandwiches and cake.** Visits also by arrangement Apr to Sept for groups of 5 to 10. Limited parking.

This lost garden, by a beautiful Dartmoor stream was overgrown and neglected. Since 2016 its mature magnolias, camellias, azaleas and other trees have been rescued. Paths and ponds cleared, archaeology preserved, borders created, bridges and terraces repaired and over 5000 bulbs planted. The meadows contain wild daffodils and bluebells, so in spring the garden is a kaleidoscope of colour. Wheelchair access limited to front and rear patios.

GROUP OPENING

24 CORSCOMBE GARDENS

Okehampton, EX20 1SD. *1m N of Dartmoor and the pretty village of Belstone. From A30 take slip rd to Okehampton. L towards Sticklepath. Past BP garage then next L to Sampford Courtenay. Over A30. At Crossways Jct take lane to Corscombe. Down hill ½m. EX20 1SD for SatNav.* **Sat 22, Sun 23 June (1-5). Combined adm £5, chd free. Home-made teas at Corscombe Barn.**

CORSCOMBE BARN
Jackie & Phil Hammans.

THE OLD COTTAGE
Mollie & Peter Fillingham.

2 very different gardens in delightful small hamlet. The Old Cottage sits, looking down on garden and slightly elevated, in one corner of ½ acre. 2 small ponds, fed by stream bordered with colourful herbaceous planting during spring, summer and autumn, and lavender walk below rose, clematis and honeysuckle arches. Behind the pretty, open-fronted stone built summerhouse, circled by various dogwoods, giving welcome winter colour, lies a well managed woodland area concentrating on the variation of colour texture and shape of the foliage. Corscombe Barn: a little bit of everything within ¾ acre. Pretty cottage garden with stone and sleeper patio and steps; orchard with a mix of trees and wildflower area; small spinney left partially wild with mix of planting; wildlife pond; bog garden and stream bordered with gunnera, skunk cabbage, astilbe; kitchen garden with raised beds and beautiful Victorian style greenhouse; lawn with summerhouse. Dogs on leads only at Corscombe Barn. Some parking available at both properties, also in adjoining field (weather permitting) and at Lower Corscombe Farm by kind permission of owners. Clearly signed. Wheelchair access only if dry. Some steps and gravel areas in both gardens.

Bulland Farm

25 THE CROFT

Yarnscombe, Barnstaple, EX31 3LW. Sam & Margaret Jewell, 01769 560535. *8m S of Barnstaple, 10m SE of Bideford, 12m W of South Molton, 4m NE of Torrington. From A377, turn W opp Chapelton railway stn. Follow Yarnscombe signs for 3m. From B3232, ¼m N of Huntshaw Cross TV mast, turn E and follow Yarnscombe signs for 2m. Parking in village hall car park.* **Sun 16 June, Sun 21 July, Sun**

18 Aug (2-6). Adm £4, chd free. Home-made teas. Visits also by arrangement June to Aug for groups of 5+. Must be arranged at least 7 days in advance. Donation to North Devon Animal Ambulance.
1 acre plantswoman's garden featuring exotic Japanese garden with tea house, koi carp pond and cascading stream, tropical garden with exotic shrubs and perennials, herbaceous borders with unusual plants and shrubs, bog garden with collection of irises, astilbes and moisture-loving plants, duck pond. Exotic borders, new beds around duck pond and bog area, large collection of rare and unusual plants.

26 ◆ DOCTON MILL

Lymebridge, Hartland, EX39 6EA. Lana & John Borrett, 01237 441369, docton.mill@btconnect.com, www.doctonmill.co.uk. *8m W of Clovelly. Follow brown tourist signs on A39 nr Clovelly.* **For NGS: Sun 9 June (10-5). Adm £4.50, chd free. Light refreshments. Cream teas and light lunches available all day.** For other opening times and information, please phone, email or visit garden website.
Situated in stunning valley location. Garden surrounds original mill pond and the microclimate created within the wooded valley enables tender species to flourish. Recent planting of herbaceous, stream and summer garden give variety through the season. Regret not suitable for wheelchairs.

GROUP OPENING

27 NEW DOLTON GARDENS

Dolton, Winkleigh, EX19 8PP. *Take B3217 towards Dolton from A3124, park in village hall car park. Tickets and maps at village hall.* **Sat 1, Sun 2 June (2-6). Combined adm £6, chd free. Home-made teas in Dolton Village Hall. Plants and local produce for sale at village hall.**

NEW COURT COTTAGE
Malcolm & Jacky Easton.

NEW COURT HOUSE
Jake Glanville & Miriam McCurdy.

HIGHER CHERUBEER
Jo & Tom Hynes.
(See separate entry)
NPC

NEW HILLSVIEW
Jenny Hicks.

NEW 1 THORNS COTTAGE
Suzanne Clarke.

NEW WEST VIEW
Penny & Derek Thorp.

Dolton is a historic and picturesque village with a lively community of shops, primary school and pubs. It has a vibrant horticultural society show each year and boasts many excellent gardens. The gardens opening include a couple of classic cottage gardens with festoons of clematis and roses, a couple of edgy sustainable gardens, a large orchard garden and a mature country garden. Greenhouses and polytunnels, rockeries and ponds, colourful herbaceous borders and shady woodland. Plenty of places to sit and relax and soak up the atmosphere of a rural Devon village. Cream teas and plant sales, also local produce and crafts in village hall.

28 DUNLEY HOUSE

Bovey Tracey, Newton Abbot, TQ13 9PW. Mr & Mrs F Gilbert. *2m E of Bovey Tracey on rd to Hennock. From A38 going W turn off slip rd R towards Chudleigh Knighton on B3344, in village follow yellow signs to Dunley House. From A38 eastwards turn off on Chudleigh K slip rd L and follow signs.* **Sat 15, Sun 16 June (2-5). Adm £5, chd free. Home-made teas.**
9 acre garden set among mature oaks, sequoiadendrons and a huge liquidambar started from a wilderness in mid eighties. Rhododendrons, camellias and over 40 different magnolias. Arboretum, walled garden with borders and fruit and vegetables, rose garden and new enclosed garden with lily pond. Large pond renovated 2016 with new plantings. Woodland walk around perimeter of property.

We open the gates to the nation's best gardens, offering a relaxing, memorable and affordable day out. A perfect experience to share with friends and family.

GROUP OPENING

29 NEW EAST CORNWORTHY GARDENS

East Cornworthy, Totnes, TQ9 7HG. *Leave A3122 at Sportsman's Arms to Dittisham. At Red Lion L to Totnes. Continue 1m into East Cornworthy.* **Sat 6, Sun 7 July (2-5). Combined adm £6, chd free. Cream teas.**

NEW BLACKNESS BARN
Andrew & Karen Davis.

NEW BROOK
John & Michelle Pain.

NEW RIVENDALE FARM
Marina Pusey.

NEW SANDFORD HOUSE
Anne Mitchell.

NEW TOAD HALL
Denis & Jacky Kerslake.

East Cornworthy is a small hamlet nestling in a valley just outside the village of Dittisham near the River Dart where 5 beautiful gardens will be opening their gates in July for the first time. Surrounded by rolling hills, with Dartmoor in the distance, you can enjoy woodland walks, streams, ponds as well as interesting planting and magnificent mixed borders in sun and shade in these very different gardens. A Devonshire cream tea and a plant stall will complete the afternoon. Limited wheelchair access. Parts of East Cornworthy are steep.

30 EAST WOODLANDS FARMHOUSE

Alverdiscott, Newton Tracey, Barnstaple, EX31 3PP. Ed & Heather Holt. *5m NE of Great Torrington, 5m S of Barnstaple, off B3232. From Great Torrington turn R into single track rd before Alverdiscott; and from Barnstaple turn L after Alverdiscott. 1m down rd R fork at Y-junction.* **Sat 11, Sun 12 May, Sat 13, Sun 14 July (2-5). Adm £4, chd free. Home-made teas. Gluten free cakes available.**
East Woodlands is a beautifully designed garden full of rooms packed with plants, shrubs and trees. Enjoy the spectacular bamboos, flowing grasses, colourful roses and newly created cottage and bog gardens (unfenced pond), all set in an acre looking out over N Devon countryside. The Koelreutaria paniculata is a feature. Sit in one of the seating areas and enjoy a cuppa. Plants for sale. Partial wheelchair access.

31 EAST WORLINGTON HOUSE

East Worlington, Witheridge, Crediton, EX17 4TS. Barnabas & Campie Hurst-Bannister. *In centre of East Worlington, 2m W of Witheridge. From Witheridge Square R to East Worlington. After 1½ m R at T-junction in Drayford, then L to Worlington. After ½ m L at T-junction. 200 yds on L. Parking nearby, disabled parking at house.* **Sun 3, Sun 10 Mar (1.30-5). Adm £4, chd free. Cream teas in thatched parish hall next to house.**
Thousands of crocuses. In 2 acre garden, set in lovely position with views down valley to Little Dart river, these spectacular crocuses have spread over many years through the garden and into the neighbouring churchyard. Cream teas in the parish hall (in aid of its modernisation fund) next door. Dogs on leads please.

32 NEW FAIRWAY

Leigh Road, Chulmleigh, EX18 7BL. R & M Barrett. *From A377 follow signs towards Chulmleigh Golf Club. Sorry, no parking at garden, please park on road.* **Suns 12, 19, 26 May; 2 June; 7, 14, 21 July (12-5). Adm £3.50, chd free. Refreshments available locally - golf club, bistro and local pubs, all of which are a short walk away.**
South-facing, sloping wildlife garden comprising perennial meadow area, pond, colourful perennial flower borders and many interesting trees and shrubs.

33 NEW FOXHOLE COMMUNITY GARDEN

Dartington, Totnes, TQ9 6EB. Zoe Jong, www.foxholecommunitygarden.org.uk. *On the Dartington Estate near the Foxhole Centre at Old School Farm.* **Sun 28, Tue 30 July (11-4). Adm £4, chd free. Home-made teas.**
Beautiful community garden and orchard on the Dartington Estate. Since 2016 it has been developed to provide a garden space for all abilities. Nature trail and garden crafts for children, talks and walks run on organic, no-dig low maintenance principles. Raised veg beds, orchard, herb, wildlife, wildflower, cutting flower, pond and potager planting areas. Full of colour, produce and wildlife. Parking directly outside the garden, main area of the garden accessible by wheelchair as is the toilet.

34 ◆ FURSDON

Cadbury, Thorverton, Exeter, EX5 5JS. David & Catriona Fursdon, 01392 860860, admin@fursdon.co.uk, www.fursdon.co.uk. *2m N of Thorverton. From Tiverton S on A396. Take A3072 at Bickleigh towards Crediton. L after 2½ m signed to Fursdon. From Exeter N on A396. L to Thorverton and R in centre of village opp Thorverton Arms.* **For NGS: Sat 8, Sun 9 June (2-5). Adm £4.50, chd free. Home-made teas in Coach Hall from 2pm, also cream teas. Teas not for NGS.** For other opening times and information, please phone, email or visit garden website.
Garden surrounds Fursdon House, home of the same family for 7 centuries. Hillside setting with extensive views S over parkland and beyond. Sheltered by house, hedges and cob walls, there are terraces of roses, herbs and perennials in mixed traditional and contemporary planting. Woodland walk, seasonal wild flowers and pond in meadow garden. Fursdon House open for guided tours on NGS days (separate entrance fee not for NGS). Some steep slopes, grass and gravel paths.

35 THE GATE HOUSE

Lee, EX34 8LR. Mrs H Booker, 01271 862409. *3m W of Ilfracombe. Park in Lee village car park. Take lane alongside The Grampus PH. Garden approx 30 metres past inn buildings. Open most days but wise to check by phoning between 7pm & 9pm.* **Daily Wed 1 May to Sat 7 Sept (9.30-3). Adm by donation.** Visits also by arrangement Apr to Sept for groups of up to 20.
Described by many visitors as a peaceful paradise, this streamside garden incl National Collection of over 100 rodgersia (at their best end of June), interesting herbaceous areas, patio gardens with semi-hardy exotics, many unusual mature trees and shrubs and large organic vegetable garden. Level gravel paths.

NPC

36 GOREN FARM

Broadhayes, Stockland, Honiton, EX14 9EN. Julian Pady, 07770 694646, gorenfarm@hotmail.com, www.goren.co.uk. *6m E of Honiton, 6m W of Axminster. Go to the Stockland television mast. Head 100 metres North signed from Ridge Cross.* **Every Sat and Sun 1 June to 16 June (10-5). Light refreshments. Evening openings Sat 1 June to Sun 23 June (5-10). Adm £3, chd free. Teas and home-made cakes, light lunches on open weekends made with local produce from the farm.** Visits also by arrangement June & July for groups of 10 to 30. Please contact by email specifying date, size and preferred time.
Wander through 50 acres of natural species rich wild flower meadows Easy access foot paths cut as well as signs. Dozens of varieties of wild flowers and grasses. Thousands of orchids from early June and butterflies July. Stunning views of Blackdown Hills. Georgian house and walled gardens, guided walks 10.30 and 2.30 on open weekends. Species information signs and picnic tables around the fields. Partial wheelchair access to meadows, dogs welcome on a lead only, please clean up after your pet.

© Ellen Rooney

GORWELL HOUSE, Barnstaple. *See Upper Gorwell House*

37 GREATCOMBE

Holne, Newton Abbot, TQ13 7SP. Robbie & Sarah Richardson. *Michelcombe, Holne, TQ13 7SP. 4m NW Ashburton via Holne Bridge and Holne Village. 4m NE Buckfastleigh via Scorriton. Narrow lanes.* **Fri 19, Sat 20, Sun 21, Mon 22 Apr, Sat 4, Sun 5, Mon 6 May, Fri 26, Sat 27, Sun 28 July (1-5). Adm £4, chd free. Home-made teas.**

Tranquil garden nestled in a Dartmoor valley, with babbling stream, swathes of colour and textual foliage. Gentle paths and lawns bordered by spring and summer flowering shrubs, herbaceous plants and ornamental grasses, plus 'The Stairway to Heaven' climbing through loosely planted banks and wild flowers. 'Wonderful combination of sights, smells, nooks and crannies.' (visitor comment). Artist's Studio featuring brightly coloured acrylic paintings, prints and cards all available to purchase along with ornamental metal plant supports in all sizes and shapes and 'Made by Robbie' metal artefacts. Sadly very limited wheelchair access.

38 HALDON GRANGE

Dunchideock, Exeter, EX6 7YE. Ted Phythian, 01392 832349. *5m SW of Exeter. From A30 through Ide Village to Dunchideock 5m. L to Lord Haldon, Haldon Grange is next L. From A38 (S) turn L on top of Haldon Hill follow Dunchideock signs, R at village centre to Lord Haldon.* **Sat 23, Sun 24, Sat 30, Sun 31 Mar, Sat 6, Sun 7, Sat 13, Sun 14, Wed 17, Sat 20, Sun 21, Mon 22, Sat 27, Sun 28 Apr, Sat 4, Sun 5, Mon 6, Wed 8, Sat 11, Sun 12, Sat 18, Sun 19, Wed 22, Sat 25, Sun 26, Mon 27 May, Sat 1, Sun 2, Sat 8, Sun 9 June (1-5). Adm £5, chd free. Home-made teas.** Visits also by arrangement Apr to June. Conducted tours by arrangement.

12 acre well established garden with camellias, magnolias, azaleas, various shrubs and rhododendrons; rare and mature trees; small lake and ponds with river and water cascades. 5 acre arboretum planted 2011 with wide range of trees, shrubs and a large lilac circle. Wisteria pergola with views over Exeter and Woodbury. Wheelchair access to main parts of garden.

39 HALSCOMBE FARM

Halscombe Lane, Ide, Exeter, EX2 9TQ. Prof J Rawlings. *From Exeter go through Ide to mini r'about take 2nd exit and continue to L turn into Halscombe Lane.* **Sat 15, Sun 16 June (2-5.30). Adm £4, chd free. Home-made teas.** Donation to The Friends of Exeter Cathedral.

Farmhouse garden created over last 6 yrs. Large collection of old roses and peonies, long and colourful herbaceous border, knot garden, productive fruit cage and vegetable garden all set within a wonderful borrowed landscape.

40 HAMBLYN'S COOMBE

Dittisham, Dartmouth, TQ6 0HE. Bridget McCrum, 01803 722228, mccrum.sculpt@waitrose.com, www.bridgetmccrum.com. *3m N of Dartmouth. From A3122 L to Dittisham. In village R at Red Lion, The Level, then Rectory Lane, past River Farm to Hamblyn's Coombe.* **Visits by arrangement Mar to Oct for groups of up to 20. Adm £5, chd free.**

7 acre garden with stunning views across the river to Greenway House and sloping steeply to R Dart at bottom of garden. Extensive planting of trees and shrubs with unusual design features accompanying Bridget McCrum's stone carvings and bronzes. Wild flower meadow and woods. Good rhododendrons and camellias, ferns and bamboos, acers and hydrangeas. Exceptional autumn colour. No wheelchair access.

41 HARBOUR LIGHTS

Horns Cross, Bideford, EX39 5DW. Brian & Faith Butler, 01237 451627, brian.nfu@gmail.com. *7m W of Bideford, 3m E of Clovelly. On main A39, so easy to find and access, between Bideford and Clovelly, halfway between Hoops Inn and Bucks Cross.* **Sat 22, Sun 23 June (11-6). Adm £4, chd free. Home-made teas. Light lunches, home-made cakes and cream teas, or perhaps a glass of wine.** Visits also by arrangement June to Aug for groups of 10+.

½ acre colourful garden with Lundy views. A garden of wit, humour, unusual ideas, artwork, volcano and many surprises. Water features, shrubs, foliage area, grasses in an unusual setting, fernery, bonsai and polytunnel, time saving ideas. You will never have seen a garden like this! Superb conservatory for cream teas. Free leaflet. We like our visitors to leave with a smile! Child friendly. A 'must visit' interactive garden. Intriguing artwork of various kinds, original plantings and ideas.

Hutswell Farm

42 THE HAVEN

Wembury Road, Hollacombe, Wembury, South Hams, PL9 0DQ. Mrs S Norton & Mr J Norton, 01752 862149, suenorton1@hotmail.co.uk. *20mins from Plymouth city centre. Use A379 Plymouth to Kingsbridge Rd. At Elburton r'about follow signs to Wembury. Parking on roadside. Bus stop nearby on Wembury Rd. Route 48 from Plymouth.* **Visits by arrangement Mar to May for groups of up to 10. Adm £4, chd free.**

½ acre sloping plantsman's garden in South Hams AONB. Tearoom and seating areas. 2 ponds. Substantial collection of large flowering Asiatic and hybrid tree magnolias. Large collection of camellias including camellia reticulata. Rare dwarf, weeping and slow growing conifers. Daphnes, early azaleas and rhododendrons, spring bulbs and hellebores. Wheelchair access to top part of garden.

43 HAYNE

Zeal Monachorum, Crediton, EX17 6DE. Tim & Milla Herniman, www.haynedevon.co.uk. *Located ½m S of Zeal Monachorum. From Zeal Monachorum, keeping church on L, drive through village. Continue on this road for ⅓m, garden drive is 1st entrance on R.* **Sun 2 June (2-6). Adm £4, chd free. Home-made teas.**

Hayne has a magical walled garden brimming with mature trees, shrubs, roses and borders. Highlights incl beautiful tree peonies, mature wisteria in both purple and white and rambling wild roses in combination with a more modern Piet Oudolf style perennial planting which surrounds the recently renovated grade II* farm buildings ... magic, mystery and soul by the spadeful! Live jazz band. Disabled WC. Wheelchair access to walled garden through orchard.

44 HEATHERCOMBE

Manaton, Nr Bovey Tracey, TQ13 9XE. Claude & Margaret Pike Woodlands Trust, 01626 354404, gardens@pike.me.uk, www.heathercombe.com. *7m NW of Bovey Tracey. From Bovey Tracey take scenic B3387 to Haytor/Widecombe. 1.7m past Haytor Rocks (before Widecombe hill) turn R to Hound Tor and Manaton. 1.4m past Hound Tor turn L at Heatree Cross to Heathercombe.* **Sun 31 Mar, Sun 12, Sun 19, Tue 21, Wed 22, Thur 23, Fri 24, Sat 25, Sun 26, Tue 28, Wed 29, Thur 30, Fri 31 May, Sat 1, Sun 2 June (1.30-5.30). Adm £5, chd free. Sat 15, Sun 16, Tue 18, Wed 19, Thur 20, Fri 21, Sat 22, Sun 23, Tue 25, Wed 26, Thur 27, Fri 28, Sat 29, Sun 30 June, Tue 2, Wed 3, Thur 4, Fri 5, Sat 6, Sun 7 July (11-5.30). Adm £6, chd free. Home-made teas in pretty cottage garden or conservatory if wet.** Visits also by arrangement Apr to Oct. No access for large coaches. Donation to Rowcroft Hospice.

Tranquil secluded valley with streams tumbling through woods, ponds & lake - setting for 30 acres of spring/summer interest (many recent changes) - daffodils, extensive bluebells, large displays of rhododendrons, many unusual specimen trees, cottage gardens, orchard, orchid/wild flower meadow, bog/fern/woodland gardens and woodland walks; sculptures. 2m mainly level sandy paths with benches. From 15 June to 7 July admission incl Heathercombe 'EDGE' Sculpture Trail - approx 50 works in woodland/garden settings. Disabled reserved parking close to tea room & toilet.

Your visits help change lives - since 1927, we've donated £55 million to nursing and caring charities

45 HIGH GARDEN

Chiverstone Lane, Kenton, EX6 8NJ. Chris & Sharon Britton, www.highgardennurserykenton.wordpress.com. *5m S of Exeter on A379 Dawlish Rd. Leaving Kenton towards Exeter, L into Chiverstone Lane, 50yds along lane. Entrance clearly marked at High Garden Nurseries. Phone for directions 01626 899106.* **Every Tue to Fri 12 Feb to 29 Nov (9-5). Adm £3.50, chd free.** Donation to Hospiscare and FORCE cancer care charities.

Very interesting and wide ranging planting of trees, shrubs, climbers and perennials in relaxed but still controlled 13 yr old garden. 70 metre summer herbaceous border, colour-themed beds, grass walkways with surprises around each corner. Always something to enjoy. Lots of unusual and different species. Self-service tea room open Mar to Nov. Garden attached to plantsman's nursery, open at same time. Slightly sloping site but the few steps can be avoided.

46 HIGHER ASH FARM

Ash, Dartmouth, TQ6 0LR. Mr Michael Gribbin & Mrs Jennifer Barwell, 07595 507516, matthew.perkins18@yahoo.co.uk, www.higherashfarm.com. *Leave A381 at Halwell for Dartmouth A3122. Turn R before Sportsman's Arms to Bugford. At T-junction go R then next L. After 1½m at Xrds go R, Higher Ash Farm entrance is 1st L.* **Sun 12, Sun 19 May (2-5). Adm £5, chd free. Tea. Opening with Ash Gardens on Sat 29, Sun 30 June.** Visits also by arrangement May & June for groups of up to 20.

Evolving garden, high up in South Devon countryside. Sitting in 2½ acres there is a large kitchen garden terraced into the hillside with adjoining orchard. Vibrant array of azaleas and rhododendrons surround the barns and courtyard. Farmhouse is surrounded by a mix of herbaceous borders, shrubs and lawns. Pond, stream, autumn interest.

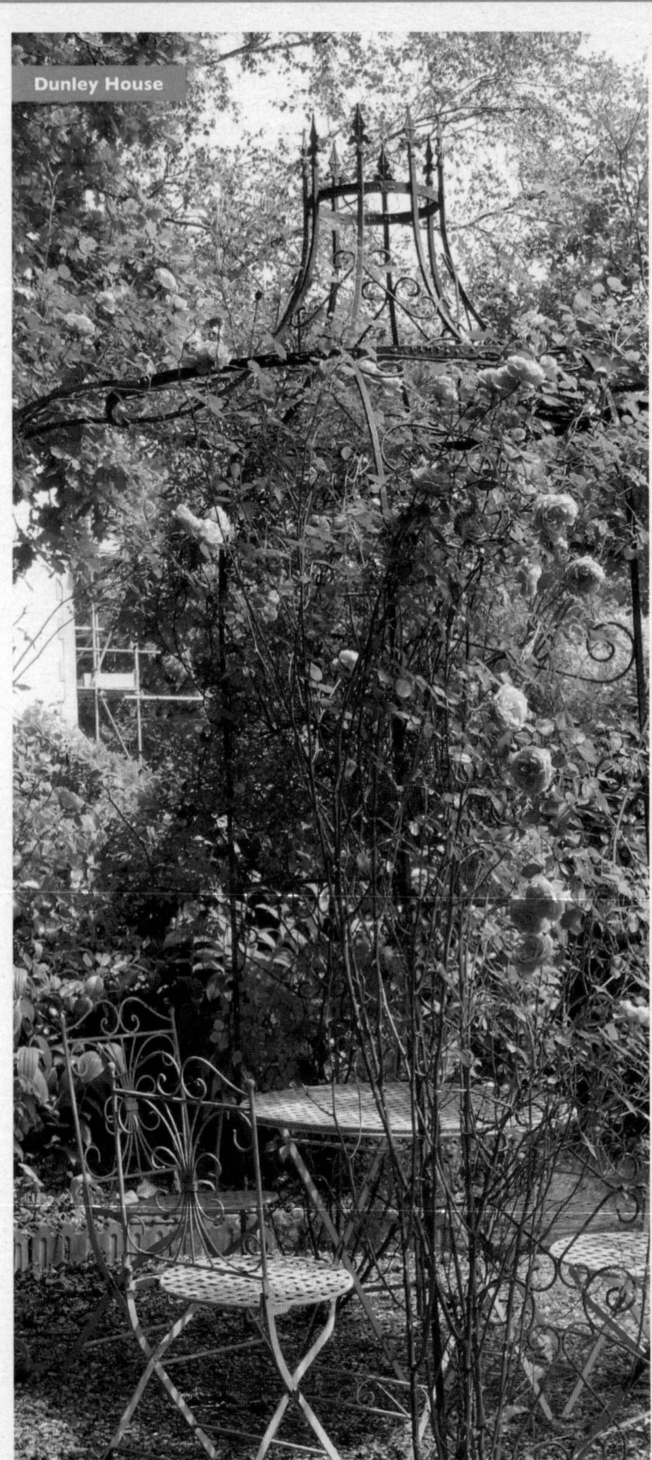
Dunley House

47 HIGHER CHERUBEER

Dolton, Winkleigh, EX19 8PP. Jo & Tom Hynes, 01805 804265, hynesjo@gmail.com, www.sites.google.com/site/cherubeergardens/the-gardens. *2m E of Dolton. From A3124 turn S towards Stafford Moor Fisheries, take 1st R, garden 500m on L.* **Fri 8, Fri 15, Sat 23 Feb (2-5); Sun 15 Sept (11-4). Adm £4, chd free. Home-made teas. 2020: Fri 7, Fri 14, Sat 22 Feb. Opening with Dolton Gardens on Sat 1, Sun 2 June.** Visits also by arrangement Feb to Oct for groups of 10+.

1¾ acre country garden with gravelled courtyard, raised beds and alpine house, lawns, large herbaceous border, shady woodland beds, potager style kitchen garden with large greenhouse and orchard. Winter openings for National Collection of cyclamen species, hellebores and over 400 snowdrop varieties. Home-made teas and plant sales available when opening outside the group.

NPC

48 HIGHER CULLAFORD

Spreyton, Crediton, EX17 5AX. Dr & Mrs Kennerley, 01837 840974, kenntoad@yahoo.com. *Approx ¾ m from centre of Spreyton, 20m W of Exeter, 10 E of Okehampton. From A30 at Whiddon Down follow signs to Spreyton. Yellow signs from A3124, centre of village and Spreyton parish church.* **Visits by arrangement May to Oct for groups of up to 20. Adm £4, chd free. Home-made teas.**

Traditional cottage style garden developed over past 12yrs from steep field and farmyard on northern edge of Dartmoor National Park. Mixed borders of herbaceous plants, roses and shrubs. 30ft pergola covered with seagull rose and many varieties of clematis. Wildlife pond. Newly planted pleached hornbeam hedge. Additional vegetable garden with polytunnel, fruit cage and fruit trees. Wheelchair access limited but can drive in to garden on request.

49 HIGHER ORCHARD COTTAGE

Aptor, Marldon, Paignton, TQ3 1SQ. Mrs Jenny Saunders, 01803 551221. *1m SW of Marldon. A380 Torquay to Paignton. At Churscombe Cross r'about R for Marldon, L towards Berry Pomeroy, take 2nd R into Farthing Lane. Follow for exactly 1m. Turn R at NGS sign for parking at Aptor Farm.* **Sat 1, Sun 2 June (11-5). Adm £4, chd free. Home-made teas. Open air teas available from 2pm to 4pm if weather permits.** Visits also by arrangement for groups of up to 10. Weekdays only. Limited parking available.

2 acre garden with generous colourful herbaceous borders, wildlife pond, productive vegetable beds and grass path walks through wild flower meadows in lovely countryside. Sculpture and art installations by local artists add excitement at every turn. Each year the garden is a showcase for local artists, in 2019 showing stone sculpture, garden iron work, wire sculpture, millinery work and paintings, textile art and pottery. Artists incl. www.jackiewills.com www.netzfineart.com www.devonartistnetwork.co.uk/artists/nicola-axe. Only area immediately at house is accessible for wheelchairs. All paths through garden are on gently sloping grass.

50 ◆ HOLBROOK GARDEN

Sampford Shrubs, Sampford Peverell, EX16 7EN. Martin Hughes-Jones & Susan Proud, 01884 821164, www.holbrookgarden.com. *1m NW from M5 J27. From M5 J27 follow signs to Tiverton Parkway. At top of slip rd off A361 follow brown sign to Holbrook Garden.* **For NGS: Fri 29, Sat 30, Sun 31 Mar, Thur 4, Fri 5, Sat 6, Sun 7, Fri 19, Sat 20, Sun 21 Apr, Fri 3, Sat 4, Sun 5 May, Fri 14, Sat 15, Sun 16 June, Fri 5, Sat 6, Sun 7 July, Thur 22, Fri 23, Sat 24 Aug, Thur 5, Fri 6, Sat 7 Sept (10-5). Adm £5, chd free. Light refreshments. home made cakes and biscuits.** For other opening times and information, please phone or visit garden website.

Lose yourself on tracks through the stone garden, the wet garden or in woodland glades. Space for nature means perfumes, songbirds and nests are everywhere in spring with many bees and butterflies in summer. Productive vegetable garden and polytunnel. Microclimates with nature inspired and diverse habitats for plants and wildlife. 2 acre S-facing garden on heavy clay, 35 yrs in the making. Coach parties by arrangement only, please phone or see holbrookgarden.com. Donation to MSF UK (Medecin sans Frontieres). Narrow paths restrict access for wheelchairs and buggies.

51 HOLE FARM

Woolsery, Bideford, EX39 5RF. Heather Alford. *11m SW of Bideford. Follow directions for Woolfardisworthy, signed from A39 at Bucks Cross. From village follow NGS signs from school for approx 2m.* **Sun 21 July, Sun 8 Sept (2-6). Adm £4, chd free. Home-made teas in converted barn. Room to sit and have a cup of tea even if its raining!**

3 acres of exciting gardens with established waterfall, ponds, vegetable and bog garden. Terraces and features incl round house have all been created using natural stone from original farm quarry. Peaceful walks through Culm grassland and water meadows border R Torridge and host a range of wildlife. Home to a herd of pedigree native Devon cattle.

52 HOLE'S MEADOW

South Zeal, Okehampton, EX20 2JS. Fi & Paul Reddaway, 07850 305040, holesmeadow@gmail.com, holesmeadow.com. *4½m from Okehampton on B3260, 4m from Whiddon Down. Signed from main street when open. Half way between the King's Arms and Oxenham Arms and opp village hall. A minute's fairly level walk along private path.* **Sat 20, Sun 21 July (12.30-5.30). Adm £4, chd free. Cream teas. Home-made cakes incl gluten free.** Visits also by arrangement in July. Evenings only from 5pm.

Below Dartmoor's Cawsand (Cosdon) Beacon, within 2 acre burgage plot. Garden features Plant Heritage National Plant Collections of both Monarda and Nepeta. Also many herbs and large naturalistic planting area, incl monardas and complementary planting. Bottom half of garden includes orchard, ornamental trees and maturing native woodland area interspersed with pathways.

NPC

53 ◆ HOTEL ENDSLEIGH

Milton Abbot, Tavistock, PL19 0PQ. Olga Polizzi, 01822 870000, mail@hotelendsleigh.com, www.hotelendsleigh.com/garden. *7m NW of Tavistock, midway between Tavistock and Launceston. From Tavistock, take B3362 to Launceston. 7m to Milton Abbot then 1st L, opp school. From Launceston & A30, B3362 to Tavistock. At Milton Abbot turn R opp school.* **For NGS: Sun 12 May, Sun 7 July (11-4). Adm £5, chd free. Light refreshments in hotel only which can be busy so please pre-book lunch/afternoon tea/ dinner beforehand.** For other opening times and information, please phone, email or visit garden website.

200 year old Repton-designed garden in 3 parts; formal gardens around house, picturesque dell with pleasure dairy and rockery and arboretum. Gardens were laid out in 1814 and have been carefully renovated over last 12yrs. Bordering River Tamar, it is a hidden oasis of plants and views. Hotel was built in 1810 by Sir Jeffry Wyattville for the 6th Duchess of Bedford in the romantic cottage Orne style. Plant Nursery adjoins hotel's 108 acres. Partial wheelchair access.

Your visits help change lives – we've donated over £16.7 million to Macmillan Cancer Support since 1984

54 HUTSWELL FARM

Blackaller Lane, Oakford, Tiverton, EX16 9JE. Paul & Jean Marcus, 01398 351241, barvanjack@aol.com. *1½m NNW of Oakford. Signed narrow lane off B3227. Turn L 12m E of S Molton. 2½m NW of Black Cat junction turn R. Signs to Hutswell.* **Sun 23 June (1.30-5.30). Adm £4.50, chd free. Home-made teas.** Visits also by arrangement May to Sept for groups of 10 to 20.

Delightful 8 acre S-facing country garden around old farmhouse. Ponds, bog garden, shrubaceous borders, prairie planting, maturing arboretum with Pyrus calleryana Chanticleer avenue, serpentine hornbeam walk, vegetable garden and orchard with local apple varieties. Walks through ancient wet woodland and recent plantation of over 11,000 native trees to viewpoints. Variety and interest all yr round.

55 IDESTONE BARTON

Dunchideock, Exeter, EX2 9UE. Mr & Mrs James Studholme. *From Ide take rd to Dunchideock. After 500m fork R (signed Idestone). Take 1st L after 1m. Follow over Xrds and down steep sided S bend. Car Park signed on R.* **Fri 28, Sat 29 June (2-6.30). Adm £5, chd free. Cream teas.**

Romantic 6-acre country garden in unspoilt countryside only 3m from Exeter. Built on 5 different levels, with several distinctive rooms, garden features yew-hedged kitchen garden, croquet lawn, rose terrace, orchard and arboretum. Picturesque kitchen garden. Garden still in development. No wheelchair access.

56 NEW KENTISBEARE HOUSE

Kentisbeare, Cullompton, EX15 2BR. Nicholas & Sarah Allan. *2m E of M5 J28 (Cullompton). Turn off A373 at Post Cross signed Kentisbeare. After ½m drive is just past cricket field on R, entrance framed by 2 low curved stone walls.* **Sat 6, Sun 7 July (10-5). Adm £5, chd free. Home-made teas.**

Surrounding the listed former Kentisbeare rectory, the gardens have been redesigned and planted by the present owners in recent years with various planting themes that complement the surrounding countryside. Formal beds, lake view, kitchen garden and glasshouse, recently established wildflower meadow. Diverse and interesting collection of trees and shrubs.

Heathercombe

GROUP OPENING

57 KENTISBURY GARDENS

Kentisbury, Barnstaple, EX31 4NT. *9m N of Barnstaple, midway between Barnstaple and Lynton. From Barnstaple take A39 to Lynton and follow signs at Kentisbury Ford. From Blackmoor Gate follow signs. From Combe Martin and Ilfracombe turn R at Easter Close Cross and follow signs on B3229.* **Sat 22, Sun 23 June (12-5). Combined adm £5, chd free. Cream teas at Beachborough Country House on Saturday 22nd June. Home made teas at Higher Patchole Farm, near Spring Cottage on Sunday 23rd June.**

BEACHBOROUGH COUNTRY HOUSE

Viviane Clout, 01271 882487, viviane@beachboroughcountryhouse.co.uk, www.beachboroughcountryhouse.co.uk.

LITTLE LEY

Jerry & Jenny Burnett.

SPRING COTTAGE

Nerys Cadvan-Jones.

Kentisbury is situated high in the North Devon countryside a few miles inland from the dramatic coastline and bordering Exmoor National Park. These 3 gardens make good use of the landscape and views, providing a variety of planting and garden habitats. Beachborough Country House is a garden created from an artist's perspective and home to hundreds of roses. Interest incl herbaceous borders, lawns, stream, pond and large ornamental kitchen garden. Little Ley is a large country garden with pond, stream, mature trees and shrubs, perennial flower and shrub beds, plus wildlife areas. Productive fruit and vegetable area. Early spring interest and superb autumn colour. Spring Cottage is a pretty cottage garden with colourful flower borders, shrubs, climbers and small trees giving yr-round interest. Devon banks, a stream and stone walls afford varying views and conditions for planting and the growing collection of hardy geraniums.

58 KENTLANDS

Whitestone, Exeter, EX4 2JR. David & Gill Oakey, 01392 811585, david.oakey3@hotmail.co.uk. *NW of Exeter mid way between Exwick and Tedburn St Mary. Follow NGS signs from centre of Whitestone village.* **Sat 18, Sun 19 May (11-5); Sun 15 Sept (11-4). Adm £4, chd free. Home-made teas.** Visits also by arrangement May to Oct for groups of 10 to 20.

Our 2 acre tucked away garden is S-facing with distant views across Exeter towards W Devon and Sidmouth. Garden was started in 2010 and is still developing. Planting is mainly perennials with some shrubs, large salvia collection, orchids and alpines, productive vegetable garden with polytunnel, fruit cage and fruit trees. Sloping garden.

Your visits help change lives – your generosity has supported unpaid carers through donations to Carers Trust totalling over £3.9 million since 1996

59 KIA-ORA FARM & GARDENS

Knowle Lane, Cullompton, EX15 1PZ. Mrs M B Disney, www.kia-orafarm.co.uk. *On W side of Cullompton and 6m SE of Tiverton. M5 J28, through town centre to r'about, 3rd exit R, top of Swallow Way turn L into Knowle Lane, garden beside Cullompton Rugby Club.* **Sun 21, Mon 22 Apr, Sun 5, Mon 6, Sun 19, Sun 26, Mon 27 May, Sun 9, Sun 23 June, Sun 7, Sun 21 July, Sun 4, Sun 18, Sun 25, Mon 26 Aug, Sun 8 Sept (2-5.30). Adm £3.50, chd free. Home-made teas at Kia-ora, inside or outside depending on personal preference and the weather! Teas and sales not for NGS charities.**

Charming, peaceful 10 acre garden with lawns, lakes and ponds. Water features with swans, ducks and other wildlife. Mature trees, shrubs, rhododendrons, azaleas, heathers, roses, herbaceous borders and rockeries. Nursery avenue, novelty crazy golf. Stroll leisurely around and finish by sitting back, enjoying a traditional home-made Devonshire cream tea or choose from the wide selection of cakes!

GROUP OPENING

60 KILMINGTON (SHUTE ROAD) GARDENS

Kilmington, Axminster, EX13 7ST. www.Kilmingtonvillage.com. *1½m W of Axminster. Signed off A35.* **Sat 18, Sun 19 May (1.30-5). Combined adm £6, chd free.**

BETTY'S GROUND
Michael & Mary-Anne Driscoll.

BREACH
J A Chapman & B J Lewis, 01297 35159, jachapman16@btinternet.com. **Visits also by arrangement.**

SPINNEY TWO
Paul & Celia Dunsford.

Set in rural E Devon in AONB yet easily accessed from A35. 3 gardens just under 1 mile apart. Spinney Two: ½ acre garden planted for yr-round colour, foliage and texture. Mature oaks and beech. Spring bulbs, hellebores, shrubs; azaleas, camellias, cornus, pieris, skimmias, viburnums. Roses, acers, flowering trees, clematis and other climbers. Vegetable patch. Breach: set in over 3 acres with woodland, partially underplanted with rhododendrons, camellia and hydrangea; rose garden, unusual and well-known trees and shrubs, expanses of grass incl wild flower area, colourful beds, vegetable garden and fruit trees. Ornamental pond and wild pond in bog garden, being extended in 2018/19. Betty's Ground, Haddon Corner: 1½ acre garden with far-reaching views. Wide selection of unusual mature trees and shrubs incl very large wisteria. Several sections to the garden with a range of differing styles providing, colour, texture and form united by repetition of 6 different plants throughout.

61 LEE FORD

Knowle Village, Budleigh Salterton, EX9 7AJ. Mr & Mrs N Lindsay-Fynn, 01395 445894, crescent@leeford.co.uk, www.leeford.co.uk/. *3½m E of Exmouth. For SatNav use postcode EX9 6AL.* **Visits by arrangement Apr to Aug for groups of 10+. Adm £6, chd free. Cream teas. Numbers and special dietary requests must be pre-booked.** Donation to Lindsay-Fynn Trust.

Extensive, formal and woodland garden, largely developed in 1950s, but recently much extended with mass displays of camellias, rhododendrons and azaleas, incl many rare varieties. Traditional walled garden filled with fruit and vegetables, herb garden, bog garden, rose garden, hydrangea collection, greenhouses. Ornamental conservatory with collection of pot plants. Lee Ford has direct access to the Pedestrian route and National Cycle Network route 2 which follows the old railway line that linked Exmouth to Budleigh Salterton. Garden is ideal destination for cycle clubs or rambling groups. Formal gardens are lawn with gravel paths. Moderately steep slope to woodland garden on tarmac with gravel paths in woodland.

62 LEWIS COTTAGE

Spreyton, nr Crediton, EX17 5AA. Mr & Mrs M Pell and Mr R Orton, 07773 785939, rworton@mac.com, www.lewiscottageplants.co.uk. *5m NE of Spreyton, 8m W of Crediton. From Hillerton Cross, keep Stone Cross to your R. Drive approx 1½m, Lewis Cottage on L, proceed across cattle grid down farm track. From Crediton follow A377 to Barnstaple for 1m turn L at NGS sign.* **Sat 25, Sun 26, Mon 27 May, Sat 22, Sun 23 June, Sat 20, Sun 21 July, Sat 24, Sun 25, Mon 26 Aug (11-5). Adm £4.50, chd free. Home made cakes, sweet & savoury tarts, tea & coffee available.** Visits also by arrangement May to Sept for groups of 10 to 20.

Located on SW-facing slope in rural Mid Devon, the 4 acre garden at Lewis Cottage has evolved primarily over the last 25 yrs, harnessing and working with the natural landscape. Using informal planting and natural formal structures to create a garden that reflects the souls of those who garden in it, it is an incredibly personal space that is a joy to share. Spring camassia cricket pitch, rose garden, large natural dew pond, woodland walks, bog garden, hornbeam rondel planted with late flowering narcissi, winter garden, hot and cool herbaceous borders, fruit & veg garden, picking garden, outdoor poetry reading room & plant nursery. Wheelchairs/motorised buggies not advised due to garden being on a slope (though many have successfully tried!).

63 LINDEN RISE

Chapel Lane, Combe Martin, Ilfracombe, EX34 0HJ. Professor Chris & Jenny Sheppard, 01272 882048, jenifer.sheppard@icloud.com. *In Combe Martin high street turn R at old PO onto Chapel lane, LInden RIse is on R opp Hollands park where parking is available.* **Sun 21 July (2-5). Adm £5, chd free. Light refreshments.** Visits also by arrangement in July.

In an area of outstanding natural beauty with countryside and sea views, 1½ acre garden of lawns, mature trees and shrubs. Children's play area, pergola, decorative ponds, small orchard and seasonal flower borders. Tarmacadam drive with wheelchair access to most areas.

64 LITTLE ASH BUNGALOW

Fenny Bridges, Honiton, EX14 3BL. Helen & Brian Brown, 01404 850941, helenlittleash@hotmail.com, www.facebook.com/littleashgarden. *3m W of Honiton. Leave A30 at Iron Bridge from Honiton 1m, Patteson's Cross from Exeter ½m and follow NGS signs.* **Sun 18 Aug (1-5). Adm £4, chd free. Light refreshments.** Visits also by arrangement May to Sept for groups of 10+. Coaches welcome, with easy access and parking.

Country garden of 1½ acres, packed with different and unusual herbaceous perennials, trees, shrubs and bamboos. Designed for yr-round interest, wildlife and owners' pleasure. Naturalistic planting in colour coordinated mixed borders, highlighted by metal sculptures, provides a backdrop to the view. Natural stream, pond and damp woodland area, mini wildlife meadows and raised gravel/alpine garden. Assorted metal sculptures. Grass paths.

65 LITTLE DORWEEKE

Silverton, Exeter, EX5 4BZ. Helen & Paul Cooper. *From Exeter take A396 towards Tiverton. Take R turn signed Butterleigh. Property approx 1½ miles up road on R.* **Sat 11, Sun 12 May (11-5). Adm £4, chd free. Light refreshments. Tea, coffee, soft drinks, home made cakes (gluten free, dairy free and vegans catered for). Hot soup and roll mid day.**

2 acre garden nestling in valley beside stream and river. It surrounds a thatched Devon longhouse where over 45 years we have developed the garden from the original smallholding. Many areas, incl koi, lily and natural ponds, bog area and vegetable garden. The natural planting, with many rhododendrons and azaleas, mature trees and shrubs provide all yr round colour. A wildlife haven.

66 LITTLE WEBBERY

Webbery, Bideford, EX39 4PS. Mr & Mrs J A Yewdall, 01271 858206, jyewdall1@gmail.com. *2m E of Bideford. From Bideford (East the Water) along Alverdiscott Rd, or from Barnstaple to Torrington on B3232. Take rd to Bideford at Alverdiscott, pass through Stoney Cross.* **Visits by arrangement May to Sept for groups of up to 30. Adm £4, chd free. Home-made teas.**

Approx 3 acres in valley setting with pond, lake, mature trees, 2 ha-has and large mature raised border. Large walled kitchen garden with yew and box hedging incl rose garden, lawns with shrubs and rose and clematis trellises. Vegetables and greenhouse and adj traditional cottage garden. Partial wheelchair access.

67 ◆ LUKESLAND

Harford, Ivybridge, PL21 0JF. Mrs R Howell and Mr & Mrs J Howell, 01752 691749, lorna.lukesland@gmail.com, www.lukesland.co.uk. *10m E of Plymouth. Turn off A38 at Ivybridge. 1½m N on Harford rd, E side of Erme valley.*

24 acres of flowering shrubs, wild flowers and rare trees with pinetum in Dartmoor National Park. Beautiful setting of small valley around Addicombe Brook with lakes, numerous waterfalls and pools. Extensive and impressive collections of camellias, rhododendrons, azaleas and acers; also spectacular Magnolia campbellii and huge Davidia involucrata. Superb spring and autumn colour. Children's trail. Open Suns, Weds and BH (11-5) 31 March - 16 June and 6 Oct - 17 November. Adm £6, Under 16s free. Group discount for parties of 20+. Group tours available by appointment. Partial wheelchair access in garden. Accessible cafe and WC.

68 ◆ MARWOOD HILL GARDEN

Marwood, EX31 4EB. Dr J A Snowdon, 01271 342528, info@marwoodhillgarden.co.uk, www.marwoodhillgarden.co.uk. *4m N of Barnstaple. Signed from A361 & B3230. Look out for brown signs. See website for map and directions. www.marwoodhillgarden.co.uk. Coach & Car park.* **For NGS: Fri 14 June (10-4.30). Adm £7, chd free. Garden Tea Room offers selection of light refreshments throughout the day, all home-made or locally**

sourced delicious food to suit most tastes. For other opening times and information, please phone, email or visit garden website.
Marwood Hill is a very special private garden covering an area of 20 acres with lakes and set in a valley tucked away in N Devon. From early spring snowdrops through to late autumn there is always a colourful surprise around every turn. National Collections of astilbe, iris ensata and tulbaghia, large collections of camellia, rhododendron and magnolia. Winner of MacLaren Cup at rhododendron and camellia show RHS Rosemoor. Partial wheelchair access.

69 MIDDLE WELL

Waddeton Road, Stoke Gabriel, Totnes, TQ9 6RL. Neil & Pamela Millward, 01803 782981, neilandpamela@talktalk.net. *A385 from Totnes towards Paignton, R at Riviera Motors signed Stoke Gabriel. Straight on for 1m to Four Cross. Straight across. From A380, R at A385 toward Totnes, L in 400m, L at Four Cross.* **Sun 9 June (11-5). Adm £5, chd free. Home-made teas. Visits by arrangement Apr to Oct. Light lunches available on request. Adm £5, chd free. Home-made teas.**
Tranquil 2 acre garden plus woodland and streams contain a wealth of interesting plants chosen for colour, form and long season of interest. Many seating places from which to enjoy the vistas. Interesting structural features (rill, summerhouse, pergola, cobbling, slate bridge). Heady mix of exciting perennials, shrubs, bulbs, climbers and specimen trees. Vegetable garden. Child friendly. Teas, produce and books in aid of Devon Air Ambulance. Mostly accessible by wheelchair.

70 MONKSCROFT

Zeal Monachorum, Crediton, EX17 6DG. Mr & Mrs Ken and Jane Hogg. *Lane opp Church.* **Sat 13, Sun 14 Apr (11-5). Adm £3.50, chd free. Home-made teas.**
Pretty, medium sized garden of oldest cottage in village. Packed with spring colours, primroses, primulas, daffodils, tulips, magnolias and camellias. Views to far hills. New exotic garden. Also tranquil fishing lake with daffodils and wild flowers in beautiful setting, home to resident kingfisher. Steep walk to lake approx 20mins, or 5mins by car. Dogs on leads welcome. Parking and WC at lake.

GROUP OPENING

71 MORETONHAMPSTEAD GARDENS

Moretonhampstead, TQ13 8PW. *12m W of Exeter, 12m N of Newton Abbot. Signs from the Xrd of A382 and B3212. On E slopes of Dartmoor National Park. Parking at both gardens.* **Fri 17, Sat 18, Sun 19 May, Sat 17, Sun 18 Aug (2-6). Combined adm £6, chd free. Home-made teas at both gardens.**

MARDON
Graham & Mary Wilson.

SUTTON MEAD
Edward & Miranda Allhusen, 01647 440296, miranda@allhusen.co.uk.
Visits also by arrangement Feb to Sept.

2 large gardens on edge of moorland town. One in a wooded valley, the other higher up with magnificent views of Dartmoor. Both have mature orchards and yr-round vegetable gardens. Substantial rhododendron, azalea and tree planting, croquet lawns, summer colour and woodland walks through hydrangeas and acers. Mardon: 4 acres based on its original Edwardian design. Long herbaceous border and formal granite terraces supporting 2 borders of agapanthus. Fernery and colourful bog garden beside stream fed pond with its thatched boathouse. Arboretum. Sutton Mead: also 4 acres, shrub lined drive. Lawns surrounding granite lined pond with seat at water's edge. Unusual planting, dahlias, grasses, bog garden, rill fed round pond, secluded seating and gothic concrete greenhouse. Sedum roofed summer house. Enjoy the views as you wander through the woods. Dogs on leads welcome, plant sale. Teas are a must. Limited wheelchair access.

72 MOTHECOMBE HOUSE

Mothecombe, Holbeton, Plymouth, PL8 1LA. Mr & Mrs A Mildmay-White, www.flete.co.uk. *12m E of Plymouth. From A379 between Yealmpton and Modbury turn S for Holbeton. Continue 2m to Mothecombe.* **Sun 5 May (2-5). Adm £5, chd free. Lunches at The Schoolhouse, Mothecombe village.**
Queen Anne house (not open) with Lutyens additions and terraces set in private estate hamlet. Walled pleasure gardens, borders and Lutyens courtyard. Orchard with spring bulbs, unusual shrubs and trees, camellia walk. Autumn garden, streams, bog garden and pond. Bluebell woods leading to private beach. Yr-round interest. Sandy beach at bottom of garden, unusual shaped large liriodendron tulipifera. Gravel paths, two slopes.

73 THE MOUNT, DELAMORE

Cornwood, Ivybridge, PL21 9QP. Mr & Mrs Gavin Dollard. *Delamore Park PL21 9QP. Please park in car park for Delamore Park Offices not in village. From Ivybridge turn L at Xrds keep PH on L, follow wall on R to sharp R bend, turn R.* **Sat 16, Sun 17 Feb (10.30-3). Adm £4.50, chd free.**
Welcome one of the first signs of spring by wandering through swathes of thousands of unusual varieties of snowdrops in this lovely wood. Closer to the village than to Delamore gardens (open only in May for the Sculpture and Art Exhibition), paths meander through a sea of these lovely plants, some of which are unique to Delamore and which were sold as posies to Covent Garden as late as 2002. Main house and garden open for sculpture exhibition every day in May. Mainly rough paths/woodland tracks so difficult wheelchair access.

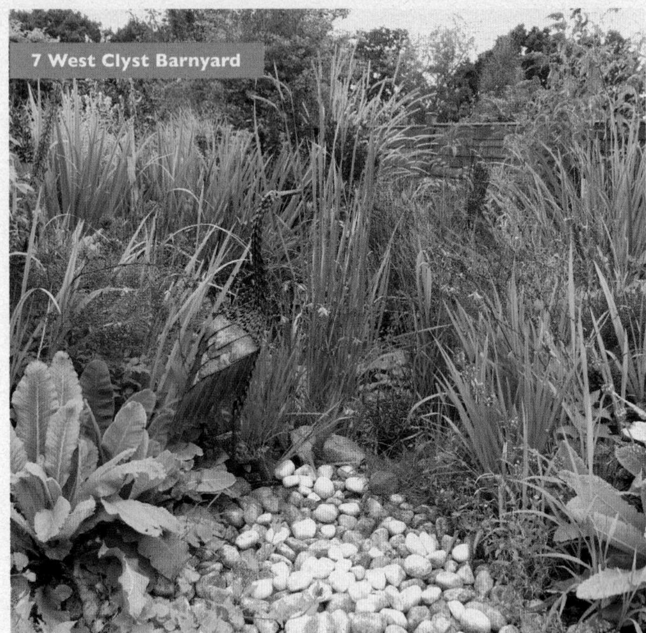
7 West Clyst Barnyard

plants from around the world. Superb mature cottage garden and Mediterranean garden will delight the visitor. Attractive viewpoint café, picnic area and shop. Open April 1st to end of Sept (9.30-5.00). Wheelchair access to café and nursery only.

74 MUSBURY BARTON

Musbury, Axminster, EX13 8BB. Lt Col Anthony Drake. *3m S of Axminster off A358. Turn E into village, follow yellow arrows. Garden next to church, parking for 12 cars, otherwise park on road in village.* **Sun 5, Mon 6 May, Sat 29, Sun 30 June (1.30-5). Adm £5, chd free. Home-made teas. Tea proceeds to Musbury Church.**
5 acres. Formal rose garden. Extensive areas of trees and shrubs, many rare or unusual. Stream. Pond. Lots of steps and bridges. Never perfect, always interesting.

75 THE OLD VICARAGE

West Anstey, South Molton, EX36 3PE. Tuck & Juliet Moss, 01398 341604, julietm@onetel.com. *9m E of South Molton. From S Molton go E on B3227 to Jubilee Inn. From Tiverton r'about take A396 7m to B3227 then L to Jubilee Inn. Follow NGS signs to garden.* **Sat 18, Sun 19 May, Sat 17, Sun 18 Aug (12-5). Adm £5, chd free. Cream teas.** Visits also by arrangement May to Sept for groups of up to 30.
Croquet lawn leads to multi-level garden overlooking 3 large ponds with winding paths, climbing roses and overviews. Brook with waterfall flows through garden past fascinating summerhouse built by owner. Benched deck overhangs first pond. Features rhododendrons, azaleas and primulas in spring and large collection of wonderful hydrangeas in Aug. New wall fountain mounted on handsome, traditional dry wall above house. Access by path through kitchen garden. A number of smaller standing stones echoing local Devon tradition.

76 ◆ PLANT WORLD

St Marychurch Road, Newton Abbot, TQ12 4SE. Ray Brown, 01803 872939, info@plant-world-seeds.com, www.plant-world-gardens.co.uk. *2m SE of Newton Abbot. 1½m from Penn Inn turn-off on A380. Follow brown tourist signs at end of A380 dual carriageway from Exeter.* **For information, please phone, email or visit garden website.**
The 4 acres of landscape gardens with fabulous views have been called Devon's 'Little Outdoor Eden'. Representing each of the five continents, they offer an extensive collection of rare and exotic

77 PROSPECT HOUSE

Lyme Road, Axminster, EX13 5BH. Peter Wadeley. *½m uphill from centre of Axminster. Just before service station.* **Fri 30, Sat 31 Aug, Sun 1 Sept (1-5). Adm £4.50, chd free. Home-made teas.**
1 acre plantsman's garden hidden behind high stone walls with Axe Valley views. Well stocked borders with rare shrubs, many reckoned to be borderline tender. 200 varieties of salvia, and other late summer perennials incl rudbeckia, helenium, echinacea, helianthus, crocosmia and grasses creating a riot of colour. A gem, not to be missed. Artist Zee Jones will be showing and selling her work. Zee uses mixed media to produce contemporary colourful semi abstract paintings. In her own words, Zee tries to portray her intuitive understanding of the way colours work together and how they can affect emotion.

78 REGENCY HOUSE

Hemyock, EX15 3RQ. Mrs Jenny Parsons, 01823 680238, jenny.parsons@btinternet.com, www.regencyhousehemyock.co.uk. *8m N of Honiton. M5 J26. From Catherine Wheel pub and church in Hemyock take Dunkeswell-Honiton Rd. Entrance ½m on R. Disabled parking (only) at house.* **Sun 9, Mon 10, Tue 11, Wed 12 June, Sun 13 Oct (2-5.30). Adm £5, chd free. Home-made teas.** Visits also by arrangement June to Oct for groups of up to 30. No coaches.
5 acre plantsman's garden approached across private ford. Many interesting and unusual trees and shrubs. Visitors can try their hand at identifying plants with the plant list or have a game of croquet. Plenty of space to eat your own picnic. Walled vegetable and fruit garden, lake, ponds, bog plantings and sweeping lawns. Horses, Dexter cattle and Jacob sheep. Gently sloping gravel paths give wheelchair access to the

walled garden, lawns, borders and terrace, where teas are served.

79 RIVERFORD FIELD KITCHEN GARDEN
Wash Farm, Buckfastleigh, TQ11 0JU. Riverford Farm, www.theriverfordfieldkitchen.co.uk. *Take A384 between Totnes and Buckfastleigh. Take turning for Riverford Organic (not the Farm Shop) and follow yellow NGS signs.* **Sat 8 June, Sat 7 Sept (11-5). Adm £4, chd free. Home-made teas. Hot and cold drinks and freshly made veg-inspired cakes! Booking essential if you want to eat in the restaurant for lunch – 01803 762074.**
An impressive 5yr old, organic kitchen garden and huge polytunnel. Planted up with an inspiring range of organic vegetables, herbs and flowers which are used daily in the farm restaurant, the award-winning Riverford Field Kitchen. Come and be inspired to grow your own! Practical demos throughout the day, guided tours of our polytunnels, plenty of fun for the kids. Mini tutorials and demo's with Penny in the polytunnel and garden. Play tractor and swings for little ones.

80 ST MERRYN
Higher Park Road, Braunton, EX33 2LG. Dr W & Mrs Ros Bradford, 01271 813805, ros@st-merryn.co.uk. *5m W of Barnstaple. On A361, R at 30mph sign, then at mini r'about, R into Lower Park Rd, then L into Seven Acre Lane, at top of lane R into Higher Park Rd. Pink house 200 yds on R.* **Sun 21 Apr, Sun 19 May, Sun 16 June (2-5.30). Adm £4, chd free. Cream teas.** Visits also by arrangement Apr to Aug for groups of up to 20.
Very sheltered, peaceful, gently sloping, S-facing, artist's garden, emphasis on shape, colour, scent and yr-round interest. A garden for pleasure with swimming pool. Thatched summerhouse leading down to herbaceous borders. Winding crazy paving paths, many seating areas. Shrubs, mature trees, fish ponds, grassy knoll, gravel areas, hens. Many environmental features. Open gallery (arts & crafts).

81 NEW SAMLINGSTEAD
Near Roadway Corner, Woolacombe, EX34 7HL. Roland & Marion Grzybek, 01271 870886, roland135@msn.com. *1m outside Woolacombe. Stay on A361 road all the way to Woolacombe. Passing through town head up Chalacombe Hill, L at T-junction, garden 200m on L.* **Sat 13 Apr (12.30-4.30). Cream teas in 'The Swallows' a purpose built out-building. Sat 6 July (12.30-4.30). Adm £4, chd free. Cream teas, home made hot sausage rolls, barbecue (weather permitting) and wine.** Visits also by arrangement Mar to Oct.
Garden is within 2 mins of N Devon coastline and Woolacombe AONB. 6 distinct areas; cottage garden at front, patio garden to one side, swallows garden at rear, meadow garden, orchard and field (a 500m walk with newly planted hedgerow). Slightly sloping ground so whilst wheelchair access is available to most parts of garden certain areas may require assistance.

82 SHAPCOTT BARTON KNOWSTONE ESTATE
(East Knowstone Manor), East Knowstone, South Molton, EX36 4EE. Anita Allen, 01398 341664. *13m NW of Tiverton. J25 M5 take Tiverton exit. 6½m to r'about take exit South Molton 10m on A361. Turn R signed Knowstone. Leave A361 travel ¼m to Roachhill through hamlet turn L at Wiston Cross, entrance on L ¼m.* **Sun 7, Sun 21 Apr, Sun 23 June, Fri 12, Sun 14 July, Sun 4 Aug (10.30-4.30). Adm £5, chd free. Light refreshments dependent on staffing. Picnics allowed.** Visits also by arrangement Apr to Aug. Donation to Cats Protection.
Large, ever developing garden of 200 acre estate around ancient historic manor house. Wildlife garden. Restored old fish ponds, stream and woodland rich in bird life. Unusual fruit orchard. Scented historic narcissi bulbs in Apr, roses in June, astilbes and phlox early July. Flowering burst July/Aug of National Plant Collections Leucanthemum superbum (shasta daisies) and buddleja davidii. Talks on Dowsing, also ghost experience talks. Very limited wheelchair access, steep slopes.
NPC

GROUP OPENING

83 SHEEPWASH GARDENS
Sheepwash, Beaworthy, EX21 5PE. Richard Coward. *1.3m N of Sheepwash. A3072 to Highampton. Take rd through Sheepwash. L on track signed Lake Farm. A386 S of Merton take road to Petrockstow. Up hill opp then L. After 350yds turn R down track signed Lake Farm.* **Sats, Suns 11, 12 May; 15, 16 June; 20, 21 July; 10, 11 Aug; 14, 15 Sept (11-5). Combined adm £5, chd free.**

LAKE FARMHOUSE
Erica Fisher, 01409 231582, erica@lakefarmhouse.co.uk, www.lakefarmhouse.co.uk.

MUSSELBROOK COTTAGE GARDEN
Richard Coward, 01409 231677, coward.richard@sky.com. **Visits also by arrangement Apr to Oct for groups of up to 30. Guided tours offered.**

2 gardens on opp sides of a track. Lake Farmhouse: A plantaholics garden with themed areas: rose garden, hosta, peony and hydrangea borders, large cut flower garden with dahlias, large productive kitchen garden, raised beds and containers. Many plants grown from seeds, cuttings and divisions. Informal, cottage style planting, Musselbrook Cottage: 1 acre naturalistic/wildlife/plantsman's garden of all season interest. Many rare/unusual plants on sloping site. 9 ponds (koi, orfe, rudd, dragonflies, lilies, aquatics). Stream, Japanese/Mediterranean gardens, oriental features. Wildflower meadow, clock golf. 1000s of bulbs. Hundreds of ericaceous plants incl acers, rhododendrons, camellias, hydrangeas and magnolias. Grasses, dierama, crocosmia. Wildlife haven. Aquatic nursery incl waterlilies.

84 SHUTELAKE

Butterleigh, Cullompton, EX15 1PG. Jill & Nigel Hall, 01884 38812, jill22hall@gmail.com. *3m W of Cullompton; 3m S of Tiverton. Between Tiverton & Cullompton, Follow signs for Silverton from Butterleigh village. Take L fork 100yds after entrance to Pound Farm. Car park sign on L after 150yds.* **Sat 13, Sun 14 July (11.30-5). Adm £4.50, chd free. Light refreshments in Studio Barn if weather inclement. Snack lunches.** Visits also by arrangement May to Aug for groups of 10 to 20.

A bridge over a stream brings you to a garden terraced into a hillside. From a natural pond full of wildlife, and a woodland walk, climb up to the herbaceous border, with colours of a Turkish carpet, and up again to discover a cobbled courtyard, sculptures, rockery, orchard and lawns surrounding a 300 year old house. Sit awhile under the pagoda and look out across Devon farmland. A place of serenity. Featured in Devon Life.

85 SIDBURY MANOR

Sidmouth, EX10 0QE. Lady Cave, www.sidburymanor.co.uk. *1m NW of Sidbury. Sidbury village is on A375, S of Honiton, N of Sidmouth.* **Fri 12, Sun 14 Apr (2-5). Adm £5, chd free. Cream teas.**

Built in 1870s this Victorian manor house built by owner's family and set within E Devon AONB comes complete with 20 acres of garden incl substantial walled gardens, extensive arboretum containing many fine trees and shrubs, a number of champion trees, and areas devoted to magnolias, rhododendrons and camellias. Partial wheelchair access.

GROUP OPENING

86 SIDMOUTH AUGUST GARDENS

Coulsdon Road, Sidmouth, EX10 9JP. *From Exeter on A3052 10m. R at Woolbrook Rd. In ½m R at St Francis Church.* **Sat 24, Sun 25, Mon 26 Aug (1.30-5.30). Combined adm £5, chd free. Home-made teas at all gardens except Fairpark. Gluten free, lactose free cakes available.**

BYES REACH
26 Coulsdon Road, Sidmouth, EX10 9JP. Lynette Talbot & Peter Endersby.

21 COULSDON ROAD
EX10 9JJ. Denise Rendell.

FAIRPARK
Knowle Drive, Sidmouth, EX10 8HP. Helen & Ian Crackston.

ROWAN BANK
44 Woolbrook Park, Sidmouth, EX10 9DX. Barbara Mence.

Situated on Jurassic Coast World Heritage Site, Sidmouth has fine beaches, beautiful gardens and magnificent coastal views. 4 contrasting ¼ acre gardens 1m apart. Byes Reach: (see separate entry). Fairpark lies behind a 12ft red brick wall, terraces, rockery, impressionist palette of colour, texture, many acres, small woodland and greenhouse. 21 Coulsdon is a contemporary take on a cottage garden in the front and a colour coordinated back garden punctuated with ornamental grasses and willow sculptures. Seating areas to enjoy homemade treats. No wheelchair access at Rowan Bank and Fairpark.

GROUP OPENING

87 SIDMOUTH JUNE GARDENS

Sidmouth, EX10 9DX. *Sidmouth. From Exeter on A3052 11m. R at Sidford T-lights. In ¾m turn L into Coulsdon Rd gardens, a short walk apart.* **Sat 8, Sun 9 June (1.30-5.30). Combined adm £4, chd free. Home-made teas. Gluten, lactose free available.**

BYES REACH
Lynette Talbot & Peter Endersby. (See separate entry)

NEW **21 COULSDON ROAD**
EX10 9JJ. Denise Rendell.

Situated on Jurassic Coast World Heritage Site, Sidmouth has fine beaches, beautiful gardens and magnificent coastal views. 2 contrasting gardens. Byes Reach: (see separate entry). 21 Coulsdon is a contemporary take on a cottage garden in the front and a colour coordinated back garden punctuated with ornamental grasses and willow sculptures. Seating areas to enjoy homemade treats. Wheelchair access at both.

88 SOCKS ORCHARD

Smallridge, Axminster, EX13 7JN. Michael & Hilary Pritchard, 01297 33693, michael.j.pritchard@btinternet.com. *2m from Axminster. From Axminster on A358 L at Weycroft Mill T-lights. Pass Ridgeway Hotel on L. Continue on lane for ½m. Park in field opp.* **Fri 5, Sat 6, Sun 7 July (1.30-5.30). Adm £4.50, chd free. Home-made teas.** Visits also by arrangement Mar to Sept for groups of up to 30.

1 acre plus plantaholic's garden designed for yr-round structure and colour. Many specimen trees, large collection of herbaceous plants, over 200 roses, woodland shrubs, dahlias, gravel and grass borders, small orchard, vegetable patch, small pond. Steep bank inset with shrubs underplanted with wild flowers with view point at top. Alpine house. Chickens. wheelchair access to most of garden.

89 SOUTH WOOD FARM

Cotleigh, Honiton, EX14 9HU. Professor Clive Potter, williamjamessmithson@gmail.com. *3m NE of Honiton. From Honiton head N on A30, take 1st R past Otter Dairy layby. Follow for 1m. Go straight over Xrds and take first L. Entrance after 1m on R.* **Sat 21, Sun 22 Sept (2-5). Adm £5, chd free. Home-made teas.** Visits also by arrangement May to July for groups of 10+.

Designed by the renowned Arne Maynard around C17 thatched farmhouse, this country garden in the Blackdown Hills exemplifies how contemporary design can be integrated into a traditional setting. Herbaceous borders, roses, yew topiary, knot garden, wildflower meadows, orchards, lean-to greenhouses and a mouthwatering kitchen garden combine to create an unforgettable sense of place. Gravel pathways, cobbles and steps.

90 SOUTHCOMBE BARN

Southcombe Barn, Widecombe-in-the-Moor, Newton Abbot, TQ13 7TU. Amanda Sabin & Stephen Hobson, 01364 621332, amandasabin1@hotmail.com. *6m W of Bovey Tracey. B3387 from Bovey Tracey after village church take rd SW for 400yds then sharp R signed Southcombe, after 200yds pass C17 farmhouse and park on L.* **Sun 26, Mon 27 May (2-5). Adm £5, chd free. Home-made teas. For £5 you very sociably make your own tea, take a slice from one of our beautiful cakes and sit out on the tea terraces among the flowers.**

2 tea lawn terraces with a super colourful rockery between 3 acre garden of crazy colourful flower meadow and flowering trees with mown grass paths running through and around and alongside the stream. The teas, too, are spectacular. Wildlife. If it is a very hardy wheelchair it can bump it's way as far as the tea terraces.

91 SPITCHWICK MANOR

Poundsgate, Newton Abbot, TQ13 7PB. Mr & Mrs P Simpson. *4m NW of Ashburton. Princetown rd from Ashburton through Poundsgate, 1st R at Lodge. From Princetown L at Poundsgate sign. Past Lodge. Park after 300yds at Xrds.* **Sat 18, Sun 19 May (11-4.30). Adm £5, chd free. Home-made teas.**

6½-acre garden with extensive beautiful views. Mature garden undergoing refreshment. A variety of different areas; lower walled garden with glasshouses, formal rose garden with fountain, camellia walk with small leat and secret garden with Lady Ashburton's plunge pool built 1763. 2.6 acre vegetable garden sheltered by high granite walls housing 9 allotments and lily pond. Mostly wheelchair access.

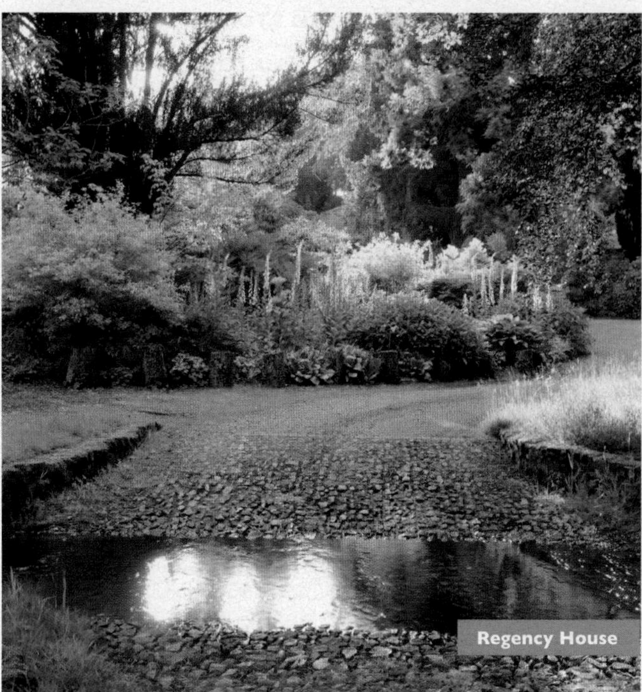

Regency House

92 SPRINGFIELD HOUSE

Seaton Road, Colyford, EX24 6QW. Wendy Pountney. *Colyford. Starting on A3052 coast rd, at Colyford PO take Seaton Rd. House 500m on R. Ample parking in field.* **Sat 1, Sat 29 June, Sat 27 July, Sat 24 Aug (10.30-5). Adm £4, chd free. Tea and cake/coffee/cream teas.**

1 acre garden of mainly fairly new planting. Numerous beds, majority of plants from cuttings and seed keeping cost to minimum, full of colour spring to autumn. Vegetable garden, fruit cage and orchard with ducks and chicken. New large formal pond. Wonderful views over R Axe and bird sanctuary, which is well worth a visit, path leads from the garden. Featured in Amateur Gardening magazine.

93 SQUIRRELS

98 Barton Road, Torquay, TQ2 7NS. Graham & Carol Starkie, 01803 329241, calgra@talktalk.net. *5m S of Newton Abbot. From Newton Abbot take A380 to Torquay. After ASDA store on L, turn L at T-lights up Old Woods Hill. 1st L into Barton Rd. Bungalow 200yds on L. Also could turn by B&Q. Parking nearby.* **Sat 20, Sun 21 July (2-5). Adm £5, chd free. Home-made teas. Visits also by arrangement in July.**

Plantsman's small town environmental garden, landscaped with small ponds and 7ft waterfall. Interlinked through abutilons to Japanese, Italianate, Spanish, tropical areas. Specialising in fruit incl peaches, figs, kiwi. Tender plants incl bananas, tree fern, brugmansia, lantanas, oleanders. Collection of fuchsia, dahlias, abutilons, bougainvillea. Enviromental and Superclass Winners. 27 cleverly hidden rain water storage containers. Advice on free electric from solar panels and solar hot water heating and fruit pruning. 3 sculptures. Many topiary birds, and balls. Huge 20ft Torbay palm. 9ft geranium. 15ft abutilons. New Moroccan and Spanish courtyard with tender succulents etc. Regret no wheelchair access. Conservatory for shelter and seating.

94 ◆ STONE LANE GARDENS

Stone Farm, Chagford, TQ13 8JU. Stone Lane Gardens Charitable Trust, 01647 231311, admin@stonelanegardens.com, www.stonelanegardens.com. *Halfway between Chagford and Whiddon Down, close to A382. Drewsteignton. 2m from Castle Drogo. 2m from A30 Whiddon Down via Long Lane.* **For NGS: Sat 14, Sat 21 Sept (10-6). Adm £6, chd £2.50. Light refreshments.** For other opening times and information, please phone, email or visit garden website.

Beautiful and unusual 5-acre arboretum and water garden on edge of Dartmoor National Park. National Collection of Birch and Alder. Our birch have lovely colourful peeling bark, from dark brown, reds, orange, pink and white. Interesting under-planting. Near by: NT Castle Drogo and garden. Featured in regional magazines. 'The Mythic Garden' sculpture exhibition from mid-May to end Oct sited among rare and unusual trees. Partial wheelchair access. WC.

♿ 🐕 ✿ NPC ☕

95 STONELANDS HOUSE

Dawlish, EX7 9BQ. Mr Kerim Derhalli (Owner) Mr Saul Walker (Head Gardener), 07815 807832, saulwalkerstonelands@outlook.com. *Outskirts of NW Dawlish. From A380 take junction for B3192 and follow signs for Teignmouth, after 2m L at Xrds onto Luscombe Hill, further 2m main gate on L.* **Visits by arrangement May to Sept for groups of 10 to 20. Weekdays only, please phone/email Head Gardener to arrange date and time. Adm £6, chd free.**

Beautiful 12 acre pleasure garden surrounding late C18 property designed by John Nash. Mature specimen trees, shrubs and rhododendrons, large formal lawn, recently landscaped herbaceous beds, vegetable garden, woodland garden, orchard with wild-flower meadow and river walk. An atmospheric and delightful horticultural secret! Featured on BBC Radio Devon and in Devon Life magazine. Wheelchair access limited to lower area of gardens as paths through woodland, meadow and riverside walk may be unsuitable for wheelchairs.

♿ D

96 SUMMERS PLACE

Little Bowlish, Whitestone, EX4 2HS. Mr & Mrs Stafford Charles, 01647 61786. *6m NW of Exeter. From M5, A30 Okehampton. After 7m R to Tedburn St Mary R at r'about past golf course 1st L after ½m signed Whitestone straight ahead at Xrds follow signs. From Exeter on Whitestone rd 1m beyond Whitestone, follow sign from Heath Cross. From Crediton follow Whitestone rd through Fordton.* **Suns 17 Mar; 7 Apr; 30 June; 29 Sept (1.30-5). Adm £5, chd free. Home-made teas. £5 includes cup of tea.** Visits also by arrangement Mar to Oct for groups of 10 to 20. Donation to Stroke Unit Royal Devon and Exeter Hospital.

Rambling rustic paths and steps (some steep) lead down a shaded woodland garden; unusual trees and shrubs (profusion of spring bulbs) and roses galore in June to ornamental orchard (berries, fruit, hip, autumn colour) with follies, sculpture, stream and ponds. Conservation as important as horticulture (wild areas). Intimate gardens round house, recently

Kentisbeare House

revamped new vistas. Animal sculptures and water features. Further new amusing features. Children and dogs love gardens. Garden related experts usually attend with sales tables.

GROUP OPENING

97 TEIGNMOUTH GARDENS

Cliff Road, Teignmouth, TQ14 8NH. *½m from Teignmouth town centre. Park in Teignmth FC for Lower Coombe Cott. Park at Bitton Hse for Orangery & 7 Coombe Ave. Park Exeter Rd for Yannon Lea. Park New Rd for High Tor, Berry Cott & 65 Teignmth Rd. Parking in Hazeldwn Rd.* **Sat 22, Sun 23 June (1-5). Combined adm £6, chd free. Home-made teas at High Tor, Cliff Road.**

BERRY COTTAGE
Alan & Irene Ward.

NEW **7 COOMBE AVENUE**
Stewart & Pat Henchie.

26 HAZELDOWN ROAD
Mrs Ann Sadler.

HIGH TOR
Gill Treweek.

NEW **LOWER COOMBE COTTAGE**
Tim & Tracy Armstrong.

NEW **THE ORANGERY**

65 TEIGNMOUTH ROAD
Mr Terry Rogers.

NEW **YANNON LEA**
Stuart Barker & Grahame Flynn.

The popular coastal town of Teignmouth has 3 new gardens joining the group this year, plus visitors can view the Teignmouth Orangery, a beautifully restored glasshouse first built in 1842, planted with exotic specimens. Lower Coombe Cottage: traditional country garden surrounding C17 thatched cottage with Bitton Brook running through the garden. Yannon Lea: newly planted with shrubs and perennials for yr round interest incl betula tree path and summer hot bed. 7 Coombe Ave: small plantsman's garden on 2 levels with wide range of exotic plants. 26 Hazeldown Rd: immaculate manicured garden with lovely sea views, beautifully clipped topiary and large koi carp pond. 65 Teignmouth Rd: stunning sea views framed by plentiful colour themed beds and pollinator friendly plants. Berry Cottage: cottage garden style planting providing a haven for wildlife. High Tor: home-made teas are served overlooking the lovely sea views in this ½-acre bee and butterfly friendly garden. Limited wheelchair access at some gardens.

98 TORVIEW

44 Highweek Village, Newton Abbot, TQ12 1QQ. Ms Penny Hammond. *On N of Newton Abbot accessed via A38. From Plymouth: A38 to Goodstone, A383 past Hele Park, L onto Mile End Rd. From Exeter: A38 to Drumbridges then A382 past Forches X, R signed Highweek. R at top of hill. Locally take Highweek signs.* **Sat 4, Sun 5, Mon 6 May (12-5). Adm £4.50, chd free. Home-made teas.**
Run by two semi-retired horticulturalists: Mediterranean formal front garden with wisteria-clad Georgian house, small alpine house. Rear courtyard with tree ferns, pots/troughs, lean-to 7m conservatory with tender plants and climbers. Steps to 30x20m walled garden - flowers, vegetables and trained fruit. Shade tunnel of woodlanders. Many rare/unusual plants. Rear garden up 7 steps, pebble areas in front garden.

99 NEW TREETOPS

Broadclyst, Exeter, EX5 3DT. Geoffrey & Margaret Gould. *From Exeter direction on B3181 drive through Broadclyst past school, next turn R. Follow signs.* **Sat 8, Sun 9 June (1-5). Adm £4, chd free. Home-made teas.**
Previously an orchard this 1-acre cottage garden, which is still evolving, is bordered by a forest and set within a beautiful borrowed landscape. Incorporating an avenue of Olivia Austin roses and an old restored brick path surrounded by borders featuring traditional and unusual cottage garden plants, grasses and pond.

100 UPPER GORWELL HOUSE

Goodleigh Rd, Barnstaple, EX32 7JP. Dr J A Marston, www.gorwellhousegarden.co.uk. *¾m E of Barnstaple centre on Bratton Fleming rd. Drive entrance between 2 lodges on L coming uphill (Bear Street) approx ¾m from Barnstaple centre. Take R fork at end of long drive. New garden entrance to R of house up steep slope.* **Sun 30 June, Sun 28 July (2-6). Adm £5, chd free. Cream teas by Goodleigh WI.**
Created mostly since 1979, this 4 acre garden overlooking the Taw estuary has a benign microclimate which allows many rare and tender plants to grow and thrive, both in the open and in walled garden. Several strategically placed follies complement the enclosures and vistas within the garden. Due to building works there will only be 2 dates this year. Mostly wheelchair access but some very steep slopes to get into garden.

101 VENN CROSS ENGINE HOUSE

Venn Cross, Waterrow, Taunton, TA4 2BE. Kevin & Samantha Anning, 01398 361392, venncross@btinternet.com. *Devon/Somerset border. Use main B3227 between Bampton and Wiveliscombe.* **Sat 20, Sun 21 July, Sat 24, Sun 25 Aug (2-5.30). Adm £5, chd free. Home-made teas. Selection of gluten-free cakes also available.** Visits also by arrangement June to Sept.
Former GWR goods yard. 4 acres of formal and less formal gardens of interest to gardeners and railway buffs alike. An acre of orchid rich wild flower meadow. Areas of mass-planted candelabra primulas start the summer with many large sweeping herbaceous borders bursting into colour as the season progresses. Sculptures, streams, ponds, vegetable beds and woodland walk, railway relics and historic pictures. Wheelchair access to main areas.

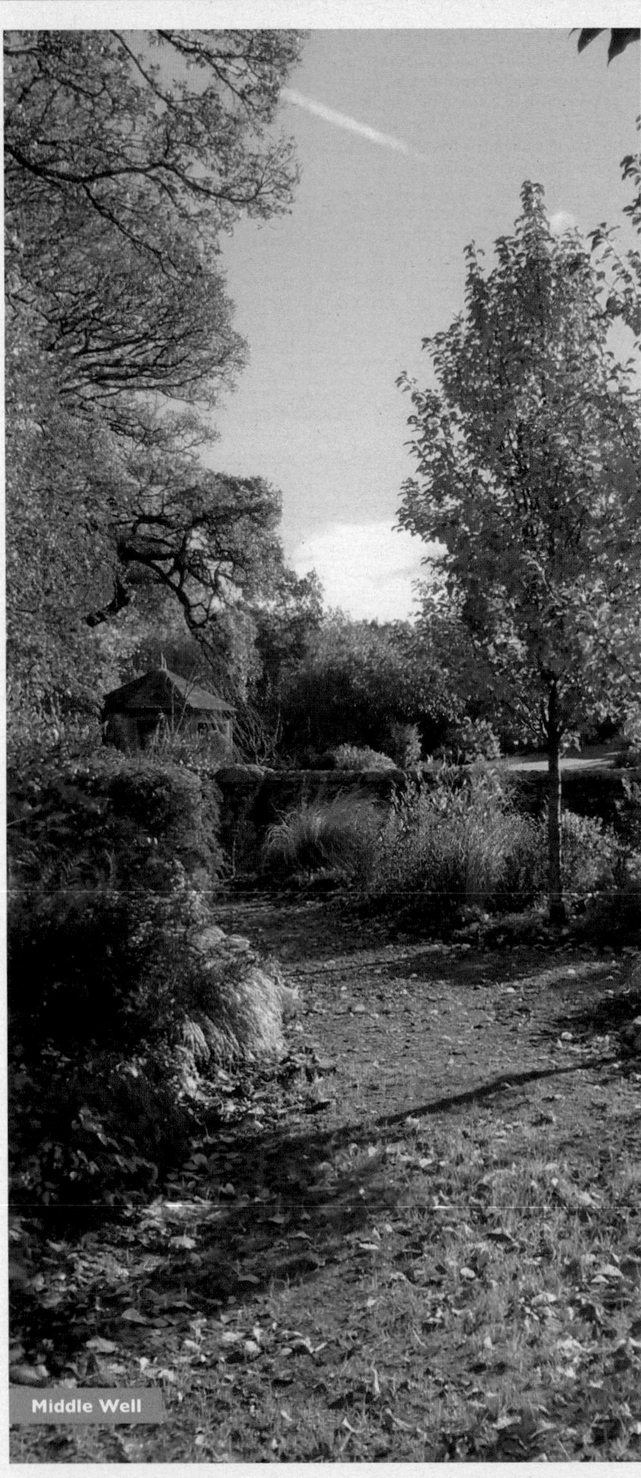
Middle Well

102 THE WALLED GARDEN, LINDRIDGE

Humber, Teignmouth, TQ14 9TE. William & Surya Patterson, 01626 870548, wspatterson@btinternet.com. *12m S of Exeter. From B3192 turn alongside Teignmouth golf course to Gipsy Corner then follow signs for Bishopsteignton. After 1m, at Rowden Cross, turn R to Lindridge. Garden 0.7m further on L.* **Visits by arrangement June to Sept for groups of 10 to 30 on 1st Friday of each month, no coaches. Adm £5, chd free. Light refreshments. Home-made cakes..** 1 acre historical walled former kitchen garden of the Lindridge Park Estate, fallow for over 50 years. Now in 4th yr of renovation, the garden has a geometric layout, lawns, mixed borders, juvenile hedges, trained fruit trees, wild flower meadow, ponds, woodland area, set in attractive countryside with far reaching views. Managed on an organic basis to provide a haven for wildlife. Sloping site with gravel paths. Some steps. Limited accessible parking.

103 NEW 7 WEST CLYST BARNYARD

West Clyst, Exeter, EX1 3TR. Malcolm & Ethel Hillier. *From Pinhoe take B3181 towards Broadclyst. At Westclyst T-lights continue straight past speed camera 1st R onto Private Road over M5 bridge, R into West Clyst Barnyard.* **Sat 22, Sun 23 June (1-5). Adm £4, chd free. Home-made teas.** Gardens and paddock extending for over an acre set in converted barnyard of medieval farm surrounded by farmland. Cottage garden, front garden with camellia and azaleas, wild life pond and bog garden, paddock with wildflower meadow. Arts and crafts for sale. Gardens and paddock accessible on same level.

104 WHITSTONE BLUEBELLS

Whitstone Farm, Bovey Tracey, TQ13 9NA. Katie & Alan Bunn, 01626 832258, katie@whitstonefarm.co.uk. *Whitstone Lane. From A382 turn towards hospital (sign opp golf range), after ⅓m L at swinging sign 'Private road leading to Whitstone'.*

Follow NGS signs. **Visits by arrangement for groups (max 30) and individuals between 15 April and 7 May. Please discuss parking when booking.** Stunning spring garden with far reaching views over Dartmoor. Bluebells throughout the garden along with camellias, rhododendrons and magnolias. Display of architectural metal sculptures and ornaments. Limited access to lower terraces for wheelchair users.

105 WHITSTONE FARM
Whitstone Lane, Bovey Tracey, TQ13 9NA. Katie & Alan Bunn, 01626 832258, katie@whitstonefarm.co.uk. *½m N of Bovey Tracey. From A382 turn towards hospital (sign opp golf range), after ⅓m L at swinging sign 'Private road leading to Whitstone'. Follow NGS signs.* **Visits by arrangement May to Sept for groups of up to 30. Contact regarding parking please. Adm £5, chd free. Tea and home-made cakes, gluten free option.**
Nearly 4 acres of steep hillside garden with stunning views of Haytor and Dartmoor. Arboretum planted 40 yrs ago, over 200 trees from all over the world incl magnolias, camellias, acers, alders, betula, davidias and sorbus. Major plantings of rhododendron and cornus. Late summer, flowering eucryphias and hydrangeas. National Collection of Eucryphias. Beautiful yr-round garden. Limited access to lower terraces for wheelchair users.

GROUP OPENING

106 WILLAND OLD VILLAGE GARDENS & ALLOTMENTS
Willand Old Village, Cullompton, EX15 2RH. *From J27 or J28 of M5 follow signs B3181 to Willand. Turn at PO sign, gardens approx 200 yds, follow yellow signs. Parking in village and at Allotments (EX15 2RG) yellow signs off B3181.* **Sat 15, Sun 16 June (2-5.30). Combined adm £5, chd free. Home-made teas.**

4 BUTTERCUP ROAD
John & Sally Holmes.

8 BUTTERCUP ROAD
Julie De-Ath-Lancaster.

CHURCH LEA
Mrs D Anderson.

COOMBE COURT
Mrs Bernice Philbrick.

THE NEW HOUSE
Celia & Bryan Holmes.

THE OLD RECTORY
Chris Borne.

THE VILLAGE ALLOTMENTS
c/o Mrs S. Statham.

The gardens and allotments and award-winning composting scheme which make up the group offer a mix from small gardens to larger ones in different parts of the village. All show what can be achieved in a more limited space, whilst meeting various owners' needs e.g. wheelchair user, and providing yr-round interest and colour. Each garden reflects differing interests and tastes. The allotment plots demonstrate a wide range of skills and production methods. St. Mary's Church and churchyard is open and interesting to explore. We can promise visitors a welcoming, full, and varied afternoon whether you plan to walk the trail or park and re-park. You can take refreshments on the way round. Start points will be indicated. Gardens, village and church have good accessibility for wheelchair users with modest slopes and few changes of level. Allotments have partial access.

107 WOOD BARTON
Kentisbeare, EX15 2AT. Mrs Rosemary Horton, 01884 266285. *8m SE of Tiverton, 3m E of Cullompton. 3m from M5 J28. A373 Cullompton to Honiton. 2m L to Bradfield/Willand, Horn Rd. After 1m at Xrds turn R. Farm drive ½m on L. Bull on sign.* **Sun 21, Mon 22 Apr (2.30-5). Adm £5, chd free. Home-made teas.** Visits also by arrangement Apr to Oct for groups of 10 to 30.
Established 2 acre arboretum with species trees on S-facing slope. Magnolias, 2 davidia, azaleas, camellias, rhododendrons, acers; several ponds and water feature. Autumn colour. New planting of woodland trees and bluebells opp house (this part not suitable for wheelchairs but dogs are welcome here). Sculptures and profiles in bronze resin. Small Japanese garden. Disabled parking in courtyard nr house.

108 YONDER HILL
Shepherds Lane, Colaton Raleigh, Sidmouth, EX10 0LP. Judy McKay, Sharon Attrell, Bob Chambers, 07864 055532, judy@yonderhill.me.uk, www.yonderhill.org.uk. *4m N of Budleigh Salterton B3178 between Newton Poppleford and Colaton Raleigh. Take turning signed Dotton and immed R into Shepherds Lane, ¼m 1st R at top of hill opp public footpath.* **Suns 7, 14, 21, Mon 22, Sun 28 Apr; Sun 5, Mon 6, Suns 12, 19, 26, Mon 27 May; Suns 2, 9, 16, 23, 30 June; Suns 7, 14, 21, 28 July; Suns 4, 11, 18, 25, Mon 26 Aug; Sun 1 Sept (1.30-4.30). Adm £3.50, chd £1. Light refreshments. Good selection of teas and coffee (make it yourself as you like it) and biscuits.** Visits also by arrangement Apr to Aug for groups of up to 30.
Enjoy a warm welcome to 3½ acres planted with love that will awaken your senses and soothe your soul. Blazing herbaceous borders buzzing with insects, cool woods, sunny glades alive with birdsong. Eucalyptus, Pittosporum, bamboo, conifer and fern collections. Rare and unusual planting, wildlife ponds, woodland walk, meadow, New features for 2019. Picnics welcome. Garden attracts great variety of birds, insects and other wildlife. Limited wheelchair access, some slopes.

Your visits help change lives – we are Hospice UK's largest charitable funder donating more than £5 million to support hospices in local communities since 1996

Volunteers

County Organiser
Alison Wright 01935 83652
wright.alison68@yahoo.com

County Treasurer
Richard Smedley 01202 528286
richard@carter-coley.co.uk

Publicity
Clare Arber 07939 071806
clarearber.ngs@gmail.com

Social Media
Di Reeds 07973 241028
digardengate@hotmail.co.uk

Booklet Editor
Judith Hussey 01258 474673
judithhussey@hotmail.com

Booklet Distributor
Alison Wright (as above)

Assistant County Organisers

Central East/Bournemouth
Trish Neale 01425 403565
trishneale1@yahoo.co.uk

North Central
Alexandra Davies 01747 860351
alex@theparishhouse.co.uk

North East/Ferndown/Christchurch
Mary Angus 01202 872789
mary@gladestock.co.uk

North West & Central
Annie Dove 01300 345450
anniedove1@btinternet.com

South Central/East
Helen Hardy 01929 471379
helliehardy@hotmail.co.uk

South Central/West
Di Reeds (as above)

South West
Debbie Bell
01297 444833
debbie@debbiebell.co.uk

Christine Corson 01308 863923
christinekcorson@gmail.com

West Central
Alison Wright (as above)

Dorset is not on the way to anywhere. We have no cathedral and no motorways. The county has been inhabited forever and the constantly varying landscape is dotted with prehistoric earthworks and ancient monuments, bordered to the south by the magnificent Jurassic Coast.

Discover our cosy villages with their thatched cottages, churches and pubs. Small historic towns including Dorchester, Blandford, Sherborne, Shaftesbury and Weymouth are scattered throughout, with Bournemouth and Poole to the east being the main centres of population.

Amongst all this, we offer the visitor a wonderfully diverse collection of gardens, found in both towns and deep countryside. They are well planted and vary in size, topography and content. In between the larger ones are the tiniest, all beautifully presented by the generous garden owners who open for the National Garden Scheme. Most of the county's loveliest gardens in their romantic settings also support us.

Each garden rewards the visitor with originality and brings joy, even on the rainiest day! They are never very far away from an excellent meal and comfortable bed.

So do come, discover and explore what the gardens of Dorset have to offer with the added bonus of that welcome cup of tea and that irresistible slice of cake, or a scone laden with clotted cream and strawberry jam!

Below: Crichel House

OPENING DATES

All entries subject to change. For latest information check www.ngs.org.uk

Extended openings are shown at the beginning of the month.

Map locator numbers are shown to the right of each garden name.

February

Snowdrop Festival

Sunday 3rd
◆ Mapperton Gardens 46

Sunday 10th
◆ Mapperton Gardens 46

Saturday 16th
Lawsbrook 41

Sunday 17th
◆ Mapperton Gardens 46

Saturday 23rd
Lawsbrook 41
Manor Farm, Hampreston 44

Sunday 24th
Manor Farm, Hampreston 44

March

Sunday 10th
Frankham Farm 22

Sunday 17th
The Old Vicarage 58
Q 61

Sunday 24th
Herons Mead 27
22 Holt Road 31
Q 61

Sunday 31st
Ivy House Garden 34

April

Wednesday 3rd
◆ Edmondsham House 19

Friday 5th
The Old Vicarage 58

Sunday 7th
Q 61

Wednesday 10th
◆ Edmondsham House 19

Saturday 13th
Chideock Manor 10
◆ Cranborne Manor Garden 16

Sunday 14th
Broomhill 8
Chideock Manor 10
Ivy House Garden 34
The Old Vicarage 58
Q 61

Wednesday 17th
◆ Edmondsham House 19

Friday 19th
Knitson Old Farmhouse 38

Saturday 20th
Knitson Old Farmhouse 38

Sunday 21st
Herons Mead 27
22 Holt Road 31
Ivy House Garden 34
Knitson Old Farmhouse 38
The Old Rectory, Netherbury 54

Monday 22nd
◆ Edmondsham House 19
Ivy House Garden 34
Knitson Old Farmhouse 38

Wednesday 24th
◆ Edmondsham House 19
Horn Park 33

Friday 26th
The Old Vicarage 58

Sunday 28th
Frankham Farm 22

May

Friday 3rd
The Old Vicarage 58

Saturday 4th
NEW Crichel House 17
The Secret Garden 64

Sunday 5th
NEW Crichel House 17
Herons Mead 27
Holworth Farmhouse 32
Ivy House Garden 34
The Old Rectory, Litton Cheney 52
The Secret Garden 64

Monday 6th
Holworth Farmhouse 32
Ivy House Garden 34

Tuesday 7th
Deans Court 18
NEW ◆ Keyneston Mill 35

Wednesday 8th
The Old Rectory, Litton Cheney 52

Sunday 12th
Chine View 11
Mayfield 47
Wolverhollow 76

Monday 13th
Wolverhollow 76

Wednesday 15th
◆ Sculpture by the Lakes 63
Wincombe Park 75

Thursday 16th
Chine View 11

Saturday 18th
NEW 22 Avon Avenue 3
Pilsdon View 59
Well Cottage 73

Sunday 19th
NEW 22 Avon Avenue 3
Chine View 11
NEW Gillans 24
22 Holt Road 31
Mayfield 47
The Old Rectory, Pulham 55
The Old Vicarage 58
Pilsdon View 59
2 Pyes Plot 60
Slape Manor 67
Well Cottage 73
Wincombe Park 75

Monday 20th
Pilsdon View 59
Well Cottage 73

Thursday 23rd
The Old Rectory, Pulham 55

Friday 24th
Knitson Old Farmhouse 38

Saturday 25th
Knitson Old Farmhouse 38

Sunday 26th
Annalal's Gallery 2
Harcombe House 26
Holworth Farmhouse 32
Knitson Old Farmhouse 38
The Old Rectory, Netherbury 54
Staddlestones 70

Monday 27th
Harcombe House 26
Holworth Farmhouse 32
Knitson Old Farmhouse 38
Mayfield 47
Staddlestones 70

Tuesday 28th
The Old Rectory, Netherbury 54

Wednesday 29th
Old Down House 51

Friday 31st
24 Carlton Road North 9
The Old Vicarage 58

June

Saturday 1st
24 Carlton Road North 9
Edwardstowe 20
Wolverhollow 76

Sunday 2nd
Annalal's Gallery 2
24 Carlton Road North 9
Edwardstowe 20
Frankham Farm 22
Old Down House 51

Monday 3rd
24 Carlton Road North 9
Wolverhollow 76

Wednesday 5th
Mayfield 47
Old Down House 51

Saturday 8th
Stable Court 69

Sunday 9th
Manor Farm, Hampreston 44
NEW Manor House Farm 45
The Old Rectory, Manston 53

Tuesday 11th
Stanbridge Mill 71

Wednesday 12th
Mayfield 47
The Old Rectory, Manston 53
Stable Court 69

Saturday 15th
Lytchett Minster Gardens 43

Sunday 16th
Broomhill 8
Lytchett Minster Gardens 43
NEW Manor House Farm 45
The Old Rectory, Litton Cheney 52
The Old School House 56
25 Richmond Park Avenue 62

Tuesday 18th
Deans Court 18
◆ Littlebredy Walled Gardens 42

Wednesday 19th
Horn Park 33
The Old School House 56

Friday 21st
◆ Knoll Gardens 39

Saturday 22nd
Chideock Manor 10
NEW Crichel House 17
The Hollow, Blandford Forum 29

Sunday 23rd
Chideock Manor 10
NEW Cliff Cottage 12
NEW Cliff Lodge 13
NEW Crichel House 17
NEW The Grange 25
The Hollow, Blandford Forum 29
22 Holt Road 31
Norwood House gardens and walks 50

Monday 24th
NEW The Grange 25

Tuesday 25th
◆ Littlebredy Walled Gardens 42

Wednesday 26th
The Hollow, Blandford Forum 29

Thursday 27th
Norwood House gardens and walks 50

Sunday 30th
Annalal's Gallery 2

July

Every Wednesday
The Hollow, Swanage 30

Saturday 6th
◆ Cranborne Manor Garden 16

Sunday 7th
Holworth Farmhouse 32
25 Richmond Park Avenue 62

Saturday 13th
NEW 22 Avon Avenue 3

Sunday 14th
NEW 22 Avon Avenue 3
NEW Black Shed 4
Broomhill 8
Hilltop 28

Thursday 18th
The Secret Garden and Serles House 65

Saturday 20th
Pilsdon View 59
Well Cottage 73

Sunday 21st
Annalal's Gallery 2
Cottesmore Farm 15
Hilltop 28
22 Holt Road 31
Pilsdon View 59
25 Richmond Park Avenue 62
The Secret Garden and Serles House 65
Well Cottage 73

Monday 22nd
Pilsdon View 59
Well Cottage 73

Sunday 28th
Cottesmore Farm 15
Hilltop 28
Manor Farm, Hampreston 44

The Secret Garden and Serles House 65

August

Every Wednesday
The Hollow, Swanage 30

Thursday 1st
The Secret Garden and Serles House 65

Saturday 3rd
10 Brookdale Close 7
Harcombe House 26

Sunday 4th
10 Brookdale Close 7
Cottesmore Farm 15
Harcombe House 26
Hilltop 28
The Old Rectory, Pulham 55
The Secret Garden and Serles House 65

Tuesday 6th
Harcombe House 26

Thursday 8th
Manor Farm, Hampreston 44
The Old Rectory, Pulham 55

Saturday 10th
10 Brookdale Close 7

Sunday 11th
Annalal's Gallery 2
10 Brookdale Close 7
Hilltop 28
Manor Farm, Hampreston 44

Thursday 15th
Broomhill 8

Sunday 18th
Hilltop 28
22 Holt Road 31
The Secret Garden and Serles House 65

Sunday 25th
The Secret Garden and Serles House 65

Monday 26th
NEW Black Shed 4
The Secret Garden and Serles House 65

Thursday 29th
The Secret Garden and Serles House 65

Saturday 31st
The Secret Garden and Serles House 65

September

Sunday 1st
NEW Brook View Care Home 6
The Secret Garden and Serles House 65

Wednesday 4th
NEW Brook View Care Home 6

Thursday 5th
The Secret Garden and Serles House 65

Saturday 7th
The Secret Garden and Serles House 65

Sunday 8th
The Secret Garden and Serles House 65

Sunday 15th
Herons Mead 27

Tuesday 17th
NEW ◆ Keyneston Mill 35

Friday 27th
◆ Knoll Gardens 39

October

Wednesday 2nd
◆ Edmondsham House 19

Wednesday 9th
◆ Edmondsham House 19

Sunday 13th
Frankham Farm 22

Wednesday 16th
◆ Edmondsham House 19

Wednesday 23rd
◆ Edmondsham House 19

November

Sunday 3rd
Lawsbrook 41

Sunday 10th
Lawsbrook 41

By Arrangement

Arrange a personalised garden visit with your club, or group of friends, on a date to suit you. See individual garden entries for full details.

THE GARDENS

1 ◆ ABBOTSBURY GARDENS

Abbotsbury, Weymouth, DT3 4LA. Ilchester Estates, 01305 871387, info@abbotsbury-tourism.co.uk, www.abbotsburygardens.co.uk. *8m W of Weymouth. From B3157 Weymouth-Bridport, 200yds W of Abbotsbury village.* **For opening times and information, please phone, email or visit garden website.**

30 acres, started in 1760 and considerably extended in C19. Much recent replanting. The maritime micro-climate enables Mediterranean and southern hemisphere garden to grow rare and tender plants. National collection of Hoherias (flowering Aug in NZ garden). Woodland valley with ponds, stream and hillside walk to view the Jurassic Coast. Open all yr except Christmas week. Featured on Countrywise and Gardeners' World and in Country Life. Limited wheelchair access, some very steep paths and rolled gravel but we have a selected wheel chair route with sections of tarmac hard surface.

♿ 🐕 ✿ 🚌 NPC ☕

2 ANNALAL'S GALLERY

25 Millhams Street, Christchurch, BH23 1DN. Anna & Lal Sims, 01202 567585, anna.sims@ntlworld.com, www.annasims.co.uk. *Town centre. Park in Saxon Square PCP - exit to Millhams St via alley at side of church.* **Suns 26 May; 2, 30 June; 21 July; 11 Aug (2-4). Adm £3, chd free. Visits also by arrangement May to Aug for groups of 10+.**

Enchanting 150 yr-old cottage, home of two Royal Academy artists. 32ft x 12½ft garden on 3 patio levels. Pencil gate leads to colourful scented Victorian walled garden. Sculptures and paintings hide among the flowers and shrubs. Unusual studio and garden room. Not suitable for wheelchairs; not suitable for dogs.

3 NEW 22 AVON AVENUE

Ringwood, BH24 2BH. Terry & Dawn Heaver, 01425 473970, terry@avongas.com. *Past Ringwood from east A31 turn L after garage, L again into Matchams Ln, Avon Castle 1m on L. A31 from west turn R into Boundary Ln, then L into Matchams Ln, Avon Ave ½m on R.* **Sat 18, Sun 19 May, Sat 13, Sun 14 July (12-5). Adm £5, chd free. Home-made teas. Visits also by arrangement May to Sept for groups of up to 10.**

Japanese themed water garden featuring granite sculptures, ponds, waterfalls, azaleas, rhododendrons cloud topiary and a collection of large koi carp. Regret, no wheelchair access due to narrow gravel path. Children only under parental supervision, due to large, deep water pond.

Norwood House Gardens and Walks

© Ellen Rooney

4 NEW BLACK SHED

Blackmarsh Farm, Dodds Cross, Sherborne, DT9 4JX. Paul & Helen Stickland, 07859 911817, info@blackshed.flowers, blackshedflowers.blogspot.com/. *On A30 just E of Sherborne. From Sherborne, follow A30 towards Shaftesbury. Black Shed approx 1m E at Blackmarsh Farm, on L, next to The Toy Barn. Large Car Park shared with The Toy Barn.* **Sun 14 July, Mon 26 Aug (1-5). Adm £4, chd free. Home-made teas.** Visits also by arrangement May to July for groups of 10+.

Over 150 colourful and productive flower beds growing a sophisticated selection of cut flowers and foliage to supply florists and the public, for weddings, events and occasions throughout the seasons. Traditional garden favourites, delphiniums, larkspur, foxgloves, scabious and dahlias alongside more unusual perennials, foliage plants and grasses, creating a stunning and unique display. A warm welcome and generous advice on creating your own cut flower garden is offered. Easy access from gravel car park. Wide grass pathways enabling access for wheelchairs. Gently sloping site.

5 BRADDOCKS

Oxbridge, Bridport, DT6 3TZ. Dr & Mrs Roger Newton, 01308 488441, rogernewton329@btinternet.com, www.braddocksgarden.co.uk. *3m N of Bridport. From Bridport, A3066 to Beaminster 3m, just before Melplash, L into Camesworth Lane signed Oxbridge. Single track rd, down steep hill. Garden signed.* **Visits by arrangement Mar to Sept for groups of 5 to 30. Mondays preferred. Adm £5, chd free. Home-made teas.**

3 acres of plant-packed sloping gardens, conceived, planted and looked after by owner. 'A feast of a garden at all times of the year'. Wild flower meadows and water. Herbaceous, underplanted shrubs and roses of all types and hues. Shady woodland garden and fine mature specimen trees. Steep slopes and gravel paths make the garden unsuitable for wheelchairs.

6 NEW BROOK VIEW CARE HOME

Riverside Road, West Moors, Ferndown, BH22 0LQ. Charles Hubberstey, www.brookviewcare.co.uk. *Past village shops, L into Riverside Road, Brook View Care Home is on R after 100 metres.* **Sun 1, Wed 4 Sept (11-5). Adm £3.50, chd free. Home-made teas. Teas in morning. Cream teas in afternoon. Payment by donation.**

Our colourful and vibrant garden is spread over two main areas, one warm and sunny, the other cooler and shadier. A fountain area is a gathering point for the sunny side, then walking past our greenhouse leads to the fruit and vegetable gardens. Produce is eagerly used by the kitchen, and residents will help out with the production of the bedding plants, all expertly managed by our gardener.

7 10 BROOKDALE CLOSE

Broadstone, BH18 9AA. Michael & Sylvia Cooper. *Located just 100yds from centre of Broadstone, Brookdale Close is on Higher Blandford Rd, with additional parking in next road, Fairview Cres.* **Sat 3, Sun 4, Sat 10, Sun 11 Aug (2-5). Adm £3.50, chd free. Home-made teas.**

Described as a 'little piece of paradise', with the 'wow' factor, our 70ft x 50ft garden is centred around a wildlife pond and tumbling waterfall. A rich kaleidoscope of colour combining both tropical and cottage garden, with tree ferns, bananas, grasses, beautiful perennials and stunning dahlia display, with a different view at every turn. Very limited wheelchair access.

8 BROOMHILL

Rampisham, Dorchester, DT2 0PU. Mr & Mrs D Parry, 01935 83266, carol.parry2@btopenworld.com. *11m NW of Dorchester. From Dorchester A37 Yeovil, 9m L Evershot. From Yeovil A37 Dorchester, 7m R Evershot. From Crewkerne A356, 1½m after Rampisham Garage L Rampisham. Follow signs.* **Sun 14 Apr, Sun 16 June, Sun 14 July, Thur 15 Aug (2-5). Adm £5, chd free. Home-made teas.** Visits also by arrangement June to Aug for groups of 10+.

Once a farmyard now a delightful, tranquil garden set in 1½ acres. Island beds and borders are planted with shrubs, roses, masses of unusual perennials and choice annuals to give vibrancy and colour into the autumn. Lawns and paths lead to less formal area with large wildlife pond, meadow, shaded areas, bog garden and late summer border. Gravel entrance, the rest is grass, some gentle slopes.

9 24 CARLTON ROAD NORTH

Weymouth, DT4 7PY. Anne & Rob Tracey. *8m S of Dorchester. A354 from Dorchester, R into Carlton Rd North. From Town Centre follow esplanade towards A354 Dorchester and L into C Rd N.* **Fri 31 May, Sat 1, Sun 2, Mon 3 June (2-5). Adm £3, chd free. Home-made teas.**

Long garden on several levels. Steps and narrow sloping paths lead to beds and borders filled with trees, shrubs and herbaceous plants incl many unusual varieties. A garden which continues to evolve and reflect an interest in texture, shape and colour. Wildlife is encouraged. Raised beds in the front garden create a space for vegetable growing.

10 CHIDEOCK MANOR

Chideock, Bridport, DT6 6LF. Mr & Mrs Howard Coates, 07885 551795, deirdrecoates9@gmail.com. *2m W of Bridport on A35. In centre of village turn N at church. The Manor is ¼m along this rd on R.* **Sat 13, Sun 14 Apr, Sat 22, Sun 23 June (2-5). Adm £6, chd free. Home-made teas.** Visits also by arrangement Feb to Dec for groups of up to 30.

6/7 acres of formal and informal gardens. Bog garden beside stream and series of ponds. Yew hedges and mature trees. Lime and crab apple walks, herbaceous borders, colourful rose and clematis arches, fernery and nuttery. Walled vegetable garden and orchard. Woodland and lakeside walks. Fine views. Partial wheelchair access.

11 CHINE VIEW

15a Cassel Avenue, Poole, BH13 6JD. Andy & Mel Leach. *2m W of Bournemouth. From centre of Westbourne turn S into Alumhurst Rd, take 8th turning on R into Mountbatten Rd then 1st L into Cassel Ave.* **Sun 12, Thur 16, Sun 19 May (1-5). Adm £4, chd free. Home-made teas.**

Unique Chine garden adjacent to public footpath leading to beach. Features incl extensive terraced rockery incorporating 330 tons of Purbeck stone, palladian rotunda, subtropical plants and profusion of azaleas and rhododendrons. Wavelength A Cappella ladies choir will be singing at 3pm on Sun 19th May. Steep steps and uneven paths make it unsuitable for the less mobile.

12 NEW CLIFF COTTAGE

West Cliff, West Bay, Bridport, DT6 4HS. Mr Asit Acharya. *Across harbour bridge in West Bay, 2nd exit at r'about, along Forty Foot Way and uphill to very top of West Walks.* **Sun 23 June (2-5). Combined adm with Cliff Lodge £5, chd free. Home-made teas.**

One acre cottage garden, originally 3 small workers' dwellings built around 1750 and set on top of West Cliff. The garden was overgrown when the present owner moved in 6 yrs ago and is still a work in progress. Some mature borders, new areas of planting, small orchard. Relaxed, informal planting. Shepherds hut and viewing deck with views towards East Cliff and Portland.

13 NEW CLIFF LODGE

West Cliff, West Bay, Bridport, DT6 4HS. Mrs Dawn Gibson. *At top of West Cliff private estate in West Bay. See directions on Cliff Cottage.* **Sun 23 June (2-5). Combined adm with Cliff Cottage £5, chd free. Home-made teas at Cliff Lodge.**

⅓ acre mature garden with good rural views. Mature camellias, hydrangeas, silver birch, old bramley apple tree with rambling fragrant roses planted through, fruit cage, geraniums, roses, lavenders, grasses, thatched summerhouse.

14 COTTAGE ROW

School Lane, Tarrant Gunville, nr Blandford Forum, DT11 8JJ. Carolyn & Michael Pawson, 01258 830212, michaelpawson637@btinternet.com. *6m NE of Blandford Forum. From Blandford take A354 towards Salisbury, L at Tarrant Hinton. After 1½m R in Tarrant Gunville into School Lane.* **Visits by arrangement Apr to Sept for groups of 6 to 25. Adm £5, chd free. Refreshments by arrangement for groups.**

Maturing ½ acre partly walled garden. Formal and informal areas separated by yew hedges. Pergola, arbours, brick paths, tree house, kitchen garden and the sound of water; bees and butterflies abound in this tranquil spot. This sophisticated cottage garden reflects the owners' love of unusual plants, structure and an artist's eye for sympathetic colour.

15 COTTESMORE FARM

Newmans Lane, West Moors, Ferndown, BH22 0LW. Paul & Valerie Guppy, 07413 925372, paulguppy@googlemail.com. *1m N of West Moors. Off B3072 Bournemouth to Verwood rd. Car parking in owner's field.* **Sun 21, Sun 28 July, Sun 4 Aug (2-5). Adm £4, chd free. Home-made teas. Visits also by arrangement July & Aug for groups of 10 to 20.**

Gardens of over an acre, created from scratch over 20 years. Wander through a plantsman's tropical paradise of giant gunneras, bananas, towering bamboos and over 100 palm trees, into a floral extravaganza. Large borders and sweeping island beds overflowing with phlox, heliopsis, helenium and much more combine to drown you in scent and colour. Wheelchair access to garden to avoid 2 lots of steps, please ask on arrival to make use of level route through main drive gate.

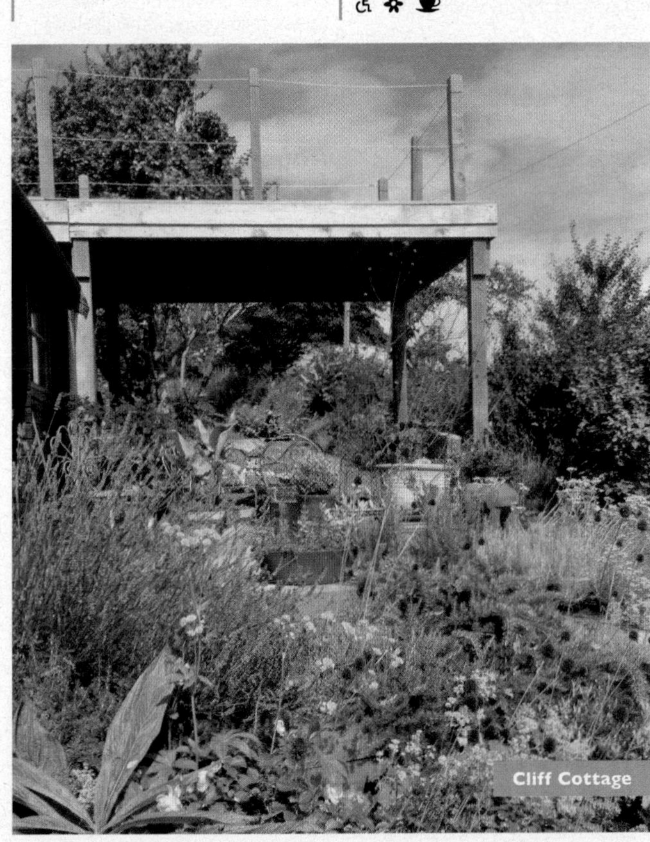

Cliff Cottage

16 ◆ CRANBORNE MANOR GARDEN

Cranborne, BH21 5PP. Viscount Cranborne, 01725 517289, info@cranborne.co.uk, www.cranborne.co.uk. *10m N of Wimborne on B3078. Enter garden via Cranborne Garden Centre, on L as you enter top of village of Cranborne.* **For NGS: Sat 13 Apr, Sat 6 July (9-4). Adm £6, chd £1. Light refreshments in Café, Cranborne Garden Centre www.cranbornegardencentre.co.uk. Breakfast, hot & cold lunches, afternoon tea.**

For other opening times and information, please phone, email or visit garden website.

Beautiful and historic garden laid out in C17 by John Tradescant and enlarged in C20, featuring several gardens surrounded by walls and yew hedges: blue and white garden, cottage style and mount gardens, water and wild garden. Many interesting plants, with fine trees and avenues. Mostly wheelchair access.

17 NEW CRICHEL HOUSE

Moor Crichel, Wimborne, BH21 5DT. Mr & Mrs R Chilton Jr. Head Gardener: Mark Lyons. *6m N of Wimborne. From B3078 turn to Witchampton and follow signs through village to gatehouse.* **Sat 4, Sun 5 May, Sat 22, Sun 23 June (10.30-4). Adm £5.50, chd free. Home-made teas.**

60 acre park, 30 acre lake and 3 acre walled garden surrounding Crichel House. Mature trees including exceptional cedars form the backdrop to the Walled Garden which was set out in 1976 and recently renovated. Box hedges and paths lead into herbaceous borders. Lime avenue flanked by orchards and tulips leads to reflecting pond completed by a stone pavilion and 7 individual secret gardens. Partial wheelchair access. Most of garden can be reached by grass pathways.

18 DEANS COURT

Deans Court Lane, Wimborne Minster, BH21 1EE. Sir William Hanham, 01202 849314, info@deanscourt.org, www.deanscourt.org. *Pedestrian Entrance (no parking) - Deans Court Lane (BH21 1EE). Vehicle Entrance (free parking) on A349, Poole Road, Wimborne (BH21 1QF).* **Tue 7 May, Tue 18 June (11-5). Adm £5, chd free. Home-made teas at our Deans Court Café on Deans Court Lane. Morning coffee, lunches, and teas.** Visits also by arrangement for groups of 20+. Donation to Friends of Victoria Hospital, Wimborne.

13 acres of peaceful, partly wild gardens in ancient monastic setting with mature specimen trees, Saxon fish pond, herb garden, orchard and apiary beside R Allen close to town centre. First Soil Association accredited garden, within C18 serpentine walls. The Permaculture system has recently been introduced here with chemical free produce supplying the Deans Court Café nearby where light lunches and teas are available. Tours of house available on National Garden Scheme open days 7 May and 18 June (2019) £5 at 12 and 2pm, book upon arrival. For disabled access, follow signs within grounds for parking closer to the gardens. Some paths have deeper gravel.

19 ◆ EDMONDSHAM HOUSE

Edmondsham, Wimborne, BH21 5RE. Mrs Julia Smith, 01725 517207, julia.edmondsham@homeuser.net. *9m NE of Wimborne. 9m W of Ringwood. Between Cranborne & Verwood. Edmondsham off B3081. Wheelchair access and disabled parking at West front door.* **For NGS: Weds 3, 10, 17 Apr (2-5), Mon 22, Wed 24 Apr (2-5); Weds 2, 9, 16, 23 Oct (2-5). Adm £2.50, chd £0.50. Tea, coffee, cake and soft drinks 3.30-4pm in Edmondsham House Weds only.** For other opening times and information, please phone or email.

6 acres of mature gardens, grounds, views, trees and shaped hedges surrounding C16/C18 house, giving much to explore incl C12 church adjacent to garden. Large Victorian walled garden is productive and managed organically (since 1984) using 'no dig' vegetable beds. Wide herbaceous borders planted for seasonal colour. Traditional potting shed and working areas. House also open on NGS days. Coaches by appointment only. Some grass and gravel paths.

20 EDWARDSTOWE

50-52 Bimport, Shaftesbury, SP7 8BA. Mike & Louise Madgwick. *Park in town's main car park. Walk along Bimport (B3091) 500mts, Edwardstowe last house on L.* **Sat 1, Sun 2 June (10.30-4.30). Adm £3.50, chd free.**

Parts of the garden have been extensively remodelled during 2018, a new greenhouse and potting shed have been added, along with changing pathways and the vegetable garden layout. Long borders have been replanted in places with trees managed letting in more light.

21 ◆ FORDE ABBEY GARDENS

Forde Abbey, Chard, TA20 4LU. Mr & Mrs Julian Kennard, 01460 221290, info@fordeabbey.co.uk, www.fordeabbey.co.uk. *4m SE of Chard. Signed off A30 Chard-Crewkerne and A358 Chard-Axminster. Also from Broadwindsor B3164.* For opening times and information, please phone, email or visit garden website.

30 acres of fine shrubs, magnificent specimen trees, ponds, herbaceous borders, rockery, bog garden containing superb collection of Asiatic primulas, Ionic temple, working walled kitchen garden supplying the tearoom. Centenary fountain, England's highest powered fountain. Gardens open daily (10am-5.30pm, last adm 4.30pm), house open from 2 April Tues to Fri incl, Suns & BH Mons. Please ask at reception for best wheelchair route. Wheelchairs available to borrow/hire, advance booking advised.

22 FRANKHAM FARM

Ryme Intrinseca, Sherborne, DT9 6JT. Susan Ross, 07594 427365, neilandsusanross@gmail.com. *3m S of Yeovil. A37 Yeovil-Dorchester; turn E; ¼m; drive is on L.* **Suns 10 Mar; 28 Apr; 2 June; 13 Oct (11.30-5). Adm £5, chd free. Home-made teas. Home produced lunch 12-2.30 pulled**

pork in roll, vegetarian soup.
3½ acre garden, created since 1960 by the late Jo Earle for yr-round interest. This large and lovely garden is filled with a wide variety of well grown plants, roses, unusual labelled shrubs and trees. Productive vegetable garden. Clematis and other climbers. Spring bulbs through to autumn colour, particularly oaks. New toilets in 2019. Sorry, no dogs.

23 FRITH HOUSE

Stalbridge, DT10 2SD. Mr & Mrs Patrick Sclater, 01963 250809, rosalynsclater@btinternet.com. *5m E of Sherborne. Between Milborne Port and Stalbridge. From A30 1m, follow sign to Stalbridge. From Stalbridge 2m and turn W by PO.* **Visits by arrangement Apr to July for groups of 10+. Monday to Friday only. Adm £5, chd free. Home-made teas.**
Approached down long drive with fine views. 4 acres of garden around Edwardian house and self-contained hamlet. Range of mature trees, lakes and flower borders. House terrace edged by rose border and featuring Lutyensesque wall fountain and game larder. Well stocked kitchen gardens.

Your visits help change lives - your generosity helps Marie Curie fund nurses to care for people night and day in their homes, with donations of more than £8.8 million

24 NEW GILLANS

Minterne Parva, Nr Dorchester, DT2 7AP. Robert & Sabina ffrench Blake, 01300 342077, sfb@gillans.net. *N of Cerne Abbas off A352, plenty of parking. Dogs on leads. Signed off main road - 200 yards to gate on L.* **Sun 19 May (2-6). Adm £5, chd free. Home-made teas.** Visits also by arrangement May & June.
Hidden 5 acre garden set in deep valley beside ponds and River Cerne; surrounded by ancient trees with borrowed landscape. Spring bulbs and blossom with species magnolia and cornus. Carpets of primroses around camellias and rhodos. Steep paths-stout footwear recommended! Partially replanted over past 6yrs. Formal beds, pots, climbing roses, wisteria and productive veg garden surround house. Wheelchair access around house.

25 NEW THE GRANGE

Burton Street, Marnhull, Sturminster Newton, DT10 1PS. Francesca Pratt. *Marnhall. 8m SW from Shaftesbury take A30 and B3092, to Marnhall turn R into Sodom lane. From south B3092 to Marnhall turn L into Church St - follow NGS signs to Grange.* **Sun 23, Mon 24 June (2-5). Adm £4.50, chd free. Home-made teas. Gluten free cakes.**
A large village garden created 4 yrs ago. Spectacular 250 yr old copper beech on lawn. Large terrace with integrated colourful borders. Extensive lawn leading to 2 herbaceous borders planted in hot colours at entry to fastigiate hornbeam avenue. Woodland garden with shade loving shrubs and ground cover, magnificent treehouse. Swimming pool garden with pool house. Wheelchair access to lawn and woodland garden - 6 steps down to terrace.

26 HARCOMBE HOUSE

Pitmans Lane, Morcombelake, Bridport, DT6 6EB. Jan & Martin Dixon, 01297 489229, harcombe@hotmail.co.uk, jdmc49.wixsite.com/harcombe-house. *4m W of Bridport - do not follow SatNav. A35 from Bridport: R to Whitchurch just past The Artwave Gallery. Immed R, bear L into Pitmans Lane. Approx 800m, park in paddock on L.* **Sun 26, Mon 27 May, Sat 3, Sun 4, Tue 6 Aug (11-5). Adm £5, chd free. Home-made teas. All cakes are home-made by Jan. Sausage rolls are home-made by Martin.** Visits also by arrangement May to Sept for groups of 5 to 30. Groups welcome, however Lane is not suitable for coaches.
Landscaped into the hillside 500ft above the Char Valley with spectacular views across Charmouth and Lyme Bay. The steeply sloped site comprises a ¾ acre formal garden and ½ acre wild garden. The beautiful ¾ acre garden has been rediscovered, restored and replanted in natural and relaxed style over last 12 yrs with an abundance of shrubs and perennials, many unusual and visually stunning. Majestic rhododendrons and azaleas complement spring bulbs in a blaze of colour in May/June and in Aug the beautiful eucryphia is the star of the garden. Whilst the garden is easily navigable, it will present a challenge to the less mobile visitor and is definitely unsuitable for wheelchairs and buggies.

27 HERONS MEAD

East Burton Road, East Burton, Wool, BH20 6HF. Ron & Angela Millington, 01929 463872, ronamillington@btinternet.com. *6m W of Wareham on A352. Approaching Wool from Wareham, turn R just before level crossing into East Burton Rd. Herons Mead ¾m on L.* **Suns 24 Mar; 21 Apr; 5 May; 15 Sept (2-5). Adm £3.50, chd free. Home-made teas.** Visits also by arrangement Mar to Sept for groups of 10 to 30.
½ acre plantlover's garden full of interest from spring (bulbs, many hellebores, pulmonaria, fritillaries) through abundant summer perennials, old roses scrambling through trees and late seasonal exuberant plants amongst swathes of tall grasses. Wildlife pond and plants to attract bees, butterflies, etc. Tiny woodland. Cacti. Small wheelchairs can gain partial access - as far as the tea house!

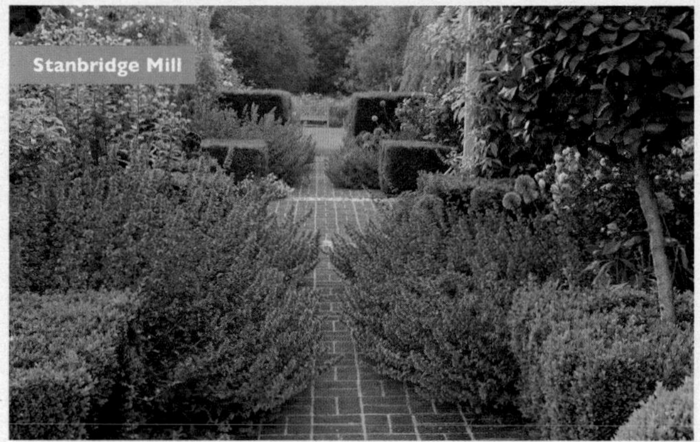
Stanbridge Mill

28 HILLTOP

Woodville, Stour Provost, Gillingham, SP8 5LY. Josse & Brian Emerson, www.hilltopgarden.co.uk. *7m N of Sturminster Newton, 5m W of Shaftesbury. On B3092 turn E at Stour Provost Xrds, signed Woodville. After 1¼m thatched cottage on R. On A30, 4m W of Shaftesbury, turn S opp Kings Arms. 2nd turning on R signed Woodville, 100 yds on L.* **Every Sun 14 July to 18 Aug (2-6). Adm £3, chd free. Home-made teas.**

Summer at Hilltop is a gorgeous riot of colour and scent, the old thatched cottage barely visible amongst the flowers. Unusual annuals and perennials grow alongside the traditional and familiar, boldly combining to make a spectacular display, which attracts an abundance of wildlife. Always something new, the unique, gothic garden loo a great success.

29 THE HOLLOW, BLANDFORD FORUM

Tower Hill, Iwerne Minster, Blandford Forum, DT11 8NJ. Sue Le Prevost. *Between Blandford and Shaftesbury. Follow signs on A350 to Iwerne Minster. Turn off at Talbot Inn, continue straight to The Chalk, bear R along Watery Lane for parking in Parish Field on R. 5 min uphill walk to house.* **Sat 22, Sun 23, Wed 26 June (2-5). Adm £3.50, chd free. Cream teas. Home-made cakes and gluten-free available.**

Hillside cottage garden built on chalk, about ⅓ acre with an interesting variety of plants in borders that line the numerous sloping pathways. Water features for wildlife and well placed seating areas to sit back and enjoy the views. Productive fruit and vegetable garden in converted paddock with raised beds and greenhouses. A high maintenance garden which is constantly evolving. Slopes, narrow gravel paths and steep steps so sadly not suitable for wheelchairs or limited mobility.

30 THE HOLLOW, SWANAGE

25 Newton Road, Swanage, BH19 2EA. Stuart & Suzanne Nutbeem, 01929 423662, gdnsuzanne@gmail.com. *½m S of Swanage town centre. From town follow signs to Durlston Country Park. At top of hill turn R at red postbox into Bon Accord Rd. 4th turn R into Newton Rd.* **Every Wed 3 July to 28 Aug (2-5.30). Adm £3, chd free.** Visits also by arrangement July & Aug for groups of up to 30.

Come and wander round a dramatic sunken garden formerly a stone quarry, a surprising find at the top of a hill above the seaside town of Swanage. Stone terraces with unusual shrubs and grasses, showing the owners' passion for plants, form a harmonious pattern of colour and foliage attracting butterflies and bees. Pieces of mediaeval London Bridge lurk in the walls and steps have elegant handrails. Exceptionally wide range of plants including succulents and airplants.

31 22 HOLT ROAD

Branksome, Poole, BH12 1JQ. Alan & Sylvia Lloyd, 01202 387509, alan.lloyd22@ntlworld.com. *2½m W of Bournemouth Square, 3m E of Poole Civic Centre. From Alder Rd turn into Winston Ave, 3rd R into Guest Ave, 2nd R into Holt Rd, at end of cul de sac. Park in Holt Rd or in Guest Ave.* **Suns 24 Mar; 21 Apr; 19 May; 23 June; 21 July; 18 Aug (2-5). Adm £3.50, chd free. Home-made teas.** Visits also by arrangement Mar to Sept for groups of 10+.

¾ acre walled garden for all seasons. Garden seating throughout the diverse planting areas, incl Mediterranean courtyard garden and wisteria pergola. Walk up slope beside rill and bog garden to raised bed vegetable garden. Return through shrubbery and rockery back to waterfall cascading into a pebble beach. Partial wheelchair access.

32 HOLWORTH FARMHOUSE

Holworth, Dorchester, DT2 8NH. Anthony & Philippa Bush, 01305 852242, bushinarcadia@yahoo.co.uk. *7m E of Dorchester. 1m S of A352. Follow signs to Holworth. Through farmyard with duckpond on R. 1st L after 200yds of rough track. Ignore No Access signs.* **Sun 5, Mon 6, Sun 26, Mon 27 May, Sun 7 July (2-5). Adm £5, chd free. Home-made teas.** Visits also by arrangement Apr to Oct.

This unusual garden is tucked away without being isolated and has an atmosphere of extraordinary peace and tranquility. At no point do visitors perceive any idea of the whole, but have to discover, by degrees and at every turn, its element of surprise, its variety of features and its appreciation of space. At all times you are invited to look back, to look round and to look up. Beautiful unspoilt views. Large vegetable garden. Ponds, fish, and water features. Many unusual trees and shrubs. Extraordinary tranquility and a space to unburden. Very limited wheelchair access.

33 HORN PARK

Tunnel Rd, Beaminster, DT8 3HB. Mr & Mrs David Ashcroft, 01308 862212, angieashcroft@btinternet.com. *1½m N of Beaminster. On A3066 from Beaminster, L before tunnel (see signs).* **Wed 24 Apr, Wed 19 June (11-5). Adm £4.50, chd free. Home-made teas. Visits also by arrangement Apr to Oct for groups of up to 30.**
Large plantsman's garden with magnificent views over Dorset countryside towards the sea. Many rare and mature plants and shrubs in terrraced, herbaceous, rock and water gardens. Woodland garden and walks in bluebell woods. Good amount of spring interest with magnolia, rhododendron and bulbs which are followed by roses and herbaceous planting, Wild flower meadow with 164 varieties incl orchids. Very limited access for wheelchair users, gravel paths and some steep slopes.

34 IVY HOUSE GARDEN

Piddletrenthide, DT2 7QF. Bridget Bowen, 07586 377675, beepeebee66@icloud.com. *9m N of Dorchester. On B3143. In middle of Piddletrenthide village, opp Village Stores near Piddle Inn.* **Sun 31 Mar, Sun 14, Sun 21, Mon 22 Apr, Sun 5, Mon 6 May (2-5). Adm £5, chd free. Home-made teas. Visits also by arrangement Mar to May for groups of 10+. An Introductory talk can be given to groups.**
Unusual and challenging ½ acre garden set on steep hillside with fine views. Wildlife friendly garden with mixed borders, ponds, propagating area, vegetable garden, fruit cage, greenhouses and polytunnel, chickens and bees, nearby allotment. Daffodils, tulips and hellebores in quantity for spring openings. Come prepared for steep terrain and a warm welcome! Run on organic lines with plants to attract birds, bees and other insects. Insect-friendly plants usually for sale. Honey and hive products available and, weather permitting, observation hive of honey bees in courtyard. Beekeeper present to answer queries!

35 NEW ◆ KEYNESTON MILL

Tarrant Keyneston, Blandford Forum, DT11 9HZ. 01258 456831, events@keynestonmill.com, www.keynestonmill.com. *From Blandford or Wimborne take the B3082. Turn into Tarrant Keynston village and continue right through to Xrds, we are straight ahead.* **For NGS: Tue 7 May, Tue 17 Sept (2-5). Adm £5, chd free. Tea and home-made cake on NGS days. For other opening times and information, please phone, email or visit garden website.**
Keyneston Mill is the creative home of Parterre Fragrances - a 50 acre estate dedicated to fragrant and aromatic plants. Enjoy the newly-created Collection Gardens, each compartment featuring plants from a different perfume family eg. floral, fern, citrus, spice. Walk through the crop fields where we grow the ingredients for our perfumes, visit the exhibition and distillery. Free guided tours on NGS days. Open all yr, please see above website for details. Compacted gravel paths in floral garden, lawns elsewhere. Wheelchair access to bistro-café and WCs. Dogs on leads allowed.

36 ◆ KINGSTON LACY

Wimborne Minster, BH21 4EA. National Trust, 01202 883402, kingstonlacy@nationaltrust.org.uk, www.nationaltrust.org.uk/kingston-lacy. *2½m W of Wimborne Minster. On Wimborne-Blandford rd B3082.* **For opening times and information, please phone, email or visit garden website.**
35 acres of formal garden, incorporating parterre and sunk garden planted with Edwardian schemes during spring and summer. 5 acre kitchen garden and allotments. Victorian fernery containing over 35 varieties. Rose garden, mixed herbaceous borders, vast formal lawns and Japanese garden restored to Henrietta Bankes' creation of 1910. 2 National Collections: Convallaria and Anemone nemorosa. Snowdrops, blossom, bluebells, autumn colour and Christmas light display. Deep gravel on some paths but lawns suitable for wheelchairs. Slope to visitor reception and South lawn.

NPC

37 ◆ KINGSTON MAURWARD GARDENS AND ANIMAL PARK

Kingston Maurward, Dorchester, DT2 8PY. Kingston Maurward College, 01305 215003, events@kmc.ac.uk, www.morekmc.com. *1m E of Dorchester. Off A35. Follow brown Tourist Information signs.* **For opening times and information, please phone, email or visit garden website.**
Stepping into the grounds you will be greeted with 35 impressive acres of formal gardens. During the late spring and summer months, our National Collection of penstemons and salvias display a lustrous rainbow of purples, pinks, blues and whites, leading you on through the ample hedges and stonework balustrades. An added treat is the Elizabethan walled garden, offering a new vision of enchantment. Open early Jan to mid Dec. Hours will vary in winter depending on conditions - check garden website or call before visiting. Partial wheelchair access only, gravel paths, steps and steep slopes. Map provided at entry, highlighting the most suitable routes.

38 KNITSON OLD FARMHOUSE

Corfe Castle, Wareham, BH20 5JB. Rachel Helfer, 01929 421681, rjehelfer@gmail.com. *2m NW of Swanage. 3m E of Corfe Castle. Signed L off A351 to Knitson. Very narrow rds for 1m. Ample parking in yard or in adjacent field.* **Fri 19, Sat 20, Sun 21, Mon 22 Apr, Fri 24, Sat 25, Sun 26, Mon 27 May (2-6). Adm £4, chd free. Cream teas. Home-made cakes. Visits also by arrangement Mar to Aug for groups of up to 30.**
Mature cottage garden nestled at base of chalk downland. Herbaceous borders, rockeries, climbers and shrubs, evolved and designed over 50yrs for yr-round colour and interest. Large wildlife friendly kitchen garden for self sufficiency. Rachel is delighted to welcome visitors, discuss all aspects of sustainable gardening and the benefits of gardening for mental and physical wellbeing. We have used a lot of local stone in the design and have interesting old stones and stone baths around the garden. Uneven, sloping paths.

39 ◆ KNOLL GARDENS

Hampreston, Wimborne, BH21 7ND. Mr Neil Lucas, 01202 873931, enquiries@knollgardens.co.uk, www.knollgardens.co.uk. *2½m W of Ferndown. ETB brown signs from A31. Large car park.* **For NGS: Fri 21 June, Fri 27 Sept (10-5). Adm £6.50, chd £4.50. Self catering drinks and pre-wrapped cakes and biscuits.** For other opening times and information, please phone, email or visit garden website.

A naturalistic haven, informal plantings of glorious grasses and flowering perennials flood the garden providing a layered transparency to this seemingly natural space. A mini-arboretum of rare and unusual trees and shrubs adds height, interest and habitat for wildlife. Renowned for its grasses, practical planting ideas surround you with plants from Knoll's onsite nursery taking the starring role. An increased event programme will mark Neil Lucas's 25th year at Knoll Gardens. Featuring walks, talks, art and horticultural workshops. 2019 will also host a series of special events celebrating the autumn glory of grasses at Knoll. Events are all bookable online at knollgardens.co.uk. Some slopes. Various surfaces incl gravel, paving, grass and bark.

40 LANGEBRIDE HOUSE

Long Bredy, DT2 9HU. Mrs J Greener, 01308 482257. *8m W of Dorchester. S off A35, midway between Dorchester and Bridport. Well signed. 1st gateway on L in village.* **Visits by arrangement Feb to July. Adm £4.50, chd free.**

This old rectory garden has carpets of spring bulbs spreading out under huge copper beech tree on lawn. A lovely place to visit in spring and early summer, with a large variety of daffodils and early spring bulbs amongst flowering shrubs, trees and herbaceous borders with kitchen garden. Limited wheelchair access if wet.

41 LAWSBROOK

Brodham Way, Shillingstone, DT11 0TE. Clive Nelson, 01258 860148, cne70bl@aol.com, www.facebook.com/Lawsbrook. *5m NW of Blandford. To Shillingstone on A357. Turn up Gunn Lane - up lane (past Wessex Avenue on L & Everetts Lane on R) then turn R as rd bends to L. Lawsbrook 250m on R.* **Sat 16, Sat 23 Feb, Sun 3, Sun 10 Nov (10-5). Adm £3.50, chd free. Home-made teas.** Visits also by arrangement Feb to Nov, full catering (lunches, teas and all day refreshments) provided on request.

Open for 10 years for NGS. Garden incl over130 different tree species spread over 6 acres. Native species and many unusual specimens incl Dawn Redwood, Damyio Oak and Wollemi Pine. Large borders, raised bed vegetable and flower garden. Wildlife, stream and meadow. You can be assured of a relaxed and friendly day out. Children's activities, all day teas/cakes and dogs are very welcome. Large scale snowdrop days in Feb, wonderful all summer (no May open days 2019/20 due to refurbishment but appointments welcome). Intense autumn hues in Nov. Enough space and interest for everyone. Gravel path at entrance, grass paths over whole garden.

42 ◆ LITTLEBREDY WALLED GARDENS

Littlebredy, DT2 9HL. The Walled Garden Workshop, 01305 898055, secretary@wgw.org.uk, www.littlebredy.com. *8m W of Dorchester. 10m E of Bridport. 1½m S of A35. NGS days: park on village green then walk 300yds. For the less mobile (and on normal open days) use gardens car park.* **For NGS: Tue 18, Tue 25 June (2-6). Adm £5, chd free. Home-made teas.** For other opening times and information, please phone, email or visit garden website.

1 acre walled garden on S-facing slopes of Bride River Valley. Herbaceous borders, riverside rose walk, lavender beds and potager vegetable and cut flower gardens.

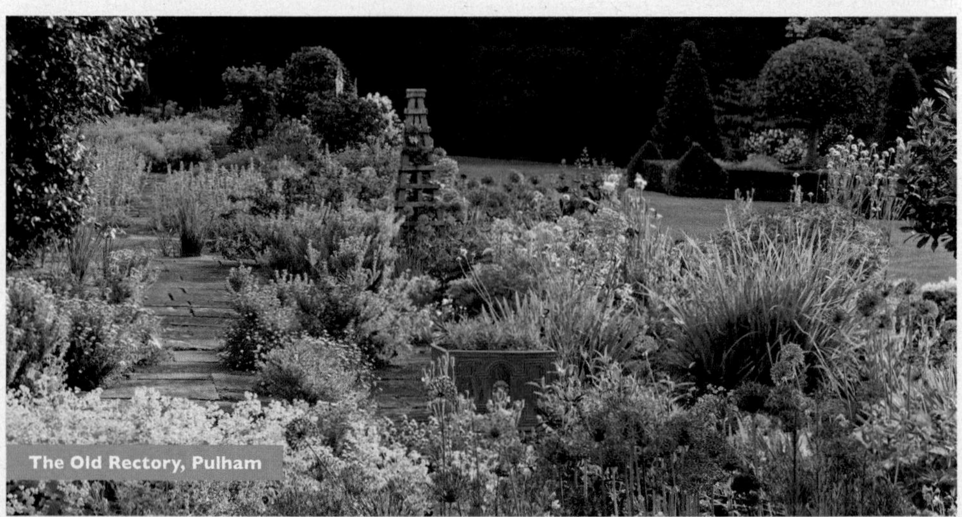

The Old Rectory, Pulham

Original Victorian glasshouses, one under renovation. Partial wheelchair access, some steep grass slopes. For disabled parking please follow signs to main entrance.

GROUP OPENING

43 LYTCHETT MINSTER GARDENS

Lytchett Minster, BH16 6JF. *3m W of Wimborne. W of Poole on old Dorchester rd. From A35 Bakers Arms Pub r'about (junction with A351), follow signs to Lytchett Minster B3067. Proceed through village to St Peters Finger Pub, then follow parking signs. Garden guide/ adm at car park.* **Sat 15, Sun 16 June (2-5). Combined adm £5.50, chd free. Home-made teas at The Old Bakehouse, 55 Dorchester Rd. Refreshments in aid of Dorset Air Ambulance.**

NEW 47 DORCHESTER ROAD
Dr Emma Alner.

57 DORCHESTER ROAD
Maureen & Stephen Kirkham.

FRIARS GREEN
Jane & Robin SeQueira.

HERON HOUSE
Geraldine & Phillip Stevens.

4 OLD FORGE CLOSE
Liz & Derek Allen.

10 ORCHARD CLOSE
Daphne Turner.

NEW WOODCUTTERS COTTAGE
Lesley & Martin Jenkins.

Mixture of old and new houses, 2 churches, 2 pubs and an ancient pound. The 7 small to medium sized gardens offer variation in cottage style planting with many varieties of herbaceous perennials and hardy geraniums, some lush waterside planting, magnificent displays of climbing roses, small fruit and vegetable plots and many other interesting features. Wheelchair access is difficult as many of the gardens have gravel drives. All gardens are in easy walking distance. Flower festival in village.

44 MANOR FARM, HAMPRESTON

Wimborne, BH21 7LX. Guy & Anne Trehane, 01202 574223, anne.trehane@live.co.uk. *2½m E of Wimborne, 2½m W of Ferndown. From Canford Bottom r'about on A31, take exit B3073 Ham Lane. ½m turn R at Hampreston Xrds. House at bottom of village.* **Sat 23 Feb (10-1); Sun 24 Feb (1-4). Light refreshments. Sun 9 June, Sun 28 July, Thur 8, Sun 11 Aug (1-5). Home-made teas. Adm £4, chd free. Soup also available at Feb openings.** Visits also by arrangement June to Sept for groups of 10 to 30.

Traditional farmhouse garden designed and cared for by 3 generations of the Trehane family through over 100yrs of farming and gardening at Hampreston. Garden is noted for its herbaceous borders and rose beds within box and yew hedges. Mature shrubbery, water and bog garden. Open for hellebores and snowdrops in Feb. Dorset Hardy Plant Society sales at openings. Hellebores for sale in Feb.

45 NEW MANOR HOUSE FARM

Ibberton, Blandford Forum, DT11 0EN. Fiona Closier. *Off A357 between Blandford Forum and Sturminster Newton. From A357 at Shillingstone take road to Okeford Fitzpaine. Follow signs for Belchalwell and Ibberton. Continue through Belchalwell to Ibberton.* **Sun 9, Sun 16 June (2-5). Adm £5, chd free. Home-made teas.**

Set in the lee of Bulbarrow Hill, this ½ acre partially terraced garden has formal yew and beech hedging interspersed with topiary, lawn, and many abundantly filled herbaceous borders. Native trees, 2 springfed ponds attracting wildlife, and walled kitchen garden also give many areas of interest. Orchard area left to meadow with spring bulbs. Wheelchair access limited in some areas due to steps, however the main parts of the garden can be seen.

46 ◆ MAPPERTON GARDENS

Mapperton, Beaminster, DT8 3NR. The Earl & Countess of Sandwich, 01308 862645, office@mapperton.com, www.mapperton.com. *6m N of Bridport. Off A356/A3066. 2m SE of Beaminster off B3163.* **For NGS: Sun 3, Sun 10, Sun 17 Feb (11-3.30). Adm £4.50, chd free. Refreshments in the Sawmill Café on Sun 3, 10 & 17 Feb.** For other opening times and information, please phone, email or visit garden website.

Terraced valley gardens surrounding Tudor/Jacobean manor house. On upper levels, walled croquet lawn, orangery and Italianate formal garden with fountains, topiary and grottoes. Below, C17 summerhouse and fishponds. Lower garden with shrubs and rare trees, leading to woodland and spring gardens. Garden & Café open 3 Mar to 31 Oct (except Fri/ Sat) (10-5); house open 3 Mar to 31 Oct (except Fri/Sat) guided tours only at 12, 1, 2 and 3pm (booking advisable). Snowdrop Sundays 3 & 10 Feb 2019. Partial wheelchair access (lawn and upper levels).

47 MAYFIELD

4 Walford Close, Wimborne Minster, BH21 1PH. Mr & Mrs Terry Wheeler, 01202 849838, terpau@talktalk.net. *½m N of Wimborne Town Centre. B3078 out of Wimborne, R into Burts Hill, 1st L into Walford Close.* **Sun 12, Sun 19, Mon 27 May, Wed 5, Wed 12 June (2-5). Adm £3.50, chd free. Home-made teas.** Visits also by arrangement May & June for groups of 5 to 30. Donation to The Friends of Victoria Hospital, Wimborne.

Town garden of approx ¼ acre. Front: formal hard landscaping planted with drought-resistant shrubs and perennials. Shaded area has wide variety of hostas. Back garden contrasts with a seductive series of garden rooms containing herbaceous perennial beds separated by winding grass paths and rustic arches. Pond, vegetable beds and greenhouses containing succulents and vines. Garden access is across a pea-shingle drive. If this is manageable, wheelchairs can access the back garden provided they are no wider than 65cms.

48 THE MILL HOUSE

Crook Hill, Netherbury, DT6 5LX. Michael & Giustina Ryan, 01308 488267, themillhouse@dsl.pipex.com. *1m S of Beaminster. Turn R off A3066 Beaminster to Bridport rd signed Netherbury. Car park at Xrds at bottom of hill.* **Visits by arrangement for groups of 6 to 30.**

6½ acres of garden around R Brit, incl mill stream and mill pond. Extensive garden consisting of formal walled, terraced and vegetable gardens and bog garden. Emphasis on spring bulbs, scented flowers, hardy geraniums, lilies, clematis and water irises. Wander through the wild garden planted with many rare and interesting trees incl conifers, magnolias, oak and fruit trees. Collection of Magnolias flowering March to Sept. Walled garden with water feature. Collection of crab apples flowering April to May and fruiting Aug to Nov. Partial wheelchair access.

49 ◆ MINTERNE GARDEN

Minterne House, Minterne Magna, Dorchester, DT2 7AU. Lord & Lady Digby, 01300 341370, enquiries@minterne.co.uk, www.minterne.co.uk. *2m N of Cerne Abbas. On A352 Dorchester-Sherborne rd.* **For opening times and information, please phone, email or visit garden website.**

As seen on BBC Gardeners' World and voted one of the 10 prettiest gardens in England by The Times. Famed for their display of rhododendrons, azaleas, Japanese cherries and magnolias in April/May. Small lakes, streams and cascades offer new vistas at each turn around the 1m horseshoe shaped gardens covering 23 acres. The season ends with spectacular autumn colour. Snowdrops in Feb. Spring bulbs, blossom and bluebells in April. Garden at its peak in April/May with historic rhododendron collection, magnolias and azaleas. Over 200 acers provide spectacular autumn colour in Sept/Oct. Regret unsuitable for wheelchairs.

50 NORWOOD HOUSE GARDENS AND WALKS

Corscombe, Dorchester, DT2 0PD. Mr & Mrs Jonathan Lewis, 07836 600185, jonathan.lewis@livegroup.co.uk. *Equidistant between Halstock and Corscombe. 1m from Fox Inn towards Halstock. 1m from national speed limit sign leaving Halstock towards Corscombe.* **Sun 23, Thur 27 June (12.30-4.30). Adm £6, chd £2. Home-made teas. Visits also by arrangement May to July for groups of 10 to 30.**

Our garden is hidden away in a stunning West Dorset Valley surrounded by our small family estate. We started our landscaping adventure from scratch in 2011. Today the glorious purple, pink and white borders surround the house and lawn. Many varieties of geranium and other perennials, grasses, shrubs and a rockery. Lake, woodland and wild flower walks thoroughly recommended, weather permitting. Steps and gravel with downhill approach from parking area, regret not suitable for wheelchairs.

51 OLD DOWN HOUSE

Horton, Wimborne, BH21 7HL. Dr & Mrs Colin Davidson, 07765 404248, pipdavidson59@gmail.com. *7½m N of Wimborne. Horton Inn at junction of B3078 with Horton Rd, pick up yellow signs leading up through North Farm. No garden access from Matterley Drove. 5min walk to garden down farm track.* **Wed 29 May, Sun 2, Wed 5 June (2-5). Adm £3.50, chd free. Home-made teas in comfortable garden room if weather inclement.**

Nestled down a farm track, this ¾ acre garden on chalk surrounds C18 farmhouse. Stunning views over Horton Tower and farmland. Cottage garden planting with formal elements, climbing roses clothe pergola and house walls along with stunning wisteria sinensis and banksia rose. Part walled potager, well stocked. Chickens. Not suitable for wheelchairs.

52 THE OLD RECTORY, LITTON CHENEY

Litton Cheney, Dorchester, DT2 9AH. Richard & Emily Cave, 01308 482266, emilycave@rosacheney.com. *9m W of Dorchester. 1m S of A35, 6m E of Bridport. Small village in the beautiful Bride Valley. Park in village and follow signs.* **Sun 5, Wed 8 May, Sun 16 June (2-5). Adm £6, chd free. Home-made teas. Visits also by arrangement.**

Steep paths lead to beguiling 4 acres of natural woodland with many springs, streams, 2 pools one a natural swimming pool planted with native plants. Front garden with pleached crabtree border, topiary and soft planting incl tulips, peonies, roses and verbascums. Walled garden with informal planting, kitchen garden, orchard and 350 rose bushes for a cut flower business. Formal front garden designed by Arne Maynard. Not suitable for wheelchairs.

53 THE OLD RECTORY, MANSTON

Manston, Sturminster Newton, DT10 1EX. Andrew & Judith Hussey, 01258 474673, judithhussey@hotmail.com. *6m S of Shaftesbury, 2½m N of Sturminster Newton. From Shaftesbury, take B3091. On reaching Manston, past Plough Inn, L for Child Okeford on R-hand bend. Old Rectory last house on L.* **Sun 9, Wed 12 June (2-5.30). Adm £5, chd free. Home-made teas. Visits also by arrangement May to Sept for groups of 5+.**

Beautifully restored 5 acre garden. S-facing wall with 120ft herbaceous border edged by old brick path. Enclosed yew hedge flower garden. Wildflower meadow marked with mown paths and young plantation of mixed hardwoods. Well maintained walled Victorian kitchen garden with new picking flower section. Large new greenhouse also installed. Knot garden now well established.

54 THE OLD RECTORY, NETHERBURY

Beaminster, DT6 5NB. Simon & Amanda Mehigan, mehigansimon@gmail.com, www.

Hilltop

© Carole Drake

oldrectorynetherbury.tumblr.com. *2m SW of Beaminster. Please park considerately in village as directed bearing in mind that large tractors need to be able to pass. Parking for the less mobile available at house.* **Sun 21 Apr, Sun 26, Tue 28 May (11-5). Adm £6, chd free. Home-made teas.** Visits also by arrangement in June. For further information please write or email mehigansimon@gmail.com.

5 acre garden designed and maintained by present owners over last 25 yrs. Formal areas with topiary near house, large drifts of naturalistic planting elsewhere. Spring bulbs incl species tulips and erythroniums are a speciality. Extensive bog garden with pond and stream, large collection of candelabra primulas and other moisture lovers. Hornbeam walk. Wild flower areas and orchards. Decorative kitchen/cutting garden. Unsuitable for wheelchairs due to steps and steep slopes.

55 THE OLD RECTORY, PULHAM

Dorchester, DT2 7EA. Mr & Mrs N Elliott, 01258 817595, gilly.elliott@hotmail.com. *13m N of Dorchester. 8m SE of Sherborne. On B3143 turn E at Xrds in Pulham. Signed Cannings Court.* **Sun 19, Thur 23 May, Sun 4, Thur 8 Aug (2-5). Adm £6, chd free. Home-made teas.** Visits also by arrangement Apr to Sept for groups of 10+.

4 acres formal and informal gardens surround C18 rectory, splendid views. Yew pyramid allées and hedges, circular herbaceous borders with late summer colour. Exuberantly planted terrace, purple and white beds. Box parterres, mature trees, pond, fernery, ha-ha, pleached hornbeam circle. 10 acres woodland walks. Flourishing extended bog garden with islands; awash with primulas and irises in May. Interesting plants for sale. Mostly wheelchair access.

56 THE OLD SCHOOL HOUSE

The Street, Sutton Waldron, Blandford Forum, DT11 8NZ. David Milanes. *Turn into Sutton Waldron from A350, continue for 300 yds, 1st house on L in The Street. Entrance past house through gates in wall.* **Sun 16, Wed 19 June (2-5). Adm £3.50, chd free. Home-made cakes and gluten free.**

Small village garden laid out in last 5 yrs with planting of hedges into rooms incl orchard, secret garden and pergola walkway. Strong framework of existing large trees, beds are mostly planted with roses and herbaceous plants. Pleached hornbeam screen. A designer's garden with interesting semi-tender plants close to house. Level lawns.

57 OLD SMITHY

Ibberton, DT11 0EN. Carol & Clive Carsley, 01258 817361, carolcarsley@btinternet.com. *9m NW of Blandford Forum. A357 Blandford to Sturminster Newton. After 6½ m L to Okeford Fitzpaine. Follow signs to Ibberton, 3m. Parking by arrangement when booking.* **Visits by arrangement for groups of 15+.**

Worth driving twisty narrow lanes to reach this rural 2½ acre streamside garden framing a thatched cottage. Back of beyond setting which inspired international best seller Mr Rosenblum's List. Succession of ponds. Mown paths. Spring bulbs in profusion, primula candelabras, aquilegia and hellebores. Sit beneath rustling trees. Views of Bulbarrow and church. Featured in regional press.

Your visits help change lives – we are the largest single funder of the Queen's Nursing Institute

58 THE OLD VICARAGE

East Orchard, Shaftesbury, SP7 0BA. Miss Tina Wright, 01747 811744, tina_lon@msn.com. *4½m S of Shaftesbury, 3½m N of Sturminster Newton. Between 90 degree bend and lay-bye with old red phone box. Parking is on opp corner towards Hartgrove.* **Sun 17 Mar (1.30-4.30); Fri 5, Sun 14, Fri 26 Apr, Fri 3, Sun 19, Fri 31 May (2-5). Adm £4, chd free. Home-made teas. Teas will be inside if raining, with wood stove if cold.** Visits also by arrangement Jan to Nov. Teas will be extra. Conducted tours if required.

1.7 acre, award-winning Dorset wildlife friendly garden with swimming pond and bog gardens. Hundreds of bulbs, herbaceous perennial, roses, clematis and autumn bulbs. Tropical cannas & Cyprus in summer. Wonderful autumn colour. Tree viewing platform with wonderful views. Children can pond dip, oak swing and hunt for hidden fairies. Children and dogs welcome. Various shelters around garden if wet. Not suitable for wheelchairs if very wet.

59 PILSDON VIEW

Junction Butts Lane and Pitman's Lane, Ryall, Bridport, DT6 6EH. D Lloyd. *5m W of Bridport, through Chideok. From E through Morecombelake A35. Take the Ryall turning opp Felicity's farm shop on A35. Garden ¾m on L at junction Butts Lane/Pitmans Lane. High hedge with PO box in wall.* **Sat 18, Sun 19, Mon 20 May, Sat 20, Sun 21, Mon 22 July (1-6). Combined adm with Well Cottage £6, chd free. Teas at Well Cottage.**

Started over 25 yrs ago, the hard landscaping provides different levels with breathtaking views over the Marshwood Vale towards Pilson Pen. Mature copper beech and evolving garden gives all yr round interest. Water features with wildlife add to the essence of the garden. Partial wheelchair access.

60 2 PYES PLOT

St. James Road, Netherbury, Bridport, DT6 5LP. Sarah & Martin Porter. *2m SW of Beaminster. Turn off A3066. Go over R Brit into centre of village. L into St James Rd, signed to Waytown, R corner Hingsdon Lane.* **Sun 19 May (2-5). Adm £3, chd free. Also open Slape Manor.**

Small but perfectly formed front and back courtyard garden, created from new in 2007. Cream walls and black paintwork make a striking framework for softer planting. Climbing plants, foliage and running water feature enhance the tranquil feel to this space, which uses every inch creatively. Home-made teas at Slape Manor.

61 Q

113 Bridport Road, Dorchester, DT1 2NH. Heather & Chris Robinson, 01305 263088, hmrobinson45@gmail.com. *Approx 300m W of Dorset County Hospital. From Top o' Town r'about head W towards Dorset County Hospital, Q 300 metres further on from Hospital on R.* **Suns 17, 24 Mar; 7, 14 Apr (2-5). Adm £3.50, chd free. Home-made teas.** Visits also by arrangement Apr to July for groups of 10 to 30. We can provide a variety of snacks as well as teas.

Q is essentially all things to all men, a modern cottage town garden, divided into rooms, with many facets, jam packed with shrubs, trees, climbers and herbaceous plants. Gazebo, statutes, water, bonsai and topiary. Planting reflects the owners' many and varied interest incl over 100 clematis, different types and varieties of spring bulbs purchased yearly. In spring the garden flourishes with bulbs from early snowdrops, herbaceous plants incl hellebores, clematis, daphne. Vegetable garden and fruit trees dotted around the garden. Small number of paths available for wheelchair users.

62 25 RICHMOND PARK AVENUE

Bournemouth, BH8 9DL. Barbara Hutchinson & Mike Roberts, 01202 531072, barbarahutchinson@tiscali.co.uk. *2½m NE Bournemouth Town Centre. From T-lights at junction with Alma Rd and Richmond Park Rd, head N on B3063 Charminster Rd, 2nd turning on R into Richmond Park Ave.* **Sun 16 June, Sun 7, Sun 21 July (2-5). Adm £3.50, chd free. Home-made teas.** Visits also by arrangement June to Aug for groups of 10 to 30.

Beautifully designed town garden with pergola leading to ivy canopy over raised decking. Cascading waterfall connects 2 wildlife ponds enhanced with domed acers. Circular lawn with colourful herbaceous border planted to attract bees and butterflies. Fragrant S-facing courtyard garden at front, sparkling with vibrant colour and Mediterranean planting. As featured in Amateur Gardening & Garden News. Partial wheelchair access.

63 ◆ SCULPTURE BY THE LAKES

Pallington Lakes, Pallington, Dorchester, DT2 8QU. Mrs Monique Gudgeon, 07720 637808, sbtl@me.com, www.sculpturebythelakes.co.uk. *6m E of Dorchester. ½m E of Tincleton, see beech hedge and security gates. From other direction ¾m from Xrds. No children under 14. No dogs allowed.* **For NGS: Wed 15 May (10-5). Adm £7.50. Light refreshments at onsite Gallery Café. Hot & cold drinks, home-made cakes, lunches and snacks, using ingredients grown onsite or from local area.** For other opening times and information, please phone, email or

visit garden website.
Recently created modern garden with inspiration taken from all over the world. Described as a modern arcadia it follows traditions of the landscape movement, but for C21. Where sculpture has been placed, the planting palette has been kept simple, but dramatic, so that the work remains the star. Home to Monique and her husband, renowned British sculptor Simon Gudgeon, sculpture park features over 30 of his most iconic pieces including Isis, which is also in London's Hyde Park. Gallery Café features smaller sculptures while newly restored Barn Gallery hosts ongoing art exhibitions. Disabled access limited though possible to go round paths on mobility scooter or electric wheelchair if care taken.

64 THE SECRET GARDEN

The Friary, Hilfield, Dorchester, DT2 7BE. The Society of St Francis, 01300 341345, hilfieldssf@franciscans.org.uk, www.hilfieldfriary.org.uk. *10m N of Dorchester, on A352 between Sherborne & Dorchester. 1st L after Minterne Magna, 1st turning on R signed The Friary. From Yeovil turn off A37 signed Batcombe, 3rd turning on L.* **Sat 4, Sun 5 May (2-5). Adm £5, chd free. Home-made cakes and teas.** Visits also by arrangement Apr to Sept.
Ongoing reclamation of neglected woodland garden. Mature trees, bamboo, rhododendrons, azaleas, magnolias, camellias, palms and other choice shrubs with stream on all sides crossed by bridges. New plantings of viburnums and further planting from Crug Farm Plants. Stout shoes recommended for woodland garden. The £5 entry fee does not include tea and cakes for which a further donation is suggested. Friary grounds open where meadows, woods and livestock can be viewed. Friary Shop selling a variety of gifts. Wheelchair access along our private road and main areas.

65 THE SECRET GARDEN AND SERLES HOUSE

47 Victoria Road, Wimborne, BH21 1EN. Ian Willis. *Centre of Wimborne. On B3082 W of town, very near hospital, Westfield car park 300yds. Off-road parking close by.* **Thur 18, Sun 21, Sun 28 July, Thur 1, Sun 4, Sun 18, Sun 25, Mon 26, Thur 29, Sat 31 Aug, Sun 1, Thur 5, Sat 7, Sun 8 Sept (2-5). Adm £3.50, chd free. Home-made teas.** Donation to Wimborne Civic Society and The Arts' Society.
Alan Titchmarsh described this amusingly creative garden as 'one of the best 10 private gardens in Britain'. The ingenious use of unusual plants complements the imaginative treasure trove of garden objects d'art. The enchanting house is also open. A feeling of a bygone age accompanies your tour as you step into a world of whimsical fantasy that is theatrical and unique. 'Deliciously bonkers'. Antiques and bric-a-brac on sale. A high summer garden with dahlias at their best late August / early September. Wheelchair access to garden only. Narrow steps may prohibit wide wheelchairs.

66 ◆ SHERBORNE CASTLE

New Rd, Sherborne, DT9 5NR. Mr E Wingfield Digby, www.sherbornecastle.com. *½m E of Sherborne. On New Rd B3145. Follow brown signs from A30 & A352.* For opening times and information, please visit garden website.
40+ acres. Grade I Capability Brown garden with magnificent vistas across surrounding landscape, incl lake and views to ruined castle. Herbaceous planting, notable trees, mixed ornamental planting and managed wilderness are linked together with lawn and pathways. Dry grounds walk. Partial wheelchair access, gravel paths, steep slopes, steps.

67 SLAPE MANOR

Netherbury, DT6 5LH. Mr & Mrs Antony Hichens. *1m S of Beaminster. Turn W off A3066 to Netherbury. House ½m S of Netherbury on back rd to Bridport signed Waytown.* **Sun 19 May (2-5). Adm £5, chd free. Home-made teas. Also open 2 Pyes Plot.**
River valley garden with spacious lawns and primula fringed streams down to lake. Walk over the stream with magnificent hostas, gunneras and horizontal Cryptomeria japonica Elegans, and around the lake. Admire the mature wellingtonias, ancient wisterias, rhododendrons and planting around the house. Mostly flat with some sloping paths and steps.

68 2 SPUR GATE

24 Spur Hill Avenue, Parkstone, Poole, BH14 9PH. Mr & Mrs R J P Butler, 01202 732342, annebbutler@icloud.com. *3m W of Bournemouth. At end of Wessex Way (A 338) take 3rd exit (Lindsay Rd). Continue to end. R at T-Lights. After next T-Lights, 2nd L into Kings Ave. Top of hill turn R into Spurhill Ave. Please park on rd.* **Visits by arrangement Apr to Oct for groups of up to 20. Weekdays only. Adm £4, chd free. Home-made teas.**
Town garden designed around modern house on steep slope. Over 10 yrs this challenging site has been converted into a series of banks and terraces which progress from the formality of pool terraces to a gravel garden, Japanese area and woodland. The Teahouse offers a peaceful and sheltered destination from which to view the house set above its bank of Stipa grasses. Regret no wheelchair access.

We help ordinary people open the gates to their extraordinary private gardens to raise impressive amounts of money through admissions, teas and slices of cake!

The Hollow, Swanage

69 STABLE COURT

Chalmington, Dorchester, DT2 0HB. Jenny & James Shanahan. *From A37 travel towards Cattistock & Chalmington for 1½m turn R at triangle to Chalmington. ½m house on R red letter box at gate. From Cattistock take first turn R then next L at triangle.* **Sat 8, Wed 12 June (2-6). Adm £4.50, chd free. Home-made teas.**

This exuberant garden was begun in 2010. Extending to about 1½ acres, it is naturalistic in style with a shrubbery, gravel garden, wild garden and pond where many trees have been planted. Overflowing with roses scrambling up trees, over hedges and walls. More formal garden closer to house with lawns and herbaceous borders. Lovely views over Dorset countryside. Exhibition of paintings in studio. Gravel path partway around garden, otherwise the paths are grass, not suitable for wheelchairs in wet weather.

70 STADDLESTONES

14 Witchampton Mill, Witchampton, Wimborne, BH21 5DE. Annette & Richard Lockwood, 01258 841405, richardglockwood@yahoo.co.uk. *5m N of Wimborne off B3078. Follow signs through village and park in sports field, 7 min walk to garden, limited disabled parking near garden.* **Sun 26, Mon 27 May (2-5). Adm £4.50, chd free. Home-made teas.** Visits also by arrangement May to Sept for groups of up to 30.

A beautiful setting for a cottage garden with colour themed borders, pleached limes and hidden gems, leading over chalk stream to shady area which has some unusual plants incl hardy orchids and arisaemas. Plenty of areas just to sit and enjoy the wildlife. Wire bird sculptures by local artist. Wheelchair access to 1st half of garden.

71 STANBRIDGE MILL

Gussage All Saints, BH21 5EP. Lord and Lady Phillimore. *7m N of Wimborne. On B3078 to Cranborne 150yds from Horton Inn on Shaftesbury road.* **Tue 11 June (10-5.30). Adm £5.50, chd free. Home-made teas.**

Hidden garden created in 1990s around C18 water mill (not open) on R Allen. Series of linked formal gardens featuring herbaceous and iris borders, pleached limes, white walk and wisteria-clad pergola. 20-acre nature reserve with reed beds and established shelter belts. Grazing meadows with wild flowers and flock of rare breed Dorset Horn sheep. Some areas around river not suitable for wheelchairs.

72 ◆ UPTON COUNTRY PARK

Upton, Poole, BH17 7BJ. Borough of Poole, 01202 262753, uptoncountrypark@poole.gov.uk, www.uptoncountrypark.com. *3m W of Poole town centre. On S side of A35/A3049. Follow brown signs.* For opening times and information, please phone, email or visit garden website.

Over 130 acres of award winning parkland incl formal gardens, walled garden, woodland and shoreline. Maritime micro-climate offers a wonderful collection of unusual trees, vintage camellias and stunning roses. Home to Upton House, Grade II* listed Georgian mansion. Regular special events. Plant centre, art gallery and tea rooms. Car parking pay + display (cash or card), free entry to the park. Open 8am - 6pm (winter) and 8am - 9pm (summer). www.facebook.com/uptoncountrypark. Surfaced paths throughout site, allowing easy access for wheelchair users.

73 WELL COTTAGE

Ryall, Bridport, DT6 6EJ. John & Heather Coley, 01297 489066, jfrcoley@btinternet.com. *Less than 1m N of A35 from Morcombelake. From E: R by farm shop in Morcombelake. Garden 0.9m on R. From W: L entering Morcombelake, immed R by village hall and L on Pitmans Lane to T junc. Turn R, Well Cott on L. Parking on site and nearby.* **Sat 18, Sun 19, Mon 20 May, Sat**

20, Sun 21, Mon 22 July (1-6). Combined adm with Pilsdon View £6, chd free. Home-made teas. Visits also by arrangement Apr to Sept for groups of up to 30. Max number dependant on car parking. Can accommodate up to 10 cars on site.
1-acre garden brought back to life over last 6½ yrs. There is now much more light after some trees were taken down and new areas have been cultivated. The planting is intended to be natural and the emphasis is very much on colour. A number of distinct areas, some quite surprising but most still enjoy wonderful views over Marshwood Vale. Heather's textile art studio will be open to view. Wheelchair access possible but there are a few hard surface paths, slopes and steps.

74 ◆ WIMBORNE MODEL TOWN & GARDENS

King Street, Wimborne, BH21 1DY. Wimborne Minster Model Town Ltd Registered Charity No 298116, 01202 881924, info@wimborne-modeltown.com, www.wimborne-modeltown.com. *2 mins walk from Wimborne Town Centre & the Minster Church. Follow Wimborne signs from A31; From Poole/Bournemouth follow Wimborne signs on A341; from N follow Wimborne signs B3082/B3078. Public parking opp in King Street Car Park.* **For opening times and information, please phone, email or visit garden website.**
Attractive garden surrounding intriguing model town buildings, incl original 1950s miniature buildings of Wimborne. Herbaceous borders, rockery, perennials, shrubs and rare trees. Miniature river system incl bog garden and other water features. Sensory area incorporates vegetable garden, grasses, a seasonally fragrant and colourful border, wind and water elements. Plentiful seating. Open 30 March - 3 November (10am - 5pm). Seniors discount; groups welcome. For admission charges see website. Tea room, shop, miniature dolls' house collection and digital model railway. Gardens, model town and facilities are wheelchair accessible. 2 wheelchairs available on site.

Stable Court

75 WINCOMBE PARK

Shaftesbury, SP7 9AB. John & Phoebe Fortescue, phoebe.fortescue@btinternet.com, www.wincombepark.com. *2m N of Shaftesbury. A350 Shaftesbury to Warminster, past Wincombe Business Park, 1st R signed Wincombe & Donhead St Mary. ¾m on R.* Wed 15, Sun 19 May (2-5). Adm £5, chd free. Home-made cakes and biscuits, tea, coffee, squash. Dairy and gluten free available. Visits also by arrangement Apr & May for groups of 10+. Coaches welcome. £10 a head incl refreshments.
Extensive mature garden with sweeping panoramic views from lawn over parkland to lake and enchanting woods through which you can wander amongst bluebells. Garden is a riot of colour in spring with azaleas, camellias and rhododendrons in flower amongst shrubs and unusual trees. Beautiful walled kitchen garden. Partial wheelchair access only, slopes and gravel paths.

76 WOLVERHOLLOW

Elsdons Lane, Monkton Wyld, DT6 6DA. Mr & Mrs D Wiscombe, 01297 560610. *4m N of Lyme Regis. 4m NW of Charmouth. Monkton Wyld is signed from A35 approx 4m NW of Charmouth off dual carriageway. Wolverhollow next to church.* Sun 12, Mon 13 May, Sat 1, Mon 3 June (11.30-4). Adm £4, chd free. Home-made teas. Visits also by arrangement Feb to Oct.
Over 1 acre of informal mature garden on different levels. Lawns lead past borders and rockeries down to a shady lower garden. Numerous paths take you past a variety of uncommon shrubs and plants. A managed meadow has an abundance of primulas growing close to stream. A garden not to be missed! Cabin in meadow area from which vintage, retro and other lovely things can be purchased.

OPENING DATES

All entries subject to change. For latest information check **www.ngs.org.uk**

Extended openings are shown at the beginning of the month.

Map locator numbers are shown to the right of each garden name.

February

Snowdrop Festival

Sunday 17th
NEW Longyard Cottage 37

Tuesday 19th
Horkesley Hall 29

Wednesday 20th
Dragons 13

Sunday 24th
Horkesley Hall 29

March

Saturday 16th
◆ The Beth Chatto Gardens 5

April

Every Thursday from Thursday 18th
Barnards Farm 3

Every Thursday and Friday
Feeringbury Manor 17

Saturday 13th
Ardleigh Gardens 1
Loxley House 38

Sunday 14th
Ardleigh Gardens 1

Tuesday 16th
Jericho Cottage (Megarry's Antiques & Teashop) 31

Sunday 21st
Tudor Roost 63

Monday 22nd
Tudor Roost 63

Friday 26th
◆ Beeleigh Abbey Gardens 4
30 Glenwood 21

Saturday 27th
St Helens 54

Sunday 28th
30 Sandford Road 55
South Shoebury Hall 60
Ulting Wick 66

May

Every Thursday
Barnards Farm 3

Every Thursday and Friday
Feeringbury Manor 17

Wednesday 1st
Furzelea 20

Friday 3rd
Ulting Wick 66

Saturday 4th
NEW West End Cottage 71

Sunday 5th
Furzelea 20
◆ Green Island 22

Monday 6th
Clavering Gardens 11
Wickets 74

Sunday 12th
Elwy Lodge 14
Sandy Lodge 56

Friday 17th
Wycke Farm 79

Sunday 19th
NEW 5 Fairfield Road 15
The White Garden 72
NEW 1 Whitehouse Cottages 73
Wycke Farm 79

Wednesday 22nd
8 Dene Court 12
Dragons 13
Writtle University College 77

Sunday 26th
Chippins 10
Field Cottage 18
Langley Village Gardens 34
Tudor Roost 63

Monday 27th
Fairwinds 16
Rookwoods 51
79 Royston Avenue 52
Tudor Roost 63
Washlands 69

Wednesday 29th
The Punchbowl 50

Friday 31st
8 Dene Court 12
Dragons 13

June

Every Thursday
Barnards Farm 3

Every Thursday and Friday
Feeringbury Manor 17

Saturday 1st
Boreham Gardens 7
St Helens 54

Sunday 2nd
Boreham Gardens 7
Furzelea 20
Havendell 26
Waltham Abbey Group Gardens 68

Tuesday 4th
8 Dene Court 12

Friday 7th
Elwy Lodge 14

Sunday 9th
Blake Hall 6
Horkesley Hall 29
Miraflores 43
Moverons 45
Peacocks 48
NEW West End Cottage 71

Tuesday 11th
Braxted Park Estate 8

Wednesday 12th
Long House Plants 36

Friday 14th
8 Dene Court 12
NEW Haytor 27

Sunday 16th
Elwy Lodge 14
NEW Haytor 27
NEW 61 Humber Avenue 30
Miraflores 43
Parsonage House 47
Wendens Ambo Gardens 70
NEW 1 Whitehouse Cottages 73
Wychwood 78

Tuesday 18th
8 Dene Court 12
Jericho Cottage (Megarry's Antiques & Teashop) 31

Saturday 22nd
NEW 9 Malyon Road 41
18 Pettits Boulevard 49

Sunday 23rd
Field Cottage 18
Fudlers Hall 19
NEW Halfway Haley's 23
NEW 9 Malyon Road 41
18 Pettits Boulevard 49
30 Sandford Road 55
Two Cottages 65
Washlands 69
The White Garden 72
Writtle Gardens 76

Wednesday 26th
Keeway 32

Friday 28th
8 Dene Court 12
Ulting Wick 66

Saturday 29th
St Helens 54
Tudor Roost 63

Sunday 30th
Barnards Farm 3
Miraflores 43
NEW 4 Shepherds Close 57
◆ Spencers 61
Tudor Roost 63
37 Turpins Lane 64
Two Cottages 65

July

Every Thursday
Barnards Farm 3

Every Thursday and Friday
Feeringbury Manor 17

Friday 5th
8 Dene Court 12
Keeway 32

Saturday 6th
16 Maida Way 39

Sunday 7th
Chippins 10
Fudlers Hall 19
262 Hatch Road 25
Hilldrop 28
Little Myles 35
Washlands 69

Friday 12th
Elwy Lodge 14

Saturday 13th
69 Rundells – The Secret Garden 53
14 Una Road 67

Sunday 14th
Elwy Lodge 14
NEW 61 Humber Avenue 30
14 Una Road 67

Tuesday 16th
8 Dene Court 12
Dragons 13

Wednesday 17th
Long House Plants 36

Saturday 20th
262 Main Road 40
14 Una Road 67

Sunday 21st
Brightlingsea Gardens 9
262 Hatch Road 25
14 Una Road 67

Friday 26th
8 Dene Court 12
30 Glenwood Avenue 21

Sunday 28th
30 Glenwood Avenue 21
NEW Harwich Gardens 24
South Shoebury Hall 60
37 Turpins Lane 64

August

Every Thursday
Barnards Farm 3

Tuesday 6th
8 Dene Court 12
Dragons 13

Saturday 10th
NEW 23 New Road 46
Tudor Roost 63

Sunday 11th
NEW 23 New Road 46
Tudor Roost 63

Wednesday 14th
Long House Plants 36

Friday 16th
8 Dene Court 12
Dragons 13

Sunday 18th
262 Main Road 40

Friday 23rd
8 Dene Court 12

Saturday 24th
NEW 23 New Road 46

Sunday 25th
NEW 23 New Road 46

Monday 26th
Ulting Wick 66

September

Every Thursday and Friday
Feeringbury Manor 17

Sunday 1st
Barnards Farm 3
Waltham Abbey Group Gardens 68

Friday 6th
Ulting Wick 66

Sunday 8th
8 Dene Court 12
Dragons 13
Horkesley Hall 29
Parsonage House 47
◆ Spencers 61
NEW Woodburn Cottage 75
Writtle University College 77

Wednesday 11th
Furzelea 20
Long House Plants 36

Saturday 14th
18 Pettits Boulevard 49

Sunday 15th
Furzelea 20
NEW Halfway Haley's 23
18 Pettits Boulevard 49

Sunday 22nd
Sandy Lodge 56

Wednesday 25th
Dragons 13

Sunday 29th
◆ The Beth Chatto Gardens 5

October

Every Thursday and Friday to Friday 4th
Feeringbury Manor 17

Saturday 12th
◆ Green Island 22

December

Saturday 7th
14 Una Road 67

Sunday 8th
14 Una Road 67

Saturday 14th
14 Una Road 67

By Arrangement

Arrange a personalised garden visit with your club, or group of friends, on a date to suit you. See individual garden entries for full details.

254 Ashurst Drive 2
Barnards Farm 3
Caynton Cottage, Boreham Gardens 7
Chippins 10
8 Dene Court 12
Dragons 13
62 Eastbrook Road, Waltham Abbey Group Gardens 68
Elwy Lodge 14
Fairwinds 16
Feeringbury Manor 17
Field Cottage 18
Fudlers Hall 19
Furzelea 20
30 Glenwood Avenue 21
39 Halfhides, Waltham Abbey Group Gardens 68
Hilldrop 28
Horkesley Hall 29
Jericho Cottage (Megarry's Antiques & Teashop) 31
Keeway 32
Kelvedon Hall 33
Long House Plants 36
NEW Longyard Cottage 37
262 Main Road 40
Miraflores 43
Monks Cottage 44
76 Monkswood Avenue, Waltham Abbey Group Gardens 68
Moverons 45
NEW 23 New Road 46
Old Bell Cottage, Langley Village Gardens 34
Peacocks 48
Piercewebbs, Clavering Gardens 11
Rookwoods 51
69 Rundells - The Secret Garden 53
St Helens 54
Shrubs Farm 58
Silver Birches, Waltham Abbey Group Gardens 68
Snares Hill Cottage 59
South Shoebury Hall 60
Strandlands 62
Tudor Roost 63
37 Turpins Lane 64
Two Cottages 65
Ulting Wick 66
Waltham Abbey Group Gardens 68
Washlands 69
Wickets 74
Wychwood 78

We open the gates to the nation's best gardens, offering a relaxing, memorable and affordable day out. A perfect experience to share with friends and family.

THE GARDENS

GROUP OPENING

1 ARDLEIGH GARDENS

Colchester, CO7 7LZ. *3½ m NE of Colchester. From Ardleigh village centre continue on A137 to Manningtree. 3rd R Tile Barn Lane. R again Hungerdown Lane. 500yds gardens on R. As narrow lane please follow this clockwise route to the gardens.* **Sat 13, Sun 14 Apr (11-4). Combined adm £6, chd free. Home-made teas at Mayfield Farm.**

CHARITY FARM
Jacqueline & Arthur Cork.

MAYFIELD FARM
Ed Fairey & Jennifer Hughes.

Two lovely, large country gardens set in the beautiful setting of nearby Constable country of north east Essex. Refreshments, and parking in paddock at Mayfield Farm. Mayfield Farm a 3 acre garden which only a few years ago was largely a field with a huge glass house and poly tunnels. Now planted with long borders, a secret garden and yew hedging for topiary. Over two hundred thousand bulbs have been planted in the last 3 years to create a wonderful spring display. Shepherds hut and potting shed. Charity Farm is a 4½ acre garden created from an open and empty site since 2001. Woodland walks and 2 avenues of trees create vistas. A large lake surrounded with natural planting and contains lots of pool frogs which sing loudly in early summer. Parts of the garden are delineated with beech and yew hedging, and the latest planting is a birch grove containing 12 different kinds of birch trees.

♿ ☕

2 254 ASHURST DRIVE

Barkingside, IG6 1EW. Maureen Keating, 0208 550 0934. *2m S of Chigwell. Nearest tube: Barkingside on Central Line approx 8 mins walk. Bus: 150 stops outside Tesco's on Cranbrook Rd. go round R side of Tescos car park. Keep R, alleyway leads to Ashurst Drive.* **Visits by arrangement for groups of 5 to 20. Adm £3.50. Home-made teas.**

Bird friendly colour filled town garden with interesting nooks and crannies each telling a story. Contains 7 water features, 6 seating areas, waterfall, pond and stream, miniature railway, model village and vibrant planting all in 40 ft square area! Regret, garden unsuitable for children.

3 BARNARDS FARM

Brentwood Road, West Horndon, Brentwood, CM13 3LX. Bernard & Sylvia Holmes & The Christabella Charitable Trust, 01268 454075, vanessa@barnardsfarm.eu, www.barnardsfarm.eu. *5m S of Brentwood. On A128 1½ m S of A127 Halfway House flyover. From Junction continue on A128 under the railway bridge. Garden on R just past bridge.* **Every Thur 18 Apr to 29 Aug (11-4.30). Adm £7.50, chd free. Light refreshments. Sun 30 June, Sun 1 Sept (1-5.30). Adm £10, chd free. Home-made teas. On Thurs Vanessa and her team serve home-made sandwich based light lunches. On Suns it's all cake!.** Visits also by arrangement Jan to Oct for groups of 30+. Donation to St Francis Church.

So much to explore! Climb the Belvedere for the wider view and take the train for a woodland adventure. Spring bulbs and blossom, summer beds and borders, ponds, lakes and streams, walled vegetable plot. 'Japanese garden', sculptures grand and quirky enhance and delight. Barnards Miniature Railway rides (BMR) :Separate charges apply. Sunday extras: Bernard's Sculpture tour 2.30pm Car collection. 1920s Cycle shop. Archery. Model T Ford Rides. Collect loyalty points on Thur visits and earn a free Sun or Thur entry. Season Tickets available Aviators welcome (PPO),. Wheelchair accessible WC Golf buggy tours available.

♿ ✽ 🚌 NPC ☕

4 ◆ BEELEIGH ABBEY GARDENS

Abbey Turning, Beeleigh, Maldon, CM9 6LL. Christopher & Catherine Foyle, 07506 867122, www.visitmaldon.co.uk/beeleigh-abbey. *1m NW of Maldon. Leaving Maldon via London Road take 1st R after Cemetery into Abbey Turning.* **For NGS: Fri 26 Apr (10.30-4.30). Adm £6, chd £2.50. Cream teas.** For other opening times and information, please phone or visit garden website.

3 acres of secluded gardens in rural historic setting. Mature trees surround variety of planting and water features, woodland walks under planted with bulbs leading to tidal river, cottage garden, kitchen garden, orchard, wild flower meadow, rose garden, wisteria walk, magnolia trees, lawn with 85yd long herbaceous border. Scenic backdrop of remains of C12 abbey incorporated into private house (not open). Refreshments including Hot and Cold Drinks, Cakes, Rolls and Quiche Salad's. Gravel paths, some gentle slopes and some steps. Large WC with ramp and handlebars.

♿ ✽ ☕

5 ◆ THE BETH CHATTO GARDENS

Elmstead Market, Colchester, CO7 7DB. The Beth Chatto Gardens, www.bethchatto.co.uk. *¼ m E of Elmstead Market. On A133 Colchester to Clacton Rd in village of Elmstead Market.* **For NGS: Sat 16 Mar (9-5). Adm £5, chd free. Sun 29 Sept (10-4). Adm £8.45, chd free. Light refreshments.** For other opening times and information, please visit garden website.

Internationally famous gardens, including dry, damp, shade, reservoir and woodland areas. The result of over 50 years of hard work and application of the huge body of plant knowledge possessed by Beth Chatto and her husband Andrew. Visitors cannot fail to be affected by the peace and beauty of the garden. The new Reservoir Garden was opened by Beth in 2017: a wonderful area, and a must-visit for those who haven't seen it yet. Large plant nursery. Tree Trail. Gift Shop. Free parking. Garden courses and events held all year. Open all year round. We have a large Tearoom overlooking the Gravel Garden and Nursery, offering homemade breakfasts, lunches and teas. It is also fully licensed. Disabled WC & parking. Wheelchair access around all of the gardens - on gravel or grass (concrete in Nursery, Giftshop and Tearoom areas).

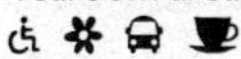

6 BLAKE HALL

Bobbingworth, CM5 0DG. Mr & Mrs H Capel Cure, **www.blakehall.co.uk.** *10m W of Chelmsford. Just off A414 between Four Wantz r'about in Ongar & Talbot r'about in North Weald. Signed on A414.* **Sun 9 June (11-4). Adm £5, chd free. Home-made teas in C17 barn.**
25 acres of mature gardens within the historic setting of Blake Hall (not open). Arboretum with broad variety of specimen trees. Spectacular rambling roses clamber up ancient trees. Traditional formal rose garden and herbaceous border. Sweeping lawns. Teas served from Essex Barn. Some gravel paths.

GROUP OPENING

7 BOREHAM GARDENS

Boreham, Chelmsford, CM3 3EF. *4m NE Chelmsford. Take B1137 Boreham Village, turn into Church Rd at Lion Inn. Caynton Cottage is 50mtrs on L. the other gardens are all within walking distance. Map will be available.* **Sat 1, Sun 2 June (1-5). Combined adm £7, chd free. Delicious home-made cakes and cream teas at Brookfield in support of Ava.**

BROOKFIELD
Bob & Linda Taylor.

CAYNTON COTTAGE
Les & Lynn Mann, 01245 463490, mannlynn15@gmail.com.
Visits also by arrangement in June for groups of up to 20.

17 FITZWALTER ROAD
Lee & Nina Marston.

MONALEE
Andrew & Debora Overington.

Four stunning, inspirational and different gardens in the lovely village of Boreham. At Brookfield a rose covered wall and perennial border greets you, a raised bed vegetable garden, perennial island beds and pond with shrub bank. A buttercup meadow, bordered by a camellia and rhododendron woodland walk. The new garden at Caynton Cottage has been designed and planted from a neglected plot with a C15 thatched cottage. It is planted with a selection of shrubs and perennials for maximum all year interest, with a small wildlife pond and dry stream. Monalee is an ever evolving garden that has many features to attract you including an oriental garden, cut flower bed, enclosed patio and summer house, with a wide variety of shrubs, trees and perennials. 17 Fitzwalter Road. is a small south west facing family garden, modern design softened with cottage style planting. Raised beds and decking made from scaffold boards, overcomes flooding issues due to underground springs. Brookfield, accessible, partial access to meadow. Caynton Cottage, gravel paths, Monalee not wheelchair friendly, 17 Fitzwalter Road partial access.

Caynton Cottage, Boreham Gardens

8 BRAXTED PARK ESTATE

Braxted Park Road, Great Braxted, Witham, CM8 3EN. Mr Duncan & Mrs Nicky Clark, www.braxtedpark.com. *A12 north, by-pass Witham,. Turn L to Rivenhall & Silver End. Turn L by closed Fox pub. Turn L to Rivenhall & Great Braxted. At T junction turn R to Gt Braxted & Witham. Follow brown sign to Braxted Pk (NOT Braxted Golf Course).* **Tue 11 June (10-4). Adm £6, chd free. You will be able to purchase lunch and refreshments from The Pavilion throughout the day.**

The wonderful gardens at Braxted Park will be open on Tuesday 11th June for the National Garden Scheme hosted by the star of BBC Radio 4's Gardener's Question Time, Bunny Guinness. Bunny will be giving a talk (priced at £15) at 12 midday, sharing her thoughtful insights into a world behind the scenes of TV, radio and of course her garden! Tickets are £15 and must be purchased in advance. Booking is simple on the Horatio's Garden website: www.horatiosgarden.org.uk/Braxted or ring 01722 326 834. Braxted Park, Grade II* park of "exceptional significance" is again opening its gardens for the NGS. Meander around the parkland's ponds, lakes and walled gardens. Experience the execution of the 10-year Parkland Restoration Management Plan. Enter walled garden 'rooms' through long Wisteria broad walk and admire Mulberry parasol trees, unique to Braxted.

♿ ✿ 🚌 ☕

GROUP OPENING

9 BRIGHTLINGSEA GARDENS

Brightlingsea, Colchester, CO7 0JF. *Approx 10m SE of Colchester. Go to Thorrington on B1027 & then head S for approx 3m towards Brightlingsea on B1029. Group gardens are either side of Church Rd. 100yds beyond Autosmith Garage.* **Sun 21 July (10-4.30). Combined adm £7, chd free. Refreshments at 44 Church Road.**

44 CHURCH ROAD
Mandy Livingstone & Steven Nicholson.

51 CHURCH ROAD
Mr & Mrs John & Maureen McAuley.

NEW **77 CHURCH ROAD**
Mr & Mrs Mick & Gill Tokley.

SANDY HOOK
Mr & Mrs Peter & Elaine Sedwell.

Four very interesting and contrasting gardens to enjoy in the unique and ancient maritime town of Brightlingsea. Sandy Hook boasts a raised rose bed, dahlias, penstemons and salvias, with a small woodland stream and a sheltered "White Garden". 44 Church Road has a traditional country garden, with gentle colours, mature trees, evergreen shrubs, a water feature and a wisteria covered pergola. The garden offers various places to relax and contemplate the different features of this quintessentially English garden. The garden at 51 Church Road is guaranteed to make you smile – and gasp! A garden that could truly be said to have some depth, with clever landscaping and use of pottery and natural stones. At 77 Church Road we have a colourful garden with an eclectic mix of trees, shrubs and perennials in borders alongside a range of hard landscaping. The garden is filled with plants and features and you can wander through pathways to hidden corners offering peaceful and tranquil seating. At Brightlingsea the spectacular award winning floral displays adorning the centre are not to be missed. There is much to see along the harbour, the marina with bracing walks along the promenade. Brightlingsea is blessed with plenty of watering holes and places to eat. Access to main border garden only at Sandy Hook and to the patio at 51 Church Rd. At No 77 the side passage is partially obstructed by a gas meter.

♿ ✿ ☕

10 CHIPPINS

Heath Road, Bradfield, CO11 2UZ. Kit & Ceri Leese, 01255 870730, ceriandkit1@btinternet.com. *3m E of Manningtree. Take A137 from Manningtree Station, turn L opp garage. Take 1st R towards Clacton. At Radio Mast turn L into Bradfield continue through village. Bungalow is opp primary school.* **Sun 26 May, Sun 7 July (11-4.30). Adm £3.50, chd free. Home-made teas. Delicious home-made cakes also available!** Visits also by arrangement May to July for groups of 5 to 30.

Artist's garden and plantaholics' paradise packed with interest. Springtime heralds irises, hostas and alliums. Stream, with wildlife pond and Horace the Huge! Summer hosts an explosion of colour with daylilies and rambling roses. Front garden with tubs, hanging baskets and exotic border with cannas, banana and cacti. Studio in conservatory with paintings and etching press. Kit is a landscape artist and printmaker, pictures always on display. Afternoon tea with delicious homemade cakes is also available for small parties (minimum of 5) on specific days if booked in advance.

♿ ✿ 🚌 ☕

Your visits help change lives – since 1927, we've donated £55 million to nursing and caring charities

GROUP OPENING

11 CLAVERING GARDENS

Middle Street, Clavering, CB11 4QL. *7m N of Bishop's Stortford. On B1038. Turn W onto B1383 at Newport. Parking at Fox & Hounds Pub & in Middle St.*
Mon 6 May (12-5). Combined adm with Wickets £8, chd free. Home-made teas at Wickets, Langley Upper Green CB11 4RY. Admission for Clavering Gardens £6 child free.

CHESTNUT COTTAGE
Carol & Mike Wilkinson.

PIERCEWEBBS
Mrs J William-Powlett, 01799 550809, jwp@william-powlett.net.
Visits also by arrangement Apr to Oct for groups of 10 to 20. Home-made refreshments will be provided if requested in advance.

Popular village with many C16/17 timber-framed dwellings. Beautiful C14 church, village green with thatched cricket pavilion and pitch. Chestnut Cottage is 1-acre cottage garden with sweeping lawns and wide flower borders, opposite Clavering Ford. Lots of pathways and seats to sit and contemplate, and stunning views over the medieval heart of the village. Come and see 'The Little House', (open), built in 1760 and reputedly the smallest thatched cottage in England. Middle Street is the medieval heart of the village with the ford crossing the River Stort. Piercewebbs has formal old walled garden and yew hedges complementing handsome red brick house. Shrubs, lawns, ha-ha, yew with topiary, stilt hedge, pond and trellised rose garden. Landscaped field walk. Best views in the village. Plant sale at Chestnut Cottage. Limited access to Piercewebbs only. Chestnut Cottage is not suitable for wheelchairs.

Tudor Roost

12 8 DENE COURT

Chignall Road, Chelmsford, CM1 2JQ. Mrs Sheila Chapman, 01245 266156. *W of Chelmsford (Parkway). Take A1060 Roxwell Rd for 1m. Turn R at T-lights into Chignall Rd. Dene Court 3rd exit on R. Parking in Chignall Rd.* **Wed 22, Fri 31 May (2-5), also open Dragons. Tue 4, Fri 14, Tue 18, Fri 28 June, Fri 5 July (2-5). Tue 16 July (2-5), also open Dragons. Fri 26 July (2-5). Tue 6, Fri 16 Aug (2-5), also open Dragons. Fri 23 Aug (2-5). Sun 8 Sept (2-5), also open Dragons. Adm £3.50, chd free.** Visits also by arrangement May to Aug for groups of 10+.

Beautifully maintained and designed compact garden (250sq yds). Owner is well-known RHS gold medal-winning exhibitor (now retired). Circular lawn, long pergola and walls festooned with roses and climbers. Large selection of unusual clematis. Densely-planted colour coordinated perennials add interest from May to Sept in this immaculate garden.

13 DRAGONS

Boyton Cross, Chelmsford, CM1 4LS. Mrs Margot Grice, 01245 248651, mandmdragons@tiscali.co.uk. *3m W of Chelmsford. On A1060. ½m W of The Hare Pub.* **Wed 20 Feb (12-3). Light refreshments. Wed 22, Fri 31 May, Tue 16 July, Tue 6, Fri 16 Aug (2-5); Sun 8 Sept (11-4). Home-made teas. Also open 8 Dene Court. Wed 25 Sept (2-5). Home-made teas. Adm £4, chd free.** Visits also by arrangement Feb to Oct for groups of 10+.

A plantswoman's ¾ acre garden, planted to encourage wildlife. Sumptuous colour-themed borders with striking plant combinations, featuring specimen plants, fernery, clematis,and grasses. Meandering paths lead to ponds, patio, scree garden and small vegetable garden. Two summerhouses, one overlooking stream and farmland.

14 ELWY LODGE

West Bowers Rd, Woodham Walter, CM9 6RZ. David & Laura Cox, 01245 222165, elwylodge@gmail.com. *Just outside Woodham Walter village. From Chelmsford, A414 to Danbury. L at 2nd mini r'about into Little Baddow Rd. From Colchester, A12 to Hatfield Peverel, L onto B1019. Follow NGS signs.* **Sun 12 May, Fri 7 June (11-5). Adm £5, chd free. Sun 16 June (10.30-5). Combined adm with 1 Whitehouse Cottages £7.50, chd free. Fri 12, Sun 14 July (11-5). Adm £5, chd free. Home-made teas. Seasonal and Special home-made cakes on Sunday openings, not to be missed.** Visits also by arrangement May to July for groups of 10+.

Tucked away in the gentle Essex countryside, the glorious garden at Elwy Lodge offers a welcome that is hard to beat. Join the growing numbers of visitors who regularly return each season to sit and savour the different sights this exceptional garden has to offer in late spring, midsummer and then again in late summer. Plenty of seating throughout the garden. Flowing lawns, herbaceous borders, scented roses, clematis, trees, wildlife pond and a small meadow area. A secluded chamomile-scented lower garden with raised veg. beds and fruit trees leads to a delightful summer house, where visitors relax and enjoy the peaceful surroundings and amazing views. Sloping uneven lawn in parts. Please check wheelchair access with garden owner before visiting.

15 NEW 5 FAIRFIELD ROAD

Leigh-On-Sea, SS9 5RZ. Rob & Gwen Evison. *Follow A127 towards Southend past Rayleigh Weir. At Progress Rd T-lights turn L. At the end turn R at the T-lights along Rayleigh Rd A1015. Fairfield Road is approx 1m on the L.* **Sun 19 May (12-4). Adm £3.50, chd free. Home-made teas, coffee and cakes or cream teas are available. Free refills of tea and coffee.**

A lovingly kept garden divided into different areas. Koi pond surrounded by climbing plants and topiary. Well tended lawn with numerous beds filled with flowering shrubs, conifers, alliums irises and peonies. Rose covered arch leads to a secluded woodland area, young birch and maple trees and many woodland plants including camellias and rhododendrons Living evergreen arches lead to a magical secret gd. Most of the garden is wheelchair accessible. There are a few shallow steps.

16 FAIRWINDS

Chapel Lane, Chigwell Row, IG7 6JJ. Sue & David Coates, 07731 796467, scoates@forest.org.uk. *2m SE of Chigwell. Grange Hill Tube, turn R at exit, 10 mins walk uphill. Car: Nr M25 J26 & N Circular Waterworks r'about. Follow signs for Chigwell. Fork R for Manor/Lambourne Rd. Park in Lodge Close Car Park.* **Mon 27 May (2-5). Adm £4, chd free. Home-made teas. Free refills of tea/coffee Soya milk available. Some green/ fruit teas and decaf on request.** Visits also by arrangement Mar to Sept fr groups of 10 to 20. Tea & cake by advance request. Guided tours on request.

Gravelled front garden and three differently styled back garden spaces with planting changes every year. Meander, sit, relax and enjoy. Flower border planting influenced by Beth Chatto, Penelope Hobhouse and Christopher Lloyd. The woodland garden includes shade planting and is home to our hens. Beyond the rustic fence, lies the wildlife pond and vegetable plot. Happy hens. Happy insects in bee house, bug house, log piles and sampling the spring pollen. Newts in pond. There be dragons a plenty!! Space for 2 disabled cars to park by the house. Wood chip paths in woodland area may require assistance.

17 FEERINGBURY MANOR

Coggeshall Road, Feering, Colchester, CO5 9RB. Mr & Mrs Giles Coode-Adams, 01376 561946, seca@btinternet.com, www.ngs.org.uk. *Between Feering & Coggeshall on Coggeshall Rd, 1m from Feering village.* **Every Thur and Fri 4 Apr to 26 July (9-4). Every Thur and Fri 5 Sept to 4 Oct (9-4). Adm £5, chd free.** Visits also by arrangement Jan to Oct. Donation to Feering Church.

There is always plenty to see in this peaceful 10 acre garden with two ponds and river Blackwater. Jewelled lawn in early April then

Field Cottage

spectacular tulips and blossom lead on to a huge number of different and colourful plants, many unusual, culminating in a purple explosion of michaelmas daisies in late Sept. Wonderful sculpture by Ben Coode-Adams. No wheelchair access to arboretum; steep slope.

18 FIELD COTTAGE

Pound Gate, Stebbing, nr Great Dunmow, CM6 3RH. Wal & Jenny Hudgell, 01371 856406, jenny_hudgell@yahoo.co.uk. *3m E of Great Dunmow. Leave Gt Dunmow on B1256. Take first L to Stebbing. At the War Memorial junction turn L, down hill to High Street. Take 2nd R past the School, signed to Garden Fields.* **Sun 26 May, Sun 23 June (1-5.30). Adm £4, chd free. Light refreshments.** Visits also by arrangement June to Sept for groups of 10 to 20. Afternoons only.

⅓ acre garden with countryside views reinvented in 2010 and still evolving. Borders packed with perennials and shrubs for all year round interest including iris, hemerocallis, hostas, roses, ferns and grasses. Approx 40 new trees planted around the garden to provide height to a very flat site. Summer house and arbour to relax in and enjoy a cuppa. A medium size vegetable garden. The garden is fully accessible to wheelchairs.

19 FUDLERS HALL

Fox Road, Mashbury, Chelmsford, CM1 4TJ. Mr & Mrs A J Meacock, 01245 231335. *7m NW of Chelmsford. Chelmsford take A1060, R into Chignal Rd. ½m L to Chignal St James approx 5m, 2nd R into Fox Rd signed Gt Waltham. Fudlers FROM GT WALTHAM. Take Barrack Lane for 3m.* **Sun 23 June, Sun 7 July (2-5). Adm £5, chd free. Home-made teas.** Visits also by arrangement June & July.

An award winning, romantic 2 acre garden surrounding C17 farmhouse with lovely pastoral views, across the Chelmer Valley. Old walls divide garden into many rooms, each having a different character, featuring long herbaceous borders, ropes and pergolas festooned with rambling old fashioned roses. Enjoy the vibrant hot border in late summer. Yew hedged kitchen garden. Ample seating.

20 FURZELEA

Bicknacre Road, Danbury, CM3 4JR. Avril & Roger Cole-Jones, 01245 225726, randacj@gmail.com. *4m E of Chelmsford, 4m W of Maldon A414 to Danbury. At village centre turn S into Mayes Lane Take 1st R. Go past Cricketers Pub, L on to Bicknacre Rd Park in NT carpark immed on L Garden 50m further on R. Extra parking 200 metres past on L.* **Wed 1 May (1-5); Sun 5 May, Sun 2 June (11-5); Wed 11 Sept (1-5); Sun 15 Sept (11-5). Adm £5, chd free. Home-made teas. All the cakes are home made many with home produced fruit, etc.** Visits also by arrangement Apr to Sept. Groups of 15+.

A Victorian house surrounded by a garden designed, created and maintained by the owners to provide all year round interest. The colour coordinated borders and beds are enhanced with topiary, grasses,and climbers. April starts with thousands of tulips followed by Alliums. By June the roses are blooming with many perennials, July is hemerocallis show time, Sept includes Dahlias Asters, late exotics. The garden has many unusual plants and shrubs. Opp Danbury Common (NT), short walk to Danbury Country Park and Lakes and short drive to RHS Hyde Hall. Very limited wheelchair access, with some steps and gravel paths and drive.

21 30 GLENWOOD AVENUE

Leigh-On-Sea, SS9 5EB.
Joan Squibb, 07543 031772, squibb44@gmail.com. *Follow A127 towards Southend. Past Rayleigh Weir. At Progress Rd T-lights turn L. At next T-lights turn L down Rayleigh Rd A1015. Past shops turn 2nd L into Glenwood Ave . Garden halfway down on R.* **Fri 26 Apr, Fri 26, Sun 28 July (11-4). Adm £3.50, chd free. Home-made teas, coffee and cakes.** Visits also by arrangement Apr to Aug for groups of 10 to 20.

Nestled next to the busy A127 lies a beautifully transformed town garden. Homemade raised beds with tulips in spring, dahlias and roses in the summer. From a corridor of Cyprus trees and grass emerges an open garden giving a vista of colour, inspiration and peaceful harmony, with many different scents to savour. Hanging baskets bloom in the fruit trees and along the fences. A paved area allows one to enjoy the view of the garden as does a deck at the back where herbs and some vegetables live alongside the flowers. A peaceful vista, to sit in and restore the batteries. Vegetables are also grown in raised beds.

22 ◆ GREEN ISLAND

Park Road, Ardleigh, CO7 7SP.
Fiona Edmond, 01206 230455, fionaedmond7@aol.com, www.greenislandgardens.co.uk. *3m NE of Colchester. From Ardleigh village centre, take B1029 towards Great Bromley. Park Rd is 2nd on R after level Xing. Garden is last on L.* **For NGS: Sun 5 May, Sat 12 Oct (10-5). Adm £7.50, chd £2.50. Light refreshments. Home-made cakes, sandwiches and baguettes.** For other opening times and information, please phone, email or visit garden website.

'A garden for all seasons' A plantsman's paradise with 20 acres packed with rare and unusual plants. Carved within mature woodland are huge island beds, Japanese garden, terrace, gravel garden, seaside garden, water gardens and extensive woodland plantings. Also tearoom with home-made cakes and snacks and nursery offering plants all seen growing in the gardens. Bluebells Bazaar weekend on the 4/5 May. Sunday 5 May is in aid of the NGS. It is a chance to see the the stunning azaleas amongst the carpets of bluebells. Bluebells and azaleas, acers and rhododendrons in May. Water gardens, island beds and tree lilies all summer. Stunning Autumn colour. Light lunches, home-made teas and cream teas served. Flat and easy walking /pushing wheelchairs. Ramps at entrance and tearoom. Disabled parking and WC.

23 NEW HALFWAY HALEY'S

26 Courtenay Gardens,, Upminster, RM14 1DD. Mr & Mrs Ed & Jan Haley. *From Upminster Station main entrance turn R, Take 1st R into Deyncourt Gardens. Take 1st rd on L which is Courtenay Gardens. The garden is aprox 5 mins walk from Upminster Station.* **Sun 23 June, Sun 15 Sept (12.30-5.30). Adm £4, chd free. Light refreshments.**

This is a long and narrow secluded garden split into 4 rooms the last being a secret garden. There are 3 mature ornamental cherry trees plus shrubs and climbing plants. There is a Hosta bed, Dahlia bed, lots of Fuchsia plants, a medium well stocked pond, Pergola and Arbours, Willow Wigwam and plenty of Seating. Although there are flower beds and borders the garden is informal and natural. Garden not suitable for wheelchairs.

GROUP OPENING

24 NEW HARWICH GARDENS

St Helens Green, Harwich, CO12 3NH. *Centre of Old Harwich. Take A120 to Harwich, continue on to The Quay. Follow the rd round into Wellington Rd. Car park is available on Wellington Rd, CO12 3DP, within 50m of St Helens Green, also available other parking on street & on The Quay.* **Sun 28 July (1-5). Combined adm £5, chd free. Home-made teas at 8 St Helens Green.**

NEW 30 CHURCH STREET
Diana Brearley.

NEW 63 CHURCH STREET
Sue & Richard Watts.

NEW QUAYSIDE COURT
Brendan & Rachel Boreham.

NEW 8 ST HELENS GREEN
Frances Vincent.

NEW THE WALLED GARDEN
Liz Fraser & Michael Pountney.

Five different gardens by the seaside. All within walking distance in the historical town of Harwich. 8 St Helens Green, just 100m from the sea. Whilst a small town garden, there is an abundance of dahlias, salvias, and hydrangeas mixed with complimentary perennials. 63 Church Street (access via Cow Lane) is a long, narrow walled courtyard with shrubs, climbers, perennials and veg packed into the garden and architectural features including an Elizabethan window with original glass. 30 Church Street (access via Customs House Lane) is a tiny courtyard reclaimed from a barren space in 18 months. Crammed with pots and climbers it is a restful space. The sunken garden is a hidden gem. Behind Quayside Court, originally a Victorian hotel and is possibly below sea level, features a pond, veg patch, roses and climbers. The Walled Garden, a garden without a house. A previous waste area enclosed by high walls planted with perennials. It's a place for plant lovers. Uneven paths and steps. Not suitable for wheelchairs.

25 262 HATCH ROAD

Pilgrims Hatch, Brentwood, CM15 9QR. Mike & Liz Thomas. *2m N of Brentwood town centre. On A128 N toward Ongar turn R onto Doddinghurst Rd at mini-r'about (to Brentwood Centre) After the Centre turn next L into Hatch Rd. Garden 4th on R.* **Sun 7, Sun 21 July (11.30-4.30). Adm £4.50, chd free. Home-made teas.**

A formal frontage with lavender. An eclectic rear garden of around an acre divided into 'rooms' with themed borders, several ponds, three green houses, fruit and vegetable plots and oriental garden. There is also a secret white garden, spring and summer wild flower folly and an exotic area. There is plenty of seating to enjoy the views and a cup of tea and cake.

26 HAVENDELL

Beckingham Street, Tolleshunt Major, Maldon, CM9 8LJ. Malcolm & Val. *5m E of Maldon 3m W of Tiptree. From B1022 take Loamy Hill rd. At the Xrds L into Witham rd. Follow NGS signs.* **Sun 2 June (11-4.30). Adm £4, chd free. Home-made teas.**

Cottage style garden set in ⅓ acre, taking you through different sections filling you with surprise. Set in this ever evolving garden we have an abundance of hosta's around a sub- tropical section with a wild life pond, fruit and vegetable plot and stumpery. Range of roses including Rambling Rector and Blue for You, Sit and relax amongst the nature this garden has to offer.

27 NEW HAYTOR

Rectory Road, Little Burstead, Billericay, CM12 9TR. Carol & Roger Savage. *From Billericay: B1007, R A176, Little Burstead, L onto Rectory Rd, Haytor is on LHS. Or A176 to Billericay, L Wash Rd 1st R, Dunton Rd. 1st R, Rectory Rd, Haytor is on RHS.* **Fri 14, Sun 16 June (11-4). Adm £4, chd free. Home-made teas.**

Lovingly cultivated over the past 30 years, its original one acre grass field is now an eclectic mix of gardeners' delights, with the lower area left to allow natural growth. There are ponds, lovely mature trees, mixed shrubs and herbaceous borders. This garden invites you to take in nature's beauty and there are many seating areas, with wild flowers and even a 'Monet' style bridge.

28 HILLDROP

Laindon Road (B1007), Horndon-On-The-Hill, Stanford-le-Hope, SS17 8QB. John Little & Fiona Crummay, 07967 733720, grassroofcompany@gmail.com, www.grassroofcompany.co.uk. *Just N of Horndon on the Hill. 80m E of junction B1007 & Lower Dunton Rd.* **Sun 7 July (2-7). Adm £5, chd free. Light refreshments. Tea and Coffee, Pimms, Cakes and Vegetarian savoury snacks. Visits also by arrangement May to July for groups of 10 to 20. Owners work full time so best after 5pm weekdays.**

Since building our turf roof house in 1995 we have trialled waste materials in our 4 acre garden to mimic brownfield habitat, one of the most undervalued places for wildlife. These are now our most beautiful and diverse habitats for plants and insects. Several green roofs and lots of ideas to create biodiverse habitats, especially for solitary bees. Views across the Thames Estuary to Kent. The garden features a self build timber house with green roof, 6 other green roofs, 3 ponds, brownfield habitat which gives ideas for difficult areas, green roof shipping container garden room, wildlife friendly hedges including laid hedges. 2 wild flower meadows and ephemeral wetland. Some wheelchair friendly paths and grass paths that may be accessible depending on rabbit damage. Garden is on a slight slope.

Horkesley Hall

29 HORKESLEY HALL

Little Horkesley, Colchester, CO6 4DB. Mr & Mrs Johnny Eddis, 078085 99290, pollyeddis@hotmail.com, www.airbnb.co.uk/rooms/10354093. *6m N of Colchester City Centre. 2m W of A134, 10 minutes from the A12. At the grass triangle with tree in middle, turn into Little Horkesley Church car park to the very far end - access is via low double black gates at the far end.* **Evening opening Tue 19 Feb (5.30-8). Light refreshments. Sun 24 Feb (1-4); Sun 9 June (11-5); Sun 8 Sept (12.30-4). Adm £6, chd free. Home-made teas, cream teas, cakes, meringues, ice creams available depending on the season.** Visits also by arrangement Feb to Oct.

8 acres in a magical setting - a romantic garden surrounding classical house in mature parkland setting. 2 lakes. Unusual, ancient and enormous trees. Largest ginkgo tree outside Kew. Walled garden, snowdrops, wild flower garden, blossom, spring bulbs, roses, hydrangeas. Formal terrace overlooking sweeping lawns to woodland. A timeless, family garden with recent and ongoing improvements. A developing lakeside Jungle Walk, appeal for all ages. Very well-stocked plant stall and home-made cakes, teas, meringues and ice creams. Stunning natural setting, jungle walk, wild flower garden, living willow, charming enclosed swimming pool garden where you can relax with teas. Traditional stable yard. Vast, unusual and ancient trees, topiary. Snowdrops, hydrangeas, roses, exotics, dahlias! A very well-stocked Plant Stall. Limited wheelchair access to some areas, gravel paths and slopes but easy access to tea area with lovely views over lake and garden. Please bring a torch for the evening opening in Feb.

30 NEW 61 HUMBER AVENUE

South Ockendon, RM15 5JW. Mr & Mrs Kasia & Greg Purton-Dmowski. *M25 - J30/31 or A13 - exit to Lakeside. J31/M25 to Thurrock Services, or Grays from A13, at the r'about take exit onto Ship Ln to Aveley, turn R and then 2nd exit at the r'about onto Stifford Rd/B1335, take Foyle Dr to Humber Ave.* **Sun 16 June, Sun 14 July (12-5). Adm £3.50, chd free. Home-made teas.**

A suburban garden close to Nature Reserve, 30m x 14m space featuring an old cherry tree from the orchard of the famous Belhus Mansion. The garden features abundant large borders planted heavily with herbaceous plants, small trees, roses, lilies, and ornamental grasses with oriental senses mixed with a traditional English feel with shady areas with hostas, tree ferns and Japanese style plants. The owners are interested in design and are members of Sogetsu International School, original arrangements will be on display during open day.

31 JERICHO COTTAGE (MEGARRY'S ANTIQUES & TEASHOP)

The Green, Blackmore, Ingatestone, CM4 0RR. Judi Wood, 01277 822170, megarrys@yahoo.co.uk, www.antique-teashop.co.uk. *4m E of Chipping Ongar 4m N of Brentwood. At centre of Blackmore village head for village green. Turn by the war memorial into Blacksmith Alley. Jericho Cottage straight ahead.* **Tue 16 Apr, Tue 18 June (1.30-5). Adm £3, chd free. Home-made teas. Megarry's Teashop scones with Rodda's clotted cream. Home-made cakes.** Visits also by arrangement Apr to Sept for groups of up to 20.

Small walled wildlife and woodland garden with mature trees, shrubs, bamboos, palms and ponds. Historic Romany Vardo and Victorian Glasshouse. Primroses, bluebells, camellias, rhododendrons and later hydrangeas, euphorbias and geraniums clothe the ground, while a canopy of wisteria, rambling roses, honeysuckle and kiwi vine shade the patio and pergola. The garden is an untamed hidden oasis. Antique shop, Teashop. A gentle paved path leads to the pergola and patio where there is access to the garden through a wrought iron gate onto the lawn.

32 KEEWAY

Ferry Road, Creeksea, nr Burnham-on-Crouch, CM0 8PL. John & Sue Ketteley, 01621 782083, sueketteley@hotmail.com. *2m W of Burnham-on-Crouch. B1010 to Burnham on Crouch. At town sign take 1st R into Ferry Rd signed Creeksea & Burnham Golf Club & follow NGS signs.* **Wed 26 June, Fri 5 July (2-5). Adm £4, chd free. Home-made teas.** Visits also by arrangement June & July. Groups of 15+.

Large, mature country garden with stunning views over the R Crouch. Formal terraces surround the house with steps leading to sweeping lawns, mixed borders packed full of bulbs and perennials, formal rose and herb garden with interesting water feature. Further afield there are wilder areas, paddocks and lake. A productive greenhouse, vegetable and cutting gardens complete the picture.

33 KELVEDON HALL

Kelvedon, Colchester, CO5 9BN. Mr & Mrs Jack Inglis, 07973 795955, v_inglis@btinternet.com. *Take Maldon Rd direction Great Braxted from Kelvedon High St. Go over R Blackwater bridge & bridge over A12 At T-junction turn R onto Kelvedon Rd. Take 1st L, single gravel road, oak tree on corner.* **Visits by arrangement Apr to July for groups of 20+. Adm £5, chd free. Home-made teas in the Courtyard Garden by the house or for larger numbers in the Pool House Walled Garden, weather permitting. Teas, Coffees and Cakes.**

Varied 6 acre garden surrounding a gorgeous C18 house. A blend of formal and informal spaces interspersed with modern sculpture. Pleached hornbeam and yew and box topiary provide structure. A courtyard walled garden juxtaposes a modern walled pool garden, both providing season long displays. Herbaceous borders offset an abundance of roses around the house. Lily covered ponds with a wet garden. Topiary, sculpture, tulips and roses. Wheelchair access not ideal as there is a lot of gravel.

GROUP OPENING

34 LANGLEY VILLAGE GARDENS

Langley Upper Green, Saffron Walden, CB11 4RY. *7m W of Saffron Walden 10m N of Bishops Stortford. At Newport take B1038. After 3m turn R at Clavering, signed Langley. Upper Green is 3m further on.* **Sun 26 May (11-5). Combined adm £7.50, chd free. Light refreshments at Village Hall on Langley Village Green. Light lunches & home-made teas.**

THE CHESTNUTS
Jane & David Knight.

OLD BELL COTTAGE
Richard Vallance, 01799 550474, r.vallance1234@gmail.com.
Visits also by arrangement May & June.

NEW **1 SPARROWS**
Kevin and Gill Shepherd.

WICKETS
Susan & Doug Copeland.
(See separate entry)

Old Bell Cottage successfully incorporates part of former field, with various herbaceous beds Spring bulbs, alliums, lupins and delphiniums. Trees frame views across valley. Greenhouse, patio area and cabinets for hardening off. Raised beds for vegetables, fruit cage. Sunken BBQ area. Natural pond. The Chestnuts features mature trees and meadow. Planting beds designed and installed by Tristen Knight, RHS Young Designer 2012. Water feature with reclaimed sleeper jetty. New productive garden with oak walkways, paving and water feature. Tranquil place to linger and enjoy. 1 Sparrows is a compact garden with fruit trees, raised vegetable beds and greenhouse. Lawn edged with buxus. Shrubs and climbers. Small water feature and wildlife friendly. A collection of Heuchera and Heucherella. Wickets has wide, mixed borders, roses, two landscaped meadows, lily pond, glasshouse, parterre and dry garden. Langley is highest Essex village set in rolling countryside. Arts & Crafts Exhibition in St John the Evangelist Church. Gravel drives at Wickets.

35 LITTLE MYLES

Ongar Road, Stondon Massey, Brentwood, CM15 0LD. Judy & Adrian Cowan. *1½m SE of Chipping Ongar. Off A128 at Stag Pub, Marden Ash, towards Stondon Massey. Over bridge, 1st house on R after 'S' bend. 400yds Ongar side of Stondon Church.* **Sun 7 July (11-4). Adm £5, chd free. Home-made teas. Seating in Tea Room, also under trees and on main lawn.**
A romantic, naturalistic garden full of hidden features, set in 3 acres. Full borders, meandering paths to Beach Garden, Perennial Prairie border, Exotic Jungle around elephant, monkeys and giraffe. Fountains, sculptures and tranquil benches. Hidden Asian garden, Slate garden, hornbeam pergola, ornamental vegetable patch and natural pond. Herb garden that inspired Little Myles herbal cosmetics. Hand painted jungle mural. Crafts and handmade herbal cosmetics for sale. Explorers sheet and map for children. Gravel paths. No disabled WC available.

36 LONG HOUSE PLANTS

Church Road, Noak Hill, Romford, RM4 1LD. Tim Carter, 01708 371719, tim@thelonghouse.net, www.longhouse-plants.co.uk. *3½m NW of J28 M25. J28 M25 take A1023 Brentwood. At 1st T-lights, turn L to South Weald after 0.8m turn L at T junction. After 1.6m turn L, over M25 after ½m turn R into Church Rd, nursery opp church.* **Wed 12 June, Wed 17 July, Wed 14 Aug, Wed 11 Sept (11-4). Adm £5, chd £3. Home-made teas.** Visits also by arrangement June to Oct for groups of 30+. Conducted tours available by arrangement for an additional fee of £50.
A beautiful garden - yes, but one with a purpose. Long House Plants has been producing home grown plants for more than 10 years - here is a chance to see where it all begins! With wide paths and plenty of seats carefully placed to enjoy the plants and views. It has been thoughtfully designed so that the collections of plants look great together through all seasons.

37 NEW LONGYARD COTTAGE

Betts Lane, Nazeing, Essex, EN9 2DA. Jackie & John Copping, 01992 892472, Nigella11@btopenworld.com. *Opposite red telephone box.* **Sun 17 Feb (11-4). Adm £4, chd free. Home-made teas.** Visits also by arrangement June to Nov for groups of 5 to 20.
Longyard Cottage is an interesting ¾ of an acre garden situated within yards of an SSSI site, an C11 Church, a myriad of footpaths and a fine display of snowdrops and spring bulbs. This conceptual garden is based on a 'journey' and depicted through the use of paths which take you through 3 distinct areas each with its own characteristics. It's a tactile garden with which you can engage or simply sit and relax.

38 LOXLEY HOUSE

49 Robin Hood Road, Brentwood, CM15 9EL. Robert & Helen Smith. *1m N of Brentwood town centre. On A128 N towards Ongar turn R onto Doddinghurst Rd at mini r'about. Take the 1st rd on L into Robin Hood Rd. 2 houses before the bend on L.* **Sat 13 Apr (11.30-3.30). Adm £4, chd free. Home-made teas.**
On entering the rear garden you will be surprised and delighted by this town garden. A colourful patio with pots and containers. Steps up onto a circular lawn surrounded by hedges, herbaceous borders, trees and climbers. 2 water features, one a Japanese theme and another with ferns in a quiet seating area. The garden is planted to offer spring colour with daffodils, tulips and perennials.

Your visits help change lives – we've donated over £16.7 million to Macmillan Cancer Support since 1984

39 16 MAIDA WAY

Chingford, E4 7JL. Clare & Steve Francis. *1m from Chingford town centre off Kings Head Hill. Maida Way is a cul-de-sac off Maida Avenue that can be accessed via Kings Head Hill or Sewardstone Rd.* **Evening opening Sat 6 July (4-9). Adm £7.50, chd free. Wine. Entrance fee incl a glass of wine and a selection of nibbles.**

There are three distinct areas to the garden. A walled patio with raised beds of ferns, climbers, hostas and planters. Steps up to middle garden with a large koi pond, seating area, with acers, shrubs, herbaceous plants, grasses and grapevine. Numerous retro artefacts creatively upcycled. The third area is a kitchen garden with raised beds of fruit trees and bushes, herbs and vegetables.

40 262 MAIN ROAD

Hawkwell, Hockley, SS5 4NW. Karen Mann, 07976 272999, karenmann10@hotmail.com. *3m NE of Rayleigh. From A127 at Rayleigh Weir take B1013 towards Hockley. Garden on L after White Hart Pub & village green.* **Sat 20 July, Sun 18 Aug (12.30-5.30). Adm £4, chd free. Home-made teas.** Visits also by arrangement July & Aug.

The garden comprises of 185 metres of island beds and borders sited on ⅓ acre. Some of the borders are elevated from the house resulting in steep banks which provide a different and interesting aspect. Salvia, dahlia, hedychium, brugmansia peak in the summer months. 'This garden features a completely new, RHS accredited Dahlia named "Jake Mann" after my late son.

41 NEW 9 MALYON ROAD

Witham, CM8 1DF. Maureen & Stephen Hicks. *Car park at bottom of High St. 5 min walk from car park cross High St by pedestrian crossing onto River Walk, follow path, take 1st R turn into Luard way Malyon Rd straight ahead.* **Sat 22, Sun 23 June (10.30-5). Adm £3.50, chd free. Home-made teas, cakes and soft drinks.**

Large town garden with mature trees and shrubs made up of a series of garden rooms. Flower beds, pond, summerhouse and greenhouse giving all year interest. Plenty of places to sit and relax with paths that take you on a tour of the garden. A quiet hidden place not expected in a busy town. Our garden is a hidden oasis, where you can escape from the hustle and bustle of busy life. Wheelchair access, but there is a step down into part of the garden.

42 ◆ MARKS HALL GARDENS & ARBORETUM

Coggeshall, CO6 1TG. Marks Hall Estate, 01376 563796, enquiries@markshall.org.uk, www.markshall.org.uk. *1½m N of Coggeshall. Follow brown & white tourism signs from A120 Coggeshall bypass.* For opening times and information, please phone, email or visit garden website.

Marks Hall Gardens and Arboretum features a tree collection from all the temperate areas of the world set in more than 200 acres of historic landscape providing interest and enjoyment throughout the year. Highlights include: the Millennium Walk designed for structure, colour and scent on the shortest days of the year; the largest planting in Europe of Wollemi pine and the inspired combination of traditional and contemporary planting in

Parsonage House

the C18 Walled Garden. Spring snowdrop and autumn colour displays are annual highlights. Tea room serving homemade cakes, hot and cold beverages, light lunches including homemade soup and daily specials. 2019 sees the return of our Bi-Annual Sculpture Exhibition from 20 July to 1 Sept. See website for opening times. Hard paths lead to all key areas of interest. Wheelchairs or staff-driven buggy available for visitors with mobility issues (booking essential).

43 MIRAFLORES

Witham, CM8 2LJ. Yvonne & Danny Owen, 07976 603863, danny@dannyowen.co.uk. *Please DO NOT go via Rowan Way, go to Forest Road as there is rear access to the garden only. Access is ONLY by rear gate at the top The Spinney, off of FOREST RD... Postcode CM8 2TP. Please follow yellow signs.* **Sun 9, Sun 16, Sun 30 June (2-5). Adm £3.50, chd free. Home-made teas, and cakes (incl gluten free), savouries, teas, coffee, soft drinks, herbal teas,.** Visits also by arrangement May & June for groups of 10 to 30.

An award-winning, medium-sized garden described as a "Little Bit of Heaven'. A blaze of colour with roses, clematis, pergola, rose arch, triple fountain with box hedging and deep herbaceous borders. See our 'Folly', exuberant and cascading hanging baskets...find our Secret Door. Featured in Garden Answers, Amateur Gardening and Essex Life. Tranquil seating areas. No access for wheelchair users as step up to garden.

44 MONKS COTTAGE

Monks Lane, Dedham nr Colchester, CO7 6DP. Nicola Baker, 07860 173214, nicola_baker@tiscali.co.uk. *6m NE of Colchester. Leave Dedham village with the church on L. Take 2nd main rd on R (Coles Oak Lane) Monks Lane is 1st rd on L.* **Visits by arrangement May to July for groups of 5 to 20. Adm £4, chd free. Home made cakes available from the Tea Shed.**

½ acre cottage garden on a sloping site in the heart of the Dedham Vale. A constantly evolving garden which features mature trees, pond, box-edged parterre beds, boggy area with strong foliage shapes, rill garden with cascade and small woodland garden. A gin-and-tonic balcony gives a high level vantage point over the garden and a raised terrace looks out over the surrounding countryside.

45 MOVERONS

Brightlingsea, CO7 0SB. Lesley & Payne Gunfield, lesleyorrock@me.com, , www.moverons.co.uk. *7m SE of Colchester. At old church turn R signed Moverons Farm. Follow lane & garden signs for approx 1m. Beware some SatNavs take you the wrong side of the river.* **Sun 9 June (10.30-5). Adm £5, chd free. Home-made teas.** Visits also by arrangement May to Sept for groups of 10+.

Beautiful tranquil 4 acre garden in touch with its surroundings and enjoying stunning estuary views. A wide variety of planting in mixed borders to suit different growing conditions and provide all year colour. Courtyard, reflection pool, large natural ponds, sculptures and barn for rainy day teas! Magnificent trees some over 300yrs old give this garden real presence. Most of the garden is accessible by wheelchair via grass and gravel paths, There are some steps and bark paths.

46 NEW 23 NEW ROAD

Dagenham, RM10 9NH. John Seaman, 07504 712818, jseaman@talktalk.net. *Leave A13 at the junction signed for A1306 - Dagenham & Hornchurch. Go around the r'about following it off at the 4th exit. Then follow the 2nd r'about straight onwards.* **Sat 10, Sun 11, Sat 24, Sun 25 Aug (12-5). Adm £4, chd free.** Visits also by arrangement July to Sept for groups of 5 to 20.

This is an exotic garden, themed on the foothills of the Himalayas in India. This garden will be like no other you may have seen before despite its modest size. It is filled with exquisite tropical plants including Canna, Gingers and Bananas. A feast for the eyes filled with good ideas for vertical space. An extravaganza of plants in all shapes, colour and form.

47 PARSONAGE HOUSE

Wiggens Green, Helions Bumpstead, Haverhill, CB9 7AD. The Hon & Mrs Nigel Turner. *3m S of Haverhill. From Xrds in the village centre go up past the Church for approx 1m. Parking on R through a five bar gate into the orchard. Garden on L of the lane.* **Sun 16 June, Sun 8 Sept (2-5). Adm £5, chd free. Home-made teas. Apple juice from the orchard for sale on day.**

C15 house (not open) surrounded by 3 acres of formal gardens with mixed borders, topiary, pond, potager and greenhouse. Further 3-acre wild flower meadow with orchids and rare trees and further 3 acre orchard of old East Anglian apple varieties in two small fields across the lane. Gravel drive and small step into WC.

48 PEACOCKS

Main Road, Margaretting, CM4 9HY. Phil Torr, 07802 472382, phil.torr@btinternet.com. *Margaretting Village Centre. From village Xrds go 75yds in the direction of Ingatestone, entrance gates will be found on L set back 50 feet from the road frontage.* **Sun 9 June (1-4). Adm £5, chd free. Light refreshments.** Visits also by arrangement May & June for groups of 20+. Please email or call owner for available dates BEFORE consulting your group. Donation to St Francis Hospice.

5-acre garden with mature native and specimen trees. Restored horticultural buildings. Series of garden rooms including Paradise Garden, Garden of Reconciliation, Alhambra fusion. Long herbaceous/mixed border. Temple of Antheia on the banks of a lily lake. Large areas for wildlife incl woodland walk, a nuttery and orchard. Traditionally managed wild flower meadow. Sunken dell with waterfall. Display of old Margaretting postcards. Small art exhibition. Garden sculpture. Wild flower meadow in traditional orchard. Most of garden wheelchair accessible.

49 18 PETTITS BOULEVARD

Rise Park, Romford, RM1 4PL. Peter & Lynn Nutley. *From M25 take A12 towards London, turn R at Pettits Lane junction then R again into Pettits Blvd or Romford Stn then 103 or 499 bus to Romford Fire Stn and follow NGS signs.* **Sat 22, Sun 23 June, Sat 14, Sun 15 Sept (1-5). Adm £4, chd free. Home-made teas.**

The garden is 80ft x 23ft on three levels with an ornamental pond, patio area with shrubs and perennials, many in pots. Large eucalyptus tree leads to a woodland themed area with many ferns and hostas. There are agricultural implements and garden ornaments giving a unique and quirky feel to the garden. There are also tranquil seating areas situated throughout. Agricultural implements on show.

50 THE PUNCHBOWL

The Street, High Easter, Chelmsford, CM1 4QW. Penny Kelsey. *Centre of High Easter. Next to the church.* **Wed 29 May (2-5). Adm £5, chd free. Home-made teas.**

Found in the village centre next to the church, this garden offers a mixture of mature shrubs and trees and coloured themed herbaceous borders. Lawns and paths lead through entertainment spaces littered with animal sculptures. With a small pond and plenty of seating the garden is accessible to wheelchairs.

51 ROOKWOODS

Yeldham Road, Sible Hedingham, CO9 3QG. Peter & Sandra Robinson, 07770 957111, sandy1989@btinternet.com, www.rookwoodsgarden.com. *8m NW of Halstead. Entering Sible Hedingham from the direction of Haverhill on A1017 take 1st R just after 30mph sign.* **Mon 27 May (10-4.30). Combined adm with Washlands £8, chd free. Home-made teas. Single adm £5.** Visits also by arrangement June to Sept fr groups of up to 30. Tuesday, Wednesday and Friday Mornings.

Rookwoods is a tranquil garden in which you can enjoy a variety of mature trees; herbaceous borders; a shrubbery; pleached hornbeam rooms; a work-in-progress wild flower bed; a buttercup meadow, and an ancient oak wood. There is no need to walk far, you can come and linger over tea, under a dreamy wisteria canopy while enjoying a view of the garden. Gravel drive.

52 79 ROYSTON AVENUE

Chingford, E4 9DE. Paul & Christine Lidbury. *From A406 Crooked Billet r'about take A112 towards Chingford. Continue ½m, across T-lights (Morrison's), Royston Ave is 3rd turn on R. Bus 97, 158, 215, 357 (Leonard Rd or Ainslie Wood Rd stops).* **Mon 27 May (12-5). Adm £3.50, chd £1. Home-made teas. Tea/coffee and home-made cakes. Quality home-brewed beer tastings available.**

A 55 x 19ft urban garden with over 600 different varieties of plants - a great many in containers, including collections of Hostas, Acers, and Sempervivums. An oasis for local birds and wildlife with two small ponds and insect habitats with further interest provided by ornaments, sculptures and artwork, where words of gardening wisdom abound. Not suitable for young children.

53 69 RUNDELLS - THE SECRET GARDEN

Harlow, CM18 7HD. Mr & Mrs K Naunton, 01279 303471, k_naunton@hotmail.com. *3m from J7 M11. A414 exit T-lights take L exit Southern Way, mini r'about 1st exit Trotters Rd leading into Commonside Rd, take 2nd L into Rundells.* **Sat 13 July (2-5). Adm £3, chd free. Home-made teas cakes, coffee and soft drinks.** Visits also by arrangement June to Sept for groups of up to 30.

As featured on Alan Tichmarsh's first 'Love Your Garden' series ('The Secret Garden') 69, Rundells is a very colourful, small town garden packed with a wide variety of shrubs, perennials, herbaceous and bedding plants in over 200 assorted containers. Hard landscaping on different levels incl's summer house, various seating areas and water features. Steep steps. Access to adjacent allotment open to view. Various small secluded seating areas. A small fairy garden has been added to give interest for younger visitors. The garden is next to a large allotment and this is open to view with lots of interesting features including a bee apiary. Honey and other produce for sale (conditions permitting).

54 ST HELENS

High Street, Stebbing, CM6 3SE. Stephen & Joan Bazlinton, 01371 856495, revbaz@phonecoop.coop. *3m E of Great Dunmow. Leave Gt Dunmow on B1256. Take 1st L to Stebbing, at T-junction turn L into High St, garden 2nd on R.* **Sat 27 Apr, Sat 1, Sat 29 June (1-5). Adm £4.50, chd free. Home-made teas.** Visits also by arrangement May to July. Refreshments included in admission fees. Donation to Dentaid.

A garden established over 40 years from a bog-ridden, cricket-bat plantation into a gently sloping woodland garden. Springs and ponds divide the garden into different areas with various shrubs and perennial planting. Partial wheelchair access.

55 30 SANDFORD ROAD

Chelmsford, CM2 6DQ. John & Mary Hawkes. *Limited parking for disabled only (gravelled). Roadside parking or park at nearby Chelmer Village Retail Park CM2 6XE. Take footpath opp Next, cross T-lights (A138) 5mins walk, follow signage.* **Sun 28 Apr, Sun 23 June (10-5). Adm £4, chd free. Home-made teas, coffee, cold drinks, home-made cakes, sausage rolls, scones.**

A surprising ⅓ acre town garden which is divided into 3 areas. A formal garden with lawn, monkey puzzle tree, flowering borders, fishpond, pergola with wisteria and a large patio. Enter through the rose arbour into a shaded area with a variety of specimen fruit and ornamental trees. Then finally, through a gate to a secret landscaped kitchen garden. Limited wheelchair access due to gravel drive and some uneven areas.

56 SANDY LODGE

Howe Drive, Hedingham Road, Halstead, CO9 2QL. Emma & Rick Rengasamy. *8m NE of Braintree. Turn off Hedingham Rd into Ashlong Grove. Howe Drive is on L. Please park in Ashlong Grove & walk up Howe Drive.* **Sun 12 May, Sun 22 Sept (11-5). Adm £4.50, chd free. Home-made teas.**

A stunning garden, with amazing views over Halstead, there is something to see every day. ¾ acre created over the last 5 years, enter to our gravel Bee Border full of irises and tulips; wander in our Winter Wedding border and the Woodlands Walk. Across the lawn you find the new double borders with flowing prairie planting. Lots of seating and viewing spots. Garden on a slight slope; gravel at front. Wheelchair access restricted due to large amount of gravel.

57 NEW 4 SHEPHERDS CLOSE

Hadleigh, Benfleet, SS7 2LR. Mr & Mrs Tracey. *Scrub Lane turn into Greenacres then into Shepherds Walk then turn R into Shepherds Close. Or, Dawes Heath Rd turn into Poors Lane, turn R Shepherds Walk.* **Sun 30 June (11-5). Adm £3.50, chd free. Home-made teas.**

A South facing, secluded garden backing on to nature reserve. Wide colourful borders feature a mixture of shrubs and herbaceous perennials. Tumbling roses over an archway lead to a productive vegetable garden and greenhouse. The terrace boasts planted terracotta pots with seasonal planting and an olive tree.

58 SHRUBS FARM

Lamarsh, Bures, CO8 5EA. Mr & Mrs Robert Erith, 01787 227520, bob@shrubsfarm.co.uk, www.shrubsfarm.co.uk. *1¼ m from Bures. On rd to Lamarsh, the drive is signed to Shrubs Farm.* **Visits by arrangement Apr to Oct for groups of 5+. Adm £7, chd free. Home-made teas. Wine & canapes by arrangement £5 per head.**

2 acres with shrub borders, lawns, roses and trees. 50 acres parkland with wild flower paths and woodland trails. Over 60 species of oak. Superb 10m views over Stour valley. Ancient coppice and pollards incl largest goat (pussy) willow (*Salix caprea*) in England. Wollemi and Norfolk pines, and banana trees. Full size black rhinoceros. Display of Bronze Age burial urns. Large grass maze. Guided Tour to incl garden, park and ancient woodland, historic items including Bronze Age Burial Urns and painting of the Stour valley 200 years ago. Restored C18 Essex barn is available for refreshment by prior arrangement. Tea proceeds to Lamarsh Church. Some ground may be boggy in wet weather.

59 SNARES HILL COTTAGE

Duck End, Stebbing, CM6 3RY. Pete & Liz Stabler, 01371 856565, petestabler@gmail.com. *Between Dunmow & Bardfield. On B1057 from Great Dunmow to Great Bardfield, ½ m after Bran End on L.* **Visits by arrangement Mar to Sept. Adm £5, chd free. Home-made teas.**

A 'quintessential English Garden' - Gardeners World. Our quirky 1½ acre garden has surprises round every corner and many interesting sculptures. A natural swimming pool is bordered by romantic flower beds, herb garden and Victorian folly. A bog garden borders woods and leads to silver birch copse, beach garden and 'Roman' temple. Natural Swimming Pond. Classic cars. Sculptures. Not wheelchair friendly as it is a hilly garden with some steep slopes.

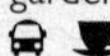

60 SOUTH SHOEBURY HALL

Church Road, Shoeburyness, SS3 9DN. Mr & Mrs M Dedman, 01702 299022, michael@shoeburyhall.co.uk. *4m E of Southend-on-Sea. Enter Southend on A127 to Eastern Ave A1159 signed Shoebury. R at r'about to join A13. Proceed S to Ness Rd. R into Church Rd. Garden on L 50 metres.* **Sun 28 Apr, Sun 28 July (2-5). Adm £4, chd free. Home-made teas.** Visits also by arrangement May to Aug for groups of 10+.

Delightful, 1-acre established walled garden surrounding Grade II listed house (not open) and bee house. Charming agapanthus and hydrangea beds. April is ablaze with 3000 tulips and fritillaria. July shows 200+ varieties of agapanthus incl 'Queen Mum' and 'Black Magic'. Unusual trees, shrubs, rose borders, with 50yr old plus geraniums, Mediterranean and Southern Hemisphere planting in dry garden. C11 St Andrews Church open to visitors (by arrangement). Garden close to sea. Bumper agapanthus sale at both open days.

61 ◆ SPENCERS

Tilbury Road, Great Yeldham, CO9 4JG. Mr & Mrs Colin Bogie, 01787 238175, lynne@spencersgarden.net, www.spencersgarden.net. *Just N of Gt Yeldham on Tilbury Rd. In village centre, turn off A1017 at the 'Blasted Oak' (huge oak stump). Keep L, following stream (signed 'The Belchamps/Tilbury Juxta Clare'). Spencers is clearly signed on L after approx ½ m.* **For NGS: Sun 30 June, Sun 8 Sept (2-5). Adm £5, chd free. Home-made teas.** For other opening times and information, please phone, email or visit garden website.

Romantic C18 walled garden laid out by Lady Anne Spencer, overflowing with blooms following Tom Stuart-Smith's renovation. Huge wisteria, armies of Lord Butler delphiniums ('Rab' lived at Spencers). Spectacular rose and herbaceous borders. Parkland with many specimen trees including Armada Oaks. Victorian woodland walk along River Colne.

62 STRANDLANDS

off Rectory Road, Wrabness, Manningtree, CO11 2TX. Jenny & David Edmunds, 01255 886260, strandlands@outlook.com. *1km along farm track from the corner of Rectory Rd. If using a SatNav, the post code will leave you at the corner of Rectory Rd. Turn onto a farm track, signed to Woodcutters Cottage & Strandlands, & continue for 1km.* **Visits by arrangement May & June for groups of 10 to 20. Adm £5, chd free. Light refreshments. Tea, coffee & a slice of home made cake.**

Cottage surrounded by 4 acres of land bordering beautiful and unspoilt Stour Estuary. One acre of decorative garden: formal courtyard with yew, box and perovskia hedges, lily pond, summerhouse and greenhouse; 2 large island beds, secret 'moon garden', madly and vividly planted 'Madison' garden, 3 acres of wildlife meadows with groups of native trees, large wildlife pond, also riverside bird hide. View the Stour Estuary from our own bird hide. Grayson Perry's 'A House for Essex' can be seen just one field away from Strandlands. Mostly accessible and flat although parking area is gravelled.

Ulting Wick

© Marcus Harpur

63 TUDOR ROOST

18 Frere Way, Fingringhoe, Colchester, CO5 7BP. Chris & Linda Pegden, 01206 729831, pegdenc@gmail.com. *5m S of Colchester. In Fingringhoe by Whalebone PH follow sign to Ballast Quay, after ½m turn R into Brook Hall Rd, then 1st L into Frere Way.* **Sun 21, Mon 22 Apr, Sun 26, Mon 27 May, Sat 29, Sun 30 June, Sat 10, Sun 11 Aug (2-5). Adm £4, chd free. Home-made teas. Large conservatory to sit in if inclement weather. Visits also by arrangement Apr to Aug for groups of 10 to 30. Adm £7 incl Tea & Cake.**

An unexpected hidden colourful ¼-acre garden. Well manicured grassy paths wind round island beds and ponds. Densely planted subtropical area with architectural and exotic plants - cannas, bananas, palms, agapanthus, agaves and tree ferns surround a colourful gazebo. Garden planted to provide yr-round colour and encourage wildlife. Many peaceful seating areas. Within 1m of Fingringhoe Wick Nature Reserve. PLEASE CONFIRM OPENING DATES ON NGS WEBSITE OR TELEPHONE.

64 37 TURPINS LANE

Chigwell, IG8 8AZ. Fabrice Aru & Martin Thurston, 0208 5050 739, martin.thurston@talktalk.net. *Between Woodford & Epping. Tube: Chigwell, 2m from North Circular Rd at Woodford, follow the signs for Chigwell (A113) through Woodford Bridge into Manor Rd & turn L, Bus 275 & W14.* **Sun 30 June, Sun 28 July (11-6). Adm £4, chd free. Visits also by arrangement May to Nov for groups of up to 10.**

An unexpected hidden, magical, part-walled garden showing how much can be achieved in a small space. An oasis of calm with densely planted rich, lush foliage, tree ferns, hostas, topiary and an abundance of well maintained shrubs complemented by a small pond and 3 water features designed for yr round interest.

65 TWO COTTAGES

Church Road, Chrishall, Saffron Walden, SG8 8QT. Michelle Thomas, 07581 745130, mrsdthomas@btinternet.com. *7m W of Saffron Walden. Continue on*

B1039, take R turn to Chrishall. Bury Lane leading into Church Rd. You will find Two Cottages on your 1st L with an old planted boat on the bank. **Sun 23, Sun 30 June (12-4). Adm £5, chd free. Home-made teas. Visits also by arrangement May to July for groups of 10 to 30.**
Magic lurks within this charming 1½ acre garden, which has evolved over 30 yrs. Many treasures hidden amongst a variety of planting. Over 215 roses showcased in island borders. Meandering lawn paths lead through the wisteria walkway to find two miniature Shetland ponies at the bottom of the garden keen to show off to guests. Tranquil seating areas, teas,cakes and gifts for sale in 'The Shed' shop. Large smoking dragon, once on display at Hampton Court garden show. Superb views over undulating countryside to the village church. Fragrance and colour that only Mother Nature can create. Gifts for sale in 'The Shed'.

66 ULTING WICK

Crouchmans Farm Road, Maldon, CM9 6QX. Mr & Mrs B Burrough, 01245 380216, philippa. burrough@btinternet.com, www.ultingwickgarden.co.uk. *3m NW of Maldon. Take R turning to Ulting off B1019 as you exit Hatfield Peverel by a green. Garden on R after 2m.* **Sun 28 Apr (11-5). Light refreshments. Fri 3 May, Fri 28 June (2-5). Home-made teas. Mon 26 Aug, Fri 6 Sept (2-5). Adm £5, chd free. Homeade soup using ingredients from the garden, filled rolls & home-made teas on 28 April. Visits also by arrangement Mar to Oct for groups of 15+. Introductory talks upon arrival. Donation to All Saints Ulting Church.**
Listed black barns provide backdrop for vibrant and exuberant planting in 8 acres. Thousands of colourful tulips, flowing innovative spring planting, herbaceous borders, pond, mature weeping willows, kitchen garden, dramatic late summer beds with zingy, tender, exotic plant combinations. Drought tolerant perennial and mini annual wild flower meadows. Woodland. Many plants propagated in-house. Lots of unusual plants for sale. All Saints Church Ulting will be open in conjunction with the garden for talks on its history. Beautiful dog walks along the R Chelmer from the garden. Some gravel around the house but main areas of interest are accessible for wheelchairs.

67 14 UNA ROAD

Bowers Gifford, Basildon, SS13 2HU. Mr & Mrs John & Barbara Spooner. *1m E of Basildon on B1464 between Pitsea & Saddlers Farm r'about (A130/A13.) From Pitsea turn L into Pound Lane. From Southend (A127) X A130/A1245 junction. 1m turn L & follow NGS signs.* **Sat 13, Sun 14, Sat 20, Sun 21 July (11-5.30). Evening opening Sat 7, Sun 8th, Sat 14 Dec (4.30-8). Adm £4, chd free. Light refreshments. Christmas refreshments will incl mulled wine, tea and coffee and mince pies.**
A beautiful ½ acre garden featuring 2 ponds. Garden divided into 'rooms' each with an interesting view, drawing you on to the next room. Small vegetable patch with greenhouse plus a family of gnomes. Summer openings plus two winter special opening events with Christmas lights, seasonal refreshments available during both openings. WC available.

GROUP OPENING

68 WALTHAM ABBEY GROUP GARDENS

Waltham Abbey, EN9 1LG. 01992 714047, frank.jewson@btconnect.com. *M25, J26 to Waltham Abbey. At T-lights by McD turn R to r'about. Take 2nd exit to next r'about. Take 3rd exit (A112) to T-lights. L to Monkswood Av.* **Sun 2 June, Sun 1 Sept (12-5.30). Combined adm £6, chd free. Home-made teas at Silver Birches, Quendon Drive. Visits also by arrangement May to Sept for groups of 10 to 20. We are able to make arrangements for a special afternoon tea event.**

62 EASTBROOK ROAD
Caroline Cassell, 07973 551196, cvcassell@gmail.com.
Visits also by arrangement June to Sept for groups of 5 to 10.

39 HALFHIDES
Chris Hamer, 01992 714047, frank.jewson@btconnect.com.
Visits also by arrangement May to Sept for groups of 10 to 20.

76 MONKSWOOD AVENUE
Cathy & Dan Gallagher, 01992 714047, frank.jewson@btconnect.com.
Visits also by arrangement May to Sept for groups of 10 to 20.

SILVER BIRCHES
Linda & Frank Jewson, 01992 714047, frank.jewson@btconnect.com.
Visits also by arrangement May to Sept for groups of 10 to 20.

Come and visit our four gardens in the historic town of Waltham Abbey. Silver Birches Lawns are surrounded by mixed borders with mature shrubs and trees. The pond is covered in water lilies and is home to much wildlife. Take a short stroll in the hidden woodland walk before enjoying tea and homemade cake. 39 Halfhides the owner has evolved her garden over 50 years. Deep perennial borders and a small pond which leads to a stream and a larger pond in the secluded shade garden. There is an opportunity to purchase many of the plants used in this garden. 76 Monkswood - a plantswomans garden with mixed borders, greenhouse and wildlife pond. You may also be tempted to purchase one of the many Victorian chimney pots which are on sale from the wildlife friendly front garden. 62 Eastbrook Road - winner of Gardeners World magazine 'Best Small Space' and 'Judges' choice 2017' and described as a 'circular seclusion' (please note limited parking and approx. 7 mins walk from other gardens). 62 Eastbrook Rd and Halfhides are not suitable for wheelchairs.

69 WASHLANDS

Prayors Hill, Sible Hedingham, CO9 3LE. Tony & Sarah Frost, 01787 460732, tony@washlands.co.uk. *¼ m NW of Sible Hedingham Church. At former Sugar Loaves Pub on A1017 turn SW into Rectory Rd, R at former White Horse Pub, pass St Peters Church on R, ¼ m NW on Prayors Hill.* **Mon 27 May (2-5). Combined adm with Rookwoods £8, chd free. Sun 23 June, Sun 7 July (2-5). Adm £5, chd free. Home-made teas.** Visits also by arrangement June & July for groups of 20+. Coach parking by arrangement.

Charming one-acre country garden surrounding a former farmhouse,with good views over rolling countryside. A former horse pond features a beach with landing stage. Rose garden, wide herbaceous, shrub and woodland borders, hidden walks and opportunities to sit and relax. Alpines, grasses and alliums. Featured in Essex Life. Come and see! Woodland walk unsuitable for wheelchairs.

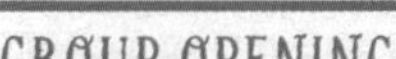

GROUP OPENING

70 WENDENS AMBO GARDENS

Saffron Walden, CB11 4JX. *Parking at village hall nr Church for 3 Church Path. Parking near Crossways. Parking next to Old Wenden Grange. All signed on day. Gardens are not within walking distance.* **Sun 16 June (2-5). Combined adm £7, chd free. Home-made teas at Crossways.**

3 CHURCH PATH
Ms Liz Hartley.

CROSSWAYS
Mrs Andrea Reynolds.

NEW **OLD WENDEN GRANGE**
Mr & Mrs Paul & Ruth Hitch.

3 Church Path, a quintessential cottage garden adjacent to historic church set behind a chocolate box thatched cottage. Terraced garden with a range of mixed shrubs, perennials, beautiful clematis and roses. Hidden vegetable garden and fruit trees. Crossways, a gently sloping garden, about 5 acres of informal 'family' garden with mixed planting for year-round interest. Some wildlife areas and wild flower area bordering part of the garden. Large pond is haven for frogs! Interesting selection of trees. Old Wenden Grange, is a young garden designed, landscaped and completed in July 2016. The garden features meandering paths past a fountain to fire pit area surrounded by planting. The path is bordered by lawn and flower beds with a mixture of hedging, grasses, bamboos and perennials. A large raised flower bed has a variety of grasses, phormium and box hedging. Wendens Ambo is a meandering historic village with a busy B road through village. Please use car parks. Beware. There is a lack of pavements in places so take great care if walking on the road. Village very close to Audley End House. Crossways and Old Wenden Grange wheelchair access to most areas. No wheelchair access to 3 Church Path.

71 NEW WEST END COTTAGE

Drury Lane, Ridgewell, nr Halstead, CO9 4SL. Louise Frayne. *On A1017 Ridgewell is 3m S of Haverhill or 2m N of Gt Yeldham. In village follow sign for village hall. Cottage on L a little way past hall.* **Sat 4 May, Sun 9 June (10-5). Adm £4.50, chd free. Home-made teas.**

A beautiful and inspiring garden set out as several "rooms" namely a knot garden, gravel garden, alpine garden with lawned areas and stunning herbaceous borders. The garden is stocked with a variety of plants, water features and hard landscaping and demonstrates just how creative a garden can be with all year round interest. Short gravel drive.

72 THE WHITE GARDEN

35 Langdon Road, Rayleigh, SS6 9HY. Mrs Louise Reed. *From A129 turn R into Langdon Rd.* **Sun 19 May, Sun 23 June (12-5). Adm £3.50, chd free. Light refreshments.**

A delightful white garden with 100 David Austin roses, unusual perennials and shrubs nestled into a tiny plot. Shady fernery walk with white hydrangeas, waterfalls, pond and blooms surrounding a lush lawn provide interest all summer long. Front garden has fragrant flowers and shrub borders, with roses, enclosed by box hedging and topiary for an evergreen curb appeal. Small back garden is a profusion of delicate cottage style planting in a scented, white, cream and pastel colour scheme. Inspiration from Beatrix Potter Tales and the White Garden at Sissinghurst. New white wooden archway clothed in roses and clematis in front entrance. Victorian greenhouse. Bird nesting boxes, unusual glass and rusted iron sculptures. New potting shed with a beautiful cedar shingle roof and stable door. Rabbit hutch with roof top miniature alpines.

73 NEW 1 WHITEHOUSE COTTAGES

Blue Mill Lane, Woodham Walter, Maldon, CM9 6LR. Mrs Shelley Rand. *In between Maldon & Danbury, a short drive from A12. From the A414 Danbury, turn L at The Anchor & continue into the village. Directly after the white village gates at the far end of the village, turn R into Blue Mill Lane.* **Sun 19 May (10.30-5). Adm £3.50, chd free. Sun 16 June (10.30-5). Combined adm with Elwy Lodge £7.50, chd free. Home-made teas.**

Nestled betwixt farmland in rural Essex, is our small secret garden, that has a wonderful charm and serenity to it. Set in 3½ acres, mostly paddocks, a little plot of loveliness wraps around our Victorian cottage, and roses smother the porch in June. A meandering lawn takes you through beds and borders softly planted with a cottage feel, a haven for wildlife and people alike. Dean Harris a local blacksmith will have a pop-up forge on-site making and selling metal plant accessories on the day of your visit. Buy plants and teas too. Parking available a short walk up the lane near The Cats pub. Unsuitable for wheelchairs unless you're intrepid.

74 WICKETS

Langley Upper Green, CB11 4RY. Susan & Doug Copeland, 01799 550553, susan.copeland@ngs.org.uk. *7m W of Saffron Walden, 10m N of Bishops Stortford. At Newport take B1038 After 3m turn R at Clavering, signed Langley. Upper Green is 3m further on. At cricket green turn R. House 200m on R.* **Mon 6 May (12-5). Combined adm with Clavering Gardens £8, chd free. Home-made teas. Single adm £5, child free. Opening with Langley Village Gardens on Sun 26 May. Visits also by arrangement in June for groups of 10+.**

Peaceful country garden 'Far from the Madding Crowd'. Wide, informal mixed borders include, shrub roses and perennials. Two landscaped meadows and shepherd's hut with fine pastoral views. Large lily pond sheltered by silver birch. Griffin Glasshouse nearby. Curvilinear design links themed planting areas. Espalier apples enclose parterre with standard weeping roses. Secluded Dry Garden. Gravel drive.

75 NEW WOODBURN COTTAGE

Borley, Sudbury, CO10 7AE. Rebecca Gorringe. *Essex/Suffolk border. Turn L immed after crossing R Stour at Rodbridge. Up hill with Borley Church on R. At top of hill small green with finger post. Carry straight on, garden is property on L.* **Sun 8 Sept (12-5). Adm £4, chd free. Home-made teas.**

A recently renovated cottage garden, with the scheme of hardy perennials devised by a professional garden designer. Planting insect friendly. Also features a copse, with a natural pond, and a beehive. Newly planted orchard. Stumpery created in 2018. Ornamental fish pond. Three resident alpacas. Has far reaching views towards the Belchamp Brook. Tea and cake.

GROUP OPENING

76 WRITTLE GARDENS

Chelmsford, CM1 3NA. *Writtle can be approached from 3 directions. From the A1060, A1016 and A414 follow the yellow signs to Writtle Village.* **Sun 23 June (12-5). Combined adm £6, chd free.**

8 THE GREEN
CM1 3DU. Andrea Johnson.

65 ONGAR ROAD
CM1 3NA. Doug & Jean Pinkney.

40 ST JOHNS ROAD
CM1 3EB. Catherine Eubanks.

Three contrasting, colourful and interesting gardens to enjoy in the delightful village of Writtle. 8 The Green offers creatively planted borders and a tapestry of colour, texture and form, with perennials, shrubs, ornamental trees, annuals and alpines, and a south-facing summerhouse. The front of the new garden at 40 St John's Road has been designed to encourage wildlife, with the rear garden offering a surprising contrast, with a more modern, landscaped Italian feel. The garden at 65 Ongar Road will transport visitors to tropical destinations, with its colour and "summer living" features. No refreshments are offered at these gardens. But Writtle offers a number of pubs and cafes, incl the renowned Tiptree Tea Room in Lordship Rd. The ancient and traditional village of Writtle, with its delightful Norman church, village green and pond, dates back to pre-Roman times, and was featured in the Doomsday Book.

77 WRITTLE UNIVERSITY COLLEGE

Writtle, CM1 3RR. Writtle University College, www.writtle.ac.uk. *4m W of Chelmsford. On A414, nr Writtle village.* **Wed 22 May, Sun 8 Sept (10-3.30). Adm £5, chd free. Light refreshments in The Garden Room (main campus) & The Lordship tea room (Lordship campus).**

15 acres; informal lawns with naturalised bulbs and wild flowers. Large tree collection, mixed shrubs, herbaceous borders. Landscaped gardens designed and built by students. Landscaped glasshouses and wide range of seasonal bedding displays. New Dry/Mediterranean garden designed and built by staff and students on our RHS courses. Herbaceous perennial borders. Extended naturalised bulb areas on front campus lawns. Renovated Rockery Open Day is coordinated by Level 3 Horticultural Students who are on hand to assist visitors. Some gravel, however majority of areas accessible to all.

78 WYCHWOOD

Epping Road, Roydon, Harlow, CM19 5DW. Mrs Madeleine Paine, 01279 792172, madeleine.paine1@btinternet.com. *At Tylers Cross r'about head in the direction of Roydon. You will find the garden on R approx 400 metres from the r'about. Parking is available in Redrick's nursery next to garden.* **Sun 16 June (12-5.30). Adm £4, chd free. Home-made teas. Visits also by arrangement May to Sept for groups of 10 to 20.**

A garden of around ¾ of an acre with a large pond, attracting much wildlife, as well as the owners resident ducks. Free ranging chickens roam in the shrubbery and budgerigar aviary. There are numerous features incl, vegetable and fruit plot, mixed shrub and herbaceous borders, 1920's summer house and Scandinavian cabin. English roses are a particular feature of the garden. Lake fully stocked with fish and inhabited by resident ducks. Sit in the Norwegian hut and enjoy your refreshments.

79 WYCKE FARM

Pages Lane, Tolleshunt D'Arcy, Maldon, CM9 8AB. Nancy & Anthony Seabrook. *5m E of Maldon, 10m SW of Colchester. B1023 from Tolleshunt D'Arcy 1m towards Tollesbury. Turn R into Pages Lane. Follow for 1m to Wycke Farm.* **Fri 17, Sun 19 May (11-5). Adm £4.50, chd free. Home-made teas.**

Large cottage style farmhouse garden situated in the peaceful Essex countryside with mature trees, mixed borders, vegetables, greenhouses and a small flock of sheep. Developed from a neglected state over 12 years ago with a fine view of the Blackwater Estuary. Walk to estuary, 1200 metres. Some gravel and grass paths.

OPENING DATES

All entries subject to change. For latest information check **www.ngs.org.uk**

Map locator numbers are shown to the right of each garden name.

January

Sunday 27th
Home Farm 39

February

Snowdrop Festival

Sunday 10th
Home Farm 39
Trench Hill 65

Sunday 17th
Trench Hill 65

March

Sunday 10th
Home Farm 39

Sunday 17th
Trench Hill 65

April

Thursday 4th
NEW Lower Slaughter 45

Saturday 6th
South Lodge 58

Sunday 7th
Highnam Court 37
Home Farm 39

Sunday 14th
Upton Wold 67

Monday 15th
◆ Kiftsgate Court 41

Tuesday 16th
Barnsley House 5

Saturday 20th
Green Bowers 33

Sunday 21st
20 Forsdene Walk 28
Green Bowers 33
Trench Hill 65

Monday 22nd
Green Bowers 33
Trench Hill 65

Saturday 27th
Green Bowers 33

Sunday 28th
Blockley Gardens 9
Charlton Down House 16
Green Bowers 33
Home Farm 39

May

Saturday 4th
South Lodge 58

Sunday 5th
Eastcombe, Bussage and Brownshill Gardens 25
Highnam Court 37

Monday 6th
Eastcombe, Bussage and Brownshill Gardens 25

Wednesday 8th
Daylesford House 24

Sunday 12th
◆ The Garden at Miserden 32
◆ Stanway Fountain & Water Garden 60

Wednesday 15th
◆ Lydney Park Spring Garden 46

Saturday 18th
Charingworth Court 15

Sunday 19th
Charingworth Court 15
20 Forsdene Walk 28
Forthampton Court 29
NEW Frith House 30
South Lodge 58

Wednesday 22nd
Charingworth Court 15
Lower Farm House 44
◆ Oxleaze Farm 50

Saturday 25th
Hookshouse Pottery 40
Longhope Gardens 43

Sunday 26th
Hookshouse Pottery 40
Longhope Gardens 43
Pasture Farm 51

Monday 27th
Hookshouse Pottery 40
Pasture Farm 51

Tuesday 28th
Hookshouse Pottery 40

Wednesday 29th
Hookshouse Pottery 40
Lower Farm House 44

Thursday 30th
Hookshouse Pottery 40

Friday 31st
Hookshouse Pottery 40

June

Saturday 1st
Hookshouse Pottery 40
Pasture Farm 51

Sunday 2nd
Blockley Gardens 9
Highnam Court 37
Hodges Barn 38
Hookshouse Pottery 40
Pasture Farm 51
South Lodge 58
Stowell Park 61

Monday 3rd
Hodges Barn 38

Wednesday 5th
Trench Hill 65

Thursday 6th
Campden House 13

Saturday 8th
Cotswold Farm 22
Longhope Gardens 43
NEW The Old Vicarage 49
Scatterford 56

Sunday 9th
Charlton Down House 16
Cotswold Farm 22
The Gables 31
Longhope Gardens 43
NEW The Old Vicarage 49
Temple Guiting Manor & Barns 62

Monday 10th
Berkeley Castle 6

Wednesday 12th
Brockworth Court 12
Eyford House 27
Rockcliffe, 55
Trench Hill 65

Thursday 13th
Campden House 13

Saturday 15th
Ashley Gardens 2
NEW Chedworth Gardens 18

Sunday 16th
Ashley Gardens 2
NEW Bisley Gardens 8
NEW Chedworth Gardens 18
20 Forsdene Walk 28
NEW Frith House 30
Stanton Village Gardens 59
NEW Weir Reach 69

Tuesday 18th
Wortley House 73

Wednesday 19th
Trench Hill 65
NEW Weir Reach 69

Thursday 20th
NEW Waterlane House 68

Saturday 22nd
Berrys Place Farm 7

Sunday 23rd
Berrys Place Farm 7
NEW Cold Aston Gardens 21
Upper Minety Open Gardens and Plant Fair 66
Winchcombe Gardens 71

Wednesday 26th
Berrys Place Farm 7
Trench Hill 65

Thursday 27th
Berrys Place Farm 7

Saturday 29th
NEW Perrywood House 54
South Lodge 58

Sunday 30th
◆ Herbs for Healing 36
The Manor 47
Moor Wood 48
NEW Perrywood House 54
◆ Sezincote 57
Stowell Park 61
NEW Thousand Acres 63

July

Saturday 6th
NEW Leckhampton Court Hospice 42

Sunday 7th
25 Bowling Green Road 11

◆ Cerney House Gardens 14
Greenfields, Little Rissington 35
Highnam Court 37

Monday 8th
25 Bowling Green Road 11

Sunday 14th
25 Bowling Green Road 11
◆ Westonbirt School Gardens 70

Monday 15th
25 Bowling Green Road 11

Sunday 21st
20 Forsdene Walk 28
Trench Hill 65

August

Sunday 4th
Highnam Court 37

Sunday 11th
◆ Bourton House Garden 10
NEW Tree Hill 64
Woodlands Farm 72

Monday 12th
◆ Kiftsgate Court 41

Sunday 18th
The Gables 31
◆ Stanway Fountain & Water Garden 60

Sunday 25th
Trench Hill 65

September

Sunday 1st
The Manor 47

Wednesday 4th
Brockworth Court 12

Sunday 8th
Highnam Court 37

Sunday 15th
Clouds Rest 19
The Patch 52
Trench Hill 65

Saturday 21st
Scatterford 56

January 2020

Sunday 26th
Home Farm 39

February 2020

Sunday 9th
Home Farm 39
Trench Hill 65

Sunday 16th
Trench Hill 65

By Arrangement

Arrange a personalised garden visit with your club, or group of friends, on a date to suit you. See individual garden entries for full details.

Ampney Brook House 1
Awkward Hill Cottage 3
Barn House, Chepstow 4
25 Bowling Green Road 11
Brockworth Court 12
Charingworth Court 15
NEW The Chase 17
NEW Cold Aston Gardens 21
Cotswold Farm 22
Daglingworth House 23
Eastleach House 26
20 Forsdene Walk 28
Forthampton Court 29
The Gables 31
Green Bowers 33
Greenfields, Brockweir Common 34
Greenfields, Little Rissington 35
Home Farm 39
Keens Cottage, Chedworth Gardens 18
Moor Wood 48
NEW Pancake Hill Flowers, Chedworth Gardens 18
Pear Tree Cottage 53
Scatterford 56
South Lodge 58
Springfield House, Longhope Gardens 43
NEW Thousand Acres 63
Trench Hill 65
NEW Weir Reach 69
Woodlands Farm 72

Barnsley House

© Carole Drake

THE GARDENS

1 AMPNEY BROOK HOUSE

School Lane, Ampney Crucis, Cirencester, GL7 5RT. Allan Hirst, 01285 851098, allan.hirst@clmail.co.uk. *From Cirencester go E on A417 toward Fairford. After passing the Crown of Crucis take 1st L and also immed L again onto School Lane and L again into the gated (open automatically) drive.* **Visits by arrangement Mar to Oct. We are happy to discuss refreshments a week or two prior to your visit. Adm £5, chd free. Light refreshments.**

Striking Grade II Cotswold country house on 4.3 acres fronting Ampney Brook. The gardens are a haven for wildlife with fun and stimulating spaces yr-round. Incl woodland, kitchen garden, herbaceous borders, meadows, newly planted arbour. Ample areas and lawns for picnicking (encouraged). No wheelchair access to kitchen garden/greenhouse.

GROUP OPENING

2 ASHLEY GARDENS

Ashley, Tetbury, GL8 8SX. *Between Tetbury and Cirencester off A433. From Tetbury A433. 2½ m turn R. R at Xrds signed Ashley ½ m. From Cirencester, take Tetbury Rd A433 after 6½ m turn L follow signs. From Malmesbury A429 L in Crudwell follow signs.* **Sat 15 June (1.30-6.30); Sun 16 June (1.30-5.30). Combined adm £6, chd free. Home-made teas at Park Cottage. Alternative disabled parking at Park Cottage, please ask at main car park in middle of village.**

ASHLEY GRANGE
Mr & Mrs D Burke.

ASHLEY MANOR
Mr & Mrs J Lodwick.

ASHLEY MANOR BARN
Michael & Liz Dallas.

NEW **BANNATREE**
Mr & Mrs C Ferns.

NEW **FIELD VIEW**
Mr & Mrs S Hedges.

NEW **FORGE COTTAGE**
Mrs S Esmond Rees.

LINCHBANK COTTAGE
Mr & Mrs S Tidman.

NEW **PARK COTTAGE**
Mr & Mrs J Nettleton.

Enjoy a quintessential Cotswold village with 8 hidden gems, several open for the first time. From cottage gardens to larger more formal gardens with a great variety of plants and designs. You will find an abundance of old fashioned climbing and shrub roses, herbaceous and perennial borders and a great variety of high quality well-stocked and much loved gardens. Specimen trees, orchards and traditional vegetable gardens abound. Natural ponds, plantsman's garden, prairie garden and wonderful views. Beautiful small C12 St James church Ashley open both days. Plants at Ashley Manor Barn (GL8 8SX). Teas at Park Cottage. Largely accessible for wheelchairs at most gardens.

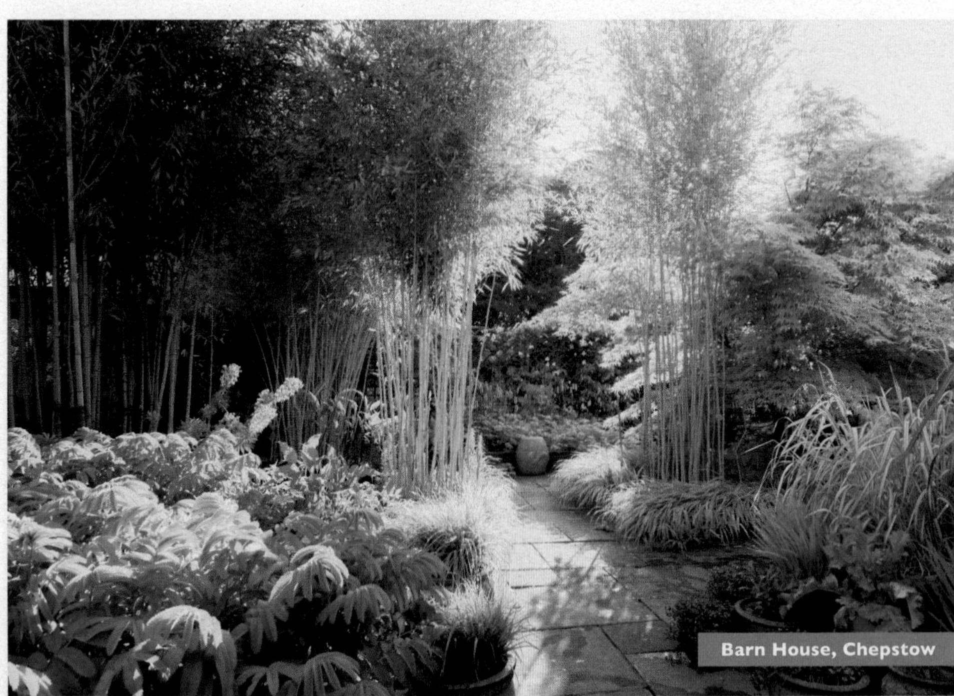

Barn House, Chepstow

3 AWKWARD HILL COTTAGE

Awkward Hill, Bibury, GL7 5NH. Mrs Victoria Summerley, v.summerley@hotmail.com, , www.awkwardhill.co.uk. *Bibury, Gloucestershire. No parking at property, best to park in village and walk past Arlington Row up Awkward Hill, or up Hawkers Hill from Catherine Wheel PH.* **Visits by arrangement June to Aug for groups of 20 to 30. Sorry, no individual appointments. Cost of entry incl refreshments. Adm £7.50, chd free. Home-made teas.**

This country Cotswold garden is a work in progress. Since 2012, when the current owner bought the property, it has been redesigned to reflect the local landscape and encourage wildlife. Planting is both formal and informal contributing yr-round interest. Pond and waterfall. Wonderful view over neighbouring meadow and woodland, small pond jetty, 2 sunny terraces and plenty of places to sit and relax.

4 BARN HOUSE, CHEPSTOW

Brockweir Common, Chepstow, NP16 7PH. Mrs Kate Patel, 01291 680041, barnhousegarden@gmail.com, www.thegardenbarnhouse.com. *10m S of Monmouth & N of Chepstow, under 1 hr from Hereford, Cheltenham & Cardiff. From Chepstow A466 to Monmouth. 2m past Tintern Abbey R Brockweir Bridge then up Mill Hill ½m, 1st L at The Rock (cottage) continue uphill 1½m. BH on R. No large coaches.* **Visits by arrangement June to Aug for groups of 10 to 30. Please book via email if possible. Adm £4.50, chd free. Light refreshments available by arrangement at additional £2.50 per person.**

Boldly and generously planted garden of an acre. Wealth of ornamental grasses plus long, late flowering perennials. Stunning mass plantings incl 70m miscanthus hedge. Imaginatively designed contrasting areas incl tranquil sunken terrace with lush Asian grasses, hot border of potted tender perennials and dramatic bamboo screening.

5 BARNSLEY HOUSE

Barnsley, Cirencester, GL7 5EE. Calcot Health & Leisure Ltd, 01285 740000, reception@barnsleyhouse.com, www.barnsleyhouse.com. *4m NE of Cirencester. From Cirencester, take B4425 to Barnsley. House entrance on R as you enter village.* **Tue 16 Apr (10-4). Adm £5, chd free. Tea.**

The beautiful garden at Barnsley House, created by Rosemary Verey, is one of England's finest and most famous gardens incl knot garden, potager garden and mixed borders in Rosemary Verey's successional planting style. The house also has an extensive kitchen garden which will be open with plants and vegetables available for purchase. Narrow paths mean restricted wheelchair access but happy to provide assistance.

6 BERKELEY CASTLE

Berkeley, GL13 9PJ. Mrs RJG Berkeley, www.berkeley-castle.com. *Half-way between Bristol & Gloucester, 10mins from J13 &14 of M5. Follow signs to Berkeley from A38 & B4066. Visitors' entrance is on L of Canonbury St, just before town centre.* **Mon 10 June (10.30-5). Adm £6, chd free. Light refreshments in yurt restaurant, next to ticket office/gift shop. Delicious home-made cakes, savouries and locally-sourced items available.**

Unique historic garden of a keen plantsman, with far-reaching views across R Severn. Gardens contain many rare plants which thrive in the warm micro-climate against stone walls of mediaeval castle. Woodland, historic trees and stunning terraced borders. Butterfly house with free-flying tropical butterflies. Difficult for wheelchairs due to terraced nature of gardens.

7 BERRYS PLACE FARM

Bulley Lane, Churcham, Gloucester, GL2 8AS. Anne Thomas, 07950 808022, gary.j.thomas1953@gmail.com. *6m W of Gloucester. A40 towards Ross. Turning R into Bulley Lane at Birdwood.* **Sat 22, Sun 23, Wed 26, Thur 27 June (11-5). Adm £4, chd free. Home-made teas. Ploughmans lunches, cream teas.**

Country garden, approx 2 acres, surrounded by farmland and old orchards. Lawns and large sweeping mixed herbaceous borders with over 100 roses. Formal kitchen garden and beautiful rose arbour leading to lake and summerhouse with a variety of water lilies and carp. All shared with peacocks and ducks.

GROUP OPENING

8 NEW BISLEY GARDENS

Wells Road, Bisley, Stroud, GL6 7AG. *Gardens & car park well signed in Bisley village. Gardens on S edge of village at head of Toadsmoor Valley, N of A419 Stroud to Cirencester road.* **Sun 16 June (2-6). Combined adm £5, chd free. Home-made teas at Paulmead.**

PAULMEAD
Judy & Philip Howard and Tom & Emma Howard.

NEW **PAX**
Mr David Holden & Mr Ramesh Mootoo.

WELLS COTTAGE
Mr & Mrs Michael Flint, 01452 770289, bisleyflints@bisleyflints.plus.com.

3 beautiful gardens with differing styles. Paulmead: 1-acre landscaped garden constructed in stages over last 25yrs. Terraced in 3 main levels. Natural stream garden, herbaceous and shrub borders, formal vegetable garden, summerhouse overlooking pond. Unusual tree house. Development of new garden around hen house, incl ha ha. Pax: Small very well kept cottage garden, in a hidden away location, with box hedging and topiary. Great views. Wells Cottage: Just under 1 acre. Terraced on several levels with beautiful views over valley. Much informal planting of trees and shrubs to give colour and texture. Lawns and herbaceous borders. Collection of grasses. Formal pond area. Rambling roses on rope pergola. Vegetable garden with raised beds.

GROUP OPENING

9 BLOCKLEY GARDENS

Blockley, GL56 9DB. *3m NW of Moreton-in-Marsh. Just off the Morton-in-Marsh to Evesham Rd A44.* **Sun 28 Apr (1-5); Sun 2 June (2-6). Combined adm £6, chd free. Home-made teas at St George's Hall on April 28, at St George's Hall & The Manor House on June 2.**

BLOCKLEY ALLOTMENTS
Blockley and District Allotment Association.
Open on Sun 2 June

CHURCH GATES
Mrs Brenda Salmon.
Open on all dates

LANDGATE
Mrs Hilary Sutton.
Open on all dates

THE MANOR HOUSE
George & Zoe Thompson.
Open on all dates

♦ MILL DENE GARDEN
Mrs B S Dare, 01386 700457, info@milldenegarden.co.uk, www.milldenegarden.co.uk.
Open on all dates

MILL GARDEN HOUSE
Andrew & Celia Goodrick-Clarke.
Open on Sun 28 Apr

THE OLD CHEQUER
Mrs G Linley.
Open on all dates

PORCH HOUSE
Mr & Mrs Johnson.
Open on Sun 28 Apr

SNUGBOROUGH MILL
Rupert & Mandy Williams-Ellis, 01386 701310, rupert.williams-ellis@talk21.com.
Open on Sun 2 June

WOODRUFF
Paul & Maggie Adams.
Open on all dates

This popular historic hillside village has a great variety of high quality, well-stocked gardens - large and small, old and new. Blockley Brook, an attractive stream which flows right through the village, graces some of the gardens; these incl gardens of former water mills, with millponds attached. From some gardens there are wonderful rural views. Shuttle coach service provided. Children welcome but close supervision is essential. Access to some gardens quite steep and allowances should be made.

10 ♦ BOURTON HOUSE GARDEN

Bourton-on-the-Hill, GL56 9AE. Mr & Mrs R Quintus, 01386 700754, info@bourtonhouse.com, www.bourtonhouse.com. *2m W of Moreton-in-Marsh. On A44.* **For NGS: Sun 11 Aug (10-5). Adm £7, chd free. Home-made teas in Grade I listed C16 Tithe Barn. Light refreshments & home-made cakes.** For other opening times and information, please phone, email or visit garden website.

Award winning 3 acre garden featuring imaginative topiary, wide herbaceous borders with many rare, unusual and exotic plants, water features, unique shade house and many creatively planted pots. Fabulous at any time of year but magnificent in summer months and early autumn. Walk in 7 acre pasture with free printed guide to specimen trees available to garden visitors. 70% access for wheelchairs.

11 25 BOWLING GREEN ROAD

Cirencester, GL7 2HD. Mrs Sue Beck, 01285 653778, zen155198@zen.co.uk. *On NW edge of Cirencester. Take A435 to Spitalgate/Whiteway T-lights, turn into The Whiteway (Chedworth turn), then 1st L into Bowling Green Rd, garden in bend in rd between Nos 23 & 27.* **Sun 7 July (2-5); Mon 8 July (11-4); Sun 14 July (2-5); Mon 15 July (11-4). Adm £3.50, chd free.** Visits also by arrangement July to Sept for groups of up to 30. Tea/coffee/ biscuits can be provided for small groups by arrangement.

Expect the unexpected as you wander at will along winding walkways and billowing borders in a naturalistic mini-jungle of heavenly hemerocallis, gorgeous grasses, curvaceous clematis, romantic roses and plentiful perennials to glimpse friendly frogs and a graceful giraffe, rated by visitors as an amazing hidden gem with a unique atmosphere. See http://thechattygardener.com/?p=2585. 2019 will mark the 40th year of opening for the National Garden Scheme. Sadly, not suitable for wheelchair access.

12 BROCKWORTH COURT

Court Road, Brockworth, GL3 4QU. Tim & Bridget Wiltshire, 01452 862938, timwiltshire@hotmail.co.uk. *6m E of Gloucester. 6m W of Cheltenham. Adj St Georges Church on Court Rd. From A46 turn into Mill Lane, turn R, L, R at T junctions. From Ermin St, turn into Ermin Park, then R at r'about then L at next r'about.* **Wed 12 June, Wed 4 Sept (2.30-5.30). Adm £5, chd free. Home-made teas in tithe barn.** Visits also by arrangement May to Oct for groups of 10 to 30. Tours of historic manor for groups of 10+. Refreshments.

This intense yet informal tapestry style garden beautifully complements the period manor house which it surrounds. Organic, naturalistic, with informal cottage-style planting areas that seamlessly blend together. Natural fish pond, with Monet bridge leading to small island with thatched Fiji house. Kitchen garden once cultivated by monks. Historic tithe barn. Views to Crickley and Coopers Hill. Adj Norman Church (open). Historic tithebarn, historic manor house visited by Henry VIII and Anne Boleyn in 1535. Partial wheelchair access.

13 CAMPDEN HOUSE

Dyers Lane, Chipping Campden, GL55 6UP. The Hon Philip & Mrs Smith. *Entrance on Chipping Campden to Weston Subedge Rd (Dyers Lane), approx ¼m SW of Campden, 1¼m drive. Do not use SatNav.* **Thur 6, Thur 13 June (2-6). Adm £6, chd free. Home-made teas.**

2 acres featuring mixed borders of plant and colour interest around house and C17 tithe barn (neither

open). Set in fine parkland in hidden valley with lakes and ponds. Woodland garden and walks, vegetable garden. Gravel paths, steep slopes.

14 ◆ CERNEY HOUSE GARDENS

North Cerney, Cirencester, GL7 7BX. Mr N W Angus & Dr J Angus, 01285 831300, janet@cerneygardens.com, www.cerneygardens.com. *4m NW of Cirencester. On A435 Cheltenham rd turn L opp Bathurst Arms, follow rd past church up hill, then go straight towards pillared gates on R (signed Cerney House).* **For NGS: Sun 7 July (10-7). Adm £5, chd £1. Home-made teas in The Bothy.** For other opening times and information, please phone, email or visit garden website.

Romantic walled garden filled with old-fashioned roses and long herbaceous borders. Knot garden filled with spring tulip display and dahlias later in the year. Working kitchen garden with heritage vegetables, scented garden and lavender walk. Drifts of naturalised snowdrops end Jan/Feb. Large collection of hellebores and woodland bluebell walk. Herb garden (in development), koi carp pond, woodland and nature walk. Dogs welcome. Limited wheelchair access.

15 CHARINGWORTH COURT

Broadway Road, Winchcombe, GL54 5JN. Susan & Richard Wakeford, 01242 603033, susanwakeford@gmail.com, www.charingworthcourtcotswoldsgarden.com. *8m NE of Cheltenham. 400 metres N of Winchcombe town centre. Limited parking along Broadway Rd. Town car parks in Bull Lane (short stay) and all day parking (£1) in Back Lane.* **Sat 18, Sun 19 May (12-6). Adm £5, chd free. Evening opening Wed 22 May (6-9). Adm £7, chd free. Home-made teas from 1pm on 18 & 19 May. Adm on 22 May incl one glass of wine (or soft drink) and nibbles.** Visits also by arrangement May & June for groups of 10 to 30.

Artistically and lovingly created 1½ acre garden surrounding restored Georgian/Tudor house (not open).

Lower Farm House

Relaxed country style with Japanese influences, large pond and walled vegetable/flower garden, created over 20 years from a blank canvas. Mature copper beech trees, Cedar of Lebanon and Wellingtonia; and younger trees replacing an earlier excess of Cupressus leylandii. Once again the garden will showcase a range of sculpture, some for sale with a percentage going to NGS charities. The garden website shows photographs of all the previous 7 exhibitions. Most paths gravelled, several areas accessible without steps. Limited disabled parking next to house.

16 CHARLTON DOWN HOUSE

Charlton Down, Tetbury, GL8 8TZ. Neil & Julie Record. *2m SW of Tetbury, Gloucs. From Tetbury, take A433 towards Bath for 1½m; turn R (north) just before the Hare and Hounds, then R again after 200yds into Hookshouse Lane. Charlton Down House is 600yds on R.* **Sun 28 Apr, Sun 9 June (11-5). Adm £5, chd free. Home-made teas.**

Extensive country house gardens in 180 acre equestrian estate. Formal terraces, perennial borders, walled topiary garden, enclosed cut flower garden and large glasshouse. Newly planted copse. Rescue animals. Ample parking. Picnickers welcome. Largely flat terrain; most garden areas accessible.

17 NEW THE CHASE

Bourton on the Hill, Moreton-In-Marsh, GL56 9AL. Mr & Mrs J Stoker, Kate Burtonwood - 07949 448483, info@cultivatedgardener.co.uk. *2m W of Moreton-in-Marsh. From Moreton, take A44 towards Evesham. Pass through Bourton on the Hill, take first L signed Longborough and Sezincote. Garden at 2nd property on R.* **Visits by arrangement May to Sept for groups of 5 to 30. Adm £5, chd free.**

5-acre private garden undergoing extensive renovation, open for the first time this year. The Chase offers areas of natural planting, with a focus on making space for wildlife. The main garden area is a disused quarry which gives challenges of access, shade and water, with areas of woodland, ponds, a new glasshouse used for propagation and tropical plants. Tulips should abound in May. Unfortunately not suitable for wheelchairs or pushchairs.

Highnam Court

GROUP OPENING

18 NEW CHEDWORTH GARDENS

Chedworth, Cheltenham, GL54 4AN. *7m NE of Cirencester. Off Fosseway, A429 between Stow-on-the-Wold (12m) & Cirencester. Park & Ride in field by village hall (signed). Tickets available from village hall.* **Sat 15, Sun 16 June (10.30-5). Combined adm £10, chd free. Home-made teas at Chedworth Village Hall.** Donation to Chedworth & District Horticultural Society.

NEW ABSOLAM'S ORCHARD
Richard & Bettina Abraham.

NEW ADAMS POOL
Bee Brockman.

NEW COBBLERS COTTAGE
Ceri Powell & Ajay Shah.

NEW HOMESIDE
Allison Oldershaw.

NEW KEENS COTTAGE
Sue & Steve Bradbury, 07831 464956, bradburydesigns@aol.com, www.bradburydesigns.co.uk.
Visits also by arrangement May & June for groups of up to 10.

NEW OLD VILLAGE STORES
Jo & Richard Todd.

THE OXBYRE
Mike & Caroline Burgess.

NEW PANCAKE HILL FLOWERS
Karen Scott, 07887 955849, karen@pancakehillflowers.co.uk, www.pancakehillflowers.co.uk.
Visits also by arrangement Apr to Sept.

NEW WINDSOR COTTAGE
Peter & Annette Seymour.

NEW WINTERWELL HOUSE
David & Gill Musgrave.

Varied collection of 10 cottage gardens, nestling throughout the mile long Chedworth Valley with tributary of R Coln running below. Stunning views. Featuring unusual water features, pretty terraces, kitchen gardens, live willow features, wild flower orchards, cut flower farm and hints from a Chelsea winning garden. Teas and lunches available (& toilet facilities) in village hall where plant sales and stalls are also available.

19 CLOUDS REST

Brockweir, Chepstow, NP16 7NW. Mrs Jan Basford. *In the Wye Valley, 6.7m N of Chepstow and 10.6m S of Monmouth, off A466, across Brockweir Bridge.* **Sun 15 Sept (1-5). Combined adm with The Patch £6, chd free. Home-made teas.**
The garden at Clouds Rest was started in 2012 from a south-westerly facing, stony paddock, with views across the Wye Valley. Its many gravel pathways meander through herbaceous beds with a mixture of roses, then later a wide selection of michaelmas daisies in September. Easy parking in our paddock. Limited wheelchair access.

20 ◆ THE COACH HOUSE GARDEN

Ampney Crucis, Cirencester, GL7 5RY. Mr & Mrs Nicholas Tanner, 01285 850256, mel@thegenerousgardener.co.uk, www.thegenerousgardener.co.uk. *3m E of Cirencester. Turn into village from A417, immed before Crown of Crucis Inn. Over hump-back bridge, parking immed to R on cricket field (weather permitting) or signed nearby field.*
For opening times and information, please phone, email or visit garden website.
Approx 1½ acres, full of structure and design. Garden is divided into rooms incl rill garden, gravel garden, rose garden, herbaceous borders, green garden with pleached lime allee and potager. Created over last 30yrs by present owners and constantly evolving. New potting shed and greenhouse added in 2018. Visitors welcome during mid March - end of June (groups of 15+), please see above website. Rare plant sales (in aid of James Hopkins Trust) and Garden Lecture Days. Limited wheelchair access. Ramp available to enable access to main body of garden, steps to other areas.

Your visits help change lives - your generosity has supported unpaid carers through donations to Carers Trust totalling over £3.9 million since 1996

GROUP OPENING

21 NEW **COLD ASTON GARDENS**

Chapel Lane, Cold Aston, Cheltenham, GL54 3BJ. 01451 821681. *In the centre of the village. Both properties within 50 yds of village green.* **Sun 23 June (2-5). Combined adm £5, chd free. Home made teas.** Visits also by arrangement.

Elmbank Farm GL54 3BJ. Elizabeth Acland: James Bolton created this garden out of the original farmyard in 2007. House faces E with herbaceous borders ending in ha-ha, framing the view. 2 large shrub beds on the drive replace a series of dilapidated concrete buildings. Malus transitoria and Irish yew border road enclosing terrace. The acacia was here before us. Springfield House, Chapel Lane GL54 3BJ. Reuben & Cathy Bodikian: Garden created from disused builders yard with overgrown trees. It is now a fully matured quintessential English cottage garden. Facing due S it was designed by renowned Cotswold garden consultant, Katie Lucas, to give yr-round foliage and colour.

22 COTSWOLD FARM

Duntisbourne Abbots, Cirencester, GL7 7JS. Mrs Mark Birchall, 01285 821857, iona@cotswoldfarmgardens.org.uk, www.cotswoldfarmgardens.org.uk. *5m NW of Cirencester off old A417. From Cirencester L signed Duntisbourne Abbots Services, R and R underpass. Drive ahead. From Gloucester L signed Duntisbourne Abbots Services. Pass Services. Drive L.* **Sat 8, Sun 9 June (2-5). Adm £5, chd free. Home-made teas by WI.** Visits also by arrangement. Donation to A Rocha.

Arts and Crafts garden in lovely position overlooking quiet valley on descending levels with terrace designed by Norman Jewson in 1930s. Snowdrops named and naturalised, aconites in Feb. Winter garden. Bog garden best in May, white border overflowing with texture and scent. Shrubs, trees, shrub roses. Allotments in old walled garden, 8 native orchids, hundreds of wild flowers and Roman snails. Family day out. Rare orchid walks. Picnics welcome. Wheelchair access to main terrace.

23 DAGLINGWORTH HOUSE

Daglingworth, nr Cirencester, GL7 7AG. David & Henrietta Howard, 01285 885626, ettajhoward@gmail.com. *3m N of Cirencester off A417/419. House with blue gate beside church in Daglingworth.* **Visits by arrangement May to Sept for groups of 5 to 30. Adm £7, chd free.**

Walled garden, temple and grotto, and pools. Classical garden of 2 acres, views and vistas with humorous contemporary twist. Hedges, topiary shapes, herbaceous borders. Pergolas, woodland, cascade and mirror canal. Lovely Cotswold village setting beside church. Numerous published articles on garden. Regretfully unsuitable for wheelchairs.

24 DAYLESFORD HOUSE

Daylesford, GL56 0YG. Lord Bamford & Lady Bamford. *5m W of Chipping Norton. Off A436. Between Stow-on-the-Wold & Chipping Norton.* **Wed 8 May (1-5). Adm £6, chd free. Home-made teas.**

Magnificent C18 landscape grounds created 1790 for Warren Hastings, greatly restored and enhanced by present owners. Lakeside and woodland walks within natural wild flower meadows. Large walled garden planted formally, centred around orchid, peach and working glasshouses. Trellised rose garden. Collection of citrus within period orangery. Secret garden with pavilion and formal pools. Very large garden with substantial distances to be walked. Partial wheelchair access.

GROUP OPENING

25 EASTCOMBE, BUSSAGE AND BROWNSHILL GARDENS

Eastcombe, GL6 7DS. *3m E of Stroud. 2m N of A419 Stroud to Cirencester Rd from turning signed to Bisley & Eastcombe. Please park considerately in villages. Not all gardens listed may be open on the day so please check before arrival.* **Sun 5, Mon 6 May (2-6). Combined adm £7, chd free. Home-made teas at Eastcombe Village Hall. Cream teas/home-made cakes.** Donation to Glos Arthritis Trust; Stroud Valleys Project; Longfield Hospice.

CADSONBURY
Natalie & Glen Beswetherick.

NEW **20 FARMCOTE CLOSE**
Ian & Dawn Sim.

21 FARMCOTE CLOSE
Mr & Mrs Robert Bryant.

HAMPTON VIEW
Geraldine & Mike Carter.

HAWKLEY COTTAGE
Helen & Gerwin Westendorp.

1 HIDCOTE CLOSE
Mr & Mrs J Southall.

12 HIDCOTE CLOSE
Mr K Walker.

HIGHLANDS
Helen & Bob Watkinson.

1 THE LAURELS
Andrew & Ruth Fraser.

MOUNT PLEASANT
Mr & Mrs R Peyton.

REDWOOD
Rita Collins.

50 STONECOTE RIDGE
Julie & Robin Marsland.

NEW **VALLEY VIEW**
Mrs Rebecca Benneyworth.

YEW TREE COTTAGE
Andy & Sue Green.

Medium and small gardens in a variety of styles, set in a picturesque hilltop location. Some approachable only by foot. Plants for sale at Eastcombe Village Hall and possibly in some gardens - see map on the day. Wheelchair access to some gardens. Please check at village hall.

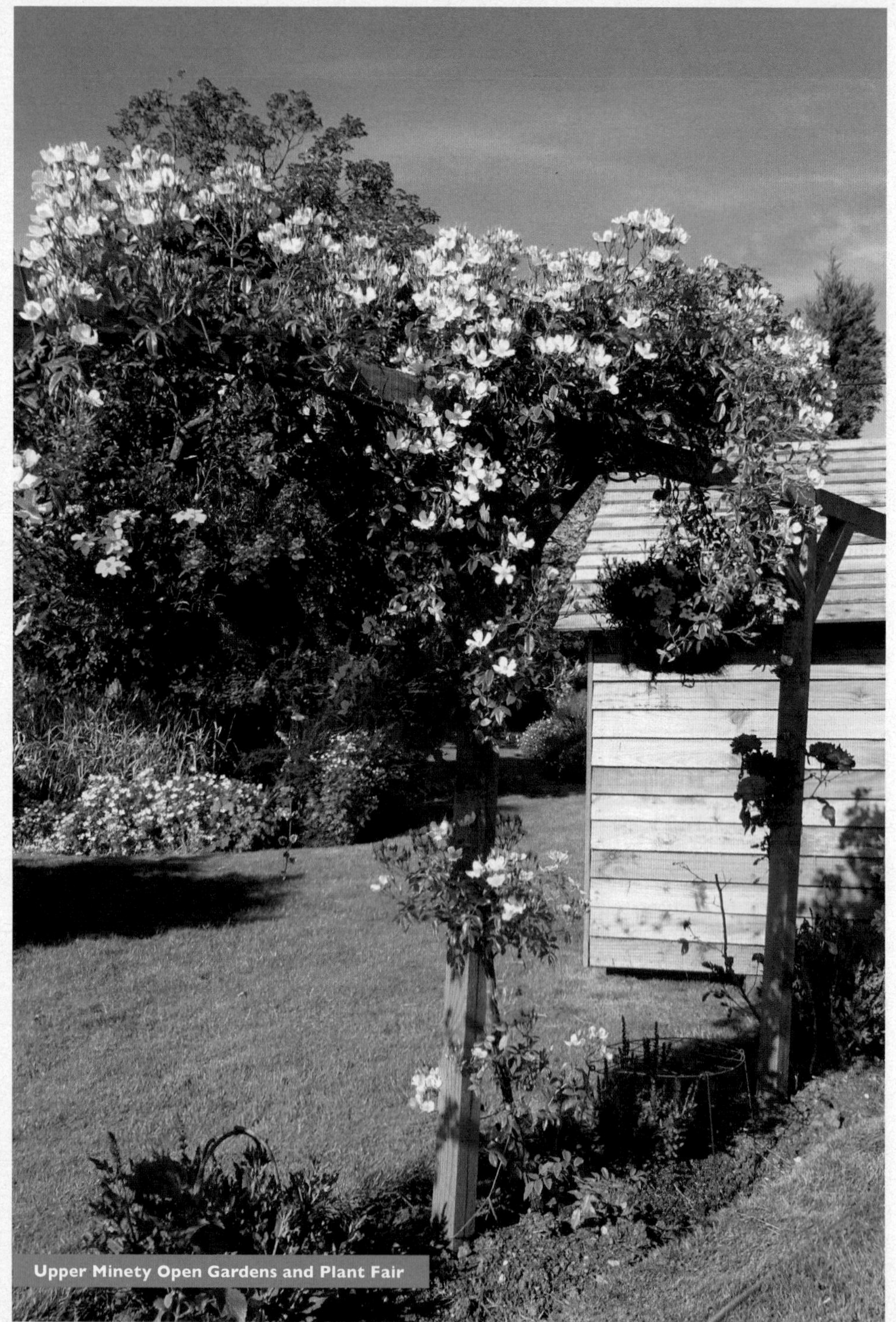

Upper Minety Open Gardens and Plant Fair

26 EASTLEACH HOUSE

Eastleach Martin, Cirencester, GL7 3NW. Mrs David Richards, garden@eastleachhouse.com, , www.eastleachhouse.com. *5m NE of Fairford, 6m S of Burford. Entrance opp church gates in Eastleach Martin. Lodge at gate, gravel driveway is quite steep and curves up to house.* **Visits by arrangement May to July.**

Large traditional all-yr-round garden. Wooded hilltop position with long views S and W. New parkland, lime avenue and arboretum. Wild flower walk, wildlife pond, lawns, walled and rill gardens, with modern herbaceous borders, yew and box hedges, iris and paeony borders, lily ponds, formal herb garden and topiary. Rambling roses into trees. Limited wheelchair access. Gravel paths.

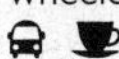

27 EYFORD HOUSE

Upper Slaughter, Cheltenham, GL54 2JN. Mrs C Heber-Percy. *2½m from Stow on the Wold on B4068 Stow to Andoversford Rd.* **Wed 12 June (10-5). Adm £5, chd free. Home-made teas. Cream teas.**

1½ acre sloping N facing garden, ornamental shrubs and trees. Laid out originally by Graham Stuart Thomas, 1976. West garden and terrace, red border, walled kitchen garden, two lakes with pleasant walks and views, boots recommended! Holy well. Walled garden now open after reconstruction.

28 20 FORSDENE WALK

Coalway, Coleford, GL16 7JZ. Pamela Buckland, 01594 837179. *From Coleford take Lydney/Chepstow Rd at T-lights. L after police station ½m up hill turn L at Xrds then 2nd R (Old Road) straight on at minor Xrds then L into Forsdene Walk.* **Sun 21 Apr (11-4); Sun 19 May, Sun 16 June, Sun 21 July (2-6). Adm £3, chd free. Light refreshments.** **Visits also by arrangement May to Sept for individuals and small groups.**

Corner garden filled with interest and design ideas to maximise smaller spaces. A series of interlinking colour themed rooms, some on different levels. Packed with perennials, grasses, ferns and bamboos. A pergola, small man-made stream, fruit and vegetables and pots in abundance on gravelled areas. Featured in Amateur Gardening.

29 FORTHAMPTON COURT

Forthampton, Tewkesbury, GL19 4RD. John Yorke, 07709 574375, alan37g@msn.com. *W of Tewkesbury. From Tewkesbury A438 to Ledbury. After 2m turn L to Forthampton. At Xrds go L towards Chaceley. Go 1m turn L at Xrds.* **Sun 19 May (12-4). Adm £5, chd free. Home-made teas. Visits also by arrangement Apr to July for groups of 10 to 20.**

Charming and varied garden surrounding North Gloucestershire medieval manor house (not open) within sight of Tewkesbury Abbey. Incl borders, lawns, roses and magnificent Victorian vegetable garden.

30 NEW FRITH HOUSE

Far Oakridge, Stroud, GL6 7PG. Mr & Mrs Jeremy Hughes. *From Bisley 2m, head S on Hayhedge Ln R onto Limekiln Ln. From Cirencester 7m, take A419, bear R to Sapperton. L at Daneway Pub, garden L, parking opp in field.* **Sun 19 May, Sun 16 June (1-5). Adm £5, chd free. Light refreshments. Refreshments in aid of Cancer Research.**

Attractive Cotswold stone house in spectacular elevated position with outstanding views across the beautiful garden and grounds and surrounding countryside. The gardens and grounds are extremely picturesque and meticulously planned and incl rose garden, formal beds, mature trees and water gardens making use of natural springs inspired by the Monet Gardens in Normandy.

31 THE GABLES

Riverside Lane, Broadoak, Newnham on Severn, GL14 1JE. Bryan & Christine Bamber, 01594 516323, bryanbamber@sky.com. *1m NE of Newnham on Severn. Park in White Hart PH overspill car park, to R of PH when facing river. Please follow signs to car park. Walk, turning R along rd towards Gloucester for approx 250yds. Access through marked gate.* **Sun 9 June, Sun 18 Aug (11-5). Adm £3.50, chd free. Home-made teas. Visits also by arrangement June to Aug for groups of 10+.**

Garden established 13 yrs ago from blank canvas. Large flat garden with formal lawns, colourful herbaceous borders, rose beds, shrubberies and long border with mini stumpery. Incl wild flower meadow incorporating soft fruits and fruit trees, allotment-size productive vegetable plot, greenhouse and composting area. Disabled parking information available at entrance. All areas of garden visible for wheelchair users but with limited access.

32 ◆ THE GARDEN AT MISERDEN

Miserden, Stroud, GL6 7JA. Mr Nicholas Wills, 01285 821303, estate.office@miserdenestate.org, www.miserden.org. *6m NW of Cirencester. Follow signs off A417 or B4070 from Stroud.* **For NGS: Sun 12 May (11-4). Adm £7, chd free. Light refreshments in separate Miserden Plant Nursery alongside. For other opening times and information, please phone, email or visit garden website.**

This lovely unspoilt garden, positioned high on the Wolds and commanding spectacular views, was created in C17 and still retains a wonderful sense of timeless peace and tranquillity. Perhaps finest features in garden are double 92metre mixed border incl roses and clematis, in different colour sections. Much of original garden is found within ancient Cotswold stone walls. Stunning gardens. Partial wheelchair access.

33 GREEN BOWERS

The Broadway, Dursley, GL11 6AG. Amanda Songer, 07791 659932, amandasonger9@gmail.com. *Up steps by white garage. With SatNav, go to The Old Spot pub. Green Bowers is 200m up a very steep hill from car park opp pub. Easier to come via town, rather than country lanes.* **Sat 20, Sun 21, Mon 22, Sat 27, Sun 28 Apr (10-3). Adm £4. Home-made teas. Proceeds to NGS, Dursley Walking Festival & GARAS - Glos based charity supporting refugees and asylum seekers.** Visits also by arrangement Apr & May for groups of up to 10. Tours guided by Amanda.

Delightful E-facing, steep woodland garden with extensive views, next to The Cotswold Way. This planted hillside takes its character from proximity of woods, wildlife activity and gradient of site. You'll find a mixture of both garden plants and wild flowers. Flower roof garden and areas with acers, pieris and camellias. Due to character of site, we would prefer no children or pets. Uneven terrain, lots of steps, not all areas have handrails. Please wear suitable footwear. Please email to make appointment to visit. Regrettably, not suitable for individuals with any access or mobility requirements.

34 GREENFIELDS, BROCKWEIR COMMON

Brockweir, NP16 7NU. Jackie Healy, 07747 186302, greenfieldsgarden@icloud.com, www.greenfieldsgarden.com. *Located in Wye valley - midway between Chepstow and Monmouth. A446: from M'mouth: Thru Llandogo. L to Brockweir, (from Chepstow, thru Tintern. R to B'weir) over bridge, pass PH up hill, 1st L, follow lane to fork, L at fork. 1st property on R. No coaches.* **Visits by arrangement May to Sept for groups of up to 30. Adm £5, chd free. Home-made teas.**

1½ acre plant person's gem of a garden set in the beautiful Wye Valley. Many mature trees and numerous unusual plants and shrubs, all planted as discrete gardens within a garden. Greenfields is the passion and work of head gardener Jackie who has a long interest in the propagation of plants. Featured in Garden Answers magazine. Mostly wheelchair access.

35 GREENFIELDS, LITTLE RISSINGTON

Cheltenham, GL54 2NA. Mrs Diana MacKenzie-Charrington, 01451 821851, dcharrington@btinternet.com. *On Rissington Road between Bourton-on-the-Water and Little Rissington, opp turn to Great Rissington (Leasow Lane). SatNav using postcode does not take you to house.* **Sun 7 July (2-5). Adm £5, chd free. Home-made teas.** Visits also by arrangement May to Aug for groups of 5 to 20.

The honey coloured Georgian Cotswold stone house sits in 2 acres of garden, created by current owners over last 17 yrs. Lawns are edged with borders full of flowers and later flowering bulbs. A small pond and stream overlook fields. Bantams roam freely. Mature apple trees in wild garden, greenhouse in working vegetable garden. Sorry no dogs. Partial wheelchair access.

36 ◆ HERBS FOR HEALING

Claptons Lane (behind Barnsley House Hotel), Barnsley, GL7 5EE. Davina Wynne-Jones, 07773 687493, davina@herbsforhealing.net, www.herbsforhealing.net. *4m NE of Cirencester. Coming into Barnsley from Cirencester - turn R after Barnsley House Hotel and R again at dairy barn. Follow signs.* **For NGS: Sun 30 June (11-5). Adm £4, chd free. Teas, herb teas and home-made cakes.** For other opening times and information, please phone, email or visit garden website.

Not a typical NGS garden, rural and naturalistic. Davina, the daughter of Rosemary Verey, has created a unique nursery, specialising in medicinal herbs and a tranquil organic garden in secluded field where visitors can enjoy the beauty of plants and learn more about properties and uses of medicinal herbs. Informative tours of the garden with Davina at 11.30 and 2.30. Products made from the herbs are available. Access to WC is difficult for wheelchair users however the garden itself is all level.

37 HIGHNAM COURT

Highnam, Gloucester, GL2 8DP. Mr & Mrs R J Head, www.HighnamCourt.co.uk. *2m W of Gloucester. On A40/A48 from Gloucester.* **Sun 7 Apr, Sun 5 May, Sun 2 June, Sun 7 July, Sun 4 Aug, Sun 8 Sept (11-5). Adm £5, chd free. Light refreshments in Orangery. Tea, coffee from 11.00am. Sandwiches available until 1.30pm. Cream teas served from 1.30 to 5pm.**

40 acres of Victorian landscaped gardens surrounding magnificent Grade I house (not open), set out by artist Thomas Gambier Parry. Lakes, shrubberies and listed Pulhamite water gardens with grottos and fernery. Exciting ornamental lakes, and woodland areas. Extensive 1-acre rose garden and many features, incl numerous wood carvings. Some gravel paths and steps into refreshment area. Disabled WC outside.

38 HODGES BARN

Shipton Moyne, Tetbury, GL8 8PR. Mr & Mrs N Hornby, www.hodgesbarn.com. *3m S of Tetbury. On Malmesbury side of village.* **Sun 2, Mon 3 June (2-6). Adm £5. Home-made teas.**

Very unusual C15 dovecote converted into family home. Cotswold stone walls host climbing and rambling roses, clematis, vines, hydrangeas and together with yew, rose and tapestry hedges create formality around house. Mixed shrub and herbaceous borders, shrub roses, water garden, woodland garden planted with cherries, magnolia and spring bulbs.

39 HOME FARM

Newent Lane, Huntley, GL19 3HQ. Mrs T Freeman, 01452 830210, torill@ukgateway.net. *4m S of Newent. On B4216 ½m off A40 in Huntley travelling towards Newent.* **Sun 27 Jan, Sun 10 Feb (11-3); Sun 10 Mar, Sun 7, Sun 28 Apr (11-4). Adm £3, chd free. 2020: Sun 26 Jan, Sun 9 Feb.** Visits also by arrangement Jan to May for groups of up to 30.

Set in elevated position with exceptional views. 1m walk through woods and fields to show carpets of spring flowers. Enclosed garden with fern border, sundial and heather bed. White and mixed shrub borders. Stout footwear advisable in winter.

40 HOOKSHOUSE POTTERY

Hookshouse Lane, Tetbury, GL8 8TZ. Lise & Christopher White, www.hookshousepottery.co.uk. *2½m SW of Tetbury. Follow signs from A433 at Hare and Hounds Hotel, Westonbirt. Alternatively take A4135 out of Tetbury towards Dursley and follow signs after ½m on L.* **Sat 25, Sun 26, Mon 27, Tue 28, Wed 29, Thur 30, Fri 31 May, Sat 1, Sun 2 June (11-5.30). Adm £4, chd free. Home-made teas.**

Garden offers a combination of dramatic perspectives and intimate corners. Planting incl wide variety of perennials, with emphasis on colour interest throughout the seasons. Borders, shrubs, woodland glade, water garden containing treatment ponds (unfenced) and flowform cascades. Kitchen garden with raised beds, orchard. Sculptural features. Run on organic principles. Pottery showroom with hand thrown wood-fired pots incl frostproof garden pots. Art & Craft exhibition incl garden furniture and sculptures. Garden games and tree house. Mostly wheelchair accessible.

41 ◆ KIFTSGATE COURT

Chipping Campden, GL55 6LN. Mr & Mrs J G Chambers, 01386 438777, info@kiftsgate.co.uk, www.kiftsgate.co.uk. *4m NE of Chipping Campden. Adj to Hidcote NT Garden.* **For NGS: Mon 15 Apr, Mon 12 Aug (2-6). Adm £9, chd £3. Home-made teas.**
For other opening times and information, please phone, email or visit garden website.

Magnificent situation and views, many unusual plants and shrubs, tree peonies, hydrangeas, abutilons, species and old-fashioned roses incl largest rose in England, Rosa filipes Kiftsgate. Steep slopes and uneven surfaces.

42 NEW LECKHAMPTON COURT HOSPICE

Church Road, Leckhampton, Cheltenham, GL53 0QJ. Sue Ryder Leckhampton Court Hospice, www.sueryder.org/care-centres/hospices/leckhampton-court-hospice. *2m SW of Cheltenham. From Church Rd take driveway by Church signed Sue Ryder Leckhampton Court Hospice and follow parking signs.* **Sat 6 July (10-4). Adm £5, chd free. Home-made teas in support of Hospice.**

Set within this Grade 2* listed medieval estate, the informal gardens at Leckhampton Court Hospice surround the buildings combining lawns and planted beds. Feature garden designed by Peter Dowle, RHS Chelsea gold medal winner. Highlights incl new walk around pond and into woodland, also numerous protected mature trees. Wheelchair access in some areas: from back of reception to Sir Charles Irving terrace; woodland walk; main courtyard.

GROUP OPENING

43 LONGHOPE GARDENS

Longhope, GL17 0NA. *10m W of Gloucester. 7m E of Ross on Wye. A40 take Longhope turn off to Church Rd. From A4136 follow Longhope signs and turn onto Church Rd. Parking available on Church Rd.* **Sat 25 May (1-5); Sun 26 May (2-6); Sat 8 June (1-5); Sun 9 June (2-6). Combined adm £5, chd free. Home-made teas.**

3 CHURCH ROAD
Rev Clive & Mrs Linda Edmonds.

SPRINGFIELD HOUSE
Sally & Martin Gibson, 01452 830406.
Visits also by arrangement May & June.

Two beautiful gardens set in the valley of Longhope. Each garden has its own style and delights for you to discover with sweeping views across the valley to May Hill and the Forest of Dean. 3 Church Road: long garden divided into rooms with large collection of hardy geraniums. Springfield House: large enclosed garden with terraced lawns, wide variety of shrubs and trees mingling with large sweeping herbaceous borders and Japanese inspired water feature. Home-made cakes, refreshments and plant sales available. Keep up to date with Longhope Gardens on our Facebook page. 3 Church Road and Springfield House featured in Amateur Gardening magazine. Springfield House also appeared in Austrian TV special 'Classic English Gardens'. Wheelchair access at Springfield House but not at 3 Church Road.

44 LOWER FARM HOUSE

Cliffords Mesne, Newent, GL18 1JT. Gareth & Sarah Williams. *2m S of Newent. From Newent, follow signs to Cliffords Mesne and Birds of Prey Centre (1½m). Approx ½m beyond Centre, turn L at Xrds (before church).* **Wed 22, Wed 29 May (2-6). Adm £4, chd free. Home-made teas.**

2½ acre garden, incl woodland, stream and large natural lily pond with rockery and bog garden. Herbaceous borders, pergola walk, terrace with ornamental fishpond, kitchen and herb garden; collections of irises, hostas and paeonies. Many interesting and unusual trees and shrubs incl magnolias and cornus. Some gravel paths.

45 NEW LOWER SLAUGHTER

Cheltenham, GL54 2HP. Jane Moore, George Leonte, 01451 820456, info@slaughtersmanor.co.uk, www.slaughtersmanor.co.uk/. *Lower Slaughter is 1m NE of Bourton on the Water.* **Thur 4 Apr (2-5). Adm £3.50, chd free. Home-made teas.**

2 individual gardens filled with spring bulbs, flowering cherries and sparkling water features. Managed by the same team of gardeners and subject to ongoing development and investment. The C17 Slaughters Manor House is set within beautiful grounds while across the road lies The Slaughters Country Inn on the banks of the River Eye with its wildlife friendly feel. Gravel paths and lawns.

46 ◆ LYDNEY PARK SPRING GARDEN

Lydney, GL15 6BU. The Viscount Bledisloe, 01594 842844/842922, www.lydneyparkestate.co.uk. *½m SW of Lydney. On A48 Gloucester to Chepstow rd between Lydney & Aylburton. Drive is directly off A48.* **For NGS: Wed 15 May (10-5). Adm £5, chd £0.50. Light lunches.** For other opening times and information, please phone or visit garden website.

Spring garden in 8 acre woodland valley with lakes, profusion of rhododendrons, azaleas and other flowering shrubs. Formal garden; magnolias and daffodils (April). Picnics in deer park which has fine trees. Important Roman Temple site and museum. Not suitable for wheelchairs due to rough pathway through garden and steps to WC.

47 THE MANOR

Little Compton, Moreton-In-Marsh, GL56 0RZ. Reed Foundation (Charity). *Next to church in Little Compton. ½m from A44 or 2m from A3400. Follow signs to Little Compton, then yellow NGS signs.* **Sun 30 June, Sun 1 Sept (2-5). Adm £5.50, chd free. Home-made teas.**

Stunning formal gardens with further meadow and arboreta. Footpaths around our fields, playground between car park and garden. In the garden you can enjoy the many garden rooms incl palette, flower garden, deer walk, Japanese garden, croquet lawn, and tennis court. Children and dogs welcome! One ramp leading to tea area. Rock garden, tennis court lawn and meadow not accessible by wheelchair.

Your visits help change lives – we are Hospice UK's largest charitable funder donating more than £5 million to support hospices in local communities since 1996

48 MOOR WOOD

Woodmancote, GL7 7EB. Mr & Mrs Henry Robinson, 01285 831397, henry@moorwoodhouse.co.uk, www.moorwoodroses.co.uk. *3½m NW of Cirencester. Turn L off A435 to Cheltenham at North Cerney, signed Woodmancote 1¼m; entrance in village on L beside lodge with white gates.* **Sun 30 June (2-6). Adm £5, chd free. Home-made teas.** Visits also by arrangement from 20th to 30th June for groups of up to 30.

2 acres of shrub, orchard and wild flower gardens in beautiful isolated valley setting. Holder of National Collection of Rambler Roses. Not recommended for wheelchairs.

NPC

49 NEW THE OLD VICARAGE

Murrells End, Hartpury, GL19 3DF. Mrs Carol Huckvale. *5m NW of Gloucester. From Over r'about on A40 N Gloucester bypass, take A417 NW to Hartpury (Ledbury Road). After Maisemore, turn L at signs for Hartpury College. House 1m on R. Follow signs for parking.* **Sat 8, Sun 9 June (11-5). Adm £5, chd free. Light refreshments.**

Tranquil garden of about 2 acres, with yew oval, mature trees, steps to croquet lawn, mixed borders around main lawn, potager, fruit trees. Work in progress developing wildflower meadow area and dry, shady woodland walk. Partial wheelchair access, disabled parking at house; gravel drive and path.

50 ◆ OXLEAZE FARM

Between Eastleach & Filkins, Lechlade, GL7 3RB. Mr & Mrs Charles Mann, 01367 850216, chipps@oxleaze.co.uk, www.oxleazebarn.co.uk. *5m S of Burford, 3m N of Lechlade off A361 to W (signed Barringtons). Take 2nd L then follow signs.* **For NGS: Wed 22 May (10-6). Adm £6, chd free. Home-made teas.** For other opening times and information, please phone, email or visit garden website.

Set amongst beautiful traditional farm buildings, plantsperson's good size garden combining formality and informality. Yr round interest; mixed borders, vegetable potager, decorative fruit cage, pond and bog garden, bees, potting shed, wild meadow, and topiary for structure when the flowers fade. Garden rooms off central lawn with reflective corners in which to enjoy this Cotswold garden. Mostly wheelchair access.

51 PASTURE FARM

Upper Oddington, Moreton-In-Marsh, GL56 0XG. Mr & Mrs John LLoyd. *3m W of Stow-on-the-Wold. Just off A436, mid-way between Upper & Lower Oddington.* **Sun 26, Mon 27 May (11-6); Sat 1, Sun 2 June (11-5). Adm £6, chd free. Home-made teas.**

Informal country garden developed over 30 yrs by current owners. Mixed borders, topiary, orchard and many species of trees. Gravel garden in 'the ruins', new concrete garden and wild flower area leads to vegetable patch. Big spring-fed pond with ducks. Also bantams, chickens and 2 kunekune pigs. Large plant sale 26/27 May with proceeds to Kate's home nursing. Public footpath across 2 small fields arrives at C11 church, St Nicholas, with doom paintings, set in ancient woodlands. Truly worth a visit. See Simon Jenkins' Book of Churches.

52 THE PATCH

Hollywell Lane, Brockweir, Chepstow, NP16 7PJ. Mrs Immy Lee. *In the Wye Valley, 6.7m N of Chepstow and 10.6m S of Monmouth, off A466, across Brockweir Bridge.* **Sun 15 Sept (1-5). Combined adm with Clouds Rest £6, chd free.**

Restructured over the last few years, this is now a well designed garden with fine borders containing a collection of 60+ repeat flowering roses and a variety of shrubs and perennials, providing colour and interest throughout the year. Partial wheelchair access.

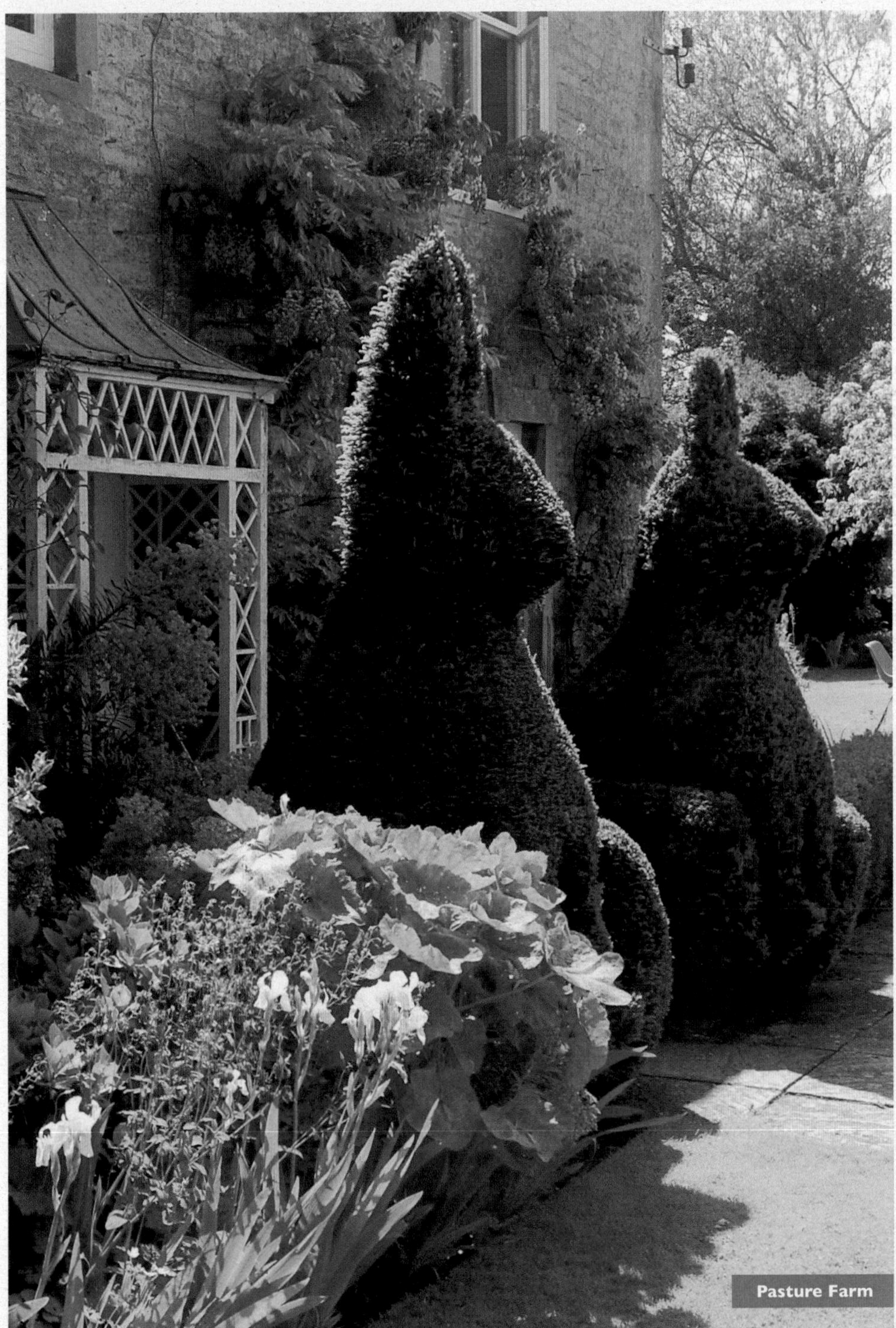

Pasture Farm

53 PEAR TREE COTTAGE

58 Malleson Road, Gotherington, GL52 9EX. Mr & Mrs E Manders-Trett, 01242 674592, edandmary@talktalk.net. *4m N of Cheltenham. From A435, travelling N, turn R into Gotherington 1m after end of Bishop's Cleeve bypass at garage. Garden on L approx 100yds past Shutter Inn.* **Visits by arrangement Mar to June for groups of up to 30. Adm £4, chd free. Light refreshments.**

Mainly informal country garden of approx ½ acre with pond and gravel garden. Herbaceous borders, trees and shrubs surround lawns and seating areas. Wild garden and orchard lead to greenhouses, vegetable garden and beehives. Spring bulbs, early summer perennials and shrubs particularly colourful. Gravel drive and several shallow steps can be overcome for wheelchair users with prior notice.

54 NEW PERRYWOOD HOUSE

Longney, Gloucester, GL2 3SN. Gill & Mike Farmer. *7m SW of Gloucester, 4m W of Quedgeley. From N: R off B4008 at Tesco Quedgeley r'about. R at end then R at 2nd mini r'about, then signed. From S: L off A38 at Moreton Valence to Epney/Longney, over canal, R at T junction then signed.* **Sat 29, Sun 30 June (11-5). Adm £4, chd free. Home-made teas.**

1 acre plant lover's garden in the Severn Vale surrounded by open farmland. Established over 20 years, an informal country garden with mature trees and shrubs, colourful herbaceous borders and containers. Plenty of places to sit and enjoy the garden and your tea. Lots of interesting plants for sale. All areas accessible with level lawns and gravel drives. Disabled parking available.

55 ROCKCLIFFE,

Upper Slaughter, Cheltenham, GL54 2JW. Mr & Mrs Simon Keswick, www.rockcliffegarden.co.uk. *2m from Stow-on-the-Wold. 1½m from Lower Swell on B4068 towards Cheltenham. Leave Stow on the Wold on B4068 through Lower Swell. Continue on B4068 for 1½m. Rockcliffe is well signed on R.* **Wed 12 June (10-5). Adm £7, chd free. Home-made teas.** Donation to Kates Home Nursing.

Large traditional English garden of 8 acres incl pink garden, white and blue garden, herbaceous borders, rose terrace, large walled kitchen garden and orchard. Greenhouses and pathway of topiary birds leading up through orchard to stone dovecot. Featured in many books and magazines, incl front cover of Gardens Illustrated. Sorry no dogs. 2 wide stone steps through gate, otherwise good wheelchair access.

56 SCATTERFORD

Newland, Gloucestershire, Coleford, GL16 8NG. Sean Swallow, 01291 675483, kelly@kellyweare.plus.com, scatterford.net. *1m S of Newland and just N of Clearwell, opp junction to Coleford. From Monmouth take A466/Redbrook Rd to Redbrook. From Chepstow take B4228 turn off to Clearwell. From Coleford take Newland Street.* **Sat 8 June, Sat 21 Sept (10-4). Adm £5, chd free. Home-made teas. Refreshments by and in aid of Mid WyeDean Churches (additional cost).** Visits also by arrangement May to Sept for groups of 20 to 30.

Well-crafted and maintained 2-acre garden between Wye valley and Forest of Dean. Formal pond, walled garden, sculpted terraces, courtyards, haha, hedges, orchards, hedgrows, natural pond and extensive borders. A contemporary design with serene atmosphere. Head Gardener: Kelly Weare. Designed by Sean Swallow and Askew Nelson Landscape Architects.

57 ◆ SEZINCOTE

Moreton-in-Marsh, GL56 9AW. Mrs D Peake, 01386 700444, enquiries@sezincote.com, www.sezincote.co.uk. *3m SW of Moreton-in-Marsh. From Moreton-in-Marsh turn W along A44 towards Evesham; after 1½m (just before Bourton-on-the-Hill) turn L, by stone lodge with white gate.* **For NGS: Sun 30 June (2-6). Adm £5, chd free. Home-made teas. Teas provided by and in aid of Longborough School.** For other opening times and information, please phone, email or visit garden website.

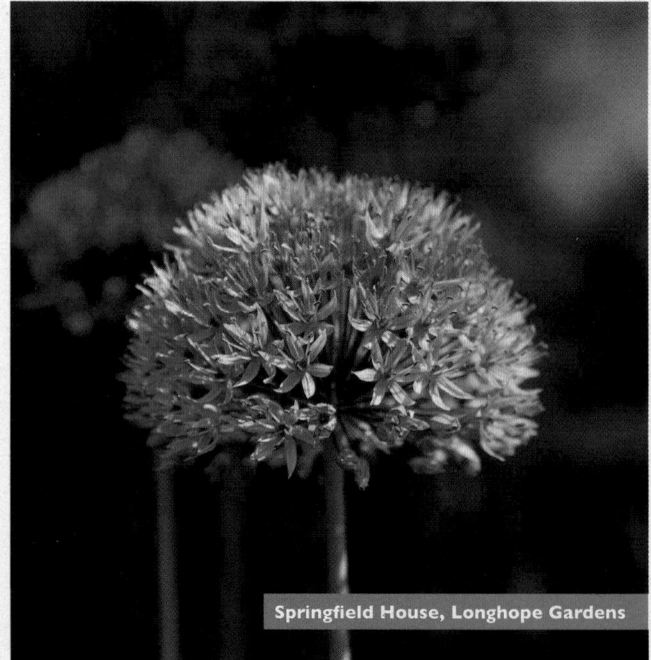

Springfield House, Longhope Gardens

Exotic oriental water garden by Repton and Daniell with lake, pools and meandering stream, banked with massed perennials. Large semi-circular orangery, formal Indian garden, fountain, temple and unusual trees of vast size in lawn and wooded park setting. House in Indian manner designed by Samuel Pepys Cockerell. Garden on slope with gravel paths, so not all areas wheelchair accessible.

58 SOUTH LODGE

Church Road, Clearwell, Coleford, GL16 8LG. Andrew & Jane MacBean, 01594 837769, southlodgegarden@btinternet.com, www.southlodgegarden.co.uk. *2m S of Coleford. Off B4228. Follow signs to Clearwell. Garden on L of castle driveway. Please park on rd in front of church or in village. No parking on castle drive.* **Sat 6 Apr, Sat 4, Sun 19 May, Sun 2, Sat 29 June (1-5). Adm £4, chd free. Home-made teas.** Visits also by arrangement Apr to June for groups of 20+. For coach parties, teas will be served in the village hall.

Peaceful country garden in 2 acres with stunning views of surrounding countryside. High walls provide a backdrop for rambling roses, clematis, and honeysuckles. Organic garden with large variety of perennials, annuals, shrubs and specimen trees with yr-round colour. Vegetable garden, wildlife and formal ponds. Rustic pergola planted with English climbing roses and willow arbour in gravel garden. Gravel paths and steep grassy slopes.

GROUP OPENING

59 STANTON VILLAGE GARDENS

Stanton, nr Broadway, WR12 7NE. *3m S of Broadway. Off B4632, between Broadway (3m) and Winchcombe (6m).* **Sun 16 June (2-6). Combined adm £7.50, chd free. Home-made teas in Burland Hall in village centre and several open gardens. Ice cream trike in village.** Donation to Village charities.

A large selection of gardens open in this picturesque, unspoilt Cotswold village. Many houses border the street with long gardens hidden behind. Gardens vary, from houses with colourful herbaceous borders, established trees, shrubs and vegetable gardens to tiny cottage gardens. Some also have attractive, natural water features fed by the stream which runs through the village. Plants for sale and book stall. Legendary home-made teas in various locations. Free parking. An NGS visit not to be missed. Few gardens suitable for wheelchair users due to gravel drives.

60 ◆ STANWAY FOUNTAIN & WATER GARDEN

Stanway, Cheltenham, GL54 5PQ. The Earl of Wemyss & March, 01386 584528, office@stanwayhouse.co.uk, www.stanwayfountain.co.uk. *9m NE of Cheltenham. 1m E of B4632 Cheltenham to Broadway rd on B4077 Toddington to Stow-on-the-Wold rd.* **For NGS: Sun 12 May, Sun 18 Aug (2-5). Adm £6, chd £2. Home-made teas in Stanway Tea Room.** For other opening times and information, please phone, email or visit garden website.

20 acres of planted landscape in early C18 formal setting. The restored canal, upper pond and fountain have re-created one of the most interesting Baroque water gardens in Britain. Striking C16 manor with gatehouse, tithe barn and church. Britain's highest fountain at 300ft, the world's highest gravity fountain which runs at 2.45 and 4.00pm for 30 mins each time. Limited wheelchair access in garden, some flat areas, able to view fountain and some of garden. House is not wheelchair suitable.

61 STOWELL PARK

Yanworth, Northleach, Cheltenham, GL54 3LE. The Lord & Lady Vestey, www.stowellpark.co.uk. *8m NE of Cirencester. Off Fosseway A429 2m SW of Northleach.* **Sun 2, Sun 30 June (2-5). Adm £6, chd free. Home-made teas.**

Magnificent lawned terraces with stunning views over Coln Valley. Fine collection of old-fashioned roses and herbaceous plants, pleached lime approach to C14 house (not open). 2 large walled gardens containing vegetables, fruit, cut flowers and range of greenhouses incl vinery, peach and orchid houses. Long rose pergola and wide, plant filled borders. Fountain garden and water features. Open continuously for over 50yrs. Plants for sale June 2nd opening only. Church open. Wheelchair access to walled gardens, terraces and teas. Limited access on some pathways.

62 TEMPLE GUITING MANOR & BARNS

Temple Guiting, Cheltenham, GL54 5RP. Mr & Mrs S Collins, www.cockahoopcollection.co.uk. *7m W of Stow-on-the-Wold. From Stow take B4077 towards Tewkesbury. On descending hill bear L to village (signed) ½m. Garden in centre of village on R.* **Sun 9 June (11-4). Adm £6.50, chd free. Home-made teas in Temple Guiting pantry. Some refreshments on site.**

5 acres of formal contemporary gardens with kitchen garden, to a private Grade I listed Historic Tudor Manor House (not open) in the Windrush Valley. Designed by Jinny Blom, gold medal winner Chelsea Flower Show. Luxury private estate can be rented privately for 10 -30 guests and small weddings. Gravel pathways.

63 NEW THOUSAND ACRES

Bournstream, Wotton-Under-Edge, GL12 7DY. Mr C Berry & Miss Y Baker, 07718 328806, dandoi@aol.com. *Just outside Wotton-under-Edge on B4060, North Nibley road. From North Nibley, entrance is immediately on R after passing 'Welcome to Wotton-under-Edge' sign. From centre of Wotton-under-Edge follow B4060 towards North Nibley.* **Sun 30 June (11-4). Adm £5, chd free. Light refreshments. Tea, coffee and a selection of home-made cakes. Visits also by arrangement Apr to Sept.**

10 acre garden with specifically different areas including orchards, several woodland areas containing some specimen trees, formal lawns and borders, field dedicated to wildlife conservation and habitat provisions incl bulbs and plants to encourage bees and other pollinators. Walled garden with box hedging and formal borders with long central pond and orangery. Veg beds and greenhouses.

64 NEW TREE HILL

76 Gretton Road, Winchcombe, Cheltenham, GL54 5EL. Mark Caswell. *½m N of Winchcombe. Leave Winchcombe via North St, straight ahead onto Gretton Rd for ½m. From M5 J9, take A46 towards Evesham, at r'about take B4077 to Stow, then R to Gretton.* **Sun 11 Aug (10-4). Combined adm with Woodlands Farm £7, chd free.**

Stepping into this garden is akin to stepping into another world. As one visitor remarked 'this is unlike any English garden I have ever seen.' On this modest plot one finds huge leaves, tall exotic plants jostling for light with the small and the delicate. Built by one man with a passion for the exotic landscapes of the Caribbean which was borne during a visit to Barbados at the tender age of 24. Two stone steps down to the garden.

65 TRENCH HILL

Sheepscombe, GL6 6TZ. Celia & Dave Hargrave, 01452 814306, celia.hargrave@btconnect.com. *1½m E of Painswick. From Cheltenham A46 take 1st turn signed Sheepscombe. Follow lane (1¼m) to bottom of hill, continue uphill towards Sheepscombe. Garden on L. SatNav leads to neighbouring garden, follow NGS signs.* **Sun 10, Sun 17 Feb, Sun 17 Mar (11-5); Sun 21, Mon 22 Apr (11-6). Every Wed 5 June to 26 June (2-6). Sun 21 July (11-5.30); Sun 25 Aug, Sun 15 Sept (11-6). Adm £4, chd free. Home-made teas. 2020: Sun 9, Sun 16 Feb. Visits also by arrangement Feb to Oct. Use of coaches must be sanctioned by the garden owners.**

Approx 3 acres set in small woodland with panoramic views. Variety of herbaceous and mixed borders, rose garden, extensive vegetable plots, wild flower areas, plantings of spring bulbs with thousands of snowdrops and hellebores, woodland walk, 2 small ponds, waterfall and larger conservation pond. Interesting wooden sculptures, many within the garden. Run on organic principles. Children's play area. Mostly wheelchair access but some steps and slopes.

GROUP OPENING

66 UPPER MINETY OPEN GARDENS AND PLANT FAIR

Upper Minety, Malmesbury, SN16 9PY. Mr & Mrs C Gallop, 01666 860286, katiegallop@btinternet.com. *7m SE of Cirencester. Follow signs from A429 (Cotswold Water Park) or alternatively from B4040 to Minety Church. Ample parking.* **Sun 23 June (11-5). Combined adm £6, chd free. Home-made teas.**

Upper Minety which takes its name from the wild mint plant found growing in and around the village will be offering 6 inspirational gardens from sweeping herbaceous borders, cottage gardens, productive fruit/veg plots, tranquil nature reserve and arboretum, open meadows with St Leonard's Church floral arrangements. Specialist plant nurseries and imaginative stalls offering accessories for your home and garden together with a display of vintage and classic cars will be hosted at Oakwood Farm with teas on the farm lawn and where garden maps can be obtained. Featured in Farmers Guardian. Some gravel, mostly grass. Disabled parking available. Coaches by arrangement only.

67 UPTON WOLD

Moreton-in-Marsh, GL56 9TR. Mr & Mrs I R S Bond, www.uptonwold.co.uk. *4½m W of Moreton-in-Marsh. On A44, ¾ mile past A424 junction at Troopers Lodge Garage, on R, opp deer warning sign. Follow road between fields, turn L at Xrds, and park in Estate Yard. Follow signs to garden.* **Sun 14 Apr (11-5). Adm £12, chd free. Home-made teas.**

Ever developing and changing garden, architecturally and imaginatively laid out around C17 house (not open) with commanding views. Yew hedges, herbaceous walk, some unusual plants and trees, vegetables, pond and woodland gardens, labyrinth. National Collections of Juglans and Pterocarya. 2 Star award from GGG.

NPC

68 NEW **WATERLANE HOUSE**

Waterlane, Oakridge, Stroud, GL6 7PN. Mr & Mrs Hall. *2m S of Bisley, turn L out of Bisley and follow rd. From Cirencester on A419 turn R towards Sapperton, through Sapperton, turn L opp Daneway pub, follow single track rd to Waterlane.* **Thur 20 June (11-4). Adm £4, chd free. Home-made teas.**

Private estate with 4 acre garden with a variety of gardening interest ranging from herbaceous borders, white garden, kitchen garden, wild flower meadows, orchard and fine lawns. The estate is set in the idyllic countryside hamlet of Waterlane. Partial wheelchair access, a lot of gravel paths and lawns. Some steps.

69 NEW **WEIR REACH**

The Rudge, Maisemore, Gloucester, GL2 8HY. Sheila & Mark Wardle, weirreach@gmail.com. *3m NW of Gloucester. Turn into The Rudge by White Hart pub. Field parking 200m from garden.* **Sun 16, Wed 19 June (11-5). Adm £4, chd free. Home-made teas.** Visits also by arrangement in June for groups of 10 to 20.

Country garden by R Severn. Approx 2 acres, half cultivated with herbaceous beds and mixed borders plus fruit and vegetable cages. Clematis and acers, stone ornaments, small sculptures, Bonsai collection. Planted rockery with waterfall and stream connect 2 ponds. Large specimen koi pond borders patio. Meadow with specimen and fruit trees and bamboo collection leading to river and country views.

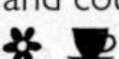

70 ◆ **WESTONBIRT SCHOOL GARDENS**

Tetbury, GL8 8QG. Holfords of Westonbirt Trust, 01666 881373, jbaker@holfordtrust.com, www.holfordtrust.com. *3m SW of Tetbury. Opp Westonbirt Arboretum, on A433. Enter via Holford wrought iron gates to Westonbirt House.* **For NGS: Sun 14 July (11-5). Adm £5, chd free. Tea, coffee & cake available to purchase in Holford Dining Room.** For other opening times and information, please phone, email or visit garden website.

28 acres. Former private garden of Robert Holford, founder of Westonbirt Arboretum. Formal Victorian gardens incl walled Italian garden now restored with early herbaceous borders and exotic border. Rustic walks, lake, statuary and grotto. Rare, exotic trees and shrubs. Beautiful views of Westonbirt House open with guided tours to see fascinating Victorian interior on designated days of the year. Afternoon tea with sandwiches and scones available for pre-booked private tours, groups of 10-60. Only some parts of garden accessible to wheelchairs. Ramps and lift allow access to house.

GROUP OPENING

71 **WINCHCOMBE GARDENS**

North Street, Winchcombe, Cheltenham, GL54 5PS. *80 North Street, and St Mary's, Cowl Lane. Winchcombe lies on B4632 mid-way between Cheltenham and Broadway. Parking behind Winchcombe Library in Back Lane car park which has steps to Cowl Lane.* **Sun 23 June (2-6). Combined adm £6, chd free. Home-made teas at St Mary's, Cowl Lane.**

THE GATE
Vanessa Berridge & Chris Evans.

ST MARY'S
Lynne & David Banks.

Two contrasting country gardens, both peaceful retreats, in the centre of an historic Cotswold town.
The Gate is a cottage-style garden planted with perennials, annuals, climbers and herbs in the walled courtyard of a former C17 Coaching Inn. Separate, productive kitchen garden with espaliers and other fruit trees. St. Mary's garden is approx ½ acre on the site of what was once part of Winchcombe Abbey. Mixed borders with repeat planting in drifts of hardy perennials providing colour all-year-round. Grasses and beds edged with box give structure and definition. Plants for sale at The Gate; home-made teas at St Mary's. Limited wheelchair access to both gardens.

72 **WOODLANDS FARM**

Rushley Lane, Winchcombe, GL54 5JE. Mrs Morag Dobbin, 01242 604261, mdobbin@btinternet.com. *6m NE of Cheltenham. Take Rushley Lane turn off B4632 N through Winchcombe, at Footbridge. Gate is 50yds behind Stancombe Lane sign. Park in field next to garden.* **Sun 11 Aug (10-4). Combined adm with Tree Hill £7, chd free. Home-made teas.** Visits also by arrangement May to Sept for groups of 10 to 20.

1½ acre garden with generously sized garden rooms. The planting and landscaping are both thoughtful and tranquil. Generous borders throughout with colourful and harmonious planting schemes. Tall hornbeam hedge creates dramatic vista to stone monolith. Long contemporary pond. New prairie style border. Cottage borders. Wheelchair assistance needed with one steepish slope to access garden.

73 **WORTLEY HOUSE**

Wortley, Wotton-Under-Edge, GL12 7QP. Simon & Jessica Dickinson. *1m from Wotton-under-Edge. Full directions will be provided with ticket.* **Tue 18 June (2-5). Adm £15, chd free. Pre-booking essential, please visit www.ngs.org.uk for information & booking. Home-made teas.**

This diverse garden of over 20 acres has been created during the last 30 yrs by the current owners and incl walled garden, pleached lime avenues, nut walk, potager, ponds, Italian garden, shrubberies and wild flower meadows. Follies, urns and statues have been strategically placed throughout to enhance extraordinary vistas, and the garden filled with plants, arbours, roses through trees and up walls and herbaceous borders. The stunning surrounding countryside is incorporated into the garden with views up the steep valley that are such a feature in this part of Gloucestershire. Wheelchair access to most areas, golf buggy also available.

Volunteers

County Organiser
Mark Porter 01962 791054
markstephenporter@gmail.com

County Treasurer
Fred Fratter 01962 776243
fred@fratter.co.uk

Publicity
Pat Beagley
01256 764772
pat.beagley@ngs.org.uk

Booklet Co-ordinator
Mark Porter (as above)

Assistant County Organisers

Central
Sue Cox 01962 732043
suealex13@gmail.com

Central West
Kate Cann 01794 389105
kategcann@gmail.com

East
Linda Smith 01329 833253
linda.ngs@btinternet.com

North
Cynthia Oldale 01420 520438
c.k.oldale@btinternet.com

North East
Lizzie Powell 01420 23185
lizzie.powell@btconnect.com

North West
Carol Pratt 01264 710305
carolacap@yahoo.co.uk

South
Barbara Sykes 02380 254521
barandhugh@aol.com

South West
Elizabeth Walker 01590 677415
elizabethwalker13@gmail.com

West
Christopher Stanford
01425 652133
stanfordsnr@gmail.com

Hampshire is a large, diverse county. The landscape ranges from clay/gravel heath and woodland in the New Forest National Park in the south west, across famous trout rivers – the Test and Itchen – to chalk downland in the east, where you will find the South Downs National Park.

Our open gardens are spread right across the county and offer a very diverse range of interest for both the keen gardener and the casual visitor.

We have a large number of gardens with rivers running through them such as those in Longstock, Bere Mill, Dipley Mill and Weir House; gardens with large vegetable kitchen gardens such as Bramdean House; and thirteen new gardens will open for the very first time.

You will be assured of a warm welcome by all our garden owners and we hope you enjoy your visits.

Below: **Ferns Lodge**

OPENING DATES

All entries subject to change. For latest information check **www.ngs.org.uk**

Extended openings are shown at the beginning of the month.

Map locator numbers are shown to the right of each garden name.

February

Snowdrop Festival

Sunday 10th
Bramdean House 17
The Down House 38

Sunday 17th
Little Court 56

Monday 18th
Little Court 56

Sunday 24th
◆ Chawton House 23
Little Court 56

Monday 25th
Little Court 56

March

Sunday 10th
Little Court 56

Wednesday 27th
Beechenwood Farm 10

Saturday 30th
The Island 54

Sunday 31st
Bere Mill 11
The Island 54

April

Every Wednesday
Beechenwood Farm 10

Sunday 7th
Old Thatch & The Millennium Barn 75

Sunday 14th
Bramdean House 17
Durmast House 39

Wednesday 17th
NEW Abbotsfield 2

Friday 19th
Crawley Gardens 32

Sunday 21st
NEW 13 Oakwood Road 71
Pylewell Park 77
28 St Ronan's Avenue 83
Terstan 91

Monday 22nd
Crawley Gardens 32
NEW 13 Oakwood Road 71

Wednesday 24th
NEW Abbotsfield 2

Saturday 27th
Moore Blatch 67

Sunday 28th
Moore Blatch 67
◆ Spinners Garden 86
Tylney Hall Hotel 93

May

Every Wednesday
Beechenwood Farm 10

Friday 3rd
Bluebell Wood 16

Saturday 4th
Bluebell Wood 16

Sunday 5th
The Cottage 29
Rotherfield Park 81

Monday 6th
Ashe Park 8
The Cottage 29

Wednesday 8th
NEW Abbotsfield 2

Thursday 9th
Tanglefoot 90

Saturday 11th
2 Sampan Close 84

Sunday 12th
Berry Cottage 12
Brick Kiln Cottage 19
The Cottage 29
The House in the Wood 52
2 Sampan Close 84
Tanglefoot 90
The Thatched Cottage 92
Walhampton 94

Monday 13th
The Cottage 29

Thursday 16th
NEW How Park Barn 53

Saturday 18th
◆ Alverstoke Crescent Garden 3
21 Chestnut Road 24
Selborne 85

Sunday 19th
21 Chestnut Road 24
Crookley Pool 33
Hinton Admiral 49
NEW How Park Barn 53
Little Court 56
Selborne 85
Tylney Hall Hotel 93

Monday 20th
Little Court 56
Selborne 85

Thursday 23rd
Bisterne Manor 14

Sunday 26th
Amport & Monxton Gardens 4
Bere Mill 11
Meon Orchard 64
NEW 13 Oakwood Road 71
Pylewell Park 77
Romsey Gardens 79
28 St Ronan's Avenue 83
West Silchester Hall 96

Monday 27th
Amport & Monxton Gardens 4
NEW 13 Oakwood Road 71
Romsey Gardens 79
West Silchester Hall 96

Thursday 30th
Bisterne Manor 14
Tanglefoot 90

June

Saturday 1st
Froyle Gardens 43
Rotherfield Greys 80
Spitfire House 87

Sunday 2nd
Dipley Mill 35
Froyle Gardens 43
Rotherfield Greys 80
Tanglefoot 90

Wednesday 5th
Beechenwood Farm 10

Thursday 6th
Lake House 55

Saturday 8th
21 Chestnut Road 24
NEW Ferns Lodge 42
Lower Baybridge House 60

Sunday 9th
Bramdean House 17
Broadhatch House 20
21 Chestnut Road 24
Conholt Park 28
Cranbury Park 31
The Dower House 36
NEW Ferns Lodge 42
NEW 108 Heath Road 47
Lake House 55
NEW Marl House 63
Romsey Gardens 79
Tylney Hall Hotel 93
Weir House 95

Monday 10th
Little Court 56

Tuesday 11th
Colemore House Gardens 26

Wednesday 12th
Colemore House Gardens 26
Down Farm House 37

Thursday 13th
Stockbridge Gardens 89

Saturday 15th
Selborne 85

Sunday 16th
Dipley Mill 35
Down Farm House 37
Little Owls 58
Longstock Park 59
NEW Marl House 63
Old Thatch & The Millennium Barn 75
Selborne 85
Spring Pond 88
Stockbridge Gardens 89

Monday 17th
Selborne 85

Saturday 22nd
NEW 5 Oakfields 70

Sunday 23rd
Durmast House 39
Oakcroft 69
NEW 5 Oakfields 70
Terstan 91
Wicor Primary School Community Garden 100

Monday 24th
Oakcroft 69

Saturday 29th
The Island 54
26 Lower Newport Road 61

Sunday 30th
19 Barnwood Road 9
Berry Cottage 12
61 Cottes Way 30
The Island 54
Little Owls 58
26 Lower Newport Road 61
The Thatched Cottage 92

July

Every Tuesday to Tuesday 23rd
Old Swan House 74

Monday 1st
61 Cottes Way 30

Wednesday 3rd
Wychwood 103

Thursday 4th
Crawley Gardens 32

Saturday 6th
NEW 15 Bruce Close 21
Oak Tree Cottage 68

Sunday 7th
Bleak Hill Nursery & Garden 15
NEW 15 Bruce Close 21
NEW Bumpers 22
Clover Farm 25
Conholt Park 28
Crawley Gardens 32
◆ The Hospital of St Cross 51
Oak Tree Cottage 68
West Silchester Hall 96

Monday 8th
Clover Farm 25

Wednesday 10th
Wychwood 103

Saturday 13th
NEW 15 Bruce Close 21
30 Compton Way 27

Sunday 14th
Bramdean House 17
NEW 15 Bruce Close 21
30 Compton Way 27
Dipley Mill 35
Little Owls 58
1 Wogsbarne Cottages 102

Monday 15th
1 Wogsbarne Cottages 102

Tuesday 16th
30 Compton Way 27

Thursday 18th
Tanglefoot 90

Saturday 20th
8 Birdwood Grove 13
21 Chestnut Road 24
Fairweather's Nursery 41

Sunday 21st
Berry Cottage 12
Bleak Hill Nursery & Garden 15
21 Chestnut Road 24
Fairweather's Nursery 41
Tanglefoot 90
Terstan 91
The Thatched Cottage 92

Saturday 27th
Rotherfield Greys 80

Sunday 28th
Meon Orchard 64
Rotherfield Greys 80

Clover Farm

© Leigh Clapp

August

Saturday 3rd
Old Camps 72
Selborne 85

Sunday 4th
Bleak Hill Nursery & Garden 15
Dipley Mill 35
Old Camps 72
Selborne 85
NEW West View 97

Monday 5th
Selborne 85

Wednesday 7th
NEW West View 97

Saturday 10th
Willows 101

Sunday 11th
Bramdean House 17
The Homestead 50
West Silchester Hall 96
Willows 101

Saturday 17th
Rotherfield Greys 80
Wheatley House 98

Sunday 18th
Berry Cottage 12
21 Chestnut Road 24
Rotherfield Greys 80
The Thatched Cottage 92
Wheatley House 98

Saturday 24th
NEW Ferns Lodge 42

Sunday 25th
NEW Ferns Lodge 42
Gilberts Dahlia Field 44

Monday 26th
Willows 101

September

Sunday 1st
Berry Cottage 12
Dipley Mill 35
Meon Orchard 64
Old Thatch & The Millennium Barn 75
The Thatched Cottage 92

Sunday 8th
Bramdean House 17
Terstan 91
Weir House 95

Tuesday 10th
◆ Apple Court Garden & Nursery 5

Sunday 15th
Bere Mill 11

Wednesday 18th
Redenham Park House 78

Thursday 19th
Redenham Park House 78

Tuesday 24th
◆ Apple Court Garden & Nursery 5

Sunday 29th
Dipley Mill 35

February 2020

Sunday 16th
Little Court 56

Monday 17th
Little Court 56

Sunday 23rd
Little Court 56

Monday 24th
Little Court 56

By Arrangement

Arrange a personalised garden visit with your club, or group of friends, on a date to suit you. See individual garden entries for full details.

80 Abbey Road 1
Appletree House 6
NEW Appleyards 7
19 Barnwood Road 9
Beechenwood Farm 10
Bere Mill 11
Berry Cottage 12
8 Birdwood Grove 13
Bramdean House 17
6 Breamore Close 18
Brick Kiln Cottage 19
Broadhatch House 20
21 Chestnut Road 24
Clover Farm 25
Colemore House Gardens 26
Conholt Park 28
The Cottage 29
Crookley Pool 33
The Deane House 34
The Dower House 36
Down Farm House 37
The Down House 38
Durmast House 39
Fairbank 40
Hambledon House 45
Hanging Hosta Garden 46
Hill Top 48
The Homestead 50
Lake House 55
Little Court 56
NEW Little Croft 57
Little Owls 58
Merdon Manor 65
Michaelmas 66
4 Mill Lane, Romsey Gardens 79
Old Camps 72
The Old Rectory 73
Redenham Park House 78
Rotherfield Greys 80
NEW Sages 82
Selborne 85
Spring Pond 88
Tanglefoot 90
Terstan 91
The Thatched Cottage 92
Walhampton 94
Weir House 95
West Silchester Hall 96
Wheatley House 98
Whispers 99
Willows 101

THE GARDENS

1 80 ABBEY ROAD

Fareham, PO15 5HW. Brian & Vivienne Garford, 01329 843939, vgarford@aol.com. *From M27 J9 take A27 E to Fareham for approx 2m. At top of hill, turn L at lights into Highlands Rd. Turn 4th R into Blackbrook Rd. Abbey Rd is 4th L.* **Visits by arrangement Apr to Aug for groups of up to 20. Light refreshments.**
The 25th year of opening our unusual small garden, with large collection of herbs and plants of botanical and historical interest. Box hedging provides structure for relaxed planting. Interesting use of containers and ideas for small gardens. Two ponds and tiny meadow for wildlife. Living willow seat, summerhouse and trained grapevine. Areas of new planting for 2019.

✿ ☕

2 NEW ABBOTSFIELD

Bennetts Lane, Burley, Ringwood, BH24 4AT. Anne Blackman. *1m W of Burley village centre. Signed from village centre. Parking in Mill Lawn Car Park or at the White Buck by kind permission. Garden approx 400 metre in each direction to both car parks. White Buck is most level.* **Wed 17, Wed 24 Apr, Wed 8 May (10.30-3.30). Adm £3.50, chd free. Home-made teas.**
Follow the Purbeck stone path past well stocked beds inter-planted with spring bulbs that hint at a display of colour as the year unfolds. Enjoy the elevated pond with a variety of fish at play and move on past a beautiful tree-scape to a rose bed and summerhouse, a newly restored raised bed vegetable garden and productive greenhouse. A welcome cup of tea is then within sight. Wheelchair access to most of the garden.

♿ ✿ ☕

3 ◆ ALVERSTOKE CRESCENT GARDEN

Crescent Road, Gosport, PO12 2DH. Gosport Borough Council, www.alverstokecrescentgarden.co.uk. *1m S of Gosport. From A32 & Gosport follow signs for Stokes Bay. Continue alongside bay to small r'about, turn L into Anglesey Rd. Crescent Garden signed 50yds on R.* **For NGS: Sat 18 May (10-4). Adm by donation. Home-made teas.** For other opening times and information, please visit garden website.

Restored Regency ornamental garden, designed to enhance fine crescent (Thomas Ellis Owen 1828). Trees, walks and flowers lovingly maintained by community and council partnership. Garden's of considerable local historic interest highlighted by impressive restoration and creative planting. Adjacent to St Mark's churchyard, worth seeing together. Heritage, history and horticulture, a fascinating package. Plant sale and teas. Green Flag Award.

GROUP OPENING

4 AMPORT & MONXTON GARDENS

Amport and Monxton, SP11 8AY. *3m SW of Andover. Turn off the A303 signed East Cholderton from the E or Thruxton village from the W. Follow signs to Amport. Car parking in a field next to Amport village green. Please drive between the two villages.* **Sun 26, Mon 27 May (2-5.30). Combined adm £6, chd free. Cream teas at village hall, Monxton.**

BRIDGE COTTAGE
John & Jenny Van de Pette.

FLEUR DE LYS
Ian & Jane Morrison.

THE WHITE COTTAGE
Mrs Angela Reckitt.

WHITE GABLES
David & Coral Eaglesham.

Monxton and Amport are two pretty villages linked by Pill Hill Brook. Visitors have four gardens to enjoy. Bridge Cottage a 2 acre haven for wildlife, with the banks of the trout stream and lake planted informally with drifts of colour, a large vegetable garden, fruit cage, small mixed orchard and arboretum with specimen trees. Fleur de Lys garden is a series of rooms with glorious herbaceous borders, leading to a large orchard. The White Cottage has a tiered garden which has recently been completely redesigned. White Gables a cottage style garden with a collection of trees, along with old roses and herbaceous plants. Amport has a lovely village green, come early and bring a picnic to enjoy the views of the thatched cottages, before the gardens open. No wheelchair access to White Gables.

5 ◆ APPLE COURT GARDEN & NURSERY

Hordle Lane, Hordle, Lymington, SO41 0HU. Mrs Emma Taylor, 07971 882317, applecourtgarden@icloud.com, www.applecourtgarden.co.uk. *4m W of Lymington. From A337 between Lymington & New Milton, follow the brown signs by turning into Hordle Lane, opp the Royal Oak at Downton Xrds.* **For NGS: Tue 10, Tue 24 Sept (10-4). Adm £5, chd free. Home-made teas.** For other opening times and information, please phone, email or visit garden website.

1 acre, exuberantly planted, sheltered walled garden, designed and planted by world-renowned horticulturists, as a series of garden rooms to provide interest throughout the seasons. Theatrical white garden, ornamental grasses, new and established subtropical borders, and many unusual specimens. Display garden of 200 varieties of daylilies and Japanese style garden with koi pond. Well stocked nursery with interesting varieties. The garden is mostly flat. WC is not accessible to wheelchair users.

6 APPLETREE HOUSE

Station Road, Soberton, SO32 3QU. Mrs J Dover, 01489 877333, jennie.dover@yahoo.co.uk. *10m N of Fareham. A32 to Droxford, at Xrds turn onto B2150. Turn R under bridge into Station Rd, follow road for 1m to garden. Roadside parking or in lay-by 300yds away.* **Visits by arrangement July & Aug.**

Designed to look larger than its 40ft x 90ft, this garden has both a shady woodland style area and also sunny areas allowing a variety of planting. Winding paths lead to different views across the garden and of the meadows beyond. Lots of ideas for the smaller garden. Large collection of over 90 clematis, mainly viticella hybrids.

7 NEW APPLEYARDS

Bowerwood Road, Fordingbridge, SP6 3BP. Mr & Mrs Bob & Jean Carr, 01425 657631, bob.carr.rtd@gmail.com. *Take Aderholt road (B3078) out of Fordingbridge centre, go past church & houses. Appleyards is 200 metres on L, just as road begins to narrow & climb slightly. Parking for 8 cars max.* **Visits by arrangement 11 Apr to 28 Apr (Thur to Sun, 1pm-5pm only). Pre-booking essential. Adm £3.50, chd free. Home-made teas.**

2 acre garden newly restored. Sloping and south facing looking over pasture. 100+ trees, sloping lawns, paths though wooded sections with massed daffodils and bluebells in spring, herbaceous beds, two rose beds, shrubberies, two wildlife ponds, orchard, sloping rockery beds, soft fruit cages, greenhouse. Large patio looking down over garden for home-made teas. Coaches welcome (drop-off & pick-up only).

8 ASHE PARK

nr Ashe, Overton, RG25 3AF. Graham & Laura Hazell. *2m E of Overton. Entrance on B3400, approx 500yds W of Deane.* **Mon 6 May (2-5). Adm £5, chd free. Home-made teas.**

An extensive developing garden within the grounds of a Georgian country house and estate, now becoming more established with further initiatives in progress. Parkland and specimen trees, mature lime avenue, woodland and bluebell walks, wild flower areas, a large contemporary potager, and a series of land sculpted features.

9 19 BARNWOOD ROAD

Fareham, PO15 5LA. Jill & Michael Hill, 01329 842156, jillhillflowers@icloud.com. *M27 J9, A27 towards Fareham. At top of Titchfield Hill, L at T-lights, 4th R Blackbrook Rd, 4th R Meadow Bank. Barnwood Rd is off Meadow Bank. Please consider neighbours when parking.* **Sun 30 June (11.30-4.30). Adm £3.50, chd free. Home-made teas.** Visits also by arrangement May to July for groups of 10 to 30.

Step through the gate to an enchanting garden designed for peace with an abundance of floral colour and delightful features. Greek style courtyard leads to natural pond with bridge and bog garden, complemented by a thatched summerhouse and jetty, designed and built by owners. Secret pathways and hexagonal greenhouse.

10 BEECHENWOOD FARM

Hillside, Odiham, Hook, RG29 1JA. Mr & Mrs M Heber-Percy, 01256 702300, beechenwood@totalise.co.uk. *5m SE of Hook. Turn S into King St from Odiham High St. Turn L after cricket ground for Hillside. Take 2nd R after 1½m, modern house ½m.* **Every Wed 27 Mar to 5 June (2-5). Adm £4, chd free. Home-made teas.** Visits also by arrangement Mar to May. Access lane not suitable for coaches.

2 acre garden in many parts. Lawn meandering through woodland with drifts of spring bulbs. Rose pergola with steps, pots with spring bulbs and later aeoniums. Fritillary and cowslip meadow. Walled herb garden with pool and exuberant planting. Orchard incl white garden and hot border. Greenhouse and vegetable garden. Rock garden extending to grasses, ferns and bamboos. Shady walk to belvedere. 8 acre copse of native species with grassed rides. Assistance available with gravel drive and some avoidable shallow steps.

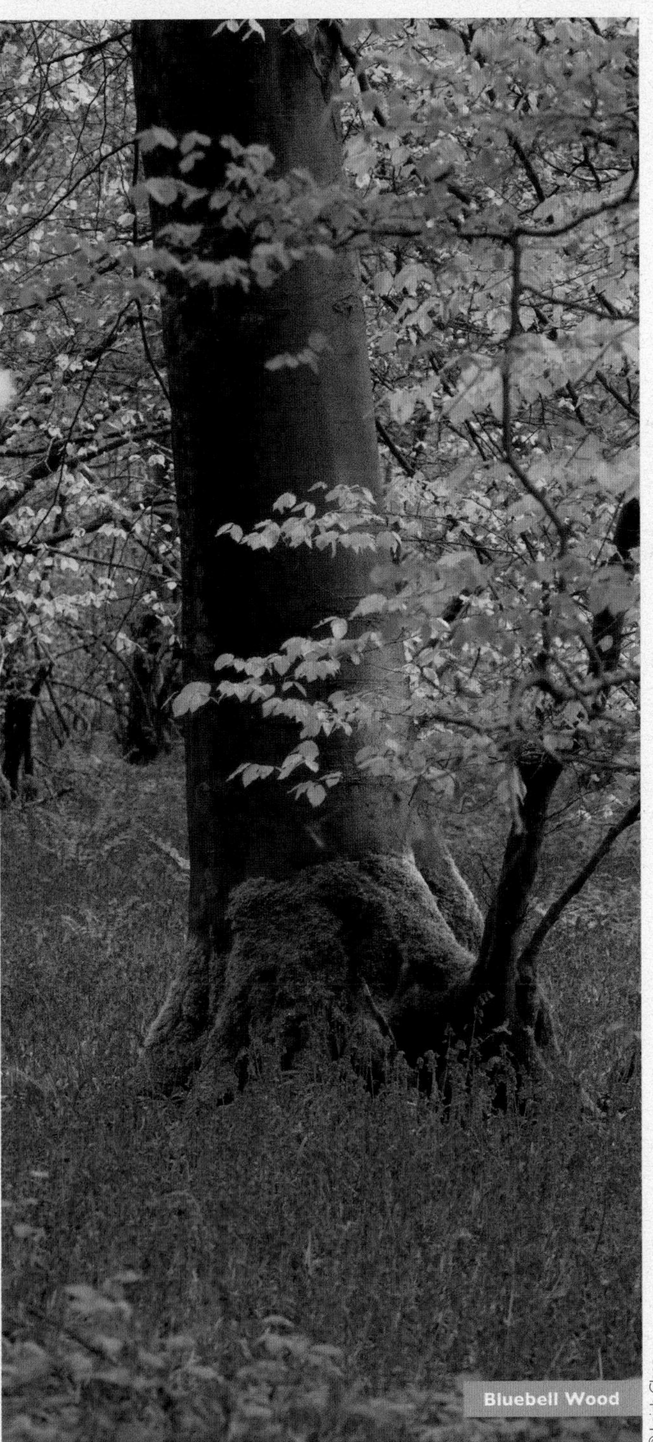

Bluebell Wood

© Leigh Clapp

11 BERE MILL

London Road, Whitchurch, RG28 7NH. Rupert & Elizabeth Nabarro, 01256 892210, rupertnab@gmail.com. *9m E of Andover, 12m N of Winchester. In centre of Whitchurch, take London Rd at r'about. Uphill 1m, turn R 50yds beyond The Gables on R. Drop-off point for disabled at garden.* **Sun 31 Mar, Sun 26 May, Sun 15 Sept (1.30-5). Adm £5, chd free. Home-made teas.** Visits also by arrangement Feb to Oct for groups of 10+. Donation to Smile Train.

On the Upper Test with water meadows and wooded valleys, this garden offers herbaceous borders, bog and Mediterranean plants, as well as a replanted orchard and two small arboretums. Features incl early bulbs, species tulips, Japanese prunus, peonies, wisteria, irises, roses, and semi-tropical planting. At heart it aims to complement the natural beauty of the site, and to incorporate elements of oriental garden design and practice. The working mill was where Portals first made paper for the Bank of England in 1716. Unfenced and unguarded rivers and streams. Wheelchair access unless very wet.

12 BERRY COTTAGE

Church Road, Upper Farringdon, Alton, GU34 3EG. Mrs P Watts, 01420 588318. *3m S of Alton off A32. Turn L at Xrds, 1st L into Church Rd. Follow road past Massey's Folly, 2nd house on R, opp church.* **Suns 12 May; 30 June; 21 July; 18 Aug; 1 Sept (2-5). Combined adm with The Thatched Cottage £8, chd free. Home-made teas.** Visits also by arrangement May to Sept for groups of 10+.

Small organic cottage garden with yr-round interest, designed and maintained by owner, surrounding C16 house (not open). Spring bulbs, roses, clematis and herbaceous borders. The borders are colour themed and contain many unusual plants. Pond, bog garden and shrubbery. Close to Massey's Folly built by the Victorian rector incl 80ft tower with unique handmade floral bricks, C11 church and some of the oldest yew trees in the county. Partial wheelchair access.

13 8 BIRDWOOD GROVE

Downend, Fareham, PO16 8AF. Jayne & Eddie McBride, 01329 280838, jayne.mcbride@ntlworld.com. *M27 J11, L lane slip to Delme r'about, L on A27 to Portchester over 2 T-lights, completely around small r'about, Birdwood Grove 1st L.* **Sat 20 July (1-5). Adm £3, chd free. Home-made teas.** Visits also by arrangement July & Aug for groups of up to 20.

The subtropics in Fareham! This small garden is influenced by the flora of Australia and New Zealand and incl many indigenous species and plants that are widely grown 'down under'. The 4 climate zones; arid, temperate, lush fertile and a shady fernery, are all densely planted to make the most of dramatic foliage, from huge bananas to towering cordylines. Fareham in Bloom gold award Small Plantsman's Back Garden and Best In Category for the 6th year running! Short gravel path not suitable for mobility scooters.

14 BISTERNE MANOR

Bisterne, Ringwood, BH24 3BN. Mr & Mrs Hallam Mills. *2½m S of Ringwood on B3347 Christchurch Rd, 500yds past church on L. Entrance signed Stable Family Home Trust on L (blue sign), just past lodge. Disabled parking signed near the house.* **Thur 23, Thur 30 May (2-5). Adm £5, chd free. Home-made teas.**

Glorious rhododendrons and azaleas form a backdrop for our C19 garden, first opened in the 1930s for the fledgling NGS. The C16 manor house (not open) overlooks a grand parterre with urns, box and yew hedges. Rare tree specimens grace fine lawns and wild flower planting, leading to a boundary woodland walk with glimpses of surrounding pastures. There is a small kitchen garden. Wheelchair access to a level garden with wide gravel paths.

15 BLEAK HILL NURSERY & GARDEN

Braemoor, Bleak Hill, Harbridge, Ringwood, BH24 3PX. Tracy & John Netherway. *2½m S of Fordingbridge. Turn off A338 at Ibsley. Go through Harbridge village to T-junction at top of hill, turn R for ¼m.* **Sun 7, Sun 21 July, Sun 4 Aug (2-5). Adm £4, chd free. Home-made teas.**

Through the moongate and concealed from view are billowing borders contrasting against a seaside scene, with painted beach huts and a boat on the gravel. Herbaceous borders fill the garden with colour wrapping around a pond and small stream. Greenhouses with cacti and sarracenias. Vegetable patch and bantam chickens. Small adjacent nursery.

16 BLUEBELL WOOD

Stancombe Lane, Bavins, New Odiham Road, Alton, GU34 5SX. Mrs Jennifer Ospici, www.bavins.co.uk. *On the corner of Stancombe Lane & the B3349 2½m N of Alton.* **Fri 3, Sat 4 May (11-4). Adm £5, chd free. Light refreshments.**

Unique 100 acre ancient bluebell woodland. If you are a keen walker you will have much to explore on the long meandering paths and rides dotted with secluded seats. Those who enjoy a more leisurely pace will experience the perfume of the carpet of blue, listen to the birdsong and watch the contrasting light through the trees nearer to the entrance of the woods. Refreshments will be served in an original rustic wooden building and incl soups using natural woodland ingredients. No wheelchair access.

17 BRAMDEAN HOUSE

Bramdean, Alresford, SO24 0JU. Mr & Mrs E Wakefield, office@bramdeanhouse.com. *4m S of Alresford. In centre of village on A272. Entrance opp sign to the church. On open days, please park over the road.* **Suns 10 Feb; 14 Apr; 9 June; 14 July; 11 Aug; 8 Sept (2-4). Adm £5, chd free. Home-made teas.** Visits also by arrangement Mar to Sept for groups of 5+.

Beautiful 5 acre garden best known for its mirror image herbaceous borders. Also carpets of spring bulbs, especially snowdrops and a large and unusual collection of plants and shrubs giving yr-round interest. 1 acre walled garden featuring prize-winning vegetables, fruit and flowers. Small arboretum. Many hardy Nerine cultivars, post recent trial in association with RHS. Features incl a wild flower meadow, boxwood castle, a large collection of old fashioned sweet peas. Home of the nation's tallest sunflower 'Giraffe'. Flowering cherries recently imported from Japan.

18 6 BREAMORE CLOSE

Boyatt Wood, Eastleigh, SO50 4QB. Mr & Mrs R Trenchard, 02380 611230, dawndavina6@yahoo.co.uk. *1m N of Eastleigh. M3 J12, follow signs to Eastleigh. Turn R at r'about into Woodside Ave, then 1st L into Broadlands Ave (park here). Breamore Close 3rd on L.* **Visits by arrangement May & June for groups of 10+. Adm £4, chd free. Home-made teas.**

Delightful plant lover's garden with coloured foliage and unusual plants, giving a tapestry effect of texture and colour. Many hostas displayed in pots and in May a wonderful wisteria scrambles over a pergola. The garden is laid out in distinctive planting themes with seating areas to sit and contemplate. In June many clematis scramble through roses and there are many varieties of phlox. Small gravel areas.

19 BRICK KILN COTTAGE

The Avenue, Herriard, Nr Alton, RG25 2PR. Barbara Jeremiah, 01256 381301, barbara@klca.co.uk. *4m NE of Alton. A339 Basingstoke to Alton, 7m out of Basingstoke turn L along The Avenue, past Lasham Gliding Club on R, then past Back Lane on L & take next track on L, one field later.* **Sun 12 May (12-4). Adm £4.50, chd free. Home-made teas.** Visits also by arrangement Apr & May.

Bluebell woodland garden with 2 acres incl treehouse, pebble garden, billabong, stumpery, ferny hollow, shepherd's hut and a traditional cottage garden filled with herbs. The garden is maintained using eco-friendly methods as a haven for wild animals, butterflies, birds and bees and English bluebells. Wildlife friendly garden in a former brick works. New bug hotel with redesigned waterpool. Excellent cream teas, home-made cakes, sandwiches and endless pots of tea. Wheelchair access to some parts of the garden.

20 BROADHATCH HOUSE

Bentley, Farnham, GU10 5JJ. Bruce & Lizzie Powell, 01420 23185, lizzie.powell@btconnect.com. *4m NE of Alton. Turn off A31 (Bentley bypass) through village, then L up School Lane. R to Perrylands, after 300yds drive on R.* **Sun 9 June (2-6). Adm £5, chd free. Home-made teas.** Visits also by arrangement May to July.

Re-opening after 12 yrs absence from NGS. 3½ acre garden set in lovely Hampshire countryside with views to Alice Holt. Divided into different areas by yew hedges and walled garden. Focussing on as long a season as possible on heavy clay. Two reflective pools help break up lawn areas; lots of flower beds. Working greenhouses and vegetable garden. Gravel paths in some areas.

21 NEW 15 BRUCE CLOSE

Fareham, PO16 7QJ. Teresa & John Greenwood. *M27 W leave J10. Under M27 bridge RH-lane, do a u-turn. At r'about 3rd exit, across T- lights. 1st R Miller Drive, 2nd R Somervell Drive. 1st R Bruce Close. Limited parking in road. Free parking at Fareham Leisure Centre (5 mins walk).* **Sat 6, Sun 7, Sat 13, Sun 14 July (11-5). Adm £3.50, chd free. Home-made teas.**

Step into a garden 88ft x 42ft with a number of secluded areas with their own character including a Mediterranean garden, decking with raised beds and a seating area with a living wall. An arched folly leads to a fireplace and summerhouse. There are a wide range of colourful plants, hanging baskets annuals and a lower patio with planted gazebo. It is ideal for entertaining and is low maintenance. Fareham in Bloom, 4 gold awards: large floral front garden (3rd year running) and overall winner, large floral back garden, floral display front garden and container and hanging basket.

22 NEW BUMPERS

Sutton Common, Long Sutton, Hook, RG29 1SJ. Stella Wildsmith. *From village of Long Sutton, turn up Copse Lane, immed opp duck pond. Follow lane for 1½m to top of steep hill, house on L.* **Sun 7 July (2-6). Adm £5, chd free. Tea.**

Large country garden with beautiful views spread over 2 acres, mixed herbaceous and shrub borders, and laid out in a series of individual areas. Some interesting sculptures and water features, with informal paths through the grounds and a number of places to sit and enjoy the views.

23 ◆ CHAWTON HOUSE

Chawton, Alton, GU34 1SJ. Andrew Bentley, 01420 595903, andrew.bentley@chawtonhouse.org, www.chawtonhouse.org. *2m S of Alton. Take the road opp Jane Austen's House museum towards St. Nicholas church. Property is at the end of this road on the L.* **For NGS: Sun 24 Feb (11-4). Adm £5, chd free. Light refreshments.** For other opening times and information, please phone, email or visit garden website.

Snowdrops are scattered through this 14 acre listed English landscape garden which is being restored. Sweeping lawns, ha-ha, wilderness, terraces, fernery and shrubbery walk surround the Elizabethan manor house. The walled garden designed by Edward Knight now includes rose garden, cutting beds, orchard and 'Elizabeth Blackwell' herb garden based on her book 'A Curious Herbal' of 1737-39. Refreshments are available in our tea room, in the old kitchen, serving hot and cold drinks, a selection of cakes and light lunches. Due to slopes and gravel paths, we regret this garden is not suitable for wheelchairs.

Your visits help change lives – since 1927, we've donated £55 million to nursing and caring charities

24 21 CHESTNUT ROAD

Brockenhurst, SO42 7RF. Iain & Mary Hayter, 01590 622009, maryiain.hayter@gmail.com, www.21-chestnut-rdgardens.co.uk. *New Forest, 4m S of Lyndhurst. At Brockenhurst turn R, B3055 Grigg Lane. Limited parking, village car park nearby. Leave M27 J2, follow Heavy Lorry Route. Mainline station less than 10 mins walk.* **Sat 18 May (11-5); Sun 19 May (1-5); Sat 8 June (11-5); Sun 9 June (1-5); Sat 20 July (11-5); Sun 21 July (1-5); Sun 18 Aug (11-5). Adm £4, chd free. Home-made teas & gluten free option.** Visits also by arrangement Apr to Aug for groups of 10+.

Welcome to our wildlife friendly garden where ponds, shrubs, perennials, bulbs, fruit and vegetables all blend to create formal and relaxed areas. Colour and scent combine artistically, all aimed to inspire. Visit the fairies and enjoy homemade refreshments. Statues, arches and creative use of water in the garden.

25 CLOVER FARM

Shalden Lane, Shalden, Alton, GU34 4DU. Tom & Sarah Floyd, 01420 86294. *Approx 3m N of Alton in the village of Shalden. Take A339 out of Alton. After approx 2m turn R up Shalden Lane. At top, turn sharp R next to church sign.* **Sun 7 July (1.30-5); Mon 8 July (2-5). Adm £5, chd free. Tea.** Visits also by arrangement June to Sept for groups of 10+.

3 acre garden with far reaching views. Herbaceous borders and sloping lawns down to reflection pond, wild flower meadow, lime avenue, rose and kitchen garden, and ornamental grass area.

26 COLEMORE HOUSE GARDENS

Colemore, Alton, GU34 3RX. Mr & Mrs Simon de Zoete, 01420 588202, simondezoete@gmail.com. *4m S of Alton (off A32). Approach from N on A32, turn L (Shell Lane), ¼m S of East Tisted. Go under bridge, keep L until you see Colemore Church. Park on verge of church.* **Tue 11, Wed 12 June (2-6). Adm £5, chd free. Home-made teas.** Visits also by arrangement May to Sept.

4 acres in lovely unspoilt countryside, featuring rooms containing many unusual plants and different aspects. A spectacular arched rose walk, water rill, mirror pond, herbaceous and shrub borders and a new woodland walk. Many admire the lawns, new grass gardens and thatched pavilion (built by students from the Prince's Trust). A small arboretum is being planted. Change and development is ongoing, and increasing the diversity of interesting plants is a prime motivation. We propagate and sell plants, many of which can be found in the garden. Some are unusual and not readily available elsewhere.

27 30 COMPTON WAY

Winchester, SO22 4HS. Susan Summers, www.summersgd.co.uk. *2m SW of Winchester. From M3 J11, follow A3090 Badger Farm Rd uphill. Turn L into Oliver's Battery Road South. Take 2nd L into Compton Way. House on R before Austin Ave. Follow directions for parking.* **Sat 13, Sun 14, Tue 16 July (2-5). Adm £4, chd free. Home-made teas.**

Contemporary garden owned by local garden designer on the outskirts of Winchester. Sunny hilltop ¼ acre plot. Themed borders of colourful mixed planting on chalky soil. Kitchen and herb gardens, and semi formal pond. Come and see our National Collection of Francoa. There will be a selection of homegrown vegetable plants, herbs and flowers for sale. Many can be seen growing in the garden.

NPC D

28 CONHOLT PARK

Hungerford Lane, Andover, SP11 9HA. Conholt Park Estate, 07917 796826, conholtgardens@btinternet.com. *7m N of Andover. Turn N off A342 at Weyhill Church, 5m N through Clanville. L at T-junction, Conholt ½m on R, opp Chute Causeway. A343, Hurstbourne Tarrant, turning for Vernham Dean, 3m L signed Conholt.* **Sun 9 June, Sun 7 July (11-5). Adm £6, chd free. Home-made teas.** Visits also by arrangement June & July for groups of 5+.

10 acres of varied garden styles and lawns with mature cedars. Large walled garden recently replanted and established beds. Orchard with wisteria walk. Formal rose garden, rhyl, secret gardens with hostas, geranium and macleaya. Other features incl large laurel maze (good for children) and croquet lawn (play if you like). Visitors welcome to picnic. Free-range chickens and guineafowl. Deep gravel and steps, not suitable for wheelchairs.

29 THE COTTAGE

16 Lakewood Road, Chandler's Ford, Eastleigh, SO53 1ES. Hugh & Barbara Sykes, 02380 254521, barandhugh@aol.com. *Leave M3 J12, follow signs to Chandler's Ford. At King Rufus on Winchester Rd, turn R into Merdon Ave, then 3rd road on L.* **Sun 5, Mon 6, Sun 12, Mon 13 May (2-6). Adm £4, chd free. Home-made teas.** Visits also by arrangement Apr & May.

¾ acre. Azaleas, rhododendrons and over 30 camellias with trilliums and erythroniums under old oaks and pines. Since 1982 we've planted 30 new trees incl P.montezuma. Herbaceous cottage style borders with unusual plants for yr-round interest. Bog garden, ponds, kitchen garden. Bantams, bees and birdsong, with over 30 bird species recorded. Wildlife areas. NGS sundial for opening for 30yrs. Childrens' quiz. 'A lovely tranquil garden', Anne Swithinbank. Hampshire Wildlife Trust Wildlife Garden Award. Honey from our garden hives for sale.

30 61 COTTES WAY

Hill Head, Fareham, PO14 3NL. Norma Matthews & Alan Stamps. *4½m S of Fareham. From Fareham follow signs to Stubbington, then Hill Head. Turn R into Bells Lane, L bend to Crofton Lane, R opp shops into Carisbrooke Ave, L into Cottes Way.* **Sun 30 June, Mon 1 July (11-4). Adm £3, chd free. Light refreshments.**

33ft x 33ft garden, designed by owner in 2015, a fine example of a low maintenance, spacious and relaxing outdoor living room. Colourful with a wide variety of shrubs, perennials and climbers. Interesting art and metal work, water features and patterned natural stone patio. Many pots and containers incl chimney pots and champagne bottles create a blaze of colour. Small vegetable patch. Fareham in Bloom, 2 gold awards, small back and front gardens.

31 CRANBURY PARK

Otterbourne, nr Winchester, SO21 2HL. Mrs Chamberlayne-Macdonald. *3m NW of Eastleigh. Main entrance on old A33 at top of Otterbourne Hill. Entrances also in Hocombe Rd, Chandlers Ford & next to Otterbourne Church.* **Sun 9 June (2-6). Adm £5, chd free. Home-made teas.** Donation to Southampton Hospital Charity.
Extensive pleasure grounds laid out in late C18 and early C19 by Papworth; fountains, rose garden, specimen trees and pinetum, lakeside walk and fern walk. Family carriages and collection of prams will be on view, also photos of King George VI, Eisenhower and Montgomery reviewing Canadian troops at Cranbury before D-Day. Disabled WC. All dogs on leads please.

GROUP OPENING

32 CRAWLEY GARDENS

Crawley, Winchester, SO21 2PR. F J Fratter, 01962 776243, fred@fratter.co.uk. *5m NW of Winchester. Between B3049 (Winchester - Stockbridge) & A272 (Winchester - Andover). Parking throughout village.* **Fri 19, Mon 22 Apr, Thur 4, Sun 7 July (2-5.30). Combined adm £7.50, chd free. Home-made teas in the village hall.**

BAY TREE HOUSE
Julia & Charles Whiteaway.
Open on all dates

LITTLE COURT
Mrs A R Elkington.
Open on Fri 19, Mon 22 Apr
(See separate entry)

PAIGE COTTAGE
Mr & Mrs T W Parker.
Open on all dates

TANGLEFOOT
Mr & Mrs F J Fratter.
Open on Thur 4, Sun 7 July
(See separate entry)

Crawley is an exceptionally pretty period village nestling in chalk downland with thatched houses, C14 church and village pond with ducks. The spring gardens are Bay Tree House, Little Court and Paige Cottage; the summer gardens are Bay Tree House, Paige Cottage and Tanglefoot; providing seasonal interest of varied character, and with traditional and contemporary approaches to landscape and planting. Most of the gardens have beautiful country views and there are other good gardens to be seen from the road. Bay Tree House has bulbs, wild flowers, a Mediterranean garden, pleached limes, a rill and contemporary borders of perennials and grasses. Little Court is a 3 acre traditional English country garden with carpets of spring bulbs and a large meadow. Paige Cottage is a 1 acre traditional English country garden surrounding a period thatched cottage (not open) with bulbs and wildflowers in spring, and old climbing roses in summer. Tanglefoot has colour themed borders, herb wheel, exceptional kitchen garden, traditional Victorian boundary wall supporting trained fruit including apricots; and a large wildflower meadow. Plants from the garden for sale at Little Court and Tanglefoot.

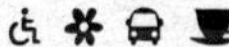

Old Camps

33 CROOKLEY POOL

Blendworth Lane, Horndean, PO8 0AB. Mr & Mrs Simon Privett, 02392 592662, jennyprivett@icloud.com. *5m S of Petersfield. 2m E of Waterlooville, off A3. From Horndean up Blendworth Lane between bakery & hairdresser. Entrance 200yds before church on L with white railings. Parking in field.* **Sun 19 May (2-5). Adm £4, chd free. Home-made teas.** Visits also by arrangement May to Sept.

Here the plants decide where to grow. Californian tree poppies elbow valerian aside to crowd round the pool. Evening primroses obstruct the way to the door and the steps to wisteria shaded terraces. Hellebores bloom under the trees. Salvias, Pandorea jasminoides, Justicia, Pachystachys lutea and passion flowers riot quietly with tomatoes in the greenhouse. Not a garden for the neat or tidy minded, although this is a plantsman's garden full of unusual plants and a lot of tender perennials. Bantams stroll throughout. Oil and watercolour paintings of flowers found in the garden will be on display and for sale in the studio.

Spring Pond

© Leigh Clapp

34 THE DEANE HOUSE

Sparsholt, Winchester, SO21 2LR. Mr & Mrs Richard Morse, 07774 863004, chrissiemorse7@gmail.com. *3½m NW of Winchester. Off A3049 Stockbridge Rd, onto Woodman Lane, signed Sparsholt. Turn L at 1st cottage on L, white with blue gables, at top of drive.* **Visits by arrangement Mar to Sept for groups of 10+. Coffee & cake offered in morning, wine & canapés for evening visits. Adm £10, chd free.**

Flowering cherry trees, statuesque copper beech and tulip trees grace the sweeping lawns at The Deane House (not open), leading the eye to the landscape beyond. This spacious garden entices you to meander from one level to another. The walled garden is best in June when the heady perfume of roses fills the air. Stained glass and modern water features abound. Water sculpture formerly seen at the Chelsea Flower Show. Sorry No Dogs.

35 DIPLEY MILL

Dipley Road, Hartley Wintney, Hook, RG27 8JP. Miss Rose McMonigall, www.dipley-mill.co.uk. *2m NE of Hook. Turn E off B3349 at Mattingley (1½m N of Hook) signed Hartley Wintney, West Green & Dipley. Dipley Mill ½m on L just over bridge.* **Suns 2, 16 June; 14 July; 4 Aug; 1, 29 Sept (2-5.30). Adm £6, chd free. Cream teas.** Donation to St Michael's Hospice.

A romantic adventure awaits as you wander by the meandering streams surrounding this Domesday Book listed mill! Explore many magical areas, such as the rust garden, the pill box grotto and the ornamental courtyard, or just escape into wild meadows. Alpacas. 'One of the most beautiful gardens in Hampshire' according to Alan Titchmarsh in his TV programme Love Your Garden. Featured on BBC TV and other press coverage as a result of a show garden at Hampton Court for Turismo De Galicia and the Spanish Tourist Office. Regret no dogs.

36 THE DOWER HOUSE

Springvale Road, Headbourne Worthy, Winchester, SO23 7LD. Mrs Judith Lywood, 01962 882848, hannahlomax@thedowerhousewinchester.co.uk, www.thedowerhousewinchester.co.uk. *2m N of Winchester. Entrance is directly opp watercress beds in Springvale Rd & near The Good Life Farm Shop. Parking at main entrance to house, following path to garden.* **Sun 9 June (2.30-5.30). Adm £4.50, chd free. Home-made teas.** Visits also by arrangement May to Sept for groups of 10 to 30.

The Dower House is set within 5½ acres of gardens with meandering paths allowing easy access around the grounds. There are plenty of places to sit, relax and enjoy the surroundings. Areas of interest incl a scented border, iris bed, geranium bed, shrubbery, a pond populated with fish and water lilies, bog garden, bluebell wood and secret courtyard garden.

37 DOWN FARM HOUSE

Whitchurch, RG28 7FB. Pat & Steve Jones, 01256 892490, patthehound@gmail.com. *1½m from the centre of Whitchurch. Please do not use SatNav. From the centre of Whitchurch take the Newbury road up the hill, over railway bridge & after approx 1m turn L over the A34, after 300 metres turn L along bridleway.* **Wed 12, Sun 16 June (1.30-5). Adm £5, chd free. Home-made teas.** Visits also by arrangement May to July for groups of 10+. Small minibuses only.

Step back in time in this 2 acre garden, created from an old walled farmyard and the surrounding land. Many of the original features are used as hard landscaping, incl organic vegetables, succulents, alpine bed created from the old concrete capped well, informal and naturalistic planting, wooded area and orchard. The garden has been created slowly over the last 34 yrs. New small stumpery for 2019. Wheelchair access by gravel drive onto lawn.

38 THE DOWN HOUSE

Itchen Abbas, SO21 1AX. Jackie & Mark Porter, 01962 791054, markstephenporter@gmail.com, www.thedownhouse.co.uk. *5m E of Winchester on B3047. 5th house on R after the Itchen Abbas village sign if coming on B3047 from Kings Worthy. 400yds on L after Plough Pub if coming on B3047 from Alresford.* **Sun 10 Feb (1-4). Adm £5, chd free. Home-made teas.** Visits also by arrangement in Feb for groups of 20+. Pre-payment is required for groups.

A 2 acre garden laid out in rooms overlooking the Itchen Valley, adjoining the Pilgrim's Way with walks to the river. In February come and see the snowdrops, winter aconites and crocus, plus borders of coloured dogwoods, willow stems and white birches. A garden of structure with pleached hornbeams, a rope-lined fountain garden and yew lined avenues, plus a pruned vineyard and a warm tea room!

39 DURMAST HOUSE

Bennetts Lane, Burley, BH24 4AT. Mr & Mrs P E G Daubeney, 01425 402132, philip@daubeney.co.uk, www.durmasthouse.co.uk. *5m SE of Ringwood. Off Burley to Lyndhurst Rd, near White Buck Hotel.* **Sun 14 Apr, Sun 23 June (2-5). Adm £4, chd free. Cream teas.** Visits also by arrangement Apr to Sept. Adm incl talk on history of garden, tour & cream teas. Donation to Delhi Commonwealth Women's Association Medical Clinic.

Designed by Gertrude Jekyll, Durmast has contrasting hot and cool colour borders, formal rose garden edged with lavender and a long herbaceous border. Many old trees, Victorian rockery and orchard with beautiful spring bulbs. Rare azaleas; Fama, Princeps and Gloria Mundi from Ghent. Features incl new rose bowers with rare French roses; Eleanor Berkeley, Psyche and Reine Olga Wurtemberg. New Jekyll border with a blue, yellow and white scheme. Many old trees incl Monterey Pine, about 140 yrs old. Many stone paths and some gravel paths.

40 FAIRBANK

Old Odiham Road, Alton, GU34 4BU. Jane & Robin Lees, 01420 86665, j.lees558@btinternet.com. *1½m N of Alton. From S, past Sixth Form College, then 1½m beyond road junction on R. From N, turn L at Golden Pot & then 50yds turn R. Garden 1m on L before road junction.* **Visits by arrangement May to Sept for groups of up to 30. Adm £3.50, chd free. Home-made teas.**

The planting in this large garden reflects our interest in trees, shrubs, fruit and vegetables. A wide variety of herbaceous plants provide colour and are placed in sweeping mixed borders that carry the eye down the long garden to the orchard and beyond. Near the house, there are rose beds and herbaceous borders, as well as a small formal pond. There is a range of acers, ferns and unusual shrubs, with 60 different varieties of fruit, along with a large vegetable garden. Please be aware of uneven ground in some areas.

41 FAIRWEATHER'S NURSERY

Hilltop, Beaulieu, SO42 7YR. Patrick Fairweather, 01590 612113, info@fairweathers.co.uk, www.fairweathers.co.uk. *1½m NE of Beaulieu village. Signed Hilltop Nursery on B3054 between Heath r'about (A326) & Beaulieu village.* **Sat 20, Sun 21 July (9.30-4). Adm £3.50, chd free. Cream teas in Aline Fairweather's garden.**

Fairweather's hold a specialist collection of over 400 Agapanthus grown in pots and display beds, incl AGM award-winning Agapanthus trialled by the RHS. Features incl guided tours of the nursery at 11am, 12.30pm and 2pm, and demonstrations of how to get the best from Agapanthus and companion planting. Agapanthus and a range of other traditional and new perennials for sale. Aline Fairweather's garden (adjacent to the nursery) will also be open, with mixed shrub and perennial borders containing many unusual plants. Also open Patrick's Patch at Fairweather's Garden Centre.

NPC

42 NEW FERNS LODGE

Cottagers Lane, Hordle, Lymington, SO41 0FE. Ms Sue Grant, www.fernslodge.co.uk. *Approx 5½m W of Lymington. From Silver St turn into Woodcock Lane, 100 metres to Cottagers Lane, parking in field ½m on L. From A337 turn into Everton Rd & drive approx 1½m, Cottagers Lane on R.* **Sat 8, Sun 9 June, Sat 24, Sun 25 Aug (2-5). Adm £3.50, chd free. Home-made teas.**

Captivating ½ acre garden! A cacophony of foxglove, camellia, azalea, tulip and lupins. Recently landscaped, brick paths guide you from cottage to summerhouse to gazebo where climbers from honeysuckle to jasmine attack the senses. Venture past the barn with its sedum roof to the 3½ acre Victorian garden in restoration (wellies are a must), with its mighty oaks, rhododendrons and Monterey pines. Visit the new wild flower meadow just planted and be surprised and delighted by what you find there. Short guided walks by Sue, enlightening visitors of the fascinating history of the wild wood! Wheelchair access to some areas.

GROUP OPENING

43 FROYLE GARDENS

Lower Froyle, Froyle, GU34 4LG. www.froyle.com/ngs. *5m NE of Alton. Access to Lower Froyle from A31 between Alton & Farnham at Bentley, or via Upper Froyle at Hen & Chicken Pub, or via B3349 & Golden Pot Pub. Park at recreation ground in Lower Froyle. Map provided.* **Sat 1, Sun 2 June (2-6). Combined adm £7.50, chd free. Home-made teas at Froyle Village Hall.**

ALDERSEY HOUSE
Nigel & Julie Southern.

DAY COTTAGE
Nick & Corinna Whines, www.daycottage.co.uk.

GLEBE COTTAGE
Barbara & Michael Starbuck.

MANOR COTTAGE
Russell Pearn & Victoria Spearing.

WARREN COTTAGE
Gillian & Jonathan Pickering.

WELL LANE CORNER
Mark & Sue Lelliott.

You will certainly receive a warm welcome as six Froyle Gardens open their gates again this year, enabling visitors to enjoy a wide variety of gardens. All the gardens have undergone development since last year and will be looking splendid. Froyle is a beautiful village with many old and interesting buildings. Froyle gardens harmonise well with the surrounding landscape and most have spectacular views. The gardens themselves are diverse with rich planting. You will see greenhouses, water features, vegetables, roses, clematis and wild flower meadows as well as a gem of a courtyard garden. Lots of ideas to take away with you, along with plants for sale. The delicious teas served in the village hall are famous, and close by there is a children's playground with a zip wire and climbing frame where younger visitors can let off steam. The main parking area is at the recreation ground, close to the village hall in Lower Froyle. Additional signed parking is available in Upper Froyle. In conjunction with Froyle Open Gardens there is an exhibition of richly decorated historic vestments to be held in St Mary's Church, Upper Froyle GU34 4LB (separate donation). Parking by the church. No wheelchair access to Glebe Cottage and Manor Cottage. Gravel area at Warren Cottage and Day Cottage with disabled access on request.

44 GILBERTS DAHLIA FIELD

Gilberts Nursery, Dandysford Lane, Sherfield English, nr Romsey, SO51 6DT. Nick & Helen Gilbert, www.gilbertsdahlias.co.uk. *Midway between Romsey & Whiteparish on A27, in Sherfield English Village. From Romsey 4th turn on L, just before small petrol station on R, visible from main road.* **Sun 25 Aug (10-4). Adm £3, chd free. Light refreshments.**

This may not be a garden but do come and be amazed by the sight of over 300 varieties of dahlias in our dedicated 1½ acre field. Prize-winning blooms are in all colours, shapes and sizes and can be closely inspected from wheelchair friendly hard grass paths. An inspiration for all gardeners.

45 HAMBLEDON HOUSE

East Street, Hambledon, PO7 4RX. Capt & Mrs David Hart Dyke, 02392 632380, dianahartdyke@talktalk.net. *8m SW of Petersfield, 5m NW of Waterlooville. In village centre, driveway leading to house in East St. Do not go up Speltham Hill even if advised by SatNav.* **Visits by arrangement Apr to Oct for groups of 5 to 30. Refreshments by prior request. Adm £5, chd free.**

3 acre partly walled plantsman's garden for all seasons. Large borders filled with a wide variety of unusual shrubs and perennials with imaginative plant combinations culminating in a profusion of colour in late summer. Hidden, secluded areas reveal surprise views of garden and village rooftops. Planting a large central area, which started in 2011, has given the garden an exciting new dimension. Partial wheelchair access as garden is on several levels.

46 HANGING HOSTA GARDEN

Narra, Frensham Lane, Lindford, Bordon, GU35 0QJ. June Colley & John Baker, 01420 489186, hanginghostas@btinternet.com. *Approx 1m E of Bordon. From the A325 at Bordon take the B3002, then B3004 to Lindford. Turn L into Frensham Lane, 3rd house on L.* **Visits by arrangement Mon 1 to Fri 5 July only for groups of up to 20. Adm £3.50, chd free.**

This garden is packed with almost 2000 plants. The collection of over 1500 hosta cultivars is one of the largest in England. Hostas are displayed at eye level to give a wonderful tapestry of foliage and colour. Islamic garden, waterfall and stream garden, cottage garden. Talks given to garden clubs.

NPC

47 NEW 108 HEATH ROAD

Petersfield, GU31 4EL. Mrs Karen Llewelyn. *A3 N & S take A272 exit (signed Midhurst). Take 1st exit from r'about (A272). 1st R into Pullens Lane (B2199). 6th road on R onto Heath Rd. Parking in lay-by, side of road or car park to Heath Pond 200 metres on L.* **Sun 9 June (2-5). Adm £3.50, chd free. Home-made teas.**

⅔ acre garden close to town centre and Heath Pond. Greenhouse and succulent collection. Tropical plants, acers, small woodland walk. 30 metre long border with shade loving plants including many hostas and ferns. Patio garden, seasonal pots and late summer herbaceous border. Newly planted driveway. Wheelchair access after a 5 metre sloping gravel drive.

48 HILL TOP

Damson Hill, Upper Swanmore, SO32 2QR. David Green, 01489 892653, tricia1960@btinternet.com. *1m NE of Swanmore. Junction of Swanmore Rd & Church Rd, up Hampton Hill, sharp L bend. After 300yds junction with Damson Hill, house on L. Disabled parking by house.* **Visits by arrangement May to Sept for groups of 20+. Adm £4, chd free. Tea.**

2 acres with extensive colourful borders and wide lawns, this garden has stunning views to the Isle of

Wight. The glasshouses produce unusual fruit and vegetables from around the world. The outdoor vegetable plots bulge with well grown produce, much for sale in season. Potted specimen plants and interesting annuals.

49 HINTON ADMIRAL

Lyndhurst Road, Hinton, Christchurch, BH23 7DY. Sir George & Lady Meyrick. *4m NE of Christchurch. On N side of A35, ¾m E of Cat & Fiddle Pub.* **Sun 19 May (1-4.30). Adm £7, chd free.** Donation to Julia's House Childrens Hospice.

Magnificent 20 acre garden within a much larger estate, now being restored and developed. Mature plantings of deciduous azaleas and rhododendrons amidst a sea of bluebells. Wandering paths lead through rockeries and beside ponds, and a stream with many cascades. Orchids appear in the large lawns. The two walled gardens are devoted to herbs and wild flowers, and a very large greenhouse. The terrace and rock garden were designed by Harold Peto. Gravel paths and some steps.

50 THE HOMESTEAD

Northney Road, Hayling Island, PO11 0NF. Stan & Mary Pike, 02392 464888, jhomestead@aol.com, www.homesteadhayling.co.uk. *3m S of Havant. From A27 Havant & Hayling Island r'about, travel S over Langstone Bridge & turn immed L into Northney Rd. Car park entrance on R after Langstone Hotel.* **Sun 11 Aug (2-5.30). Adm £4, chd free. Home-made teas.** Visits also by arrangement June to Sept for groups of 10+.

1¼ acre garden surrounded by working farmland with views to Butser Hill and boats in Chichester Harbour. Trees, shrubs, colourful herbaceous borders and small walled garden with herbs, vegetables and trained fruit trees. Large pond and woodland walk with shade-loving plants. A quiet and peaceful atmosphere with plenty of seats to enjoy the vistas within the garden and beyond. Some gravel paths.

51 ◆ THE HOSPITAL OF ST CROSS

St Cross Road, Winchester, SO23 9SD. The Hospital of St Cross & Almshouse of Noble Poverty, 01962 851375, porter@hospitalofstcross.co.uk, www.hospitalofstcross.co.uk. *½m S of Winchester. From city centre take B3335 (Southgate St & St Cross Rd) S. Turn L immed before The Bell Pub. If on foot follow riverside path S from Cathedral & College, approx 20 mins.* **For NGS: Sun 7 July (2-5). Adm £4, chd free. Home-made teas in the Hundred Men's Hall in the Outer Quadrangle.** For other opening times and information, please phone, email or visit garden website.

The Medieval Hospital of St Cross nestles in water meadows beside the River Itchen and is one of England's oldest almshouses. The tranquil, walled Master's Garden, created in the late C17 by Bishop Compton, now contains colourful herbaceous borders, old fashioned roses, interesting trees and a large fish pond. The Compton Garden has unusual plants of the type he imported when Bishop of London. Wheelchair access, but surfaces are uneven in places.

52 THE HOUSE IN THE WOOD

Beaulieu, SO42 7YN. Victoria Roberts. *New Forest. 8m NE of Lymington. Leaving the entrance to Beaulieu Motor Museum on R (B3056), take next R signed Ipley Cross. Take 2nd gravel drive on RH-bend, approx ½m.* **Sun 12 May (2-5). Adm £5, chd free. Cream teas.**

Peaceful 12 acre woodland garden with continuing progress and improvement. Very much a spring garden with mature azaleas and rhododendrons interspersed with acers and other woodland wonders. A magical garden to get lost in with many twisting paths leading downhill to a pond and with a more formal layout of lawns around the house. Used in the war to train the Special Operations Executive. A wonderful setting for cream teas. Partial wheelchair access.

53 NEW HOW PARK BARN

Kings Somborne, Stockbridge, SO20 6QG. Kate & Chris Cann. *2m from Stockbridge, just outside Kings Somborne. Take A3057 from Stockbridge & just before village of Kings Somborne turn R into Cow Drove Hill, turn L at top of hill at bench, at end of road fork L, where we are situated on the Clarendon Way.* **Thur 16, Sun 19 May (2-5). Adm £5, chd free. Home-made teas.**

2 acre country garden in elevated position with uninterrupted panoramic views over the Test Valley. Set within 12 acres of chalk grassland. Large borders of naturalistic planting and shrubs with some slopes. Sweeping lawns connect different levels of garden interest. A tranquil setting within the landscape of C17 listed barn (not open). Walkers and cyclists welcome from nearby Test Way. Gravel drive and some slopes, but wheelchair access to most of the garden.

54 THE ISLAND

Greatbridge, Romsey, SO51 0HP. Mr & Mrs Christopher Saunders-Davies. *1m N of Romsey on A3057. Entrance alongside Greatbridge (1st bridge Xing the River Test), flanked by row of cottages on roadside.* **Sat 30, Sun 31 Mar, Sat 29, Sun 30 June (2-5). Adm £5, chd free. Home-made teas.**

6 acres either side of the River Test. Fine display of paeonies, wisteria and spring flowering trees. Main garden has herbaceous and annual borders, fruit trees, rose pergola, lavender walk and extensive lawns. An arboretum planted in the 1930s by Sir Harold Hillier contains trees and shrubs providing interest throughout the yr. Please Note: No Dogs Allowed.

55 LAKE HOUSE

Northington, SO24 9TG. Lord Ashburton, 07795 364539, lukeroeder@hotmail.com. *4m N of Alresford. Off B3046. Follow English Heritage signs to The Grange, and then to Lake House.* **Thur 6, Sun 9 June (12.30-5). Adm £5, chd free. Home-made teas.** Visits also by arrangement May to Oct for groups of 10+.

Two large lakes in Candover Valley set off by mature woodland with waterfalls, abundant birdlife, long landscaped vistas and folly. 1½ acre walled garden with rose parterre, mixed borders, long herbaceous border, rose pergola leading to moongate. Flowering pots, conservatory and greenhouses. Picnicking by lakes. Grass paths and slopes to some areas of the garden.

56 LITTLE COURT

Crawley, Winchester, SO21 2PU. Mrs A R Elkington, 01962 776365, elkslc@btinternet.com. *5m NW of Winchester. Between B3049 (Winchester - Stockbridge) & A272 (Winchester - Andover) 400yds from either pond or church.* **Sun 17, Mon 18, Sun 24, Mon 25 Feb, Sun 10 Mar (2-4.30); Sun 19, Mon 20 May, Mon 10 June (2-5.30). Adm £5, chd free. Home-made teas in the village hall. 2020: Sun 16, Mon 17, Sun 23, Mon 24 Feb. Opening with Crawley Gardens on Fri 19, Mon 22 Apr.** Visits also by arrangement Feb to July.

3 acres, dating from C19, aiming to give continuous calm and enjoyment throughout the seasons, from thousands of crocuses in Feb to full herbaceous borders in summer with beautiful colours and contrasting textures. The garden is sheltered and in 7 walled sections. There is a traditional kitchen garden, free range bantams, treehouse, many seats with good views and a south facing wildlife field. Good butterflies in early July.

57 NEW LITTLE CROFT

Church Grove, Fleet, GU51 4LA. Graham & Pauline Bowyer, graham.bowyer@me.com. *Less than ½m from Fleet town centre. When entering Fleet from M3 J4A, turn R into Church Rd. Where the road bends to the L, turn L into Church Grove. Little Croft is the 2nd house on the L.* **Visits by arrangement in May for groups of 10 to 30. Adm £4, chd free. Home-made teas on request.**

A garden with features inspired by Japanese garden design principles. There are 3 main Japanese style features; a pond and stream garden, a tea garden with stepping stone pathway leading to an arbour and a dry stone garden.

58 LITTLE OWLS

27 Russell Road, Lee-on-the-Solent, PO13 9HR. Kerry & Neil Littleales, 07727 657246, kerrylittleales@outlook.com. *4½m S of Fareham. From Fareham on B3385 follow signs for Lee-on-the-Solent. Continue S past The Bun Penny Pub on L. Turn L after pub into Grove Rd & L again into Russell Rd.* **Sun 16, Sun 30 June, Sun 14 July (11-4). Adm £3, chd free. Home-made teas.** Visits also by arrangement June to Aug for groups of 10 to 30. Weekdays & evenings only. Art groups welcome.

A suburban 40ft x 40ft plot championing the small garden. A variety of shrubs and perennials for shade and sun in a colourful and exuberant style, attracting bees and butterflies, a pond full of newts with hovering damsel flies, a sedum green roof with solitary bee house and a bonsai collection. There are quirky recycled pieces created by the owners and a small craft studio open for viewing and sales. NGS quilt on display.

59 LONGSTOCK PARK

Leckford, Stockbridge, SO20 6EH. Leckford Estate Ltd, part of John Lewis Partnership, www.longstockpark.co.uk. *4m S of Andover. From Leckford village on A3057 towards Andover, cross the river bridge & take 1st turning to the L signed Longstock.* **Sun 16 June (1-4). Adm £6, chd £2. Light refreshments.**

Famous water garden with extensive collection of aquatic and bog plants set in 7 acres of woodland with rhododendrons and azaleas. A walk through the park leads to National Collections of *Buddleja* and *Clematis viticella*; arboretum and herbaceous border. Light refreshments at Leckford Farm Shop, at Longstock Nurseries (last orders at 3.45pm). Assistance dogs only.

60 LOWER BAYBRIDGE HOUSE

Lower Baybridge Lane, Owslebury, Winchester, SO21 1JN. Sophie & Jon Adams. *5m S of Winchester. Take the Morestead Rd out of Winchester, turn R at Xrds towards Owslebury, 1st L after the cricket pitch into Baybridge Lane & take next R. Parking in field opp. Disabled drop off at house.* **Sat 8 June (1-5). Adm £3.50, chd free. Home-made teas.**

A garden on chalk designed and planted by the owner. Features incl a sunken lawn bordered by classical flower border, a hummocky shaded evergreen border and a hillock meadow. A lavender walk leads to a kitchen garden enclosed by espalier fruit trees. Also open grassland with mown pathways and a wilderness area for bees. Warm sheltered walls for climbers, a choice of areas to sit and enjoy.

61 26 LOWER NEWPORT ROAD

Aldershot, GU12 4QD. Mr & Mrs P Myles. *From the A331 coming off at the Aldershot junction, head towards Aldershot. Take the 1st R turn, opp the Fiat Showroom into North Lane & then 1st L into Lower Newport Rd.* **Sat 29, Sun 30 June (11-4). Adm £3, chd free. Light refreshments.**

A 'T' shaped small town garden full of ideas, split into four distinct sections; a semi-enclosed patio area with pots and water feature; a free-form lawn with a tree fern, perennials, bulbs and shrubs; secret garden with a 20ft x 6ft raised pond, exotic planting backdrop and African carvings; and a potager garden with a selection of vegetable, roses and plant storage. We also have over 89 named varieties of hosta.

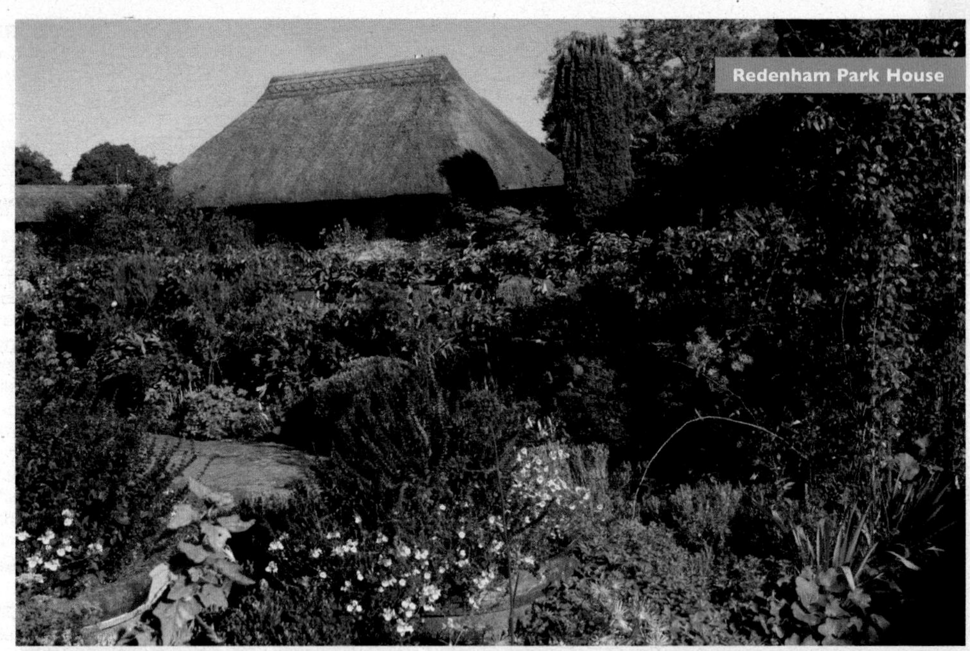

Redenham Park House

© Leigh Clapp

62 ◆ MACPENNYS WOODLAND GARDEN & NURSERIES

Burley Road, Bransgore, Christchurch, BH23 8DB. Mr & Mrs T M Lowndes, 01425 672348, office@macpennys.co.uk, www.macpennys.co.uk. *6m S of Ringwood, 5m NE of Christchurch. From Crown Pub Xrds in Bransgore take Burley Rd, following sign for Thorney Hill & Burley. Entrance ¼m on R.* **For opening times and information, please phone, email or visit garden website.**

4 acre woodland garden originating from worked out gravel pits in the 1950s, offering interest yr-round, but particularly in spring and autumn. Attached to a large nursery that offers for sale a wide selection of home-grown trees, shrubs, conifers, perennials, hedging plants, fruit trees and bushes. Tearoom offering home-made cakes, afternoon tea (pre-booking required), and light lunches using locally sourced produce wherever possible. Nursery closed Christmas through to the New Year. Partial wheelchair access.

63 NEW MARL HOUSE

Burley Street, Burley, Ringwood, BH24 4DD. Mr Richard Rowney & Mrs Helen Wilson-Rowney. *From the A31 at Picket Post follow the Burley turn off. Continue on the Ringwood Rd towards Burley for approx 2m travelling through Burley St. Follow the yellow signs. Marl House is positioned on the RH-side, directly opp Longmead Rd.* **Sun 9, Sun 16 June (1-5). Adm £5, chd free. Home-made teas.**

National award-winning garden designed by Sarah Eberle covers 11 acres in the New Forest. A formal area surrounds the house with traditional planting of roses, a pergola, fountains and some contemporary surprises. Herbaceous borders with perennials and ornamental grasses lead the visitor to a natural lake and a path through the woods. There is much to explore in this magical garden before enjoying a welcome cup of tea. Wheelchair access to most of the gardens, however uneven surfaces in some areas.

64 MEON ORCHARD

Kingsmead, North of Wickham, PO17 5AU. Doug & Linda Smith, 01329 833253, meonorchard@btinternet.com. *5m N of Fareham. From Wickham take A32 N for 1½m. Turn L at Roebuck Inn. Garden in ½m. Park on verge or in field N of property.* **Sun 26 May, Sun 28 July, Sun 1 Sept (2-6). Adm £5, chd free. Home-made teas.**

1½ acre garden designed and constructed by current owners. An exceptional range of rare, unusual and architectural plants incl National Collection of Eucalyptus. Dramatic foliage plants from around the world, see plants you have never seen before! Flowering shrubs in May and June; perennials in July; bananas, tree ferns, cannas, gingers, palms dominate in Sept; and streams and ponds, plus an extensive range of planters complete the display. Visitors are welcome to explore the 20 acre meadow and ½m of Meon River frontage attached to the garden. Extra big plant sale of the exotic and rare on Sun 1 Sept. Garden fully accessible by wheelchair, reserved parking.

NPC

72 OLD CAMPS

Newbury Road, Headley, Thatcham, RG19 8LG. Mr & Mrs Adam & Heidi Vetere, 07720 449702, gardens@oldcamps.co.uk, www.oldcamps.co.uk. *Turn off the A339 into Galley Lane & after 100yds turn R into Plumtrees Farm. Follow the concrete road to the car park (signed). Walk 400yds to garden.* **Sat 3, Sun 4 Aug (10-5). Adm £6.50, chd free. Home-made teas. BBQ cooked burgers are served from 11-2 (weather permitting).** Visits also by arrangement June to Sept for groups of 20+.

As featured on Gardeners' World, a breathtaking garden set over an acre, which benefits from panoramic views of Watership Down. Surprises await, ranging from traditional herbaceous borders through desert/prairie planting, an enchanted knot garden, potager to exuberant subtropical schemes; featuring bananas, cannas, hedychiums and more. Enjoy teas surrounded by Brugmansia, Figs and Citrus. The garden is built on the site of a Roman Camp and Bath House. Partial wheelchair access. Non-disabled WC, though there is enough room for a wheelchair.

73 THE OLD RECTORY

East Woodhay, Newbury, RG20 0AL. David & Victoria Wormsley, 07801 418976. *6m SW of Newbury. Turn off A343 between Newbury & Highclere to Woolton Hill. Turn L to East End, continue ¾m beyond East End. Turn R, garden opp St Martin's Church.* **Visits by arrangement May to Sept for groups of 20+. Adm £10. Home-made teas.**

A classic English country garden of about 2 acres surrounding a Regency former rectory (not open). Formal lawns and terrace provide tranquil views over parkland. A large walled garden with grass paths, full of interesting herbaceous plants including topiary, roses and unusual perennials. A Mediterranean pool garden, wildflower meadow and fruit garden. Explore and enjoy. Gravel drive and some steps.

74 OLD SWAN HOUSE

High Street, Stockbridge, SO20 6EU. Mr Herry Lawford. *9m W of Winchester. The garden is accessed from Recreation Ground Lane which runs off the eastern end of the High St, next to the Framing Shop.* **Every Tue 2 July to 23 July (2-5). Adm £4, chd free. Lemonade & biscuits included. Opening with Stockbridge Gardens on Thur 13, Sun 16 June.**

This town garden is designed around seven areas defined by the sun at different times of the day. Planting is modern perennial with euphorbias, rosemary and box used extensively. Surprise is provided by a grass and gravel garden and a small wildflower meadow. There is an ancient hazel against a brick and flint wall, a loggia hung with creeper, an orchard and a pond.

GROUP OPENING

75 OLD THATCH & THE MILLENNIUM BARN

Sprats Hatch Lane, Winchfield, Hook, RG27 8DD. *3m W of Fleet. 1½m E of Winchfield Station, follow NGS signs. Sprats Hatch Lane is opp the Barley Mow Pub. Public canal car park at Barley Mow slipway is ½m from garden. Parking available in adjacent field to Old Thatch, if dry. Parking info will be displayed.* **Sun 7 Apr, Sun 16 June, Sun 1 Sept (2-6). Combined adm £4, chd free. Home-made teas. Pimms if hot & mulled wine if cool.**

THE MILLENNIUM BARN
Mr & Mrs G Carter.

OLD THATCH
Jill Ede, www.old-thatch.co.uk.

Who could resist visiting Old Thatch, a chocolate box thatched cottage, featured on film and TV, a smallholding with a 5 acre garden and woodland alongside the Basingstoke Canal (unfenced). A succession of spring bulbs, a profusion of wild flowers, perennials and homegrown annuals pollinated by our own bees and fertilised by the donkeys, who await your visit. Over 30 named clematis and rose cultivars. Sometimes lambs in April and donkey foals in summer. Children enjoy our garden quiz, adults enjoy tea and home-made cakes. Arrive by narrow boat! Trips on 'John Pinkerton' may stop at Old Thatch on NGS days www.basingstoke-canal.org.uk. Also Accessible Boating shuttle available from Barley Mow wharf, approx every 45 mins. Parking for Blue badge holders: please use entrance by the red telephone box. Paved paths and grass slopes give access to the whole garden.

76 ◆ PATRICK'S PATCH

Fairweather's Garden Centre, High Street, Beaulieu, SO42 7YB. Patrick Fairweather, 01590 612307, info@fairweathers.co.uk, www.fairweathers.co.uk. *SE of New Forest at head of Beaulieu River. Leave M27 at J2 & follow signs for Beaulieu Motor Museum. Go up High St & park in Fairweather's on LH-side.* **For opening times and information, please phone, email or visit garden website.**

Model kitchen garden with a full range of vegetables, trained top and soft fruit and herbs. Salads in succession used as an educational project for all ages. Maintained by volunteers, primary school children and a part-time head gardener. Open daily by donation from dawn to dusk. Gravelled site.

77 PYLEWELL PARK

South Baddesley, Lymington, SO41 5SJ. Lord Teynham. *Coast road 2m E of Lymington. From Lymington follow signs for Car Ferry to Isle of Wight, continue for 2m to South Baddesley.* **Sun 21 Apr, Sun 26 May (2-5). Adm £4, chd free.**

A large parkland garden laid out in 1890. Enjoy a walk along the extensive informal grass and moss paths, bordered by fine rhododendrons, magnolias, embothriums and cornus. Wild daffodils in bloom at Easter and bluebells in May. Large lakes are bordered by giant gunnera. Distant views of the Isle of Wight across the Solent. Lovely for families and dogs. Bring your own tea or picnic and wellingtons! Old glasshouses and other out buildings are not open to visitors. Wear suitable footwear for muddy areas.

Fairbank

78 REDENHAM PARK HOUSE

Redenham Park, Andover, SP11 9AQ. Lady Olivia Clark, 01264 772511, oliviaclark@redenhampark.co.uk. *Approx 1½m from Weyhill on the A342 Andover to Ludgershall road.* **Wed 18, Thur 19 Sept (2.30-4.30). Adm £5.50, chd free. Cream teas in the thatched Pool House.** Visits also by arrangement Sept & Oct for groups of 5 to 30.

Redenham Park built in 1784. The garden sits behind the house (not open). The formal rose garden is planted with white flowered roses. Steps lead up to the main herbaceous borders which peak in late summer. A calm green interlude, a gate opens into gardens with espaliered pears, apples, mass of scented roses, shrubs and perennial planting surrounds the swimming pool. A door opens onto a kitchen garden.

GROUP OPENING

79 ROMSEY GARDENS

Town Centre, Romsey, SO51 8LD. *All gardens are within walking distance of each other & are clearly signed. Use Lortemore Place public car park (SO51 8LD), free on Sundays & BH.* **Sun 26, Mon 27 May, Sun 9 June (10.30-4). Combined adm £6, chd free. Home-made teas (May) & Teas (June) at King John's Garden.**

KING JOHN'S GARDEN
Friends of King John's Garden & Test Valley Borough, www.facebook.com/KingJohnsGarden/.

4 MILL LANE
Miss J Flindall, 01794 513926. **Visits also by arrangement May to Sept for groups of 10+. Combined opening with The Old Thatched Cottage.**

THE NELSON COTTAGE
Margaret Prosser.

OLD THATCHED COTTAGE
Genevieve & Derek Langford.

Romsey is a small, unspoilt, historic market town with the majestic C12 Norman Abbey as a backdrop to 4 Mill Lane, a garden described by Joe Swift as 'the best solution for a long thin garden with a view'. King John's Garden, with its fascinating listed C13 house (not open), has all period plants that were available before 1700; it also has an award-winning Victorian garden with a courtyard (no dogs, please). The Old Thatched Cottage (C15) has a cottage garden with hollyhocks, wisteria and roses; it features a variety of shrubs, vegetable patch, fruit cordons, rockery, water features and gazebo. The Nelson Cottage was formally a pub; the ½ acre garden has a variety of perennial plants and shrubs, with a wild grass meadow bringing the countryside into the town. No wheelchair access at 4 Mill Lane.

80 ROTHERFIELD GREYS

Fernhill Lane, New Milton, BH25 5ST. Dr Peter Clode & Dr David Smith, 07899 895215 / 01425 627679, pclode@gmail.com. *Approx 1m N of New Milton Station. Leave New Milton on B3058, on L just N of Ballard School, before junction of B3055. Disabled parking only on-site.* **Sat 1, Sun 2 June, Sat 27, Sun 28 July (1.30-5); Sat 17, Sun 18 Aug (1.30-4.30). Adm £4, chd free. Home-made teas.** Visits also by arrangement May to Oct for groups of 10 to 30.

1 acre garden featuring vibrant borders of Sanguisorba, salvia, lobelia, dahlia, canna and helenium. Stunning ancient olives trees. Large oak pergola, bog gardens oozing with interest, romantic white garden, hosta and begonia gazebo, gushing water features, wildflower meadow, woodland walk with spotting trail. Come relax, soak up the beauty and enjoy teas in many seating areas. Wheelchair access to most areas. N.B. gravel paths, summerhouse and gazebo accessed by steps only.

81 ROTHERFIELD PARK

East Tisted, Alton, GU34 3QE. Sir James & Lady Scott. *4m S of Alton on A32. Please turn off your SatNav. Entry from A32 only.* **Sun 5 May (2-5). Adm £5, chd free. Home-made teas. Visitors may picnic in the park from noon.**

Take some ancient ingredients: ice house, lime avenue and walled garden. Add fruit, vegetables, trees and topical topiary (will the rabbit eat the carrot?). Set this 12 acre plot in an early C19 park. Mix in a bluebell wood, a willow chapel and Kim Wilkie's take on an amphitheatre. A good day out for all the family. Retail therapy from top local growers including, Marcus Dancer. Wheelchair access to walled garden.

82 NEW SAGES

Sages Lane, Privett, Alton, GU34 3NP. Joanne Edmonds, 07739 680052, sagesprivett@gmail.com. *Turn off A32 opp The Angel Hotel, then Sages is ½m down the road on the L.* **Visits by arrangement Sun 14 July to Sun 4 Aug (pm only) for groups of 10 to 30. Refreshments on request. Adm £5, chd free.**

A charming courtyard garden with a raised pond, pots of lilies and hydrangeas cascading over tiered flint walls, leads you up to the 2½ acre garden. Newly developed, designed and maintained by the owners in a setting of mature trees. Enjoy soft coloured planting, a glasshouse with unusual orchids, a tranquil Japanese style pond and jungle walk.

83 28 ST RONAN'S AVENUE

Southsea, Portsmouth, PO4 0QE. Ian & Liz Craig. *St Ronan's Rd can be found off Albert Rd, Southsea. Follow signs from Albert Rd or Canoe Lake on seafront. Parking in Craneswater School.* **Sun 21 Apr, Sun 26 May (2-6). Adm £3.50, chd free. Home-made teas.**

Town garden 145ft x 25ft, 700 metres from the sea. A mixture of tender, exotic and dry loving plants, along with more traditional incl king protea, bananas, ferns, agaves, echeverias, echium and puya. Wild flower area and wildlife pond. Two different dry gardens showing what can be grown in sandy soil. Recycled items have been used to create sculptures.

84 2 SAMPAN CLOSE

Warsash, Southampton, SO31 9BU. Amanda & Robert Bailey. *4½m W of Fareham. M27 J9 take A27 W, L at Park Gate into Brook Lane by Esso garage. Straight over 3 r'abouts, L at 4th r'about into Schooner Way. Sampan Close, 4th on R. Please park in Schooner Way.* **Sat 11, Sun 12 May (1-4). Adm £3, chd free. Light refreshments.**

Sited on former strawberry fields this compact garden 50ft x 27ft was designed by the owner, an enthusiastic horticulturalist, to give yr-round interest. Inspirational design ideas for tiny plots with perennials, grasses, old roses, trough planting and raised vegetable beds. A small brick rill edges a circle of lawn. A blue, lean-to glasshouse, against a brick garden wall is an attractive feature.

85 SELBORNE

Caker Lane, East Worldham, Alton, GU34 3AE. Brian & Mary Jones, 01420 83389, mary.trigwell-jones@outlook.com, www.worldham.org. *2m SE of Alton. On B3004 at Alton end of the village of East Worldham, near The Three Horseshoes Pub. Please note: 'Selborne' is the name of the house, it is not in the village of Selborne. Parking signed.* **Sat 18, Sun 19, Mon 20 May, Sat 15, Sun 16, Mon 17 June, Sat 3, Sun 4, Mon 5 Aug (2-5). Adm £3.50, chd free. Home-made teas in the orchard with plenty of seating. Visits also by arrangement May to Aug. Donation to East Worldham Church & Tafara Mission Zimbabwe (Aug).**

This much-loved ½ acre mature garden with views across farmland provides visitors with surprises around every corner. It features a productive 60 yr old orchard of named varieties, densely-planted borders, shrubs and climbers, especially clematis. Metal and stone sculptures enhance the borders. Bug mansion. Enjoy tea in the shade of the orchard. Summerhouses and conservatory provide shelter. Book stall, garden quizzes for children and a sandpit for small children. At our June opening, there will be a Surrey Artists Open Studios art exhibition in the village hall. Wheelchair access, please note some gravel paths.

86 ◆ SPINNERS GARDEN

School Lane, Pilley, Lymington, SO41 5QE. Andrew & Vicky Roberts, 07545 432090, info@spinnersgarden.co.uk, www.spinnersgarden.co.uk. *1½m N of Lymington. Follow sign to Boldre off the A337 between Brockenhurst & Lymington. At top of Pilley Hill turn R into School Lane. Spinners Garden is at the end of a row of houses on the R.* **For NGS: Sun 28 Apr (2-5). Adm £5, chd free. Cream teas. For other opening times and information, please phone, email or visit garden website.**

Peaceful woodland garden overlooking the Lymington valley with many rare and unusual plants. The garden continues to be developed with new plants added to the collections and the layout changed to enhance the views. The house was rebuilt in 2014 to reflect its garden setting. Come and enjoy tea on the patio. Andy will take groups of 20 on tours of the hillside with its woodland wonders and draw attention to the treats at their feet - trilliums, wood anemones and erythroniums! Partial wheelchair access.

87 SPITFIRE HOUSE

Chattis Hill, Stockbridge, SO20 6JS. Tessa & Clive Redshaw. *2m from Stockbridge. Follow the A30 W from Stockbridge for 2m. Go past the Broughton/Chattis Hill Xrds & take the next R towards the Wallops, then next R up private drive to Spitfire House.* **Sat 1 June (2-5). Adm £4, chd free. Home-made teas.**

A country garden situated high on chalk downland. On the site of a WW11 Spitfire assembly factory with Spitfire tethering rings still visible. Established garden including vegetables and an orchard, but with several recently developed areas including large wildflower meadow. Wander through woodland to the wild flowers and on across the downs to be rewarded with extensive views. Some areas of gravel and a slope up to wildflower meadow.

88 SPRING POND

Laverstoke, Whitchurch, RG28 7PD. Julian & Carolyn Sheffield, info@springpondgarden.co.uk, , www.springpondgarden.co.uk. *1m S of the B3400 in Laverstoke. 8m W of Basingstoke, 3m W of Overton. In Laverstoke turn L opp Bombay Sapphire brick building on B3400 to Micheldever Station. Spring Pond is 1m along road on the L.* **Sun 16 June (2-5). Adm £6, chd free. Home-made teas. Visits also by arrangement May to Sept for groups of 5+.**

Spring Pond is full of colour coordinated borders, with an abundance of roses and clematis, while hornbeam, yew and box hedges add structure to the garden.

There is a pond with a wide variety of marginal plants, an arboretum full of ornamental trees, and a conservatory with Mediterranean and tropical plants. Hardy Garden Plants Nursery is 1m from Spring Pond.

GROUP OPENING

89 STOCKBRIDGE GARDENS

Stockbridge, SO20 6EX. *9m W of Winchester. On A30, at the junction of A3057 & B3049. Parking on High St. All gardens on High St.* **Thur 13, Sun 16 June (2-5). Combined adm £7, chd free. Home-made teas on the lawn at St Peter's Church.**

LITTLE WYKE
Mrs Mary Matthews.

THE OLD RECTORY
Robin Colenso & Chrissie Quayle.

OLD SWAN HOUSE
Mr Herry Lawford.
(See separate entry)

TROUT COTTAGE
Mrs Sally Milligan.

Stockbridge with its wide High St on a Roman causeway across the Test has excellent shops and hostelries. Four gardens will open this yr, located off the High St, offering a variety of styles and character. Little Wyke, next to the Town Hall has a long mature town garden with mixed borders and fruit trees. Trout Cottage is a small walled garden, which will inspire those with small spaces and little time to achieve tranquillity and beauty. There are two seating areas and approx 180 plants flowering for almost 10 mths of the yr, all set round a rectangular lawn. The Old Rectory has a partially walled garden with formal pond, fountain and planting near the house, with a stream-side walk under trees, many climbing and shrub roses and a woodland area. Old Swan House, at the east end of the High St has lawn under a huge hazel and modern mixed planting alongside an ancient flint wall. There is a gravel grass garden and an orchard, as well as a mature fish pond flanked by box pyramids.

90 TANGLEFOOT

Crawley, Winchester, SO21 2QB. Mr & Mrs F J Fratter, 01962 776243, fred@fratter.co.uk. *5m NW of Winchester. Between B3049 (Winchester - Stockbridge) & A272 (Winchester - Andover). Lane beside Crawley Court (Arqiva). Parking in adjacent mown field.* **Thur 9, Sun 12, Thur 30 May, Sun 2 June, Thur 18, Sun 21 July (2-5.30). Adm £4, chd free. Soft drinks & biscuits included. Opening with Crawley Gardens on Thur 4, Sun 7 July.** Visits also by arrangement May to July.

Developed by owners since 1976, Tanglefoot's ½ acre garden is a blend of influences, from Monet-inspired rose arch and small wildlife pond to Victorian boundary wall with trained fruit trees. Highlights include a raised lily pond, herbaceous bed (a riot of colour later in the summer), herb wheel, large productive kitchen garden and unusual flowering plants. In contrast to the garden, a 2 acre field with views over the Hampshire countryside has recently been converted into spring and summer wildflower meadows, with mostly native trees and shrubs; it has delighted visitors in recent summers. Watercolour flower paintings. Plants from the garden for sale. Narrow paths in vegetable area.

91 TERSTAN

Longstock, Stockbridge, SO20 6DW. Alexander & Penny Burnfield, paburnfield@gmail.com, www.pennyburnfield.wordpress.com. *¾m N of Stockbridge. From Stockbridge (A30) turn N to Longstock at bridge. Garden ¾m on R.* **Suns 21 Apr; 23 June; 21 July; 8 Sept (2-6). Adm £5, chd free. Home-made teas.** Visits also by arrangement Apr to Sept for groups of 10+.

A garden for all seasons, developed over 45 yrs into a profusely planted, contemporary cottage garden in peaceful surroundings. There is a constantly changing display in pots, starting with tulips and continuing with many unusual plants. Gravel garden, water features, cutting garden and Showman's Caravan. Art Groups welcome. Live music for NGS openings. Wheelchair access, but some gravel paths and steps.

92 THE THATCHED COTTAGE

Church Road, Upper Farringdon, Alton, GU34 3EG. Mr David & Mrs Cally Horton, 01420 587922, dwhorton@btinternet.com. *3m S of Alton off A32. From the A32, take the road to Upper Farringdon. At the top of the hill turn L into Church Rd, follow round corner, past Masseys Folly & we are the 1st house on the R.* **Suns 12 May; 30 June; 21 July; 18 Aug; 1 Sept (2-5). Combined adm with Berry Cottage £8, chd free.** Visits also by arrangement May to Sept for groups of 10+. Donation to Jubilee Sailing Trust.

A 1½ acre garden hidden behind a C16 thatched cottage (not open). Borders burst with cottage garden plants and the pond provides the soothing sound of water. This garden encourages exploration. Chickens and ducks wander under a walnut tree. Fruit trees, raised vegetable beds, roses and a fruit cage are to be found at the far end. The vegetable patch is being transformed in the winter to make less work. Fully accessible by wheelchair after a short gravel drive.

93 TYLNEY HALL HOTEL

Ridge Lane, Rotherwick, RG27 9AZ. Elite Hotels, 01256 764881, sales@tylneyhall.com, www.tylneyhall.co.uk. *3m NW of Hook. From M3 J5 via A287 & Newnham, M4 J11 via B3349 & Rotherwick.* **Sun 28 Apr, Sun 19 May, Sun 9 June (10-4). Adm £5, chd free. Light refreshments in the Chestnut Suite from 12pm.**

Large garden of 66 acres with extensive woodlands and beautiful vista. Fine avenues of wellingtonias; rhododendrons and azaleas, Italian garden, lakes, large water and rock garden, dry stone walls originally designed with assistance of Gertrude Jekyll. Partial wheelchair access.

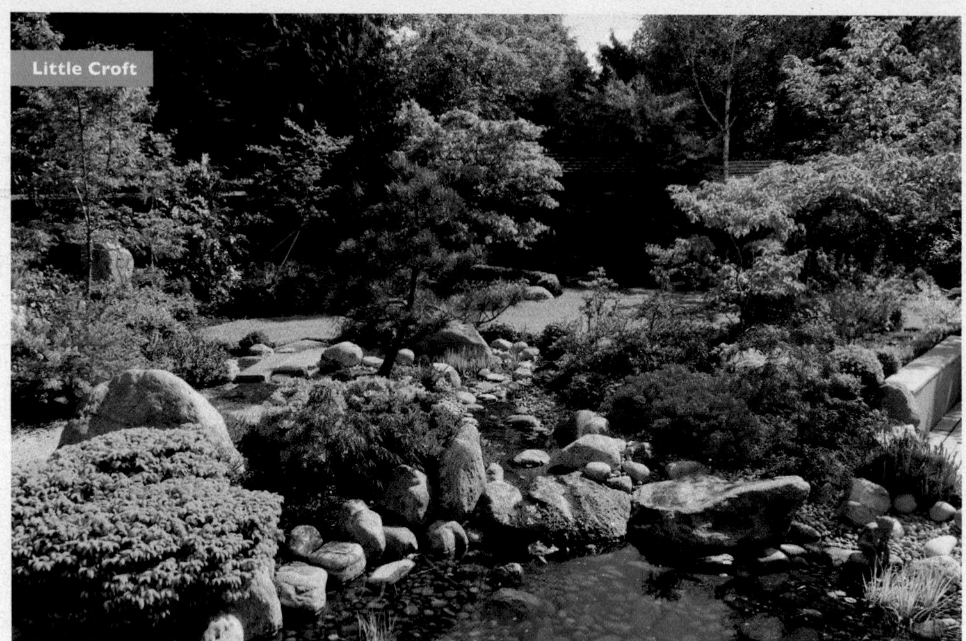
Little Croft

94 WALHAMPTON

Beaulieu Road, Walhampton, Lymington, SO41 5ZG. Walhampton School Trust Ltd, 07928 385694, d.hill@walhampton.com. *1m E of Lymington. From Lymington follow signs to Beaulieu (B3054) for 1m & turn R into main entrance at 1st school sign, 200yds after top of hill.* **Sun 12 May (2-6). Adm £5, chd free. Home-made teas in school dining room.** Visits also by arrangement May to July for groups of up to 20. Donation to St John's Church, Boldre.

Glorious walks through large C18 landscape garden surrounding magnificent mansion (not open). Visitors will discover three lakes, serpentine canal, climbable prospect mount, period former banana house and orangery, fascinating shell grotto, plantsman's glade and Italian terrace by Peto (c1907), drives and colonnade by Mawson (c1914) with magnificent views to the Isle of Wight. Excedrae and sunken garden, rockery, Roman arch, and fountain. Seating. Guided Tours with garden history available on the day. Gravel paths, some slopes.

95 WEIR HOUSE

Abbotstone Road, Old Alresford, SO24 9DG. Mr & Mrs G Hollingbery, 01962 735549, jhollingbery@me.com. *½m N of Alresford. From New Alresford down Broad St (B3046), past Globe Pub, take 1st L signed Abbotstone. Weir House is 1st drive on L. Park in signed field.* **Sun 9 June, Sun 8 Sept (2-5). Adm £5, chd free. Home-made teas.** Visits also by arrangement for groups of 10+.

Spectacular riverside garden with sweeping lawn backed by old walls, yew buttresses and mixed perennial beds. Contemporary vegetable garden at its height in Sept. Also incl contemporary garden around pool area, bog garden (at its best in May/June) and wilder walkways through wooded areas. Children welcome. Wheelchair access to most of the garden.

96 WEST SILCHESTER HALL

Bramley Road, Silchester, RG7 2LX. Mrs Jenny Jowett, 01189 700278, www.jennyjowett.com. *8m N of Basingstoke. 9m S of Reading, off A340 (signed from centre of village).* **Sun 26, Mon 27 May, Sun 7 July, Sun 11 Aug (2-5.30). Adm £4, chd free. Home-made teas.** Visits also by arrangement May to Sept for groups of 10+.

This much loved 2 acre garden is full of fascinating colour combinations inspired by the artist owner, with many spectacular herbaceous borders filled with rare and unusual plants. Pots with half hardies, a wild garden with orchids surrounding a pond, banks of rhododendrons and a kitchen garden. Always a large plant sale with a tempting selection of plants propagated from the garden. Large studio with exhibition of the owner's botanical, landscape and portrait paintings, cards and prints. Near Roman site. Wheelchair access to large part of the garden, gravel drive.

97 NEW WEST VIEW

Old London Road, Stockbridge, SO20 6EL. Rebecca Ferris. *Old London Rd is directly opp The White Hart Pub at the E end of Stockbridge High St. West View is 300yds on R opp the school.* **Sun 4 Aug (10-4); Wed 7 Aug (1.30-4.30). Adm £3.50, chd free.**

½ acre garden designed and constructed by the current owners, built into the natural chalk cliff on levels. 60 steep steps take you up through a series of small garden rooms from pool area, to sun deck, copper garden and white garden. The garden opens up as you get higher, culminating in a field with wildlife pond, shepherds hut, wild flower area, orchard and spectacular views of the Test Valley.

98 WHEATLEY HOUSE

Wheatley Lane, between Binsted & Kingsley, Bordon, GU35 9PA. Mr & Mrs Michael Adlington, 01420 23113, adlingtons36@gmail.com. *4m E of Alton, 5m SW of Farnham. Take A31 to Bentley, follow sign to Bordon. After 2m, R at Jolly Farmer Pub towards Binsted, 1m L & follow signs to Wheatley.* **Sat 17, Sun 18 Aug (1.30-5.30). Adm £5, chd free. Home-made teas.** Visits also by arrangement June to Oct for groups of 10+.

Situated on a rural hilltop with panoramic views over Alice Holt Forest and the South Downs. The owner admits to being much more of an artist than a plantswoman, but has had great fun creating this 1½ acre garden full of interesting and unusual planting combinations. The sweeping, mixed borders and shrubs are spectacular with colour throughout the season, particularly in late summer. The black and white border, now with bright red accents, is very popular with visitors. Local variety of craft, produce and home-made teas in Old Barn. Wheelchair access with care on lawns, good views of garden and beyond from terrace.

99 WHISPERS

Chatter Alley, Dogmersfield, Hook, RG27 8SS. Mr & Mrs John Selfe, 01252 613568, Sally.selfe@googlemail.com. *3m W of Fleet. Turn N to Dogmersfield off A287 Odiham to Farnham Rd. Turn L by Queen's Head Pub.* **Visits by arrangement July & Aug for groups of 20+. Adm £6, chd free.**

Come and discover new plants in this 2 acre garden of manicured lawns surrounded by large borders of colourful shrubs, trees and long flowering perennials. Wild flower area, water storage system, greenhouse, kitchen garden and living sculptures. Spectacular waterfall cascades over large rock slabs and magically disappears below the terrace. A garden not to be missed. Gravel entrance.

100 WICOR PRIMARY SCHOOL COMMUNITY GARDEN

Portchester, Fareham, PO16 9DL. Louise Moreton. *Halfway between Portsmouth & Fareham on A27. Turn S at Seagull Pub r'about into Cornaway Lane, 1st R into Hatherley Drive. Entrance to school is almost opp. Parking on-site, pay at main gate.* **Sun 23 June (12-4). Adm £3.50, chd free. Home-made teas.**

As shown on Gardeners' World in 2017. Beautiful school gardens tended by pupils, staff and community gardeners. Wander along Darwin's path to see the new coastal garden, Jurassic garden, orchard, tropical bed, wildlife areas, allotment and apiary, plus one of the few camera obscuras in the south of England. Wheelchair access to all areas, flat ground.

101 WILLOWS

Pilley Hill, Boldre, Lymington, SO41 5QF. Elizabeth & Martin Walker, 01590 677415, elizabethwalker13@gmail.com, www.willowsgarden.co.uk. *New Forest. 2m N Lymington off A337. To avoid traffic in Lyndhurst, leave M27 at J2 & follow Heavy Lorry Route. Disabled parking at gate.* **Sat 10, Sun 11, Mon 26 Aug (2-5). Adm £4, chd free. Cream teas.** Visits also by arrangement July & Aug for groups of 20+.

Golden bamboo greets you as you enter our vibrant front garden. Borders overflow with colourful dahlias, cannas, crocosmias, swathes of heleniums and rudbeckias. Exciting exotics contrast with a jungly mix of gunneras, ferns and giant hostas around the tranquil pond and bog garden. Sunny upper borders have dark leaved dahlias with billowing grasses, interesting topiary and wonderful hydrangeas. Willows will hold Dahlia Demo Days on each open day at 3pm. Elizabeth will demonstrate how to plant seeds, take cuttings and plant and separate mature tubers. Also, how to over winter mature tubers in the ground, protect them, dig them up and store if ground is unsuitable, feed and protect them from slugs. Wheelchairs usually manage to access all parts of Willows garden.

102 1 WOGSBARNE COTTAGES

Rotherwick, RG27 9BL. Miss S & Mr R Whistler. *2½m N of Hook. M3 J5, M4 J11, A30 or A33 via B3349.* **Sun 14, Mon 15 July (2-5). Adm £3, chd free. Home-made teas.**

Small traditional cottage garden with a roses around the door look, much photographed for calendars, jigsaws and magazines. Mixed flower beds and borders. Vegetables grown in abundance. Ornamental pond and alpine garden. Views over open countryside to be enjoyed whilst you take afternoon tea on the lawn. The garden has been open for the NGS for more than 30 yrs. Some gravel paths.

103 WYCHWOOD

Silchester Road, Little London, Tadley, RG26 5EP. Jenny Inwood. *Please do not park in The Plough car park. Access to Wychwood garden is by rear access with Limited Parking. Follow the signs opp Beach's Crescent.* **Wed 3, Wed 10 July (2-5). Adm £3.50, chd free. Light refreshments.**

A joyful garden comprising a stunning water feature with statuary and countless containers brimming with annuals. A tranquil and peaceful atmosphere invites you to sit and enjoy the many seating areas, amidst shrubs, roses and trees. The garden offers gentle access to different levels and habitats, and extends into a natural wooded area with views over the fields beyond. Wheelchair access may be difficult on gravel path and through the woods.

OPENING DATES

All entries subject to change. For latest information check **www.ngs.org.uk**

Extended openings are shown at the beginning of the month.

Map locator numbers are shown to the right of each garden name.

February

Snowdrop Festival

Every Thursday
Ivy Croft 21

Sunday 17th
The Old Corn Mill 32

Friday 22nd
◆ The Picton Garden 36

March

Saturday 16th
◆ Ralph Court Gardens 38

Sunday 17th
The Old Corn Mill 32
◆ The Picton Garden 36
◆ Ralph Court Gardens 38

April

Wednesday 3rd
◆ Stockton Bury Gardens 47

Saturday 6th
◆ Ralph Court Gardens 38
Seabournes 42

Sunday 7th
Bury Court Farmhouse 9
Lower Hope 26
◆ The Picton Garden 36
◆ Ralph Court Gardens 38
Whitfield 49

Sunday 14th
Whitfield 49

Monday 15th
◆ Moors Meadow Gardens 28

Friday 19th
Aulden Farm 2
Ivy Croft 21

Saturday 20th
Aulden Farm 2
Ivy Croft 21
◆ The Picton Garden 36

Sunday 21st
Coddington Vineyard 13
Hill House Farm 19
The Old Corn Mill 32
Revilo 39
Woodview 51

Monday 22nd
Coddington Vineyard 13
The Old Corn Mill 32
Revilo 39

Saturday 27th
Shuttifield Cottage 45

May

Every Tuesday and Wednesday from Tuesday 28th
Church Cottage 12

Friday 3rd
Rhodds Farm 40

Saturday 4th
Rhodds Farm 40

Sunday 5th
◆ The Picton Garden 36
Southbourne & Pine Lodge 46

Monday 6th
◆ The Picton Garden 36
Southbourne & Pine Lodge 46

Friday 10th
◆ Perrycroft 35

Saturday 11th
Shuttifield Cottage 45

Sunday 12th
Lower House Farm 27
The Old Corn Mill 32
Shuttifield Cottage 45

Monday 13th
◆ Bryan's Ground 8
◆ Moors Meadow Gardens 28

Sunday 19th
Hill House Farm 19
Lower Hope 26

Saturday 25th
Shuttifield Cottage 45

Sunday 26th
Kentchurch Court 22
The Old Corn Mill 32
◆ The Picton Garden 36
Sheepcote 43

Monday 27th
The Old Corn Mill 32

June

Every Tuesday and Wednesday
Church Cottage 12

Every day from Monday 10th to Friday 14th
Newport House 30

Saturday 1st
NEW Castle Moat House 10

Friday 7th
Rhodds Farm 40

Saturday 8th
Rhodds Farm 40

Sunday 9th
Brockhampton Cottage 5
The Brooks 6
Broxwood Court 7
◆ Caves Folly Nurseries 11
Grendon Court 16
Kentchurch Court 22
NEW Longacre 25

Friday 14th
◆ Hereford Cathedral Gardens 18

Saturday 15th
The Old Rectory 34
◆ The Picton Garden 36
◆ Ralph Court Gardens 38
Wolferlow House 50

Sunday 16th
Hill House Farm 19
The Old Rectory 34
◆ The Picton Garden 36
◆ Ralph Court Gardens 38
NEW Rosedale Court 41
Seabournes 42

Monday 17th
◆ Moors Meadow Gardens 28

Tuesday 18th
Hillcroft 20

Wednesday 19th
Hillcroft 20

Thursday 20th
Hillcroft 20

Friday 21st
◆ Perrycroft 35

Saturday 22nd
Newton St Margarets Gardens 31
Shuttifield Cottage 45

Sunday 23rd
Lower House Farm 27
Newton St Margarets Gardens 31

Saturday 29th
Aulden Arts and Gardens 1
◆ The Garden of the Wind at Middle Hunt House 15
◆ Ralph Court Gardens 38

Sunday 30th
Aulden Arts and Gardens 1
◆ The Garden of the Wind at Middle Hunt House 15
◆ Ralph Court Gardens 38
Whitfield 49

July

Every Tuesday and Wednesday
Church Cottage 12

Friday 5th
Rhodds Farm 40

Saturday 6th
Rhodds Farm 40

Sunday 7th
Hill House Farm 19
Lower Hope 26
Woodview 51

Monday 8th
◆ Moors Meadow Gardens 28

Sunday 14th
◆ The Picton Garden 36
Poole Cottage 37

Saturday 20th
Shuttifield Cottage 45

Sunday 21st
The Laskett Gardens 23
Woodview 51

August

Every Tuesday and Wednesday to Wednesday 14th
Church Cottage 12

Sunday 4th
Aulden Farm 2
Ivy Croft 21

Monday 5th
Aulden Farm 2
Ivy Croft 21
◆ Moors Meadow Gardens 28

Wednesday 7th
◆ The Picton Garden 36

Sunday 11th
Hill House Farm 19

Saturday 17th
Shuttifield Cottage 45

Sunday 18th
◆ The Picton Garden 36

Saturday 24th
◆ The Garden of the Wind at Middle Hunt House 15
NEW Hatterall Herbs 17

Sunday 25th
◆ The Garden of the Wind at Middle Hunt House 15
NEW Hatterall Herbs 17

Monday 26th
◆ The Picton Garden 36

September

Sunday 1st
Mulberry House 29

Sunday 8th
The Brooks 6
NEW Old Grove 33

Sunday 15th
Bury Court Farmhouse 9
Hill House Farm 19
Lower Hope 26
◆ The Picton Garden 36

Friday 20th
◆ Perrycroft 35

Saturday 21st
Dovecote Barn 14

Sunday 22nd
Dovecote Barn 14

October

Saturday 5th
Southbourne & Pine Lodge 46

Sunday 6th
Southbourne & Pine Lodge 46

Tuesday 8th
◆ The Picton Garden 36

Saturday 12th
◆ Ralph Court Gardens 38

Sunday 13th
◆ Ralph Court Gardens 38

Sunday 20th
Hill House Farm 19
◆ The Picton Garden 36

February 2020

Thursday 6th
Ivy Croft 21

Thursday 13th
Ivy Croft 21

Thursday 20th
Ivy Croft 21

Thursday 27th
Ivy Croft 21

By Arrangement

Arrange a personalised garden visit with your club, or group of friends, on a date to suit you. See individual garden entries for full details.

Aulden Farm 2
Bachefield House 3
Brighton House, Newton St Margarets Gardens 31
Brilley Court 4
Bury Court Farmhouse 9
Church Cottage 12
Coddington Vineyard 13
Grendon Court 16
NEW Hatterall Herbs 17
Hill House Farm 19
Hillcroft 20
Ivy Croft 21
Lawless Hill 24
Newport House 30
The Old Corn Mill 32
The Old Rectory 34
Poole Cottage 37
Revilo 39
Shucknall Court 44
Shuttifield Cottage 45
Weston Hall 48
Whitfield 49
Woodview 51

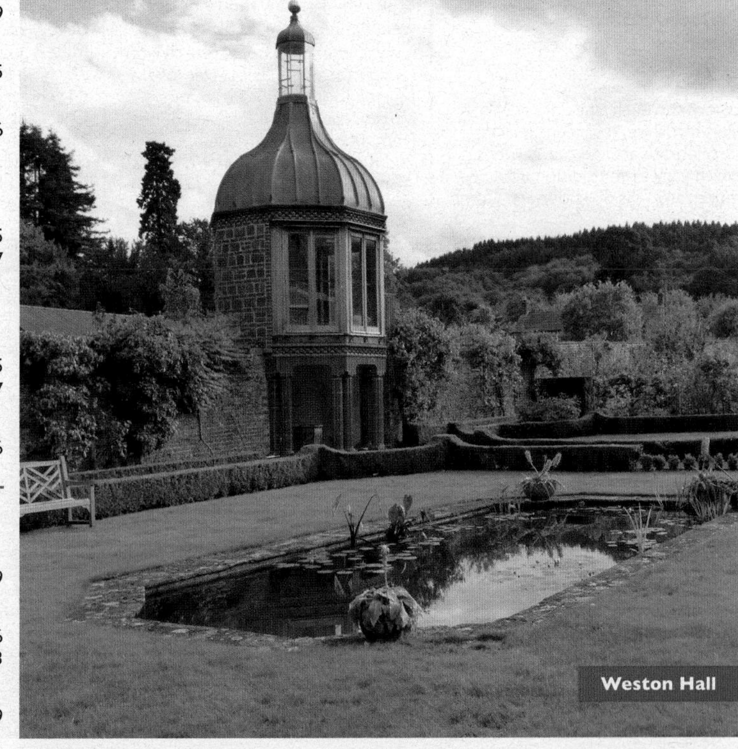
Weston Hall

THE GARDENS

GROUP OPENING

1 AULDEN ARTS AND GARDENS

Aulden, Leominster, HR6 0JT. www.auldenfarm.co.uk/auldenarts. *4m SW of Leominster. From Leominster, take Ivington/Upper Hill rd, ¾m after Ivington church turn R signed Aulden. From A4110 signed Ivington, take 2nd R signed Aulden.* **Sat 29, Sun 30 June (2-5.30). Combined adm £7, chd free. Home-made teas.**

AULDEN FARM
Alun & Jill Whitehead.
(See separate entry)
NPC

HILL VIEW
Tricia & Andy Mitchell.

HONEYLAKE COTTAGE
Jennie & Jack Hughes.

OAK HOUSE
Bob & Jane Langridge, 01568 720577, oakcroft16@gmail.com.

Lost in the back lanes of Herefordshire, 4 gardens looking to celebrate art and our gardens, which vary from traditional to more zany – as does our art! Come and explore, sit awhile and enjoy yummy cakes! Aulden Farm art will be on display in our barn - canvases inspired by walks, stitchery by Nature. We are drawn to that fertile ground where realism meets abstraction. Hill View: a tranquil garden with art by Tricia Mitchell. Honeylake Cottage; mature peaceful garden that encourages wildlife with a pond and numerous nest boxes. Cottage flowers predominate interspersed with fragrant English roses, lawns and a well-stocked traditional vegetable garden - the garden is an inspiration for artwork using a variety of media. Oak House: ⅔ acre of evolving garden with amazing views towards Upper Hill. Currently has good bones but is fraying round the edges, divided into several areas including borders, ponds, chickens and a vegetable plot. Photography and textiles will be displayed throughout the garden.

2 AULDEN FARM

Aulden, Leominster, HR6 0JT. Alun & Jill Whitehead, 01568 720129, web@auldenfarm.co.uk, www.auldenfarm.co.uk. *4m SW of Leominster. From Leominster take Ivington/Upper Hill rd, ¾m after Ivington church turn R signed Aulden. From A4110 signed Ivington, take 2nd R signed Aulden.* **Fri 19, Sat 20 Apr, Sun 4, Mon 5 Aug (2-5.30). Combined adm with Ivy Croft £7, chd free. Single garden opening £4. Homemade teas and ice cream. Opening with Aulden Arts and Gardens on Sat 29, Sun 30 June. Visits also by arrangement Apr to Sept.**
Informal country garden surrounding old farmhouse, 3 acres planted with wildlife in mind. Emphasis on structure and form, with a hint of quirkiness, a garden to explore with eclectic planting. Irises thrive around a natural pond, shady beds and open borders, seats abound, feels mature but ever evolving. Our own ice cream and home-burnt cakes, Lemon Chisel a speciality! National Collection of Siberian Iris and plant nursery.
NPC

3 BACHEFIELD HOUSE

Kimbolton, HR6 0EP. Jim & Rowena Gale, 01568 615855, rowena.jimgale@btinternet.com. *3m E of Leominster. Take A4112 off A49 (signed Leysters), after 10yds 1st R (signed Stretford/Hamnish). 1st L to Grantsfield, over Xrds (signed Bache), continue for approx 1m, garden on R 200yds past rd to Gorsty Hill.* **Visits by arrangement May & June for groups of up to 20. Mid-May - end of June. Adm £4, chd free. Home-made teas.**
Charming traditional cottage-style garden of 1 acre on gentle hill slope. Beds and borders bulge with beautiful blooms and foliage. Part-

Shuttifield Cottage

© Alan Wilkes

walled kitchen and cutting garden, gravel and herbaceous beds, rockery and pond. Good collections of roses, peonies, heritage pinks and irises. Summerhouse with fine views.

4 BRILLEY COURT

Whitney-on-Wye, HR3 6JF. Mr & Mrs David Bulmer, 01497 831467, rosebulmer@hotmail.com. *6m NE of Hay-on-Wye. 5m SW of Kington. 1½m off A438 Hereford to Brecon rd signed to Brilley.* **Visits by arrangement Mar to Sept. Refreshments by request. Adm £5, chd free.**

Garden created 40 years ago, 7 acres in total, wild valley stream garden with special trees, ornamental walled kitchen garden, tulips and wild flower areas. Summer roses and herbaceous . Wonderful views to the Black Mountains. Regret no dogs (except guide dogs). Limited wheelchair access.

5 BROCKHAMPTON COTTAGE

Brockhampton, HR1 4TQ. Peter Clay. *8m SW of Hereford. 5m N of Ross-on-Wye on B4224. In Brockhampton take rd signed to B Crt nursing home, pass N Home after ¾m, go down hill and turn L. 'Drop-off' at gate, car park 500yds downhill on L in orchard.* **Sun 9 June (1-4). Combined adm with Grendon Court £10, chd free. Single garden adm £6. Teas at Grendon Court.**

Created from scratch in 1999 by the owner and Tom Stuart-Smith, this beautiful hilltop garden looks S and W over miles of unspoilt countryside. On one side a woodland garden and 5 acre wild flower meadow, on the other side a Perry pear orchard and in valley below: lake, stream and arboretum. The extensive borders are planted with drifts of perennials in the modern romantic style. Allow 1hr 30 mins. Picnic parties welcome by the lake . Visit Grendon Court (2 - 5.30) after your visit to us.

6 THE BROOKS

Pontrilas, HR2 0BL. Marion & Clive Stainton, www.marionet.co.uk/the_brooks. *12m SW of Hereford. From the A465 Hereford to Abergavenny rd, turn L at Pontrilas onto B4347, take next R, then immediate L signed Orcop & Garway Hill. Garden 1¾m on L.* **Sun 9 June, Sun 8 Sept (2-5). Adm £5, chd free. Home-made teas.**

This 2½ acre Golden Valley garden incl part-walled enclosed vegetable garden and greenhouse (wind/solar-powered), orchard, ornamental, perennial, shade and shrub borders, wildlife pond, evolving arboretum cum coppice, and meadows with stunning views. Surrounding a stone 1684 farmhouse (not open), the garden has mature elements, but much has been created since 2006, with future development plans.

7 BROXWOOD COURT

Broxwood, nr Pembridge, Leominster, HR6 9JJ. Richard Snead-Cox & Mike & Anne Allen. *From Leominster follow signs to Brecon A44/A4112. After approx 8m, just past Weobley turn off, go R to Broxwood/Pembridge. After 2m straight over Xrds to Lyonshall. 500yds on L over cattle grid.* **Sun 9 June (2-5.30). Adm £5, chd free. Tea.**

Stunning 29 acre garden and arboretum, designed in 1859 by W. Nesfield for great-grandfather of present owner. Magnificent yew hedges and km long avenue of cedars and Scots pines. Spectacular view of Black Mountains, sweeping lawns, rhododendrons, gentle walks to summer house, chapel and ponds. Rose garden, mixed borders, rill, gazebo and fountain. Peacocks and white doves. Some gravel, but mostly lawn. Gentle slopes. Disabled WC.

8 ◆ BRYAN'S GROUND

Letchmoor Lane, Stapleton, Presteigne, LD8 2LP. David Wheeler & Simon Dorrell, 01544 260001, simonjdorrell@gmail.com, www.bryansground.co.uk. *12m NW of Leominster. Between Kinsham & Stapleton. At Mortimer's Cross take B4362 signed Presteigne. At Combe, follow signs. SATNAV is misleading. Coaches: please pre-book.* **For NGS: Mon 13 May (2-5). Adm £6, chd £2. Home-made teas. Please pre-book for coaches.** For other opening times and information, please phone, email or visit garden website.

8 acre internationally renowned contemporary reinterpretation of an Arts and Crafts garden dating from 1912, conceived as series of rooms with yew and box topiary, parterres, colour-themed flower and shrub borders, reflecting pools, potager, Edwardian greenhouse, heritage apple orchard, follies. Arboretum of 400 specimen trees and shrubs with wildlife pool beside R Lugg. Home of Hortus, garden journal. The majority of the garden is accessible by wheelchair, though there are some steps adjoining the terrace.

9 BURY COURT FARMHOUSE

Ford Street, Wigmore, Leominster, HR6 9UP. Margaret & Les Barclay, 01568 770618, l.barclay@zoho.com. *10m from Leominster, 10m from Knighton, 8m from Ludlow. On A4110 from Leominster, at Wigmore turn R just after shop & garage. Follow signs to parking and garden.* **Sun 7 Apr, Sun 15 Sept (2-5). Adm £4, chd free. Home-made teas. Visits also by arrangement Feb to Oct. Individuals and groups up to 50.**

¾ acre garden, 'rescued' since 1997, surrounds the 1820's stone farmhouse (not open). The courtyard contains a pond, mixed borders, fruit trees and shrubs, with steps up to a terrace which leads to lawn and vegetable plot. The main garden (semi-walled) is on two levels with mixed borders, greenhouse, pond, mini-orchard with daffodils in spring, and wildlife areas. Year-round colour. Mostly accessible for wheelchairs by arrangement.

10 NEW CASTLE MOAT HOUSE

Dilwyn, Hereford, HR4 8HZ. Mr & Mrs T Voogd. *6m W of Leominster. A44, after 4m take A4112 to Dilwyn. Garden by the village green.* **Sat 1 June (11-5). Adm £4, chd free. Home-made teas.**

A 2 acre plot consisting of a more formal cottage garden that wraps around the house. The remaining area is a tranquil wild garden which includes paths to a Medieval Castle Motte, part filled Moat and Medieval fish and fowl ponds. A haven for wildlife and people alike. The garden contains some steep banks and deep water, with limited access to Motte, Moat and ponds.

11 ◆ CAVES FOLLY NURSERIES

Evendine Lane, Colwall, WR13 6DX. Wil Leaper & Bridget Evans, 01684 540631, bridget@cavesfolly.com, www.cavesfolly.com. *1¼m NE of Ledbury. B4218. Between Malvern & Ledbury. Evendine Lane, off Colwall Green.* **For NGS: Sun 9 June (2-5). Combined adm with Longacre £7, chd free. Home-made teas. Single garden adm £3.50.** For other opening times and information, please phone, email or visit garden website.

Organic nursery and display gardens. Specialist growers of cottage garden plants herbs and alpines. All plants are grown in peat free organic compost. This is not a manicured garden! It is full of drifts of colour and wild flowers and a haven for wildlife.

12 CHURCH COTTAGE

Hentland, Ross-on-Wye, HR9 6LP. Sue Emms & Pete Weller, 01989 730222, sue.emms@mac.com, www.wyegardensbydesign.com. *6m from Ross-on-Wye. A49 from Ross. R turn Hentland/Kynaston. Sharp R to St Dubricius at bottom of hill. Narrow lane with few passing places - please take care. Unsuitable for motor homes. We are just before church.* **Every Tue and Wed 28 May to 14 Aug (2-5). Adm £3, chd free. Home-made teas.** Visits also by arrangement May to Aug for groups of up to 30.

Garden designer and plantswoman's ½ acre evolving garden packed with plants, many unusual varieties mixed with old favourites, providing interest over a long period. Wildlife pond, rose garden, potager, mixed borders, white terrace, gravel garden. Interesting plant combinations and design ideas to inspire.

13 CODDINGTON VINEYARD

Coddington, HR8 1JJ. Sharon & Peter Maiden, 01531 641817, sgmaiden@yahoo.co.uk, www.coddingtonvineyard.co.uk. *4m NE of Ledbury. From Ledbury to Malvern A449, follow brown signs to Coddington Vineyard.* **Sun 21, Mon 22 Apr (12-4). Adm £3.50, chd free. Home-made teas. Wine can also be served, homemade ice cream and our own apple juice. Visits also by arrangement Feb to Oct for groups of 10+. Lunches can be arranged pre booking essential We are licensed.**

5 acres incl 2 acre vineyard, listed farmhouse, threshing barn and cider mill. Garden with terraces, wild flower meadow, woodland with massed spring bulbs, large pond with wildlife, stream garden with masses of primula and hosta. Hellebores and snowdrops, hamamelis and parottia. Azaleas followed by roses and perennials. Lots to see all year.

14 DOVECOTE BARN

Stoke Lacy, Bromyard, HR7 4HJ. Gill Pinkerton & Adrian Yeeles. *4m S of Bromyard on A465. Turn into lane running alongside Stoke Lacy Church. Parking in 50 meters.* **Sat 21, Sun 22 Sept (2-5). Adm £4, chd free. Home-made teas at Stoke Lacy Church adjacent to Dovecote Barn.**

Nestling in the unspoilt Lodon Valley, 2 acre, organic, wildlife-friendly garden designed in 2008. Featuring ornamental vegetable and fruit gardens, peaceful and romantic pond area, copse with specimen trees for spring and autumn colour, winter walk, wild flower meadow and prairie banks. The C17 barn, framed by cottage garden planting, looks out over the garden to the Malvern Hills beyond. Gravel paths.

15 ◆ THE GARDEN OF THE WIND AT MIDDLE HUNT HOUSE

Middle Hunt House, Walterstone, Hereford, HR2 0DY. Rupert & Antoinetta Otten, 01873 860359, rupertotten@gmail.com. *4m W of Pandy, 17m S of Hereford, 10m N of Abergavenny. A465 to Pandy, West towards Longtown, turn R at Clodock Church, 1m on R. Disabled parking available.* **For NGS: Sat 29, Sun 30 June (2-5). Adm £5, chd free. Sat 24, Sun 25 Aug (2-5). Combined adm with Hatterall Herbs £7.50, chd free. Home-made teas.** For other opening times and information, please phone or email.

A modern garden using swathes of herbaceous plants and grasses, surrounding stone built farmhouse and barns with stunning views of the Black Mountains. Special features: rose border, hornbeam alley, formal parterre and bespoke water rill and fountains, William Pye water feature, architecturally designed greenhouse complex, vegetable gardens. Carved lettering and sculpture throughout, garden covering about 4 acres. Garden seating throughout the site on stone, wood and metal benches including some with carved lettering. The garden is also the home of part of the National Collection of Contemporary Memorial Art on loan from the Lettering and Commemorative Arts Trust. Partial wheelchair access. Disabled WC facilities not easily accessible for wheelchair users due to gravel.

16 GRENDON COURT

Upton Bishop, Ross on Wye, HR9 7QP. Mark & Kate Edwards, 07971 339126, kate@grendoncourt.co.uk. *3m NE of Ross-on-Wye. M50, J3 . Hereford B4224 Moody Cow PH, 1m open gate on R. From Ross. A40, B449, Xrds R Upton Bishop. 100yds on L by cream cottage.* **Sun 9 June (2-5.30). Combined adm with Brockhampton Cottage £10, chd free. Single garden adm £5. Home made teas in the barn.** Visits also by arrangement. Lunch provided for groups up to 65. Private functions.

A contemporary garden designed

by Tom Stuart-Smith. Planted on 2 levels, a clever collection of mass-planted perennials and grasses of different heights, textures and colour give all-yr interest. The upper walled garden with a sea of flowering grasses makes a highlight. Views of the new pond and valley walk. Visit Brockhampton Cottage (1-4) before you visit us (picnic in parking field). Please note that Grendon Court garden does not open until 2pm. Wheelchair access possible but some gravel.

17 NEW HATTERALL HERBS

Longtown, Hereford, HR2 0LT. Hanneke van der Werf, hatterallherbs@gmail.com. *Longtown, HR2 0LT. From Abergavenny/the South: turn L off A465 at Pandy, follow signs for the gardens. From Hereford/the North: turn R off A465 in Pontrilas, to Ewyas Harold, follow signs to the gardens.* **Sat 24, Sun 25 Aug (2-6). Combined adm with The Garden of the Wind at Middle Hunt House £7.50. Single garden admission £3.50.** Visits also by arrangement May to Sept for groups of up to 10. Group visits will be guided and last at least 1 hour.

A ½ acre organic working garden started in 2014 applying permaculture and no dig principles. Divided into distinct areas, the garden contains annual medicinal herbs, edible flowers, cut flowers, a large collection of medicinal plants, pleached lime and fruit trees, raised vegetable beds, soft fruit, wild flower meadow, an orchard with unusual fruit trees and a 'food forest'. Herb Labyrinth, Views over Hatterall Ridge and the Black Mountains. Medicinal plants. Butterflies. Fantastic walks from the car park. Teas at The Garden of the Wind.

We open the gates to the nation's best gardens, offering a relaxing, memorable and affordable day out. A perfect experience to share with friends and family.

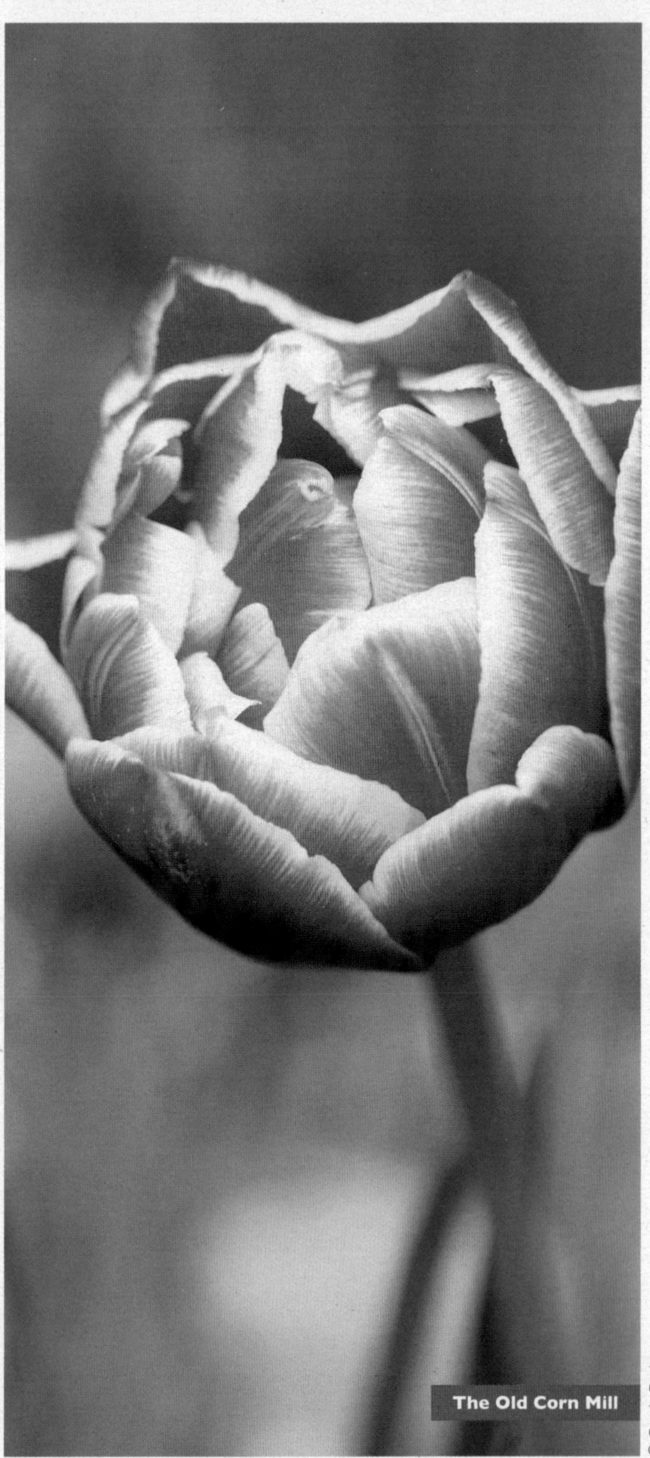

The Old Corn Mill

© Carole Drake

18 ◆ HEREFORD CATHEDRAL GARDENS

Hereford, HR1 2NG. Dean of Hereford Cathedral, 01432 374202, Peter.Challenger@herefordcathedral.org, www.herefordcathedral.org. *Centre of Hereford. Approach rds to the Cathedral are signed. Tours leave from information desk in the cathedral building or as directed.* **For NGS: Fri 14 June (10-4). Adm £5, chd free. Light refreshments in Cathedral's Cloister Café.** For other opening times and information, please phone, email or visit garden website.

A guided tour of late 15th century historic award-winning gardens. Tours include colourful courtyard garden, an atmospheric cloisters garden enclosed by C15 buildings, the Vicars Choral garden, with plants with ecclesiastical connections and roses, the private Dean's Garden and the Bishop's Garden with fine trees and an outdoor chapel for meditation in ancient surroundings. College Hall holding 100 people available for teas and other refreshments. Collection of plants with ecclesiastical connections in College Garden. Open every Wed & Sat 1 May to 30 Sept, guided tours 2.30. Please see website for other dates and information on booked and guided tours. Partial wheelchair access.

19 HILL HOUSE FARM

Knighton, LD7 1NA. Simon & Caroline Gourlay, 01547 528542, simongourlay@btinternet.com, www.hillhousefarmgarden.com. *4m SE of Knighton. S of A4113 via Knighton (Llanshay Lane, 4m) or Bucknell (Reeves Lane, 3m).* **Sun 21 Apr, Sun 19 May, Sun 16 June, Sun 7 July, Sun 11 Aug, Sun 15 Sept, Sun 20 Oct (2-5.30). Adm £5, chd free. Light refreshments. Self service teas, coffee and soft drinks.** Visits also by arrangement Apr to Oct for groups of up to 20.

5 acre south facing garden developed over 50 years, set in magnificent hilly countryside. Some herbaceous and extensive lawns around the house. Mown paths lead through shrubs, roses and specimen trees down to the half acre Oak Pool 200ft below. There are 11 sculptures and as many sitting places scattered around this very peaceful garden. Good range of snack bars and biscuits. Suggested contributions into an honesty box. Surrounded by pastureland with distant views of the Black Mountains. Wheelchair access limited to the top of the garden. Disabled parking at the side of the house.

20 HILLCROFT

Coombes Moor, Presteigne, LD8 2HY. Liz O'Rourke & Michael Clarke, 01544 262795, lorconsulting@hotmail.co.uk. *North Herefordshire. 10m from Leominster. Coombes Moor is under Wapley Hill on the B4362, between Shobdon & Presteigne. The house is on R just beyond Byton Cross when heading west.* **Tue 18, Wed 19, Thur 20 June (11-5). Adm £4, chd free. Tea, coffee and cold drinks along with delicious home-made cakes can be enjoyed in the garden or the conservatory.** Visits also by arrangement in June for groups of up to 30.

The garden is part of a 5 acre site on the lower slopes of Wapley Hill in the beautiful Lugg Valley. The highlight in mid summer is the romantic Rose Walk, combining sixty roses with mixed herbaceous planting set in an old cider apple orchard. In addition to the garden area around the house, there is a secret garden, wild flower meadow and a vegetable and fruit area.

21 IVY CROFT

Ivington Green, Leominster, HR6 0JN. Sue & Roger Norman, 01568 720344, ivycroft@homecall.co.uk, www.ivycroftgarden.co.uk. *3m SW of Leominster. From Leominster take Ryelands Rd to Ivington. Turn R at church, garden ¾m on R. From A4110 signed Ivington, garden 1¾m on L.* **Every Thur 7 Feb to 28 Feb (9-4.30). Adm £4, chd free. Fri 19, Sat 20 Apr, Sun 4, Mon 5 Aug (2-5.30). Combined adm with Aulden Farm £7, chd free. Home-made teas. Single garden adm £4. 2020: Thur 6, Thur 13, Thur 20, Thur 27 Feb.** Visits also by arrangement. All year. Conducted tours.

A maturing rural garden with areas of meadow, wood and orchard, blending with countryside and providing habitat for wildlife. The cottage is surrounded by borders, raised beds, trained pears and containers giving all year interest. Paths lead to the wider garden including herbaceous borders, vegetable garden framed with espalier apples and seasonal pond with willows, ferns and grasses. Snowdrops. Partial wheelchair access.

The Picton Garden

© Leigh Clapp

22 KENTCHURCH COURT

Pontrilas, HR2 0DB. Mrs Jan Lucas-Scudamore, 01981 240228, jan@kentchurchcourt.co.uk, www.kentchurchcourt.co.uk. *12m SW of Hereford. From Hereford A465 towards Abergavanny, at Pontrilas turn L signed Kentchurch. After 2m fork L, after Bridge Inn. Garden opp church.* **Sun 26 May, Sun 9 June (11-5). Adm £5, chd free. Home-made teas.**
Kentchurch Court is sited close to the Welsh border. The large stately home dates to C11 and has been in the Scudamore family for over 1000yrs The deer-park surrounding the house dates back to the Knights Hospitallers of Dinmore and lies at the heart of an estate of over 5000 acres. Historical characters associated with the house incl Welsh hero Owain Glendower, whose daughter married Sir John Scudamore. The house was modernised by John Nash in 1795. First opened for NGS in 1927. Formal rose garden, traditional vegetable garden redesigned with colour, scent and easy access. Walled garden and herbaceous borders, rhododendrons and wild flower walk. Deer-park and ancient woodland. Extensive collection of mature trees and shrubs. Stream with habitat for spawning trout. Some slopes, shallow gravel.

23 THE LASKETT GARDENS

Much Birch, Hereford, HR2 8HZ. Sir Roy Strong, www.thelaskettgardens.co.uk. *Approx 7m from Hereford; 7m from Ross. On A49, midway between Ross-on-Wye & Hereford, turn into Laskett Lane towards Hoarwithy. The drive is approx 350yds on L.* **Sun 21 July (10-4). Adm £10, chd free. Light refreshments. Coffee, light lunches & afternoon teas.**
The Laskett Gardens are the largest private formal gardens to be created in England since 1945 consisting of 4 acres of stunning garden rooms incl rose and knot garden, fountains, statuary, topiary and a Belvedere from which to view the gardens on high. Partial wheelchair access.

24 LAWLESS HILL

Sellack, Ross-on-Wye, HR9 6QP. Katalin & Keith Meehan, 07595 678837, Lawlesshill@gmail.com, www.facebook.com/Lawless-Hill-315093135189525. *4m NW of Ross-on-Wye. Western end of M50. On A49 to Hereford, take 2nd R, signed Sellack. After 2m, turn R by white house, to Sellack church. At next church sign, turn L. Garden halfway down lane, before church.* **Car parking facility: max 10 car space on site. Adm £5, chd free. Visits by arrangement Mar to Oct for groups of up to 30. Teas/coffees and cakes on request for extra charge.**
Modernist Japanese-influenced garden with dramatic views over R Wye. Collection of 'rooms' sculpted from the steep hillside using network of natural stone walls and huge rocks. Among exotic and unusual plantings, natural ponds are held within the terracing, forming waterfalls between them. Due to steep steps and stepping stones by open water, the garden is unsuitable for the less mobile and young children. - magical views overlooking waterfall and the river Wye - infinity pond offers great photographic opportunities - cloud shaped pines and taxus trees from Japan - zen meditation/ gravel garden - dry river garden - sophisticated stone walls- exquisite engineering works.

25 NEW LONGACRE

Evendine Lane, Colwall Green, WR13 6DT. Mr & Mrs C Hellowell. *3m S of Malvern. Off Colwall Green. Off B4218. Car parking at Caves Folly Nursery.* **Sun 9 June (2-5). Combined adm with Caves Folly Nursery £7, chd free. Single garden adm £4.50.**
2-acre garden-cum-arboretum developed since 1970. Island beds of trees and shrubs, some underplanted with bulbs and herbaceous perennials, present a sequence of contrasting pictures and views through the seasons. There are no 'rooms' - rather long vistas lead the eye and feet, while the feeling of spaciousness is enhanced by glimpses caught between trunks and through gaps in the planting. Over 50 types of conifer provide the background to maples, rhododendrons, azaleas, dogwoods, eucryphias etc. over gravel paths and lawns.

26 LOWER HOPE

Lower Hope Estate, Ullingswick, Hereford, HR1 3JF. Mr & Mrs Clive Richards, www.lowerhopegardens.co.uk. *5m S of Bromyard. A465 N from Hereford, after 6m turn L at Burley Gate onto A417 towards Leominster. After approx 2m turn R to Lower Hope. After ½m garden on L. Disabled parking available.* **Sun 7 Apr, Sun 19 May, Sun 7 July, Sun 15 Sept (2-5). Adm £6, chd £1. Tea and cakes.**
Outstanding 5 acre garden with wonderful seasonal variations. Impeccable lawns with herbaceous borders, rose gardens, white garden, Mediterranean, Italian and Japanese gardens. Natural streams, man-made waterfalls, bog gardens. Woodland with azaleas and rhododendrons with lime avenue to lake with wild flowers and bulbs. Glasshouses with exotic plants and breeding butterflies. Prizewinning Hereford cattle and Suffolk sheep. Wheelchair access to most areas.

We help ordinary people open the gates to their extraordinary private gardens to raise impressive amounts of money through admissions, teas and slices of cake!

27 LOWER HOUSE FARM

Vine Lane, Sutton, Tenbury Wells, WR15 8RL. Mrs Anne Durston Smith, 01885 410233, www.kyre-equestrian.co.uk. *3m SE of Tenbury Wells; 8m NW of Bromyard. From Tenbury take A4214 to Bromyard. After approx 3m turn R into Vine Lane, then R fork to Lower House Farm.* **Sun 12 May, Sun 23 June (2-6). Adm £3.50, chd free. Home-made teas.**

Award-winning country garden surrounding C16 farm-house (not open) on working farm. Herbaceous borders, roses, box-parterre, productive kitchen and cutting garden, spring garden, ha-ha allowing wonderful views. Wildlife pond and children's activities in adjoining field. Walkers and dogs can enjoy numerous footpaths across the farm land. Home to Kyre Equestrian Centre with access to safe rides and riding events.

28 ◆ MOORS MEADOW GARDENS

Collington, Bromyard, HR7 4LZ. Ros Bissell, 01885 410318/07812 041179, moorsmeadow@hotmail.co.uk, www.moorsmeadow.co.uk. *4m N of Bromyard, on B4214. ½m up lane follow yellow arrows.* **For NGS: Mon 15 Apr, Mon 13 May, Mon 17 June, Mon 8 July, Mon 5 Aug (11-5). Adm £6.50, chd £1.50.** For other opening times and information, please phone, email or visit garden website.

7-acre organic hillside garden brimming with rarely seen plant species, an emphasis on working with nature to create a wildlife haven. With intriguing features and sculptures it is an inspiration to the garden novice as well as the serious plantsman. Wander through fernery, grass garden, extensive shrubberies, herbaceous beds, meadow, dingle, pools and kitchen garden. Resident Blacksmith. Huge range of unusual and rarely seen plants from around the world. Unique home-crafted sculptures.

29 MULBERRY HOUSE

Knapp Close, Goodrich, Ross-on-Wye, HR9 6JW. Tina & Adrian Barber. *Centre of Goodrich. 5m from Ross on Wye 7m from Monmouth. Close to Goodrich Castle in Wye Valley AONB. Goodrich signed from A40 or take B4234 from Ross on Wye. Park in village & follow signs to the garden.* **Sun 1 Sept (11-5). Adm £4, chd free. Home-made teas.**

Mulberry House: a beautiful ½ acre garden created from scratch 12 years ago. Imaginatively planted and nurtured by a professional gardener with an artistic eye. Themed herbaceous borders, areas of shrub planting including clipped box and ornamental grasses all provide a long season of interest. Also a potager area and a series of garden rooms with views out to beautiful listed village buildings.

30 NEWPORT HOUSE

Almeley, HR3 6LL. David & Jenny Watt, 07754 234903, david.gray510@btinternet.com. *5m S of Kington. 1m from Almeley Church, on rd to Kington. From Kington take A4111 to Hereford. After 4m turn L to Almeley, continue 2m, garden on L.* **Daily Mon 10 June to Fri 14 June (11-5). Adm £5, chd free. Light refreshments.** Visits also by arrangement May to Sept.

20 acres of garden, woods and lake (with walks). Formal garden set on 3 terraces with large mixed borders framed by formal hedges, in front of Georgian House (not open). 2½-acre walled organic garden in restoration since 2009.

GROUP OPENING

31 NEWTON ST MARGARETS GARDENS

Newton St. Margarets, Hereford, HR2 0JU. Sue Londesborough. *17m SW of Hereford, 9m SE of Hay-on-Wye. A465 S from Hereford, R onto B4348, then L to Vowchurch & Michaelchurch Escley. After approx. 3m take either 1st or 3rd L turns. Follow yellow signs. From Hay B4348, R to Vowchurch, then as above.* **Sat 22, Sun 23 June (2-6). Combined adm £6, chd free. Home-made teas at Brighton House.**

BRIGHTON HOUSE

Sue & Richard Londesborough, 01981 510148, slondesborough138@btinternet.com.

Visits also by arrangement Apr to Sept.

NEW **OLD FARM COTTAGE**

Jane Wake & Alan McCardle.

Two country gardens with very different styles in the picturesque Herefordshire Golden valley. Brighton House: a plantswoman's garden of just over an acre, divided into several distinct areas crammed with many unusual and interesting plants. Herbaceous borders, ornamental and fruit trees, kitchen garden, two small ponds. The garden is planted to encourage wildlife. Views to the Black Mountains. Children's garden trail and play area. Plants for sale propagated from the garden. Old Farm Cottage: cottage garden, with herbaceous borders, shrubs, vegetable garden and greenhouse. Rill and bog garden. Brook side walk with wild flowers and mature oak trees. Secluded seating areas with views to the Black Mountains. Garden not suitable for wheelchairs due to steep access and gravel. Plants for sale at Brighton House.

32 THE OLD CORN MILL

Aston Crews, Ross-on-Wye, HR9 7LW. Mrs Jill Hunter, 01989 750059, www.theoldcornmillgarden.com. *5m E of Ross-on-Wye. A40 Ross to Gloucester. Turn L at T-lights at Lea Xrds onto B4222 signed Newent, Garden ½m on L. Parking for disabled down drive. DO NOT USE THE ABOVE POSTCODE IN YOUR SATNAV - try HR9 7LA.* **Sun 17 Feb, Sun 17 Mar, Sun 21, Mon 22 Apr, Sun 12, Sun 26, Mon 27 May (1-5). Adm £5, chd free. Adm incl tea or coffee and cake.** Visits also by arrangement Feb to Oct.

4 acres of woodland, meadows, ponds and streams. A tranquil and relaxed country garden of scents, sights and sounds. Interest all year with drifts of tulips, wild daffodils and common spotted orchids in spring. Good Autumn colour. Pop-up Art Exhibition in house. Sculpture in the garden by Simon Probym.

Lower Hope

33 NEW OLD GROVE

Llangrove, Ross-On-Wye, HR9 6HA. Ken & Lynette Knowles. *Between Ross & Monmouth. 2m off A40 at Whitchurch. Disabled parking at house. Park in village hall car park. Five minute walk to garden following NGS signs.* **Sun 8 Sept (2-5). Adm £4, chd free. Home-made teas.**
1 ½ acre garden plus two fields. SW facing with unspoilt views. Lots of mixed beds with plenty of late summer colour and many unusual plants. Large collection of dahlias and salvias. Wild life pond. Formal herb garden. Masses of pots. Seating throughout. Interesting trees. Gentle slopes, some steps but accessible.

34 THE OLD RECTORY

Thruxton, Hereford, HR2 9AX. Mr & Mrs Andrew Hallett, 01981 570401 & 07774 129690, ar.hallett@gmail.com, www.thruxtonrectory.co.uk. *6m SW of Hereford. A465 to Allensmore. At Locks (Shell) garage take B4348 towards Hay-on-Wye. After 1½m turn L towards Abbey Dore & Cockyard. Car park 150yds on L.* **Sat 15, Sun 16 June (1-5). Adm £5, chd free. Home-made teas. Visits also by arrangement May to Sept. Min adm £70 if less than 14 people.**
With breathtaking views over Herefordshire countryside this four acre garden - two acres formal and two acres paddock with ornamental trees and shrubs, and heritage fruit trees- has been created since 2007. Constantly changing plantsman's garden stocked with unusual perennials and roses, together with woodland borders, gazebo, vegetable parterre, glasshouse and natural pond. Many places to sit. Most plants labelled. Mainly level with some gravel paths.

35 ◆ PERRYCROFT

Jubilee Drive, Upper Colwall, Malvern, WR13 6DN. Gillian & Mark Archer, 07858 393767, gillianarcher@live.co.uk, www.perrycroft.co.uk. *Between Malvern & Ledbury. On B4232 between British Camp & Wyche cutting. Park in Gardiners Quarry pay & display car park on Jubilee Drive, short walk to the garden.* **For NGS: Fri 10 May, Fri 21 June, Fri 20 Sept (11-4). Adm £5, chd free. Tea.** For other opening times and information, please phone, email or visit garden website.
Perrycroft is an Arts and Crafts house designed by CFA Voysey in 1895. High on the Malvern Hills, with magnificent views to the south and west, the garden has been developed over the past 20 years. Yew and box hedges, topiary, mixed and herbaceous borders, shrubs and roses, meadows, ponds and woodland combine to create a relaxed and varied garden with traditional and contemporary planting styles. Self-serve tea, coffee and cake in the Coach House. This garden is unsuitable for wheelchairs, due to steep and uneven grass and gravel paths.

36 ◆ THE PICTON GARDEN

Old Court Nurseries, Walwyn Road, Colwall, WR13 6QE. Mr & Mrs Paul Picton, 01684 540416, oldcourtnurseries@btinternet.com, www.autumnasters.co.uk. *3m W of Malvern. On B4218 (Walwyn Rd) N of Colwall Stone. Turn off A449 from Ledbury or Malvern onto the B4218 for Colwall.* **For NGS: Fri 22 Feb, Sun 17 Mar, Sun 7, Sat 20 Apr, Sun 5, Mon 6, Sun 26 May, Sat 15, Sun 16 June, Sun 14 July, Wed 7, Sun 18, Mon 26 Aug, Sun 15 Sept, Tue 8, Sun 20 Oct (11-5). Adm £3.50, chd free.** For other opening times and information, please phone, email or visit garden website.
1½ acres W of Malvern Hills. Bulbs and a multitude of woodland plants in spring. Interesting perennials and shrubs in Aug. In late Sept and early Oct colourful borders display the National Plant Collection of Michaelmas daisies, backed by autumn colouring trees and shrubs. Many unusual plants to be seen, incl bamboos, more than 100 different ferns and acers. Features raised beds and silver garden. National Plant Collection of autumn-flowering asters and an extensive nursery that has been growing them since 1906. Wheelchair access gravel paths but all fairly level, no steps.

NPC

37 POOLE COTTAGE

Coppett Hill, Goodrich, Ross on Wye, HR9 6JH. Jo Ward-Ellison & Roy Smith, 01600 890148, jo@ward-ellison.com, www.herefordshiregarden.wordpress.com. *5m from Ross on Wye, 7m from Monmouth. Above Goodrich Castle in Wye Valley AONB. Goodrich signed from A40 or take B4234 from Ross. No parking close to garden on 14 July. Park in village & follow signs. Shuttle service available up to garden or walk 10-15 mins up from village.* **Sun 14 July (11-6). Adm £4, chd free. Home-made teas. Visits also by arrangement Aug & Sept for groups of up to 20. Parking for up to 5 cars at the garden for by arrangement visitors.**
Home to designer Jo Ward-Ellison this 2 acre hillside garden created just 8 years ago is now maturing into the landscape. Predominately naturalistic in style and with a contemporary feel it has a long season of interest with many grasses and later flowering perennials. Some steep slopes, steps and uneven paths. Features include grass hedges, small orchard and kitchen garden with fabulous views.

38 ◆ RALPH COURT GARDENS

Edwyn Ralph, Bromyard, Hereford, HR7 4LU. Mr & Mrs Morgan, 01885 483225, ralphcourtgardens@aol.com, www.ralphcourtgardens.co.uk. *From Bromyard follow the Tenbury rd for approx 1m. On entering the village of Edwyn Ralph take 1st turning on R towards the church.* **For NGS: Sat 16, Sun 17 Mar, Sat 6, Sun 7 Apr, Sat 15, Sun 16, Sat 29, Sun 30 June, Sat 12, Sun 13 Oct (10-5). Adm £9, chd £6. Light refreshments.** For other opening times and information, please phone, email or visit garden website.
12 amazing gardens set in the grounds of a gothic rectory. A family orientated garden with a twist, incorporating an Italian Piazza, an African Jungle, Dragon Pool, Alice in Wonderland and the elves in their conifer forest and our new section 'The Monet Garden'. These are just a few of the themes

within this stunning garden. Overlooking the Malvern Hills 120 seater Licenced Restaurant. Offering a good selection of daily specials, delicious Sunday roasts, Afternoon tea and our scrumptious homemade cakes. All areas ramped for wheelchair and pushchair access. Some grass areas, without help can be challenging during wet periods.

39 REVILO

Wellington, Hereford, HR4 8AZ. Mrs Shirley Edgar, 01432 830189, Shirleyskinner@btinternet.com. *6m N of Hereford. On A49 from Hereford turn L into Wellington village, pass church on R. Then just after barn on L, turn L up driveway in front of The Harbour, to furthest bungalow.* **Sun 21, Mon 22 Apr (2-5). Adm £3.50, chd free. Home-made teas.** Visits also by arrangement Apr to Sept for groups of 5+.

Third of an acre garden surrounding bungalow includes mixed borders, meadow and woodland areas, scented garden, late summer bed, gravelled herb garden and vegetable/fruit garden. Flower arranger's garden. Wheelchair access to all central areas of the garden from the garage side.

40 RHODDS FARM

Lyonshall, HR5 3LW. Richard & Cary Goode, 01544 340120, cary.goode@russianaeros.com, www.rhoddsfarm.co.uk. *1m E of Kington. From A44 take small turning S just E of Penrhos Farm, 1m E of Kington. Continue 1m, garden straight ahead.* **Fri 3, Sat 4 May, Fri 7, Sat 8 June, Fri 5, Sat 6 July (11-5). Adm £5, chd free. Home-made teas and cake available for guests to help themselves in return for a donation.**

Created by the owner, a professional garden designer, the garden contains an extensive range of interesting plants. Formal garden leads to dovecote and through to mixed borders with interest throughout the year. Double herbaceous borders of hot colours, several ponds, new arboretum, woodland planting, large gravel garden. A natural garden that fits the setting. Not suitable for wheelchairs

41 NEW ROSEDALE COURT

Pudleston, Leominster, HR6 0RF. Mr & Mrs Charles Ingleby. *7m E of Leominster. A49 N from Leominster, turn R onto A4112 (Tenbury). At Leysters turn R at Xrds (after Duke of York) & take 1st R to Rosedale/Pudleston. After 1½m, L up drive, opp green railings on R.* **Sun 16 June (2-5). Adm £5, chd free. Home-made teas.**

South facing sloping lawns are partially enclosed within Edwardian yew hedges clipped into architectural shapes overlooking a large lake. Mown paths lead to the woodland gardens which include 100 year old acers and other specimen trees. Ornamental gardens surround the house, including a white rose garden and other enclosed areas within the old farm buildings. Partial wheelchair access due to some steep slopes.

42 SEABOURNES

Fawley, Hereford, HR1 4SP. Karen Birch, 01432 840 217, karen@riverseaholdings.com. *10m from Hereford. 7m from Ross-on-Wye. From Hereford B4224, via Fownhope, on 3.4m, turn R in How Caple. 2.2m, then L to Seabournes. From Ross/M50 take B4224, turn L at How Caple. After 2.2m turn L to Seabournes.* **Sat 6 Apr (9.30-1.30); Sun 16 June (12-4). Adm £5, chd free. Light refreshments, wine, coffee, tea (in the chapel if wet).**

10 acre garden on gentle slope on banks of R. Wye. Magnificent mature Magnolia, Acers, Ginko, Katsura and other fine trees and shrubs. Arts and Crafts summerhouse, original A&C garden layout under reconstruction. Ornamental pond with pagoda from Kerala. Woodland walk with views to the river. C12 chapel open. The beauty of the garden is in its setting overlooking the Wye. Romantic but not perfect ! Teas in aid of Fawley Chapel Trust.

Southbourne & Pine Lodge

43 SHEEPCOTE

Putley, Ledbury, HR8 2RD. Tim & Julie Beaumont. *5m W of Ledbury off the A438 Hereford to Ledbury Rd. Passenger drop off; parking 200 yards.* **Sun 26 May (12-5.30). Adm £5, chd free. Home-made teas.**

⅓ acre garden taken in hand from 2011 retaining many quality plants, shrubs and trees from earlier gardeners. Topiary holly, box, hawthorn, privet and yew formalise the varied plantings around the croquet lawn and gravel garden; beds with heathers, azaleas, lavender surrounded by herbaceous perennials and bulbs; v small ponds; kitchen garden with raised(?) beds. Not suitable for wheelchairs.

44 SHUCKNALL COURT

Hereford, HR1 4BH. Mrs Cessa Moore, 01432 850230. *5m E of Hereford. On A4103, signed (southerly) Weston Beggard, 5m E of Hereford towards Worcester.* **Visits by arrangement for groups of up to 20. 10 April to 30 June. Adm £6, chd free.**

Tree paeonies in May. Large collection of species, old-fashioned and shrub roses. Mixed borders in old walled farmhouse garden. Wild garden, vegetables and fruit. Himalayan type roses growing into trees, from mid June. Partial wheelchair access.

♿ ✿ 🚌

45 SHUTTIFIELD COTTAGE

Birchwood, Storridge, WR13 5HA. Mr & Mrs David Judge, 01886 884243, judge.shutti@btinternet.com. *15m E of Hereford. Turn R off A4103 at Storridg opp the Church to Birchwood. After 1¼m L down steep tarmac drive. Please park on roadside at the top of the drive but drive down if walking is difficult (150 yards).* **Sat 27 Apr, Sat 11, Sun 12, Sat 25 May, Sat 22 June, Sat 20 July, Sat 17 Aug (1.30-5). Adm £5, chd free. Home-made teas. Visits also by arrangement Apr to Sept for groups of 10+.**

Superb position and views. Unexpected 3-acre plantsman's garden, extensive herbaceous borders, primula and stump bed, many unusual trees, shrubs, perennials, colour-themed for all-yr interest. Anemones, bluebells, rhododendrons and azaleas are a particular spring feature. Large old rose garden with many spectacular climbers. Small deer park, vegetable garden. Wildlife ponds, wild flowers and walks in 20 acres of ancient woodland. Some sloping lawns and steep paths in wooded area.

46 SOUTHBOURNE & PINE LODGE

Dinmore, Hereford, HR1 3JR. Lavinia Sole & Frank Ryding. *8m N of Hereford; 8m S of Leominster. From Hereford on A49, turn R at bottom of Dinmore Hill towards Bodenham, gardens 1m on L. From Leominster on A49, L onto A417,*

Hill House Farm

2m turn R & through Bodenham, following NGS signs to garden. **Sun 5, Mon 6 May, Sat 5, Sun 6 Oct (11-5). Adm £5, chd free. Tea/ coffee and homemade cakes.**
2 south facing linked gardens totalling 4½ acres with panoramic views over Bodenham Lakes to the Black Mountains and Malvern Hills. Southbourne: Steep access to 2 acres of terraced lawns, herbaceous beds, shrubs, pond and ornamental woodland. Pine Lodge: Goblin Wood is 2½ acres featuring most of Britain's native trees plus unusual oaks with the emphasis on tree history and folklore. Not suitable for wheelchair access.

47 ◆ STOCKTON BURY GARDENS

Kimbolton, HR6 0HA. Raymond G Treasure, 07880 712649, twstocktonbury@outlook.com, www.stocktonbury.co.uk. *2m NE of Leominster. From Leominster to Ludlow on A49 turn R onto A4112. Gardens 300yds on R.* **For NGS: Wed 3 Apr (12-5). Adm £7, chd free. Home-made teas in Tithe Barn.** For other opening times and information, please phone, email or visit garden website.
Superb, sheltered 4-acre garden with colour and interest from April until October. Extensive collection of plants, many rare and unusual set amongst medieval buildings. Features pigeon house, tithe barn, grotto, cider press, auricula theatre, pools, secret garden, garden museum and rill, all surrounded by unspoilt countryside. We pride ourselves in offering great plant and gardening advice to our visitors. Café serves coffee, tea, homemade cakes and lunches made from local and seasonal produce open 11-4.30. Last lunches served at 2.45. Stockton Bury has a small garden school - all classes to be found at www.stocktonbury.co.uk. Partial wheelchair access.

48 WESTON HALL

Weston-under-Penyard, Ross-on-Wye, HR9 7NS. Mr P & Miss L Aldrich-Blake, 01989 562597, aldrichblake@btinternet.com. *1m E of Ross-on-Wye. on A40 towards Gloucester.* **Visits by arrangement Apr to Sept for groups of 5+. Light refreshments by request at modest extra cost. Adm £5, chd free.**
6 acres surrounding Elizabethan house (not open). Large walled garden with herbaceous borders, vegetables and fruit, overlooked by Millennium folly. Lawns and mature and recently planted trees and shrubs, with many unusual varieties. Orchard, ornamental ponds and lake. 4 generations in the family, but still evolving year on year. Wheelchair access to walled garden only.

49 WHITFIELD

Wormbridge, HR2 9BA. Mr & Mrs Edward Clive, 01981 570202, tclive@whitfield-hereford.com, www.whitfield-hereford.com. *8m SW of Hereford. The entrance gates are off the A465 Hereford to Abergavenny rd, ½m N of Wormbridge.* **Sun 7, Sun 14 Apr, Sun 30 June (2-5). Adm £5, chd free. Home-made teas. Visits also by arrangement Mar to Sept for groups of 10 to 30. Light refreshments can be arranged for a small extra cost.**
Parkland, wild flowers, ponds, walled garden, many flowering magnolias (species and hybrids), 1780 ginkgo tree, 1½m woodland walk with 1851 grove of coastal redwood trees. Picnic parties welcome. Dogs on leads welcome. Delicious teas. Partial access to wheelchair users, some gravel paths and steep slopes.

50 WOLFERLOW HOUSE

Wolferlow, nr Upper Sapey, HR7 4QA. Stuart & Jill Smith, 01886 853311, hillheadfm@aol.com, www.holidaylettings.co.uk/rentals/worcester/210892. *5m N of Bromyard. Off B4203 or B4214 between Upper Sapey & Stoke Bliss. Disabled parking at the house.* **Sat 15 June (10.30-5). Adm £5, chd free. Home-made teas.**
Surrounded by farmland this former Victorian rectory is set within formal and informal gardens with planting to attract wildlife. Walks through the old orchard and ponds to sit by, space to relax and reflect taking in the views of borrowed landscape. Fruit, vegetable and cutting garden and wild flower meadow. Gravel paths.

51 WOODVIEW

Great Doward, Whitchurch, Ross-on-Wye, HR9 6DZ. Janet & Clive Townsend, 01600 890477, clive.townsend5@homecall.co.uk. *6m SW of Ross-on-Wye, 4m NE of Monmouth. A40 Ross/Mon At Whitchurch follow signs to Symonds Yat west, then to Doward Park campsite. Take forestry rd 1st L garden 2nd L - follow NGS signs. (Don't rely on satnav).* **Sun 21 Apr, Sun 7, Sun 21 July (1-6). Adm £5, chd free. Home-made teas. Visits also by arrangement Apr to Sept.**
Formal and informal gardens approx 4 acres in woodland setting. Herbaceous borders, hosta collection, mature trees, shrubs and seasonal bedding. Gently sloping lawns. Statuary and found sculpture, local limestone, rockwork and pools. Woodland garden, wild flower meadow and indigenous orchids. Collection of vintage tools and memorabilia. Croquet, clock golf and garden games.

HERTFORDSHIRE

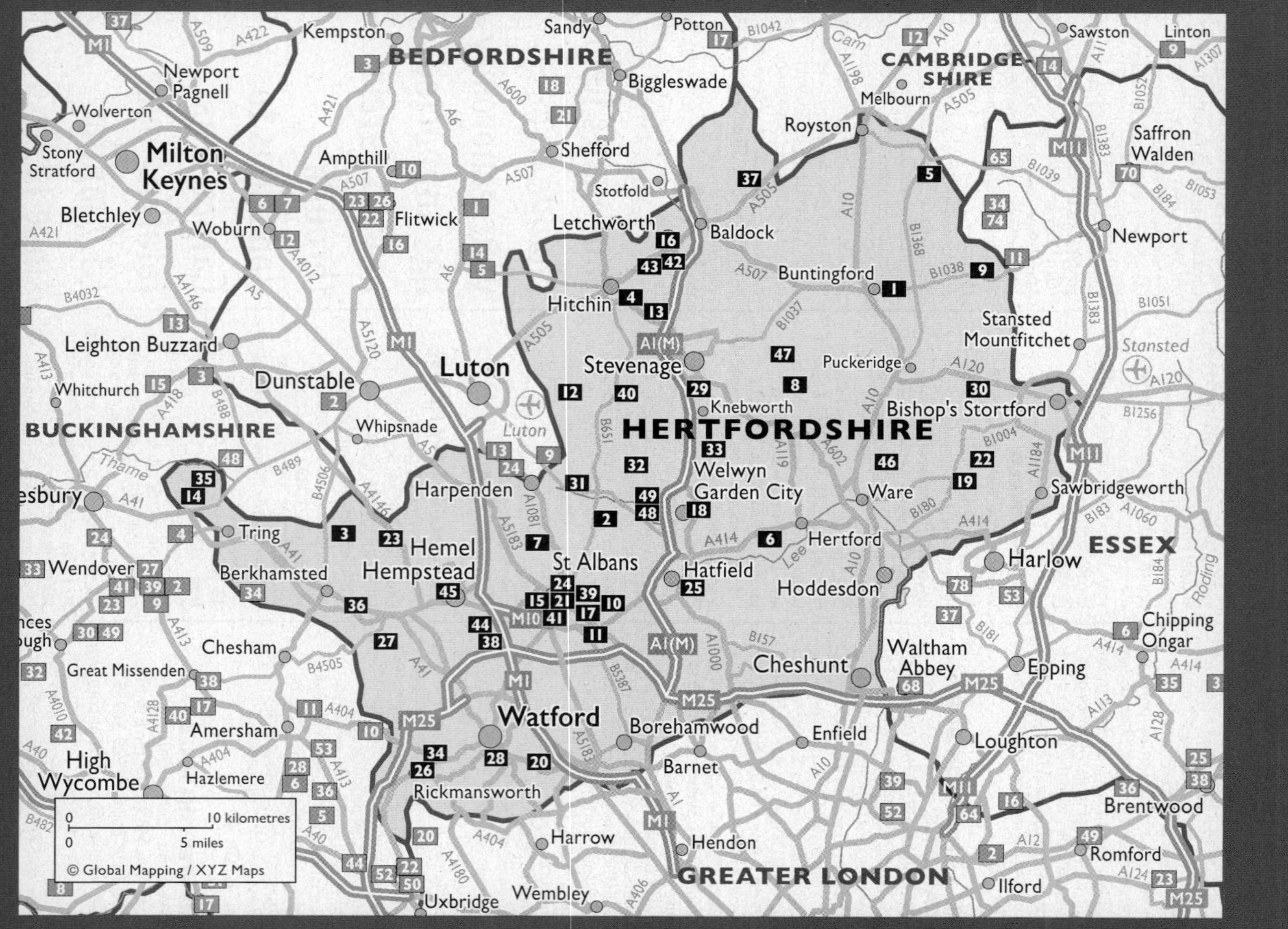

With its proximity to London, Hertfordshire became a breath of country air and a retreat for wealthy families wishing to escape the grime of the city – hence the county is peppered with large and small country estates, some of which open their garden gates for the NGS.

Hertfordshire was home for a long time to a flourishing fruit, vegetable and cut-flower trade, with produce sent up from nurseries and gardens to the London markets. There is a profusion of inviting rural areas with flower-filled country lanes and some of the best ancient woodlands carpeted with bluebells in late spring. Pretty villages sit in these rural pockets, with farmhouse, manor house and cottage gardens to visit.

Our diverse urban areas, such as St Albans with its abbey, the 'new town' of Hemel Hempstead, and Welwyn and Letchworth, the original garden cities, provide an array of interesting town gardens, both modern and traditional in their approach.

We have many gardens open 'by arrangement', and we are happy to arrange tours for large groups.

Our open gardens are each a unique reflection of the character and style of their owner, and on every visit you'll be sure to find inspiration and ideas to take home.

Below: Pie Corner

Volunteers

County Organiser
Julie Knight
01727 752375
julie.knight@ngs.org.uk

County Treasurer
Peter Barrett
01442 393508
peter.barrett@ngs.org.uk

Publicity
Kerrie Lloyd-Dawson
07736 442883
kerrield@yahoo.co.uk

Photography
Barbara Goult
07712 131414
barbara.goult@gmail.com

Social Media
Helene Iley
07805 454310
iley.helene@gmail.com

Booklet Coordinator
Julie Knight (as above)

New Gardens
Julie Wise
01438 821509
juliewise@f2s.com

Group Tours
Sarah Marsh
07813 083126
sarahkmarsh@hotmail.co.uk

Assistant County Organisers
Kate de Boinville
07973 558838
katedeboinville@btconnect.com

Christopher Melluish
01920 462500
c.melluish@btopenworld.com

Karen Smith 07850 406403
hertsgardeningangel@gmail.com

OPENING DATES

All entries subject to change. For latest information check **www.ngs.org.uk**

Map locator numbers are shown to the right of each garden name.

February

Snowdrop Festival

Saturday 9th
Walkern Hall 47

Sunday 10th
Walkern Hall 47

Friday 15th
1 Elia Cottage 19

Saturday 16th
Old Church Cottage 35

Sunday 17th
1 Elia Cottage 19
Old Church Cottage 35

March

Saturday 23rd
◆ Hatfield House West Garden 25

Saturday 30th
Walkern Hall 47

Sunday 31st
Walkern Hall 47

April

Sunday 7th
◆ St Paul's Walden Bury 40

Sunday 14th
Alswick Hall 1

Sunday 28th
Amwell Cottage 2
Serendi 43

May

Sunday 5th
Patchwork 36
Pie Corner 38

Sunday 12th
◆ St Paul's Walden Bury 40

Sunday 19th
The Manor House, Ayot St Lawrence 32
◆ Pembroke Farm 37
Thundridge Hill House 46

Saturday 25th
Beechleigh 6

Sunday 26th
15 Gade Valley Cottages 23
Huntsmoor 27

Monday 27th
Beechleigh 6
43 Mardley Hill 33

June

Sunday 2nd
The Cherry Tree 13

Friday 7th
1 Elia Cottage 19

Sunday 9th
1 Elia Cottage 19
Foxglove Cottage 22
NEW Grove House 24
◆ St Paul's Walden Bury 40
Serge Hill Gardens 44

Sunday 16th
◆ Ashridge House 3
Barley Gardens 5
8 Chapel Road 12
Serendi 43

Friday 21st
NEW Railway Cottage 39
Serendi 43
The White Cottage 49

Saturday 22nd
NEW Brent Pelham Hall 9

Sunday 23rd
NEW Brent Pelham Hall 9
NEW Railway Cottage 39

Friday 28th
The Cherry Tree 13
28 Fishpool Street 21
Mackerye End House 31

Saturday 29th
124 Highfield Way 26

Sunday 30th
◆ Benington Lordship 8
28 Fishpool Street 21
124 Highfield Way 26
9 Lloyd Taylor Close 30
St Stephens Avenue Gardens 41
Scudamore 42

July

Saturday 6th
Kearns & Meiring Physic Garden 28

Sunday 7th
Kearns & Meiring Physic Garden 28
Mackerye End House 31
9 Tannsfield Drive 45

Friday 12th
102 Cambridge Road 10

Saturday 13th
42 Falconer Road 20

Sunday 14th
102 Cambridge Road 10
42 Falconer Road 20

Friday 19th
NEW 11 Culver Road 17

Saturday 20th
42 Falconer Road 20
Kearns & Meiring Physic Garden 28

Sunday 21st
Beesonend Gardens 7
NEW 11 Culver Road 17
42 Falconer Road 20
15 Gade Valley Cottages 23
Kearns & Meiring Physic Garden 28

Sunday 28th
35 Digswell Road 18

August

Friday 2nd
22a The Avenue 4

Sunday 4th
9 Tannsfield Drive 45

Sunday 18th
Patchwork 36

Monday 26th
10 Cross Street 16

September

Every day from Saturday 7th to Sunday 15th
◆ The Celebration Garden 11

Sunday 1st
St Stephens Avenue Gardens 41

Sunday 22nd
35 Digswell Road 18
◆ Pembroke Farm 37

Saturday 28th
Waterend House 48

Sunday 29th
Church Barn 14

November

Saturday 9th
42 Falconer Road 20

By Arrangement

Arrange a personalised garden visit with your club, or group of friends, on a date to suit you. See individual garden entries for full details.

102 Cambridge Road 10
NEW 14 Corinium Gate 15
35 Digswell Road 18
1 Elia Cottage 19
42 Falconer Road 20
Huntsmoor 27
Kearns & Meiring Physic Garden 28
9 Lloyd Taylor Close 30
Morning Light 34
Patchwork 36
Pie Corner 38
Serendi 43
9 Tannsfield Drive 45
Thundridge Hill House 46
Waterend House 48
The White Cottage 49

THE GARDENS

1 ALSWICK HALL

Hare Street Road, Buntingford, SG9 0AA. Mike & Annie Johnson, www.alswickhall.co.uk/gardens. *1m from Buntingford on B1038. From the S take A10 to Buntingford, drive into town & take B1038 E towards Hare Street Village. Alswick Hall is 1m on R.* **Sun 14 Apr (12-4.30). Adm £5, chd free. Home-made teas and cake. Bar and Hog Roast.**

Listed Tudor House with 5 acres of landscaped gardens set in unspoiled farmland. Two well established natural ponds with rockeries. Herbaceous borders, shrubs, woodland walk and wild flower meadow with a fantastic selection of daffodils, tulips, camassias and crown imperial. Spring blossom, formal beds, orchard and glasshouses. Licensed Bar, Hog Roast, Teas, delicious home-made cakes, plant stall and various other trade stands, children's entertainment. Good access for disabled with lawns and wood chip paths. Slight undulations.

2 AMWELL COTTAGE

Amwell Lane, Wheathampstead, AL4 8EA. Colin & Kate Birss. *½m S of Wheathampstead. From St Helen's Church, Wheathampstead turn up Brewhouse Hill. At top L fork (Amwell Lane), 300yds down lane, park in field opp.* **Sun 28 Apr (2-5). Adm £4, chd free. Home-made teas.**

Informal garden of approx 2½ acres around C17 cottage. Large orchard of mature apples, plums and pear laid out with paths. Extensive lawns with borders, framed by tall yew hedges and old brick walls. A large variety of roses, stone seats with views, woodland pond, greenhouse, vegetable garden with raised beds and fire-pit area. Gravel drive.

3 ◆ ASHRIDGE HOUSE

Berkhamsted, HP4 1NS. Ashridge (Bonar Law Memorial) Trust, 01442 843491, events@ashridge.hult.edu, www.ashridgehouse.org.uk. *3m N of Berkhamsted. A4251, 1m S of Little Gaddesden.* **For NGS: Sun 16 June (11-4). Adm £4.50, chd £2.50. Light refreshments.**

For other opening times and information, please phone, email or visit garden website.

The gardens cover 190 acres forming part of the Grade II Registered Landscape of Ashridge Park. Based on designs by Humphry Repton in 1813 modified by Jeffry Wyatville. Small secluded gardens, as well as a large lawn area leading to avenues of trees. 2013 marked the 200th anniversary of Repton presenting Ashridge with the Red Book, detailing his designs for the estate. In 2019 Ashridge House will be holding a plant sale on the same day as the National Garden Scheme Open Day. Plants are all provided by local growers and gardens and will be reasonably priced.

4 22A THE AVENUE

Hitchin, SG4 9RL. Martin Woods, www.mwgardendesign.co.uk. *½m E of town centre. Opposite St Mary's Church head up Windmill Hill, continue to top, crossing Highbury Rd into Wymondley Rd. The Avenue is 1st turning on L. There is plenty of on rd parking.* **Evening opening Fri 2 Aug (5-9). Adm £4, chd free. Wine.**

Contemporary town garden combining clever design with knowledgeable plantsmanship. A patio area is bordered by a formal raised pond. Pots of unusual and interesting succulents, alpines, species pelargoniums and other tender plants line the steps which lead up to the lawn and garden beyond. The garden is not wheelchair accessible.

GROUP OPENING

5 BARLEY GARDENS

Barley, Royston, SG8 8LL. *Smiths End Lane, Barley. From M11, exit J10 (at Duxford) take A505 towards Royston. Follow A505 to intersection at Flint Cross, turn L for Barley (B1368). When in Barley, turn L onto Smiths End Lane. Sat Nav SG8 8LL.* **Sun 16 June (11-5). Combined adm £6, chd free. Home-made teas at Dovehouse Shott. Pinkster Gin and Tonics too!**

DOVEHOUSE SHOTT
Stephen & Justine Marsh.

THE HOOPS
Georgie McMahon.

SMITHS END BARN
Kristin & Sam Macdonald.

A group of 3 lovely family gardens all located along Smith's End Lane, a charming winding lane with spectacular far-reaching views over Hertfordshire. The three gardens share a variety of features, including lavender walks, luscious pink roses, deep herbaceous borders, small orchards, wildlife meadows, pond plantings and a courtyard garden. Wheelchair access is limited. Several steps to deal with but mostly manageable.

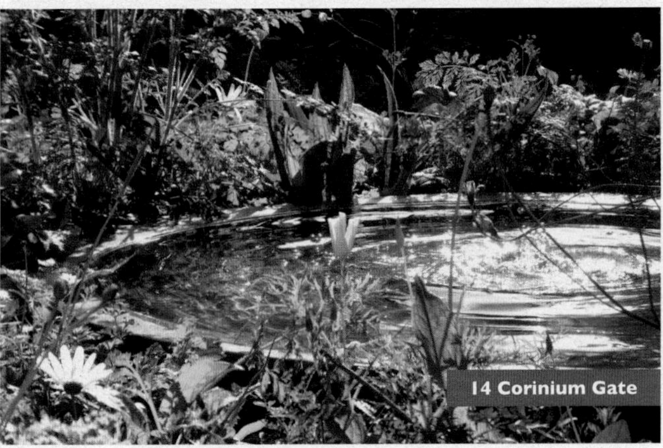

14 Corinium Gate

6 BEECHLEIGH

Birch Green, Hertford, SG14 2LP. Jacky & Gary O'Leary, www.jackyodesign.co.uk. *From A1M follow signs to Hertford along A414. From Hertford on A414, take 1st L after Hertingfordbury r'about & immed R along Old Coach Rd. House is mid way along Old Coach Rd.* **Evening opening Sat 25 May (5-7). Wine. Mon 27 May (11-4.30). Home-made teas. Adm £5, chd free. Additional Artisan Stalls.**

Set in 2½ acres, the garden combines bold confident lines of contemporary planting with more traditional herbaceous borders. The house and outbuildings formed part of the historic Panshanger Estate with the new design incorporating reclaimed stone and red brick from the original buildings. Long beds of perennial grasses surround the 13m reflective pool, forming a focal point to the main house. Contemporary perennial grass borders. Integrated fire pit and surrounding area.

Artisan stalls, children's quiz. Some gravelled/stone areas.

GROUP OPENING

7 BEESONEND GARDENS

Harpenden, AL5 2AN. *1m S of Harpenden. Take A1081 S from Harpenden, after 1m turn R into Beesonend Lane, bear R into Burywick to T-junction. Follow signs to Barlings Road.* **Sun 21 July (2-5.30). Combined adm £6, chd free. Home-made teas at both gardens.**

2 BARLINGS ROAD

Liz & Jim Machin.

NEW **7 BARLINGS ROAD**

Chris Berendt.

Set in a mature development these two gardens reflect their owners individual interests and needs. 2 Barlings Road is packed with plants, shrubs, climbers and formal pond to provide yr-round structure. The courtyard garden and shade garden add extra interest. 7 Barlings Road is a new and beautifully designed garden by Heartwood Garden Design with minimal maintenance and maximum impact. Mature trees, climbers, water feature, seating areas, wisteria and rose covered pagoda, informal borders packed with plants and a children's play area complete with Wendy house and mud kitchen. Plants for sale at No.2. Level gardens accessed via side paths.

8 ◆ BENINGTON LORDSHIP

Stevenage, SG2 7BS. Mr & Mrs R Bott, 01438 869668, garden@beningtonlordship.co.uk, www.beningtonlordship.co.uk. *4m E of Stevenage. In Benington Village, next to church. Signs off A602.* **For NGS: Sun 30 June (12-5). Adm £5, chd free. Light refreshments at Benington parish hall, next door to garden entrance.**

For other opening times and information, please phone, email or visit garden website.

7 acre garden incl historic buildings, kitchen garden, lakes. Spectacular herbaceous borders, unspoilt panoramic views. Wheelchair access is limited as garden is on a steep slope. Accessible WC available in parish hall only.

Serendi

9 NEW BRENT PELHAM HALL

Brent Pelham, Buntingford, SG9 0HF. Alexandra Carrell. *From Buntingford take the B1038 E for 5m. From Clavering take the B1038 W for 3m.* **Sat 22, Sun 23 June (2-5). Adm £5, chd free. Home-made teas will be served in the Estate Office.** Donation to St. Mary's Church, Brent Pelham.

Surrounding a beautiful grade I listed property, the gardens consist of 12 acres of formal gardens, redesigned 10 years ago by the renowned landscaper Kim Wilkie. They include two walled gardens, a potager, a walled kitchen garden, greenhouses, an orchard and a new double herbaceous border. The further 14 acres of parkland include wildflower meadows and two lakes. It is all gardened organically. Access by wheelchair to most areas of the garden, including paths of paving, gravel and grass.

10 102 CAMBRIDGE ROAD

St. Albans, AL1 5LG. Anastasia & Keith, arezanova@gmail.com. *Nr Ashley Road end of Cambridge Road in The Camp neighbourhood on east side of city. S of the A1057 (Hatfield Rd). Take the A1057 from the A1(M) J3. Take the A1081 from M25 J22.* **Evening opening Fri 12 July (6-9). Wines and authentic homemade samosas. Sun 14 July (2-6). Adm £4, chd free. Selection of teas, barista/coffee-shop coffee, homemade cakes.** Visits also by arrangement May to Sept for groups of up to 20. Cake available on request. Video presentation available as part of visit. Donation to Alzheimer's Society.

Contemporary space sympathetically redesigned in 2017 to keep as much of the existing plants, trees and shrubs in a 1930s semi's garden. Modern take on the classic garden in two halves: ornamental and vegetable. All-year interest gabion borders packed with perennials and annuals, central bed featuring a pond and a mature Japanese maple. All vegetables, annuals, and some perennials, grown from seed. 'Count the Frog' activity for children and young-at-heart. The garden features steps - there is no wheelchair access.

11 ◆ THE CELEBRATION GARDEN

Aylett Nurseries Ltd, North Orbital Road, St Albans, AL2 1DH. 01727 822255, info@aylettnurseries.co.uk, www.aylettnurseries.co.uk. *The Celebration Garden is adjacent to the Garden Centre. Aylett Nurseries is situated on the eastbound carriageway of the A414 S of St Albans, between the Park Street r'about & London Colney r'about. Drive through green gates at end of carpark.* **For NGS: Daily Sat 7 Sept to Sun 15 Sept (9-4.30). Adm by donation. Home-made teas in the Festival tea tent 7-15 Sept.** For other opening times and information, please phone, email or visit garden website.

The Celebration Garden is sited next to our famous Dahlia Field. Dahlias are planted amongst other herbaceous plants and shrubs. We also have a wild flower border complete with insect hotel. The garden is open all year to visit, during the garden centre opening hours, but it is especially spectacular from July to early autumn when the Dahlias are in flower. Annual Autumn Festival between 7 and 15 Sept. Refreshments available in the Dahlia Coffee House open all year round. Grass paths.

12 8 CHAPEL ROAD

Breachwood Green, Hitchin, SG4 8NU. Mr & Mrs Melvin Gore. *Midway between Hitchin, Harpenden & Luton, Breachwood Green is well signed. We are just 2 doors from Red Lion Pub.* **Sun 16 June (12-5). Adm £4, chd free. Home-made teas.**

Standing in the heart of the village surrounding a C17 cottage is an informal garden having no lawns or straight level pathways with a good selection of perennials, shrubs and alpines. The paths meander past ponds and waterfalls. With one of the largest collections of vintage garden tools and machinery on display as featured in Garden Answers.

13 THE CHERRY TREE

Stevenage Road, Little Wymondley, Hitchin, SG4 7HY. Patrick Woollard & Jane Woollard. *½m W of J8 off A1M. Follow sign to Little Wymondley; under railway bridge & house is R at central island flower bed opp Bucks Head Pub. Parking in adjacent rds.* **Sun 2 June (1-5). Light refreshments. Evening opening Fri 28 June (6-8.30). Wine. Adm £4, chd free.**

The Cherry Tree is a small, secluded garden on several levels containing shrubs, trees and climbers, many of them perfumed. Much of the planting, including exotics, is in containers that are cycled in various positions throughout the seasons. A heated greenhouse and summerhouse maintain tender plants in winter. The garden has been designed to be a journey of discovery as you ascend.

14 CHURCH BARN

Church Road, Puttenham, Tring, HP23 4PR. R Barker, digwithdorris.wordpress.com. *Set in the heart of Puttenham, this is one of the 51 Thankful Villages of England and Wales. From A41 take B4009 Tring/ Wendover exit. Take 1st exit on to Tring Hill towards Aston Clinton. At r'about exit to Lower Icknield Way. After 0.9m turn L. Follow signs from here.* **Sun 29 Sept (1.30-5). Adm £4, chd free. Home-made teas.**

Started from scratch in 2014, rural crafts and bee-friendly plants have been chosen to blend the garden within its rural setting. Willow stock fencing, woven in situ, a shelter crafted in locally grown sweet chestnut, hedges of Hornbeam give structure to tall, wild, colourful borders. Later flowering perennials and grasses self-seed amongst roses, annuals and dahlias. Mainly flat with lawn and stone path.

Your visits help change lives – we are Hospice UK's largest charitable funder donating more than £5 million to support hospices in local communities since 1996

15 NEW 14 CORINIUM GATE

St. Albans, AL3 4HX. Amanda Shipman, 07787 554 900, amanda@amandashipman.com, www.amandashipman.com/projects/2671945/small-town-garden-no-lawn. *1m SW of central St Albans, nr Waitrose. From King Harry Lane, take r'about into Mayne Avenue (signed 'supermarket'), then 1st L into Corinium Gate. Follow rd as it turns R, no. 14 is on L. Parking in rd or nearby.* **Visits by arrangement Apr to Nov for groups, between 4 and 12 adults, including light refreshments. Adm £7.50.**

Designed for relaxation, this low maintenance garden makes the most of a 10m x 10m urban plot. Features include a south-facing terrace, gazebo, an ornamental water feature surrounded by wild flower turf, shed with sedum roof, planting for dappled shade and zonal lighting. The garden is best appreciated from one of the seating areas. Practical, space-saving features for every-day living are built into the design. Soft fruit bushes, small fruit trees and vegetables are integrated amongst herbaceous planting in the front garden.

16 10 CROSS STREET

Letchworth Garden City, SG6 4UD. Renata & Colin Hume, www.cyclamengardens.com. *Nr town centre. From A1(M) J9 signed Letchworth, across 2 r'abouts, R at 3rd, across next 3 r'abouts L into Nevells Rd, 1st R into Cross St.* **Mon 26 Aug (2-6). Adm £4.50, chd free. Home-made teas.**

A garden with mature fruit trees is planted for interest throughout the year. The structure of the garden evolved around three circular lawns, one of which has been turned into a wildlife pond. Borders connect the different levels of the garden. There is also a large pond near the house. Featured in 'Garden News' and the 2017 Chelsea Special Edition of 'Garden Answers'. Not suitable for wheelchairs.

17 NEW 11 CULVER ROAD

St Albans, AL1 4EB. Frances Mason. *½m N from St Albans City Centre. Take A1081 N from City Centre. Turn R onto B651 (Stonecross & Sandridge Rd) then turn 2nd R into Sandpit Lane. Take 1st L (one way) into Culver Rd.* **Evening opening Fri 19 July (4-8). Sun 21 July (1-5). Adm £3.50, chd free. Light refreshments. Home made cakes and scones.**

60` by 14` terraced house garden packed with colour and texture. Annuals, perennials and flowering shrubs provide colour and interest from Spring through to late Summer including exotics such as Brugmansia and Coconut Palms and wonderful evening scents in July from, for example, Nicotiana and Tree lilies all framed by over sixteen varieties of clematis and a wealth of hanging baskets.

18 35 DIGSWELL ROAD

Welwyn Garden City, AL8 7PB. Adrian & Clare de Baat, 01707 324074, adrian.debaat@ntlworld.com, www.adriansgarden.org. *½m N of Welwyn Garden City centre. From the Campus r'about in city centre take N exit just past the Public Library into Digswell Rd. Over the White Bridge, 200yds on L.* **Sun 28 July (2-5.30); Sun 22 Sept (2-5). Adm £4, chd free. Home-made teas. Cream teas (July). Visits also by arrangement July to Oct for groups of up to 20. Adm £7 incl tea or coffee and home-made cakes.**

Town garden of around a third of an acre with naturalistic planting inspired by the Dutch garden designer, Piet Oudolf. The garden has perennial borders plus a small meadow packed with herbaceous plants and grasses. The contemporary planting gives way to the exotic, incl a succulent bed and under mature trees, a lush jungle garden incl bamboos, bananas, palms and tree ferns. Daisy Roots Nursery will be selling plants at July opening. Grass paths and gentle slopes to all areas of the garden.

19 1 ELIA COTTAGE

Nether Street, Widford, Ware, SG12 8TH. Margaret & Hugh O'Reilly, 01279 843324, hughoreilly56@yahoo.co.uk. *B1004 from Ware, Wareside to Widford past Green Man Pub into dip at Xrd take R Nether St. 8m W of Bishop's Stortford on B1004 through Much Hadham at Widford sign turn L. B180 from Stanstead Abbots.* **Fri 15, Sun 17 Feb (12-4). Light refreshments. Fri 7, Sun 9 June (12.30-5.30). Home-made teas. Adm £3.50, chd free. Visits also by arrangement Feb to Sept for groups of up to 10.**

Third acre garden reflecting the seasons. Snowdrops are our first welcome visitors. Stream with Monet-style bridge, pond and cascade. Water features. Plenty of seats. Snowdrop time warm baguettes available. In June clematis and roses abound inc. 60ft Pauls Himalayan Musk. Small wild flower meadow. Teas, cakes and Fairy Trail! Steep nature of garden means we are sorry no wheelchair access.

20 42 FALCONER ROAD

Bushey, Watford, WD23 3AD. Mrs Suzette Fuller, 077142 94170, suzettesdesign@btconnect.com. *M1 J5 follow signs for Bushey. From London A40 via Stanmore towards Watford. From Watford via Bushey Arches, through to Bushey High St, turn L into Falconer Rd, opp St James church.* **Sat 13, Sun 14, Sat 20, Sun 21 July (12-6). Adm £3.50, chd free. Light refreshments. Evening opening Sat 9 Nov (6-8). Adm £3, chd free. Wine. Visits also by arrangement for groups of up to 10.**

Enchanting magical unusual Victorian style space. Children so very welcome. Winter viewing for fairyland lighting, for all ages, bring a torch. Bird cages and chimneys a feature, plus a walk through conservatory with orchids.

21 28 FISHPOOL STREET

St. Albans, AL3 4RT. Jenny & Antony Jay. *A5183 to St Albans city centre. Turn into George St. onto Romeland then Fishpool St. At The Lower Red Lion pub walk through archway to the end of the pub car park.* **Evening opening Fri 28 June (6-8). Wine. Sun 30 June (2-5). Home-made teas. Adm £5, chd free.**

Sculpted box and yew hedging and a C17 Tripe House feature strongly in this tranquil oasis set in the vicinity of St Albans Cathedral. Gravel paths lead to a lawn surrounded by late flowering sustainable herbaceous perennial

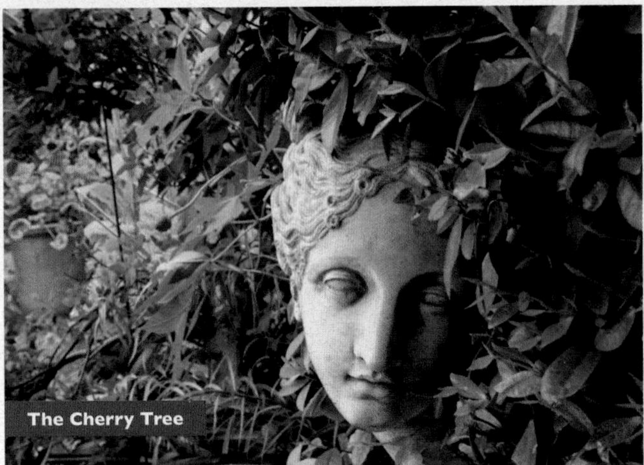
The Cherry Tree

borders and a relaxed woodland retreat. Imaginative planting in these areas offer unique perspectives. Not suitable for wheelchairs due to differing levels.

22 FOXGLOVE COTTAGE

Perry Green, Much Hadham, SG10 6EF. Jennifer & John Flexton. *6m SW of Bishops Stortford. Follow brown signs to Henry Moore Foundation. Foxglove is 2 mins walk from Hoops Inn Pub & Henry Moore Foundation Satnav postcode SG10 6EE Free Parking at Hoops Inn Pub.* **Sun 9 June (2-5). Adm £4, chd free. Home-made teas.**

A beautiful thatched cottage in an idyllic setting on ⅔ of an acre, the epitome of English country charm. Colourful abundant successional planting and classic cottage garden plants fill the overflowing herbaceous borders. A hardworking greenhouse is bordered by organic vegetables, herbs and rose garden. Vibrant blooms attract bees, butterflies and bird boxes abound. Foxgloves pop up everywhere!

23 15 GADE VALLEY COTTAGES

Dagnall Road, Great Gaddesden, Hemel Hempstead, HP1 3BW. Bryan Trueman. *3m N of Hemel Hempstead. Follow B440 N from Hemel Hempstead. Past Water End. Go past turning for Great Gaddesden. Gade Valley Cottages on R. Park in village hall car park.* **Sun 26 May, Sun 21 July (1.30-5). Adm £3.50, chd free. Home-made teas.**

165ft x 30ft sloping rural garden. Patio, lawn, borders and pond. Paths lead through a woodland area emerging by wildlife pond and sunny border. A choice of seating offers views across the beautiful Gade valley or quiet shady contemplation with sounds of rustling bamboos and bubbling water.

24  GROVE HOUSE

Waverley Road, St. Albans, AL3 5QX. Rennie Grove Hospice Care, www.renniegrove.org/opengarden. *Located in the grounds of St Albans City Hospital. Turn immed R into Lavender Crescent then follow road round to the L.* **Sun 9 June (1-5). Adm £5, chd free. Home-made teas.**

A tranquil garden with a number of different areas including a rose garden, shrubs, herbaceous plants and herbs, which create a year round interest for all. We have a new area which includes some new specimen trees and grasses. The garden is forever changing to reflect the seasons, starting with our earliest flowers, Hellebores. The garden is maintained by a wonderful dedicated team of Volunteers. There is easy wheelchair access and plenty of parking.

25 ◆ HATFIELD HOUSE WEST GARDEN

Hatfield, AL9 5HX. The Marquess of Salisbury, 01707 287010, visitors@hatfield-house.co.uk, www.hatfield-house.co.uk. *Pedestrian Entrance to Hatfield House is opp Hatfield Railway Stn, from here you can obtain directions to the gardens. Free parking is available, please use AL9 5HX with a sat nav.* **For NGS: Sat 23 Mar (11-5). Adm £6, chd free.** For other opening times and information, please phone, email or visit garden website. Donation to Another charity (to be decided by the Garden Owner).

Visitors can enjoy the spring bulbs in the lime walk, sundial garden and view the famous Old Palace garden, childhood home of Queen Elizabeth I. The adjoining woodland garden is at its best in spring with masses of naturalised daffodils and bluebells. Beautifully designed gifts, jewellery, toys and much more can be found in the Stable Yard shops. Visitors can also enjoy relaxing at the River Cottage Restaurant which serves a variety of delicious foods throughout the day. There is a good route for wheelchairs around the West garden and a plan can be picked up at the garden kiosk.

26 124 HIGHFIELD WAY

Rickmansworth, WD3 7PH. Mrs Barbara Grant. *1m E of J18 M25, 1m NW of Rickmansworth. Easily accessible from J17 or J18 M25.* **Sat 29, Sun 30 June (2-5.30). Adm £5, chd free. Home-made teas.**

Now well established, this gently sloping garden with a plethora of plants and trees provides an ever-changing burst of colour and interest throughout the year. Mixed shrub and perennial borders as well as 'cutting garden', woodland area, bog garden, fruit patch, greenhouse and an enormous pond with many fish including koi. May include sale of artworks on Open Days. Also plant sales, home-made cakes, tea and musical entertainment. Wide paths - although they are gently sloping and a little bumpy in places.

27 HUNTSMOOR

Stoney Lane, Bovingdon, Hemel Hempstead, HP3 0DP. Mr & Mrs Brian & Jane Bradnock, 01442 832014, b.bradnock@btinternet.com. *Between Bovingdon & Hemel Hempstead. Do not follow SatNav directions along Stoney Lane. Huge pot holes & ruts in lane. Approach from Bushfield Rd. Huntsmoor is facing you at the end of Bushfield Road.* **Sun 26 May (2-5). Adm £6, chd free. Home-made teas. Gluten free provided.** Visits also by arrangement May to July for groups of 10+. Adm incl tea and biscuits.

Rose garden, rhododendron border, arboretum, Koi pond, nature pond, shrub and herbaceous borders. Also has a 'cave', and lots of places to sit. Full access to garden including easy access to WC.

28 KEARNS & MEIRING PHYSIC GARDEN

89 Mildred Avenue, Watford, WD18 7DU. Victoria Kearns & Pieter Meiring, 07864 945 086, info@kmherbalists.co.uk, www.kmherbalists.co.uk. *Metered parking is available at top of Mildred Ave (opp church) & limited free parking is available on Shepherds Rd (opp Watford Grammar School for Boys) or at Cassiobury Park.* **Sat 6, Sun 7, Sat 20, Sun 21 July (11-4). Adm £5, chd free. Light refreshments. We offer a selection of herbal teas and home made cakes.** Visits also by arrangement June & July for groups of 5 to 20.

The Kearns & Meiring Physic Garden – an impressive display of medicinal herbs from Europe and beyond by practising herbalists Victoria Kearns & Pieter Meiring, based in Watford, Hertfordshire. The garden is divided into medicinal plants by body system and features ~70 different herbs. Talks about the medicinal plants in the garden with teas and cakes. Wheelchair access is available through the side passage. Contact us for parking arrangements.

29 ◆ KNEBWORTH HOUSE GARDENS

Knebworth, SG1 2AX. The Hon Henry Lytton Cobbold, 01438 812661, info@knebworthhouse.com, www.knebworthhouse.com. *nr Stevenage. Direct access from A1(M) J7 at Stevenage.* For opening times and information, please phone, email or visit garden website.

The present layout of Knebworth House's delightful Formal Gardens dates largely from the Edwardian era. Sir Edwin Lutyens' garden rooms and pollarded lime walks, Gertrude Jekyll's herb garden, the restored maze, yew hedges, roses and herbaceous borders are key features of the formal gardens with peaceful woodland walks beyond. The Garden Terrace Tea Room is available for visitors to the Park and Gardens, offering a selection of snacks and locally produced hot and cold lunches. The Gift Shop stocks a wide range of affordable gifts and souvenirs, seasonal plants and concert memorabilia, much of which is unique to Knebworth. For more details please see the website.

30 9 LLOYD TAYLOR CLOSE

Little Hadham, Ware, SG11 2NB. Anne & David Willett, 01279 771564, annemread@msn.com. *3m W of Bishop Stortford, 4m E of Standon. From A10 follow A120 to Bishop Stortford through Standon to Little Hadham lights. Turn R towards Much Hadham. Within 100yds turn R - The Smithy - then R, then L & through white gate.* **Sun 30 June (2-5). Adm £4, chd free. Home-made teas.** Visits also by arrangement May to Sept for groups of 10 to 30.

A colourful contemporary garden completely redesigned by the owners in 2013 with a small woodland garden to the side. The garden is planted to provide year round interest and colour through careful planting of bulbs, perennials, shrubs, trees and unusual plants. Also a water feature, pergola, wind spinner, garden ornaments and insect hotel with various seating areas. Step into woodland.

31 MACKERYE END HOUSE

Mackerye End, Harpenden, AL5 5DR. Mr & Mrs G Penn. *3m E of Harpenden. A1 J4 follow signs Wheathampstead, then turn R Marshalls Heath Lane. M1 J10 follow Lower Luton Road B653. Turn L Marshalls Heath Lane. Follow signs.* **Evening opening Fri 28 June (6-9). Wine. Sun 7 July (12-5). Home-made teas. Adm £6, chd free. Friday evening wine with canapés.**

C16 (Grade I listed) Manor House (not open) set in 15 acres of formal gardens, parkland and woodland, front garden set in framework of formal yew hedges. Victorian walled garden with extensive box hedging and box maze, cutting garden, kitchen garden and lily pond. Courtyard garden with extensive yew and box borders. West garden enclosed by pergola walk of old English roses. All proceeds from the refreshments will be donated to the Isabel Hospice. Walled garden access by gravel paths.

32 THE MANOR HOUSE, AYOT ST LAWRENCE

Welwyn, AL6 9BP. Rob & Sara Lucas. *4m W of Welwyn. 20 mins J4 A1M. Take B653 Wheathampstead. Turn into Codicote Rd follow signs to Shaws Corner. Parking in field, short walk to garden. A disabled drop-off point is available at the end of the drive.* **Sun 19 May (11-5). Adm £5, chd free. Home-made cakes and tea for sale.**

A 6-acre garden set in mature landscape around Elizabethan Manor House (not open). 1-acre walled garden incl glasshouses, fruit and vegetables, double herbaceous borders, rose and herb beds. Herbaceous perennial island beds, topiary specimens. Parterre and temple pond garden surround the house. Gates and water features by Arc Angel. Garden designed by Julie Toll. Home-made cakes and tea/coffee and produce for sale.

33 43 MARDLEY HILL

Welwyn, AL6 0TT. Kerrie & Pete, www.agardenlessordinary.blogspot.co.uk. *5m N of Welwyn Garden City. On B197 between Welwyn & Woolmer Green, on crest of Mardley Hill by bus stop for Arriva 300/301.* **Mon 27 May (1-5). Adm £4, chd free. Home-made teas.**

An unexpected garden created by plantaholics and packed with unusual plants. Focus on foliage and long season of interest. Constantly being developed and new plants sourced. Various areas: alpine bed;

sunny border; deep shade; white-stemmed birches and woodland planting; naturalistic stream, pond and bog; chicken house and potted vegetables; potted exotics. Seating areas on different levels. Featured in Garden News and Garden Answers.

34 MORNING LIGHT

7 Armitage Close, Loudwater, Rickmansworth, WD3 4HL. Roger & Patt Trigg, 01923 774293, roger@triggmail.org.uk. *From M25 J18 take A404 towards Rickmansworth, after ¾m turn L into Loudwater Lane, follow bends, then turn R at T-junction & R again into Armitage Close.* **Visits by arrangement Apr to Sept for groups of up to 30. Adm £4, chd free. Home-made teas.**

Compact, south-facing plantsman's garden, densely planted with mainly hardy and tender perennials and shrubs in shady environment. Features include island beds, pond, chipped cedar paths and raised deck. Tall perennials can be viewed advantageously from the deck. Large conservatory (450 sq ft) stocked with sub-tropicals.

35 OLD CHURCH COTTAGE

Chapel Lane, Long Marston, Tring, HP23 4QT. Dr John & Margaret Noakes. *A41 to Aylesbury take Tring exit. On outskirts of Tring take B488 towards Ivinghoe. At 1st r'about go on to Long Marston. Park in village - accessible parking & drop off only at house.* **Sat 16, Sun 17 Feb (11.30-3). Adm £5, chd free. At venue mulled wine and shortbreads served, incl in the adm.**

Small garden around a 400yr old thatched cottage adjoining a disused churchyard with ancient yews and Norman tower being the remnant of a Chapel of Ease. Garden laid out with raised beds with many species and varieties of snowdrops together with cyclamen, crocuses, irises and other early spring bulbs. Garden is at the end of a very narrow country lane, hence request to park in village. Ancient listed buildings in a conservation zone. Garden laid out with raised beds with many unusual snowdrops. Difficult for wheelchairs but we can help.

36 PATCHWORK

22 Hall Park Gate, Berkhamsted, HP4 2NJ. Jean & Peter Block, 01442 864731. *3m W of Hemel Hempstead. Entering E side of Berkhamsted on A4251, turn L 200yds after 40mph sign.* **Sun 5 May, Sun 18 Aug (2-5). Adm £4, chd free. Light refreshments. Visits also by arrangement Mar to Oct for groups of 10 to 30.**

¼-acre garden with lots of year-round colour, interest and perfume, particularly on opening days. Sloping site containing rockeries, 2 small ponds, herbaceous border, island beds with bulbs in Spring and dahlias in Summer, roses, fuchsias, hostas, patio pots and tubs galore - all set against a background of trees and shrubs of varying colours. Seating and cover from the elements. Not suitable for wheelchairs, as side entrance is narrow, and there are many steps and levels.

37 ◆ PEMBROKE FARM

Slip End, Ashwell, Baldock, SG7 6SQ. Krysia Selwyn-Gotha, 01462 743102, Pembrokefarmgarden@gmail.com, www.pembrokefarmgarden.co.uk. *½m S of Ashwell. Turn off A505 (The Ashwell turn opp the Wallington & Rushden junction.) Go under railway bridge & past a cottage on R, after 200 yards enter the white farm gates on R. Car park close to garden entry.* **For NGS: Sun 19 May, Sun 22 Sept (12-5). Adm £4.50, chd free.** For other opening times and information, please phone, email or visit garden website.

A country house garden in a bosquet setting, with formal gardens intermingled with nature. You are invited to meander through changing spaces creating a palimpsest of nature and structure. Wheelchair access is available through the blue door off the car-park entering the garden through the potager.

38 PIE CORNER

Millhouse Lane, Bedmond, Abbots Langley, WD5 0SG. Bella & Jeremy Stuart-Smith, piebella1@gmail.com. *Between Watford & Hemel Hempstead. 1½m from J21 M25. 3m from J8 of M1. Go to the centre of Bedmond. Millhouse Lane is opp the shops. Entrance is 50m down Millhouse Lane.* **Sun 5 May (2-5). Adm £4.50, chd free. Home-made teas.** Visits also by arrangement Apr to Sept.

A garden designed to complement the modern classical house. Formal areas near the house, with views down the valley, include lawns and a formal pool. The garden becomes more informal towards the woodland edge. A dry garden leads through new meadow planting to the vegetable garden. Enjoy blossom, bulbs, wild garlic, bluebells and rhododendrons in late spring. Access to all areas on grass or gravel paths except the formal pond where there are steps.

39 NEW RAILWAY COTTAGE

16 Sandpit Lane, St Albans, AL1 4HW. Siobhan & Barry Brindley. *½m N of St Albans city centre. J 21a of M25, follow St Albans A5183. Through town centre on A1081. Please use on-street parking in Battlefield, Lancaster, & Gurney Court Roads.* **Evening opening Fri 21 June (5-8). Wine. Sun 23 June (2-5). Home-made teas. Adm £4, chd free.**

Sandwiched between a main road and railway line this urban cottage garden is a hidden gem. Little paths are bordered by plants and flowers of all descriptions creating a mass of colour and a haven for insects and birds. There is seating throughout the garden with an eclectic collection of reclaimed items old and new. Raised bed vegetable plot with greenhouse and summerhouses.

40 ◆ ST PAUL'S WALDEN BURY

Whitwell, Hitchin, SG4 8BP. The Bowes Lyon family, stpaulswalden@gmail.com, , www.stpaulswaldenbury.co.uk. *5m S of Hitchin. On B651; ½m N of Whitwell village. From London leave A1(M) J6 for Welwyn (not Welwyn Garden City). Pick up signs to Codicote, then Whitwell.* **For NGS: Sun 7 Apr, Sun 12 May, Sun 9 June (2-7). Adm £5, chd £1. Home-made teas.** For other opening times and information, please email or visit garden website. Donation to St Paul's Walden Charity.

Spectacular formal woodland garden, Grade I listed, laid out 1720, covering over 50 acres. Long rides lined with clipped beech hedges lead to temples, statues, lake and a terraced theatre. Seasonal displays of snowdrops, daffodils, cowslips, irises, magnolias, rhododendrons, lilies. Wild flowers are encouraged. This was the childhood home of the late Queen Mother. Children welcome. 9 June, Open Garden combined with Open Farm Sunday with free tours of the farm. Wheelchair access to part of the garden. Steep grass slopes in places.

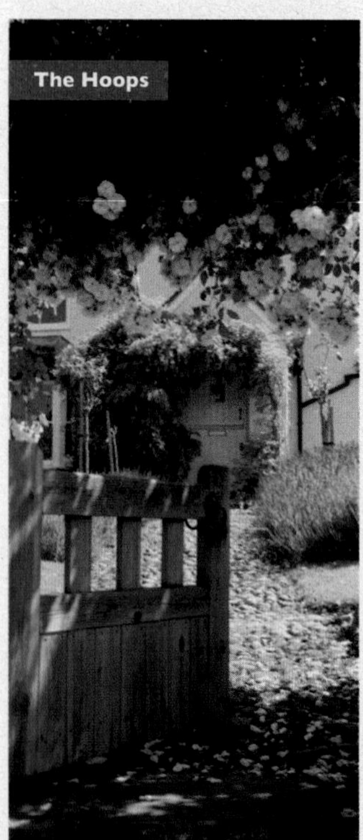
The Hoops

GROUP OPENING

41 ST STEPHENS AVENUE GARDENS

St Albans, AL3 4AD. *1m S of St Albans City Centre. From A414 take A5183 Watling St. At double mini-r'about by St Stephens Church/ King Harry Pub take B4630 Watford Rd. St Stephens Ave is 1st R.* **Sun 30 June, Sun 1 Sept (2.30-5.30). Combined adm £5, chd free. Home-made teas at No 20. WC Gluten free cake available.**

20 ST STEPHENS AVENUE

Heather & Peter Osborne.

30 ST STEPHENS AVENUE

Carol & Roger Harlow.

Two gardens of similar size and the same aspect, developed in totally different ways. The wildlife friendly plantswoman's garden at number 20 is designed to blur the boundaries of a long and narrow plot. Paths meander through the carefully maintained borders packed with unusual plants, which supply successional waves of coordinated colour. Specimen trees, and fences clothed with climbers contribute to the peaceful seclusion. Varied plant habitats include cool shade, hot dry gravel and lush pondside displays. Seating in both sun and shade is positioned to appreciate different views, a large conservatory provides shelter. Number 30 has a southwest facing gravelled front garden that has a Mediterranean feel. Herbaceous plants, such as sea hollies and achilleas, thrive in the poor, dry soil. Clipped box, beech and hornbeam in the back garden provide a cool backdrop for the strong colours of the herbaceous planting. A gate beneath a beech arch frames the view to the park beyond. Plants for sale at June opening only. Compost making demonstrations.

42 SCUDAMORE

1 Baldock Road, Letchworth Garden City, SG6 3LB. Michael & Sheryl Hann. *Opp Spring Rd, between Muddy Lane & Letchworth Lane. J9 A1M. Follow directions to Letchworth. Turn L to Hitchin A505. After 1m House on L after Muddy Lane.. Parking in Muddy Lane & Spring Rd.* **Sun 30 June (11-5). Adm £5, chd free. Home-made teas.**

½ acre garden surrounding early C17 cottages that were converted and extended in 1920s to form current house. Garden of mature trees, mixed herbaceous borders with shrubs, pond and stream, wet bed, wilder garden and orchard/ vegetable area. Many sculptures add interest to the garden.

43 SERENDI

22 Hitchin Road, Letchworth Garden City, SG6 3LT. Valerie, 01462 635386, valerie.aitken@ntlworld.com. *1m from city centre. A1(M) J9 signed Letchworth on A505. At 2nd r'about take first exit Hitchin A505. Straight over T-lights. Garden 1m on R.* **Sun 28 Apr, Sun 16 June (11-5). Home-made teas. Evening opening Fri 21 June (6-8.30). Wine. Adm £5, chd free. Visits also by arrangement Apr to Aug for groups of 10 to 20.**

A garden for all seasons. Spring bulbs and trees in abundance in large beds. Four different gravel areas, water rill surrounded by pots, a 'dribble of stones' home to Stipa and Dierama, contemporary knot garden and dry planted area with arch and bench. Later in the year an abundance of roses climbing 5 pillars, perennials and grasses. A greenhouse for over wintering and a Griffin glass house. Refreshment proceeds donated to Garden House Hospice Care. Gravel entrance driveway and paths, can be difficult. Plenty of lawns.

GROUP OPENING

44 SERGE HILL GARDENS

Serge Hill Lane, Bedmond, Watford, WD5 0RT. *½m E of Bedmond. Go to Bedmond & take Serge Hill Lane, where you will be directed past the lodge & down the drive.* **Sun 9 June (2-5). Combined adm £8, chd free. Home-made teas at Serge Hill.**

THE BARN
Sue & Tom Stuart-Smith.
D

SERGE HILL
Kate Stuart-Smith.

Two very diverse gardens. At its entrance the Barn has an enclosed courtyard, with tanks of water, herbaceous perennials and shrubs tolerant of generally dry conditions. To the N there are views over the 5-acre wild flower meadow, and the West Garden is a series of different gardens overflowing with bulbs, herbaceous perennials and shrubs. The house at Serge Hill results principally from the work of Charles Augustin Busby (1786-1817), an architect and engineer perhaps most renowned for a development west of Brighton christened Brunswick Town and for his 1808 publication: A series of designs for villas and country houses. In 1811 Busby exhibited his designs for Serge Hill House at the Royal Academy. It has wonderful views over the ha-ha to the park; a walled vegetable garden with a large greenhouse, roses, shrubs and perennials leading to a long mixed border. At the front of the house there is an outside stage used for family plays, and a ship.

45 9 TANNSFIELD DRIVE

Hemel Hempstead, HP2 5LG. Peter & Gaynor Barrett, 01442 393508, tterrabjp@ntlworld.com, www.peteslittlepatch.co.uk. *Approx 1m NE of Hemel Hempstead town centre & 2m W of J8 on M1. From M1, J8 cross r'about, A414 to Hemel Hempstead. Under ftbridge, cross r'about then 1st R across dual c'way to Leverstock Green Rd then on to High St Green. L into Ellingham Rd then follow signs.* **Sun 7 July, Sun 4 Aug (1.30-4.30). Adm £3.50, chd free. Home-made teas.** Visits also by arrangement June to Aug for groups of 5 to 10.

This small, town garden is decorated with over 450 plants which, together with the ever-present sound of water, create a welcoming oasis of calm for visitors to savour. Narrow paths divide, leading visitors on a voyage of discovery of the garden's many features. The owners regularly experiment with the garden planting scheme which ensures the look of the garden alters from year to year. Water features, metal sculptures, wall art and mirrors run throughout the garden. As a time and cost saving experiment all hanging baskets are planted with hardy perennials most of which are normally used for ground cover.

46 THUNDRIDGE HILL HOUSE

Cold Christmas Lane, Ware, SG12 0UE. Christopher & Susie Melluish, 01920 462500, c.melluish@btopenworld.com. *2m NE of Ware. ¾m from The Sow & Pigs Pub off the A10 down Cold Christmas Lane, crossing bypass.* **Sun 19 May (2-5.30). Adm £5, chd free. Cream teas.** Visits also by arrangement May to Sept for groups of 20+.

Well-established garden of approx 2½ acres; good variety of plants, shrubs and roses, attractive hedges. Visitors often ask for the unusual yellow-only bed. Several delightful places to sit. Wonderful views in and out of the garden especially down to the Rib Valley to Youngsbury, visited briefly by Lancelot 'Capability' Brown. 'A most popular garden to visit'.

47 WALKERN HALL

Walkern, Stevenage, SG2 7JA. Mrs Kate de Boinville. *4m E of Stevenage. Turn L at War Memorial as you leave Walkern, heading for Benington (immed after small bridge). Garden 1m up hill on R.* **Sat 9, Sun 10 Feb (12-4); Sat 30, Sun 31 Mar (12-5). Adm £5, chd free. Home-made teas. Warming homemade soup.**

Walkern Hall is essentially a winter woodland garden. Set in 8 acres, the carpet of snowdrops and aconites is a constant source of wonder in Jan/Feb. This medieval hunting park is known more for its established trees such as the tulip trees and a magnificent London plane tree which dominates the garden. Following on in March and April is a stunning display of daffodils and other spring bulbs. There is wheelchair access but quite a lot of gravel. No disabled WC.

48 WATEREND HOUSE

Waterend Lane, Wheathampstead, St Albans, AL4 8EP. Mr & Mrs J Nall-Cain, 07736 880810, sj@nallcain.com. *2m E of Wheathampstead. Approx 10 mins from J4 of A1M. Take B653 to Wheathampstead, past Crooked Chimney Pub, after ½m turn R into Waterend Lane. Cross river, house is immed. on R.* **Sat 28 Sept (12-6). Adm £5, chd free. Home-made teas. Wine and savoury snacks.** Visits also by arrangement Mar to June for groups of 20 to 30.

A hidden garden of 4 acres sets off an elegant Jacobean Manor House (not open). Stunning Autumn display. Steep grass slopes and fine views of glorious countryside. Formal flint-walled garden. Mature specimen trees. New pond, formal vegetable garden, bantams and Indian runner ducks. Access to a 7 acre Arboretum of close to 100 species of trees, planted in 1999. Hilly garden. Wheelchair access to lower gardens only. No accessible WC.

49 THE WHITE COTTAGE

Waterend Lane, Wheathampstead, St.Albans, AL4 8EP. Sally Trendell, 07775 897713, 01582 834617, sallytrendell@me.com. *2m E of Wheathampstead. Approx 10 mins from J5 A1M Take B653 to Wheathampstead. Soon after Crooked Chimney Pub turn R into Waterend Lane, garden 300yds on L. Parking in field opp.* **Evening opening Fri 21 June (5-9.30). Adm £5, chd free. Wine. Picnickers are welcome.** Visits also by arrangement.

An idyllic and atmospheric setting. A riverside retreat of over an acre in rural position adjacent to a ford. The River Lea widens and forms the boundary to this wildlife haven which could be a setting for 'Wind in the Willows'. Sally's cottage garden reflects her unique eclectic style.

ISLE OF WIGHT

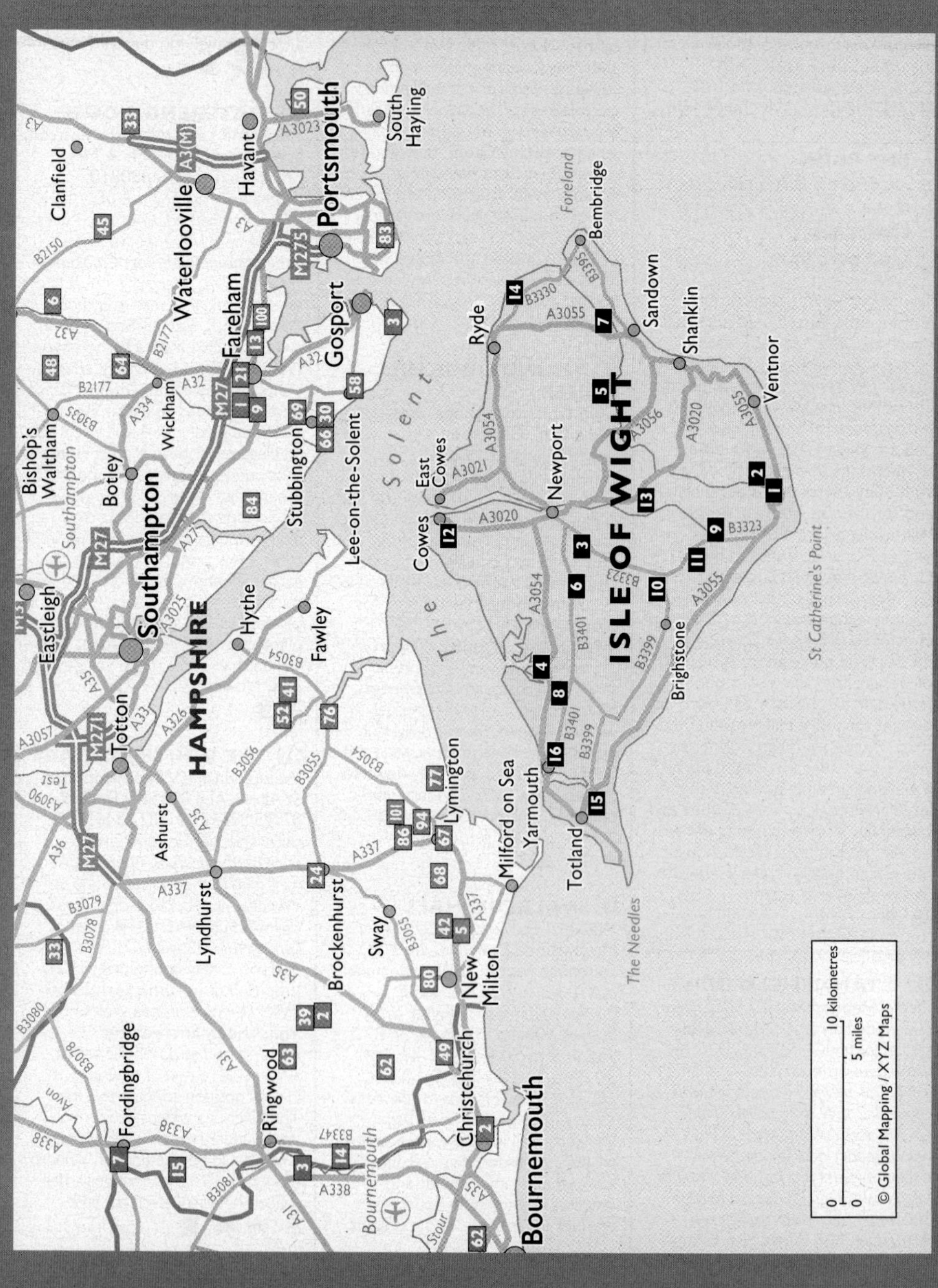

The island is a very special place to those who live and work here and to those who visit and keep returning. We have a range of natural features, from a dramatic coastline of cliffs and tiny coves to long sandy beaches.

Inland, the grasslands and rolling chalk downlands contrast with the shady forests and woodlands. Amongst all of this beauty nestle the picturesque villages and hamlets, many with gardens open for the National Garden Scheme. Most of our towns are on the coast and many of the gardens have wonderful sea views.

The one thing that makes our gardens so special is our climate. The moderating influence of the sea keeps hard frosts at bay, and the range of plants that can be grown is therefore greatly extended.

Conservatory plants are planted outdoors and flourish. Pictures taken of many island gardens fool people into thinking that they are holiday snaps of the Mediterranean and the Canaries.

Our gardens are very varied and our small enthusiastic group of garden owners are proud of their gardens, whether they are small town gardens or large manor gardens, and they love to share them for the National Garden Scheme.

Below: Salterns Cottage

Volunteers

County Organiser
Jennie Fradgley
01983 730805
jenniemf805@yahoo.co.uk

County Treasurer
Jennie Fradgley
(as above)

Publicity
Jennie Fradgley
(as above)

Booklet Co-ordinator
Jennie Fradgley
(as above)

Assistant County Organisers
Mike Eastwood
01983 721060
mike@aristia.co.uk

Sally Parker
01983 612495
sallyparkeriow@btinternet.com

OPENING DATES

All entries subject to change. For latest information check **www.ngs.org.uk**

Map locator numbers are shown to the right of each garden name.

May

Sunday 5th
Morton Manor 7

Sunday 19th
Badminton 3

Saturday 25th
NEW North Grounds Farm 9
Sunny Patch 15

Sunday 26th
NEW North Grounds Farm 9
Sunny Patch 15

June

Sunday 2nd
Meadowsweet 6
Thorley Manor 16

Saturday 8th
NEW Knighton Farmhouse 5

Sunday 9th
NEW Knighton Farmhouse 5
Rookley Manor 13

Sunday 16th
The Old Rectory 11

Saturday 22nd
Ashknowle House 2

Sunday 23rd
Ashknowle House 2

July

Sunday 7th
Amelia Cottage Garden 1

Sunday 14th
324 Park Road 12

Sunday 21st
Crab Cottage 4

August

Sunday 11th
Morton Manor 7

September

Sunday 15th
Northcourt Manor Gardens 10

By Arrangement

Arrange a personalised garden visit with your club, or group of friends, on a date to suit you. See individual garden entries for full details.

Crab Cottage 4
Morton Manor 7
Ningwood Manor 8
Northcourt Manor Gardens 10
The Old Rectory 11
324 Park Road 12
Salterns Cottage 14
Sunny Patch 15

THE GARDENS

1 AMELIA COTTAGE GARDEN

Lower Fields, Niton, Isle Of Wight, PO38 2DX. Kathy & David Yates. *5m W of Ventnor. Turn into Allotment Rd from the Niton/ Whitwell road. Follow road to the end for field parking, or park in Allotment Rd.* **Sun 7 July (11.30-4.30). Adm £3.50, chd free. Home-made teas.**
Country garden with several areas of interest, which just 14 yrs ago was farmland. Cottage-style area, vegetable plot with glasshouse, large borders, small wild flower meadow, orchard and young native trees. A haven for wildlife, butterflies and birds, and development is still ongoing.

2 ASHKNOWLE HOUSE

Ashknowle Lane, Whitwell, Ventnor, PO38 2PP. Mr & Mrs K Fradgley. *4m W of Ventnor. Take the Whitwell Rd from Ventnor or Godshill. Turn into unmade lane next to Old Rectory. Field parking. Disabled parking at house.* **Sat 22, Sun 23 June (12-4). Adm £4, chd free. Home-made teas.**
A variety of features to explore in the grounds of this Victorian house (not open). Woodland walks, wildlife and fish ponds, many colourful beds and borders. The large, well maintained, kitchen garden is highly productive and boasts a wide range of fruit and vegetables grown in cages, tunnels, glasshouses and raised beds. Diversely planted and highly productive orchard incl protected cropping of strawberries, peaches and apricots.

3 BADMINTON

Clatterford Shute, Carisbrooke, Newport, PO30 1PD. Mr & Mrs G S Montrose. *1½m SW of Newport. Parking in Carisbrooke Castle car park. Garden signed approx 200yds. Parking for disabled can be arranged, please phone 01983 526143, prior to opening.* **Sun 19 May (2-5). Adm £4, chd free. Home-made teas.**
1 acre garden on sheltered south and west facing site with good vistas. Planted for yr-round interest with many different shrubs, trees and perennials to give variety, structure and colour. Natural stream with bridges and waterfall. Pond being developed alongside kitchen garden.

4 CRAB COTTAGE

Mill Road, Shalfleet, PO30 4NE. Mr & Mrs Peter Scott, 07768 065756, mencia@btinternet.com. *4½m E of Yarmouth. At New Inn, Shalfleet, turn into Mill Rd. Continue 400yds, drive through open NT gates. Park where indicated.* **Sun 21 July (11-5). Adm £4, chd free. Home-made teas.** Visits also by arrangement May to Aug.
1¼ acres on gravelly soil. Part glorious views across croquet lawn over Newtown Creek and Solent, leading through wild flower meadow to hidden water lily pond and woodland walk. Part walled garden protected from westerlies with mixed borders, leading to terraced sunken garden with ornamental pool and pavilion, planted with exotics, tender shrubs and herbaceous perennials. Croquet, plant sales, book sales, and excellent teas, soft drinks and cakes. Gravel and uneven grass paths.

5 NEW KNIGHTON FARMHOUSE

Knighton Shute, Newchurch, Sandown, PO36 0NT. Mr & Mrs David & Ali Cripps. *Approx 1m N of Newchurch. Newchurch is accessed from the A3056 Newport to Sandown road, or Knighton from the Downs road via Knighton Shute.* **Sat 8, Sun 9 June (2-5). Adm £4, chd free. Home-made teas.**
This family garden has evolved over the past 8 yrs and is continuing to be developed. The C17 farmhouse (not open) was surrounded only by grass when we came here, and now there are mixed beds and borders, a productive organic vegetable garden, cutting garden and fruit cage. There are two small courtyard areas and plans for a third. Not suitable for wheelchairs as there are a number of steps.

6 MEADOWSWEET

5 Great Park Cottages, off Betty-Haunt Lane, Carisbrooke, PO30 4HR. Gunda Cross. *4m SW of Newport. From A3054 Newport/ Yarmouth road, turn L at Xrd Porchfield/Calbourne, over bridge into 1st lane on R. Parking along one side, on grass verge & past house.* **Sun 2 June (11.30-4.30). Adm £4, chd free. Home-made teas.**
From windswept barren 2 acre cattle field to developing tranquil country garden. Natural, mainly native planting and wild flowers. Cottagey front garden, herb garden, orchard, fruit cage and large pond. The good life and a haven for wildlife! Creative planting, wildlife pond and woodland. Very popular and unusual plants for sale. Flat level garden with grass paths.

7 MORTON MANOR

Morton Manor Road, Brading, Sandown, PO36 0EP. Mr & Mrs G Godliman, 07768 605900, patricia.godliman@yahoo.co.uk. *Off A3055 5m S of Ryde, just out of Brading. At Yarbridge T-lights turn into The Mall. Take next L into Morton Manor Rd.* **Sun 5 May, Sun 11 Aug (11-4). Adm £4, chd free. Light refreshments.** Visits also by arrangement May to Oct.
A colourful garden of great plant variety. Mature trees incl many acers with a wide variety of leaf colour. Early in the season a display of rhododendrons, azaleas and camellias and later hydrangeas and hibiscus. Ponds, sweeping lawns, roses set on a sunny terrace and much more to see in this extensive garden surrounding a picturesque C16 manor house (not open). Gravel driveway.

8 NINGWOOD MANOR

Station Road, Ningwood, Nr Newport, PO30 4NJ. Nicholas & Claire Oulton, 01983 761352, claireoulton@gmail.com. *Nr Shalfleet. From Newport, turn L opp the Horse & Groom Pub. Ningwood Manor is 300-400yds on the L. Please use 2nd set of gates.* **Visits by arrangement May to Sept for groups of up to 30. Adm £5, chd free. Light refreshments.**
A 3 acre, landscape designed country garden divided into several rooms; a walled courtyard, croquet lawn, white garden and kitchen garden. They flow into each other, each with their own gentle colour schemes, the exception to this is the croquet lawn garden which is a riot of colour, mixing oranges, reds, yellows and pinks. Much new planting has taken place over the last few yrs. The owners have several new projects underway, so the garden is a work in progress. Features incl a vegetable garden with raised beds and a small summerhouse, part of which is alleged to be Georgian.

The Old Rectory

© Carole Drake

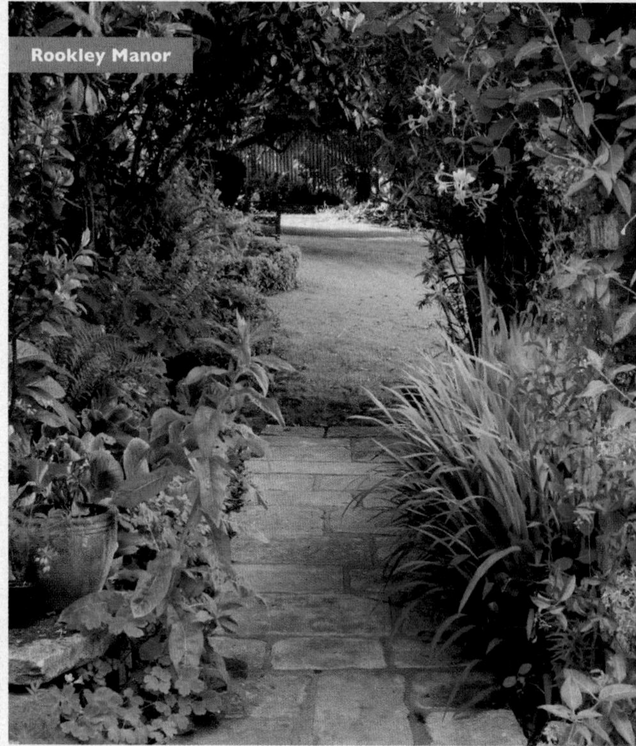
Rookley Manor

© Heather Edwards

9 NEW NORTH GROUNDS FARM

Appleford Road, Chale Green, Ventnor, PO38 2AP. Michael & Miranda Acland. *Located opp the Chale Green village sign as you approach from the E. From the W, go through Chale Green, past the village shop & the farm is ½m along, on the L.* **Sat 25, Sun 26 May (2-6). Adm £4, chd free. Home-made teas.**

Stunning landscaped garden with mature borders and a wide range of unusual plants, currently being restored by new owners with gardener Steve Cawthorne. Ornamental garden, cottage garden, spring garden, orchard, greenhouses, vegetable and herb garden, rose pergola, gazebo and wild flower meadow. Small lake with boathouse and duckhouse, planted with willows, lilies and shrubs. Barns, old piggery, woodland and sheep. Grass from parking in field to garden. Parts of garden only accessible via steps.

10 NORTHCOURT MANOR GARDENS

Main Road, Shorwell, PO30 3JG. Mr & Mrs J Harrison, 01983 740415, john@northcourt.info, www.northcourt.info. *4m SW of Newport. On entering Shorwell from Newport, entrance at bottom of hill on R. If entering from other directions head through village in direction of Newport. Garden on the L, on bend after passing the church.* **Sun 15 Sept (12-5). Adm £5, chd free. Home-made teas. Visits also by arrangement Mar to Oct for groups of 5+.**

15 acre garden surrounding large C17 manor house (not open). Boardwalk along jungle garden. A large variety of plants enjoying the different microclimates. Subtropical planting of bananas, cannas, palms tetrapanax, and a large range of salvias and hydrangeas. 1 acre walled kitchen garden with double borders, fruit and vegetables. Terraced walks, downland views, leading to chalk stream. Picturesque wooded valley around the stone manor house. Bathhouse and snail mount leading to terraces. 1 acre walled garden being restored. Last yr the house celebrated its 403rd yr anniversary. Wheelchair access on main paths only, some paths are uneven and the terraces are hilly.

11 THE OLD RECTORY

Kingston Road, Kingston, PO38 2JZ. Derek & Louise Ness, louiseness@gmail.com, www.theoldrectorykingston.co.uk. *8m S of Newport. Entering Shorwell from Carisbrooke, take L turn at mini-r'about towards Chale (B3399). Follow road, house 2nd on L, after Kingston sign. Park in adjacent field.* **Sun 16 June (2-5). Adm £4, chd free. Home-made teas. Visits also by arrangement in June for groups of up to 30.**

Constantly evolving romantic country garden surrounding the late Georgian Rectory (not open). Areas of interest incl the walled kitchen garden, orchard, formal and wildlife ponds, a wonderfully scented collection of old and English roses and two perennial wild flower meadows. Partial wheelchair access, some gravel and grass paths.

12 324 PARK ROAD

Cowes, PO31 7NN. Andrea Richter, 07970 433905, andrea@richters.co.uk. *Park Rd is the route to the Red Jet passenger ferry terminal. The property is towards the top of the road on the R as you travel from The Roundhouse r'about.* **Sun 14 July (10.30-4.30). Adm £3.50, chd free. Light refreshments. Visits also by arrangement May to Sept for groups of 5 to 20. Guided tour & tea & cake.**

This garden is an escape to the Mediterranean and Madeira. The hard landscaping takes inspiration from Moorish design. The plants are a mixture of origin from all over the world, with particular attention to the Antipodes. The garden changes dynamic throughout the year and there is always something unusual in flower. A microclimate using planting means less hardy species thrive. Wheelchair access to main parts of the garden, some smaller pathways may prove difficult.

13 ROOKLEY MANOR

Niton Road, Rookley, PO38 3NR. Mr M Eastwood & Mr M von Brasch. *Enter Niton Rd from Rookley Village. Manor is 8th house on R.* **Sun 9 June (10-4). Adm £4, chd £1. Light refreshments.**
A private, romantic, 1 acre garden developed over 15 yrs by an artist and a writer, respecting the older trees and Georgian house built in 1782 (not open). Within the framework of the garden is a continuous exploration of the possibilities of new planting ideas that take into account shade, light and space.

14 SALTERNS COTTAGE

Salterns Road, Seaview, PO34 5AH. Susan & Noël Dobbs, 01983 612132, sk.dobbs@icloud.com. *Enter Seaview from W via Springvale, Salterns Rd links the Duver Rd with Bluett Ave.* **Visits by arrangement Apr to Oct. Adm £4, chd free. Light refreshments.**
A glasshouse, a potager, exotic borders and fruit trees are some of the many attractions in this 33ft x 131ft plot. Salterns Cottage (not open), a listed building built in 1640 was bought in 1927 by Noel's grandmother Florence, married to Bram Stoker the author of Dracula. The garden was created by Susan in 2005. Flooding and sandy soil poses a constant challenge to the planting. The greenhouse and potager all raised to cope with floods. A flood step makes it difficult for wheelchair access.

15 SUNNY PATCH

Victoria Road, Freshwater, PO40 9PP. Mrs Eileen Pryer, 01983 752974, Freshair33@hotmail.com. *Halfway between Freshwater Village & Freshwater Bay. Down Afton Rd, L at garage up Stroud Rd. Keep L, just up from Parish Hall on same side. Parking in road outside house.* **Sat 25, Sun 26 May (9.30-4.30). Adm £4, chd free. Light refreshments.** Visits also by arrangement May to Aug.
A garden of an eccentric plantaholic and sculpture collector. This large and constantly evolving area has been created over 30 yrs to accommodate and reflect the owner's passion. Seasonal interest is sustained and nurtured through an extensive and interesting collection of trees, shrubs, perennials and bulbs incl some rare specimens. Features incl a fairy wood, two ponds and a variety of seated areas from which to view the landscape. This garden is a celebration of fun, fantasy and life, so look closely to appreciate its diversity. There are no paved paths and yrs of mole activity has made the ground uneven.

16 THORLEY MANOR

Thorley, Yarmouth, PO41 0SJ. Mr & Mrs Anthony Blest. *1m E of Yarmouth. From Bouldnor take Wilmingham Lane, house ½m on L.* **Sun 2 June (2-5). Adm £3.50, chd free. Home-made teas.**
Mature informal gardens of over 3 acres surrounding manor house (not open). Garden set out in a number of walled rooms incl herb garden, perennial and colourful self-seeding borders, shrub borders, lawns, large old trees, and an unusual island croquet lawn all seamlessly blending in to the surrounding farmland.

Your visits help change lives – we are the largest single funder of the Queen's Nursing Institute

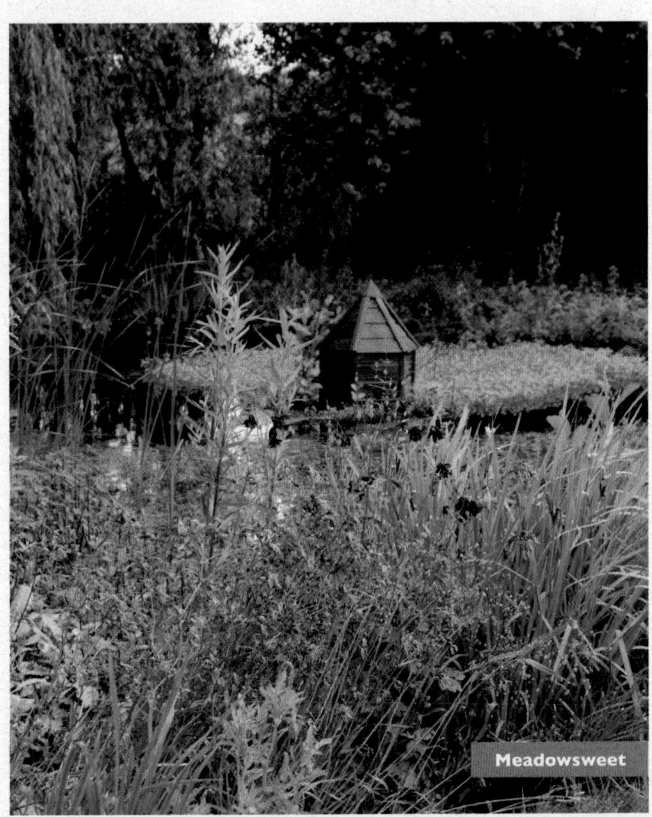
Meadowsweet

© Heather Edwards

KENT

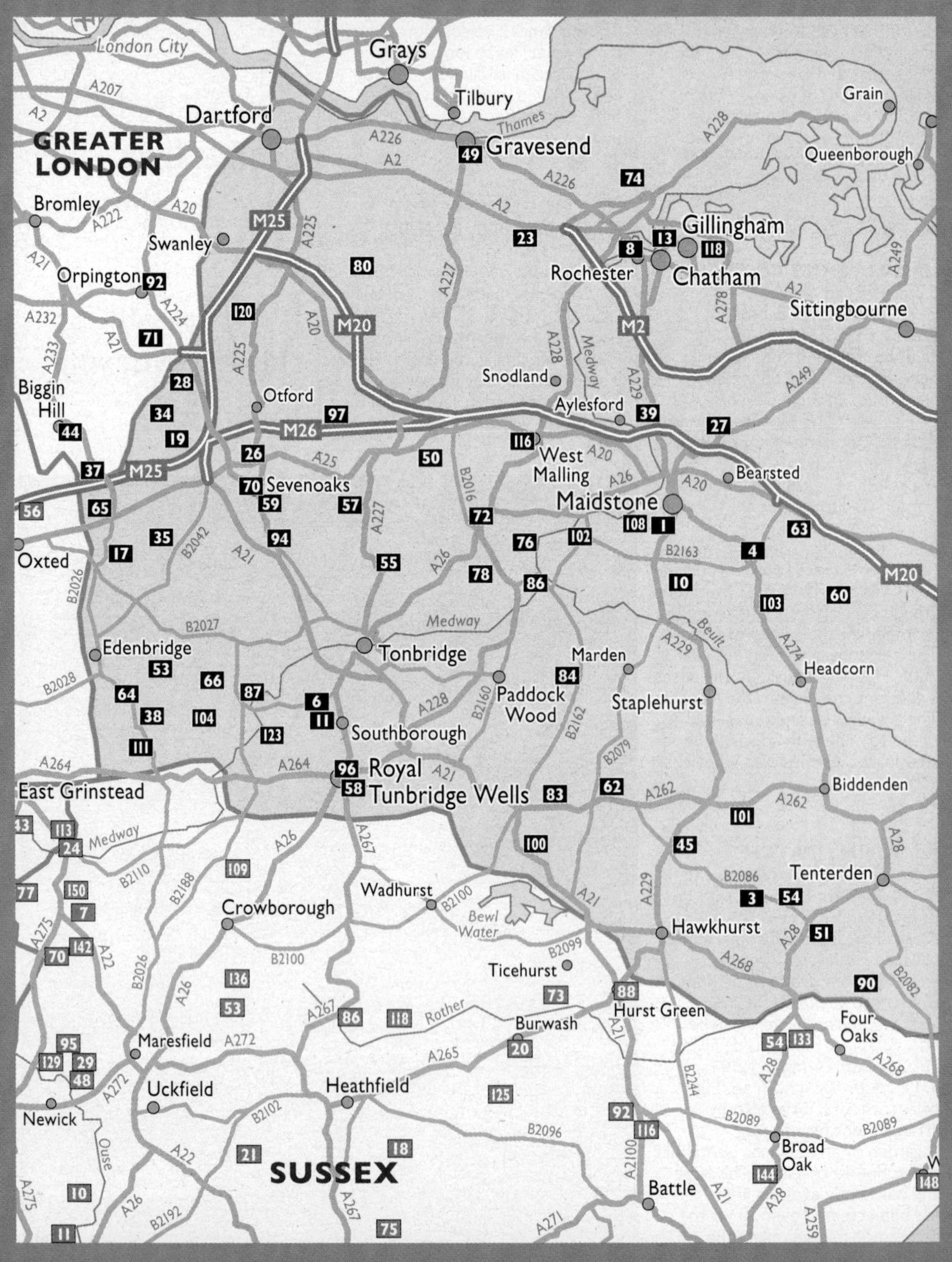
London City
Grays
Tilbury
Thames
Grain
Dartford
GREATER LONDON
Gravesend
Queenborough
Bromley
Swanley
Gillingham
Rochester
Chatham
Orpington
Sittingbourne
Snodland
Medway
Biggin Hill
Otford
Aylesford
West Malling
Bearsted
Sevenoaks
Maidstone
Oxted
Edenbridge
Tonbridge
Marden
Headcorn
Paddock Wood
Staplehurst
Southborough
Royal Tunbridge Wells
East Grinstead
Biddenden
Tenterden
Wadhurst
Crowborough
Bewl Water
Hawkhurst
Ticehurst
Hurst Green
Rother
Burwash
Four Oaks
Maresfield
Uckfield
Heathfield
Newick
Ouse
Broad Oak
SUSSEX
Battle
Beult
M25
M20
M26
M2
A2
A20
A21
A26
A28
A207
A226
A228
A229
A249
A227
A225
A25
A264
A262
A267
A268
A272
A22
A275
A2100
A265
A271
A259
A278
A232
A233
A224
A222
A274
B2042
B2026
B2027
B2028
B2016
B2163
B2160
B2162
B2079
B2086
B2082
B2110
B2188
B2100
B2099
B2244
B2089
B2096
B2102
B2192

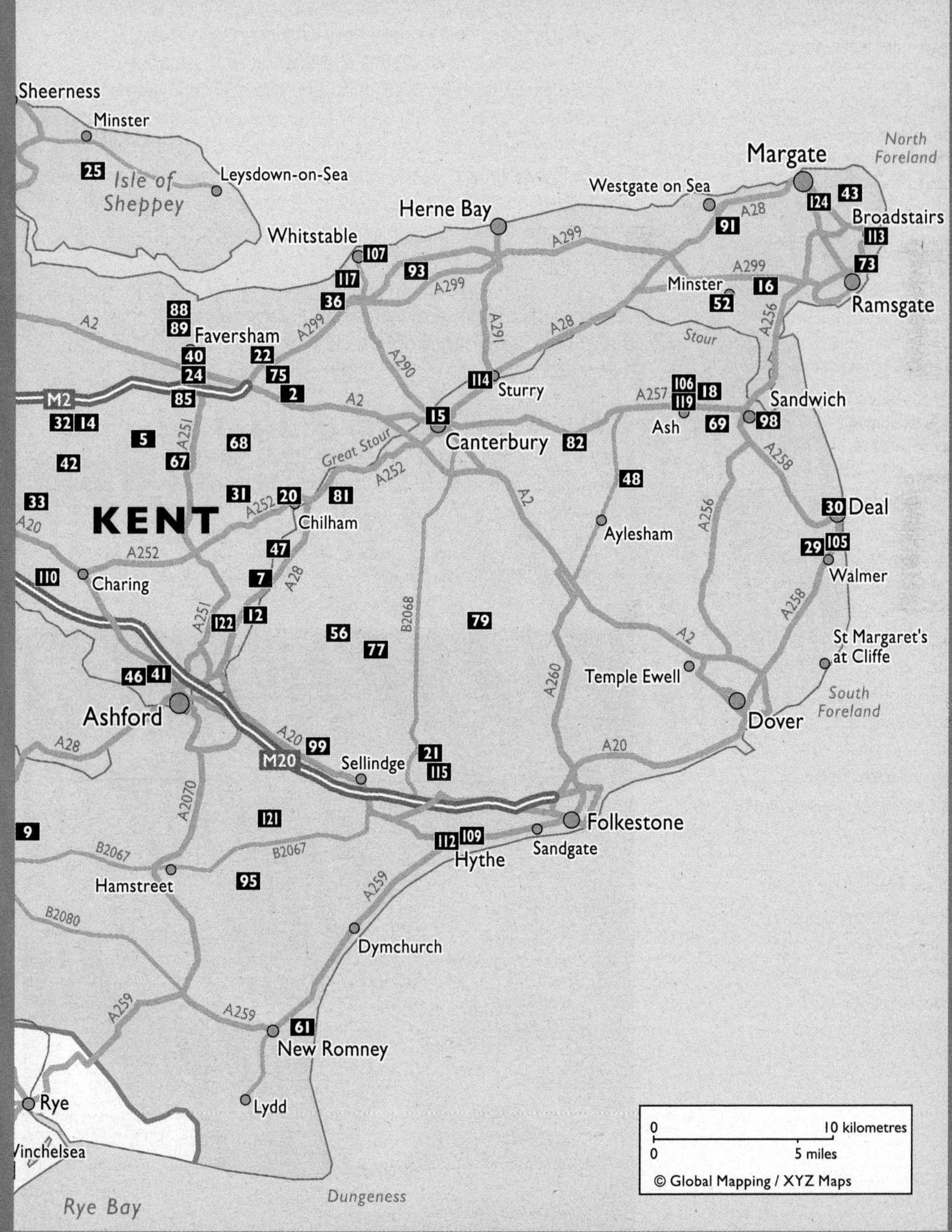
Sheerness
Minster
Isle of Sheppey
Leysdown-on-Sea
Whitstable
Herne Bay
Margate
North Foreland
Westgate on Sea
Broadstairs
Minster
Ramsgate
Faversham
Sturry
Stour
Sandwich
Ash
Canterbury
Great Stour
KENT
Chilham
Charing
Aylesham
Deal
Walmer
St Margaret's at Cliffe
Temple Ewell
South Foreland
Dover
Ashford
Sellindge
Folkestone
Sandgate
Hythe
Hamstreet
Dymchurch
New Romney
Lydd
Rye
Winchelsea
Rye Bay
Dungeness
M2
M20
A2
A20
A28
A251
A252
A256
A257
A258
A259
A260
A290
A291
A299
A2070
B2067
B2068
B2080
0 10 kilometres
0 5 miles
© Global Mapping / XYZ Maps

Volunteers

County Organiser
Jane Streatfeild 01342 850362
janestreatfeild@btinternet.com

County Treasurer
Andrew McClintock 01732 838605
mcclintockandrew@gmail.com

Publicity
Jane Streatfeild (as above)

Booklet Advertising
Marylyn Bacon 01797 270300
ngsbacon@ramsdenfarm.co.uk

Booklet Co-ordinator
Ingrid Morgan Hitchcock
01892 528341
ingrid@morganhitchcock.co.uk

Booklet Distribution
Diana Morrish 01892 723905
diana.morrish@hotmail.co.uk

Group Tours
Sue Robinson 01622 729568
suerobinson.timbers@gmail.com

Assistant County Organisers
Jacqueline Anthony 01892 518879
jacqueline.anthony@ngs.org.uk

Marylyn Bacon (as above)

Clare Barham 01580 241386
clarebarham@holepark.com

Mary Bruce 01795 531124
mary.bruce@churchmans.co.uk

Bridget Langstaff 01634 842721
bridget.langstaff@btinternet.com

Virginia Latham 01303 862881
lathamvj@gmail.com

Andrew Montgomery 01843 822971,
andrew.montgomery2012@btinternet.com

Diana Morrish (as above)

Sue Robinson (as above)

Julia Stanton 01227 700421
familystanton@hotmail.com

Nicola Talbot 01342 850526
nicola@falconhurst.co.uk

Famously known as 'The Garden of England', Kent is a county full of natural beauty, special landscapes and historical interest.

Being England's oldest county, Kent unsurprisingly boasts an impressive collection of castles and historic sites, notably the spectacular Canterbury Cathedral, and the medieval Ightham Mote.

Twenty eight per cent of the county forms two Areas of Outstanding Natural Beauty: the Kent Downs and the High Weald. The landscapes of Kent are varied and breathtaking, and include haunting marshes, rolling downs, ancient woodlands and iconic white cliffs.

The gardens of Kent are well worth a visit too, ranging from the landscaped grounds of historic stately homes and castles, to romantic cottage gardens and interesting back gardens.

Never has a county been so close to London and yet feels so far away, so why not escape to the peace of a Kent garden? The variety of the gardens and the warmth of the garden owners will ensure a memorable and enjoyable day out.

Below: **Ladham House**

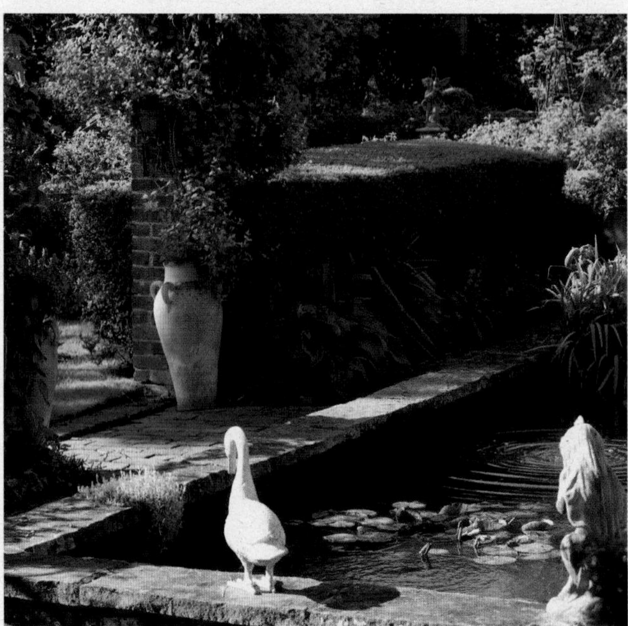

© Leigh Clapp

OPENING DATES

All entries subject to change. For latest information check www.ngs.org.uk

Map locator numbers are shown to the right of each garden name.

January

Wednesday 30th
Yew Tree Cottage 123

February

Snowdrop Festival

Sunday 10th
Copton Ash 24

Tuesday 12th
◆ Hever Castle & Gardens 53

Wednesday 13th
Yew Tree Cottage 123

Saturday 16th
Knowle Hill Farm 60

Sunday 17th
Copton Ash 24
Knowle Hill Farm 60
Mere House 72

Monday 18th
Knowle Hill Farm 60

Sunday 24th
◆ Doddington Place 32
◆ Goodnestone Park Gardens 48

Wednesday 27th
Yew Tree Cottage 123

By Arrangement:
The Old Rectory 80
Spring Platt 103

March

Sunday 3rd
Mere House 72

Sunday 10th
Stonewall Park 104

Wednesday 13th
Yew Tree Cottage 123

Sunday 17th
Copton Ash 24
Haven 52

Saturday 23rd
NEW The Old Barn 78

Sunday 24th
◆ Godinton House & Gardens 46
Mere House 72
◆ Mount Ephraim 75
NEW The Old Barn 78

Wednesday 27th
Yew Tree Cottage 123

Thursday 28th
◆ The Salutation Garden 98

Sunday 31st
Copton Ash 24
◆ Great Comp Garden 50
Haven 52

April

Wednesday 3rd
Copton Ash 24

Thursday 4th
◆ Ightham Mote 57

Sunday 7th
14 Anglesey Avenue 1
Balmoral Cottage 3
Godmersham Park 47

Wednesday 10th
Great Maytham Hall 51
Yew Tree Cottage 123

Sunday 14th
34 Cross Road 29
Frith Old Farmhouse 42
◆ Hole Park 54
Mere House 72

Friday 19th
Haven 52
Oak Cottage and Swallowfields Nursery 77

Saturday 20th
Oak Cottage and Swallowfields Nursery 77

Sunday 21st
Haven 52

Monday 22nd
◆ Cobham Hall 23
Haven 52

Wednesday 24th
Yew Tree Cottage 123

Saturday 27th
Watergate House 114

Sunday 28th
Bilting House 7
Boldshaves 9
Calico House 14
Copton Ash 24
The Courtyard 25
Frith Old Farmhouse 42
Hurst House 56
Potmans Heath House 90

Tuesday 30th
◆ Riverhill Himalayan Gardens 94

May

Wednesday 1st
◆ Hole Park 54

Friday 3rd
14 Anglesey Avenue 1

Saturday 4th
14 Anglesey Avenue 1

Sunday 5th
14 Anglesey Avenue 1
Balmoral Cottage 3
Haven 52
NEW May Cottage 70

Monday 6th
Haven 52

Wednesday 8th
Yew Tree Cottage 123

Saturday 11th
NEW Avalon 2
Copton Ash 24

Sunday 12th
NEW Avalon 2
◆ Boughton Monchelsea Place 10
Copton Ash 24
Elgin House 34
Sandown 99
Stonewall Park 104

Wednesday 15th
◆ Scotney Castle 100

Saturday 18th
NEW Brompton Village Gardens 13
Little Gables 65
NEW 18 Royal Chase 96

Sunday 19th
Bilting House 7
NEW Brompton Village Gardens 13
◆ Doddington Place 32
Frith Old Farmhouse 42
◆ Godinton House & Gardens 46
Ladham House 62
Little Gables 65
12 The Meadows 71
The Orangery 81
NEW 18 Royal Chase 96
St Clere 97
Whitstable Gardens 117

Wednesday 22nd
Great Maytham Hall 51
Yew Tree Cottage 123

Saturday 25th
Canterbury Cathedral Gardens 15
Orchard End 83

Sunday 26th
NEW Bankside 4
Canterbury Cathedral Gardens 15
The Coach House 22
The Courtyard 25
NEW The Farmhouse Garden at Tyland Barn 39
Haven 52
Old Bladbean Stud 79
Orchard End 83
◆ Orchard House, Spenny Lane 84
Sandown 99

Monday 27th
NEW Bankside 4
The Coach House 22
Falconhurst 38
Haven 52

June

Saturday 1st
14 Anglesey Avenue 1
NEW Avalon 2
Churchfield 21
Faversham Gardens 40
Tram Hatch 110
West Court Lodge 115
Wyckhurst 121

Sunday 2nd
14 Anglesey Avenue 1
◆ Boughton Monchelsea Place 10

Chevening 19
Churchfield 21
The Courtyard 25
◆ Goodnestone Park Gardens 48
◆ Hole Park 54
West Court Lodge 115
West Malling Early Summer Gardens 116
Wyckhurst 121

Tuesday 4th
14 Anglesey Avenue 1

Wednesday 5th
14 Anglesey Avenue 1
Yew Tree Cottage 123

Friday 7th
La Mouette 61
Oak Cottage and Swallowfields Nursery 77

Saturday 8th
Denne Manor Farm 31
NEW Enchanted Gardens 36
Little Gables 65
Oak Cottage and Swallowfields Nursery 77
NEW The Old Barn 78
Wyckhurst 121

Sunday 9th
Denne Manor Farm 31
NEW Enchanted Gardens 36
Haven 52
La Mouette 61
Little Gables 65
Nettlestead Place 76
NEW The Old Barn 78
Old Bladbean Stud 79
43 The Ridings 93
Rock Cottage 95
Wyckhurst 121

Wednesday 12th
◆ Riverhill Himalayan Gardens 94

Saturday 15th
NEW Cherry Tree Cottage 18
43 The Ridings 93
NEW Tankerton Gardens 107
NEW Topgallant 109
NEW Vergers 112
Watergate House 114

Sunday 16th
NEW Cherry Tree Cottage 18
NEW The Croft 27
Falconhurst 38
Godmersham Park 47
Haven 52
Ivy Chimneys 58
Potmans Heath House 90
NEW Topgallant 109
NEW Vergers 112
◆ The World Garden at Lullingstone Castle 120

Wednesday 19th
Upper Pryors 111
Yew Tree Cottage 123

Thursday 20th
◆ Mount Ephraim 75

Friday 21st
◆ Godinton House & Gardens 46

Saturday 22nd
Bishopscourt 8
Sunnybank 105

Sunday 23rd
Bishopscourt 8
Cromlix 28
Knowle Hill Farm 60
Leydens 64
Lords 67
Old Bladbean Stud 79
Sunnybank 105
Wye Gardens 122

Wednesday 26th
Great Maytham Hall 51

Saturday 29th
◆ Belmont 5

Sunday 30th
◆ Belmont 5
The Courtyard 25
Deal Gardens 30
Smiths Hall 102

July

Wednesday 3rd
◆ Doddington Place 32
◆ Leeds Castle 63

Saturday 6th
NEW Avalon 2

Sunday 7th
Bidborough Gardens 6
NEW 31 Forest Avenue 41
Goddards Green 45
Old Bladbean Stud 79
Rock Cottage 95
Tram Hatch 110

Tuesday 9th
◆ Knole 59

Saturday 13th
The Mount 74
NEW Ouden 85

Sunday 14th
Haven 52
The Mount 74
◆ Quex Gardens 91
86 Ramsden Road 92

Saturday 20th
142 Cramptons Road 26
Eureka 37
Gravesend Gardens Group 49
Hurst House 56
Orchard End 83

Sunday 21st
3 Bramble Close 12
142 Cramptons Road 26
Eureka 37
Gravesend Gardens Group 49
Hurst House 56
Old Bladbean Stud 79
Orchard End 83
Yoakley House 124

Saturday 27th
The Courtyard 25
The Orangery 81
NEW Woodlands Road Allotments 118

Sunday 28th
The Courtyard 25
The Orangery 81
Sweetbriar 106
NEW Woodlands Road Allotments 118
12 Woods Ley 119

Monday 29th
The Courtyard 25

Wednesday 31st
Great Maytham Hall 51

August

Saturday 3rd
Eureka 37
NEW 5 Montefiore Avenue 73
The Watch House 113

Sunday 4th
Eureka 37
NEW 5 Montefiore Avenue 73
Old Bladbean Stud 79
◆ Orchard House, Spenny Lane 84
The Watch House 113

Tuesday 6th
◆ Knole 59

Saturday 10th
The Garden Gate 43

Sunday 11th
Haven 52
Tram Hatch 110

Saturday 17th
◆ Chilham Castle 20

Sunday 18th
◆ Cobham Hall 23
Gardenview 44
Old Bladbean Stud 79
Sweetbriar 106
12 Woods Ley 119

Saturday 24th
Eureka 37

Sunday 25th
The Courtyard 25
Eureka 37
Haven 52

Monday 26th
The Courtyard 25
Haven 52
Long Meadow 66

September

Sunday 1st
Falconhurst 38
NEW 31 Forest Avenue 41

Wednesday 4th
NEW Ouden 85

Sunday 8th
◆ Doddington Place 32

Thursday 12th
◆ Penshurst Place & Gardens 87

Sunday 15th
Chapel House 16

Wednesday 18th
◆ Emmetts Garden 35
◆ The Salutation Garden 98

Sunday 22nd
Balmoral Cottage 3
Haven 52

Wednesday 25th
◆ Chartwell 17

Saturday 28th
NEW Enchanted Gardens 36

Sunday 29th
NEW Avalon 2
Balmoral Cottage 3
The Courtyard 25
NEW Enchanted Gardens 36
◆ Mount Ephraim 75
Sweetbriar 106
12 Woods Ley 119

October

Tuesday 1st
◆ Sissinghurst Castle Garden 101

Thursday 3rd
◆ Ightham Mote 57

Sunday 6th
Nettlestead Place 76

Sunday 13th
◆ Hole Park 54

Sunday 20th
Haven 52

Sunday 27th
◆ Great Comp Garden 50

January 2020

Sunday 26th
Copton Ash 24

February 2020

Saturday 8th
Knowle Hill Farm 60

Sunday 9th
Knowle Hill Farm 60

Sunday 16th
Copton Ash 24

By Arrangement

Arrange a personalised garden visit with your club, or group of friends, on a date to suit you. See individual garden entries for full details.

14 Anglesey Avenue 1
Bilting House 7
Boundes End 11
The Coach House 22
Copton Ash 24
142 Cramptons Road 26
Eagleswood 33
Falconhurst 38
NEW 31 Forest Avenue 41
Frith Old Farmhouse 42
The Garden Gate 43
Gardenview 44
Goddards Green 45
Godmersham Park 47
Haven 52
Hookwood House 55
Hurst House 56
Knowle Hill Farm 60
La Mouette 61
Lords 67
Luton House 68
Marshborough Farmhouse 69
The Old Rectory 80
The Orangery 81
The Orchard 82
Parsonage Oasts 86
Pheasant Barn 88
Pheasant Farm 89
43 The Ridings 93
Sandown 99
Spring Platt 103
Sweetbriar 106
Timbers 108
Wyckhurst 121

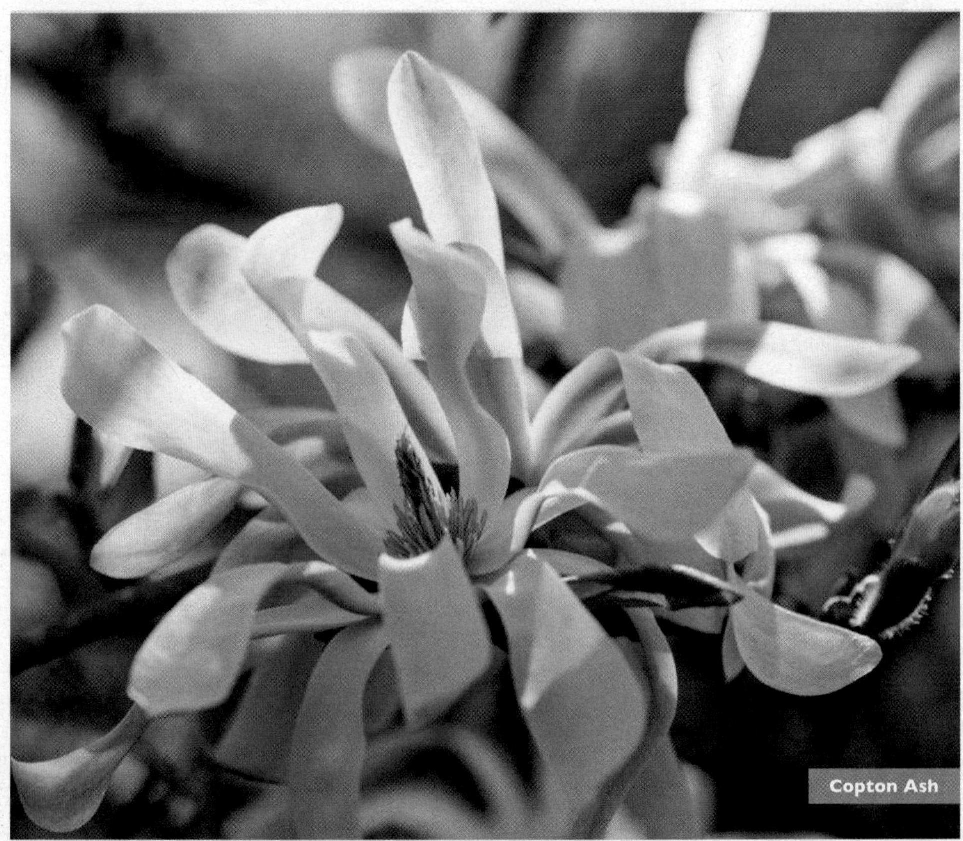
Copton Ash

© Bennet Smith

THE GARDENS

1 14 ANGLESEY AVENUE

Maidstone, ME15 9SH. Mike & Hazel Brett, 01622 299932, mandh.brett@tiscali.co.uk. *2m S of Maidstone. From Maidstone take A229 (bus routes 5 & 89) and after Swan pub take 1st R into Anglesey Avenue. Limited street parking.* **Sun 7 Apr, Fri 3, Sat 4, Sun 5 May, Sat 1, Sun 2, Tue 4, Wed 5 June (11-5). Adm £3, chd free. Light refreshments.** Visits also by arrangement Apr to June for groups of up to 20.

Plantsman's 120ft x 30ft garden with many unusual plants. Raised beds, rockeries and troughs accommodating alpine/rock garden plants. Herbaceous and shrub borders plus a shady woodland area at the end of the garden with Hellebores, Erythroniums, Trilliums, Anemones etc.

2 NEW AVALON

57 Stoney Road, Dunkirk, ME13 9TN. Mrs Croll. *4m E of Faversham, 5m W of Canterbury, 2.5m W of J7 M2. M2 J7 or A2 W of Faversham take A299, first L, Staplestreet, then L, R past Mt Ephraim, turn L, R. From A2 Canterbury, turn off Dunkirk, bottom hill turn R, Staplestreet then R, R. Park in side roads.* **Sat 11, Sun 12 May (11-6). Sat 1 June (11-6), also open Faversham Gardens. Sat 6 July (11-6). Sun 29 Sept (11-6), also open Mount Ephraim. Adm £4, chd free. Light refreshments.**

½ acre sheltered woodland garden planted for all seasons on a NW slope with views of Thames estuary. Collections of roses, hostas and ferns plus rhododendrons, shrubs, trees, vegetables, fruit, unusual plants and cut flowers for local shows. It is planted by feeling, making it a reflective space and a plant lovers' garden. Plenty of seating for taking in the garden and resting from lots of steps.

3 BALMORAL COTTAGE

The Green, Benenden, Cranbrook, TN17 4DL. Charlotte Molesworth, thepottingshedholidaylet@gmail.com. *Few 100 yds down unmade track to W of St George's Church, Benenden.* **Sun 7 Apr, Sun 5 May, Sun 22, Sun 29 Sept (12-6). Adm £6, chd £2.50. Refreshments available at Hole Park, April and May (separate additional price).**

An owner created and maintained garden now 33yrs mature. Varied, romantic and extensive topiary form the backbone for mixed borders. Vegetable garden, organically managed. Particular attention to the needs of nesting birds and small mammals lend this artistic plantswoman's garden a rare and unusual quality. No hot borders or dazzling dahlias here, where September exemplifies the 'season of mists and mellow fruitfulness'.

4 NEW BANKSIDE

Orchard Close, Langley, Maidstone, ME17 3LL. Mr & Mrs Peter and Pat Barnes. *6m S of Maidstone. From J8 M20 follow Lenham A20. At 3rd r'about take B2163 through Leeds village towards Langley. Take 2R into Heath Rd L into Shepherds Way & L into Orchard Cl. Park in Shepherds Way or Orchard Close.* **Sun 26, Mon 27 May (11-4). Adm £4. Home-made teas.**

The garden is on 2 levels & steps are used to lead you into this pretty relaxed cottage style garden. Most of the borders can be viewed on all sides. Several archways lead to areas with beds full of hostas, poppies, delphiniums, roses, clematis etc. Pond surrounded by several varieties of tall grasses. Many seating areas to enjoy a cream tea. No children due to deep pond.

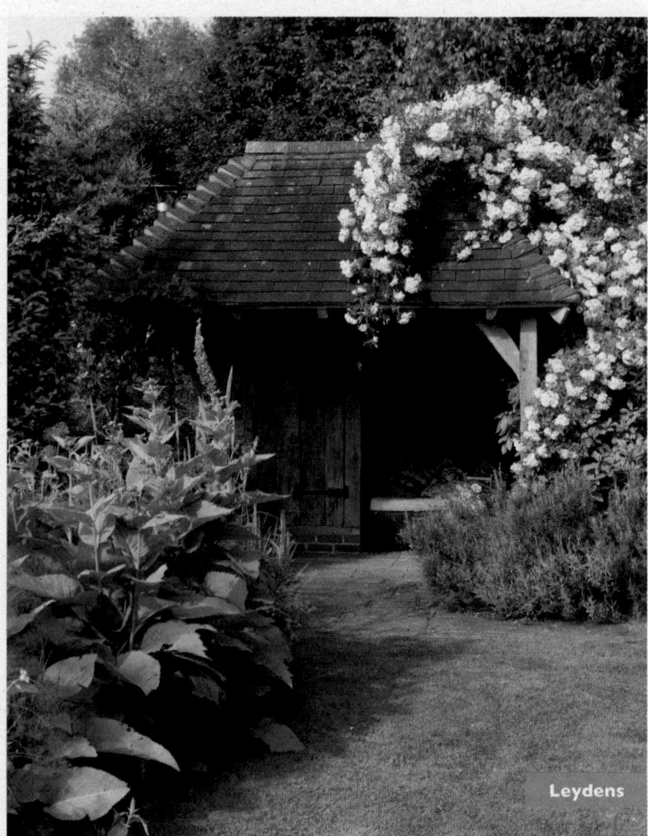

Leydens

© Leigh Clapp

5 ◆ BELMONT

Belmont Park, Throwley, Faversham, ME13 0HH. Harris (Belmont) Charity, 01795 890202, administrator@belmont-house.org, www.belmont-house.org. *4½m SW of Faversham. A251 Faversham-Ashford. At Badlesmere, brown tourist signs to Belmont.* **For NGS: Sat 29, Sun 30 June (12-5). Adm £5, chd free. Light refreshments. For other opening times and information, please phone, email or visit garden website.**

Belmont House is surrounded by large formal lawns that are landscaped with fine specimen trees, a pinetum and a walled garden containing long borders, wisteria and large rose border. There is a second walled kitchen garden, restored in 2000 (to a design by Arabella Lennox Boyd), featuring lawns, hop arbours, pleached fruit, vegetables and flowers. During the season (April-Sept) the tea room is open on Wednesdays from 12pm for light lunches and afternoon teas. At the weekend tea and home-made cake available between 1-5pm. Out of season the tea room is open on a self service basis and welcomes visitors.

GROUP OPENING

6 BIDBOROUGH GARDENS

Bidborough, Tunbridge Wells, TN4 0XB. *3m N of Tunbridge Wells, between Tonbridge & Tunbridge Wells W off A26. Take B2176 Bidborough Ridge signed to Penshurst. Take 1st L into Darnley Drive, then 1st R into St Lawrence Ave.* **Sun 7 July (1-5). Combined adm £5, chd free. Home-made teas. Gluten and dairy free cake available. Donation to Hospice in the Weald.**

The Bidborough gardens (collect garden list from Boundes End, 2 St Lawrence Avenue) are in a small village at the heart of which are The Kentish Hare pub (book in advance), the church, village store and primary school. It is a thriving community with many clubs incl a very active Garden Association! In the surrounding countryside there are several local walks. The gardens are owner designed. Enjoy a variety of formal and informal features in front and main gardens, raised beds, a pebble bed, terraces and pergolas. There are specimen trees, interesting plants and plenty of places to sit and enjoy the peaceful surroundings. Partial wheelchair access, some gardens have steps.

7 BILTING HOUSE

nr Ashford, TN25 4HA. Mr John Erle-Drax, 07764 580011, jdrax@marlboroughfineart.com. *5m NE of Ashford. A28, 9m S from Canterbury. Wye 1½m.* **Sun 28 Apr, Sun 19 May (2-6). Adm £5, chd free. Home-made teas. Visits also by arrangement Apr to Sept for groups of 10+.**

6 acre garden with ha-ha set in beautiful part of Stour Valley. Wide variety of rhododendrons, azaleas and ornamental shrubs. Woodland walk with spring bulbs. Mature arboretum with recent planting of specimen trees. Rose garden and herbaceous borders. Conservatory.

8 BISHOPSCOURT

24 St Margaret's Street, Rochester, ME1 1TS. Mrs Bridget Langstaff. *Central Rochester, nr castle & cathedral. On St Margaret's St at junction with Vines Lane. Rochester train stn 7 mins walk. Disabled parking only at garden but many car parks within 5-7 mins walk.* **Sat 22, Sun 23 June (1-5). Adm £4, chd free. Home-made teas.**

The residence of the Bishop of Rochester, this 1 acre historic walled garden is a peaceful oasis in the heart of Rochester with views of the castle from a raised lookout. Mature trees, lawns, yew hedges, rose garden, sculptures, fountain, wild flowers and mixed borders with perennials. Greenhouse and small vegetable garden. WC incl disabled.

9 BOLDSHAVES

Woodchurch, nr Ashford Kent, TN26 3RA. Mr & Mrs Peregrine Massey, 01233 860283, masseypd@hotmail.co.uk, www.boldshaves.co.uk. *Between Woodchurch & High Halden off Redbrook St. From centre of Woodchurch, with church on L and Bonny Cravat/Six Bells PH on R, 2nd L down Susan's Hill, then 1st R after ½ mile before L after a few 100 yards to Boldshaves. P as indicated.* **Sun 28 Apr (2-6). Adm £7.50, chd free. Home-made teas in Cliff Tearoom or 17C Barn (weather dependent). Donation to Kent Minds.**

7-acre garden developed over past 25 years, partly terraced, S-facing, with wide range of ornamental trees and shrubs, walled garden, Italian garden, Diamond Jubilee garden, camellia dell, herbaceous borders (incl flame bed, red borders and rainbow border), vegetable garden, bluebell walks in April, woodland and ponds. **For details of other opening times see garden website www.boldshaves.co.uk**

Home of the Wealden Literary Festival. Grass paths.

10 ◆ BOUGHTON MONCHELSEA PLACE

Church Hill, Boughton Monchelsea, Maidstone, ME17 4BU. Mr & Mrs Dominic Kendrick, 01622 743120, mk@boughtonplace.co.uk, www.boughtonplace.co.uk. *4m SE of Maidstone. From Maidstone follow A229 (Hastings Rd) S for 3½m to major T-lights at Linton Xrds, turn L onto B2163, house 1m on R; or take J8 off M20 & follow Leeds Castle signs to B2163, house 5½m on L.* **For NGS: Sun 12 May, Sun 2 June (2-5.30). Adm £5, chd £1. Home-made teas. For other opening times and information, please phone, email or visit garden website.**

150 acre estate mainly park & woodland, spectacular views over own deer park & the Weald. Grade I manor house (not open). Courtyard herb garden, intimate walled gardens, box hedges, herbaceous borders, orchard. Planting is romantic rather than manicured. Terrace with panoramic views over bluebell woods, wisteria tunnel, David Austin roses, traditional greenhouse & kitchen garden. Visit St. Peter's Church next door to see the huge stained glass Millennium Window designed by renowned local artist Graham Clark & the tranquil rose garden overlooking the deer park of Boughton Place.

11 BOUNDES END

2 St Lawrence Avenue, Bidborough, Tunbridge Wells, TN4 0XB. Carole & Mike Marks, 01892 542233, carole.marks@btinternet.com, www.boundesendgarden.co.uk. *Between Tonbridge & Tunbridge Wells off A26. Take B2176 Bidborough Ridge signed to Penshurst. Take 1st L into Darnley Drive, then 1st R into St Lawrence Ave.* **Visits by arrangement June to Aug for groups of up to 20. Adm £3, chd free. Home-made teas. Home-made teas incl gluten and dairy free.** Donation to Hospice in the Weald.

Garden, designed by owners, on an unusually shaped ⅓ acre plot formed from 2 triangles of land. Front garden features raised beds, and the main garden divided into a formal area with terrace, pebble bed and 2 pergolas, an informal area in woodland setting with interesting features and specimen trees. Plenty of places to sit and enjoy the garden. Some uneven ground in lower garden.

12 3 BRAMBLE CLOSE

Wye, TN25 5QA. Dr M Copland. *two min walk from Wye Station car park. Bramble Close is off Bramble Lane, nearly opp Wye Motors and close to Wye Stn where parking is available.* **Sun 21 July (2-6). Adm £3, chd free. Opening with Wye Gardens on Sun 23 June.**

A very wild, experimental garden sown from seed 1987-89. Wild flower meadow, pond and ditches, mown paths, native copse and hedges buzzing with wildlife - a unique experience. Demonstrating how plants manipulate diseases, insects and other animals to establish and maintain their natural population density. Featured on BBC Gardeners World. A completely wild meadow cut each year in September but supporting a large populations of butterflies, moths and other insects, amphibians, reptiles, birds, mammals including bats. Some soft ground with some uneven pathways.

GROUP OPENING

13 NEW BROMPTON VILLAGE GARDENS

Garden Street and Prospect Row, Brompton, Gillingham, ME7 5AL. Jennifer Jones. *Brompton is between Chatham & Gillingham A231 - Dock Rd next to Historic Dockyard. At r'about take A231 Wood St, opp. RSME Barracks enter Mansion Row, 1st L Garden St. Road parking in village.* **Sat 18, Sun 19 May (2-5). Combined adm £6, chd free. Home-made teas at 17 Prospect Row.**

NEW 26 GARDEN STREET
Mrs Lissie Larkin.

NEW 7 PROSPECT ROW
Ms Elaine Fowler.

NEW 13 PROSPECT ROW
Ms Nettie Iles.

NEW 14 PROSPECT ROW
Ms Audrey Iles.

NEW 16 PROSPECT ROW
Jennifer Jones.

NEW 20 PROSPECT ROW
Clive and Karen Perry.

NEW 26 PROSPECT ROW
Ms Shelagh Burroughs.

In Brompton, the 'village in the Towns' on the Saxon Shore Way, and a stone's throw from the Historic Dockyard and other historic attractions, there are 7 town gardens in two adjacent streets showing different ideas for small plots. Most of these have been re-designed in recent years, and form a combination of formal and informal designs giving alternative views about how to make interesting use of small spaces. These ideas incl what can be done when the builders do not leave enough top soil, differing approaches to ponds, planting schemes, and hard landscaping. The gardens range from low maintenance (No. 20), creative use of pots and containers (No. 26), Italianate style gardens (No's 13, 20 and 26 Garden St) and a more established garden with mature trees and all year colour attracting wildlife (No. 14), a plantswoman garden with unusual plants (No. 16) to a recently re-designed garden where plants are still establishing themselves, (No. 7).

14 CALICO HOUSE

The Street, Newnham, Sittingbourne, ME9 0LN. Graham Lloyd-Brunt, www.lloydbrunt.com. *Garden located in middle of village on rd that runs through Newnham from A2 to A20.* **Sun 28 Apr (11-5). Adm £5, chd free. Cream teas. Also open Frith Old Farmhouse.**

The garden at Calico House was made over the past decade utilising yew hedges and topiary dating from the 1920s. Terraced lawns and themed flower borders are set within a traditional English garden framework of hedges and walks. In the Spring the borders have contemporary plantings of tulips set under cherry blossom in distinct pastel, cool and hot palettes.

GROUP OPENING

15 CANTERBURY CATHEDRAL GARDENS

Canterbury, CT1 2EP. 01227 762862, events@canterbury-cathedral.org, www.canterbury-cathedral.org. *Canterbury Cathedral Precincts.* **Enter precincts via main Christchurch gate.** *No access for cars, use park & ride or public car parks.* **Entry Info: Sat 25 May general precinct & gardens entry £17. Precinct pass holders £5 gardens entry. Sun 26 May £5 gardens entry (no precinct charge). Light refreshments.**

ARCHDEACONRY
Archdeacon Jo Kelly-Moore.

THE DEANERY
The Dean.

15 THE PRECINCTS
Canon Treasurer.

19 THE PRECINCTS
Canon Librarian.

22 THE PRECINCTS
Canon Pastor.

A wonderful opportunity to visit and enjoy the private gardens within the historic precincts of Canterbury Cathedral. The Deanery Garden with scented roses, kitchen garden, unusual trees and wild fowl enclosure; the Archdeaconry includes the ancient mulberry tree, contrasting traditional and modern planting and now both a Japanese and New World influence. Other gardens offer sweeping herbaceous banks, delightful enclosed spaces, and areas planted to attract and support wildlife. Step back in time and see the herb garden, which shows the use of herbs grown for many purposes in the Middle Ages. The walled Memorial Garden has wonderful wisteria, formal roses, mixed borders and the stone war memorial at its centre, and the hidden Bastion Chapel in the city wall. A garden planted in the Friends' name surrounds the Buffs' statue. New plant fair incorporating specialist nurseries with unusual plants for sale. Cathedral Gardeners' herb stall. Home-made refreshments. Dover Beekeepers' Association, up close and personal opportunity with Birds of Prey and unique access to Bastion Chapel. Classic cars on Green Court. All gardens are wheelchair accessible.

NPC

16 CHAPEL HOUSE

Thorne Hill, Ramsgate, CT12 5DS. Andrew Montgomery. *3m W of Ramsgate. From Canterbury take A253 towards Ramsgate, from Sandwich take A256 towards Ramsgate. At Sevenscore r'about take slip rd turn R, Cottington Rd, follow Thorne Farm signs.* **Sun 15 Sept (12-5). Adm £5, chd free. Home-made teas.**

Arts and Crafts style garden within flint and brick walls surrounding converted thirteenth century chapel, orchard and vegetable garden. Teas served from granary by horse pond. Uneven paving and steps may cause difficulties.

17 ◆ CHARTWELL

Mapleton Road, Westerham, TN16 1PS. National Trust, 01732 868381, chartwell@nationaltrust.org.uk, www.nationaltrust.org.uk/chartwell. *4m N of Edenbridge, 2m S of Westerham. Fork L off B2026 after 1½m.* **For NGS: Wed 25 Sept (10-4). Adm £7.75, chd £4.50. For other opening times and information, please phone, email or visit garden website.**

Informal gardens on hillside with glorious views over Weald of Kent. Water features and lakes together with red brick wall built by Sir Winston Churchill, former owner of Chartwell. Lady Churchill's rose garden. Avenue of golden roses runs down the centre of a must see productive kitchen garden. Hard paths to Lady Churchill's rose garden and the terrace. Some steep slopes and steps.

18 NEW CHERRY TREE COTTAGE

Brookestreet, Ash, Canterbury, CT3 2NP. Mr & Mrs Kate and Neil Dymant. *8m from Canterbury. Turn off A257 into Hill's Court Rd (opp side of bypass to Ash village), continue ¾m past Brookestreet Farmhouse, garden entrance on L after sharp L bend. Ample parking.* **Sat 15, Sun 16 June (11-5). Adm £5, chd free. Home-made teas.**

One acre garden created from scratch in 2008. Stream-side woodland garden with shepherd's hut leads to formal vegetable garden flanked by outdoor kitchen adjoining mixed borders, gravel and Japanese gardens, orchard and ponds. Full of wildlife. Families welcome, games lawn, plenty of places to sit. Homemade refreshments. Most of the garden is wheelchair accessible, fairly flat with gravel paths except sloping woodland garden.

We help ordinary people open the gates to their extraordinary private gardens to raise impressive amounts of money through admissions, teas and slices of cake!

19 CHEVENING

Nr Sevenoaks, TN14 6HG. The Board of Trustees of the Chevening Estate, www.cheveninghouse.com. *4m NW of Sevenoaks. Turn N off A25 at Sundridge T-lights on to B2211; at Chevening Xrds 1½m turn L.* **Sun 2 June (2-5). Adm £7, chd £1. Home-made teas.**

The pleasure grounds of the Earls Stanhope at Chevening House are today characterised by lawns and wooded walks around an ornamental lake. First laid out between 1690 and 1720 in the French formal style, in the 1770s a more informal English design was introduced. In early C19 lawns, parterres and a maze were established and many specimen trees planted to shade woodland walks. A new cascade, modelled on a 1718 predecessor, commemorates 250 years of the Stanhope family's ownership of Chevening and 50 years stewardship by the Board of Trustees. Group guided tours of park and gardens can sometimes be arranged with the Estate Office when the house is unoccupied. Gentle slopes, gravel paths throughout.

20 ◆ CHILHAM CASTLE

Canterbury, CT4 8DB. Mr Stuart Wheeler, 01227 733100, enquiries@chilham-castle.co.uk, www.chilham-castle.co.uk. *6m SW of Canterbury, 7m NE of Ashford, centre of Chilham Village. Follow NGS signs from A28 or A252 up to Chilham village square & through main gates of Chilham Castle.* **For NGS: Sat 17 Aug (10-4). Adm £5, chd free. Home-made teas. For other opening times and information, please phone, email or visit garden website.**

The garden surrounds Jacobean house 1616 (not open). C17 terraces with herbaceous borders. Topiary frames the magnificent views with lake walk below. Extensive kitchen and cutting garden beyond spring bulb filled quiet garden. Established trees and ha-ha lead onto park. Check website for other events and attractions. Partial wheelchair access.

21 CHURCHFIELD

Pilgrims Way, Postling, Hythe, CT21 4EY. Chris and Nikki Clark. *2m NW of Hythe. From M20 J11 turn S onto A20. 1st L after ½m on bend take rd signed Lyminge. 1st L into Postling.* **Sat 1 June (1-5), also open Wyckhurst. Sun 2 June (1-5). Combined adm with West Court Lodge £6, chd free. Home-made teas in Village Hall.**
At the base of the Downs, springs rising in this garden form the source of the East Stour. Two large ponds are home to wildfowl and fish and the banks have been planted with drifts of primula, large leaved herbaceous bamboo and ferns. The rest of the 5 acre garden is a Kent cobnut platt and vegetable garden, large grass areas and naturally planted borders and woodland. Postling Church open for visitors. Areas around water may be slippery. Children must be carefully supervised.

22 THE COACH HOUSE

Kemsdale Road, Hernhill, Faversham, ME13 9JP. Alison & Philip West, 07801 824867, alison.west@kemsdale.plus.com. *3m E of Faversham. At J7 of M2 take A299, signed Margate. After 600 metres take 1st exit signed Hernhill, take 1st L over dual carriageway to T-junction, turn R & follow yellow NGS signs.* **Sun 26, Mon 27 May (11-6). Adm £4, chd free. Cream teas. Visits also by arrangement May to Sept.**
The ¾ acre garden has views over surrounding fruit-producing farmland. Sloping terraced site, and island beds with yr-round interest, a pond room, herbaceous borders containing bulbs, shrubs, perennials, and a tropical bed. The different areas are connected by flowing curved paths. Unusual planting on light sandy soil where wildlife is encouraged. Kent Wild for Wildlife gold award winner. Gold Award from Kent Wildlife Trust - Wild about Wildlife. Most of garden accessible to wheelchairs. Seating available in all areas.

23 ◆ COBHAM HALL

Cobham, DA12 3BL. Mr D Standen (Bursar), 01474 823371, www.cobhamhall.com. *3m W of Rochester, 8m E of M25 J2. Ignore SatNav directions to Lodge Lane. Entrance drive is off Brewers Rd, 50 metres E from Cobham/Shorne A2 junction.* **For NGS: Mon 22 Apr, Sun 18 Aug (2-5). Adm £3, chd free. Home-made teas in the Gilt Hall. For other opening times and information, please phone or visit garden website.**
1584 brick mansion (open for tours) and parkland of historical importance, now a boarding and day school for girls. Some herbaceous borders, formal parterres, drifts of daffodils, C17 garden walls, yew hedges and lime

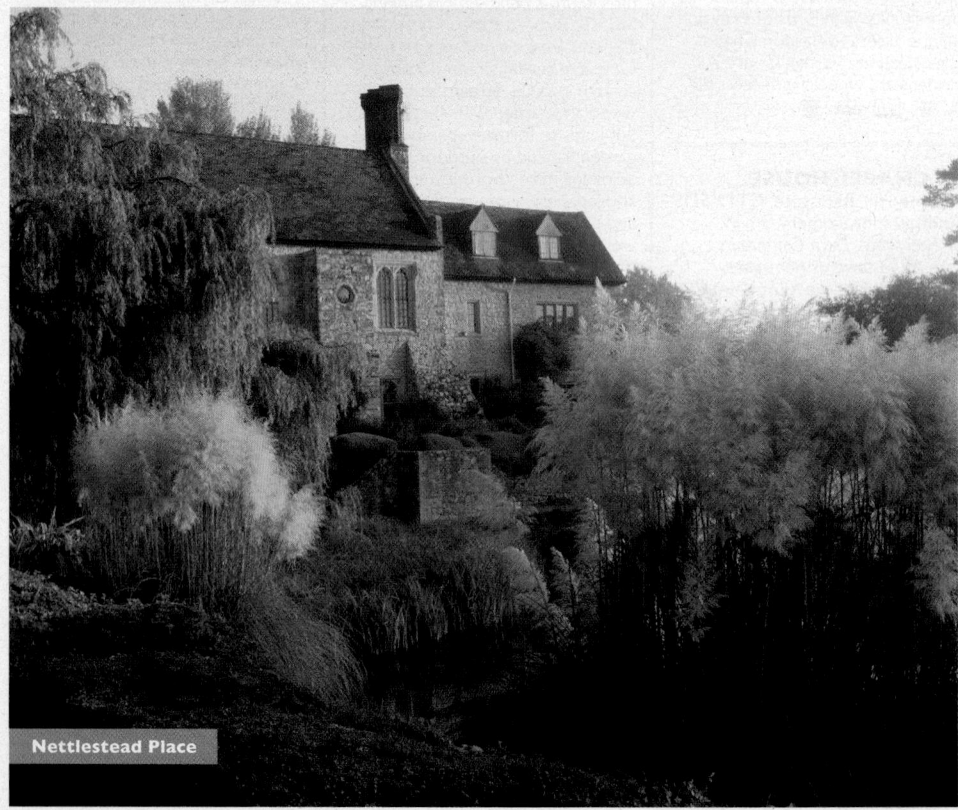

Nettlestead Place

© Leigh Clapp

avenue. Humphry Repton designed 50 hectares of park, most garden follies restored in 2009. Film location for BBC's Bleak House series and films by MGM and Universal. ITV serial The Great Fire. CBBC filmed serial 1 & 2 of Hetty Feather. Gravel and slab paths through gardens. Land uneven, many slopes. Stairs and steps in Main Hall. Please call in advance to ensure assistance.

24 COPTON ASH

105 Ashford Road, Faversham, ME13 8XW. Drs Tim & Gillian Ingram, 01795 535919, coptonash@yahoo.co.uk, www.coptonash.plus.com. *½m S of A2, Faversham. On A251 Faversham to Ashford rd. Opp E bound J6 with M2. Park in nearby laybys.* **Sun 10, Sun 17 Feb (12-4); Sun 17, Sun 31 Mar, Wed 3 Apr (12-5). Sun 28 Apr (12-5), also open Calico House. Sat 11, Sun 12 May (12-5). Adm £4, chd free. Home-made teas. Home-made soup (Jan and Feb only). 2020: Sun 26 Jan, Sun 16 Feb.** Visits also by arrangement Jan to June. Coaches offload and park nearby.

Garden grown out of a love and fascination with plants. Contains very wide collection incl many rarities and newly introduced species raised from wild seed. Special interest in woodland flowers, snowdrops and hellebores with flowering trees and shrubs of spring. Refreshed Mediterranean plantings to adapt to a warming climate. Raised beds with choice alpines and bulbs. Small alpine nursery. Gravel drive, shallow step by house and some narrow grass paths.

25 THE COURTYARD

Elmley Road, Minster On Sea, Sheerness, ME12 3SS. Kyle Ratcliffe. *Located on The Isle of Sheppey, 11m from the M2. From the A2500, travel past the rugby club, over the small r'about & turn immediately R after the 2nd hand car lot. Our garden is situated to the rear of the 5th bungalow on the L.* **Sun 28 Apr, Sun 26 May, Sun 2, Sun 30 June, Sat 27, Sun 28, Mon 29 July, Sun 25, Mon 26 Aug, Sun 29 Sept (10.30-3). Adm £5, chd free. Home-made teas.**

A young garden and home created in October 2016 by the BBC DIY SOS team. This is our family garden and smallholding which is enjoyed by our four young children daily. Our family garden has planted borders and raised beds. Having raised flower beds aids our two young sons who are full-time wheelchair users, to enjoy their garden too. Sensory based, family focused garden. We are a smallholding with a few hens, pigs, sheep, honey bees and hives, a small raised fish pond and a little pony. We welcome all families - especially those with children with special needs. Tarmac and hard stone pathways and drive.

26 142 CRAMPTONS ROAD

Sevenoaks, TN14 5DZ. Mr Bennet Smith, bennet.smith@hotmail.co.uk. *3½m from M25 J5. 1½m N of Sevenoaks, off Otford Road (A225) between Bat & Ball T-lights & Otford. Access to garden via side/rear passage. Limited parking in Cramptons Rd.* **Sat 20, Sun 21 July (11-5.30). Adm £3.50, chd free. Home-made teas.** Visits also by arrangement July to Sept for groups of 5 to 20. Weekends only.

A very small, lush & leafy plantsman's oasis. A tapestry of plants selected for texture, elegance, leaf shape, long-season interest, or perhaps for unusual habit or rarity: schefflera, wildlife-friendly umbellifers, trochodendron, tetrapanax, pseudopanax & Aesculus wangii. Immerse yourself in plants & discover what can be created and combined in a tiny space! Gardeners' World Small Space Finalist.

27 NEW THE CROFT

Pilgrims Way, Detling, Maidstone, ME14 3JY. Mr & Mrs Blair Gulland. *Detling village. J7 M20. Head N up A249 towards Sittingbourne. 1st R to Detling. 3rd R along Pilgrim's Way. House on R after de-restriction zone sign (100 yds).* **Sun 16 June (11-5). Adm £5, chd free. Home-made teas.**

Wild flower meadow, orchard with bee hives & small pond installed last year for amphibians. Walled kitchen garden designed 30 years ago to reflect the age of the house, containing a deep herbaceous border with nectar rich flowers & wide path with box hedge round vegetable area. Relaxed planting management provides haven for wildlife. Plenty of seating areas and views of the N. Downs. Local Pub and walks. Visit St Martin's medieval church in the middle of the village. Parking in meadow but access via drive for wheelchairs if necessary.

28 CROMLIX

Otford Lane, Halstead, Sevenoaks, TN14 7EB. The Kitchener family. *5m NW of Sevenoaks, 3m from M25 J4. Exit M25 at J4 for A21/A224. After ½m, 1st exit at r'bout for Badgers Mount A224. At next r'bout 3rd exit to Shoreham Ln, past PH, turn L at Xrds to Otford Ln. Field access to garden 400yds on L.* **Sun 23 June (1-5). Adm £5, chd free. Home-made teas.** Donation to West Kent Cruse Bereavement Care.

13 acre grounds, of which 7 acres are a botanist's garden with some unusual plants. Colourful herbaceous borders, scented garden, croquet and tennis lawns contrast with informal wooded walks opening up varied vistas. Laid out in the 1960s with specimen trees incl Giant Redwood and further enhanced since 2010; many bamboos. Wisteria covers tree tops and shaded areas accommodate c.400 ferns.

We open the gates to the nation's best gardens, offering a relaxing, memorable and affordable day out. A perfect experience to share with friends and family.

29 34 CROSS ROAD

Walmer, CT14 9LB. Mr Peter Jacob & Mrs Margaret Wilson. *A258 Dover to Deal. In Upper Walmer turn L into Station Rd. Under railway bridge, Cross Rd is 2nd R. Do not approach from Ringwould as SatNav suggests.* **Sun 14 Apr (11-5). Adm £4, chd free.**

An exciting and lovely garden combining great artistic sensibility with an extensive and fascinating variety of plants. ⅓ acre plantsman's garden. Collection of daphnes, hardy geraniums, herbaceous beds, unusual trees, shrubs and alpines.

GROUP OPENING

30 DEAL GARDENS

Deal, CT14 6EB. *A258 to Deal. Signs from all town car parks, maps & tickets at all gardens.* **Sun 30 June (11-5). Combined adm £5, chd free. Light refreshments at 8 Robert Street. Cafes in Town Centre.**

4 GEORGE ALLEY
Lyn Freeman & Barry Popple, 07889572676, lynandbarry10@yahoo.co.uk, www.gleaners.co.uk.

THE LANDMARK GARDEN
Imogen Jenkins on behalf of the DWCA, www.facebook.com/thelandmarkgarden.

NEW **PORTOBELLO COURT**
Mr Graham Jordan & Mr Peter Hoadley.

4 ROBERT STREET
Christine Hayes-Watkins.

NEW **8 ROBERT STREET**
Mrs Gill Walshe.

10 ST GEORGES ROAD
Peter Tullo, 01304694144, bearswell@gmail.com.

88 WEST STREET
Lyn & Peter Buller.

Start from any town car park (signs from here). 88 West Street: Cottage garden, perennials, shrubs, clematis and roses. Finalist, Kent Life Amateur Gardener Award. Landmark Community Garden: Natural planting and useful native plants, edible annuals, fruiting perennials and useful foliage. 4 George Alley: A pretty alley leads to a secret garden with courtyard and a vibrant cottage garden with summer house. 4 Robert Street: A small walled garden divided into four areas. Bedding plants, perennials, shrubs, trees, mature bamboos and water feature. 8 Robert Street: Walled wildlife friendly garden. Grape vine, rambling roses, lawn and pond. An added bonus side verge that overflows with colour. 10 St Georges Rd: North facing walled garden attached to 18 Century house. Lawn, borders, pond and majestic willow tree. Portobello Court: a pretty atmospheric narrow alley. Pots provide a colourful display of roses, hydrangeas, dahlias, begonias and other summer bedding. Limited capacity for teas. Partial wheelchair access at 4 Robert Street, 8 Robert Street, 88 West Street. No access at 4 George Alley or Portobello Court.

31 DENNE MANOR FARM

Denne Manor Lane, Shottenden, Canterbury, CT4 8JJ. Louisa Mills, www.dennemanorfarm.com. *Drive into the centre of the Hamlet of Shottenden, turn at the only 4 way X-road which is signposted to Denne Manor Lane - continue to the very end of Denne Manor Lane.* **Sat 8, Sun 9 June (12-4). Adm £5, chd free. Cream teas.**

Denne Manor House & Barn is a mid-17th and 18th Century farm house and restored barn. It is set in approx 10 acres of parkland with 2 rare breed sheep paddocks. The Manor Gardens are intricate and at the front have a Kentish apple tree and designed Buxus topary miniature maze. Further information at www.dennemanorfarm.com. Toilet with wheelchair access is available but not specifically a disabled toilet.

32 ◆ DODDINGTON PLACE

Church Lane, Doddington, Sittingbourne, ME9 0BB. Mr & Mrs Richard Oldfield, 01795 886101, enquiries@doddingtonplacegdns.co.uk, www.doddingtonplacegardens.co.uk. *6m SE of Sittingbourne. From A20 turn N opp Lenham or from A2 turn S at Teynham or Ospringe (Faversham), all 4m.* **For NGS: Sun 24 Feb (11-4); Sun 19 May (11-5). Cream teas. Wed 3 July (11-5). Light refreshments. Sun 8 Sept (10-5). Cream teas. Adm £8, chd £2. For other opening times and information, please phone, email or visit garden website.**

10 acre garden, landscaped with wide views; trees and cloud clipped yew hedges; woodland garden with azaleas and rhododendrons; Edwardian rock garden recently renovated (not wheelchair accessible); formal garden with mixed borders. A flint and brick late 20th-century gothic folly. Snowdrops in February. Wheelchair access possible to majority of gardens except rock garden.

33 EAGLESWOOD

Slade Road, Warren Street, Lenham, ME17 2EG. Mike & Edith Darvill, 01622 858702, mike.darvill@btinternet.com. *Going E on A20 nr Lenham, L into Hubbards Hill for approx 1m then 2nd L into Slade Rd. Garden 150yds on R. Coaches permitted.* **Visits by arrangement Apr to Oct for groups of 10 to 30. Adm £4, chd free. Light refreshments.** Donation to Demelza House Hospice.

2 acre plantsman's garden situated high on N-Downs, developed over the past 31yrs. Wide range of trees and shrubs (many unusual), herbaceous material and woodland plants grown to give yr-round interest, particularly in spring and for autumn colour.

34 ELGIN HOUSE

Main Road, Knockholt, Sevenoaks, TN14 7LH. Mrs Avril Bromley. *Off A21 between Sevenoaks/Orpington at Pratts Bottom r'about road signed Knockholt (Rushmore Hill) 3m on R, follow yellow NGS signs. Main Road is continuation of Rushmore Hill.* **Sun 12 May (12-5). Adm £5, chd free. Home-made teas.**

Victorian family house surrounded by a garden which has evolved over the last 50 years rhododendrons, azaleas, wisteria, camellias, magnolias, mature trees, incl a magnificent cedar tree and spacious lawns. This garden is on the top of the North Downs.

35 ◆ EMMETTS GARDEN

Ide Hill, Sevenoaks, TN14 6BA. National Trust, 01732 751507, emmetts@nationaltrust.org.uk, www.nationaltrust.org.uk/emmetts-garden. *5m SW of Sevenoaks. 1½m S of A25 on Sundridge-Ide Hill Rd. 1½m N of Ide Hill off B2042.* **For NGS: Wed 18 Sept (10-4). Adm £9, chd £4.50.**

For other opening times and information, please phone, email or visit garden website.

5 acre hillside garden, with the highest tree top in Kent, noted for its fine collection of rare trees and flowering shrubs. The garden is particularly fine in spring, while a rose garden, rock garden and extensive planting of acers for autumn colour extend the interest throughout the season. Hard paths to the Old Stables for light refreshments and WC. Some steep slopes. Volunteer driven buggy available for lifts up steepest hill.

36 NEW ENCHANTED GARDENS

Sonoma House, Pilgrims Lane, Seasalter, Whitstable, CT5 3AP. Mrs Donna Richardson, www.enchantedgardenskent.co.uk. *2m from Whitstable Town. Whitstable: At r'about, take exit onto A290 Canterbury. At r'about, take 3rd exit onto A299 ramp London/Faversham Merge onto A299. Take slip rd offered on L, turn R for Pilgrims Lane.* **Sat 8, Sun 9 June, Sat 28 Sept (10-5.30). Sun 29 Sept (10-5.30), also open Avalon. Adm £4, chd free. Light refreshments.**

It has taken 25 years to create Enchanted Gardens from open farmland to the traditional cottage style gardens it is today. I am passionate about the loss of our pollinating insects and am organic. I have collections of roses, shrubs and perennials in herbaceous borders for all garden situations to provide colour and interest from February to December.

37 EUREKA

Buckhurst Road, Westerham Hill, TN16 2HR. Gordon & Suzanne Wright. *Off A233, 1½m N of Westerham, 1m S from centre of Biggin Hill. 5m from J5 & J6 of M25 Parking at Westerham Heights Garden Centre at top of Westerham Hill on A233, 300yds from garden. Satnav use TN16 2HW. Parking at house for those with walking difficulties.* **Sat 20, Sun 21 July, Sat 3, Sun 4, Sat 24, Sun 25 Aug (11-4). Adm £5, chd free. Home-made teas.**

Approx 1 acre garden with a blaze of colourful displays in perennial borders and the 8 cartwheel centre beds. Hundreds of annuals in 100 tubs and troughs and 50 hanging baskets. Sculptures, garden art, chickens, lots of seating, and stairs to a viewing platform. Many quirky surprises at every turn. Great fun for children incl a free Treasure Trail with prizes for all, bubbles & small watering cans. Garden art incl 12ft dragon, a horse's head carved out of a 200yr old yew tree stump and a 10ft dragonfly on a reed. 2 'Secret' paths through Rhododendrons & Bamboos and a 'Spooky' walk inside the 20ft high Laurel hedge. Wheelchair access to most of the garden.

38 FALCONHURST

Cowden Pound Road, Markbeech, Edenbridge, TN8 5NR. Mr & Mrs Charles Talbot, 01342 850526, nicola@falconhurst.co.uk, www.falconhurst.co.uk. *3m SE of Edenbridge. B2026 at Queens Arms pub turn E to Markbeech. 2nd drive on R before Markbeech village.* **Mon 27 May, Sun 16 June, Sun 1 Sept (1.30-5). Adm £5, chd free. Home-made teas.** Visits also by arrangement May to Oct for groups of 10+.

4 acre garden with fabulous views devised and cared for by the same family for 160yrs. Deep mixed borders with old roses, peonies, shrubs and a wide variety of herbaceous and annual plants; ruin garden; walled garden; interesting mature trees and shrubs; kitchen garden; wildflower meadows with woodland and pond walks. Woodland pigs; orchard chickens; lambs in the paddocks.

The Mount

© Leigh Clapp

39 NEW THE FARMHOUSE GARDEN AT TYLAND BARN

Chatham Road, Sandling, Maidstone, ME14 3BD. Kent Wildlife Trust, www.kentwildlifetrust.org.uk/nature-reserves/tyland-barn. *2½m N of Maidstone. From M20 J6 take A229 to Chatham. Take 2nd L signposted Tyland Barn, R at Lower Bell Pub. Go under A229, R back onto A229 towards Maidstone. L at Esso Garage & follow Tyland Barn sign & Yellow Signs.* **Sun 26 May (10-4). Adm £4, chd free. Light refreshments.**

The Farmhouse Garden is managed chemical free & always with wildlife in mind. Relaxed borders contain pollinator friendly flowers throughout the seasons. For the herbivores there are wildflower banks & wild plants seed around. Stepover apples line path edged with geraniums. Small wildlife pond. Bee hotels, log piles. Plants labelled. Garden normally closed to the public. In Nature Park many native plants and wildflower meadows. Large pond. Tours with Head Gardener around the Nature park & gardeners on hand to answer questions. Cafe on site. Parking for blue badge users. Wheelchair access to the Farmhouse Garden is possible but with care. Wheelchair accessible path around Nature park.

GROUP OPENING

40 FAVERSHAM GARDENS

Faversham, ME13 8QN. *On edge of town, short distance from A2 & train stn. From M2 J6 take A251, L into A2, R into The Mall, cont along Forbes Rd, then L before zebra crossing/into Athelstan Rd. Combined tickets & maps from No 54.* **Sat 1 June (10-5). Combined adm £5, chd free.**

54 ATHELSTAN ROAD
Sarah Langton-Lockton OBE.

19 NEWTON ROAD
Posy Gentles, www.posygentles.co.uk.

17 NORMAN ROAD
Mary & John Cousins.

3 distinctive walled gardens in historic Faversham. Start at 54 Athelstan Road. Recently planted on a neglected site, the garden mirrors the angular 1922 house. Ornamental vegetable beds take centre stage. Climbing roses, clematis, thalictrums, Regale lilies, sibirica irises and unusual shrubs thrive, sheltered by old walls. On to 17 Norman Road, an established town garden offering privacy and delight. A large apple tree gives dappled shade, wisteria and clematis clothe the walls. Small ponds teem with wildlife. Vegetables and herbs are near the kitchen door; perennials interwoven with mature shrubs throughout. 19 Newton Road, a long, thin town garden, where the plant loving owner has used billowing roses, shrubs, climbers and perennials to blur boundaries. The judicious planting of trees, and curving paths, veil rather than conceal the garden as you move through it. Predominately soft colour scheme of creams, peaches and faded lilacs. Teas widely available in Faversham. Level access to 54 Athelstan Road.

41 NEW 31 FOREST AVENUE

Orchard Heights, Ashford, TN25 4GB. Tony and Wendy Green, 01233650710, tony.green41@yahoo.co.uk. *From Drovers Island Ashford take A20 Maidstone L @ 1st r'about Orchard Heights, R @ next r'about cont. to next r'about L into Forest Ave follow NGS signs.* **Sun 7 July, also open Tram Hatch. Sun 1 Sept (11-4). Adm £3, chd free. Home-made teas.**
Visits also by arrangement in Aug for groups of 5 to 20. Week days only 12pm-4pm.

Small suburban garden evolved since May 2017 containing unusual and rare tress, shrubs and plants e.g. Multi-stemmed Ginkgo Biloba, Japanese Redwood, Wollemi Pine and a collection of Salvias. Instead of a hot tub immerse yourself in a Japanse and exotic space.

42 FRITH OLD FARMHOUSE

Frith Road, Otterden, Faversham, ME13 0DD. Drs Gillian & Peter Regan, 01795 890556, peter.regan@cantab.net. *½m off Lenham to Faversham rd. From A20 E of Lenham turn N up Hubbards Hill, follow signs Eastling; after 4m turn L into Frith Rd. From A2 in Faversham turn S (Brogdale Rd); continue 7m (thro' Eastling), turn R into Frith Rd.* **Sun 14 Apr (11-5). Sun 28 Apr (11-5), also open Copton Ash. Sun 19 May (11-5). Adm £5, chd free. Home-made teas.** Visits also by arrangement Apr to Sept. Please contact owners in advance.

A riot of plants growing together as if in the wild, developed over 40 yrs. No neat edges or formal beds, but several hundred interesting (& some very unusual) plants. Trees and shrubs chosen for year-round appeal. Special interest in bulbs and woodland plants. Visitor comments - 'one of the best we have seen, natural & full of treasures', 'a plethora of plants', 'inspirational', 'a hidden gem'. Altered habitat areas to increase the range of plants grown. Areas for wildlife.

43 THE GARDEN GATE

Northdown Park, Northdown Park Road, Margate, Kent, CT9 3TP. The Garden Gate Project Ltd, 07714742456, info@thegardengateproject.co.uk, www.thegardengateproject.co.uk. *Located within Northdown Park, opp Friends Corner on Northdown Park Rd B2052 between Margate and Broadstairs, nr Northdown House.* **Sat 10 Aug (2-5). Adm £3, chd free. Light refreshments. Wood fired pizzas with toppings from the garden will be on sale.** Visits also by arrangement.

The Garden Gate is a community garden based in Northdown Park, growing a mixture of plants, flowers and vegetables using organic methods. We also have a wildlife pond, two polytunnels, a shade house, some coppiced woodland and a green roof on one of our buildings. The garden is flat and on one level with grass or wood chip paths.

44 GARDENVIEW

6 Edward Road, Biggin Hill, Westerham, TN16 3HL. Freda Davis, 07958534074, fredagdavis@aol.com, www.fredasgarden.co.uk. *Off A233, 7½m S of Bromley, 3½m N of Westerham. Edward Rd is located at the southern end of Main Rd, Biggin Hill by the pedestrian crossing. Parking available on rd. Buses 246 (Village Green Way stop) and 320 (Lebanon Gardens stop).* **Sun 18 Aug (12-4). Adm £5, chd free. Light refreshments. Visits also by arrangement July & Aug for groups of 10+.**

Full of interest with a wide variety of shrubs, small orchard, veg beds and tranquil seating areas with beautifully placed statuary, this garden has been transformed into a beautiful, peaceful and welcoming oasis. There is also a small art exhibition available to view. Various musicians will entertain visitors during the main opening.

45 GODDARDS GREEN

Angley Road, Cranbrook, TN17 3LR. John & Linde Wotton, 01580 715507, jpwotton@gmail.com, www.goddardsgreen.btck.co.uk. *½m SW of Cranbrook. On W of Angley Rd. (A229) at junction with High St, opp War Memorial.* **Sun 7 July (12.30-4.30). Adm £5, chd free. Home-made teas. Visits also by arrangement May to Sept for groups of 10+. The owner normally conducts each visit.**

Gardens of about 5 acres, surrounding beautiful 500+yr old clothier's hall (not open), laid out in 1920s and redesigned since 1992 to combine traditional and modern planting schemes. Fountain and rill, water garden, fern garden, mixed borders of bulbs, perennials, shrubs, trees and exotics; birch grove, grass border, pond, kitchen garden, meadows, arboretum and mature orchard. Our opening on Sunday 7th July will feature an exhibition of both outdoor and indoor art works, presented by Grierson Galleries of Sevenoaks. Some slopes and steps, but most areas are wheelchair accessible. Disabled parking is reserved near the house.

46 ◆ GODINTON HOUSE & GARDENS

Godinton Lane, Ashford, TN23 3BP. The Godinton House Preservation Trust, 01233 643854, info@godintonhouse.co.uk, www.godintonhouse.co.uk. *1½m W of Ashford. M20 J9 to Ashford. Take A20 towards Charing & Lenham, then follow brown tourist signs.* **For NGS: Sun 24 Mar, Sun 19 May, Fri 21 June (1-6). Adm £5, chd free. Home-made teas. For other opening times and information, please phone, email or visit garden website.**

12 acres complement the magnificent Jacobean house. Terraced lawns lead through herbaceous borders, rose garden and formal lily pond to intimate Italian garden and large walled garden with delphiniums, potager, cut flowers and iris border. March/April the wild garden is a mass of daffodils, fritillaries, other spring flowers. Large collection of Bearded Iris flowering late May. Delphinium Festival (14 June - 23 June). Garden workshops and courses throughout the yr. Partial wheelchair access to ground floor of house and most of gardens.

Your visits help change lives – since 1927, we've donated £55 million to nursing and caring charities

47 GODMERSHAM PARK

Godmersham, CT4 7DT. Mrs Fiona Sunley, 01227 730293, ben@godmershampark.com. *5m NE of Ashford. Off A28, midway between Canterbury & Ashford.* **Sun 7 Apr, Sun 16 June (1-5). Adm £5, chd free. Home-made teas in The Mansion Orangery. Visits also by arrangement Mar to Sept for groups of 5+. Donation to Godmersham Church.**

24 acres of restored wilderness and formal gardens set around C18 mansion (not open). Topiary, rose garden, herbaceous borders, walled kitchen garden and recently restored Italian & swimming pool gardens. Superb daffodils in spring and roses in June. Historical association with Jane Austen. Also visit the Heritage Centre. Deep gravel paths.

48 ◆ GOODNESTONE PARK GARDENS

Wingham, Canterbury, CT3 1PL. Francis Plumptre, 01304 840107, enquiries@goodnestoneparkgardens.co.uk, www.goodnestoneparkgardens.co.uk. *6m SE of Canterbury. Village lies S of B2046 from A2 to Wingham. Brown tourist signs off B2046.* **For NGS: Sun 24 Feb (12-4). Home-made teas. Sun 2 June (11-5). Light refreshments. Adm £7, chd £2. Light lunches are available at June opening. Only Tea & homemade cake at Feb opening. For other opening times and information, please phone, email or visit garden website.**

One of Kent's outstanding gardens and the favourite of many visitors. 14 acres around C18 house (not open) and with views over cricket ground and parkland. Something special yr-round from snowdrops and spring bulbs to the famous walled garden with old fashioned roses and kitchen garden. Outstanding trees and woodland garden with cornus collection and hydrangeas later. 2 arboretums, contemporary gravel garden. Picnics welcome.

GROUP OPENING

49 GRAVESEND GARDENS GROUP

Gravesend, DA12 1JZ. *Approx ½m from Gravesend town centre. From A2 take A227 towards Gravesend. At T-lights with Cross Lane turn R then L at next T-lights following yellow NGS signs. Park in Sandy Bank Rd or Leith Park Rd.* **Sat 20, Sun 21 July (12-5). Combined adm £5, chd free. Cream teas.**

58A PARROCK ROAD
Mr Barry Bowen.

68 SOUTH HILL ROAD
Judith Hathrill.

Enjoy two lovely gardens, very different in character, close to Windmill Hill which has extensive views over the Thames estuary. 58A Parrock Road is a beautiful, well established town garden, approx 120ft x 40ft, nurtured by owner for 55yrs. There is a stream running down to a pond, luscious planting along the rocky banks, fascinating water features, mature trees and shrubs, magnificent display of hostas and succulents. 68 South Hill Road is an award winning wildlife garden, showing that wildlife friendly gardens need not be wild. Flowers, herbs and vegetables in the raised beds. Ferns, grasses, perennials and shrubs in the borders and fruit and vegetables grown in containers on the terrace. Tender vegetables thrive in the greenhouse, two ponds planted with native species and wild flowers. Jazz Trio at 58A Parrock Road.

50 ◆ GREAT COMP GARDEN

Comp Lane, Platt, nr Borough Green, Sevenoaks, TN15 8QS. Great Comp Charitable Trust, 01732 885094, office@greatcompgarden.co.uk, www.greatcompgarden.co.uk. *7m E of Sevenoaks. 2m from Borough Green Station. Accessible from M20 & M26 motorways. A20 at Wrotham Heath, take Seven Mile Lane, B2016; at 1st Xrds turn R; garden on L ½m.* **For NGS: Sun 31 Mar, Sun 27 Oct (11-5). Adm £8, chd £3. For other opening times and information, please phone, email or visit garden website.**

Skilfully designed 7 acre garden of exceptional beauty. Spacious setting of well maintained lawns and paths lead visitors through plantsman's collection of trees, shrubs, heathers and herbaceous plants. Early C17 house (not open). Magnolias, hellebores and snowflakes (leucojum), hamamellis and winter flowering heathers are a great feature in the spring. A great variety of perennials in summer incl salvias, dahlias and crocosmias. Tearoom open daily for morning coffee, home-made lunches and afternoon teas. Most of garden accessible to wheelchair users. Disabled WC.

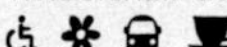

51 GREAT MAYTHAM HALL

Maytham Road, Rolvenden, Tenterden, TN17 4NE. The Sunley Group. *3m from Tenterden. Maytham Rd off A28 at Rolvenden Church, ½m from village on R. Designated parking for visitors.* **Wed 10 Apr, Wed 22 May, Wed 26 June, Wed 31 July (1-4). Adm £6, chd free.**

Lutyens designed gardens famous for having inspired Frances Hodgson Burnett to write The Secret Garden (pre Lutyens). Parkland, woodland with bluebells. Walled garden with herbaceous beds and rose pergola. Pond garden with mixed shrubbery and herbaceous borders. Interesting specimen trees. Large lawned area, rose terrace with far reaching views.

52 HAVEN

22 Station Road, Minster, Ramsgate, CT12 4BZ. Robin Roose-Beresford, 01843 822594, robin.roose@hotmail.co.uk. *Off A299 Ramsgate Rd, take Minster exit from Manston r'bout, straight rd, R fork at church is Station Rd.* **Sun 17, Sun 31 Mar, Fri 19, Sun 21, Mon 22 Apr, Sun 5, Mon 6, Sun 26, Mon 27 May, Sun 9, Sun 16 June (10-4.30). Sun 14 July (10-4.30), also open Quex Gardens. Sun 11, Sun 25, Mon 26 Aug, Sun 22 Sept, Sun 20 Oct (10-**

Balmoral Cottage

4.30). Adm £4, chd free. Visits also by arrangement Feb to Nov for groups of up to 20.
Award winning 300ft garden, designed in the Glade style, similar to Forest gardening but more open and with use of exotic and unusual trees, shrubs and perennials, with wildlife in mind, devised and maintained by the owner, densely planted in a natural style with stepping stone paths. Two ponds (one for wildlife, one for fish with water lilies), gravel garden, rock garden, fernery, Japanese garden, cactus garden, hostas and many exotic, rare and unusual trees, shrubs and plants incl tree ferns and bamboos and yr-round colour. Greenhouse cactus garden.

53 ◆ HEVER CASTLE & GARDENS

Edenbridge, TN8 7NG. Hever Castle Ltd, 01732 865224, info@hevercastle.co.uk, www.hevercastle.co.uk. *3m SE of Edenbridge. Between Sevenoaks & East Grinstead off B2026. Signed from J5 & J6 of M25, A21, A264.* For NGS: Tue 12 Feb (10.30-4.30). Adm £14.95, chd £9.40.
For other opening times and information, please phone, email or visit garden website.
Romantic double-moated castle, the childhood home of Anne Boleyn, set in 125 acres of formal and natural landscape. Topiary, Tudor herb garden, magnificent Italian gardens with classical statuary, sculpture and fountains. 38-acre lake, yew and water mazes. Walled rose garden with over 4000 roses, 110 metre-long herbaceous border. Fine snowdrop displays in Feb. Partial wheelchair access.

54 ◆ HOLE PARK

Benenden Road, Rolvenden, Cranbrook, TN17 4JB. Mr & Mrs Edward Barham, 01580 241344, info@holepark.com, www.holepark.com. *4m SW of Tenterden. Midway between Rolvenden & Benenden on B2086. Follow brown tourist signs from Rolvenden.* For NGS: Sun 14 Apr, Wed 1 May, Sun 2 June, Sun 13 Oct (11-6). Adm £7.50, chd £1. Cream teas. Home-made cakes and light lunches served in The Coach House. **For other opening times and information, please phone, email or visit garden website.**
Hole Park is proud to stand amongst the group of gardens which first opened in 1927 soon after it was laid out by my great grandfather. Our 15 acre garden is surrounded by parkland with beautiful views and contains fine yew hedges, large lawns with specimen trees, walled gardens, pools and mixed borders combined with bulbs, rhododendrons and azaleas. Massed bluebells in woodland walk, standard wisterias, orchids in flower meadow and glorious autumn colours make this a garden for all seasons. Wheelchairs are available for free hire and may be reserved.

55 HOOKWOOD HOUSE

Puttenden Road, Shipbourne, Tonbridge, TN11 9RJ. Mr & Mrs Nicholas Ward, 01732 810525, hookwood1@yahoo.co.uk. *2m N of Tonbridge. From A227 1m N of Tonbridge, turn on to Puttenden Rd. After 1m Hookwood House is on R.* Visits by arrangement Apr to June for groups of 10+.
Charming country garden of 2 acres of formal features; old brick paths lead through small garden rooms enclosed by clipped native and yew hedges; tulips, mixed and herbaceous border, topiary, herb and vegetable garden, nut plat, chickens, fruit orchard, cobbled Kentish ragstone yard and planted containers.

56 HURST HOUSE

Waltham Road, Hastingleigh, Ashford, TN25 5JD. Mrs Lynn Smith, 01233 750120, btclynn@aol.com. *On the top of the downs above Wye Village, between Ashford and Canterbury, 10 mins from A28. From A28 go through Wye towards Hastingleigh. Follow road over Downs to x-roads, L towards Waltham. Ignore first R. 2nd house on R set back off rd.* Sun 28 Apr (2-4.30); Sat 20, Sun 21 July (12.30-5). Adm £4, chd free. Home-made teas. Visits also by arrangement May to Aug.
3 acre idyllic secluded garden surrounded by bluebell woods. Mature borders, winding beds, ponds/ornamental trees perennials/shrubs/annuals designed for year round colours. Damp shady borders/dry sunny borders, unusual plants, huge pieris, acers and rhododendrons. Newly formed stumpery planted with ferns/shade loving plants – woodland walk/ painted forest, intriguing features and sculptures. Whilst it is possible to use a wheelchair - the drive is gravel and there can be muddy paths around and through the woods.

57 ◆ IGHTHAM MOTE

Mote Road, Ivy Hatch, Sevenoaks, TN15 0NT. National Trust, 01732 810378, ighthammote@nationaltrust.org.uk, www.nationaltrust.org.uk/ightham-mote. *6m E of Sevenoaks. Off A25, 2½m S of Ightham. Buses from train stations Sevenoaks or Borough Green to Ivy Hatch & Ightham Mote on weekdays.* For NGS: Thur 4 Apr, Thur 3 Oct (10-5). Adm £14, chd £7. Light refreshments in The Mote Café. **For other opening times and information, please phone, email or visit garden website.**
Lovely 14 acre garden surrounding a moated medieval manor house c1320, open for NGS since 1927. Herbaceous borders, lawns, C18 cascade, pools, courtyard and cutting gardens provide formal interest, while the informal north lake, pleasure grounds, fernery, stumpery and orchard all contribute to the sense of charm and tranquillity. Ticket incl admission to garden & house. Garden tours incl a visit to the South Lake. We have a small natural play area at the north end of the garden. Wheelchairs available from visitor reception and shop. Please ask for wheeled access guide at visitor reception. Last admission 16.30.

58 IVY CHIMNEYS

Mount Sion, Tunbridge Wells, TN1 1TW. Laurence and Christine Smith. *At the end of Tunbridge Wells High St, with Pizza Express on the corner, turn L up Mount Sion. Ivy Chimneys is a red brick Queen Anne house at the top of the hill on the R.* **Sun 16 June (11-5). Adm £5, chd free. Light refreshments. Pimms.**

Town centre garden with herbaceous borders and masses of roses set on three layers of lawns enclosed in an old walled garden. This property also boasts a large vegetable garden with flowers for cutting and chickens for eggs! The property dates back to the late 1600's. Parking in public carparks near the Pantiles. Winner of best back garden in Tunbridge Wells in Bloom competition.

59 ◆ KNOLE

Knole, Sevenoaks, TN15 0RP. Lord Sackville, 01732 462100, knole@nationaltrust.org.uk, www.nationaltrust.org.uk/knole. *1½m SE of Sevenoaks. Leave M25 at J5 (A21). Park entrance S of Sevenoaks town centre off A225 Tonbridge Rd (opp St Nicholas Church). For SatNav use TN13 1HU.* **For NGS: Tue 9 July, Tue 6 Aug (11-3.30). Adm £15, chd £7.50. For other opening times and information, please phone, email or visit garden website.**

Lord Sackville's private garden at Knole is a magical space, featuring sprawling lawns, a walled garden, an untamed wilderness area and a medieval orchard. Access is through the beautiful Orangery, off Green Court, where doors open to reveal the secluded lawns of the 26 acre garden and stunning views of the house. Last entry at 3.30pm. Refreshments are available in the Brewhouse Café. Bookshop in Green Court. Gift shop and plant sales in the Brewhouse Café. Wheelchair access via the bookshop into the Orangery. Some paths may be difficult in poor weather. Assistance dogs are allowed in the garden.

60 KNOWLE HILL FARM

Ulcombe, Maidstone, ME17 1ES. The Hon Andrew & Mrs Cairns, 01622 850240, elizabeth@knowlehillfarm.co.uk, www.knowlehillfarmgarden.co.uk. *7m SE of Maidstone. From M20 J8 follow A20 towards Lenham for 2m. Turn R to Ulcombe. After 1½m, L at Xrds, after ½m 2nd R into Windmill Hill. Past Pepper Box PH, ½m 1st L to Knowle Hill.* **Sat 16, Sun 17, Mon 18 Feb (11-3). Light refreshments. Sun 23 June (2-5). Home-made teas. Adm £5, chd free. Hot food in February. 2020: Sat 8, Sun 9 Feb. Visits also by arrangement Feb to Sept for groups of up to 30. Access only for 25-30 seater coaches.**

2 acre garden created over 35yrs on S-facing slope of N Downs. Spectacular views. Snowdrops and hellebores, many tender plants, china roses, agapanthus, verbenas, salvias and grasses flourish on light soil. Topiary continues to evolve with birds at last emerging. Lavender ribbons hum with bees. Pool and rill enclosed in small walled white garden. A green garden is nearly complete. Some steep slopes.

♿ 🐕 ✿ 🚌 ☕

61 LA MOUETTE

Blenheim Road, Littlestone, New Romney, TN28 8PR. Sheila Georgiades, 01797 369189. *From A259 at New Romney take B2071 for approx. 1m, then follow NGS signs.* **Fri 7 June (2-5). Sun 9 June (2-5), also open Wyckhurst. Adm £3.50, chd free. Visits also by arrangement Apr to Sept for groups of up to 10.**

Interestingly designed densely planted small south facing garden making the most of the available space to create different areas and microclimates. Mixed planting within the constraints of the dry, windy coastal location to provide all year interest. Many grasses and Med. plants. The low maintenance front garden was landscaped 6 years ago and planted with a scheme of white and lime green. Partial access.

♿ ✿

62 LADHAM HOUSE

Ladham Road, Goudhurst, TN17 1DB. Guy & Nicola Johnson. *8m E of Tunbridge Wells. On NE of village, off A262. Through village towards Cranbrook, turn L at The Goudhurst Inn. 2nd R into Ladham Rd, main gates approx 500yds on L.* **Sun 19 May (2-5). Adm £5, chd free. Light refreshments.**

Ten acres of garden with many interesting plants, trees and shrubs, incl rhododendrons, camellias, azaleas and magnolias. A beautiful rose garden, arboretum, an Edwardian sunken rockery, a woodland walk leading to bluebell woods, ponds & a vegetable garden. The garden also has spectacular 60 meter twin borders and a white pool garden designed by Chelsea Flower Show Gold Medal winner, Jo Thompson. Small Classic Car Display.

63 ◆ LEEDS CASTLE

Maidstone, ME17 1PL. Leeds Castle Trustees, 01622 765400, enquiries@leeds-castle.co.uk. *Off J8 of M20.* **For NGS: Evening opening Wed 3 July (6-8). Adm £15, chd free. Pre-booking essential, please visit www.ngs.org.uk for information & booking. Refreshments available before Garden Tour. For other opening times and information, please phone or email.**

Visitors to the 'loveliest castle in the world' are often surprised and enchanted by the glorious gardens which surround this magnificent moated building. Natural woodland walks, the Culpeper Garden - a quintessential English cottage garden - and the Lady Baillie Garden - a Mediterranean style terraced garden overlooking the Great Water - are complemented by the beautiful surrounding parkland. Fully wheelchair accessible with smooth paths through gardens, disabled WC and mobility bus.

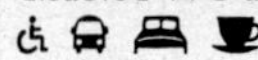

64 LEYDENS

Hartfield Road, Edenbridge, TN8 5NH. Roger Platts, www.rogerplatts.com. *1m S of Edenbridge. On B2026 towards Hartfield (use Nursery entrance & car park).* **Sun 23 June (12-5). Adm £5, chd free. Home-made teas.**

Small private garden of garden designer, nursery owner and author who created NGS Garden at Chelsea in 2002, winning Gold and Best in Show, and in 2010 Gold and People's Choice for the M&G Garden and Gold in 2013. A wide range of roses, shrubs and perennials adjoining wild flower hay meadow and plant nursery. Kitchen garden and orchard. Plants clearly labelled and fact sheet available.

65 LITTLE GABLES

Holcombe Close, Westerham, TN16 1HA. Mrs Elizabeth James. *Centre of Westerham. Off E side of London Rd A233, 200yds from The Green. Please park in public car park. No parking available at house.* **Sat 18, Sun 19 May, Sat 8, Sun 9 June (2-5). Adm £4, chd free. Home-made teas.**

¾ acre plant lover's garden extensively planted with a wide range of trees, shrubs, perennials etc, incl many rare ones. Collection of climbing and bush roses. Large pond with fish, water lilies and bog garden. Fruit and vegetable garden. Large greenhouse.

66 LONG MEADOW

1 Bourne Row, Wellers Town Road, Chiddingstone, TN8 7BQ. Ian & Jo Peel. *5m SE of Edenbridge via B2027. 1m S of Chiddingstone Village. Garden on L.* **Mon 26 Aug (11-4.30). Adm £4, chd free. Home-made teas.**

A contemporary cottage garden of ⅓ of an acre that wraps around the house with a pond and wonderful countryside views. A gorgeous mix of traditional and modern varieties of late summer perennials and grasses. The colour palette is kept simple but the planting is dense and many plants are designed to peak at the end of summer with shades of pink, purple, copper and bronze.

67 LORDS

Sheldwich, Faversham, ME13 0NJ. John Sell CBE & Barbara Rutter, 01795 536900, john@sellwade.co.uk. *On A251 4m S of Faversham & 3½m N of Challock Xrds. From A2 or M2 take A251 towards Ashford. ½m S of Sheldwich church find entrance lane on R adjacent to wood.* **Sun 23 June (2-5). Adm £5, chd free. Home-made teas.** Visits also by arrangement Mar to July for groups of 10 to 30.

C18 walled garden and greenhouse. Mediterranean terrace and citrus standing. Flowery mead beneath fruit trees including medlars and quinces. Across a grass tennis court a cherry orchard grazed by Jacob sheep. Pleached hornbeams, clipped yew hedges and topiary, lawns, ponds and wild area. Fine old sweet chestnuts, planes, copper beech and 120ft tulip tree. Some gravel paths.

68 LUTON HOUSE

Selling, ME13 9RQ. Lady Swire, 07866 601230, wendyestokes@gmail.com. *4m SE of Faversham. From A2 (M2) or A251 make for White Lion in Selling, entrance 30yds E on same side of rd.* **Visits by arrangement Apr to Oct. Adm £4, chd free.**

6 acres. C19 landscaped garden with ornamental ponds, trees underplanted with azaleas, camellias, woodland plants, hellebores, spring bulbs, magnolias, cherries, daphnes, halesias, maples, Judas trees and cyclamen. Depending on the weather, those interested in camellias, early trees and bulbs may like to visit in late Mar/early April.

69 MARSHBOROUGH FARMHOUSE

Farm Lane, Marshborough, Sandwich, CT13 0PJ. David & Sarah Ash, 01304 813679. *1½m W of Sandwich, ½m S of Ash. From Ash take R fork to Woodnesborough. After 1m Marshborough sign. L into Farm Lane at white thatched cottage, garden 100yds on L. Coaches must phone for access information.* **Visits by arrangement June to Aug for groups of 5+. Adm £5, chd free. Home-made teas.**

Interesting 2½ acre plantsman's garden, developed enthusiastically over 20yrs by the owners. Paths and lawns lead to many unusual shrubs, trees and perennials in island beds, borders, rockery and raised dry garden creating yr-round colour and interest. Tender pot plants, succulents in glass house, pond and water features. Over 70 varieties of Salvia both hardy and tender.

70 NEW MAY COTTAGE

52, St Botolphs Road, Sevenoaks, TN13 3AG. Graham & Maggie Moat. *Central Sevenoaks, close to the historic Vine cricket ground & Knole Park. Easy walking distance from mainline railway station with trains direct from London & the local bus station. 2m from J5 M25, on the B2020. Park for free on either side of the rd.* **Sun 5 May (11-4). Adm £4, chd free. Light refreshments.**

A ⅓ of an acre family spring garden, comprising mature shrubs and specimen plants, with spring bulbs, a vegetable patch and local trees that shield the garden. Close to the historic Knole deer Park & House, which can be explored on foot after your visit. Please ask for directions.

71 12 THE MEADOWS

Chelsfield, Orpington, BR6 6HS. Mr Roger & Mrs Jean Pemberton. *3m from J4 on M25. 10 mins walk from Chelsfield station. Exit M25 at J4. At r'about 1st exit for A224, next r'about 3rd exit - A224, ½m, take 2nd L, Warren Rd. Bear L into Windsor Drive. 1st L The Meadway, follow signs to garden.* **Sun 19 May (11-5.30). Adm £4, chd free. Light refreshments.**

Front garden Mediterranean style gravel with sun loving plants. Rear ¾ acre garden in 2 parts. Semi-formal Japanese style area with two ponds, one Koi and one natural (lots of spring interest). Mature bamboos, acers, grasses etc and semi wooded area, children's path with 13ft high giraffe, Sumatran tigers and lots of points of interest. Designated children's area. Adults only admitted if accompanied by responsible child! Wheelchair access to all parts except small stepped area at very bottom of garden.

Your visits help change lives – we've donated over £16.7 million to Macmillan Cancer Support since 1984

72 MERE HOUSE

Mereworth, ME18 5NB.
Mr & Mrs Andrew Wells,
www.mere-house.co.uk. *7m E of Tonbridge. From A26 turn N on to B2016 & then R into Mereworth village. 3½m S of M20/M26 junction, take A20, then B2016 to Mereworth.* **Sun 17 Feb, Sun 3, Sun 24 Mar, Sun 14 Apr (2-5). Adm £5, chd free. Home-made teas.**

C18 landscape surrounding 6 acre garden, completely replanted since 1958, bounded to the south by lake created 1780 and park to west. Increasing areas of snowdrops and daffodils in spring. Extensive lawns set off herbaceous borders, ornamental shrubs and trees with yr-round foliage contrast. Major tree planting since 1987 storm; woodland, park and lake walks can be enjoyed beyond the garden.

73 NEW 5 MONTEFIORE AVENUE

Ramsgate, CT11 8BD. Pauline and Mike Ashley. *Opposite Thanet Bowls Club. A255 Hereson Rd from Ramsgate to Broadstairs. Turn R (L if from Broadstairs) at Garden Centre into Montefiore Av. Cross Dumpton Pk Dr into continuation of Montefiore Av. House on R.* **Sat 3, Sun 4 Aug (12-5). Adm £4, chd free. Home-made teas. Also open The Watch House.**

An Edwardian walled garden densely planted with a wide variety of herbaceous and tropical plants. A courtyard with over 90 pots features acers, hostas and aeoniums. Through an arch, a lawned area with gazebo, borders, large informal koi pond with waterfall and two small wildlife ponds. A pergola leads to a vegetable garden and treehouse garden with a mix of roses, Mediterranean and tropical plants. A highlight of the garden is the koi pond with a mix of fish incl large Koi, and the wide variety of plants, both Mediterranean and tropical. The garden is situated in a cul-de-sac with an entrance to King George VI park where the famous Italianate Greenhouse is located. Gravel paths.

74 THE MOUNT

Haven Street, Wainscott, Rochester, ME3 8BL. Marc Beney & Susie Challen. *3½m N of Rochester. At M2 J1, take A289 twds Grain. At r'bout, R into Wainscott. Co-op ahead, turn R into Higham Rd. R into Islingham Farm Rd, parking in field on corner of Woodfield Way. House 7min walk up slight hill.* **Sat 13, Sun 14 July (12-4). Adm £5, chd free. Home-made teas.**

Approx. 2 acres incl a walled kitchen garden with espaliered fruit trees, climbing roses, vegetable beds and colourful herbaceous border; old grass tennis court traversed by a mown labyrinth with a small nuttery at one end; yellow and white terrace garden with steps up to a grassed mound above it. Wide ranging views of countryside from different parts of the garden. Mature specimen trees. Finalist in Kent Life Amateur Garden competition. Gravel drive, uneven paths and steps.

Orchard End

© Carole Drake

75 ◆ MOUNT EPHRAIM

Hernhill, Faversham, ME13 9TX. Mr & Mrs E S Dawes & Mr W Dawes, 01227751496, info@mountephraimgardens.co.uk, www.mountephraimgardens.co.uk. *3m E of Faversham. From end of M2, then A299 take slip rd 1st L to Hernhill, signed to gardens.* **For NGS: Sun 24 Mar, Thur 20 June (11-5). Sun 29 Sept (11-5), also open Avalon. Adm £7, chd £2.50. Afternoon teas, lunches, wine. For other opening times and information, please phone, email or visit garden website.**

Herbaceous border, topiary, daffodils and rhododendrons, rose terraces leading to small lake. Rock garden with pools, water garden, young arboretum. Rose garden with arches and pergola planted to celebrate the Millennium. Magnificent trees. Grass maze. Superb views over fruit farms to Swale estuary. Tea Room Small Play area for children. Partial wheelchair access; top part manageable, but steep slope. Disabled WC. Full access to tea room.

76 NETTLESTEAD PLACE

Nettlestead, ME18 5HA. Mr & Mrs Roy Tucker, www.nettlesteadplace.co.uk. *6m W/SW of Maidstone. Turn S off A26 onto B2015 then 1m on L, next to Nettlestead Church.* **Sun 9 June, Sun 6 Oct (2-5). Adm £6, chd free. Home-made teas.**

C13 manor house in 10 acre plantsman's garden. Large formal rose garden. Large herbaceous garden of island beds with rose and clematis walkway leading to a newly planned garden of succulents. Fine collection of trees and shrubs; sunken pond garden, a maze of Thuja, terraces, bamboos, glen garden, Acer lawn. Young pinetum adjacent to garden. Sculptures. Wonderful open country views. maze. Gravel paths, partial access: sunken pond garden. Large steep bank and lower area accessible with some difficulty.

77 OAK COTTAGE AND SWALLOWFIELDS NURSERY

Elmsted, Ashford, TN25 5JT. Martin & Rachael Castle. *6m NW of Hythe. From Stone St (B2068) turn W opp the Stelling Minnis turning. Follow signs to Elmsted. Turn L at Elmsted village sign. Limited parking at house, further parking at Church (7mins walk).* **Fri 19, Sat 20 Apr, Fri 7, Sat 8 June (11-4). Adm £4, chd free. Cream teas.**

Get off the beaten track and discover this beautiful ½ acre cottage garden in the heart of the Kent countryside. This plantsman's garden is filled with unusual and interesting perennials, incl a wide range of salvias. There is a small specialist nursery packed with herbaceous perennials.

78 NEW THE OLD BARN

Bells Farm Road, East Peckham, Tonbridge, TN12 5NA. John Greenslade. *Follow Bells Farm Rd, look out for brick walls with black sign saying 'The Old Barn'.* **Sat 23, Sun 24 Mar, Sat 8, Sun 9 June (11-4). Adm £3.50, chd free. Light refreshments.**

The Old Barn is a beautiful family garden surrounded by outbuildings and fields. In the last few years this garden has gone from neglected site to stunning gardens, with plenty more changes still to happen in the future. Thousands of spring bulbs already planted! This garden has a deep gravel drive, which may not be suitable for wheelchairs. The courtyard has a few steps within, so may not be accessible.

79 OLD BLADBEAN STUD

Bladbean, Canterbury, CT4 6NA. Carol Bruce, www.oldbladbeanstud.co.uk. *6m S of Canterbury. From B2068, follow signs into Stelling Minnis, turn R onto Bossingham Rd, then follow yellow NGS signs through single track lanes.* **Sun 26 May, Sun 9, Sun 23 June, Sun 7, Sun 21 July, Sun 4, Sun 18 Aug (2-6). Adm £6, chd free. Home-made teas.**

5 interlinked gardens all designed and created from scratch by the garden owner on 3 acres of rough grassland between 2003 and 2011. Romantic walled rose garden with over 90 labelled old fashioned rose varieties, tranquil yellow and white garden, square garden with blended pastels borders and Victorian style greenhouse, 300ft long colour schemed symmetrical double borders. An experimental self sufficiency project comprises a wind turbine, rain water collection, solar panels and a ground source heat pump, an organic fruit and vegetable garden. The gardens are maintained entirely by the owner and were designed to be managed as an ornamental ecosystem with a large number of perennial species encouraged to set seed, and with staking, irrigation, mulching and chemical use kept an absolute minimum. Each garden has a different season of interest – please see the garden website for more information.

80 THE OLD RECTORY

Valley Road, Fawkham, Longfield, DA3 8LX. Karin & Christopher Proudfoot, 01474 707513, keproudfoot@gmail.com. *1m S of Longfield. Midway between A2 & A20, on Valley Rd 1½m N of Fawkham Green, 0.3m S of Fawkham church, opp sign for Gay Dawn Farm/Corinthian Sports Club. Parking on drive only. Not suitable for coaches.* **Visits by arrangement in Feb for groups of up to 20. Also open by arrangement Feb 2020. Adm £5, chd free. Home-made teas.**

1½ acres with impressive display of long-established naturalised snowdrops and winter aconites; over 100 named snowdrops added more recently. Garden developed around the snowdrops over 30yrs, incl hellebores, pulmonarias and other early bulbs and flowers, with foliage perennials, shrubs and trees, also natural woodland. Gentle slope, gravel drive, some narrow paths.

81 THE ORANGERY

Mystole, Chartham, Canterbury, CT4 7DB. Rex Stickland & Anne Prasse, 01227 738348, rex.mystole@btinternet.com. *5m SW of Canterbury. Turn off A28 through Shalmsford Street. In 1½m at Xrds turn R downhill. Cont, ignoring rds on L & R. Ignore drive on L (Mystole House only). At sharp RH bend in 600yds turn L into private drive.* **Sun 19 May (1-6); Sat 27, Sun 28 July (1-5). Adm £5, chd free. Home-made teas.** Visits also by arrangement Mar to Sept for groups of 5+. By arrangement groups of 5-60.

1½ acre gardens around C18 orangery, now a house (not open). Magnificent extensive herbaceous border & impressive ancient wisteria. Large walled garden with a wide variety of shrubs, mixed borders & unusual specimen trees. Water features & intriguing collection of modern sculptures in natural surroundings. Refreshments on terrace with splendid views over ha-ha to the lovely Chartham Downs. Ramps to garden.

82 THE ORCHARD

Bramling, Canterbury, CT3 1NB. Mark Lane, 01227 722172, mark@marklanedesigns.com, www.marklanedesigns.com. *5m E of Canterbury. Please call for further directions. Limited parking available.* **Visits by arrangement July to Sept for groups of up to 10. Adm £4, chd free. Light refreshments.**

The Orchard is the home to Mark Lane, the UK's first wheelchair-bound garden designer, published gardening writer and BBC TV presenter, and his civil partner Jasen. The one acre garden incl: herb garden, blue and yellow border, white garden, grass borders with stepped granite water feature, roses and peonies, as well as a small orchard, lawn and the large colourful herbaceous borders. Limited wheelchair access - gravel paths. A complete circle of the garden can be done using an alternative route.

83 ORCHARD END

Cock Lane, Spelmonden Road, Horsmonden, TN12 8EQ. Mr Hugh Nye. *8m E of Tunbridge Wells. From A21 going S turn L at r'bout onto B2162 to Horsmonden. After 2m turn R onto Spelmonden Rd. After ½m turn R into Cock Lane. Garden on R.* **Sat 25, Sun 26 May, Sat 20, Sun 21 July (11-5). Adm £5, chd free. Home-made teas.** Donation to The Amyloidosis Foundation.

Contemporary classical garden within a 4 acre site. Made over 15yrs by resident landscape designer. Divided into rooms with linking vistas. Incl hot borders, white garden, exotics, oak and glass summerhouse amongst magnolias. Dramatic changes in level. Formal pool with damp garden, ornamental vegetable potager. Wildlife orchards and woodland walks.

84 ◆ ORCHARD HOUSE, SPENNY LANE

Claygate, Marden, Tonbridge, TN12 9PJ. Mr & Mrs Lerwill, 01892 730662, jeanette@lerwill.com. *Just off B2162 between Collier St & Horsmonden. Spenny Lane is adjacent to White Hart PH. Orchard House is 1st house on R about 400m from PH.* **For NGS: Sun 26 May, Sun 4 Aug (11-4). Adm £5, chd free. Home-made teas. For other opening times and information, please phone or email.**

A relatively new garden created within the last 13yrs. Gravel garden with potted tender perennials, cottage garden and herbaceous borders. Potager with vegetables, fruit and flowers for cutting. Bee friendly borders. Tropical style planting with breeze house added 2018. Hornbeam avenue underplanted with camassia. Small nursery on site specialising in herbaceous perennials and ornamental grasses. Productive beehives and honey for sale. Access for wheelchairs, some pathways are gravel, grassed areas uneven in places.

85 NEW OUDEN

Brogdale Road, Ospringe, Faversham, ME13 8XY. Frances & Paul Moskovits. *Close to Faversham. From A2 in Faversham turn S along Brogdale Rd for ¾m, Ouden is on R. Parking on roadside or at Brogdale Farm 100 yds before property.* **Sat 13 July, Wed 4 Sept (11-4). Adm £3.50, chd free. Limited teas at Ouden. Courtyard Restaurant at Brogdale serving teas.**

A variety of mature shrubs and trees form the backbone of this ¼ acre garden. The front garden features a shrubbery and cottage planting. The rear garden has a well stocked colourful long border leading to two working greenhouses. Exotic planting intermingles with traditional garden favourites. Small paths allow time for a closer look. Situated close to National Fruit Collection at Brogdale Farm.

86 PARSONAGE OASTS

Hampstead Lane, Yalding, ME18 6HG. Edward & Jennifer Raikes, 01622 814272, jmraikes@parsonageoasts.plus.com. *6m SW of Maidstone. On B2162 between Yalding village & stn, turn off at Boathouse PH. over lifting bridge, cont 100 yds up lane. House and car park on L.* **Visits by arrangement Apr to Sept for groups of 10 to 30. Admission price incl cream tea. Adm £6, chd free. Cream teas.**

Our garden has a lovely position on the bank of the R Medway. Typical Oast House (not open) often featured on calendars and picture books of Kent. 70yr old garden now looked after by grandchildren of its creator. ¾ acre garden with walls, daffodils, crown imperials, shrubs, clipped box and a spectacular magnolia. Small woodland on river bank. Best in spring, but always something to see. Unfenced river bank. Gravel paths.

87 ◆ PENSHURST PLACE & GARDENS

Penshurst, TN11 8DG. Lord & Lady De L'Isle, 01892 870307, contactus@penshurstplace.com, www.penshurstplace.com. *6m NW of Tunbridge Wells. SW of Tonbridge on B2176, signed from A26 N of Tunbridge Wells.* **For NGS: Thur 12 Sept (10.30-6). Adm £10, chd £6. For other opening times and information, please phone, email or visit garden website.**

11 acres of garden dating back to C14. The garden is divided into a series of rooms by over a mile of yew hedge. Profusion of spring bulbs, formal rose garden and famous peony border. Woodland trail and arboretum. Yr-round interest. Toy museum. Some paths not paved and uneven in places; own assistance will be required. 2 wheelchairs available for hire.

88 PHEASANT BARN

Church Road, Oare, ME13 0QB. Paul & Su Vaight, 07843 739301, paul.vaight@btinternet.com. *2m NW of Faversham. Entering Oare from Faversham, turn R at Three Mariners PH towards Harty Ferry. Garden 400yds on R, before church. Parking on roadside.* **Visits by arrangement May to July for groups of up to 30. Adm £5, chd free. refreshments by prior arrangement only..**

Series of smallish gardens around award-winning converted farm buildings in beautiful situation overlooking Oare Creek. Main area is nectar-rich planting in formal design with a contemporary twist inspired by local landscape. Also vegetable garden, dry garden, water features, wild flower meadow and labyrinth. July optimum for wild flowers. Kent Wildlife Trust Oare Marshes Bird Reserve within 1m. Two village inns serving lunches/dinners.

89 PHEASANT FARM

Church Road, Oare, Faversham, ME13 0QB. Jonathan & Lucie Neame, 01795 535366, neamelucie@gmail.com. *2m NW of Faversham. Enter Oare from Western Link Road. L at T-junction. R at Three Mariners PH into Church Road. Garden 450yds on R, beyond Pheasant Barn, before church. Parking on roadside & as directed.* **Visits by arrangement Apr to June for groups of 10 to 30. Adm £8, chd free. Home-made teas. Entry price includes cream tea and cakes..**

A walled garden surrounding C17 farmhouse with outstanding views over Oare marshes and creek. Main garden with shrubs and herbaceous plants. Infinity lawn overlooking Oare marshes and creek. Circular walk through orchard and adjoining churchyard. Two local public houses serving lunches. Wheelchair access in main garden only.

Watergate House

© Leigh Clapp

90 POTMANS HEATH HOUSE

Wittersham, TN30 7PU. Dr Alan & Dr Wilma Lloyd Smith. *1½m W of Wittersham. Between Wittersham & Rolvenden, 1m from junction with B2082. 200yds E of bridge over Potmans Heath Channel.* **Sun 28 Apr, Sun 16 June (2-6). Adm £5, chd free. Home-made teas.**

Large country garden divided into compartments each with a different style. Daffodils, tulips and many blossoming ornamental cherry and apple trees in Spring, often spectacular. Many and varied rose species; climbers a speciality. Early summer beds and borders. Orchards, some unusual trees, lawns, vegetable garden, 2 greenhouses. Some awkward slopes but generally accessible.

91 ◆ QUEX GARDENS

Quex Park, Birchington, CT7 0BH. Powell-Cotton Museum, 01843 842168, enquiries@quexmuseum.org, www.quexpark.co.uk/museum/quex-gardens. *3m W of Margate. Follow signs for Quex Park on approach from A299 then A28 towards Margate, turn R into B2048 Park Lane. Quex Park is on L.* **For NGS: Sun 14 July (10-5). Adm £4.95, chd £3.50. Light refreshments in Mama Feelgoods Café and Quex Barn. For other opening times and information, please phone, email or visit garden website.**

10 acres of woodland and gardens with fine specimen trees unusual on Thanet, spring bulbs, wisteria, shrub borders, old figs and mulberries, herbaceous borders. Victorian walled garden with cucumber house, long glasshouses, cactus house, fruiting trees. Peacocks, dovecote, woodland walk, wildlife pond, children's maze, croquet lawn, picnic grove, lawns and fountains. Head Gardener will be available on NGS open days to give tours and answer questions. Mama Feelgood's Boutique Café serving morning coffee, lunch or afternoon tea. Quex Barn farmers market selling local produce and serving breakfasts to evening meals. Picnic sites available. Garden almost entirely flat with tarmac paths. Sunken garden has sloping lawns to the central pond.

92 86 RAMSDEN ROAD

Orpington, BR5 4LT. Patricia Dow. *from M25 take J4 follow A21 for Bromley then at r'about take 4th exit (A224) for about 1½m and at 2nd set of T-lights turn R into Ramsden Rd.* **Sun 14 July (1-5). Adm £3.50, chd free. Home-made teas.**

Driving down Ramsden Road offers no clue of the colourful plant lover's garden to the rear of the house. Many plants grown from seed and cuttings from our greenhouse, filling pots and troughs front of the house too. New patio pond for 2019. Very personal small garden designed over many years by owners with ingenious economical solutions to garden needs, incl solar powered fairy water feature.

93 43 THE RIDINGS

Chestfield, Whitstable, CT5 3QE. David & Sylvie Buat-Menard, 01227 500775, sylviebuat-menard@hotmail.com. *Nr Whitstable. From M2 heading E cont onto A299. In 3m take A2990. From r'about on A2990 at Chestfield, turn onto Chestfield Rd, 5th turning on L onto Polo Way which leads into The Ridings.* **Sun 9 June (11-5). Sat 15 June (11-5), also open Tankerton Gardens. Adm £4, chd free. Visits also by arrangement Apr to Sept for groups of 5 to 20.**

Delightful small garden brimming with interesting plants both in the front and behind the house. Many different areas. Dry gravel garden in front, raised beds with alpines and bulbs and borders with many unusual perennials and shrubs. The garden ornaments are a source of interest for visitors. The water feature will be of interest for those with a tiny garden as well as the smoky cauldron. Many alpine troughs & raised beds as well as dry shade & mixed borders all in a small space. Kent Life First prize amateur garden.

94 ◆ RIVERHILL HIMALAYAN GARDENS

Riverhill, Sevenoaks, TN15 0RR. The Rogers Family, 01732 459777, info@riverhillgardens.co.uk, www.riverhillgardens.co.uk. *2m South of Sevenoaks on A225. Leave A21 at A225 & follow signs for Riverhill Himalayan Gardens.* **For NGS: Tue 30 Apr, Wed 12 June (10.30-5). Adm £9, chd £6.50.**
For other opening times and information, please phone, email or visit garden website.
Beautiful hillside garden, privately owned by the Rogers family since 1840. Extensive views across the Weald of Kent. Spectacular rhododendrons, azaleas and fine specimen trees. Bluebell and natural woodland walks. Rose garden. Walled garden with planting, terracing and water feature. Children's adventure playground, den building trail, hedge maze and Yeti spotting. Rock Garden is now open. Café serving freshly-ground coffee, speciality teas, light lunches, home-made cream teas, cakes, gluten free cakes and soya milk. Wheelchair access to Walled Garden only. Good access to café, shop and tea terrace (no disabled WC).

95 ROCK COTTAGE

New Church Road, Bilsington, Ashford, TN25 7LA. Bill & Penny Sisley, 01233 720416, hello@kentcottageholiday.co.uk, www.kentcottageholiday.co.uk/ngs. *6½m SE of Ashford. From M20, J10 take A2070 to Hastings. Join B2067 to Hamstreet, turn L on B2067 towards Bilsington, at White Horse PH turn R, onto New Church Rd. After 1m Rock Cottage is on L.* **Sun 9 June (10.30-4.30), also open La Mouette. Sun 7 July (10.30-4.30). Adm £5, chd free. Home-made teas.**
Runners up in Kent Life Garden of the Year. Tranquil 2 acre garden with a surprise around every corner, a series of garden rooms and a mixture of styles. Collections of clematis, rambling roses, wisteria walk, topiary garden, lime avenue, arboretum, meadow, living willow & native hedges, restored pond, fruit orchard, dahlia bed, Specimen trees & shrubs, Mediterranean garden, Agaves. Partial wheelchair access.

96 NEW 18 ROYAL CHASE

Tunbridge Wells, TN4 8AY. Eithne Hudson. *Situated at the top of Mount Ephraim and The Common. Leave A21 at Southborough, follow signs for Tunbridge Wells. After St John's Rd take R turn at junction on Common and sharp R again. From South, follow A26 through town up over Common. Last turn on L.* **Sat 18, Sun 19 May (1.30-5). Adm £4, chd free. Home-made teas.**
Town garden of a ¼ of acre on sandy soil which was originally Common and woodland. Lovely in late Spring with Camellias, Acers, Rhododendrons and Alliums. Large lawn with island beds planted with roses and herbaceous perennials and a small pond with lilies and goldfish. The owner is a florist and has planted shrubs and annuals specifically with flower arranging in mind. Access through right hand side gate.

97 ST CLERE

Kemsing, Sevenoaks, TN15 6NL. Mr & Mrs Simon & Eliza Ecclestone, www.stclere.com. *6m NE of Sevenoaks. 1m E of Seal on A25, turn L signed Heaverham. In Heaverham turn R signed Wrotham. In 75yds straight ahead marked Private Rd; 1st L to house.* **Sun 19 May (2-5). Adm £5, chd £1. Home-made teas in The Garden Room.**
4 acre garden, full of interest. Formal terraces surrounding C17 mansion (not open), with beautiful views of the Kent countryside. Herbaceous and shrub borders, productive kitchen and herb gardens, lawns and rare trees. Garden tours with Head Gardener at 2.30pm and 3.45pm (£1 per person). Some gravel paths and small steps.

98 ◆ THE SALUTATION GARDEN

Knightrider Street, Sandwich, CT13 9EW. Mr J Fothergill, 01304 619919, enquiries@the-salutation.com, www.the-salutation.com. *In the heart of Sandwich. Turn L at Bell Hotel & into Quayside car park. Entrance in far R corner of car park.* **For NGS: Thur 28 Mar, Wed 18 Sept (10-5). Adm £8, chd free. Home-made teas. For other opening times and information, please phone, email or visit garden website.**
3½ acres of ornamental and formal gardens designed by Sir Edwin Lutyens in 1911 surrounding Grade I listed house. Designated historic park and garden. White, yellow, spring, woodland, gardens, vegetable garden, herbaceous borders and exotic garden, Designed to provide yr-round changing colour. Unusual plants for sale.

99 SANDOWN

Plain Road, Smeeth, nr Ashford, TN25 6QX. Pamela Woodcock, 01303813478, pmwoodcock078@gmail.com. *4m SE of Ashford. Exit J10 onto A20, take 2nd L signed Smeeth, turn R Woolpack Hill, past garage on L, past next L, garden on L. From A20 in Sellindge at Church, turn R carry on 1m. Park in layby on hill.* **Sun 12, Sun 26 May (11-4). Adm £5, chd free. Tea. Visits also by arrangement Apr & May for groups of 10 to 20.**
My small compact Japanese style garden and pond has visitor book comments such as: inspirational, just like Japan, a stunning hidden gem. There is a Japanese arbour, tea house/veranda, waterfall and stream. Acers, bamboos, ginkgo, fatsia japonica, clerodendrum trichotomum, pinus mugos, wisterias, hostas and mind your own business for ground cover. WC available. Regret no small children owing to deep pond. Wheelchair access to top section of garden only.

100 ◆ SCOTNEY CASTLE

Lamberhurst, TN3 8JN. National Trust, 01892 893820, scotneycastle@nationaltrust.org.uk, www.nationaltrust.org.uk/scotneycastle. *6m SE of Tunbridge Wells. On A21 London - Hastings, brown tourist signs. Bus: (Mon to Sat) Tunbridge Wells - Wadhurst, alight Lamberhurst Green.* **For NGS: Wed 15 May. For other opening times and information, please phone, email or visit garden website.**
The medieval moated Old Scotney Castle lies in a peaceful wooded valley. In C19 its owner Edward Hussey III set about building a new house, partially demolishing the

Old Castle to create a romantic folly, the centrepiece of his picturesque landscape. From the terraces of the new house, sweeps of rhododendron and azaleas cascade down the slope in summer, mirrored in the moat. In the house three generations have made their mark, adding possessions and character to the homely Victorian mansion which enjoys far reaching views out across the estate. Wheelchairs available for loan.

101 ◆ SISSINGHURST CASTLE GARDEN

Sissinghurst, TN17 2AB. National Trust, 01580 710700, sissinghurst@nationaltrust.org.uk, www.nationaltrust.org.uk/sissinghurst-castle-garden. *2m NE of Cranbrook, 1m E of Sissinghurst on Biddenden Rd (A262), see our website for more information.* **For NGS: Tue 1 Oct (11-5.30). Adm £15.20, chd £7.60. For other opening times and information, please phone, email or visit garden website.**

Historic, poetic, iconic; a refuge dedicated to beauty. Vita Sackville-West and Harold Nicolson fell in love with Sissinghurst Castle and created a world renowned garden. More than a garden, visitors can also find Elizabethan and Tudor buildings, find out about our history as a Prisoner of War Camp and see changing exhibitions. Free welcome talks and estate walks leaflets. Café, restaurant, gift, secondhand book and plant shops are open from 10am-5.30pm. Some areas unsuitable for wheelchair access due to narrow paths and steps.

102 SMITHS HALL

Lower Road, West Farleigh, ME15 0PE. Mr S Norman, www.smithshall.com. *3m W of Maidstone. A26 towards Tonbridge, turn L into Teston Lane B2163. At T-junction turn R onto Lower Rd B2010. Opp Tickled Trout PH.* **Sun 30 June (11-5). Adm £5, chd free. Light refreshments. Donation to Heart of Kent Hospice.**

Delightful 3 acre gardens surrounding a beautiful 1719 Queen Anne House (not open). Lose yourself in numerous themed rooms: sunken garden, iris beds, scented old fashioned rose walk, formal rose garden, intense wild flowers, peonies, deep herbaceous borders and specimen trees. Walk 9 acres of park and woodland with great variety of young native and American trees and fine views of the Medway valley. Cakes available. Gravel paths.

103 SPRING PLATT

Boyton Court Road, Sutton Valence, Maidstone, ME17 3BY. Mr & Mrs John Millen, 01622 843383, carolyn.millen1@gmail.com, www.kentsnowdrops.com. *5m SE of Maidstone. From A274 nr Sutton Valence follow yellow NGS signs. Limited parking.* **Visits by arrangement Jan & Feb. Adm £5, chd free. Light refreshments.**

One acre garden under continual development with panoramic views of the Weald. Over 600 varieties of snowdrop grown in tiered display beds with spring flowers in borders. An extensive collection of alpine plants in a large greenhouse. Vegetable garden and natural spring fed water feature. Home-made soup, home-made bread, tea/coffee and cake. Garden on a steep slope and many steps.

104 STONEWALL PARK

Chiddingstone Hoath, nr Edenbridge, TN8 7DG. Mr & Mrs Fleming. *4m SE of Edenbridge. Via B2026. ½way between Markbeech & Penshurst.* **Sun 10 Mar, Sun 12 May (2-5). Adm £8, chd free. Home-made teas in the conservatory (Teas incl in admission fee). Donation to Sarah Matheson Trust & St Mary's Church, Chiddingstone.**

Even from the driveway you can see a vast amount of self seeded daffodils, leading down to a romantic woodland garden in historic setting featuring species such as rhododendrons, magnolias, azaleas, bluebells and a range of interesting trees and shrubs, sandstone outcrops, wandering paths and lakes. Historic parkland with cricket ground.

105 SUNNYBANK

12 Herschell Road East, Walmer, Deal, CT14 7SQ. Mr & Mrs James & Flora Cockburn. *Turn off Dover Rd at Corner Café onto Herschell Rd East. Sunnybank is the last house on R before Herschell Sq.* **Sat 22, Sun 23 June (2-5.30). Adm £3.50, chd free. Home-made teas in the garden.**

Sunnybank's small town garden has been rejuvenated since 2016. Whilst retaining many of the original high walls and hedges the gardens have been transformed with new planting throughout. From the entrance at the front via the side garden leading into the back garden and beyond to the studio garden there are a series of surprises which keep visitors engaged and delighted. James Cockburn is an artist whose studio is surrounded by the shade garden.

106 SWEETBRIAR

69 Chequer Lane, Ash, nr Sandwich, CT3 2AX. Miss Louise Dowle & Mr Steven Edney, 01304 448476, lou.dowle@hotmail.co.uk. *8m from Canterbury, 3m from Sandwich. Turn off A257 into Chequer Lane, 100 meters from junction opp field.* **Sun 28 July, Sun 18 Aug, Sun 29 Sept (11-5). Adm £4.50, chd free. Home-made teas. Also open 12 Woods Ley. Visits also by arrangement July to Sept for groups of 10 to 20.**

An average sized back garden transformed into an exotic jungle paradise full of fabulous foliage. A real plantsman's collection of many rare hardy and tender exotics to transport you into a lawn free tropical oasis. The front garden is a traditional cottage kitchen garden combining flowers and vegetables with fruit and herbs. Wildlife friendly, chemical free with 3 small ponds and eco grass drive. Gold award from Kent wildlife trust. As seen as BBC Gardeners' World (Sept 2018).

GROUP OPENING

107 NEW TANKERTON GARDENS

Whitstable, CT5 2EP. *31 Strangford Rd is parallel to Northwood Rd and is one of the turnings off Castle Rd. Tickets & map of participating gardens at the above.* **Sat 15 June (10-5). Combined adm £5, chd free. Also open 43 The Ridings. Local cafes are available in Tankerton High Street, Tower Parade and the Sea Front.**

NEW 17A BADDLESMERE ROAD
Mr Derek Scoones.

NEW 16 NORTHWOOD ROAD
Mr Simon Courage.

NEW 12 STRANGFORD ROAD
Sarah Yallop.

Three very different town gardens within a mile of the sea, so enjoying a mild climate, Baddlesmere densely planted for colour all year round, Strangford a more traditional garden and Northwood Road, a very contemporary garden space.

108 TIMBERS

Dean Street, East Farleigh, nr Maidstone, ME15 0HS. Mrs Sue Robinson, 07905281764, suerobinson.timbers@gmail.com, www.timbersgardenkent.co.uk. *2m S of Maidstone. From Maidstone take B2010 to East Farleigh. After Tesco's on R follow Dean St for ½m. Timbers on L behind 8ft beech hedge. Parking through gates.* **Visits by arrangement Apr to July for groups of 20+. Adm £6, chd free. Home-made teas.**
Beautiful 5 acre garden surrounding house designed with flower arranger's eye and with colour a priority. Unusual perennials, annuals and shrubs. Tulips in spring. New partly walled garden, parterre, arbour, pergola, island beds, lawns and mature specimen trees plus 100yr old Kentish cobnut plat, wildflower meadows and woodland. Rock pool with waterfalls. Valley views. Plant List. Tea room. Variety of plants, colour combinations & design a priority. 2 acre meadows, 5 orchid species, cobnuts. Most of garden is flat, some steep slopes to rear.

109 NEW TOPGALLANT

5 North Road, Hythe, CT21 5UF. Mary Sampson. *M20 exit 11, take A259 to Hythe, then going towards Folkestone at r'about, take 2nd L up narrow hill signed to Saltwood. L at junction with North Rd. House on L.. Parking in Church car park.* **Sat 15, Sun 16 June (2-5). Combined adm with Vergers £6, chd free.**
Opening with Vergers, also in Hythe, Topgallant is one of two very different South West facing gardens on the hillside with views over the sea. Both terraced and developed to cope with the prevailing winds and the slope. A secluded Sculptors garden, with mature trees and planting for year round interest. Sloping hillside garden with many steps.

110 TRAM HATCH

Charing Heath, Ashford, TN27 0BN. Mrs P Scrivens, Tramhatch.com. *10m NW of Ashford. A20 turn towards Charing Railway Stn on Pluckley Rd, over motorway then 1st R signed Barnfield to end, turn L carry on past Barnfield, Tram Hatch ahead.* **Sat 1 June, Sun 7 July, also open 31 Forest Avenue, Sun 11 Aug (12-5). Adm £5, chd free. Home-made teas.**
Meander your way off the beaten track to a mature, extensive garden changing through the seasons. You will enjoy a garden laid out in rooms - what surprises are round the corner? Large selection of trees, vegetable, rose and gravel gardens, colourful containers. The River Stour and the Angel of the South enhance your visit. Please come and enjoy, then relax in our lovely garden room for tea. The garden is totally flat, apart from a very small area which can be viewed from the lane.

111 UPPER PRYORS

Butterwell Hill, Cowden, TN8 7HB. Mr & Mrs S G Smith. *4½m SE of Edenbridge. From B2026 Edenbridge-Hartfield, turn R at Cowden Xrds & take 1st drive on R.* **Wed 19 June (12-6). Adm £5, chd free. Home-made teas.**
10 acres of English country garden surrounding C16 house - a garden of many parts; colourful profusion, interesting planting arrangements, immaculate lawns, mature woodland, water and a terrace on which to appreciate the view, and tea!

112 NEW VERGERS

Church Road, Hythe, CT21 5DP. Nettie & John Wren. *As above. M20 exit 11,take A259 to Hythe, then going towards Folkestone at r'about, take 2nd L up narrow hill. L at junction into North Rd, 1st L again into Church Road. Vergers is at the end of this short rd, next door to St. Leonards Church, Church and Ossuary open, parking in Church car park* **Sat 15, Sun 16 June (2-5). Combined adm with Topgallant £6, chd free. Home-made teas at Vergers.**
South facing hillside garden which has been reclaimed and developed over the past five years by the present owners. Steps from car park lead up to the garden terrace, goldfish pond and lawn. Winding paths slope up to many seating areas with spectacular views of the town and Channel. Kitchen garden, wildlife area and pond, bug hotels, mixed planting for year round interest.

113 THE WATCH HOUSE

7 Thanet Road, Broadstairs, CT10 1LF. Dan Cooper, www.frustratedgardener.com. *Off Broadstairs High St on narrow side rd. At Broadstairs station, cont along High St (A255) towards sea front. Turn L at Terence Painter Estate Agent then immed turn R.* **Sat 3, Sun 4 Aug (12-4). Adm £4, chd free. Home-made teas. Also open 5 Montefiore Avenue.**
Adjoining an historic fishermen's cottage, two small courtyard gardens shelter an astonishing array of unusual plants. Thanks to a unique microclimate, the east-facing garden is home to a growing collection of exotics, chosen principally for exuberant, jungly foliage. In the west-facing courtyard a garden room leads onto a terrace where flowering plants jostle for space around a greenhouse. Within a few mins walk of Viking Bay, The Dickens Museum and Bleak House.

114 WATERGATE HOUSE

King Street, Fordwich, Canterbury, CT2 0DB. Fiona Cadwallader, www.cadwallader.co.uk. *2m E of Canterbury. From Canterbury A257 direction, Sandwich, 1m L to Fordwich. 1m L on Moat Lane, direct to Watergate House bottom of High St. Follow parking instructions.* **Sat 27 Apr, Sat 15 June (2-6). Adm £4.50, chd free.**

Magical walled garden by the River Stour: Defined areas of formal, spring, woodland, vegetable and secret garden reveal themselves in a naturally harmonious flow, each with its own colour combinations. Ancient walls provide the garden's basic structure, while a green oak pergola echoes a monastic cloister. The garden is mainly on one level with one raised walkway under pergola.

115 WEST COURT LODGE

Postling Court, The Street, Postling, nr Hythe, CT21 4EX. Mr & Mrs John Pattrick. *2m NW of Hythe. From M20 J11 turn S onto A20. Immed 1st L. After ½m on bend take rd signed Lyminge. 1st L into Postling.* **Sat 1 June (1-5), also open Wyckhurst. Sun 2 June (1-5). Combined adm with Churchfield £6, chd free. Home-made teas in Village Hall or garden.**

S-facing one acre walled garden at the foot of the N Downs, designed in 2 parts: main lawn with large sunny borders and a romantic woodland glade planted with shadow loving plants and spring bulbs, small wildlife pond. Lovely C11 church will be open next to the gardens.

GROUP OPENING

116 WEST MALLING EARLY SUMMER GARDENS

West Malling, ME19 6LW. *On A20, nr J4 of M20. Park (Ryarsh Lane and Station) in West Malling. Maps and directions to 1&2 New Barns Cottages (parking) & New Barns Oasts are available from gardens in town.* **Sun 2 June (12-5). Combined adm £7, chd free. Home-made teas at New Barns Cottages.** Donation to St Mary's Church, West Malling.

ABBEY BREWERY COTTAGE
Dr & Mrs David and Lynda Nunn.

BROME HOUSE
John Pfeil & Shirley Briggs.

LUCKNOW, 119 HIGH STREET
Ms Jocelyn Granville.

NEW BARNS COTTAGES
Mr & Mrs Anthony Drake.

2 NEW BARNS OAST
Nick Robinson & Becky Robinson Hugill.

TOWN HILL COTTAGE
Mr & Mrs P Cosier.

WENT HOUSE
Alan & Mary Gibbins.

West Malling is an attractive small market town with some fine buildings. Enjoy seven lovely gardens that are entirely different from each other and cannot be seen from the road. Brome House and Went House have large gardens with specimen trees, old roses, mixed borders, attractive kitchen gardens and garden features incl a coach house, Roman temple, fountain and parterre. Lucknow and Town Hill Cottage are walled town gardens with mature and interesting planting. Abbey Brewery Cottages is a recent jewel-like example of garden restoration and development. New Barns Cottages has serpentine paths leading through woodland to roomed gardens: tea and cakes in the courtyard garden of the cottages. New Barns Oasts has bespoke landscape features and is a child friendly adults' garden. Town Hill Cottage garden, Abbey Brewery Cottages and New Barns Cottages are difficult to access but the other gardens have wheelchair access.

Rock Cottage

© Leigh Clapp

GROUP OPENING

117 WHITSTABLE GARDENS

Whitstable, CT5 4LT. *Off A299, or A290. Down Borstal Hill, L by garage into Joy Lane to collect map of participating gardens (also available at other gardens). Parking at Joy Lane School and Gorrell Tank.* **Sun 19 May (10-5). Combined adm £6, chd free. Light refreshments at Stream Walk Community Gardens and Umbrella Centre Cafe.**

6 ALEXANDRA ROAD
Andrew Mawson & Sarah Rees.

56 ARGYLE ROAD
Emma Burnham & Mel Green.

NEW **69 CROMWELL ROAD**
Mark Baker.

THE GUINEA, 31 ISLAND WALL
Sheila Wyver.

19 JOY LANE
Francine Raymond, www.kitchen-garden-hens.co.uk.

NEW **67A JOY LANE, JUPITER HOUSE & SHERRIN'S COTTAGE**
Ed Lamb, Shelagh O'Riordan and Ric Horner.

96 JOY LANE
Vernon & Terrie Brown.

OCEAN COTTAGE
Katherine Pickering.

STREAM WALK TRUST
Stream Walk Community Gardens.

NEW **UMBRELLA COMMUNITY GARDEN**
Whitstable Umbrella Community Centre.

Enjoy a day of eclectic gardens by the sea. 10 people are showing off their gardens, but others, marked with yellow balloons, are there to admire from the street. From fishermen's yards to formal gardens, the residents of Whitstable are making the most of quirky plots, enjoying the mild climate and the range of plants we can grow. Drop in and admire contemporary gardens (Alexandra Rd & Cromwell Rd), wildlife (96 & 19 Joy Lane), gravel gardens (The Guinea), those recently established (56 Argyle Rd) and fabulous sea views (67 Joy Lane). We're maximising our space, be it tiny (Ocean Cottage), on a busy road or in deep shade. We garden on heavy Kent clay and are prone to northerly winds. Stream Walk and the Umbrella Centre are the heart of our community, where residents can learn new skills & buy surplus produce - the ideal spot for those without outside space of their own. By opening, we're hoping to encourage those new to gardening with our ingenuity and style, rather than rolling acres. Combined adm £6 per adult or £10 for 2. Plant stalls at 19 Joy Lane and the Umbrella Centre.

142 Cramptons Road

© Bennet Smith

118 NEW WOODLANDS ROAD ALLOTMENTS

48 Tangmere Close, Gillingham, ME7 2TN. John Jones. *From A278 onto Lower Woodlands Rd 2nd L onto Hazlemere Dr, 1st R onto Tangmere Cl. Public Transport Bus 176 to Hazlemere Dr.* **Sat 27, Sun 28 July (12-4). Adm £4, chd free. Home-made teas.**

At least 10-12 of the total 160 plots in this large allotments site will be open for visiting. Visitors will have an opportunity to see a working gardening community growing fresh food, flowers and fruit for home use. Evidence of the health and social benefits to be expected. Exhibition of this Dig for Victory group founded in 1940. Concrete level path round much of the site.

119 12 WOODS LEY

Woods Ley, Ash, Canterbury, CT3 2HF. Philip Oostenbrink. *20 mins from Canterbury. From A257 turn R at Chequer Lane. Go down Chequer Lane & turn L into Chilton Field. Keep going down the rd and turn the 2nd L into Woods Ley.* **Sun 28 July, Sun 18 Aug, Sun 29 Sept (11-5). Adm £3, chd free. Wine. Also open Sweetbriar. Prosecco served in the garage.**

A tropical style garden, showing what can be achieved in the smaller modern garden, filled with colourful flowers and unusual foliage. The side garden has a selection of ferns and shade loving plants. The back garden is full of tropical plants and a selection of the National Collection of Hakonechloa macra/ Ophiopogon japonicus. Indoors you will find the National Collection of Aspidistra elatior. Private garden of the Head Gardener of Canterbury Cathedral.

NPC

120 ◆ THE WORLD GARDEN AT LULLINGSTONE CASTLE
Eynsford, DA4 0JA. Mrs Guy Hart Dyke, 01322 862114, info@lullingstonecastle.co.uk, www.lullingstonecastle.co.uk. *1m from Eynsford. Over Ford Bridge in Eynsford Village. Follow signs to Roman Villa. Keep Roman Villa immed on R then follow Private Rd to Gatehouse.* **For NGS: Sun 16 June (12-5). Adm £9, chd £4.50. Light refreshments. For other opening times and information, please phone, email or visit garden website.**
The World Garden is located within a two-acre, 18th-century Walled Garden in the stunning grounds of Lullingstone Castle, where heritage meets cutting-edge horticulture. The garden is laid out in the shape of a miniature map of the world. Thousands of species are represented, all planted out in their respective beds. The World Garden Nursery offers a host of horticultural and homegrown delights, to reflect the unusual and varied planting of the garden. New for 2019 is our Hot 'n' Juicy Cactus House. Wheelchairs available upon request.
NPC

121 WYCKHURST
Mill Road, Aldington, Ashford, TN25 7AJ. Mr & Mrs Chris Older, 01233 720395, cdo@rmfarms.co.uk. *4m SE of Ashford. From M20 J10 take A20 2m E to Aldington turning; turn R at Xrds & proceed 1½m to Aldington Village Hall. Turn R & immed L by Walnut Tree Inn down Forge Hill. After ¼m turn R into Mill Rd.* **Sat 1 June (12-5), also open West Court Lodge. Sun 2, Sat 8 June (12-5). Sun 9 June (12-5), also open Rock Cottage. Adm £5, chd free. Home-made teas on the Sun Terrace. Visits also by arrangement in June for groups of 5 to 20. No access for large vehicles & coaches. Car parking in field.**
Delightful C16 Kent Cottage (not open) nestles in romantic seclusion at the end of a drive. This enchanting 1 acre garden is a mixture of small mixed herbaceous borders, roses and much unusual topiary incl a wildflower meadow. There is plenty of seating round the lawns to enjoy the garden and teas with extensive views of the Kent countryside across to the Romney Marsh on towards the sea. There is a dell with a small water feature and in the wildflower meadow is a shepherd's hut to enjoy rest after a stroll. The garden is under continuous redesign and development with fresh plantings each year to provide changing interest for every visitor. A gentle slope which limits wheelchair access in a small area.

GROUP OPENING

122 WYE GARDENS
Wye, TN25 5BP. *3m NE of Ashford. From A28 take turning signed Wye. Bus: Ashford to Canterbury via Wye. Train: Wye. Parking at Spring Grove School, Station Car Park and in centre of village. Maps available from Wye Church & all gardens.* **Sun 23 June (2-6). Combined adm £5, chd free. Home-made teas at Wye Church.**

3 BRAMBLE CLOSE
TN25 5QA. Dr M Copland.
(See separate entry)

MIDDLEFIELD HOUSE
TN25 5EP. Kathy and Steve Bloom.

3 ORCHARD DRIVE
TN25 5AU. Liz Coulson.

NEW **32 OXENTURN ROAD**
TN25 5BE. Rosemary Fitzpatrick.

SPRING GROVE FARM HOUSE
TN25 5EY. Heather Van den Bergh.

The gardens open in the Historic Market Town of Wye this year are all very different in character: 3 Bramble Close: a very wild experimental garden buzzing with wildlife demonstrates how plants maintain their natural population density. Middlefield House: a half-acre plot with sweeping views over open fields, woodland, borders, wildlife meadow, raised vegetable beds, sculpture and huge wildlife photographs peering through foliage. 3 Orchard Drive: a relatively new garden packed with plants and features (rose arches, benches, raised beds), a great example of what can be achieved in a modest plot. 32 Oxenturn Road: a wildlife garden featuring a wild flower meadow, a green-roofed shed and worm composting as well as shrubs, flowers and raised vegetable beds. Spring Grove Farm House: a large country garden full of colour and many interesting features including a lake, pond and a gravel garden. Wye Gardens opening coincides with Stour Music Festival. Wheelchair access to 32 Oxenturn Rd & Spring Grove Farm House only.

123 YEW TREE COTTAGE
Penshurst, TN11 8AD. Mrs Pam Tuppen, 01892 870689. *4m SW of Tonbridge. From A26 Tonbridge to Tunbridge Wells, join B2176 Bidborough to Penshurst Rd. 2m W of Bidborough, 1m before Penshurst. Unsuitable for coaches.* **Wed 30 Jan, Wed 13, Wed 27 Feb, Wed 13, Wed 27 Mar, Wed 10, Wed 24 Apr, Wed 8, Wed 22 May, Wed 5, Wed 19 June (12-5). Adm £3, chd free. Light refreshments.**
Small, romantic cottage garden with steep hillside entrance. Lots of seats and secret corners, many unusual plants - hellebores, spring bulbs, old roses, many special perennials. Small pond; something to see in all seasons. Created and maintained by owner, a natural garden full of plants.

124 YOAKLEY HOUSE
Drapers Close, Margate, CT9 4AH. Michael Yoakley's Charity, www.yoakleycare.co.uk. *Drapers Close, Margate. Near Margate QEQM Hospital, Drapers Cl is a cul de sac turning off St Peters Rd. At the end of Drapers Cl is access to the Yoakley car park, through the hedge.* **Sun 21 July (2.30-4.30). Adm £5, chd £2.50. Home-made teas in Yoakley House Care Home on site.**
Set in 2½ acres of grounds, cultivated the old fashioned way to complement the ancient almshouses it serves. Well-manicured lawns with extensive borders and densely planted display beds: summer bedding, carpet bedding, specimen trees, shrubs and rockery plants, herbaceous planting, shrub rose beds with standard roses. Magnificent hanging baskets. Accessible pathways from the main car park throughout the grounds.

LANCASHIRE

Merseyside, Greater Manchester

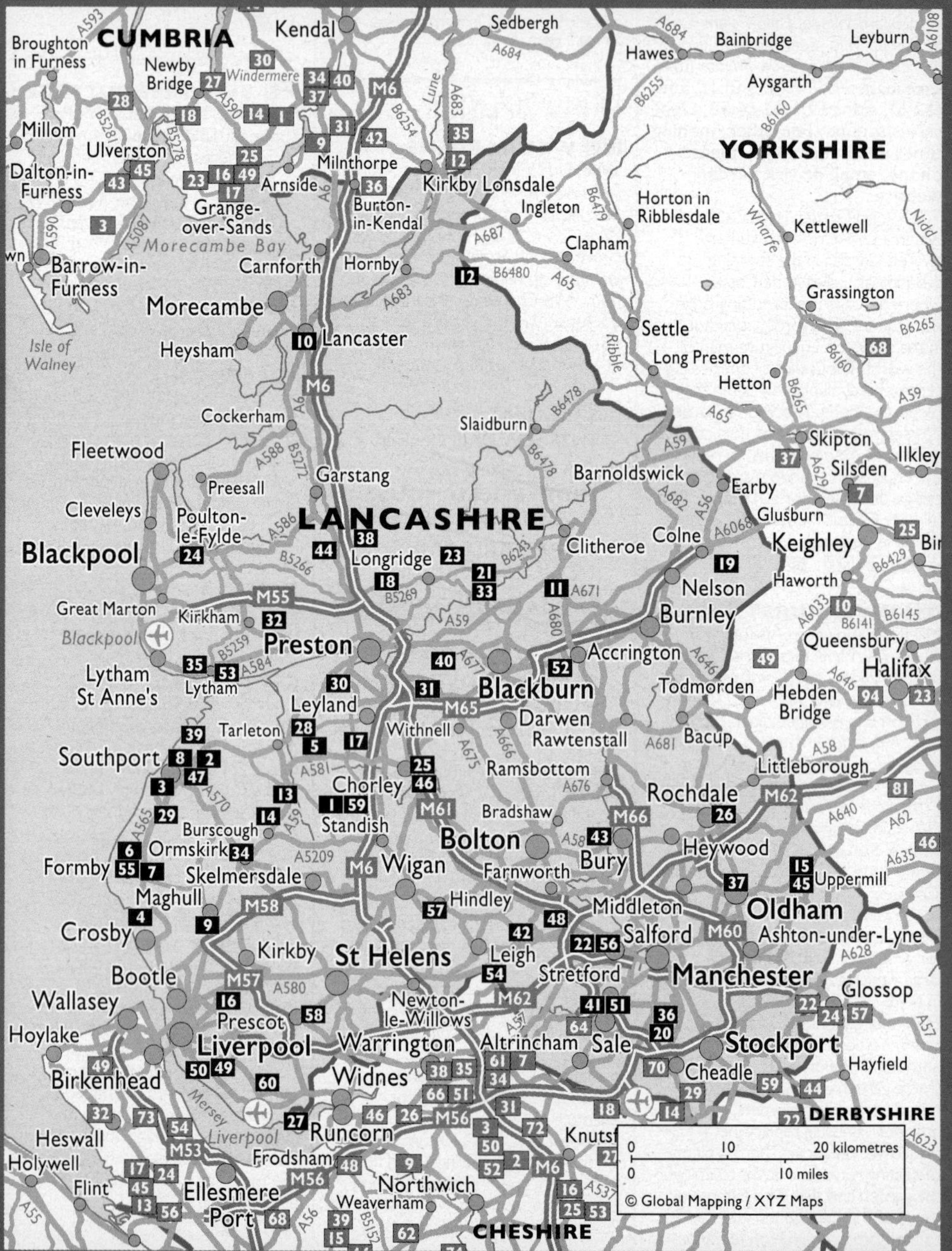

The gardens of the Red Rose County of Lancashire offer a wide range of horticultural excellence and inspiration.

Hidden behind walls, hedges and fences lie some of the most exquisite private gardens in the country; a range of expertly tended plots full of colour, innovation and seasonal interest. There is something here to inspire all the family, whether it be allotments, wildlife sanctuaries, rows of back to back terrace gardens, inner city sanctuaries with water features or rolling acres with lakes.

So, whatever size your own patch, why not visit some of our stunning gardens and maybe take away a few brilliant ideas to copy at home- all with the added pleasure of home- made cakes and tea, and often plants for sale too.

Our gardeners look forward to welcoming you!

Below: Wigan & Leigh Hospice

Volunteers

County Organiser
Margaret Fletcher
01704 567742
margaret.fletcher@ngs.org.uk

County Treasurer
Geoff Fletcher
01704 567742
geoffwfletcher@hotmail.co.uk

Publicity
Barbara & Richard Farbon
01772 600750
farbons@btinternet.com

Christine Ruth
01517 274877
caruthchris@aol.com

Booklet Co-ordinator
Brenda Doldon
01704 834253
doldon@btinternet.com

Assistant County Organisers
Anne & Jim Britt
01614 458100
annebritt@btinternet.com

Peter & Sandra Curl
01704 893713
peter.curl@btinternet.com

Deborah Jackson
debs136@icloud.com

John & Jennifer Mawdsley
01704 564708

Carole Ann & Stephen Powers
01254 824903
chows3@icloud.com

Eric & Sharon Rawcliffe
01253 883275
ericrawk@talktalk.net

OPENING DATES

All entries subject to change. For latest information check **www.ngs.org.uk**

Extended openings are shown at the beginning of the month.

Map locator numbers are shown to the right of each garden name.

February

Snowdrop Festival

Sunday 17th
Weeping Ash Garden 54

Sunday 24th
Weeping Ash Garden 54

April

Saturday 27th
Dale House Gardens 18

Sunday 28th
Dale House Gardens 18

May

Saturday 4th
Warton Hall 53

Sunday 5th
Warton Hall 53

Monday 6th
◆ The Ridges 46
Warton Hall 53

Saturday 18th
NEW Matshead Lodge 38

Sunday 19th
NEW Blundell Gardens 4
79 Crabtree Lane 14
◆ Hazelwood 28
Hillside Gardens 29

Sunday 26th
Bretherton Gardens 5
◆ Clearbeck House 12
Parkers Lodge 43

Monday 27th
◆ Clearbeck House 12

June

Saturday 1st
The Old Vicarage 42

Sunday 2nd
Birkdale Gardens 3
NEW Kington Cottage 32
Maggie's Oldham 37
The Old Vicarage 42
The Secret Valley 48

Saturday 8th
136 Buckingham Road 9

Sunday 9th
136 Buckingham Road 9
31 Cousins Lane 13
Didsbury Village Gardens 20
NEW 45 Grey Heights View 25
NEW 6 Menivale Close 39
NEW 120 Roe Lane 47
Sefton Park June Gardens 49

Saturday 15th
Giles Farm 23
Mill Barn 40

Sunday 16th
8 Andertons Mill 1
79 Crabtree Lane 14
Giles Farm 23
◆ Hazelwood 28
Mill Barn 40

Saturday 22nd
Carr House Farm 10
5 Crib Lane 15
Dale House Gardens 18
35 Ellesmere Road 22
Mill Barn 40
11 Platt Lane 45
11 Westminster Road 56

Sunday 23rd
Bridge Inn Community Farm 7
Carr House Farm 10
5 Crib Lane 15
Dale House Gardens 18
Green Farm Cottage 24
Mill Barn 40
11 Platt Lane 45

Friday 28th
Dutton Hall 21

Saturday 29th
Hale Village Gardens 27
Jack Green Cottage 31

Sunday 30th
◆ Clearbeck House 12
Dutton Hall 21
Hale Village Gardens 27
Jack Green Cottage 31

July

Saturday 6th
NEW Kington Cottage 32

Sunday 7th
Birkdale Gardens 3
Bretherton Gardens 5
NEW 33 Brewery Lane 6
◆ Clearbeck House 12
NEW Hutton Gardens 30
NEW Kington Cottage 32
Parkers Lodge 43
6 West Lane 55

Sunday 14th
NEW 45 Grey Heights View 25
72 Ludlow Drive 34
Woolton Village Gardens 60

Saturday 20th
Willowbrook Hospice Gardens 58

Sunday 21st
Hillside Gardens 29
NEW Lytham Hall 35
Maggie's Manchester 36
Southlands 51
Wigan & Leigh Hospice 57
Willowbrook Hospice Gardens 58

Sunday 28th
Moss Park Allotments 41

August

Saturday 3rd
Lower Dutton Farm 33

Sunday 4th
19 Cumberland Avenue 17
NEW Kington Cottage 32
Lower Dutton Farm 33

Saturday 10th
The Growth Project 26

Sunday 11th
19 Cumberland Avenue 17
NEW Gresgarth Hall
Plant World 44

Sunday 18th
NEW 45 Grey Heights View 25
Weeping Ash Garden 54

Sunday 25th
Bretherton Gardens 5
Croxteth Park Walled Garden 16

Monday 26th
◆ The Ridges 46

September

Sunday 8th
NEW Sefton Park September Gardens 50
Weeping Ash Garden 54

October

Sunday 20th
Weeping Ash Garden 54

Weeping Ash Garden

By Arrangement

Arrange a personalised garden visit with your club, or group of friends, on a date to suit you. See individual garden entries for full details.

THE GARDENS

1 8 ANDERTONS MILL

Mawdesley, Ormskirk, L40 3TW. Mr & Mrs R Mercer, 01257 450636, margaret.mercer6@btinternet.com. *9m E of Ormskirk. M6 J27 A5209 over Parbold Hill, R Lancaster Lane/Chorley Rd, L after Farmers Arms to Bentley Lane/Andertons Mill. Garden 500yds on R. From Burscough A59,A5209 towards Parbold, L Lancaster Lane.* **Sun 16 June (12.30-5.30). Adm £3.50, chd free. Home-made teas.** Visits also by arrangement June to Aug for groups of 10 to 30.

This ½ acre cottage garden started in 2010, has many colourful borders of perennials, shrubs, and roses. A patio with raised beds, secluded potted plant area, large vegetable garden. Rose and clematis covered arches and many wrought iron features. An extensive bed of scented roses and a wonderful view of Harrock Hill Group openings with Woodstock Barn by arrangement.

2 12 BANKFIELD LANE

Churchtown, Southport, PR9 7NJ. Alan & Eileen Brannigan, 07528 027943, abrannigan@sky.com. *2½m N of Southport. Turn R at T-lights on A565 in Churchtown 1st L at r'about, then past Hesketh Arms pub & Botanic Gardens main entrance on L. Garden is 220yds on R.* **Visits by arrangement May to Sept fr groups of 10 to 20. Adm incl refreshments. Individuals may be added to groups. Adm £6, chd free. Light refreshments. incl tea, coffee and home-made cakes.** Donation to Woodlands Animal Sanctuary.

This attractive walled garden has been lovingly landscaped by current owners over 30yrs and is continually evolving. It has a well stocked pond with waterfalls, a stone bed, alpine troughs, mixed borders with magnolias, and rhododendrons. Open aspect to rear. Greenhouse and patio areas. A small stumpery has recently been created. The front garden has a stone bed and mixed borders. Level paths but entrance gate to rear garden too narrow for wheelchairs.

GROUP OPENING

3 BIRKDALE GARDENS

Birkdale, Southport, PR8 2AX. *1m S of Southport. Gardens signed from A565 Southport to Liverpool rd & A5267 S through Birkdale Village. Maps available at each location.* **Sun 2 June, Sun 7 July (11-5). Combined adm £5, chd free. Home-made teas at 14 Saxon Rd. Bacon sandwiches at 22 Hartley Cres.**

22 HARTLEY CRESCENT
Sandra & Keith Birks.
Open on Sun 7 July

10 MEADOW AVENUE
John & Jenny Smith.
Open on all dates

14 SAXON ROAD
Margaret & Geoff Fletcher, 01704 567742, margaret.fletcher@ngs.org.uk.
Open on all dates
Visits also by arrangement May to July for groups of 10+.

66 SHAWS ROAD
Vivienne Rimmer.
Open on Sun 2 June

An established group of gardens surrounding the bustling Victorian village of Birkdale, reached by a short car journey. Gardens feature a delightful plants woman's L shaped garden with a very special secret garden, a walled garden with an array of tender plants amongst informal island beds and a family garden full of surprises with imaginative use of reclaimed materials. Wheelchair access to some gardens.

GROUP OPENING

4 NEW BLUNDELL GARDENS

Blundell Road, Hightown, Liverpool, L38 9EF. *11m N of Liverpool, 11m S of Southport. M57/58 .A5758,keep L at r'bout ,Take 2nd exit A565. 2nd L onto B5193.Turn R Moss Lane. L onto Alt Rd. R onto Kerslake Way.At r'bout 2nd exit onto Thornbeck, 1st L onto Village Way.R onto Blundell Rd.* **Sun 19 May (1-5). Combined adm £3.50, chd free. Home-made teas at 75 Blundell Road.**

11 BLUNDELL AVENUE
Karen Rimmer.

5 BLUNDELL AVENUE
Denise & Dave Ball.

NEW **75 BLUNDELL ROAD**
Shirley & Phil Roberts.

A group of gardens in the village of Hightown.One is a well stocked courtyard with a 'quaint sweet shop'.Nearby a quirky garden full of surprises and a wide variety of plants .Thirdly a wildlife-friendly garden with pond,pergola and fairy glen.

GROUP OPENING

5 BRETHERTON GARDENS

South Road, Bretherton, Leyland, PR26 9AD. *8m SW of Preston. Between Southport & Preston, from A59, take B5247 towards Chorley for 1m. Gardens signed from South Rd (B5247).* **Sun 26 May, Sun 7 July, Sun 25 Aug (12-5). Combined adm £5, chd free. Home-made teas all dates, also light lunches 7 July.**

GLYNWOOD HOUSE
Terry & Sue Riding.

HAZEL COTTAGE
John & Kris Jolley, 01772 600896, jolley@johnjolley.plus.com. **Visits also by arrangement May to Oct for groups of 10+.**

OWL BARN
Richard & Barbara Farbon, 01772 600750, farbons@btinternet.com. **Visits also by arrangement May to Aug for groups of up to 20.**

PEAR TREE COTTAGE
John & Gwenifer Jackson.

Four contrasting gardens spaced across attractive village with conservation area. Glynwood House has ¾ acre mixed borders, pond with drystone-wall water feature, woodland walk, patio garden with pergola and raised beds, all in a peaceful location with spectacular open aspects. Pear Tree Cottage garden blends seamlessly into its rural setting with informal displays of ornamental and edible crops, water and mature trees, against a backdrop of open views to the West Pennine Moors. Owl Barn has herbaceous borders with cottage garden and hardy plants, a productive kitchen garden providing fruit, vegetables and cut flowers, and two ponds with fountains which complement the C18 converted barn (not open). Hazel Cottage garden has evolved from a Victorian subsistence plot to encompass a series of themed spaces packed with plants to engage the senses and the mind. Live music at Glynwood. Home-made preserves for sale at Pear Tree Cottage. Narrow or uneven paths in some parts of all the gardens.

6 NEW 33 BREWERY LANE

Formby, Liverpool, L37 7DY. Susan Hughes. *7m S of Southport. S on Formby by-pass A565 past RAF Woodvale R at r'about to Southport Rd , R to Green Ln continues to Massams Ln, first R into West Ln continues to Brewery Ln.* **Sun 7 July (11-4). Combined adm with 6 West Lane £3.50, chd free. Home-made teas.**

We started planting up the garden in 2015 with perennials, shrubs and climbers. There are colour themed raised beds with lawns and a paved terrace. Seating throughout the garden. Productive area with raised beds of vegetables and cut flowers raised from seed in the greenhouse. Delicious cakes and plants for sale.

7 BRIDGE INN COMMUNITY FARM

Moss Side, Formby, Liverpool, L37 0AF. Bridge Inn Community Farm, www.bridgeinncommunityfarm.co.uk. *7m S of Southport. Formby by-pass A565, L onto Moss Side.* **Sun 23 June (10-4). Adm £3.50, chd free. Light refreshments in canteen.**

Bridge Inn Community Farm was established in 2010 in response to a community need. Our farm sits on a beautiful 4 acre small holding with views looking out over the countryside. We provide a quality service of training in a real life work environment and experience in horticulture, conservation and animal welfare.

8 4 BROCKLEBANK ROAD

Southport, PR9 9LP. Heather Sidebotham, 01704 543389, alansidebotham@yahoo.co.uk. *1¼ m N of Southport. Off A565 Southport to Preston Rd, opp North entrance to Hesketh Park.* **Visits by arrangement May to Aug for groups of 10+. Adm £3.50, chd free. Home-made teas.**

A walled garden incorporating a church folly. Landscaped with reclaimed materials from historic sites in the Southport area. There are several water features, an extensive herbaceous border and various areas of differing planting, thus creating a garden with much interest.

9 136 BUCKINGHAM ROAD

Maghull, L31 7DR. Debbie & Mark Jackson. *7m N of Liverpool. End M57/M58, take A59 towards Ormskirk. Turn L after car superstore onto Liverpool Rd Sth, cont' on past Meadows Pub, 3rd R into Sandringham Rd, L into Buckingham Rd.* **Sat 8, Sun 9 June (12-5). Adm £2.50, chd free. Home-made teas.** Donation to The Walton Centre.

A profusion of plants within a small suburban garden, cottage style planting, shrubs, climbers, perennials and containers brimming with hostas, acers and much more. Rose bed, wisteria covered pergola and fishpond. The garden is planted to attract butterflies and bees. Plenty of seating available and exceedingly good cakes.

10 CARR HOUSE FARM

Carr House Lane, Lancaster, LA1 1SW. Robin & Helen Loxam. *SW of Lancaster City. From A6 Lancaster city centre turn at hospital, past B&Q & 1st R, straight under railway bridge into farm.* **Sat 22, Sun 23 June (10-5). Adm £4, chd free. Home-made teas.** Donation to Fairfield Flora & Fauna Association.

A hidden gem in historic City of Lancaster. Farmhouse gardens incl Mediterranean, rustic and cottage flowers and trees intertwined beautifully with 2 ponds fed naturally by 'Lucy Brook' attracting all manner of wildlife. Apple, pear, plum, lemon and orange trees mix well within the scene. See rare breed cattle and enjoy nature walk in adjoining fields. Slope towards pond.

11 CASA LAGO

1 Woodlands Park, Whalley, BB7 9UG. Carole Ann & Stephen Powers, 01254 824903, chows3@icloud.com. *2½ m S of Clitheroe. From M6 J31, take A59 to Clitheroe. 9m take 2nd exit at*

r'about for Whalley. After 2m reach village & follow yellow signs. Parking in village car parks or nearby. **Visits by arrangement May to Aug for groups of up to 30. Adm £4, chd free. Home-made teas.**
Traverse the globe with hints of The Far East, Italy and England… Bonsai Trees, Koi Ponds, Succulent Collection, Miniature/Adult Olive trees, Trough Alpine displays, black limestone wall, Hostas, bamboos, oak pergolas. Decked elevated glass areas and The Chow Chows! Consistent visitor comments: "Inspirational, Stunning, Immaculate, Excellent, Oasis, Admiration, such lovely welcoming hosts"

12 ◆ CLEARBECK HOUSE

Mewith Lane, Higher Tatham via Lancaster, LA2 8PJ. Peter & Bronwen Osborne, 01524 261029, www.clearbeckgarden.org.uk. *13m NE of Lancaster. Signed from Wray (M6 J34, A683, B6480) & Low Bentham.* **For NGS: Sun 26, Mon 27 May, Sun 30 June, Sun 7 July (11-5). Adm £4, chd free. Light refreshments. For other opening times and information, please phone or visit garden website.**
We celebrate our 30th year with NGS 'A surprise round every corner' say visitors. They can enjoy streams, ponds, sculptures, boathouses and follies: Rapunzel's tower, temple, turf maze, giant fish made of CDs, walk-through pyramid. 2 acre wildlife lake attracts many species of insects and birds. Planting incl herbaceous borders, grasses, bog plants and many roses. Vegetable and fruit garden. Painting studio open. Children- friendly incl quiz. Artists and photographers welcome by arrangement. Wheelchair access -many grass paths, some sloped.

13 31 COUSINS LANE

Rufford, Ormskirk, L40 1TN. Brenda & Roy Caslake. *From M6 J27, follow signs for Parbold then Rufford. Turn L onto the A59. Turn R at Hesketh Arms Pub. 4th turn.* **Sun 9 June (10.30-4.30). Adm £3.50, chd free. Home-made teas in Rufford Cricket Club adjacent to garden. take time to re-energise with a glass of prosecco, a cream tea whilst enjoying the best of English pastimes.**
The garden contrasts open views with intimate spaces. Each space offers different planting themes and plays with texture and colour. The competing demands of a family garden are managed in a sensitive way to allow both the expert and the amateur to feel at ease.

14 79 CRABTREE LANE

Burscough, L40 0RW. Sandra & Peter Curl, 01704 893713, peter.curl@btinternet.com, www.youtube.com/watch?v=TqpxW7_8HT4. *3m NE of Ormskirk. A59 Preston - Liverpool Rd. From N before bridge R into Redcat Lane signed for Martin Mere. From S over 2nd bridge L into Redcat Lane after ¾m L into Crabtree Lane.* **Sun 19 May, Sun 16 June (11-4). Adm £4, chd free. Home-made teas. Visits also by arrangement May to July. Short talk on how the garden developed.**
¾ acre all year round plants person's garden with many rare and unusual plants. Herbaceous borders and colour themed island beds leading to a pond and rockery, rose garden, spring area and autumn hot bed. Many stone features built with reclaimed materials. Shrubs and rhododendrons, Koi pond with waterfall, hosta and fern walk. Gravel garden with Mediterranean plants. Patio, surrounded by shrubs and raised alpine bed. Trees giving areas for shade loving plants. Flat grass and bark paths.

15 5 CRIB LANE

Dobcross, Oldham, OL3 5AF. Helen Campbell. *5m E of Oldham. From Dobcross village-head towards Delph on Platt Lane, Crib Lane opp Dobcross Band Club - about 100 metres up, limited parking for disabled visitors only opp double green garage door, signed NGS.* **Sat 22, Sun 23 June (1-4). Combined adm with 11 Platt Lane £3.50, chd free. Home-made teas.**
Open with 11 Platt Lane - a well loved and used family garden which is challenging as on a high terraced hillside and visited by deer, hares and the odd cow ! Of additional interest are wildlife ponds, a vegetable garden, a poly tunnel, four bee hives and an art gallery and sculptures. Areas are always being re thought, dug up and changed depending on time and aged bodies aches and pains! Art gallery and stone sculptures in the garden. Four bee hives and local honey for sale. Plants for sale by the National Trust.

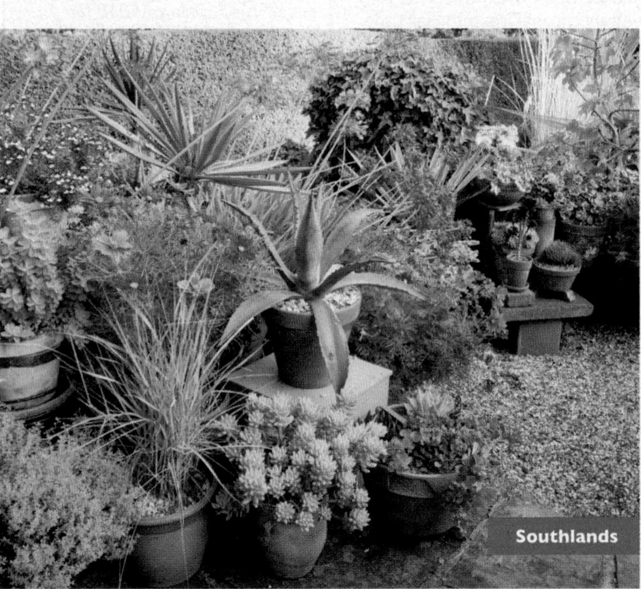

Southlands

16 CROXTETH PARK WALLED GARDEN

Liverpool, L11 1EH. Liverpool City Council, Dina Younis, www.liverpoolcityhalls.co.uk/croxteth-hall/about/victorian-walled-garden. *6m NE of Liverpool. From M57 Exit J4 take A580 towards Liverpool. Look for brown tourist signs directing L. Hall is off r'about at junction of Dwerryhouse Lane & Muirhead Av.* **Sun 25 Aug (11.30-5). Adm £3.50, chd free. Home-made teas.**

The two acre Victorian Walled Garden at Croxteth Hall was built around 1850. It produced a year round supply of fresh fruit, vegetable and cut flowers for the Hall until the last Earl died in 1972. Bedding display, herbaceous and mixed borders, trained fruit trees, herb garden, roses, soft fruits and a fuchsia collection. The garden houses part of Liverpool's historic botanical collection under glass. The estate offers ample opportunities for walking. Earlier in the summer Croxteth Park hosts the CBBC summer festival so there will be some surprises for younger visitors to the walled garden. There is disabled permit parking available near to the Hall and Garden – use the service entrance from Croxteth Hall Lane (Satnav postcode L12 0HB). There is disabled permit parking available near to the Hall and Garden – use the service entrance from Croxteth Hall Lane (Satnav postcode L12 0HB).

NPC

17 19 CUMBERLAND AVENUE

Leyland, PR25 1BE. Maureen Duggan. *M6 J28 to town centre on Turpin Green Lane (B5256) then Towngate (B5254). R on Church Rd (B5248) follow to Fox Lane. After Tennis club L Royal Ave, 2nd L Cumberland Ave.* **Sun 4, Sun 11 Aug (1-5). Adm £3, chd free. Light refreshments.**

Well planted garden with island flower beds. Trees and shrubs with some unusual perennials. Also a pond and a view of Worden Park and woods. Visited by a lot of wildlife. Partial wheelchair access but some paths are too narrow.

18 DALE HOUSE GARDENS

off Church Lane, Goosnargh, Preston, PR3 2BE. Caroline & Tom Luke, 01772 862464, tomlukebudgerigars@hotmail.com. *2½ m E of Broughton. M6 J32 signed Garstang Broughton, T-lights R at Whittingham Lane, 2½ m to Whittingham at PO turn L into Church Lane garden between nos 17 & 19.* **Sat 27, Sun 28 Apr, Sat 22, Sun 23 June (10-4). Adm £3.50, chd free. Home-made teas. Visits also by arrangement Apr to June. Donation to St Francis School, Goosnargh.**

½ acre tastefully landscaped gardens comprising of limestone rockeries, well stocked herbaceous borders, raised alpine beds, well stocked koi pond, lawn areas, greenhouse and polytunnel, patio areas, specialising in alpines rare shrubs and trees, large collection unusual bulbs. All year round interest. New features for 2019. Large indoor budgerigar aviary. 300+ budgies to view. Gravel path, lawn areas.

19 DENT HALL

Colne Road, Trawden, Colne, BB8 8NX. Mr Chris Whitaker-Webb & Miss Joanne Smith, 01282 861892, denthall@tiscali.co.uk. *Turn L at end of M65. Follow A6068 for 2m; just after 3rd r'about turn R down B6250. After 1½ m, in front of church, turn R, signed Carry Bridge. Keep R, follow road up hill, garden on R after 300yds.* **Visits by arrangement June to Aug for groups of 10+. Adm £5, chd free. Home-made teas. Donation to MIND.**

Nestled in the oldest part of Trawden villlage and rolling Lancashire countryside, this mature and evolving country garden surrounds a 400 year old grade II listed hall (not open); featuring a parterre, lawns, herbaceous borders, shrubbery, wildlife pond with bridge to seating area and a hidden summerhouse in a woodland area. Plentiful seating throughout. Some uneven paths and gradients.

GROUP OPENING

20 DIDSBURY VILLAGE GARDENS

Tickets: Any Village Garden, or Moor Cottage, Grange Lane, Didsbury, Manchester, M20 6RW. *5m S of Manchester. From M60 J5 follow signs to Northenden. Turn R at T-lights onto Barlow Moor Rd to Didsbury. From M56 follow A34 to Didsbury.* **Sun 9 June (12-5). Combined adm £6, chd free. Home-made teas at Moor Cottage & 68 Brooklawn Drive.**

68 BROOKLAWN DRIVE
Anne & Jim Britt, www.thefruitygardener.com.

3 THE DRIVE
Peter Clare & Sarah Keedy, www.theshadegarden.com.

MOOR COTTAGE
William Godfrey.

38 WILLOUGHBY AVENUE
Simon Hickey.

Didsbury is an attractive South Manchester suburb which retains its village atmosphere. There are interesting shops, cafes and restaurants, well worth a visit in themselves! This year we have 4 gardens demonstrating a variety of beautiful spaces- one is a large walled family garden surrounding a Georgian cottage, divided into several enchanting areas with towering Echiums and free range chickens. Another is an expertly planted shade garden with many choice rarities, whilst another reflects the charm of the cottage garden ethos with rose covered pergola, old fashioned perennials and tranquil raised pool. Our smaller gardens show beautifully how suburban plots, with limited space, can be packed full of interesting features and a range of planting styles. Dogs allowed at some gardens. Wheelchair access to some gardens.

21 DUTTON HALL

Gallows Lane, Ribchester, PR3 3XX. Mr & Mrs A H Penny, www.duttonhall.co.uk. *2m NE of Ribchester. Signed from B6243 & B6245 also directions on website.* **Evening opening Fri 28 June (5-8). Wine. Sun 30 June (1-5). Home-made teas. Adm £5, chd free.**

An increasing range of interesting trees and shrubs have been added to the existing collection of old fashioned roses, including rare and unusual varieties and Plant Heritage National Collection of Pemberton Hybrid Musk roses. Formal garden at front with backdrop of C17 house (not open). A range of other features and extensive views over the Ribble Valley. Analemmatic Sundial, pond, meadow areas all with extensive views over Ribble Valley. Teas provided by St John's Church. Plant Heritage Plant Stall with unusual varieties for sale. Disabled access difficult due to different levels and steps.

22 35 ELLESMERE ROAD

Eccles, Salford, Manchester, M30 9FE. Enid Noronha. *3m W of Salford, 4m W of Manchester. From M60 exit at M602 for Salford.Take A576 for Trafford Park & Eccles, stay on A576. Turn L onto Half Edge Lane, keep L to Monton on Half Edge Lane. Turn R onto Stafford Rd & L onto Ellesmere Rd.* **Sat 22 June (12-5). Combined adm with 11 Westminster Road £5, chd free. Home-made teas.**

Amidst the busy urban environment of Eccles in Salford, lies a hidden pocket of grand houses with wide roads,and these two havens of tranquillity. 35 Ellesmere Road is a peaceful country garden with deep herbaceous borders filled with shrubs, scented roses, and perennials. A climber covered pergola leads to a productive vegetable garden where raised beds and fruit trees add to the feeling of abundance.

23 GILES FARM

Four Acre Lane, Thornley, Preston, PR3 2TD. Kirsten & Phil Brown. *3m NE of Longridge. From J31A or J32 of M6 follow signs for Longridge. Pass through Longridge & follow signs for Chipping. Pass the Derby Arms on the L & then turn R at the old school for 1m. Parking at the farm.* **Sat 15, Sun 16 June (12-5). Adm £4, chd free. Light refreshments. A selection of sandwiches & home baked cakes.**

Nestled high on the side of Longridge fell, with beautiful long-reaching views across the Ribble Valley, the gardens surround the old farmhouse and buildings. The gardens are ever evolving and include an acre of perennial wildflower meadows, wildlife pond, woodland areas and cottage gardens. There are plentiful areas to sit and take in the views. There are steps and uneven surfaces in the gardens. Disabled access difficult due to different levels, surface areas and steps.

24 GREEN FARM COTTAGE

42 Lower Green, Poulton-le-Fylde, FY6 7EJ. Eric & Sharon Rawcliffe. *500yds from Poulton-le-Fylde Village. M55 J3 follow A585 Fleetwood. T- lights turn L. Next lights bear L A586. Poulton 2nd set of lights turn R Lower Green. Cottage on L.* **Sun 23 June (10-5). Adm £4, chd free. Home-made teas.**

½ acre well established formal cottage gardens. Feature koi pond, paths leading to different areas. Lots of climbers and rose beds. Packed with plants of all kinds. Many shrubs and trees. Well laid out lawns. Collections of unusual plants. A surprise round every corner. Said by visitors to be 'a real hidden jewel'.

NEW GRESGARTH HALL

Caton, Lancaster LA2 9NB. Sir Mark & Lady Lennox-Boyd. *Take the M6 to J34 then A683 to Caton (2m), turn R on the Quernmore Road & after half a mile you reach the entrance.*

Sun 11 Aug (11-5). Adm £9, chd free. Home-made teas.

One of Lancashire's secret garden gems, Arabella Lennox-Boyd renowned garden designer 's own garden at Gresgarth Hall, Caton, Lancaster is certainly worth a visit to see the extensive plant collections. The garden at Gresgarth has been the testing ground for Arabella's design work since she moved there in 1978. Here is displayed her innate Italian style combined with her famous skills as a plantswoman. The impressive tree collection including magnolias, prunus, and also rhododendrons and azaleas are maturing - with many rare specimens, often grown from seeds collected on Arabella's Far Eastern plant hunting trips. There is so much to see, the main gardens have herbaceous borders, terraces down to the Lake billowing with roses and shrubs, overflowing pots with novel plant combinations everywhere and the formal entrance forecourt with its topiary and statuary give way to bog and lakeside gardens, the walled kitchen garden a nuttery and orchard, the serpentine beech walk, the lilac walk and much more. Wheelchair access to the majority of the garden.

25 NEW 45 GREY HEIGHTS VIEW

Off Eaves Lane, Chorley, PR6 0TN. Barbara Ashworth, 07941339702. *1m from Chorley Hospital. From Wigan/Coppull B5251. At (town centre) Xrds straight across . At r'about across to Lyons Ln and follow NGS signs. From M61, J8 follow signs A6 Town Centre to Lyons Ln signed from here.* **Sun 9 June, Sun 14 July, Sun 18 Aug (11-5). Adm £3, chd free. Cream teas. Visits also by arrangement June to Aug for groups of 10 to 30.**

A small suburban garden with cottage garden style planting including fruit trees. Heavily planted with a profusion of perennials, roses and clematis. No repeat planting. Including a greenhouse, small vegetable and fruit area. An abundance of recycling and space saving ideas. Back drop of Healey Nab, and a stones throw from the Leeds - Liverpool Canal. Craft items for sale.

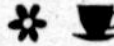

Your visits help change lives – your generosity has supported unpaid carers through donations to Carers Trust totalling over £3.9 million since 1996

26 THE GROWTH PROJECT

Kellett Street Allotments, Rochdale, OL16 2JU. Karen Hayday, 01706 810245, k.hayday@hourglass.org.uk, www.rochdalemind.org.uk/growth-project. *From A627M. R A58 L Entwistle Rd R Kellett St.* **Sat 10 Aug (11.30-4). Adm £3.50, chd free. Home-made teas.** Visits also by arrangement June to Oct. Weds and Thurs only. Donation to The Growth Project.

Providing homemade lunches, cut flowers, veg, preserves and gifts plus guides to give horticultural advice. The Growth Project is set on over an acre and incl organic veg varieties, wildlife pond, insect hotels, formal flower and wildflower borders, and potager. Visit the Elizabethan straw bale house, stroll down the pergola walk and under the handcrafted arches to the wild flower meadow and orchard. Afternoon tea served in the Victorian style ornate 'Woodland Green' woodworking station. Jams and cakes to buy. The new attraction this year is the wildflower meadow and orchard The Growth Project is a partnership between Hourglass and Rochdale and District mind. No disabled WC, ground can be uneven.

GROUP OPENING

27 HALE VILLAGE GARDENS

Liverpool, L24 4BA. *6m S of M62 J6. Take A5300, A562 towards Liverpool, then A561, L for Hale opp the RSPCA. From S L'pool head for the airport then L sign for Hale. The 82A bus runs through the village from Widnes/Runcorn to L'pool.* **Sat 29, Sun 30 June (2-5). Combined adm £4, chd free. Light refreshments at 2 Pheasant Field & 66 Church Rd.**

54 CHURCH ROAD
Norma & Ray Roe.

66 CHURCH ROAD
Liz Kelly-Hines & David Hines.

2 PHEASANT FIELD
Roger & Tania Craine.

The delightful village of Hale, is set in rural S Merseyside between Widnes and Liverpool Airport. It is home to the cottage, sculpture and grave of the famous giant known as the Childe of Hale. Gardens at different ends of the village have been fully developed by the present owners. No 2 Pheasant Field at the west of the village has a lovely waterfall in a well-planted area and lots of summer colour . Nos 54 and 66 Church Road at the south of the village are on the way to the old lighthouse at Hale Point and have wonderful views over the river Mersey and the distant Welsh Hills. A wildlife pond and mixed planting for structure, colour and fragrance, along with a substantial allotment, all feature.

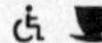

Giles Farm

28 ◆ HAZELWOOD

North Road, Bretherton, Leyland, PR26 9AY. Jacqueline Iddon & Thompson Dagnall, 01772 601433, jacquelineiddon@gmail.com, www.jacquelineiddon.co.uk. *8m SW of Preston. Between Southport & Preston, from A59, take B5247 for 1m then L onto (B5248) Garden signed from North Rd.* **For NGS: Sun 19 May, Sun 16 June (1-5). Adm £3.50, chd free. Cream teas.** For other opening times and information, please phone, email or visit garden website.

1½ acre garden and hardy plant nursery, originally orchard, now has gravel garden with pots and seating area bottle wall and folly, shrubs, herbaceous borders, large stream-fed pond with woodland walk. Sculpture, Victorian fern house. Oak-framed, summerhouse, log cabin as sculpture gallery fronted by cottage garden beds. Sculpture demonstration at 2 pm, Beach area. Teas in Coach house in aid of Queenscourt Hospice. Extensive sculpture collection, the work of Thompson Dagnall. The majority of the garden is accessible to wheel chairs.

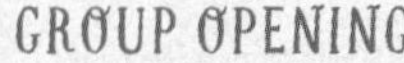

GROUP OPENING

29 HILLSIDE GARDENS

Liverpool Road, Southport, PR8 3DE. *3m S of Southport. Gardens signed from A565 Waterloo Rd & A5267 Liverpool Rd.* **Sun 19 May, Sun 21 July (11-5). Combined adm £5, chd free. Home-made teas at 339 Liverpool Rd. WC facilities available.**

23 ASHTON ROAD
John & Jennifer Mawdsley.

33 CLOVELLY DRIVE
Bob & Eunice Drummond.

LINKS VIEW, 18 CLOVELLY DRIVE
Christine & Dave McGarry.

339 LIVERPOOL ROAD
Ian & Sue Dexter.

The gardens of Hillside are full of variety and interest, each having ponds or water features which create a relaxed atmosphere. Ashton Road is separated into three rooms with interesting shrubs, herbaceous plants and a vegetable plot. Featured in Lancashire Life. 18 Clovelly Drive is a developing new garden with a patio. Glass features around the perimeter walls add a different dimension, with chain saw carvings interspersed amongst plants. At 33 Clovelly Drive mature trees and shrubs set off the circular lawn with sweeping colour-themed herbaceous borders. Rhododendrons and azaleas give colour in spring. Featured in Amateur Gardening . Liverpool Road was a neglected landscape garden full of beautiful and unusual trees and shrubs. It is now being brought back to life and developed with herbaceous planting and grasses. Excellent spring colour. Limited wheelchair access to gardens.

GROUP OPENING

30 NEW HUTTON GARDENS

Tolsey Drive, Hutton, Preston, PR4 5SH. Heather & John Lund. *2m SW of Preston. Take A59 towards Southport, at the r'about head towards Longton on Liverpool Road. Tolsey Drive is 100 yds on the L. Signed from A59 r'about.* **Sun 7 July (12-4). Combined adm £5, chd free. Home-made teas at 10 Tolsey Dr. Wine.**

NEW 1 TOLSEY DRIVE
Lynn & Simon Pinder.

NEW 2 TOLSEY DRIVE
Vicki & Alex Cullen.

NEW 5 TOLSEY DRIVE
Marilyn & James Woods.

NEW 10 TOLSEY DRIVE
Heather & John Lund.

NEW 13 TOLSEY DRIVE
Joan & Arthur Marshall.

NEW 107 LIVERPOOL ROAD
Jackie & Chris Procter.

Hutton is a small village on the outskirts of Preston. There are 6 gardens, one is a small, private cottage style garden and the other 5 are long, narrow gardens which vary in style. Some have an open aspect with sweeping lawns and mature trees and shrubs, others have cottage style or perennial herbaceous planting with some unusual features. Most gardens have wheelchair access limited to the initial patio area, one is inaccessible.

---

31 JACK GREEN COTTAGE

Mill House Lane, Brindle, Chorley, PR6 8NS. Aurelia & Peter McCann. *5m N Chorley. From Chorley A6 turn R at r'about on B5256 Westwood Rd then L at r'about on B5256 Sandy Lane through Brindle for 2m, then L on Hill House Lane for ¾m. Turn L on Oram Rd for 200yd.* **Sat 29, Sun 30 June (11-4). Adm £5, chd free. Home-made teas.**

This 2¾ acre garden has been developed in the last 8 years by a young family and it is still 'work in progress'. With long borders of cottage style plants, Japanese garden, herb garden, small parterre, orchards, fruit cage and vegetable plots, there is a surprise around every corner. Chicken pen, secluded BBQ area, greenhouse and children's play area with willow tunnel and den. Not all areas are suitable for wheelchair use, users should ideally be accompanied as some parts of the garden may be difficult to navigate.

32 NEW KINGTON COTTAGE

Treales Village, Treales, Preston, PR4 3SD. Mrs Linda Kidd. *M55 J3. Take A585 to Kirkham, exit Preston St ,L into Carr Lane to Treales Village. Cottage on L in front of Derby Arms. Parking here.* **Sun 2 June, Sat 6, Sun 7 July, Sun 4 Aug (10-5). Adm £3.50, chd free. Home-made teas.**

Nestling in the beautiful village of Treales this generously sized Japanese garden has many authentic and unique Japanese features, along side its 2 ponds linked by a river. The stroll garden leads down to the tea house garden.The planting and the meandering pathway blend together to create a tranquil meditative garden in which to relax. Runner up in Daily Mail Best Kept Garden Competition. Wheelchair access to some areas, uneven paths.

33 LOWER DUTTON FARM

Gallows Lane, Ribchester, PR3 3XX. Mr R Robinson, 01254 878405, aforrest_50@outlook.com. *1½m NE of Ribchester. Leave M6 J31. Take A59 towards Clitheroe, turn L at T-lights towards Ribchester. Signed from B6243 & B6245. Ample car parking in adjacent field.* **Sat 3, Sun 4 Aug (1-5). Adm £4, chd free. Home-made teas.** **Visits also by arrangement May to Aug for groups of 10+.**

Traditional long Lancashire farmhouse and barn, with 2 acre gardens. Formal gardens nr house with mixed herbaceous beds and shrubs. Sweeping lawns lead down past island beds to wildlife area and established large pond with small woodland. Small orchard at rear of house with mix of fruit-trees and shrubs. Several seating areas. Lawns may be difficult in very wet weather.

34 72 LUDLOW DRIVE

Ormskirk, L39 1LF. Marian & Brian Jones. *½m W of Ormskirk on A570. From M58 J3 follow A570 to Ormskirk town centre. Continue on A570 towards Southport. At A570 junction with A59 cross T-lights after ½m turn R at garage onto Heskin Lane then R Ludlow Drive.* **Sun 14 July (11-4). Adm £3.50, chd free. Home-made teas.**

A beautiful town garden overflowing with a wide variety of bee friendly planting. Developed over the last 10 years it includes a gravel garden, colourful herbaceous and shrub borders, raised shade and rose borders with old and new rose varieties and many clematis. There is also an attractive raised pond, alpine troughs, succulent pots and wall baskets a summer house and greenhouse. Wheelchair access to front garden but limited access to rear garden.

35 NEW LYTHAM HALL

Ballam Rd, Lytham, Lytham St. Annes, FY8 4JX. Paul Lomax. *Follow the brown tourist signs for Lytham Hall Sat Nav users use postcode FY8 4TQ.* **Sun 21 July (10-4.30). Adm £4, chd free. Light refreshments. There are picnic tables on the East Lawn.**

Lytham Hall is a C18 Georgian house set in 78 acres of historic woodlands, with a new parterre, herbaceous border, south prospect garden, a lake and a wildlife pond. A mount, that can be climbed and 4km of paths. There is a newly built RHS award winning vegetable garden and potager adjacent to an apiary. 1m drive from the main gates to the Hall, part of the way there is a separate designated path for pedestrians past fields and through woodland. An outside catering vehicle will be available for hot drinks and snacks in addition to the cafe Wheelchair access available to most areas. Gravel paths in woodland. Coaches by appointment only.

36 MAGGIE'S MANCHESTER

Kinnaird Road, Manchester, M20 4QL. Jemma Halman. *At the end of Kinnaird Rd which is off Wilmslow Rd opposite the Christie Hospital.* **Sun 21 July (11-4). Adm £3, chd free. Light refreshments.**

The architecture of Maggie's Manchester, designed by world-renowned architect Lord Foster, is complemented by gardens designed by Dan Pearson, Best in Show winner at Chelsea Flower Show. Combining a rich mix of spaces, including the working glass house and vegetable garden, the garden provides a place for both activity and contemplation. The colours and sensory experience of nature becomes part of the Centre through micro gardens and internal courtyards, which relate to the different spaces within the building. Wheelchair access to most of the garden from the front entrance.

37 MAGGIE'S OLDHAM

The Royal Oldham Hospital, Rochdale Road, Oldham, OL1 2JH. Maggie's Centres, 0161 989 0550, oldham@maggiescentres.org, www.maggiescentres.org/oldham. *Maggie's is in the grounds of the Royal Oldham Hospital, next door to A&E. It's the wooden building on stilts and the garden lies underneath the building.* **Sun 2 June (11-5). Adm by donation. Home-made teas.** Visits also by arrangement May to Sept.

The garden is framed by enclosing walls. The building 'floating' aloft is like a drop curtain to the scene, creating a picture window effect. The trees soar upwards filling the volume of space. A woodland understorey weaves between the structure of the numerous white birch and crispy bark of the pine trunks. The garden could be described as an ornamental woodland. Please introduce yourself to a member of the team on arrival who will guide you to the wheelchair entrance to the garden.

38 NEW MATSHEAD LODGE

Brock Side, Bilsborrow, Preston, PR3 0GL. Sheila & Nick Baines. *2m N of Bilsborrow. Parking at Barton Grange Garden Centre on A6 (permission granted), cross A6 to car sales yard follow public footpath, over railway bridge along river and foot bridge to NGS signage.* **Sat 18 May (10.30-4.30). Adm £3.50, chd free. Light refreshments.**

Set in approx 2 acres, a garden of mixed herbaceous borders, with shrubs, orchard and loose stone pathways.Hidden away on the banks of river Brock featuring Japanese area, walled vegetable garden, pond, many seating areas. Disabled access at address only.

39 NEW 6 MENIVALE CLOSE

Southport, PR9 9RY. Ann-Marie Hutson. *4m N of Southport. A565 from Preston at BP garage turn R. Then 3rd R. At T junction turn R, then 1st L. A565 from Southport at BP garage turn L. Then 3rd R. At T junction turn R. then 1st L.* **Sun 9 June (11-5). Combined adm with 120 Roe Lane £3.50, chd free. Home-made teas.**

Set in a 1970's housing estate, the garden follows a cottage garden style with brick edged island beds, each bed having a seasonal focus. Surrounded by neighbouring trees, the garden is sheltered from the NW winds. ⅔ of the garden has access for wheelchairs.

40 MILL BARN

Goosefoot Close, Samlesbury, Preston, PR5 0SS. Chris Mortimer, 01254 853300, chris@millbarn.net, www.millbarn.net. *6m E of Preston. From M6 J31 2½m on A59/A677 B/burn. Turn S. Nabs Head Lane, then Goosefoot Lane.* **Sat 15, Sun 16, Sat 22, Sun 23 June (1-5). Adm £5, chd free. Cream teas.** Visits also by arrangement May to July for groups of 5+.

The unique and quirky garden at Mill Barn is a delight: or rather a series of delights. Along the R Darwin, through the tiny secret grotto, past the suspension bridge and view of the fairytale tower, visitors can a stroll past folly, sculptures, lily pond, and lawns, enjoy the naturally planted flowerbeds, then enter the secret garden and through it the pathways of the wooded hillside beyond. A garden developed on the site of old mills gives a fascinating layout which evolves at many levels. Partial wheelchair access, visitors have not been disappointed in the past.

ALLOTMENTS

41 MOSS PARK ALLOTMENTS

Lesley Road, Stretford, Manchester, M32 9EE. Allison Sterlini. *3m SW of Manchester. From M60 J7 (Manchester), A56 (Manchester), A5181 Barton Road, L onto B5213 Urmston Lane, ½m L onto Lesley Rd signed Stretford Cricket Club. Parking at second gate.* **Sun 28 July (11-4). Adm £4, chd free. Home-made teas.**

Moss Park is a stunning, award winning allotment site in Stretford, Manchester. Wide grass paths flanked by pretty flower borders give way to a large variety of well-tended plots bursting with ideas to try at home, from insect hotels to unusual fruits and vegetables. Take tea and cake on the lawn outside the quirky society clubhouse that looks like a beamed country pub. WC facilities. Limited wheelchair access.

42 THE OLD VICARAGE

Church Road, Astley, Manchester, M29 7FS. Susan & Neil Kinsella. *½ way between Leigh & Worsley*

off A580 East Lancs Rd. Opp the site of the old St Stephens Astley CE Church & next to Dam House, 250 yds from the mini r'about junction at Church Rd (A5082) & Manchester Rd(A572). Close to the Bull's Head. **Sat 1, Sun 2 June (10-4). Adm £4, chd free. Cream teas.**
Recently restored medium sized gardens of Grade 2* vernacular Georgian vicarage comprising both formal and informal planting and statuary as the garden narrows to follow the woodland stream which runs through it. There are six separate areas/rooms which gradually merge into the surrounding trees ending several hundred yards from the frontage to the property. Most of the garden is flat with some gravel paths.

43 PARKERS LODGE

28 Lodge Side, Bury, BL8 2SW. Keith Talbot, wcp1964@gmail.com. *2m W of M66 J2. From A58 then B6196 Ainsworth Rd turn R onto Elton Vale Rd, drive past the sports club onto a small estate, and follow the road round to car park.* **Sun 26 May, Sun 7 July (11-4). Adm £4, chd free. Light refreshments.** Visits also by arrangement.
Parkers Lodge is set on the site of a demolished Victorian Mill that was used for bleaching. Since the houses were completed in 2014 a small group of volunteers have been working to transform what was a jungle into a manicured wild space that still allows the local wildlife to flourish. Set in 12 acres with 2 lakes with 50 percent of them open for a leisurely stroll round.

44 PLANT WORLD

Myerscough College, St Michaels Road, Bilsborrow, Preston, PR3 0RY. Myerscough college. *5m N J32 M6. From the S on A6 turn L into St Michaels Rd take the 2nd entrance to the college.* **Sun 11 Aug (11-4). Adm £3.50, chd free. Light refreshments.**
A gardener's paradise with an acre of RHS gold award winning gardens and glasshouses, including tropical, temperate and desert zones. Themed and herbaceous borders, pinetum, fruit garden, bog garden, pond and woodland garden. With many plants labelled for identification purposes. Plant sales with many rare and unusual specimens. Myerscough Tea rooms overlook the stunning gardens serving a wide range of delicious locally produced cakes and sandwiches. Indoor and outdoor seating. Guided tours throughout the day. Dogs welcome in the gardens, sales area and the cafés outdoor seating area.

45 11 PLATT LANE

Dobcross, Oldham, OL3 5AD. Marilyn McNeill. *5m E of Oldham. From Dobcross village square the exit to Platt Lane, the garden is last house on L. From Delph take the turning opposite the Bell Inn & continue the garden is on the R.* **Sat 22, Sun 23 June (1-4). Combined adm with 5 Crib Lane £3.50, chd free. Cream teas.**
This cottage garden has a front garden planted with shrubs. The main garden has herbaceous borders with shrubs, roses and perennials. There is a wildlife pond and a summerhouse with an exhibition of textiles. The rear garden has a mixture of flowers, vegetables and fruit. There is also a small wildlife pond and a greenhouse.

46 ◆ THE RIDGES

Weavers Brow (cont. of Cowling Rd), Limbrick, Chorley, PR6 9EB. Mr & Mrs J M Barlow, 01257 279981, barbara@barlowridges.co.uk, www.bedbreakfast-gardenvisits.com. *2m SE of Chorley town centre. From M6 J27. From M61 J8. Follow signs for Chorley A6 then signs for Cowling & Rivington. Passing Morrison's up Brook St, mini r'about 2nd exit, Cowling Brow. Pass Spinners Arms on L. Garden on R.* **For NGS: Mon 6 May, Mon 26 Aug (11-5). Adm £4.50, chd free. Cream teas.** For other opening times and information, please phone, email or visit garden website.
3 acres, incl old walled orchard garden, cottage-style herbaceous borders, with perfumed rambling roses and clematis thru fruit trees. Arch leads to formal lawn, surrounded by natural woodland, shrub borders and specimen trees with contrasting foliage. Woodland walks and dell. Natural looking stream, wildlife ponds. Walled water feature with Italian influence, and walled herb garden. Classical music played. Home made cakes, baked and served by ladies of St James Church, Chorley. Wheelchair access some gravel paths and woodland walks not accessible.

The Growth Project

47 NEW 120 ROE LANE

Southport, PR9 7PJ. Mrs Mavis Standing. *2m N Southport. A565 N on Lord St at r'about 3rd exit to Manchester Rd continue to Roe Lane.* **Sun 9 June (11-5). Combined adm with 6 Menivale Close £3.50, chd free. Cream teas.**

Mature garden encouraged to develop over 25 years and includes trees, shrubs, succulents and perennials. Diverse corners and wildlife.

48 THE SECRET VALLEY

Christ the King Primary School Carpark, Worsley, Manchester, M28 3DW. Sally Berry, 0161 7300128, info@thesecretvalley.com, www.thesecretvalley.com. *7½ m from central Manchester. 1½ m from J13 M60. Straight over r'about onto Walkden Rd, at 1st T-lights turn R onto A580 Take 2nd L onto Holly Ave, park in Christ the King Primary School. No parking on 'Hopefold Drive' or 'The Reach'.* **Sun 2 June (10-4). Adm £5, chd free. Light refreshments.** Visits also by arrangement Apr to Oct for groups of 5 to 30. Groups will have access to WC, large Pagoda and a tea making cabin.

As featured on gardeners world. Large 2 acre water garden with ponds, streams, waterfalls, islands and lake. High variety of trees, plants and climbers. It is a haven for waterfowl and local wildlife (incl swans, ducks, geese, coots, moorhens, grebes, herons and kingfishers). Adjoining gardens and allotment are also open. Waterfall, 1 acre lake, smaller ponds, streams, fountain, statues, wild swans and ducks, lots of seating and areas to relax. The entrance, central area are wheelchair friendly. Many paths are not if there is rain.

Your visits help change lives – we are Hospice UK's largest charitable funder donating more than £5 million to support hospices in local communities since 1996

GROUP OPENING

49 SEFTON PARK JUNE GARDENS

Arundel Avenue, Liverpool, L17 2AT. *1m S of Liverpool city centre. From end of M62 take A5058 Queens Drive ring rd S through Allerton to Sefton Park. Parking roadside in Arundel Ave.* **Sun 9 June (12-5). Combined adm £5, chd free. Home-made teas at Fern Grove Community Garden, Community Orchard and Wildlife Garden in Arundel Avenue.**

THE COMMUNITY ORCHARD AND WILDLIFE GARDEN
The Society of Friends, www.tann.org.uk.

FERN GROVE COMMUNITY GARDEN
Liverpool City Council.

NEW **17 SYDENHAM AVE**
Fatima Aabbar-Marshall.

THAT BLOOMIN' GREEN TRIANGLE, DUCIE ST
Mrs Helen Hebden.

This is a fascinatingly varied group of Liverpool gardens. In That Bloomin' Green Triangle, Architecture group Assemble won the Turner Prize 2015 for their work with the four streets. It was the guerrilla gardening of local residents which led to the area's regeneration. See the wild flower meadow in Ducie Street at its peak in June, and beautifully kept back alleys and yards. Two local gardening projects to see: Fern Grove Community garden has raised beds for abundant vegetable growing and the Community Orchard is a quiet haven with glorious planting in early summer at the former Quaker Burial Ground in Arundel Avenue. And opening for the first time, the exquisitely laid out and planted private garden in Sydenham Avenue. Children's activities at Fern Grove Community Garden and a beekeeping demonstration at 2pm. Tours of the Bloomin' Green Triangle at 1 and 3 pm.

GROUP OPENING

50 NEW SEFTON PARK SEPTEMBER GARDENS

Sefton Drive, Sefton Park, Liverpool, L8 3SD. *From end of M62, take A5058 Queens Drive ring road S through Allerton to Sefton Park and follow the yellow signs. Parking roadside in Sefton Park.* **Sun 8 Sept (12-5). Combined adm £5, chd free. Home-made teas at Sefton Park Allotments, Sefton Villa and 37 Prince Alfred Rd.**

PARKMOUNT
L17 3BP. Jeremy Nicholls.

NEW **37 PRINCE ALFRED ROAD**
Jane Hammett.

SEFTON PARK ALLOTMENTS
L17 1AS. Sefton Park Allotments Society.

SEFTON VILLA
L8 3SD. Patricia Williams, 0151 281 3687, seftonvilla@live.co.uk.

Three beautiful gardens planted for late summer colour and interest, and nearly 100 allotments full of abundant produce and flowers. The secret garden at 37 Prince Alfred Road opens its gates to the public for the first time. It's so hidden away, you'd never guess it was there. And inside the sandstone walled space is glorious planting, a lovely greenhouse, summerhouse and bothy. The long borders at Park Mount reach their peak in late summer, with a flaming hot colour scheme, and hidden woodland paths. And the plantswoman's garden in Sefton Drive delights with perfect colour blending, and rare and unusual plants. At the allotments, vegetable production will be at its peak, and many of the gardeners have lovely dahlia displays. No wheelchair access at 37 Prince Alfred Road. Disabled WC at Sefton Park allotments.

38 Willoughby Avenue, Didsbury Village Gardens

51 SOUTHLANDS

12 Sandy Lane, Stretford, M32 9DA. Maureen Sawyer & Duncan Watmough, www.southlands12.com. *3m S of Manchester. Sandy Lane (B5213) is situated off A5181 (A56) ¼m from M60 J7.* **Sun 21 July (12-5.30). Adm £4, chd free. Home-made teas. Cake-away service (take a slice of your favourite cake home).**

Described by visitors as 'totally inspirational', this artists' multi-award winning garden unfolds into a series of beautiful spaces including Mediterranean, Ornamental and Woodland gardens. Organic kitchen garden with large glasshouse. Extensive herbaceous borders,hanging baskets and stunning container plantings throughout the garden, 2 ponds and a water feature. BBC North west tonight.

53 WARTON HALL

Lodge Lane, Lytham, Lytham, FY8 5RP. Nicola & David Thompson, www.total-art.co.uk. *J3 exit M55. L for Kirkham, follow signs for Wrea Green, L towards Warton to the BAE T-lights, R, Lodge Lane on R after The Golf Academy & 2m before Lytham town centre.* **Sat 4, Sun 5, Mon 6 May (10-5). Adm £4, chd free. Light refreshments. Some Gluten Free Baking.**

Georgian Manor House (not open) set in10 acre garden with Bluebell woodland walk, Bog Garden and Sculpture Trail. Japanese Water Garden and Dry Garden. Art/Design Classes in the Garden and Studio, Yoga classes under the 400 year old Weeping Hornbeam tree. The Tearoom will be serving light refreshment incl homemade cakes, plants and garden gifts for sale. Woodland walk and Sculpture Trail. Craft and Art classes in the Garden and Art Studio can be booked online at www.total-art.co.uk 'Gardens of Warton Hall' on Facebook for updates and Booking Classes Free craft sessions in the Garden Outdoor Yoga NO PICNICS. Wheelchair access to most of the garden on light gravel paths.

Maggie's Oldham

54 WEEPING ASH GARDEN

Bents Garden & Home, Warrington Road, Glazebury, WA3 5NS. John Bent, www.bents.co.uk. *15m W of Manchester. Located next to Bents Garden & Home, just off the A580 East Lancs Rd at Greyhound r'about near Leigh. Follow brown 'Garden Centre' signs.* **Sun 17, Sun 24 Feb, Sun 18 Aug, Sun 8 Sept, Sun 20 Oct (10-4). Adm £5, chd free.**
Created by retired nurseryman and photographer John Bent, Weeping Ash is a garden of all-year interest with a beautiful display of early snowdrops. Broad sweeps of colour lend elegance to this stunning garden which is much larger than it initially seems with hidden paths and wooded areas creating a sense of natural growth. Weeping Ash Garden is located immed adjacent to Bents Garden & Home with its award winning Fresh Approach Restaurant and Dining Destinations. It also offers an Indoor Beach, Outdoor Play Area and Jurassic Cove Adventure Golf Course for those looking for a complete day out. Partial wheelchair access and weather dependent.

55 6 WEST LANE

Formby, L37 7BA, L37 7BA. Laurie & Sue Lissett. *Freshfield. From Formby By-pass turn into Southport Rd (Esso at junction). Proceed to mini r'about and turn R into Green Ln (Grapes pub on corner). Follow road to West Lane which is 2nd on R.* **Sun 7 July (11-4). Combined adm with 33 Brewery Lane £3.50, chd free. Light refreshments.**
Suburban garden on sandy soil near to NT Nature Reserve home to red squirrels and Formby Sand Dunes. Garden with pergola and arches with mixed planting to rockeries and borders. Large selection of baskets and containers with decking and patio areas.

56 11 WESTMINSTER ROAD

Eccles, Manchester, M30 9HF. Lynne Meakin. *3m W of Salford, 4m W of Manchester. 1st exit M602 Manchester direction 1st exit (r'about) 2nd T-lights turn L. After Xing turn R, Victoria Rd 2nd R (Westminster Rd) no. 11 on L.* **Sat 22 June (12-5). Combined adm with 35 Ellesmere Road £5, chd free. Wine. Homemade teas at the Ellesmere Road.**
There is pretty front garden with topiary chickens and well stocked with perennials, mature trees, and box hedging. The garden is divided by a trellis and rose arch which separates the flower beds and lawn from the fruit growing area, and there are a large number of fuchsias grown in pots. A coach house to the rear of the garden where wine/ nibbles will be served. The garden is on the flat except for a small area in the front garden, care will need to be taken in case the path is slippy.

57 WIGAN & LEIGH HOSPICE

Kildare Street, Hindley, Wigan, WN2 3HZ. Wigan & Leigh Hospice, 01942 525566, j.nicholson@wlh.org.uk, thehospicegardener.com. *1½m SW of Wigan. From Wigan on A577 Leigh/Manchester Rd. In Hindley turn R at St Peter's Church onto Liverpool Rd A58. After 250 metres turn R into Kildare St.* **Sun 21 July (11-4). Adm £3.50, chd free. Home-made teas.** Visits also by arrangement Apr to Sept.
Large attractive gardens surround the Hospice creating a place of tranquillity. At the front are beautiful raised beds, at the rear 3 large ponds and a Chinese bridge. Outside patients' rooms are colourful tubs and flower beds.

A memorial daisy garden and 2 courtyards also feature. A new wild flower garden has been created - 'The Amberswood Garden'. The gardens are a haven for wildlife. Fully accessible, including WC.

58 WILLOWBROOK HOSPICE GARDENS

Portico Lane, Eccleston Park, Prescot, L34 2QT.Willowbrook Hospice. *Leave M6 at exit 21A to M62. At J7 take A57 to Prescot/Liverpool. Continue on A57, turn R onto B5201 Willowbrook is on the R.* **Sat 20, Sun 21 July (11-4). Adm £3, chd free. Home-made teas. On site café available for light lunches.**

An oasis containing three distinctive National Japanese Garden Society built gardens; a "willowbrook" flower bed designed by RHS Wisley students and a community vegetable garden.

59 WOODSTOCK BARN

Andertons Mill, Mawdesley, Ormskirk, L40 3TW. Mr & Mrs J Bean, 01772 641033, johnpatbean@sky.com. *9m E of Ormskirk. M6 J27 A5209 over Parbold hill, R Lancaster Lane/ Chorley Rd, L after Farmers Arms to Bentley Lane/Andertons Mill. Garden 500 yds on L. From Burscough A59, A5209 towards Parbold, L Lancaster Lane.* **Visits by arrangement May to Sept for groups of 10 to 30. With 8 Andertons Mill. Textile exhib.Dems/workshops inspired by garden. Home-made teas. Some seating under cover available for up to 30 people.**

An established country garden of over ¾ acre with form, texture and a green tapestry all year round. Developed from a barren wilderness to one with wildlife, amidst tall trees, shrubs, mixed borders, pond, vegetable patch, woodland area and stream. There are several seating areas to enjoy the tranquil atmosphere of this relaxing garden.

GROUP OPENING

60 WOOLTON VILLAGE GARDENS

Woolton, Liverpool, L25 8QF. *7m S of Liverpool. Woolton Rd B5171 or Menlove Ave A562 follow signs for Woolton.* **Sun 14 July (12-5). Combined adm £5, chd free. Light refreshments. at 23 Hillside Drive and Bishops Lodge.**

NEW **BISHOPS LODGE**
Bishop Paul & Kate Bayes.

NEW **23 HILLSIDE DRIVE**
Bruce & Fiona Pennie.

71 MANOR ROAD
John & Maureen Davies.

NEW **231 SPEKE ROAD**
Paul & Helen Ekoku, 07765379967, iekoku@yahoo.co.uk.

A group of gardens surrounding the NW and Britain in Bloom award winning Woolton Village, all within a short walk or drive.. The contrasting gardens show what can be achieved in a suburban garden all different and reflecting their owners gardening styles A family garden with raised patio and decked area planted with roses, clematis and passion flowers, wildlife pond with hostas, ferns, trees and shrubs. A garden with unusual veg, well stocked borders and domed seating area. Another interesting garden with mature trees, fruit and beautiful flowers. The Bishops Lodge has herbaceous borders, mature trees and shrubs, with a pond and impressive waterfall, also a lavender hedge with rose beds and a croquet lawn. Wheelchair access to some gardens.

Glynwood House

LEICESTERSHIRE & RUTLAND

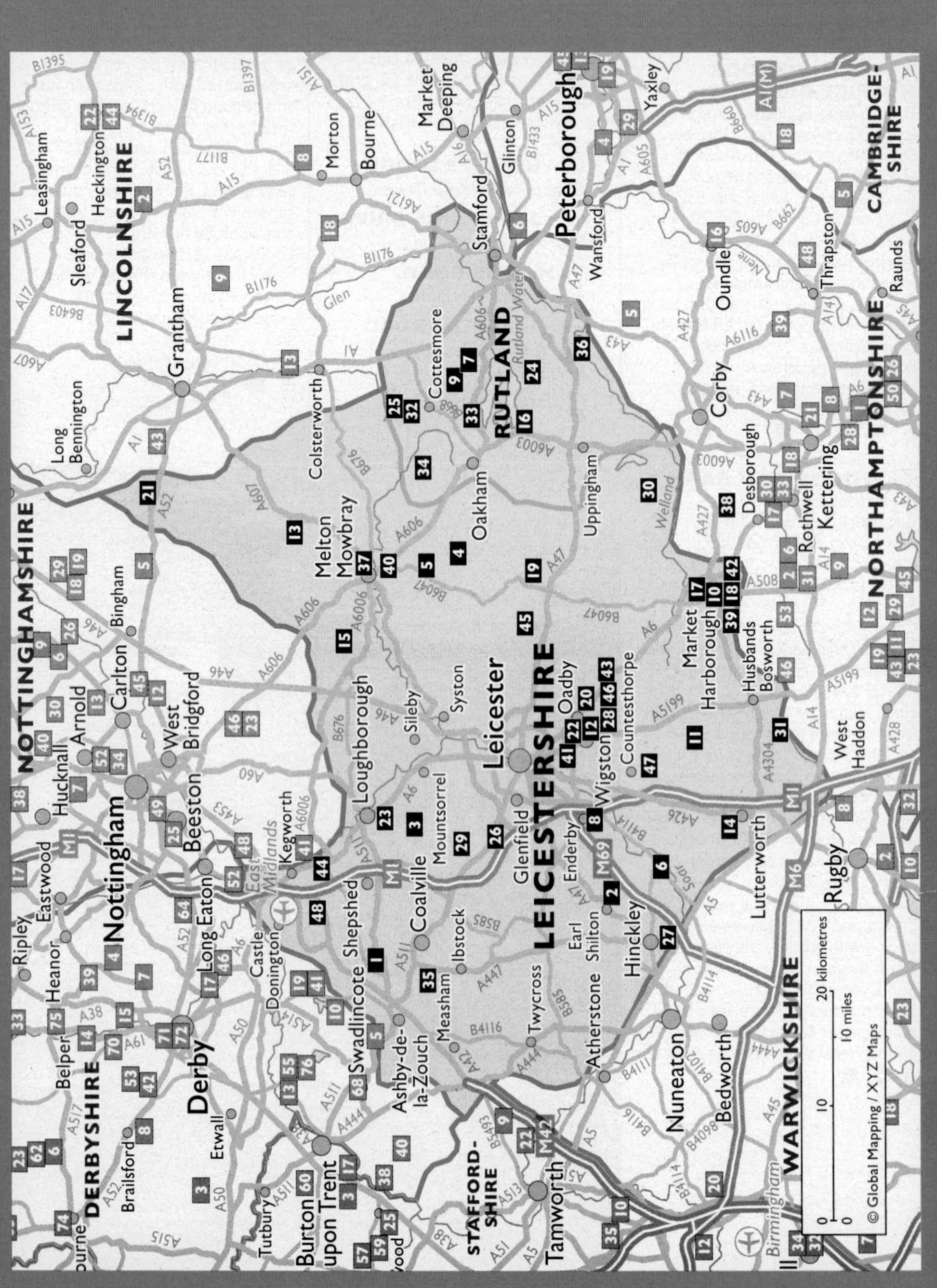

Leicestershire is a landlocked county in the Midlands with a diverse landscape and fascinating heritage providing a range of inspiring city, market town and village gardens.

Our gardens include Victorian terraces that make the most of small spaces and large country houses with historic vistas. We have an arboretum with four champion trees and a city allotment with over 100 plots. We offer something for everyone, from the serious plants person to the casual visitor.

You'll receive a warm welcome at every garden gate. Visit and get ideas for your own garden or to simply enjoy spending time in a beautiful garden. Most gardens sell plants and offer tea and cake, many are happy to take group bookings. We look forward to seeing you soon!

'Much in Little' is Rutland's motto. They say small is beautiful and never were truer words said.

Rutland is rural England at its best. Honey-coloured stone cottages make up pretty villages nestling amongst rolling hills; the passion for horticulture is everywhere you look, from stunning gardens to the hanging baskets and patio boxes showing off seasonal blooms in our two attractive market towns of Oakham and Uppingham.

There's so much to see in and around Rutland whatever the time of year, including many wonderful National Garden Scheme gardens.

Below: Kapalua, Willoughby Gardens

Volunteers

Leicestershire

County Organiser
Pamela Shave 01858 575481
pamelashave@btconnect.com

County Treasurer
Martin Shave 01455 556633
martinshave@kilworthaccountancy.co.uk

Talks
Pat Beeson 07940771185
pat.beeson@ngs.org.uk

Assistant County Organisers
Janet Rowe 0116 2597339
janetnandrew@btinternet.com

Gill Hadland, 01162 592170
gillhadland1@gmail.com

Roger Whitmore and Shirley Jackson 01162 787179
whitmorerog@hotmail.co.uk

Booklet Co-ordinator (Leicestershire & Rutland):
Sharon Maher 01162 711680
sharon@wildebeast.plus.com

Publicity
Carol Bartlett 01616 261053
carol@dekbe.plus.com

Social Media
Zoe Lewin 07810 800 007
zoe.lewin@ngs.org.uk

Rutland

County Organiser
Sally Killick 01572 737816
sally.killick@aol.co.uk

Lucy Hurst 01780 444845,
lucyjhurst@gmail.com

County Treasurer
David Wood 01572 737465
rdavidwood1@gmail.com

Publicity
Jane Alexander-Orr 01572 737368
janealexanderorr@hotmail.com

Assistant County Organiser
Rose Dejardin 01572 737788
rosedejardin@btopenworld.com

OPENING DATES

All entries subject to change. For latest information check **www.ngs.org.uk**

Extended openings are shown at the beginning of the month.

Map locator numbers are shown to the right of each garden name.

February

Snowdrop Festival

Saturday 23rd
Hedgehog Hall 19
Westview 43

Sunday 24th
Hedgehog Hall 19
Mary's Garden 27
Westview 43

April

Sunday 7th
Gunthorpe Hall 16

Sunday 28th
NEW 44 Fairfield Road 10
The Old Hall 32
Tresillian House 40

May

Sunday 5th
Burrough Hall 4
Hedgehog Hall 19
Westbrooke House 42

Monday 6th
Hedgehog Hall 19

Sunday 12th
NEW Exton Hall 9

Saturday 18th
Grimston Gardens 15

Sunday 19th
Grimston Gardens 15
Mill House 28
The Old Vicarage, Whissendine 34
◆ Whatton Gardens 44

Wednesday 22nd
Thorpe Lubenham Hall 39

Sunday 26th
NEW 10 Brook Road 3
The Old Vicarage, Burley 33

Monday 27th
NEW 10 Brook Road 3
Westview 43

June

Every Wednesday
Stoke Albany House 38

Sunday 2nd
Enderby Gardens 8
Manton Gardens 24
Nevill Holt Hall 30

Tuesday 4th
NEW 10 Brook Road 3

Wednesday 5th
NEW 10 Brook Road 3

Saturday 8th
28 Gladstone Street 12
Goadby Marwood Hall 13
13 Highcroft Avenue 20

Sunday 9th
28 Gladstone Street 12
13 Highcroft Avenue 20

Sunday 16th
NEW 44 Fairfield Road 10
Market Overton Gardens 25

Saturday 22nd
Loughborough Gardens 23
Oak Tree House 31

Sunday 23rd
Empingham Gardens 7
Loughborough Gardens 23
Oak Tree House 31
119 Scalford Road 37
NEW 15 The Woodcroft 48

Sunday 30th
Redhill Lodge 36
Tresillian House 40
Westbrooke House 42

July

Every Wednesday
Stoke Albany House 38

Saturday 6th
28 Gladstone Street 12
Tresillian House 40
NEW Wigston Gardens 46

Sunday 7th
28 Gladstone Street 12
NEW Harborough Allotments Group 18
NEW Wigston Gardens 46
Willoughby Gardens 47

Sunday 14th
Green Wicket Farm 14
Mill House 28

Wednesday 17th
Green Wicket Farm 14

August

Saturday 3rd
221 Markfield Road 26

Sunday 4th
Honeytrees Tropical Garden 21
221 Markfield Road 26

Monday 5th
221 Markfield Road 26

Tuesday 6th
221 Markfield Road 26

Wednesday 7th
221 Markfield Road 26

Thursday 8th
221 Markfield Road 26

Friday 9th
Honeytrees Tropical Garden 21
221 Markfield Road 26

Saturday 10th
221 Markfield Road 26

Sunday 11th
The Firs 11
221 Markfield Road 26

Sunday 18th
Honeytrees Tropical Garden 21

Sunday 25th
Honeytrees Tropical Garden 21
Tresillian House 40

September

Sunday 1st
Washbrook Allotments 41
Westview 43

October

Sunday 13th
Hammond Arboretum 17

Sunday 20th
Tresillian House 40

By Arrangement

Arrange a personalised garden visit with your club, or group of friends, on a date to suit you. See individual garden entries for full details.

Aqueduct Cottage 1
Barracca 2
Crossfell House 5
Dairy Cottage 6
Farmway, Willoughby Gardens 47
The Firs 11
Goadby Marwood Hall 13
Green Wicket Farm 14
Honeytrees Tropical Garden 21
Knighton Sensory 22
221 Markfield Road 26
Mary's Garden 27
Mill House 28
Mountain Ash 29
Ravenstone Hall 35
Redhill Lodge 36
119 Scalford Road 37
Tresillian House 40
Westbrooke House 42
Westview 43
The White House Farm 45

THE GARDENS

1 AQUEDUCT COTTAGE

Gelsmoor Road, Coleorton, Coalville, LE67 8JF. Jayne Wright, 07713 624595, jaynewright38@yahoo.co.uk. *Nr Ashby de la Zouch. Corner of Gelsmoor Rd and Aqueduct Rd. Access is via gate on Aqueduct Rd.* **Visits by arrangement June to Sept. Opening for June and September only (not opening July & Aug). Adm £7.50, chd free. Home-made teas.**

Mature, classic English garden, in excess of 3 acres. It is flanked by a disused (1836) railway line which is wooded and boasts a large variety of specimen trees. There are formal perennial beds and specimen rose beds with a lot of roses! A small classic fish pond in the formal part of the garden and a 30m open pond in a wildlife friendly setting. Please advise if dietary requirements are needed at time of booking an appointment.

2 BARRACCA

Ivydene Close, Earl Shilton, LE9 7NR. Mr & Mrs John & Sue Osborn, 01455 842609, susan.osborn1@btinternet.com, www.barraccagardens.co.uk. *10m W of Leicester. From A47 after entering Earl Shilton, Ivydene Close is 4th on L from Leicester side of A47.* **Visits by arrangement Feb to July for groups of 10+. Homemade teas incl. in price. Additional refreshments considered on request. Adm £7.50, chd free.**

1 acre garden with lots of different areas, silver birch walk, wildlife pond with seating, apple tree garden, Mediterranean planted area and lawns surrounded with herbaceous plants and shrubs. Patio area with climbing roses and wisteria. There is also a utility garden with greenhouse, vegetables in beds, herbs and perennial flower beds, lawn and fruit cage. Part of the old gardens owned by the Cotton family who used to open approx 9 acres to the public in the 1920's. Partial wheelchair access.

3 NEW 10 BROOK ROAD

Woodhouse Eaves, Loughborough, LE12 8RS. Geoff & Carol Fowle. *4m south of Loughborough, opp Bulls Head PH. Parking at pub.* **Sun 26, Mon 27 May, Tue 4, Wed 5 June (12-5.30). Adm £4, chd free. Light refreshments.**

1 acre mature country garden with different and interesting areas incl a stream & clay lined pond, lawn areas with island beds containing roses, rhododendrons, azaleas & Japanese maples, created by the owners over 20 yrs from a neglected Victorian garden. Many ornaments and recycled quirky materials made into garden features with a traditional summer house for you to enjoy your refreshments. Partial wheelchair access.

4 BURROUGH HALL

Burrough on the Hill, LE14 2QZ. Richard & Alice Cunningham. *Somerby Rd, Burrough on the Hill. Close to B6047. 10 mins from A606. 20 mins from Melton Mowbray.* **Sun 5 May (2-5). Adm £4, chd free. Home-made teas.**

Burrough Hall was built in 1867 as a classic Leicestershire hunting lodge. The garden, framed by mature trees and shrubs, was extensively redesigned by garden designer George Carter in 2007. The garden continues to develop. This family garden designed for all generations to enjoy and is surrounded by magnificent views across High Leicestershire. Gravel paths and lawn. In addition to the garden there will be a small collection of vintage and classic cars on display.

5 CROSSFELL HOUSE

4d Nether End, Great Dalby, Melton Mowbray, LE14 2EY. Jane & Ian West, 07912 066976 01664 500585, janeawest@gmail.com. *3m S of Melton Mowbray on B6047. On entering Great Dalby from Melton Mowbray remain on B6047. Crossfell House is on L approx 300 yards from village 30mph sign.* **Visits by arrangement in June for groups of 10 to 30. Adm £6, chd free. Home-made teas. Refreshments are incl in admission.**

A formal garden consisting of a terraced herbaceous border and rockery, flanked by a border of shrubs, two small areas of lawn and a sweeping path leading to a two acre meadow with wild grasses, flowers and a recently created wildlife pond. Paths crisscross the meadows, culminating in spectacular countryside views from our Shepherd's Hut and picnic area. Wheelchair access to patio and garden area, only partial wheelchair access to meadow.

6 DAIRY COTTAGE

15 Sharnford Road, Sapcote, LE9 4JN. Mrs Norah Robinson-Smith, 01455 272398, nrobinsons@yahoo.co.uk. *9m SW of Leicester. Sharnford Rd joins Leicester Rd in Sapcote to B4114 Coventry Rd. Follow NGS signs at both ends.* **Visits by arrangement May & June for groups of 10+. Adm £3.50, chd free. Tea and cakes £2.00.** Donation for Sapcote in Bloom Group.

From a walled garden with colourful mixed borders to a potager approached along a woodland path, this mature cottage garden combines extensive perennial planting with many unusual shrubs and specimen trees. More than 90 clematis and climbing roses are trained up pergolas, arches and into trees 50ft high – so don't forget to look up!

Your visits help change lives – your generosity helps Marie Curie fund nurses to care for people night and day in their homes, with donations of more than £8.8 million

Market Overton Gardens

GROUP OPENING

7 EMPINGHAM GARDENS

Empingham, LE15 8PS. *Empingham Village. 5m E of Oakham, 5m W of Stamford on A606.* **Sun 23 June (2-5.30). Combined adm £6, chd free. Home-made teas at Prebendal House.**

HONEYLEA

Mr & Mrs Barry & Janet Chalmers-Stevens.

LAVANDER COTTAGE

Virginia Todd.

PREBENDAL HOUSE

Matthew & Rebecca Eatough.

3 very different gardens in a lovely village. Park and start your visit at Prebendal House, next door to the Church and standing in four acres of garden with open parkland views to the River Gwash. Included are extensive herbaceous borders, topiary and a sunken water garden. The tiny garden of Lavander Cottage in Nook Lane has been developed over 10yrs into a series of rooms linked by rose and honeysuckle arches and packed with climbing, shrub and standard roses, richly underplanted with lavender, alliums and clematis and full of colour & scent. Honeylea, opposite, is an 'Enabled Garden'. The owner is registered disabled and has designed it for maximum accessibility & relaxation with yr round interest. Wheelchair access only at Prebendal House and Honeylea.

GROUP OPENING

8 ENDERBY GARDENS

Enderby, Leicester, LE19 4NA. Mrs Pat Beeson. *4m south of Leicester. From M1 J21 take A5460 to Fosse Park, turn R on B4114. Turn R to Enderby at next r'about, straight on to church then follow yellow NGS signs.* **Sun 2 June (11-5). Combined adm £4, chd free. Home-made teas. at 12 Alexander Ave.**

12 ALEXANDER AVENUE

Mr & Mrs J Beeson.

13 BANTLAM LANE
Clive and Helen Biggs.

A large Parish with a long history incl the Roman Fosse Way, the church of St. John the Baptist and modern retail outlets. The two small town gardens are quite different with interesting features and many creative ideas.

---

9 NEW EXTON HALL

Cottesmore Road, Exton, LE15 8AN. Viscount & Viscountess Campden, www.extonpark.co.uk. *Exton, Rutland. 5m E of Oakham. 8m from Stamford off A1 (A606 turning).* **Sun 12 May (2-5). Adm £5, chd free. Home-made teas.**
Extensive park, lawns, specimen trees and shrubs, lake, private chapel and C19 house (not open). Pinetum, woodland walks, lakes, ruins, dovecote and formal herbaceous garden. Whilst there is wheelchair access, areas of the garden are accessible along grass or gravel paths which, weather dependent, may make access difficult.

10 NEW 44 FAIRFIELD ROAD

Market Harborough, LE16 9QJ. Steve Althorpe and Judith Rout. *Opp primary school.* **Sun 28 Apr, Sun 16 June (11.30-5). Adm £3, chd free. Home-made teas. Hot drinks (incl hot chocolate) & home made cakes.**
This wildlife friendly, ⅓ acre plot in the heart of Market Harborough, is a garden in which you can relax. There are large borders informally planted with a good variety of perennials and shrubs, a substantial pond full of amphibians and invertebrates and a copse under-planted with a host of spring flowers. There's also plenty of seating at which to enjoy homemade refreshments. Block paved drive and patio with gentle slope down on to lawn.

11 THE FIRS

Main Street, Bruntingthorpe, LE17 5QF. Howard & Carmel Grant, thefirsgarden@gmail.com. *5m NE of Lutterworth. Exit J20 M1 to Lutterworth A426. Turn R to Gilmorton & Bruntingthorpe opp petrol station. From Leicester A5199 to Arnesby. Turn R & follow rd 2m to T-junction. Turn L to Bruntingthorpe.* **Sun 11 Aug (11-5). Adm £4, chd free. Home-made teas.** Visits also by arrangement July & Aug for groups of 10+.
A tranquil garden of 1½ acres with views over open countryside. The front garden features terraced borders and paving. The main rear garden has large areas of sweeping lawn and grass walkways around many flowing borders. There is a large variety of themed coloured planting, shrubs and trees. In amongst the borders can be found many unusual design features, artefacts and seating areas. Large sequoia tree at the front of the property was damaged by a bomber returning from a night training flight during the WWII. Short gravel drive, some paving, rest grass.

12 28 GLADSTONE STREET

Wigston Magna, LE18 1AE. Chris & Janet Huscroft. *4m S of Leicester. Off Wigston by-pass (A5199) follow signs off McDonalds r'about.* **Sat 8, Sun 9 June (11-5). Combined adm with 13 Highcroft Avenue £4.50, chd free. Sat 6, Sun 7 July (11-5). Combined adm with Wigston Gardens £5, chd free. Home-made teas.**
Our mature 70'x15' town garden is divided into rooms and bisected by a pond with a bridge. It is brimming with unusual hardy perennials, incl collections of ferns and hostas. David Austin roses chosen for their scent feature throughout, incl a 30' rose arch. A shade house with unusual hardy plants. Regular changes to planting and new for 2019, a Hosta Theatre! Frameworks Knitters Museum nearby - open Sundays.

13 GOADBY MARWOOD HALL

Goadby Marwood, LE14 4LN. Mr & Mrs Westropp, 01664 464202. *4m NW of Melton Mowbray. Between Waltham-on-the-Wolds & Eastwell, 8m S of Grantham. Plenty of parking space available.* **Sat 8 June (10.30-5). Adm £5, chd £3.50. Home-made teas in Village Hall.** Visits also by arrangement Apr to Oct. Extra £5 if tea required.
Redesigned in 2000 by the owner based on C18 plans. A chain of 5 lakes (covering 10 acres) and several ironstone walled gardens all interconnected. Lakeside woodland walk. Planting for yr-round interest. Landscaper trained under plantswoman Rosemary Verey at Barnsley House. Beautiful C13 church open. Gravel paths and lawns.

14 GREEN WICKET FARM

Ullesthorpe Road, Bitteswell, Lutterworth, LE17 4LR. Mrs Anna Smith, 01455 552646, greenfarmbitt@hotmail.com. *2m NW of Lutterworth J20 M1. From Lutterworth follow signs through Bitteswell towards Ullesthorpe. Garden situated behind Bitteswell Cricket Club. Use this as a landmark rather than relying totally on your satnav.* **Sun 14, Wed 17 July (2-5). Adm £3.50, chd free. Home-made teas.** Visits also by arrangement June to Sept for groups of 10 to 30.
Created in 2008 on a working farm with clay soil and a very exposed site. Many unusual hardy plants along with a lot of old favourites have been used to provide a long season of colour and interest. Anemone nemorosa, Pacific coast iris and Salvias are of particular interest. Formal pond and water features. Some gravel paths.

Your visits help change lives – we are the largest single funder of the Queen's Nursing Institute

GROUP OPENING

15 GRIMSTON GARDENS

Main Street, Grimston, Melton Mowbray, LE14 3BZ. Brian & Monica Ravenscroft. *5m NW Melton Mowbray. Follow Yellow NGS signs. The gardens are situated either side of the Church on Main Street/Perkins Lane.* **Sat 18, Sun 19 May (10-5). Combined adm £5, chd free. Home-made teas in Grimston Village Hall.**

FOURWINDS
Monica and Brian Ravenscroft.

NEW **THE YEWS FARM**
Mr & Mrs Tony & Claire Moore.

Grimston is a small village with a c13 church restored in 1856. The village green has a large stone and stocks set under a mature Chestnut. Fourwinds is approx. 1 acre, with mature trees and shrubs, extensive flower beds, vegetable garden and long stretches of lawns. The Yews Farm is thought to be the oldest house in the village and the garden of approx 1 acre contains 2 notable Yew trees considered to be 500+ years old. The peaceful garden has mixed borders, fruit trees and a productive vegetable garden as well as a glorious wisteria on the house. The adjoining paddock boasts extensive views over the countryside as well as an ancient 'holloway'. Fourwinds Drive rather uneven in places, with a rather sharp slope. The Yews Farm has gravel drive and uneven lawn.

16 GUNTHORPE HALL

Gunthorpe, Nr Oakham, LE15 8BE. Tim Haywood. *A6003 between Oakham & Uppingham; 1m from Oakham, up drive between lodges. Proceed over railway bridge to gardens, 600 yards ahead. Please follow the signs for parking.* **Sun 7 Apr (2-5.30). Adm £5, chd free. Home-made teas.**
Large garden in a country setting with extensive views across the Rutland landscape with the carpets of daffodils being the outstanding feature. A great deal of recent re-design has transformed this garden with more recent works being undertaken on the kitchen garden and around the (former) stable yard.

17 HAMMOND ARBORETUM

Burnmill Road, Market Harborough, LE16 7JG. The Robert Smyth Academy, www.hammondarboretum.org.uk. *15m S of Leicester on A6. From High St, follow signs to The Robert Smyth Academy via Bowden Lane to Burnmill Rd. Park in 1st entrance on L.* **Sun 13 Oct (2-4.30). Adm £4, chd free. Home-made teas.**
A site of just under 2½ acres containing an unusual collection of trees and shrubs, many from Francis Hammond's original planting dating from 1913 to 1936 whilst headmaster of the school. Species from America, China and Japan with malus and philadelphus walks and a moat. Proud owners of 4 champion trees identified by national specialist. Guided walks and walk plans available. Some steep slopes.

18 NEW HARBOROUGH ALLOTMENTS GROUP

Stevens St LE16 9BB, Northampton Rd LE16 9HB, Market Harborough, LE16 9BB. Mr John Howell. *Northampton Road 1/2 mile S of town on A508 Stevens St off Coventry Rd Follow Yellow signs for both sites.* **Sun 7 July (11-3). Adm £4, chd free. Home-made teas.**
Stevens St has over 130 plots growing a variety of vegetables, fruit & flowers, a dedicated composting area (demos on the day), ponds, wild life area & small orchards. Northampton Rd is a smaller flatter site of 50 plots with polytunnel. Plots show variety of veg, fruit & flowers. Both sites have good wide paths, most are suitable for wheelchairs. Compost making, plot holders interaction & activities on the day.

19 HEDGEHOG HALL

Loddington Road, Tilton on the Hill, LE7 9DE. Janet & Andrew Rowe. *8m W of Oakham. 2m N of A47 on B6047 between Melton & Market Harborough. Follow yellow NGS signs in Tilton towards Loddington.* **Sat 23, Sun 24 Feb (11-4). Light refreshments. Also open Westview. Sun 5, Mon 6 May (11-4). Home-made teas. Adm £4, chd free.**
½ acre organically managed plant lover's garden. Steps leading to three stone walled terraced borders filled with shrubs, perennials, bulbs and a patio over looking the valley. Lavender walk, herb border, beautiful spring garden, colour themed herbaceous borders. Courtyard with collection of hostas and acers and terrace planted for yr-round interest with topiary and perennials. Snowdrop collection. Homemade soup and a roll February opening. Cake, tea or coffee May opening. Regret, no wheelchair access to terraced borders.

20 13 HIGHCROFT AVENUE

Oadby, Leicester, LE2 5UH. Sharon Maher & Mike Costall. *Just off A6, 5m S Leicester & 9m N Market Harborough. Follow NGS yellow arrows.* **Sat 8, Sun 9 June (11-5). Combined adm with 28 Gladstone Street £4.50, chd free. Home-made teas.**
Our garden continues to evolve and develop. It is approx 22m x 14m. We have a bed of David Austin roses, a herbaceous border, a wildlife area, alpine bed, patio planters and a small wildlife pond. There are four raised beds for vegetables which is supplemented by a small greenhouse. We also have a herb area. There's plenty of room on the patio to sit and enjoy the tea and cake too!

21 HONEYTREES TROPICAL GARDEN

85 Grantham Road, Bottesford, NG13 0EG. Julia Madgwick & Mike Ford, 01949 842120, Julia_madgwick@hotmail.com. *7m E of Bingham on A52. Turn into village. Garden is on L on slip road behind hedge going out of village towards Grantham. Parking on grass opp property.* **Sun 4 Aug (11-4). Home-made teas. Evening opening Fri 9 Aug (5-9). Wine. Sun 18, Sun 25 Aug (11-4). Home-made teas. Adm £4, chd free.** Visits also by arrangement July & Aug for groups of 10+.

The garden is on a S-facing slope which has evolved over 15 yrs into a tropical escape. Exotic planting as you enter the garden gives way on a gentle incline to more surprises to incl glass houses dedicated to various climatic zones interspersed with more exotic planting. There are steps and some gravel but plenty to view and enjoy from a wheelchair.

22 KNIGHTON SENSORY

Knighton Park, Leicester, LE2 3YQ. Mike Chalk, 0116 2104217, kpgc@hotmail.co.uk, www.knightonparkgardeningclub.com. *Off A563 (Outer Ring Rd) S of Leicester. From Palmerston Blvd, turn into South Kingsmead Rd then 1st L into Woodbank Rd. Park entrance at end of rd. Enter park, follow path to R, garden on R.* **Visits by arrangement May to Sept for groups of 10 to 30. Adm £3. Light refreshments.**

This ¼ acre community garden stands in a secluded corner of Knighton Park away from the bustle of the city. It is a feast for all the senses incl shrubs, some traditional bedding, herbaceous borders, bog garden with bridge, dry riverbed, wildflower meadow and wildlife area, Separate area contains raised beds for edibles. Awarded outstanding by the It's Your Neighbourhood Scheme.

GROUP OPENING

23 LOUGHBOROUGH GARDENS

Herrick Road, Loughborough, LE11 2BU. www.growloughborough.org.uk. *1m SW Loughborough. From M1 J23 take A512 Ashby Rd to Loughborough. At r'about R onto A6004 Epinal Way. At Beacon Rd r'about L, Herrick Rd 1st on R.* **Sat 22 and Sun 23 June (11-3). Combined adm £3, chd free. Light refreshments.**

94 HERRICK ROAD
Marion Smith.

134 HERRICK ROAD
Janet Currie, www.thesecateur.com.

Herrick Road, Loughborough is a quiet leafy area with a mix of Victorian and mid-century homes. The gardens in this group contain plenty of horticultural and creative interest and offer a warm welcome to all visitors. 134 Herrick Road is a long garden, cleverly designed to make use of the space, full of attractive planting and brimming with artistic flair. The excellent Secret Craft Fair held during the open gardens weekend provides delight and surprises for visitors. 94 Herrick Road is a traditional old-fashioned English garden at the rear of the Victorian house. Mainly perennial planting with interest in hardy geraniums and heucheras, small pond and three active beehives, this walled garden also has a Coach House. Check the website for more details of the open gardens and other featured events as they become available.

The White House Farm

GROUP OPENING

24 MANTON GARDENS

Oakham, LE15 8SR. *3m N of Uppingham and 3m S of Oakham. Manton is on S shore of Rutland Water ¼m off A6003. Please park carefully in village.* **Sun 2 June (12.30-5.30). Combined adm £6, chd free. Home-made teas in Village Hall (1.30 - 5.30).**

HALL COTTAGE
Mary Stenson.

NEW **THE HOLLIES**
Richard & Barbara Camp.

22 LYNDON ROAD
Chris & Val Carroll.

MANTON GRANGE
Anne & Mark Taylor.

SHAPINSAY
Tony & Jane Bews.

3 ST MARY'S ROAD
Ruth Blinch.

6 gardens in small village on S shore of Rutland Water. Manton Grange - 2½ acre garden with interesting trees, shrubs and herbaceous borders, incl a rose garden, water features, a lime tree walk and clematis pergola. Shapinsay - ⅔ acre garden with mature trees framing views over the Chater Valley, incl a woodland walk, perennial borders, island shrub borders and a stream linking numerous ponds. 22 Lyndon Rd - a beautiful combination of cottage garden and unusual plants in overflowing borders, hanging baskets and decorative pots. 3 St Mary's Road - a tiny garden where the use of every available space is maximised to create a series of areas within which to sit and enjoy beds, and numerous pots, packed with plants. The Hollies-a mature terraced garden with a stunning view over Rutland Water. Hall Cottage - a delightful small walled cottage garden full of clever planting and hidden nooks. Wheelchair access to Manton Grange and Shapinsay only.

GROUP OPENING

25 MARKET OVERTON GARDENS

59 Thistleton Road, Market Overton, Oakham, LE15 7PP. *Last house leaving village towards Thistleton. 7m NE of Oakham. Turn R off Ashwell/Wymondham rd at Teigh.* **Sun 16 June (2.30-5.30). Combined adm £6, chd free. Home-made teas at the Bowls Club on Thistleton Road.**

NEW **2 BERRYBUSHES**
Mr John Deacon.

7 MAIN STREET
Ann Tibbert.

THE OLD HALL
Mr & Mrs Timothy Hart.
(See separate entry)

59 THISTLETON ROAD
Wg Cdr Andrew Stewart JP.

1 THISTLETON ROAD
Martin Debenham.

49 THISTLETON ROAD
Alan Hubbard.

47 THISTLETON ROAD
Jane Smeetem.

A village group opening of 7 gardens. At one end of the village, 59 Thistleton Rd, is a 1.8 acre garden providing a haven for wildlife with large pond, shrubbery, orchard, large colourful perennial beds and a short woodland walk. Next door, are 2 tiny cottage gardens overlooking the cricket green. At the further end of the road is No.1 a small, enclosed garden with a lawn meandering through borders packed with plants. Close by, 7 Main St is a delightful garden divided into a series of areas richly planted to provide yr-round interest and featuring specimen trees, unusual shrubs and colourful planted pots and containers. At the furthest end of Main Street, The Old Hall offers views over the countryside from its terraced garden with stone walls and yew hedges enclosing herbaceous borders and mature shrubs & trees. Between them is 2 Berrybushes, once the home of Sir Issac Newton, a stone head of whom is visible on the stone gazebo in this formal garden which incl a sunken rose area. Wheelchair access at 59 Thistleton Rd, 2 Berrybushes and The Old Hall only.

Mountain Ash

26 221 MARKFIELD ROAD

Groby, Leicester, LE6 0FT. Jackie Manship, 01530 249363, jmanship@btinternet.com. *From M1 J22 take A50 towards Leicester. In approx 3m at the T-lights junction with Lena Drive turn L. Parking available along this road, no parking on A50.* **Sat 3, Sun 4, Mon 5, Tue 6, Wed 7, Thur 8, Fri 9, Sat 10, Sun 11 Aug (10-4). Adm £4, chd free. Cream teas.** **Visits also by arrangement in Aug for groups of 20 to 30. Group visit dates 3rd - 11th August only 6.00pm - 10.00pm.**

A S facing plot of land nestled between the village of Groby and Markfield approx 1 acre in size. The hidden treasures are deceptive from the front of the property which sits on one of the main trunk roads out of Leicester. Packed with interest and created over the last 20 years from a dishevelled overgrown plot you will be presented with a garden full of delight. We are happy to provide light refreshments (e.g. ploughman's lunches) but would ask that these are ordered prior to arrival.

27 MARY'S GARDEN

7 Hall Road Burbage, Hinckley, Leics, LE10 2LU. Don Baker, donmary7@tiscali.co.uk. *Sketchley Manor Estate. From M69 J1, take B4109 signed Hinckley. At 2nd r'about follow NGS yellow arrows.* **Sun 24 Feb (11-4). Adm £3, chd free.** Visits also by arrangement Feb to June for groups of 10 to 30.

Medium sized garden with a good mix of shrubs large selection snowdrops, erythroniums, spring bulbs and hellebores. Partial wheelchair access.

28 MILL HOUSE

118 Welford Road, Wigston, LE18 3SN. Mr & Mrs P Measures, 01162 885409, petemeasures@hotmail.co.uk. *4m S of Leicester. From Leicester to Wigston Magna follow A5199 Welford Rd S towards Kilby, up hill past Mercers Newsagents, 100yds on L.* **Sun 19 May, Sun 14 July (12-5). Adm £2.50, chd free. Home-made teas.** Visits also by arrangement June & July for groups of up to 20.

Walled town garden with an extensive plant variety, many rare and unusual. A plant lovers garden, with interesting designs incorporated in the borders, rockery and scree. It is full of surprises with memorabilia and bygones as reminders of our past. Good variety of reasonably priced plants on sale both open days.

29 MOUNTAIN ASH

140 Ulverscroft Lane, Newtown Linford, LE6 0AJ. Mike & Liz Newcombe, 01530 242178, mjnew12@gmail.com. *7m SW of Loughborough, 7m NW of Leicester, 1m NW of Newtown Linford. Head ½m N along Main St towards Sharpley Hill, fork L into Ulverscroft Lane and Mountain Ash, is about ½m along on the L. Parking is along the opp verge.* **Visits by arrangement May to Aug for groups of 20+. Adm £6.50, chd free. Home-made teas.**

2 acre garden with stunning views across Charnwood countryside. Nr the house are patios, lawns, water feature, flower & shrub beds, fruit trees, soft fruit cage, greenhouses & vegetable plots. Lawns slope down to a gravel garden, large wildlife pond and small areas of woodland with walks through many species of trees. Many statues and ornaments. Several places to sit and relax around the garden. Only the top part of the garden around the house is reasonably accessible by wheelchair.

30 NEVILL HOLT HALL

Drayton Road, Nevill Holt, Market Harborough, LE16 8EG. Mr David Ross. *5m NE of Market Haborough. Signed off B664 at Medbourne.* **Sun 2 June (12-4). Adm £5, chd free. Tea.**

The gardens are at their peak in June. Whilst the walled kitchen garden shows signs of a harvest to come, our two other walled gardens and adjoining cedar lawn garden are full of colour and texture, all working together to create a summer scene that feels warm and summery, even on the dullest days. Please do join us for tea and cake – we would love to share our garden with you.

31 OAK TREE HOUSE

North Road, South Kilworth, LE17 6DU. Pam & Martin Shave. *15m S of Leicester. From M1 J20, take A4304 towards Market Harborough. At North Kilworth turn R, signed South Kilworth. Garden on L after approx 1m.* **Sat 22 June (1-5); Sun 23 June (11-5). Adm £4, chd free. Home-made teas.**

⅔ acre beautiful country garden full of colour, formal design, softened by cottage style planting. Modern sculptures. Large herbaceous borders, vegetable plots, pond, greenhouse, shady area, colour-themed borders. Extensive collections in pots, incl pelargoniums and hostas. Trees with attractive bark. Many clematis and roses. Dramatic arched pergola. Constantly changing garden as borders enlarge.

32 THE OLD HALL

Main Street, Market Overton, LE15 7PL. Mr & Mrs Timothy Hart. *6m N of Oakham. Beyond Cottesmore, 6m N of Oakham; 5m from A1 via Thistleton. 10m E from Melton Mowbray via Wymondham.* **Sun 28 Apr (2-5.30). Adm £5, chd free. Home-made teas. incl Hambleton Bakery cakes. Opening with Market Overton Gardens on Sun 16 June.**

Set on a southerly ridge overlooking Catmose Vale. Stone walls and yew hedges divide the garden into enclosed areas with herbaceous borders, shrubs, and young and mature trees. In 2006 the lower part of garden was planted with new shrubs to create a walk with mown paths.There are interesting plants flowering most of the time. Partial wheelchair access. Gravel and mown paths. Return to house is steep.

33 THE OLD VICARAGE, BURLEY

Church Road, Burley, Nr Oakham, LE15 7SU. Jonathan & Sandra Blaza, www.theoldvicarageburley.com. *1m NE of Oakham. In Burley just off B668 between Oakham & Cottesmore. Church Rd is opp village green.* **Sun 26 May (11-5). Adm £5, chd free. Home-made teas.**

Country garden, planted for year round interest, incl a walled garden (with vine house) producing fruit, herbs, vegetables and cut flowers. Formal lawns and borders, lime walk, rose gardens and a rill with an avenue of standard wisteria. Wildlife garden with pond, 2 orchards and mixed woodland. Some gravel and steps between terraces.

34 THE OLD VICARAGE,

WHISSENDINE
2 Station Road, Whissendine, LE15 7HG. Prof Peter & Dr Sarah Furness, www.pathology.plus.com/Garden. *Garden situated up hill from St Andrew's church in Whissendine. 1st gate on L in Station Rd.* **Sun 19 May (2-5). Adm £5, chd free. Home-made teas in St Andrew's Church, Whissendine.**
⅔ acre packed with variety. Terrace with topiary, a formal fountain courtyard and raised beds backed by small gothic orangery with tender plants. Herbaceous borders surround main lawn. Wisteria tunnel leads to raised vegetable beds and large ornate greenhouse, four beehives, Gothic hen house plus rare breed hens. Hidden white walk, unusual plants. New Victorian style garden room and much more! Teas served in the Lady Chapel of the Church and outside if clement. Access to the church can be gained directly from the garden or from Main Street.

35 RAVENSTONE HALL
Ashby Road, Ravenstone, Coalville, LE67 2AA. Jemima Wade, 07976 302260, jemimawade@hotmail.com. *Ravenstone village is situated off the A511 between Ashby de la Zouch and Coalville. The house is 1st on the L if approached from Ashby.* **Visits by arrangement Apr to Sept for groups of 10 to 20. Adm £5, chd free. Home-made teas.**
The garden was transformed in 2009 when the new owners moved to the house and planting and development has been on-going since that time. Azaleas and rhododendrons are planted on the bank of the drive. Beech trees and a beech hedge line the main front lawn. There is a woodland walk planted with bluebells. The main garden comprises a sunken garden, a rose garden, gravel path with herbaceous planting one side and iris and tulip on the other, a vegetable garden, an orchard, and a koi pond situated in a courtyard with white flowering plants and mixed foliage. Bluebell walk for groups from mid April, please call for details.

36 REDHILL LODGE
Seaton Road, Barrowden, Oakham, LE15 8EN. Richard & Susan Moffitt, 07894 064789, s.moffitt@yahoo.co.uk, www.m360design.co.uk. *Redhill Lodge is 1m from village of Barrowden along Seaton Rd.* **Sun 30 June (12-5.30). Adm £5, chd free. Home-made teas.** Visits also by arrangement May to Oct for groups of up to 30.
Bold contemporary design with formal lawns, grass amphitheatre and turf viewing mound, herbaceous borders & new rose garden. Prairie style planting showing vibrant colour in late summer. Also natural swimming pond surrounded by Japanese style planting, bog garden and fernery.

37 119 SCALFORD ROAD
Melton Mowbray, LE13 1JZ. Richard & Hilary Lawrence, 01664 562821, randh1954@me.com. *½m N of Melton Mowbray. Take Scalford Rd from town centre past Cattle Market. Garden 100yds after 1st turning on L (The Crescent). Some parking available on the drive but The Crescent is an easy walk.* **Sun 23 June (11-5). Adm £3, chd free. Home-made teas. incl gluten free cakes.** Visits also by arrangement May to Aug for groups of 10 to 30.
Larger than average town garden which has evolved over the last 30 yrs. Mixed borders with traditional and exotic plants, enhanced by container planting particularly begonias. Vegetable parterre and greenhouse. Various seating areas for viewing different aspects of the garden. Water features incl ponds. New additions to the garden are a White Border and a Succulents bed. Partial wheelchair access. Gravelled drive, ramp provided up to lawn but paths not accessible.

38 STOKE ALBANY HOUSE
Desborough Road, Stoke Albany, Market Harborough, LE16 8PT. Mr & Mrs A M Vinton, www.stokealbanyhouse.co.uk. *4m E of Market Harborough. Via A427 to Corby, turn to Stoke Albany, R at the White Horse (B669) garden ½m on the L.* **Every Wed 5 June to 31 July (2-4.30). Adm £5, chd free.** Donation to Marie Curie Cancer Care.
4 acre country house garden; fine trees and shrubs with wide herbaceous borders and sweeping striped lawn. Good display of bulbs in spring, roses June and July. Walled grey garden; nepeta walk arched with roses, parterre with box and roses. Mediterranean garden. Heated greenhouse, potager with topiary, water feature garden and sculptures.

39 THORPE LUBENHAM HALL
Farndon Road, Lubenham, LE16 9TR. Sir Bruce & Lady MacPhail. *2m W of Market Harborough. From Market Harborough take 3rd L off main rd, down Rushes Lane, past church on L, under old railway bridge & straight on up private drive.* **Wed 22 May (10.30-4). Adm £6, chd free. Home-made teas.**
15 acres of formal and informal garden surrounded by parkland and arable. Many mature trees. Traditional herbaceous borders and various water features. Walled pool garden with raised beds. Ancient moat area along driveway. Gravel paths, some steep slopes and steps.

We help ordinary people open the gates to their extraordinary private gardens to raise impressive amounts of money through admissions, teas and slices of cake!

Empingham Gardens

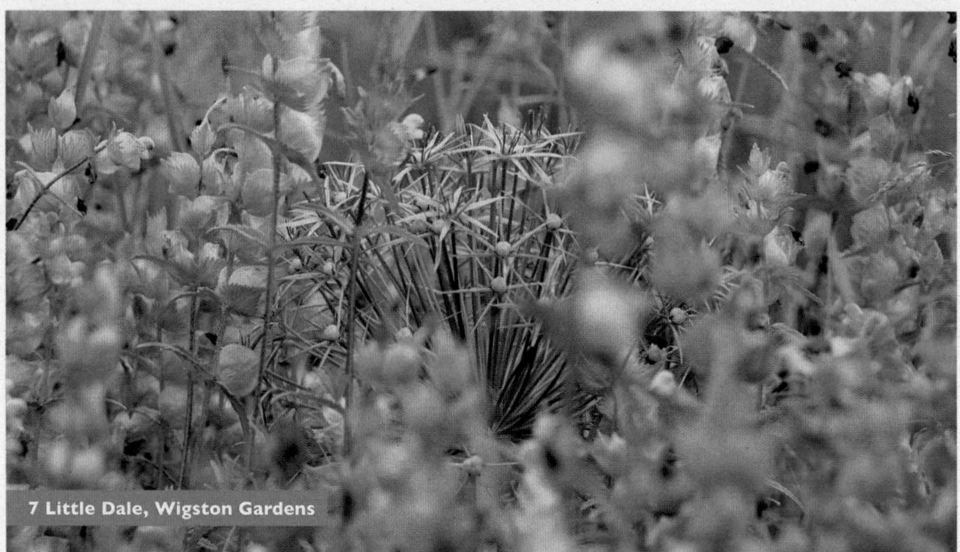
7 Little Dale, Wigston Gardens

40 TRESILLIAN HOUSE

67 Dalby Road, Melton Mowbray, LE13 0BQ. Mrs Alison Blythe, 01664 481997, alisonblythe@tresillianhouse.com, www.tresillianhouse.com. *Situated on B6047 Dalby Rd, S of Melton town centre. (Melton to Gt Dalby/ Market Harborough rd). Parking on site.* **Sun 28 Apr, Sun 30 June (11-4). Evening opening Sat 6 July (6.30-9). Sun 25 Aug, Sun 20 Oct (11-4). Adm £3.50, chd free. Light refreshments.** Visits also by arrangement Apr to Oct for groups of up to 30.

¾ acre garden re-established by current owner since 2009. Beautiful blue cedar trees, excellent specimen tulip tree. Parts of garden original, others reinstated with variety of plants and bushes. Original bog garden and natural pond. Koi pond added in 2015. Vegetable plot. Cowslips and bulbs abound in Springtime. Variety of unusual plants and shrubs. Quiet and tranquil oasis now maturing well. Ploughmans lunches, cream teas, home-made cakes. October opening offers stew & dumplings or soup and cream teas. New in 2019 : Summer evening open garden will offer a relaxing visit with live - but gentle - jazz. Slate paths, steep in places but manageable.

41 WASHBROOK ALLOTMENTS

Welford Road, Leicester, LE2 6FP. Sharon Maher. *Approx 2½ m S of Leicester, 1½ m N of Wigston. Regret no onsite parking. Welford Rd difficult to park on. Please use nearby side rds & Pendlebury Drive (LE2 6GY).* **Sun 1 Sept (11-3). Adm £3, chd free. Home-made teas.**

Our allotment gardens are a hidden oasis off the main Welford Road. There are over 100 whole, half and quarter plots growing a wide variety of fruit, vegetables and flowers. We have a wildflower meadow, other wildlife friendly areas and a composting toilet! Look out for the remains of Anderson Shelters, and other 'Heath Robinson' constructions. Circular route around the site is uneven in places but is suitable for wheelchairs.

42 WESTBROOKE HOUSE

52 Scotland Road, Little Bowden, Market Harborough, LE16 8AX. Bryan & Joanne Drew, 07872 316153, Jwsd1980@hotmail.co.uk. *½ m S Market Harborough. From Northampton Rd follow NGS arrows.* **Sun 5 May, Sun 30 June (11-5). Adm £5, chd free. Cream teas in the Courtyard Cafe.** Visits also by arrangement May & June for groups of 10+.

Westbrooke House is a late Victorian property built in 1887. The gardens comprise 6 acres in total and are approached through a tree lined driveway of mature limes and giant redwoods. Key features are walled flower garden, walled kitchen garden, lower garden, pond area, spring garden, lawns, woodland paths and a meadow with a wild flower area, ha-ha and hornbeam avenue.

43 WESTVIEW

1 St Thomas's Road, Great Glen, Leicester, LE8 9EH. Gill & John Hadland, 01162592170, gillhadland1@gmail.com. *7m S of Leicester. Take either r'about from A6 into village centre then follow NGS signs. Please park in Oaks Rd.* **Sat 23, Sun 24 Feb (11-4), also open Hedgehog Hall. Mon 27 May, Sun 1 Sept (12-5). Adm £3, chd free. Home-made teas. Hot soup and homemade bread rolls also available in Feb.** Visits also by arrangement Feb to Sept for groups of 5 to 20.

Organically managed small walled cottage garden with year-round interest. Rare and unusual plants, many grown from seed. Formal box parterre herb garden, courtyard garden, herbaceous borders, woodland garden, small wildlife pond, greenhouse, vegetable and fruit garden. Display of alpines. Collection of Galanthus (Snowdrops.) Recycled materials used to make quirky garden ornaments. Restored Victorian outhouse functions as a garden office and houses a collection of old garden tools and ephemera.

44 ◆ WHATTON GARDENS

Long Whatton, Loughborough, LE12 5BG. Lord & Lady Crawshaw, 01509 842225, whattonhouse@gmail.com, www.whattonhouseandgardens.co.uk. *4m NE of Loughborough. On A6 between Hathern & Kegworth; 2½m SE of M1J24.* **For NGS: Sun 19 May (11-5). Adm £4, chd free. Home-made teas. Refreshments 2pm - 5pm. For other opening times and information, please phone, email or visit garden website.**

Often described by visitors as a hidden gem, this 15 acre C19 Country House garden is a relaxing experience for all the family. Listen to the birds, and enjoy walking through the many fine trees, spring bulbs and shrubs, large herbaceous border, traditional rose garden, ornamental ponds and lawns. Available for group bookings. Gravel paths.

45 THE WHITE HOUSE FARM

Billesdon Road, Ingarsby, nr Houghton-on-the-Hill, LE7 9JD. Pam & Richard Smith, 0116 259 5448, Pamsmithtwhf@aol.com. *7m E of Leicester. 12m W of Uppingham. Take A47 from Leicester through Houghton-on-the-Hill towards Uppingham. 1m after Houghton, turn L (signed Tilton). After 1m turn L (signed Ingarsby), garden is 1m further on.* **Visits by arrangement May to Sept for groups of up to 30. Groups of 15 minimum. Home-made teas.**

Former Georgian farm in 2 acres of country garden. Beautiful views. Box, yew & beech hedges divide a cottage garden of gaily coloured perennials and roses; a formal herb garden; a pergola draped with climbing plants; an old courtyard with roses, shrubs & trees. Herbaceous borders lead to pools with water lilies & informal cascade. Orchard, wild garden and lake. Home for lots of wildlife.

GROUP OPENING

46 NEW WIGSTON GARDENS

Wigston, LE18. Zoe Lewin. *Just south of Leicester off A5199.* **Sat 6, Sun 7 July (11-4.30). Combined adm with 28 Gladstone Street £5, chd free. Home-made teas. Vegan and gluten free catered for at 7 Little Dale.**

7 LITTLE DALE, LE18 3LF
Zoe Lewin & Neil Garner.

NEW 40 ROLLESTON ROAD, LE18 2EP
Jenni & Glen Proudman.

7 Little Dale is a maturing wildlife friendly garden with meadow lawn, greenhouse and upcycled pieces. New wildlife pond. 40 Rolleston Road is a small town garden packed with interest incl. willow arbour, mixed beds, scented arch pergola and many pots. Great teas and cakes at each garden.

GROUP OPENING

47 WILLOUGHBY GARDENS

Willoughby Waterleys, LE8 6UD. *9m S of Leicester. From A426 heading N turn R at Dunton Bassett lights. Follow signs to Willoughby. From Blaby follow signs to Countesthorpe. 2m S to Willoughby.* **Sun 7 July (11-5). Combined adm £5, chd free. Home-made teas.**

1 CHURCH FARM LANE
Kathleen & Peter Bowers.

2 CHURCH FARM LANE
Valerie & Peter Connelly.

FARMWAY
Eileen Spencer, 01162 478321, eileenfarmway9@msn.com.
Visits also by arrangement July & Aug for groups of up to 20. Admission price inclusive of light refreshments.

HIGH MEADOW
Phil & Eva Day.

JOHN'S WOOD
John & Jill Harris.

KAPALUA
Richard & Linda Love.

3 ORCHARD ROAD
Diane Brearley.

Willoughby Waterleys lies in the South Leicestershire countryside. The Norman Church will be open, hosting a film of the local bird population filmed by a local resident. 7 gardens will be open. John's Wood is a 1½ acre nature reserve planted to encourage wildlife. 1, Church Farm Lane is a well stocked garden with lawn, trees and shrubs, roses and climbers. 2 Church Farm Lane has been professionally designed with many interesting features. Farmway is a plant lovers garden with many unusual plants in colour themed borders. High Meadow has been evolving over 10yrs. Incl mixed planting and ornamental vegetable garden. 3 Orchard Road is a small garden packed with interest. Kapalua has an interesting planting design incorporating views of open countryside. Willoughby embroidery on display in village hall. 30mins film of local wildlife in the church.

48 NEW 15 THE WOODCROFT

Diseworth, Derby, DE74 2QT. Nick & Sue Hollick. *The Woodcroft is off The Green, parking on The Woodcroft.* **Sun 23 June (11-5). Adm £4, chd free. Home-made teas.**

⅓ acre garden developed over 38 years with mature trees and shrubs, old and modern shrub roses, ferns, wildlife area and mixed herbaceous borders.

LINCOLNSHIRE

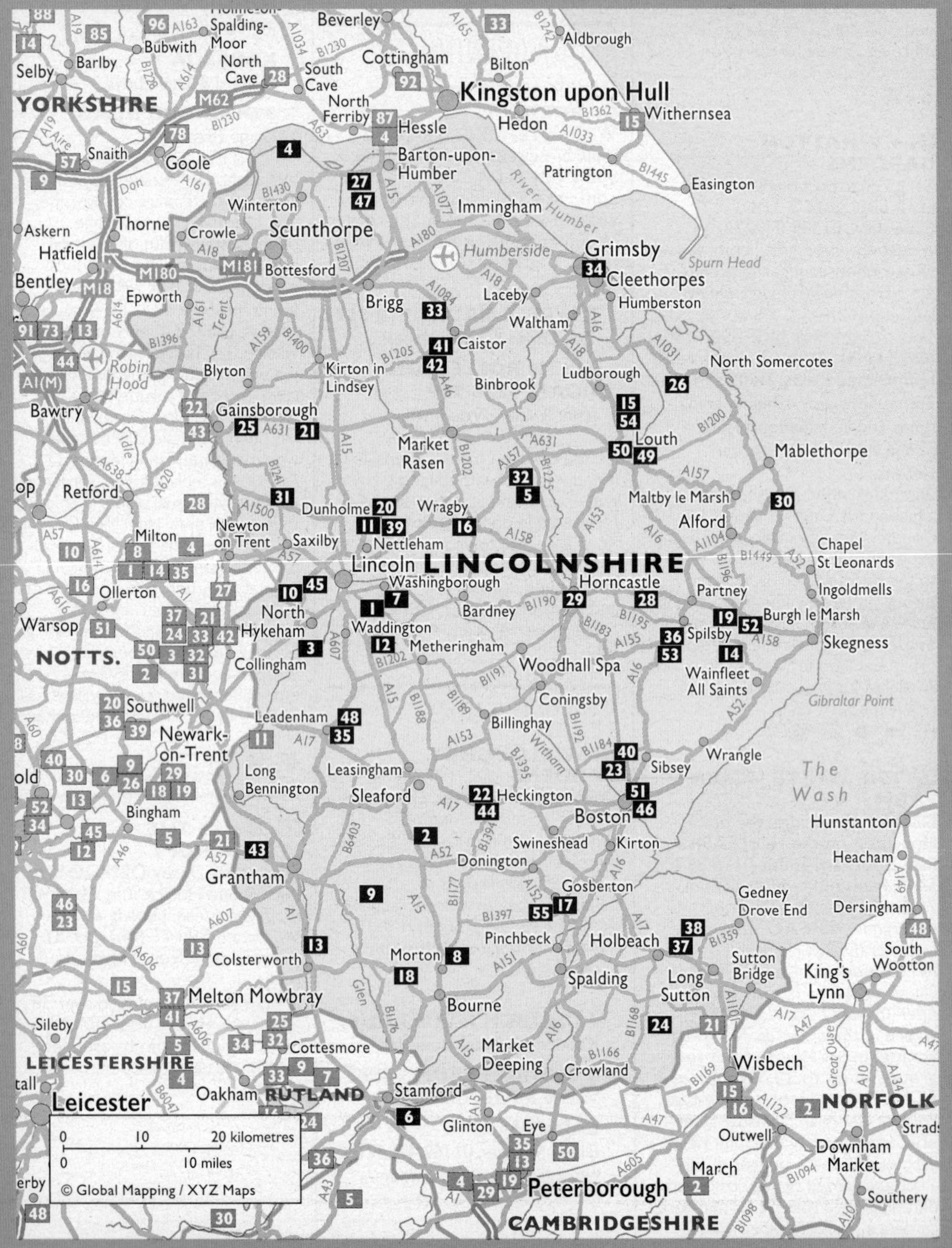

Lincolnshire is a county shaped by a rich tapestry of fascinating heritage, passionate people and intriguing traditions; a mix of city, coast and countryside.

The city of Lincoln is dominated by the iconic towers of Lincoln Cathedral. The eastern seaboard contains windswept golden sands and lonely nature reserves. The Lincolnshire Wolds is a nationally important landscape of rolling chalk hills and areas of sandstone and clay, which underlie this attractive landscape.

To the south is the historic, religious and architectural heritage of The Vales, with river walks, the fine Georgian buildings of Stamford and historic Burghley House. In the east the unqiue Fens landscape thrives on an endless network of waterways inhabited by an abundance of wildlife.

Beautiful gardens of all types, sizes and designs are cared for and shared by their welcoming owners. Often located in delightful villages, a visit to them will entail driving through quiet roads often bordered by verges of wild flowers.

Lincolnshire is rural England at its very best. Local heritage, beautiful countryside walks, aviation history and it is the home of the Red Arrows.

Volunteers

County Organisers

Helen Boothman
01652 628424
boothmanhelen@gmail.com

Sally Grant
01205 750486
sallygrant50@btinternet.com

County Treasurer

Helen Boothman
(as above)

Publicity

Margaret Mann
01476 585905
marg_mann2000@yahoo.com

Erica McGarrigle
01476 585909
ericamcg@hotmail.co.uk

Assistant County Organisers

Tricia Elliot 01427 788517
t.elliott575@gmail.com

Colin & Janet Johnson 01775 822808
colinj04@hotmail.com

Stephanie Lee 01507 442151
marigoldlee@btinternet.

Jenny Leslie 01529 497317
jenny@collegefarmbraceby.co.uk

Rita Morgan 01472 597529
rita.morgan1@sky.com

Sylvia Ravenhall 01507 526014
sylvan@btinternet.com

Jo Rouston 01673 858656
jo@rouston-gardens.co.uk

Lesley Wykes 01673 86035
lesley@wykeslodge.co.uk

Left: **Easton Walled Gardens**

OPENING DATES

All entries subject to change. For latest information check **www.ngs.org.uk**

Map locator numbers are shown to the right of each garden name.

February

Snowdrop Festival

Saturday 16th
21 Chapel Street 8

Sunday 17th
21 Chapel Street 8

Sunday 24th
Ashfield House 1

April

Saturday 6th
◆ Burghley House Private South Gardens 6

Sunday 7th
NEW Aswarby Park 2
◆ Burghley House Private South Gardens 6
Woodlands 54

Thursday 11th
◆ Grimsthorpe Castle 18

Saturday 13th
The Manor House 29

Sunday 14th
The Old Rectory 36

Friday 19th
◆ Easton Walled Gardens 13

Monday 22nd
Firsby Manor 14

Saturday 27th
Marigold Cottage 30

Sunday 28th
◆ Goltho House 16
Marigold Cottage 30

May

Sunday 5th
Dunholme Lodge 11
Fotherby Gardens 15

Sunday 12th
NEW Cantello Cottage 7
The Old Vicarage 37
Old White House 38
66 Spilsby Road 46

Saturday 18th
NEW Bumble Bee Cottage 5
2 Mill Cottage 32
Willoughby Road Allotments 51

Sunday 19th
Holly House 23
The Old Rectory 36
NEW The Poplars 40

Saturday 25th
Marigold Cottage 30

Sunday 26th
Manor House 28
Marigold Cottage 30
Pottertons Nursery 41

June

Saturday 1st
Oasis Garden – Your Place 34

Sunday 2nd
Hackthorn Hall 20
Ludney House Farm 26
Oasis Garden - Your Place 34
NEW Skellingthorpe Hall 45
Woodlands 54

Wednesday 5th
◆ Grimsthorpe Castle 18

Sunday 9th
Inner Lodge 25
Manor Farm 27
Springfield 47
48 Westgate 50

Sunday 16th
Ashfield House 1
Aubourn Hall 3
NEW East Mere House 12
Gosberton Gardens 17
Shangrila 44

Saturday 22nd
Marigold Cottage 30

Sunday 23rd
◆ Hall Farm 21
Ludney House Farm 26
Marigold Cottage 30
Windrush 53

Sunday 30th
Dunholme Lodge 11
Firsby Manor 14

July

Every Sunday from Sunday 21st
68 Watts Lane 49

Sunday 7th
The Old House 35
Walnut Tree Cottage 48
Woodlands 54

Sunday 14th
Inner Lodge 25

Saturday 20th
Marigold Cottage 30

Sunday 21st
Ballygarth 4
Marigold Cottage 30
Sedgebrook Manor 43
Yew Tree Farm 55

August

Every Sunday
68 Watts Lane 49

Sunday 4th
NEW Cantello Cottage 7
◆ Gunby Hall & Gardens 19
Woodlands 54

Sunday 18th
Inner Lodge 25
Willoughby Road Allotments 51

Saturday 24th
Marigold Cottage 30

Sunday 25th
Manor House 28
Marigold Cottage 30

September

Sunday 1st
Fotherby Gardens 15
◆ Hall Farm 21

Wednesday 18th
◆ Doddington Hall Gardens 10

Saturday 21st
Inley Drove Farm 24

Sunday 22nd
◆ Goltho House 16
Inley Drove Farm 24

October

Sunday 6th
Woodlands 54

By Arrangement

Arrange a personalised garden visit with your club, or group of friends, on a date to suit you. See individual garden entries for full details.

Ashfield House 1
NEW Aswarby Park 2
Aubourn Hall 3
Ballygarth 4
21 Chapel Street 8
Corner House Farm 9
Firsby Manor 14
Hackthorn Hall 20
23 Handley Street 22
Inley Drove Farm 24
Ludney House Farm 26
Manor House 28
Marigold Cottage 30
Mere House 31
The Old Rectory 36
The Old Vicarage 37
Overbeck 39
School House 42
68 Watts Lane 49
Willow Cottage 52

THE GARDENS

1 ASHFIELD HOUSE

Lincoln Road, Branston, Lincoln, LN4 1NS. John & Judi Tinsley, 07977 505682, john@tinsleyfarms.co.uk. *3m S of Lincoln on B1188. Northern outsirts of Branston on B1188 Lincoln Rd. Signed 'TINSLEY FARMS - ASHFIELD' near bus stop, follow signs down drive.* **Sun 24 Feb (11-3); Sun 16 June (11-4.30). Adm £4, chd free. Home-made teas.** Visits also by arrangement Feb to Oct for groups of 10 to 30. Tea & cake incl in adm.

10 acre garden with sweeping lawns constructed around a planting of trees and shrubs. The main feature in the spring is the collection of some 110 flowering cherries of 40 different varieties along with massed plantings of spring flowering bulbs. We recently planted a magnolia collection in a newly constructed woodland garden. In the autumn the colours can be amazing. Fairly level garden. Grass paths.

2 NEW ASWARBY PARK

Aswarby, Sleaford, NG34 8SD. Mr & Mrs George Playne, 01529 455222/07770 721646, cgp@playne.co.uk. *5m S of Sleaford on A15 Take signs to Aswarby. Entrance is straight ahead by Church through black gates.* **Sun 7 Apr (1-5). Adm £4.50, chd free. Home-made teas.** Visits also by arrangement.

Formal and woodland garden in a parkland setting of approx 20 acres. Yew Trees form a backdrop to borders and lawns surrounding the house which is a converted stable block. Walled garden contains a greenhouse with a Muscat vine, which is over 300 years old. Large display of daffodils, snowdrops and climbing roses in season. Partial wheelchair access on gravel paths and drives.

Hall Farm

© Clive Nicholls

3 AUBOURN HALL

Harmston Road, Aubourn, Lincoln, LN5 9DZ. Mr & Mrs Christopher Nevile, 01522 788224, paula@aubournhall.co.uk, www.aubournhall.co.uk. *7m SW of Lincoln. Signed off A607 at Harmston & off A46 at Thorpe on the Hill.* **Sun 16 June (2-5). Adm £5.50, chd free. Home-made teas.** Visits also by arrangement May to Sept.

Approx 9 acres. Lawns, mature trees, shrubs, roses, mixed borders, rose garden, large prairie and topiary garden, spring bulbs, woodland walk and ponds. C11 church adjoining. Access to garden is fairly flat and smooth. Depending on weather some areas may be inaccessible to wheelchairs. Parking in field not on tarmac.

4 BALLYGARTH

Post Office Lane, Whitton, Scunthorpe, DN15 9LF. Joanne & Adrian Davey, 07871 882339, joanne.davey1971@gmail.com. *From Scunthorpe on A1077 follow signs to West Halton. Through West Halton approx 3m to Whitton. Follow signs for parking at Village Hall.* **Sun 21 July (11-4). Adm £3.50, chd free. Home-made teas in Whitton Village Hall.** Visits also by arrangement June & July for groups of 5 to 20.

Set in the rural village of Whitton our end terraced house has approx ⅓ acre garden with large herbaceous and grass borders and two water features. Seating areas overlooking the garden, countryside. Many home-made garden artifacts using recycled materials incl a small folly. Everything in wood, brick and metal has been made by us. Drop off for those with limited mobility but parking is at village hall.

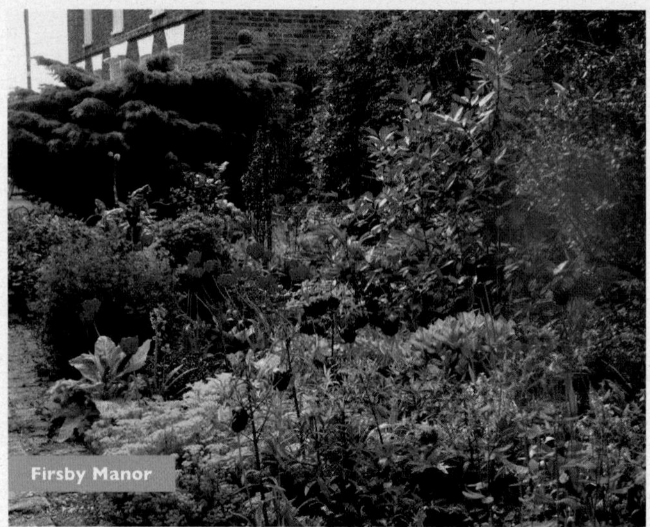
Firsby Manor

5 NEW BUMBLE BEE COTTAGE

Barkwith Road, South Willingham, Market Rasen, LN8 6NN. Dennis & Christine Washer. *10ms from Louth & Horncastle. 50 yards from the T junction in the centre of South Willingham.* **Sat 18 May (1-5). Combined adm with 2 Mill Cottage £5, chd free. Home-made teas at 2 Mill Cottage.**
Well established garden of approximately ⅔ acre. The garden includes several mature trees and has been extensively developed over the past 17 yrs, including a formal gravel garden, orchard with island beds and through a gate to a more relaxed garden with vegetable plot. The garden is on a slight incline and access is via a staggered paved path then grass, which could prove difficult in wet or damp weather.

6 ♦ BURGHLEY HOUSE PRIVATE SOUTH GARDENS

Stamford, PE9 3JY. Burghley House Preservation Trust, 01780 752451, burghley@burghley.co.uk, www.burghley.co.uk. *1m E of Stamford. From Stamford follow signs to Burghley via B1443.* **For NGS: Sat 6, Sun 7 Apr (11-4). Adm £5, chd £3. Light refreshments in The Orangery Restaurant.** For other opening times and information, please phone, email or visit garden website.
On 6 and 7 April the Private South Gardens at Burghley House will open for the NGS with spectacular spring bulbs in park like setting with magnificent trees and the opportunity to enjoy Capability Brown's famous lake and summerhouse. Entry to the Private South Gardens via Orangery. The Garden of Surprises, Sculpture Garden and House are open as normal. (Regular adm prices apply). Fine Food Market. Gravel paths.

7 NEW CANTELLO COTTAGE

56 High Street, Heighington, Lincoln, LN4 1JS. Robert & Gillian How. *4m SE of Lincoln. From Lincoln take B1188 to Branston. At furthest end of village turn L onto Moor Lane, L at x-roads, 3rd L in Heighington* **Sun 12 May, Sun 4 Aug (10.30-4.30). Adm £3, chd free. Home-made teas.**
C18 Grade II listed cottage. Garden developed from a blank canvas. Twenty-one foot original stone-lined well with wrought iron cover. Yew tree cut in heart shape. Mixed perennials. Pergolas with clematis, roses and other climbers. Seating areas for refreshments. Craft garden room open with plants for sale. Gravel paths and some steps.

8 21 CHAPEL STREET

Hacconby, Bourne, PE10 0UL. Joan Curtis & Sharon White, 01778 570314, cliffordcurtis@btinternet.com. *3m N of Bourne. A15, turn E at Xrds into Hacconby, L at village green.* **Sat 16, Sun 17 Feb (11-4). Adm £3, chd free. Home-made teas. Hot soup (Feb).** Visits also by arrangement Feb & Mar.
This snowdrop garden of the late Cliff Curtis will be open this year for its final time. Joan, his wife, and Sharon, his daughter, are opening it as a tribute to him. A cottage garden behind a 300yr old cottage. Snowdrops, primroses, hellebores and many different spring flowering bulbs. Part gravel and part grass paths.

9 CORNER HOUSE FARM

Little Humby, Grantham, NG33 4HW. Colin & Erica McGarrigle, 01476 585909, ericamcg@hotmail.co.uk. *6m SE of Grantham. Turn off A52 signed Ropsley. ½m E of Ropsley, turn R to Humby.* **Visits by arrangement May & June for groups of 10+. Adm £6 incl refreshments. Evening visits also welcome, glass of wine incl.**
This garden offers diversity and a wealth of interesting features. Behind the Grade 2 listed farmhouse (C17) is a stunning rose garden, a timeless tribute to rose lovers. To the front rise sweeping lawns, mixed borders, a majestic ash tree and a mystical bog garden. The orchard includes a raised vegetable plot and beyond an ancient farmyard lies a paddock fringed by a varied selection of trees. Parking in field.

10 ♦ DODDINGTON HALL GARDENS

Doddington, Lincoln, LN6 4RU. Claire & James Birch, 01522 694308, info@doddingtonhall.com, www.doddingtonhall.com. *5m W of Lincoln on B1190. Signed from the A46 Newark to Lincoln rd. Also from the A57 between the A1 & Lincoln. If you are using 'sat nav', the post- code to enter is LN6 4RU.* **For NGS: Wed 18 Sept (11-4.30). Adm £7, chd £3.50.**

For other opening times and information, please phone, email or visit garden website.
5 acres of romantic walled and wild gardens. Naturalised autumn crocus and colchicums, cyclamen, shrubs, grasses, roses and late flowering perennials. Turf maze and ancient chestnut trees. Fully productive working walled kitchen garden with pleached, espaliered and fan-trained fruit trees, dahlias, herbs and plants for butterflies and bees. Wheelchair access possible via gravel paths. Ramps also in use. Access map available from Gatehouse Shop.

11 DUNHOLME LODGE

Dunholme, Lincoln, LN2 3QA. Hugh & Lesley Wykes. *4m NE of Lincoln. Turn off A46 towards Welton at hand car wash garage. After ½m turn L up long private road. Garden at top.* **Sun 5 May (11-5). Home-made teas. Sun 30 June (11-5). Cream teas. Adm £3.50, chd free.**
3 acre garden. Spring bulb area, shrub borders, fern garden, topiary, large natural pond, wild flower area, orchard and vegetable garden. RAF Dunholme Lodge Museum and War Memorial in the grounds. Most areas wheelchair accessible but some loose stone and gravel.

12 NEW EAST MERE HOUSE

East Mere, Bracebridge Heath, Lincoln, LN4 2HU. James Dean. *From A15 take B1178 towards Bardney & Mere. Follow B1178 for 1m to sharp L hand bend & take the lane to the R at the bend. East Mere House drive is on your R.* **Sun 16 June (11.30-5). Adm £4, chd free. Home-made teas.**
2 acre formal country garden, recently redesigned by Angel Collins, surrounding a stone farmhouse. Box-edged borders planted with grasses, perennials and seasonal bedding. Lawns, ornamental trees, crab apple avenue and small rose garden. Parterre planted with rosemary, lavender, santolina and alliums. Kitchen garden with raised vegetable beds and fruit trees on the walls. Wild flower meadow.

13 ◆ EASTON WALLED GARDENS

Easton, NG33 5AP. Sir Fred & Lady Cholmeley, 01476 530063, info@eastonwalledgardens.co.uk, www.visiteaston.co.uk. *7m S of Grantham. 1m from A1, off B6403.* **For NGS: Fri 19 Apr (11-4). Adm £7.70, chd £3.50. Light refreshments & lunches.**
For other opening times and information, please phone, email or visit garden website.
A 400-year-old, restored, 12 acre garden set in the heart of Lincolnshire. Home to snowdrops, sweet peas, roses and meadows. The tearoom serves delicious light lunches and cream teas and there is a well-stocked gift shop and plants for sale. Other highlights include a turf maze, swing, yew tunnel and bird hide. Regret no wheelchair access to lower gardens but tearoom, shop and upper gardens all accessible.

14 FIRSBY MANOR

Firsby, Spilsby, PE23 5QJ. David & Gill Boldy, 01754 830386, gillboldy@gmail.com. *5m E of Spilsby. From Spilsby take B1195 to Wainfleet all Saints. In Firsby, turn R into Fendyke Rd. Firsby Manor is 0.8m along lane on L.* **Mon 22 Apr, Sun 30 June (1-4.30). Adm £3, chd free.** Visits also by arrangement Feb to Sept for groups of 10 to 20.
Firsby Manor is a lovely garden which has been developed to provide peace and pleasure for humans as well as a restful haven for wildlife. Snowdrops appear in February, followed by over a hundred daffodil cultivars in April. By June the garden is full of cottage garden perennials. Partial wheelchair access due to large areas of shingle and uneven ground and no toilet access.

GROUP OPENING

15 FOTHERBY GARDENS

Peppin Lane, Fotherby, Louth, LN11 0UW. *2m N of Louth on A16 signed Fotherby. Limited parking on Peppin Lane where signed. Further space in village but please park considerately. Ltd space for B Badge holders at each site. Free taxi service between Woodlands & Nut Tree Farm.* **Sun 5 May, Sun 1 Sept (11-5). Combined adm £5, chd free. Home-made teas at Woodlands.**

NUT TREE FARM
Tim & Judith Hunter.

SHEPHERDS HEY
Barbara Chester.

WOODLANDS
Ann & Bob Armstrong.
(See separate entry)
NPC

Start your visit at Shepherds Hey, a small garden packed with unusual and interesting perennials. Its open frontage gives a warm welcome, with a small pond, terraced border and steep bank side to a stream. The rear garden, with colour themed borders, takes advantage of the panoramic views over open countryside. 350yds along Peppin Lane is Woodlands, a lovely mature woodland garden with many unusual plants set against a backdrop of an ever changing tapestry of greenery. A peaceful garden where wildlife thrives. The front garden is a crevice area of sand for alpine plants. There is a Plant Heritage collection of Codonopsis and the nursery, featured in RHS Plantfinder, gives visitors the opportunity to purchase plants seen in the garden. An award winning professional artist's studio/gallery is also open. Complete your visit at Nut Tree Farm. The garden, established in 2007, is over an acre and enjoys stunning views of Lincolnshire Wolds. A sweeping herbaceous border frames the lawn and a double wall, planted with seasonal annuals, surrounds the house. From the raised terrace a rill runs to the large pond. There is also a raised brick edged vegetable garden. Surrounding the garden are fields with a flock of pedigree Hampshire Down sheep and a small herd of Lincoln Red cattle. Local honey (Nut Tree Farm produced) for sale. Limited access at each garden.
NPC

16 ♦ GOLTHO HOUSE

Lincoln Road, Goltho, Wragby, Market Rasen, LN8 5NF. Mr & Mrs S Hollingworth, 01673 857768, bookings@golthogardens.com, www.golthogardens.com. *10m E of Lincoln. On A158, 1m before Wragby. Garden on L (not in Goltho Village).* **For NGS: Sun 28 Apr, Sun 22 Sept (10-4). Adm £5, chd free. Light refreshments.** For other opening times and information, please phone, email or visit garden website.

4½ acre garden started in 1998 but looking established with long grass walk flanked by abundantly planted herbaceous borders forming a focal point. Paths and walkway span out to other features incl nut walk, prairie border, wild flower meadow, rose garden and large pond area. Snowdrops, hellebores and shrubs for winter interest.

GROUP OPENING

17 GOSBERTON GARDENS

Gosberton, Spalding, PE11 4NQ. *Entering Gosberton on A152, from Spalding , Salem St on L & Mill Lane on R opp the War Memorial. 21 Quadring Rd is located at the end of the village on main road on R.* **Sun 16 June (12-5). Combined adm £5, chd free. Home-made teas at Salem Street.**

MILLSTONE HOUSE
Mrs J Chatterton.

NEW **21 QUADRING ROAD**
Julie Crunkhorn.

4 SALEM STREET
Roley and Tricia Hogben.

The village of Gosberton welcomes visitors to 3 private houses to view their gardens. We hope that everyone will find interesting features during their tour and enjoy the 3 locations. Millstone House. Colourful herbaceous borders are hidden by a privet hedge. Dappled shade creates a feeling of relaxation at the rear of the house. 4 Salem Street. Delightful secluded garden. Mixed borders including a small water feature lead to a productive vegetable plot. 21 Quadring Road has a large herbaceous front garden and secluded garden rooms. Partial wheelchair access.

18 ♦ GRIMSTHORPE CASTLE

Grimsthorpe, Bourne, PE10 0LZ. Grimsthorpe & Drummond Castle Trust, 01778 591205, ray@grimsthorpe.co.uk, www.grimsthorpe.co.uk. *3m NW of Bourne. 8m E of A1 on A151 from Colsterworth junction. Main entrance gates indicated by brown tourist sign.* **For NGS: Thur 11 Apr, Wed 5 June (10.30-5). Adm £7, chd £3. Light refreshments.** For other opening times and information, please phone, email or visit garden website.

The Grade I listed gardens encompass nearly 65 acres and incl large formal lawns, fine topiary and formal hedges, ornamental and productive kitchen garden, large herbaceous borders, rose parterre and woodland walks with spring bulb displays. Visitors can explore the surrounding 3000 acre estate that encompasses a Capability Brown landscape, in addition to the tranquil and relaxing gardens. Home-made lunches, afternoon tea and cakes. Gift shop, cycle hire and adventure playground, historic house, park trails. Gravel paths.

19 ♦ GUNBY HALL & GARDENS

Spilsby, PE23 5SS. National Trust, 01754 890102, gunbyhall@nationaltrust.org.uk, www.nationaltrust.org.uk. *2½m NW of Burgh-le-Marsh. 7m W of Skegness. On A158. Signed off Gunby r'about.* **For NGS: Sun 4 Aug (11-5). Adm £6.75, chd £3.75. Light refreshments in Gunby tea-room.** For other opening times and information, please phone, email or visit garden website.

Eight acres of formal and walled gardens. Old roses, herbaceous borders, herb garden and kitchen garden with fruit trees and vegetables. Greenhouses, carp pond and sweeping lawns. Tennyson's Haunt of Ancient Peace. House built by Sir William Massingberd in 1700. Wheelchair access in gardens and with Gunby's dedicated wheelchair on ground floor of house.

20 HACKTHORN HALL

Hackthorn, Lincoln, LN2 3PQ. Mr & Mrs William Cracroft-Eley, 01673 860423, office@hackthorn.com, www.hackthorn.com. *6m N of Lincoln. Follow signs to Hackthorn. Approx 1m off A15 N of Lincoln.* **Sun 2 June (1-5). Adm £4, chd free. Home-made teas at Hackthorn Village Hall.** Visits also by arrangement Feb to Sept for groups of 20+.

Formal and woodland garden, productive and ornamental walled gardens surrounding Hackthorn Hall and church extending to approx 15 acres. Parts of the formal gardens designed by Bunny Guinness. The walled garden boasts a magnificent Black Hamburg vine, believed to be second in size to the vine at Hampton Court. Partial wheelchair access, gravel paths, grass drives.

21 ♦ HALL FARM

Harpswell, Gainsborough, DN21 5UU. Pam & Mark Tatam, 01427 668412, pam.tatam@gmail.com, www.hall-farm.co.uk. *7m E of Gainsborough. On A631, 1½m W of Caenby Corner.* **For NGS: Sun 23 June, Sun 1 Sept (1-5). Adm £4, chd free. Home-made teas.** For other opening times and information, please phone, email or visit garden website.

The 3 acre garden encompasses formal and informal areas, incl a parterre, a sunken garden, a courtyard with rill, a walled Mediterranean garden, double herbaceous borders for late summer, lawns, pond, giant chess set, and a flower and grass meadow. It is a short walk to the medieval moat, which surrounds over an acre of wild semi-woodland garden with picnic table, benches and 'beach'. Free seed collecting on Sun 1 Sept. Most of garden suitable for wheelchairs.

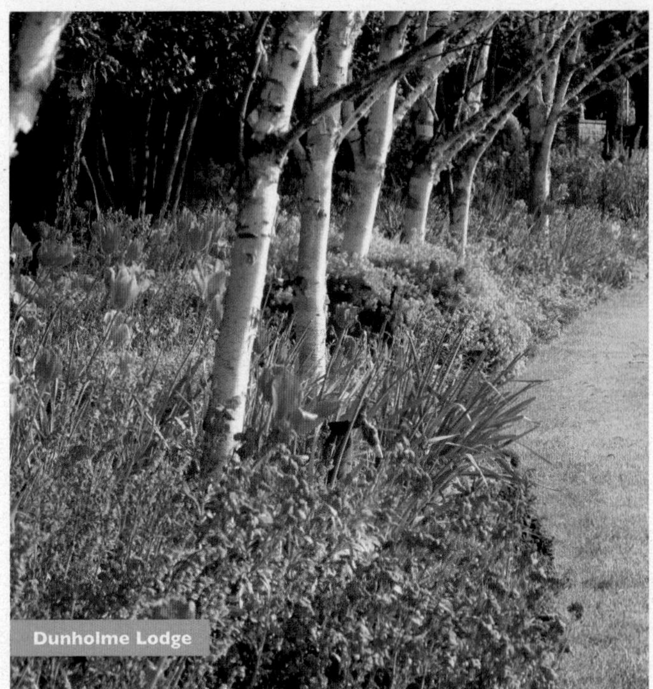
Dunholme Lodge

22 23 HANDLEY STREET

Heckington, nr Sleaford, NG34 9RZ. Stephen Donnison, 01529 460097, donno5260@gmail.com. *A17 from Sleaford, turn R into Heckington. Follow road to the Green. L, follow road past Church, R into Cameron St. At end of this road L into Handley St.* **Visits by arrangement June & July for groups of up to 20. Adm £3, chd free. Home-made teas.**
Compact, quirky garden, large fish pond. Further 5 small wildlife ponds. Small wooded area and Jurassic style garden with Tree ferns. Densely planted flower borders featuring Penstemons. Large patio with seating.

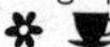

23 HOLLY HOUSE

Fishtoft Drove, Frithville, Boston, PE22 7ES. Sally & David Grant. *3m N of Boston. 1m S of Frithville. Unclassified rd. On W side of West Fen Drain. Marked on good maps.* **Sun 19 May (12-5). Combined adm with The Poplars £6, chd free. Home-made teas.**
Approx 1 acre informal mixed borders, steps leading down to pond with cascade and stream. Small woodland area. Quiet garden with water feature. Extra 2½ acres devoted to wildlife, especially bumble bees and butterflies. Partial wheelchair access with some steep slopes and steps.

24 INLEY DROVE FARM

Inley Drove, Sutton St James, Spalding, PE12 0LX. Francis & Maisie Pryor, 01406 540088, www.pryorfrancis.wordpress.com/. *Just off rd from Sutton St James to Sutton St Edmund. 2m S of Sutton St James. Look for yellow NGS signs on double bend.* **Sat 21, Sun 22 Sept (11-4). Adm £4.50, chd free. Home-made teas.** Visits also by arrangement Apr to July for groups of 10 to 30. Restricted parking.
Over 3 acres of Fenland garden and meadow plus 6½ acre wood developed over 20yrs. Garden planted for colour, scent and wildlife. Double mixed borders and less formal flower gardens all framed by hornbeam hedges. Unusual shrubs and trees, incl fine stand of Black Poplars, vegetable garden, woodland walks and orchard. Disabled WC outside. Some gravel and a few steps but mostly flat grass.

25 INNER LODGE

Somerby, Gainsborough, DN21 3HG. Paul & Karen Graves. *On A631 Gainsborough to Grimsby rd. From Gainsborough, track on R at Very end of the dual carriageway, follow ½m track to find marked parking areas in small woodland glades.* **Sun 9 June, Sun 14 July, Sun 18 Aug (11-4). Adm £3, chd free. Home-made cakes by Karen (Chocolate Cake a must) Hot & Cold Drinks.**
Set in woodland our colourful cottage garden of approx 1 acre was started in 2013 and is still developing. We have mixed borders, shrubs, fernery, several quirky features, and small secret garden. Plenty of seating around the garden but regret it is not suitable for wheelchairs. There will also be Craft sales (open on all the days) with a percentage of takings donated to the NGS.

26 LUDNEY HOUSE FARM

Ludney, Louth, LN11 7JU. Jayne Bullas, 07733 018710, jayne@theoldgatehouse.com. *Between Grainthorpe & Conisholme.* **Sun 2, Sun 23 June (1-4). Adm £6, chd free. Light refreshments. Home-made teas and cakes incl.** Visits also by arrangement Apr to Sept for groups of 5 to 30.
A beautiful landscaped garden of several defined spaces containing formal and informal areas. There is an excellent mix of trees, shrubs, perennials and roses, also a long wild grass area which is home to the bee hives. In spring there is a nice selection of bulbs and spring flowers. There are plenty of seats positioned around to sit and enjoy a cuppa and piece of cake! Wheelchair access to most parts.

27 MANOR FARM

Horkstow Road, South Ferriby, Barton-upon-Humber, DN18 6HS. Geoff & Angela Wells. *3m from Barton-upon-Humber on A1077, turn L onto B1204, opp Village Hall.* **Sun 9 June (11-5). Combined adm with Springfield £5, chd free. Home-made teas.**

A garden which is much praised by visitors. Set within approx 1 acre with mature shrubberies, herbaceous borders, gravel garden and pergola walk. Rose bed, white garden and fernery. Many old trees with preservation orders. Wildlife pond set within a paddock.

28 MANOR HOUSE

Manor Road, Hagworthingham, Spilsby, PE23 4LN. Gill Maxim & David O'Connor, 01507 588530, vcagillmaxim@aol.com. *5m E of Horncastle. S of A158 in Hagworthingham, turn into Bond Hayes Lane downhill, becomes Manor Rd. Please follow signs down gravel track to parking area.* **Sun 26 May, Sun 25 Aug (2-5). Adm £3.50, chd free. Home-made teas.** Visits also by arrangement May to Sept for groups of 10+.

2 acre garden on S-facing slope, partly terraced and well protected by established trees and shrubs. Redeveloped over 18yrs with natural and formal ponds. Shrub roses, laburnum walk, hosta border, gravel bed and other areas mainly planted with hardy perennials, trees and shrubs.

29 THE MANOR HOUSE

Manor House Street, Horncastle, LN9 5HF. Mr Michael & Dr Marilyn Hieatt. *Manor House St runs off the Market Square in middle of Horncastle, beside St Mary's Church. The Manor House is approx 100 metres from the Market Square (on R).* **Sat 13 Apr (12.30-4.30). Adm £4, chd free.**

An informal spring garden and orchard bordered by the River Bain, hidden in the middle of Horncastle. The garden includes a short section of the 3rd/4th Century wall that formed part of a Roman fort (Scheduled Ancient Monument) with the remnants of an adjacent medieval well. Restricted wheel chair access (some parts not accessible).

30 MARIGOLD COTTAGE

Hotchin Road, Sutton-on-Sea, LN12 2NP. Stephanie Lee & John Raby, 01507 442151, marigoldlee@btinternet.com, www.rabylee.uk/marigold/. *16m N of Skegness on A52. 7m E of Alford on A1111. 3m S of Mablethorpe on A52. Turn off A52 on High St at Cornerhouse Cafe. Follow rd past playing field on R. Rd turns away from the dunes. House 2nd on L.* **Sat 27, Sun 28 Apr, Sat 25, Sun 26 May, Sat 22, Sun 23 June, Sat 20, Sun 21 July, Sat 24, Sun 25 Aug (2-5). Adm £3, chd free. Home-made teas.** Visits also by arrangement Apr to Sept for groups of 10+.

Slide open the Japanese gate to find secret paths, lanterns, a circular window in a curved wall, water lilies in pots and a gravel garden, vegetable garden and propagation area. Take the long drive to see the sea. Back in the garden, find a seat, enjoy the birds and bees. We face the challenges of heavy clay and salt ladened winds but look for unusual plants not the humdrum for these conditions. Most of garden accessible to wheelchairs along flat, paved paths.

31 MERE HOUSE

Stow Road, Sturton by Stow, Lincoln, LN1 2BZ. Nigel & Alice Gray, 07932 442349, alice@merehome.uk. *10m NW of Lincoln between Sturton & Stow. 1m from centre of Sturton village heading to Stow, house on L. NB: Postcode will not bring you far enough out of Sturton village.* **Visits by arrangement Mar to Sept. We have a large car park with room for coaches. Adm £5, chd free. Home-made teas.**

Approx 1½ acres of established garden planted for the first time in 1975, redesigned in 1996. Renovated over the last 5yrs to incl new beds with drift planting but still incl the formal parterre. Spring bulbs and late summer colour are highlights. There is also a cutting garden, pleached hedges, vegetable garden and orchard. Work in progress incl a new garden project and long herbaceous border. There is the highly acclaimed Cross Keys Pub in Stow Village that does a very good lunch. The garden is wheelchair accessible on grass.

Inner Lodge

32 2 MILL COTTAGE

Barkwith Road, South Willingham, Market Rasen, LN8 6NN. Mrs Jo Rouston. *5m E of Wragby. On A157 turn R at pub in East Barkwith then immed L to South Willingham. Cottage 1m on L.* **Sat 18 May (12-5). Combined adm with Bumble Bee Cottage £5, chd free. Home-made teas.**

A garden of several defined spaces, packed with interesting features, unusual plants and well placed seating areas, created by garden designer Jo Rouston. Original engine shed, a working well, raised beds using local rock with small pond. Clipped box, alpines, roses, summerhouses and water feature. Greenhouse and herb garden. Woven metal and turf tree seat. New outdoor bar-b-q area with log wall. Partial wheelchair access. Gravel at far end of garden. Steps down to main greenhouse.

33 ◆ MILL FARM

Caistor Road, Grasby, Caistor, DN38 6AQ. Mike & Helen Boothman, 01652 628424, boothmanhelen@gmail.com, www.millfarmgarden.co.uk. *3m NW of Caistor on A1084. Between Brigg & Caistor. From Cross Keys pub towards Caistor for approx 200yds. Do not go into Grasby village.* **For opening times and information, please phone, email or visit garden website.**

This is a garden which continues to be developed. Over 3 acres of garden with many diverse areas. Formal frontage with shrubs and trees. The rear is a plantsman haven with a peony and rose garden, specimen trees, vegetable area, old windmill adapted into a fernery, alpine house and shade house with a variety of shade loving plants. Herbaceous beds with different grasses and hardy perennials. Small nursery on site with home grown plants available. Open by arrangement for groups. Mainly grass, but with some gravelled areas.

34 OASIS GARDEN - YOUR PLACE

Wellington Street, Grimsby, DN32 7JP. Grimsby Neighbourhood Church, www.yourplacegrimsby.com. *Enter Grimsby (M180) over flyover, along Cleethorpes Rd. Turn R into Victor St, Turn L into Wellington St. Your Place is on the R on junction of Wellington St & Weelsby St.* **Sat 1, Sun 2 June (11-3). Adm £3, chd free. Light refreshments.**

The multi award winning Oasis Garden, Your Place, recently described by the RHS as the 'Most inspirational garden in the six counties of the East Midlands', is approximately 1½ acres and nestles in the heart of Great Grimsby's East Marsh Community. A working garden producing 15k plants per year, grown by local volunteers of all ages and abilities. Lawns, fruit, vegetable, perennial and annual beds.

35 THE OLD HOUSE

1 The Green, Welbourn, Lincoln, LN5 0NJ. Mr & Mrs David Close. *11m S of Lincoln or 12m N of Grantham on A607. From Newark A17 then A607. Turn off A607 into S end of village, on village green opp red phone box.* **Sun 7 July (2-6). Combined adm with Walnut Tree Cottage £4, chd free. Home-made teas at Welbourn Village Hall, LN5 0LZ. Ice creams at The Old House.**

The formal front garden of this listed Georgian house was redesigned by Guy Petheram. Gravel, paving and pebble mosaics provide hard landscaping around beds with box hedging, clipped Portuguese laurel, lavender and roses. Herbaceous border, white hydrangea bed, and small enclosed paved garden. Welbourn Blacksmiths shop and forge dating from 1864 and still in full working order open with Friends of Forge on hand to answer questions. Plant stall by Plantazia of Lincoln, artisan honey and bee products, metal sculpture, will have stands within the gardens. Some gravel.

36 THE OLD RECTORY

Church Lane, East Keal, Spilsby, PE23 4AT. Mrs Ruth Ward, 01790 752477, rfjward@btinternet.com. *2m SW of Spilsby. Off A16. Turn into Church Lane by PO.* **Sun 14 Apr, Sun 19 May (2-4.30). Adm £3.50, chd free. Home-made teas. Visits also by arrangement Mar to Oct. Individuals or small groups at short notice.**

Beautifully situated, with fine views, rambling cottage garden on different levels falling naturally into separate areas, with changing effects and atmosphere. Steps, paths and vistas to lead you on, seats well placed for appreciating special views or relaxing and enjoying the peace. Dry border, vegetable garden, orchard, woodland walk, wild flower meadow. Yr-round interest. Welcoming to wildlife. Limited wheelchair access.

We open the gates to the nation's best gardens, offering a relaxing, memorable and affordable day out. A perfect experience to share with friends and family.

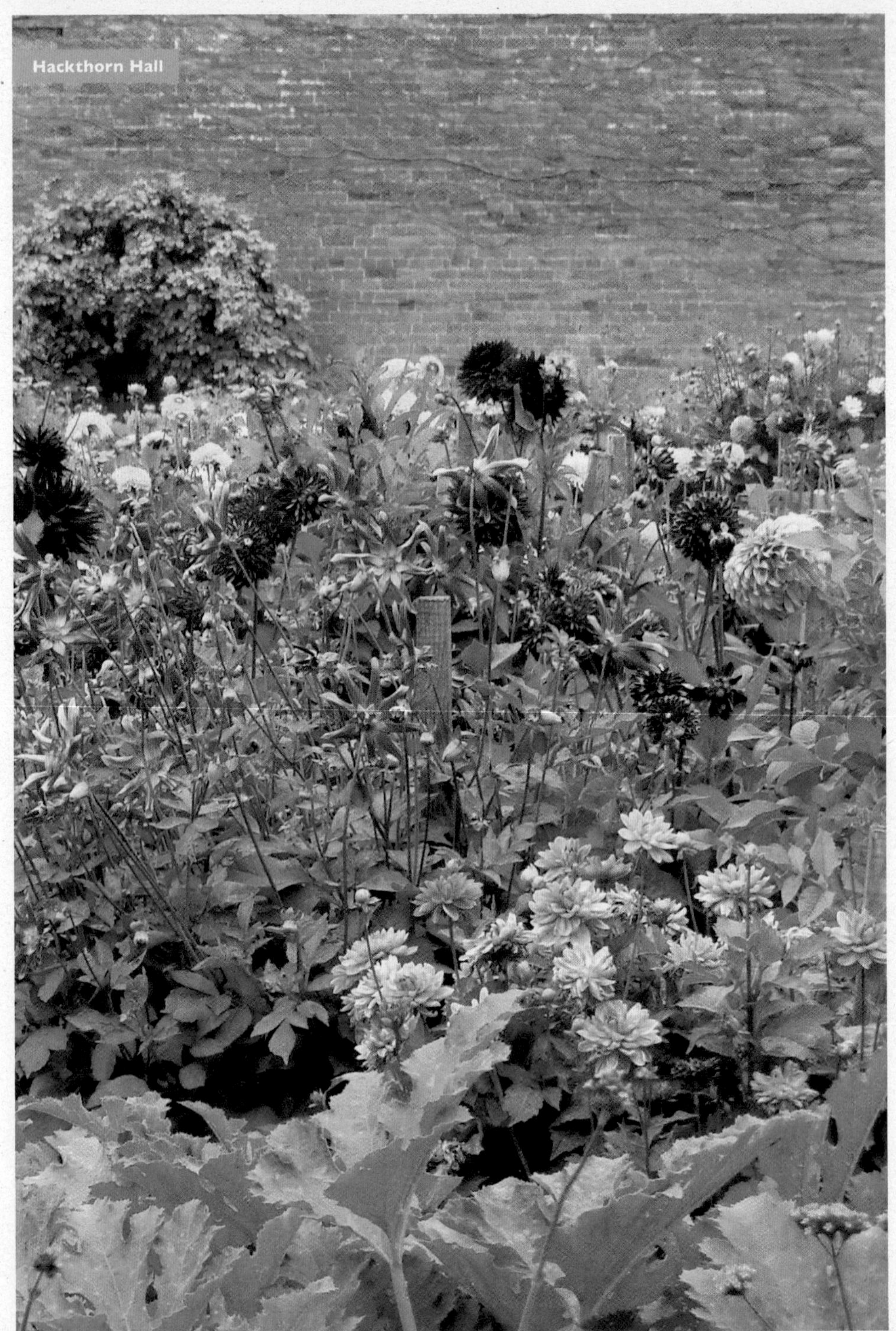

Hackthorn Hall

37 THE OLD VICARAGE

Low Road, Holbeach Hurn, PE12 8JN. Mrs Liz Dixon-Spain, 01406 424148, lizdixonspain@gmail.com. *2m NE of Holbeach. Turn off A17 N to Holbeach Hurn, past post box in middle of village, 1st R at war memorial into Low Rd. Old Vicarage is on R approx 400yds Parking in grass paddock.* **Sun 12 May (1-5). Combined adm with Old White House £5, chd free.** Visits also by arrangement Apr to Sept for groups of up to 30.

2 acres of garden with 150yr old tulip, plane and beech trees: borders of shrubs, roses, herbaceous plants. Shrub roses and herb garden in old paddock area, surrounded by informal areas with pond and bog garden, wild flowers, grasses and bulbs. Small fruit and vegetable gardens. Kids love exploring winding paths through the wilder areas. Garden is managed environmentally. Fun for kids! Gravel drive, some paths, mostly grass access.

38 OLD WHITE HOUSE

Baileys Lane, Holbeach Hurn, PE12 8JP. Mrs A Worth. *2m N of Holbeach. Turn off A17 N to Holbeach Hurn, follow signs to village, cont through, turn R after Rose & Crown Pub at Baileys Lane.* **Sun 12 May (1-5). Combined adm with The Old Vicarage £5, chd free. Home-made teas.**

1½ acres of mature garden, featuring herbaceous borders, roses, patterned garden, herb garden and walled kitchen garden. Large catalpa, tulip tree that flowers, ginko and other specimen trees. Flat surfaces, some steps, wheelchair access to all areas without using steps.

39 OVERBECK

46 Main Street, Scothern, LN2 2UW. John & Joyce Good, 01673 862200, jandjgood@btinternet.com. *4m E of Lincoln. Scothern signed from A46 at Dunholme & A158 at Sudbrooke. Overbeck is E end of Main St.* **Visits by arrangement May to July for groups of 10+. Day time or Evening visits welcome mid May to mid July. Adm £3, chd free. Light refreshments.**

Situated in an attractive village this approx ⅔ acre garden is a haven for wildlife. Long herbaceous borders and colour themed island beds with some unusual perennials. Hosta border, gravel bed with grasses, fernery, trees, numerous shrubs, small stumpery, climbers, a developing parterre and large prolific vegetable and fruit area.

40 NEW THE POPLARS

Church Lane, Frithville, Boston, PE22 7ET. James & Zoe Mitchell. *3m N of Boston. 1m S of Frithville. Unclassified rd. On W side of West Fen Drain. Marked on good maps.* **Sun 19 May (12-5). Combined adm with Holly House £6, chd free.**

Previously used as paddock and later a pig farm, our garden has had a variety of uses over the years. Work on the garden in its current form began in 2010 after the site was completely cleared of rubbish, and the main house renovated. The garden today has a mix of formal spaces and semi-mature borders, and features a large ornamental pond with a rock waterfall and reed bed.

41 POTTERTONS NURSERY

Moortown Road, Nettleton, Caistor, LN7 6HX. Rob & Jackie Potterton, www.pottertons.co.uk. *1m W of Nettleton. From A46 at Nettleton turn onto B1205 (Moortown). Nursery 1¼m, turn by edge of wood.* **Sun 26 May (9-5). Adm £3, chd free. Home-made teas. We will be offering excellent cream teas and homemade light refreshments & drinks.**

5 acre garden of alpine rockeries, stream and waterfall, raised beds, troughs, tufa bed, crevice garden, woodland beds, extensively planted with alpines, bulbs and woodland plants, which will be at their flowering peak. On the day we have invited Plant Hunters Fairs to the garden, with 10 specialist nurseries offering a range incl Acers, shrubs, alpines, rare perennials and cottage garden plants. Access mostly on mixed grass surfaces.

43 SEDGEBROOK MANOR

Church Lane, Sedgebrook, Grantham, NG32 2EU. Hon James & Lady Caroline Ogilvy. *2m W of Grantham on A52. In Sedgebrook village by church.* **Sun 21 July (1-5). Adm £4.50, chd free. Home-made teas.**

Yew and box topiary surround this charming Manor House (not open). Croquet lawn, herbaceous border and summer house. Bridge over small pond and two larger ponds. Ancient mulberry tree. Tennis court, vegetable garden and area with chickens. Swimming pool in enclosed garden. Wheelchair access to most areas.

44 SHANGRILA

Little Hale Road, Great Hale, Sleaford, NG34 9LH. Marilyn Cooke & John Knight. *On B1394 between Heckington & Helpringham.* **Sun 16 June (11-5). Adm £4.50, chd free. Home-made teas.**

Approx 3 acre garden with sweeping lawns long herbaceous borders, colour themed island beds, hosta collection, lavender bed with seating area, topiary, acers, small raised vegetable area, 3 ponds and new exotic borders. Wheelchair access to all areas.

Your visits help change lives – since 1927, we've donated £55 million to nursing and caring charities

45 NEW SKELLINGTHORPE HALL

Lincoln Road, Skellingthorpe, Lincoln, LN6 5UU. Charlie & Anne Coltman. *4m W of Lincoln, 500 yds from A46 Lincoln relief rd. At the r'about (mid way between A57 & B1190) signed Skellingthorpe take the NW exit. Skellingthorpe Hall entrance is circa. 500yds on the R opposite Waterloo Lane.* **Sun 2 June (10-4.30). Adm £3.50, chd free. Home-made teas. Some allergies are not catered for please ask.**

A 3½ acre landscaped garden with long views across the ha-ha to the park and beyond. Extensive lawns with mature trees. Shrubs and perennial borders created over the last 25yrs. Spring bulbs naturalised in the grass and tulips in the borders. Pond and paved area by the small conservatory and a larger one in the main garden, A large vegetable garden with green houses. Some paths can be an effort to navigate.

46 66 SPILSBY ROAD

Boston, PE21 9NS. Rosemary & Adrian Isaac. *From Boston town take A16 towards Spilsby. On L after Trinity Church. Parking on Spilsby Rd.* **Sun 12 May (11-4). Adm £4, chd free. Home-made teas.**

1⅓ acre with mature trees, moat, Venetian Folly, summer house and orangery, lawns and herbaceous borders. Children's Tudor garden house, gatehouse and courtyard. Wide paths.

47 SPRINGFIELD

Main Street, Horkstow, Barton-Upon-Humber, DN18 6BL. Mr & Mrs G Allison. *4m from Barton on Humber. Take the A1077 towards Scunthorpe & in South Ferriby bear L onto the B1204, after 2m Springfield is on the hillside on L.* **Sun 9 June (11-5). Combined adm with Manor Farm £5, chd free.**

This beautiful hillside garden on the edge of the Wolds was renovated and redesigned in 2011 from an overgrown state. It features many shrubs and perennials with a rose pergola and stunning views over the Ancholme Valley.

Your visits help change lives – we've donated over £16.7 million to Macmillan Cancer Support since 1984

48 WALNUT TREE COTTAGE

6 Hall Lane, Welbourn, Lincoln, LN5 0NN. Nina & Malcolm McBeath. *Approx 11m S of Lincoln, 12m N of Grantham on A607. From Newark A17 then A607. On A607 from Lincoln turn R into Hall Lane by Welbourn Hall Nursing Home. From Leadenham take L turn after W Hall Nursing Home. Garden is 3rd gate on L. Please park at Village Hall (Beck Street),.* **Sun 7 July (2-6). Combined adm with The Old House £4, chd free. Home-made teas at Welbourn Village Hall LN5 0LZ.**

A peaceful ½ acre garden full of interesting perennials planted in long, curved and colour themed borders. Winding paths surrounded by shrubs and climbing roses provide varied vistas and secluded seating areas. Many old varieties of roses feature throughout, with spectacular displays in June of Paul's Himalayan Musk, Adelaide d'Orleans and Climbing Cecil Brunner dominating three trees. Plant stall by Plantazia, Lincoln, and Artisan honey and bee products for sale in this garden. Nearby, Welbourn Blacksmith's shop and forge, dating from 1864 and still in full working order (open 2pm until 4.30pm), with the fire lit and Friends of the Forge on hand to answer questions. Accessible gravel drive to front of house, with some steps and some narrow paths at the rear.

49 68 WATTS LANE

Louth, LN11 9DG. Jenny & Rodger Grasham, 07977 318145, sallysing@hotmail.co.uk, www.facebook.com/thesecretgardenoflouth. *½m S of Louth town centre. For Sat Nav and to avoid opening/closing gate on Watts Lane, use postcode LN11 9DJ this is Mount Pleasant Ave, leads straight to our house front.* **Every Sun 21 July to 25 Aug (11-4). Adm £2.50, chd free. Home-made teas.** Visits also by arrangement July to Sept for groups of up to 30.

Blank canvas of ⅕ acre in early 90s. Developed into lush, colourful, exotic plant packed haven. A whole new world on entering from street. Exotic borders, raised exotic

Inley Drove Farm

island, long hot border, ponds, stumpery . Intimate seating areas along garden's journey. Facebook page - The Secret Garden of Louth. Children, find where the frogs are hiding! Butterflies and bees but how many different types? Feed the fish, find Cedric the spider, Simon the snake, Colin the Crocodile. Grass pathways, main garden area accessible. Wheelchairs not permitted on bridge over pond, both sides can be reached via pathways.

50 48 WESTGATE

Louth, LN11 9YD. Kenneth Harvey. *Approx 100 yrds before The Wheatsheaf Pub, nr to Church.* **Sun 9 June (11-4). Adm £3.50, chd free. Home-made teas. Teas, cakes, sandwiches, quiches etc will be available on the terrace by the R Ludd.**

Large town garden of about 1½ acres that crosses the R Ludd. Hidden away behind the high Georgian facades of Louth is a good example of a town garden of trees, herbaceous borders, two small ponds, a fern and white garden and formal vegetable parterre. Wonderful views of Louth church spire. The garden was originally planted in the late 1950s, but has been remodelled over the last 7yrs. Because of the steps and steep slope from the street down to the river level, it might not be an ideal garden for those in wheelchairs.

ALLOTMENTS

51 WILLOUGHBY ROAD ALLOTMENTS

Willoughby Road, Boston, PE21 9HN. Willoughby Road Allotments Association, willoughbyroadallotments.org.uk. *Entrance is adjacent to 109 Willoughby Road, Boston, PE21 9HN. Street Parking only.* **Sat 18 May, Sun 18 Aug (10.30-4). Adm £3.50, chd free. Light refreshments.**

Set in 5 acres the allotments comprise 60 plots growing fine vegetables, fruit, flowers and herbs. There is a small orchard and wild flower area and a community space adjacent. Grass paths run along the site. Several plots will be open to walk round. There will be a seed and plant stall. Light refreshments are available. Small orchard and wild flower beds Community area with kitchen and disabled toilet.

52 WILLOW COTTAGE

Gravel Pit Lane, Burgh le Marsh, Lincs, PE24 5DW. Bob & Karen Ward, 01754 811450, robertward055@aol.com, www.Birdsongtouringpark.com. *6m W of Skegness. S of Gunby r'about on A158, take 1st R signed Bratoft & Burgh-le-Marsh. 1st R again onto Bratoft Lane. L at T-junction, parking on R 25yds.* **Visits by arrangement Apr to June fr groups of 20+. Afternoons 2 until 5 or evenings 6:30 to 9. Adm £4, chd free. Home-made teas on the terrace. Sumptuous home-made cakes, tea in china pots or drinks and canapés.**

Amidst the hustle n bustle that surrounds us everyday, to find a place of peace, search indeed we may. An oasis of calm, tranquility, nature at its best, wildlife and fauna, altogether here at rest. So much to discover, the hours simply do fly by, to uplift and refresh you, inspire you we will try! So get a group of friends visit us and see, you'll be delighted by ALL you'll find, even the cake and tea. Woodland walk and Victorian glasshouse, new prairie border and caravan site pond walk now open. Partial wheelchair access. For assistance please phone ahead of visit.

53 WINDRUSH

Main Road, East Keal, Spilsby, PE23 4BB. Ian & Suzie MacDonald. *On A16, 4m S of Spilsby, opp A155 turning signed West Keal.* **Sun 23 June (11-4). Adm £4, chd free. Home-made teas.**

Country garden of approx 4 acres with herbaceous borders, shrub and climbing roses, clematis and grasses. Woodland walk and ponds, and vegetable garden. Meadow planted in 2018 with orchard of Lincolnshire apples. Shallow steps and some uneven ground and paths.

54 WOODLANDS

Peppin Lane, Fotherby, Louth, LN11 0UW. Ann & Bob Armstrong, www.woodlandsplants.co.uk. *2m N of Louth off A16 signed Fotherby. Please park on R verge opp allotments & walk approx 350 yds to garden. If full please park considerately elsewhere in the village. No parking at garden. Please do not drive beyond designated area.* **Sun 7 Apr, Sun 2 June, Sun 7 July, Sun 4 Aug (11-5); Sun 6 Oct (11-4). Adm £3, chd free. Home-made teas. Opening with Fotherby Gardens on Sun 5 May, Sun 1 Sept.**

A lovely mature woodland garden where a multitude of unusual plants are the stars, many of which are available from the well stocked RHS listed nursery. The two new areas completed recently have developed well and this year there will be a new border for late interest to coincide with an October opening. Award winning professional artist's studio/gallery open to visitors. Specialist collection of Codonopsis for which Plant Heritage status has been granted. Possible to access most areas with care.

NPC

55 YEW TREE FARM

Westhorpe Road, Gosberton, Spalding, PE11 4EP. Robert & Claire Bailey-Scott. *Nr Spalding. Enter the village of Gosberton. Turn into Westhorpe Rd, opp The Bell Inn, cont for approx. 1½m. Property is 3rd on R after bridge.* **Sun 21 July (11-5). Adm £4, chd free. Home-made teas.**

A lovely country garden, 1½ acres. Large herbaceous and mixed borders surround the well kept lawns. Wildlife pond with two bog gardens, woodland garden and shaded borders containing many unusual plants. A mulberry tree forms the centre piece of one lawn. Picturesque annual flower meadow, orchard, wild flower meadow and large vegetable plot. Gardeners World 2018 finalist and featured in Garden News. Gravel driveway, some gravel paths.

LONDON

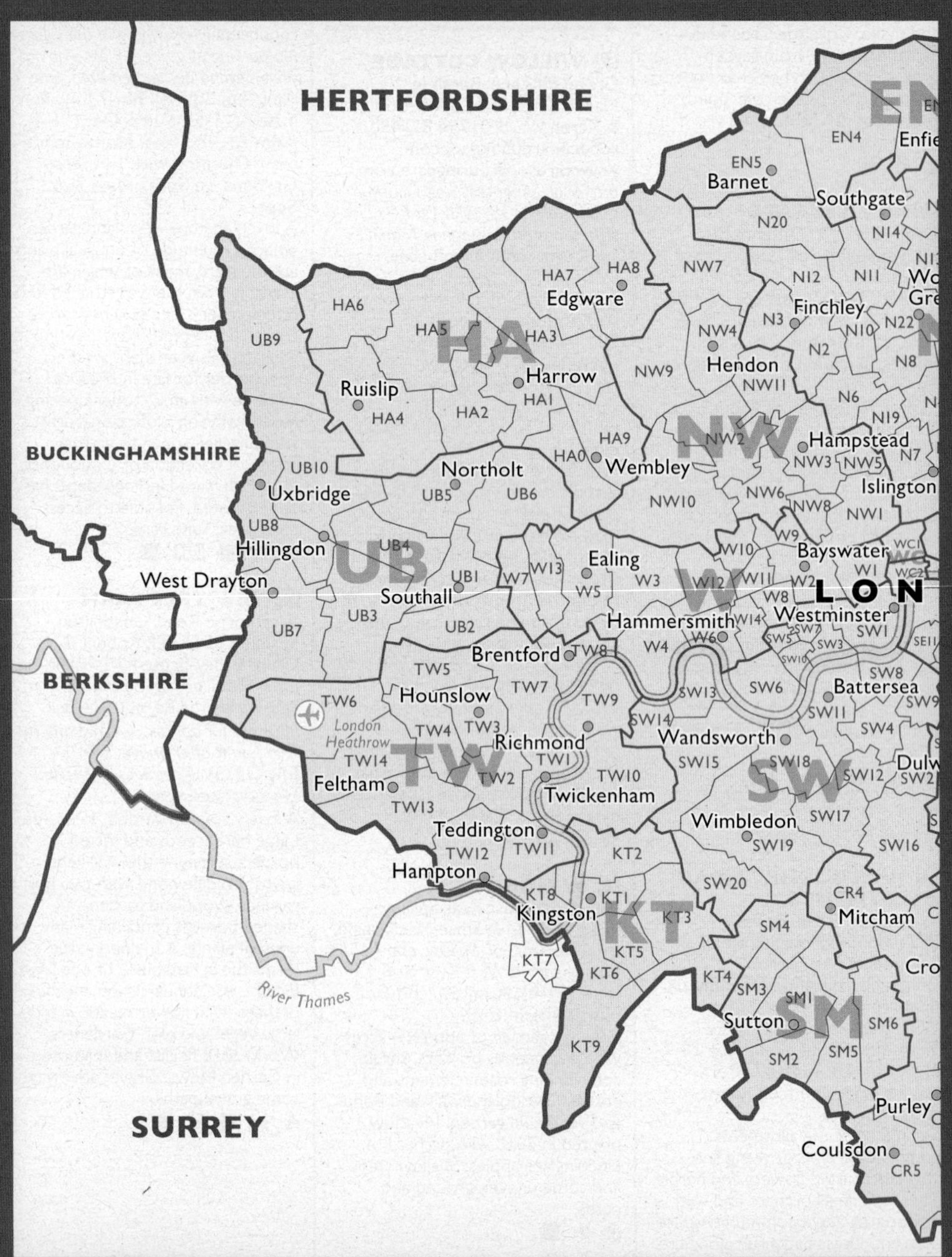
HERTFORDSHIRE
BUCKINGHAMSHIRE
BERKSHIRE
SURREY
River Thames
London Heathrow
EN4
EN5
Barnet
Enfie
Southgate
N20
N14
NW7
N12
N11
HA7
HA8
Edgware
HA6
HA5
HA
HA3
UB9
Finchley
N3
N10
N22
NW4
Hendon
NW11
N2
N8
NW9
Harrow
HA1
Ruislip
HA4
HA2
N6
N19
NW
NW2
Hampstead
HA9
HA0
Wembley
NW3
NW5
N7
BUCKINGHAMSHIRE
UB10
Northolt
UB5
UB6
Uxbridge
Islington
NW6
NW10
NW8
NW1
UB8
Hillingdon
UB4
UB
W9
W10
Bayswater
WC1
W1
Ealing
W13
W7
W5
W3
W12
W11
W2
WC2
West Drayton
UB1
Southall
W8
LON
UB3
UB7
UB2
Hammersmith
W14
Westminster
SW1
W6
W4
SW5
SW7
SW3
SW10
Brentford
TW8
TW5
SW8
Battersea
TW6
TW7
SW13
SW6
Hounslow
TW9
SW11
SW14
SW4
TW4
TW3
Richmond
Wandsworth
TW14
TW1
SW15
SW18
SW
SW12
Dulw
SW2
TW
TW2
TW10
Feltham
Twickenham
TW13
SW17
Wimbledon
Teddington
SW19
SW16
TW12
TW11
KT2
Hampton
SW20
CR4
Mitcham
KT8
KT1
Kingston
KT
KT3
SM4
KT5
KT7
KT6
KT4
Cro
SM3
SM1
SM
Sutton
SM6
KT9
SM2
SM5
Purley
Coulsdon
CR5

ESSEX
KENT
River Thames
Chingford
Edmonton
Woodford Green
Tottenham
Walthamstow
Ilford
Romford
Upminster
Stratford
Barking
Rainham
London City
Thamesmead
Greenwich
Peckham
Lewisham
Eltham
Bexleyheath
Bexley
Sidcup
Chislehurst
Bromley
Orpington
Addington
Biggin Hill
E
IG
RM
SE
DA
BR
CR
TN
0 5 10 kilometres
0 5 miles
© Global Mapping / XYZ Maps

Volunteers

County Organiser
Penny Snell
01932 864532
pennysnellflowers@btinternet.com

County Treasurer
John McNicholas
07785 701770
john@jandjmcnicholas.com

Publicity
Penny Snell (as above)

Booklet Co-ordinator
Sue Phipps
07771 767196
sue@suephipps.com

Booklet Distributor
Joey Clover
020 8870 8740
joeyclover@hotmail.com

Assistant County Organisers

Central London
Eveline Carn
07831 136069
evelinecbcarn@icloud.com

Clapham & surrounding area
Sue Phipps
(as above)

Croydon & outer South London
Ben & Peckham Carroll
0208 777 9012
b.j.carroll@btinternet.com

Dulwich & surrounding area
Clive Pankhurst
07941 536934
alternative.ramblings@gmail.com

E London
Teresa Farnham
07761 476651
farnhamz@yahoo.co.uk

Hackney
Philip Lightowlers
020 8533 0052
plighto@gmail.com

Hampstead
Joan Arnold
020 8444 8752
joan.arnold40@gmail.com

Hampstead Garden Suburb, Finchley & Barnet
Caroline Broome
020 8444 2329
carosgarden@virginmedia.com

Islington
Penelope Darby Brown
020 7226 6880
pendarbybrown@blueyonder.co.uk

Gill Evansky
020 7359 2484
gevansky@gmail.com

Northwood, Pinner, Ruislip & Harefield
Hasruty Patel
07815 110050
hasruty@gmail.com

NW London
Susan Bennett & Earl Hyde
020 8883 8540
suebearlh@yahoo.co.uk

Outer NW London
James Duncan Mattoon
020 8830 7410
jamesmattoon@msn.com

Outer W London
Julia Hickman
020 8339 0931
julia.hickman@virgin.net

SE London
Janine Wookey
07711 279636
j.wookey@btinternet.com

SW London
Joey Clover
(as above)

W London, Barnes & Chiswick
Siobhan McCammon
07952 889866
siobhan.mccammon@gmail.com

From the tiniest to the largest, London gardens offer exceptional diversity. Hidden behind historic houses in Spitalfields are exquisite tiny gardens, while on Kingston Hill there are 9 acres of landscaped Japanese gardens.

The oldest private garden in London boasts 5 acres, while the many other historic gardens within these pages are smaller – some so tiny there is only room for a few visitors at a time – but nonetheless full of innovation, colour and horticultural excellence.

London allotments have attracted television cameras to film their productive acres, where exotic Cape gooseberries, figs, prizewinning roses and even bees all thrive thanks to the skill and enthusiasm of city gardeners.

The traditional sit comfortably with the contemporary in London – offering a feast of elegant borders, pleached hedges, topiary, gravel gardens and the cooling sound of water – while to excite the adventurous there are gardens on barges and green roofs to explore.

The season stretches from April to October, so there is nearly always a garden to visit somewhere in London. Our gardens opening this year are the beating heart of the capital just waiting to be visited and enjoyed.

LONDON GARDENS LISTED BY POSTCODE

Inner London Postcodes

E and EC London

Spitalfields Gardens E1
Lower Clapton Gardens E5
84 Lavender Grove E8
Mapledene Gardens E8
17 Greenstone Mews E11
37 Harold Road E11
10 Wellesley Road E11
51 Tweedmouth Road E13
87 St Johns Road E17
46 Cheyne Avenue E18
25 Mulberry Way E18
The Charterhouse EC1
The Inner and Middle Temple Gardens EC4

N and NW London

37 Alwyne Road N1
Arlington Square Gardens N1
Barnsbury Group N1
4 Canonbury Place N1
13 College Cross N1
De Beauvoir Gardens N1
Diespeker Wharf N1
91 Englefield Road N1
58 Halliford Street N1
King Henry's Walk Garden N1
2 Lonsdale Square N1
20 St Mary's Grove N1
19 St Peter's Street N1
131 Southgate Road N1
66 Abbots Gardens N2
12 Lauradale Road N2
24 Twyford Avenue N2
18 Park Crescent N3
7 The Grove N6
3 The Park N6
Southwood Lodge N6
5 Blackthorn Av Apartment 5 N7
33 Huddleston Road N7
1a Hungerford Road N7
60 & 62 Hungerford Road N7
23 & 24b Penn Road N7
19 Coolhurst Road N8
12 Fairfield Road N8
11 Park Avenue North N8
35 Weston Park N8
Princes Avenue Gardens N10
5 St Regis Close N10
25 Springfield Avenue N10
33 Wood Vale N10
94 Brownlow Road N11
9 Churston Gardens N11
Golf Course Allotments N11
46 Ollerton Road N11
2 Conway Road N14
70 Farleigh Road N16
53 Manor Road N16
15 Norcott Road N16
21 Gospatrick Road N17
36 Ashley Road N19
21 Oakleigh Park South N20
20 Hillcrest N21
91 Vicar's Moor Lane N21
95 Woodland Way N21
Railway Cottages N22
Garden of Medicinal Plants NW1
69 Gloucester Crescent NW1
70 Gloucester Crescent NW1
The Holme NW1
4 Park Village East (Tower Lodge Garden) NW1
98 Parkway NW1
106 Dartmouth Rd Flat 1 NW2
93 Tanfield Avenue NW2
58A Teignmouth Road NW2
208 Walm Lane The Garden Flat NW2
Fenton House NW3
Marie Curie Hospice Hampstead NW3
27 Nassington Road NW3
Tudor Herbalist Garden NW3
Copthall Group NW7
Highwood Ash NW7
Hampstead Garden Suburb Gardens NW11
5 Hill Close NW11

SE and SW London

Garden Barge Square at Downings Roads Moorings SE1
The Garden Museum SE1
Lambeth Palace SE1
35 Camberwell Grove SE5
Camberwell Grove Gardens SE5
24 Grove Park SE5
226 Conisborough Crescent SE6
41 Southbrook Road SE12
Blackheath Gardens SE13
101 Pepys Road SE14
Choumert Square SE15
Lyndhurst Square Group SE15
4 Becondale Road SE19
Court Lane Gardens SE21
103 and 105 Dulwich Village SE21
4 Cornflower Terrace SE22
86 Underhill Road SE22
Forest Hill Gardens Group SE23
5 Burbage Road SE24
2 Shardcroft Avenue SE24
South London Botanical Institute SE24
Cadogan Place South Garden SW1
Eaton Square Garden SW1
Eccleston Square SW1
Chelsea Physic Garden SW3
51 The Chase SW4
4 Franconia Road SW4
2 Littlebury Road SW4
Royal Trinity Hospice SW4
35 Turret Grove SW4
The Hurlingham Club SW6
7 Spencer Road SW18
97 Arthur Road SW19
123 South Park Road SW19
Paddock Allotments & Leisure Gardens SW20

W and WC London

Rooftopvegplot W1
Hyde Park Estate Gardens W2
41 Mill Hill Road W3
65 Mill Hill Road W3
Zen Garden at Japanese Temple W3
Chiswick Mall Gardens W4
Park Road Gardens W4
All Seasons W5
38 York Road W5
10 Loris Road W6
Maggie's West London W6
27 St Peters Square W6
White Cottage W7
1 York Close W7
Edwardes Square W8
57 St Quintin Avenue W10
Arundel & Elgin Gardens W11
Arundel & Ladbroke Gardens W11
12 Lansdowne Road W11
49 Loftus Road W12
57 Tonbridge House WC1H

Outer London Postcodes

12 Overbrae BR3
209 Worsley Bridge Road BR3
2 Springhurst Close CR0
Whitgift School CR2
West Lodge Park EN4
190 Barnet Road EN5
45 Great North Road EN5
57 King Edward Road EN5
26 Normandy Avenue EN5
36 Potters Lane EN5
31 Arlington Drive HA4
4 Manningtree Road HA4
12 Haywood Close HA5
470 Pinner Road HA5
4 Ormonde Road HA6
74 Glengall Road IG8
20 Goldhaze Close IG8
The Watergardens KT2
The Circle Garden KT3
Hampton Court Palace KT8
5 Pemberton Road KT8
61 Wolsey Road KT8
40 Ember Lane KT10
9 Imber Park Road KT10
40 The Crescent SM2
7 St George's Road TW1
20 Beechwood Avenue TW9
Kew Green Gardens TW9
Marksbury Avenue Gardens TW9
20 Taylor Avenue TW9
28 Taylor Avenue TW9
Trumpeters House & Sarah's Garden TW9
31 West Park Road TW9
Ormeley Lodge TW10
Petersham House TW10
Stokes House TW10
12 Gloucester Road TW12
16 Links View Road TW12
Dragon's Dream Grove Lane UB8
Church Gardens UB9
Swakleys Cottage 2 The Avenue UB10

OPENING DATES

All entries subject to change. For latest information check **www.ngs.org.uk**

February

Snowdrop Festival

Sunday 17th

7 The Grove, N6

March

Sunday 31st

4 Canonbury Place, N1

April

Monday 1st

◆ Chelsea Physic Garden, SW3

Sunday 7th

NEW Hyde Park Estate Gardens, W2

Royal Trinity Hospice, SW4

Sunday 14th

Edwardes Square, W8

7 The Grove, N6

South London Botanical Institute, SE24

Thursday 18th

◆ Hampton Court Palace, KT8

Sunday 28th

51 The Chase, SW4

5 St Regis Close, N10

May

Thursday 2nd

51 The Chase, SW4

12 Lansdowne Road, W11

Sunday 5th

27 St Peters Square, W6

Southwood Lodge, N6

The Watergardens, KT2

Monday 6th

King Henry's Walk Garden, N1

Saturday 11th

Cadogan Place South Garden, SW1

The Circle Garden, KT3

Sunday 12th

5 Burbage Road, SE24

74 Glengall Road, IG8

58 Halliford Street, N1

Princes Avenue Gardens, N10

20 St Mary's Grove, N1

86 Underhill Road, SE22

West Lodge Park, EN4

Saturday 18th

The Circle Garden, KT3

Eaton Square Garden, SW1W

Garden of Medicinal Plants, NW1

69 Gloucester Crescent, NW1

70 Gloucester Crescent, NW1

NEW 12 Gloucester Road, TW12

The Hurlingham Club, SW6

NEW 98 Parkway, NW1

Sunday 19th

Arundel & Elgin Gardens, W11

Arundel & Ladbroke Gardens, W11

Eccleston Square, SW1

Forest Hill Gardens Group, SE23

NEW 12 Gloucester Road, TW12

15 Norcott Road, N16

3 The Park, N6

Royal Trinity Hospice, SW4

Whitgift School, CR2

Monday 20th

Lambeth Palace, SE1

Friday 24th

Chiswick Mall Gardens, W4

Saturday 25th

16 Links View Road, TW12

Sunday 26th

36 Ashley Road, N19

Chiswick Mall Gardens, W4

Dragon's Dream, Grove Lane, UB8

NEW 91 Englefield Road, N1

Garden Barge Square at Downings Roads Moorings, SE1

37 Harold Road, E11

Kew Green Gardens, TW9

16 Links View Road, TW12

NEW 36 Potters Lane, EN5

NEW White Cottage, W7

Monday 27th

36 Ashley Road, N19

June

Saturday 1st

Maggie's West London, W6

Zen Garden at Japanese Temple, W3

Sunday 2nd

66 Abbots Gardens, N2

37 Alwyne Road, N1

31 Arlington Drive, HA4

190 Barnet Road, EN5

Barnsbury Group, N1

35 Camberwell Grove, SE5

Choumert Square, SE15

NEW 9 Churston Gardens, N11

13 College Cross, N1

19 Coolhurst Road, N8

4 Cornflower Terrace, SE22

Diespeker Wharf, N1

12 Fairfield Road, N8

21 Gospatrick Road, N17

Kew Green Gardens, TW9

2 Lonsdale Square, N1

NEW 10 Loris Road, W6

Lower Clapton Gardens, E5

Marksbury Avenue Gardens, TW9

Park Road Gardens, W4

NEW 101 Pepys Road, SE14

19 St Peter's Street, N1

123 South Park Road, SW19

Stokes House, TW10

208 Walm Lane, The Garden Flat, NW2

NEW White Cottage, W7

Zen Garden at Japanese Temple, W3

Tuesday 4th

◆ Fenton House, NW3

Wednesday 5th

The Charterhouse, EC1

Saturday 8th

41 Southbrook Road, SE12

Spitalfields Gardens, E1

Trumpeters House & Sarah's Garden, TW9

Sunday 9th

Arlington Square Gardens, N1

Blackheath Gardens, SE13

Copthall Group, NW7

De Beauvoir Gardens, N1

7 The Grove, N6

12 Haywood Close, HA5

NEW 20 Hillcrest, N21

1a Hungerford Road, N7

60 & 62 Hungerford Road, N7

84 Lavender Grove, E8

49 Loftus Road, W12

Mapledene Gardens, E8

27 Nassington Road, NW3

NEW 5 Pemberton Road, KT8

NEW Swakleys Cottage, 2 The Avenue, UB10

NEW 20 Taylor Avenue, TW9

NEW 28 Taylor Avenue, TW9

91 Vicar's Moor Lane, N21

31 West Park Road, TW9

61 Wolsey Road, KT8

Sunday 16th

97 Arthur Road, SW19

40 The Crescent, SM2

103 and 105 Dulwich Village, SE21

5 Hill Close, NW11

Ormeley Lodge, TW10

5 St Regis Close, N10

25 Springfield Avenue, N10

2 Springhurst Close, CR0

Saturday 22nd

Zen Garden at Japanese Temple, W3

Sunday 23rd
20 Beechwood Avenue, TW9
5 Blackthorn Av, Apartment 5, N7
NEW 40 Ember Lane, KT10
NEW Court Lane Gardens, SE21
9 Imber Park Road, KT10
57 King Edward Road, EN5
Lyndhurst Square Group, SE15
12 Overbrae, BR3
11 Park Avenue North, N8
18 Park Crescent, N3
209 Worsley Bridge Road, BR3
Zen Garden at Japanese Temple, W3

Tuesday 25th
The Inner and Middle Temple Gardens, EC4

Saturday 29th
All Seasons, W5
The Holme, NW1
Paddock Allotments & Leisure Gardens, SW20
10 Wellesley Road, E11
1 York Close, W7

Sunday 30th
All Seasons, W5
NEW 70 Farleigh Road, N16
Highwood Ash, NW7
The Holme, NW1
NEW 131 Southgate Road, N1
57 Tonbridge House, WC1H
1 York Close, W7

July

Saturday 6th
Rooftopvegplot, W1

Sunday 7th
Camberwell Grove Gardens, SE5
46 Cheyne Avenue, E18
Hampstead Garden Suburb Gardens, NW11
33 Huddleston Road, N7
Marie Curie Hospice, Hampstead, NW3
23 & 24b Penn Road, N7
Railway Cottages, N22
Rooftopvegplot, W1
57 St Quintin Avenue, W10
Tudor Herbalist Garden, NW3

Saturday 13th
NEW 226 Conisborough Crescent, SE6

Sunday 14th
94 Brownlow Road, N11
NEW 226 Conisborough Crescent, SE6
NEW 25 Mulberry Way, E18
26 Normandy Avenue, EN5
46 Ollerton Road, N11
2 Shardcroft Avenue, SE24
93 Tanfield Avenue, NW2
24 Twyford Avenue, N2

Thursday 18th
◆ Hampton Court Palace, KT8

Friday 19th
41 Mill Hill Road, W3
65 Mill Hill Road, W3

Sunday 21st
190 Barnet Road, EN5
4 Manningtree Road, HA4
46 Ollerton Road, N11
18 Park Crescent, N3
57 St Quintin Avenue, W10
5 St Regis Close, N10
35 Turret Grove, SW4
38 York Road, W5

Sunday 28th
NEW 4 Becondale Road, SE19

August

Saturday 3rd
4 Franconia Road, SW14
The Holme, NW1

Sunday 4th
69 Gloucester Crescent, NW1
70 Gloucester Crescent, NW1
45 Great North Road, EN5
The Holme, NW1

Monday 5th
87 St Johns Road, E17

Sunday 11th
20 Goldhaze Close, IG8
17 Greenstone Mews, E11

Sunday 18th
41 Mill Hill Road, W3
65 Mill Hill Road, W3
51 Tweedmouth Road, E13
NEW 35 Weston Park, N8

Monday 26th
Church Gardens, UB9

Thursday 29th
NEW 7 Spencer Road, SW18

September

Sunday 1st
2 Conway Road, N14
Golf Course Allotments, N11
24 Grove Park, SE5
Royal Trinity Hospice, SW4
33 Wood Vale, N10

Saturday 7th
NEW 226 Conisborough Crescent, SE6
◆ The Garden Museum, SE1

Sunday 8th
NEW 12 Lauradale Road, N2
2 Littlebury Road, SW4
NEW 21 Oakleigh Park South, N20
NEW 95 Woodland Way, N21

Wednesday 11th
NEW 4 Becondale Road, SE19

Sunday 15th
190 Barnet Road, EN5
NEW 106 Dartmouth Rd, Flat 1, NW2
53 Manor Road, N16
4 Ormonde Road, HA6
58A Teignmouth Road, NW2

Sunday 22nd
470 Pinner Road, HA5

October

Sunday 20th
The Watergardens, KT2
West Lodge Park, EN4

By Arrangement

Arrange a personalised garden visit with your club, or group of friends, on a date to suit you. See individual garden entries for full details.

8 Almack Road, Lower Clapton Gardens, E5
Arundel & Ladbroke Gardens, W11
36 Ashley Road, N19
190 Barnet Road, EN5
20 Beechwood Avenue, TW9
5 Burbage Road, SE24
35 Camberwell Grove, SE5
40 The Crescent, SM2
48 Erskine Hill, NW11, Hampstead Garden Suburb Gardens, NW11
Garden of Medicinal Plants, NW1
69 Gloucester Crescent, NW1
70 Gloucester Crescent, NW1
20 Goldhaze Close, IG8
21 Gospatrick Road, N17
45 Great North Road, EN5
7 The Grove, N6
5 Hill Close, NW11
27 Horniman Drive, Forest Hill Gardens Group, SE23
1a Hungerford Road, N7
Kew Green Gardens, TW9
84 Lavender Grove, E8
49 Loftus Road, W12
53 Mapledene Road, Mapledene Gardens, E8
41 Mill Hill Road, W3
65 Mill Hill Road, W3
94 Oakwood Road, Hampstead Garden Suburb Gardens, NW11

4 Park Village East (Tower Lodge Garden), NW1
3 The Park, N6
Petersham House, TW10
7 St George's Road, TW1
27 St Peters Square, W6
57 St Quintin Avenue, W10
5 St Regis Close, N10
41 Southbrook Road, SE12
Southwood Lodge, N6
Stokes House, TW10
58A Teignmouth Road, NW2
74 Willifield Way, NW11, Hampstead Garden Suburb Gardens, NW11
86 Willifield Way, NW11, Hampstead Garden Suburb Gardens, NW11
61 Wolsey Road, KT8
33 Wood Vale, N10

THE GARDENS

66 ABBOTS GARDENS, N2

East Finchley, N2 0JH. Stephen & Ruth Kersley. *6 mins walk from rear exit East Finchley tube on Causeway to East End Rd. 2nd L into Abbots Gardens. 143 stops at Abbots Gardens on East End Rd. 102, 263 & 234 all go to East Finchley High Rd.* **Sun 2 June (2-5.30). Adm £4, chd free. Home-made teas.**

Combining grass and glass: Stephen studied garden design at Capel Manor and Ruth is a glass artist. Designed for yr round interest, this garden creates a calming yet dramatic environment through plant form, colour, texture and asymmetrical geometry. Glass amphorae and feathers catch the eye suspended amongst grasses, ornamental shrubs, perennials, a vegetable plot, mosaics and water features.

ALL SEASONS, W5

97 Grange Road, Ealing, W5 3PH. Dr Benjamin & Mrs Maria Royappa. *Tube: Ealing Broadway/ South Ealing/Ealing Common: 10-15 mins walk.* **Sat 29, Sun 30 June (1-6). Adm £4, chd free.**

Garden designed, built and planted by owners, with several interesting plants ,some of them acclamatised to London weather, incl ponds, pergolas, Japanese garden, Tropical house for orchids, exotics and aviaries. Several recycled features, composting and rain water harvesting, orchard with fruiting kiwi and grape vines,several Clematis architectural and unusual plants. Partial wheelchair access.

37 ALWYNE ROAD, N1

London, N1 2HW. Mr & Mrs J Lambert. *Buses: 38, 56, 73, 341 on Essex Rd; 4, 19, 30, 43 on Upper St, alight at Town Hall; 271 on Canonbury Rd, A1. Tube: Highbury & Islington.* **Sun 2 June (2-5). Adm £5, chd free. Home-made teas. Also open 13 College Cross.** Donation to The Friends of the Rose Bowl.

The New River curves around the garden, freeing it from the constraints of the usual London rectangle and allowing differing degrees of formality - roses along the river, topiary, a secluded spot where the life of the river is part of the charm. Visitors return to see what's new and to enjoy the spectacular array of very good home-made cakes. Shelter if it rains. Wheelchair access only with own assistant for 3 shallow entrance steps.

31 ARLINGTON DRIVE, HA4

Ruislip, HA4 7RJ. John & Yasuko O'Gorman. *Tube: Ruislip. Then bus H13 to Arlington Drive, or 15 mins walk up Bury St. Arlington Drive is opp Millar & Carter Steakhouse on Bury St.* **Sun 2 June (2-5.30). Adm £3.50, chd free. Home-made teas.**

Cottage garden at heart with a wonderful oriental influence. Traditional cottage garden favourites have been combined with Japanese plants - a reflection of Yasuko's passion for plants and trees of her native Japan. Acers, paeonies, rhododendrons and flowering cherries underplanted with hostas, ferns and hellebores, create a lush exotic scheme. Emphasis on structure and texture.

GROUP OPENING

ARLINGTON SQUARE GARDENS, N1

London, N1 7DP. www.arlingtonassociation.org.uk. *South Islington. Off New North Rd via Arlington Ave or Linton St. Buses: 21, 76, 141, 271.* **Sun 9 June (2-5.30). Combined adm £6, chd free. Home-made teas at St James' Vicarage, 1A Arlington Square.**

26 ARLINGTON AVENUE, N1

Thomas Blaikie.

27 ARLINGTON SQUARE

Geoffrey Wheat & Rev Justin Gau.

25 ARLINGTON SQUARE

Michael Foley.

30 ARLINGTON SQUARE

James & Maria Hewson.

ST JAMES' VICARAGE, 1A ARLINGTON SQUARE

John & Maria Burniston.

Behind the early Victorian facades of Arlington Square and Arlington Avenue are 5 contrasting town gardens; 4 plantsmen's gardens and a delightful spacious garden at the Vicarage with an impressive herbaceous border created over the last few years, and mature London Plane trees. The group reflects the diverse tastes and interests of each garden owner, who know each other through the community gardening of Arlington Square. It is hard to believe you are minutes from the bustle of the City of London. Live Music at St James' Vicarage.

97 ARTHUR ROAD, SW19

Wimbledon, SW19 7DP. Tony & Bella Covill. *Wimbledon Park tube, then 200yds up hill on R.* **Sun 16 June (2-6). Adm £5, chd free. Light refreshments.**

½ acre garden of an Edwardian house. Garden est. for more than 25yrs, constantly evolving with a large variety of plants and shrubs. It has grown up around several lawns with ponds and fountains, encouraging an abundance of wildlife and a bird haven. A beautiful place with much colour, foliage and texture. New gravel garden, planting to attract butterflies.

ARUNDEL & ELGIN GARDENS, W11

Kensington Park Road, Notting Hill, W11 2JD. Residents of Arundel Gardens & Elgin Crescent, www.arundelandelgingardens.org. *Entrance opp 174 Kensington Park Rd. Nearest tube within walking distance: Ladbroke Grove (3mins) or Notting Hill (8mins). Buses: 52, 452, 23, 228 all stop opp garden entrance.* **Sun 19 May (12-5). Adm £5, chd free. Home-made teas. Also open Arundel & Ladbroke Gardens.**

A friendly and informal garden square with mature and rare trees, plants and shrubs laid out according to the original Victorian design of 1862, one of the best preserved gardens of the Ladbroke estate. The central hedged garden area is an oasis of tranquillity with extensive and colourful herbaceous borders. The garden incl several topiary hedges, a rare Mulberry tree, a pergola and benches from which the vistas can be enjoyed. Gardeners Chris Jelston & Anna Park. Play areas for young children.

ARUNDEL & LADBROKE GARDENS, W11

Kensington Park Road, Notting Hill, W11 2EP. Arundel & Ladbroke Gardens Committee, 07941 296375 (texts preferred), susan.lynn1@ntlworld.com, www.arundelladbrokegardens.co.uk. *Entrance on Kensington Park Rd, between Ladbroke & Arundel Gardens. Tube: Notting Hill Gate or Ladbroke Grove. Buses: 23, 52, 228, 452. Alight at stop for Portobello Market/Arundel Gardens.* **Sun 19 May (2-6). Adm £4, chd free. Home-made teas. Also open Arundel & Elgin Gardens.** Visits also by arrangement.

This private communal garden is one of the few that retains its attractive mid Victorian design of lawns and winding paths. A woodland garden at its peak in spring, with rhododendrons, flowering dogwoods, early roses, bulbs, ferns and rare exotics. Live music on the lawn during tea. Playground for small children. A few steps and gravel paths to negotiate.

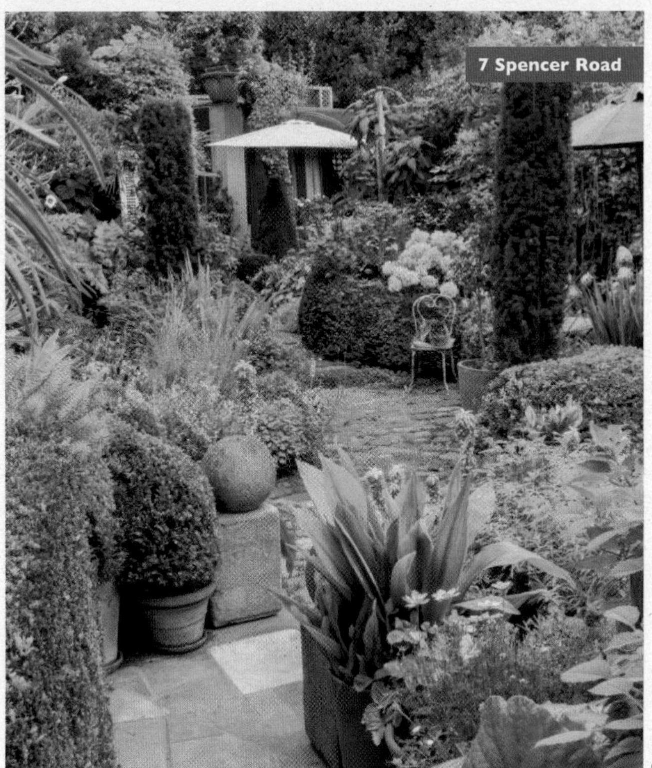

7 Spencer Road

© Marianne Majerus

36 ASHLEY ROAD, N19

London, N19 3AF. Alan Swann & Ahmed Farooqui, 07506 128638, swann.alan@googlemail.com. *Between Stroud Green & Crouch End. Underground: Archway or Finsbury Park. Overground: Crouch Hill. Buses: 210 or 41 from Archway to Hornsey Rise. W7 from Finsbury Park to Heathville Road. Car: Free parking in Ashley Road at weekends.* **Sun 26, Mon 27 May (2-6). Adm £3.50, chd free. Home-made teas. Home-brewed ginger beer also available.** Visits also by arrangement May to Sept. Groups are offered a short talk on the design and development of the garden.

A lush town garden rich in textures, colour and forms. At its best in late spring as Japanese maple cultivars display great variety of shape and colour whilst ferns unfurl fresh, vibrant fronds over a tumbling stream and alpines and clematis burst into flower on the rockeries and pergola. The garden has a number of micro habitats incl. ferneries, a bog garden, stream and pond plantings, rockeries, alpines and shade plantings. Young ferns and plants propagated from specimens in the garden for sale. Indoor pop-up cafe with views over the garden when wet. Entrance to the garden is down a flight of 7 steps.

190 BARNET ROAD, EN5
Arkley, Barnet, EN5 3LF. Hilde & Lionel Wainstein, 07949764007, hildewainstein@hotmail.co.uk. *1m S of A1, 2m N of High Barnet tube. Garden located on corner of A411 Barnet Rd & Meadowbanks cul-de-sac. Nearest tube: High Barnet, then 107 bus, Glebe Lane stop. Ample unrestricted roadside parking.* **Sun 2 June, Sun 21 July, Sun 15 Sept (2-6). Adm £4, chd free. Home-made teas.** Visits also by arrangement Apr to Sept.
Garden designer's walled garden, 90ft x 36ft. Modern, idiosyncratic design, year round interest. Flowing herbaceous drifts around trees, shrubs, central pond. Spring, Summer, Autumn bulbs. Upcycled containers, recycled objects and homemade sculptures. Copper trellis divides space into contrasting areas. Garden continues to evolve as planted areas are expanded. Rusty tin can 'Derek Jarman' garden. Selection of home-made cakes worthy of Mary Berry! Favourite at last opening was raspberry and white chocolate layer cake. Gluten free cakes also available. Wide range of interesting plants for sale, all propagated from the garden. Single steps within garden.

GROUP OPENING

BARNSBURY GROUP, N1
Islington, N1 1DB. *Barnsbury, London N1. Tube: King's Cross, Caledonian Rd or Angel. Overground: Caledonian Rd & Barnsbury. Buses: 17, 91, 259 to Caledonian Rd.* **Sun 2 June (2-6). Combined adm £8, chd free. Home-made teas at 57 Huntingdon Street N1 1BX. Also open 13 College Cross.**

BARNSBURY WOOD
London Borough of Islington, ecologycentre@islington.gov.uk.

44 HEMINGFORD ROAD
Peter Willis & Haremi Kudo.

57 HUNTINGDON STREET
Julian Williams.

36 THORNHILL SQUARE
Anna & Christopher McKane.

Within Barnsbury's historic Georgian squares and terraces, discover these four contrasting spaces. Barnsbury Wood is London's smallest nature reserve, a hidden secret and Islington's only site of mature woodland, a tranquil oasis of wild flowers and massive trees just minutes from Caledonian Road. Wildlife info available. The gardens have extensive collections of unusual plants; 57 Huntingdon St is a secluded garden room - an understorey of silver birch and hazel, ferns, native perennials and grasses and two container ponds to encourage wildlife. 44 Hemingford Road is a small, dense composition of trees (some unusual), shrubs, perennials and lawns – and a small pond. 36 Thornhill Square, a 120 ft garden with a country atmosphere, filled with old and new roses and many herbaceous perennials. A bonsai collection will astound! These gardens have evolved over many years and show what can be achieved in differing spaces with the right plants growing in the right conditions, surmounting the difficulties of dry walls and shade. Plants for sale at 36 Thornhill Square.

NEW **4 BECONDALE ROAD, SE19**
Gipsy Hill, Norwood, SE19 1QJ. Mr & Mrs Christopher & Wendy Spink. *Off Gipsy Hill. Nearest stn Gipsy Hill. Buses 3 & 322. Some parking on Becondale rd.* **Sun 28 July (2.30-5). Adm £3.50, chd free. Home-made teas. Evening opening Wed 11 Sept (5-8). Adm £5, chd free. Wine. Canapes.**
This garden takes vertical planting to new heights - but is not for those who are afraid to walk a gangplank. It is packed with a mass of exotic and rich planting with a Mediterranean feel from Bougainvillea to bananas and palms to plumbago. Steeply sloping it maximises every bit of height with plants cascading over high rise balconies and dropping down to a theatrically styled well of a garden. Mediterranean planting on four levels. Regret, that because of narrow paths and verticality this garden is not suitable for small children or mobility challenged.

20 BEECHWOOD AVENUE, TW9
Kew, Richmond, TW9 4DE. Dr Laura de Beden, 02083921969, lauradebeden@hotmail.com, www.lauradebeden.co.uk. *Within walking distance of Kew Gardens Tube Station on East side exit.* **Evening opening Sun 23 June (5-7.30). Adm £5.50, chd free. Wine.** **Visits also by arrangement May & June for groups of 5 to 10.**
Delightful town garden minutes away from Royal Botanic Gardens and Kew Retail Park. Minimalist layout by the designer owner offsets exquisite favourite plant combinations. Writing shed holds pride of place as safe refuge & main idea production centre. Topiary, pots, sculpture, surprises (the latest in the new small fernery) and good humour are all on offer for an inspiring innovative visit.

GROUP OPENING

BLACKHEATH GARDENS, SE13
Lewisham, London, SE13 7EA. *Gardens sit between Lewisham, Lee & Blackheath stns. DLR: Buses 54, 89, 108, 202, 122, 178, 261, 321, 621 Free parking on Sundays but space limited.* **Sun 9 June (2-5). Combined adm £7, chd free. Home-made teas at Lee Rd, Michael's Cl & Southbrook Rd.**

28 GRANVILLE PARK
Joanna Herald, www.joannaherald.com.
D

49 LEE ROAD
Jane Glynn & Colin Kingsnorth.

1 MICHAEL'S CLOSE
Jeffrey Warren.

41 SOUTHBROOK ROAD
Barbara & Marek Polanski, 020 8333 2176, polanski101@yahoo.co.uk. Visits also by arrangement May to Aug for groups of 10 to 20.

Grouped together for the 1st time are four lovely gardens, set among the gentle hills and winding roads of Blackheath area. A love of roses is a common thread. In Michael's Cl, a magnificent Rambling Rector rose blankets a hawthorn hedge with densely planted borders defined by paths, steps and low retaining walls. Shade rules in the garden designer's softly contoured family space in Granville Park which offers a wildlife friendly pool, herbaceous and lush shrub plantings. A sunken terrace provides a suntrap seating area. A generous oasis of calm in Lee Rd. Benches are set beneath rambling roses overlooking sweeps of formal lawns with flowerbeds. Paths through silver birches and grasses reveal a treehouse clad with roses and clematis. Incl a prolific vegetable garden. A little further lies a well bedded in garden in Southbrook Rd with an abundance of big rambling roses. An abundance of everything in fact from Indian pergolas to lily ponds , box parterres and ancient pear trees & seating. Plants for sale at Granville Park, Lee Road and Michael's Close. See NGS website for trail map

5 BLACKTHORN AV, APARTMENT 5, N7

London, N7 8AQ. Juan Carlos Cure Hazzi. *Barnsbury. 5 min walk from Highbury & Islington Stn. Building is on south side of Arundel Sq.* **Sun 23 June (11-5). Adm £5, chd free. Pre-booking essential, please visit www.ngs.org.uk for information & booking. Light refreshments.**

Small patio garden with lush tropical, sub-tropical and temperate plants. The garden has been featured frequently in BBC Gardeners' World magazine, the English Garden magazine and a finalist in the Small Space category competition as well as on YouTube. It has a beautiful connection with the house, not wasting an inch of space, with plenty of colour, texture and year-round interest.

94 BROWNLOW ROAD, N11

Bounds Green, N11 2BS. Spencer Viner, www.northeleven.co.uk. *Close to N Circular. Tube: Bounds Green then 5 mins walk, direction N Circular. Corner of Elvendon Rd & Brownlow Rd.* **Sun 14 July (2-6). Adm £3, chd free. Light refreshments. Also open 46 Ollerton Road.**

A small courtyard for meditation. The conception of this garden by a designer transports the visitor to a different, foreign place of imagination and tranquillity, far away from the suburbs. Features incl reclaimed materials, trees, water, pergola, pleached limes, seating and a strong theme of pared back simplicity. Design and horticultural advice available.

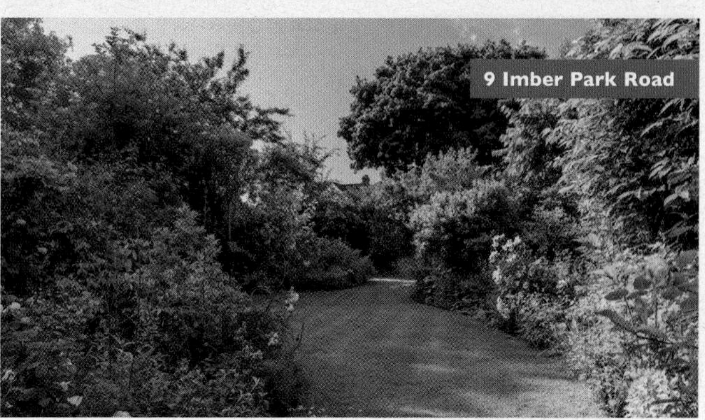
9 Imber Park Road
© Matthew Bruce

5 BURBAGE ROAD, SE24

Herne Hill, SE24 9HJ. Crawford & Rosemary Lindsay, 020 7274 5610, rl@rosemarylindsay.com, www.rosemarylindsay.com. *Nr junction with Half Moon Lane. Herne Hill & N Dulwich mainline stns, 5 mins walk. Buses: 3, 37, 40, 68, 196, 468.* **Sun 12 May (2-5). Adm £4, chd free. Home-made teas.** Visits also by arrangement Mar to June.

Much photographed garden of a member of The Society of Botanical Artists. 150ft x 40ft with varied range of plants. Herbaceous borders for sun and shade, climbers, pots, terraces, lawns. Gravel areas to reduce watering. Diseased box has beenreplaced with alternatives. A garden for all seasons. See our website for what the papers say. Incl in The London Garden book A-Z. Popular plants sale.

CADOGAN PLACE SOUTH GARDEN, SW1

Sloane Street, Chelsea, SW1X 9PE. The Cadogan Estate, www.cadogan.co.uk. *Entrance to garden opp 97 Sloane St.* **Sat 11 May (10-4). Adm £4, chd free. Home-made teas.**

Many surprises and unusual trees and shrubs are hidden behind the railings of this large London square. The first square to be developed by architect Henry Holland for Lord Cadogan at the end of C18, it was then called the London Botanic Garden. Mulberry trees planted for silk production at end of C17. Cherry trees, magnolias and bulbs are outstanding in spring. Beautiful 300 year old Black Mulberry Tree (originally planted to produce silk, but incorrect variety!). Once home to the Royal Botanic Garden. Also features a Bug Hotel & Children's playground.

35 CAMBERWELL GROVE, SE5

London, SE5 8JA. Lynette Hemmant & Juri Gabriel, 020 7703 6186, juri@jurigabriel.com. *Backing onto St Giles Church, Camberwell Church St. From Camberwell Green go down Camberwell Church St. Turn R into Camberwell Grove.* **Sun 2 June (12-6.30). Adm £3.50, chd free. Light refreshments.** Visits also by arrangement May to July for groups of 20 to 30. Minimum fee £70. Donation to St Giles Church.

Plant packed 120ft x 20ft garden with charming backdrop of St Giles Church. Evolved over 30yrs into a romantic country style garden brimming with colour and overflowing with pots. In June, spectacular roses stretch the full length of the garden, both on the artist's studio and festooning an old iron staircase. Artist's studio open. Lynette has painted the garden obsessively for the past 20yrs; see her (lynettehemmant.com) and NGS websites.

GROUP OPENING

CAMBERWELL GROVE GARDENS, SE5

Camberwell, SE5 8JE. *10 mins from Denmark Hill mainline & overgound stn. Buses: 12, 36, 68, 148, 171, 176, 185, 436. Entrance through garden rooms at rear.* **Sun 7 July (2-6). Combined adm £5, chd free. Home-made teas. Wine available.**

81 CAMBERWELL GROVE
Jane & Alex Maitland Hudson.

83 CAMBERWELL GROVE
Robert Hirschhorn & John Hall.

These neighbouring walled gardens behind C18 houses in this beautiful tree lined street open in July. At No.81 a tall Trachycarpus Palm and a magnolia grandiflora shade York stone paving and borders filled with herbaceous perennials and shade loving ground cover. There is a pond and bog garden. Pots of all sizes line the steps to the kitchen door and the terrace outside the garden room and greenhouse. No. 83 is a mature garden, with abundant, unusual planting within a structure of box hedging, providing varied and interesting areas of peace and privacy. As trees mature the nature of the garden is changing, and more shade tolerant perennials are being introduced. Contemporary garden room, gravel and York stone paths and seating areas, calming pool and lovely views of parish church. Home-made cakes and tea at No. 81 and sparkling wine at No. 83.

4 CANONBURY PLACE, N1

London, N1 2NQ. Mr & Mrs Jeffrey Tobias. *Highbury & Islington Tube & Overground. Buses: 271 to Canonbury Square. Located in old part of Canonbury Place, off Alwyne Villas, in a cul de sac.* **Sun 31 Mar (2-5.30). Adm £3.50, chd free. Home-made teas.**

A paved, 100ft garden, with interesting architectural features, echoing the date of the house -1780. Spectacular mature trees enclosed in a walled garden. Mostly pots and also interesting shrubs and climbers. Daffodlils, tulips and bluebells abound for this early springtime opening. Artisan pastries and sourdough bread as supplied to Fortnum & Mason.

THE CHARTERHOUSE, EC1

Charterhouse Square, London, EC1M 6AN. The Governors of Sutton's Hospital, www.thecharterhouse.org. *Buses: 4, 55. Tube: Barbican. Turn L out of stn, L into Carthusian St & into square. Entrance around or through Charterhouse Square.* **Evening opening Wed 5 June (6-9). Adm £5, chd free. Wine. Evening to incl BBQ (additional charge).**

Enclosed courtyard gardens within the grounds of historic Charterhouse, which dates back to 1347. English country garden style featuring roses, herbaceous borders, ancient mulberry trees and small pond. Various garden herbs found here are still used in the kitchen today. In addition, two other areas are being opened for the NGS. Pensioners Court, which is partly maintained by the private tenants and Master's Garden, the old burial ground which now consists of lawns, borders and wildlife garden planted to camouflage a war time air raid shelter. A private garden for the Brothers of Charterhouse, not usually open to the public. (Buildings not open).

51 THE CHASE, SW4

London, SW4 0NP. Mr Charles Rutherfoord & Mr Rupert Tyler, www.charlesrutherfoord.net. *Off Clapham Common Northside. Tube: Clapham Common. Buses: 137, 452.* **Sun 28 Apr (12-5). Evening opening Thur 2 May (5.30-8). Adm £4, chd free. Light refreshments.**

Member of the Society of Garden Designers, Charles has created the garden over 30yrs. In 2015 the main garden was remodelled, to much acclaim. Spectacular in spring, when 2000 tulips bloom among irises and tree peonies. Scented front garden. Rupert's geodetic dome shelters seedlings, succulents and subtropicals.

◆ CHELSEA PHYSIC GARDEN, SW3

66 Royal Hospital Road, London, SW3 4HS. Chelsea Physic Garden Company, 020 7352 5646, www.chelseaphysicgarden.co.uk. *Tube: Sloane Square (10 mins). Bus: 170. Parking: Battersea Park (charged). Entrance in Swan Walk.* **For NGS: Mon 1 Apr (11-6). Adm £11, chd £7.50. Brunches, lunch and afternoon tea at The Physic Garden Café.** For other opening times and information, please phone or visit garden website.

Come and explore London's oldest botanic garden situated in the heart of Chelsea. With a unique living collection of around 5000 plants, this walled garden is a celebration of the importance of plants and their beauty. Highlights incl Europe's oldest pond rockery, the Garden of Edible and Useful Plants, the Garden of Medicinal Plants and the World Woodland Garden. Tours available. Wheelchair access is via 66 Royal Hospital Rd.

46 CHEYNE AVENUE, E18

South Woodford, Essex, E18 2DR. Helen Auty. *Nearest tube S Woodford. Short walk. From station take Clarendon Rd. Cross High Rd into Broadwalk, 3rd on L Bushey Ave. 1st R Cheyne Ave.* **Sun 7 July (12-5). Adm £4, chd free. Home-made teas.**

On site of Lord Cheyne's original market garden, typical suburban garden with lawn and borders of shrubs, climbers and perennials - greenhouse and productive fruit and vegetable garden.

GROUP OPENING

CHISWICK MALL GARDENS, W4

Chiswick, W4 2PR. *Car: Towards Hogarth r'about, A4 (W) turn Eyot Grds S. Tube: Stamford Brook or Turnham Green. Buses: 27, 190, 267 & 391 to Young's Corner. From Chiswick High Rd or Kings St S under A4 to river.* **Evening opening Fri 24 May (6-8). Combined adm £12.50, chd free. Sun 26 May (2-5.30). Combined adm £8, chd free. Tea at 16 Eyot Gardens. On Friday wine at Swan House & Field House.**

16 EYOT GARDENS
Dianne Farris.
Open on all dates

FIELD HOUSE
Rupert King, www.fieldhousegarden.co.uk.
Open on all dates

LONGMEADOW
Charlotte Fraser.
Open on all dates

ST PETERS WHARF
Barbara Brown.
Open on Sun 26 May

SWAN HOUSE
Mr & Mrs George Nissen.
Open on all dates

Five gardens on or nr the River Thames: An exotic water garden, featured in the RHS 'Garden' magazine and in Gardener's World, a riverside garden in an artists' complex, a town house garden with an extensive vegetable garden, a large walled garden with the emphasis on foliage and shade-loving plants, and a small walled garden demonstrating the clever use of restricted space.

CHOUMERT SQUARE, SE15

Peckham, SE15 4RE. The Residents. *Off Choumert Grove. Trains from London Victoria, London Bridge, London Blackfriars, Clapham Junction to Peckham Rye; buses (12, 36, 37, 63, 78, 171, 312, 345). Free Car park (1 min) in Choumert Grove.* **Sun 2 June (1-6). Adm £4, chd free. Light refreshments. We will be serving afternoon teas, a variety of homemade cakes & Pimms.** Donation to St Christopher's Hospice.
About 46 mini gardens with maxi planting in Shangri-la situation that the media has described as a Floral Canyon, which leads to small communal secret garden. The day is primarily about gardens and sharing with others our residents' love of this little corner of the inner city; but it is also renowned for its demonstrable community spirit. Stalls in the style of a village fete and Live Music. The popular open gardens will combine this year with our own take on a village fete with home produce stalls, arts, crafts and music. No steps within the Square just a tiny step to a raised paved space in the communal garden area.

CHURCH GARDENS, UB9

Church Hill, Harefield, Uxbridge, UB9 6DU. Patrick McHugh. *If coming from Harefield Village, continue for ¼ mile down Church Hill. If coming from A40 Uxbridge junction, follow signs to Harefield.* **Mon 26 Aug (2-5). Adm £5, chd £2. Light refreshments.**
Harefield's own 'secret garden'. 17th Century Renaissance walled gardens on the outskirts of Harefield, incl a traditional organic kitchen garden, consisting of 56 geometrically arranged raised beds, 60m long herbaceous borders, trained fruit trees, alpines, herb garden and an orchard with rare arcaded wall, dating back to the early 1600's. Unique opportunity to view ongoing restoration project.

NEW 9 CHURSTON GARDENS, N11

New Southgate, N11 2NJ. Pauline Hamilton. *Tube Bounds Green or Overground Bowes Park both 10 mins walk. Buses 102, 184, 299 and 221.* **Sun 2 June (2-6). Adm £4, chd free. Home-made teas.**
A charming new garden created by the owner over three years combining elegant & contemporary hard landscaping with informal pretty planting. Structure is provided by several specimen trees, evergreens and grasses. These are interspersed with bulbs, roses, clematis and herbaceous perennials in a palette of strong pinks, plums and purples with splashes of orange.

THE CIRCLE GARDEN, KT3

33 Cambridge Avenue, New Malden, KT3 4LD. Vincent & Heidi Johnson-Paul-McDonnell, www.thecirclegarden.com. *1¼m N of A3 Malden junction. Bus: 213. 10 mins walk from New Malden train stn; A3 signposted for Kingston; 213 bus stop located a short distance from end of rd; our house is pink!* **Sat 11, Sat 18 May (2-6). Adm £3.50, chd free. Home-made teas.**
A welcoming front garden with cottage style planting leading to an unexpected rear garden with intriguing vistas where you will find herbaceous and annuals in mixed borders. Relax in the Japanese area, stroll through the potager and chat to our suburban hens. An ever evolving garden with plans for further developments.

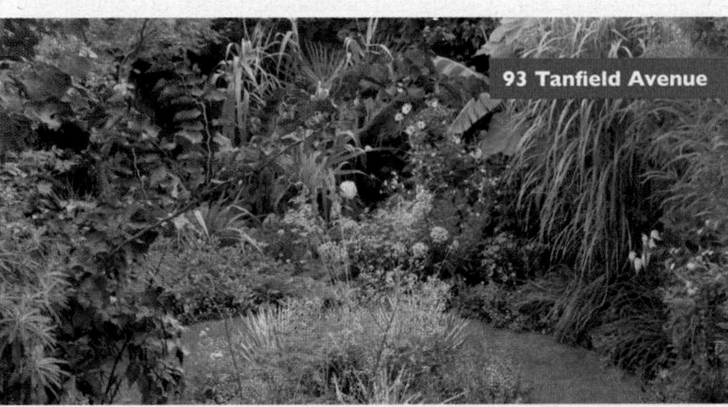

93 Tanfield Avenue

13 COLLEGE CROSS, N1
London, N1 1YY. Diana & Stephen Yakeley. *Barnsbury, Islington. Tube: Highbury & Islington. Buses: 19, 73, 277.* **Sun 2 June (2-6). Adm £3.50, chd free. Also open 2 Lonsdale Square.**
An award winning paved and walled garden 5m x 17m, behind a Georgian terraced house, enclosed by evergreen climbers with mature Bay, Box, Olive and Fig trees. Architectural plants chosen for form and texture in shades of green, enlivened by pots of white flowers. Black slate bench and a glass balustrade provide contemporary design interest.

NEW **226 CONISBOROUGH CRESCENT, SE6**
Catford, SE6 2SF. Alex Redfern & Joe Shannon, www.thegardeningguys.co.uk. *Rail: Bellingham (10 mins) or Catford (15 mins). Approach via Bellingham Road or Daneswood Ave, short walk from A21. Parking in nearby streets.* **Sat 13, Sun 14 July, Sat 7 Sept (11-5). Adm £4, chd free. Home-made teas.**
Award winning Garden, hidden behind this terraced house in South London lies an unexpected tropical oasis. Towering bamboos, bananas, cannas, palms and other lush exotic planting transport you to the tropics. The garden reveals a hidden spa area as you venture through. In contrast the front garden is overflowing with colour from an interesting mix of annuals, perennials and collection of Dahlias. Lush tropical planting.

2 CONWAY ROAD, N14
Southgate, N14 7BA. Eileen Hulse. *Buses: 121 & W6 from Palmers Green or Southgate to Broomfield Park stop. Walk up Aldermans Hill R into Ulleswater Road 1st L into Conway Road.* **Sun 1 Sept (2-6). Adm £4, chd free. Home-made teas.**
A passion, nurtured from childhood, for growing unusual plants has culminated in two contrasting gardens. The original, calming with lawn, pond and greenhouse, compliments the adjoining, Mediterranean terraced rooms with pergolas clothed in exotic climbers, vegetable beds and cordon fruit. Tumbling Achoqcha, figs, datura and Rosa banksiae mingle creating a horticultural adventure. Those unsteady on their feet need to take care.

19 COOLHURST ROAD, N8
Hornsey, Hornsey, London, N8 8EP. Jane Muirhead. *Exit tube at Highgate onto Priory Gardens, L on Shepherd's Hill, R on Stanhope Road, L on Hurst Ave, R on Coolhurst Road (15mins) W7 from Finsbury Park to Crouch End & 5min walk 41 & 91 busses nearby.* **Sun 2 June (2-6). Adm £4, chd free. Home-made teas. Also open 12 Fairfield Road.**
Evolving, organic and wildlife garden with dappled sunlight, bees, birds and butterflies. Informal woodland planting under magnificent deciduous trees with interesting shrubs, box shapes and perennials. Small vegetable patch & wild flower garden where knapweed, campion, honesty, wild carrot & sweet rocket have naturalised. Large lawn with seating. Some steps and uneven surfaces.

GROUP OPENING

COPTHALL GROUP, NW7
Mill Hill, London, NW7 2NB. *Short bus ride (221) from Edgware tube, Mill Hill East and Mill Hill Broadway.* **Sun 9 June (2-5.30). Combined adm £5, chd free. Home-made teas at 2 Copthall Drive.**

2 COPTHALL DRIVE
Janet Jomain.

13 COPTHALL GARDENS
Lise Marshfield.

Two small town gardens enthusiastically gardened by their plantaholic owners. 13 Copthall Gardens is a mature leafy garden in a quiet cul-de-sac. Emphasis on form and texture. Clipped shrubs, topiary, perennials and roses. Small pond. Portal to third dimension. Traditional Finnish swing seat. 2 Copthall Drive is a small east-facing town garden with more than 60 roses and many clematis, alliums, hydrangeas and a wildlife pond. A small but productive fruit and vegetable patch incl nectarines and kiwi fruit, with other exotic plants in the greenhouse.

4 CORNFLOWER TERRACE, SE22
East Dulwich, London, SE22 0HH. Clare Dryhurst. *5 mins walk from 363 & 63 bus stop at bottom of Forest Hill Rd. Turn into Dunstans Rd, then 2nd on L. Stn: Peckham Rye or Honor Oak Park.* **Sun 2 June (2-5.30). Adm £3, chd free. Home-made teas. Also open 101 Pepys Road.**
Among the smallest front and back gardens featured, both have proven powerful, offering a calm retreat to help heal mind and body. Surrounding this East Dulwich terraced cottage are star jasmine, climbing roses, lavender and annuals providing colour & scent. Heucheras & huge bamboo weave cool and shade. Every inch is a tapestry of planting, sculpture, texture and spaces to sit, talk and reflect.

GROUP OPENING

NEW **COURT LANE GARDENS, SE21**
Dulwich Village, SE21 7EA. Jean & Charles Cary-Elwes. *Court Lane, Dulwich. Buses P4, 12, 40, 176, 185 (to Dulwich Library) 37. Mainline; North Dulwich then 12 mins walk. Ample free parking.* **Sun 23 June (2-5.30). Combined adm £8, chd free. Home-made teas.**

122 COURT LANE, SE21
Jean & Charles Cary-Elwes.

125 COURT LANE, SE21
Stephen Henden & Neil Ellis.

NEW **164 COURT LANE**
Mrs Katie Dawes.

Three beautifully tended and contrasting gardens. 164, backing on the Park, is newly designed. Intimate zones wind through an enchanting space with colourful abundant borders, vegetables, a cottage garden with rose arch and an impressive mature oak. 125, developed over 15 years and renowned for delicious cakes and tea, has winding paths that weave between eclectic, deep herbaceous borders with a broad palette of colours and plants of vibrant interest. 122 is a generously proportioned garden with deep, colourful herbaceous borders.

Backing onto the Park, it has a countryside feel with live Jazz on the terrace, a children's trail, plant sales and a wormery demonstration. Jazz at 122.

40 THE CRESCENT, SM2

Belmont, Sutton, SM2 6BJ. Mrs Barbara Welch, 02086421030. *Train: 5 min walk from Belmont Stn, from Sutton Stn take Bus 280 to Belmont. Over bridge into Station Rd, 1st L into The Crescent. No 40 ½ way up on R. Street parking.* **Sun 16 June (1-5). Adm £4, chd free. Home-made teas.** Visits also by arrangement Feb & Mar for groups of 5 to 10.

The structured layout of this rectangular suburban garden, 80' x 50', contains beds and island borders surrounded by clipped box hedges with box and yew topiary, many different shrubs including philadelphus, deutzias, weigela, lilacs, and borders filled with cottage-style planting. Small paths dissect the borders and central lawn leading to various enclosed areas, some with seating, including a circular tree seat, a water feature, and a rose-covered pergola. Terrace with second water feature, many pots for ericaceous-loving plants, fuchsias and seasonal planting. New snowdrop collection, hellebores, early flowering shrubs to be seen in Feb & Mar.

NEW 106 DARTMOUTH RD, FLAT 1, NW2

Willesden Green, London, NW2 4HB. Ms Hester Coley. *2 mins walk from Willesden Green tube stn.* **Sun 15 Sept (2-5). Combined adm with 58A Teignmouth Road £7, chd free. Home-made teas.**

A garden on three levels with flowing paths of stone and gravel, dense planting of shrubs and perennials and a large box parterre. There are several small trees and seating areas. In the centre is a pergola of reclaimed wrought iron railings, smothered in grapevine and clematis. In September many flowering plants are still looking great, along with the start of some warm autumn colour. Visitors can also choose to visit just one of the two gardens - price £4.

GROUP OPENING

DE BEAUVOIR GARDENS, N1

London, N1 4HU. *Highbury & Islington tube then 30 or 277 bus; Angel tube then 38, 56 or 73 bus; Bank tube then 21, 76 or 141 bus. 10 mins walk from Dalston Overground Stns. Street parking available.* **Sun 9 June (11-3). Combined adm £6, chd free. Home-made teas at 158 Culford Road.**

158 CULFORD ROAD
Gillian Blachford.

NEW 64 LAWFORD ROAD

21 NORTHCHURCH TERRACE
Nancy Korman.

Three gardens to explore in De Beauvoir, a leafy enclave of Victorian villas near to Islington and Dalston. The area boasts some of Hackney's keenest gardeners and a thriving garden club. The walled garden at 21 Northchurch Terrace has a formal feel, with deep herbaceous borders, pond, fruit trees, pergola, patio pots and herb beds. 64 Lawford Road is a small 18ftx40ft cottage style garden with old fashioned roses, espaliered apples and scented plants. 158 Culford Road is a long narrow garden with a path winding through full borders with shrubs, small trees, perennials and many unusual plants.

DIESPEKER WHARF, N1

38 Graham Street, London, N1 8JX. Pollard Thomas Edwards. *Beside Regents Canal, Angel, Islington. Underground & Buses: 5 mins from Angel.* **Sun 2 June (2-5.30). Adm £4, chd free. Home-made teas. Also open 19 St Peter's Street.**

An intriguing and unexpected garden in an historic industrial setting alongside the Regents Canal owned and converted by a firm of architects. The garden has become an enticing and unique space enjoyed both socially and for business. Interesting climbers clothe the high wall. Canalside beds incl aster monarch, verbena bonariensis, acanthus spinosis, astrantia major and euphorbia silver edge. The garden has won numerous awards from Islington in Bloom and London in Bloom. Trips along the canal in a narrow boat available.

DRAGON'S DREAM, GROVE LANE, UB8

Grove Lane, Uxbridge, UB8 3RG. Chris and Meng Pocock. *Garden is in a small lane that is very close to Hillingdon Hospital. Parking is available in the nearby Royal Lane. Buses from Uxbridge Tube Station: U1,U3,U4,U5,U7. Buses from West Drayton: U1, U3.* **Sun 26 May (2-5). Adm £3.50, chd free. Home-made teas. Malaysian curry puffs also available.**

This is a secluded, mature garden with two contrasting areas. It is a quiet oasis planted with cordon fruit trees and herbaceous shrubs. The main features are an unusually large wisteria, a huge gunnera manicata and a rare dawn redwood tree. Other features incl a romneya poppy, ferns, rose and herb beds, tree peony, acers and a pond. This garden has won an award for promoting wildlife.

We help ordinary people open the gates to their extraordinary private gardens to raise impressive amounts of money through admissions, teas and slices of cake!

GROUP OPENING

103 AND 105 DULWICH VILLAGE, SE21

London, SE21 7BJ. Mr & Mrs A Rutherford, Mr and Mrs N Annesley. *Rail: N Dulwich or W Dulwich then 10 -15 mins walk. Tube: Brixton then P4 bus, alight Dulwich Picture Gallery stop. Street parking.* **Sun 16 June (2-5). Combined adm £7, chd free. Home-made teas at 103 Dulwich Village.** Donation to Macmillan Cancer Care.

103 DULWICH VILLAGE
Mr & Mrs N Annesley.

105 DULWICH VILLAGE
Mr & Mrs A Rutherford.

2 Georgian houses with large gardens, 3 mins walk from Dulwich Picture Gallery and Dulwich Park. 103 Dulwich Village is a country garden in London with a long herbaceous border, lawn, pond, roses and fruit and vegetable gardens. 105 Dulwich Village is a very pretty garden with many unusual plants, lots of old fashioned roses, fish pond and water garden. Amazing collection of plants for sale from both gardens.

EATON SQUARE GARDEN, SW1W

South Cenral Garden, Eaton Square, London, SW1W 9BD. The Grosvenor Estate, www.grosvenorlondon.com. *Entry to garden via gate opp no. 42 Eaton Sq. Easy walk from Victoria Stn or Sloane Sq. Many bus routes pass close to the square incl C1, 16, 38 and 52. Follow the yellow signs & garden open signs to the South Central Garden.* **Sat 18 May (10-2). Adm £3, chd free. Cream teas.**
Thomas Cubitt laid out the 6 formal gardens flanking either side of the Kings Rd in 1826 in what was the main approach to Buckingham Palace. Eaton Square Garden today combines well-manicured lawns, shady pathways and mixed borders with quiet seating and contemporary sculptures.The fabulously preserved regency buildings form a fine backdrop, complemented by the square's mature London planes. This is a level access site with paths suitable for wheelchairs running the perimeter of the garden and a hard landscaped central area.

ECCLESTON SQUARE, SW1

London, SW1V 1NP. Roger Phillips & the Residents. *Off Belgrave Rd nr Victoria Stn, parking allowed on Suns.* **Sun 19 May (2-5). Adm £5, chd free. Home-made teas.**
Planned by Cubitt in 1828, the 3 acre square is subdivided into mini gardens with camellias, iris, ferns and containers. Dramatic collection of tender climbing roses and 20 different forms of tree peonies. National Collection of ceanothus incl more than 70 species and cultivars. Notable important additions of tender plants being grown and tested. World collection of ceanothus, tea roses and tree peonies.

NPC

EDWARDES SQUARE, W8

South Edwardes Square, Kensington, London, W8 6HL. Edwardes Square Garden Committee. *Tube: Kensington High St & Earls Court. Buses: 9, 10, 27, 28, 31, 49 & 74 to Odeon Cinema. Entrance in South Edwardes Square.* **Sun 14 Apr (11-4). Adm £4, chd free. Cream teas.**
One of London's prettiest secluded garden squares. 3½ acres laid out differently from other squares, with serpentine paths by Agostino Agliothe, Italian artist and decorator who lived at No.15 from 1814-1820, and a beautiful Grecian temple which is traditionally the home of the head gardener. Romantic rose tunnel winds through the middle of the garden. Good displays of bulbs and blossom. Pimms available if sunny. Children's play area. WC.

NEW 40 EMBER LANE, KT10

Esher, KT10 8EP. Sarah and Franck Corvi. *½ mile from centre of Esher. From the A307, turn into Station Rd which becomes Ember Lane.* **Sun 23 June (1-5). Combined adm with 9 Imber Park Road £5, chd free. Home-made teas.**
A contemporary family garden designed and maintained by the owners with distinct areas for outdoor living. A 70ft East facing plot with some unusual planting and several ornamental trees including a Stewartia Rostrata. The owners are currently experimenting with the planting of a new dry border.

NEW 91 ENGLEFIELD ROAD, N1

London, N1 3LJ. Antoinette and Michael. *East Canonbury. Highbury & Islington tube or Canonbury Overground stn; 30 bus to Southgate Rd stop, 5 min wk. Angel tube; 38, 56 or 73 bus to Ockendon Rd, 5 min wk.* **Sun 26 May (2-6). Adm £3, chd free. Light refreshments.**
This garden surprises. South facing yet shaded by a 40ft magnolia and a mature apple tree, a hammock slung between, making a sublime place to relax and read. The philosophy is 'if you like a plant you can find a space', so dense and varied planting, more at home in a country garden, creates an eclectic mix and it works! A patio crammed with pots and hanging baskets seeks to entertain. Garden is approached via steep steps at side of house.

12 FAIRFIELD ROAD, N8

Hornsey, N8 9HG. Christine Lane. *Tube: Finsbury Park & then W3 (Weston Park stop) or W7 (Crouch End Broadway), alternatively Archway & then 41 bus (Crouch End Broadway) it's then a short walk.* **Sun 2 June (2-5.30). Adm £3.50, chd free. Also open 19 Coolhurst Road.**
This peaceful and secluded garden has been created on two levels with year-round interest and is packed with a variety of trees, shrubs and flowers, as well as succulents, palms and bamboos. There is a woodland garden with sculptures, a cobbled Zen garden and a raised pond - made by a Vietnamese family - which creates different atmospheres whilst seating provides places to contemplate and enjoy.

NEW 70 FARLEIGH ROAD, N16

STOKE NEWINGTON, N16 7TQ.

Mr Graham Hollick. *Short walk from junction of Stoke Newington High St & Amhurst Rd.* **Sun 30 June (11-6.30). Adm £3.50, chd free. Home-made teas.**
A diverse garden in a Victorian terrace with an eclectic mix of plants, many in vintage pots reflecting the owner's interests. A small courtyard leads onto a patio surrounded by pots followed by a lawn flanked by curving borders. At the rear is a paved area with raised beds containing vegetables.

◆ FENTON HOUSE, NW3

Hampstead Grove, Hampstead, NW3 6SP. National Trust, www.nationaltrust.org.uk. *300yds from Hampstead tube. Entrances: Top of Holly Hill & Hampstead Grove.* **For NGS: Evening opening Tue 4 June (6.30-7.30). Adm £15. Pre-booking essential, please visit www.ngs.org.uk for information & booking. Wine.** For other opening times and information, please visit garden website.
Join the Gardener-in-Charge for a special evening tour. Andrew Darragh who brings over 10yrs experience from Kew to Fenton House will explore this timeless 1½ acre walled garden. Laid out over 3 levels and featuring formal areas, a small sunken rose garden, a 300yr old orchard and kitchen garden, Andrew will present the garden and the changes he has made over the past 7 years.

Your visits help change lives – we are Hospice UK's largest charitable funder donating more than £5 million to support hospices in local communities since 1996

GROUP OPENING

FOREST HILL GARDENS GROUP, SE23

Forest Hill, London, SE23 3BP. *Off S Circular (A205) behind Horniman Museum & Gardens. Station: Forest Hill, 10 mins walk. Buses: 176, 185, 312, P4.* **Sun 19 May (1-6). Combined adm £8, chd free. Home-made teas. Teas available at 53 Ringmore Rise.** Donation to St Christopher's Hospice and Marsha Phoenix Trust.

7 CANONBIE ROAD
June Wismayer.

THE COACH HOUSE, 3 THE HERMITAGE
Pat Rae.

HILLTOP, 28 HORNIMAN DRIVE
Frankie Locke.

27 HORNIMAN DRIVE
Rose Agnew, 020 8699 7710, roseandgraham@talktalk.net. **Visits also by arrangement Apr to Oct for groups of up to 30.**

53 RINGMORE RISE
Valerie Ward.

25 WESTWOOD PARK
Beth & Steph Falkingham-Blackwell.

Six character-packed gardens (one returning with a makeover!) on the highest hill in SE London, nr Horniman Gdns, with spectacular views over London and South Downs. All within a short walk of each other. Help available (for small donation) for those with mobility problems. See a plantswoman's sunny, dry, prairie planting contrasting with a watery fern garden. Admire the new white border in a tiered, organic bee-enticing garden. Wander in a country-style garden with new planting to cope with climate change, a meadow, children's story trail and assorted chicken breeds. Watch for tame robins in the walled courtyard of an 18thC coach house that feels spacious after hedging removed (box moth)! Owner's sculptures, fountain, birdbath and decorative pots give interest all year. Relax in a haven of peace and harmony amid an embroidery of vibrant colours and enjoy breathtaking views! Unwind with delicious cakes and listen to music amid drifting pastel hues of a garden inspired by Beth Chatto. Great views everywhere. Plants for sale: 27 Horniman Dr and 7 Canonbie Rd. Garden ceramics and sculptures for sale: The Coach House. Teas and music: 53 Ringmore Rise.

4 FRANCONIA ROAD, SW14

Abbeville Village, Clapham, London, SW4 9ND. Paul Harris. *Abbeville Village. From Clapham Common tube, walk 600 metres S to Elms Rd (opp The Windmill hotel) walk along Elms Rd 400 metres to Abbeville Rd, then turn L. Franconia Rd is next on R after 100 metres.* **Sat 3 Aug (10-5). Adm £5, chd free. Light refreshments.**
A private residential garden with a SW aspect. Soil type heavy clay. The garden is a tranquil spot despite the close proximity of neighbours. Receiving sunshine throughout the day, the design offers a shady terrace as well as a sun terrace, separated by a sunken lawn. An exotic planting scheme helps one to escape, whilst being practical for the growing conditions found in a London climate. Floating pergola offering shade to the wildlife hotel and concealing the working area.

GARDEN BARGE SQUARE AT DOWNINGS ROADS MOORINGS, SE1

31 Mill Street, London, SE1 2AX. Mr Nick Lacey. *5 mins walk from Tower Bridge. Mill St off Jamaica Rd, between London Bridge & Bermondsey Stns, Tower Hill also nearby. Buses: 47, 188, 381, RV1.* **Sun 26 May (2-5). Adm £4, chd free. Home-made teas.** Donation to RNLI.
Series of seven floating barge gardens connected by walkways and bridges. Gardens have an eclectic range of plants for yr-round seasonal interest. Marine environment: suitable shoes and care needed. Small children must be closely supervised.

◆ THE GARDEN MUSEUM, SE1

Lambeth Palace Road, London, SE1 7LB. The Garden Museum, www.gardenmuseum.org.uk. *E side of Lambeth Bridge. Tube: Lambeth North, Vauxhall, Waterloo. Buses: 507 Red Arrow from Victoria or Waterloo mainline & tube stns, also 3, 77, 344.* **For NGS: Sat 7 Sept (10.30-4). Adm £6, chd free. For other opening times and information, please visit garden website.**

Britain's only Museum of Gardens re-opened in spring 2017 after a £6.5 million refurbishment. The centre piece of a new extension will be a garden designed by Dan Pearson as a contemporary re-interpretation of plant collectors' lust for plants, inspired by the life of John Tradescant, who is buried here. The new extension incl a cafe. The Museum curates three major exhibitions each year on the art and design of gardens, and has over fifty events in its public programme. The Museum is accessible for wheelchair users via ramps and access lift.

♿ D

GARDEN OF MEDICINAL PLANTS, NW1

11 St Andrews Place, Regents Park, London, NW1 4LE. Royal College of Physicians of London, www.garden.rcplondon.ac.uk. *Tubes: Great Portland St & Regent's Park. Garden is one block N of stn exits, on Outer Circle opp SE corner of Regent's Park.* **Sat 18 May (2-5.30). Adm £5, chd free. Also open 70 Gloucester Crescent. Visits also by arrangement.**

One of several individual and distinctive gardens opening in NW1. Here are 1,100 different plants used in medicines around the world and throughout history: plants named after physicians; plants which make modern medicines and plants used by herbalists. Unique beds with the plants used medicinally in the College's Pharmacopoeia of 1618. Guided tours by physicians explaining the uses of the plants, their histories and stories about them. Books about the plants in the medicinal garden will be on sale. The entry to the garden is at far end of St Andrews Place. Wheelchair ramps at steps. Wheelchair lift for lavatories. No parking on site.

♿ 🚌

Rooftopvegplot

74 GLENGALL ROAD, IG8
Woodford Green, IG8 0DL. Mr & Mrs J Woolliams. *5 mins walk from Woodford Central line, off Snakes Lane West. Buses nearby incl 275,179,W13 & 20. No parking restrictions on Suns.* **Sun 12 May (1.30-5). Adm £4, chd free. Home-made teas.**
A secluded S-facing cottage style garden, developed over 25 years for yr-round interest. Areas incl 2 lawns, a rock garden, small wildlife pond with bog garden, shade borders and a gravel garden, linked by several paths. Throughout are mixtures of trees shrubs perennials bulbs bamboos grasses and climbers. Some steps but mostly wheelchair accessible.

69 GLOUCESTER CRESCENT, NW1
Camden, London, NW1 7EG. Sandra Clapham, 020 7485 5764, set69@gloscres.com. *Between Regent's Park & Camden Town tube station. Tube: Camden Town 2 mins, Mornington Crescent 10 mins. Metered parking in Oval Rd.* **Sat 18 May (2-5.30), also open 98 Parkway. Sun 4 Aug (2-5.30), also open The Holme. Adm £4, chd free.** Visits also by arrangement Apr to Oct for groups of up to 30.
Delightful little cottage front garden, opening jointly with No. 70 next door. It shows what can be done with a front garden as an attractive alternative to a paved parking space. Ursula Vaughan Williams lived here and the very old iceberg rose at the front, the yellow roses, the border of London pride and the Crinum powellii Rosea lily in a pot are all inherited from her. Many plants have been added since, incl a bed of tomatoes and a delicious 22yr-old grape vine, trained up and along the balcony, that produces generous amounts of grape jelly! One of several local gardens opening for the NGS in NW1.

70 GLOUCESTER CRESCENT, NW1
London, NW1 7EG. Lucy Gent, 07531 828752 (texts please), gent.lucy@gmail.com. *Between Regent's Park & Camden Town tube station. Tube: Camden Town 2 mins, Mornington Crescent 10 mins. Metered parking in Oval Rd.* **Sat 18 May (2-5.30), also open 98 Parkway. Sun 4 Aug (2-5.30), also open The Holme. Adm £4, chd free.** Visits also by arrangement Apr to Oct for groups of up to 30.
Here is an oasis in Camden's urban density, where resourceful planting outflanks challenges of space and shade, and Mrs Dickens who once lived here is an amiable ghost. May open day occurs alongside other distinctive local gardens while an August opening shows how wonderful the month can be in a town garden. Other unexpected times of the year also worth another visit, especially September.

NEW **12 GLOUCESTER ROAD, TW12**
Gloucester Road, Hampton, TW12 2UH. Lindy Cumming. *Hampton. Hampton station. Cross over footbridge north side. Turn R, past shops straight on. 285 Bus from Feltham. Off stop before Hampton Hill R70 Richmond to Hampton Broad Lane. 111 Kingston-Hampton.* **Sat 18, Sun 19 May (11-4). Adm £4, chd free. Cream teas.**
Carefully planned garden, immaculately maintained. Interesting planting with many unusual plants. Sunny terrace. Olive trees The garden is secluded and surprising. An unexpected oasis. Wheelchair Access to view whole garden but steps up and down to tour garden.

20 GOLDHAZE CLOSE, IG8
Woodford Green, IG8 7LE. Jenny Richmond, 07801 628799, oscar.singh@ntlworld.com. *Off A1009 Broadmead Rd, Orchard Estate Bus Stop for W14 then forward and L into Underwood Rd and L then R into Goldhaze Cl. Tube: Woodford Stn.* **Sun 11 Aug (12.30-5.30). Adm £5, chd free. Home-made teas.** Visits also by arrangement in Aug.
100ft L-shaped landscaped garden bursting with over 100 plants grown in different types of conditions. A huge 35 yr-old eucalyptus resembles a mature oak with beautiful bark. Paths lined with a strawberry tree, roses, campsis, penstemons, crocosmia and variety of other plants. Vegetables (in pots grown from seed in a greenhouse) leads to a secret decked garden for relaxation.

GOLF COURSE ALLOTMENTS, N11
Winton Avenue, London, N11 2AR. GCAA Haringey, www.golfcourseallotments.co.uk. *Junction of Winton Av & Blake Rd. Tube: Bounds Green. Buses: 102, 184, 299 to Sunshine Garden Centre, Durnsford Rd. Through park to Bidwell Gdns. Straight on up Winton Ave. No cars on site.* **Sun 1 Sept (1-4.30). Adm £4, chd free. Home-made teas. Also open 2 Conway Road. Light lunches also available.**
Large, long established allotment with over 200 plots, some organic. Maintained by culturally diverse community growing wide variety of fruit, vegetables and flowers enjoyed by the bees. Picturesque corners and quirky sheds - a visit feels like being in the countryside. Autumn Flower and Produce Show features prize winning horticultural and domestic exhibits and beehives. Tours of best plots. Fresh allotment produce, chutneys, jams, honey, cakes and light refreshments for sale. Wheelchair access to main paths only. Gravel and some uneven surfaces. WC incl disabled.

21 GOSPATRICK ROAD, N17
London, N17 7EH. Matthew Bradby, 020 8352 2354, mattbradby@hotmail.com. *Nearest underground station Turnpike Lane or Wood Green, overland station Bruce Grove. Bus routes 144, 217, 231, 444 to Gospatrick Rd, or 123, 243 to Waltheof Ave, or 318 to Gt Cambridge Rd.* **Sun 2 June (2-5.30). Adm £4, chd free. Home-made teas.** Visits also by arrangement Mar to Sept for groups of up to 10. Light refreshment/wine with donation.
Diverse 40 metre plot with lawn dominated by large weeping willow, giving dappled shade over fan palms, grasses, ferns and climbers. Fruit and vegetable garden with large Japanese banana, grapevine, olive and bay trees, climbing roses, greenhouse and pond. Patio with exotics in pots. Mainly organic and managed for nature, this is a very tranquil and welcoming garden.

45 GREAT NORTH ROAD, EN5
Barnet, EN5 1EJ. Ron & Miriam Raymond, 07880 500617, ron.raymond91@yahoo.co.uk. *1m S of Barnet High St, 1m N of Whetstone. Tube: Midway between High Barnet & Totteridge & Whetstone stns. Buses 34, 234, 263, 326, alight junction Great N Rd & Lyonsdown Rd. 45 Great North Rd is on the corner of Cherry Hill.* **Sun 4 Aug (2-5.30). Adm £3.50, chd free. Home-made teas.** Visits also by arrangement July & Aug.
45 Great North Road is designed to give a riot of colour in late summer. The 90ft x 90ft cottage style front garden is packed with interesting perennials. Tiered stands line the side entrance with over 64 pots displaying a variety of flowering and foliage plants.The rear garden incl nearly 100 tubs and hanging baskets. Small pond surrounded by tiered beds. Magnificent named tuberous begonias. Children's fun trail for 3-6yr olds and adult garden quiz with prizes. Partial wheelchair access.

17 GREENSTONE MEWS, E11
Wanstead, London, E11 2RS. Mrs T Farnham. *Wanstead. Tube: Snaresbrook or Wanstead, 5 mins walk. Bus: 101, 308, W12, W14 to Wanstead High St. Greenstone Mews is accessed via Voluntary Place which is off Spratt Hall Road.* **Sun 11 Aug (12-5). Adm £5, chd free.**
Coloured Slate paved garden (20ft x 17ft). Height provided by a mature strawberry tree. Sunken reused bath now a fishpond surrounded by climbers clothing fences underplanted with herbs, vegetables, shrubs and perennials grown from cuttings. Ideas aplenty for small space gardening. Regret garden unsuitable for children. Wheelchair access through garage. Limited turning space.

7 THE GROVE, N6
Highgate Village, London, N6 6JU. Mr Thomas Lyttelton, 07713 638161. *Between Highgate West Hill & Hampstead Lane. Tube: Archway or Highgate. Buses: 143, 210, 214 and 271.* **Sun 17 Feb (11-3). Light refreshments. Sun 14 Apr, Sun 9 June (2-6). Home-made teas. Adm £5, chd free.** Visits also by arrangement Feb to Dec for groups of up to 30. Donation to The Harington Scheme.
½ acre garden designed for yr-round interest making a tapestry of greens and yellows. A wild garden with mature trees giving a woodland feel. Large lawn, perfect for teas. Water garden, 20 paths, vistas and views galore. Brilliant for hide and seek, Pooh-sticks and young explorers. Snowdrops in February. Exceptional camellias and magnolia in the spring, 'hidden' cyclamen in early autumn. Hot soup incl with entry for Snowdrop opening. Cup of tea incl with entry for Spring/Summer openings.

24 GROVE PARK, SE5
Camberwell, SE5 8LH. Clive Pankhurst, www.alternative-planting.blogspot.com. *Chadwick Rd end of Grove Park. Stns: Peckham Rye or Denmark Hill, both 10 mins walk. Good street parking.* **Sun 1 Sept (2-5.30). Adm £4.50, chd free. Home-made teas.**
An exotic jungle of lush big leafed plants, ponds and Southeast Asian influences. Towering paulownias, bananas, dahlias, tetrapanax and exotica transport you to the tropics. Huge hidden garden created from the bottom halves of two neighbouring gardens gives the 'wow' factor and unexpected size. Lawn and lots of hidden corners give spaces to sit and enjoy. Renowned for delicious home-made cake.

Your visits help change lives – your generosity helps Marie Curie fund nurses to care for people night and day in their homes, with donations of more than £8.8 million

58 HALLIFORD STREET, N1
London, N1 3NQ. Jennifer Tripp Black. *Canonbury. Tube: Highbury & Islington or Essex Rd. From Essex Rd, house numbers consecutive on LH side by 3rd speed bump.* **Sun 12 May (1-6). Adm £4, chd free. Home-made teas. Also open 20 St Mary's Grove. Vegan & full fat cakes.**
An English country garden in the heart of Islington. Lush planting: cytisus battandieri 'Yellow Tail' tree, two apple trees, one quince. Roses: bush and climbing, clematis, rhododendrons, exotic palms, cannas, abutilons, heucheras, salvias, cordelines. Small greenhouse, antique pergola, pots containing hosta collection and window boxes. The front garden welcomes with special roses and agapanthus. Donation to Katie's Lymphoedema Fund.

GROUP OPENING

HAMPSTEAD GARDEN SUBURB GARDENS, NW11
London, NW11 6YJ. *Golders Green. Car A1 & A406 Henley's Corner. Tube Golders Green, Bus H2, 82,102,460 to Temple Fortune. Tickets & map from Fellowship House, Willifield Way via Hampstead Way.* **Sun 7 July (11.30-5.30). Combined adm £12, chd free. Home-made teas at Fellowship House, Willifield Way. Light refreshments at Willifield Way allotments**

NEW **43 ADDISON WAY**
Mr Christopher Matthews.

4 ASMUNS HILL
Peter & Yvonne Oliver.

48 ERSKINE HILL, NW11
Marjorie & David Harris, 020 8455 6507, marjorieharris@btinternet.com.
Visits also by arrangement May to Sept for groups of up to 20. Tea and cake included in entry price (food allergies catered for).

121 ERSKINE HILL, NW11
Mike & Heather Collins.

94 HAMPSTEAD WAY
Patsy Larsen.

85 NORTHWAY
Susan Fischgrund.

94 OAKWOOD ROAD
Michael & Adrienne Franklin, 07836 541383, mikefrank@onetel.com. **Visits also by arrangement May to Aug for groups of 5 to 20.**

NEW **102 WILLIFIELD WAY**
Dr Gerald Weinbrenn.

74 WILLIFIELD WAY, NW11
David Weinberg, 020 8201 9052, davidwayne@hotmail.co.uk. **Visits also by arrangement June to Aug.**

86 WILLIFIELD WAY, NW11
Diane Berger, 020 8455 0455, dianeberger@hotmail.co.uk. **Visits also by arrangement June to Sept for groups of 5 to 20.**

WILLIFIELD WAY TF HILL ALLOTMENT
Peter Hodgson.

NEW **10 WORDSWORTH WALK**
Augusta & Laurence Wolff.

32 WORDSWORTH WALK
Chris Page.

A unique opportunity to explore one of the best known garden suburbs in England. Surrounded by ancient woods and adjacent to Hampstead Heath. Noted for its Arts and Crafts architecture. A riot of colour and array of planting schemes behind the artisan cottages, emerging from the borrowed woodland landscape beyond. Discover a hidden allotment site enclosed within the Suburb's signature hedges. Many gardens can be accessed through a network of leafy twittens, or footpaths, that traverse the Suburb. Take afternoon tea by the village green. Specialist nurseries, and home propagated plants for sale. London Gardens' Society award winning gardens 86 Willifield Way, 48 Erskine Hill and 4 Asmuns Hill. 74 Willifield Way, 32 Wordsworth Walk & 94 Oakwood Road are regular winners of Suburb in Bloom. Partial wheelchair access to several gardens.

◆ HAMPTON COURT PALACE, KT8

East Molesey, KT8 9AU. Historic Royal Palaces, www.hrp.org.uk. *Follow brown tourist signs on all major routes. Junction of A308 with A309 at foot of Hampton Court Bridge.* **For NGS: Evening opening Thur 18 Apr, Thur 18 July (6-8). Adm £12, chd free. Pre-booking essential, please visit www.ngs.org.uk for information & booking. Wine.** For other opening times and information, please visit garden website.

Take the opportunity to join 2 special NGS private tours, after the wonderful historic gardens have closed to the public. Spring Walk in April and Mid-Summer abundance in July in the wonderful gardens of Hampton Court Palace. Some unbound gravel paths.

NPC

37 HAROLD ROAD, E11

Leytonstone, London, E11 4QX. Dr Matthew Jones Chesters. *Tube: Leytonstone exit L subway 5 mins walk. Overground: Leytonstone High Rd 5 mins walk. Buses: 257 & W14. Parking at station or limited on street.* **Sun 26 May (1-5). Adm £4, chd free. Home-made teas.**

50ft x 60ft pretty corner garden arranged around 7 fruit trees. Fragrant climbers, woodland plants and shade-tolerant fruit along north wall. Fastigiate trees protect raised vegetable beds and herb rockery. Long lawn bordered by roses and perennials on one side; prairie plants on the other. Patio with raised pond, palms and rhubarb. Planting designed to produce fruit, fragrance and lovely memories. Plant list and garden plan available.

12 HAYWOOD CLOSE, HA5

Pinner, HA5 3LQ. Brenda & Roy Jakes. *Approx ½m from Pinner Met Line Stn. off Elm Park Rd. From Northwood, Stanmore, Harrow & Watford head towards Pinner Green & look for signs. Park in Elm Park Road as Haywood Close narrow.* **Sun 9 June (2-5). Adm £4.50, chd free. Home-made teas. Incl gluten free cakes.**

A beautiful suburban garden created by enthusiastic, plantaholic owners. Herbaceous borders containing many interesting species surround the lawn. The garden contains over 100 varieties of roses and clematis, a rose walk, rose covered gazebo, water features, sink garden, pleached hornbeam trees with box collars and a fruit and veg plot. There are seating areas and a summerhouse to sit and relax. Most of garden wheelchair accessible.

HIGHWOOD ASH, NW7

Highwood Hill, Mill Hill, NW7 4EX. Mr & Mrs R Gluckstein. *Totteridge & Whetstone on Northern line, then bus 251 stops outside - Rising Sun/Mill Hill stop. By car: A5109 from Apex Corner to Whetstone. Garden located opp The Rising Sun PH.* **Sun 30 June (2-5.30). Adm £5, chd free. Home-made teas.**

Created over the last 50yrs, this 3¼ acre garden features rolling lawns, two large interconnecting ponds with koi, herbaceous and shrub borders and a modern gravel garden. A garden for all seasons with many interesting plants and sculptures. A country garden in London. Partial access for wheelchairs, lowest parts too steep.

5 HILL CLOSE, NW11

London, NW11 7JP. Leanne & Winston Newman, lafnewman@hotmail.co.uk. *1m N of Golders Green. Off Hampstead Way between Meadway and Willifield Way, also off South Square. No parking in Hill Close. Tube: Golders Green then H2 'Hail & Ride' to bottom of Hill Close.* **Sun 16 June (2-5.30). Adm £3, chd free. Home-made teas. Visits also by arrangement for groups of 5 to 10.**

Delightful garden of a unique Arts and Crafts house set amidst the distinctive spreading cedar tree and bordered by mature oak and poplars.

NEW 20 HILLCREST, N21

Winchmore Hill, N21 1AT. Gwyneth & Ian Williams. *Tube: Southgate then W9 to Winchmore Hill Green followed by a short walk via Wades Hill. Train: Winchmore Hill, turn R towards the Green, then short walk via Wades Hill.* **Sun 9 June (1.30-5.30). Adm £4, chd free. Home-made teas. Also open 91 Vicar's Moor Lane. Dairy-free options. Herbal teas.**
A secluded NW facing hillside garden in a quiet road offers a broad horizon and afternoon sun. A terrace provides seating under iron-work gazebo. Wide stone steps lead to a wooden climber clad pergola with seating and dappled sunlight. A lawn, mature borders, scented rose arches, perennials, rockery and meandering path lead to a pretty summer house with alpines and a small secret garden. Steep Steps!

THE HOLME, NW1

Inner Circle, Regents Park, NW1 4NT. Lessee of The Crown Commission. *In centre of Regents Park on The Inner Circle. Within 15 mins walk from Great Portland St or Baker St Underground Stations, opp Regents Park Rose Garden Cafe.* **Sat 29, Sun 30 June, Sat 3, Sun 4 Aug (2.30-5.30). Adm £5, chd free.**
4 acre garden filled with interesting and unusual plants. Sweeping lakeside lawns intersected by islands of herbaceous beds. Extensive rock garden with waterfall, stream and pool. Formal flower garden with unusual annual and half hardy plants, sunken lawn, fountain pool and arbour. Gravel paths and some steps which gardeners will help wheelchair users to negotiate.

33 HUDDLESTON ROAD, N7

London, N7 0AD. Gilly Hatch & Tom Gretton. *5 mins from Tufnell Park Tube. Tube: Tufnell Park. Buses: 4, 134, 390 to Tufnell Park. Follow Tufnell Park Rd to 3rd rd on R.* **Sun 7 July (2-6). Adm £3.50, chd free. Home-made teas. Also open 23 & 24b Penn Road.**
The rambunctious front garden weaves together perennials, grasses and ferns, while the back garden makes a big impression in a small space. After 40yrs, the lawn is now a wide curving path, a deep sunny bed on one side; mixing shrubs and perennials in an ever changing blaze of colour, on the other; a screen of varied greens and textures. This flowery passage leads to a secluded sitting area.

1A HUNGERFORD ROAD, N7

London, N7 9LA. David Matzdorf, davidmatzdorf@blueyonder.co.uk, , www.growingontheedge.net. *Between Camden Town & Holloway. Tube: Caledonian Rd. Buses: 17, 29, 91, 253, 259, 274, 390 & 393. Parking free on Sundays.* **Sun 9 June (1-6). Adm £3, chd free. Also open 60 & 62 Hungerford Road. Visits also by arrangement Apr to Oct for groups of up to 10.**
Unique eco house with walled, lush front garden in modern exotic style, densely planted with palms, acacia, bamboo, ginger lilies, bananas, ferns, yuccas, abutilons and unusual understorey plants. Floriferous and ambitious green roof resembling Mediterranean or Mexican hillside, planted with yuccas, dasylirions, agaves, aloes, flowering shrubs, euphorbias, grasses, alpines, sedums and aromatic herbs. Sole access to roof is via built in ladder. Garden and roof each 50ft x 18ft.

60 & 62 HUNGERFORD ROAD, N7

London, N7 9LP. John Gilbert, Lynne Berry & Frances Pine. *Between Camden Town & Holloway. Tube: Caledonian Rd, 6 mins walk. Buses: 29 & 253 to Hillmarton Rd stop in Camden Rd. Also 17, 91, 259, 393 to Hillmarton Rd. 10 to York Way.* **Sun 9 June (2-6). Adm £5, chd free. Tea. Also open 1a Hungerford Road.**
Two contrasting gardens behind a Victorian terrace. No. 62 is densely planted and mature, designed to maximise space for planting and create several different sitting areas, views and moods. Professional garden designer's own garden. No 60 is a family garden with large lawn and a good range of shrubs, flowering perennials and trees. Together they form an inspiring oasis, connected by a secret door.

THE HURLINGHAM CLUB, SW6

Ranelagh Gardens, London, SW6 3PR. The Members of the Hurlingham Club, www.hurlinghamclub.org.uk. *Main gate at E end of Ranelagh Gardens. Tube: Putney Bridge (110yds). NB: No onsite parking. Meter parking on local streets & restricted parking on Sats (9-5).* **Sat 18 May (10-4.30). Adm £5, chd free. Light refreshments in the Napier Servery in the East Wing.**
Rare opportunity to visit this 42 acre jewel with many mature trees, 2 acre lake with water fowl, expansive lawns and a river walk. Capability Brown and Humphry Repton were involved with landscaping. The gardens are renowned for their roses, herbaceous and lakeside borders, shrubberies and stunning bedding displays. The riverbank is a haven for wildlife with native trees, shrubs and wild flowers. Garden Tours at 11am and 2pm - ticketed event, tickets available at entrance.

GROUP OPENING

NEW HYDE PARK ESTATE GARDENS, W2

Kendal Street, London, W2 2AN. Church Commissioners for England, www.hydeparkestate.com. *The Hyde Park Estate is bordered by Sussex Gardens, Bayswater Road and Edgware Road. Nearest tube stations include Marble Arch, Paddington and Edgware Road.* **Sun 7 Apr (10-2). Combined adm £10, chd free. Pre-booking essential, please visit www.ngs.org.uk for information & booking.**

NEW CONISTON COURT
Church Commissioners for England, www.hydeparkestate.com.

NEW DEVONPORT
Church Commissioners for England.

NEW THE QUADRANGLE
Church Commissioners for England.

NEW THE WATER GARDENS
Church Commissioners for England.

Four newly designed gardens, never before open to the public. Each garden planted sympathetically to reflect the surroundings. Uniquely The Watergardens feature vast expanses of open water. The gardens on the Hyde Park Estate are owned and managed by the Church Commissioners for England and play a key part in the environmental and ecological strategy on the Hyde Park Estate. In 2018 we met the target we had set of ensuring that 10% of the Estate was 'green' - not only with the garden spaces but by installing planters on unused paved areas, green roofs on new developments and olive trees throughout Connaught Village. Pre-booking essential. Most of the gardens can be accessed by wheelchairs. There are some steps at The Water Gardens for the upper levels.

9 IMBER PARK ROAD, KT10

Esher, KT10 8JB. Jane & John McNicholas. *½ m from centre of Esher. From the A307, turn into Station Rd which becomes Ember Lane. Go past Esher train station on R. Take 3rd rd on R into Imber Park Rd.* **Sun 23 June (1-5). Combined adm with 40 Ember Lane £5, chd free. Home-made teas.**
An established cottage style garden, always evolving, and designed and maintained by the owners who are passionate about gardening and collecting plants. The garden is S-facing, with well stocked, large, colourful herbaceous borders containing a wide variety of perennials, evergreen and deciduous shrubs, a winding lawn area and a small garden retreat. There is a short gravel path at the side of the house.

THE INNER AND MIDDLE TEMPLE GARDENS, EC4

Crown Office Row, Inner Temple, London, EC4Y 7HL. The Honourable Societies of the Inner and Middle Temples, www.innertemple.org.uk/www.middletemple.org.uk. *Entrance: Main Garden Gate on Crown Office Row, access via Tudor Street gate or Middle Temple Lane gate.* **Tue 25 June (11.30-3). Adm £50, chd free. Pre-booking essential, please visit www.ngs.org.uk for information & booking. Light refreshments.**
Inner Temple Garden is a haven of tranquillity and beauty with sweeping lawns, unusual trees and charming woodland areas. The well known herbaceous border shows off inspiring plant combinations from early spring through to autumn. The award winning gardens of Middle Temple are comprised of a series of courtyards and one larger formal garden. **Adm incl conducted tour of the gardens by Head Gardeners. Light lunch in Middle Hall, one of the finest examples of an Elizabethan hall in the country**. Please advise in advance if wheelchair access is required.

GROUP OPENING

KEW GREEN GARDENS, TW9

Kew, TW9 3AH. 020 8940 2426, linda@bpethick.me.uk. *NW side of Kew Green. Tube: Kew Gardens. Mainline Stn: Kew Bridge. Buses: 65, 391. Entrance via riverside.* **Sun 26 May (2-5). Combined adm £6, chd free. Evening opening Sun 2 June (6-8). Combined adm £8, chd free. Teas at St Anne's Church (May). Wine at Gardens (June).** Visits also by arrangement in June.

65 KEW GREEN
Giles & Angela Dixon.

67 KEW GREEN
Lynne & Patrick Lynch.

69 KEW GREEN
John & Virginia Godfrey.

71 KEW GREEN
Mr & Mrs Jan Pethick.

73 KEW GREEN
Sir Donald & Lady Elizabeth Insall.

These five adjacent long gardens run for 100 yds from the back of historic houses on Kew Green down to the Thames towpath. Together they cover nearly 1½ acres, and in addition to the style and structure of the individual gardens they can be seen as one large space, exceptional in London. The borders between the gardens are mostly relatively low and the trees and large shrubs in each contribute to viewing the whole, while roses and clematis climb between gardens giving colour to two adjacent gardens at the same time. On open days we try to have music as the sound carries through the five gardens. Difficult for wheelchairs.

33 Huddleston Road

57 KING EDWARD ROAD, EN5

Barnet, EN5 5AU. Ms Pam Mitchell & Ms Sandy Kaufman. *New Barnet. High Barnet tube, 15 mins walk. Bus 263 & others to Everyman Cinema. Turn up Potters Lane opposite BP Garage then 1st L. Plenty of free parking. Entry also via Meadway if coming from Nth.* **Sun 23 June (2-6). Adm £4, chd free. Home-made teas.**

Our garden combines plenty of space for relaxing and entertaining. It also provides endless opportunities for me to indulge my passion for gardening and creative projects. There are many different areas to explore incl a shade garden, wildlife area and a working veg patch. It is a constantly evolving space.

KING HENRY'S WALK GARDEN, N1

11c King Henry's Walk, London, N1 4NX. Friends of King Henry's Walk Garden, www.khwgarden.org.uk. *Buses incl: 21, 30, 38, 56, 141, 277. Behind adventure playground on KHW, off Balls Pond Rd.* **Mon 6 May (2-4.30). Adm £3.50, chd free. Home-made teas.** Donation to Friends of KHW Garden.

Vibrant ornamental planting welcomes the visitor to this hidden oasis and leads you into a verdant community garden with secluded woodland area, bee hives, wildlife pond, wall trained fruit trees, and plots used by local residents to grow their own fruit and vegetables. Disabled WC.

LAMBETH PALACE, SE1

Lambeth Palace Rd, London, SE1 7JU. The Church Commissioners, www.archbishopofcanterbury.org. *Entrance via Main Gatehouse facing Lambeth Bridge. Station: Waterloo. Tube: Westminster, Vauxhall all 10 mins walk. Buses: 3, C10, 77, 344, 507.* **Evening opening Mon 20 May (5.30-8). Adm £6, chd free. Wine.**

Lambeth Palace has one of the oldest and largest private gardens in London. It has been occupied by Archbishops of Canterbury since 1197. Formal courtyard boasts historic White Marseilles fig planted in 1556. Parkland style garden features mature trees, woodland and native planting, orchard and pond. There is a formal rose terrace, summer gravel border, scented chapel garden and active beehives. Garden Tours will be available. Ramped path to rose terrace, disabled WC.

12 LANSDOWNE ROAD, W11

London, W11 3LW. The Lady Amabel Lindsay. *Tube: Holland Park. Buses: 12, 88, 94, 148, GL711, 715 to Holland Park, 4 mins walk up Lansdowne Rd.* **Thur 2 May (2.30-6.30). Adm £5, chd free. Light refreshments. Soft drinks.**

A country garden in the heart of London. An old mulberry tree, billowing borders, rambling Rosa banksiae, and a greenhouse of climbing pelargoniums. Partial wheelchair access to level paved surfaces.

NEW 12 LAURADALE ROAD, N2

FORTIS GREEN, N2 9LU. David Gilbert and Mary Medyckyj. *300 metres from 102 & 234 bus stops. 500 metres from 43 & 134 bus stops. 10 min walk from East Finchley Underground Stn.* **Sun 8 Sept (12-6). Adm £4, chd free. Home-made teas.**

Exotic, large, newly-designed garden, featuring tropical/ Mediterranean-zone plants. Dramatic, architectural planting including bananas, tree ferns and rare palms, weaves along curving stone paths, culminating in a paradise garden. A modern take on the rockery embeds glacial boulders amid dry zone plants incl dasylirion, beschorneria and many succulents. Sculptures by artist owner.

84 LAVENDER GROVE, E8

Hackney, E8 3LS. Anne Pauleau, a.pauleau@hotmail.co.uk. *Short walk from Haggerston or London Fields overground stations.* **Sun 9 June (2-5). Adm £3.50, chd free. Cream teas.** Visits also by arrangement Apr to Sept for groups of up to 20.

Two gardens for the price of one! Country meets town in the heart of Hackney. Courtyard garden with tropical backdrop of bamboos and palms, foil to clipped shrubs leading to wilder area , the cottage garden mingling roses, lilies, alliums, grasses, clematis, poppies, star jasmine and jasmine. A very highly scented garden with rampant ramblers and billowing vegetation enchanting all senses. Children's quiz offered with prize on completion.

16 LINKS VIEW ROAD, TW12

Hampton Hill, Hampton, TW12 1LA. Guy & Virginia Lewis. *5 mins walk from Fulwell station. On 281,267,285 and R70 bus routes.* **Sat 25, Sun 26 May (2-5). Adm £4.50, chd free. Home-made teas.**

A surprising garden featuring acers, hostas and fern collection and other unusual shade loving plants. Many climbing roses, clematis and herbaceous border. Rockery and folly with waterfall, bog garden and small pond, with grotto. A formal pond. A mini meadow with chickens. Raised veg and fruit plot. Summer house and Greenhouse with tender pelargonium collection. A verandah with planted pots. Wheelchair access with help.

2 LITTLEBURY ROAD, SW4

Clapham, SW4 6DN. Jack Wallington & Christopher Anderson, www.jackwallington.com. *2 mins from Clapham High St station, 4 mins walk from Clapham N & Clapham Common. From main High St, head down Clapham Manor St, turn R down Voltaire Rd past leisure centre. Take 1st L on Littlebury Rd, house on R.* **Sun 8 Sept (1-6). Adm £4.50, chd free. Home-made teas.**

Small garden, creatively packed with bright colours and interesting plants. Features a living wall of 50 fern species, a micro-pond, tropical plants and quirky indoor plants. September opening sees Dahlias in triumphant, unmissable glory plus canna, persicaria, salvia, clematis and many exotics. Owned by a garden designer/writer who uses his garden as a trial ground for new ideas. Plants in every part of the house, from the front, through rooms and out to the garden. Cut flowers from Jack's allotment.

49 LOFTUS ROAD, W12
London, W12 7EH. Emma Plunket, emma@plunketgardens.com, , www.plunketgardens.com. *Shepherds Bush or Shepherds Bush Market tube, train or bus to Uxbridge Rd. Free street parking.* **Sun 9 June (3-7.30). Adm £4, chd free. Tea. Visits also by arrangement May to Sept for groups of up to 10.**
Professional garden designer, Emma Plunket, opens her acclaimed walled garden. Richly planted, it is the ultimate hard working city garden with all year structure and colour incorporating fruit and herbs. Set against a backdrop of trees, this city haven is unexpectedly open and peaceful. Garden plan, plant list and advice available.

2 LONSDALE SQUARE, N1
London, N1 1EN. Jenny Kingsley. *Barnsbury. Tube: Highbury & Islington or Angel. Along Liverpool Rd, walk up Richmond Ave. 1st R, entrance via passageway on R.* **Sun 2 June (2-6). Adm £2.50, chd free. Also open Barnsbury Group.**
One could describe our garden as a person: small and unpretentious. Attractively formed by yew and box hedges and faithful beds with hellebores, fatsia, erysimum, euonymous, euphorbia and the lively climbing roses, star jasmine and solanium. Planters with olive trees, herbs and pansies are fine companions, mauve, white and emerald favoured colours. She walks on cobblestones, a most tranquil soul.

NEW **10 LORIS ROAD, W6**
Hammersmith, W6 7QA. Mrs Cordelia Fraser Trueger. *Loris Rd is a cul-de-sac off Lena Gardens, located behind Shepherds Bush Road, midway between Hammersmith Underground and Shepherds Bush Underground stations.* **Evening opening Sun 2 June (5-7.30). Adm £5, chd free. Wine. Home made pizza.**
Long narrow garden designed by award winning Jo Thompson. This garden is separated into four distinct rooms by clever use of 3D hardscaping, so as to obscure surrounding houses. Espaliered apple trees, steel-framed pergolas, seating areas & a mix of ground textures together with a working pizza oven. Host to more than 20 different roses and 15 clematis as well as many perennials.

GROUP OPENING

LOWER CLAPTON GARDENS, E5
Hackney, London, E5 0RL. *12 mins walk from Hackney Central or Hackney Downs stns. Buses 38, 55, 106, 242, 253, 254 or 425, alight Lower Clapton Rd or Powerscroft Rd.* **Sun 2 June (2-5). Combined adm £5, chd free. Home-made teas at 77 Rushmore Rd.**

8 ALMACK ROAD
Philip Lightowlers, 07910 850276, plighto@gmail.com.
Visits also by arrangement Apr to Aug for groups of up to 20.

77 RUSHMORE ROAD
Penny Edwards.

Lower Clapton is an area of mid Victorian terraces sloping down to the River Lea. These gardens reflect their owner's tastes and interests. No. 77 Rushmore Rd features a fruit and vegetable garden and wildlife pond. 8 Almack Rd is a long thin garden with two different rooms, one cool and peaceful the other with hot colours and tropical foliage.

GROUP OPENING

LYNDHURST SQUARE GROUP, SE15
Lyndhurst Square, London, SE15 5AR. Group Gardens. *Overground & National Rail services to Peckham Rye Station; numerous bus routes.* **Sun 23 June (1.30-5). Combined adm £6, chd free. Light refreshments in the small garden in the square.** Donation to MIND, Mental Health Charity.

5 LYNDHURST SQUARE
Martin Lawlor & Paul Ward.

6 LYNDHURST SQUARE
Iain Henderson & Amanda Grygelis.

7 LYNDHURST SQUARE
Pernille Ahlström & Barry Joseph.

Three very attractive gardens open in this small, elegant square of 1840s listed villas located in Peckham SE London. Each approx 90ft x 50ft has its own shape and style as the Square curves in a U shape. No. 5, the design combines Italianate and Gothic themes with roses, lavender, olives, euphorbia and ferns within yew and box parterres. Plants for sale here. No. 6 is an up to date family garden given drama with architectural plants. A wisteria pergola frames the vegetables bordered by espaliered apples. Check out the treehouse! Simplicity, Swedish style, is key at No. 7, with roses and raised beds, framed by yew hedges. Some uneven surfaces.

MAGGIE'S WEST LONDON, W6
Charing Cross Hospital, Fulham Palace Road, Hammersmith, W6 8RF. Miss Anna Wall-Budden. *Follow Fulham Palace Rd from the station towards Charing Cross Hospital. The centre is on the corner of St Dunstan's Rd and is painted tomato-orange so is very visible.* **Sat 1 June (10-2). Adm £4, chd free. Home-made teas.**
The garden at Maggie's West London was designed by the great Dan Pearson in 2008. It is now a well-established space offering therapy and peace to those affected by cancer each year. The gardens surround the vivid orange walls of the Centre. The path leading to the Centre meanders through scented beds and mature trees. Visitors have access to various courtyards with a wonderful array of flora including fig trees, grape vines and even a mature pink silk mimosa. Ground floor gardens & courtyards are accessible. Roof gardens not accessible.

4 MANNINGTREE ROAD, HA4

Ruislip, HA4 0ES. Costas Lambropoulos & Roberto Haddon. *Manningtree Rd is just off Victoria Rd, 10 mins walk from South Ruislip tube station.* **Sun 21 July (2-6). Adm £4, chd free. Home-made teas. Cakes and savouries. Home-made jams and biscuits also for sale.**

Compact garden with an exotic feel that combines hardy architectural plants with more tender ones.
A feeling of a small oasis incl plants like Musa Basjoo, Ensette Montbelliardii, tree ferns, black bamboo etc. Potted mediterranean plants on the patio incl a fig tree and two olive trees.

53 MANOR ROAD, N16

Stoke Newington, N16 5BH. Jonathan Trustram. *Nr Stoke Newington station & Heathland Rd 106 bus stop.* **Sun 15 Sept (1-5). Adm £3.50, chd free. Home-made teas. Also jams and chutneys for sale.**

Big garden for London, thickly enclosed by ivy, roses and jasmine, crowded with plants, many unusual: eryngiums, thalictrums, salvias, pelargoniums, eucomis, inulas, lilies, indigofera, azara, myrtle. Small sculptural rock garden. Soft fruit. Lots of poorly policed self-seeders. Organic credentials finally lost in 30 years war against slugs. Popular plant sale.

Your visits help change lives – we are the largest single funder of the Queen's Nursing Institute

GROUP OPENING

MAPLEDENE GARDENS, E8

Mapledene Road, Hackney, E8 3JW. *7 mins walk from 67, 149, 242, 243 bus stop Middleton Rd, 10 mins from 30, 38, 55 stops on Dalston Lane. 7 mins from Haggerston Overground or 10 mins walk through London Fields from Mare St buses.* **Sun 9 June (2-6). Combined adm £5, chd free. Home-made teas at 61 Mapledene Road.**

53 MAPLEDENE ROAD

Tigger Cullinan, 020 7249 3754, tiggerine8@blueyonder.co.uk. **Visits also by arrangement June & July for groups of up to 10.**

55 MAPLEDENE ROAD

Amanda & Tony Mott.

61 MAPLEDENE ROAD

Katja & Ned Staple.

63 MAPLEDENE ROAD

Helen Hunsperger & Simon Mathews.

With much the same space, these 4 strongly contrasting N-facing neighbouring gardens have very different design intentions and styles. No. 53 is an established plantaholic's garden, with jewel-like planting where clematis take pride of place. No. 55 is a garden with Moorish influenced terrace leading to a wildlife garden planted to attract birds, butterflies and bees. No. 61 is a newly planted family garden with large open lawn, wildflower meadow and delicate, ethereal planting and 63 has a romantic feel with repeat planting of roses, hydrangeas and box balls.

MARIE CURIE HOSPICE, HAMPSTEAD, NW3

Lyndhurst Gardens, London, NW3 5NS. Tracy Annunziato. *In the heart of Hampstead. Nearest tube: Belsize Park. Buses: 46, 268 & C11 all stop nr the Hospice.* **Sun 7 July (2-5.30). Adm £3.50, chd free. Cream teas. Also open Tudor Herbalist Garden. In addition to Cream Teas there will also be a range of other refreshments and sweet treats available.**

This peaceful and secluded two part garden surrounds the Marie Curie Hospice, Hampstead. A garden, tended to by dedicated volunteers, makes for a wonderful space for patients to enjoy the shrubs and seasonal colourful flowers.
The garden has seating areas for relaxation either in the shade or in the sunshine with great views of the garden, and in company with squirrels running through the trees. Step free access to garden and toilets.

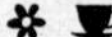

GROUP OPENING

MARKSBURY AVENUE GARDENS, TW9

Richmond, TW9 4JE. *Approx 10 mins walk from Kew Gardens tube. Exit westbound platform to North Rd. Take 3rd L into Atwood Ave. Marksbury Ave is 3rd R. Buses 190, 419 or R68.* **Sun 2 June (3-6). Combined adm £7, chd free. Home-made teas at 60 Marksbury Avenue.**

60 MARKSBURY AVENUE

Gay Lyle.

34 MARKSBURY AVENUE

Annette Parshotam.

61 MARKSBURY AVENUE

Siobhan McCammon.

26 MARKSBURY AVENUE

Sue Frisby.

59 MARKSBURY AVENUE

Clarissa Fletcher.

Five neighbouring gardens reflecting the enthusiasm and knowledge of their owners. One features many New Zealand natives and a variety of fruit trees incl figs, apricots and vines. A trampoline is cleverly screened by black stemmed bamboo and copper beech. There is calming water and a camomile lawn. Another garden has evolved over 11yrs and features separate areas not all visible from the house. There is a continuing process of experimenting with plants. The group provides variety and charm for the visitors.

✽ ☕

41 MILL HILL ROAD, W3

London, W3 8JE. Marcia Hurst, 020 8992 2632/07989 581940, marcia.hurst@sudbury-house.co.uk. *Tube: Acton Town, cross zebra crossing, turn R, Mill Hill Rd second R off Gunnersbury Lane. Many local Buses and London Overground.* **Evening opening Fri 19 July (7-9). Combined adm with 65 Mill Hill Road £6, chd free. Wine. Sun 18 Aug (2-6). Combined adm with 65 Mill Hill Road £5, chd free. Home-made teas.** Visits also by arrangement June to Aug for groups of up to 20.

120ft x 40ft garden. A surprisingly large and sunny garden, with lavender and hornbeam hedges, herbaceous planting and climbers, incl unusual and rare plants as the owner is a compulsive plantaholic. Good in July and August, with many salvias, clematis, dahlias and late flowering hardy and half hardy annuals. Lots of space to sit and enjoy the garden. Good selection of the plants growing in the garden are for sale in pots with planting and growing advice from the knowledgeable owner.

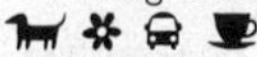

65 MILL HILL ROAD, W3

London, W3 8JF. Anna Dargavel, 07802 241965, annadargavel@mac.com. *Tube: Acton Town, turn R, Mill Hill Rd on R off Gunnersbury Lane.* **Evening opening Fri 19 July (7-9). Combined adm with 41 Mill Hill Road £6, chd free. Wine. Sun 18 Aug (2-6). Combined adm with 41 Mill Hill Road £5, chd free.** Visits also by arrangement June to Aug for groups of up to 20.

Garden designer's own garden. A secluded and tranquil space, paved, with changes of level and borders. Sunny areas, topiary, a greenhouse and interesting planting combine to provide a wildlife haven. A pond and organic principles are used to promote a green environment and give a stylish walk to a studio at the end of the garden.

NEW 25 MULBERRY WAY, E18

South Woodford, E18 1EB. Mrs Laura Piercy-Farley. *100 metres from South Woodford tube station. ¼M M11 JW. Public transport central line to South Woodford use westbound exit. Cross the pedestrian crossing and turn L. Garden is 100 meters on the R opp public car park.* **Sun 14 July (1-5). Adm £3, chd free. Home-made teas. Tea coffee homemade cakes & wine.**

A pretty Victoria terrace London house with a dog friendly Italian patio style garden. The garden has a tranquil white theme with a preference for white hydrangeas. The garden has all year interest with box hedges, bay trees evergreen shrubs & climbers. There are places to sit, lounge, eat and relax.

36 Park Road, Park Road Gardens

© Matthew Bruce

27 NASSINGTON ROAD, NW3

Hampstead, London, NW3 2TX. Lucy Scott-Moncrieff. *From Hampstead Heath rail stn & bus stops at South End Green, go up South Hill Pk, then Parliament Hill, R into Nassington Rd.* **Sun 9 June (2-6). Adm £5, chd free. Home-made teas.**

Double width town garden planted for colour and to support wildlife. Spectacular ancient wisteria, prolific roses; herbs and unusual fruit and vegetables in with the flowers. The main feature is a large eco pond with colourful planting in and out of the water and lots of mini-beasts. Pots and planters, arches, bowers, view of allotments and very peaceful location give a rural feel in the city. Pond dipping for newts and mini beasts all afternoon. Live music from the Secret Life Sax Quartet from 4:30 to 5:30pm. Cakes incl lemon drizzle made with lemons from the garden and gluten free cakes; teas incl rose hips from the garden but also real tea.

15 NORCOTT ROAD, N16

Stoke Newington, N16 7BJ. Amanda & John Welch. *Buses: 67, 73, 76, 106, 149, 243, 393, 476, 488. Clapton & Rectory Rd mainline stns. One way system: by car approach from Brooke Rd which crosses Norcott Rd, garden in S half of Norcott Rd.* **Sun 19 May (2-6). Adm £3.50, chd free. Home-made teas.**

A large walled garden developed by the present owners over the last forty years with pond, aged fruit trees and an abundance of herbaceous plants including irises, columbines, day lilies, many available in our plant sale. We enjoy opening at different times of the year. After a September opening in 2018, this year we are opening in May.

26 NORMANDY AVENUE, EN5

Barnet, EN5 2JA. Derek Epstein & Jo Vargas. *Tube: High Barnet then 5 mins walk. Buses: 34, 184, 84, 107, 307, 263, 326, 234. Ample parking. Normandy Ave is opp QE Girls School with Old Court House on corner.* **Sun 14 July (2-6). Adm £4, chd free. Home-made teas.**

120ft garden with three water features, two lawns, two 1920s garden buildings, two terraces, 40 pots, woodland walk, a veggie patch, sculptures and ornaments. A host of plants incl roses, hydrangeas, begonias, shrubs. Some of owners' sculpture and pottery will be on display. Sit on one of the terraces, in the lovely summerhouse, or by the pond while you enjoy tea and delicious cakes.

NEW **21 OAKLEIGH PARK SOUTH, N20**

London, N20 9JS. Carol and Robin Tullo. *Totteridge and Whetstone tube on N. Line (15 min walk or 251 bus) & Oakleigh Park station (10 mins). Also 34 and 125 from High Rd. Plenty of street parking.* **Sun 8 Sept (2-6). Adm £4, chd free. Home-made teas.**

Opening for the first time, a mature 200ft garden with large lawn area and borders. A magnificent 100 year old ash tree frames the garden. Path leads to a pond area fed by a natural spring within landscaped terraced paving. Beyond is a herb and vegetable area, orchard and the working part of the garden. A mix of sunny borders, pond marginals and woodland shade areas with seating. Level access to terrace and lawn. Path up to pond area but raised levels beyond.

46 OLLERTON ROAD, N11

Boundsgreen, New Southgate, N11 2LA. Mr & Mrs J Richardson. *Close to North circular. Tube: Bounds Green then 10 mins walk direction, N circular corner of Evesham Rd.* **Sun 14, Sun 21 July (2-5.30). Adm £3.50, chd free. Home-made teas.**

A herringbone brick garden that has been created from scratch in just 3yrs. Its owner has built raised flower beds out of reclaimed wooden tracks & managed to create an oasis of calm & tranquillity by using Hollyhocks & other colourful and tall plants. A lovely pergola covered in vines makes for a shady spot to sit and enjoy the garden. Artist studio will be open showing the owner's paintings.

ORMELEY LODGE, TW10

Ham Gate Avenue, Richmond, TW10 5HB. Lady Annabel Goldsmith. *From Richmond Park exit at Ham Gate into Ham Gate Ave, 1st house on R. From Richmond A307, after 1½m, past New Inn on R. At T-lights turn L into Ham Gate Ave.* **Sun 16 June (3-6). Adm £5, chd free. Tea.**

Large walled garden in delightful rural setting on Ham Common. Wide herbaceous borders and box hedges. Walk through to orchard with wild flowers. Vegetable garden, knot garden, aviary and chickens. Trellised tennis court with roses and climbers. A number of historic stone family dog memorials. Dogs not permitted.

4 ORMONDE ROAD, HA6

Moor Park, Northwood, HA6 2EL. Hasruty & Yogesh Patel. *Approx 5m from J17 & 18, M25; 6½m from J5, M1. From Batchworth Lane take Wolsey Rd exit at mini r'about. Ormonde Rd is 2nd turning on L. Ample parking on Ormonde Rd & surrounding rds.* **Sun 15 Sept (2-5). Adm £5.50, chd free. Home-made teas.**

Beautifully planted frontage entices visitors to a large rear garden. A calm oasis enclosed by mature hedging. A rare variegated flowering tulip tree provides dappled shade alongside rhododendrons, peonies, magnolias and diverse acers. Lavender hues of phlox foam along the raised patio. There is much interest throughout the whole garden due to attention paid to successional planting.

12 OVERBRAE, BR3

Beckenham, BR3 1SX. Mrs Alix Branch. *Off Worsley Bridge Rd, nr Kent Cricket Ground. Nearest stations, Beckenham Junction, Lower Sydenham or Beckenham Hill. Each approx 1m. Bus 352.* **Sun 23 June (2-5). Combined adm with 209 Worsley Bridge Road £5, chd free. Home-made teas.**

An award winning garden (Bromley in Bloom) of two parts with a delightful woodland area of mature trees to the rear and an open south facing lawn and flower beds offering a complete contrast. Vivid colour and variety of planting with patio area fully used for vegetables and hanging flower baskets. Some steep slopes require care.

PADDOCK ALLOTMENTS & LEISURE GARDENS, SW20

51 Heath Drive, Raynes Park, SW20 9BE. Paddock Horticultural Society. *Bus: 57, 131, 200 to Raynes Pk station then 10 min walk or bus 163. 152 to Bushey Rd 7 min walk; 413, 5 min walk from Cannon Hill Lane. Street parking.* **Sat 29 June (12-5). Adm £3.50, chd free. Light refreshments.**

An allotment site not to be missed, over 150 plots set in 5½ acres. Our tenants come from diverse communities growing a wide range of flowers, fruits and vegetables, some plots are purely organic others resemble English country gardens. Winner of London in Bloom Best Allotment. Plants, jams and produce for sale. Ploughman's Lunch available. Display of arts and crafts by members of the Paddock Hobby Club. Paved and grass paths, mainly level.

93 PALACE ROAD

London SW2 3LB. Charlotte & Matthew Vaight. *Stn: Tulse Hill. Buses: 2, 68, 322, 415, 432, 468. Sun 5 May (2-5).* **Adm £4.50, chd free. Home-made teas.**

The strong structural lines and oval lawns are framed by mixed borders. Evergreen shrubs act as backing singers to the tulip divas, floating on a froth of forget me nots. The garden makes the most of its north facing, multi level site and features a wild life pond, shady planted terraces and several contemporary sculptures. Includes a well planted front garden. A rare spring opening to coincide with the garden appearing in Gardeners World magazine.

11 PARK AVENUE NORTH, N8

Crouch End, London, N8 7RU. Mr Steven Buckley & Ms Liz Roberts. *Tube: Finsbury Park & Turnpike Lane, nearest bus stop W3, 144, W7.* **Sun 23 June (11.30-5.30). Adm £4, chd free. Home-made teas.**

An exotic 250ft garden. Dramatic, mainly spiky, foliage dominates with the focus on palms, agaves, dasylirions, aeoniums, tree ferns, nolinas, cycads, bamboo, yuccas, cacti and several hundred types of succulent. Aloes are a highlight. Fruit trees incl banana, peach and apricot. Rocks and terracotta pots lend a Mediterranean accent. Vegetables grow in oak raised beds and a modern glasshouse.

18 PARK CRESCENT, N3

Finchley, N3 2NJ. Rosie Daniels. *Tube: Finchley Central. Buses: 13 to Victoria Park, also 125, 460, 626, 683. Walk from Ballards Lane into Etchingham Pk Rd, 2nd L Park Crescent.* **Sun 23 June, Sun 21 July (2-6). Adm £4, chd free. Home-made teas.**

This charming constantly evolving "Secret Garden" is designed and densely planted by the owner. Tumbling roses & clematis in June, salvias, rudbeckia, helenium in July. Two very small ponds, tub water features, bird haven. Stepped terrace with lots of pots. New glass installations and sculptures by owner. Hidden seating with view through garden. Children's treasure hunt. Extensive collection of clematis and salvias. London Gardens Society: Awarded Gold

GROUP OPENING

PARK ROAD GARDENS, W4

London, W4 3HH. *Arrive by overground train at Chiswick Stn, follow Park Rd (opp the stn, N side) for approx ½m north.* **Sun 2 June (2-6). Combined adm £5, chd free. Tea.**

34 PARK ROAD
Simon Lockett.

36 PARK ROAD, W4
Meyrick & Louise Chapman.

These two gardens are next door to each other on the northern end of Park Road. No 36 is a city garden with distinct structure and formality based on a series of rooms within hedging. Designed to create a flavour to each room; one hot, one cool and one dark using perennials, roses, hostas and ferns against a repeated background of yew, azalea and camellia. Green wall and reflective pool. No 34 is a modern garden design built on creating different spaces using architectural walls to separate the areas. Planting incl mature olive trees as a centre piece in each area with bee friendly flowers integrated with pre-existing trees. Partial wheelchair access.

4 PARK VILLAGE EAST (TOWER LODGE GARDEN), NW1

Regents Park, London, NW1 7PX. Eveline Carn, 07831 136069, evelinecbcarn@icloud.com. *Tube: Camden Town or Mornington Crescent 7 mins. Bus: C2 or 274 3 mins. Opp The York & Albany, just off junction of Parkway/Prince Albert Rd.* **Visits by arrangement Apr to Oct for groups of 5+. Group visits welcome for coffee, cakes, afternoon teas, wine evenings.**
An unexpectedly large, tranquil garden behind a John Nash house, screened by mature trees and descending over 3 terraces with stepped ponds to the original foundations of the Regents Canal. Emphasis on shapes, textures, shades of green and bold foliage set in strong landscape architecture. Sculptures. Lots of places to sit and enjoy the garden incl a tree hung swing!

3 THE PARK, N6

off Southwood Lane, London, N6 4EU. Mr & Mrs G Schrager, 020 8348 3314, buntyschrager@gmail.com. *3 mins from Highgate tube, up Southwood Lane. The Park is 1st on R. Buses: 43, 134, 143, 263.* **Sun 19 May (2.30-5.30). Adm £3.50, chd free. Home-made teas. Visits also by arrangement Apr to June for groups of 5 to 20.**
Established large garden with informal planting for colour, scent and bees. Pond with fish, frogs and tadpoles. Tree peonies, Crinodendron hookerianum and Paulownia. Plants, tea and home-made jam for sale. Children particularly welcome - a treasure hunt with prizes!

NEW 98 PARKWAY, NW1

Camden Town, NW1 7AN. Fanny Calder. *A short walk from Camden Tube Station - the entrance is at basement level, next door to the Rock and Roll Charity Shop.* **Sat 18 May (2-5.30). Adm £2, chd free. Home-made teas. Also open 70 Gloucester Crescent.**
A small, walled townhouse garden hidden away unexpectedly behind a busy street of shops and cafes in Camden. The garden is predominantly a very diverse collection of white flowers in several raised beds and large pots - roses, allium, iris, peonies, clematis, aquilegia, geraniums, dicentra and more will be out in May. Accessed by steep steps so not suitable for people with mobility problems.

NEW 5 PEMBERTON ROAD, KT8

East Molesey, KT8 9LG. Armi Maddison. *Please enter the garden down the side path to the RHS of the house.* **Sun 9 June (2-5). Adm £4.50, chd free. Light refreshments. Also open 61 Wolsey Road.**
An artist's sheltered and secluded gravel garden designed alongside our new build in 2015. Many grasses, pink blue and white planting with occasional 'pops' of bright colour, a galvanised drinking trough with bullrushes and water lilies, a large mature central acer tree combine with several sitting areas to extend our living space into fabulous outdoor room.

21 Gospatrick Road

23 & 24B PENN ROAD, N7

London, N7 9RD. Pierre Delarue & Mark Atkinson. *Between Camden Town & Holloway. Buses: 29 or 253 to Hillmarton Rd or 91 to Camden Rd stops. Tube: Caledonian Road on Piccadilly line, 6 mins walk.* **Sun 7 July (2-6). Adm £4.50, chd free. Also open 33 Huddleston Road.**
2 neighboring gardens famous for their planting as well as delicious teas & home-made cakes. Access through a leafy passage at No.23, fronted with prairie wilderness. The main 25x70ft back garden presents a mixture of old-fashioned roses & Mediterranean plants to achieve an exotic feel. Specimen plants incl a Red Barked Arbutus, a Santa Cruz Ironwood, an Orange Barked Myrtle & a tall 'stripped' Trachycarpus. A neoclassic studio with patio and newly installed water feature act as focal point. The 25X46ft 'pleasure garden' at 24b is now accessible through a gate & features three contrasting borders: dry, woodland & roses. A selection of refreshments will be served inside the Garden Studio alongside a wide range of delicious homemade Bundt cakes in a variety of interesting flavours, now integral to the NGS experience at 23 Penn Road.

NEW 101 PEPYS ROAD, SE14

New Cross, SE14 5SE. Mrs Helen Le Fevre. *Entrance via side gate. Situated at the top of Telegraph Hill, off the A2. Overground New Cross Gate 15mins walk. Buses to New Cross Bus garage: 21,36,53,136,171,172,453. Street parking available.* **Sun 2 June (2-5.30). Adm £3.50, chd free. Home-made teas. Also open 4 Cornflower Terrace.**
This garden will surprise you with its unexpected length (160ft) and beautiful individual 'rooms' on different levels. Features incl informal planting with splendid mature trees, shrubs and an emphasis on colourful foliage, many raised organic veg beds, a hidden greenhouse and nature pond. Bee and pollinator friendly borders, with ingenious snail defences create a charming haven for wildlife.

PETERSHAM HOUSE, TW10

Petersham Road, Petersham, Richmond, TW10 7AA. Francesco & Gael Boglione, 020 8940 5230, info.richmond@petershamnurseries.com, www.petershamnurseries.com. *Stn: Richmond, then 65 bus to Dysart PH. Entry to garden off Petersham Rd, through nursery. Parking very limited on Church Lane.* **Visits by arrangement May to Sept. Adm £12, chd free. Light refreshments in the nursery.**
Broad lawn with large topiary, generously planted double borders. Productive vegetable garden with chickens. Adjoins Petersham Nurseries with extensive plant sales, shop and café serving lunch, tea and cake.

470 PINNER ROAD, HA5

Pinner, HA5 5RR. Nitty Chamcheon. *N Harrow Station, L to T-lights, L at next T-lights, cross to be on Pinner Rd. L - 3rd house from T-lights. Parking: Pinner Rd & George V Av - yellow lines stop after 15 yds.* **Sun 22 Sept (2-6). Adm £4, chd free. Home-made teas.**
Once (20 yrs ago) a back yard with just a lawn in the first half and the second half a jungle with a very mature apple and pear tree; now a beautiful garden. A path passing through fruit and vegetable garden to the secret log cabin after a bridge over the pond with waterfall in front of a tree house in the pear tree. An attempt has been made to extend the season as far as possible.

NEW 36 POTTERS LANE, EN5

Barnet, EN5 5BE. Roderick Muir & Laurence Little. *New Barnet. High Barnet tube 15 min walk down Meadway. R into King Edward Rd and 2nd R into Potters Lane. Buses: from N get off opp BP garage. From S Everyman cinema. 7min walk up Potters Lane.* **Sun 26 May (2-6). Adm £5, chd free. Home-made teas.**
Our garden has evolved, and is still evolving, over the 30 years that we have been working on it. The garden is unusually long for a suburban garden and is on a gentle slope away from the house. It is divided into different areas, a formal garden, a working garden, a less formal area leading to a gate through a purple beech hedge into a secret garden and wildlife pond.

GROUP OPENING

PRINCES AVENUE GARDENS, N10

Muswell Hill, N10 3LS. *Buses: 43 & 134 from Highgate tube; also W7, 102, 144, 234, 299. Princes Ave opp M&S in Muswell Hill Broadway, or John Baird PH in Fortis Green.* **Sun 12 May (2-6). Combined adm £5, chd free. Home-made teas.**

17 PRINCES AVENUE
Patsy Bailey & John Rance.

28 PRINCES AVENUE
Ian & Viv Roberts.

In a beautiful Edwardian avenue in the heart of Muswell Hill Conservation Area, two very different gardens reflect the diverse life styles of their owners. The charming garden at No 17 is designed for relaxing and entertaining . Although south facing it is shaded by large surrounding trees - among which is a ginko. The garden features a superb hosta and fern display. No 28 is a well established traditional garden reflecting the charm typical of the era. Mature trees, shrubs, mixed borders and woodland garden creating an oasis of calm just off the bustling Broadway.

GROUP OPENING

RAILWAY COTTAGES, N22

2 Dorset Road, Alexandra Palace, London, N22 7SL. *Tube: Wood Green, 10 mins walk. Overground: Alexandra Palace, 3 mins. Buses W3, 184. 3 mins. Free parking in local streets on Suns.* **Sun 7 July (2-5.30). Combined adm £4.50, chd free. Home-made teas at 2 Dorset Rd.**

24A DORSET ROAD
Eddie & Jane Wessman.

2 DORSET ROAD
Jane Stevens.

4 DORSET ROAD
Mark Longworth.

14 DORSET ROAD
Cathy Brogan.

22 DORSET ROAD
Mike & Noreen Ainger.

A row of historical railway cottages, tucked away from the bustle of Wood Green nr Alexandra Palace, takes the visitor back in time.The tranquil country style garden at 2 Dorset Rd flanks three sides of the house. Clipped hedges contrast with climbing roses, clematis, honeysuckle, abutilon, grasses and ferns. Trees include mulberry, quince, fig, apple and a mature willow creating an interesting shady corner with a pond. There is an emphasis on scented flowers that attract bees and butterflies and the traditional medicinal plants found in cottage gardens. No 4 is a pretty secluded garden (accessed through the rear of no 2), and sets off the sculptor owners figurative and abstract work. There are three front gardens open for view. No 14. An informal, organic, bee friendly garden, planted with fragrant and useful herbs, flowers and shrubs. No 22 is nurtured by the grandson of the original railway worker occupant. A lovely place to sit and relax and enjoy the varied planting. No.24a reverts to the potager style cottage garden with raised beds overflowing with vegetables and flowers.

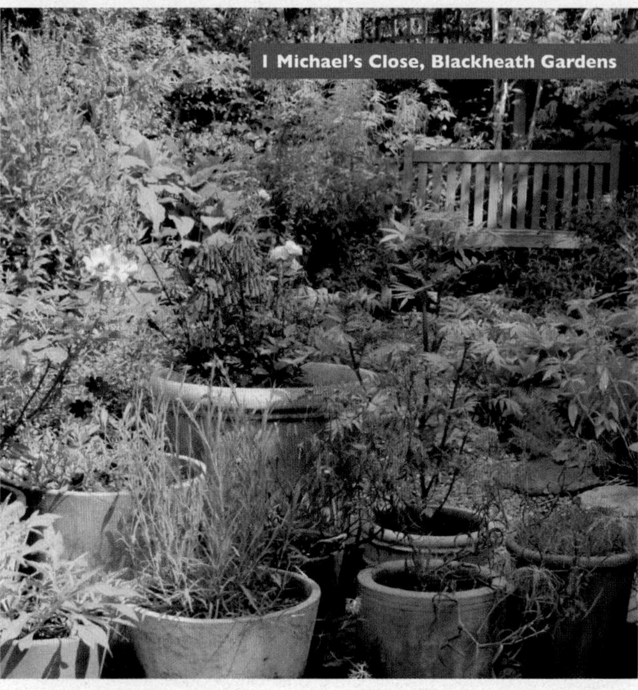
I Michael's Close, Blackheath Gardens

ROOFTOPVEGPLOT, W1
122 Gt Titchfield Street, London, W1W 6ST. Miss Wendy Shillam, www.rooftopvegplot.com. *Fitzrovia. Located on the 5th floor, flat roof of a private house. Ring the doorbell marked Shillam & Smith to be let into the building.* **Sat 6, Sun 7 July (11-4). Adm £5, chd free. Home-made teas. Cakes and drinks using garden ingredients where possible. Pre-booking essential, please visit www.ngs.org.uk for information & booking.**
A nutritional garden, where fruit and veg grow amongst complementary flowers in six inches of soil, in raised beds on a flat roof. This is a tiny garden, so tours are restricted to six persons. Home made cakes and growing and nutritional tips from Wendy Shillam, a keen environmentalist with an extensive knowledge of green nutrition. Tomatoes and cucumber growing in a greenhouse. Grapevine from Le Moulin Gif-sur-Yvette, France. Elder, Jasmine, Japanese wineberry. Potatoes. Edible honeysuckle (Henrii) Salads, artichokes, garlic, annuals, roses, marigolds, nasturtiums, hyssop, sweet and garden peas, climbing beans and courgettes.

ROYAL TRINITY HOSPICE, SW4
30 Clapham Common North Side, London, SW4 0RN. Royal Trinity Hospice, www.royaltrinityhospice.org.uk. *Tube: Clapham Common. Buses: 35, 37, 345,137 stop outside.* **Sun 7 Apr, Sun 19 May, Sun 1 Sept (10.30-4.30). Adm £3, chd free.**
Royal Trinity's beautiful, award winning gardens play an important therapeutic role in the life and function of Royal Trinity Hospice. Over the years, many people have enjoyed our gardens and today they continue to be enjoyed by patients, families and visitors alike. Set over nearly 2 acres, they offer space for quiet contemplation, family fun and make a great backdrop for events. Picnics welcome. Ramps and pathways.

7 ST GEORGE'S ROAD, TW1
St Margarets, Twickenham, TW1 1QS. Richard & Jenny Raworth, 020 8892 3713, jraworth@gmail.com, www.raworthgarden.com. *1½m SW of Richmond. Off A316 between Twickenham Bridge & St Margarets r'about.* **Visits by arrangement May to July for groups of 10 to 30. Home-made teas.**
Exuberant displays of Old English roses and vigorous climbers with unusual herbaceous perennials. Massed scented crambe cordifolia. Pond with bridge converted into child safe lush bog garden and waterfall. Large N-facing luxuriant conservatory with rare plants and climbers. Pelargoniums a speciality. Sunken garden Pergola covered with climbing roses and clematis. New white garden. Water feature and fernery. Reading Garden.

87 ST JOHNS ROAD, E17
London, E17 4JH. Andrew Bliss. *15 mins walk from W'stow tube/ overground or 212/275 bus. Alight at St Johns Rd stop. 10 mins walk from Wood St overground. Very close to N Circular.* **Mon 5 Aug (1.30-5.30). Adm £3.50, chd £0.50. Home-made teas.**
My garden epitomises what can be achieved with imagination, design and colour consideration in a small typical terraced outdoor area.
Its themes are diverse and incl a fernery, Jardin Majorelle, a water feature and 3 individual seating areas. All enhanced with circles, mirrors and over planting to create an atmosphere of tranquility within an urban environment.

20 ST MARY'S GROVE, N1
London, N1 2NT. Mrs B Capel. *Canonbury, Islington. Highbury & Islington Tube & Overground. Buses: 4, 19, 30, 393 to St Paul's Rd. 271 to Canonbury Square.* **Sun 12 May (2.30-5.30). Adm £3, chd free. Also open 58 Halliford Street.**
Come and discover this delightful small garden with sweet smelling spring shrubs and flowers - akebia, coronilla, tree peony, camellias, lilac, azalea and climbing roses. Preserves and plants for sale.

27 ST PETERS SQUARE, W6
London, W6 9NW. Oliver & Gabrielle Leigh Wood, oliverleighwood@hotmail.com. *Tube to Stamford Brook exit station & turn S down Goldhawk Rd. At T-lights cont ahead into British Grove. Entrance to garden at 50 British Grove 100 yds on L.* **Sun 5 May (2-6). Adm £4.50, chd free. Home-made teas.** Visits also by arrangement Apr to July.
This long, secret space, is a plantsman's eclectic semi-tamed wilderness. Created over the last 10yrs it contains lots of camellias, magnolias and fruit trees. Much of the hard landscaping is from skips and the whole garden is full of other people's unconsidered trifles of fancy incl a folly and summer house.

19 ST PETER'S STREET, N1
Islington, London, N1 8JD. Adrian Gunning. *Angel, Islington. Tube: Angel. Bus: Islington Green.* **Sun 2 June (2.30-5.30). Adm £3.50, chd free. Also open Diespeker Wharf.**
Charming secluded town garden with climbing roses, trees, shrubs, climbers, pond, patio with containers, and a gazebo with a trompe l'oeil mural.

57 ST QUINTIN AVENUE, W10
London, W10 6NZ. Mr H Groffman, 020 8969 8292. *Less than 1m from Ladbroke Grove or White City tube. Buses: 7, 70, 220 all to North Pole Rd. Free parking on Sundays.* **Sun 7, Sun 21 July (2-6). Adm £4.50, chd free. Home-made teas.** Visits also by arrangement July & Aug.
A 30 x 40 ft garden with a diverse selection of plants incl evergreen and deciduous shrubs for foliage effects. Patio with colour themed bedding material. Focal points throughout. Clever use of mirrors and plant associations. First phase major refurbishment planned for 2019. Recipient 2018 Mayoral Award for Services to Horticulture. Brighter Kensington & Chelsea Special Award for WW1 Commemoration. Look out for the garden theme for 2019 announcement on the NGS website!

5 ST REGIS CLOSE, N10
Alexandra Park Road, Muswell Hill, N10 2DE. Ms S Bennett & Mr E Hyde, 020 8883 8540, suebearlh@yahoo.co.uk. *Tube: Bounds Green then 102 or 299 bus, or E. Finchley take 102. Alight St Andrews Church. 134 or 43 bus stop at end of Alexandra Pk Rd, follow arrows.* **Sun 28 Apr (2-6.30). Sun 16 June (2-6.30), also open 25 Springfield Avenue. Sun 21 July (2-6.30). Adm £4, chd free. Home-made teas. Gluten free available. Herbal teas.** Visits also by arrangement Apr to Oct for groups of 10+. Short talks available.
Cornucopia of sensual delights. Artist's garden famous for architectural features and delicious cakes. New Oriental Tea House. Baroque temple, pagodas, Raku tiled mirrored wall conceals plant nursery. American Gothic shed overlooks Liberace Terrace and stairway to heaven. Maureen Lipman's favourite garden, combines colour, humour, trompe l'oeil with wildlife friendly ponds, waterfalls, weeping willow, lawns, abundant planting. A unique experience awaits! Unusual architectural features including Oriental Tea House overlooking carp pond. Mega plant sale. Open

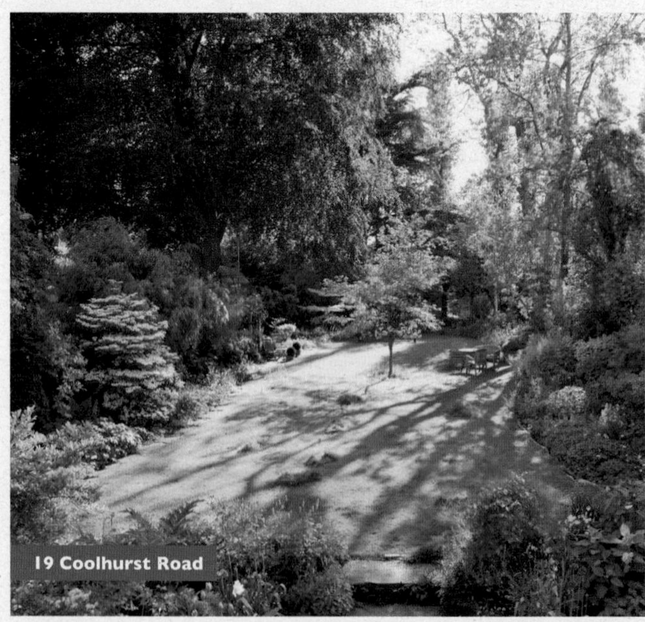
19 Coolhurst Road

Studio with ceramics and cards. Wheelchair access to all parts of garden unless waterlogged.

2 SHARDCROFT AVENUE, SE24

Herne Hill, London, SE24 0DT. Catriona Andrews. *Short walk from Herne Hill rail station & bus stops. Buses: 3, 68, 196, 201, 468 to Herne Hill. Closest tube Brixton. Parking in local streets.* **Sun 14 July (2-6). Adm £4, chd free. Home-made teas.**

A designer's garden with loose, naturalistic planting. Geometric terracing accommodates a natural slope, framing vistas from the house. Drought tolerant beds with cascading perennials and grasses, scented courtyard, formal wildlife pond, woodland glade with fire pit and green roofed shed provide wildlife habitats and a feast for the senses. Planted ecologically to benefit wildlife. Nesting boxes and log piles.

SOUTH LONDON BOTANICAL INSTITUTE, SE24

323 Norwood Road, London, SE24 9AQ. South London Botanical Institute, www.slbi.org.uk. *Mainline stn: Tulse Hill. Buses: 68, 196, 322 & 468 stop at junction of Norwood & Romola Rds.* **Sun 14 Apr (2-5). Adm £3.50, chd free. Home-made teas. Donation to South London Botanical Institute.**

London's smallest botanical garden, densely planted with 500 labelled species grown in a formal layout of themed borders. Wildflowers flourish beside medicinal herbs. Carnivorous, scented, native and woodland plants are featured, growing among rare trees and shrubs. Spring highlights incl mosses, unusual bulbs and flowering trees. The fascinating SLBI building is also open.

123 SOUTH PARK ROAD, SW19

Wimbledon, London, SW19 8RX. Susan Adcock. *Mainline & tube: Wimbledon, 10 mins; S Wimbledon tube 5 mins. Buses: 57, 93, 131, 219 along High St. Entrance in Bridges Rd (next to church hall) off South Park Rd.* **Sun 2 June (2-6). Adm £3.50, chd free. Light refreshments.**

This small L-shaped garden has a high treetop deck overlooking a woodland area, paving from the garden room with pots and seating, several small water containers, a fish pond and a secluded courtyard with raised beds for flowers and herbs, as well as a discreet hot tub. Lots of ideas for giving a small space atmosphere and interest.

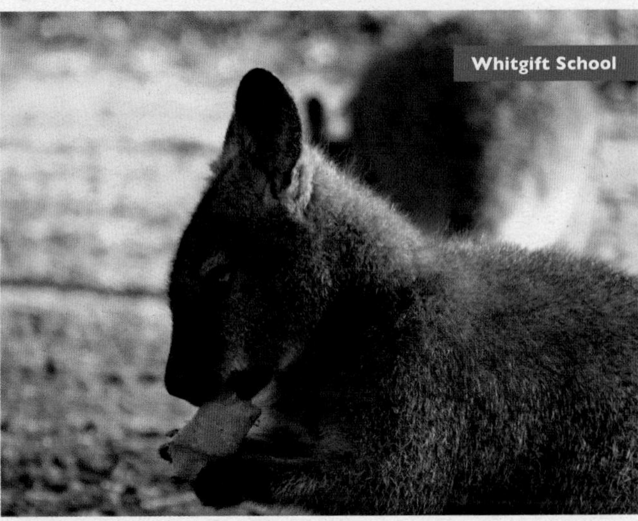

Whitgift School

41 SOUTHBROOK ROAD, SE12

Lee, London, SE12 8LJ. Barbara & Marek Polanski, 020 8333 2176, polanski101@yahoo.co.uk. *Southbrook Rd is situated off S Circular, off Burnt Ash Rd. Train: Lee & Hither Green, both 10 mins walk. Bus: P273, 202.* **Sat 8 June (2-5.30). Adm £3.50, chd free. Home-made teas. orange squash. Visits also by arrangement May to Aug for groups of 10 to 20. Afternoons only. Also opens as part of Blackheath Gardens on Sun 9 June.**

Developed over 14yrs, this large garden has a formal layout, with wide mixed herbaceous borders full of colour and interest, surrounded by mature trees, framing sunny lawns, a central box parterre and an Indian pergola. Ancient pear trees festooned in June with clouds of white Kiftsgate and Rambling Rector roses. Discover fish and damselflies in 2 lily ponds. Many sheltered places to sit and relax. Enjoy refreshments in a small classical garden building with interior wall paintings, almost hidden by roses climbing way up into the trees. Orangery. Side access available for standard wheelchairs.

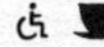

NEW 131 SOUTHGATE ROAD, N1

London, N1 3JZ. John Le Huquet and Vicki Primm-Sexton. *East Canonbury. Bank or Old St tube then 21 or 141 bus to Englefield Rd stop (outside house). Highbury & Islington tube, 30 bus to Southgate Rd stop, 5 min wk. Angel tube, 38, 56 or 73 bus to Ockendon Rd, 5 min walk.* **Sun 30 June (12-6). Adm £3, chd free. Light refreshments. A selection of hot and cold drinks, some with a botanical theme.**

Open for the first time, this vivacious little walled town garden is densely planted with over 50 species of sun-loving perennials, creating an intense visual experience. The lush, naturalistic planting showcases a jamboree of jewel-like blooms weaving through softly waving grasses and delicate umbellifers. Specially commissioned Corten steel wall screens and a charming idiosyncratic shed. Garden reached by staircase.

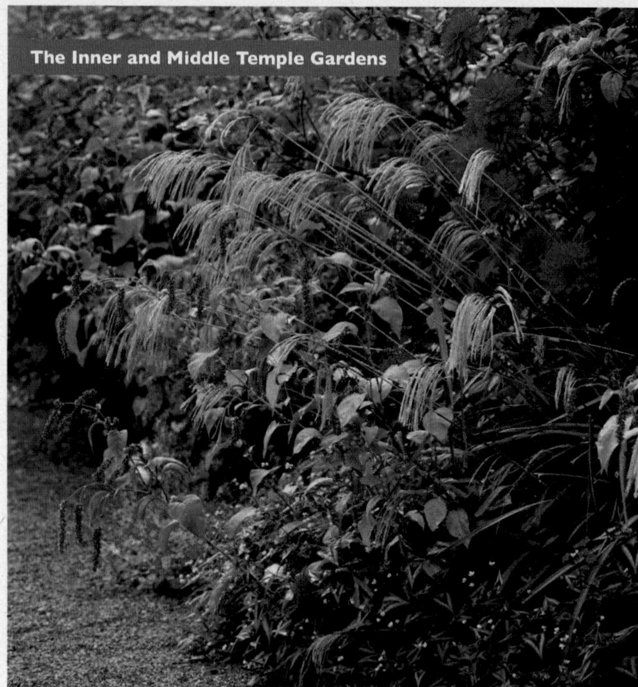

SOUTHWOOD LODGE, N6
33 Kingsley Place, Highgate, N6 5EA. Mrs S Whittington, 020 8348 2785, suewhittington@hotmail.co.uk. *Tube: Highgate then 6 mins uphill walk along Southwood Lane. 4 min walk from Highgate Village along Southwood Lane. Buses: 143, 210, 214, 271.* **Sun 5 May (2-5.30). Adm £4, chd free. Home-made teas. Visits also by arrangement Apr to July. Lunch for groups of 10+ or teas (any number) by arrangement.**
Densely planted garden hidden behind C18 house (not open). Many unusual plants, some propagated for sale. Ponds, waterfall, frogs, toads, newts. Topiary shapes formed from self sown yew trees. Sculpture carved from three trunks of a massive conifer which became unstable in a storm. Hard working greenhouse! Only one open day this year so visits by appointment especially welcome. Toffee hunt for children. Secret Life Sax Quartet will perform in the garden from 2.30pm.

 **7 SPENCER ROAD, SW18**
Wandsworth, SW18 2SP. Christopher Masson. *12 mins from upper exit Clapham Junction station Buses 170, 37, 39,219,337,87,77,156. Parking free after 4.30pm.* **Evening opening Thur 29 Aug (5.30-8). Adm £6, chd free. Wine.**
Garden designer's experimental ground. Long narrow north-facing paved garden with water. Dense planting of varying evergreen textures plus an array of potted perennials, constantly changing. Sunny garden room with terrace and overhead cover in rain. Garden lighting at dusk. Narrow side access and difficult level changes.

GROUP OPENING

SPITALFIELDS GARDENS, E1
London, E1 6QE. *Nr Spitalfields Market. 10 mins walk from Aldgate E Tube & 5 mins walk from Liverpool St stn. Overground: Shoreditch High St - 3 mins walk.* **Sat 8 June (11-4). Combined adm £15, chd free. Home-made teas at Town House, 5 Fournier St, 29 & 30 Fournier St. Maps available.**

26 ELDER STREET
The Future Laboratory.

 **FLAT 1, 30 CALVIN STREET**
Susan Young.

20 FOURNIER STREET
Ms Charlie de Wet.

29 FOURNIER STREET
Juliette Larthe.

31 FOURNIER STREET
Tom Holmes.

21 PRINCELET STREET
Marianne & Nicholas Morse.

37 SPITAL SQUARE
Society for the Protection of Ancient Buildings.

21 WILKES STREET
Rupert Wheeler.

23 WILKES STREET
Juliet McKoen.

Hidden treasures behind some of the finest merchants and weavers houses in Spitalfields. Visit the courtyard of the Society for the Protection of Ancient Buildings at 37 Spital Square, founded by William Morris in 1877. The other gardens are in nearby Elder Street, two in Wilkes Street, one in Princelet Street and three in Fournier Street, and a new intriguing garden in Calvin St, behind a former warehouse. Be enchanted by how each garden owner has adapted their urban space to complement an historic house. Vegetables, herbs, layered vertical and ground beds with 'very English planting', ornamental pots, statuary and architectural artefacts greet you. The area has fertile roots: once a field beside the 12th century St Mary's Spital priory. In the 17th century French Huguenots brought their silk-weaving skills to the area and built the elegant houses with lofts. The herbalist physician Nicholas Culpeper set up a pharmacy in Spitalfields, using herbs collected nearby. Walk back in time!

25 SPRINGFIELD AVENUE, N10
Muswell Hill, N10 3SU. Nigel Ragg & Heather Hampson. *Off Muswell Hill. Buses 102 299 W7 134 43 From main r'about at Muswell Hill descend towards Crouch End . Springfield Av 1st L.* **Sun 16 June (2-6). Adm £4, chd free. Home-made teas. Also open 5 St Regis Close.**
We re-landscaped our town garden in 2013, transforming it's plain incline to individual terraces, mixing an aura of spirituality with a country atmosphere. The mature trees of Alexander Palace lend the garden a spectacular backdrop and together with pot and chimney planting, summerhouse and decking, make it unique. New for 2019 - one of the terraces has been redesigned. Environmentally friendly parking in front garden. Steep steps.

2 SPRINGHURST CLOSE, CR0
Shirley Church Road, Croydon, CR0 5AT. Ben & Peckham Carroll. *2m S of Croydon. Off A2022 from Selsdon. Off A232 from Croydon. Ent to Close opp The Addington Golf Club. Parking at Golf Club. Tramline 3 to Addington Village. East Croydon Station.* **Sun 16 June (2-5.30). Adm £4, chd free. Home-made teas.**
Popular garden reopened, designer terrace beds with specimen grasses, topiary, periennials, decorative trees and elegant water feature with extensive hosta collection. Planting in a soft colour palette designed to attract bees with border of unusual black plants. Vegetable garden in raised beds, bug hotel, fernery, woodland hydrangea walk add interest and variety all in a secluded woodland setting. All cakes home-made. Extensive plant sale. Wheelchair friendly level garden with grass and gravel paths with only a few steps, WC facilities with low step.

STOKES HOUSE, TW10
Ham Street, Ham, Richmond, TW10 7HR. Peter & Rachel Lipscomb, 020 8940 2403, rlipscomb@virginmedia.com. *2m S of Richmond off A307. Trains & tube to Richmond & train to Kingston which link with 65 bus stopping at Ham Common every 6 mins.* **Sun 2 June (2-5). Adm £4, chd free. Home-made teas.** Visits also by arrangement Apr to Oct for groups of 10+. Stokes House Ham St Light lunch or tea available.
Originally an orchard, this ½ acre walled country garden surrounding Georgian house (not open) is abundant with roses, clematis and perennials. There are mature trees incl ancient mulberries and wisteria. The yew hedging, pergola and box hedges allow for different planting schemes throughout the year. Supervised children are welcome to play on the slide and swing. Herbaceous borders, brick garden, wild garden, large compost area and interesting trees. Teas, garden tour, history of house and area for group visits. Wheelchair access via double doors from street with 2 wide steps. Unfortunately no access for larger motorised chairs.

We help ordinary people open the gates to their extraordinary private gardens to raise impressive amounts of money through admissions, teas and slices of cake!

NEW **SWAKLEYS COTTAGE, 2 THE AVENUE, UB10**
Ickenham, Uxbridge, UB10 8NP. Lady Singleton Booth. *Take the B466 to Ickenham from the A40 at Hillingdon Circus. Go 1m into Ickenham village. Coach and Horses PH on R, turn L into Swakeley's Rd. After the shops, The Avenue is on L.* **Sun 9 June (2-6). Adm £4, chd free. Home-made teas.**
Classic English cottage garden. The garden has been designed by Lady Booth and her late husband Sir Christopher Booth. The garden is charming and wraps around a 600 year old cottage. It consists of herbaceous borders which are dotted with vegetables, garden herbs & fruit trees. There is an abundance of colour and some very interesting plants incorporating different styles.

93 TANFIELD AVENUE, NW2
Dudden Hill, London, NW2 7SB. Mr James Duncan Mattoon. *Dudden Hill - Neasden. Nearest station: Neasden - Jubilee line then 10 mins walk; or various bus routes to Neasden Parade or Tanfield Ave.* **Sun 14 July (2-6). Adm £4, chd free. Home-made teas.**
New Chamomile lawn and newly finished Arabic style watercourse, complete an 8 year development of this Plantsman's hillside paradise garden! Raised Deco deck with panoramic views, plunges down steps into Mediterranean and subtropical oasis, overflowing with many rare and exotic plants e.g. Hedychium, Puya, Strobilanthes! To rear, jungle shade terrace offers cool views of paradise on sunny days. Previous garden was Tropical Kensal Rise (Doyle Gardens), featured on BBC2 Open Gardens and in Sunday Telegraph.

NEW **20 TAYLOR AVENUE, TW9**
Richmond, TW9 4ED. Mrs Caroline Perkins. *Turn R off the South Circular Rd.* **Sun 9 June (1-4). Combined adm with 28 Taylor Avenue £3.50, chd free. Also open 31 West Park Road.**
Situated near Kew Gardens, this is a very verdant garden with mature trees and shrubs, a small water feature attracting frogs and newts, a large pergola covered by a mature wisteria, a 'zen' inspired area and a recent professional re-design of the garden reclaiming the rear area from the (now grown up) children. This re-design involved re-shaping and new planting around existing planting.

NEW 28 TAYLOR AVENUE, TW9

Kew, Richmond, TW9 4ED. Inma Lapena. *10 mins walk from Kew Gardens Station. Follow North Rd until Atwood Ave. Turn L & then follow to end where it becomes Taylor Ave. If driving turn R off the South Circular.* **Sun 9 June (1-4). Combined adm with 20 Taylor Avenue £3.50, chd free. Home-made teas. Also open 31 West Park Road.**

The garden is about 30 metres long and about 10 metres wide. It is an urban garden typical of any semi-detached house in London. There are borders on both sides with many varieties of plants.

58A TEIGNMOUTH ROAD, NW2

Cricklewood, NW2 4DX. Drs Elayne & Jim Coakes, 020 8208 0082, elayne.coakes@btinternet.com, www.facebook.com/gardening4bees. *Cricklewood (Willesden Green). Tube: Willesden Green or Kilburn 10 mins walk. Buses: 16, 32, 189, 226, 260, 266, 316, 332, 460. Teignmouth Rd just off Walm Lane.* **Sun 15 Sept (2-5). Combined adm with 106 Dartmouth Rd, Flat 1 £7, chd free. Home-made teas at 106 Dartmouth Road. Cold drinks available at Teignmouth Rd.** Visits also by arrangement Mar to Oct for groups of up to 20.

Front and back gardens with eclectic planting schemes incl restrained palate coordinated beds, pergola with wisteria, climbing roses and 40+ clematis, 2 ponds, water features, acers, hardy and unusual plants. Rainwater harvesting with integral watering system, native plants and organic treatment means a home for frogs, newts and bees. Won Silver in the London in Bloom Fresh Air awards. Under the terrace is a 3½ ton tank for the water harvesting system that feeds water to taps around the garden; Clematis & other climbing plants clothe the pergola, woodland walk & the fences. This is an energetic garden attracting wildlife and wild flowers. Entry price to this garden only is £4. Some areas only accessible by stepping stones. Deep ponds.

57 TONBRIDGE HOUSE, WC1H

Tonbridge Street, London, WC1H 9PG. Sue Heiser. *S of Euston Road. Tube: King's Cross & St Pancras Stn & Russell Sq. Behind Camden Town Hall off Judd St. Turn into Bidborough St which becomes Tonbridge St. Side entrance to garden.* **Sun 30 June (2-5.30). Adm £3.50, chd free. Home-made teas.**

Unexpected oasis off the Euston Road, overlooked on all sides by tall buildings. Mixed informal planting, with seating, rockery, pergola and shady areas. Mature magnolia, sycamore, holly and some long established shrubs and perennials incl ferns, hostas and heuchera. Small vegetable beds and herbs. Evolved over 35yrs on a low budget with plenty of help from friends. Wheelchair access from street and throughout garden.

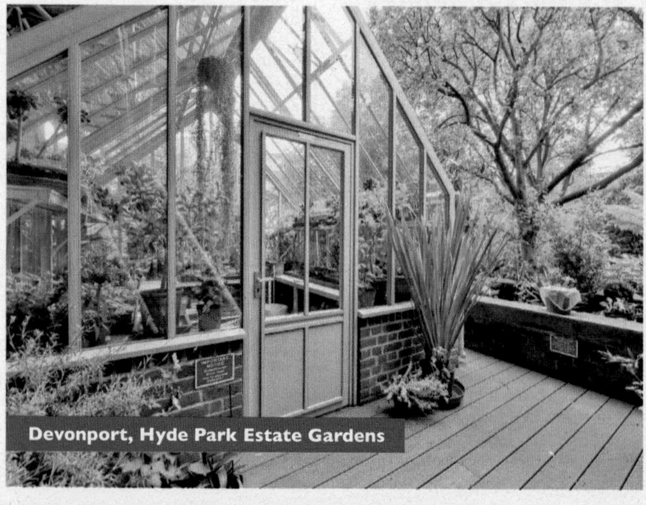

Devonport, Hyde Park Estate Gardens

TRUMPETERS HOUSE & SARAH'S GARDEN, TW9

Richmond, TW9 1PD. Baroness Van Dedem. *Richmond riverside. 5 mins walk from Richmond Station via Richmond Green in Trumpeter's Yard. Parking on Richmond Green & Old Deer Park car park only.* **Sat 8 June (2-5). Adm £5, chd free. Home-made teas.**

The 2 acre garden is on the original site of Richmond Palace. Long lawns stretch from the house to banks of the River Thames. There are clipped yews, a box parterre and many unusual shrubs and trees, a rose garden and oval pond with carp. The ancient Tudor walls are covered with roses and climbers. Discover Sarah's secret garden behind the high walls. Wheelchair access on grass and gravel.

TUDOR HERBALIST GARDEN, NW3

37 Christchurch Hill, Hampstead, NW3 1LA. Paul & Hazelanne Lewis. *7 mins from Hampstead Underground, 10 mins from Hampstead Heath Overground Stn. L out of Hampstead Underground, L into Flask Walk, straight to Christchurch Hill, and R to 37. From Hampstead Heath Stn, walk uphill bearing L onto South End Rd and Willow Rd at Horse trough.* **Sun 7 July (1-5.30). Adm £3.50, chd free. Home-made teas. Also open Marie Curie Hospice, Hampstead.**

A narrow informal garden with a SW aspect, developed to meet the requirements of a Tudor Herbalist re-enactor. The garden is on four levels. The first level is predominantly flower beds with herbs being introduced progressively on the second and third levels. The informal layout means that herbs mix with plants like the mature Melianthus and Clematis climb over other plants. Entrance is via basement staircase.

35 TURRET GROVE, SW4

Clapham Old Town, SW4 0ES. Wayne Amiel, www.turretgrove.com. *Off Rectory Grove. 10 mins walk from Clapham Common Tube & Wandsworth Rd Mainline. Buses: 87, 137.* **Sun 21 July (10-5). Adm £4.50, chd free. Home-made teas.**

As featured on BBC Two - Gardeners' World, 2018, this north facing garden shows what can be achieved in a small space (8m x 20m). The owner, who makes no secret of disregarding the rule book, describes this visual feast of intoxicating colours as Clapham meets Jamaica. This is gardening at its most exuberant, where bananas, bamboos, tree ferns and fire bright plants flourish beside the traditional. Children very welcome.

36 Potters Lane

51 TWEEDMOUTH ROAD, E13

Plaistow, London, E13 9HT. Cary Rajinder Sawhney. *51 Tweedmouth Road, Plaistow, London E13 9HT. 10 mins walk from Plaistow District Line & Hammersmith & City Line Stn. From Stratford stn 15 mins by bus (262,473). Balaam St stop. Parking free on Sundays.* **Sun 18 Aug (1-5). Adm £3.50, chd £1. Light refreshments in 20 Edinburgh Road E139HS.(next door to 51 Tweedmouth Road).**

Hidden away in the East End of London - a micro tropical garden with formal islamic garden accents in terms of design and Asian influences incl Indian vegetables grown for foliage. Plantains meld with Black Mulberry, Loquat, Windmill palms and ginger and many other species in this secret 10m x 4m plot, incl canal-style pond which is home to koi carp and terrapins. The garden access is via the house only and has some low single steps.

24 TWYFORD AVENUE, N2

East Finchley, London, N2 9NJ. Rachel Lindsay and Jeremy Pratt. *Twyford Avenue runs parallel to Fortis Green, between East Finchley and Muswell Hill. Tube: Northern line to East Finchley. Buses 102, 143, 234, 263 to East Finchley. Buses 43, 134, 144, 234 to Muswell Hill. Buses 102 and 234 stop at end of rd. Garden signposted from Fortis Green.* **Sun 14 July (2-6). Adm £4, chd free. Home-made teas.**

A very sunny, 120 foot south-facing garden, planted for colour. Brick-edged borders and over-flowing containers packed with masses of traditional herbaceous and perennial cottage garden plants and shrubs. Shady area at the bottom evolving as much by happy accident as by design. Uneven ground in places. Water feature. Greenhouse bursting with cuttings. Lots of places to sit and think, chat or doze.

86 UNDERHILL ROAD, SE22

East Dulwich, SE22 0QU. Claire & Rob Goldie. *Between Langton Rise & Melford Rd. Stn: Forest Hill. Buses: P13, 363, 63, 176, 185 & P4.* **Sun 12 May (2-6). Adm £3.50, chd free. Home-made teas.**

A generous family space bursting with tulips and spring colour. Step down from the elegant slate terrace to the bustling gravel garden and then wind your way through to a green embrace. Feast on delicious cakes and relax in secluded seating areas.

91 VICAR'S MOOR LANE, N21

Winchmore Hill, N21 1BL. Mr David & Dr Malkanthie Anthonisz. *Tube: Southgate then W9 to Winchmore Hill Green then short walk. Train: Winchmore Hill then short walk via Wades Hill.* **Sun 9 June (2-6). Adm £4, chd free. Light refreshments. Also open 20 Hillcrest.**

Established characterful garden. Paths wind through species acers, clematis, climbers shrubs, perennials planted for colour and form. Waterfall and stream flows under raised pergola, viewing platform to home bred koi carp pond. Exotic elements, and art abound in this much loved evolving paradise. Summerhouse, terraces, sunken garden provide tranquil, comfortable places to sit and contemplate.

208 WALM LANE, THE GARDEN FLAT, NW2

London, NW2 3BP. Miranda & Chris Mason, www.thegardennw2.co.uk. *Tube: Kilburn. Garden at junction of Exeter Rd & Walm Lane. Buses: 16, 32, 189, 226, 245, 260, 266, 316 to Cricklewood Broadway, then consult A-Z.* **Sun 2 June (2-6). Adm £3.50, chd free. Home-made teas.**

Tranquil oasis of green. Meandering lawn with island beds, curved and deeply planted borders of perennials, scented roses and flowering shrubs. An ornamental fishpond with fountain. Shaded mini woodland area of tall trees underplanted with rhododendrons, ferns, hostas and lily of the valley with winding path from oriental inspired summerhouse to secluded circular seating area. Live music and raffle prizes.

Coniston Court, Hyde Park Estate Gardens

THE WATERGARDENS, KT2

Warren Road, Kingston-upon-Thames, KT2 7LF. The Residents' Association. *1m E of Kingston. From Kingston take A308 (Kingston Hill) towards London; after approx ½m turn R into Warren Rd. No. 57 bus along Coombe Lane West, alight at Warren Rd.* **Sun 5 May, Sun 20 Oct (2-4.30). Adm £5, chd free.**
Japanese landscaped garden originally part of Coombe Wood Nursery, planted by the Veitch family in the 1860s. Approx 9 acres with ponds, streams and waterfalls. Many rare trees which, in spring and autumn, provide stunning colour. For the tree lover this is a must see garden. Gardens attractive to wildlife.

10 WELLESLEY ROAD, E11

Wanstead, E11 2HF. Mrs Ann Holmes. *Short walk from Snaresbrook or Wanstead tube station. Buses W12, W13, W14, 101 & 145 stop nearby.* **Sat 29 June (1-5). Adm £3, chd free. Home-made teas.**
An evergreen T-shaped garden, bringing a little of the Mediterranean into East London. A large Silver birch commands a raised bed of Trachycarpus, Chamaerops and ferns, with a Rock water feature. You can sit beneath a grapevine or a Magnolia grandiflora, surrounded by vibrant pots of summer colour, listen to the bubbling water feature and - Salud! You could be in Spain! Entrance via side gate to allow wheelchair access. Paved area with a gentle slope to end of garden leading to decking area all on same level.

WEST LODGE PARK, EN4

Cockfosters Road, Hadley Wood, EN4 0PY. Beales Hotels, 020 8216 3904, headoffice@bealeshotels.co.uk, www.bealeshotels.co.uk/westlodgepark/. *1m S of Potters Bar. On A111. J24 from M25 signed Cockfosters.* **Sun 12 May (2-5); Sun 20 Oct (1-4). Adm £5, chd free. Light refreshments.**
Open for the NGS for over 30yrs, the 35 acre Beale Arboretum consists of over 800 varieties of trees and shrubs, incl National Collection of Hornbeam cultivars (Carpinus betulus) and National collection of Swamp Cypress (Taxodium). Network of paths through good selection of conifers, oaks, maples and mountain ash - all specimens labelled. Beehives and 2 ponds. Stunning collection within the M25. Guided tours available. Breakfasts, morning coffee/biscuits, restaurant lunches, light lunches, dinner all served in the hotel. Please see website.
NPC

31 WEST PARK ROAD, TW9

Kew, Richmond, TW9 4DA. Anna Anderson. *Just by Kew Gardens station.* **Sun 9 June (1-5). Adm £3. Also open 28 Taylor Avenue.**
Modern botanical garden with an oriental twist. Emphasis on foliage and an eclectic mix of unusual plants, a reflecting pool and rotating willow screens which provide varying views or privacy. Dry bed, shady beds, mature trees and a private paved dining area with dappled light and shade.

NEW 35 WESTON PARK, N8

London, N8 9SY. Mrs Theresa & Mr Keith Rutter. *Tube Finsbury Park then W3 bus (Weston Park stop) or W7 (Crouch End Broadway.) Or tube to Archway then 41 bus (Crouch End Broadway). Short walk from each one.* **Sun 18 Aug (2-6). Adm £4, chd free.**
SE facing large garden with a wide range of plants, shrubs and trees suited to varying conditions incl a bog garden. Summer colour in the densely planted beds and pots incl dahlias, cannas and salvias. Elements such as golden bamboo, phormiums, grasses and sculptures provide structure. A curving path leads up to an artists's studio.

NEW WHITE COTTAGE, W7

208 Church Road, Hanwell, W7 3BP. Dawn Keep. *Entrance through side gate. White Cottage is opp Church Fields.* **Sun 26 May, Sun 2 June (2-6). Adm £3, chd free. Home-made teas.**
Tightly packed 20' x 40' north facing garden. Box edged beds brimming with David Austin roses. A mature wisteria drapes the wall and pergola. The side entrance to the garden features many shade loving plants in pots and hanging baskets.

WHITGIFT SCHOOL, CR2

Haling Park, South Croydon, CR2 6YT. James Mallett, www.whitgift.co.uk. *Train: South Croydon then 5 mins walk. Buses: 119, 197, 312, 466. School entrance on Nottingham Rd.* **Sun 19 May (2-4.30). Adm £4, chd free. Home-made teas.**
Whitgift Gardens are a series of fascinating, well-maintained gardens in a number of original

styles within the extensive grounds of the school, all of which help to provide a stimulating environment for students. The gardening team have added various new planting schemes over the course of the past year incl beautiful wildflower beds and some new mixed herbaceous and shrub borders. Wildlife and birds (wallabies, flamingos, peacocks in an enclosed area) are a feature of the school grounds. Most garden areas accessible by wheelchair. The Andrew Quadrangle can be accessed, but non accessible steps within the garden.

61 WOLSEY ROAD, KT8

East Molesey, KT8 9EW. Jan & Ken Heath, janheath61@gmail.com. *Less than 10 mins walk from Hampton Court Palace & station - very easy to find.* **Sun 9 June (2-6). Adm £4, chd free. Home-made teas. Also open 5 Pemberton Road.** Visits also by arrangement June & July for groups of 20+.
Romantic, secluded and peaceful garden of two halves designed and maintained by the owners. Part is shaded by two large copper beech trees with woodland planting. The second reached through a beech arch has cottage garden planting, pond and wooden obelisks covered with roses. Beautiful octagonal gazebo overlooks pond plus an oak framed summerhouse designed and built by the owners. Extensive seating throughout the garden to sit quietly and enjoy your tea and cake, either in the cool shade of the gazebo under the copper beech trees, relaxing in the summerhouse or enjoying the full sunshine elsewhere in the garden.

33 WOOD VALE, N10

Highgate, N10 3DJ. Mona Abboud, 020 8883 4955, monaabboud@hotmail.com, www.monasgarden.co.uk. *Tube: Highgate, 10 mins walk. Buses: W3, W7 to top of Park Rd.* **Sun 1 Sept (1.30-6). Adm £3.50, chd free. Light refreshments.** Visits also by arrangement May to Aug for groups of 5+. Group visits particularly welcome.
This 100m-long unique and award winning garden is home to the Corokia National Collection along with a great number of other unusual Australasian, Mediterranean and exotic plants complemented by perennials and grasses which thrive thanks to 250 tons of topsoil, gravel and compost brought in by wheelbarrow. Emphasis on structure, texture, shapes and contrasting foliage.

NPC

NEW 95 WOODLAND WAY, N21

Winchmore Hill N21 3PY. David Sherlock & Gilbert Hopley. *Tube. Southgate. Then W9 bus to Winchmore Hill Green then 10 min. walk. Train. Winchmore Hill. Walk to Green then L onto Hoppers Rd past Salisbury pub R into Downes Ct. Next L Woodland Way.* **Sun 8 Sept (2-6). Adm £4, chd free. Home-made teas.**
Ambitious restoration in progress. Two steps up to gently sloping lawn. Classic English design with colourful romantic borders. Experimental gravel & dry quadrant & little or no feed but good results. Speed composting & woodland collection under old fruit trees. Tiny potager planned.

209 WORSLEY BRIDGE ROAD, BR3

Beckenham, BR3 1RW. Mrs Lizzy Spencer. *100 metres from junction of Copers Cope Rd & Worsley Bridge Rd. 352 Bus route. Opp Kent County Cricket Ground. Unrestricted Parking. Nearest station Lower Sydenham.* **Sun 23 June (2-5). Combined adm with 12 Overbrae £5, chd free. Light refreshments.**
150ft suburban garden with a meandering path taking visitors from the patio, through lawned area with mixed borders of roses, climbers, perennials shrubs and grasses, a paved shady area with a gargantuan bay tree and an ancient recumbent apple tree, up past more roses and mixed planting to a gravel area, and the upper pergola, covered in akebia, roses and clematis.

1 YORK CLOSE, W7

Hanwell, W7 3JB. Tony Hulme & Eddy Fergusson. *By road only, entrance to York Close via Church Rd. Nearest station Hanwell mainline. Buses E3, 195, 207.* **Sat 29 June (2-6). Adm £6, chd free. Sun 30 June (2-6). Adm £5, chd free.**
Tiny quirky, prize winning garden extensively planted with eclectic mix incl hosta collection, many unusual and tropical plants. Plantaholics paradise. Many surprises in this unique and very personal garden. Pimms on Saturday (incl in adm), Bar on Sunday for a donation!

38 YORK ROAD, W5

Ealing, W5 4SG. Nick & Elena Gough, www.thedistinctivegardener.com. *Northfields & South Ealing Tube - 5 mins. Buses: E3, 65. 5 mins. Free parking in local streets. Off Northfield Av & South Ealing Rd.* **Sun 21 July (2-6). Adm £4, chd free. Home-made teas.**
A hidden oasis full of surprises and built on several different levels. This walled corner garden was restored and expanded by its garden designer owner, having been acquired in 2014. There are a number of beautiful and diverse areas within it, all of which add to its special atmosphere, incl a woodland dell path, circular sun terrace, large pond with waterfalls and flower filled parterre.

ZEN GARDEN AT JAPANESE TEMPLE, W3

Three Wheels, 55 Carbery Avenue, London, W3 9AB. Reverend Prof K T Sato, www.threewheels.org.uk. *Tube: Acton Town 5 mins walk, 200yds off A406.* **Sat 1, Sun 2, Sat 22, Sun 23 June (2-5). Adm £3.50, chd free. Matcha tea ceremony £3.**
Pure Japanese Zen garden (so no flowers) with 12 large and small rocks of various colours and textures set in islands of moss and surrounded by a sea of grey granite gravel raked in a stylised wave pattern. Garden surrounded by trees and bushes outside a cob wall. Oak framed wattle and daub shelter with Norfolk reed thatched roof. Talk on the Zen garden between 3-4pm. Buddha Room open to public.

NORFOLK

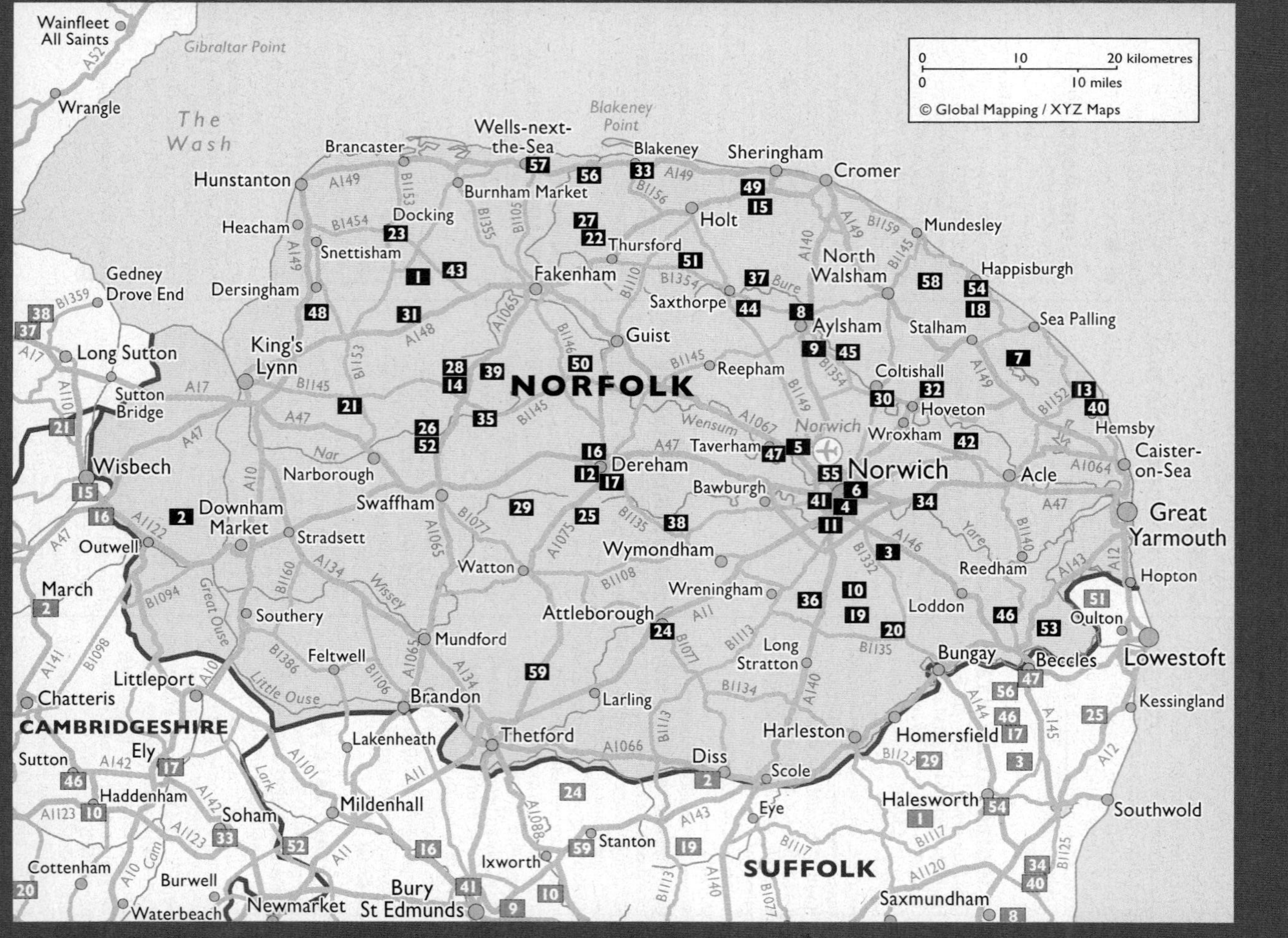

0 10 20 kilometres
0 10 miles
© Global Mapping / XYZ Maps
NORFOLK
SUFFOLK
CAMBRIDGESHIRE
The Wash
Gibraltar Point
Blakeney Point
Wainfleet All Saints
Wrangle
Gedney Drove End
Long Sutton
Sutton Bridge
Wisbech
Outwell
March
Chatteris
Sutton
Hunstanton
Heacham
Dersingham
King's Lynn
Downham Market
Littleport
Ely
Haddenham
Cottenham
Brancaster
Snettisham
Docking
Burnham Market
Wells-next-the-Sea
Fakenham
Narborough
Swaffham
Stradsett
Southery
Feltwell
Lakenheath
Mildenhall
Soham
Burwell
Waterbeach
Newmarket
Bury St Edmunds
Brandon
Mundford
Watton
Thetford
Ixworth
Stanton
Larling
Attleborough
Blakeney
Thursford
Guist
Dereham
Wymondham
Wreningham
Diss
Eye
Scole
Holt
Saxthorpe
Reepham
Taverham
Bawburgh
Long Stratton
Harleston
Sheringham
Cromer
North Walsham
Aylsham
Norwich
Coltishall
Hoveton
Wroxham
Mundesley
Happisburgh
Stalham
Sea Palling
Hemsby
Caister-on-Sea
Acle
Great Yarmouth
Reedham
Loddon
Bungay
Homersfield
Halesworth
Saxmundham
Hopton
Oulton
Beccles
Lowestoft
Kessingland
Southwold
Bure
Wensum
Yare
Nar
Wissey
Little Ouse
Great Ouse
Lark
Cam

Norfolk is a lovely low-lying county, predominantly agricultural with a relatively small population.

Visitors come to Norfolk because they are attracted to the peaceful countryside, the medieval churches, the coastal area and the large network of rivers and waterways of the Broads. Norwich the capital is a fine city.

Our garden owners are a loyal group; Sandringham, one of the original gardens to open for the scheme has been supporting us continuously since 1927. Several gardens have been opening their gates for over 50 years, whilst others will be opening for the very first time. The variety is enormous from those of the large estates and manor houses, to the smaller cottages, courtyards and town gardens. Located throughout the county, styles vary too from the old and traditional, to the contemporary and naturalistic.

So why not come and experience for yourself the rich tapestry of big skies, rural countryside and beautiful gardens.

Below: The Old Rectory

Volunteers

County Organiser
Julia Stafford Allen
01760 755334
julia.staffordallen@ngs.org.uk

County Treasurer
Neil Foster
01328 701288
neilfoster@lexhamestate.co.uk

Publicity
Graham Watts
01362 690065
graham.watts@ngs.org.uk

Social Media
Claire Reinhold
01485 576221
reinholdclaire@googlemail.com

Photographer
Simon Smith
01362 860530
simon.smith@ngs.org.uk

Booklet Co-ordinator
Sally Bate
07881 907735
sally.bate@ngs.org.uk

New Gardens Organiser
Fiona Black
01692 650247
fiona.black@ngs.org.uk

Assistant County Organisers
Jenny Clarke 01508 550261
jenny.clarke@ngs.org.uk

Nick Collier 07733 108443
nick.collier@ngs.org.uk

Jennifer Dyer 01263 761811
jennifer.dyer.16@outlook.com

Sue Guest 01362 858317
guest63@btinternet.com

Sue Roe 01603 455917
sueroe8@icloud.com

OPENING DATES

All entries subject to change. For latest information check **www.ngs.org.uk**

Map locator numbers are shown to the right of each garden name.

February

Snowdrop Festival

Saturday 16th
Horstead House 30

Sunday 24th
Bagthorpe Hall 1
Chestnut Farm 15

March

Sunday 3rd
Chestnut Farm 15

Saturday 9th
◆ East Ruston Old Vicarage 18

Sunday 10th
◆ Raveningham Hall 46

April

Sunday 7th
Gayton Hall 21

Sunday 14th
◆ Mannington Estate 37

Sunday 21st
Wretham Lodge 59

Monday 22nd
Wretham Lodge 59

Sunday 28th
Chestnut Farm 15
The Old House 42

May

Monday 6th
Witton Hall 58

Saturday 11th
Greenways 22

Sunday 12th
Greenways 22
Holme Hale Hall 29

Thursday 16th
◆ Sheringham Park 49

Sunday 19th
Blickling Lodge 8
Lexham Hall 35

Tuesday 21st
◆ Stody Lodge 51

Sunday 26th
Bank House 2
Warborough House 56

Monday 27th
Chestnut Farm 15

June

Thursday 6th
◆ Sheringham Park 49

Saturday 8th
Elm House 19
Kettle Hill 33

Sunday 9th
Bolwick Hall 9
High House Gardens 25
Oulton Hall 44

Wednesday 12th
High House Gardens 25

Sunday 16th
NEW Broadway Farm 12
NEW Grove House 23
NEW The Old Rectory 43
Walcott House 54

Thursday 20th
◆ Mannington Estate 37

Sunday 23rd
Manor House Farm, Wellingham 39

Saturday 29th
The Bear Shop 4

Sunday 30th
The Bear Shop 4
Bishop's House 6
Manor Farm, Coston 38

July

Saturday 6th
NEW The Firs 20

Sunday 7th
9 Bellomonte Crescent 5
NEW The Firs 20
27 St Edmunds Road 47
Tyger Barn 53
Wells-Next-The-Sea Gardens 57

Sunday 21st
NEW Burnley Hall 13
Dunbheagan 17
NEW 30 Hargham Road 24
NEW North Corner 40

Sunday 28th
Dale Farm 16
Holme Hale Hall 29
NEW 33 Waldemar Avenue 55

Wednesday 31st
Lexham Hall 35

August

Sunday 4th
The Long Barn 36
North Lodge 41

Sunday 11th
Brick Kiln House 10
Highfield House 26
North Lodge 41
Tudor Lodgings 52

Sunday 18th
◆ Hoveton Hall Gardens 32
NEW 33 Waldemar Avenue 55

Sunday 25th
Bank House 2

September

Sunday 1st
Chapel Cottage 14
7 Holly Close 28

Sunday 8th
High House Gardens 25

Wednesday 11th
High House Gardens 25

Sunday 15th
Silverstone Farm 50

Sunday 29th
◆ Hindringham Hall 27

October

Saturday 12th
◆ East Ruston Old Vicarage 18

Sunday 20th
The Barn Arboretum 3

By Arrangement

Arrange a personalised garden visit with your club, or group of friends, on a date to suit you. See individual garden entries for full details.

Bank House 2
Black Horse Cottage 7
Brick Kiln House 10
21 Broadhurst Road 11
Chestnut Farm 15
Dale Farm 16
Dunbheagan 17
Elm House 19
Gayton Hall 21
Greenways 22
Holme Hale Hall 29
Horstead House 30
Lake House 34
Manor House Farm, Wellingham 39
Oxnead Hall 45
Wretham Lodge 59

We open the gates to the nation's best gardens, offering a relaxing, memorable and affordable day out. A perfect experience to share with friends and family.

THE GARDENS

1 BAGTHORPE HALL

Bagthorpe, Bircham, King's Lynn, PE31 6QY. Mr & Mrs D Morton, 01485 578528, dgmorton@hotmail.com. *3½ m N of East Rudham, off A148. Take turning opposite The Crown in East Rudham.* **Sun 24 Feb (11-4). Adm £5, chd free. Home-made teas. Home-made soups made with organic vegetables from the farm.**

Stunning display of snowdrops carpeting a circular woodland walk which returns through the walled -garden. Limited access for wheelchairs in the garden, but not the woodland walk.

2 BANK HOUSE

Middle Drove, Marshland St James, PE14 8JT. Teresa Lovick & Andrew Stephens, 07950 362221, teresajoylovick@gmail.com. *A1122 in Outwell turn onto Langhorn's Lane at Crown Motel. Bear L onto Marsh Rd. R onto Stow Rd for 5 mins. Turn L at sign onto Middle Drove. Cross bridge with T-lights. Parking on L in paddock.* **Sun 26 May, Sun 25 Aug (10-4). Adm £4.50, chd free. Home-made teas. Visits also by arrangement May to July for groups of 10 to 30.**

Exuberant and established 2 acres, packed with plants from damp shade to dry gravel. Veg and fruit, ornamental grasses, bog garden, lawn, mixed borders, patios and secret spaces. Year-round interest. An oasis in the fens. Regret there is no wheelchair access. Gravel paths and changes of level.

3 THE BARN ARBORETUM

Framingham Earl, Norwich, NR14 7SA. Mr James Colman. *3m SE of Norwich. From A47 take A146 for 1½ m. Turn R at Old Feathers signed Framingham Pigot Business Centre. Follow the signs to Poringland after 1m the entrance is on L.* **Sun 20 Oct (10-3). Adm £5, chd free. Light refreshments.**

The Arboretum at Framingham currently some 14 hectares, lies on the south slope of a 50 metre hill from which there are extensive views to the north east across some ornamental ponds built in the C18, and towards Great Yarmouth and the sea. In the middle distance St Andrew's Church, Framingham Pigot is framed.

4 THE BEAR SHOP

Elm Hill, Norwich, NR3 1HN. Robert Stone. *Norwich City Centre. From St Andrews, L to Princes St, then L to Elm Hill. Garden at side of shop through large wooden gate & along alleyway.* **Sat 29 June (11-4). Sun 30 June (11-4), also open Bishop's House. Adm £4, chd free. Home-made teas.**

Considered to be based on a design by Gertrude Jekyll, The famous Bear Shop has a small terraced garden hidden behind a C15 house in the historic Cathedral Quarter of Norwich. Enjoy the tranquillity of the riverside and beautiful, cobbled Elm Hill. The walled garden is full of flowering plants, old roses and yew topiary with plenty of places to sit and enjoy this secret space. Wheel chair access is limited to the upper level of the garden.

5 9 BELLOMONTE CRESCENT

Drayton, Norwich, NR8 6EJ. Wendy & Chris Fitch. *5m N of Norwich. Drayton, off A1067. Access from Bellomonte Crescent or through Drayton churchyard.* **Sun 7 July (11-5). Combined adm with 27 St Edmunds Road £6, chd free. Home-made teas. Single adm £3**

Approx ¼ acre plot the garden, lovingly created from scratch by the owners, is a mix of traditional, exotic/Mediterranean and shady planting. A large deck overlooks main lawn with planted pergolas and arbour. Views across to Drayton Church gives interest and privacy. Terraced upper garden with fruit and vegetables and secluded courtyard area. Home-made cakes and plants for sale. Money raised from sale of refreshments and plants is donated to Cystic Fibrosis Trust. No wheelchair access to upper levels.

6 BISHOP'S HOUSE

Bishopgate, Norwich, NR3 1SB. The Bishop of Norwich, www.dioceseofnorwich.org/gardens. *City centre. Located in the city centre near the Law Courts & The Adam & Eve Pub.* **Sun 30 June (1-5). Adm £4, chd free. Home-made teas. Also open The Bear Shop.**

4 acre walled garden dating back to the C12. Extensive lawns with specimen trees. Borders with many rare and unusual shrubs. Spectacular herbaceous borders flanked by yew hedges. Rose beds, meadow labyrinth, kitchen garden, woodland walk and long border with hostas and bamboo walk. Popular plant sales. Gravel paths and some slopes.

Burnley Hall

7 BLACK HORSE COTTAGE

The Green, Hickling, Norwich, NR12 0YA. Yvonne Pugh, 01692 598691, yvonne.pugh@intamail.com. *3m E of Stalham. Turn E off A149 at Catfield, turn L onto Heath Rd, 1½m to centre of Hickling village. Next to The Greyhound Inn (Good food!).* **Visits by arrangement March to end October. Individuals & groups welcome. Adm £5, chd free. Refreshments by prior arrangement..**

Thatched house with traditional barn ½m from Hickling Broad. Plantsman's garden over 2 acres professionally redesigned. Spacious borders and islands with diverse range of characterful planting. Particular emphasis on achieving full year round interest. Wide range of managed mature specimen trees. Many long two-way vistas. Wide mown walkways through large meadow. Various sitting opportunities! No dogs allowed.

8 BLICKLING LODGE

Blickling, Norwich, NR11 6PS. Michael & Henrietta Lindsell. *½m N of Aylsham. Leave Aylsham on Old Cromer Rd towards Ingworth. Over hump back bridge & house is on R.* **Sun 19 May (11-5). Adm £5, chd free. Home-made teas.**

Georgian house (not open) set in 17 acres of parkland including cricket pitch, mixed border, walled kitchen garden, yew garden, woodland/water garden.

9 BOLWICK HALL

Marsham, NR10 5PU. Mr & Mrs G C Fisher. *8m N of Norwich off A140. From Norwich, heading N on A140, just past Marsham take 1st R after Plough Pub, signed 'By Road' then next R onto private drive to front of Hall.* **Sun 9 June (1-5). Adm £5, chd free. Home-made teas.**

Landscaped gardens and park surrounding a late Georgian hall. The original garden design is attributed to Humphry Repton. The current owners have rejuvenated the borders, planted gravel and formal gardens and clad the walls of the house in old roses. Enjoy a woodland walk around the lake as well as as stroll through the working vegetable and fruit garden with its double herbaceous border. Please ask at gate for wheelchair directions.

10 BRICK KILN HOUSE

Priory Lane, Shotesham, Norwich, NR15 1UJ. Jim & Jenny Clarke, jennyclarke@uwclub.net. *6m S of Norwich. From Shotesham All Saints church Priory Lane is 200m on R on Saxlingham Rd.* **Sun 11 Aug (11-5). Adm £5, chd free. Home-made teas.** Visits also by arrangement June to Sept.

2 acre country garden with a large terrace, lawns and colourful herbaceous boarders. There is an intimate rose garden, garden sculptures and a stream running through a diversely planted wood. Parking in field but easy access to brick path.

30 Hargham Road

11 21 BROADHURST ROAD

Eaton Rise, Norwich, NR4 6RD. David & Beverly Woods, 07909 504769, dwoods054@icloud.com. *1m S of Norwich. Take A140 S from Norwich city centre to outer ring rd T-lights. Stay on A140 & Broadhurst Rd is 3rd turning on R opp tennis courts.* **Visits by arrangement July to Sept for groups of up to 20. Adm £3.50, chd free. Home-made teas.**

Around the world in 80 steps! This south facing suburban garden takes you from the Mediterranean to Japan. Mature trees from adjoining gardens create a 'borrowed landscape' feel. Olive trees, lavenders, palms, salvias, Japanese maples, pines and tree ferns in an unusual planting layout. Interesting topiary and stones throughout the garden. Drive and garden paths are mainly gravel.

12 NEW BROADWAY FARM

The Broadway, Scarning, Dereham, NR19 2LQ. Michael & Corinne Steward. *16m W of Norwich. 12m E of Swaffham From A47 W take a R into Fen Rd, opposite Drayton Hall Lane. From A47 E take L into Fen Rd, then immediate L at T-junction, immediate R into The Broadway.* **Sun 16 June (11-5). Adm £3.50, chd free. Home-made teas.**

Half acre cottage garden surrounding a C14 clapboard farmhouse. Colourful herbaceous borders with a wide range of perennial and woody plants and a well planted pond,providing habitat for wildlife. A plantswoman's garden !

13 NEW BURNLEY HALL

East Somerton, Great Yarmouth, NR29 4DZ. Lady Agnew. *10m N of Gt Yarmouth. On Winterton Rd between W Somerton & Winterton, turn sharp N on tight corner by our (signed) front gate. Go up concrete road following signs. Ample parking in farmyard and park.* **Sun 21 July (11-5). Combined adm with North Corner £5, chd free. Home-made teas.**

Large mixed beds around two lawns form the view from the H shaped C18 house (not open). An elderly thatched and a new wooden-roofed summerhouse. Some new planting in front of the house and around western approaches, including hydrangeas, hellebores and crocosmias. Victorian greenhouse under restoration Lawn, drive and some paths wheelchair accessible, depending on the weather.

14 CHAPEL COTTAGE

Rougham, King's Lynn, PE32 2SE. Sarah Butler, 01328 838347, sarahbutler4@gmail.com. *15m E from King's Lynn, 8m SW from Fakenham. On B1145. Parking in the centre of the village.* **Sun 1 Sept (10.30-5). Combined adm with 7 Holly Close £4, chd free. Home-made teas.**

A naturalistic cottage garden created by owner to encourage wildlife. Divided into charming peaceful areas that include pond, vegetables, herbs, wild flower lawns, and beehives. Plenty of shade and seating. Attractive village with Church open.

15 CHESTNUT FARM

Church Road, West Beckham, Holt, NR25 6NX. Mr & Mrs John McNeil Wilson, 01263 822241, judywilson100@gmail.com. *2½m S of Sheringham. From A148 opp Sheringham Park entrance. Take the rd signed BY WAY TO WEST BECKHAM, about ¾m to the Village Sign and garden.* **Sun 24 Feb, Sun 3 Mar (11-4); Sun 28 Apr, Mon 27 May (11-5). Adm £5, chd free. Light refreshments.** Visits also by arrangement Feb to Aug for groups of 10+.

Mature 3-acre garden with collections of many rare and unusual plants and trees. 100+ varieties of snowdrops, drifts of crocus with seasonal flowering shrubs. Later, wood anemones, fritillary meadow, wild flower walk, pond, small arboretum, croquet lawn and colourful herbaceous borders. New planting opportunities have arisen from losing a tree in 2018 winter. Garden sculpture display by local blacksmith Toby Winterbourne. Usually visiting nurseries and plants for sale. Wheelchair access tricky if wet.

16 DALE FARM

Sandy Lane, Dereham, NR19 2EA. Graham & Sally Watts, 01362 690065, grahamwatts@dsl.pipex.com. *16m W of Norwich. 12m E of Swaffham. From A47 take B1146 signed to Fakenham, turn R at T-junction, ¼m turn L into Sandy Lane (before pelican crossing).* **Sun 28 July (11-5). Adm £5, chd free. Home-made teas.** Visits also by arrangement June & July for groups of 10+.

2-acre plant lovers' garden with a large spring-fed pond. Over 1000 plant varieties in exuberantly planted borders with sculptures. Also, gravel, vegetable, nature and waterside gardens. Collection of 130 hydrangeas! Music during the afternoon and remote-controlled model boats on pond for children. Some grass paths and gravel drive. Wide choice of plants for sale.

17 DUNBHEAGAN

Dereham Road, Westfield, NR19 1QF. Jean & John Walton, 01362 696163, jandjwalton@btinternet.com. *2m S of Dereham. From Dereham turn L off A1075 into Westfield Rd by the Vauxhall garage/Premier food store. straight ahead at Xrds into lane which becomes Dereham Rd. garden on L.* **Sun 21 July (12.30-5). Adm £5, chd free. Home-made teas.** Visits also by arrangement June & July. Last day for visits 18 July.

Relax and enjoy walking among extensive borders and island beds - a riot of colour all summer. Vast collection of rare, unusual and more recognisable plants in this ever changing plantsman's garden. If you love flowers, you'll love it here. We aim for the WOW factor. Lots of changes for 2019. Featured in Nick Bailey's book 365 Days of Colour. Music during the afternoon. Gravel driveway.

18 ◆ EAST RUSTON OLD VICARAGE

East Ruston, Norwich, NR12 9HN. Alan Gray & Graham Robeson, 01692 650432, erovoffice@btconnect.com, www.eastrustonoldvicarage.co.uk. *3m N of Stalham. Turn off A149 onto B1159 signed Bacton, Happisburgh. After 2m turn R 200yds N of East Ruston Church (ignore sign to East Ruston).* **For NGS: Sat 9 Mar, Sat 12 Oct (12-5.30). Adm £9.50, chd £1.** For other opening times and information, please phone, email or visit garden website.

Large garden with traditional borders and modern landscapes inc. Walled Gardens, Rose Garden, Exotic Garden, Topiary and Box Parterres, Water Features, Mediterranean Garden, a monumental Fruit Cage, Containers to die for in spring and summer. Cornfield and Meadow Gardens, Vegetable and Cutting Gardens, Parkland and Heritage Orchard, in all 32 acres. Rare and unusual plants abound.

NPC

19 ELM HOUSE

The Green, Saxlingham Nethergate, Norwich, NR15 1TH. Mrs Linda Woodwark, lyncwpoppyland@live.co.uk. *8m S of Norwich. From Norwich take A140 to Ipswich, at Newton Flotman turn L at sign post to Saxlingham Nethergate, continue to the end of the rd, turn R & travel through the village, follow NGS signs.* **Sat 8 June (11.30-5). Adm £4.50, chd free. Home-made teas.** Visits also by arrangement June to Aug.

A family country garden whose owner loves plants. There are several island beds, 2 autumn long borders, filled with herbaceous perennials, arbours with roses and a natural wildlife pond for ducks and moorhens. There is also a paddock/play area for grandchildren, chickens and 3 goats. There is a certain amount of wheelchair access.

20 NEW THE FIRS

Church Road, Woodton, nr Bungay, NR35 2NB. Alan & Shirley Steadman. *9m S of A47 (A146 junction). Take the B1332 from Norwich. Continue until passed the Woodton sign. Turn R at sign for B15527 to Hempnall. Follow signs for NGS.* **Sat 6, Sun 7 July (11-5.30). Adm £4, chd free. Home-made teas.**

From field to landscaped garden, it takes you through a journey of flowers, secrets, and fruits. Developed and maintained purely by the owners, the acre garden comprises of secret areas, fish pond, ornamental pond, wildlife pond, orchard, borders, formal kitchen garden, rose garden, lawn, and much more. Many seating areas. Refreshments available in aid of National Oesteoporosis Society.

21 GAYTON HALL

Gayton, King's Lynn, PE32 1PL. Viscount & Viscountess Marsham, 01485 528432, ciciromney@icloud.com. *6m E of King's Lynn. Off the B1145.* **Sun 7 Apr (1-5). Adm £5, chd free. Home-made teas.** Visits also by arrangement Mar to Oct for groups of 10 to 30.

This rambling semi-wild 20 acre water garden, has over 2m of paths, and contains lawns, lakes, streams, bridges and woodland. Primulas, astilbes, hostas, lysichiton and gunnera. Spring bulbs. A variety of unusual trees and shrubs, many labelled, have been planted over the years. Wheelchair access to most areas, gravel and grass paths.

22 GREENWAYS

Blacksmiths Lane, Hindringham, Fakenham, NR21 0QB. Geraldine Maelzer & Anne Callow, 01328 878354. *Close to village centre. A148 Holt to Fakenham Rd, turn by Crawfish Pub at Thursford, after 2m turn L Blacksmiths Lane after village hall. Parking at village hall.* **Sat 11, Sun 12 May (11-4). Adm £4, chd free. Light home-made refreshments .** Visits also by arrangement Apr to Sept for groups of 10+.

A mature 1 acre garden with a meandering stream, developed by the owners with informal planting to give continuous colour and interest; a delight for all gardeners. Sit and listen to birdsong and enjoy the variety of wildlife habitats and the many species of bumble bees. Enjoy the display of tulips and geums. Not suitable for wheelchairs.

23 NEW GROVE HOUSE

High Street, Docking, King's Lynn, PE31 8NH. Mr & Mrs Charles Polito. *Limited parking at house.* **Sun 16 June (11-5). Adm £4.50, chd free. Home-made teas. Also open The Old Rectory, Syderstone.**

Village garden just over an acre, created during the last four years by the owners. Includes fine lawn surrounded by flower borders, vegetable and cutting garden with extensive sweet peas. Small orchard. Difficult for wheelchairs due to extent of gravelled paths etc.

24 NEW 30 HARGHAM ROAD

Attleborough, NR17 2ES. Darren & Karen Spencer. *Turn off A11 at Breckland Lodge, continue 2m into Attleborough, turn R opp Sainsbury's into Hargham Road and we're 200 yds on the R.* **Sun 21 July (11-5). Adm £3.50, chd free. Home-made teas.**

Step into a vibrant, colourful haven in just under a ⅓ acre. Created from scratch with self built structures and homemade water features. Borders filled with perennials and annuals with a variety of exotics. Follow the pathway round to a modern allotment area.

25 HIGH HOUSE GARDENS

Blackmoor Row, Shipdham, Thetford, IP25 7PU. Sue & Fred Nickerson. *6m SW of Dereham. Take the airfield or Cranworth Rd off A1075 in Shipdham. Blackmoor Row is signed.* **Sun 9, Wed 12 June, Sun 8, Wed 11 Sept (2-5.30). Adm £4.50, chd free. Home-made teas.**

3 acre plantsman's garden developed and maintained by the current owners, over the last 40 years. Garden consists of colour themed herbaceous borders with an extensive range of perennials, box edged rose and shrub borders, woodland garden, pond and bog area, orchard and small arboretum. Plus large vegetable garden. Gravel paths.

26 HIGHFIELD HOUSE

Back Lane, Castle Acre, King's Lynn, PE32 2AR. David & Jackie Moss. *Off A1065 4m N Swaffham. Follow Signs.* **Sun 11 Aug (11-5). Combined adm with Tudor Lodgings £6, chd free.**

A ¾ acre garden begun over 30 years ago. Planted for all seasons with large herbaceous borders, lawn sloping down to pond and summerhouse. Patio, vegetable plot and south facing gravel garden,. Wheelchair access limited. Please enquire beforehand.

27 ◆ HINDRINGHAM HALL

Blacksmiths Lane, Hindringham, NR21 0QA. Mr & Mrs Charles Tucker, 01328 878226, **info@hindringhamhall.org, www.hindringhamhall.org.** *7m from Holt/Fakenham/Wells. Turn off A148 at Crawfish Pub. L into Blacksmiths Lane in Hindringham.* **For NGS: Sun 29 Sept (10-4). Adm £6, chd free. Home-made teas.** For other opening times and information, please phone, email or visit garden website.

Grade 2* Tudor Manor House (not open) surrounded by moat. Medieval site with fishponds. Working walled vegetable garden, Victorian nut walk, formal beds, bog and stream gardens. Something of interest throughout the year continuing well into autumn. Some access for wheelchairs able to cope with gravel paths.

28 7 HOLLY CLOSE

Rougham, King's Lynn, PE32 2SJ. Derek Barker. *15m E of King's Lynn, 8m SW of Fakenham on B1145. Holly Close is ¼ m from the church.* **Sun 1 Sept (11-5). Combined adm with Chapel Cottage £4, chd free.**

The front garden has a variety of planting, with well stocked borders filled with colour and structure. Rear garden is laid out in potager style, with fruit trees, flowers and vegetables encouraging bees and wildlife. The garden shows how much can be achieved in a small plot providing late summer colour.

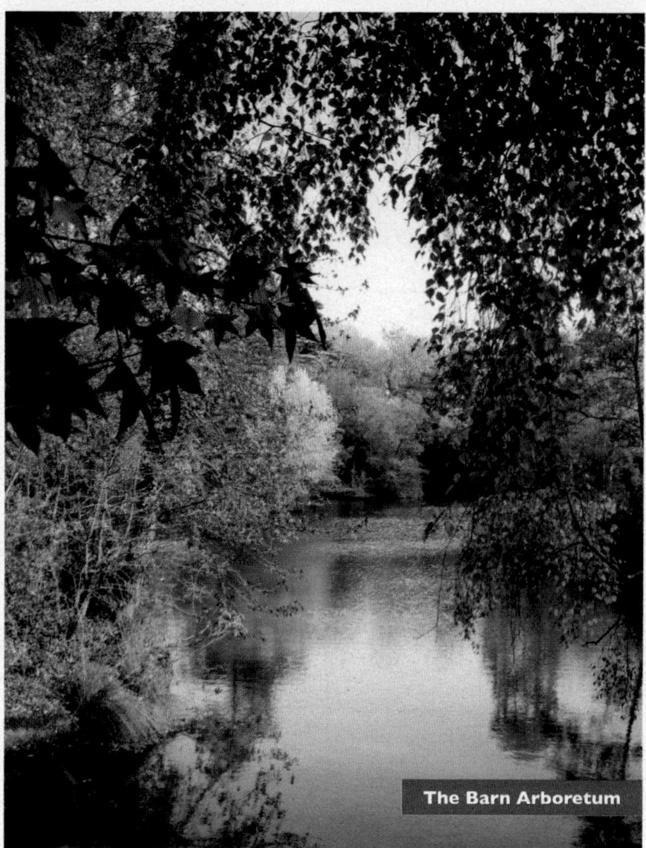

The Barn Arboretum

29 HOLME HALE HALL

Holme Hale, Swaffham, Thetford, IP25 7ED. Mr & Mrs Simon Broke, 01760 440328, simon.broke@hotmail.co.uk. *2m S of Necton off A47. 1m E of Holme Hale village.* **Sun 12 May, Sun 28 July (12-4). Adm £6, chd free. Light refreshments in tea room. savoury, sweet and gluten free.** Visits also by arrangement Apr to Sept. Guided by owner.

Noted for its Spring display of tulips, alliums and historic wisteria. Walled kitchen garden and front garden designed by Chelsea winner Arne Maynard in 2000. Trained fruit, vegetables and traditional greenhouse. Mid and late summer colour with herbaceous borders rejuvenated over the past two years by Maynard. Wheelchair access available to the Front Garden, Kitchen Garden and tearoom.

30 HORSTEAD HOUSE

Mill Road, Horstead, Norwich, NR12 7AU. Mr & Mrs Matthew Fleming, 07771 655 637, caro.fleming@sky.com. *6m NE of Norwich on North Walsham rd, B1150. Down Mill Rd opp the Recruiting Sergeant Pub.* **Sat 16 Feb (11-4). Adm £4, chd free. Home-made teas. We will be serving drinks and cakes.** Visits also by arrangement in Feb for groups of up to 20.

A beautiful display of snowdrops carpet the woodland setting with winter flowering shrubs. A stunning feature are the dogwoods growing on a small island in R. Bure, which flows through the garden. Small walled garden. Wheelchair access to main snowdrop area.

31 ◆ HOUGHTON HALL WALLED GARDEN

Bircham Road, New Houghton, King's Lynn, PE31 6TY. The Cholmondeley Gardens Trust, 01485 528569, info@houghtonhall.com, www.houghtonhall.com. *11m W of Fakenham. 13m E of King's Lynn. Signed from A148.* For opening times and information, please phone, email or visit garden website.

The award-winning, 5 acre walled garden includes a spectacular double-sided herbaceous border, rose parterre, wisteria pergola and glasshouses. Mediterranean garden and kitchen garden with arches and espaliers of fruit trees. Antique statues, fountains and contemporary sculptures by Jeppe Hein, Richard Long and Stephen Cox. Plants on sale. Gravel and grass paths. Electric buggies available in the walled garden.

♿ ✿ 🚌 ☕

32 ◆ HOVETON HALL GARDENS

Hoveton Hall Estate, Hoveton, Norwich, NR12 8RJ. Mr & Mrs Harry Buxton, 01603 784297, office@hovetonhallestate.co.uk, www.hovetonhallestate.co.uk. *8m N of Norwich. 1m N of Wroxham Bridge. Off A1151 Stalham Rd - follow brown tourist signs.* **For NGS: Sun 18 Aug (10.30-5). Adm £7.50, chd £4. Light lunches and afternoon tea from our on-site Garden Kitchen Cafe.** For other opening times and information, please phone, email or visit garden website.

15-acre gardens and woodlands taking you through the seasons. Mature walled herbaceous and kitchen gardens. Informal woodlands and lakeside walks. Nature Spy activity trail for our younger visitors. A varied events programme runs throughout the season. Please visit our website for more details. The gardens are approximately 75% accessible to wheelchair users. We offer a reduced entry price for wheelchair users and their carers.

♿ ✿ 🚌 🛏 ☕

33 KETTLE HILL

The Downs, Langham Road, Blakeney, NR25 7PN. Mrs R Winch. *½m from Blakeney off the B1156 to Langham.* **Sat 8 June (11.30-4). Adm £5, chd free. Home-made teas.**

A garden with herbaceous borders, wild flower meadows and a secret garden. Stunning rose garden and grass paths through woods, a real treat for any garden lover. Excellent views across Morston to the sea, framed by lavender, roses and sky. Gardens have been developed by the owner with design elements from George Carter and Tamara Bridge. Gravel drive way and lawns but hard paving near the house. Ramps are situated around the garden making all except the wood accessible for wheelchairs.

♿ 🐕 ✿ D ☕

34 LAKE HOUSE

Postwick Lane, Roman Drive, Brundall, NR13 5LU. Mrs Janet Muter, 01603 712933. *5m E of Norwich. On A47; take Brundall turn at r'about. Turn R into Postwick Lane at T-junction.* **Visits by arrangement for groups of up to 30. Adm £5, chd free.**

In the centre of Brundall Gardens, a series of ponds descends through a wooded valley to the shore of a lake. Steep paths wind through a variety of shrubs and flowers in season, which attract many kinds of rare birds, dragonflies and mammals. Water features, great variety of bird life, dragonflies, pond life and forest trees.

🐕 ✿ 🚌

35 LEXHAM HALL

nr Litcham, PE32 2QJ. Mr & Mrs Neil Foster, www.lexhamestate.co.uk. *6m N of Swaffham off B1145. 2m W of Litcham.* **Sun 19 May, Wed 31 July (11-5). Adm £6, chd free. Home-made teas.**

Parkland with lake and river walks surround C17/18 Hall (not open). Formal garden with terraces, roses and mixed borders. Traditional working kitchen garden with crinkle-crankle wall. Year round interest with rhododendrons, azaleas, camellias and magnolias in the 3 acre woodland garden in May. July sees the walled garden borders at their peak. A reed thatched summerhouse. The 15' wisteria clad 'Dome' is the centrepiece in the walled garden.

✿ 🚌 ☕

36 THE LONG BARN

Flordon Road, Newton Flotman, Norwich, NR15 1QX. Mr & Mrs Mark Bedini. *6m S of Norwich along A140. Leave A140 in Newton Flotman towards Flordon. Exit Newton Flotman & approx 150 yards beyond 'passing place' on L, turn L into drive. Note that SatNav does not bring you to destination.* **Sun 4 Aug (11-5). Adm £5, chd £2. Home-made teas.**

Beautiful setting with new haha creating infinity views across ancient parkland. Strong Mediterranean influences throughout large paved courtyard, outdoor pool and unique walled group of 4 venerably gnarled olive trees. Herbaceous borders, tiered lawns and woodland garden set around a stunning barn conversion with woodland walks to a stretch of the River Tas - serene! Wheelchair drop off at front of house. Gradual lawn slope provides access to upper tier of garden except woodland walk to river. WC requires steps.

♿ ☕

37 ◆ MANNINGTON ESTATE

Mannington, Norwich, NR11 7BB. The Lord & Lady Walpole, 01263 584175, enquiries@manningtonestate.co.uk, www.manningtonestate.co.uk. *18m NW of Norwich. 2m N of Saxthorpe via B1149 towards Holt. At Saxthorpe/Corpusty follow signs to Mannington.* **For NGS: Sun 14 Apr (11-5). Evening opening Thur 20 June (6-8.30). Adm £6, chd free. Light refreshments at Greedy Goose Tearooms.** For other opening times and information, please phone, email or visit garden website.

20 acres feature shrubs, lake, trees and roses. Heritage rose and period gardens. Borders. Sensory garden. Extensive countryside walks and trails. Moated manor house and Saxon church with C19 follies. Wild flowers and birds. The Greedy Goose tearooms offer home made locally sourced food with light lunches and home made teas. Gravel paths, one steep slope.

♿ ✿ 🚌 🛏 ☕

38 MANOR FARM, COSTON

Coston Lane, Coston, Barnham Broom, NR9 4DT. Mr & Mrs J D Hambro. *10m W of Norwich. Off B1108 Norwich - Watton Rd. Take B1135 to Dereham at Kimberley. After approx 300yds sharp L bend, go straight over down Coston Lane, house & garden on L.* **Sun 30 June (11-5). Adm £5, chd free. Home-made teas.**

Wonderful 3 acre country garden set in larger estate. Several small garden rooms with both formal and informal planting. Climbing roses, walled kitchen garden, white, grass and late summer themes, classic herbaceous and shrub borders, box parterres and large areas of wildflowers. Various sculptures dotted round the garden. Dogs and picnics most welcome. 1 mile field walk. Something for everyone. Some gravel paths and steps.

39 MANOR HOUSE FARM, WELLINGHAM

Fakenham, Kings Lynn, PE32 2TH. Robin & Elisabeth Ellis, 01328 838227, libbyelliswellingham@gmail.com, www.manor-house-farm.co.uk. *7m W from Fakenham. 8m E from Swaffham, ½m off A1065. By the Church.* **Sun 23 June (11.30-5). Adm £6, chd free.** Visits also by arrangement Apr to Sept for groups of 10+.

Charming 4 acre country garden surrounds an attractive farmhouse: Formal quadrants. 'Hot spot' of grasses and gravel. Small arboretum, pleached lime walk, vegetable parterre and rose tunnel. Unusual walled 'Taj' garden with old-fashioned roses, tree peonies, lilies and a pond. A variety of herbaceous plants. Small herd of Formosan Sika deer. Dogs on leads. Some wheelchair access.

Your visits help change lives - your generosity has supported unpaid carers through donations to Carers Trust totalling over £3.9 million since 1996

9 Bellomonte Cresecent

Broadway Farm

40 NEW **NORTH CORNER**
Market Place, Winterton-on-Sea, Great Yarmouth, NR29 4BE. David and Julia King. *8m N of Great Yarmouth. Enter Winterton-on-Sea by the church & follow Black St until the roads open out into the old market place. North Corner is on the L at the junction between Back Path & North Market Rd.* **Sun 21 July (11-5). Combined adm with Burnley Hall £5, chd free.**
Newly designed, small village garden which has been divided into defined areas to maximise the space. Originally a butcher's shop, this property is half a mile from the beach and has varied planting in beds, with collections of hostas, bonsais and agapanthus. Large greenhouse full of exotic plants. The garden is mainly level for wheelchair access but has some woodchip paths. Gardening books and magazines available for sale/ donation in aid of NGS. Parking at Burnley Hall, but if you need to park closer to garden, please park sensitively in the village.

41 **NORTH LODGE**
51 Bowthorpe Road, Norwich, NR2 3TN. Bruce Bentley & Peter Wilson. *1½m W of Norwich City Centre. Turn into Bowthorpe Rd off Dereham Rd, garden 150 metres on L. By bus: 5, 21, 22, 23, 23A/B, 24 & 24A from City centre, Old Catton, Heartsease, Thorpe & most of W Norwich. Parking available outside.* **Sun 4, Sun 11 Aug (11-5). Adm £4, chd free. Home-made teas.**
Delightful town garden surrounding Victorian Gothic Cemetery Lodge. Full of follies created by current owners, including a classical temple, oriental water garden and formal ponds. Original 80ft-deep well! Predominantly herbaceous planting. House extension won architectural award. Slide show of house and garden history. Wheelchair access possible but difficult. Sloping gravel drive followed by short, steep, narrow, brickweave ramp. WC not easily wheelchair accessible.

Your visits help change lives – since 1927, we've donated £55 million to nursing and caring charities

42 **THE OLD HOUSE**
Ranworth, NR13 6HS. The Hon Mrs Jacquetta Cator. *9m NE of Norwich. Nr South Walsham, below historic Ranworth Church.* **Sun 28 Apr (11-4). Adm £5, chd free. Home-made teas.**
Attractive linked and walled gardens alongside Ranworth Inner Broad. Bulbs, shrubs and Villandry inspired potager with interesting sculptures throughout. Mown rides through arboretum with spectacular views of the church and the broad. Some rough grass and gravel. Dogs allowed in arboretum but not in the garden itself. Teas in aid of St Helen's Church Ranworth. Wheelchair access some rough grass and gravel.

43 NEW **THE OLD RECTORY**
Creake Road, Syderstone, King's Lynn, PE31 8SF. Mr & Mrs Tom White. *The Old Rectory. Access from Creake Road, or side gate opposite Village Hall.* **Sun 16 June (11-5). Adm £4.50, chd free. Home-made teas. Also open Grove House, Docking**
Garden designed by Arne Maynard, with lawns; box, hornbeam, yew and beach hedging; pleached crab apple; wisteria and climbing roses; parterre of English shrub roses (David Austin); herbaceous beds; shrubbery and orchard.

44 **OULTON HALL**
Oulton, Aylsham, NR11 6NU. Bolton Agnew. *4m NW of Aylsham. From Aylsham take B1354. After 4m turn L for Oulton Chapel, Hall ½m on R. From B1149 (Norwich/Holt rd) take B1354, next R, Hall ½m on R.* **Sun 9 June (1-5). Adm £5, chd free. Home-made teas.**
C18 manor house (not open) and clocktower set in 6-acre garden with lake and woodland walks. Chelsea designer's own garden - herbaceous, Italian, bog, water, wild, verdant, sunken and parterre gardens all flowing from one tempting vista to another. Developed over 25 yrs with emphasis on structure, height and texture, with a lot of recent replanting in the contemporary manner.

45 OXNEAD HALL

Oxnead, Norwich, NR10 5HP. Mr & Mrs David Aspinall, beverley@oxneadhall.co.uk. *3m from Aylsham. From Norwich take A140 to Cromer. After Aylsham turn R to Burgh-next-Aylsham. After Burgh take R turn at next Xrds signed Brampton & Buxton .After the Oxnead sign take 1st L.* **Visits by arrangement Apr to Oct. Groups of 20 to 50. Tea and cake will be provided on request.**

The 14 acre gardens were laid out by the Pastons between 1580 and 1660 and are largely intact. The design consists of a series of Italianate courtyards and terraces which are embellished with statuary. The gardens are undergoing renovation with guidance from George Carter and now incl a parterre, viewing mound, water garden, lake, herbaceous borders, walled kitchen garden, and woodland. There are slopes to most parts of the garden, but some areas cannot be accessed by wheelchair.

46 ◆ RAVENINGHAM HALL

Raveningham, Norwich, NR14 6NS. Sir Nicholas & Lady Bacon, 01508 548480, sonya@raveningham.com, www.raveningham.com. *14m SE of Norwich. 4m from Beccles off B1136.* **For NGS: Sun 10 Mar (11-4). Adm £5, chd free. Light refreshments in our own Gardens Tea Room.** For other opening times and information, please phone, email or visit garden website.

Traditional country house garden in glorious parkland setting. Restored Victorian conservatory, walled kitchen garden, herbaceous borders, newly planted stumpery, an arboretum established after the 1987 gale and lake created to mark the Millennium. A Time Garden inspired by Sir Francis Bacon, herb and rose gardens, and sculpture by Susan Bacon throughout the gardens. February sees drifts of snowdrops followed by daffodils, other spring bulbs and flowering shrubs. In May there are meadow flowers and the herbaceous borders fill out. Summer months showcase the walled kitchen garden and the agapanthus collection for which the garden is known. Tea Room. Gravel paths allow wheelchair access.

47 27 ST EDMUNDS ROAD

Taverham, Norwich, NR8 6NY. Alan Inness & Sue Collins. *6m N of Norwich, just off the Fakenham Road A1067. Coming from Norwich on A1067, drive through the village of Drayton. Carry on up hill to Taverham, turn L into Roeditch Drive. The property will then be on your R at T-junction.* **Sun 7 July (11-5). Combined adm with 9 Bellomonte Crescent £6, chd free. Home-made teas. Single adm £3**

Half acre garden featuring part woodland setting and view over the Wensum valley via raised decking area. The garden has undergone substantial redevelopment over the past nine years as it was originally two separate gardens. Redevelopment has included the addition of vine covered pergola, two summerhouses, herbaceous borders, small vegetable plot with greenhouse and potting shed. Plant sales. No Wheelchair Access.

48 ◆ SANDRINGHAM GARDENS

Sandringham, PE35 6EH. Her Majesty The Queen, 01485 545408, visits@sandringhamestate.co.uk, www.sandringhamestate.co.uk. *6m NW of King's Lynn. By gracious permission, the House, Museum & Gardens will be open.* For opening times and information, please phone, email or visit garden website.

60 acres of glorious gardens and woodland with lakes, rare plants and trees. Colour and all year round interest; spring-flowering bulbs, rhododendrons and azaleas, lavender and roses. Dazzling autumn colour. Donations are given from the Estate to various charities. Open daily from Mon 1 Apr to Sun 20 Oct inclusive except Good Friday 19 Apr and Wed 31 July. Gravel paths (not deep), long distances - please tel or visit website for our Accessibility Guide.

49 ◆ SHERINGHAM PARK

Wood Farm Visitors Centre, Upper Sheringham, NR26 8TL. National Trust, 01263 820550, sheringhampark@nationaltrust.org.uk, www.nationaltrust.org.uk/sheringham. *2m SW of Sheringham. Access for cars off A148 Cromer to Holt Rd, 5m W of Cromer, 6m E of Holt, signs in Sheringham town.* **For NGS: Thur 16 May, Thur 6 June (10-5). Light refreshments in Courtyard Cafe.** For other opening times and information, please phone, email or visit garden website.

80 acres of species rhododendron, azalea and magnolia. Also numerous specimen trees incl handkerchief tree. Viewing towers, waymarked walks, sea and parkland views. No admission charge to Sheringham Park, car park charge £6 for non NT members Special walkway and WCs for disabled. 1½ m route is accessible for wheelchairs, mobility scooters available to hire.

50 SILVERSTONE FARM

North Elmham, Dereham, NR20 5EX. George Carter Design Limited, georgecartergardens.co.uk. *Nearer to Gateley than North Elmham. From North Elmham church head N to Guist. Take 1st L onto Great Heath Rd. L at T-junction. Take 1st R signed Gateley, Silverstone Farm is 1st drive on L by a wood.* **Sun 15 Sept (1-5). Adm £5, chd free. Home-made teas.**

Garden belonging to George Carter described by the Sunday Times as 'one of the 10 best garden designers in Britain'. 1830s farmyard and formal gardens in 2 acres. Inspired by C17 formal gardens, the site consists of a series of interconnecting rooms with framed views and vistas designed in a simple palette of evergreens and deciduous trees and shrubs such as available in that period. Books by the owner for sale. Level site mostly wheelchair accessible.

51 ◆ STODY LODGE

Melton Constable, NR24 2ER. Mr & Mrs Charles MacNicol, 01263 860572, enquiries@stodyestate.co.uk, www.stodylodgegardens.co.uk. *16m NW of Norwich, 3m S of Holt. Off B1354. Signed from Melton Constable on Holt Rd. For SatNav NR24 2ER. Gardens signed as you approach.* **For NGS: Tue 21 May (1-5). Adm £7, chd free. Home-made teas.** For other opening times and information, please phone, email or visit garden website.

Spectacular gardens with one of the largest concentrations of rhododendrons and azaleas in East Anglia. Created in the 1920s, the gardens also feature magnolias, camellias, a variety of ornamental and specimen trees, late daffodils, tulips and bluebells. Expansive lawns and magnificent yew hedges. Woodland walks and 4 acre Water Gardens filled with over 2,000 vividly-coloured azalea mollis. Home-made teas provided by selected local and national charities. Access to most areas of the garden. Gravel paths to Azalea Water Gardens with some uneven ground.

52 TUDOR LODGINGS

Castle Acre, King's Lynn, PE32 2AN. Gus & Julia Stafford Allen. *4m N of Swaffham off A1065. Parking in the field below the house.* **Sun 11 Aug (11-5). Combined adm with Highfield House £6, chd free. Light refreshments in the Barn.**

The C15 house (not open), incorporates part of the Norman earthworks. The 2 acre garden contains C18 dovecote, abstract topiary, lawns and a 'Mondrian' knot garden. Ornamental grasses and hot border. Productive fruit cage and cutting garden. A natural wild area includes a shepherd's hut and informal pond. Bantams and Ducks. Wheelchair access is limited, please ask for assistance beforehand. Disabled WC.

53 TYGER BARN

Wood Lane, Aldeby, Beccles, NR34 0DA. Julianne Fernandez. *Approx 1m from Toft Monks. From A143 towards Great Yarmouth at Toft Monks turn R into Post Office Lane opp White Lion Pub, after ¼m turn L into Wood Lane. After ½m Tyger Barn is 2nd house on L.* **Sun 7 July (11-5). Adm £5, chd free. Light refreshments.**

A 'work in progress', started in 2007 on the site of a former farmyard, the garden incl extensive densely planted borders with hot, exotic and 'ghost' themes, a secret cottage garden, wild flower swathes and colonies of bee orchids. A traditional hay meadow and ancient woodland provide a beautiful setting. Garden is mainly level, but is divided by a shingle drive which wheelchairs without wide wheels will find difficult to cross.

D

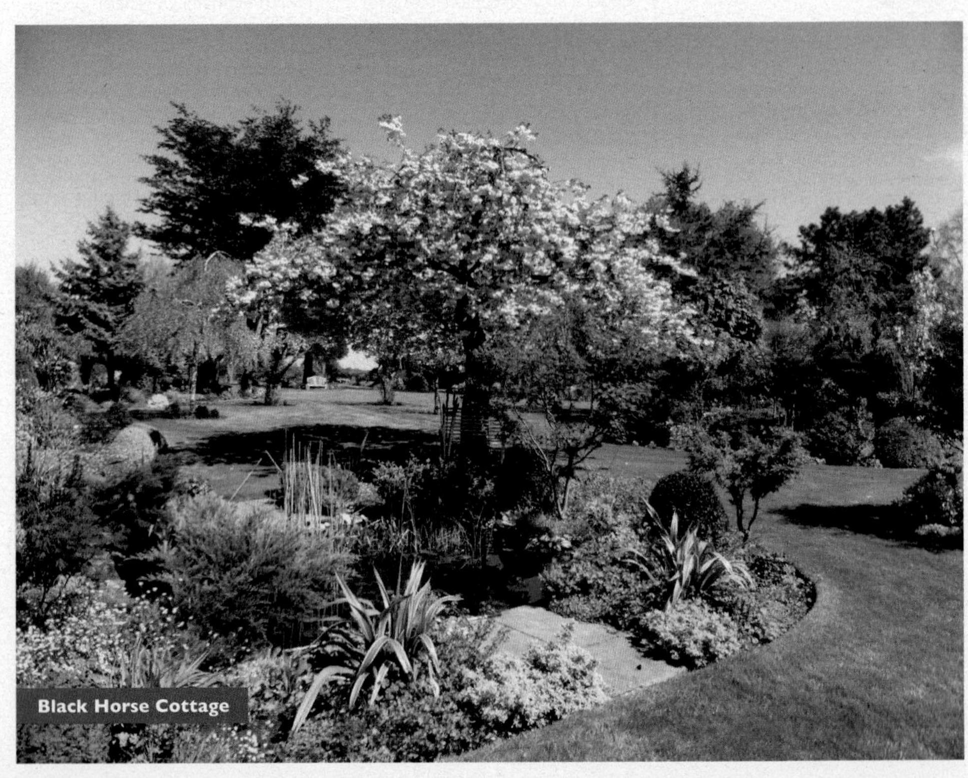

Black Horse Cottage

54 WALCOTT HOUSE
Walcott Green, Walcott, Norwich, NR12 0NU. Mr & Mrs Nick Collier. *3m N of Stalham. Off the Stalham to Walcott rd (B1159).* **Sun 16 June (11-5). Adm £4, chd free. Light refreshments.**
A 12 acre site with over 1 acre of formal gardens based on model C19 Norfolk farm buildings. Woodland and damp gardens; arboretum; vistas with tree lined avenues; woodland walks. Small single steps to negotiate when moving between gardens in the yards.

55 NEW 33 WALDEMAR AVENUE
Hellesdon, Norwich, NR6 6TB. Sonja Gaffer. *Waldemar Ave is situated about 400 yards off Norwich ring road towards Cromer on the A140.* **Sun 28 July, Sun 18 Aug (11-5). Adm £4, chd free. Home-made teas.**
A surprising and large suburban garden of many parts with an exciting mix of exotic and tropical plants combined with unusual perennials, many grown from seed. A quirky palm-thatched Tiki hut is an eye catching feature. Teas will be served and you can sit by the pond which is brimming with wildlife and rare plants. A large collection of succulents will be on show and there will be plants to buy. Wheelchair access surfaces are mostly of lawn and concrete and are on one level. Two entrance gates are 33 and 39 inches wide respectively.

56 WARBOROUGH HOUSE
2 Wells Road, Stiffkey, NR23 1QH. Mr & Mrs J Morgan. *13m N of Fakenham, 4m E of Wells-Next-The-Sea on A149 in the centre of village. Please DO NOT park on main rd as this causes congestion. Parking is available & signed at garden entrance. Coasthopper bus stop outside garden.* **Sun 26 May (1-5). Adm £5, chd free. Home-made teas.**
7 acre garden on a steep chalk slope, surrounding C19 house (not open) with views across the Stiffkey valley and to the coast. Woodland walks, formal terraces, shrub borders, lawns and walled garden create a garden of contrasts. Garden slopes steeply in parts. Paths are gravel, bark chip or grass. Disabled parking allows access to garden nearest the house and teas.

GROUP OPENING

57 WELLS-NEXT-THE-SEA GARDENS
NR23 1DP. *10m N of Fakenham. All gardens near Coasthopper 'Burnt Street' or 'The Buttlands' bus stops. Car-parking for all gardens in Market Lane area.* **Sun 7 July (11-5). Combined adm £5, chd free. Home-made teas at Caprice.**

CAPRICE
Clubbs Lane. David & Joolz Saunders.

NEW HIRAETH
11 Burnt street
Jen Davies.

7 MARKET LANE
Hazel Ashley.

NORFOLK HOUSE
17 Burnt Street.
Katrina & Alan Jackson.

POACHER COTTAGE
15 Burnt Street. Roger & Barbara Oliver.

Wells-next-the-Sea is a small, friendly coastal town on the North Norfolk Coast. Popular with families, walkers and bird watchers. The harbour has shops, cafes, fish and chips. Beach served by a narrow gauge railway. Fine parish church. The five town gardens, though small, demonstrate a variety of design and a wide selection of planting. Wheelchair access at all gardens except Norfolk House which has limited access.

58 WITTON HALL
Old Hall Road, North Walsham, NR28 9UF. Sally Owles. *3½m from North Walsham. From North Walsham take Happisburgh Rd or Byway to Edingthorpe Rd off North Walsham bypass. Situated nr to Bacton Woods.* **Mon 6 May (12-4). Adm £5, chd free. Light refreshments.**
A natural woodland garden. Walk past the handkerchief tree and wander through carpets of English bluebells, rhododendrons and azaleas. Walk from the garden down the field to the church. Stunning views over farmland to the sea. Sensible footwear required as deer, rabbits and badgers inhabit this garden! Witton Park laid out by Humphrey Repton. Wheelchair access difficult if wet.

59 WRETHAM LODGE
East Wretham, IP24 1RL. Mr Gordon Alexander & Mr Ian Salter, 01953 498997. *6m NE of Thetford. A11 E from Thetford, L up A1075, L by village sign, R at Xrds then bear L.* **Sun 21, Mon 22 Apr (11-5). Adm £5, chd free. Home-made teas in Church. Visits also by arrangement Apr to Sept.**
10 acre garden surrounding former Georgian rectory (not open). In spring masses of species tulips, hellebores, fritillaries, daffodils and narcissi; bluebell walk and small woodland walk. Topiary pyramids and yew hedging lead to double herbaceous borders. Shrub borders and rose beds (home of the Wretham Rose). Traditionally maintained walled garden with fruit, vegetables and perennials.

NORTH EAST

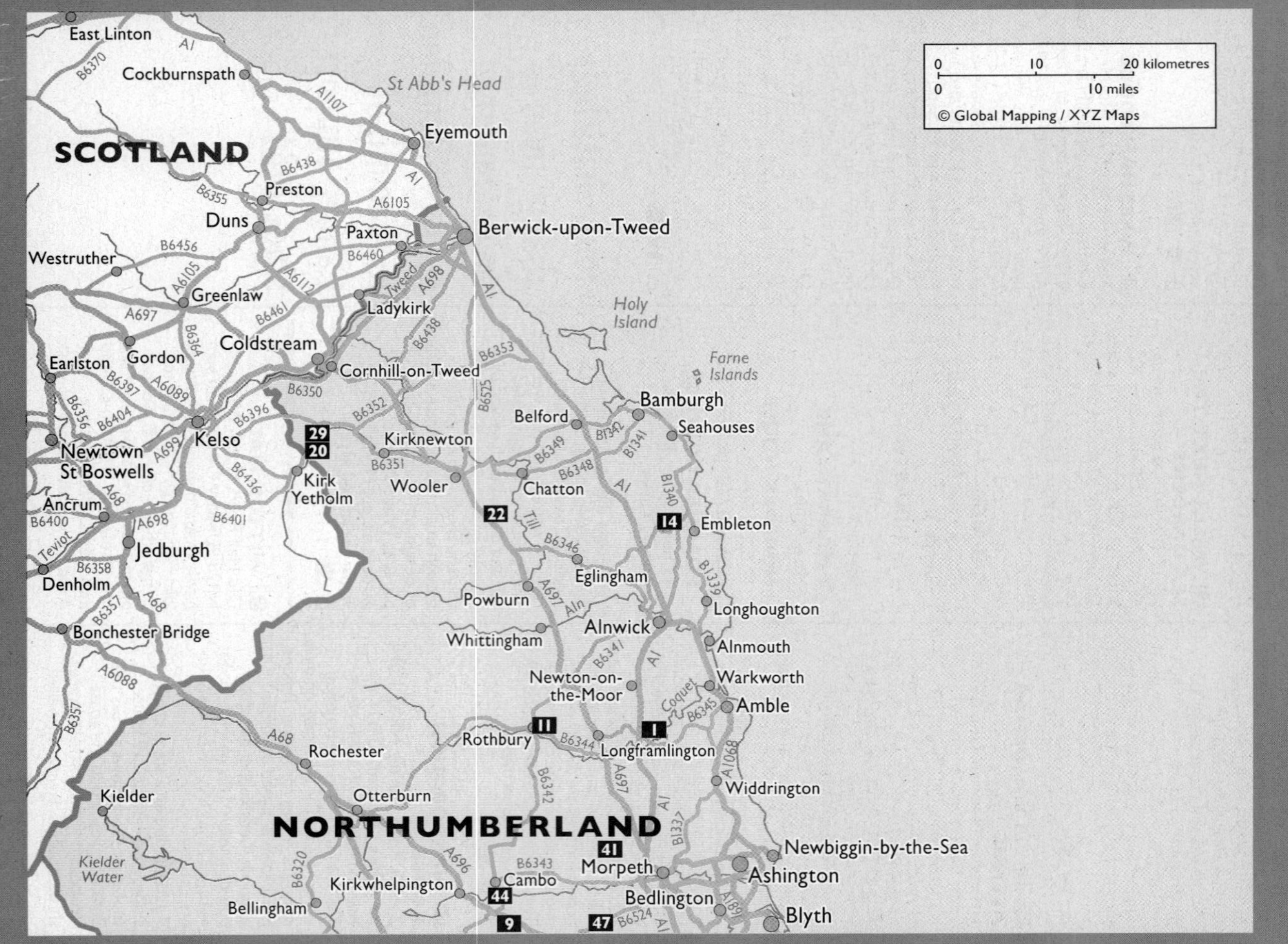

0 10 20 kilometres
0 10 miles
© Global Mapping / XYZ Maps
SCOTLAND
NORTHUMBERLAND
St Abb's Head
Eyemouth
Berwick-upon-Tweed
Holy Island
Farne Islands
Bamburgh
Seahouses
Embleton
Longhoughton
Alnmouth
Warkworth
Amble
Widdrington
Newbiggin-by-the-Sea
Ashington
Blyth
Bedlington
Morpeth
Longframlington
Alnwick
Eglingham
Newton-on-the-Moor
Belford
Chatton
Powburn
Whittingham
Rothbury
Cambo
Kirkwhelpington
Otterburn
Rochester
Bellingham
Kielder
Kielder Water
Wooler
Kirknewton
Cornhill-on-Tweed
Ladykirk
Paxton
Coldstream
Kirk Yetholm
Kelso
Preston
Duns
Greenlaw
Cockburnspath
East Linton
Westruther
Gordon
Earlston
Newtown St Boswells
Ancrum
Jedburgh
Denholm
Bonchester Bridge
Tweed
Till
Aln
Coquet
Teviot

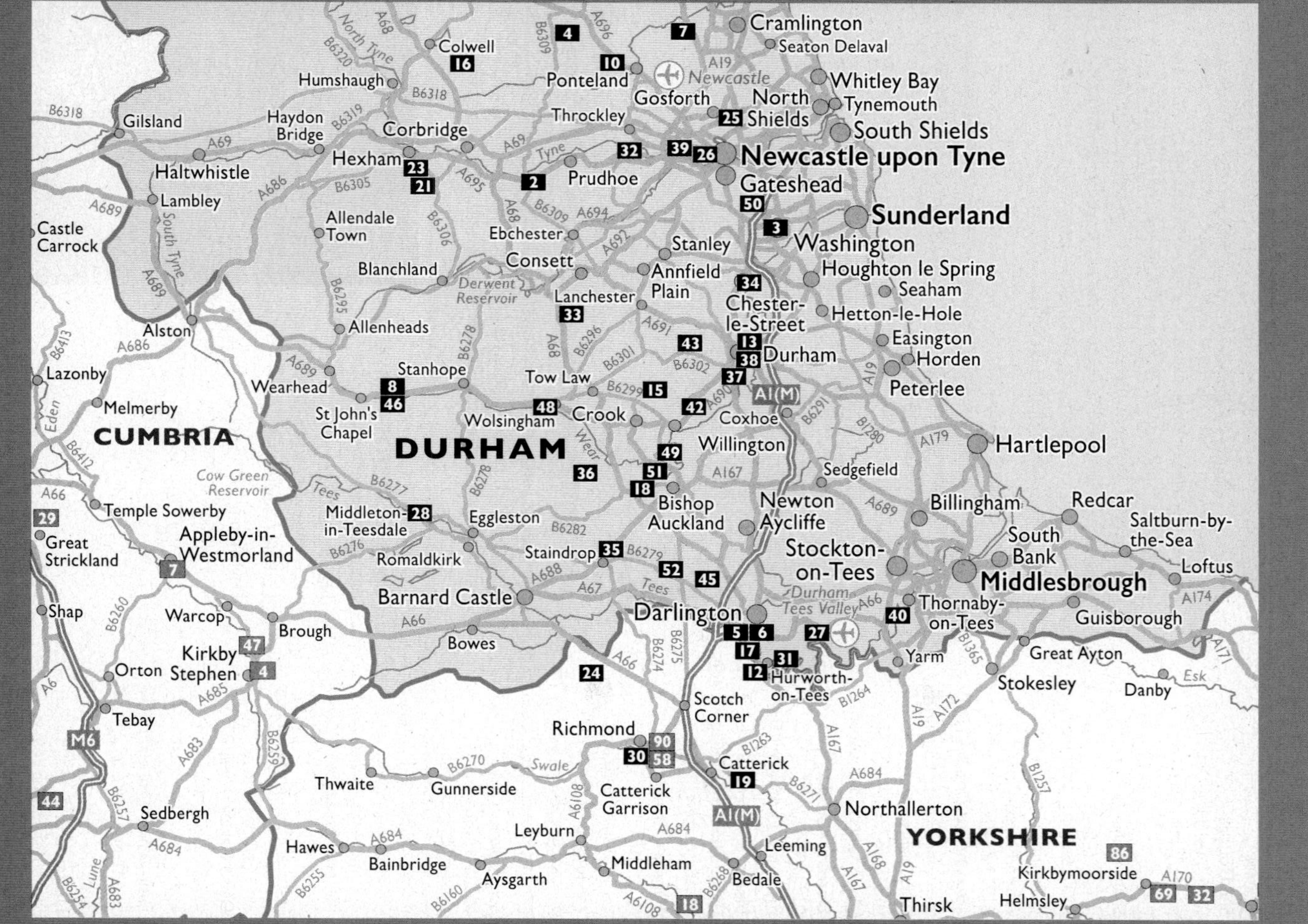
Cramlington
Seaton Delaval
Whitley Bay
Tynemouth
North Shields
South Shields
Newcastle upon Tyne
Gateshead
Sunderland
Washington
Houghton le Spring
Seaham
Hetton-le-Hole
Easington
Horden
Peterlee
Chester-le-Street
Durham
Coxhoe
Willington
Hartlepool
Billingham
Sedgefield
Newton Aycliffe
Stockton-on-Tees
Redcar
Saltburn-by-the-Sea
Loftus
South Bank
Middlesbrough
Guisborough
Thornaby-on-Tees
Yarm
Great Ayton
Danby
Stokesley
Darlington
Durham Tees Valley
Hurworth-on-Tees
Scotch Corner
Catterick
Northallerton
YORKSHIRE
Thirsk
Kirkbymoorside
Helmsley
Leeming
Bedale
Catterick Garrison
Richmond
Middleham
Leyburn
Aysgarth
Bainbridge
Hawes
Gunnerside
Thwaite
Sedbergh
Bishop Auckland
Crook
Tow Law
Wolsingham
DURHAM
Stanhope
St John's Chapel
Wearhead
Eggleston
Middleton-in-Teesdale
Romaldkirk
Barnard Castle
Bowes
Staindrop
Brough
Kirkby Stephen
Warcop
Appleby-in-Westmorland
Orton
Tebay
Shap
Great Strickland
Temple Sowerby
CUMBRIA
Melmerby
Lazonby
Alston
Castle Carrock
Gilsland
Lambley
Haltwhistle
Haydon Bridge
Humshaugh
Hexham
Corbridge
Colwell
Allendale Town
Allenheads
Blanchland
Consett
Ebchester
Lanchester
Annfield Plain
Stanley
Prudhoe
Throckley
Ponteland
Gosforth
Newcastle
Derwent Reservoir
Cow Green Reservoir
Tyne
North Tyne
South Tyne
Wear
Tees
Swale
Eden
Lune
Esk

Volunteers

County Durham
County Organiser
Iain Anderson
01325 778446
iain.anderson@ngs.org.uk

County Treasurer
Sue Douglas
07712 461002
pasm.d@btinternet.com

Booklet Co-ordinator
Sheila Walke
07837 764057
sheila.walke@ngs.org.uk

Publicity
Alison Morgan
01913 843842
alison.morgan@ngs.org.uk

Assistant County Organisers
Gill Knights
01325 483210
gillianknights55@gmail.com

Dorothy Matthews
01325 354434
matthews.dorothy@googlemail.com

Monica Spencer
01325 286215 monicaspencer@btinternet.com

Margaret Stamper
01325 488911
margaretstamper@tiscali.co.uk

Gill Naisby
01325 381324
gillnaisby@gmail.com

Sue Walker
01325 481881
walker.sdl@gmail.com

County Durham: an unsung county.

County Durham lies between the river Wear and the river Tees and is varied and beautiful.

Our National Garden Scheme gardens are to be found in the city, high up in the dales, in the attractive villages of South Durham and the outskirts of Teesside industrial heartland. Something different for you every week.

So join the allotmenteers in St Margaret's Allotments set in the spectacular backdrop of Durham Cathedral and cultivated since the middle ages. Then visit the wide variety of gardens in the Weardale village of Wolsingham. You can experience stunning modern garden design in Killerby at Woodside or the High Victorian style gardens at Southlands in Eaglescliffe.

Choose old favourites from our gardens and also check out our new gardens – Neasham Abbey, Middleton Hall retirement village or Wolsingham village. All of our garden owners are looking forward to welcoming you.

Northumberland is a county rich in history with sturdy castles, stunning coastline and a wild landscape threaded with sheltered valleys.

Gardeners have learnt how to make the most of the land; terracing hillsides, enhancing the soil and often using the wonderful architecture as a backdrop, such as at Lilburn Tower.

Garden owners have managed to create gardens whatever the conditions. At Blagdon the solution has been to plant within an old quarry, and at Wallington to use a long narrow valley for shelter.

An eclectic range of gardens open for the National Garden Scheme. Each reflects the style and character of their owners, with the extra attraction of home-made teas and plant sales.

Northumberland & Tyne and Wear
County Organiser
& Booklet Coordinator
Maureen Kesteven
01914 135937
kestevenmaureen@gmail.com

County Treasurer
David Oakley 07941 077594
david.oakley@ngs.org.uk

Publicity
Susie White 07941 077595
susie@susie-white.co.uk

Talks Co-ordinator & Social Media
Liz Reid 01914 165981
lizreid52@ntworld.com

Assistant County Organisers
Maxine Eaton 077154 60038
acottagegardener@gmail.com

Natasha McEwen 07917 754155
natashamcewengd@aol.co.uk

Liz Reid (as below left)

David Young 01434 600699
davyoung0601@me.com

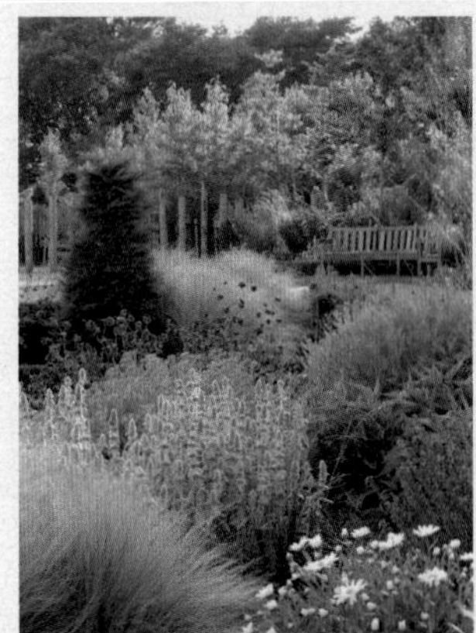

Right: Coldcotes Moor Farm

OPENING DATES

All entries subject to change. For latest information check **www.ngs.org.uk**

Map locator numbers are shown to the right of each garden name.

March

Sunday 3rd
◆ Crook Hall & Gardens 13

April

Saturday 27th
◆ Wallington 44

Sunday 28th
45 Blackwell 5
46 Blackwell 6

May

Friday 3rd
◆ Cragside 11

Sunday 5th
Hillside Cottages 18

Sunday 19th
Blagdon 7

Saturday 25th
Ushaw College 43

Sunday 26th
Croft Hall 12
Lilburn Tower 22

Monday 27th
Woodbine House 49

June

Saturday 1st
Maggie's 25

Sunday 2nd
Loughbrow House 23
NEW Neasham Abbey 31

Sunday 9th
The Beacon 2
Oliver Ford Garden 33

Saturday 15th
Middleton in Teesdale Garden Group 28
◆ Wallington 44

Sunday 16th
NEW The Shilling House Garden 39

Saturday 22nd
NEW Wolsingham Village Gardens 48

Sunday 23rd
Hidden Gardens of Croft Road 17
◆ Mindrum Garden 29
No. 2 Ferndene 32

Saturday 29th
Fallodon Hall 14
Woodlands 50

Sunday 30th
Southlands 40
Stanton Fence 41
Westgate Gardens 46

Mr Yorke's Walled Garden

July

Thursday 4th
Woodlands 50

Friday 5th
The Fold 15

Saturday 6th
The Fold 15
Kirky Cottage 20

Sunday 7th
Marie Curie Hospice Newcastle on Tyne 26
St Margaret's Allotments 38
◆ Whalton Manor Gardens 47

Thursday 11th
24 Bede Crescent 3

Saturday 13th
◆ Raby Castle 35

Sunday 14th
24 Bede Crescent 3
Bichfield Tower 4

Wednesday 17th
Coldcotes Moor Farm 10

Saturday 20th
Coldcotes Moor Farm 10

Sunday 21st
Kiplin Hall 19
Lambshield 21

Sunday 28th
Gardener's Cottage Plants 16
St Cuthbert's Hospice 37

August

Saturday 3rd
Woodside, Killerby 52

Sunday 4th
Ravensford Farm 36

Saturday 10th
NEW Middleton Hall Retirement Village 27

Sunday 11th
Capheaton Hall 9

Sunday 18th
Walworth Gardens 45

By Arrangement

Arrange a personalised garden visit with your club, or group of friends, on a date to suit you. See individual garden entries for full details.

Acton House 1
The Beacon 2
24 Bede Crescent 3
Breckon Hill 8
Coldcotes Moor Farm 10
The Fold 15
Hillside Cottages 18
Kirky Cottage 20
Lambshield 21
Lilburn Tower 22
Loughbrow House 23
Lowbridge House 24
Mr Yorke's Walled Garden 30
No. 2 Ferndene 32
25 Park Road South 34
Ravensford Farm 36
Southlands 40
4 Stockley Grove 42
Westgate Gardens 46
Woodlands 50
Woodside House 51

THE GARDENS

1 ACTON HOUSE

Felton, Morpeth, NE65 9NU. Mr Alan & Mrs Eileen Ferguson, Head Gardener 07779 860217, jane@actonhouseuk.com. *N of Morpeth. Directions given when booking confirmed.* **Visits by arrangement May to Aug. Adm £5, chd free.**

This stunning walled garden has structure, colour and variety of planting, with abundant herbaceous perennials and different grasses. Planted in the spring of 2011, it has sections devoted to fruit and vegetables, David Austin rose borders, standard trees and climbers spreading over the brick walls. There are additional mixed borders, a ha-ha, and developing woodland planting, in total extending over 5 acres. Herbaceous perennial plantings include species and varieties favoured by butterflies and bees.

2 THE BEACON

10 Crabtree Road, Stocksfield, NE43 7NX. Derek & Patricia Hodgson, 01661 842518, patandderek@hotmail.com. *12m W of Newcastle upon Tyne. From A69 follow signs into village. Station & cricket ground on L . Turn R into Cadehill Rd then 1st R into Crabtree Rd (cul de sac) Park on Cadehill.* **Sun 9 June (2-6). Adm £5, chd free. Home-made teas.** Visits also by arrangement for groups of 10+.

This garden illustrates how to make a cottage garden on a steep site with loads of interest at different levels. Planted with acers, roses and a variety of cottage garden and formal plants. Water runs gently through it and there are tranquil places to sit and talk or just reflect. Stunning colour and plant combinations. Wildlife friendly - numerous birds, frogs, newts, hedgehogs. Haven for butterflies and bees. Steep, so not wheelchair friendly but wheelchair users have negotiated the drive and enjoyed the view of the main garden. Owner available for entertaining group talks.

3 24 BEDE CRESCENT

Washington, NE38 7JA. Sheila Brookes, 0191 417 9702, sheilab24@hotmail.co.uk. *From Old Hall to Cenotaph, 600yds up Village Lane past R C Church, turn onto Bede Cres before Black Bush pub. End house, facing grassed oval. On foot, walk PAST Black Bush, through cut into Bede Cres.* **Thur 11 July (12.30-4.30). Sun 14 July (12.30-4.30). Adm £2.50, chd free. Cold drinks, biscuits & crisps available if desired.** Visits also by arrangement May to Aug for groups of up to 10.

A lesson in how to make a small shady place colourful and interesting. Small 'courtyard style' garden, with central paved area, surrounded by borders containing shrubs and box balls for year round structure, and packed with colourful Astilbes, lilies and clematis for summer impact. Small patio front garden, with gravel border planted with box balls and containerised shrubs. Light refreshments at cafes & pubs around our pretty Village Green (gold medal winner in Northumbria in Bloom). Access into paved 'courtyard garden' via a side gate, (which should accommodate a small wheelchair, although not a wide entrance).

4 BICHFIELD TOWER

Belsay, Newcastle Upon Tyne, NE20 0JP. Lesley & Stewart Manners, 075114 39606, lesleymanners@gmail.com, www.bitchfieldtower.co.uk. *Private rd off B6309, 4m N of Stamfordham and SW of Belsay village.* **Sun 14 July (1-4). Adm £5, chd free. Home-made teas.**

6 acre maturing garden in it's 4th year of rejuvenation. Set around a Medieval Pele Tower, there is an impressive stone water feature, large trout lake,mature woodland, Pear Orchard, and 2 Walled gardens. Extensive herbaceous borders, prairie borders and contemporary grass borders. Delicious home-made teas provided by the 6th Morpeth Scout Group in the carriage house garden and building. Historic building, tennis court, woodlands, fairy walk for kids, sculpture walk throughout the grounds, croquet lawn and set, trout lake, pop-up shops of local businesses.

5 45 BLACKWELL

Darlington, DL3 8QT. Cath & Peter Proud. *SW Darlington, next to R.Tees. ½ way along Blackwell in Darlington, which links Bridge Rd (on A66 just past Blackwell Bridge) & Carmel Rd South. Alternatively, turn into Blackwell from Post Office on Carmel Rd South.* **Sun 28 Apr (1-5). Combined adm with 46 Blackwell £4, chd free. Home-made teas, coffees and soft drinks and a selection of scones with home-made jams will be available.**

No. 45 Blackwell rises from the River Tees up to a garden with many mature trees, wildlife meadow, pond with waterfall, herb and Mediterranean garden, camellia border, lawns and colourful Spring borders and containers full of Spring bulbs. Refreshments, preserves and plants for sale. Well behaved dogs on leads welcome. Wheelchair access to patios and to lawn with assistance.

6 46 BLACKWELL

Darlington, DL3 8QT. Christopher & Yvonne Auton. *(Please refer to directions to 45 Blackwell, Darlington - joint garden opening).* **Sun 28 Apr (1-5). Combined adm with 45 Blackwell £4, chd free. Teas at 45 Blackwell Road.**

46 Blackwell is a plantsman's garden - compact, but full of unusual specimens and collections of plants and trees, with a pond and summerhouse in the back garden. Full wheelchair access to front garden, but limited access to back garden.

7 BLAGDON

Seaton Burn, NE13 6DE. Viscount Ridley, www.blagdonestate.co.uk. *5m S of Morpeth on A1. 8m N of Newcastle on A1, N on B1318, L at r'about (Holiday Inn) & follow signs to Blagdon. Entrance to parking area signed.* **Sun 19 May (1-4.30). Adm £5, chd free. Home-made teas.**

Unique 27 acre garden encompassing formal garden with Lutyens designed 'canal', Lutyens structures and walled kitchen garden. Valley with stream and various follies, quarry garden and woodland walks. Large numbers of ornamental trees and shrubs planted over many generations. National Collections of Acer, Alnus and Sorbus. Trailer rides around the estate (small additional charge) and stalls selling local produce. Partial wheelchair access.

NPC

8 BRECKON HILL

Westgate, Bishop Auckland, DL13 1PD. Jennie & David Henderson, 01388 517735, lefontanil@gmail.com. *Approaching Westgate from Stanhope, on A689 you will come to Breckon Hill. It is accessed up a ½m tarmac rd to the R which will be clearly marked. Parking for 6 cars.* **Visits by arrangement June & July for groups of up to 10. Adm £4, chd free. Home-made teas. Gluten free to order. Wine available if evening viewing..**

Breckon Hill is perched on the fellside at 1100ft above sea level, just outside the village of Westgate in Weardale, part of the North Pennines AONB. There are fabulous views of Weardale from our walled garden.

9 CAPHEATON HALL

Capheaton, Newcastle Upon Tyne, NE19 2AB. William & Eliza Browne-Swinburne, 01830 530159, capheatonhall@gmail.com, www.capheatonhall.co.uk/accomodation. *24m N of Newcastle off A696. From S turn L onto Silver Hill rd signed Capheaton. From N, past Wallington/Kirkharle junction, turn R.* **Sun 11 Aug (2-5). Adm £5, chd free. Home-made teas.**

Set in parkland, Capheaton Hall has magnificent views over the Northumberland countryside. Formal ponds sit south of the house, which has an C19 conservatory, and a walk to a Georgian folly of a chapel. The outstanding feature is the very productive walled kitchen garden, at its height in late summer, mixing colourful vegetables, espaliered fruit with annual and perennial flowering borders. Walled Kitchen Garden; fruit and vegetable production; annual and perennial borders; Victorian glasshouse and conservatory. Wheelchair access to the walled garden and teas in the house is limited by steps and gravel paths, but the lawns are closely mown and generally flat.

10 COLDCOTES MOOR FARM

Ponteland, Newcastle Upon Tyne, NE20 0DF. Ron & Louise Bowey, info@theboweys.co.uk. *Off A696 N of Ponteland. From S, leave Ponteland on A696 towards Jedburgh, after 1m take L turn marked 'Milbourne 2m'. After 400yds turn L into drive.* **Wed 17, Sat 20 July (1-5). Adm £10, chd £2. Light refreshments incl in adm. Go to www.coldcotesmoorgarden.org.uk to book your tickets. Adm includes home-made afternoon tea. Visits also by arrangement in July for groups of 20+. Individual and small groups can book on one of our all ticket days on 17 and 20 July.**

Please note, this garden requires you to pre- book tickets. Go to www.coldcotesmoorgarden.org.uk to book. The garden, landscaped grounds and woods cover around 15 acres. The wooded approach opens out to lawned areas surrounded by ornamental and woodland shrubs and trees. A courtyard garden leads to an ornamental walled garden, beyond which is an orchard, vegetable garden, flower garden and rose arbour. To the south the garden looks out over a lake and field walks, with woodland walk to the west. Small children's play area. Most areas can be accessed though sometimes by circuitous routes or an occasional step. WC access involves three steps.

11 ◆ CRAGSIDE

Rothbury, NE65 7PX. National Trust, 01669 620333, cragside@nationaltrust.org.uk, www.nationaltrust.org.uk/cragside. *13m SW of Alnwick. (B6341); 15m NW of Morpeth (A697).* **For NGS: Fri 3 May (10-4). Adm £18, chd £9. Light refreshments at Cragside Tea Rooms or Still Room. For other opening times and information, please phone, email or visit garden website.**

The Formal Garden is in the 'High Victorian' style created by the 1st Lord and Lady Armstrong. Incl orchard house, carpet bedding, ferneries, Italian terrace and Rose borders. The largest sandstone Rock Garden in Europe with its tumbling cascades. Extensive grounds of over 1000 acres famous for rhododendrons in June, large lakes and magnificent conifer landscape. The House, mainly the design of Norman Shaw, with its very fine arts and crafts interiors is worth a separate visit. Limited wheelchair access to formal garden.

12 CROFT HALL

Croft-on-Tees, DL2 2TB. Mr & Mrs Trevor Chaytor Norris. *3m S of Darlington. On A167 to Northallerton, 6m from Scotch Corner. Croft Hall is 1st house on R as you enter village from Scotch Corner.* **Sun 26 May (2-5). Adm £5, chd free. Home-made teas.**

A lovely lavender walk leads to a Queen Anne-fronted house (not open) surrounded by a 5 acre garden, comprising a stunning herbaceous border, large fruit and vegetable plot, two ponds and wonderful topiary arched wall. Pretty rose garden and mature box Italianate parterre are beautifully set in this garden offering peaceful, tranquil views of open countryside. Wheelchair access, some gravel paths.

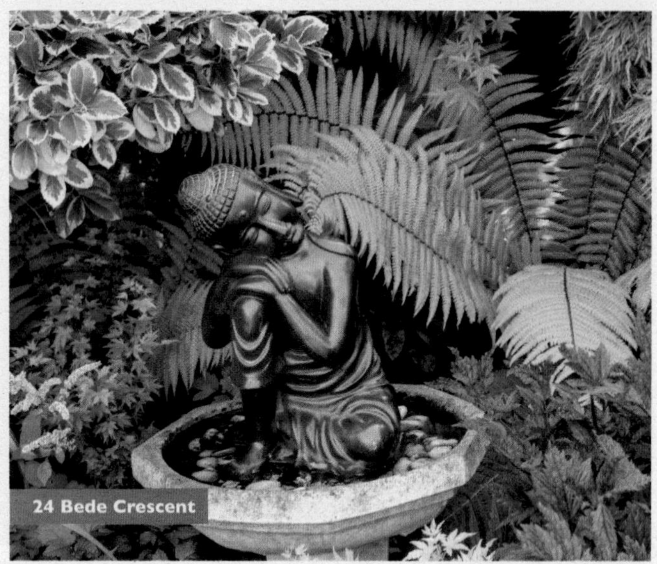

24 Bede Crescent

© Susie White

13 ◆ CROOK HALL & GARDENS

Sidegate, Durham City, DH1 5SZ. Maggie Bell, 0191 384 8028, info@crookhallgardens.co.uk, www.crookhallgardens.co.uk. *Centre of Durham City. Crook Hall is short walk from Durham's Market Place. Follow the tourist info signs. Pay and display parking available at entrance.* **For NGS: Sun 3 Mar (10-4). Adm £6, chd £3. incl Hall. For other opening times and information, please phone, email or visit garden website.**

Described in Country Life as having 'history, romance and beauty'. Intriguing medieval manor house surrounded by 4 acres of fine gardens. Visitors can enjoy magnificent cathedral views from the 2 walled gardens. Other garden 'rooms' incl the silver and white garden. An orchard, moat pool, maze and Sleeping Giant give added interest! Refreshments in the Tea Room (main building) and the Café (entrance building). Wheelchair accessible and disabled WC.

14 FALLODON HALL

Alnwick, NE66 3HF. Mr & Mrs Mark Bridgeman, www.bruntoncottages.co.uk. *5m N of Alnwick, 2m off A1. From the A1 turn onto the B6347 signed Christon Bank & Seahouses. Turn into the Fallodon gates after exactly 2m, at Xrds. Follow drive for 1m.* **Sat 29 June (2-5). Adm £5, chd free. Home-made teas.**

Extensive, well established garden, with a hot greenhouse beside the bog garden. The late C17 walls of the kitchen garden surround cutting and vegetable borders and the fruit greenhouse. The sunken garden from 1898 has been replanted by Natasha McEwen. Woodlands, pond and arboretum extend over 10 acres to explore. Renowned home-made teas in stable yard, and plant sale. Partial wheelchair access.

15 THE FOLD

High Wooley, Stanley Crook, DL15 9AP. Mr & Mrs G Young, 01388 768412, gfamyoung@gmail.com. *Turn R at Xrds in Brancepeth, opp turn to Castle, drive 3m along the single track rd until you reach the junction on bend with the main rd. Entrance 100yards on L.* **Fri 5, Sat 6 July (10.30-4.30). Adm £4, chd free. Home-made teas. Visits also by arrangement May to Sept for groups of 10 to 30. Visit the Comedian for lunch close by in Sunniside 730029.**

Garden, approx ½ acre created over 20 years in an area that had been extensively mined. It stands at 700ft and enjoys splendid views over countryside. Herbaceous borders, alpine bed, island beds, ponds, numerous mature trees and small roof garden. Wide range of plants, mostly perennials, many grown from seed and cuttings. Emphasis on colour, harmony and texture to create all year interest. No disabled access as steep slopes and gravel paths.

16 GARDENER'S COTTAGE PLANTS

Gardener's Cottage, Bingfield, Newcastle Upon Tyne, NE19 2LE. Andrew Davenport, www.gcplants.co.uk. *6m N of Corbridge. From N turn L off A68 signed Bingfield, after approx. 0.6m turn L at T junction, garden on R approx. 0.9m. From S turn R off A68 signed Bingfield, garden on R approx. 1.8m.* **Sun 28 July (11-4). Adm £4, chd free. Variety of home-made cakes and scones.**

This compact (¼ acre) experimental garden and nursery provides an education in organic and sustainable gardening. Organic vegetable, fruit, herb and floral gardens show the use of mulching, hen assisted composting and other ideas from the garden's inventive creator. Pollinator friendly wild flowers thrive amongst cultivated varieties in a range of attractive ornamental borders. Collection of unusual, historic and rare plants of the mid-Tyne valley.

GROUP OPENING

17 HIDDEN GARDENS OF CROFT ROAD

Darlington, DL2 2SD. Mrs Gypsy Nichol. *2m S of Darlington on A167. ¾m S from A167/A66 r'about between Darlington & Croft.* **Sun 23 June (1-5). Combined adm £5, chd free. Home-made teas at Oxney Flatts & Orchard Gardens.** Donation to Great North Air Ambulance.

NAGS HEAD FARM
Jo & Ian Fearnly.

NEW COTTAGE
Jane & John Brown.

ORCHARD GARDENS
Gill & Neil Segger.

OXNEY COTTAGE
Gypsy Nicol.

OXNEY FLATTS FARM
Carol & Chris Pratt.

5 very different and interesting gardens, well named as 'Hidden Gardens'. All are behind tall hedges. Oxney Cottage is a very pretty cottage garden with lawns, herbaceous borders and roses, colourful and varied unusual plants. Nags Head Farm has a wonderful rill running alongside a sloping garden with a variety of plants leading to a quiet, peaceful courtyard. There is a large vegetable garden in which stands a magnificent glass-house with prolific vines and chilli plants. A woodland walk enhances the tranquility of this garden. Orchard Gardens is a large interesting garden of mixed planting, stump sculptures, colourful themed beds, fruit trees and different imaginative ornaments. Oxney Flatts has well-stocked herbaceous borders and a wild life pond. New Cottage a recently acquired garden has a new fruit and vegetable area, original herbaceous border, pond and small alpine garden. Partial wheelchair access.

GROUP OPENING

18 HILLSIDE COTTAGES

Low Etherley, Bishop Auckland, DL14 0EZ. Mary Smith, Eric & Delia Ayres, 01388 832727, mary@maryruth.plus.com. *Off the B6282 in Low Etherley, nr Bishop Auckland. To reach the gardens walk down the track opp number 63 Low Etherley. Please park on main rd. Limited disabled parking at the cottages.* **Sun 5 May (1.30-5). Combined adm £4. Home-made teas at No.2. We provide tea coffee and other beverages, cakes and savoury snacks.** Visits also by arrangement Feb to Nov for groups of up to 30. We welcome groups with specialist interests e.g. painting.

1 HILLSIDE COTTAGE
Eric & Delia Ayres.

2 HILLSIDE COTTAGE
Mrs M Smith.

The gardens of these two C19 cottages offer contrasting styles. At Number 1, grass paths lead you through a layout of trees and shrubs including many interesting specimens. Number 2 is based on island beds and has a cottage garden feel with a variety of perennials among the trees and shrubs and also incl a wild area, vegetables and fruit. Both gardens have ponds and water features. This year we are opening to show off spring flowers and Rhododendrons and pond life. There is a good sized Wollomi pine and Monkey puzzle tree and other unusual trees. Children will be able to see pond life close up. At number 2 there are two stone railway sleepers from the nearby 1825 Stockton and Darlington railway. There are steps in both gardens.

19 KIPLIN HALL

nr Scorton, Richmond, North Yorkshire, DL10 6AT. Kiplin Hall Trustees, www.kiplinhall.co.uk. *Between Richmond & Northallerton on B6271. Approx 5m E of A1. Exit at junction 52 towards Brompton on Swale, and follow signs to Scorton and Kiplin Hall.* **Sun 21 July (10-5). Adm £6.20, chd £3.50. Home-made teas. Home baking, lunches and teas using fresh garden produce. Hot/cold drinks, wine, beer.**
Fabulous lake views, gardens, woodland and parkland. These beautiful grounds, once in decline, are being restored to their former beauty in this lovely setting. Topiary surrounds the White and Rose Gardens. Perennial and Hot Borders, Knot and Sensory Gardens. Mayflies dance in the Bog Garden and the Walled Garden is once more productive. From snowdrops to glorious autumn colours, this garden is a joy! Wheelchair access. The gardens close to the house and Walled Garden are accessible. Coaches must be booked in advance.

20 KIRKY COTTAGE

12 Mindrum Farm Cottages, Mindrum, TD12 4QN. Mrs Ginny Fairfax, 01890 850246, Ginny@mindrumgarden.co.uk. *6m SW of Coldstream. 9m NW of Wooler on B6352. 4m N of Yetholm village.* **Sat 6 July (11-5). Adm £4, chd free. Home-made teas.** Visits also by arrangement for groups.
It is 6 years since Ginny Fairfax created Kirky Cottage Garden in the beautiful Bowmont Valley surrounded, and protected by, the Border Hills. A gravel garden in cottage garden style, old roses, violas and others jostle with favorites from Mindrum. It is a lovely, abundant garden and, with Ginny's new and creative ideas, ever evolving.

21 LAMBSHIELD

Hexham, NE46 1SF. David Young, 01434 600699, davyoung0601@me.com. *2m S of Hexham. Take the B6306 from Hexham. After 1.6m turn R at chevron sign. Lambshield drive is 2nd on L after 0.6m.* **Sun 21 July (1-4.30). Adm £5, chd free. Home-made teas.** Visits also by arrangement May to Aug for groups of 10+.

2 acre country garden with strong structure and exciting plant combinations, begun in 2010 around a working farm. Distinct areas and styles with formal herbaceous, grasses, contemporary planting, cottage garden, pool and orchard. Cloud hedging, pleached trees, and topiary create a backdrop to colourful and exuberant planting. Modern sculpture. Oak building and fencing by local craftsmen. Level ground but gravel paths not suitable for wheelchairs.

22 LILBURN TOWER

Alnwick, NE66 4PQ. Mr & Mrs D Davidson, 01668 217291, lilburntower@outlook.com. *3m S of Wooler. On A697.* **Sun 26 May (2-5). Adm £5, chd free. Home-made teas.** Visits also by arrangement May to Sept for groups of 10+.

10 acres of magnificent walled and formal gardens set above river; rose parterre, topiary, scented garden, Victorian conservatory, wild flower meadow. Extensive fruit and vegetable garden, large glasshouse with vines. 30 acres of woodland with walks. Giant lilies, meconopsis around pond garden. Rhododendrons and azaleas. Also ruins of Pele Tower, and C12 church. Partial wheelchair access.

23 LOUGHBROW HOUSE

Hexham, NE46 1RS. Mrs K A Clark, 01434 603351, patriciaclark351@hotmail.com. *1m S of Hexham on B6306. Dipton Mill Rd. Rd signed Blanchland, ¼m take R fork; then ¼m at fork, lodge gates & driveway at intersection.* **Sun 2 June (2-5). Adm £5, chd free. Home-made teas.** Visits also by arrangement.

A real country house garden with sweeping, colour themed herbaceous borders set around large lawns. Unique Lutyens inspired rill with grass topped bridges and climbing rose arches. Part walled kitchen garden and paved courtyard. Bog garden with pond. Developing new border and rose bed. Wild flower meadow with specimen trees. Woodland quarry garden with rhododendrons, azaleas, hostas and rare trees. Home-made jams and chutneys for sale.

24 LOWBRIDGE HOUSE

Dalton, Richmond, DL11 7FB. Mrs Clarissa Milbank, 01833 621228, clarissamilbank@btinternet.com. *From W turn R off A66 at Rokeby Inn. In 1½m turn L to Dalton. Straight over Xrds. 100yds. Lowbridge House is on L. From E 6½m from Scotch Corner on A66 take L turn to Dalton. L at Xrds 100yds on L is Lowbridge House.* **Visits by arrangement June to Sept for groups of up to 30. Price of visit on application. Light refreshments on patio area by pond, to be discussed on booking.**

Rural setting with wonderful panoramic views of local countryside. Garden consists of mixed borders, roses and sweet peas. Large pond (small lake) stocked with ghost carp and trout, with natural planting including candelabra primulas and wild flower banks. Island has ducks, coots and moorhens nesting. Patio area suitable for wheelchairs . Woodland and streamside walk with dippers and kingfishers. Most areas are accessible with care.

25 MAGGIE'S

Melville Grove, Newcastle Upon Tyne, NE7 7NU. Marissa Magee, www.maggiescentres.org/newcastle. *Driving into the grounds of the Freeman Hospital, Maggie's can be found opp entrance to the Northern Centre for Cancer Care. Nearest parking the Freeman Hospital multi-storey.* **Sat 1 June (11-3). Adm by donation. Home made cakes and scones, teas and coffees. Garden inspired mocktails.**

The garden, by Chelsea medal winning designer, Sarah Price, is a sheltered sun trap. There are banked wild flower beds and multiple planters, with seasonal displays, at ground level, plus two roof gardens. This gives a choice of outside spaces for visitors to enjoy. Copper beech, cherry blossom, crocus, bulbs, wild flowers and herbs give a colourful seasonal planting palette. A tranquil oasis. Homemade cakes and scones will be available. Partial wheelchair access, gravel in the garden and roof garden, but the main section can be accessed.

26 MARIE CURIE HOSPICE NEWCASTLE ON TYNE

Marie Curie Hospice, Marie Curie Drive, Newcastle Upon Tyne, NE4 6SS. Marie Curie Organisation, www.mariecurie.org.uk/help/hospice-care/hospices/newcastle/about. *In West Newcastle just off Elswick rd. At the bottom of a housing estate. The turning is between MA brothers & Dallas Carpets.* **Sun 7 July (2-4.30). Adm by donation. Light refreshments served in our Garden Café.**

The landscaped gardens of the purpose-built Marie Curie Hospice overlook the Tyne and Gateshead and offer a beautiful, tranquil place for patients and visitors to sit and chat. Rooms open onto a patio garden with gazebo and fountain. There are climbing roses, evergreens and herbaceous perennials.The garden is well maintained by volunteers. Come and see the work NGS funding helps make possible. Plant sale and refreshments available. The Hospice and Gardens are wheelchair accessible.

27 NEW MIDDLETON HALL RETIREMENT VILLAGE

Middleton St. George, Darlington, DL2 1HA. MHRV, www.middletonhallretirementvillage.co.uk. *From A67 D'ton/Yarm, turn at 2nd r'about signed to Middleton St George. Turn L at the mini r'about & immediately R after the railway bridge, signed Low Middleton. Main entrance is ¼m on L.* **Sat 10 Aug (10-4). Adm £5, chd free. Home-made teas in The Orangery, on-site.**

Like those in our retirement community, the extensive grounds are gloriously mature, endlessly interesting and with many hidden depths. 45 acres of features beckon; natural woodland and parkland, Japanese, Mediterranean and Butterfly Gardens, an Enchanted Forest, croquet lawn, putting green, allotments, ponds, wetland and bird hide. (all wheelchair accessible and linked by a series of Woodland Walks).

GROUP OPENING

28 MIDDLETON IN TEESDALE GARDEN GROUP

Market Place, Middleton-In-Teesdale, Barnard Castle, DL12 0ST. *Middleton-in-Teesdale Open Gardens are all located in & near the village. Tickets & map with directions to each garden available from the Tourist Information Centre, in the centre of the village.* **Sat 15 June (11-5). Combined adm £5, chd free. Home-made teas in Masonic Hall. Gluten free scones available.**

Middleton in Teesdale sits amongst the outstanding scenery of Upper Teesdale. It welcomes Pennine Way walkers, and is just 4m to the E of the famous High Force on the R Tees. 6 + gardens will be open in and around this delightfully picturesque village, covering a variety of sizes, designs and planting. The gardens, in and near the village, range in elevation from 1,200ft - 750ft above sea level, and present both alpine and cottage planting. Plants available for sale and teas offered in the Masonic Hall in the centre of the village. Wheelchair access to most gardens.

29 ◆ MINDRUM GARDEN

Mindrum, Northumberland, TD12 4QN. Mr & Mrs T Fairfax, 01890 850228, tpfairfax@gmail.com, www.mindrumestate.com. *6m SW of Coldstream, 9m NW of Wooler. Off B6352, 4m N of Yetholm. 5m from Cornhill on Tweed. Disabled parking close to house.* **For NGS: Sun 23 June (2-5). Adm £5, chd free. Home-made teas.** For other opening times and information, please phone, email or visit garden website.

7 acres of romantic planting with old fashioned roses, violas, hardy perennials, lilies, herbs, scented shrubs, and intimate garden areas flanked by woodland and river walks. Glasshouses with vines, jasmine. Large hillside limestone rock garden with water leading to a pond, delightful stream, woodland and wonderful views across Bowmont valley. Large plant sale, mostly home grown. Partial wheelchair access due to landscape. Wheelchair accessible WC available.

30 MR YORKE'S WALLED GARDEN

Cravengate, Richmond, DL10 4RE. Mr & Mrs Dennis & Marcia McLuckie, 01748 825525, marcia@yorkshirecountryholidays.co.uk. *5 min walk from Richmond Market Place. Third of way down Cravengate on rd out to Leyburn. From Market Place go up Finkle St, past Black Lion into cobbled Newbiggin. L into Cravengate. Garden on R. No parking at the garden.* **Visits by arrangement Apr to Sept for groups of 20+. Please pre-book dates with owner before making other arrangements. Adm £5.50, chd free. Home-made teas. Either pre-ordered homemade cakes and scones, tea and coffee OR wine and nibbles.**

Charming C18 walled garden, redesigned with herbaceous border, ponds, mature trees, standard and climbing roses, vegetable garden, fruit trees, lawns and grassy paths. This is a garden in change and work has progressed since the garden opened for the first time for the NGS in 2017. The owners continue to further enhance and develop this one acre pleasant, tranquil town garden. Fabulous views of Billy Banks Woods, Richmond Castle and Culloden Tower. The garden is on a hill. Main grass paths accessible with a wheelchair, but they are quite steep.

31 NEW NEASHAM ABBEY

Neasham, Near Darlington, DL2 1QW. Barbara-Anne Johnson. *At the Football Stadium r'about on A66 take direction Neasham/ Hurworth. At the end of this rd (approx. 2m) at the T-junction head straight across into the drive of Neasham Abbey.* **Sun 2 June (1-5). Adm £5, chd free. Home-made teas.**

A country house garden with views of the river Tees. Interesting paths lead to different areas including a walled garden of beautiful old red brick surrounding shady borders. A walk between a newly planted orchard and a sunny herbaceous border. A rose garden leads to a shady garden surrounding an old ornamental pond. A new feature of the garden is a rustic children's adventure play area. Wheelchair access very limited as all the paths are gravelled - sorry.

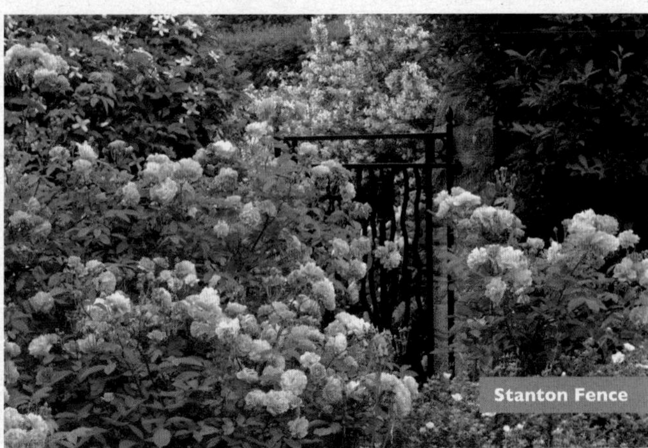

Stanton Fence

32 NO. 2 FERNDENE

2 Holburn Lane Court, Holburn Lane, Ryton, NE40 3PN. Maureen Kesteven, 0191 413 5937, kestevenmaureen@gmail.com, www.facebook.com/northeastgardenopenforcharity/. *In Ryton Old Village, 8m W of Gateshead. Off B6317, on Holburn Lane in Old Ryton Village. Park in Co-op carpark on High St, cross rd & walk through Ferndene Park following yellow signs.* **Sun 23 June (1-4.30). Adm £5, chd free. Home-made teas. Light lunch available.** Visits also by arrangement Mar to Aug for groups of 10+.

¾ acre garden, developing since 2009, surrounded by trees. Informal areas of herbaceous perennials, more formal box bordered area, sedum roof, wildlife pond, cutting, bog and fern gardens. Willow work. Early interest - hellebores, snowdrops, daffodils, bluebells and tulips. Summer interest from wide range of flowering perennials. 1½ acre mixed broadleaf wood. 2018 new gravel garden.

33 OLIVER FORD GARDEN

Longedge Lane, Rowley, Consett, DH8 9HG. Bob & Bev Tridgett, www.gardensanctuaries.co.uk. *5m NW of Lanchester. Signed from A68 in Rowley. From Lanchester take rd towards Sately. Garden will be signed as you pass Woodlea Manor.* **Sun 9 June (1-5). Adm £4, chd free. Home-made teas.**

A peaceful, contemplative 3 acre garden developed and planted by the owner and BBC Gardener of the Year as a space for quiet reflection. Arboretum specialising in bark, stream, wildlife pond and bog garden. Semi-shaded Japanese maple and dwarf rhododendron garden. Rock garden and scree bed. Insect nectar area, orchard and 1½ acre meadow. Annual wild flower area. Terrace and ornamental kitchen garden,. Has a number of sculptures around the garden. Unfortunately not suitable for wheelchairs.

34 25 PARK ROAD SOUTH

Chester le Street, DH3 3LS. Mrs A Middleton, 0191 388 3225. *4m N of Durham. Located at S end of A167 Chester-le-St bypass rd. Precise directions provided when booking visit.* **Visits by arrangement May to July. Adm £3, chd free. Light refreshments.**

A stunning town garden with all year round interest. Herbaceous borders with unusual perennials, grasses, shrubs surrounding lawn and paved area. Courtyard planted with foliage and small front gravel garden. The garden owner is a very knowledgeable plantswoman who enjoys showing visitors around her inspiring garden. No minimum size of group. Plants for sale.

35 ◆ RABY CASTLE

Staindrop, Darlington, DL2 3AH. Lord Barnard, 01833 660202, admin@rabycastle.com, www.rabycastle.com. *12m NW of Darlington, 1m N of Staindrop. On A688, 8m NE of Barnard Castle.* **For NGS: Sat 13 July (9-4.30). Adm £7.50, chd £3.50.** For other opening times and information, please phone, email or visit garden website.

Raby Castle is one of the founding gardens of the NGS and has been opening for charity since 1927. C18 walled gardens set within the grounds of Raby Castle. Designers such as Thomas White and James Paine have worked to establish the gardens, which now extend to 5 acres, displaying herbaceous borders, old yew hedges, formal rose gardens and informal heather and conifer gardens. Tearoom is located just outside the entrance gate to the Walled Gardens. Assistance will be needed for wheelchairs.

36 RAVENSFORD FARM

Hamsterley, DL13 3NH. Jonathan & Caroline Peacock, 01388 488305, caroline@ravensfordfarm.co.uk. *7m W of Bishop Auckland. From A68 at Witton-le-Wear turn off W to Hamsterley. Go through village & turn L just before tennis courts at west end.* **Sun 4 Aug (2-5). Adm £4, chd free. Home-made teas.** Visits also by arrangement Mar to Nov for groups of up to 30.

This large garden offers colour and interest throughout the year. Beyond the large lawn and herbaceous beds are two ponds, a sunken garden, a wood with shade-loving plants, an orchard and a good number of unusual plants, shrubs and trees. Early August is often a peak time for colour - and on NGS day we sell plants, we serve home-made teas. Some gravel, so assistance will be needed for wheelchairs. Assistance dogs only in the garden, but others okay in the field.

37 ST CUTHBERT'S HOSPICE

Park House Road, Durham, DH1 3QF. Paul Marriott, CEO, www.stcuthbertshospice.com. *1m SW of Durham City on A167. Turn into Park House Rd, the Hospice is on the L after bowling green car park. Parking available.* **Sun 28 July (11-4). Adm £4, chd free. Light refreshments. Hot & cold drinks, homemade cakes served in the Victorian style greenhouse and coffee shop.**

5 acres of mature gardens surround this CQC outstanding-rated Hospice. In development since 1988, the gardens are cared for by volunteers. Incl a Victorian-style greenhouse and large vegetable, fruit and cut flower area. Lawns surround smaller scale specialist planting, and areas for patients and visitors to relax. Woodland area with walks, sensory garden, and an 'In Memory' garden with stream. Plants and produce for sale. We are active participants in Northumbria in Bloom and Britain in Bloom, with several awards in recent years, including overall winner in 2015 & 2018 for the Care/ Residential / Convalescent Homes / Day Centre / Hospices category. Almost all areas are accessible for wheelchairs.

ALLOTMENTS

38 ST MARGARET'S ALLOTMENTS

Margery Lane, Durham, DH1 4QU. *From A1 take A690 to City Centre/ Crook. Straight ahead at T-lights after 4th r'about. 10mins walk from bus or rail station.* **Sun 7 July (2-5). Adm £4, chd free.**

5 acres of over 100 allotments against the spectacular backdrop of Durham Cathedral. This site has been cultivated since the Middle Ages. Enthusiastic gardeners, many

using organic methods, cultivate plots which display a great variety of fruit, vegetables and flowers. Guided tours available. Many unusual vegetables. Display of creative and fun competition for plot holders. The site has some steep and narrow paths.

39 NEW THE SHILLING HOUSE GARDEN

342 West Road, Fenham, Newcastle Upon Tyne, NE4 9JU. David Wallace. *On the West Rd. Nearest side street, Grange Rd. Park on West Rd (when no restrictions in force) or in Grange Rd.* **Sun 16 June (3-6). Adm £8, chd free. Pre-booking essential, please visit www.ngs.org.uk for information & booking. Light refreshments.**

An unusual terraced garden begun in 1996 and still evolving. A calm green space characterised by its structural form, strongly related to the distinctive architecture of the house. Clipped hedging and topiary create a verdant framework. Mainly white flowers, including a mature Kiftsgate and standard roses, plus a limited range of shrubs, perennials, bulbs and seasonal annuals highlight the form. Opening to a limited number of visitors by pre-booking only. There will be a display about the history of the unique house and gardens, with original garden plans and photographs.

40 SOUTHLANDS

The Avenue, Eaglescliffe, Stockton-On-Tees, TS16 9AS. Ian Waller, 01642 899199, ian.waller@theakstonestates.com. *1½m from Yarm on A135. JA66 signed A135 Stockton West/Yarm. South towards Yarm for approx 1½ m past Preston Park. From Yarm on A135 for 1½ m passing Golf Course. The Avenue is opposite junction to Railway Station.* **Sun 30 June (2-5.30). Adm £5, chd free. Light refreshments, cakes and scones.** Visits also by arrangement in June.

South facing High Victorian Gardens created by Sir Samuel and Lady Sadler. Elevated site with sloping lawns, herbaceous borders, orchards and woodland areas. A natural stream runs through this 10 acre garden with a miniature lake and island. Established Rhododendrons and Azaleas, specimen trees with gingko, maples, beech, pines and redwoods. Coaching house (serving teas), Bothy, old Greenhouse and fountain. Steeply sloping site.

41 STANTON FENCE

Stanton, Morpeth, NE65 8PP. Sir David & Lady Kelly. *5m NW of Morpeth. Nr Stanton on the C144 between Pigdon & Netherwitton. OS map ref NZ 13588.* **Sun 30 June (1-5). Adm £6, chd free. Home-made teas.**

Contemporary 4.7 acre country garden designed by Chelsea Gold Medal winner, Arabella Lennox-Boyd, in keeping with its rural setting. A strong underlying design unites the different areas from formal parterre and courtyard garden to orchard, wild flower meadows and woodland. Romantically planted rose covered arbours and long clematis draped pergola walk. Nuttery, kitchen garden and greenhouse. Delightful views. Robert Iley, the garden builder, and Steve Grimwood, the gardener, will be present. Featured in Country Life August 2018. Wheelchair access for those chairs that can use mown paths as well as hard paving.

42 4 STOCKLEY GROVE

Brancepeth, DH7 8DU. Mr & Mrs Bainbridge, 079439 40708, fabb633@gmail.com. *5m W of Durham City. Situated on A690 between Durham & Crook. From Durham direction turn L at village Xrds & park at castle at end of rd. There is no parking available in Stockley Grove. Lifts to the garden will be available if required.* **Visits by arrangement May to Sept. Adm £5, chd free. Home-made teas.**

A stunning ½ acre garden with inspirational planting to provide yr-round colour and interest. Landscaped with hidden grassy paths with many unusual trees, shrubs and plants incl wildlife pond, rockery area and water features. 5 times winners of The Beautiful Durham Competition.

43 USHAW COLLEGE

Woodland Road, Durham, DH7 9BJ. The Trustees of Ushaw College, 0191 373 8500, meet@ushaw.org, www.ushaw.org. *3m W of Durham City. From A167 N of Neville's Cross turn on to minor road signed Bearpark & Ushaw College. The College entrance is signed to the R in 2½m.* **Sat 25 May (10-4). Adm £4, chd free. Home-made teas in the College.**

Part of the 50 acre landscape within open countryside around Ushaw College, the gardens were originally laid out in 1840 in front of the Georgian house and feature a formal rhododendron garden with herbaceous borders and rose beds. Extensive renovations to the garden have been under way for the last 5 years and continue, with some wild areas, a former pond, and extensive areas of woodland. Wheelchair access to concentric paths, but not to more overgrown areas.

44 ◆ WALLINGTON

Cambo, NE61 4AR. National Trust, 01670 773600, simon.thompson@nationaltrust.org.uk, www.nationaltrust.org.uk/wallington. *12m W of Morpeth 20m NW Newcastle. From N B6343; from S via A696 from Newcastle, 6m W of Belsay, B6342 to Cambo.* **For NGS: Sat 27 Apr, Sat 15 June (10-5). Adm £14.50, chd £7.30. Light refreshments at Courtyard Cafe.** For other opening times and information, please phone, email or visit garden website.

Magical walled, terraced garden with herbaceous and mixed borders. Packed with colour. Edwardian conservatory with unusual plants. 100 acres of woodland. Pleasure grounds, river and lakes. Set in a stunning landscape, with opportunities for walking and cycling. House dates from 1688. Wheelchair access limited to top terrace in Walled Garden but elsewhere possible with care and support.

GROUP OPENING

45 WALWORTH GARDENS

Walworth, Darlington, DL2 2LY. *Approx 5m W of Darlington on A68 or ½m E of Piercebridge on A67. Follow brown signs to Walworth Castle Hotel. Just up the hill from the Castle entrance, follow NGS yellow signs down private track. Tickets & Teas at Quarry End.* **Sun 18 Aug (1-5). Combined adm £5.50, chd free. Home-made teas. Teas at Quarry End.**

THE ARCHES
Stephen & Becky Street-Howard.

CASTLE BARN
Joe and Sheila Storey.

THE DOVECOTE
Tony & Ruth Lamb.

QUARRY END
Iain & Margaret Anderson.

A NEW garden is added to this group opening for 2019. Castle Barn has 2 small gardens, lawns surrounded by borders with a range of plants which are attractive to bees and butterflies. In addition there are fruit trees, raised beds for vegetables, a greenhouse, a herb garden and maturing grape vines. The Dovecote has a Japanese garden with a Koi pond and a large collection of specimen Acers, an interesting vegetable garden and also an english garden with lawn, flower border and a chicken run. The Arches' expansive garden comprises an orchard, a large vegetable garden, a wildlife pond, an ornamental garden and a new arboretum. There is also a large play area available so bring the family! In contrast to these young gardens, Quarry End is a 1½ acre woodland garden developed over 19 years on the site of an ancient quarry. It incorporates a newly developed woodland, a wide variety of trees, shrubs, perennials, a fernery and potager. The site includes an C18 ice house. Some areas of the Quarry End garden are not accessible, though the main garden area is.

GROUP OPENING

46 WESTGATE GARDENS

Westgate in Weardale, County Durham, Bishop Auckland, DL13 1PD. 01388 517735, lefontanil@gmail.com. *Approach Westgate from Stanhope, passing through the village of Eastgate, on the A689. Look out for the NGS yellow parking signs.* **Sun 30 June (11-4.30). Combined adm £5, chd free. Home-made teas. Each garden can offer teas with home made scones and jam, or cake. Visits also by arrangement June to Aug for groups of up to 10.**
Westgate in Weardale is in the North Pennines AONB, little known to many but with wonderful views of the wild and lovely fells in particular from Hill House B & B at an elevation of 1150 ft. Other gardens include Finn's Flowers, garden and allotment and a pretty bungalow with plenty of baskets and pots. The Dale is famous for lead mining in days now gone and, of course, sheep, amongst them our famous Swaledales. For walkers, The Weardale Way runs through the village and along the banks of the beautiful Wear, so the visits can be done on foot for the fit. The gardens are quite spread out, so maps and tickets are available at each one. Owners in Westgate are very friendly so allow lots of time. We have special challenges to our growing season here, from snow until as late as April and early autumns with buffeting west winds. Come and see how we do it! (Since our last opening, several owners have moved away from Westgate, but we'd still love to share with you the love of our gardens). Pub in the village - Sunday roasts by booking only. Excellent playground by the Weardale and beautiful riverside walk.

47 ◆ WHALTON MANOR GARDENS

Whalton, Morpeth, NE61 3UT. Mr T R P S Norton, 01670 775205, gardens@whaltonmanor.co.uk, www.whaltonmanor.co.uk. *5m W of Morpeth. On the B6524, the house is at E end of the village & will be signed.* **For NGS: Sun 7 July (2-5). Adm £5, chd free. For other opening times and information, please phone, email or visit garden website.**
The historic Whalton Manor, altered by Sir Edwin Lutyens in 1908, is surrounded by 3 acres of magnificent walled gardens, designed by Lutyens with the help of Gertrude Jekyll. The gardens have been developed by the Norton family since the 1920s and incl extensive herbaceous borders, 30yd peony border, rose garden, listed summerhouses, pergolas and walls, festooned with rambling roses and clematis. Partial wheelchair access, some stone steps.

GROUP OPENING

48 NEW WOLSINGHAM VILLAGE GARDENS

Wolsingham, Bishop Auckland, DL13 3AY. Janette Kelly. *Gardens are spread throughout the village. Parking is available in village centre& at the recreation field. Refreshments are also available at the recreation hall, St Anne's Centre.* **Sat 22 June (1-5). Combined adm £5, chd free. Home-made teas at St Anne's community centre in the recreation field.**
8 gardens mainly centred around the recreation field. One is a short walk/drive to the edge of the village . They vary between traditional gardens, more unusual gardens and allotments. One borders the river Wear, another has ponds and water features. Owing to the number of gardens not all are accessible for wheelchair users.

49 WOODBINE HOUSE

22 South View, Hunwick, Crook, DL15 0JW. Stewart Irwin & Colin Purvis. *On main rd through the village opp village green. B6286 off A689 Bishop Auckland - Crook or A690 Durham - Crook. On street parking, entrance to the rear of the property RHS of house.* **Mon 27 May (1-5). Adm £4, chd free. Light refreshments. All refreshments are home-made.**
The garden is approx a quarter

of an acre, divided into two, one half used as a vegetable garden with large greenhouse. The other half of the garden is lawn with well stocked (and some unusual planting) herbaceous borders and small pond. Bees are kept in the vegetable garden. Wheelchair access to refreshment area but paths in garden are not wide enough for wheelchairs.

50 WOODLANDS

Peareth Hall Road, Springwell Village, Gateshead, NE9 7NT. Liz Reid, 07719 875750, lizreid52@ntlworld.com. *3½m N Washington Galleries. 4m S Gateshead town centre. On B1288 turn opp Guide Post pub (NE9 7RR) onto Peareth Hall Rd. Continue for ½m passing 2 bus stops on L. 3rd drive on L past Highbury Ave.* **Sat 29 June, Thur 4 July (1.30-4.30). Adm £3.50, chd free. Home-made teas. beer and wine available. Visits also by arrangement June to Aug for groups of 10 to 30.**

Mature garden on a site of approx one seventh acre- quirky, with tropical themed planting and Caribbean inspired bar. Also an area of cottage garden planting. A fun garden with colour throughout the year, interesting plants, informal beds and borders, pond area and deck. On the 29 June 2019 Springwell Village is hosting a 'Forties Weekend' with many events and attractions. Eg: 2nd WW battle re-enactments and a military camp are planned on the nearby Bowes Railway (SAM) site. There are also plans for craft and other stalls and live music throughout the village.

51 WOODSIDE HOUSE

Witton Park, Bishop Auckland, DL14 0DU. Charles & Jean Crompton, 01388 609973, ctjcrompton@gmail.com, www.woodsidehousewittonpark.com. *2m N of Bishop Auckland. From Bishop Auckland take A68 to Witton Park. In village DO NOT follow SatNav. park on main st, walk down track next to St Pauls Church.* **Visits by arrangement Apr to Oct. Adm £5, chd free. Home-made teas.**

Stunning 2 acre, mature, undulating garden full of interesting trees, shrubs and plants. Superbly landscaped (by the owners) with island beds, flowing herbaceous borders, an old walled garden, rhododendron beds, fernery, 3 ponds, grass bed and vegetable garden. Delightful garden full of interesting and unusual features: much to fire the imagination. featured in the Telegraph, Amateur gardening. Winner of Bishop Auckland in Bloom. Partial wheelchair access.

52 WOODSIDE, KILLERBY

North Lane, Killerby, Darlington, DL2 3UH. Dr Satinder Faulkner. *Killerby sits between Summerhouse & Ingleton. We can offer parking in our fields & if ground very wet, vehicles can also park on the main road in Killerby village & walk the ¼m up North Lane.* **Sat 3 Aug (1-5). Adm £5, chd free. Home-made teas.**

Woodside is set in 12 acres of which 2 acres have been developed into garden. The owner had a stroke 32 years ago yet has designed and executed the works mostly single handed. The garden includes prairie bed, woodland beds, rose garden, bog garden over 100 trees, a wood, wildlife pond, vegetable and cut flower beds and runs horticultural therapy for adults with disability. Nature trail for children and live music. The garden sits mostly on one level although paths in the woods are narrow for wheelchair access.

Bichfield Tower

NORTHAMPTONSHIRE

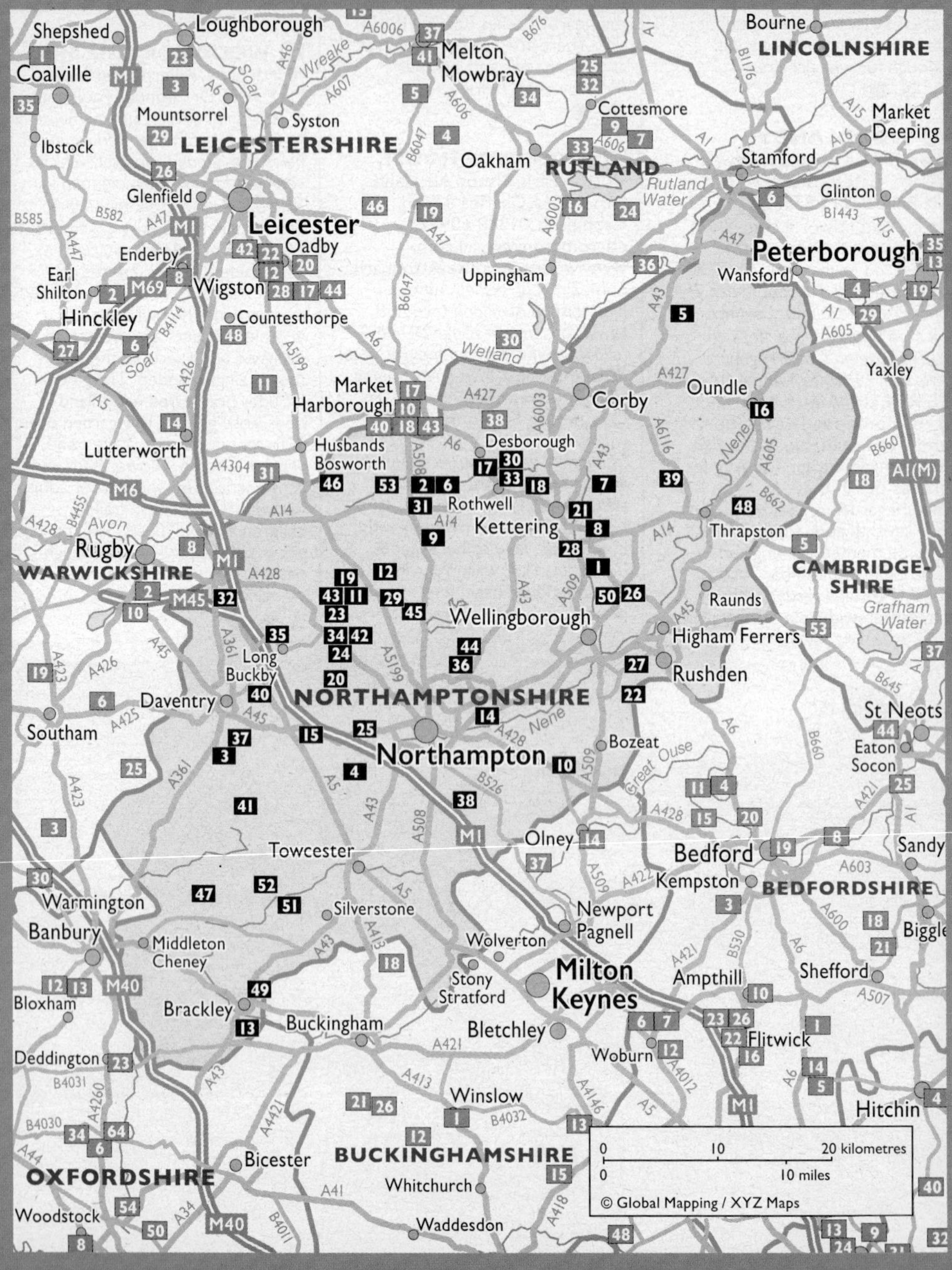

The county of Northamptonshire is famously known as the 'Rose of the Shires', but is also referred to as the 'Shire of Spires and Squires', and lies in the East Midlands area of the country bordered by eight other counties.

Take a gentle stroll around charming villages with thatch and stone cottages and welcoming inns. Wander around stately homes, discovering art treasures and glorious gardens open for the National Garden Scheme: Kelmarsh Hall, Holdenby House, Castle Ashby, Cottesbrooke Hall and Boughton House. In contrast visit some village groups, which include small imaginatively designed gardens.

Explore historic market towns such as Oundle and Brackley in search of fine footwear, antiques and curiosities. Or visit wildlife sanctuaries such as Sulby Gardens with 12 acres of interesting flora and fauna.

The serenity of our waterways will delight, and our winding country lanes and footpaths will guide you around a rural oasis, far from the pressures of modern living, where you can walk knee-deep in bluebells and snowdrops in spring at gardens such as Boughton House and Bosworth House, or view the late autumn colours of Sulby Gardens.

Our first garden opens in February and the final opening occurs in November, giving a glimpse of gardens throughout the seasons.

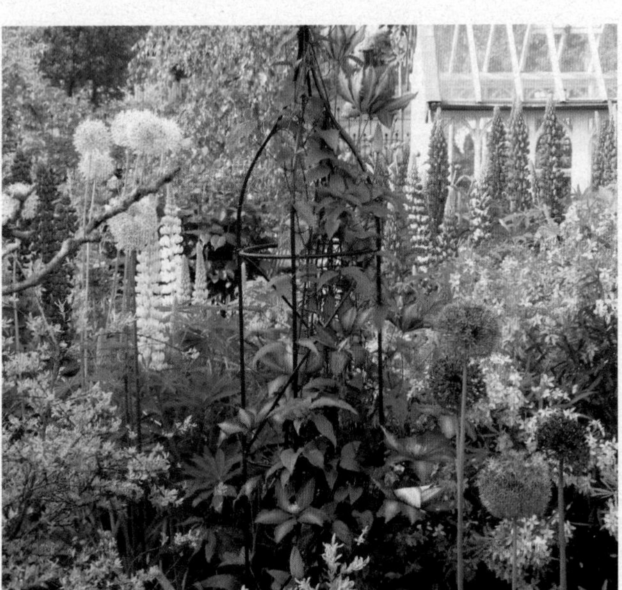

Volunteers

County Organisers
David Abbott
01933 680363
d_j_abbott@btinternet.com

Gay Webster
01604 740203
gay.webster6@gmail.com

County Treasurer
Michael Heaton
01865 425909
ngs@mimomul.co.uk

Publicity
David Abbott
(as above)

Photographer
Snowy Ellson
07508 218320
snowyellson@yahoo.co.uk

Booklet Coordinators
David Abbott
(as above)

Michael Heaton
(as above)

Assistant County Organisers
Amanda Bell
01327 860651
asrbell@btinternet.com

Lindsey Cartwright
01327 860056
lindsey@loisweedon.net

Philippa Heumann
01327 860142
pmheumann@gmail.com

Elaine & William Portch
01536 522169
elaine.portch@yahoo.com

Geoff Sage
01788 510334
sagegw@gmail.com

Left: **The Cottage, Newnham Gardens**

OPENING DATES

All entries subject to change. For latest information check **www.ngs.org.uk**

Map locator numbers are shown to the right of each garden name.

February

Snowdrop Festival

Sunday 17th
Bosworth House 6

Sunday 24th
◆ Boughton House 7
67-69 High Street 26

April

Sunday 7th
Flore Gardens 15

Sunday 14th
Briarwood 8
◆ Kelmarsh Hall & Gardens 31

Thursday 25th
Sulby Gardens 46

Sunday 28th
Bosworth House 6
◆ The Old Rectory, Sudborough 39
The Old Vicarage 40

May

Sunday 5th
◆ Cottesbrooke Hall Gardens 12
Great Brington Gardens 20
Greywalls 22

Monday 6th
NEW Limetrees 34
Titchmarsh House 48

Sunday 12th
NEW 3 Baptists Close 4
Guilsborough Gardens 23

Sunday 19th
Badby Gardens 3
◆ Kelmarsh Hall & Gardens 31
Titchmarsh House 48

Saturday 25th
NEW 1 Hinwick Close 28

Sunday 26th
NEW 50 Alexandra Street 1
Newnham Gardens 37

June

Sunday 2nd
Evenley Gardens 13
67-69 High Street 26
Old Rectory, Quinton 38

Saturday 8th
Titchmarsh House 48

Sunday 9th
Foxtail Lilly 16
◆ Haddonstone Show Gardens 24
Harpole Gardens 25
Hostellarie 30
16 Leys Avenue 33
Moulton College Horticulture Unit 36
NEW Ravenswood 43
Spratton Gardens 45
Sulgrave Gardens 47
Turweston Gardens 49
Weedon Lois & Weston Gardens 52

Sunday 16th
Kilsby Gardens 32
Rosearie-de-la-Nymph 44
Wappenham Gardens 51

Thursday 20th
Sulby Gardens 46

Saturday 22nd
Flore Gardens 15

Sunday 23rd
Flore Gardens 15
◆ Holdenby House Gardens 29
Rosearie-de-la-Nymph 44

Sunday 30th
Arthingworth Open Gardens 2
The Green Patch 21
67-69 High Street 26
The Vicarage 50

Titchmarsh House

© Leigh Clapp

July

Sunday 7th
◆ Castle Ashby Gardens 10

Saturday 13th
NEW 1 Hinwick Close 28

Sunday 14th
Ravensthorpe Gardens 42

Sunday 21st
Blatherwycke Estate 5
Long Buckby Gardens 35

Sunday 28th
Froggery Cottage 17
136 High Street 27
Hostellarie 30

August

Sunday 11th
NEW The Bungalow 9

Thursday 22nd
Sulby Gardens 46

September

Sunday 1st
Old Rectory, Quinton 38

Sunday 8th
◆ Coton Manor Garden 11
16 Leys Avenue 33
NEW Ravenswood 43

October

Thursday 10th
Sulby Gardens 46

Friday 11th
Sulby Gardens 46

Sunday 13th
Briarwood 8

Sunday 20th
◆ Boughton House 7

By Arrangement

Arrange a personalised garden visit with your club, or group of friends, on a date to suit you. See individual garden entries for full details.

NEW 50 Alexandra Street 1
NEW 3 Baptists Close 4
Bosworth House 6
Briarwood 8
NEW The Bungalow 9
The Close, Harpole Gardens 25
Dripwell House, Guilsborough Gardens 23
NEW 48 The Fairoaks 14
Foxtail Lilly 16
Glendon Hall 18
Gower House 19
Greywalls 22
67-69 High Street 26
Hostellarie 30
16 Leys Avenue 33
19 Manor Close, Harpole Gardens 25
Old West Farm 41
Ravensthorpe Nursery, Ravensthorpe Gardens 42
4 Skinyard Lane, Long Buckby Gardens 35
Titchmarsh House 48
Woodcote Villa, Long Buckby Gardens 35
The Wooden Owl 53

THE GARDENS

1 NEW 50 ALEXANDRA STREET

Burton Latimer, Kettering, NN15 5SF. Adrian & Sue Watts, 01536 675495, wildmagick@ntlworld.com. *5½m S of Kettering. J10 A14 Burton Latimer or A6 Burton Latimer. Use Library/ Civic centre car park on Piggott's Lane opp Sainsbury's. Follow signs to Alexandra St (5 min walk).* **Sun 26 May (10.30-6). Adm £3.50, chd free. Home-made teas.** **Visits also by arrangement Apr to Aug for groups of up to 10. Tour with owner dependent on numbers.**
The garden is situated at the back of an end-of-terrace built in 1893. It is a long narrow garden of 150ft with a range of planting and habitat areas including livestock, greenhouse, outdoor cooking/living area, sun-room and workshops. Plant habitats incl pots, shaded areas, full sun, vertical growing, soft and hard fruit, nut trees, miniature forest garden, lawn and trial meadow area. Small scale aquaponics and permaculture principles. Photographic story of garden.

GROUP OPENING

2 ARTHINGWORTH OPEN GARDENS

Arthingworth, nr Market Harborough, LE16 8LA. *6m S of Market Harborough. From Market Harborough via A508, after 4m take L to Arthingworth. From Northampton, A508 turn R just after Kelmarsh. Park your car in Arthingworth village & tickets for sale in the village hall.* **Sun 30 June (1-5). Combined adm £6, chd free. Home-made teas at village hall & Bosworth House.**
Arthingworth has been welcoming NGS visitors for more than 8 yrs. It is a village affair with 8 to 9 gardens opening and 2 pop-up tearooms with home baked cakes. We now have some regulars who keep us on our toes and we love it. Come and enjoy the diversity, we aim to give visitors an afternoon of discovery. Our gardens have been chosen because they are all different in spirit, and tended by young and weathered gardeners. We have gardens with stunning views, traditional with herbaceous borders and vegetables, walled, and artisan. The village is looking forward to welcoming you. St Andrew's Church, Grade II* listed will be open and the village is next to the national cycle path. Wheelchair access to some gardens.

GROUP OPENING

3 BADBY GARDENS

Badby, Daventry, NN11 3AR. *3m S of Daventry on E-side of A361.* **Sun 19 May (2-6). Combined adm £5, chd free. Teas & home-made cakes in St Mary's Church.**

NEW CHAPEL HOUSE
Moira & Peter Cooper.

THE OLD HOUSE
Mr & Mrs Robert Cain.

SHAKESPEARES COTTAGE
Jocelyn Hartland-Swann.

SOUTHVIEW COTTAGE
Alan & Karen Brown.

TRIFIDIA
Colin & Shirley Cripps.

Delightful hilly village with attractive old houses of golden coloured Hornton stone, set around a C14 church and two village greens (no through traffic). There are five gardens of differing styles; a wisteria-clad thatched cottage (not open) with a sloping garden and modern sculptures; a traditional garden featuring a spectacular view across fields to Badby Wood; an elevated garden with views over the village; a hillside garden focussing on unusual and interesting plants that aim for yr-round interest, with a conservatory and vegetable garden; and newly opening this year, a secluded garden with five distinct areas, pond and fernery, patio, lawn, small orchard and formal vegetable garden. We look forward to welcoming you to our lovely village!

4 NEW 3 BAPTISTS CLOSE

Bugbrooke, Northampton, NN7 3RU. Claire Smith, 07798 905563, smithsgarden16@gmail.com. *2mins from A5, 5m from J16 M1. From A5 signs to Bugbrooke, follow road to village that becomes Church St. Park close to Five Bells Pub on L. Baptists Close is on L (no parking in close).* **Sun 12 May (1.30-5). Adm £4, chd free. Light refreshments.** **Visits also by arrangement Apr to Sept for groups of up to 10.**
A medium sized plant lover's garden with tranquil pastoral farmland behind. Designed and planted about 10 yrs ago from a previous farmyard site, the garden has fully mature lime trees down one side and is a mix of shrubs with foliage interest and colourful herbaceous borders. Spring garden under the walnut tree, n-facing potager, traditional borders and short woodland walk. Pathway around the house and lawned area. Some large gravel paths and woodland walk not easily accessible.

5 BLATHERWYCKE ESTATE

Blatherwycke, Peterborough, PE8 6YW. Mr George, Owner & S Bonney, Head Gardener. *Blatherwycke is signed off the A43 between Stamford & Corby. Follow road through village & the gardens entrance is next to the large river bridge.* **Sun 21 July (11-4). Adm £4, chd free. Home-made teas.**
Blatherwycke Hall was demolished in the 1940s and its gardens lost. In 2011 the renovation of the derelict 4 acre walled gardens started. So far a large kitchen garden, wall trained fruit trees, extensive herbaceous borders, parterre, wild flower meadows, tropical bed, shrub borders and large arboretum have been planted. Restoration of the crinkle crankle wall has also begun. Grass and gravel paths, some slopes and steps.

6 BOSWORTH HOUSE

Oxendon Road, Arthingworth, Nr Market Harborough, LE16 8LA. Mr & Mrs C E Irving-Swift, 01858 525202, irvingswift@btinternet.com. *From the phone box, when in Oxendon Rd, take the little lane with no name, 2nd to the R.* **Sun 17 Feb (12-4); Sun 28 Apr (2-6). Adm £4, chd free. Home-made teas at village hall.** Visits also by arrangement May to July for groups of 10 to 20. For groups of 15+ guided tour by Cecile Irving-Swift for 1½ hours.

Just under 3 acres, almost completely organic garden and paddock with fabulous panoramic views. Early in the season a pleasing display of snowdrops, wood anemones, fritillaries, daffodils, bluebells and tulips. The garden also incl herbaceous borders, orchard, cottage garden with greenhouse, vegetable garden, herbs and strawberries, and little spinney. There is a magnificent Wellingtonia. Partial wheelchair access.

7 ◆ BOUGHTON HOUSE

Geddington, Kettering, NN14 1BJ. Duke of Buccleuch & Queensberry, KT, 01536 515731, info@boughtonhouse.co.uk, www.boughtonhouse.org.uk. *3m NE of Kettering. From A14, 2m along A43 Kettering to Stamford, turn R into Geddington, house entrance 1½m on R.* **For NGS: Sun 24 Feb, Sun 20 Oct (11-3). Adm £6, chd £3. Light refreshments in C18 Stable Block.** For other opening times and information, please phone, email or visit garden website.

The Northamptonshire home of the Duke and Duchess of Buccleuch. The garden opening incl opportunities to see the historic walled kitchen garden and herbaceous border, and the sensory and wildlife gardens. The wilderness woodland will open for visitors to view the spring flowers or the autumn colours. As a special treat the garden originally created by Sir David Scott (cousin of the Duke of Buccleuch) will also be open.

8 BRIARWOOD

4 Poplars Farm Road, Barton Seagrave, Kettering, NN15 5AF. William & Elaine Portch, 01536 522169, elaine.portch@yahoo.com, www.elaineportch-gardendesign.co.uk. *1½m SE of Kettering Town Centre. J10 off A14 turn onto Barton Rd (A6) towards Wicksteed Park. R into Warkton Lane, after 200 metres R into Poplars Farm Rd.* **Sun 14 Apr (10-4); Sun 13 Oct (11-3). Adm £4.50, chd free. Light refreshments.** Visits also by arrangement Apr to July for groups of 10 to 30.

A garden for all seasons with quirky original sculptures and many faces. Firstly, a south aspect lawn and borders containing bulbs, shrubs, roses and rare trees with yr-round interest; hedging, palms, climbers, a wildlife, fish and lily pond, terrace with potted bulbs and unusual plants in odd containers. Secondly, a secret garden with summerhouse, small orchard, raised bed potager and greenhouse. Crafts for sale and children's quiz.

9 NEW THE BUNGALOW

Harborough Road, Maidwell, Northampton, NN6 9JA. David & Ann Sharman, 01604 686243. *Approx 10m N of Northampton. On A508 between Northampton & Market Harborough, opp Westaways Garage.* **Sun 11 Aug (11-4). Adm £4, chd free. Light refreshments in village hall (1-4).** Visits also by arrangement May to Aug for groups of 10 to 20.

The garden is on a steep, terraced site, which tumbles down to a stream. Bridges lead to a recently acquired wooded area, equally steep. Ann has artistically incorporated a quirky collection of car boot finds, which adds interest to the exuberant planting. Self-seeding is encouraged, giving a natural effect. There are several secluded seating areas for relaxation. A steep site and many steps, sadly not suitable for the less mobile.

10 ◆ CASTLE ASHBY GARDENS

Castle Ashby, Northampton, NN7 1LQ. Earl Compton, 01604 695200, petercox@castleashby.co.uk, www.castleashbygardens.co.uk. *6m E of Northampton. 1½m N of A428, turn off between Denton & Yardley Hastings. Follow brown tourist signs (SatNav will take you to the village, look for brown signs).* **For NGS: Sun 7 July (10-5.30). Adm £8.50, chd £3.75 (5-16 yrs).** For other opening times and information, please phone, email or visit garden website.

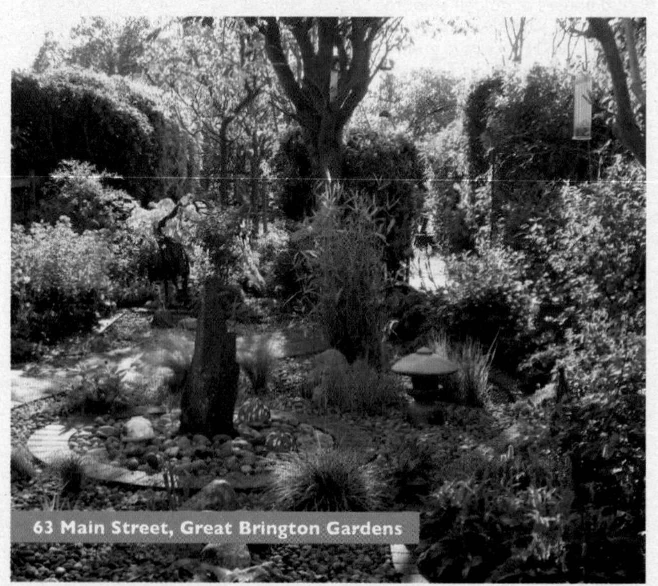

63 Main Street, Great Brington Gardens

35 acres within a 10,000 acre estate of both formal and informal gardens, incl Italian gardens with orangery and arboretum with lakes, all dating back to the 1860s, as well as a menagerie which incl meerkats and marmosets. Play area, tearooms and gift shop. Gravel paths within gardens.

11 ◆ COTON MANOR GARDEN

Coton, Northampton, NN6 8RQ. Mr & Mrs Ian Pasley-Tyler, 01604 740219, www.cotonmanor.co.uk. *10m N of Northampton, 11m SE of Rugby. From A428 & A5199 follow tourist signs.* **For NGS: Sun 8 Sept (12-5.30). Combined adm with Ravenswood £7.50, chd free. Light refreshments at Stableyard Cafe.** For other opening times and information, please phone or visit garden website.

10 acre garden set in peaceful countryside with old yew and holly hedges and extensive herbaceous borders, containing many unusual plants. One of Britain's finest throughout the season, the garden is at its most magnificent in September, and is an inspiration as to what can be achieved in late summer. Adjacent specialist nursery with over 1000 plant varieties propagated from the garden. Partial wheelchair access as some paths are narrow and the site is on a slope.

12 ◆ COTTESBROOKE HALL GARDENS

Cottesbrooke, Northampton, NN6 8PF. Mr & Mrs A R Macdonald-Buchanan, 01604 505808, welcome@cottesbrooke.co.uk, www.cottesbrooke.co.uk. *10m N of Northampton. Signed from J1 on A14. Off A5199 at Creaton, A508 at Brixworth.* **For NGS: Sun 5 May (2-5.30). Adm £7, chd £4. Home-made teas.** For other opening times and information, please phone, email or visit garden website.

Award-winning gardens by Geoffrey Jellicoe, Dame Sylvia Crowe, James Alexander Sinclair and more recently Arne Maynard. Formal gardens and terraces surround Queen Anne house, with extensive vistas onto the lake and C18 parkland containing many mature trees. Wild and woodland gardens, a short distance from the formal areas, are exceptional in spring. Partial wheelchair access as paths are grass, stone and gravel. Access map identifies best route.

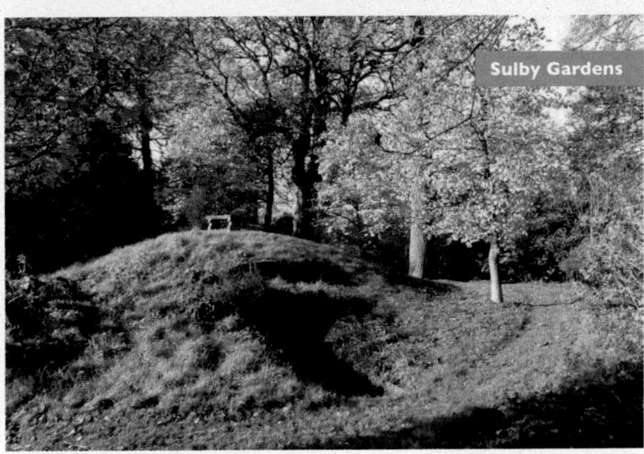
Sulby Gardens

GROUP OPENING

13 EVENLEY GARDENS

Evenley, Brackley, NN13 5SG. *From Brackley 1m S on A43. Gardens situated on Broad Lane, the village green & Church Lane. Follow signs around the village. Tickets cover entry to all gardens & are available at each garden.* **Sun 2 June (2-6). Combined adm £5, chd free. Home-made teas in St George's Church (2.30-5.30).**

CHRISTMAS COTTAGE
Stuart & Wendy Freestone.

15 CHURCH LANE
Carrie & Kevin O'Regan.

FINCH COTTAGE
Cathy & Chris Ellis.

NEW **14 THE GREEN**
Nic Hamblin.

NEW **38 THE GREEN**
Anna & Matt Brown.

Evenley is a charming village situated approx 1m south of Brackley off the A43. It has a central village green surrounded by many period houses (not open), an excellent village shop and The Red Lion Pub which offers first class food and a warm welcome. Evenley gardens are a mix of established gardens and those being developed over the past 5 yrs. They all have mixed borders with established shrubs and trees. There are also orchards and vegetable gardens in some. Partial wheelchair access to most gardens across gravel drives and narrow paths, with steps to reach some areas.

14 NEW 48 THE FAIROAKS

The Fairoaks, Northampton, NN3 9UZ. Lucie Oko, 07936 552494, nanalucie@btinternet.com. *A43 Lumbertubs Way, turn onto Standens Barn Rd, R onto Flaxwell Court, at r'about 2nd exit onto The Fairoaks.* **Visits by arrangement for groups of 10 to 30. Afternoons only. Adm by donation.**

My 'labour of love' is an unconventional garden that I started from scratch back in 1993. Since then I have built up a green sanctuary for my children and grandchildren through intuition and a lot of salvaging! Fellow garden enthusiasts are most welcome to come and share banter and tips with me. 'Russian Vine and Mile a Minute' plant is one of the expansive features of the garden. Wheelchair access via side gate.

GROUP OPENING

15 FLORE GARDENS

Flore, Northampton, NN7 4LQ. *Off A45 2m West of M1 J16. Avoid By-Pass. Garden maps provided at free car park, SatNav NN7 4LS. Coaches welcome, please phone 01327 341225 for parking information.* **Sun 7 Apr (2-6). Combined adm £5, chd free. Sat 22, Sun 23 June (11-6). Combined adm £6, chd free. Home-made teas in Chapel School Room (Apr). Morning coffee & teas in Church & light lunches & teas in Chapel School Room (June).** Donation to All Saints Church & United Reform Church, Flore.

24 BLISS LANE
John & Sally Miller.
Open on all dates

BUTTERCUP COTTAGE
Mrs Elizabeth Chignell.
Open on Sat 22, Sun 23 June

THE CROFT
John & Dorothy Boast.
Open on all dates

OAKLANDS
Martin & Rose Wray.
Open on Sun 7 Apr

PRIVATE GARDEN OF BLISS LANE NURSERY
Christine & Geoffrey Littlewood.
Open on all dates

ROCK SPRINGS
Tom Higginson & David Foster.
Open on all dates

RUSSELL HOUSE
Peter Pickering & Stephen George, 01327 341734, peterandstephen@btinternet.com, www.RussellHouseFlore.com.
Open on all dates

17 THE GREEN
Mrs Wendy Amos.
Open on Sat 22, Sun 23 June

Flore gardens have been open since 1963 as part of the Flore Flower Festival and the partnership with the NGS started in 1992. Flore is an attractive village with views over the Upper Nene Valley. We have a varied mix of gardens, developed by friendly, enthusiastic and welcoming owners. Our gardens range from the traditional to the eccentric providing yr-round interest. There are greenhouses, gazebos and summerhouses, with seating providing opportunities to rest while enjoying the gardens. In spring there are early flowering perennials, interesting trees, shrubs, and bulbs in pots and border drifts. There is planting for all situations from shade to full sun. June gardens open in association with Flore Flower Festival. The gardens incl formal and informal designs with lots of roses, clematis and many varieties of trees, shrubs, perennials, herbs, fruit and some vegetables. Partial wheelchair access to most gardens, some assistance may be required.

16 FOXTAIL LILLY

41 South Road, Oundle, PE8 4BP. Tracey Mathieson, 01832 274593, foxtaillilly41@gmail.com, www.foxtail-lilly.co.uk. *1m from Oundle town centre. From A605 at Barnwell Xrds take Barnwell Rd, 1st R to South Rd.* **Sun 9 June (11-4). Adm £4.50, chd free. Home-made teas.** Visits also by arrangement May to Sept for groups up to 60.

A cottage garden where perennials and grasses are grouped creatively together amongst gravel paths, complementing one another to create a natural look. Some unusual plants and quirky oddities create a different and colourful informal garden. Lots of flowers for cutting and a shop in the barn. New meadow pasture turned into new cutting garden.

17 FROGGERY COTTAGE

85 Breakleys Road, Desborough, NN14 2PT. Mr John Lee, www.froggerycottage.com. *6m N of Kettering. 5m S of Market Harborough. Signed off A6 & A14.* **Sun 28 July (11.30-5). Combined adm with Hostellarie £4, chd free. Home-made teas, a gluten free option & light lunches.**

1 acre plantsman's garden full of rare and unusual plants. NCCPG Collection of 435 varieties of penstemons incl dwarfs and species. Mediterranean and water gardens with large herbaceous borders. Artifacts on display incl old ploughs and garden implements. Penstemon workshops throughout the day.

NPC

18 GLENDON HALL

Kettering, NN14 1QE. Rosie Bose, 01536 711732, rosiebose@googlemail.com. *1½m E of Rothwell. A6003 to Corby (A14 J7) W of Kettering, turn L onto Glendon Rd signed Rothwell, Desborough, Rushton. Entrance 1½m on L past turn for Rushton.* **Visits by arrangement for groups of up to 30. Adm £4, chd free. Tea.**

Mature specimen trees, topiary, box hedges and herbaceous borders stocked with many unusual plants. Large walled kitchen gardens with glasshouse and a shaded area, well stocked with ferns. Some gravel and slopes, but wheelchair access via longer route.

19 GOWER HOUSE

Guilsborough, Northampton, NN6 8PY. Ann Moss, 01604 740140, cattimoss@aol.com. *Off High St by The Witch & Sow Pub, through pub car park.* **Visits by arrangement May & June for groups of 10 to 30. Combined visit with Dripwell House, next door included. Adm £6, chd free. Light refreshments.**

Although Gower House garden is small, it is closely planted with specimen trees, shrubs, perennials, orchids, thyme lawn, wild flowers and alpines; some rare or unusual, with foliage colour being important. Several seating areas designed for elderly relatives incorporating recycled materials. Soft fruit and vegetable garden shared with Dripwell House is an important part of our gardening.

GROUP OPENING

20 GREAT BRINGTON GARDENS

Northampton, NN7 4JJ. *7m NW of Northampton. Off A428 Rugby Rd. From Northampton, 1st L turn past main gates of Althorp. Free parking. Programmes & maps available at car park.* **Sun 5 May (11-5). Combined adm £5, chd free. Home-made teas & cakes in Parish Church & morning coffee & lunches in Reading Room.**

FOLLY HOUSE
Sarah & Joe Sacarello.

15 HAMILTON LANE
Mr & Mrs Robin Matthews.

63 MAIN STREET
Kim Robinson & Michael Carter.

ROSE COTTAGE
David Green & Elaine MacKenzie.

THE STABLES
Mrs A George.

SUNDERLAND HOUSE
Mrs Margaret Rubython.

Great Brington is proud of its nearly 25 yrs association with the NGS and arguably one of the most successful one day scheme events in the county. This yr we offer six gardens open to view. Our gardens provide superb quality and immense variety; many of the gardens continue to evolve each yr and most are designed, planted and maintained by their owners on a scale which is eminently practical and rewarding. Our particularly picturesque, predominately stone and thatch village is well worth a day out in its own right, and its configuration is perfect for the occasion; compact, self-contained, circular and virtually flat. On offer on the day, including our memorable gardens; a warm welcome, free car parking, programmes and maps, morning coffee, lunches and teas, plant stalls and a local history exhibition. Small coaches of groups up to 26 max welcome by prior arrangement only, please call 01604 770939.

21 THE GREEN PATCH

Valley Walk, Kettering, NN16 0LU. Sue McKay. *Junction of Valley Walk & Margret Rd, signed from A4300 Stamford Rd.* **Sun 30 June (11.30-2.30). Adm £3, chd free. Light refreshments.**

The Green Patch is a 2½ acre, Green Flag award-winning community garden, situated on the edge of Kettering. We have hens, ducks, beehives, ponds, children's play area, orchard and so much more. We rely on our wonderful volunteers to make our friendly and magical garden the warm and welcoming place it is. Run by the environmental charity Groundwork Northamptonshire. Sandwiches, cakes and drinks on sale - bring a blanket for a picnic. Wheelchair access and disabled WC facilities.

22 GREYWALLS

Farndish, NN29 7HJ. Mrs P M Anderson, 01933 353495, greywalls@dbshoes.co.uk. *2½m SE of Wellingborough. A609 from Wellingborough, B570 to Irchester, turn to Farndish by cenotaph. House adjacent to church.* **Sun 5 May (2-5). Adm £3.50, chd free. Light refreshments.** Visits also by arrangement for groups of 10 to 30. Coaches welcome.

A 2 acre mature garden surrounding the old vicarage (not open). The garden features an alpine house with raised alpine beds, stunning water features and natural ponds with views over open countryside. You can also meet the rare breed hens and two rescue donkeys.

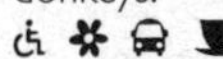

Beeches House, Wappenham Gardens

GROUP OPENING

23 GUILSBOROUGH GARDENS

High Street, Guilsborough, NN6 8RA. *10m NW of Northampton. 10m E of Rugby. Between A5199 & A428. J1 off A14. Car parking in field on Hollowell Rd out of Guilsborough. Information & maps from village hall, next to primary school.* **Sun 12 May (1-5.30). Combined adm £6, chd free. Home-made teas in village hall.**

DRIPWELL HOUSE
Mr J W Langfield & Dr C Moss, 01604 740140, cattimoss@aol.com.
Visits also by arrangement May & June for groups of 10 to 30.

FOUR ACRES
Mark & Gay Webster.

NEW **FOURWAYS**
Phil & Charles Mynard.

THE GATE HOUSE
Mike & Sarah Edwards.

GUILSBOROUGH HOUSE
Mr & Mrs John McCall.

THE OLD HOUSE
Richard & Libby Seaton Evans.

THE OLD VICARAGE
John & Christine Benbow.

NEW **PEACE GARDEN**
Guilsborough Church of England Primary School.

Enjoy a warm welcome in this village with its very attractive rural setting of rolling hills and reservoirs. Eight village gardens, including two new gardens at the primary school and a revitalised mature garden at Fourways, a charming walled garden at The Gate House and several large gardens with sweeping lawns, mature trees and wonderful views. There is plenty of room to sit and relax and picnics can be spread out in the car park field. Several of us are interested in growing fruit and vegetables, and walled kitchen gardens and a potager are an important part of our gardening. Plants both rare and unusual from our plantsmen's gardens are for sale, a true highlight here. Dripwell House has opened for the NGS since 1986, originally an individual garden and is a destination in its own right. There is thus a lot to see and visitors find that they need the whole afternoon. Bug hunt for children. No wheelchair access at Dripwell House and The Gate House.

24 ◆ HADDONSTONE SHOW GARDENS

The Forge House, Church Lane, East Haddon, Northampton, NN6 8DB. Haddonstone Ltd, 01604 770711, info@haddonstone.co.uk, www.haddonstone.com. *7m NW of Northampton. The Show Gardens are signposted via brown tourism signs from the A428. They are located in the centre of the village, near the church & opp the primary school.* **For NGS: Sun 9 June (11-5). Adm £4, chd free. Light refreshments. For other opening times and information, please phone, email or visit garden website.**

The beautiful walled manor gardens feature Haddonstone ornaments including planters, fountains, statues, bird baths and sundials. These mature gardens incl roses, clematis, climbers, herbaceous borders, ornamental flowers, topiary, specimen shrubs and trees. Designs from the Sir John Soane's Museum and busts of Capability Brown and Humphrey Repton are also featured. The gardens incorporate planting, structures and ornaments used at the company's acclaimed Chelsea Flower Show exhibits. Wheelchair access to all key features of main garden.

Vale View, Spratton Gardens

GROUP OPENING

25 HARPOLE GARDENS

Harpole, NN7 4BX. *On A45 4m W of Northampton towards Weedon. Turn R at The Turnpike Hotel into Harpole. Village maps given to all visitors.* **Sun 9 June (1-6). Combined adm £5, chd free. Home-made teas at The Close.**

BRYTTEN-COLLIER HOUSE
James & Lucy Strickland.

NEW **CEDAR COTTAGE**
Spencer & Joanne Hannam.

THE CLOSE
Michael Orton-Jones, 07714 896500, michael@orton-jones.com. **Visits also by arrangement Apr to July.**

19 MANOR CLOSE
Caroline & Andy Kemshed, 01604 830512, carolinekemshed@live.co.uk. **Visits also by arrangement in June for groups of up to 20.**

THE MANOR HOUSE
Mrs Katy Smith.

MILLERS
Mrs M Still.

THE OLD DAIRY
David & Di Ballard.

We welcome everyone to join in the Harpole Gardens experience. Harpole is an attractive village nestling at the foot of the Harpole Hills, with many houses built of the local sandstone. Visit us and delight in a wide variety of gardens of all shapes, sizes and content. We have interesting and quirky artifacts dotted around, a variety of garden structures and plenty of seating for the weary. You will see luxuriant lawns, mixed borders with plants for sun and shade, mature trees, herbs, vegetables and alpines. You can enjoy views over neighbouring farmland and perhaps best of all, enjoy delicious home-made teas at The Close. Wheelchair access at Brytten-Collier House, The Close and The Old Dairy only.

26 67-69 HIGH STREET

Finedon, NN9 5JN. Mary & Stuart Hendry, 01933 680414, sh_archt@hotmail.com. *6m SE Kettering. Garden signed from A6 & A510 junction.* **Sun 24 Feb (11-3); Sun 2 June (2-6). Adm £3.50, chd free. Sun 30 June (2-6). Combined adm with The Vicarage £3.50, chd free. Soup & roll in Feb (incl in adm). Cream teas in June.** Visits also by arrangement Feb to Sept.

⅓ acre rear garden of C17 cottage (not open). Early spring garden with snowdrops and hellebores, summer and autumn mixed borders, many obelisks and containers, kitchen garden, herb bed, rambling roses, and at least 60 different hostas. All giving varied interest from Feb through to Oct. Large selection of home raised plants for sale (all proceeds to NGS). St Mary's Church open on all dates with tea and biscuits in Feb only.

27 136 HIGH STREET

Irchester, Wellingborough, NN29 7AB. Mr & Mrs Ade & Jane Parker. *At end of High St, about ½m before junction with A45. Please park on High St. Disabled parking in driveway.* **Sun 28 July (11-4). Adm £3.50, chd free. Light refreshments.**

½ acre garden with various different borders including those planted for shade, sun and bee friendly situations. Alpine houses, raised beds and planted stone sinks. Wildlife pond. Seasonally planted tubs. Mostly lawn, some gravel pathways.

28 NEW 1 HINWICK CLOSE

Kettering, NN15 6GB. Mrs Pat Cole-Ashton. *J9 A14 A509 Kettering. At Park House r'about take 4th exit to Holdenby. Hinwick Close 3rd exit on R. From Kettering A509, at Park House r'about take the 1st exit to Holdenby, Hinwick Close 3rd exit on R.* **Sat 25 May, Sat 13 July (12-5). Adm £3.50, chd free. Tea, home-made cakes & savouries.**

A garden reclaimed from rubble surrounding a new build house (not open). In the past 6 years Pat and Snowy have transformed this space into a wildlife haven. The garden has numerous influences; seaside, woodland and English country gardens. Ponds and waterfalls add to the delights. Vintage signs, numerous figures and seating areas at different vantage points are dotted throughout the garden.

29 ◆ HOLDENBY HOUSE GARDENS

Holdenby House, Holdenby, Northampton, NN6 8DJ. Mr & Mrs James Lowther, 01604 770074, events@holdenby.com, www.holdenby.com. *7m NW of Northampton. Off A5199 or A428 between East Haddon & Spratton.* **For NGS: Sun 23 June (1-5). Adm £5, chd free. Cream teas & light refreshments.** For other opening times and information, please phone, email or visit garden website.

Holdenby has a historic Grade I listed garden. The inner garden incl Rosemary Verey's renowned Elizabethan Garden and Rupert Golby's Pond Garden and long borders. There is also a delightful walled kitchen garden with original Victorian greenhouse. Away from the formal gardens, the terraces of the original Elizabethan Garden are still visible, one of the best preserved examples of their kind. Connie's Vintage Tea Parlour and Gift Shop. The estate includes gravel paths.

Your visits help change lives – your generosity helps Marie Curie fund nurses to care for people night and day in their homes, with donations of more than £8.8 million

30 HOSTELLARIE

78 Breakleys Road, Desborough, NN14 2PT. Stella Freeman, stelstan78@aol.com. *6m N of Kettering. 5m S of Market Harborough. From church & war memorial turn R into Dunkirk Ave, then 3rd R. From cemetery L into Dunkirk Ave, then 4th L.* **Sun 9 June (1-5). Combined adm with 16 Leys Avenue £4, chd free. Sun 28 July (11.30-5). Combined adm with Froggery Cottage £4, chd free. Home-made teas & a gluten free option.** Visits also by arrangement June & July for groups of 10 to 30.

Over 180ft long town garden. Divided into rooms of different character; courtyard garden with a sculptural clematis providing shade, colour themed flower beds, ponds and water features, cottage gardens and gravel borders, clematis and roses, all linked by lawns and grass paths. The collection of hostas, over 50 different varieties, are taking up more space each year and are the pride of the garden.

31 ◆ KELMARSH HALL & GARDENS

Main Road, Kelmarsh, Northampton, NN6 9LY. The Kelmarsh Trust, 01604 686543, enquiries@kelmarsh.com, www.kelmarsh.com. *Kelmarsh is 5m S of Market Harborough & 11m N of Northampton. From A14, exit J2 & head N towards Market Harborough on the A508.* **For NGS: Sun 14 Apr, Sun 19 May (11-5). Adm £6, chd £3.50. The tearoom offers light lunches, cream teas & cakes.** For other opening times and information, please phone, email or visit garden website.

Kelmarsh Hall is an elegant Palladian house set in glorious Northamptonshire countryside with highly regarded gardens, which are the work of Nancy Lancaster, Norah Lindsay and Geoffrey Jellicoe. Hidden gems incl an orangery, sunken garden, long border, rose gardens and, at the heart of it all, a historic walled garden. Highlights throughout the seasons incl fritillaries, tulips, roses and dahlias. Beautiful interiors brought together by Nancy Lancaster in the 1930s, in a palladian style hall designed by James Gibbs. The recently restored laundry and servant's quarters in the Hall are open to the public, providing visitors the incredible opportunity to experience life 'below stairs'. Blue badge disabled parking is available close to the Visitor Centre entrance. Paths are loose gravel, wheelchair users advised to bring a companion.

GROUP OPENING

32 KILSBY GARDENS

Middle Street, Kilsby, CV23 8XT. *5m SE of Rugby. 6m N of Daventry on A361. The road through Kilsby village is the B4038.* **Sun 16 June (2-6). Combined adm £5, chd free. Light refreshments at Kilsby Village Hall (1-5).**

12 DAVENTRY ROAD
Julie Bunyan.

GRAFTON HOUSE
Andy & Sally Tomkins.

MANOR COTTAGE
Helen & Tom Jones.

ORCHARD HOUSE
Barbara & Frank Almond.

PYTCHLEY GARDENS
Kathy Jenkins & Neighbours.

RAINBOW'S END
Mr & Mrs J Madigan.

NEW **SUMMERHILL**
Diana & Ron Smith.

SUNDIAL COTTAGE
Richard & Sue Haslett.

As a special treat, the trail of open gardens in our village will be enlivened by a decorated wheelbarrow competition, trialled last year and back by popular demand. Kilsby's name has long been associated with Stephenson's famous railway tunnel and an early skirmish in the Civil War. The houses and gardens of the village offer a mixture of sizes and styles, which reflect its development through time. We welcome you to test the friendliness for which we are renowned. No wheelchair access to 7 Middle Street, narrow access to Pytchley Gardens & partial access to other gardens.

33 16 LEYS AVENUE

Desborough, Kettering, NN14 2PY. Mr & Mrs Keith & Beryl Norman, 01536 760950, bcn@stainer16.plus.com. *6m N of Kettering, 5m S of Market Harborough. From church & War Memorial turn R into Dunkirk Ave & 5th R into Leys Ave.* **Sun 9 June (1-5). Combined adm with Hostellarie £4, chd free. Sun 8 Sept (1-6). Adm £3, chd free. Light refreshments.** Visits also by arrangement June to Sept for groups of 20 to 30.

A town garden with two water features, plus a stream and a pond flanked by a 12ft clinker built boat. There are six raised beds which are planted with vegetables and dahlias. A patio lined with acers has two steps down to a gravel garden with paved paths. Mature trees and acers give the garden yr-round structure and interest. Access by two steps from patio to main garden.

34 NEW LIMETREES

1 Priestwell Court, East Haddon, Northampton, NN6 8BT. Barry & Sally Hennessey. *15 mins from J16 or J18 on M1, or J1 on A14 just off A428. Approach East Haddon from A428, or Holdenby Rd, or Ravensthorpe Rd. Garden is at the junction of Tilbury Rd, Main St & Ravensthorpe Rd. Strictly no parking allowed in Priestwell Court.* **Mon 6 May (2-6). Adm £4, chd free. Home-made teas.**

Limetrees is a medium sized garden, only 2 yrs in the making by the current owners, but already looking mature and well established thanks to the existing mature Birch, Oak, Hawthorn, Holly, Laburnum and pollarded lime trees around the mostly ironstone and cob-walled boundaries. Several hundred herbaceous plants and shrubs from previous gardens have been planted and added to. Plants propagated from those in the garden and raised from seed will be on sale. Some paths may be narrow for wheelchairs but you can view most of the mainly level garden.

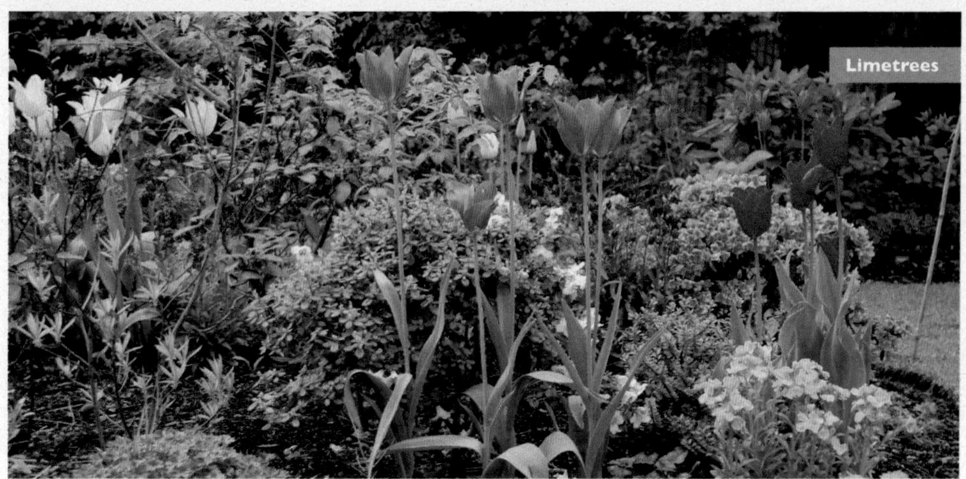

Limetrees

GROUP OPENING

35 LONG BUCKBY GARDENS

Northampton, NN6 7RE. *8m NW of Northampton, midway between A428 & A5. Long Buckby is signed from A428 & A5. 10 mins from J18 M1. Long Buckby train station is ½m from centre of the village.* **Sun 21 July (1-6). Combined adm £5, chd free. Home-made teas.**

25 BERRYFIELD
Mandy Morley & Jane Harrison.

3 COTTON END
Roland & Georgina Wells.

4 COTTON END
Sue & Giles Baker.

NEW **3A KNUTSFORD LANE**
Tim & Jan Hunt.

LAWN COTTAGE, 36 EAST STREET
Michael & Denise Nichols.

10 LIME AVENUE
June Ford.

NEW **MEADOW VIEW, SALEM CLOSE**
Trish & John York.

4 SKINYARD LANE
William & Susie Mitchell, 01327 843426, mitchewi52@gmail.com.
Visits also by arrangement May to Sept for groups of 10 to 20.

WOODCOTE VILLA
Sue & Geoff Woodward, geoff.and.sue@btinternet.com.
Visits also by arrangement Mar to Sept for groups of 10+.

Nine gardens in the historic villages of Long Buckby and Long Buckby Wharf, incl two new gardens this yr. One shows just what can be created in a small space and the other has a bit of everything including spectacular views. The gardens in the group vary in size and style, from courtyard and canal side to cottage garden, some are established and others evolving. They incl water features, pergolas, garden structures, chickens and pigs, but the stars are definitely the plants. Bursting with colour, visitors will find old favourites and the unusual, used in a variety of ways; trees, shrubs, perennials, climbers, annuals, fruit and vegetables. Of course there will be teas and plants for sale to complete the visit. Come and see us for a friendly welcome and a good afternoon out. Full or partial wheelchair access to all gardens, except 4 Skinyard Lane.

36 MOULTON COLLEGE HORTICULTURE UNIT

Holcot Site (Gate 3), Pitsford Road, Moulton, NN3 7RR. Moulton College, www.moulton.ac.uk. *Horticulture Unit via the Garden Centre. Turn off A43 Northamton to Kettering Rd at small r'about to Overstone Rd. In village centre follow yellow signs. The car park is on the Pitsford Rd out of the village.* **Sun 9 June (10-4). Adm £5, chd free. Tea, coffee & cake.**

Moulton College started life as an agricultural college and has a strong horticultural dept. There are show gardens, allotments, a 2½ hectare millenium arboretum, more formal areas around the original 1920s buildings and interesting specimen trees, maintained by the students, in an attractive rural setting. Wide tarmac path from carpark to village centre via arboretum.

GROUP OPENING

37 NEWNHAM GARDENS

Newnham, Daventry, NN11 3HF. *2m S of Daventry on B4037 between the A361 & A45. Continue to the centre of the village & follow signs for the car park, just off the main village green.* **Sun 26 May (11-5). Combined adm £5, chd free. Light lunches, drinks & cakes in the village hall.**

THE BANKS
Sue & Geoff Chester, www.suestyles.co.uk.

THE COTTAGE
Jacqueline Minor.

HILLTOP
David & Mercy Messenger.

KEY COTTAGE
David & Janet Woodford.

WREN COTTAGE
Mr & Mrs Jim Dorkins.

Five lovely gardens set in a beautiful ancient village cradled between the gentle hills of south Northamptonshire. The varied gardens, set around traditional village houses look enchanting at this special time of year. Spend the day with us enjoying the gardens, buying plants, strolling around the old village lanes, visiting our C14 church and its exhibition and indulging yourself with tasty light lunches and scrumptious refreshments and cakes. Please note that the village and gardens are hilly in parts and while most gardens are accessible to wheelchairs, others are more restricted.

38 OLD RECTORY, QUINTON

Preston Deanery Road, Quinton, Northampton, NN7 2ED. Alan Kennedy & Emma Wise. www.quintonoldrectory.co.uk. *M1 J15, 1m from Wootton towards Salcey Forest. House is next to the church.* **Sun 2 June, Sun 1 Sept (10-5). Adm £10, chd free. Pre-booking essential, please visit www.ngs.org.uk for information & booking. Teas & light lunches.**

A beautiful contemporary 3 acre rectory garden designed by multi-award-winning designer, Anoushka Feiler. Taking the Old Rectory's C18 history and its religious setting as a key starting point, the main garden at the back of the house has been divided into six parts; a kitchen garden, glasshouse and flower garden, a woodland menagerie, a pleasure garden, a park and an orchard. Elements of C18 design such as formal structures, parterres, topiary, long walks, occasional seating areas and traditional craft work have been introduced, however with a distinctly C21 twist through the inclusion of living walls, modern materials and features, new planting methods and abstract installations. Wheelchair access, but there are gravel paths.

39 ◆ THE OLD RECTORY, SUDBOROUGH

Kettering, NN14 3BX. Mr & Mrs G Toller, 01832 734085, contact@theoldrectorygardens.co.uk, www.theoldrectorygardens.co.uk. *8m NE of Kettering. Exit 12 off A14. Village just off A6116 between Thrapston & Brigstock. Free private parking in a small paddock adjacent to the house.* **For NGS: Sun 28 Apr (11-5). Adm £7, chd free. Home-made teas & cake.**

For other opening times and information, please phone, email or visit garden website.

A charming 3 acre village garden situated next to a church, including extensive herbaceous borders, a rose garden, gravel border and highly regarded potager, designed by Rosemary Verey. This is a garden for all seasons with early spring bulbs, a wide variety of old roses, tree peonies, standard Lycianthes Rantonnetii, a small lily pond and charming woodland walk alongside Harpers Brook. Set in a tranquil conservation area with stunning views and setting. Partial wheelchair access as some gravel paths. Guide dogs welcome.

40 THE OLD VICARAGE

Daventry Road, Norton, Daventry, NN11 2ND. Mr & Mrs Barry & Andrea Coleman. *Norton is about 2m E of Daventry, 11m W of Northampton. From Daventry follow signs to Norton for 1m. On A5 N from Weedon follow road for 3m, take L turn signed Norton. On A5 S take R at Xrds signed Norton, 6m from Kilsby. Garden is R of All Saints Church.* **Sun 28 Apr (1-4). Adm £4, chd free. Home-made teas.**

The vicarage days bequeathed dramatic and stately trees to the modern garden. The last 40 yrs of evolution and the happy accidents of soil-type, and a striking location with lovely vistas have shaped the garden around all the things that make April so thrilling, including prodigious sweeps of primulas of many kinds. The trees are in blossom and tea and cakes will be waiting for you in the orangery. The interesting C14 church of All Saints will be open to visitors. Gravel drive.

41 OLD WEST FARM

Little Preston, Daventry, NN11 3TF. Mr & Mrs G Hoare, caghoare@gmail.com. *7m SW Daventry, 8m W Towcester, 13m NE Banbury. ¾m E of Preston Capes on road to Maidford. Last house on R in Little Preston with white flagpole.* **Visits by arrangement May & June for groups of 10 to 30.**

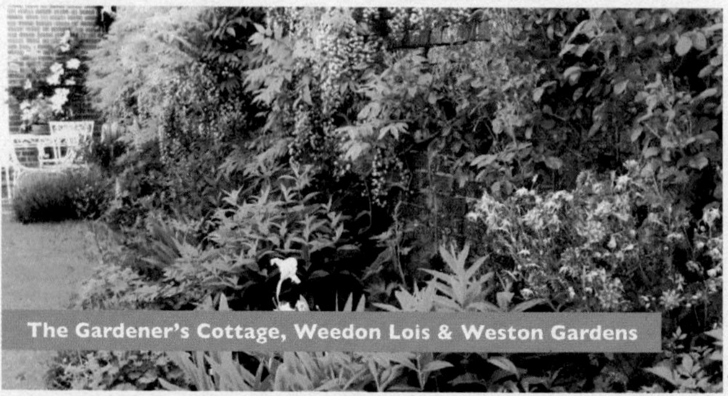

The Gardener's Cottage, Weedon Lois & Weston Gardens

Adm £4, chd free. Home-made teas.
Large rural garden developed over the past 39 yrs on a very exposed site, planted with hedges and shelter. Roses, shrubs and borders aiming for yr-round interest. Partial wheelchair access on grass.

GROUP OPENING

42 RAVENSTHORPE GARDENS

Ravensthorpe, NN6 8ES. *7m NW of Northampton. Signed from A428. Wigley Cottage is in The Hollows off Bettycroft.* **Sun 14 July (1.30-5.30). Combined adm £5, chd free. Home-made teas at village hall.**

CORNERSTONE
Lorna Jones.

QUIETWAYS
Russ Barringer.

RAVENSTHORPE NURSERY
Mr & Mrs Richard Wiseman, 01604 770548, ravensthorpenursery@hotmail.com.
Visits also by arrangement Apr to Oct.

TREETOPS
Ros & Gordon Smith.

WIGLEY COTTAGE
Mr & Mrs Dennis Patrick.

Attractive village in Northamptonshire uplands near to Ravensthorpe reservoir and Top Ardles Wood Woodland Trust, which have bird watching and picnic opportunities. Established and developing gardens set in beautiful countryside displaying a wide range of plants, many of which are available from the Nursery. Offering inspirational planting, quiet contemplation, beautiful views, water features, gardens encouraging wildlife and a flower arranger's garden. Partial wheelchair access to Wigley Cottage. Disabled WC available at the village hall.

43 NEW RAVENSWOOD

Coton, Northampton, NN6 8RG. Jean & Mike Percival. *1m S of Guilsborough. Follow sign on lane, nr Coton Manor indicating 'Village only' & 'No Through Road', garden 100yds on R. Car park in field as signed.* **Sun 9 June (2-5.30). Adm £5, chd free. Sun 8 Sept (12-5.30). Combined adm with Coton Manor Garden £7.50, chd free. Home-made teas at St. Etheldreda Church, Guilsborough (9 June). Light refreshments at Coton Manor (8 Sept).**
Since purchase, the owners have redeveloped the garden to take advantage of the sloping site overlooking woods and farmland. A wide variety of herbaceous plants, shrubs and maturing trees have been planted to provide colour throughout the gardening year.

44 ROSEARIE-DE-LA-NYMPH

55 The Grove, Moulton, Northampton, NN3 7UE. Peter Hughes, Mary Morris, Irene Kay, Steven Hughes & Jeremy Stanton. *N of Northampton town. Turn off A43 at small r'about to Overstone Rd. Follow NGS signs in village. The garden is on the Holcot Rd out of Moulton.* **Sun 16, Sun 23 June (11-5). Adm £4.50, chd free. Light refreshments.**
We have been developing this romantic garden for about 10 yrs and now have over 1800 roses, incl English, French and Italian varieties. Many unusual water features and specimen trees. Roses, scramblers and ramblers climb into trees, over arbours and arches. Collection of 140 Japanese maples. Mostly flat, but there is a standard width doorway to negotiate.

We help ordinary people open the gates to their extraordinary private gardens to raise impressive amounts of money through admissions, teas and slices of cake!

GROUP OPENING

45 SPRATTON GARDENS

Smith Street, Spratton, NN6 8HP. *6½m NNW of Northampton. On A5199 between Northampton & Welford. S from J1, A14. Car Park at Spratton Hall School with close access to gardens.* **Sun 9 June (11-5). Combined adm £7, chd free. Home-made teas at St Andrew's Church, Church Road.**

THE COTTAGE
Mr & Mrs Andrew Elliott.

FORGE COTTAGE
Daniel & Jo Bailey.

NEW **28 GORSE ROAD**
Lee Miller.

11 HIGH STREET
Philip & Frances Roseblade.

MULBERRY COTTAGE
Kerry Herd.

NORTHBANK HOUSE
Helen Millichamp.

STONE HOUSE
John Forbear.

VALE VIEW
John Hunt.

WALTHAM COTTAGE
Norma & Allan Simons.

1 WILLOW CLOSE
Ken & Lorraine Bennett.

As well as attractive cottage gardens alongside old Northampton stone houses, Spratton also has unusual gardens, including those showing good use of a small area; one dedicated to encouraging wildlife with views of the surrounding countryside; newly renovated gardens; courtyard garden; gravel garden with sculpture; mature gardens with fruit trees and herbaceous borders. There will be a 'Bug Hunt' for children. Tea, cakes and rolls will be available in the Norman St. Andrew's Church. The King's Head Pub will be open, lunch reservations recommended.

46 SULBY GARDENS

Sulby, Northampton, NN6 6EZ. Mrs Alison Lowe. *16m NW of Northampton, 2m NE of Welford off A5199. Past Wharf House Hotel, take 1st R signed Sulby. After R & L bends, turn R at sign for Sulby Hall Farm. Turn R at junction, garden is 1st L. Parking limited, no vans or buses please.* **Thur 25 Apr, Thur 20 June, Thur 22 Aug (2-5); Thur 10 Oct (1-4); Fri 11 Oct (11-4). Adm £4, chd free. Home-made teas.**

Interesting and unusual property, on the Leicestershire border between Welford and Husbands Bosworth, covering 12 acres comprising working Victorian kitchen garden, orchard, and late C18 icehouse, plus species-rich nature reserve incl woodland, feeder stream to River Avon, a variety of ponds and established wild flower meadows. Open Day features incl April: snakeshead fritillaries, cowslips, bluebells. June: wildflower meadows in full bloom. Aug: butterflies, dragonflies, aquatic plants. Oct: two-day Apple Event. Regular plant sales. NB: Children welcome but under strict supervision because of deep water.

GROUP OPENING

47 SULGRAVE GARDENS

Banbury, OX17 2RP. *8m NE of Banbury. Just off B4525 Banbury to Northampton road, 7m from J11 off M40. Car parking at church hall.* **Sun 9 June (2-6). Combined adm £5, chd free. Home-made teas.**

FORGE COTTAGE
Anna Faure.

MILL HOLLOW BARN
David & Judith Thompson.

RECTORY FARM
Charles & Joanna Smyth-Osbourne, 01295 760261, sosbournejm@gmail.com.

THREEWAYS
Alison & Digby Lewis.

NEW **VINECROFT**
Claire & Jon Sadler.

THE WATERMILL
Mr & Mrs T Frost.

Sulgrave is a small historic village having recently celebrated its strong American connections as part of the 150 yrs of the signing of the Treaty of Ghent. Six gardens opening; Threeways, a small walled cottage garden packed with interest. Rectory Farm has lovely views, a rill, well, and planted arbours. Mill Hollow Barn, a large garden with lakes, streams, ponds and many rare and interesting trees, shrubs and perennials. The Watermill, a contemporary garden designed by James Alexander Sinclair, set around a C16 watermill and mill pond. Forge Cottage, a walled cottage garden, recently remodelled, and Vinecroft, a contemporary garden by Alexander John Design with roses, climbers, perennials and shrubs. An award-winning community owned and run village shop will be open.

48 TITCHMARSH HOUSE

Chapel Street, Titchmarsh, NN14 3DA. Sir Ewan & Lady Harper, 01832 732439, ewan@ewanh.co.uk, www.titchmarsh-house.co.uk. *2m N of Thrapston. 6m S of Oundle. Exit A14 at junction signed A605, Titchmarsh signed as turning E towards Oundle & Peterborough.* **Mon 6, Sun 19 May (2-6); Sat 8 June (12.30-5). Adm £4, chd free. Teas at parish church (May). BBQ lunch & teas at village fete (June).** Visits also by arrangement Apr to June for groups of 5+.

4½ acres extended and laid out since 1972. Special collections of magnolias, spring bulbs, iris, peonies and roses with many rare trees and shrubs. Walled ornamental vegetable garden and ancient yew hedge. Some newly planted areas; please refer to the website. Collections of flowering trees and other unusual plants such as rare Buddleias, Philadelphus, Deutzias and Abelias. Wheelchair access to most of the garden without using steps. No dogs.

GROUP OPENING

49 TURWESTON GARDENS

Brackley, NN13 5JY. *2m E of Brackley. A43 from M40 J10. On Brackley bypass turn R on A422 towards Buckingham, ½m turn L signed Turweston.* **Sun 9 June (2-5). Combined adm £3, chd free. Home-made teas at Turweston House.**

TURWESTON HOUSE
Mr & Mrs C Allen.

TURWESTON LODGE
Mr & Mrs B P Collins.

TURWESTON MILL
Mr Harry Leventis.

Charming unspoilt stone built village in a conservation area. Three very different beautiful gardens. The Mill with bridges over the millstream and a spectacular waterfall, wildlife pond and a kitchen garden. At Turweston House there are landscaped gardens with borders, woodlands, lake and parkland and Turweston Lodge with a lovely cottage garden and spectacular rambling roses. Some gravel and slopes, but generally good access.

50 THE VICARAGE

Church Hill, Finedon, NN9 5NR. Revds Richard & David Coles. *Garden signed from A6 & A510 junction.* **Sun 30 June (2-6). Combined adm with 67-69 High Street £3.50, chd free. Cream teas at 67-69 High Street.**

Built in the original Vicarage rose garden in 2000 and landscaped 8 yrs ago. Front surrounded by tall deciduous trees and old preserved hedge. The walled garden is rooms of raised beds, living willow arch, summerhouse, Italian pizza oven, and Zen inspired meditation zone, as featured on the RHS Chelsea Flower Show 2018. Planting is English country and cottage garden sympathetic to local eco environment.

GROUP OPENING

51 WAPPENHAM GARDENS

Wappenham, NN12 8SJ. *4m W of Towcester, 6m N of Brackley, 8m E of Banbury. Tickets & map available at each garden. Limited off street parking in village.* **Sun 16 June (2-6). Combined adm £7.50, chd free. Home-made teas in the village hall.**

NEW **BEECHES HOUSE**
Alastair & Kate Judge.

NEW **ELM LODGE FARMHOUSE**
Charlotte Supple, 07976 406641, charlotte@charlottesupple.com.

HOME FARM
Mr & Mr Robert Tomkinson.

PITTAMS FARM
Hilary & John Wickham.

STONE COTTAGE
Diane & Brian Watts.

WAPPENHAM MANOR
Mr & Mrs Fordham.

A fabulous collection of six diverse gardens all set around beautiful C17, C18 and C19 Northamptonshire stone houses. Expect packed perennial borders, topiary, bulging vegetable gardens and productive orchards. The gardens range in size from several acres to ones that offer great ideas for smaller gardens. Two are designed by James Alexander-Sinclair. Not all gardens are accessible to wheelchairs due to steps.

GROUP OPENING

52 WEEDON LOIS & WESTON GARDENS

Weedon Lois, Towcester, NN12 8PJ. *7m W of Towcester. 7m N of Brackley. Turn off A43 at Towcester towards Abthorpe & Wappenham & turn R for Weedon Lois. Or turn off A43 at Brackley, follow signs to Helmdon & Weston.* **Sun 9 June (1-5.30). Combined adm £6, chd free. Home-made teas in Baptist Chapel, Weston.**

THE GARDENER'S COTTAGE
Mrs Sitwell.

HILLSIDE
Mrs Karen Wilcox.

LOIS WEEDON HOUSE
Lady Greenaway.

OLD BARN
Mr & Mrs John Gregory.

NEW **PRIMROSE HILL**
Terry & Hugh Tyler.

RIDGEWAY COTTAGE
Jonathan & Elizabeth Carpenter.

4 VICARAGE RISE
Ashley & Lindsey Cartwright.

Two adjacent villages in south Northamptonshire with a handsome Medieval church in Weedon Lois. The extension churchyard contains the grave of the poet Dame Edith Sitwell who lived in Weston Hall (not open), marked with a gravestone by Henry Moore. There are seven very different gardens open this year, some large and well established, some more recently planted. There is a plantsman garden with many unusual perennials, others with interesting herbaceous beds, terracing, country views, woodland planting, fruit trees and vegetables. We hope you will join us for our open day, enjoy looking round our gardens, and tuck into our famous home-made teas.

53 THE WOODEN OWL

10A The Green, Clipston, Market Harborough, LE16 9RS. Mrs Julie Connell, 01858 525336, j.connell118@btinternet.com. *Clipston is on the Daventry, West Haddon, Naseby Market Harborough road. Approx 15m W of Kettering, NW of Northampton & SSE of Leicester. Off A14 J1 take the A5199 to Naseby then Clipston. Off A14 J2 take the A508 to Kelmarsh then Clipston.* **Visits by arrangement May & June for groups of 10+. Adm £4, chd free. Cream teas.**

A garden in the making around owner's new house (not open), built in the stableyard of The Maltings, the garden the owner opened for the NGS for 10 yrs. The garden is within the owner's old plantsman's garden, full of unusual plants, shrubs and clematis. Many different fruit trees and bushes, vegetables and a new water garden. A garden with great interest, especially to people who used to visit The Maltings. It will be interesting to see how it develops over the coming yrs. Most of the garden is wheelchair friendly.

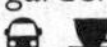

Your visits help change lives – since 1927, we've donated £55 million to nursing and caring charities

Hostellarie

NOTTINGHAMSHIRE

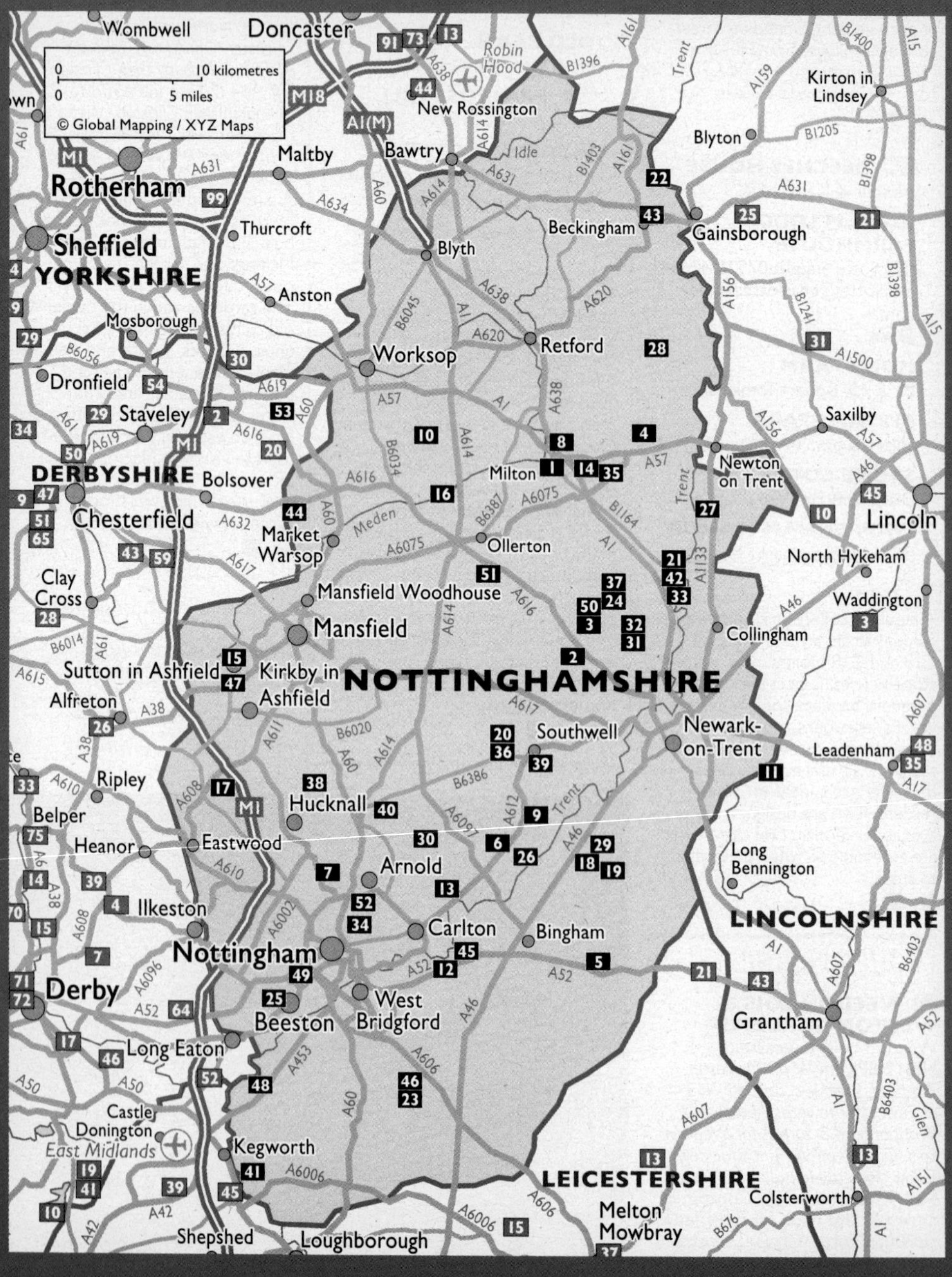

Nottinghamshire is best known as Robin Hood country. His legend persists and his haunt of Sherwood Forest, now a nature reserve, contains some of the oldest oaks in Europe. The Major Oak, thought to be 800 years old, still produces acorns.

Civil War battles raged throughout Nottinghamshire, and Newark's historic castle bears the scars. King Charles I surrendered to the Scots in nearby Southwell after a night at The Saracen's Head, which is still an inn today.

The Dukeries in the north of the county provide an unmatched landscape of lakes, parks and woods, so called because four dukes lived there, and their estates were contiguous. The dukes are gone, but their estates at Clumber, Thoresby and Welbeck continue to offer a pre-industrial haven in a thickly populated county.

Oaks in Sherwood, apples in Southwell (where the original Bramley tree still stands) and 100 kinds of rhubarb in the ducal kitchen garden at Clumber Park – they await your visit.

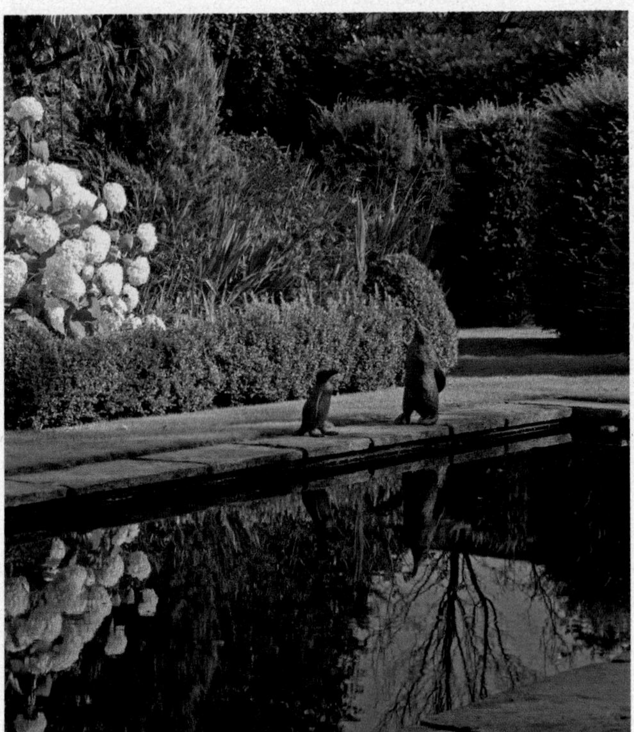

Volunteers

County Organiser
Georgina Denison
01636 821385
campden27@aol.com

County Treasurer
Nicola Cressey
01159 655132
nicola.cressey@gmail.com

Publicity
Julie Davison
01302 719668
julie.davison@ngs.org

Social Media
Malcolm Turner
01159 222831
malcolm.turner14@btinternet.com

Booklet Co-ordinators
Malcolm and Wendy Fisher
0115 966 4322
wendy.fisher111@btinternet.com.

Assistant County Organisers
Judy Geldart
01636 823832
judygeldart@gmail.com

Beverley Perks
01636 812181
perks.family@talk21.com

Mary Thomas
01509 672056
nursery@piecemealplants.co.uk

Andrew Young
01623 863327
andrew.young@ngs.org.uk

Left: The Coach House

OPENING DATES

All entries subject to change. For latest information check **www.ngs.org.uk**

Map locator numbers are shown to the right of each garden name.

February

Snowdrop Festival

Saturday 16th
The Beeches 1

Sunday 17th
The Beeches 1
Church Farm 8

Sunday 24th
Holmes Villa 22

March

Sunday 10th
NEW Upper Grove Farm 50

April

Sunday 14th
Capability Barn 6

Sunday 21st
◆ Felley Priory 17

May

Sunday 5th
Capability Barn 6
NEW Long Acres 29

Monday 6th
The Old Vicarage 36

Sunday 12th
NEW Bridge Farm 3

Sunday 19th
Church House 9
6 Hope Street 25
NEW Hunters Moon 26
Ivy Bank Cottage 27
38 Main Street 30
◆ Norwell Nurseries 32
Rose Cottage 46
University Park Gardens 49

Sunday 26th
Papplewick Hall 38
Patchings Art Centre 40

Monday 27th
Halam Gardens and Wildflower Meadow 20
Holmes Villa 22

June

Saturday 1st
The Echium Garden 16

Sunday 2nd
Broadlea 4
5 Burton Lane 5

Sunday 9th
The Chimes 7
NEW Flintham Hall 18
Flintham House 19
The Poplars 42
Primrose Cottage 43

Sunday 16th
NEW East Meets West 15
Park Farm 39
Spring Bank House 47

Saturday 22nd
The Old Vicarage 36

Sunday 23rd
The Chimes 7
Hopbine Farmhouse, Ossington 24
Ossington House 37
Riseholme, 125 Shelford Road 45
NEW Whitwell Open Gardens 53

Sunday 30th
Beesthorpe Hall Farm 2
East Markham Gardens 14
Norwell Gardens 31
Rose Cottage 46
Thrumpton Hall 48

July

Wednesday 3rd
Norwell Gardens 31
Rhubarb Farm 44

Sunday 7th
Lodge Mount 28
Wellow Village Gardens 51
6 Weston Close 52

Saturday 13th
◆ Clumber Park Walled Kitchen Garden 10

Sunday 21st
The Coach House 11
Cornerstones 12

Sunday 28th
5a High Street 21
Norwood 33

August

Sunday 4th
Nottinghamshire Hospice 34

Sunday 11th
The Old Vicarage 36

Sunday 18th
Piecemeal 41

Monday 26th
5 Burton Lane 5

September

Sunday 1st
NEW East Meets West 15
Oak Barn Exotic Garden 35
Spring Bank House 47

Sunday 29th
◆ Norwell Nurseries 32

October

Sunday 13th
◆ Norwell Nurseries 32

By Arrangement

5 Burton Lane 5
Capability Barn 6
The Coach House 11
Cornerstones 12
Dumbleside 13
5a High Street 21
Holmes Villa 22
Home Farm House, 17 Main Street 23
Lodge Mount 28
The Manor, East Markham Gardens 14
The Old Vicarage 36
Park Farm 39
Piecemeal 41
Riseholme, 125 Shelford Road 45
Rose Cottage 46
6 Weston Close 52

Wellow Village Gardens

THE GARDENS

1 THE BEECHES

The Avenue, Milton, Newark, NG22 0PW. Margaret & Jim Swindin. *1m S A1 Markham Moor. Exit A1 at Markham Moor, take Walesby sign into village (1m). From Main St, L up The Avenue.* **Sat 16, Sun 17 Feb (11-4). Adm £3, chd free. Home-made teas.**

One acre garden full of colour and interest to plant enthusiasts looking for unusual and rare plants. Spring gives some 250 named snowdrops together with hellebores and early daffodils. The lawn is awash with crocus, fritillarias, anemones, narcissi and cyclamen. Large vegetable garden on raised beds. Lovely views over open countryside. Sadly, this will be our last year opening. Newcastle Mausoleum (adjacent) open. Local guides present history. Some slopes and gravel paths - seats in garden.

2 BEESTHORPE HALL FARM

Caunton, Newark, NG23 6AT. Pamela & Peter Littlewood. *On the Maplebeck rd. ½way between Caunton & Maplebeck. From A616 at Caunton take the Maplebeck/ Eakring rd. 1m farm on R. 2 fields off the rd.* **Sun 30 June (1-5). Adm £3.50, chd free. Home-made teas.**

Large country garden full of exciting planting including an extensive ecologically designed, unique gravel garden. Walk through wildflower meadow to large pond.

3 NEW BRIDGE FARM

Norwell Woodhouse, Newark, NG23 6NG. Rachel Cook. *If entering the village from Norwell , the property is on the R just after the dairy farm.* **Sun 12 May (1-4). Adm £3, chd free. Home-made teas.**

A large country garden in a quiet village (work in progress) with a wide variety of plants providing flower and foliage colour all year round. A contemporary swimming pond with a tranquil decking area to sit and ponder, views of open fields to the rear. Patio and courtyard, along with raised flower and vegetable beds Plenty of seats available to relax and enjoy tea and a slice of cake.

4 BROADLEA

North Green, East Drayton, Retford, DN22 0LF. David & Jean Stone. *Broadlea. From A1 take A57 E towards Lincoln. East Drayton is signed L off A57, approx 2m from A1. North Green runs N from church. Garden last gate on R.* **Sun 2 June (2-5). Adm £3, chd free. Home-made teas. Tea and cakes £2.50.**

Our aim in this 1 acre garden is to have interest throughout the yr and attract wildlife. There is plenty to see, woodland walk, many perennials, shrubs and spring bulbs. Large pond is a haven for wildlife and a kitchen garden together with wild bank and dyke add attraction to the formal vistas. Partial wheelchair access.

5 5 BURTON LANE

Whatton in the Vale, NG13 9EQ. Ms Faulconbridge, 01949 850942, jpfaulconbridge@hotmail.co.uk, www.ayearinthegardenblog.wordpress.com. *3m E of Bingham. Follow signs to Whatton from A52 between Bingham & Elton. Garden nr Church in old part of village. Follow yellow NGS signs.* **Sun 2 June, Mon 26 Aug (12.30-4.30). Adm £3.50, chd free. Home-made teas. Visits also by arrangement May to Sept for groups of up to 30.**

Modern cottage garden which is productive and highly decorative.

We open the gates to the nation's best gardens, offering a relaxing, memorable and affordable day out. A perfect experience to share with friends and family.

We garden organically and for wildlife. The garden is full of colour and scent from spring to autumn. Several distinct areas, incl fruit and vegetables. Large beds are filled with over 500 varieties of plants with paths through so you can wander and get close. Also features seating, gravel garden, pond, shade planting and sedum roof. Historic church, attractive village with walks.

6 CAPABILITY BARN

Gonalston Lane, Hoveringham, NG14 7JH. Malcolm & Wendy Fisher, 01159 664322, wendy.fisher111@btinternet.com, www.capabilitybarn.com. *8m NE of Nottingham. A612 from Nottingham through Lowdham. Take 1st R into Gonalston Lane. 1m on L.* **Sun 14 Apr (11.30-4.30). Home-made teas. Sun 5 May (11.30-4.30). Adm £4, chd free. Visits also by arrangement Apr & May for groups of 20+. Admission price incl refreshments.**

Imaginatively planted large country garden with something new each year. April brings displays of Daffodils, Hyacinths and Tulips along with erythroniums, brunneras and primulas. Wisteria, Magnolia, Rhodos and apple blossom greet May. A backdrop of established trees, shrubs and shady paths give a charming country setting. Large vegetable/fruit gardens with orchard/meadow completes the picture.

7 THE CHIMES

37 Glenorchy Crescent, Heronridge, NG5 9LG. Stan & Ellen Maddock. *4m N of Nottingham. A611 towards Hucknall on to Bulwell Common. Turn R at Tesco Top Valley up to island. Turn L 100 yds. 1st L then 2nd L onto Glenorchy Crescent to bottom.* **Sun 9, Sun 23 June (1-5). Adm £3, chd free. Home-made teas.**

We would like to invite you to pass through our archway and into our own little oasis on the edge of a busy city. Come and share our well-stocked small garden, full of roses, peonies, lilies and much more. Visit us and be surprised. We look forward to seeing you.

8 CHURCH FARM

Church Lane, West Drayton, Retford, DN22 8EB. Robert & Isobel Adam. *A1 exit Markham Moor. A638 Retford 500 yds signed West Drayton. 1m Church Lane, 1st R past church. Ample parking in farm yard.* **Sun 17 Feb (11-4.30). Adm £3, chd £1.50. Light refreshments at St Pauls Church.**

The garden is essentially a spring garden and a little on the wild side. We have a small woodland area which is carpeted with many snowdrops, aconites and cyclamen which have seeded into the adjoining churchyard, with approx 180 named snowdrops growing in island beds. Limited amount of snowdrops and miniature iris for sale.

9 CHURCH HOUSE

Hoveringham, NG14 7JH. Alex & Sue Allan. *6m NE of Nottingham. To the R of the church and church hall in the centre of the village.* **Sun 19 May (1-5). Combined adm with Hunters Moon £4.50, chd free. Home-made teas in Hoveringham Village Hall served by Hoveringham WI.**

Small, walled, cottage-style garden with herbaceous borders, auricula theatre, Japanese area and vegetable plot. This charming garden offers a delighful setting in which to relax and is packed with ideas for those gardeners with limited space. Gravel driveway and paths.

10 ◆ CLUMBER PARK WALLED KITCHEN GARDEN

Clumber Park, Worksop, S80 3BE. National Trust, 01909 476592, clumberpark@nationaltrust.org.uk, www.nationaltrust.org.uk/clumber-park. *4m S of Worksop. From main car park or main entrance follow directions to Walled Kitchen Garden.* **For NGS: Sat 13 July (10-5). Adm £4.50, chd £2.50. Light refreshments at Garden Tea House.** For other opening times and information, please phone, email or visit garden website.

Beautiful 4 acre walled kitchen garden, growing unusual and heritage varieties of vegetables and fruits. Herbs and flower beds, incl the magnificent 400ft double herbaceous borders. 450ft glasshouse with grapevines. Museum of gardening tools. Soft fruit garden, rose garden. National Collections of culinary rhubarbs (130 varieties) and apples from the East Midlands and Yorkshire (72 varieties). Some paths on slopes.

NPC

11 THE COACH HOUSE

Fosse Road, Farndon, Newark, NG24 2SF. Sir Graeme & Lady Svava Davies, Graeme.davies@london.ac.uk. *On old A46 W of Farndon approx 250yds on R past new overbridge turn off to Hawton. Entrance driveway marked Private Road.* **Sun 21 July (1-5). Adm £5, chd free. Home-made teas.** Visits also by arrangement July & Aug.

The Coach House has two major garden areas set in approximately 0.9 acres. Both have several distinct sections and the planting throughout is designed to give color and interest through the seasons. There are many rare and unusual species among the mainly perennial plants, shrubs, grasses and trees. The planting in each area of the garden is fully detailed in a brochure for visitors.

12 CORNERSTONES

15 Lamcote Gardens, Radcliffe-on-Trent, Nottingham, NG12 2BS. Judith & Jeff Coombes, 0115 8458055, judithcoombes@gmail.com, www.cornerstonesgarden.co.uk. *4m E of Nottingham. From A52 take Radcliffe exit at RSPCA junction, then 2nd L just before hairpin bend.* **Sun 21 July (1.30-5). Adm £3.50, chd free. Home-made teas.** Visits also by arrangement July & Aug for groups of 10+.

Plant lovers' garden, approaching ½ acre. Flowing colour themed and specie borders, with rare, exotic and unusual plants, provide a wealth of colour and interest, whilst the unique fruit and vegetable garden generates an abundance of produce. Bananas, palms, fernery, fish pond, bog garden, lovely summerhouse area and greenhouse. Enjoy tea and delicious home-made cake in a beautiful setting. Wheelchair access but some bark paths and unfenced ponds.

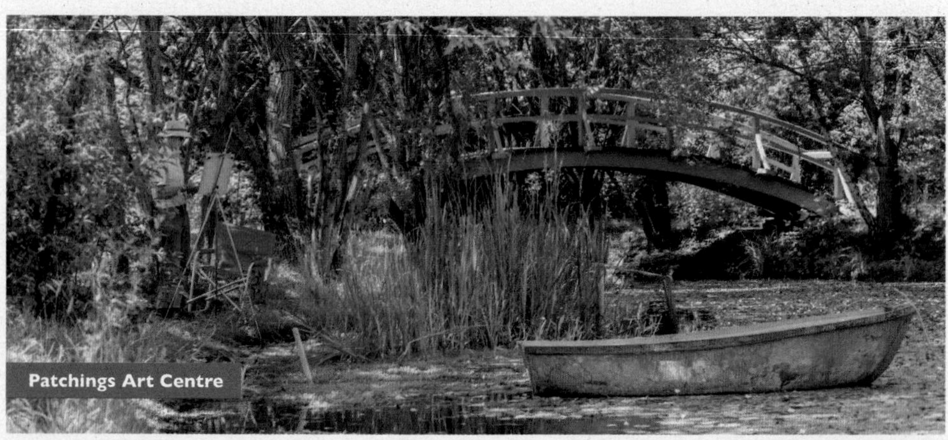

Patchings Art Centre

13 DUMBLESIDE

17 Bridle Road, Burton Joyce, NG14 5FT. Mr P Bates, 01159 313725, cpbates2015@gmail.com. *5m NE of Nottingham. The Bridle Rd is an unsurfaced, single track, R hand fork off Lambley Ln. Leave passengers at our gate and park 50 yds beyond where the rd branches 3 ways.* **Visits by arrangement Feb to Oct. Admission price incl refreshments - confirm on booking. Adm £6, chd free. Home-made teas.**

Gorgeous 2 acres of varied habitat. Stream with primulas, iris, tree ferns and the like; 50yds of mixed herbaceous borders; gardening in grass with wild flowers, Spring and Autumn bulbs; woodland walks of massed cyclamen, snowdrops & anemones and a nice sunny raised gravel bed for alpines and small plants. Plant lovers' delight! Steep slopes towards stream therefore partial access only for wheelchairs.

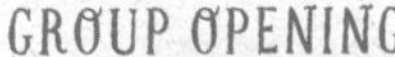

14 EAST MARKHAM GARDENS

Church Street, East Markham, Newark, NG22 0SA. Anne Beeby, anne.beeby@sky.com. *East Markham Newark NG22 0SA. 7m S of Retford. Take A1 Markham Moor r'about exit for A57 Lincoln. Turn at East Markham junction & follow signs for the church.* **Sun 30 June (1-5). Combined adm £5, chd free. Home-made teas in the grounds of The Manor.**

THE MANOR
Ms Christine Aldred, 01777 872719, clownsca@yahoo.co.uk.
Visits also by arrangement for groups of 10 to 20.

NORWOOD COTTAGE
Anne Beeby.

OAK BARN EXOTIC GARDEN
Simon Bennett & Laura Holmes. (See separate entry)

SPRINGFIELD HOUSE
Graham & Sue White.

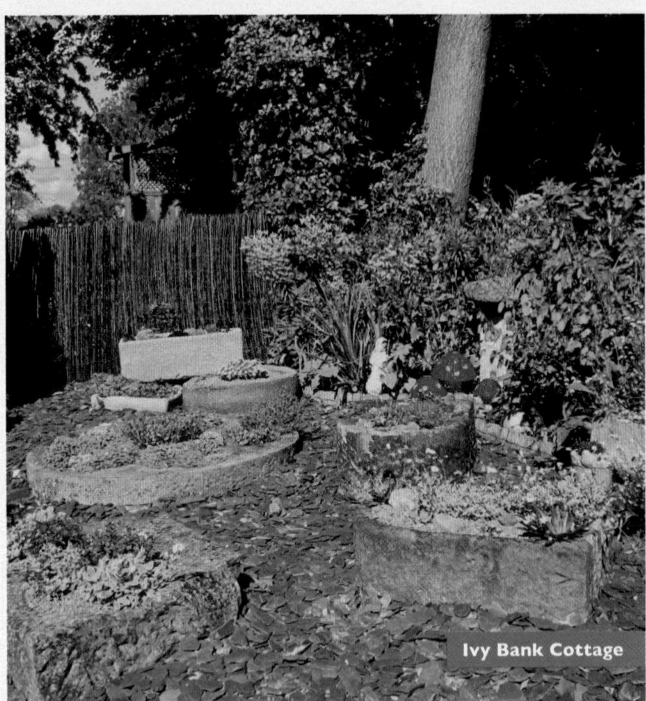
Ivy Bank Cottage

Norwood Cottage is an outstanding example of a plantswoman's take on a cottage garden, combining plants to create a visual feast of texture, colour and form. The Manor, an extensive colour themed garden on different levels, incl a sunken garden and pond, surrounded by glorious agapanthus and lavender. Climbing roses .adorn the old stone house. Springfield House features fantastic roses with the garden wrapping around the house, with contemporary water feature and newly created herbaceous borders. Oak Barn - a densely planted exotic oasis incorporating lush green unusual foliage plants, tree ferns and many more plants. Wheelchair access to some parts of the gardens only.

15 NEW EAST MEETS WEST

85 Cowpes Close, Sutton-In-Ashfield, NG17 2BU. Kate and Mel Calladine. *Close to Quarrydale School entrance to Carsic Housing Estate. The Cl has limited parking. Parking on Stoneyford Rd, Sutton-in-Ashfield NG17 2DU would relieve congestion. Cross on zebra and walk down jitty into Cowpes Cl following NGS signposting.* **Sun 16 June, Sun 1 Sept (12-5). Combined adm with Spring Bank House £4, chd free. Light refreshments at Spring Bank House.**

East: We have a number of sizable acers, bamboos and Japanese lanterns. A stream flows past a deer scarer and cloud tree into a pond with goldfish and water lilies. West: A trompe d'oeil arch creates a magical garden illusion with an arch shaped 'rainbow' flower bed providing a flamboyant colour arrangement. The front drive has pink/white borders, hanging baskets and 'green' camouflage for bins. No steps from pavement to garden. Cobbled path allows wheelchair access to full length of garden.

16 THE ECHIUM GARDEN

Walled Garden, Thoresby Park, Nr Ollerton, Newark, NG22 9EP. Linda & Ray Heywood, www.echiumworld.co.uk. *From Nottingham: A614 at Ollerton r'about take turn to A1 in 2m turn L at Thoresby r'about along the County Rd for 1m turn L for Thoresby Courtyard (just before Thoresby Hall Hotel entrance).* **Sat 1 June (12-4). Adm £5, chd free.**

A short walk to The Echium Garden that occupies a corner of the partially restored five acre walled kitchen garden at Thoresby Park dating from 1700s. Featuring the National Plant Collection of Echium incl the Giant Tree Echium growing to over 14ft, endemic to the Canary Islands. The garden designed in 2018 features herbaceous borders with some unusual & heritage plants grown in Victorian times. Uneven surfaces & gravel paths.

NPC

17 ◆ FELLEY PRIORY

Underwood, NG16 5FJ. Ms Michelle Upchurch for the Brudenell Family, 01773 810230, michelle@felleypriory.co.uk, www.felleypriory.co.uk. *8m SW of Mansfield. Off A608 ½m W M1 J27.* **For NGS: Sun 21 Apr (10-4). Adm £6, chd free. Light refreshments.** For other opening times and information, please phone, email or visit garden website.

Garden for all seasons with yew hedges and topiary, snowdrops, hellebores, herbaceous borders and rose garden. There are pergolas, a white garden, small arboretum and borders filled with unusual trees, shrubs, plants and bulbs. The grass edged pond is planted with primulas, bamboo, iris, roses and eucomis. Bluebell woodland walk. Orchard with extremely rare daffodils.

18 NEW FLINTHAM HALL

Flintham, Newark, Nottinghamshire, NG23 5LE. Sir Robert and Lady Hildyard. *5m SW of Newark. Flintham is signposted off A46. Follow twisting road past cricket ground and school. At next bend turn R towards church for ample parking.* **Sun 9 June (1-5). Combined adm with Flintham House £7.50, chd free. Home-made teas in the village hall adjacent to the gardens.** Donation to St. Augustine's Church, Flintham.

18c walled gardens with rose borders and espaliered fruit trees. Range of trees and shrubs with a profusion of shrub and rambling roses. Views of Grade I listed house impressively remodelled in 1850s by TC Hine in the Italianate style with an adjoining conservatory said to be the finest of its type in England. Balustraded terrace with views across park and lake. A place of true romance.

19 FLINTHAM HOUSE

Main Street, Flintham, Newark, NG23 5LA. Mr & Mrs Digby Burley. *5m S of Newark on A46. Flintham E junction off A46 past cricket club down Inholmes Rd to Main St. Please park carefully in village.* **Sun 9 June (1-5). Combined adm with Flintham Hall £7.50, chd free. Home-made teas in the village hall.** Donation to Village Hall/School/St Augustine's Church.

Our family home for 50+yrs. Come, enjoy peace within a walled garden of formal area, apple orchard, herb garden and seated arbour for quiet moments. Views across the Vale of Belvoir - unusual rockery built from volcanic rock brought to England by a former resident - a merchant seaman. Flintham has many listed buildings within the largest conservation area in Rushcliffe. Some gravel in yard area.

GROUP OPENING

20 HALAM GARDENS AND WILDFLOWER MEADOW

Nr Southwell, NG22 8AX. *Village gardens within walking distance of one another. Hill's Farm wildflower meadow is a short drive of ½m towards Edingley village, turn R at brow of hill as signed.* **Mon 27 May (1-5). Combined adm £5.50, chd free. Home-made teas at The Old Vicarage, Halam.**

HILL FARM HOUSE
Victoria Starkey.

HILL'S FARM
John & Margaret Hill.

THE OLD VICARAGE
Mrs Beverley Perks.
(See separate entry)

Lovely mix of a very popular beautiful, well-known, organic, rural plant lovers' garden with bounteous roses, clematis, campanula and lots else with sweeping lawns, lots of pond life; a small wrap-around village cottage garden and a 6 acre wildflower meadow - part of an organic farm - visitors can be assured of an inspiring discussion with the farmer; passionate about the benefits of this method of farming for our environment. 12th Century Church open - surrounded by freely planted, attractive churchyard - all welcome to enjoy this peaceful haven in English rural village setting.

21 5A HIGH STREET

Sutton-on-Trent, Newark, NG23 6QA. Kathryn & Ian Saunders, kathrynsaunders.optom@gmail.com. *6m N of Newark. Leave A1 at Sutton on Trent, follow Sutton signs. L at Xrds. 1st R turn (approx 1m) onto Main Street. 2nd L onto High Street. Garden 50 yds on R. Park on road.* **Sun 28 July (1-5). Combined adm with Norwood £5, chd free. Light refreshments.** Visits also by arrangement June to Aug for groups of 10+. Refreshments incl in admission.

This hidden plot started as a field 30 years ago. Trees form a frame for this plantsman's garden. Ponds run through the area which ranges from tropical to naturalistic. 600 named plants incl over 100 types of fern in the woodland areas. Herbaceous borders add a riot of colour. Ornamental grass borders and succulents add further interest. All shown off to great effect by well manicured lawns.

22 HOLMES VILLA

Holmes Lane, Walkeringham, Gainsborough, DN10 4JP. Peter & Sheila Clark, 01427 890233,

clarkshaulage@aol.com. *4m NW of Gainsborough. A620 from Retford or A631 from Bawtry/Gainsborough & A161 to Walkeringham then towards Misterton. Follow NGS signs for 1m. Plenty of parking. Reserved disabled parking.* **Sun 24 Feb (12-4). Light refreshments. Mon 27 May (12-4). Home-made teas. Adm £2.50, chd free. Feb opening offers hot food.** Visits also by arrangement May to July. Coach parking at garden.
1¾ acre plantsman's garden offering yr-round interest and inspiration starting with carpets of snowdrops, mini daffodils, hellebores and spring bulbs. Unusual collection of plants and shrubs for winter. Come and be surprised at the different fragrant and interesting plants in early spring. Places to sit and ponder, gazebos, arbours, wildlife pond, hosta garden, old tools on display and scarecrows. A flower arranger's artistic garden. February opening has home made soup and hot sausage rolls. Special parking for those requiring wheelchair access in yard.

23 HOME FARM HOUSE, 17 MAIN STREET

Keyworth, Nottingham, NG12 5AA. Graham & Pippa Tinsley, 01159 377122, Graham_Tinsley@yahoo.co.uk, www.homefarmgarden.wordpress.com. *7m S of Nottingham. Follow signs for Keyworth from A60 or A606 & head for church. Garden about 50yds down Main St. Parking on the street or at village hall or Bunny Lane car parks.* **Visits by arrangement May to July for groups of up to 30. Adm £4, chd free. Tea.**
A large garden hidden behind old farmhouse in the village centre with views over open fields. Many trees incl cedars, limes, oaks and chestnuts which, with high beech and yew hedges, create hidden places to be explored. Old orchard, ponds, turf mound, rose garden, winter garden and old garden with herbaceous borders. Pergolas with wisteria, ornamental vine and roses. Access via gravel yard. Some steps and slopes.

24 HOPBINE FARMHOUSE, OSSINGTON

Hopbine Farmhouse, Main Street, Ossington, NG23 6LJ. Mr & Mrs Geldart. *From A1 N take exit marked Carlton, Sutton-on-Trent, Weston etc. At T-Junction turn L to Kneesall. Drive 2m to Ossington. In village turn R to Moorhouse & park in field.* **Sun 23 June (2-5). Combined adm with Ossington House £4, chd free. Home-made teas at The Hut, Ossington.**
A small garden in two parts, the south garden has a long herbaceous border with spring, summer and autumn planting, with clematis, roses and honeysuckle climbing a brick wall. The intimate walled north garden has a full rose bed under planted with cranesbill. One wall is covered with white roses, clematis and hydrangea. There are shrubs and herbaceous plants incl many astrantias and hostas. Some narrow paths.

25 6 HOPE STREET

Beeston, Nottingham, NG9 1DR. Elaine Liquorish. *From M1 J25, A52 for Nottm. After 2 r'abouts, turn R for Beeston at The Nurseryman (B6006). Beyond hill, turn R into Bramcote Dr. 3rd turn on L into Bramcote Rd, then immediately R into Hope St.* **Sun 19 May (1.30-5.30). Adm £3, chd free. Cream teas.**
A small garden packed with a wide variety of plants providing flower and foliage colour year round. Collections of alpines, bulbs, mini, small and medium size hostas, ferns, grasses, carnivorous plants, succulents, perennials, shrubs and trees. A pond and a greenhouse with subtropical plants. Troughs and pots. Home made crafts. There is a small step down into the front part of the garden and a step up into the greenhouse.

26 NEW HUNTERS MOON

Gonalston Lane, Hoveringham, Nottingham, NG14 7JH. David & Lorraine Hook. *Opp the church hall in the centre of the village - parking in the village.* **Sun 19 May (1-5). Combined adm with Church House £4.50, chd free. Home-made teas at Hoveringham Village Hall opp Hunters Moon. served by Hoveringham WI.**
A newly designed rear garden which is still a work in progress. Birch woodland area with contemporary under planting. Parterre featuring a combination of alliums, roses and edged with pleached photinia. Vegetable area with greenhouse. Mature front garden with feature Monkey Puzzle tree. Gravel driveway and steps.

27 IVY BANK COTTAGE

The Green, South Clifton, Newark, NG23 7AG. David & Ruth Hollands. *12m N of Newark. From S, exit A46 N of Newark onto A1133 towards Gainsborough. From N, exit A57 at Newton-on-Trent onto A1133 towards Newark.* **Sun 19 May (1-5). Adm £3, chd free. Home-made teas.**
A traditional cottage garden, with herbaceous borders, fruit trees incl a Nottinghamshire Medlar, vegetable plots and many surprises incl a stumpery, a troughery, dinosaur footprints and even fairies! Many original features: pigsties, double privy and a wash house. Children can search for animal models and explore inside the shepherd's van. Seats around and a covered refreshment area.

28 LODGE MOUNT

Town Street, South Leverton, Retford, DN22 0BT. Mr A Wootton-Jones, 07730004646, jane1.windsor@gmail.com. *4m E of Retford. Opp Miles Garage on Town Street.* **Sun 7 July (1-5). Adm £4, chd free. Home-made teas.** Visits also by arrangement May to Sept for groups of 10 to 30.
Lodge Mount Garden is the vision founded and established by Helen just before she died of cancer in 2012. The garden has been open to the public for the past 6 years since her death. Helen's original plans can be seen through the flourishing growth and development of her plants and trees which now grow strong displaying the vibrant colours which she hoped they would. Access is via a long sloping driveway. There is one step into the main garden which is flat.

29 NEW LONG ACRES

Moor Lane, Syerston, Newark, NG23 5NA. Iain and Marie Nicholson. *The garden is situated ½ way between Newark and Bingham off the A46. Exit A46 either N/S follow directions to Syerston and 'Syerston village only'. The house is 1st you come to if you keep L after passing the village church. Parking as directed in field/village.* **Sun 5 May (1-5). Adm £3.50, chd free. Home-made teas in Syerston Village Hall.**

Welcome to our Spring garden of hellebores, narcissi, bluebells, exchordia, clematis and an abundance of beautiful tulips - both old favourites and unusual varieties. Large, mature cottage garden incl atmospheric walled garden, box edged parterre with a cutting garden and vegetable plots. The Norman village church will be open to visitors with floral displays. Paths are grass and stone.

30 38 MAIN STREET

Woodborough, Nottingham, NG14 6EA. Martin Taylor & Deborah Bliss. *Turn off Mapperley Plains Rd at sign for Woodborough. Alternatively, follow signs to Woodborough off A6097 (Epperstone bypass). Property is between Park Av & Bank Hill.* **Sun 19 May (1-5). Adm £3.50, chd free. Home-made teas.**

Varied ⅓ acre. Bamboo fenced Asian species area with traditional outdoor wood fired Ofuro bath, herbaceous border, raised rhododendron bed, vegetables, greenhouse, pond area and art studio and terrace.

GROUP OPENING

31 NORWELL GARDENS

Newark, NG23 6JX. *6m N of Newark. Halfway between Newark & Southwell. Off A1 at Cromwell turning, take Norwell Rd at bus shelter. Or off A616 take Caunton turn.* **Sun 30 June (1-5). Evening opening Wed 3 July (6.30-9). Combined adm £5, chd free. Home-made teas in Village Hall (30 June) and Norwell Nurseries (3 July).**

NEW BRICKYARD COTTAGE
Bernadette McBreen.

FAUNA FOLLIES
Mr Roy Pilgrim.

JUXTA MILL
Janet McFerran.

NORWELL ALLOTMENT / PARISH GARDENS
Norwell Parish Council.

NORWELL NURSERIES
Andrew & Helen Ward.
(See separate entry)

THE OLD MILL HOUSE, NORWELL
Mr & Mrs M Burgess.

SOUTHVIEW COTTAGE
Margaret & Les Corbett.

WILLOUGHBY HOUSE
Mrs Suzannah Edward-Jones, 01636 636266, willoughbyhousebandb@gmail.com.

This is the 23rd yr that Norwell has opened a range of different, very appealing gardens all making superb use of the beautiful backdrop of a quintessentially English countryside village. It incl a garden and nursery of national renown and the rare opportunity to walk around vibrant allotments with a wealth of gardeners from seasoned competition growers to plots that are substitute house gardens, bursting with both flower colour and vegetables in great variety. To top it all there are a plethora of breathtaking village gardens showing the diversity that is achieved under the umbrella of a cottage garden description! The beautiful medieval church and its peaceful churchyard with grass labyrinth will be open for quiet contemplation.

32 ◆ NORWELL NURSERIES

Woodhouse Road, Norwell, NG23 6JX. Andrew & Helen Ward, 01636 636337, wardha@aol.com, www.norwellnurseries.co.uk. *6m N of Newark halfway between Newark & Southwell. Off A1 at Cromwell turning, take rd to Norwell at bus stop. Or from A616 take Caunton turn.* **For NGS: Sun 19 May, Sun 29 Sept, Sun 13 Oct (2-5). Adm £3, chd free. Home-made teas in the Pavillion, Norwell Nurseries. Opening with Norwell Gardens on Sun 30 June, Wed 3 July.** For other opening times and information, please phone, email or visit garden website.

Jewel box of over 2,500 different, beautiful and unusual plants sumptuously set out in a one acre plantsman's garden incl shady garden with orchids, woodland gems, cottage garden borders, alpine and scree areas. Pond with opulently planted margins. Extensive herbaceous borders and effervescent colour themed beds. Sand beds showcase Mediterranean, North American and alpine plants. Nationally renowned nursery open with over 1,000 different rare plants for sale. Autumn opening features UK's largest collection of hardy chrysanthemums for sale and the National Collection of Hardy Chrysanthemums. New borders incl the National Collection Of Astrantias. Grass paths, no wheelchair access to woodland paths.

NPC

33 NORWOOD

Carlton Lane, Sutton-On-Trent, Newark, NG23 6PH. Linda & Danny Mellors. *When coming into Sutton on Trent via A1 take the exit signed posted Carlton on Trent come onto Great North Rd, onto Main St., Carlton Ln can be found on the sharp bend. Follow the signs.* **Sun 28 July (1-5). Combined adm with 5a High Street £5, chd free.**

Our quirky oriental themed garden with its tea room and green houses is open to you. Come and walk round the gravel paths and discover a variety of ferns and palms alongside native and non-native plants. Take a peep in the cave and look in the nooks and crannies of the stone built walls where you will find a few surprises.

34 NOTTINGHAMSHIRE HOSPICE

384 Woodborough Road, Nottingham, NG3 4JF. Nottinghamshire Hospice, www.nottshospice.org. *Located*

on the B684, Woodborough Rd, served by the bus route no. 45, Sky Blue Line, from the city centre towards Mapperley. No public parking allowed onsite, plenty of on-street parking. **Sun 4 Aug (1-4). Adm £3, chd free. Light refreshments.**
Large enclosed area, with various protected trees, shrubs, planting, rockeries and lawn. Within our garden there is a beautiful pond and water feature. There are raised vegetable beds, and a terraced area. Some sloping areas, with steps. The garden is designed to be a relaxing space and give therapeutic benefit to hospice patients. You are very welcome to bring your own picnic to enjoy.

35 OAK BARN EXOTIC GARDEN

Oak Barn Church Street, East Markham, Newark, NG22 0SA. Simon Bennett & Laura Holmes, www.facebook.com/OakBarn1. *From A1 Markham Moor junction take A57 to Lincoln. Turn R at Xrds into E Markham. L onto High St & R onto Plantation Rd. Enter farm gates at T-Junction, garden located on L.* **Sun 1 Sept (1-5). Adm £3, chd free. Home-made teas. Opening with East Markham Gardens on Sun 30 June.**
On entering the Oak Lych style gate you will be met with the unexpected dense canopy of greenery and tropical foliage. The gravel paths wind under towering palms and bananas which are underplanted with cannas and gingers. On the lowest levels houseplants are bedded out from the large greenhouse to join the summer displays. They surround the Jungle Hut which is used for dining and socialising. Private visits and plant sales by arrangement.

36 THE OLD VICARAGE

Halam Hill, Halam, NG22 8AX. Mrs Beverley Perks, 01636 812181, perks.family@talk21.com. *1m W of Southwell. Please park diagonally into beech hedge on verge with speed interactive sign or in village - a busy road so no parking on roadside.* **Mon 6 May (12-4); Sat 22 June (12-4.30); Sun 11 Aug (1-5). Adm £4, chd free. Home-made teas. Opening with Halam Gardens and Wildflower Meadow on Mon 27 May.** Visits also by arrangement May to Aug for groups of 20+.
Celebrating 22yrs since arrival and major planting transformation. Single handed labour of love has grown out of hillside pony paddocks into much admired landscape gardens. One-time playground for children, a source of shared pleasure for village openings and 17yrs for NGS. An artful eye for design/texture/colour and love of unusual plants/trees makes this a gem to visit. Beautiful C12 Church open only a short walk into the village or across field through attractively planted churchyard - rare C14 stained glass window. Gravel drive - undulating levels as on a hillside - plenty of cheerful help available.

37 OSSINGTON HOUSE

Moorhouse Road, Ossington, Newark, NG23 6LD. Georgina Denison. *10m N of Newark, 2m off A1. From A1 N take exit marked Carlton, Sutton-on-Trent, Weston etc. At T-junction turn L to Kneesall. Drive 2m to Ossington. In village turn R to Moorhouse & park in field next to Hopbine Farmhouse.* **Sun 23 June (2-5). Combined adm with Hopbine Farmhouse, Ossington £4, chd free. Home-made teas in The Hut, Ossington.**
Vicarage garden redesigned in 1960 and again in 2014. Chestnuts, lawns, formal beds, woodland walk, poolside planting, orchard. Terraces, yews, grasses. Ferns, herbaceous perennials, roses. Disabled parking available in drive to Ossington House.

38 PAPPLEWICK HALL

Hall Lane, Papplewick, Nottinghamshire, NG15 8FE. Mr & Mrs J R Godwin-Austen, www.papplewickhall.co.uk. *7m N of Nottingham. 300yds out N end of Papplewick village, on B683 (follow signs to Papplewick from A60 & B6011). Free parking at Hall.* **Sun 26 May (2-5). Adm £4, chd free.** Donation to St James' Church.
This historic, mature, 8 acre garden, mostly shaded woodland, abounds with rhododendrons, hostas, ferns, and spring bulbs. Suitable for wheelchair users, but sections of the paths are gravel.

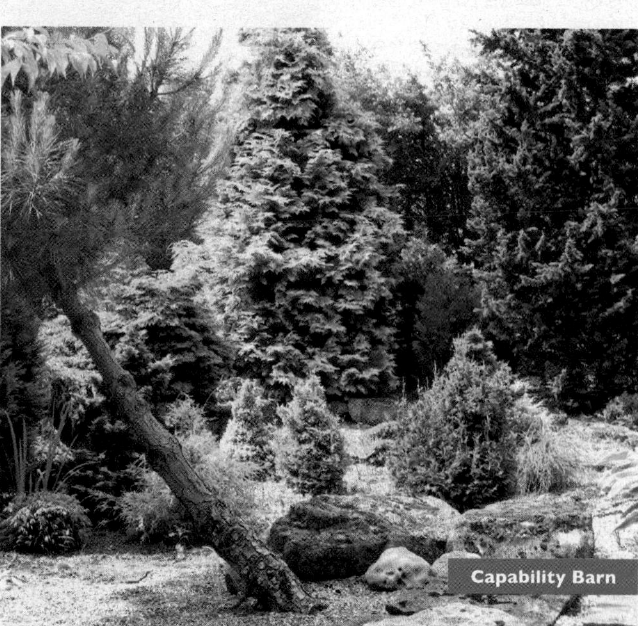
Capability Barn

39 PARK FARM

Crink Lane, Southwell, NG25 0TJ. Ian & Vanessa Johnston, 01636 812195, v.johnston100@gmail.com. *1m SE of Southwell. From Southwell town centre go down Church St, turn R on Fiskerton Rd & 200yds up hill turn R into Crink Lane. Park Farm is on 2nd bend.* **Sun 16 June (2-5.30). Adm £4, chd free. Home-made teas.** Visits also by arrangement Apr to Aug for groups of 10+. Guided tours offered for groups of 10 or more, additional 50p per person.

3 acre garden remarkable for its extensive variety of trees, shrubs and perennials, many rare or unusual. Long colourful herbaceous borders, roses, woodland garden, alpine/scree garden and a large wildlife pond. Spectacular views of the Minster across a wildflower meadow and ha-ha.

40 PATCHINGS ART CENTRE

Oxton Road, Calverton, Nottingham, NG14 6NU. Chas & Pat Wood, www.patchingsartcentre.co.uk. *N of Nottingham city take A614 towards Ollerton. Turn R on to B6386 towards Calverton and Oxton. Patchings is on L before turning to Calverton. Brown tourist directional signs.* **Sun 26 May (10.30-3.30). Adm £3, chd free. Light refreshments at Patchings Cafe.**

Patchings Art Centre celebrated 30 years last year, when we opened new areas and walks in celebration. 50 acres to incl wild flowers, woodland and meadow landscapes. The aim is to inspire and encourage artists to paint in the open, whilst providing enjoyment and tranquillity for visitors. The day also incls a variety of free art and craft activities for all ages. Four exhibition galleries featuring paintings, photography, jewellery, ceramics and glass. Card gallery, gift shop and art materials. Studio artists in residence. Patchings Cafe. In the Pavilion free 'have a go' opportunity, being creative with a variety of painting and craft materials. Grass paths, with some undulations and uphill sections accessible to wheelchairs with help. Please enquire for assistance.

38 Main Street

41 PIECEMEAL

123 Main Street, Sutton Bonington, Loughborough, LE12 5PE. Mary Thomas, 01509 672056, nursery@piecemealplants.co.uk. *2m SE of Kegworth (M1 J24). 6m NW of Loughborough. Almost opp St Michael's Church & Sutton Bonington Hall at the N end of the village.* **Sun 18 Aug (12-5). Adm £3, chd free. Tea. Visits by arrangement June to Aug for groups; min 4, max 10. For 10+ please contact to discuss. Adm £3, chd free. Tea.**
Pots of (mainly terracotta) pots - around 400 in total! All in a tiny, sheltered walled garden and featuring a wide range of shrubs, some flowering, many unusual. Also climbers, perennials and even a few trees! Focus is on distinctive form, foliage shape and colour combination. Collection of ferns around well. Conservatory more for plants than seating!

42 THE POPLARS

60 High Street, Sutton-on-Trent, Newark, NG23 6QA. Sue & Graham Goodwin-King. *7m N of Newark. Leave A1 at Sutton/Carlton/Normanton-on-Trent junction. In Carlton turn L onto B1164. Turn R into Hemplands Ln then R into High St. 1st house on R. Limited parking.* **Sun 9 June (1-5). Adm £3.50, chd free. Home-made teas.**
Mature ½ acre garden on the site of a Victorian flower nursery, now a series of well planted areas each with its own character. Exotics courtyard with late summer colour. Iron balcony overlooking pond and oriental style gravel garden. 'Jungle' with thatched shack. Black and white garden. Woodland area. Walled potager. Fernery and hidden courtyard. Lawns, borders and charming sitting places. Some gravel paths and shallow steps, but most areas accessible.

43 PRIMROSE COTTAGE

Bar Road North, Beckingham, Doncaster, DN10 4NN. Terry & Brenda Wilson. *8m N of Retford. A631 to Beckingham r'about, enter village, L to village green, L to Bar Rd.* **Sun 9 June (2-5). Adm £3, chd free. Home-made teas in Recreation Room - Village Green.**
Old fashioned cottage garden. Walled herbaceous border, well stocked shrubbery, many old roses, kitchen garden, summerhouse and greenhouse. Secret fernery and courtyard, herb garden. Central dome over water feature supporting varied clematis.

44 RHUBARB FARM

Hardwick Street, Langwith, Mansfield, NG20 9DR. Community Interest Company, www.rhubarbfarm.co.uk. *On NW border of Nottinghamshire in village of Nether Langwith. From A632 in Langwith, by bridge (single file traffic) turn up steep Devonshire Drive. N.B. Turn off SatNav. Take 2nd L into Hardwick St. Rhubarb Farm at end. Parking to R of gates.* **Wed 3 July (10.30-4). Adm £2.50, chd free. Home-made teas made by Rhubarb Farm volunteers available in our on-site cafe.**
52 varieties of fruit and vegetables organically grown not only for sale but for therapeutic benefit. This 2 acre social enterprise provides training and volunteering opportunities to 90 ex offenders, drug and alcohol misusers, and people with mental and physical ill health and learning disability. Timed tours at 11.00am, 2.00pm. 3x 65ft polytunnels, outdoor classroom, willow domes and willow arches, 100 hens, sensory garden, outdoor pizza ovens, comfrey bed and comfrey fertiliser factory, composting toilet. Chance to meet and chat with volunteers with a variety of needs, who come to gain skills, confidence and training. Main path down site suitable for wheelchairs but bumpy. Not all of site accessible. Cafe and composting toilet wheelchair accessible.

Your visits help change lives – we've donated over £16.7 million to Macmillan Cancer Support since 1984

45 RISEHOLME, 125 SHELFORD ROAD

Radcliffe on Trent, NG12 1AZ. John & Elaine Walker, 01159 119867. *4m E of Nottingham. From A52 follow signs to Radcliffe. In village centre take turning for Shelford (by Co-op). Approx ¾m on L.* **Sun 23 June (1.30-5). Adm £3.50, chd free. Home-made teas. Visits also by arrangement June to Sept for groups of 10+.**
Imaginative and inspirational is how the garden has been described by visitors. A huge variety of perennials, grasses, shrubs and trees combined with an eye for colour and design. Jungle area with exotic lush planting contrasts with tender perennials particularly salvias thriving in raised beds and in gravel garden with stream. Unique and interesting objects complement planting. Gravel drive and paths.

46 ROSE COTTAGE

81 Nottingham Road, Keyworth, Nottingham, NG12 5GS. Richard & Julie Fowkes, rosecottagedesign@yahoo.co.uk. *7m S of Nottingham. Follow signs for Keyworth from A606. Garden (white cottage) on R 100yds after Sainsburys. From A60, follow Keyworth signs & turn L at church, garden is 400yds on L.* **Sun 19 May, Sun 30 June (12-5). Adm £3.50, chd free. Home-made teas. Visits also by arrangement May to Aug for groups of 10 to 30.**
Small cottage garden (300sqm) informally designed and packed full with butterfly and bee friendly plants. Sedum roof, mosaics and water features add unique interest. There is a decked seating area and summerhouse. A wildlife stream meanders down between two ponds and bog gardens. Some narrow paths and steps. A woodland area leads to the fruit, veg and a herb spiral. Art studio will be open. Paintings and art cards designed by Julie will be on sale.

47 SPRING BANK HOUSE

84 Kirkby Road, Sutton-in-Ashfield, NG17 1GH. Mr Peter Robinson. *From Mansfield take A38 to Sutton-in-Ashfield. Turn R on to Station Rd, turn L on to High Pavement and continue on to Kirkby Rd.* **Sun 16 June, Sun 1 Sept (12-5). Combined adm with East Meets West £4, chd free. Home-made teas.**

Mediterranean planting, a bog garden, a summerhouse and a white garden, a water table from India and lion statues from Nepal, this garden offers much variety. Dug from wasteland in 2012 its clear design displays hundreds of rare plants. Two terraces punctuate its slope and a woodland area with hardy exotics and a wildlife pond offer cobbled paths and mown grass for a choice of garden circuits. Coaches may be possible but will need to park elsewhere.

48 THRUMPTON HALL

Thrumpton, NG11 0AX. Miranda Seymour, www.thrumptonhall.com. *7m S of Nottingham. M1 J24 take A453 towards Nottingham. Turn L to Thrumpton village & cont to Thrumpton Hall.* **Sun 30 June (1.30-4.30). Adm £5, chd free. Home-made teas.**

2 acres incl. lawns, rare trees, lakeside walks, flower borders, rose garden, new pagoda, and box-bordered sunken herb garden, all enclosed by C18 ha-ha and encircling a Jacobean house. Garden is surrounded by C18 landscaped park and is bordered by a river. Rare opportunity to visit Thrumpton Hall (separate ticket). Jacobean mansion, unique carved staircase, Great Saloon, State Bedroom, Priest's Hole.

49 UNIVERSITY PARK GARDENS

Nottingham, NG7 2RD. University of Nottingham, www.nottingham.ac.uk/estates/grounds/. *Approx 4m SW of Nottingham city centre & opp Queens Medical Centre. NGS visitors: Please purchase admission tickets in the Millennium Garden (in centre of campus), signed from N & W entrances to University Park & within internal road network.* **Sun 19 May (12-4). Adm £4, chd free. Light refreshments at Lakeside Arts Centre and The Hemsley.**

University Park has many beautiful gardens incl the award winning Millennium garden with its dazzling flower garden, timed fountains and turf maze. Also the huge Lenton Firs rock garden, the dry garden and the Jekyll garden. During summer, the walled garden is alive with exotic plantings. In total, 300 acres of landscape and gardens. Picnic area, cafe, walking tours, information desk, workshop, accessible minibus to feature gardens within campus. Plants for sale in Millennium garden. Some gravel paths and steep slopes.

50 NEW UPPER GROVE FARM

Norwell Woodhouse, Newark, NG23 6NG. Kathryn Wiltshire. *A616 either from Newark (10m) or Ollerton (7m) at Xroads turn to Laxton R to Norwell 1st white farmhouse on R, look out for the big chimney pots!* **Sun 10 Mar (12-3). Adm £3, chd free. Light refreshments.**

We are a country garden around a farmhouse. It is a spring garden with colour from the daffodils. Hot soup, tea and homemade cake in the barn or courtyard if fine. Bring sturdy footwear to walk down to a small wood. Most of garden accessible to wheelchairs, some gravel paths.

GROUP OPENING

51 WELLOW VILLAGE GARDENS

Potter Lane, Wellow, Newark, NG22 0EB. *12m NW of Newark. Wellow is on A616 between Ollerton & Newark approx 1m from Ollerton. Parking available around village green & as indicated by car park signs.* **Sun 7 July (10-5). Combined adm £5, chd free. Home-made teas in Wellow Memorial Hall.** Donation to Wellow Memorial Hall.

Norwood Cottage, East Markham Gardens

MAYFIELD
Leslie & Brenda Acutt.

4 POTTER LANE
Anne & Fred Allsop.

TITHE BARN
Andrew & Carrie Young.

Wellow, formerly Wellah, from the number of wells, has a green and a famous maypole. Not so well known is the Wellow Dyke, which surrounds the village and can still be seen in some places. Now come and see some Wellow gardens: Mayfield. This eclectic garden is both family and wildlife friendly. The wide variety of plants is a smorgasbord of pollen for insects and bees. 4 Potter Lane: Created over more than 20 yrs, this series of gardens has a section of the Wellow Dyke at the top and has a well tended vegetable garden. Shade garden at side and colourful pleasure garden in centre. Tithe Barn: The approach to this garden between yew hedges sets the tone to the wide sweeps of lawn and generous terrace. Herbaceous beds, roses and rambling roses. Mature planting of shrubs and weeping trees.

52 6 WESTON CLOSE

Woodthorpe, Nottingham, NG5 4FS. Diane & Steve Harrington, 0115 9857506, mrsdiharrington@gmail.com. *3m N of Nottingham. A60 Mansfield Rd. Turn R at T-lights into Woodthorpe Drive. 2nd L Grange Road. R into The Crescent. R into Weston Close. Please park on The Crescent.* **Sun 7 July (1-5). Adm £3, chd free. Home-made teas. incl gluten free cakes.** Visits also by arrangement June to Aug for groups of 10 to 30. Note minimum group charge £60.
Set on a substantial slope with 3 separate areas, dense planting creates a full, varied yet relaxed display incl many scented roses, clematis and a collection of over 80 named mature hostas in the impressive colourful rear garden. Large plant sale packed with good value home propagated plants. Occasional craft stalls.

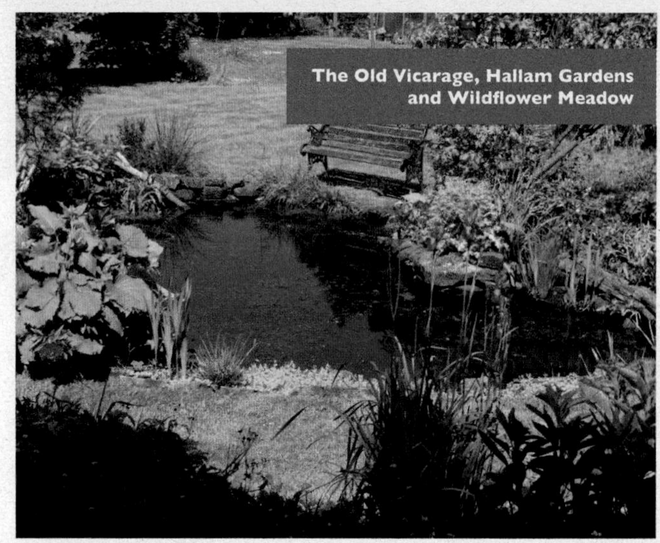

The Old Vicarage, Hallam Gardens and Wildflower Meadow

GROUP OPENING

53 NEW WHITWELL OPEN GARDENS

High Street, Whitwell, Worksop, S80 4QZ. Wendy Birch. *Whitwell is off A619 Barlborough to Worksop. It is 4m from M1 J30 at Barlborough or A57 Worksop. Parking is opp the Co Op, postcode is S80 4QR. There is street parking around the village.* **Sun 23 June (2-5). Combined adm £5, chd free.**

NEW **GREENWELL COTTAGE**
Ruth & Jack Denston.

NEW **4 MANOR FARM COURT**
Kate & John Taylor.

NEW **5 MANOR FARM COURT**
Denise Watts.

NEW **ORCHARD BUNGALOW**
Wendy Birch.

NEW **RED WALLS**
Harry & Nannette Brown.

NEW **15 SCOTLAND STREET**
Iris Walker.

NEW **17 SOUTH VIEW**
Sue Marks.

NEW **THE STABLES**
Victoria & Neil Truman.

Whitwell is close to the famous Creswell Crags. There is variety of front and large gardens. Orchard Bungalow: There are perennials, shrubs and lawns, a pond that is wildlife friendly, a veg and herb garden and fruit trees. Greenwell Cottage: The yard has been lovingly tended and is full of surprises. Begonias, shrubs and potted plants. Red Walls: A mature garden, herbaceous borders and a 100-year-old Wisteria. 4 Manor Farm Court: The front garden has pots and shrubs, hanging baskets and a water feature a great small space. The Stables: A family front garden with a mix of shrubs and perennials, roses and pots and colour. 5 Manor Farm Court: This cottage garden has an eclectic mix of perennials and shrubs. It is full of little surprises. Scotland Street: A small front garden that is bee and insect friendly with grape vines and poppies in the walls. Southfield View: Magnolias, Japanese Acers and a Tree Fern. Small shrubs and bedding plants, wall baskets and water features.

OXFORDSHIRE

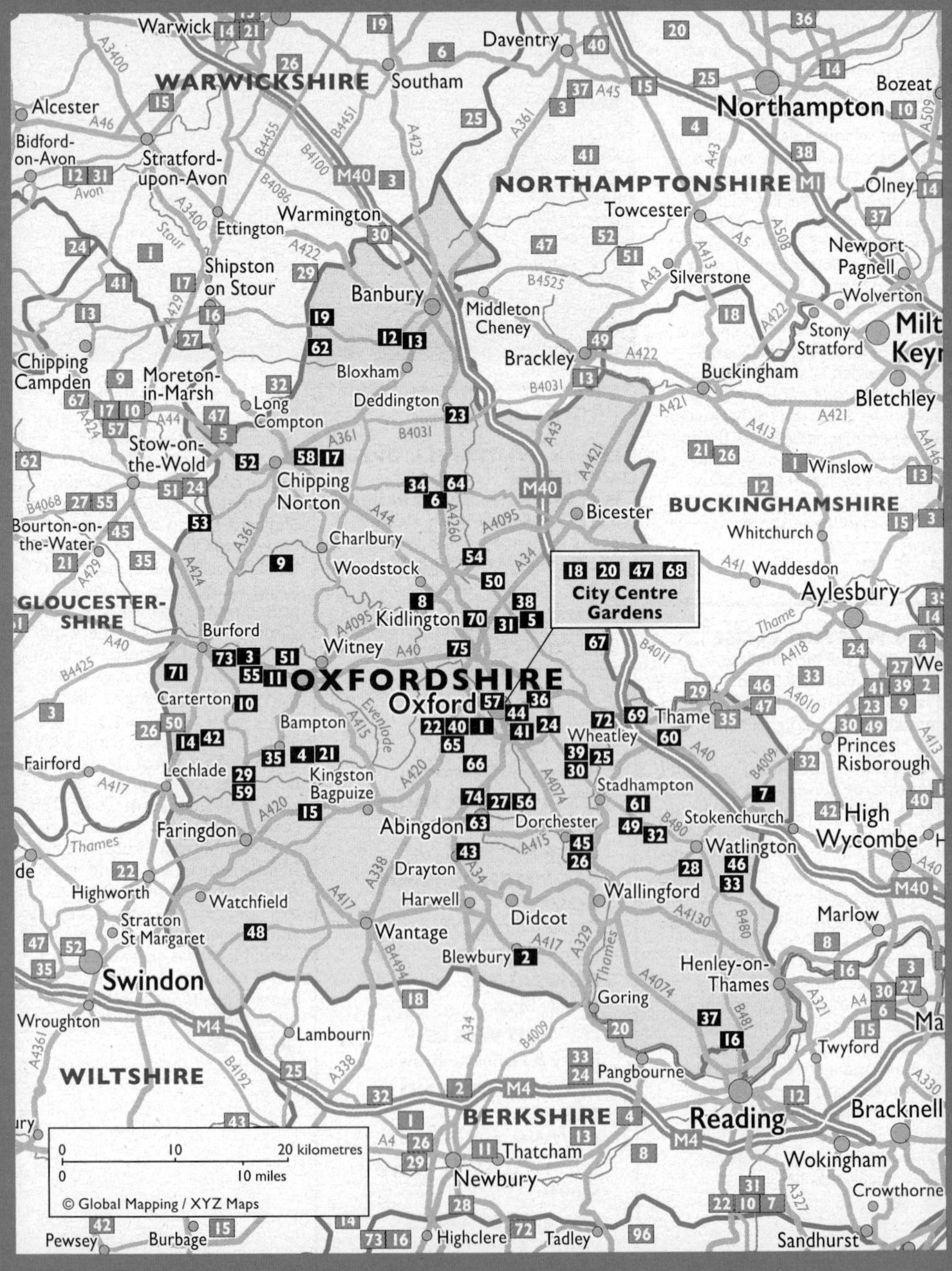

In Oxfordshire we tend to think of ourselves as one of the most landlocked counties, right in the centre of England and furthest from the sea.

We are surrounded by Warwickshire, Northamptonshire, Buckinghamshire, Berkshire, Wiltshire and Gloucestershire, and, like these counties, we benefit from that perfect British climate which helps us create some of the most beautiful and famous gardens in the world.

Many gardens open in Oxfordshire for the National Garden Scheme between spring and late-autumn. Amongst these are the perfectly groomed college gardens of Oxford University, and the grounds of stately homes and palaces designed by a variety of the famous garden designers such as William Kent, Capability Brown, Rosemary Verey, Tom Stuart-Smith and the Bannermans of more recent fame.

But we are also a popular tourist destination for our honey-coloured mellow Cotswold stone villages, and for the Thames which has its spring near Lechlade. More villages open as 'groups' for the National Garden Scheme in Oxfordshire than in any other county, and offer tea, hospitality, advice and delight with their infinite variety of gardens.

All this enjoyment benefits the excellent causes that the National Garden Scheme supports.

Volunteers

County Organiser
Marina Hamilton-Baillie
01367 710486
marina_hamilton_baillie@hotmail. com

County Treasurer
David White
01295 812679
davidwhite679@btinternet.com

Publicity
Priscilla Frost
01608 810578
info@oxconf.co.uk

Social Media
Lara Cowan
lara.cowan@ngs.org.uk

Petra Hoyer Millar
petra.hoyermillar@ngs.org.uk

Photographer
Alexandra Davies
07833 461120
hello@alexandrajdavies.co.uk

Booklet Co-ordinator
Petra Hoyer Millar
(as above)

Assistant County Organisers
Lynn Baldwin
01608 642754
elynnbaldwin@gmail.com

Lara Cowan
(as above)

Petra Hoyer Millar
(as above)

John & Joan Pumfrey
01189 722848
joanpumfrey@lineone.net

Lyn Sanders
01865 739486
sandersc4@hotmail.com

Left: **Bolters Farm**

OPENING DATES

All entries subject to change. For latest information check **www.ngs.org.uk**

Map locator numbers are shown to the right of each garden name.

February

Snowdrop Festival

Sunday 10th
Stonehaven 65

Sunday 17th
Hollyhocks 38
Monks Head 50

March

Sunday 17th
Asthall Manor 3

Thursday 21st
Yarnton Manor 75

April

Sunday 7th
Ashbrook House 2
Wadham College 68

Sunday 14th
Buckland Lakes 15
Lime Close 43
Magdalen College 44
◆ Waterperry Gardens 69

Sunday 21st
The Old Vicarage, Bledington 53

Monday 22nd
Kencot Gardens 42

Saturday 27th
50 Plantation Road 57

Sunday 28th
◆ Broughton Grange 13
50 Plantation Road 57

May

Thursday 2nd
NEW Garsington Manor 30

Friday 3rd
NEW Garsington Manor 30

Saturday 4th
50 Plantation Road 57

Sunday 5th
Hollyhocks 38
50 Plantation Road 57

Monday 6th
Meadow Cottage 46

Sunday 19th
The Grove 34
Headington Gardens 36
Steeple Aston Gardens 64
Westwell Manor 71

Saturday 25th
Deddington Gardens 23

Sunday 26th
Barton Abbey 6
Old Whitehill Barn 54

Monday 27th
Friars Court 29

Wednesday 29th
NEW The Grange, Islip 32

June

Sunday 2nd
Cumnor Village Gardens 22
Lime Close 43
Wayside 70
Whitehill Farm 73

Saturday 8th
Rivendel 60

Sunday 9th
Brize Norton Gardens 10
Cote Manor House Garden 21
Failford 27
Iffley Gardens 41
Orchard House 55
116 Oxford Road 56
The Priory Garden 58
Rivendel 60

Thursday 13th
Wootton Gardens 74

Sunday 16th
Asthall Manor 3
◆ Broughton Castle 12
Denton House 25
Manor House 45
The Old Vicarage, Bledington 53
Wheatley Gardens 72

Wednesday 19th
Midsummer House 48

Friday 21st
Appleton Dene 1

Sunday 23rd
◆ Broughton Grange 13
Broughton Poggs & Filkins Gardens 14
Chalkhouse Green Farm 16
Sibford Gardens 62

Thursday 27th
Rofford Manor 61

Saturday 29th
◆ Blenheim Palace 8

Sunday 30th
Corpus Christi College 20

July

Sunday 7th
NEW 113 Brize Norton Road 11
Dorchester Gardens 26
Ham Court 35
NEW The Old Bakehouse 51

Sunday 14th
Wadham College 68

Sunday 21st
Merton College Oxford Fellows' Garden 47

Sunday 28th
◆ Broughton Grange 13

August

Sunday 18th
Manor House 45
Radcot House 59

Sunday 25th
Aston Pottery 4

Monday 26th
Aston Pottery 4

September

Sunday 1st
Bolters Farm 9

Saturday 7th
Christ Church Masters', Pocock & Cathedral Gardens 18

Sunday 8th
Ashbrook House 2

Wednesday 11th
Midsummer House 48

Sunday 15th
◆ Broughton Grange 13
◆ Waterperry Gardens 69

October

Sunday 6th
Radcot House 59

February 2020

Sunday 16th
Hollyhocks 38

By Arrangement

Arrange a personalised garden visit with your club, or group of friends, on a date to suit you. See individual garden entries for full details.

Appleton Dene 1
Ashbrook House 2
Bannisters 5
6 Bennetts Yard 7
Bolters Farm 9
Carter's Yard, Sibford Gardens 62
Chivel Farm 17
Church Farm Field 19
103 Dene Road 24
Denton House 25
Failford 27
Foxington 28
The Grange 31
NEW The Grange, Islip 32
Greenfield Farm 33
Hearns House 37
Hollyhocks 38
Home Close 39
86 Hurst Rise Road 40
10 Kennett Road, Headington Gardens 36
Lime Close 43
Manor House 45
The Manor House, Wheatley Gardens 72
Meadow Cottage 46
Midsummer House 48
Mill Barn 49
Monks Head 50

Your visits help change lives – your generosity has supported unpaid carers through donations to Carers Trust totalling over £3.9 million since 1996

THE GARDENS

1 APPLETON DENE

Yarnells Hill, Botley, Oxford, OX2 9BG. Mr & Mrs A Dawson, 07701 000977, annrobe@aol.com. *3m W of Oxford. Take W road out of Oxford, through Botley Rd, pass under A34, turn L into Westminster Way, Yarnells Hill 2nd on R, park at top of hill. Walk 200 metres. Disabled parking at the house.* **Evening opening Fri 21 June (4-8). Adm £4. Home-made teas. Wine. Visits also by arrangement May to Sept for groups of 5 to 30.**

Beautiful secluded garden set in a hidden valley. The ¼ acre garden on a steeply sloping site surrounds a mature tulip tree. There is a skillfully incorporated level lawn area overlooked by deep colour themed borders incl a wide variety of plants for long seasonal interest. There will be a short floral demonstration at 6.30pm. Not suitable for wheelchairs as there is a steep slope and steps.

2 ASHBROOK HOUSE

Blewbury, OX11 9QA. Mr & Mrs S A Barrett, 01235 850810, janembarrett@me.com. *4m SE of Didcot. Turn off A417 in Blewbury into Westbrook St. 1st house on R. Follow yellow signs for parking in Boham's Rd.* **Sun 7 Apr, Sun 8 Sept (2-5.30). Adm £5, chd free. Tea. Visits also by arrangement Mar to Sept for groups of up to 20.**

The garden where Kenneth Grahame read Wind in the Willows to local children and where he took inspiration for his description of the oak doors to Badger's House. Come and see, you may catch a glimpse of Toad and friends in this 3½ acre chalk and water garden, in a beautiful spring line village. In spring the banks are a mass of daffodils and in late summer the borders are full of unusual plants.

3 ASTHALL MANOR

Asthall, Burford, OX18 4HW. Rosanna Pearson, www.onformsculpture.co.uk/asthall-manor. *3m E of Burford. Going from Witney to Burford on A40, turn R at r'about. Coming from Chipping Norton, come through Shipton-under-Wychwood & Swinbrook. The nearest bus stop (a 10 min walk) is on route 233.* **Sun 17 Mar (1.30-5). Sun 16 June (2-6). Home-made teas in the village. Adm £7.50, chd free.**

6 acres of dramatic planting surround this C17 Cotswolds manor house (not open), once home to the Mitford family. The gardens, designed by I & J Bannerman in 1998, offer 'a beguiling mix of traditional and contemporary' as described by the Good Gardens Guide. Exuberant scented borders, sloping box parterres, wild flowers, a gypsy wagon, 2 earth mounds and a hidden lake all contribute to the mix. Partial wheelchair access.

4 ASTON POTTERY

Aston, Bampton, OX18 2BT. Mr Stephen Baughan, www.astonpottery.co.uk. *4m S of Witney. On the B4449 between Bampton & Standlake.* **Sun 25, Mon 26 Aug (12-5). Adm £5, chd free. Home-made teas in the café.**

5 stunning borders flower from June until November, set around Aston Pottery's Gift Shop and Cafe. Featuring a 72 metre hornbeam walk with summerhouse, an 80 metre hot bank with kniphofia, alstroemeria, cannas, salvias, a double dahlia border with over 600 dahlias and a border full of over 5000 annuals.

5 BANNISTERS

Middle Street, Islip, Kidlington, OX5 2SF. Wendy Price, 01865 375418. *2m E of Kidlington & approx 5m N of Oxford. From A34, exit Bletchingdon & Islip. B4027 direction Islip, turn L into Middle St, beside Great Barn.* **Visits by arrangement July & Aug for groups of up to 20. Light refreshments.**

A hidden garden of perennials and grasses, naturalistic planting contrasted with trained fruit trees and shrubs. A contemporary interpretation of an old garden. Gravel paths and some shallow steps.

6 BARTON ABBEY

Steeple Barton, OX25 4QS. Mr & Mrs P Fleming. *8m E of Chipping Norton. On B4030, ½m from junction of A4260 & B4030.* **Sun 26 May (2-5). Adm £5, chd free. Home-made teas.**

15 acre garden with views from house (not open) across sweeping lawns and picturesque lake. Walled garden with colourful herbaceous borders, separated by established yew hedges and espalier fruit, contrasts with more informal woodland garden paths with vistas of specimen trees and meadows. Working glasshouses and fine display of fruit and vegetables.

7 6 BENNETTS YARD

Kingston Blount, Chinnor, OX39 4RQ. Ms Emma Rogers, Emma.kb@outlook.com. *Bennetts Yard is a small cul-de-sac off Brook St in Kingston Blount. Please park in Brook St only.* **Visits by arrangement May to July for groups of 10+. Adm £3, chd free.**

Follow the path down the side of this semi-detached house (not open) and enter a delightful small cottage garden, packed with colour and interest. A new build 14 yrs ago, Emma has transformed it into her oasis, featuring patio area, raised bed, small pond, rockery, lawn and herbaceous border packed with colour. Even a small greenhouse tucked to one side. Dogs on short leads. Wheelchair access to a level site with one shallow step.

8 ◆ BLENHEIM PALACE

Woodstock, OX20 1PX. His Grace the Duke of Marlborough, 01993 810530, operations@blenheimpalace.com, www.blenheimpalace.com. *8m N of Oxford. The S3 bus runs every 30 mins from Oxford train station & Oxford's Gloucester Green bus station to Blenheim. Oxford Bus Company's 500 leaves from Oxford Parkway & stops at Blenheim.* **For NGS: Sat 29 June (10-6). Adm £4, chd £2.** For other opening times and information, please phone, email or visit garden website.

Blenheim Gardens, originally laid out by Henry Wise, incl the formal Water Terraces and Italian Garden by Achille Duchêne, Rose Garden, Arboretum, and Cascade. The Secret Garden offers a stunning garden paradise in all seasons. Blenheim Lake, created by Capability Brown and spanned by Vanburgh's Grand Bridge, is the focal point of over 2,000 acres of landscaped parkland. The Pleasure Gardens complex incl the Herb and Lavender Garden and Butterfly House. Other activities incl the Marlborough Maze, adventure play area, giant chess and draughts. Some gravel paths, terrain can be uneven in places, incl some steep slopes. Dogs allowed in park only.

9 BOLTERS FARM

Chilson, Pudlicote Lane, Chipping Norton, OX7 3HU. Robert & Amanda Cooper, 07778 476517, art@amandacooper.co.uk. *Centre of Chilson village. On arrival in the hamlet of Chilson, heading N, we are the last in an old row of cottages on R with old white gates. Please drive past & park considerately on the L in the lane.* **Sun 1 Sept (2-5). Adm £5, chd free. Home-made tea & gluten free options.** Visits also by arrangement May, June & Sept for groups of 5 to 20. Donation to Hands Up Foundation.

A cherished old cottage garden restored over the last 10 yrs. Tumbly moss covered walls and sloping lawns down to a stream with natural planting and character. Wheelchairs have to negotiate sloping deep gravel and numerous steps.

GROUP OPENING

10 BRIZE NORTON GARDENS

Brize Norton, OX18 3LY. www.bncommunity.org/ngs. *3m SW of Witney. Brize Norton Village, S of A40, between Witney & Burford. Parking at Elderbank Hall & Mason Arms in Burford Rd. Coaches welcome with plenty of parking nearby.* **Sun 9 June (1-6). Combined adm £5, chd free. Home-made teas at Elderbank Village Hall & Grange Farm.**

BARNSTABLE HOUSE
Mr & Mrs P Butcher, www.ourgarden.org.uk.

NEW **THE CHAPEL**
Chris & Jayne Woodward.

CHURCH FARM HOUSE
Philip & Mary Holmes.

CLUMBER
Mr & Mrs S Hawkins.

GRANGE FARM
Mark & Lucy Artus.

MIJESHE
Mr & Mrs M Harper.

MILLSTONE
Bev & Phil Tyrell.

PAINSWICK HOUSE
Mr & Mrs T Gush.

ROOKERY FARM
Ian & Fiona Roberts.

NEW **ROSE COTTAGE**
Brenda & Brian Trott.

95 STATION ROAD
Mr & Mrs P A Timms.

STONE COTTAGE
Mr & Mrs K Humphris.

Doomsday village on the edge of the Cotswold's offering a number of gardens open for your enjoyment. You can see a wide variety of planting incl ornamental trees, herbaceous borders, ornamental grasses and traditional fruit and vegetable gardens. Features incl a Mediterranean style patio, courtyard garden, water features; plus gardens where you can just sit, relax and enjoy the day. Tickets and maps available at Elderbank Village Hall and each garden. Plants will be available for sale at individual gardens. A Flower Festival will take place in the Brize Norton St Britius Church. Partial wheelchair access to some gardens.

11 NEW 113 BRIZE NORTON ROAD

Minster Lovell, Witney, OX29 0SQ. David & Lynn Rogers. *Approx 2½ m W of Witney. On main village road (B4447), ½ m N of A40 Witney Bypass intersection on the R.* **Sun 7 July (2-5). Adm £3, chd free. Home-made teas. Also open The Old Bakehouse.**

Mixed variety garden of over 1 acre including quirky features for added interest. Lawns, meadow grass area, small woodland, native mixed hedging, wildlife pond, fish pond, huge mix of plants and trees with emphasis on yr-round colour. The whole garden has been developed with wildlife in mind.

Your visits help change lives – we are Hospice UK's largest charitable funder donating more than £5 million to support hospices in local communities since 1996

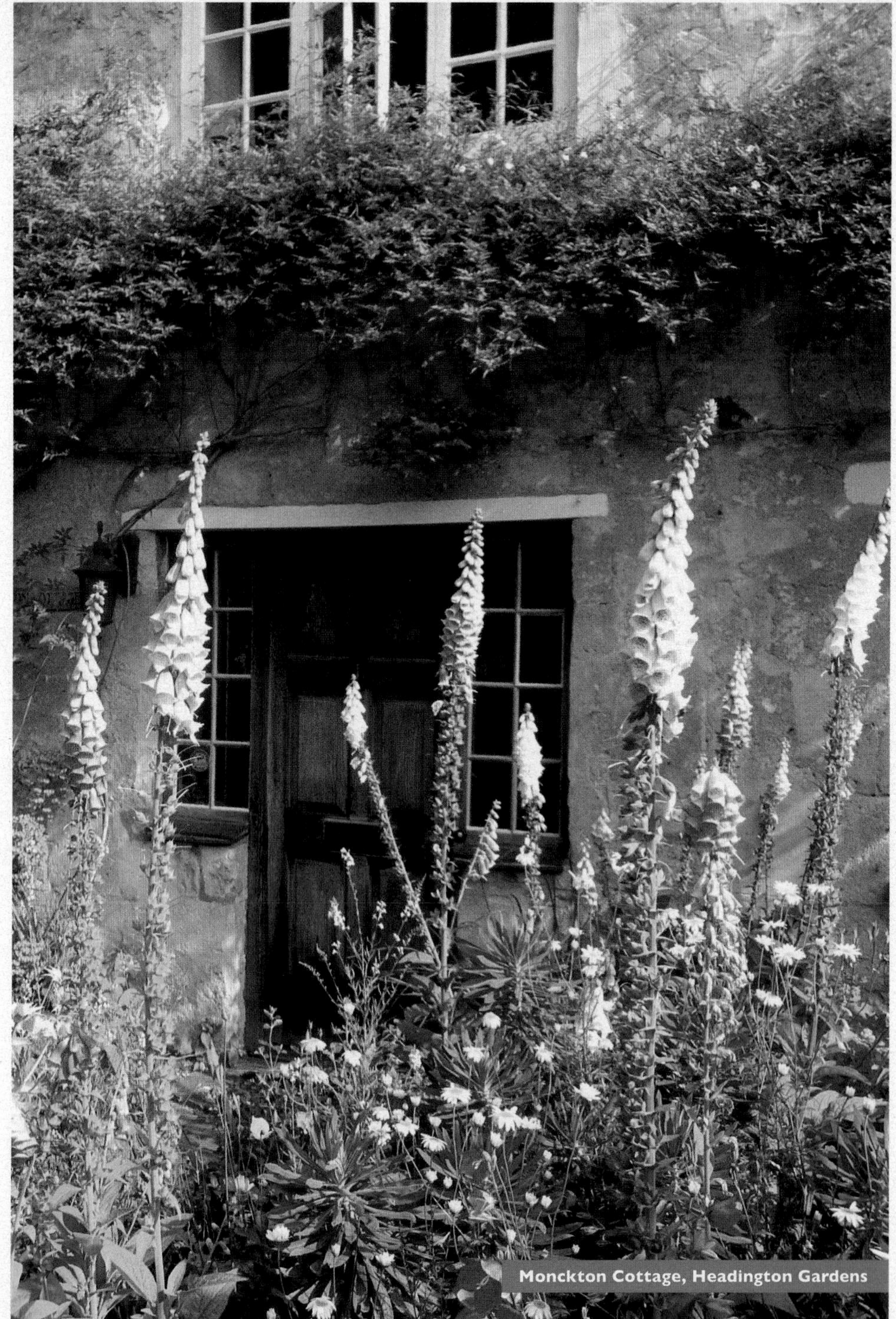

Monckton Cottage, Headington Gardens

12 ◆ BROUGHTON CASTLE

Banbury, OX15 5EB. Martin Fiennes, 01295 276070, info@broughtoncastle.com, www.broughtoncastle.com. *2½ m SW of Banbury. On Shipston-on-Stour road (B4035).* **For NGS: Sun 16 June (2-4.30). Adm £5, chd £5. Home-made teas.** For other opening times and information, please phone, email or visit garden website.

1 acre; shrubs, herbaceous borders, walled garden, roses, climbers seen against background of C14-C16 castle surrounded by moat in open parkland. House also open (additional charge).

13 ◆ BROUGHTON GRANGE

Wykham Lane, Broughton, Banbury, OX15 5DS. S Hester, www.broughtongrange.com. *¼ m out of village. From Banbury take B4035 to Broughton. Turn L at Saye & Sele Arms Pub up Wykham Lane (one way). Follow road out of village for ¼ m. Entrance on R.* **For NGS: Suns 28 Apr; 23 June; 28 July; 15 Sept (10-5). Adm £8, chd free. Light refreshments.** For other opening times and information, please visit garden website.

An impressive 25 acres of gardens and light woodland in an attractive Oxfordshire setting. The centrepiece is a large terraced walled garden created by Tom Stuart-Smith in 2001. Vision has been used to blend the gardens into the countryside. Good early displays of bulbs followed by outstanding herbaceous planting in summer. Formal and informal areas combine to make this a special site incl newly laid arboretum with many ongoing projects. Limited wheelchair and mobility scooter access.

GROUP OPENING

14 BROUGHTON POGGS & FILKINS GARDENS

Lechlade, GL7 3JH. www.filkins.org.uk. *3m N of Lechlade. 5m S of Burford. Just off A361 between Burford & Lechlade on the B4477. Map of the gardens available.* **Sun 23 June (2-6). Combined adm £6, chd free. Home-made teas in Filkins Village Hall.**

ANSTRUTHER
Julian & Caroline Alder.

BROUGHTON POGGS MILL
Charlie & Avril Payne.

THE CORN BARN
Ms Alexis Thompson.

FILKINS ALLOTMENTS
Filkins Allotments.

LITTLE PEACOCKS
Colvin & Moggridge.

PIGEON COTTAGE
Lynne Savege.

PIP COTTAGE
G B Woodin.

THE TALLOT
Ms M Swann & Mr Don Stowell.

TAYLOR COTTAGE
Mr & Mrs Ian & Ronnie Bailey.

WELL COTTAGE
Christiaan Richards & Michelle Woodworth.

WILLOW COTTAGE
Emma Sparks.

11 gardens and flourishing allotments in these beautiful and vibrant Cotswold stone twin villages. Scale and character vary from the grand landscape setting of Filkins Hall, to the small but action packed Pigeon Cottage, Taylor Cottage and The Tallot. Broughton Poggs Mill has a rushing mill stream with an exciting bridge; Pip Cottage combines topiary, box hedges and a fine rural view. In these and the other equally exciting and varied gardens horticultural interest abounds. Features incl plant stall by professional local nursery, Swinford Museum of Cotswolds tools and artefacts, and Cotswold Woollen Weavers. Many gardens have gravel driveways, but most are suitable for wheelchair access. Most gardens welcome dogs on leads.

15 BUCKLAND LAKES

Nr Faringdon, SN7 8QW. The Wellesley Family. *3m NE of Faringdon. Buckland is midway between Oxford (14m) & Swindon (15m), just off the A420. Faringdon 3m, Witney 8m. Follow the yellow NGS signs which will lead you to driveway & car park by St Mary's Church.* **Sun 14 Apr (2-5). Adm £5, chd free. Home-made teas at Memorial Hall.** Donation to RWMT (community bus).

Descend down wooded path to two large secluded lakes with views over undulating historic parkland, designed by Georgian landscape architect Richard Woods. Picturesque mid C18 rustic icehouse, cascade with iron footbridge, thatched boathouse and round house, and renovated exedra. Many fine mature trees, drifts of spring bulbs and daffodils amongst shrubs. Norman church adjoins. Cotswold village. Children must be supervised due to large expanse of unfenced open water.

16 CHALKHOUSE GREEN FARM

Chalkhouse Green, Kidmore End, Reading, RG4 9AL. Mr & Mrs J Hall, www.chgfarm.com. *2m N of Reading, 5m SW of Henley-on-Thames. Situated between A4074 & B481. From Kidmore End take Chalkhouse Green Rd. Follow NGS yellow signs.* **Sun 23 June (2-6). Adm £3, chd free. Cream teas.**

1 acre garden and open traditional farmstead. Herbaceous borders, herb garden, shrubs, old fashioned roses, trees incl medlar, quince and mulberries, and walled ornamental kitchen garden. New cherry orchard. Rare breed farm animals incl British White cattle, Suffolk Punch horses, donkeys, pigs, geese, chickens, ducks and turkeys. Plant and jam stall, donkey and pony rides, swimming in covered pool, grass tennis court, trailer rides, farm trail, WWII bomb shelter, heavy horse and bee display. Partial wheelchair access.

17 CHIVEL FARM

Heythrop, OX7 5TR. Mr & Mrs J D Sword, 01608 683227, rosalind.sword@btinternet.com. *4m E of Chipping Norton. Off A361 or A44.* **Visits by arrangement May to Sept. Light refreshments.**

Beautifully designed country garden with extensive views, designed for continuous interest that is always evolving. Colour schemed borders with many unusual trees, shrubs and herbaceous plants. Small formal white garden and a conservatory.

18 CHRIST CHURCH MASTERS', POCOCK & CATHEDRAL GARDENS

St Aldate's, Oxford, OX1 1DP. Christ Church, www.chch.ox.ac.uk/gardens-and-meadows. *5 mins walk from Oxford city centre. Entry from St Aldate's through the Memorial Gardens, into Christ Church Meadow, then turn L into Masters' Garden gate after main visitor entrance. No parking available.* **Sat 7 Sept (10-4). Adm £5, chd free.**

Three gardens, not normally open to visitors, with herbaceous, shrub, Mediterranean and tropical borders. Includes the magnificent 'Jabberwocky' Tree, an Oriental Plane planted in the mid 1600s, as well as other links to Alice in Wonderland, St Frideswide and Harry Potter. Gravel paths.

♿

19 CHURCH FARM FIELD

Church Lane, Epwell, Banbury, OX15 6LD. Mrs D V D Castle, 01295 788473. *7½m W of Banbury on N side of Epwell village.* **Visits by arrangement Apr to Oct. Adm £2, chd free. Tea & cakes.**

Woods, arboretum with wild flowers (planting started 1992), over 90 different trees and shrubs in 4½ acres. Paths cut through trees for access to various parts. Lawn tennis court and croquet lawns. Light refreshments (weather permitting).

20 CORPUS CHRISTI COLLEGE

Merton Street, Oxford, OX1 4JF. Domestic Bursar, www.ccc.ox.ac.uk. *Entrance from Merton St.* **Sun 30 June (6.30-10.30am). Adm £2, chd free. Home-made teas in the Old Lodgings.**

As an experiment, after 27 yrs of NGS afternoon openings, why not instead come in as early as you like, between 6.30am and 10.30am? Have tea, coffee and Danish pastries in the Old Lodgings and enjoy our informal, and, I think, beautiful organic garden with the added bonus of great views from the old town wall, across Christ Church gardens, meadows and Cathedral. The garden incl one slope.

♿

21 COTE MANOR HOUSE GARDEN

Cote, Bampton, OX18 2EG. Annabel & James Salter. *3m from Bampton. 4m from Witney. Cote village is next to Aston village on B4449. The postcode will stop in middle of Cote village, keep on this road for about ½m past Chimney turn until you see a very high wall on the RH-side. Parking signposted on R in field.* **Sun 9 June (1-5). Adm £5, chd free. Cream teas. Ice creams.**

6 acres of beautiful ancient gardens dating from medieval times, set around Grade II* moated Elizabethan Manor House (not open). The formal Irish yew garden leads to a lake filled with waterlillies and surrounded by lavender, a knot garden with topiary 'Fox & Hounds'; a heart shaped secret garden, summerhouse and woodland garden containing some rare tree specimens, vegetable and herb garden.

GROUP OPENING

22 CUMNOR VILLAGE GARDENS

Leys Road, Cumnor, Oxford, OX2 9QF. *4m W of central Oxford. From A420, exit for Cumnor & follow B4017 into the village. Parking on road & side roads, behind PO, or behind village hall in Leys Rd. Additional parking in Bertie & Norreys Rd.* **Sun 2 June (2-6). Combined adm £5, chd free. Home-made teas in United Reformed Church Hall, Leys Road.**

36 BERTIE ROAD
Esther & Neil Whiting.
D

10 LEYS ROAD
Penny & Nick Bingham.

41 LEYS ROAD
Philip & Jennie Powell.

STONEHAVEN
Dr Dianne & Prof Keith Gull.
(See separate entry)

The four gardens feature a wide variety of plants, shrubs, trees, vegetables, fruit and wild flowers. Two of the gardens are cottage style with unusual perennials and many shrubs and trees; one is professionally designed with three structured rooms and relaxed planting; another has a Japanese influence exhibiting unusual plants many with black or bronze foliage and gravel areas. Wheelchair access to 36 Bertie Road and 41 Leys Road. WC facilities in United Reformed Church Hall.

GROUP OPENING

23 DEDDINGTON GARDENS

Castle Street, Deddington, Banbury, OX15 0TE. *Deddington is about 6m S of Banbury on the A4260 Oxford to Banbury road.* **Sat 25 May (2-5). Combined adm £5, chd free. Home-made teas.**

CASTLE END HOUSE
Petra Hoyer Millar.

RUSHALL HOUSE
Lynda Lake-Stewart.

SATIN LANE ALLOTMENTS
Deddington Allotment Society.

Beautiful ironstone village on the edge of the Cotswolds. Deddington is centred around a charming, bustling market place, church and chapel square. Two lovely village gardens and the flourishing village allotments are opening their gates to visitors this year. All are in close proximity, located to the east of the village. Castle End House, a new garden now three years in the making; one acre dry-stone walled garden, featuring formal lawns, ha-ha, substantial herbaceous borders, terraced orchard, woodland garden and (in development) herb garden. Rushall House, delightful small walled garden containing intensively planted perennial beds to cover all seasons and filled with family plant and sculpture treasures. Satin Lane Allotments are a thriving community treasure, established in 1925. The site accommodates 47 beautiful individual plots that have been worked over generations.

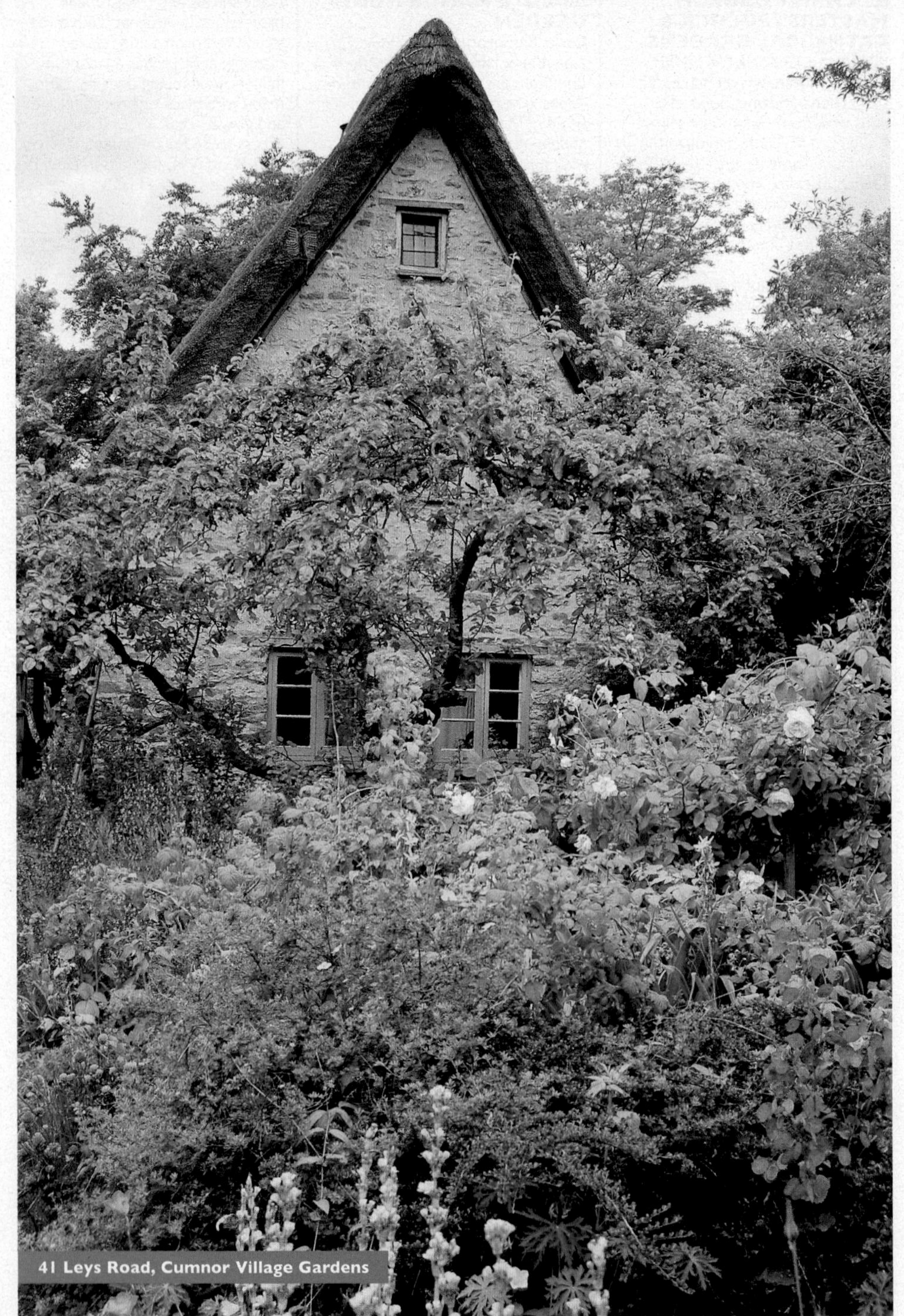

41 Leys Road, Cumnor Village Gardens

24 103 DENE ROAD

Headington, Oxford, OX3 7EQ. Mr & Mrs Steve & Mary Woolliams, 01865 764153, stevewoolliams@gmail.com. *S Headington nr Nuffield. Dene Rd accessed from The Slade from the N, or from Hollow Way from the S. Both access roads are B4495. Garden on sharp bend.* **Visits by arrangement Apr to Sept for groups of up to 10. Adm £3.50, chd free. Home-made teas.**

A surprising eco-friendly garden with borrowed view over the Lye Valley Nature Reserve. Lawns, a wild flower meadow, pond and large kitchen garden are incl in a suburban 60ft x 120ft sloping garden. Fruit trees, soft fruit and mixed borders of shrubs, hardy perennials, grasses and bulbs, designed for seasonal colour. This garden has been noted for its wealth of wildlife incl a variety of birds and butterflies and other insects, incl the rare Brown Hairstreak butterfly, the rare Currant Clearwing moth and the Grizzled Skipper.

25 DENTON HOUSE

Denton, Oxford, OX44 9JF. Mr & Mrs Luke, 01865 874440, waveney@jandwluke.com. *In a valley between Garsington & Cuddesdon.* **Sun 16 June (1.30-6). Adm £5, chd free. Home-made teas.** Visits also by arrangement May to Oct for groups of up to 30.

Large walled garden surrounds a Georgian mansion (not open) with shaded areas, walks, topiary and many interesting mature trees, large lawns, herbaceous borders and rose beds. The windows in the wall were taken in 1864 from Brasenose College Chapel and Library. Wild garden and a further walled fruit garden.

GROUP OPENING

26 DORCHESTER GARDENS

Dorchester-On-Thames, Wallingford, OX10 7HZ. *Off A4074 or A415 signed to Dorchester. Parking at Old Bridge Meadow, at SE end of Dorchester Bridge. Disabled parking at 26 Manor Farm Road (OX10 7HZ). Tickets available at each garden.* **Sun 7 July (2-5). Combined adm £5, chd free.**

26 MANOR FARM ROAD
David & Judy Parker.

6 MONKS CLOSE
Leif & Petronella Rasmussen.

7 ROTTEN ROW
Michael & Veronica Evans.

Three contrasting gardens in a historic village surrounding the medieval Abbey and the scene of many Midsomer Murders. 26 Manor Farm Road (OX10 7HZ) was part of an old, neglected garden which now has a formal lawn and planting, vegetable garden and greenhouse. Children should be accompanied. From the yew hedge down towards the River Thame, which often floods in winter, is an apple orchard underplanted with spring bulbs. 6 Monks Close (OX10 7JA) is idyllic and surprising. A small spring-fed stream and sloping lawn surrounded by naturalistic planting runs down to a monastic fish pond. Bridges over this deep pond lead to the River Thame with steep banks; children should be accompanied. 7 Rotten Row (OX10 7LJ) is Dorchester's lawnless garden, a terrace with borders leads to a lovely geometric garden supervised by a statue of Hebe. Access is from the allotments. Wheelchair access to 26 Manor Farm Road, partial access to other gardens.

27 FAILFORD

118 Oxford Road, Abingdon, OX14 2AG. Miss R Aylward, 01235 523925, aylwardsdooz@hotmail.co.uk. *118 is on the LH-side of Oxford Rd when coming from Abingdon Town, or on the RH-side when approaching from the N. Entrance to this garden is via 116 Oxford Road.* **Sun 9 June (11-4). Combined adm with 116 Oxford Road £5, chd free. Home-made teas.** Visits also by arrangement June to Sept for groups of up to 20.

A town garden, an extension of the home with many rooms both formal and informal. Features incl walkways through shaded areas, arches, kitchen garden, grasses, roses, topiaries, acers, hostas and heucheras. A wide variety of planting with many quirky features, all within an area 570 sq ft. Partial wheelchair access due to gravel areas, narrow pathways and uneven surfaces.

28 FOXINGTON

Britwell Salome, Watlington, OX49 5LG. Mrs Mary Roadnight, 01491 612418, mary@foxington.co.uk. *At Red Lion Pub take turning to Britwell Hill. After 350yds turn into drive on L.* **Visits by arrangement Apr to Sept for groups of 5 to 20. Adm £6, chd free. Home-made teas. Special dietary options by prior request.**

Stunning views to the Chiltern Hills provide a wonderful setting for this impressive garden, remodelled in 2009. Patio, heather and gravel gardens enjoy this view, whilst the back and vegetable gardens are more enclosed. The relatively new planting is maturing well and the area around the house (not open) is full of colour. There is an orchard, a flock of white doves and possibly some vintage tractors on display by prior request. Well behaved dogs are welcome, but they must be kept on a lead at all times as there are many wild animals in the garden, wildflower meadow, wood and neighbouring fields. Wheelchair access on level paths and no steps.

29 FRIARS COURT

Clanfield, OX18 2SU. Charles Willmer, www.friarscourt.com. *5m N of Faringdon. On A4095 Faringdon to Witney. ½m S of Clanfield.* **Mon 27 May (2-6). Adm £4, chd free. Home-made teas.**

Over 3 acres of formal and informal gardens with flower beds, borders and specimen trees, lie within the remaining arms of a C16 moat which partially surrounds the large C17 Cotswold stone house. Bridges span the moat with waterlily filled ponds to the front whilst beyond the gardens is a woodland walk. A museum about Friars Court is located in the old Coach House. A level path goes around part of the gardens and is suitable for wheelchairs.

30 NEW GARSINGTON MANOR
28 Southend, Garsington, Oxford, OX44 9DH. Sam Wilson, Head Gardener. *3m SE of Oxford. N of B480. 1½m S of Wheatley.* **Thur 2, Fri 3 May (1-5). Adm £5, chd free. Tea.**
C17 Manor House of architectural, literary and musical interest (not open). Early monastic fish ponds, water garden, dovecote c1700. Ornamental pool and flower parterre, Italianate terrace and loggia and Italian statues laid out by Philip and Lady Ottoline Morrell c1915-1923. The garden has a large spring bulb display and is currently in a period of extensive renovation. Please come to see how the garden evolves over the coming years. Gravel paths, steps, steep slopes, uneven surfaces and water features.

31 THE GRANGE
Berrick Road, Chalgrove, OX44 7RQ. Mrs Vicky Farren, 01865 400883, vickyfarren@mac.com. *12m E of Oxford & 4m from Watlington, off B480. The entrance to The Grange is at the grass triangle between Berrick Rd & Monument Rd.* **Visits by arrangement June to Oct. Adm £5, chd free. Home-made teas on request (additional £3 pp).**
11 acre plot with an evolving garden including herbaceous borders and a field turned to prairie with many grasses inspired by the Dutch style. There is a lake with bridges and a planted island, a brook running through the garden, wild flower meadow, a further pond, arboretum, an old orchard and partly walled vegetable garden. There is deep water and bridges, which may be slippery when wet. Partial wheelchair access due to grass paths in many areas, bridges, island and steps.

32 NEW THE GRANGE, ISLIP
Mill Street, Islip, Kidlington, OX5 2SY. Ann & Jon Conibear, 01865 373494 (weekdays only), annconibear494@gmail.com. *2m E of Kidlington & approx 5m N of Oxford. The Grange is 400yds down Mill St on the R. The garden is 200yds from the car park.* **Wed 29 May (2-5.30). Adm £4, chd free. Home-made teas. Visits also by arrangement Mar to Oct for groups of up to 20.**
A 2½ acre garden in a former quarry with landscaped banks and cloud pruned hedges. The garden is naturalistic and combines wild planting with more formal planting of shrubs and perennials. The woodland garden is planted with rare plants and there are wildflower meadows which look especially colourful in the spring. There is a small pond and bog garden edged by a rockery with interesting ferns. The garden has steep gravel paths and is on several levels.

33 GREENFIELD FARM
Christmas Common, Nr Watlington, OX49 5HG. Andrew & Jane Ingram, 01491 612434, andrew@andrewbingram.com. *4m from J5 M40, 7m from Henley. J5 M40, A40 towards Oxford for ½m, turn L signed Christmas Common. ¾m past Fox & Hounds Pub, turn L at Tree Barn sign.* **Visits by arrangement May to Sept for groups of up to 30. Adm £4, chd free.**
10 acre wild flower meadow surrounded by woodland, established 22 yrs ago under the Countryside Stewardship Scheme. Traditional Chiltern chalkland meadow in beautiful peaceful setting with 100 species of perennial wild flowers, grasses and 5 species of orchids. ½m walk from parking area to meadow. Opportunity to return via typical Chiltern beechwood.

34 THE GROVE
North Street, Middle Barton, Chipping Norton, OX7 7BZ. Ivor & Barbara Hill. *7m E Chipping Norton. On B4030, 2m from junction A4260 & B4030, opp Cinnamon Stick restaurant. Parking in street.* **Sun 19 May (1.30-5). Adm £3.50, chd free. Home-made teas.**
Mature informal plantsman's ⅓ acre garden, planted for yr-round interest around C19 Cotswold stone cottage (not open). Numerous borders with wide variety of unusual shrubs, trees and hardy plants; several species weigela, syringe, viburnum and philadelphus. Pond area, well stocked greenhouse. Plant list and garden history available. Home-made preserves for sale. Wheelchair access to most of garden.

35 HAM COURT
Ham Court Farm, Weald, Bampton, OX18 2HG. Emma Bridgewater & Matthew Rice. *Drive through the village towards Clanfield. The drive is on the R, exactly opp Weald St.* **Sun 7 July (2-5). Adm £5, chd free. Home-made teas.**
Ham Court was once the gate house of a major C14 castle. Emma Bridgewater and Matthew Rice found it with no garden at all and have been making progress in the project of putting this to rights. Beginning by digging a moat, planting thousands of trees, hiding thousands of tonnes of rubble and laying down the plans for their future garden. Now a productive kitchen garden and a lot of bright flowers. This is a garden in development, no two years are the same. Come early as delicious teas run out quick!

Your visits help change lives - your generosity helps Marie Curie fund nurses to care for people night and day in their homes, with donations of more than £8.8 million

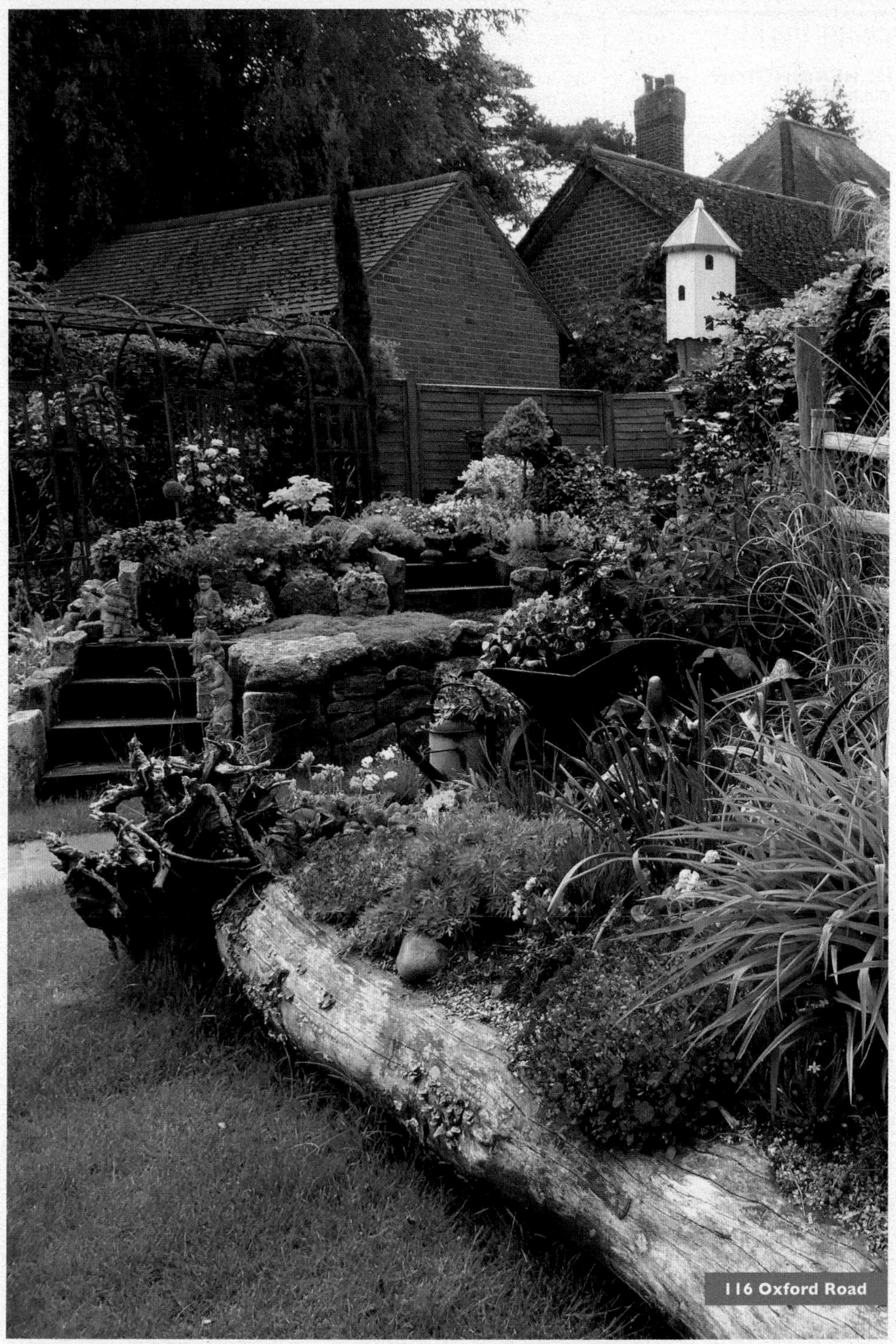

116 Oxford Road

GROUP OPENING

36 HEADINGTON GARDENS

Old Headington, Oxford, OX3 9BT. *2m E from centre of Oxford. After T-lights in the centre of Headington, heading towards Oxford, take the 2nd turn on R into Osler Rd. Gardens at end of road in Old Headington, in Kennett Rd & Beech Rd nearby.* **Sun 19 May (2-6). Combined adm £6, chd free. Home-made teas at Ruskin College.**

11 BEECH ROAD
Lucy & David Lawrence.

THE COACH HOUSE
David & Bryony Rowe.

10 KENNETT ROAD
Linda & David Clover, 01865 765881, lindaclover@yahoo.co.uk.
Visits also by arrangement for groups of up to 10.

MONCKTON COTTAGE
Julie Harrod & Peter McCarter, 01865 751471, petermccarter@msn.com.

40 OSLER ROAD
Nicholas & Pam Coote, 07804 932748, pamjcoote@gmail.com.
Visits also by arrangement May to Aug for groups of up to 30.

RUSKIN COLLEGE
Ruskin College, ruskincrinklecrankle.org.

7 ST ANDREWS ROAD
Monique Halloran.

9 STOKE PLACE
Clive Hurst.

WHITE LODGE
Catharine Macksmith.

Situated above Oxford, Headington is an old village with high stone walls, narrow lanes and a Norman church. The 9 gardens offer wide variety. 40 Osler Road is a well-established garden with an Italian theme brimming with exotic planting. White Lodge provides a large park-like setting for a Regency property. The Coach House combines a formal setting with hedges, flowers and lawn and a courtyard with a water garden. 9 Stoke Place has a traditional lawn and mixed border on one side and a formal garden on the other. The walled vegetable garden in the grounds of Ruskin College incorporates a Grade II listed Crinkle Crankle Wall. Monckton Cottage is a walled, woodland garden with a meadow area, topiary, and unusual plants. 7 St Andrews Road is a small town garden with mixed borders and a unique water feature. No 10 Kennett Road is a well-planned small garden with lawns and borders, a pond, a fernery and greenhouse. 11 Beech Road is a recently planted garden in its third full season. Partial wheelchair access to most gardens due to gravel paths and steps.

37 HEARNS HOUSE

Gallowstree Common, RG4 9DE. John & Joan Pumfrey, 01189 722848, joanpumfrey@lineone.net. *5m N of Reading, 5m W of Henley. From A4074 turn E at Cane End. Car parking available on-site.* **Visits by arrangement May to Sept for groups of 5 to 20. Adm £5, chd free. Home-made teas.**

An inspiration for artists and gardeners with unusual hard landscaping, sculpture and indigenous and exotic planting designed to suit specific areas including dry shade under trees, a hot bank and a low maintenance courtyard. New for 2018 was a wild flower area, and a display of the National Collection of brunnera and omphalodes. The nursery is full of wonderful plants propagated from the garden. Within the 2 acres is an almost entirely paved walled garden with many self-seeding plants to give a pretty effect with low maintenance. Groups of gardeners and artists are welcome to enjoy/paint inspirational hard landscaping and planting. Grass lawn access generally, with occasional single steps at terrace.

NPC

38 HOLLYHOCKS

North Street, Islip, Kidlington, OX5 2SQ. Avril Hughes, 01865 377104, ahollyhocks@btinternet.com. *3m NE of Kidlington. From A34, exit Bletchingdon & Islip. B4027 direction Islip, turn L into North St.* **Sun 17 Feb (1.30-4.30). Light refreshments. Sun 5 May (2-5). Home-made teas. Adm £3.50, chd free. Combined adm with Monks Head on 17 Feb only £5.00, chd free. 2020: Sun 16 Feb.** Visits also by arrangement Feb to Sept for groups of up to 20. Combined visits with Monks Head or Bannisters may be possible.

Plantswoman's small Edwardian garden brimming with yr-round interest, especially planted to provide winter colour, scent and snowdrops. Divided into areas with bulbs, May tulips, herbaceous borders, roses, clematis, shade and woodland planting especially Trillium, Podophyllum and Arisaema, late summer salvias and annuals give colour. Large pots and troughs add colour and seasonal interest. Some steps into the garden.

39 HOME CLOSE

Southend, Garsington, OX44 9DH. Mrs M Waud & Dr P Giangrande, 01865 361394. *3m SE of Oxford. N of B480, opp Garsington Manor.* **Visits by arrangement Apr to Sept. Adm £4, chd free. Refreshments by prior request.**

2 acre garden with listed house (not open), listed granary and 1 acre mixed tree plantation with fine views. Unusual trees and shrubs planted for yr-round effect. Terraces, stone walls and hedges divide the garden and the planting reflects a Mediterranean interest. Vegetable garden and orchard.

40 86 HURST RISE ROAD

Cumnor Hill, Oxford, OX2 9HH. Ms P Guy & Mr L Harris, 07762 342238, penny.theavon@virginmedia.com. *W side of Oxford. Take Botley interchange off A34 from N or S. Follow signs for Oxford & then turn R at Botley T-lights, opp MacDonalds & follow NGS yellow signs.* **Visits by arrangement June & July for groups of 5 to 30. Tea & cake by prior request. Adm £4, chd free.**

A small town garden designed and planted by the owners in 2013. Good use of a 40ft x 40ft space brimming with herbaceous perennial plants, roses, clematis, shrubs and small trees. Seasonal use of containers and hanging baskets incl tender succulents. An unusual stone water feature, two raised beds packed with interesting plants, an arch and pergola all add to a plantaholic's garden. Partial wheelchair access as path is partly pebble.

GROUP OPENING

41 IFFLEY GARDENS

Iffley, Oxford, OX4 4EF. *2m S of Oxford. Within Oxford's ring road, off A4158 Iffley road, from Magdalen Bridge to Littlemore r'about, to Iffley village. Map provided at each garden.* **Sun 9 June (2-6). Combined adm £5, chd free. Home-made teas in village hall.**

17 ABBERBURY ROAD
Mrs Julie Steele.

25 ABBERBURY ROAD
Rob & Bridget Farrands.

29 ABBERBURY ROAD
Sarah North & Andrew Rathmell.

86 CHURCH WAY
Helen Beinart & Alex Coren.

122 CHURCH WAY
Sir John & Lady Elliott.

THE MALT HOUSE
Helen Potts.

NEW **400 MEADOW LANE**
David & Jo Goode.

Secluded old village with renowned Norman church, featured on cover of Pevsner's Oxon Guide. Visit 7 gardens ranging in variety and style from the large Malt House garden and a thatched C17 cottage garden to mixed family gardens with shady borders and vegetables. Varied planting throughout the gardens including herbaceous borders, shade loving plants, roses, fine specimen trees and plants in terracing. Features incl water features, statues, formal gardens, small lake and Thames riverbank. Plant Sale at 17 Abberbury Road. Wheelchair access to some gardens only.

GROUP OPENING

42 KENCOT GARDENS

Kencot, Lechlade, GL7 3QT. *5m NE of Lechlade. E of A361 between Burford & Lechlade.* **Mon 22 Apr (2-6). Combined adm £5, chd free. Home-made teas at village hall.**

THE ALLOTMENTS
Amelia Carter Charity.

BELHAM HAYES
Mr Joseph Jones.

IVY NOOK
Gill & Wally Cox.

KENCOT HOUSE
Tim & Katie Gardner.

MANOR FARM
Henry & Kate Fyson.

WELL HOUSE
Janet & Richard Wheeler.

In 2019, 5 gardens and the allotments will open as part of Kencot Gardens. The Allotments, tended by 8 people, growing a range of vegetables, flowers and fruit. Ivy Nook with spring flowers, shrubs, rockery, small pond, waterfall, magnolia and fruit trees. Belham Hayes, a mature cottage garden with mixed herbaceous borders, two old fruit trees, small vegetable patch and an emphasis on scent and colour coordination. Manor Farm has a 2 acre walled garden with bulbs, wood anemones, fritillaria in mature orchards, old English fruit trees, pleached lime walk, 130yr old yew ball and Black Hamburg vine. Also you will see chickens and occasionally pigs and lambs. Kencot House, a 2 acre garden and a haven for wildlife incl a gingko tree, shrubs, spring bulbs, clockhouse, summerhouse and a carved C13 archway. Well House, a ⅓ acre garden with mature trees, hedges, wildlife pond, waterfall, small bog area, bulbs giving early colour, mixed borders and rockeries. Plant sale at Manor Farm. No wheelchair access to The Allotments.

43 LIME CLOSE

35 Henleys Lane, Drayton, Abingdon, OX14 4HU. M C de Laubarede, mail@mclgardendesign.com, , www.mclgardendesign.com. *2m S of Abingdon. Henleys Lane is off main road through Drayton.* **Sun 14 Apr, Sun 2 June (2-5). Adm £5, chd free. Cream teas.** Visits also by arrangement in Feb for groups of 10+. Donation to CLIC Sargent Care for Children.

4 acre mature plantsman's garden with rare trees, shrubs, roses and bulbs. Mixed borders, raised beds, pergola, topiary and shade borders. Herb garden by Rosemary Verey. Listed C16 house (not open). Cottage garden by MCL Garden Design, planted for colour, an iris garden with 100 varieties of tall bearded irises. Winter bulbs. New arboretum with exotic trees from Asia and USA planted for autumn colour.

44 MAGDALEN COLLEGE

Oxford, OX1 4AU. Magdalen College, www.magd.ox.ac.uk. *Entrance in High St.* **Sun 14 Apr (1-6). Adm £6, chd £5 (chd under 7 yrs free). Light refreshments in the Old Kitchen.**

60 acres incl deer park, college lawns, numerous trees 150-200 yrs old; notable herbaceous and shrub plantings. Magdalen meadow where purple and white snake's head fritillaries can be found is surrounded by Addison's Walk, a tree lined circuit by the River Cherwell developed since the late C18. Ancient herd of 60 deer. Press bell at the lodge for porter to provide wheelchair access.

We help ordinary people open the gates to their extraordinary private gardens to raise impressive amounts of money through admissions, teas and slices of cake!

Primrose Gardens, Steeple Aston Gardens

45 MANOR HOUSE

Manor Farm Road, Dorchester-on-Thames, OX10 7HZ. Simon & Margaret Broadbent, 01865 340101, manor@dotoxon.uk. *8m SSE of Oxford. Off A4074, signed from village centre. Parking at Bridge Meadow (400 metres). Disabled parking at house.* **Sun 16 June, Sun 18 Aug (2-4.30). Adm £4, chd free. Home-made teas in Dorchester Abbey Guesthouse (90 metres).** Visits also by arrangement June to Sept for groups of 10+.

2 acre garden in beautiful setting around Georgian house (not open) and medieval abbey. Spacious lawn leading to riverside copse of towering poplars with fine views of Dorchester Abbey. Terrace with rose and vine covered pergola around lily pond. Colourful herbaceous borders, small orchard and vegetable garden. Gravel paths.

♿ 🐕 ✿ ☕

46 MEADOW COTTAGE

Christmas Common, Watlington, OX49 5HR. Mrs Zelda Kent-Lemon, 01491 613779, zelda_kl@hotmail.com. *1m from Watlington. Coming from Oxford M40 to J6. Turn R & go to Watlington. Turn L up Hill Rd to top. Turn R after 50yds, turn L into field.* **Mon 6 May (12-5). Adm £5, chd free. Home-made teas.** Visits also by arrangement Feb to Sept for groups of 10 to 30.

1¾ acre garden adjoining ancient bluebell woods, created by the owner from 1995 onwards.

Many areas to explore including a professionally designed vegetable garden, large composting areas, wild flower garden and pond, old and new fruit trees, many shrubs, much varied hedging and a tall treehouse which children can climb under supervision. Indigenous trees and C17 barn (not open). Wonderful snowdrops in Feb and during the month of May visit the bluebell woodland. Partial wheelchair access as gravel driveway and lawns.

♿ 🐕 ✿ 🚌 ☕

47 MERTON COLLEGE OXFORD FELLOWS' GARDEN

Merton Street, Oxford, OX1 4JD. Merton College, 01865 276310. *Merton St runs parallel to High St.* **Sun 21 July (10-5). Adm £6, chd free.**

Ancient mulberry, said to have associations with James I. Specimen trees, long mixed border, recently established herbaceous bed. View of Christ Church meadow.

♿

48 MIDSUMMER HOUSE

Woolstone, Faringdon, SN7 7QL. Anthony & Penny Spink, 01367 820219, pennyspink@gmail.com. *7m W & 7m S of Faringdon. Woolstone is a small village off B4507, below Uffington White Horse Hill. Take the road towards Uffington from the White Horse Pub.* **Wed 19 June, Wed 11 Sept (2-6). Adm £4, chd free. Home-made teas.** Visits also by arrangement May to Oct for groups of 5 to 20.

On moving to Midsummer House four years ago, the owners created the garden using herbaceous plants brought with them from their previous home at Woolstone Mill House (not open this year). Herbaceous border, parterre with new topiary, and espaliered Malus Everest. The garden designed by owner's son Justin Spink, a renowned garden designer and landscape architect. Short gravel drive at the entrance.

49 MILL BARN

25 Mill Lane, Chalgrove, OX44 7SL. Pat Hougham, 01865 890020, pat@gmec.co.uk. *12m E of Oxford. Chalgrove is 4m from Watlington off B480. Mill Barn is in Mill Lane on the W of Chalgrove, 300yds S of Lamb Pub. Parking in lane or gravel entrance yard.* **Visits by arrangement May to Sept for groups of 5 to 30. Adm £4, chd free. Home-made teas.**

Mill Barn has an informal cottage garden with a variety of flowers, shrubs and fruit trees including medlar, mulberry and quince in sunny and shaded beds. Rose arches and a pergola lead to a vegetable plot surrounded by a cordon of fruit trees all set in a mill stream landscape.

50 MONKS HEAD

Weston Road, Bletchingdon, OX5 3DH. Sue Bedwell, 01869 350155, bedwell615@btinternet.com. *Approx 4m N of Kidlington. From A34 take B4027 to Bletchingdon, turn R at Xrds into Weston Rd.* **Sun 17 Feb (1.30-5). Adm £3, chd free. Home-made teas. Combined adm with Hollyhocks £5.00, chd free.** Visits also by arrangement.

Plantaholics' garden for all year interest. Bulb frame and alpine area, greenhouse. Changes evolving all the time.

51 NEW THE OLD BAKEHOUSE

Old Minster Lovell, Minster Lovell, Witney, OX29 0RN. Michael Brodtman & Naomi Fine. *The Old Bakehouse is halfway up on the RH-side going from the Old Swan towards the Church in Old Minster Lovell.* **Sun 7 July (2-5). Adm £5, chd free. Home-made teas. Also open 113 Brize Norton Road.**

At approx 1½ acres, this village garden in the pretty Cotswold village of Minster Lovell has evolved over the last few yrs. Through a curious wooden gate, the original cottage garden now opens out into a former paddock, now with an orchard, vegetable garden, long prairie border and pond. Beyond, a newly designed rose garden connects through to a second tranquil apple orchard. Many steps and garden levels may be challenging for wheelchair users.

52 OLD RECTORY

Salford, Chipping Norton, OX7 5YL. Mr & Mrs N M Chambers, 01608 643969. *Approx 3m W of Chipping Norton. Off the A44, on the W side of the small village of Salford, next to the church.* **Visits by arrangement Feb to Oct for groups of up to 10. Adm £4, chd free.**

1½ acre cottage garden with yr-round interest. Early flowering shrubs and bulbs, some snowdrops, mixed borders and old roses. Small orchard and vegetable garden. Salford Inn open for lunch from 12.00-2.30pm (closed on Mondays). No dogs.

53 THE OLD VICARAGE, BLEDINGTON

Main Road, Bledington, Chipping Norton, OX7 6UX. Sue & Tony Windsor, 01608 658525, tony.g.windsor@gmail.com. *6m SW of Chipping Norton. 4m SE of Stow-on-the-Wold. On the main street B4450 through Bledington. Not next to church.* **Sun 21 Apr (11-5); Sun 16 June (2-6). Adm £4, chd free.** Visits also by arrangement May to July for groups of up to 40.

1½ acre garden around a late Georgian vicarage (1843) not open. Borders and beds filled with spring bulbs, hardy perennials, shrubs and trees. Informal rose garden with over 300 David Austin roses. Small pond and vegetable garden. Paddock with trees, shrubs and herbaceous border. Planted for yr-round interest. Gravel driveway and gently sloped garden can be hard work.

54 OLD WHITEHILL BARN

Old Whitehill, Tackley, Kidlington, OX5 3AB. Gill & Paul Withers. *10m N of Oxford. 3m from Woodstock. Hamlet ¾m S of Tackley. Signed from A4260 & A4095.* **Sun 26 May (2-5.30). Adm £4, chd free. Home-made teas.**

1 acre country garden on a sloping site around a stone barn conversion. Created by the owners from a farmyard and surrounding field over last 17 yrs. Sunny walled courtyard. Colour themed borders. Field of formal and informal areas, mature hedging, orchard, meadow grass and enclosed vegetable garden.

55 ORCHARD HOUSE

Asthall, Burford, OX18 4HH. Dr Elizabeth Maitreyi, 07939 111605, oneconsciousbreath@gmail.com. *3m E of Burford. 1st house on R as you come downhill into Asthall.* **Sun 9 June (1.30-6). Adm £5, chd free. Home-made teas.** Visits also by arrangement Apr to Sept for groups of 5 to 20. Donation to MS Society.

A 5 acre garden in the making. Formal borders and courtyard. New paths and hedges created since 2018 add more character and planting opportunities. The whole design is now visible. We are creating an English garden finely balanced between the formal and the wild. Beautiful sculptures add to the planting and there is woodland to walk in beyond. Two large black pigs. One step down from the driveway. No WC available.

We open the gates to the nation's best gardens, offering a relaxing, memorable and affordable day out. A perfect experience to share with friends and family.

56 116 OXFORD ROAD

Abingdon, OX14 2AG. Mr & Mrs P Aylward, 01235 523925, aylwardsdooz@hotmail.co.uk. *116 Oxford Road is on the RH-side if coming from A34 N exit, or on the LH-side after Picklers Hill, turn if approaching from Abingdon town centre.* **Sun 9 June (11-4). Combined adm with Failford £5, chd free. Home-made teas. Visits also by arrangement June to Sept for groups of up to 20.**

New town garden opening for its third year, a creation that started in July 2014. The garden is wedge-shaped, 70ft top 37ft at the bottom and 80ft in length. The challenge was it had to be interesting and look as though it had been there for many years. It has a folly greenhouse and other unusual features, plus raised beds, lawns, herbaceous borders and a diverse collection of plants and trees. Limited access by gravel driveway. Uneven surfaces and paths.

57 50 PLANTATION ROAD

Oxford, OX2 6JE. Philippa Scoones. *Central Oxford. N on Woodstock Rd take 2nd L. Coming into Oxford on Woodstock Rd turn R after Leckford Rd. No disabled parking near house.* **Sat 27, Sun 28 Apr, Sat 4, Sun 5 May (2-5). Adm £3.50, chd free. Home-made teas.**

Surprisingly spacious city garden designed in specific sections. N-facing front garden, side alley filled with shade loving climbers. S-facing rear garden with hundreds of tulips in spring, unusual trees incl Mount Etna Broom, conservatory, terraced area and secluded water garden with water feature, woodland plants and alpines.

58 THE PRIORY GARDEN

Charlbury, OX7 3PX. Dr D El Kabir & Colleagues. *6m SE of Chipping Norton. Large Cotswold village on B4022 Witney-Enstone Rd, near St Mary's Church.* **Sun 9 June (2-5). Adm £5, chd free. Home-made teas.**

1½ acre of formal terraced topiary gardens with Italianate features. Foliage colour schemes, shrubs, parterres with fragrant plants, old roses, water features, sculpture and inscriptions aim to produce a poetic, wistful atmosphere. Formal vegetable and herb garden. Arboretum of over 3 acres borders the River Evenlode and incl wildlife garden and pond. Home-made teas in the new Charlbury Community Centre (limited parking nearby). Partial wheelchair access.

59 RADCOT HOUSE

Radcot, OX18 2SX. Robin & Jeanne Stainer, 01367 810231, rstainer@radcothouse.co.uk, www.radcothouse.com. *1¼m S of Clanfield. On A4095 between Witney & Faringdon, 300yds N of Radcot bridge.* **Sun 18 Aug, Sun 6 Oct (2-5.30). Adm £5, chd free. Home-made teas. Visits also by arrangement July to Oct for groups of 10+. Refreshments on request.**

Approx 3 acres of dramatic yet harmonious planting in light and shade, formal pond, fruit and vegetable cages. Convenient seating at key points enables relaxed observation and reflection. Extensive use of grasses and unusual perennials and interesting sculptural surprises. Spectacular autumn display.

60 RIVENDEL

Old London Road, Milton Common, Thame, OX9 2JR. Anthony & Lynn Ussher. *Milton Common is 5m SW of Thame at junction of A329, A40 & J7 of M40.* **Sat 8, Sun 9 June (2-5.30). Adm £4, chd free. Home-made teas.**

When moving to Rivendel 8 yrs ago we took over a family garden used as a football pitch and children's playground. We have made successive changes resulting in our garden today, made up of varied planting with small trees, shrubs, herbs and herbaceous with a strong emphasis on quirky architectural features to moving water.

61 ROFFORD MANOR

Rofford Lane, Little Milton, Oxford, OX44 7QQ. Mr & Mrs Jeremy Mogford. *10m SE of Oxford. 1m from Little Milton on Chalgrove Rd. Signposted Rofford only. Parking on verges outside garden.* **Evening opening Thur 27 June (5.30-7.30). Adm £25. Pre-booking essential, please visit www.ngs.org.uk for information & booking. Evening drinks & canapés.**

Discover one of Oxfordshire's secret treasures in this 2 acre garden created since 1985 around the venerable gabled house and within old walls, with some design and planting by Michael Balston. From the cloud-clipped box garden to the burgeoning vegetable garden, and including deep herbaceous borders and herb, rose and swimming pool gardens, it is all designed and planted to an exceptional standard, with the bonus of many memorable views out over the surrounding countryside. Yew hedges and pleached limes provide enclosures and frame borders and there is a feast of interesting plants to enjoy.

GROUP OPENING

62 SIBFORD GARDENS

Sibford Gower, OX15 5RX. *7m W of Banbury. Near the Warwickshire border, S of B4035, in centre of village near Wykham Arms Pub.* **Sun 23 June (2-6). Combined adm £7, chd free. Home-made teas at Sibford Gower Village Hall (opp the church).**

BUTTSLADE HOUSE
James & Sarah Garstin.

CARTER'S YARD
Sue & Malcolm Bannister, 01295 780365, sebannister@gmail.com. **Visits also by arrangement May to Oct for groups of 5 to 30.**

HOME CLOSE
Graham & Carolyn White.

HOME FARM
Professor Stephen & Mrs Jean Kennedy.

In two charming small villages of Sibford Gower and Sibford Ferris, off the beaten track with thatched stone cottages, four contrasting gardens ranging from an early C20 Arts and Crafts house (not open) and garden, to varied cottage gardens bursting with bloom, interesting planting and some unusual plants. No wheelchair access to Carter's Yard, partial access to Buttslade House and Home Close.

63 64 SPRING ROAD

Abingdon, OX14 1AN. Janet Boulton, 01235 524514, j.boulton89@btinternet.com, www.janetboulton.co.uk. *S Abingdon from A34 take L turn after police station into Spring Rd. Minute's drive to number 64 on L.* **Visits by arrangement July to Sept for groups of up to 5. Adm £5. Tea.**

A very special small but unique artist's garden (4½ x 30½ metres) behind a Victorian terrace house. Predominantly green with numerous inscribed sculptures relating to art, history and the human spirit. Inspired by gardens the owner has painted, especially Little Sparta in Scotland. Visitors are invited to watch a film about this celebrated garden before walking around the garden itself. Narrow steps to property and garden are not suitable for wheelchairs.

GROUP OPENING

64 STEEPLE ASTON GARDENS

Steeple Aston, OX25 4SP. *14m N of Oxford, 9m S of Banbury. ½m E of A4260.* **Sun 19 May (2-6). Combined adm £6, chd free. Home-made teas in village hall.**

ACACIA COTTAGE
Jane & David Stewart.

CEDAR COTTAGE
Josephine Meddings & Robert Scott.

COMBE PYNE
Chris & Sally Cooper.

KRALINGEN
Mr & Mrs Roderick Nicholson.

THE LONGBYRE
Mr Vaughan Billings.

PRIMROSE GARDENS
Richard & Daphne Preston, 01869 340512, richard.preston5@btopenworld.com.
Visits also by arrangement May to July for groups of 10+. Talk on the garden history by prior request.

Steeple Aston, often considered the most easterly of the Cotswold villages, is a beautiful stone built village with gardens that provide a huge range of interest. A stream meanders down the hill as the landscape changes from sand to clay. The 6 open gardens include small floriferous cottage gardens, large landscaped gardens, natural woodland areas, ponds and bog gardens, and themed borders. No wheelchair access at Primrose Gardens.

65 STONEHAVEN

6 High Street, Cumnor, Oxford, OX2 9PE. Dr Dianne & Prof Keith Gull. *4m from central Oxford. Exit to Cumnor from the A420. In centre of village opp PO. Parking at back of PO.* **Sun 10 Feb (2-5). Adm £3, chd free. Tea. Opening with Cumnor Village Gardens on Sun 2 June.**

Front, side and rear garden of a thatched cottage (not open). Front is partly gravelled and side courtyard has many pots. Rear garden overlooks meadows with old apple trees underplanted with ferns, wildlife pond, unusual plants, many with black or bronze foliage, planted in drifts and repeated throughout the garden. Planting has mild Japanese influence; rounded, clipped shapes interspersed with verticals. Snowdrops in February. There are two pubs in the village serving food; The Bear & Ragged Staff and The Vine. Gravel drive to access garden.

Your visits help change lives – since 1927, we've donated £55 million to nursing and caring charities

66 UPLANDS

Old Boars Hill, Oxford, OX1 5JF. Lyn Sanders, 01865 739486, sandersc4@hotmail.com. *3m S of Oxford. From S ring road towards A34 at r'about follow signs to Wootton & Boars Hill. Up Hinksey Hill take R fork. 1m R into Berkley Rd. Follow road around 2 bends, garden opp 3rd bend. Parking in lane.* **Visits by arrangement July to Oct for groups of 5 to 30. Home-made teas.**

A hidden ½ acre garden with borrowed views and colour throughout the year. The long sloping lawn leads to a new sunny formal garden. There is a wildlife pond inhabited by great crested and smooth newts in spring and damselflies and dragonflies later, plus an extensive range of perennial plants, spring bulbs, roses, dahlias, Michaelmas daisies and clematis. Some steps can be avoided by using the sloping lawns.

67 UPPER GREEN

Brill Road, Horton cum Studley, Oxford, OX33 1BU. Susan & Peter Burge, 01865 351310, sue.burge@ndm.ox.ac.uk, www.uppergreengarden.co.uk. *6½m NE of Oxford. Enter village, turn R up Horton Hill. At T-junction turn L into Brill Rd. Upper Green 250yds on R, 2 gates before pillar box. Roadside parking.* **Visits by arrangement Feb to Oct for groups of up to 30. Light refreshments.**

Mature ½ acre wildlife friendly garden packed with interest and colour throughout the year. Over 1500 plants in garden database. Wildlife friendly. Includes drought-resistant gravel bed, rock bed, ferns, hot border, potager, bog and pond. Snowdrop collection. Alpines. Old apple trees support rambling roses. Autumn fruit and berries. Spectacular views. Great compost! Sorry, no dogs. Gravel drive limits wheelchair access.

68 WADHAM COLLEGE

Parks Road, Oxford, OX1 3PN. The Warden & Fellows. *Central Oxford. Wadham College gardens are accessed through the main entrance of the College on Parks Rd.* **Sun 7 Apr, Sun 14 July (2-5). Adm £2, chd free.**

5 acres, best known for trees, spring bulbs and mixed borders. In Fellows' main garden, fine ginkgo and *Magnolia acuminata*; bamboo plantation; in Back Quadrangle very large *Tilia tomentosa* 'Petiolaris'; in Mallam Court white scented garden est 1994; in Warden's garden an ancient tulip tree; in Fellows' private garden, Civil War embankment with period fruit tree cultivars, recently established shrubbery with unusual trees and ground cover amongst older plantings.

69 ◆ WATERPERRY GARDENS

Waterperry, Wheatley, OX33 1JZ. School of Economic Science, 01844 339226, office@waterperrygardens.co.uk, www.waterperrygardens.co.uk. *7½m from Oxford city centre. From E M40 J8, from N M40 J8a. Follow brown tourist signs. For SatNav please use OX33 1LA.* **For NGS: Sun 14 Apr, Sun 15 Sept (10-5.30). Adm £8.50, chd free. Light refreshments in the teashop (10-5).** For other opening times and information, please phone, email or visit garden website.

Waterperry gardens are extensive, well-maintained and full of interesting plants. From The Virgin's Walk with its shade-loving plants to the long classical herbaceous border, brilliantly colourful from late May until Oct. The Mary Rose Garden illustrates modern and older roses, and the formal garden is neatly designed and colourful with a small knot garden, herb border and wisteria tunnel. Newly redesigned walled garden, river walk, statues and pear orchard. Riverside walk may be inaccessible to wheelchair users if very wet.

NPC

70 WAYSIDE

82 Banbury Road, Kidlington, OX5 2BX. Margaret & Alistair Urquhart, 01865 460180, alistairurquhart@ntlworld.com. *5m N of Oxford. On R of A4260 travelling N through Kidlington.* **Sun 2 June (2-6). Adm £3, chd free. Tea. Visits also by arrangement May & June for groups of up to 20.**

¼ acre garden shaded by mature trees. Mixed border with some rare and unusual plants and shrubs. A climber clothed pergola leads past a dry gravel garden to the woodland garden with an extensive collection of hardy ferns. Conservatory and large fern house with a collection of unusual species of tree ferns and tender exotics. Important collection of hardy garden ferns. Partial wheelchair access.

71 WESTWELL MANOR

Westwell, Nr Burford, OX18 4JT. Mr Thomas Gibson. *2m SW of Burford. From A40 Burford-Cheltenham, turn L ½m after Burford r'about signed Westwell. After 1½m at T-junction, turn R & Manor is 2nd house on L.* **Sun 19 May (2-6.30). Adm £5, chd free.** Donation to Aspire.

7 acres surrounding old Cotswold manor house (not open) with knot garden, potager, shrub roses, herbaceous borders, topiary, earth works, moonlight garden, auricula ladder, rills and water garden.

GROUP OPENING

72 WHEATLEY GARDENS

High Street, Wheatley, OX33 1XX. *5m E of Oxford. Leave A40 at Wheatley, turn into High St. Gardens at W end of High St, S side.* **Sun 16 June (2-6). Combined adm £5, chd free. Cream teas at The Manor House.**

BREACH HOUSE GARDEN
Liz Parry.

THE MANOR HOUSE
Mrs Elizabeth Hess, echess@hotmail.co.uk. **Visits also by arrangement Mar to July. A historic presentation about the Manor House on request.**

THE STUDIO
S & A Buckingham.

Three adjoining gardens in the historic coaching village of Wheatley. Breach House Garden has an established main area with extensive shrubs and perennials, a more contemporary reflective space and a wild meadow with ponds. The Studio, cottage style walled garden developed from previous farmyard. Herbaceous borders, climbing roses and clematis, shrubs, vegetable plot and fruit trees. The Manor House is a 1½ acre garden surrounding an Elizabethan manor house (not open). Formal box walk, herb garden, cottage garden with rose arches and a shrubbery with old roses. A romantic oasis. All in all a lovely collection of gardens set in the heart of the busy village of Wheatley. Various musical events. Wheelchair access with assistance due to gravel paths, two shallow steps and grass.

73 WHITEHILL FARM

Widford, Burford, OX18 4DT. Mr & Mrs Paul Youngson, 01993 822894, anneyoungson@btinternet.com. *1m E of Burford. From A40 take road signed Widford. Turn R at the bottom of the hill, 1st house on the L with ample car parking.* **Sun 2 June (2-6). Adm £4, chd free. Home-made teas. Visits also by arrangement May to Sept.**

2 acres of hillside gardens and woodland with spectacular views overlooking Burford and Windrush valley. Informal plantsman's garden built up by the owners over 20 yrs. Herbaceous and shrub borders, ponds and bog area, old fashioned roses, ground cover, ornamental grasses, bamboos and hardy geraniums. Large cascade water feature, pretty tea patio and wonderful Cotswold views.

GROUP OPENING

74 WOOTTON GARDENS

Wootton, OX13 6DP. *Wootton is 3m SW of Oxford. From the Oxford ring road S, take the turning to Wootton. Parking for all gardens at the Bystander Pub & on the road.* **Thur 13 June (2-6). Combined adm £5, chd free. Home-made teas.**

13 AMEY CRESCENT
Sylv & Liz Gleed.

60 BESSELSLEIGH ROAD
Freda East.

NEW **67 BESSELSLEIGH ROAD**
Jean Beedell.

NEW **14 HOME CLOSE**
Kev & Sue Empson.

22 SANDLEIGH ROAD
Peter & Jennie Debenham.

35 SANDLEIGH ROAD
Hilal Baylav Inkersole.

6 inspirational small gardens, all with very different ways of providing a personal joy. 13 Amey Cresent is a gravel garden with grasses and prairie plants. The garden has a small wildlife pond, alpine house and troughs. 14 Home Close is a garden containing mainly shrubs with an unusually shaped lawn. There is also a pond, raised bed and a vegetable garden. 67 Besselsleigh Road is a compact and vibrant garden. Its deep borders are brimming with a variety of colourful plants shaped around a pathway. 60 Besselsleigh Road has 'The Deadwood Stage' with toadstools and a secret garden with many creatures to find. 22 Sandleigh Road is packed with cottage garden favourites including an experimental wildflower area and recently planted white border. Hidden fairy doors wait to be found! 35 Sandleigh Road is a mature garden, laid to lawn on two levels. Grown mostly from cuttings the garden is brimming with vibrant flowers, pondside planting and glass art. Partial wheelchair access.

75 YARNTON MANOR

Church Lane, Yarnton, OX5 1PY. Yarnton Manor, 01865 809400, events@yarntonmanor.com, www.yarntonmanor.com. *From M40 J9, follow A34 towards Oxford for approx 6m until A44 exit. At Peartree Interchange, follow A44 N towards Woodstock, at r'about take 1st L onto Cassington Rd. Follow road for ½m & then take L onto Church Lane. Yarnton Manor signed 500 metres on R.* **Thur 21 Mar (11-2). Adm £5, chd free. Home-made teas.**

7 acres of gardens incl a large back lawn, walled garden, sunken garden, kitchen garden and lime tree avenue. The gardens feature a large variety of shrubs, herbaceous borders, mature trees, climbers and seasonal bedding against a backdrop of a C17 Manor House. The gardens are designed and overseen by Robin Lane Fox. House tours available on request for an additional charge (not for NGS). Croquet and garden games available on the lawn. Garden and estate team onsite. Plant sale and tea shop. Access via a gravel path with several small steps in the majority of the gardens. No wheelchair accessible facilities.

Radcot House

SHROPSHIRE

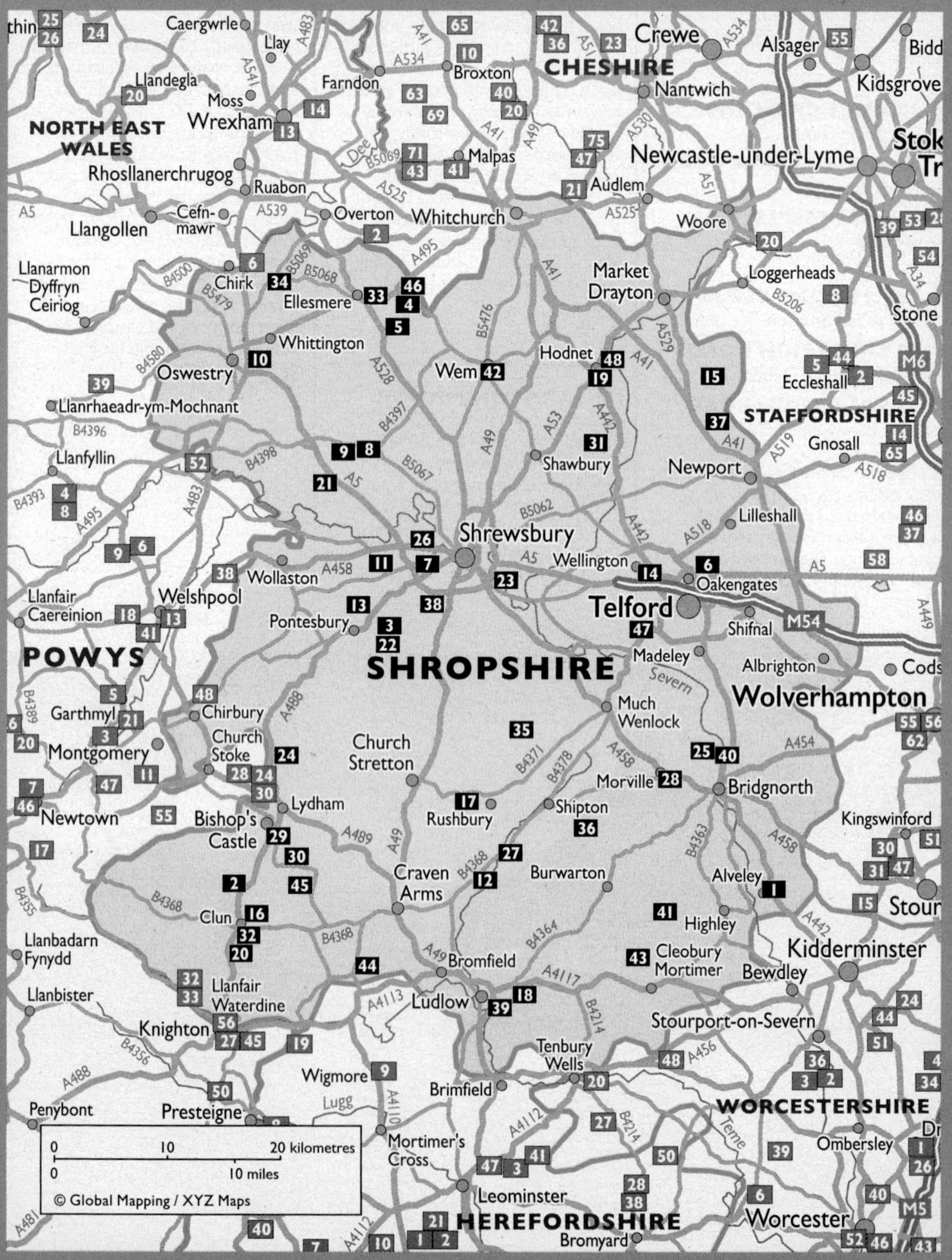

CHESHIRE
NORTH EAST WALES
SHROPSHIRE
STAFFORDSHIRE
POWYS
WORCESTERSHIRE
HEREFORDSHIRE
Crewe
Nantwich
Wrexham
Newcastle-under-Lyme
Whitchurch
Market Drayton
Oswestry
Wem
Shrewsbury
Telford
Wolverhampton
Welshpool
Church Stretton
Bridgnorth
Ludlow
Kidderminster
Worcester
Leominster
0 10 20 kilometres
0 10 miles
© Global Mapping / XYZ Maps

Welcome to Shropshire! One of Britain's hidden gems and home to some of the best gardens in the country! Our historic county town of Shrewsbury not only stages the world oldest Flower Show but has a great horticultural history:

Shrewsbury sons include the original "celebrity" gardener, Percy Thrower and the ultimate plantsman, Charles Darwin. Horticultural passion is reflected throughout the county with a multitude of exquisite gardens, both large and small, in town and country, that open for the National Garden Scheme.

Some of Shropshire's historic estates first opened in 1927 when the National Garden Scheme started and are still opening today. As well as being able to visit our grand estates, such as Walcot Hall, Oteley, Hodnet Hall, Millichope Park, Stanley Hall and the nationally acclaimed, Wollerton Old Hall, there are many other beautiful private gardens that can only be visited on National Garden Scheme days.

This year we have many new gardens for visitors to enjoy alongside old favourites. You will be most welcome in a Shropshire garden this year.

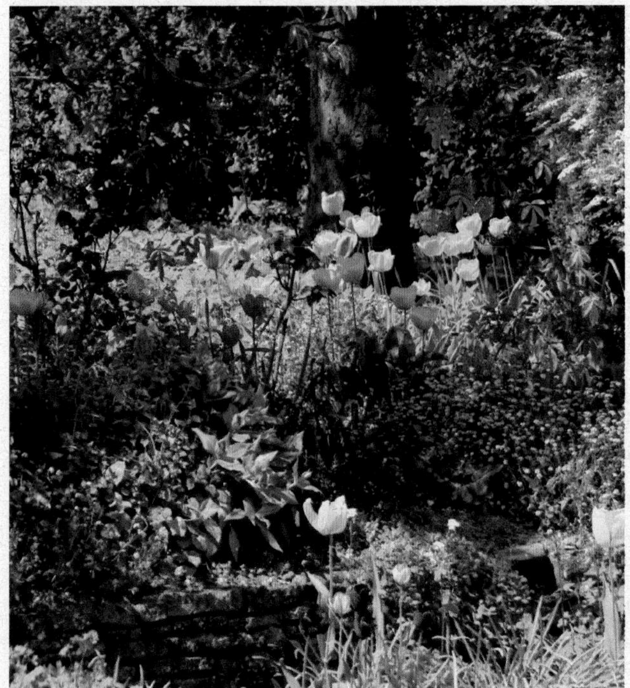

Volunteers

County Organiser
Allison Walter
01743 627900
allison.walter@ngs.org.uk

County Treasurer
Suzanne Stevens
01588 660314
harrystevens@btconnect.com

Publicity
Allison Walter
(as above)

Social Media
Victoria Kirk
01743 821429
victoria.kirk@ngs.org.uk

Booklet Co-ordinator
Fiona Chancellor
01952 507675
fionachancellor@btinternet.com

Talks Organiser
Chris Neil
01743 821651

Photographer
Julie Stanley
jaajstan@aol.com

Assistant County Organisers
Ruth Dinsdale
ruth.dinsdale@btinternet.com

Sue Griffiths
sue.griffiths@btinternet.com

Sheila Jones
smaryjones@icloud.com

Penny Tryhorn
pennypottingshed@icloud.com

Left: **The Mount**

OPENING DATES

All entries subject to change. For latest information check **www.ngs.org.uk**

Map locator numbers are shown to the right of each garden name.

February

Snowdrop Festival

Sunday 17th
Millichope Park 27

March

Saturday 30th
NEW Balmer Cottage 4

April

Sunday 7th
Edge Villa 13

Saturday 27th
NEW The Mount 29

Tuesday 30th
Brownhill House 8

May

Sunday 5th
NEW Longden Manor 22
Lyndale House 25
Millichope Park 27

Monday 6th
Ruthall Manor 36

Saturday 11th
NEW Kinton Grove 21
Upper Shelderton House 44

Sunday 12th
Delbury Hall Walled Garden 12
NEW Kinton Grove 21
Oteley 33
Upper Shelderton House 44

Friday 17th
Ruthall Manor 36
◆ Wollerton Old Hall 48

Saturday 18th
Ruthall Manor 36

Sunday 19th
Guilden Down Cottage 16
NEW Henley Hall 18
Longner Hall 23
Stanley Hall 40

Tuesday 21st
NEW Pooh Corner 34

Thursday 23rd
NEW 3 Oakeley Mynd 30

Sunday 26th
NEW The Gardeners Lodge 14
Sunningdale 42
Walcot Hall 45

Monday 27th
Walcot Hall 45

Tuesday 28th
Brownhill House 8

Wednesday 29th
Goldstone Hall Gardens 15

June

Saturday 1st
NEW Beaufort 6

Sunday 2nd
Edge Villa 13
2 School Cottages 38
Windy Ridge 47

Saturday 8th
NEW The Old Vicarage 32

Sunday 9th
NEW Hargrove 17
Hodnet Hall Gardens 19
Morville Hall Gardens 28

Wednesday 12th
Goldstone Hall Gardens 15

Friday 14th
Ruthall Manor 36

Saturday 15th
NEW The Mount 29
Ruthall Manor 36

Sunday 16th
NEW 5 Church Street 9
Preen Manor 35
Ruthall Manor 36

Saturday 22nd
Secret Garden 39

Sunday 23rd
Delbury Hall Walled Garden 12

Tuesday 25th
Brownhill House 8

Wednesday 26th
Goldstone Hall Gardens 15

Sunday 30th
NEW Beam Cottage 5

July

Saturday 6th
Cruckfield House 11
Ruthall Manor 36

Sunday 7th
Ruthall Manor 36
2 School Cottages 38
NEW Upper Marshes 43
Windy Ridge 47

Wednesday 10th
Goldstone Hall Gardens 15

Sunday 14th
Lower Brookshill 24
NEW Welshampton Gardens 46

Wednesday 17th
Oakgate Nursery & Garden Centre 31

Sunday 21st
Sambrook Manor 37

Sunday 28th
Delbury Hall Walled Garden 12
NEW Merton 26

Tuesday 30th
Goldstone Hall Gardens 15

August

Tuesday 6th
Goldstone Hall Gardens 15

Saturday 10th
NEW 27 Croxon Rise 10

Sunday 11th
Windy Ridge 47

Wednesday 14th
Goldstone Hall Gardens 15

Sunday 18th
Delbury Hall Walled Garden 12

Sunday 25th
Sambrook Manor 37

September

Wednesday 4th
Goldstone Hall Gardens 15

Sunday 8th
Edge Villa 13
Windy Ridge 47

Saturday 14th
Ruthall Manor 36

Sunday 15th
Ruthall Manor 36

Saturday 21st
NEW Balmer Cottage 4

October

Sunday 13th
Millichope Park 27

By Arrangement

Arrange a personalised garden visit with your club, or group of friends, on a date to suit you. See individual garden entries for full details.

Ancoireán 1
Argoed House 2
Avocet 3
NEW Balmer Cottage 4
Bowbrook Allotment Community 7
Brownhill House 8
Cruckfield House 11
Edge Villa 13
Goldstone Hall Gardens 15
Guilden Down Cottage 16
The Hollies 20
NEW Kinton Grove 21
NEW Merton 26
NEW The Mount 29
Oteley 33
NEW Pooh Corner 34
Ruthall Manor 36
Sambrook Manor 37
2 School Cottages 38
Secret Garden 39
NEW 12 Station Road 41
Sunningdale 42
Windy Ridge 47

THE GARDENS

1 ANCOIREÁN

24 Romsley View, Alveley, WV15 6PJ. Judy & Peter Creed, 01746 780504, pdjc@me.com. *6m S Bridgnorth off A442 Bridgnorth to Kidderminster rd. N from Kidderminster turn L just after Royal Oak PH. S from Bridgnorth turn R after Squirrel Pub. Take 3rd turning on R & follow NGS signs.* **Visits by arrangement June & July for groups of 20+. Adm £4, chd free. Light refreshments by arrangement with groups.**

Natural garden layout on several levels, developed over 30yrs, with a large variety of herbaceous plants and shrubs, water features, wooded area with bog garden containing numerous varieties of ferns and hostas, and colourful alpine scree. Features, wooded area, stumpery, ornamental grass border and Spring bulb collection, clematis collection, acer and azalea beds. Selection of plants, bird and insect boxes for sale. Close to Severn Valley Railway and Country Park and Dudmaston Hall NT.

2 ARGOED HOUSE

Bryn, Bishops Castle, SY9 5LE. Roger & Jane Fairweather, 01588 630663, janefairweather1@icloud.com. *Bishop's Castle A488 S for 3m. Take lane on R "Bryn 1, Cefn Einion 2, Mainstone 3" for ½m past Captain's Coppice. At fork go R up hill. Garden 200yds on L. Email for map.* **Visits by arrangement June to Sept for groups of up to 20. (Closed in Aug). Limited parking - max 6 cars. Adm £4, chd free. Home-made teas.**

1 acre garden approx. 700ft high, nestled amongst hills and surrounded by woods. The front garden was professionally landscaped in 2002 with large beds of spring bulbs, perennial plants and shrubs, living willow structures and a sizeable pond with informal planting. This opens out into a sloping mown areas with specimen trees. To the rear, the garden goes uphill and is left for wild flowers.

3 AVOCET

3 Main Road, Plealey, Shrewsbury, SY5 0UZ. Malc & Jude Mollart, 01743 791743, malcandjude@btinternet.com. *6m SW of Shrewsbury. From A5 take A488 signed Bishops Castle, approx ½m past Lea Cross Tandoori turn L signed Plealey. In ¾m turn L, garden on R. SatNav unreliable!* **Visits by arrangement Apr to Aug for groups of up to 30. Adm £4, chd free. Home-made teas.**

Cottage style garden with modern twists owned by plantaholics and shared with wildlife. Designed around a series of garden compartments and for year round interest. Features include a wildlife pool, mixed borders, seaside garden, gravel garden, succulents, trained fruit trees, and sculpture. This is a constantly evolving garden so something new every year. Countryside views from garden. Collection of vintage garden tools.

4 NEW BALMER COTTAGE

The Balmer, Welshampton, Ellesmere, SY12 0PP. Mr & Mrs Geoff & Valerie Barrow, 01948 710888, geoffbarrow@btinternet.com. *3m outside Ellesmere, Shropshire, on the edge of the village of Welshampton. From Ellesmere, SE approx ½m on A528. L on A495 towards Whitchurch for approx 2m. In village of Welshampton, R on B5063, towards Wem. Balmer Cottage is approx ½m on L.* **Sat 30 Mar, Sat 21 Sept (10-4). Adm £5, chd free. Light refreshments.** Visits also by arrangement Mar to Oct.

One acre of landscaped garden originally designed by Chelsea Flower Show gold medal winner Richard Lucas. An avenue of Malus red sentinels leads to mowed pathways in a paddock with fruit trees. The main garden features a woodland area, a variety trees and shrubs, spring bulb plantings, dry stone walled terraces with winding pathways and interesting shady areas and strong autumn colour.

5 NEW BEAM COTTAGE

Colemere, Ellesmere, SY12 0QW. Rob & Barbara Platt. *Follow signs off A495 (Shrewsbury/Ellesmere Rd) to Colemere Country Park. After 1m Beam Cottage is on R just before T- junction opp phone box.* **Sun 30 June (12-6). Adm £4, chd free. Light refreshments at St. John the Evangelist Church, Colemere.**

Garden of approx. ¾ acres surrounding half-timbered 400 year old thatched cottage. Mainly herbaceous borders with vegetable patch, herb garden and 2 small ponds. Situated in picturesque village of Colemere. Large Davidia involucrata, Liriodendron tulipifera and Taxus baccata. Several rose species climbing through holly and apple trees. Not suitable for wheelchairs as paths are uneven.

6 NEW BEAUFORT

Coppice Drive, Moss Road Wrockwardine Wood, Telford, TF2 7BP. Mike King, www.carnivorousplants.uk.com. *Approx 2m N from Telford town centre. From Asda Donnington, turn L at lights on Moss rd, ⅓m, turn L into Coppice Drive. 4th Bungalow on L with solar panels.* **Sat 1 June (10-5). Adm £4, chd free. Light refreshments.**

If carnivorous plants are your thing, then come and visit our National Collection of Sarracenia (pitcher plants); also over 100 different Venus flytrap clones (Dionaea muscipula), Sundews (Drosera) and Butterworts (Pinguicula.) - over 6000 plants in total. Large greenhouses at Telford's first carbon negative house; a great place to visit - kids will love it! Not wheelchair accessible into greenhouses.

NPC

Your visits help change lives – we've donated over £16.7 million to Macmillan Cancer Support since 1984

ALLOTMENTS

7 BOWBROOK ALLOTMENT COMMUNITY

Mytton Oak Road, Shrewsbury, SY3 5BT. Bowbrook Allotment Community, 01743 363605, pete-haycox@hotmail.co.uk, bowbrookallotments.wordpress.com. *On western edge of Shrewsbury between A5 Bypass & Royal Shrewsbury Hospital. From A5 Shrewsbury Bypass take B4386 (Mytton Oak Road) towards Shrewsbury, following signs to Royal Shrewsbury Hospital. The allotment entrance is ½m from A5 r'about, on R, opp Oak Lane.* **Visits by arrangement Apr to Sept for groups of 10 to 30. Min charge £60. Combined adm £6, chd free. Light refreshments. Tea/ Coffee and Cakes provided for visitors - cost included in entry fee..**

Recipient of RHS National Certificate of Distinction, this 5 acre site, comprising 93 plots, displays wide ranging cultivation methods. The site has featured on BBC TV, local radio programmes and in several magazines. Members cultivate organically with nature in mind using companion planting and attracting natural predators. Green spaces flourish throughout and include Gardens of the 4 Seasons, orchards, and many wildlife features including wild flower meadows and pond. Children are encouraged to be part of the community and have their own special places such as a story telling willow dome, willow tunnel, sensory garden and turf spiral. See how the Contemplation Garden and the Prairie Garden have developed. Wheelchair access possible with care. Generally flat wide grass paths allow access to all the main areas of the site, although paths may be bumpy!

8 BROWNHILL HOUSE

Ruyton XI Towns, Shrewsbury, SY4 1LR. Roger & Yoland Brown, 01939 261121, brownhill@eleventowns.co.uk, www.eleventowns.co.uk. *9m NW of Shrewsbury on B4397. On the B4397 in the village of Ruyton XI Towns.* **Tue 30 Apr, Tue 28 May, Tue 25 June (1.30-5). Adm £4, chd free. Home-made teas.** Visits also by arrangement May to July.

A unique 2 acre hillside garden with many steps and levels bordering R Perry. Visitors can enjoy a wide variety of plants and styles from formal terraces to woodland paths. The lower areas are for the sure-footed and mobile while the upper levels with a large kitchen garden have many places to sit and enjoy the views. Kit cars on show.

9 NEW 5 CHURCH STREET

Ruyton X1 Towns, Shrewsbury, SY4 1LA. Steve & Jill Owen. *Village of Ruyton XI Towns. From A5 take B4397 to Ruyton XI Towns. Enter the village, carry straight on passing The Talbot pub on the R. House is on the L. 50m further on, opposite school.* **Sun 16 June (12-5). Adm £4, chd free. Home-made teas.**

Long village garden divided into sections affording different styles of planting: herbaceous borders with a wide variety of plants, shrubs and trees giving year-round interest through texture and colour; wild flower area and wildlife pond. Summer house, vegetable area and greenhouse. Not suitable for wheelchairs.

10 NEW 27 CROXON RISE

Oswestry, SY11 2YQ. Natalie & Tony Bainbridge. *Eastern Oswestry. ½m from A5 Oswestry Bypass. Take B4580 to Oswestry. Take 1st L Harlech Rd, 1st exit r'about Cabin lane. Take 5th L Aston Way, 1st L & 1st L again Croxon Rise. Please park courteously in surrounding rds.* **Sat 10 Aug (10-4). Adm £4, chd free. Home-made teas.**

Packing a lot into a small space, this secluded, beautifully planted town garden offers interest at every turn. Mixed borders provide colour through to late summer. A raised bed vegetable garden, greenhouse and cut flower garden, soft fruit cage, seating areas, and water features. A rose garden surrounds a mature cherry tree and south facing wall protects step-over and cordon fruits.

11 CRUCKFIELD HOUSE

Shoothill, Ford, Shrewsbury, SY5 9NR. Geoffrey Cobley, 01743 850222. *5m W of Shrewsbury. A458, turn L towards Shoothill.* **Sat 6 July (2-6). Adm £6, chd free. Home-made teas.** Visits also by arrangement June & July for groups of 30+.

3 acre romantic S-facing garden, formally designed, informally and intensively planted with a great variety of unusual herbaceous plants. Nick's garden, with many species trees and shrubs, surrounds a large pond with bog and moisture-loving plants. Ornamental kitchen garden with pretty outbuildings. Rose and peony walk. Courtyard fountain garden and large shrubbery and extensive clematis collection Extensive topiary, and lily pond.

12 DELBURY HALL WALLED GARDEN

Delbury Hall Estate, Mill Lane, Diddlebury, Craven Arms, SY7 9DH. Mr & Mrs Rallings, www.myndhardyplants.co.uk. *8m W of Craven Arms. 1m off B4368, Craven Arms to Bridgnorth, through village of Diddlebury, turn R at Mynd Hardy Plants sign.* **Sun 12 May, Sun 23 June, Sun 28 July, Sun 18 Aug (11-5). Adm £5, chd free. Home-made teas. English wine from our own vineyard.**

A two acre early Victorian Walled Garden with large herbaceous borders, a vegetable and a herb garden, shrubbery, vines and very old fruit trees. In addition there is a large Penstemon and Hemerocallis collection. The gardens of Delbury Hall will be accessible unless a private function is being held. Please check our website for details. Gravel and grass paths. Dogs are welcome in the Walled Garden but not in the Hall Gardens.

13 EDGE VILLA

Edge, nr Yockleton, SY5 9PY. Mr & Mrs W F Neil, 01743 821651, billfneil@me.com. *6m SW of Shrewsbury. From A5 take either A488 signed to Bishops Castle or B4386 to Montgomery for approx 6m then follow NGS signs.* **Sun 7 Apr, Sun 2 June, Sun 8 Sept (2-5). Adm £5, chd free. Home-made teas.** Visits also by arrangement Apr to Sept for

groups of 10+.
Two acres nestling in South Shropshire hills. Self-sufficient vegetable plot. Chickens in orchard, foxes permitting. Large herbaceous borders. Dewpond surrounded by purple elder, irises, candelabra primulas and dieramas. Large selection of fragrant roses. Teas in sheltered courtyard. Wendy House and Teepee for children. Many unusual plants propagated for sale. Some German and French spoken. Some gravel paths.

14 NEW THE GARDENERS LODGE

2 Roseway, Wellington, Telford, TF1 1JA. Amanda Goode, www.lovegrowshereweb.wordpress.com/. *1½m (4 mins) from J7 (M54). B5061 Holyhead Rd 2nd L after NT 'Sunnycroft'. (New Church Rd) We are the cream house on corner of NCR & Roseway.* **Sun 26 May (9.30-4.30). Adm £4, chd free.**
There was just one tree in the garden when the current owners purchased The Gardener's Lodge, the ground having been cleared, ready to sell as a building plot. However the owners had other plans for it: the garden is now eclectically divided, arranged and planted into areas: Mediterranean, Cottage, Indian etc but, seamlessly, each section merges and leads into the next developing idea. A small urban garden with seating, water features and shade.

15 GOLDSTONE HALL GARDENS

Goldstone, Market Drayton, TF9 2NA. Mr John Cushing, 01630 661202, enquiries@goldstonehall.com, www.goldstonehall.com. *5m N of Newport on A41. Follow brown & white signs from Hinstock. From Shrewsbury A53, R for A41 Hinstock & follow brown & white signs & NGS signs.* **Wed 29 May, Wed 12, Wed 26 June, Wed 10, Tue 30 July, Tue 6, Wed 14 Aug, Wed 4 Sept (2-5). Adm £5, chd free. Home-made teas. Teas served in award winning oak framed pavilion in the midst of the garden.**
Visits also by arrangement May to Sept for groups of 10+. All tours welcomed with introductory talk and garden maps for each visitor.
5 acres with highly productive beautiful kitchen garden. Unusual vegetables and fruits - alpine strawberries; heritage tomatoes, salad, chillies, celeriac. Roses in Walled Garden from May; Double herbaceous in front of old English garden wall at its best July and August; Sedums and Roses stunning in September. Teas in Pavilion with cakes created by award-winning Chef. Lawn aficionados will enjoy the stripes. Rosetted and award winning restaurant, AA Red Star Country House Hotel, Good Hotel Guide listed. Majority of garden can be accessed on gravel and lawns.

16 GUILDEN DOWN COTTAGE

Guilden Down, Clun, Craven Arms, SY7 8NZ. Mike Black & Sue Wilson, 07795 275557, sue.guilden@gmail.com, www.facebook.com/teaontheway. *In Clun Signs for YHA. Continue 1m up hill. Past cottages on L. At farm bear R through farm buildings. 100 yds at end of road .Garden on L.* **Sun 19 May (2-6). Adm £5, chd free. Home-made teas. Guilden Down Cottage also operates as a tea garden under the name of TEA on the WAY.**
Visits also by arrangement May to Aug for groups of up to 30. Book for morning coffee, light lunches, afternoon tea or evening snacks.
With spectacular views, this one acre organic garden has been developed over the past 14 years to be in harmony and its surroundings. Divided into many rooms, there are vibrant herbaceous borders and terraces, rose trellises and a large vegetable plot. Our wild garden includes a natural pond, living willow structures, wild flower orchard, trees, shrubs and planted borders. Partial wheelchair access, front garden only but worth it for the views.

17 NEW HARGROVE

Wall-Under-Heywood, Church Stretton, SY6 7DP. Sally & Gerard Wainwright. *Hargrove - grid ref SO 5013 9286. Approached by a drive directly off B4371 on Wall Bank. Proceed over cattle grid down ⅔m.* **Sun 9 June (1-6). Adm £6, chd free. Cream teas at cottage in the grounds. Tea, coffee and soft drinks with home baked cream teas and cakes.**
Approached by a ⅔m tree lined drive through parkland bordered by ancient woodland. Varied 2 acre gardens surround a contemporary country house. Water features, walled herb and soft fruit garden with cascading roses. Orchard and extensive random flower beds created for family, friends and six dogs. Short woodland walk bordering lake with swans. Teas available at cottage in grounds with plant and local china sales.

Argoed House

18 NEW HENLEY HALL

Henley, Ludlow, SY8 3HD. Helen &. Sebastian Phillips. *2½m E of Ludlow. 1½m from the A49. Off the A4117 - signed Bitterley. Gates on the R when travelling in the direction toward Clee Hill.* **Sun 19 May (12-4). Adm £5, chd free. Light refreshments.**

The historic elements of the gardens – mature specimen trees, rock garden, water features, yew hedges, balustrades and Ha-ha – are complemented by a naturalistic planting scheme. Highlights include: fern river walk, organic kitchen garden, daffodil 'slang', cedar collection and green garden. Guided tour from leading ecologist on how to make your garden friendly for wildlife.

19 HODNET HALL GARDENS

Hodnet, Market Drayton, TF9 3NN. Sir Algernon & The Hon Lady Heber-Percy, www.hodnethallgardens.org. *5½m SW of Market Drayton. 12m NE Shrewsbury. At junction of A53 & A442.* **Sun 9 June (11-5). Adm £7.50, chd £1. Light refreshments.**

60 acre landscaped garden with series of lakes and pools; magnificent forest trees, great variety of flowers, shrubs providing colour throughout season. Unique collection of big-game trophies in C17 tearooms. Kitchen garden. For details please see website and Facebook page. Maps are available to show access for our less mobile visitors.

20 THE HOLLIES

Rockhill, Clun, SY7 8LR. Pat & Terry Badham, 01588 640805, patbadham@btinternet.com. *10m W of Craven Arms. 8m S of Bishops Castle. From A49 Craven Arms take B4368 to Clun. Turn L onto A488 continue for 1½m. Bear R signed Treverward. After 50 yards turn R at Xrds, property is 1st on L.* **Visits by arrangement June to Sept for groups of up to 30. Refreshments available in Clun. Adm £4, chd free.**

A garden of approx 2 acres at 1000ft which was started in 2009. Features include a kitchen garden with raised beds and fruit cage. Large island beds and borders with perennials, shrubs and grasses, specimen trees. Wildlife dingle with stream. Wheelchair access is available to the majority of the garden over gravel and grass.

21 NEW KINTON GROVE

Kinton, Nesscliffe, Shrewsbury, SY4 1AZ. Tim & Judy Creyke, 01743 741263, judycreyke@icloud.com. *Off A5, between Shrewsbury & Oswestry. Take either of the r'abouts at the two ends of the Nesscliffe by-pass, signed either Nesscliffe or Kinton. Then follow the yellow signs.* **Sat 11, Sun 12 May (1-5). Adm £4, chd free. Home-made teas.** Visits also by arrangement May & June for groups of 5 to 30.

A garden of ¾ acre, with colourful herbaceous borders, roses and many interesting trees and shrubs. Lovely views across the Briedden Hills from the garden and plenty of pleasant places to sit and admire the views.

22 NEW LONGDEN MANOR

Plealey, Pontesbury, Shrewsbury, SY5 0XH. Karen Lovegrove. *Longden Manor. Post Code: SY5 0XG From Shrewsbury: Take Longden Rd from A4380 Through Hook-a-Gate & Annscroft to Longden. Pass Village Shop & Post Office on L & Turn R opposite The Tankerville Arms Car Park.* **Sun 5 May (10-4.30). Adm £5, chd free. Home-made teas.**

Large estate garden with lots of character and interest: woodland walks and grass paths; humorous topiary; wide variety of specimen trees; rhododendrons and azaleas; wildflowers; panoramic vistas of surrounding countryside; holly garden. Also, children's treasure hunt, giant Jenca, Skittles and Croquet - a great place for all the family to visit.

23 LONGNER HALL

Atcham, Shrewsbury, SY4 4TG. Mr & Mrs R L Burton. *4m SE of Shrewsbury. From M54 follow A5 to Shrewsbury, then B4380 to Atcham. From Atcham take Uffington rd, entrance ¼m on L.* **Sun 19 May (2-5). Adm £5, chd free. Home-made teas.**

A long drive approach through parkland designed by Humphry Repton. Walks lined with golden yew through extensive lawns, with views over Severn Valley. Borders containing roses, herbaceous and shrubs, also ancient yew wood. Enclosed walled garden containing mixed planting, garden buildings, tower and game larder. Short woodland walk around old moat pond. 1 acre walled garden currently being restored now open to visitors. Woodland walk not suitable for wheelchairs.

Beam Cottage

24 LOWER BROOKSHILL

Nind, Lydham, (near) Bishops Castle, SY5 0JW. Patricia & Robin Oldfield, robin.oldfield@live.com. *3m N of Lydham on A488. Take signed turn to Nind & after ½m sharp L & follow narrow rd for another ½m.* **Sun 14 July (2-6). Adm £5, chd free. Home-made teas.**

10 acres of hillside garden and woods at 950ft within the AONB with fine views, described by one visitor last year as 'A Shropshire idyll'. Begun in 2010 from a derelict and overgrown site, it includes brookside walks, a 'pocket' park, four ponds (one inspired by Monet's lily pond), mixed borders and lawns, cottage garden and annual wild flowers. Unfortunately not really suitable for wheelchairs.

25 LYNDALE HOUSE

Astley Abbotts, Bridgnorth, WV16 4SW. Bob & Mary Saunders. *2m out of Bridnorth off B4373. From High Town Bridgnorth take B4373 Broseley Rd for 1½m, then take lane signed Astley Abbotts & Colemore Green.* **Sun 5 May (1-5). Adm £4, chd free. Home-made teas.**

1½ acre garden which has been lovingly tended for 25yrs. Rose terrace under planted with tulips and alliums. Large lawns interspersed with well planted flower beds. For 2019 revamped pool and waterfall, courtyard with topiary. Masses of tulips in the spring, which all overlooks the Shropshire countryside. Topiary garden, waterfall to pool, many unusual trees. Please ask owner about wheelchair friendly access.

26 NEW MERTON

Shepherds Lane, Bicton, Shrewsbury, SY3 8BT. David & Jessica Pannett, 01743 850773, jessicapannett@hotmail.co.uk. *3m W of Shrewsbury. Follow B4380 from Shrewsbury past Shelton for 1m Shepherd's Lane turn L garden signed on R or from A5 by pass at Churncote r'about turn towards Shrewsbury 2nd turn L Shepherds Lane.* **Sun 28 July (1-5). Adm £4, chd free. Home-made teas. Visits also by arrangement May to Sept.**

Mature ½ acre botanical garden with a rich collection of trees and shrubs including unusual conifers from around the world. Hardy perennial borders with seasonal flowers and grasses plus an award winning collection of hosta varieties in a woodland setting. Outstanding gunneras in a waterside setting with moisture loving plants. Level paths and lawns.

27 MILLICHOPE PARK

Munslow, Craven Arms, SY7 9HA. Mr & Mrs Frank Bury, www.wildegoosenursery.co.uk. *8m NE of Craven Arms. off B4368 Craven Arms to Bridgnorth Rd. Nr Munslow then follow yellow signs.* **Sun 17 Feb (2-5); Sun 5 May (1-6); Sun 13 Oct (2-5). Adm £6, chd free. Light refreshments in the walled garden tea room.**

Historic landscape gardens covering 14 acres with lakes, cascades dating from C18, woodland walks and wildflowers. Snowdrops in February, Bluebells and Violas in May, Roses and Autumn colour in October. Also open the Walled Garden at Millichope, an exciting restoration project bringing the walled gardens and C19 glasshouses back to life. There is the opportunity to see the Bouts Viola collection. UK's largest collection of hardy, perennial, scented violas. Many varieties for sale during the May opening. Wildegoose nursery and the walled garden at Millichope will also be open.

Your visits help change lives – your generosity has supported unpaid carers through donations to Carers Trust totalling over £3.9 million since 1996

GROUP OPENING

28 MORVILLE HALL GARDENS

Bridgnorth, WV16 5NB. *3m W of Bridgnorth. On A458 at junction with B4368.* **Sun 9 June (2-5). Combined adm £6, chd free. Home-made teas in Morville Church.**

THE COTTAGE
Ms A Nichol-Smith.

THE DOWER HOUSE
Dr Katherine Swift.

1 THE GATE HOUSE
Mr & Mrs Rowe.

2 THE GATE HOUSE
Mrs G Medland.

MORVILLE HALL
Mr & Mrs C Hodsoll & The National Trust.

SOUTH PAVILION
Mr & Mrs B Jenkinson.

An interesting group of gardens that surround a beautiful Grade I listed mansion (house not open). The Cottage has a pretty walled garden with plenty of colour. The Dower House is a horticultural history lesson about Morville Hall which includes a turf maze, cloister garden, Elizabethan knot garden, C18 canal garden, Edwardian kitchen garden and more. It is the setting of Katherine Swift's bestselling book 'The Morville Hours', and the sequel 'The Morville Year'. 1 and 2 The Gate House are cottage-style gardens with colourful borders, formal areas, lawns and wooded glades. The three acre Morville Hall (NT) garden has a parterre, medieval stew pond, shrub borders and large lawns, all offering glorious views across the Mor Valley. South Pavilion features new thoughts and new designs in a small courtyard garden. Please note that National Trust membership does not give admission to this NGS opening. Mostly level ground, but plenty of gravel to negotiate.

Goldstone Hall Gardens

29 NEW THE MOUNT

Bull Lane, Bishops Castle, SY9 5DA. Heather Willis, 01588 638288, adamheather@btopenworld.com. *Bishops Castle off A488 Shrewsbury to Knighton Rd. The Mount is at the top of the town, 130 metres up Bull Lane on R hand side. No parking at the property itself, but parking is free in Bishops Castle.* **Sat 27 Apr, Sat 15 June (11-6). Adm £4, chd free. Home-made teas.** Visits also by arrangement Apr to Aug for groups of up to 20.

An acre of garden that has evolved over 24 years, with 4 lawns, a rosebed in the middle of the drive with pink and white English roses, and herbaceous and mixed shrub borders. There are roses planted throughout the garden and in the spring daffodils and tulips abound. Two large beech trees frame the garden with a view that sweeps down the valley over fields and then up to the Long Mynd. Access easy to the garden itself, but not to WC which is in the house up steps.

30 NEW 3 OAKELEY MYND

Stank Lane, Bishops Castle, SY9 5EX. Derek & Eileen Mattey. *Approx 2m E of Bishop's Castle, off B4385. Follow B4385 for approx ½m, turn L at NGS sign. Garden located on R, 1m up the hill. Limited parking at garden, please park in Bishop's Castle & use free shuttle bus (5mins) from Market car park.* **Thur 23 May (12.30-5.30). Adm £5, chd free. Home-made teas.**

Just under 1 acre, south facing, wildlife-friendly country garden. Informal planting, with wildflowers, herbaceous perennials, shrubs, small wildlife pond, produce garden, greenhouses and fruit trees. Hillside setting at 935'/285m with lovely views over the Shropshire Hills. Please note that whilst the garden is all on one level, the ground is very uneven in places and therefore not suitable for wheelchair users.

31 OAKGATE NURSERY & GARDEN CENTRE

Ellerdine Heath, nr Telford, TF6 6RL. Oakgate Garden Centre, www.oakgatenursery.co.uk. *Signed A53 between Shawbury & Hodnet. A442 Between Shawbirch & Hodnet.* **Wed 17 July (10-4). Adm £5, chd free. Light refreshments. Adm includes tea/coffee & cake.**

The original site of the nursery was a Pick Your Own Farm, over the years it has been transformed into what it is today: a delightful haven of trees, shrubs, herbaceous and seasonal bedding. All dug by hand, including 2 ponds! The gardens are still maintained by the family who live on site but welcome visitors to share the peaceful setting, relaxing in our tearoom overlooking the pond. Limited wheelchair access.

32 NEW THE OLD VICARAGE

Vicarage Road, Clun, Craven Arms, SY7 8JG. Peter & Jay Upton. *16m NW of Ludlow. Over bridge at Clun towards Knighton (parking in public car park by bridge); walk up to church, turn L into Vicarage Rd; house on R next to church.* **Sat 8 June (2-6). Adm £5, chd free. Home-made teas in Hightown Community Hall next door.**
A revived, old vicarage garden: a slow retrieval and recovery revealing a wealth of features and plants chosen by plantsmen vicars: buddleia globosa fascinates bees and butterflies; glorious oriental poppies fascinate visitors. 'The Tree', an enormous Leyland cypress (5th biggest girth in the world); the most dramatic feature is a formal wisteria allee with alliums - a symphony of mauve and purple. Teas in aid of Church

33 OTELEY

Ellesmere, SY12 0PB. Mr R K Mainwaring, 01691 622514. *1m SE of Ellesmere. Entrance out of Ellesmere past Mere, opp Convent nr to A528/495 junction.* **Sun 12 May (2-5). Adm £5, chd free. Light refreshments. Visits also by arrangement May to Oct for groups of 10+. Coaches by arrangement.**
10 acres running down to The Mere. Walled kitchen garden, architectural features, many old interesting trees. Rhododendrons, azaleas, wild woodland walk and views across Mere to Ellesmere. First opened in 1927 when the National Garden Scheme started. Wheelchair access if dry.

34 NEW POOH CORNER

6 Laburnum Close, St Martins, Oswestry, SY11 3HU. Sue Napper, 01691 774368, suenapper@talktalk.net. *5m NE of Oswestry in St Martin's village. In St Martins Village. NGS yellow signs from A5. Please park courteously outside property and in surrounding roads.* **Tue 21 May (10.30-5). Adm £4, chd free. Light refreshments. Visits also by arrangement Apr to Sept for groups of up to 30.**
A plants-woman's garden giving particular emphasis to shade loving perennials and unusual shrubs and climbers, some of which are rarely grown outdoors. Relatively compact in size and divided into 4 distinct areas providing diverse growing conditions for a wide variety of plants including ferns, primulas and alpines. Partial wheelchair access only but mainly level throughout.

35 PREEN MANOR

Church Preen, SY6 7LQ. Mr & Mrs J Tanner. *6m W of Much Wenlock. From A458 Shrewsbury to Bridgnorth rd turn off at Harley follow signs to Kenley & Church Preen. From B4371 Much Wenlock to Church Stretton road go via Hughley to Church Preen.* **Sun 16 June (2-5). Adm £6, chd free. Home-made teas.**
6-acre garden on site of Cluniac monastery and Norman Shaw mansion. Kitchen, chess, water and wild gardens. Fine trees in park; woodland walks. Developed for over 30yrs with changes always in progress.

36 RUTHALL MANOR

Ditton Priors, Bridgnorth, WV16 6TN. Mr & Mrs G T Clarke, 01746 712608, clrk608@btinternet.com. *7m SW of Bridgnorth. Ruthall Rd signed on Derrington Rd near Garage.* **Mon 6, Fri 17, Sat 18 May, Fri 14, Sat 15, Sun 16 June, Sat 6, Sun 7 July, Sat 14, Sun 15 Sept (1-6). Adm £5, chd free. Home-made teas. Visits also by arrangement Apr to Oct. Refreshments by arrangement.**
Offset by a mature collection of specimen trees, the garden is divided into intimate sections, carefully linked by winding paths. The front lawn flanked by striking borders, extends to a gravel, art garden and ha-ha. Clematis and roses scramble through an eclectic collection of wrought-iron work, unique pottery and secluded seating. A stunning horse pond features primulas, iris and bog plants. Lots of lovely shrubs to see. Jigsaws for sale Bring or buy. Wheelchair access to most parts.

> Your visits help change lives - we are Hospice UK's largest charitable funder donating more than £5 million to support hospices in local communities since 1996

37 SAMBROOK MANOR

Sambrook, Newport, TF10 8AL. Mrs E Mitchell, 01952 550256, eileengran@hotmail.com . *Between Newport & Ternhill. 1m off A41 in the village of Sambrook.* **Sun 21 July, Sun 25 Aug (12.30-5). Adm £4, chd free. Home-made teas. Visits also by arrangement May to Sept for groups of 10+.**
Deep, colourful, well-planted borders offset by sweeping lawns surrounding an early C18 manor house (not open). Wide ranging herbaceous planting with plenty of roses to enjoy; the arboretum below the garden, with views across the river, has been further extended with new trees. The waterfall and Japanese garden are now linked by a pretty rill. Lovely garden to visit for all the family. Woodland area difficult for wheelchairs.

38 2 SCHOOL COTTAGES

Hook-a-Gate, Shrewsbury, SY5 8BQ. Andrew Roberts & Dru Yarwood, andyrobo@hotmail.co.uk. *From B4380 Roman Rd in Shrewsbury by cemetery take the Longden Rd island. 1.8m past school's continue to the village Hook-a-Gate. Garden is situated on L past Hill Side Nursery. Parking at Nursery.* **Sun 2 June, Sun 7 July (1-5). Adm £4.50, chd free. Home-made teas. Visits also by arrangement May to July.**
A 3 acre garden set on a slope with steps and inclines. A mixture of various herbaceous beds, shrubs, trees, sunken garden and formal planting. Orchard, vegetable, soft fruit cage, greenhouse, chickens and pigs. Large oriental garden with surprises leading you to pasture with wildlife-friendly hedging and spectacular views of the Welsh Hills.

39 SECRET GARDEN

21 Steventon Terrace, Steventon New Road, Ludlow, SY8 1JZ. Mr & Mrs Wood, 01584 876037, carolynwood2152@yahoo.co.uk. *Park & Ride if needed, stops outside garden.* **Sat 22 June (12.30-4.30). Adm £3.50, chd free. Home-made cakes, tea, coffee, ice cream.** Visits also by arrangement June to Sept.

½-acre of very secret south facing garden, Developed over 30yrs with enthusiasm creativity and the love of gardening by the present owners. Divided up into different sections: rose garden, herbaceous borders, koi fish pond with gazebo, summer house, poly tunnel and chickens. Mediterranean style terrace garden with views of the Shropshire hills. Heart of England in Bloom Chairman's Award.

40 STANLEY HALL

Bridgnorth, WV16 4SP. Mr & Mrs M J Thompson. *½m N of Bridgnorth. Leave Bridgnorth by N gate B4373; turn R at Stanley Lane. Pass Golf Course Club House on L & turn L at Lodge.* **Sun 19 May (2-6). Adm £4, chd free. Home-made teas.**

Drive ½m with rhododendrons, fine trees and pools. Restored ice-house. Woodland walks. Also open Dower House (Mr & Mrs Colin Wells) 4 acre woodland and shrub garden with contemporary sculpture and walled vegetable garden. The Granary (Mr & Mrs Jack Major) Small trellis garden with flowers in hanging baskets and herbaceous borders and South Lodge (Mr Tim Warren) Cottage hillside garden.

41 NEW 12 STATION ROAD

Stottesdon, Kidderminster, DY14 8TT. Wade Muggleton, 07771 842 863, stationroadpermaculture@hotmail.com. *Findable via Sat Nav with the above postcode and look for yellow signs.* **Visits by arrangement May to Oct for groups of up to 20. As parking is limited please try to car share or minbus etc. Adm £4, chd free. Light refreshments.**

A small plot behind an ex local authority semi, designed along Permaculture principles the garden grows 30 types of fruit and 20 odd types of vegetables and contains a collection of 30 varieties of apples. 2 greenhouses, chickens, guinea pigs and 2 ponds. all in 80ft x 40ft rectangle. The garden has a flight of steps so is not very wheelchair friendly.

42 SUNNINGDALE

9 Mill Street, Wem, Shropshire, SY4 5ED. Mrs Susan Griffiths, 01939 236733, sue.griffiths@btinternet.com. *Town centre. Wem is on B5476. Parking in public car park Barnard St. The property is opp the purple house below the church.* **Sun 26 May (11-4). Adm £3, chd free. Home-made teas.** Visits also by arrangement.

A good half acre town garden. A wildlife haven for a huge variety of birds including nesting gold crests. A profusion of excellent nectar rich plants means that butterflies and other pollinators are in abundance. Interesting plantings with carefully collected rare plants and unusual annuals means there is always something new to see, in a garden created for all year round viewing. Koi pond and natural stone waterfall rockery. Antique and modern sculpture. Sound break yew walkway. Large perennial borders, with rare plants, unusual annuals, exotic climbers, designed by owner as an all year round garden. Although the garden is on the level there are a number of steps mostly around the pond area; paths are mainly gravel or flags; there is a flat lawn.

43 NEW UPPER MARSHES

Catherton Common, Hopton Wafers, Kidderminster, DY14 0JJ. Jo & Chris Bargman. *3m NW of Cleobury Mortimer. From A4117 follow signs to Catherton. Property is on Common land 100yds at end of track.* **Sun 7 July (12-5). Adm £4, chd free. Home-made teas**

Commoner's stone cottage and 3 acre small holding. 800' high. Garden has been developed to complement its unique location on edge of Catherton common with herbaceous borders, vegetable plot, herb garden. Short walk down to a spring fed wildlife pond. Plenty of seats to stop and take in the tranquillity. Optional circular walk across Wildlife Trust common to SSI field. Various animals and poultry.

44 UPPER SHELDERTON HOUSE

Shelderton, Clungunford, Craven Arms, SY7 0PE. Andrew Benton & Tricia McHaffie, 01547 540525, triciamchaffie@googlemail.com. *Between Ludlow & Craven Arms. Heading from Shrewsbury to Ludlow on A49, take 1st R after Onibury railway crossing. Take 3rd R signed Shelderton. After approx 2½m the house is on L. Garden will be signed.* **Sat 11, Sun 12 May (1.30-5). Adm £5, chd free. Home-made teas.**

Set in a stunning tranquil position, our naturalistic and evolving 6½ acre garden was originally landscaped in 1962. Most of the trees, azaleas and rhododendrons were planted then. There is a wonderful new kitchen garden designed and planted by Jayne and Norman Grove. Ponds and woodland walk encourage wildlife. A large sweeping lawn leads in various directions revealing a multitude of colourful rhododendron and azalea beds, ponds a varied collection of trees and a very productive kitchen garden. There are plenty of tranquil seating areas from which to enjoy a moment in our garden. unfortunately our garden isn't flat and there are gravel paths, however if you contact us beforehand we may be able to offer a solution.

45 WALCOT HALL

Lydbury North, SY7 8AZ. Mr & Mrs C R W Parish, 01588 680570, secretary@walcothall.com, www.walcothall.com. *4m SE of Bishop's Castle. B4385 Craven Arms to Bishop's Castle, turn L by Powis Arms, in Lydbury North.* **Sun 26, Mon 27 May (1.30-5.30). Adm £5, chd free.**

Arboretum planted by Lord Clive of India's son, Edward. Cascades of rhododendrons, azaleas amongst specimen trees and pools. Fine views of Sir William Chambers' Clock Towers, with lake and hills beyond. Walled kitchen garden; dovecote; meat safe; ice house and mile-long lakes. Outstanding ballroom where excellent teas are served. Russian wooden church, grotto and fountain now complete and working; tin chapel. Relaxed borders and rare shrubs. Lakeside replanted, and water garden at western end re-established. The garden adjacent to the ballroom is accessible via a sloping bank, as is the walled garden and arboretum.

Walcot Hall

GROUP OPENING

46 NEW WELSHAMPTON GARDENS

Welshampton, Ellesmere, SY12 0QA. *A495 ½m E of Welshampton towards Whitchurch. Holly House Welshampton Shropshire SY12 0QA Located on the A495 E of Welshampton Shropshire. From Welshampton head towards Whitchurch ½m. Follow Yellow Signs.* **Sun 14 July (11-5). Combined adm £5, chd free. Light refreshments.**

NEW THE HOLLIES
Andrew & Marie Haydon.

NEW HOLLY HOUSE
Mike & Ruth Dinsdale.

The Hollies: 3 acres around Victorian house; mature and new specimen trees, roses; woodland area; old established orchard with some heritage varieties; duck pond. Pls use car parking in the Hollies, giving access to neighbouring garden. Holly House: densely planted, plants-woman's garden developed over last 5yrs; eclectic planting with some rare and unusual plants; shady woodland area, herbaceous borders, lawns and ornamental pond leading to 1-acre field with both mature and newly planted specimen trees, large natural wildlife pond, floating duck house well used by wild moor hens. A wild flower "project", vegetable garden, croquet lawn and is surrounded with rural views. Lots of seating; "Garden Trail Quiz" for children; small nursery offering plants for sale. Not suitable for wheelchairs.

47 WINDY RIDGE

Church Lane, Little Wenlock, Telford, TF6 5BB. George & Fiona Chancellor, 01952 507675, fionachancellor@btinternet.com. *2m S of Wellington. Follow signs for Little Wenlock from N (J7, M54) or E (off A5223 at Horsehay). Parking signed. Do not rely on SatNav.* **Sun 2 June, Sun 7 July, Sun 11 Aug, Sun 8 Sept (12-5). Adm £6, chd free. Home-made teas. Visits also by arrangement May to Sept for groups of 10+.**
Universally admired for its structure, inspirational planting and balance of texture, form and all-season colour, the garden more than lives up to its award-winning record. Developed over 30 years, 'open plan' garden rooms display over 1000 species (mostly labelled) in a range of colour-themed planting styles, beautifully set off by well-tended lawns, plenty of water and fascinating sculpture. Some gravel paths but help available.

48 ◆ WOLLERTON OLD HALL

Wollerton, Market Drayton, TF9 3NA. Lesley & John Jenkins, 01630 685760, info@wollertonoldhallgarden.com, www.wollertonoldhallgarden.com. *4m SW of Market Drayton. On A53 between Hodnet & A53-A41 junction. Follow brown signs.* **For NGS: Fri 17 May (12-5). Adm £7.50, chd free. Light refreshments.** For other opening times and information, please phone, email or visit garden website.
4-acre garden created around C16 house (not open). Formal structure creates variety of gardens each with own colour theme and character. Planting is mainly of perennials, the large range of which results in significant collections of salvias, clematis, crocosmias and roses. Ongoing lectures by Gardening Celebrities including Chris Beardshaw, and other garden designers and personalities. For refreshments, food is freshly prepared in the Tea Room for each open day. Home-cooked, hot and cold lunches which have a reputation for quality, licensed to sell alcohol. Free Head Gardener's Walks. Partial wheelchair access.

SOMERSET, BRISTOL AREA & SOUTH GLOUCESTERSHIRE incl BATH

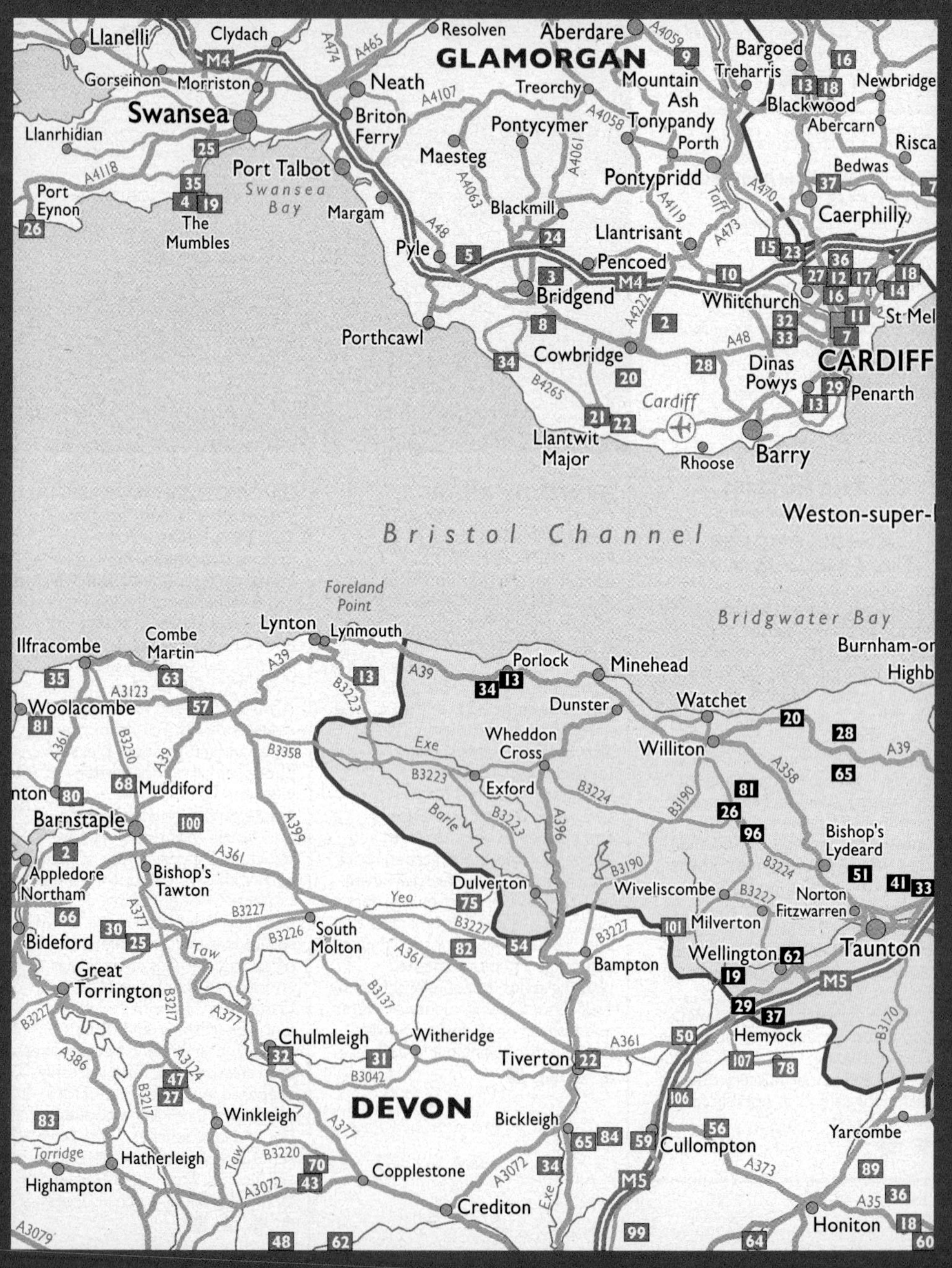

SOMERSET, BRISTOL AREA & S. GLOUCESTERSHIRE
GLOUCESTERSHIRE
GWENT
WILTSHIRE
DORSET
Usk
Tintern Parva
Pontypool
Cwmbran
Chepstow
Caerleon
Newport
Caldicot
Thornbury
Stone
Dursley
Nailsworth
Wotton-under-Edge
Tetbury
Cricklade
Malmesbury
Chipping Sodbury
Yate
Patchway
Avonmouth
Portishead
Mangotsfield
Kingswood
Bristol
Clevedon
Nailsea
Yatton
Congresbury
Keynsham
Chew Magna
Bath
Corsham
Chippenham
Calne
Lyneham
Bradford-on-Avon
Melksham
Devizes
Potterne
Trowbridge
Blagdon
Cheddar
Radstock
Midsomer Norton
Wedmore
Wells
Shepton Mallet
Frome
Westbury
West Lavington
Warminster
Shrewton
Longbridge Deverill
Glastonbury
Bridgwater
Street
North Petherton
Bruton
Castle Cary
Mere
Wylye
Wilton
Somerton
Langport
Wincanton
Gillingham
Shaftesbury
Ilchester
Martock
Yeovil
Sherborne
Stalbridge
Ilminster
South Petherton
Sturminster Newton
Merriott
Chard
Crewkerne
Middlemarsh
Beaminster
Axminster
Maiden Newton
0 10 20 kilometres
0 10 miles
© Global Mapping / XYZ Maps

Somerset, Bristol, Bath and South Gloucestershire make up an NGS 'county' of captivating contrasts, with castles and countryside and wildlife and wetlands, from amazing cities to bustling market towns, coastal resorts and picturesque villages.

Bristol's stunning location and famous landmarks offer a wonderful backdrop to our creative and inspiring garden owners who have made tranquil havens and tropical back gardens in urban surroundings. The surrounding countryside is home to gardens featuring contrasting mixtures of formality, woodland, water, orchard and kitchen gardens.

Bath is a world heritage site for its Georgian architecture and renowned for its Roman Baths. Our garden visitors can enjoy the quintessentially English garden of Bath Priory Hotel with its billowing borders and croquet lawn, or venture further afield and explore the hidden gems in nearby villages.

Somerset is a rural county of rolling hills such as the Mendips, the Quantocks and Exmoor National Park contrasted with the low-lying Somerset Levels. Famous for cheddar cheese, strawberries and cider; agriculture is a major occupation. It is home to Wells, the smallest cathedral city in England, and the lively county town of Taunton.
Visitors can explore more than 150 diverse gardens, mostly privately owned and not normally open to the public ranging from small urban plots to country estates.

Gardens on windswept hilltops, by the seaside, hidden in lush green countryside, in idyllic villages as well as communal town allotments are all to be visited, as well as historic gardens designed by Gertrude Jekyll, Margery Fish and Harold Peto.

Somerset Volunteers

County Organiser
Laura Howard 01460 282911
laura.howard@ngs.org.uk

County Treasurer
Sue Youell 01984 656741
sue.youell@ngs.org.uk

Publicity
Roger Peacock
jrogerpeacock@btinternet.com

Social Media
Rae Hick 07972 280083
raehick@gmail.com

Photographer
Sue Sayer 07773 181891
suesayer58@hotmail.com

Presentations
Dave & Prue Moon 01373 473381
davidmoon202@btinternet.com

Booklet Co-ordinator
Bill Hodgson 07711 715311
somersetngs@outlook.com

Booklet Distributor
Ash Warne 07548 889705
ashwarne@btinternet.com

Assistant County Organisers
Marsha Casely 07854 882616
marjac321@hotmail.com

Patricia Davies-Gilbert 01823 412187
pdaviesgilbert@gmail.com

Alison Highnam 01258 821576
allies1@btinternet.com

Marion Jay 01643 841486
marion.jay@icloud.com

Julie Nelson 07774 021517
julienelson.ngs@gmail.com

Judith Stanford 01761 233045
judithstanford.ngs@hotmail.co.uk

Ash Warne (as above)

Bristol Area Volunteers

County Organiser
Su Mills 01454 615438
susanlmills@gmail.com

County Treasurer
Ken Payne 01275 333146
kg.payne@outlook.com

Publicity
Myra Ginns 01454 415396
m.ginns1@btinternet.com

Booklet Co-ordinator
Bill Hodgson 07711 715311
somersetngs@outlook.com

Booklet Distributor
Graham Guest 01275 472393
gandsguest@btinternet.com

Assistant County Organisers
Angela Conibere 01454 413828
aeconibere@hotmail.com

Graham Guest (as above)

Tracey Halladay 07956 784838
thallada@icloud.com

Christine Healey 01454 612795
christine.healey@uwclub.net

Margaret Jones 01225 891229
ian@weircott.plus.com

Jeanette Parker 01454 299699
jeanette_parker@hotmail.co.uk

Jane Perkins 01454 414570
janekperkins@gmail.com

Irene Randow 01275 857208
irene.randow@sky.com

OPENING DATES

All entries subject to change. For latest information check **www.ngs.org.uk**

Extended openings are shown at the beginning of the month.

Map locator numbers are shown to the right of each garden name.

February

Snowdrop Festival

Every day
◆ Ston Easton Park 82

Sunday 3rd
◆ Elworthy Cottage 26
Rock House 70
Vine House 90

Saturday 9th
◆ Elworthy Cottage 26

Sunday 10th
Rock House 70
◆ Sherborne Garden 74

Monday 11th
◆ Sherborne Garden 74

Friday 15th
◆ Elworthy Cottage 26

Sunday 17th
◆ East Lambrook Manor Gardens 25

Thursday 21st
Southfield Farm 78

Sunday 24th
Rock House 70

Sunday 31st
Rock House 70

March

Every day
◆ Ston Easton Park 82

Sunday 3rd
NEW Hill House 42
Nynehead Court 62

Tuesday 5th
◆ Hestercombe Gardens 41

Saturday 23rd
Lower Shalford Farm 52

April

Every day to Friday 12th
◆ Ston Easton Park 82

Every day from Friday 26th
◆ Ston Easton Park 82

Thursday 11th
Bath Priory Hotel 8
◆ Elworthy Cottage 26

Friday 12th
Tormarton Court 87

Sunday 14th
Fairfield 28
Hangeridge Farmhouse 37
Rose Cottage 71

Wednesday 17th
◆ Greencombe Gardens 34

Saturday 20th
Westbrook House 95

Monday 22nd
◆ Elworthy Cottage 26

Thursday 25th
◆ Elworthy Cottage 26

Saturday 27th
◆ East Lambrook Manor Gardens 25
The Walled Gardens of Cannington

Sunday 28th
Algars Manor 3
Algars Mill 4
The Walled Gardens of Cannington
Watcombe 91
◆ The Yeo Valley Organic Garden at Holt Farm 100

May

Every day
◆ Ston Easton Park 82

Thursday 2nd
◆ Elworthy Cottage 26

Saturday 4th
Hillcrest 43
NEW Lane End House 49

Sunday 5th
Hillcrest 43
NEW Lane End House 49

Thursday 9th
◆ Kilver Court Gardens 48

Friday 10th
Little Yarford Farmhouse 51

Saturday 11th
Little Yarford Farmhouse 51

Sunday 12th
◆ Court House 20
Greystones 36
Little Yarford Farmhouse 51
◆ Milton Lodge 58

Monday 13th
Little Yarford Farmhouse 51

Saturday 18th
Forest Lodge 30
Lower Shalford Farm 52

Sunday 19th
4 Haytor Park 39
Laughing Water 50
Lucombe House 53
The Old Vicarage, Over Stowey 65
The Red Post House 69
Watcombe 91
Wayford Manor 93

Wednesday 22nd
Waverley 92

Saturday 25th
NEW John's Corner 47
The Miller's House 57
Woodlea Bottom 97

Sunday 26th
Babbs Farm 6
NEW John's Corner 47
Woodlea Bottom 97

Monday 27th
Babbs Farm 6
◆ Elworthy Cottage 26
Glebe Court 33
◆ Stoberry Garden 80

Tuesday 28th
Wellfield Barn 94

Thursday 30th
◆ Elworthy Cottage 26

June

Every day
◆ Ston Easton Park 82

Saturday 1st
NEW American Museum & Gardens 5
◆ East Lambrook Manor Gardens 25
Stoneleigh Down 83

Sunday 2nd
Acton Court 2
◆ Milton Lodge 58
Nynehead Court 62
Stoneleigh Down 83

Tuesday 4th
◆ Hestercombe Gardens 41

Wednesday 5th
Laughing Water 50

Thursday 6th
Watcombe 91

Saturday 8th
The Old Rectory, Doynton 63
South Cary House 76

Sunday 9th
Acton Court 2
NEW Hill House 42
Model Farm 59
16 Montroy Close 60
Yeo Meads 99

Wednesday 12th
Waverley 92
NEW Wrington Gardens 98

Saturday 15th
NEW Holland Farm 44
Lympsham Gardens 54
Westbrook House 95

Sunday 16th
Acton Court 2
NEW Batcombe House 7
9 Catherston Close 15
Crete Hill House Garden 22
Laughing Water 50
Lympsham Gardens 54
The Old Rectory, Limington 64
Penny Brohn UK 68
Stogumber Gardens 81
NEW Wrington Gardens 98

Thursday 20th
9 Catherston Close 15
Forest Lodge 30
◆ Special Plants 79

Friday 21st
Tormarton Court 87

Sunday 23rd
Doynton House 23
Frome Gardens 31
Swift House 86
Truffles 88

Thursday 27th
◆ Elworthy Cottage 26

Sunday 30th
NEW Coombe House 18
NEW 70 Entry Hill 27
Vine House 90
Yews Farm 101

July

Every day
◆ Ston Easton Park 82

Wednesday 3rd
9 Catherston Close 15

Thursday 4th
◆ Elworthy Cottage 26

Sunday 7th
Brent Knoll Gardens 11
Gants Mill & Garden 32
Honeyhurst Farm 45
◆ Milton Lodge 58

Monday 8th
Honeyhurst Farm 45

Tuesday 9th
Muriel Jones Field Allotments 61

Thursday 11th
◆ Elworthy Cottage 26

Saturday 13th
NEW The Hay Barn 38
NEW Willett Farm 96

Sunday 14th
◆ Court House 20
◆ University of Bristol Botanic Garden 89
NEW Willett Farm 96

Wednesday 17th
◆ Greencombe Gardens 34

Thursday 18th
◆ Special Plants 79

Sunday 21st
Benter Gardens 9
Stowey Gardens 84
Sutton Hosey Manor 85

Saturday 27th
NEW 9 Greenpark Road 35
NEW John's Corner 47
Park Cottage 67

Sunday 28th
◆ Cothay Manor & Gardens 19
NEW 9 Greenpark Road 35
Hangeridge Farmhouse 37
NEW John's Corner 47

August

Every day
◆ Ston Easton Park 82

Saturday 3rd
Park Cottage 67

Sunday 4th
◆ Jekka's Herbetum 46

Sunday 11th
◆ Elworthy Cottage 26
Parish's House 66

Thursday 15th
◆ Special Plants 79

Sunday 18th
Fernhill 29

Sunday 25th
Babbs Farm 6
NEW 1 The Crescent 21

Monday 26th
Babbs Farm 6
◆ Elworthy Cottage 26

Thursday 29th
◆ Elworthy Cottage 26

Saturday 31st
NEW John's Corner 47

September

Every day
◆ Ston Easton Park 82

Sunday 1st
NEW 1 The Crescent 21
NEW John's Corner 47

Tuesday 3rd
◆ Hestercombe Gardens 41

Thursday 5th
◆ Kilver Court Gardens 48

Saturday 7th
Stoneleigh Down 83

Sunday 8th
NEW 70 Entry Hill 27
Stoneleigh Down 83

Saturday 14th
NEW The Hay Barn 38

Sunday 15th
NEW Maes Knoll Gardens 55

Thursday 19th
◆ Special Plants 79

Friday 20th
◆ Midney Gardens 56

Saturday 21st
The Walled Gardens of Cannington

Sunday 22nd
The Walled Gardens of Cannington

October

Every day
◆ Ston Easton Park 82

Thursday 17th
◆ Special Plants 79

Sunday 27th
St Monica Trust 72

November

Every day to Friday 29th
◆ Ston Easton Park 82

February 2020

Sunday 2nd
Rock House 70

Sunday 9th
Rock House 70

Saturday 15th
◆ East Lambrook Manor Gardens 25

By Arrangement

Arrange a personalised garden visit with your club, or group of friends, on a date to suit you. See individual garden entries for full details.

Abbey Farm 1
Bradon Farm 10
Brewery House 12
Broomclose 13
Cameley House 14
Cherry Bolberry Farm 16
Coldharbour Cottage 17
College Barn, Benter Gardens 9
NEW Coombe House 18
East End Farm 24
Forest Lodge 30
Glebe Court 33
Hangeridge Farmhouse 37
4 Haytor Park 39
Henley Mill 40
Hillcrest 43
Honeyhurst Farm 45
NEW John's Corner 47
Knoll Cottage, Stogumber Gardens 81
Laughing Water 50
Little Yarford Farmhouse 51
Lucombe House 53
Nynehead Court 62
The Old Rectory, Limington 64
The Red Post House 69
Rock House 70
Rose Cottage 71
Serridge House 73
Sole Retreat 75
South Kelding 77
Sutton Hosey Manor 85
Tormarton Court 87
Truffles 88
Watcombe 91
Waverley 92
Wellfield Barn 94
Westbrook House 95
Whitewood Lodge, Maes Knoll Gardens 55
NEW Willett Farm 96
Yews Farm 101

THE GARDENS

1 ABBEY FARM

Montacute, TA15 6UA. Elizabeth McFarlane, 01935 823556, abbey.farm64@gmail.com. *4m from Yeovil. Follow A3088, take slip rd to Montacute, turn L at T-junction into village. Turn R between Church & King's Arms (no through rd).* **Visits by arrangement May to Sept for groups of 10 to 20. Adm £5, chd free. Light refreshments.**

2½ acres of mainly walled gardens on sloping site provide the setting for Cluniac Medieval Priory gatehouse. Interesting plants incl roses, shrubs, grasses, clematis. Herbaceous borders, white garden, gravel garden. Small arboretum. Pond for wildlife - frogs, newts, dragonflies. Fine mulberry, walnut and monkey puzzle trees. Seats for resting. Restored Grade 2 listed dovecote. Gravel area and one steep slope.

2 ACTON COURT

Latteridge Road, Iron Acton, Bristol, BS37 9TL. 01454 228224, info@actoncourt.com, www.actoncourt.com. *10m NE of Bristol. On B4059 near junction with B4058. Brown sign for Acton Court. For SatNav use BS37 9TJ.* **Sun 2, Sun 9, Sun 16 June (11-5). Adm £5, chd free. Home-made teas.**

3 acres: Beautiful walled wildflower meadow and apple orchard with an abundance of old English and wild roses on the grounds of a grade I listed Tudor Manor House (restricted access). Organic kitchen garden producing vegetables, culinary and medicinal herbs, with lavender centrepiece. The site is Soil Association certified and promotes wildlife. Acton Court will be sponsoring several special events on the themes of The Tudors, wildlife and music in support of our NGS days. Details on our website and social media. Charges may be made for additional activities. Uneven ground, grass paths, kitchen garden not accessible - gravel path and step.

3 ALGARS MANOR

Station Rd, Iron Acton, BS37 9TB. Mrs B Naish. *9m N of Bristol, 3m W of Yate/Chipping Sodbury. Turn S off Iron Acton bypass B4059, past village green and past White Hart PH, 200yds, then over level Xing. No access from Frampton Cotterell via lane; ignore SatNav. Parking at Algars Manor.* **Sun 28 Apr (2-5). Combined adm with Algars Mill £5, chd free. Home-made teas.**

2 acres of woodland garden beside River Frome, mill stream, native plants mixed with collections of 60 magnolias and 70 camellias, rhododendrons, azaleas, eucalyptus and other unusual trees and shrubs. Daffodils and other early spring flowers. Partial wheelchair access only, gravel paths, some steep and uneven slopes.

4 ALGARS MILL

Frampton End Rd, Iron Acton, Bristol, BS37 9TD. Mr & Mrs John Wright. *9m N of Bristol, 3m W of Yate/Chipping Sodbury. (For directions see Algars Manor).* **Sun 28 Apr (2-5). Combined adm with Algars Manor £5, chd free. Home-made teas.**

2 acre woodland garden bisected by R Frome; spring bulbs, shrubs; very early spring feature (Feb-Mar) of wild Newent daffodils. 300-400yr-old mill house (not open) through which millrace still runs.

5 NEW AMERICAN MUSEUM & GARDENS

Claverton Manor, Bath, BA2 7BD. Jon Ducker, www.americanmuseum.org. *Signposted from Bath city centre and from A36 Warminster road.* **Sat 1 June (10-5). Adm £7.50, chd £5 (garden only). Light refreshments.**

The American Museum & Gardens takes you on a journey through the history of America, from its early settlers to the C20 with its remarkable collection of folk and decorative arts. The New American Garden follows a free form planting style featuring many native American plants. The Winding Way encircles the lawn, threads through the American Rose Collection, and skirts the natural amphitheatre. We have a full access statement available on our website.

6 BABBS FARM

Westhill Lane, Bason Bridge, Highbridge, TA9 4RF. Sue & Richard O'Brien, www.babbsfarm.co.uk. *1½m E of Highbridge, 1½m SSE of M5 exit 22. Turn into Westhill Lane off B3141 (Church Rd), 100yds S of where it joins B3139 (Wells-Highbridge rd).* **Sun 26, Mon 27 May, Sun 25, Mon 26 Aug (2-5). Adm £5, chd free. Home-made teas.**

¾ acre plantsman's garden on Somerset Levels, gradually created out of fields surrounding old farmhouse over last 20 yrs and still being developed. Trees, shrubs and herbaceous perennials planted with an eye for form and shape in big flowing borders. Various ponds (formal and informal), box garden, patio area and conservatory.

7 NEW BATCOMBE HOUSE

Gold Hill, Batcombe, Shepton Mallet, BA4 6HF. Libby Russell, www.mazzullorussell landscapedesign.com. *In centre of Batcombe, 3m from Bruton. Please park in field just down from church as signed.* **Sun 16 June (2-5.30). Adm £6, chd £2. Home-made teas.**

A designer's garden of two parts – one a riot of colour through kitchen terraces, potager leading to wildflower orchard; the other a calm contemporary amphitheatre with large herbaceous borders and interesting trees and shrubs. Designer garden, plantswoman's garden. Interesting herbaceous planting, naturalistic planting, wildflowers and roses, interesting pots, always changing. Wheelchairs are welcome but we are a steep garden with steps and difficult access to some of the garden for wheelchairs.

Your visits help change lives – your generosity helps Marie Curie fund nurses to care for people night and day in their homes, with donations of more than £8.8 million

8 BATH PRIORY HOTEL

Weston Rd, Bath, BA1 2XT. Jane Moore, Head Gardener, 01225 331922, info@thebathpriory.co.uk, www.thebathpriory.co.uk. *Close to centre of Bath. Metered parking in Royal Victoria Park. No 4, 14, 39 and 37 buses from City centre. Please note: Disabled parking only in Hotel grounds.* **Thur 11 Apr (2-5). Adm £3.50, chd free. Home-made teas.**

Discover 3 acres of mature walled gardens. Quintessentially English, the garden has billowing borders, croquet lawn, wild flower meadow and ancient specimen trees. Spring is bright with tulips and flowering cherries. Perennials and tender plants provide summer highlights while the kitchen garden supplies herbs, fruit and vegetables to the restaurant. Gravel paths and some steps.

GROUP OPENING

9 BENTER GARDENS

Benter, Oakhill, Radstock, BA3 5BJ. *Between the villages of Chilcompton, Stratton on the Fosse and Oakhill, narrow lanes. A37, from Bristol and Shepton Mallet, turn to gardens by village shop in Gurney Slade. Follow lane for approx 1m, turn R at grass triangle before incline. From Bath A367, after S on F, 2nd R to Benter.* **Sun 21 July (10-5). Combined adm £5, chd free. Tea. Variety of home-made cakes to choose from.**

COLLEGE BARN
Alex Crossman & Jen Weaver, 01761 233414, alex@crossmanassociates.co.uk. **Visits also by arrangement in July for groups of 5+.**

FIRE ENGINE HOUSE
Patrick & Nicola Crossman.

2 contrasting gardens in beautiful, rural setting. The garden at Fire Engine House is mature and established, with lawns, generous borders and narrow, enticing paths; through a garden door and tumble-down bothy is a small orchard with specimen trees. College Barn garden is 5 yrs old and draws upon the surrounding meadows and woods with hazel and hornbeam hedges, swathes of perennials and prairie planting with ornamental grasses. Intimate walled garden filled with vegetables, herbs, flowers and fruit. Peace and tranquillity surrounds.

10 BRADON FARM

Isle Abbotts, Taunton, TA3 6RX. Mr & Mrs Thomas Jones, deborahjstanley@hotmail.com. *Take turning to Ilton off A358. Bradon Farm is 1½m out of Ilton on Bradon Lane.* **Visits by arrangement June to Sept for groups of 10+. Adm £6, chd free. Home-made teas.**

Classic formal garden created in recent years, demonstrating the effective use of structure. Much to see incl parterre, knot garden, pleached lime walk, formal pond, herbaceous borders, orchard and wildflower planting.

GROUP OPENING

11 BRENT KNOLL GARDENS

Highbridge, TA9 4DF. *2m N of Highbridge. Off A38 & M5 J22. From M5 take A38 N (Cheddar etc) first L into Brent Knoll.* **Sun 7 July (2-5). Combined adm £6, chd free. Home-made teas at Ball Copse Hall, also cream teas.**

BALL COPSE HALL
Mrs S Boss & Mr A J Hill.

LABURNUM COTTAGE
Catherine Weber.

The distinctive hill of Brent Knoll, an iron age hill fort, is well worth climbing 449ft for the 360° view of surrounding hills incl Glastonbury Tor and the Somerset Levels. Lovely C13 church renowned for its bench ends. Ball Copse Hall: S-facing Edwardian house (not open) on lower slopes of Knoll. Front garden maturing well with curving slopes and paths. Ha-ha, wild area and kitchen garden. Views to Quantock and Polden Hills. Kitchen garden enclosed by crinkle crankle wall. Flock of Soay sheep. Laburnum Cottage: ½ acre garden developed over 15 yrs with over 100 varieties of hemerocallis (day lilies) incl many unusual forms and spider types. Large, sweeping borders with mixed plantings of shrubs and herbaceous plants. Wheelchair access in both gardens, some restricted.

12 BREWERY HOUSE

Southstoke, Bath, BA2 7DL. John & Ursula Brooke, 01225 833153, jbsouthstoke@gmail.com. *2½m S of Bath. A367 Radstock Rd from Bath. At top of dual carriageway turn L onto B3110. Straight on at double r'about. Next R into Southstoke.* **Visits by arrangement May to Aug for groups of 5 to 20. Adm £3.50, chd free. Cream teas. Refreshments by arrangement.**

¾ acre garden in centre of village. The garden is organic. There are splendid views to S over rolling countryside. Long established walled garden with fine, mature trees, shrubs and climbers. The mature planting gives a sense of mystery as one explores the contrast of colours and shapes. There are a number of unusual plants. Wheelchair access restricted to lower part of garden.

13 BROOMCLOSE

Porlock, Minehead, TA24 8NU. David & Nicky Ramsay, 01643 862078, nickyjamesramsay@gmail.com. *Off A39 on Porlock Weir Rd, between Porlock and West Porlock. From Porlock take rd signed to Porlock Weir. Leave houses of Porlock behind, pass 3 fields, we are 1st drive on L. NB Some SatNavs direct wrongly from Porlock - so beware!* **Visits by arrangement Apr to Sept for groups of up to 30. Adm £4, chd free. Home-made teas.**

Large, varied garden set around early 1900s Arts and Crafts house overlooking the sea. Original stone terraces, Mediterranean garden, long borders, copse, camellia walk, orchard with bee hives and vegetable garden. Maritime climate favours unusual sub-tropical trees, shrubs and herbaceous plants.

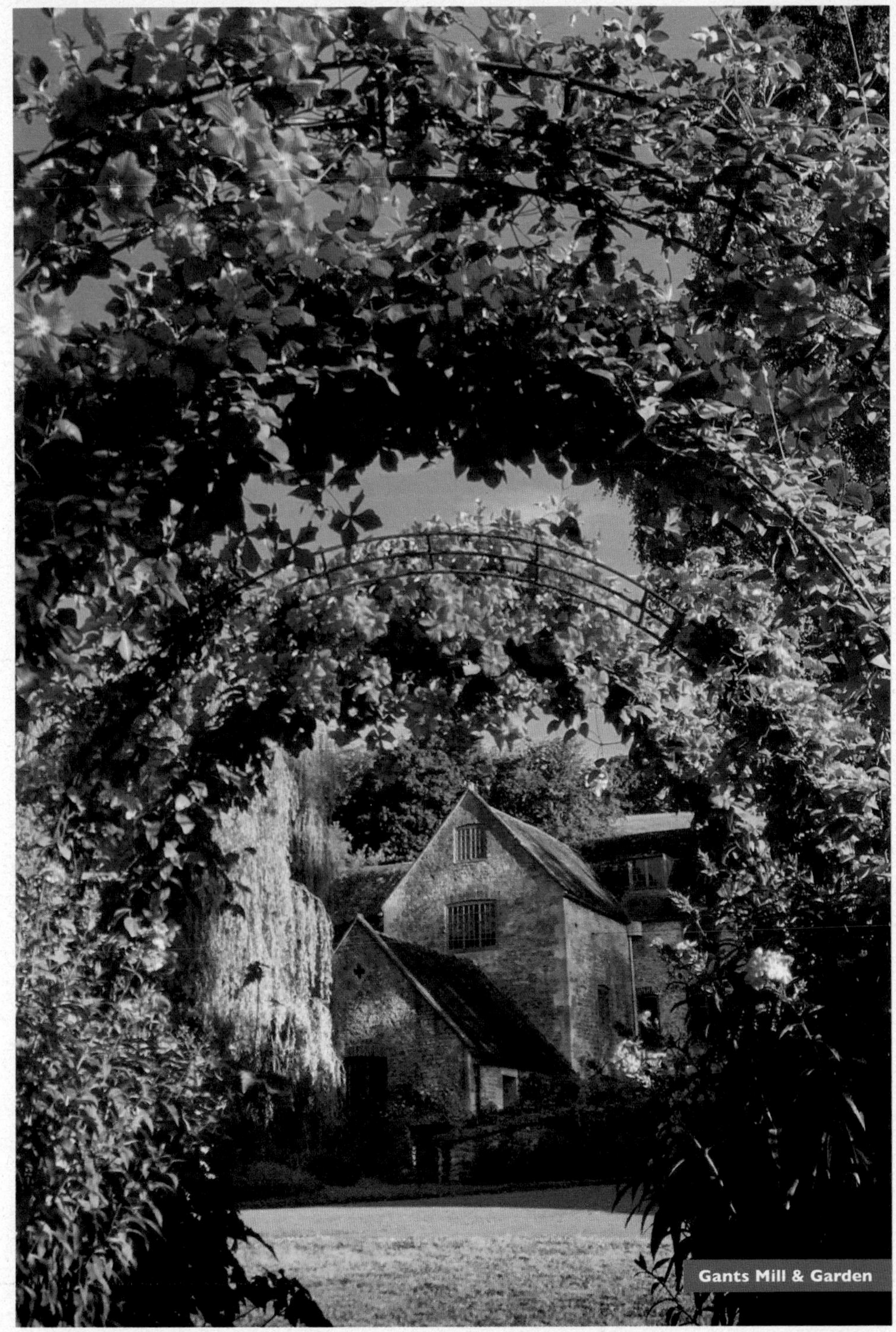

Gants Mill & Garden

14 CAMELEY HOUSE

Cameley, Temple Cloud, Bristol, BS39 5AJ. Fiona & Jonathan Hayward, 01761 451111, flodden@btconnect.com. *10m from Bristol, Bath and Wells. In Temple Cloud turn off A37 onto Cameley Road/Cameley Lane. 1½m on L.* **Visits by arrangement for groups of 10 to 30 from mid April to mid May (smaller groups considered). Adm £7.50, chd free. Home-made teas. £2.50.**

3 acre garden surrounding C18 Strawberry Hill Gothic house (not open). An established garden on a sloping site developed and re-planted by owners over the last 9 years. The Cam Brook runs through the garden with woodland including ginkgo and tulip trees. Borders with tulips, hellebores, geums, camassias and magnolias. White garden. Cherry orchard with topiary and sculpture. Alpine troughs. Limited wheelchair access.

15 9 CATHERSTON CLOSE

Frome, BA11 4HR. Dave & Prue Moon. *15m S of Bath. Town centre W towards Shepton Mallet (A361). R at Sainsbury's r'about, follow lane for ½m. L into Critchill Rd. Over Xrds, 1st L Catherston Close.* **Sun 16, Thur 20 June, Wed 3 July (12-5). Adm £4, chd free. Opening with Frome Gardens on Sun 23 June.**

Walk around the corner and see the unexpected, a small town garden which has grown to ⅓ acre! Colour-themed shrub and herbaceous borders, pond, patios, pergolas and wild meadow areas lead to wonderful far reaching views. Productive 'no dig' vegetable and fruit garden with greenhouse. Exhibition of garden photography by garden owner, from near and far, displayed in summerhouse. Gold winner Frome-in-Bloom. Several shallow steps, gravel paths.

16 CHERRY BOLBERRY FARM

Furge Lane, Henstridge, BA8 0RN. Mrs Jenny Raymond, 01963 362177, cherrybolberryfarm@tiscali.co.uk. *6m E of Sherborne. In centre of Henstridge, R at small Xrds signed Furge Lane. Continue straight up lane, over 2 cattle grids, garden at top of lane on R.* **Visits by arrangement in June for groups of 5+. Adm £5, chd free. Home-made teas.**

40 yr-old award winning, owner designed and maintained, 1 acre garden planted for yr-round interest with wildlife in mind. Colour themed island beds, shrub and herbaceous borders, unusual perennials and shrubs, old roses and an area of specimen trees. Lots of hidden areas, brilliant for hide and seek! Vegetable and flower cutting garden, greenhouses, nature ponds. Wonderful extensive views. Garden surrounded by our dairy farm which has been in the family for nearly 100 years. You will see Jersey cows, sheep, horses and hens!

17 COLDHARBOUR COTTAGE

Radford Hill, Radford, Radstock, BA3 2XU. Ms Amanda Cranston, 01761 470600, amanda.cranston@yahoo.co.uk. *Bath & NE Somerset. South of Bath, please ask for directions when booking.* **Visits by arrangement May to July for groups of 5 to 20. Adm £5.50, chd £2.50. Light refreshments. Please confirm visitor numbers 2 weeks prior to visit.**

¾ acre rural garden with mature trees, wild areas, vegetable garden, open lawns and borders with secluded seating areas. Interesting out-buildings, hen house, small ponds and stumpery. Pretty lavender and rose path in summer. Designed to attract wildlife all yr round. This hidden garden is a great place to gather your thoughts and unwind. Dementia groups and carers particularly welcome as are groups from our beneficiaries, residential and care homes. Wheel-chair access to grassed areas may be weather-dependant. Some narrow and uneven paths.

18  COOMBE HOUSE

102 Bove Town, Glastonbury, BA6 8JG. Mr Alan Gloak, 07860 463647, a.gloak@btinternet.com, www.coombehouse.org. *½m from town centre. Take shuttle bus from town hall car park. Coombe House in Bove Town is at top of hill which is top of the High St.* **Sun 30 June (2-6). Adm £4. Home-made teas.** Visits also by arrangement June to Aug for groups of 10 to 20. Donation to TS5C.

2-acre romantic and lavishly-planted garden, incl unusual and tender plants. Dramatic scenes, pools, terraces and Abbots' retreat.

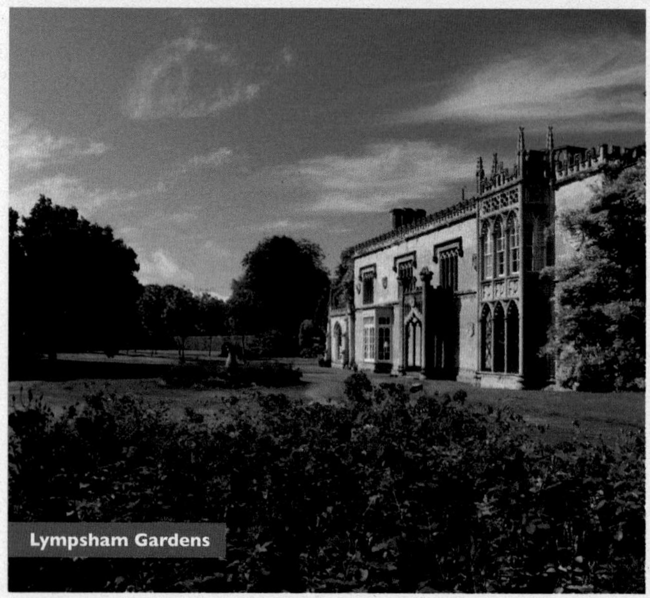

Lympsham Gardens

Kitchen garden, orchards, nut walk and lots to see and ponder on. An English garden in a mystical town with lots of country views It is a garden of colour, a rich liqueur distilled from the elements that surround it. Partial help at hand to assist.

19 ◆ COTHAY MANOR & GARDENS

Greenham, Wellington, TA21 0JR. Mrs Alastair Robb, 01823 672283, cothaymanor@btinternet.com, www.cothaymanor.co.uk. *5m SW of Wellington. 7m off M5 via A38, signed Greenham, follow brown signs for Cothay Manor & Gardens. See website for more detailed directions.* **For NGS: Sun 28 July (1-5). Adm £7.80, chd £3.60. Cream teas. For other opening times and information, please phone, email or visit garden website.**
Few gardens are as evocatively romantic as Cothay. Laid out in 1920s and replanted in 1990s within the original framework, Cothay encompasses a rare blend of old and new. Plantsman's paradise set in 12 acres of magical gardens. Small nursery and tea room. Sorry no dogs or picnicking in gardens. House tour 3.00pm (separate admission cost). Partial wheelchair access, gravel paths.

20 ◆ COURT HOUSE

East Quantoxhead, TA5 1EJ. East Quantoxhead Estate (Hugh Luttrell Esq), 01278 741271, hugh_luttrell@yahoo.co.uk. *12m W of Bridgwater. Off A39, house at end of village past duck pond. Enter by Frog Street (Bridgwater/ Kilve side from A39). Car park £1 in aid of church.* **For NGS: Sun 12 May, Sun 14 July (2-5). Adm £5, chd free. Cream teas. For other opening times and information, please phone or email.**
Lovely 5 acre garden, trees, shrubs (many rare and tender), herbaceous and 3 acre woodland garden with spring interest and late summer borders. Traditional kitchen garden (chemical free). Views to sea and Quantocks. Gravel, stone and some mown grass paths.

21 NEW 1 THE CRESCENT

Worlebury, Weston-Super-Mare, BS22 9SR. Jane & Stephen Sands. *4m from J21 of M5. At M5 J21 take B3440. After 2.7m turn R at r'about signed Worlebury & Golf Course. Proceed for 0.9m to top of hill. L at Golf Club. The Crescent is 150yds on L with very limited parking.* **Sun 25 Aug, Sun 1 Sept (2-5). Adm £4, chd free. Home-made teas.**
½ acre garden developed over 20 yrs by present owners and still not complete. Divided into 7 areas of distinctly different character. Lawns with colour themed borders, ponds and cascading water features, vegetable garden, copse and orchard. Mendip views. Half the garden is on the level, the other half drops downhill with sloping paths and steps. Partial wheelchair access.

22 CRETE HILL HOUSE GARDEN

Cote House Lane, Durdham Down, Bristol, BS9 3UW. John Burgess. *2m N of Bristol city centre/3m S J16 M5. A4018 Westbury Rd from city centre, L at White Tree r'about, R into Cote Rd, continue into Cote House Lane across the Downs. 2nd house on L. Parking on street.* **Sun 16 June (1-5). Adm £4, chd free. Home-made teas.**
C18 house in hidden corner of Bristol. Mainly SW facing garden, 80'x40', with shaped lawn, heavily planted traditional mixed shrub, rose, clematis and herbaceous borders. Pergola with climbers, terrace with pond, several seating areas.

23 DOYNTON HOUSE

Bury Lane, Doynton, Bristol, BS30 5SR. Frances & Matthew Lindsey-Clark. *5m S of M4 J18, 6m N of Bath, 8m E of Bristol. Doynton is NE of Wick (turn off A420 opp Bath Rd) and SW of Dyrham (signed from A46). Doynton House is at S end of Doynton village, opp Culleysgate/Horsepool Lane. Park in signed field.* **Sun 23 June (1-5). Adm £6, chd free. Home-made teas.**
A variety of garden areas separated by old walls and hedges. Mixed borders, wall planting, parterre, rill garden, walled vegetable garden, cottage beds, pool garden, dry garden, peach house and greenhouse. Bees. Chickens. Meadow area in 2nd year. Paths are of hoggin, stone and gravel. The grade of the gravel makes it a hard push in places but all areas are wheelchair accessible.

24 EAST END FARM

Pitney, Langport, TA10 9AL. Mrs A M Wray, 01458 250598. *2m E of Langport. Please telephone for directions.* **Visits by arrangement in June. Adm £3.50, chd free. Light refreshments.**
Approx ⅓ acre. Timeless small garden of many old-fashioned roses in beautiful herbaceous borders set amongst ancient listed farm buildings. Mostly wheelchair access.

25 ◆ EAST LAMBROOK MANOR GARDENS

Silver Street, East Lambrook, TA13 5HH. Mike & Gail Werkmeister, 01460 240328, enquiries@eastlambrook.com, www.eastlambrook.com. *2m N of South Petherton. Follow brown tourist signs from A303 South Petherton r'about or B3165 Xrds with lights N of Martock.* **For NGS: Sun 17 Feb, Sat 27 Apr, Sat 1 June (10-5). Adm £6, chd free. Tea and cake with gluten free options. 2020: Sat 15 Feb. For other opening times and information, please phone, email or visit garden website.**
The quintessential English cottage garden created by C20 gardening legend Margery Fish. Plantsman's paradise with old-fashioned and contemporary plants grown in a relaxed and informal manner to create an extraordinary garden of great beauty and charm. With noted collections of snowdrops, hellebores and geraniums and the excellent specialist Margery Fish Plant Nursery. Also open 1 Feb - 31 Oct, Tues to Sat and BH Mons plus Suns in Feb and May to July; (10-5). Main features not accessible to wheelchair users due to narrow paths and steps.

26 ◆ ELWORTHY COTTAGE

Elworthy, Taunton, TA4 3PX. Mike & Jenny Spiller, 01984 656427, mike@elworthy-cottage.co.uk, www.elworthy-cottage.co.uk. *12m NW of Taunton. On B3188 between Wiveliscombe and Watchet.* **For NGS: Sun 3, Sat 9, Fri 15 Feb, Thur 11, Mon 22, Thur 25 Apr, Thur 2, Mon 27, Thur 30 May, Thur 27 June, Thur 4, Thur 11 July, Sun 11, Mon 26, Thur 29 Aug (11-4). Adm £4, chd free. Home-made teas.** Visits also by arrangement Apr – Sept and also Feb for snowdrops. Tea proceeds to Children's Hospice South West. For other opening times and information, please phone, email or visit garden website.

1 acre plantsman's garden in tranquil setting. Island beds, scented plants, clematis, unusual perennials and ornamental trees and shrubs to provide yr-round interest. In spring, pulmonarias, hellebores and more than 350 varieties of snowdrops. Planted to encourage birds, bees and butterflies, lots of birdsong. Wild flower areas, decorative vegetable garden, living willow screen. Seats for visitors to enjoy the peaceful countryside. Garden attached to plantsman's nursery, open at the same time.

27 NEW 70 ENTRY HILL

Bath, BA2 5NA. Nyla Abraham & Paul Sadler. *Approx 100m up hill from entrance to Entry Hill Golf Course, on opp side of road. On street parking is available a short walk away on Entry Hill Park.* **Sun 30 June, Sun 8 Sept (10-5). Adm £3, chd free. Home-made teas. Selection of cakes available, incl gluten and dairy free. Tea/ coffee.**

A suburban garden with a difference. Step through our garden gate to find a secret garden full of treasures. Home to three pekin bantams who get free range of the shade garden, gravel garden, lawn with colourful herbaceous border, mini orchard, vegetable garden with the secret garden shelter and two restored stone turrets. Come and explore with the pekins and who knows what you will find. Bath in Bloom Silver Gilt winner 2016. Narrow gates, and some gravelled areas make wheelchair access quite difficult. One elevated section, not accessible by wheelchair.

28 FAIRFIELD

Stogursey, Bridgwater, TA5 1PU. Lady Acland Hood Gass. *7m E of Williton. 11m W of Bridgwater. From A39 Bridgwater to Minehead rd turn N. Garden 1½m W of Stogursey on Stringston rd. No coaches.* **Sun 14 Apr (2-5). Adm £4, chd free. Home-made teas.**

Woodland garden with bulbs, roses shrubs and fine trees. Paved maze. Views of Quantocks and sea.

29 FERNHILL

Whiteball, Wellington, TA21 0LU. Peter Bowler, www.sampfordarundel.org.uk/fernhill. *3m W of Wellington. At top of Whiteball hill on A38 on L going West, just before dual carriageway, parking on site.* **Sun 18 Aug (2-5). Adm £4, chd free. Home-made teas.**

In approx 2 acres, a delightful garden to stir your senses, with a myriad of unusual plants and features. Intriguing almost hidden paths leading through English roses and banks of hydrangeas. Scenic views stretching up to the Blackdowns and its famous monument. Truly a Hide and Seek garden ..... for all ages. Well stocked herbaceous borders, octagonal pergola and water garden with slightly wild boggy area. Wheelchair access to terrace and other parts of garden from drive.

30 FOREST LODGE

Pen Selwood, BA9 8LL. Mr & Mrs James Nelson, 07974 701427, lucillanelson@gmail.com. *1½m N of A303, 3m E of Wincanton. Leave A303 at B3081 (Wincanton to Gillingham rd), up hill to Pen Selwood, L towards church. ½m, garden on L - low curved wall and sign saying Forest Lodge Stud.* **Sat 18 May (11.30-4.30). Combined adm with Lower Shalford Farm £7, chd free. Thur 20 June (11.30-4.30). Adm £6, chd free. Home-made teas.** Visits also by arrangement May to Sept for groups of 5 to 20. Donation to Heads Up Wells, Balsam Centre Wincanton.

3 acre mature garden with many camellias and rhododendrons in May. Lovely views towards Blackmore Vale. Part formal with pleached hornbeam allée and rill, part water garden with lake. Wonderful roses in June. Unusual spring flowering trees such as Davidia involucrata, many beautiful cornus. Interesting garden sculpture. Wheelchair access to front garden only, however much of garden viewable from there.

GROUP OPENING

31 FROME GARDENS

Frome, BA11 4HR. *15m S of Bath. 9 Catherston Cl signed Sainsbury r'about A361 W of town to S/ Mallet. 3 Lynfield Rd A362 Frome to Radstock r'bout turn L Nunney Rd take 2nd R in 400m, Lynfield Rd. 84 Weymouth Rd off Badcox on A362.* **Sun 23 June (12-5). (84 Weymouth Rd 1-4pm only). Combined adm £6, chd free.**

9 CATHERSTON CLOSE
Dave & Prue Moon.
(See separate entry)

NEW **3 LYNFIELD ROAD**
Sharon Rossiter & Dinah Randall.

84 WEYMOUTH ROAD
Amanda Relph.

More than a warm welcome awaits you at 9 Catherston Close, you will be bowled over on seeing how this small town garden has grown into ⅓ acre! 3 Lynfield Road: Conifer and rock front garden, fruit and veg growing midst borders. Scree bed. 3 yrs after moving in, 1970's garden is rejuvenated. Walled Mediterranean themed back garden, combining hard landscaping and soft planting, water features, pergola with roses and clematis, gravel paths to paved terrace. Thriving olive, fig and lemon trees. 84 Weymouth Road: designed and planted by Simon Relph to celebrate his life and work. Architectural design of metal arches and geometrical raised beds made by his son Alex Relph with other artists surround a raised pond. Choice shrubs surround the walled garden. Maturing ferns, roses and camellias add to the central courtyard. Raised veg beds, greenhouse and soft fruits. Catherston Close has some gravel paths, slopes and shallow steps. 3 Lynfield Rd has some gravel and steps in back garden. No dogs in the gardens pls.

32 GANTS MILL & GARDEN

Gants Mill Lane, Bruton, BA10 0DB. Elaine & Greg Beedle. *½m SW of Bruton. From Bruton centre take Yeovil rd, A359, under railway bridge, 100yds uphill, fork R down Gants Mill Lane. Parking for wheelchair users.* **Sun 7 July (2-5). Adm £6, chd free. Home-made teas.**

¾ acre garden. Clematis, rose arches and pergolas, streams, ponds, waterfalls. Riverside walk to top weir, delphiniums, day lilies, 100+ dahlia varieties, vegetable, soft fruit and cutting flower garden. Garden is overlooked by the historic watermill, open on NGS day. Firm wide paths round garden. Narrow entrance to mill not accessible to wheelchairs. WC.

33 GLEBE COURT

West Monkton, Taunton, TA2 8QT. Mark & Mary Thomas, 07866 232044, marydressage@gmail.com. *2m NE of Taunton. Follow signs to W Monkton from A38. In village take driveway (entrance marked by 2 large 5 mph signs) leading to church.* **Mon 27 May (1-5). Adm £6, chd free. Cream teas. Home-made cakes, soft drinks.** Visits also by arrangement May to Oct for groups of 10 to 20. Light refreshments £3 per person.

Walled garden with greenhouses, orchard, vegetable plots, fruit tree cages and flower beds; herbaceous and shrub borders; copse and paddocks with some unusual trees; series of ponds. 11 acres in all surrounding Georgian Rectory. (House not open to the public). Dogs must be on leads. Partial wheelchair access: some uneven steps. Access to walled garden up slope and through gate with couple of low steps.

34 ◆ GREENCOMBE GARDENS

Porlock, TA24 8NU. Greencombe Garden Trust, 01643 862363, info@greencombe.org, www.greencombe.org. *Between Porlock and West Porlock, off road to Porlock Weir. Follow A39 W through Porlock and fork R onto B3225 to Porlock Weir. Drive ½m and turn L at Greencombe Gardens sign. Go up drive; parking signed.* **For NGS: Wed 17 Apr, Wed 17 July (2-6). Adm £7, chd £1.** For other opening times and information, please phone, email or visit garden website.

An organic woodland garden of international renown, Greencombe stretches along a sheltered hillside and offers outstanding views over Porlock Bay. Moss-covered paths meander through a collection of ornamental plants that flourish beneath a canopy of oaks, hollies, conifers and chestnuts. Camellias, rhododendrons, azaleas, lilies, roses, clematis, and hydrangeas blossom among 4 National Collections. Champion English Holly tree (Ilex aquifolium), the largest and oldest in the UK. A millennium chapel hides in the wood. An ecologically constructed Green Room holds garden records, collection information, and paintings by Exmoor artist Jon Hurford.

NPC

Abbey Farm

35 NEW 9 GREENPARK ROAD

Southmead, Bristol, BS10 5NQ. Clarie & Simon Miles. *From M32 turn onto Filton Rd, 3rd exit at r'about on Station Rd/Link Rd, 2nd exit at r'about onto Southmead Rd. 3rd turning on L.* **Sat 27, Sun 28 July (2-5). Adm £3.50, chd free. Home-made teas.**

This city garden (260 sq m) overflows with interest and contains some unusual plants. Created by the current owners 3 yrs ago, the clever design of this family garden caters for all. Incl a potage garden with raised veg beds, pot theatres, contemplative space, play area, herbaceous display beds, forest garden hedgerow, stumpery, and working garden. Featured in Modern Gardens. Children's quiz offered with a prize on completion.

36 GREYSTONES

Hollybush Lane, Bristol, BS9 1JB. Mr & Mrs P Townsend. *2m N of Bristol city centre, close to Durdham Down in Bristol, backing onto the Botanic Garden. A4018 Westbury Rd, L at White Tree r'about, L into Saville Rd, Hollybush Lane 2nd on R. Narrow lane, parking limited, recommended to park in Saville Rd.* **Sun 12 May (2-5). Adm £4, chd free. Home-made teas.**

Peaceful garden with places to sit and enjoy a quiet corner of Bristol. Interesting courtyard with raised beds and large variety of conifers and shrubs leads to secluded garden of contrasts - from sun drenched beds with olive tree and brightly coloured flowers to shady spots, with acers, hostas and a fern walk. Small apple orchard, espaliered pears and koi pond. Paved footpath provides level access to all areas.

37 HANGERIDGE FARMHOUSE

Wrangway, Wellington, TA21 9QG. Mrs J M Chave, 07812 648876, hangeridge@hotmail.co.uk. *2m S of Wellington. Off A38 Wellington bypass signed Wrangway. 1st L towards Wellington monument, over motorway bridge 1st R.* **Sun 14 Apr, Sun 28 July (2-5). Adm £3, chd free. Home-made teas.** Visits also by arrangement May to Aug for groups of 10+.

Rural fields and mature trees surround this 1 acre informal garden offering views of the Blackdown and Quantock Hills. Magnificent hostas and heathers, colourful flower beds, cascading wisteria and roses and a trickling stream. Relax with home-made refreshments on sunny or shaded seating admiring the views and birdsong.

38 NEW THE HAY BARN

Kingstone, Ilminster, TA19 0NS. Philippa Sage. *Kingstone is 1m out of Ilminster on Crewkerne road. Coming from Ilminster take Crewkerne road, at Kingstone Church turn L, road turns to gravel follow round to L. The Haybarn is first house on R.* **Sat 13 July, Sat 14 Sept (1-5.30). Adm £4.50, chd free. Home-made teas.**

Delightful garden created over past 7 years, wrapping around an attractive ham stone barn conversion creating a wonderful sense of peace and tranquility. Paths invite you around the garden to view the collection of unusual plants, shrubs and trees providing yr-round colour and interest. Gravel areas provide ideal planting for drought loving plants. Trees link the garden into the country. Front of house and driveway gravel, making pushing a wheelchair hard. Please ask for assisted parking.

Sutton Hosey Manor

39 4 HAYTOR PARK

Bristol, BS9 2LR. Mr & Mrs C J Prior, 07779 203626, p.l.prior@gmail.com. *3m NW of Bristol city centre. From A4162 Inner Ring Rd take turning into Coombe Bridge Ave, Haytor Park is 1st on L. Please no parking in Haytor Park.* **Sun 19 May (2-5). Combined adm with Lucombe House £6, chd free.** Visits also by arrangement May to Aug for groups of 10 to 30.

Enter past the sun-baked, pot - laden patio, seeking dragons through a tracery of arches and cascading climbers. Along meandering paths to plant packed, secret spaces. Discover hidden seats to dream upon. Search for the rare boot tree and arty paraphernalia, via ponds and a plethora of plants.

40 HENLEY MILL

Henley Lane, Wookey, BA5 1AW. Peter & Sally Gregson, 01749 676966, millcottageplants@gmail.com, www.millcottageplants.co.uk. *2m W of Wells, off A371 towards Cheddar. Turn L into Henley Lane, 50 yds turn L through stone pillars, continue to end of drive. Henley Mill is on R of building, garden visitor entry through garage doors, car sharing advised.* **Visits by arrangement 1st April to 30 September, please confirm visitor numbers 2wks before visit. Adm £5, chd free. Home-made teas.**

Beside River Axe, with a zigzag boardwalk at river level, lies 2½ acres of scented garden with roses, hydrangea borders, shady folly garden and late summer borders with grasses and perennials. Kitchen and cutting garden. Deck overhangs mill leat and looks down onto gunneras, Siberian iris and miscanthus. Wild area of native English daffodils, fritillaries and cowslips in spring. Rare Japanese hydrangeas and new Chinese epimediums. We hold a collection of Benton bearded irises by Cedric Morris, some may well be in flower in May/June. Plants, as seen in the garden, are on sale. Garden is on 1 level but paths can get a bit muddy after heavy rain.

41 ◆ HESTERCOMBE GARDENS

Cheddon Fitzpaine, Taunton, TA2 8LG. Hestercombe Gardens Trust, 01823 413923, info@hestercombe.com, www.hestercombe.com. *4m N of Taunton, less than 6m from J25 of M5. Follow brown tourist signs. SatNav postcode TA2 8LQ.* **For NGS: Tue 5 Mar, Tue 4 June, Tue 3 Sept (10-5). Adm £12.50, chd £6.25. Light refreshments in Stables Café offering light lunches, teas and cakes and covered courtyard seating.** For other opening times and information, please phone, email or visit garden website.

Georgian landscape garden designed by Coplestone Warre Bampfylde, Victorian terrace and shrubbery and stunning exquisite example of Lutyens/Jeykll designed formal garden. These together make up 50 acres of woodland walks, temples, terraces, pergolas, lakes and cascades. Hestercombe House is also now open comprising a contemporary art gallery and second-hand book shop. 3 eras of garden design, contemporary art gallery, restored watermill and barn, historic house and family garden trails. Gravel paths, steep slopes, steps. All abilities route marked. Tramper mobility scooter available, booking required.

42 NEW HILL HOUSE

West End, Wickwar, Wotton-Under-Edge, GL12 8JZ. Joanna Hellen & Mark Allan. *20m N of Bristol. M5 junction 14. Follow B4509 to Wickwar, past Quarry and rd on R to West End and Hall End. Hill House on R after Wickwar village sign and 30mph sign. Parking next right at playing fields.* **Sun 3 Mar (1-4); Sun 9 June (1-5). Adm £5, chd free. Home-made teas.**

Mature garden originally created by Sally, Duchess of Westminster. Currently under restoration. Specimen trees in arboretum setting. Pleached lime tree walk, herbaceous borders, kitchen garden. Lovely bulbs and snowdrops. Roses are spectacular in early June. Gravel drive may make access challenging, but help will be available.

43 HILLCREST

Curload, Stoke St Gregory, Taunton, TA3 6JA. Charles & Charlotte Sundquist, 01823 490852, chazfix@gmail.com. *At top of Curload. From A358 turn L along A378, then branch L to North Curry and Stoke St. Gregory. L ½m after Willows & Wetlands centre. Hillcrest is 1st on R with parking directions.* **Sat 4, Sun 5 May (1-5). Combined adm with Lane End House £6, chd free. Home-made teas.** Visits also by arrangement Apr to Sept for groups of 5 to 30. Home-made tea available at £2.50 per person.

The garden boasts stunning views of the Somerset Levels, Burrow Mump and Glastonbury Tor, but even on a hazy day this 5 acre garden offers plenty of interest. Woodland walks, varied borders, flowering meadow and several ponds; also kitchen garden, greenhouses, orchards and unique standing stone as focal point. Most of garden is level. Long gently sloping path through flower meadow to lower pond and wood.

44 NEW HOLLAND FARM

South Brewham, Bruton, BA10 0JZ. Mrs Nickie Gething. *Postcode will not take you to Holland Farm, please follow yellow signs.* **Sat 15 June (10-4). Adm £6, chd free. Home-made teas in the Garden Room.**

The house and garden at Holland Farm were built from scratch in 2007. What was a derelict farmyard has been transformed into a beautiful house (not open) and garden which sit comfortably in the surrounding countryside. Designed courtyard garden, large ornamental pond and lake. Limited wheelchair access.

D

We help ordinary people open the gates to their extraordinary private gardens to raise impressive amounts of money through admissions, teas and slices of cake!

45 HONEYHURST FARM

Honeyhurst Lane, Rodney Stoke, Cheddar, BS27 3UJ. Don & Kathy Longhurst, 01749 870322, donlonghurst@btinternet.com, www.ciderbarrelcottage.co.uk. *4m E of Cheddar. From A371 between Wells and Cheddar, turn into Rodney Stoke signed Wedmore. Pass church on L and continue for almost 1m.* **Sun 7, Mon 8 July (2-5). Adm £3.50, chd free. Home-made teas. Cream teas.** Visits also by arrangement May to Sept for groups of 10 to 30.

⅔ acre part walled rural garden with babbling brook and 4 acre traditional cider orchard, with views. Specimen hollies, copper beech, paulownia, yew and poplar. Pergolas, arbour and numerous seats. Mixed informal shrub and perennial beds with many unusual plants. Many pots planted with shrubs, hardy and half-hardy perennials. Level, grass and some shingle.

46 ◆ JEKKA'S HERBETUM

Shellards Lane, Alveston, Bristol, BS35 3SY. Mrs Jekka McVicar, 01454 418878, sales@jekkasherbfarm.com, www.jekkasherbfarm.com. *7m N of M5 J16 or 6m S from J14 of M5. 1m off A38 signed Itchington. From M5 J16, A38 to Alveston, past church turn R at junction signed Itchington. M5 J14 on A38 turn L after T-lights to Itchington.* **For NGS: Sun 4 Aug (10-4). Adm £5, chd free. Home-made teas.** For other opening times and information, please phone, email or visit garden website.

Jekka's Herbetum is a living encyclopaedia of herbs, displaying the largest collection of culinary herbs in Europe. A wonderful resource for plant identification for the gardener and a gastronomic experience for chefs and cooks. Wheelchair access possible however terrain is rough from car park to Herbetum.

47 NEW JOHN'S CORNER

2 Fitzgerald Road, Bedminster, Bristol, BS3 5DD. John Hodge, 0117 9720558. *3m from city centre. S of Bristol, off St.John's Lane, Totterdown end. 1st house on R, entrance at side of house. On number 50 bus route. Parking in residential street.* **Sats, Suns 25, 26 May; 27, 28 July; 31 Aug, 1 Sept (1-5). Adm £3.50, chd free. Home-made teas.** Visits also by arrangement May to Oct for groups of up to 20.

Unusual and interesting city garden in Bedminster with a mixture of exciting plants and features. Ponds, ferns and much more. Eden project style greenhouse with collection of cacti. Paths, no steps. Not all areas accessible by wheelchair.

48 ◆ KILVER COURT GARDENS

Kilver Street, Shepton Mallet, BA4 5NF. Roger & Monty Saul, 01749 340410, info@kilvercourt.com, www.kilvercourt.com. *Directly off A37 rd to Bath, opp cider factory in Shepton Mallet. Disabled parking in lower car park.* **For NGS: Thur 9 May, Thur 5 Sept (10-4). Adm £7.50, chd free. Discount/ prepaid vouchers are not valid on the 2 NGS charity days kindly donated by Kilver Court.** For other opening times and information, please phone, email or visit garden website.

Visitors can wander by the millpond, explore the formal and informal Gardens and enjoy a replica of the splendid Chelsea Flower Show Gold Medal winning rockery where a gushing recirculated stream flows from pool to pool with waterfalls into the lake. All set against stunning backdrop of Charlton viaduct. Recently replanted 100m border. Featured on BBC Gardeners' World and in regional and national press. Some slopes, rockery not accessible for wheelchairs but can be viewed.

49 NEW LANE END HOUSE

Curload, Stoke St. Gregory, Taunton, TA3 6JA. Eric & Veronica Martin. *Curload, Stoke St Gregory, Taunton TA3 6JA. Taunton A358 turn L on A378, Fork L to North Curry & Stoke St Gregory. L ½m after Willows & Wetlands Centre. 1st house on L. Parking at Hillcrest Garden opp.* **Sat 4, Sun 5 May (1-5). Combined adm with Hillcrest £6, chd free. Refreshments at Hillcrest.**

A mature Somerset Levels garden set on heavy clay with mixed borders, orchard, veg patch, greenhouses and free range chickens. The recent introduction of a ½ acre field into the garden sees mature trees and shrubs sharing the garden with newly planted specimen trees, a pond and wildflower areas that support our own honey bees and a variety of wildlife. Unique sculptures enhance the 1 acre plot. Level gardens with gravel courtyard.

50 LAUGHING WATER

Weir Lane, Yeovilton, Yeovil, BA22 8EU. Peter & Joyce Warne, 01935 841933, p.j.warne@btinternet.com. *2m from A303, 7m N of Yeovil. Leave A303 signed Ilchester, take B3151 dir RNAS Yeovilton, take Bineham Lane, signed Yeovilton village, Laughing Water last house on R at end of village. Park at weir just past house.* **Sun 19 May, Wed 5 June (2-5). Adm £3.50, chd free. Sun 16 June (2-5). Combined adm with The Old Rectory, Limington £6, chd free. Home-made teas 16 June.** Visits also by arrangement May to July for groups of up to 30.

½ acre+ garden hidden behind Grade II listed house (not open). A mature garden, remodelled since 2011, it reflects the owner's love of flowers and foliage with sweeping grass paths through mixed beds packed with shrubs, herbaceous perennials, annuals and bulbs. Floriferous from early spring through to autumn frosts. Large wildlife pond and other ornamental water features. Picturesque weir (after which the house is named) on river 20 mtrs past house. Fleet Air Arm Memorial Church, with C13 Nave, in village worth a visit. Limited wheelchair access.

51 LITTLE YARFORD FARMHOUSE

Kingston St Mary, Taunton, TA2 8AN. Brian Bradley, 01823 451350, yarford@ic24.net. *1½m W of Hestercombe, 3½m N of Taunton. From Taunton on Kingston St Mary rd. At 30mph sign turn L at Parsonage Lane. Continue 1¼m W, to Yarford sign. Continue 400yds. Turn R up concrete rd.* **Fri 10 May (11-5). Light refreshments. Sat 11,**

Sun 12 May (2-5.30). Cream teas. Mon 13 May (11-5). Light refreshments. Adm £5, chd free. Weekdays incl coffee, soup, bread & cheese. Visits also by arrangement May to Sept.
This unusual 5 acre garden embraces a C17 house (not open) overgrown with climbing plants. 3 ponds and waterlilies. Its special interest are its 300+ rare and unusual tree cultivars: the best collection of broad leaf and conifer cultivars in Somerset West (listed on NGS website); those trees not available to Bampfylde Warre at Hestercombe in C18. It is 'like stepping into Eden'. Guided tree tours 2 & 3.30pm. On Google map. Mostly wheelchair access. An exercise in landscaping and creating views both within the garden and without to the vale and the Quantock Hills. Mostly wheelchair access.

52 LOWER SHALFORD FARM

Shalford Lane, Charlton Musgrove, Wincanton, BA9 8HE. Mrs Suki Posnett. *Lower Shalford is 2m NE of Wincanton. Leave A303 at Wincanton go N on B3081 towards Bruton. Just beyond Otter Nursery, Turn R Shalford Lane, Lower Shalford is ½m on L. Parking opp house.* **Sat 23 Mar (10-4). Adm £5, chd free. Sat 18 May (10-4). Combined adm with Forest Lodge (open 11.30 to 4.30) £7, chd free. Light refreshments.**
Fairly large open garden with extensive lawns and wooded surroundings with drifts of daffodils in spring. Small winterbourne stream running through with several stone bridges. Walled rose/parterre garden, hedged herbaceous garden and several ornamental ponds. Partial wheelchair access.

53 LUCOMBE HOUSE

12 Druid Stoke Ave, Stoke Bishop, Bristol, BS9 1DD. Malcolm Ravenscroft, 01179 682494, famrave@gmail.com. *4m NW of Bristol centre. At top of Druid Hill. Garden on R 200m from junction.* **Sun 19 May (2-5). Combined adm with 4 Haytor Park £6, chd free. Home-made teas.** Visits also by arrangement Apr to Sept.
A garden for tree lovers of all ages!! In addition to the 250 yr old Lucombe Oak - now registered as one of the most significant trees in the SW - there are over 30 mature English trees planted together with ferns and bluebells to create an urban woodland. Also for 2019, a newly designed Arts & Craft front garden. A landscape gardener will be available to answer questions. Rough paths in woodland area, 2 steps to patio.

GROUP OPENING

54 LYMPSHAM GARDENS

Church Road, Lympsham, Weston-super-Mare, BS24 0DT. *5m S of Weston-super-Mare and 5m N of Burnham on Sea. 2m M5 J22. Entrance to all 3 gardens initially from main gates of Manor at junction of Church Rd and Lympsham Rd.* **Sat 15, Sun 16 June (2-5). Combined adm £6, chd free. Cream teas at The Manor.**

CHURCH FARM
Andy & Rosemary Carr.

LYMPSHAM MANOR
James & Lisa Counsell.

NEW **WORTHY HOUSE**
Julia Carr.

At the heart of the stunning village of Lympsham next to C15 church of St Christopher's are the gardens of 3 of the village's most historic homes. The Manor is a 200-year old gothic rectory manor house with 2 octagonal towers, built by the Stephenson family who were rectors in Lympsham for 3 generations, and is set in 10 acres of formal and semi-formal garden, surrounded by paddocks and farmland. It boasts a fully working Victorian kitchen garden and greenhouse, an arboretum of trees from all parts of the world, a large pond and a beautiful old rose garden. Church Farm has a ¾ acre informal English country garden with herbaceous borders, shrub-lined paths, raised beds and a small courtyard garden. The garden of Worthy House, first time opener this year, has well-stocked herbaceous borders, shrubs, climbing roses, clematis and hydrangeas, small woodland area leading to kitchen garden boasting vegetables, kiwi, potting shed and greenhouse.

Hillcrest

GROUP OPENING

55 NEW MAES KNOLL GARDENS

Norton Lane, Whitchurch, Bristol, BS14 0BU. Selena Gray. *6m S of Bristol, 3 gardens at northern edge of village. Norton Malrewood outside Whitchurch. Leave Bristol on A37, R down Norton Lane for approx 1m. Parking in field on R, behind Whitewood Lodge.* **Sun 15 Sept (1-4). Combined adm £6, chd free. Home-made teas.**

NEW NEW BARN FARMHOUSE
Fiona & Chris Carter.

NEW NEW BARN LODGE
Jo Haywood.

WHITEWOOD LODGE
Guy & Selena Norfolk, 07753 322318, selena.gray@btopenworld.com. **Visits also by arrangement Mar to Oct for groups of 6-10 weekends or evenings.**

3 contrasting gardens nestle in this hidden valley just outside Bristol. On the slopes of Maes Knoll, an ancient hill fort, is Whitewood Lodge, offering stunning garden design, enticing walks through wildlife gardens and a pond. Many seats allow time to relax and take in the stunning views and varied flower beds. Next door lies New Barn Lodge, a vibrant small holding where ponies and chickens live in an ancient Somerset orchard. Vegetables and soft fruit grow in the polytunnel, and there is a walk through an arboretum with swathes of perennials and prairie planting in the style of Piet Oudoulf, leading to a grove of silver birches. At New Barn Farm beautiful stone walls and gravel walkways lead you through this terraced garden bordered by beech and hornbeam hedges. At the end of the garden an orchard overlooks fields that dip steeply down to a wildlife pond, with the old Bristol to Pensford railway in the distance. Wheelchair access at Whitewood Lodge and New Barn Lodge.

♿ 🐕 ✿ ☕

56 ◆ MIDNEY GARDENS

Mill Lane, Midney, Somerton, TA11 7HR. David Chase & Alison Hoghton, 01458 274250, www.midneygardens.co.uk. *1m SE of Somerton. 100yds off B3151. From Podimore r'about on A303 take A372. After 1m R on B3151 towards Street. After 2m L on bend into Mill Lane.* **For NGS: Fri 20 Sept (11-5). Adm £6, chd £1.50. Cream teas.** For other opening times and information, please phone or visit garden website.

1.4 acre plantsman's garden, where unusual planting combinations, interesting use of colour, subtle themes and a natural flowing style create a garden full of variety and inspiring ideas. Increasingly known for it's wildlife friendly planting. Incl seaside garden, white garden, kitchen garden, woodland walk, wildlife pond and undercover world gardens. Nursery offers herbaceous perennials, alpines, herbs and grasses.

✿ ☕

College Barn, Benter Gardens

57 THE MILLER'S HOUSE

17 Horn Street, Nunney, Frome, BA11 4NP. Caroline Toll. *3m SW of Frome off the A361. Nunney Catch, A361 between Frome and Shepton Mallet, follow signs to Nunney (1m).* **Sat 25 May (12.30-4). Adm £4, chd free.**
Garden of person who considers herself to be an untidy planter! Mostly perennial garden, terraced borders, rockeries, large romantic mill pond and wild area designed for butterfly attraction and perfume, areas to sit and enjoy views of garden. Don't miss the terraced veg patch and small modern sculptures. Caution needed around mill pond steps and paths, stout footwear advisable. Wild paddock along the valley between the leat and Nunney Brook. There are several corners to rest in from which to enjoy the different views. Partial access, small steps into top garden accessible to visitors with restricted mobility, part of remaining garden and millpond can be viewed here.

58 ◆ MILTON LODGE

Old Bristol Road, Wells, BA5 3AQ. Simon Tudway Quilter, 01749 672168, www.miltonlodgegardens.co.uk. *½m N of Wells. From A39 Bristol-Wells, turn N up Old Bristol Rd; car park 1st gate on L signed.* **For NGS: Sun 12 May, Sun 2 June, Sun 7 July (2-5). Adm £5. Home-made teas. Children under 14 no entry charge. Discount/prepaid vouchers are not valid on the 3 NGS charity days kindly donated by Milton Lodge.** For other opening times and information, please phone or visit garden website.
Mature Grade II terraced garden. Architectural terraces transformed from sloping land with profusion of plants capitalising on views of Wells Cathedral and Vale of Avalon. Garden was restored to its former glory by current owner's parents who moved here in 1960, orchard replaced with collection of ornamental trees. Cross Old Bristol Rd to 7 acre woodland garden, the Combe, a natural peaceful contrast to formal garden of Milton Lodge. Now a peaceful, serene and relaxing atmosphere within the garden following the ravages of two World Wars. Unsuitable for wheelchairs/pushchairs or those with limited mobility due to slopes and differing levels.

59 MODEL FARM

Perry Green, Wembdon, Bridgwater, TA5 2BA. Mr & Mrs Dave & Roz Young, 01278 429953, daveandrozontour@hotmail.com, www.modelfarm.com. *4m from J23 of M5. Follow Brown signs from r'about on A39 2m W of Bridgwater.* **Sun 9 June (2-5.30). Adm £4, chd free. Light refreshments.**
4 acres of flat gardens to S of Victorian country house. Created from a field in last 9 yrs and still being developed. A dozen large mixed flower beds planted in cottage garden style with wildlife in mind. Wooded areas, lawns, wildflower meadows and wildlife pond. Plenty of seating throughout the gardens. Lawn games incl croquet.

60 16 MONTROY CLOSE

Henleaze, Bristol, BS9 4RS. Sue & Rod Jones. *3½ m N of Bristol city centre. From Bristol, on B4056 (Henleaze Rd) continue past all Henleaze shops, R into Rockside Dr (opp Eastfield Inn). Up hill, across Xrds into The Crescent. Montroy Close is 3rd turning on L.* **Sun 9 June (2-5.30). Adm £3.50, chd free. Home-made teas in the tearoom, overlooking the garden. Tea, coffee & home-made lemonade and cakes.**
Large SW-facing town garden on corner plot. 20 ft stream, informal pond with pebble beach, pergola and seats. Lawn with curving flower beds incl ferns, shrubs, perennials, climbers, small rock garden with water feature, unusual partitioned greenhouse with alpine bench. 8ft wide arch with climbers. Hanging baskets and many pots of fuchsias. Width of gateway: 79cm.

61 MURIEL JONES FIELD ALLOTMENTS

Birchill Lane, Feltham, Frome, BA11 5ND. Frome Allotment Association, fromeallotments.co.uk. *15m S of Bath. On Frome by-pass (take A361). At r'about exit B3092 signed Blatchbridge. Drive approx ½m towards Frome, turn R into Birchill Lane, signed. Continue to allotments on R, parking onsite.* **Tue 9 July (11-5). Adm £4.50, chd free. Light refreshments. Delicious home-made cakes, gluten free option, filled rolls. Produce from allotments available.**
Hidden in a rural setting on the outskirts of Frome are 98 pretty allotments on a charming 5 acre gently sloping site. On show are a range of gardening styles from the traditional to a more relaxed approach. 8 accessible raised beds for less mobile gardeners to develop and share their love of gardening. Wonderful views of Longleat Forest across the River Frome with Cley Hill in the distance. Flowers, fruit and vegetables in abundance. Visitors are welcome to bring a picnic. Well behaved dogs on short leads welcome. Viewing area over allotments designated for wheelchair users. Accessible compost toilet.

62 NYNEHEAD COURT

Nynehead, Wellington, TA21 0BN. Nynehead Care Ltd, 01823 662481, nyneheadcare@aol.com, www.nyneheadcourt.co.uk. *1½m N of Wellington. M5 J26 B3187 towards Wellington. R on r'about marked Nynehead & Poole, follow lane for 1m, take Milverton turning at fork.* **Sun 3 Mar, Sun 2 June (2-4.30). Adm £5, chd free. Home-made teas in Orangery.** Visits also by arrangement for groups of 10 to 30.
The house is a private residential care home for the elderly, once the home of the Sandford family from 1590-1902. There was a stone house in late C14 but it was rebuilt in 1675 by John Sandford. The gardens are noted for many superb specimen trees, a pinetum and ice house built in 1803. Taunton Deane Borough Council also awarded the gardens an historic landscape award. A garden tour, approx 45mins, will be conducted by Justin Cole, Head Gardener, at 2pm. Limited wheelchair access: cobbled yards, gentle slopes, chipped paths, lilable to puddle during or after rain - Please wear suitable footware.

63 THE OLD RECTORY, DOYNTON

18 Toghill Lane, Doynton, Bristol, BS30 5SY. Edwina & Clive Humby, www.doyntongardens.tumblr.com. *At heart of village of Doynton, between Bath and Bristol. Follow Toghill Lane up from The Holy Trinity Church about 500 metres, around cricket field to car park field. Signs to garden.* **Sat 8 June (11-4). Adm £5, chd free. Home-made teas. The local WI will be on site selling tea, coffee and home-made cakes.**

Doynton's Grade II-listed Georgian Rectory's walled garden and extended 15 acre estate. Renovated over 12 yrs, it sits within AONB. Garden has diversity of modern and traditional elements, fused to create an atmospheric series of garden rooms. Large landscaped kitchen garden featuring canal, vegetable plots, fruit cages and tree house. Partial wheelchair access, some narrow gates and uneven surfaces.

64 THE OLD RECTORY, LIMINGTON

Church St, Limington, Yeovil, BA22 8EQ. John Langdon & Paul Vintner, 01935 840127, jdlpv@aol.com. *2m E of Ilchester. From A303 exit on A37 to Yeovil/Ilchester. At 1st r'about L to Ilchester/Limington. 2nd R to Limington. Continue 1½m and house is immediately past church on R. Please park on drive.* **Sun 16 June (2-5). Combined adm with Laughing Water £6, chd free. Teas available only at Laughing Water. Visits also by arrangement Apr to Sept. Hot/cold drinks, cream teas/ploughmans lunches available by prior arrangement & wine for eve visits.**

Romantic walled gardens of 2 acres. Formal beds and herbaceous borders. Many unusual shrubs and trees incl 200 yr-old lucombe oak, liriodendron, laburnocytisus, trochdendron, leycesteria and poncirus. New meadow and wildlife pond and trees. A variety of peaceful seating areas where refreshments can be taken. Gravel drive, one gentle slope only into rear garden.

65 THE OLD VICARAGE, OVER STOWEY

Over Stowey, Bridgwater, TA5 1HA. Mrs Sally Jago. *10m W of Bridgwater. A39 from Bridgwater, L fork at Cottage Inn to Over Stowey. Over Xrds, opp church, car park in field.* **Sun 19 May (2-5). Adm £5, chd free. Home-made teas in gazebo at back of house. Assorted cakes and scones.**

Set in the beautiful Quantock Hills, and developed from an original 1-acre garden to nearly 3 acres. A quirky garden with a huge, eclectic variety of shrubs, trees, grasses, agapanthus, sub-tropical palms, phormiums, exotic ornaments, together with an arboretum, large pond and willow arbour. Original drystone ha-ha, built in 1780 by Rev William Holland and discovered by owner 25 yrs ago. A truly loved space. Due to steep slopes, upper part of garden has only partial wheelchair access.

66 PARISH'S HOUSE

Hook Hill, Timsbury, Bath, BA2 0ND. Aisha Bangura. *On B3115 North Road to Hook Hill entrance on R or from Camerton/Tunley take Timsbury exit at mini r'about, follow rd bend R. Garden is at E edge of village.* **Sun 11 Aug (2-5). Adm £5, chd free. Home-made teas.**

8-acre garden surrounding Regency house (not open) with beautiful views across open countryside. Lawns sweep down to ha-ha. Colour themed herbaceous and shrub borders. Elegant water feature. Arboretum of specimen trees and more recently planted acer glade. New woodland walk taking you from native British woodland to more exotic woodland planting. Walled kitchen garden: vegetables, fan trained and cordoned fruit trees of significant age and cut flower beds. Parts of the garden are being developed so we invite you to share our vision, anticipation and excitement!

67 PARK COTTAGE

Wrington Hill, Wrington, Bristol, BS40 5PL. Mr & Mrs J Shepherd. *Halfway between Bristol & Weston S Mare. 10m S of Bristol on A370 at Cleeve turn L onto Cleeve Hill Rd (opp sports field). Continue on Cleeve Hill Road for 1½ miles. Car park in paddock on R 50m from garden on L.* **Sat 27 July, Sat 3 Aug (11-5). Adm £5, chd free. Home-made teas provided by Wrington Pop-Up Vintage Café, proceeds to Weston Hospicecare.**

Take a colourful journey through 1¼ acres of this 'Alice in Wonderland' garden. Divided by high hedges is an established perennial flower garden developed over 26 yrs. Explore the many different areas incl potager, jungle garden, rainbow border, white garden, green gallery and 90 ft of double herbaceous borders. A large Victorian-style greenhouse displays tender plants. Countryside views and plenty of seating. Sorry no dogs and no WC. Mostly good wheelchair access, some narrow bark chip paths. Narrow flagstone bridge with steps.

68 PENNY BROHN UK

Chapel Pill Lane, Pill, North Somerset, BS20 0HH. Penny Brohn UK, 01275 370076, ian.riddell@pennybrohn.org.uk, www.pennybrohn.org.uk. *4m W of Bristol. Off A369 Clifton Suspension Bridge to M5 (J19 Gordano Services). Follow signs to Penny Brohn UK and to Pill/Ham Green (5 mins).* **Sun 16 June (10-4). Adm £4, chd free. Light refreshments. Lunch also available.**

3½ acre tranquil garden surrounds Georgian mansion with many mature trees, wild flower meadow, flower garden, cedar summerhouse, fine views from historic gazebo overlooking River Avon, courtyard gardens with water features. Garden is maintained by volunteers and plays an active role in the Charity's Living Well with Cancer approach. Plants, teas, music and plenty of space to enjoy a picnic. Gift shop. Tours of centre to find out more about the work of Penny Brohn UK. Some gravel and grass paths.

69 THE RED POST HOUSE

Fivehead, Taunton, TA3 6PX. The Rev Mervyn & Mrs Margaret Wilson, 01460 281558, margaretwilson426@gmail.com. *10m E of Taunton. On the corner of A378 and Butcher's Hill, opp garage. From M5 J25, take A358 towards Langport, turn R at T-lights at top of hill onto A378. Garden is at Langport end of Fivehead.* **Sun 19 May (2-5). Adm £4, chd free. Home-made teas. Visits also by arrangement Apr to Oct for groups of up to 20. Refreshments by arrangement.**

⅓ acre walled garden with shrubs, borders, trees, circular potager, topiary. We combine beauty and utility. Further 1½ acres, lawn, orchard and vineyard. Plums, 40 apple and 20 pear, walnut, quince, medlar, mulberry, fig. Fruit trees may be in blossom. Mown paths, longer grass. Views aligned on Ham Hill. Summerhouse with sedum roof, belvedere. Garden in its present form developed over last 15 yrs. Paths are gravel and grass, belvedere is not wheelchair accessible. Dogs on leads.

70 ROCK HOUSE

Elberton, BS35 4AQ. Mr & Mrs John Gunnery, 01454 413225. *10m N of Bristol. 3½m SW Thornbury. From Old Severn Bridge on M48 take B4461 to Alveston. In Elberton, take 1st turning L to Littleton-on-Severn and turn immed R.* **Suns 3, 10 Feb; 24, 31 Mar (11-4). Adm £3.50, chd free. 2020: Suns 2 & 9 Feb. Visits also by arrangement for groups of up to 10.**

2 acre garden. Pretty woodland vistas with many snowdrops and daffodils, some unusual. Spring flowers, cottage garden plants and roses. Old yew tree and pond. Limited wheelchair access.

71 ROSE COTTAGE

Smithams Hill, East Harptree, Bristol, BS40 6BY. Bev & Jenny Cruse, 01761 221627, bandjcruse@gmail.com. *5m N of Wells, 15m S of Bristol. From B3114 turn into High St in EH. L at Clock Tower and immed R into Middle St, up hill for 1m. From B3134 take EH rd opp Castle of Comfort, continue 1½m. Car parking in field opp cottage.* **Sun 14 Apr (2-5). Adm £4.50, chd free. Home-made teas. Visits also by arrangement Apr to Aug for groups of up to 30. Please confirm visitor number 2 weeks prior to visit.**

This 1-acre hillside cottage garden, carpeted with seasonal bulbs, primroses and hellebores, welcomes spring. Bordered by stream and established mixed hedges. The garden continues to evolve with new planting. Plenty of seating areas to enjoy panoramic views over Chew Valley, home-made teas and the music of the Congresbury Brass Band. Wildlife area and pond in corner of car park field. Limited wheelchair access, hillside setting.

We open the gates to the nation's best gardens, offering a relaxing, memorable and affordable day out. A perfect experience to share with friends and family.

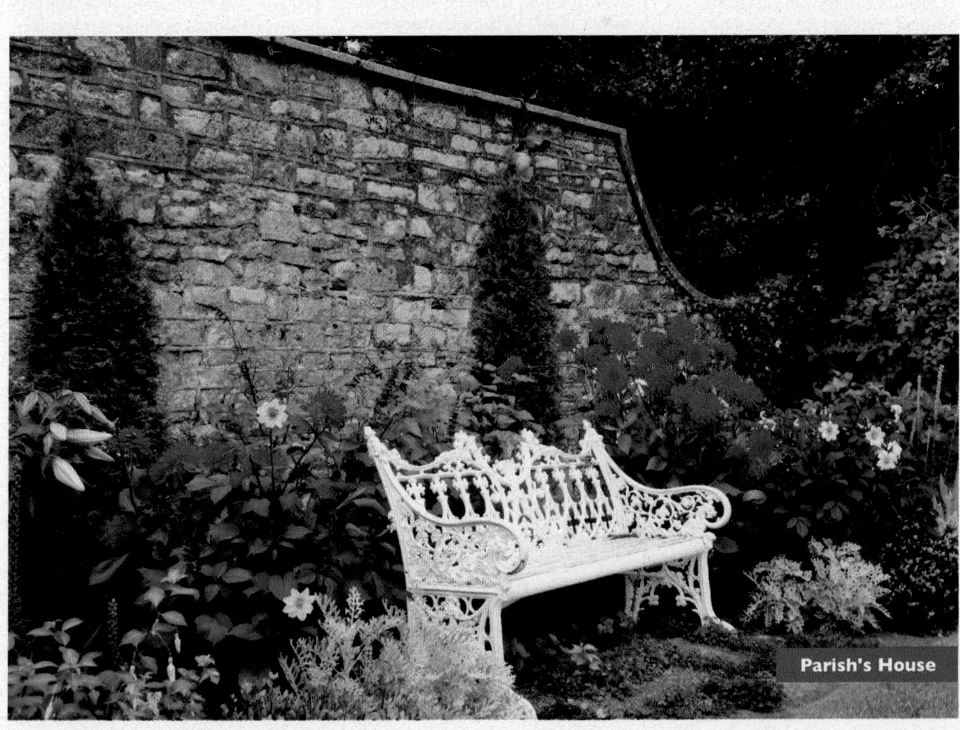

Parish's House

72 ST MONICA TRUST

Cote Lane, Westbury on Trym, Bristol, BS9 3UN. St Monica Trust. *A4018 towards Bristol from M5/Cribbs Causeway, St Monica Trust is on R, just before start of Durdham Downs.* **Sun 27 Oct (10.30-3). Adm £5, chd free. Light refreshments. Teas, cold drinks and cakes.**

The gardens of the St Monica Trust retirement community are a mix of old established borders and new planting. The tree collection, documented in a tree guide, is extensive and impressive, with many unusual specimens. The scented garden is the centrepiece of the gardens and provides yr-round interest. The ponds and woodland wildlife areas benefit from being closed to traffic, and are home to a wide range of bird, mammal and insect species.

73 SERRIDGE HOUSE

Henfield Rd, Coalpit Heath, BS36 2UY. Mrs J Manning, 01454 773188. *9m N of Bristol. On A432 at Coalpit Heath T-lights (opp church), turn into Henfield Rd. R at PH, ½m small Xrds, garden on corner with Ruffet Rd, park on Henfield Rd.* **Visits by arrangement July & Aug for groups of 10 to 30. Adm £5, chd free. Adm incl home-made teas afternoons. Wine available evenings.**

2½ acre garden with mature trees, heather and conifer beds, island beds mostly of perennials, woodland area with pond. Colourful courtyard with old farm implements. Lake views and lakeside walks. Unique tree carvings. Mostly flat grass and concrete driveway. Wheelchair access to lake difficult.

74 ◆ SHERBORNE GARDEN

Litton, Radstock, BA3 4PP. Mrs Pamela Southwell, 01761 241220. *15m S of Bristol. 15m W of Bath, 7m N of Wells. On B3114 Chewton Mendip to Harptree rd, ½m past The Litton (PH).* **For NGS: Sun 10, Mon 11 Feb (11-4). Adm £4, chd free. Tea/coffee and home-made biscuits.** For other opening times and information, please phone.

4½ acre gently sloping garden with small pinetum, holly wood and many unusual trees and shrubs. Cottage garden leading to privy. 3 ponds linked by wadi and rills with stone and wooden bridges. Snowdrops and hellibores. Hosta walk leading to pear and nut wood. Rondel and gravel gardens with grasses and phormiums. Collections of day lilies, rambling and rose species. Good labelling. Plenty of seats. Garden open for private visits and parties. Grass and gentle slopes.

75 SOLE RETREAT

Haydon Drove, Haydon, nr West Horrington, Wells, BA5 3EH. Jane Clisby, 01749 672648/07790 602906, janeclisby@aol.com, www.soleretreat.co.uk. *3m NE of Wells. From Wells take B3139 towards the Horringtons and keep on main road for 3m. L into Haydon Drove and Sole Retreat Reflexology, signed, garden 50yds on L.* **Visits by arrangement May to Aug for groups of up to 20. Car sharing advisable. Adm £4, chd free. Tea. Please confirm numbers 2 weeks prior to agreed date.**

Described as 'stepping into a piece of paradise'. What a challenge to garden at 1000' on the Mendip Hills AONB. Laid out with tranquillity and healing in mind, garden is full of old favourites set in ⅓ acre. 10 differing areas within dry stone walls and raw face bedrock incl herbaceous borders, labyrinth, water feature, vegetable plot, contemplation garden and recent addition of the Gothic corner. Tranquil, contemplation garden with corners for relaxation and mindful thinking. Some gravel, narrow paths.

76 SOUTH CARY HOUSE

South Street, Castle Cary, BA7 7ES. Sally Walford. *For South St, from Station Rd turn L then R onto B3152 into Castle Cary, turn R down high street, pass church on R onto South St. The house has black rails and is opp local pub.* **Sat 8 June (2-5). Adm £5, chd £3. Cream teas.**

Approx 1 acre of gardens in grounds of Grade II listed Georgian house. In our third year of development, semi walled garden with small woodand walk with views of Lodge Hill, specimen trees, rose gardens, box-edging, colour border and pots and extensive lawns. Wheelchair access by arrangement.

77 SOUTH KELDING

Brewery Hill, Upton Cheyney, Bristol, BS30 6LY. Barry & Wendy Smale, 0117 9325145, wendy.smale@yahoo.com. *Halfway between Bristol and Bath. Upton Cheyney lies ½m up Brewery Hill off A431 just outside Bitton. Detailed directions and parking arrangements given when appt made. Restricted access means pre-booking essential.* **Visits by arrangement Apr to Oct for groups of up to 30. Adm £4.50, chd free. Home-made cakes and tea/coffee are an additional £2.50 per person.**

7 acre hillside garden offering panoramic views from its upper levels, with herbaceous and shrub beds, prairie-style scree beds, orchard, native copses and small arboretum grouped by continents. Large wildlife pond, boundary stream and wooded area featuring shade and moisture-loving plants. In view of slopes and uneven terrain this garden is unsuitable for disabled access.

78 SOUTHFIELD FARM

Farleigh Rd, Backwell, Bristol, BS48 3PE. Pamela & Alan Lewis. *6m S of Bristol. On A370, 500yds after George Inn towards WsM. Farm directly off main rd on R, large car park.* **Thur 21 Feb (10-1). Adm £4, chd free. Home-made teas.**

2 acre owner-designed garden of rooms. Mixed shrub and herbaceous borders. Much winter colour and scent. Aconites, heathers, snowdrops, hellebores and more. Courtyards, terrace, orchard, vegetable and herb gardens. Paths through native meadow to woodland garden and large wildlife pond with bird hides. Indoor tearooms in old stable yard. Wheelchair access to most areas on grass paths. Some gravel and steps.

79 ◆ SPECIAL PLANTS

Greenway Lane, Cold Ashton, SN14 8LA. Derry Watkins, 01225 891686, derry@specialplants.net, www.specialplants.net. *6m N of Bath. From Bath on A46, turn L into Greenways Lane just before r'about with A420.* **For NGS: Thurs 20 June; 18 July; 15 Aug; 19 Sept; 17 Oct (11-5). Adm £5, chd free. Home-made teas.** For other opening times and information, please phone, email or visit garden website.

Architect-designed ¾ acre hillside garden with stunning views. Started autumn 1996. Exotic plants. Gravel gardens for borderline hardy plants. Black and white (purple and silver) garden. Vegetable garden and orchard. Hot border. Lemon and lime bank. Annual, biennial and tender plants for late summer colour. Spring fed ponds. Bog garden. Woodland walk. Allium alley. Free list of plants in garden.

80 ◆ STOBERRY GARDEN

Stoberry Park, Wells, BA5 3LD. Frances & Tim Young, 01749 672906, stay@stoberry-park.co.uk, www.stoberryhouse.co.uk. *½m N of Wells. From Bristol - Wells on A39, L into College Rd and immed L through Stoberry Park, signed.* **For NGS: Mon 27 May (2-5.30). Adm £5, chd free. Light refreshments. Discount/prepaid vouchers are not valid on NGS charity days kindly donated by Stoberry Garden.** For other opening times and information, please phone, email or visit garden website.

With breathtaking views over Wells Cathedral, this 6 acre family garden planted sympathetically within its landscape provides stunning combinations of vistas accented with wildlife ponds, water features, sculpture, 1½ acre walled garden, gazebo, and lime walk. Colour and interest every season; spring bulbs, irises, salvias, wild flower circles, new wild flower meadow walk and fernery. Interesting sculpture artistically integrated. Regret no wheelchair access. No dogs.

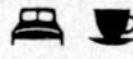

GROUP OPENING

81 STOGUMBER GARDENS

Station Road, Stogumber, TA4 3TQ. *11m NW of Taunton. 3m W of A358. Signed to Stogumber, W of Crowcombe. Village maps given to all visitors.* **Sun 16 June (2-6). Combined adm £6, chd free. Home-made teas in Village Hall.**

CRIDLANDS STEEP
Audrey Leitch.

HIGHER KINGSWOOD
Fran & Tom Vesey.

KNOLL COTTAGE
Elaine & John Leech, 01984 656689, john@Leech45.com, www.knoll-cottage.co.uk. **Visits also by arrangement June to Oct for groups of 5 to 30.**

ORCHARD DEANE
Brenda & Peter Wilson.

POUND HOUSE
Barry & Jenny Hibbert.

NEW **WYNES**
Paul & Trish Haines.

6 delightful and very varied gardens in picturesque village at edge of Quantocks. 4 surprisingly large gardens in village centre, one semi-wild garden, and 2 very large gardens on outskirts of village, with many rare and unusual plants. Conditions range from waterlogged clay to well-drained sand. Walled garden, ponds, bog gardens, rockery, vegetable and fruit gardens, collection of over 80 different roses, even an apple orchard. Fine views of surrounding countryside. Dogs on leads allowed in 4 gardens. Wheelchair access to main features of all gardens.

82 ◆ STON EASTON PARK

Ston Easton, Radstock, BA3 4DF. Ston Easton Ltd, www.stoneaston.co.uk. *On A37 between Bath & Wells. Entrance to Park through high metal gates set back from main road, A37, in centre of village, opp bus shelter.* **For NGS: Daily Fri 1 Feb to Fri 12 Apr (10.30-4). Daily Fri 26 Apr to Fri 29 Nov (10.30-4). Adm £5.** For other information, please visit the website.

Walk the glorious parkland of historic Repton landscape along the quietly cascading River Norr. Garden team diligently work 36 acres of C18 parkland and Victorian Kitchen Garden. Visit late winter/early spring for snowdrops, cyclamen and hellebore, summer brings roses, clematis, herbaceous borders, veg sowing incl some giant veg, autumn for loofah growing and surrounding changing colours. Please mention the NGS when you visit. Deep gravel paths, steep slopes, shallow steps.

83 STONELEIGH DOWN

Upper Tockington Road, Tockington, Bristol, BS32 4LQ. Su & John Mills. *12m N of Bristol. On LH side of Upper Tockington Road when travelling from Tockington towards Olveston. Set back from the road up a gravel drive. Parking in village.* **Sat 1, Sun 2 June, Sat 7, Sun 8 Sept (2-5). Adm £5, chd free. Home-made teas.**

Approaching ⅔ acre, the south-facing garden has curved gravel pathways around an S-shaped lawn that connects themed areas. On a level site, it has been densely planted with a wide variety of trees, shrubs, perennials and bulbs for yr-round interest. Plenty of places to sit. Steps into courtyard. Finalist in BBC Gardeners' World Magazine 'Gardens of the Year 2018', and filmed for BBC Gardeners' World and ITV's 'Love Your Garden'.

Your visits help change lives – we've donated over £16.7 million to Macmillan Cancer Support since 1984

GROUP OPENING

84 STOWEY GARDENS

Stowey, Bishop Sutton, Bristol, BS39 5TL. *10m W of Bath. Stowey Village on A368 between Bishop Sutton and Chelwood. From Chelwood r'about take A368 to Weston-s-Mare. At Stowey Xrds turn R to car park, 150yds down lane, ample off road parking opp Dormers. Limited disabled parking at each garden which will be signed.* **Sun 21 July (2-6). Combined adm £5, chd free. Home-made teas at Stowey Mead, pedestrian entrance for teas via lower gate at Stowey Xrds on A368, entrance to R of seat, diagonally opp lane to Dormers.**

DORMERS
Mr & Mrs G Nicol.

◆ MANOR FARM
Richard Baines & Alison Fawcett, 01275 332297.

STOWEY MEAD
Mr Victor Pritchard.

3 very different gardens, not to be missed, each with its individual style and planting. A broad spectrum of interest and styles developing year on year. But there is far more than this in these gardens, the visitor's senses will be aroused by the sights, scents and diversity of these 3 gardens in the tiny, ancient village of Stowey. Flower-packed beds, borders and pots, roses, topiary, hydrangeas, exotic garden, many unusual trees and shrubs, orchards, vegetables, ponds, specialist sweet peas, lawns, Stowey Henge, and ha ha. An abundant collection of mature trees and shrubs. Ample seating areas, wonderful views from each garden. Something of interest for everyone, all within a few minutes walk of car park at Dormers. Plant sales at Dormers. Well behaved dogs on short leads welcome. Wheelchair access restricted in places, many grassed areas in each garden.

85 SUTTON HOSEY MANOR

Long Sutton, TA10 9NA. Roger Bramble, 0203 9066213, rbramble@bdbltd.co.uk. *2m E of Langport, on A372. Gates N of A372 at E end of Long Sutton.* **Sun 21 July (2.30-6). Adm £5, chd £3. Home-made teas.** Visits also by arrangement Aug & Sept for groups of 10 to 30.
3 acres, of which 2 walled. Lily canal through pleached limes leading to amelanchier walk past duck pond; rose and juniper walk from Italian terrace; judas tree avenue; ptelea walk. Ornamental potager. Drive-side shrubbery. Music by Young Musicians Symphony Orchestra.

86 SWIFT HOUSE

9 Lyndale Avenue, Stoke Bishop, Bristol, BS9 1BS. Mark & Jane Glanville, www.bristolgarden.weebly.com. *NW Bristol - 4m from city centre. 2m from M5 J18 Portway (A4). Turn into Sylvan Way. At lights take R onto Shirehampton Rd. After ¾m turn R into Sea Mills Lane. Lyndale Ave is 2nd rd on L - we're half way up.* **Sun 23 June (2-5). Adm £3.50, chd free.**
We've designed our city garden to look beautiful, provide fruit and vegetables and to be a haven for wildlife. Plants are grown to provide food and shelter throughout the year with the emphasis on flowers that are nectar rich. We have the largest breeding colony of swifts in Bristol www.bristolswifts.co.uk. See inside our swift boxes via live cameras and learn about swift conservation. Plants for Sale.

87 TORMARTON COURT

Church Road, Tormarton, GL9 1HT. Noreen & Bruce Finnamore, 01454 218236, home@thefinnamores.com. *3m E of Chipping Sodbury, off A46 at J18 M4. Follow signs to Tormarton from A46 then follow signs for car parking.* **Fri 12 Apr, Fri 21 June (10-3.30). Adm £5, chd free. Coffee/Tea and cakes available for small charge.** Visits also by arrangement for groups of 10+.
11 acres of formal and natural gardens in stunning Cotswold setting. Features incl roses, herbaceous, kitchen garden, Mediterranean garden, mound and natural pond. Extensive walled garden, spring glade and meadows with young and mature trees.

88 TRUFFLES

Church Lane, Bishop Sutton, Bristol, BS39 5UP. Sally Monkhouse, 01275 333665, sallymonkhouse961@gmail.com. *10m W of Bath. On A368 Bath to Weston-super-Mare. Take rd opp PO/stores uphill towards Top Sutton/ Hinton Blewett. 1st R Church Lane. Please park carefully on nearby rds, 1 level disabled parking place top of drive.* **Sun 23 June (11.30-5.30). Adm £4.50, chd free. Home-made teas.** Visits also by arrangement for groups of 10+ from 17 to 28 June incl. Please confirm visitor numbers 2 weeks in advance.
Now over 3 acres, lake views and surprises. Formal and wildlife planting linked with meandering paths, lots of sturdy seating. Magical wooded valley, ephemeral stream, wildflower meadows, hens. Wildlife pond with visiting dragon flies, formal flower beds, some sculpture. Unique ¼ acre kitchen garden with several 21 ft long x 4 ft wide waist high raised beds. New field this year, wonderful views. Slope up to the house, grass and gravel paths for partial wheelchair access.

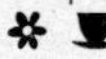

89 ◆ UNIVERSITY OF BRISTOL BOTANIC GARDEN

Stoke Park Road, Stoke Bishop, Bristol, BS9 1JG. University of Bristol Botanic Garden, 0117 4282041, botanic-gardens@bristol.ac.uk, www.bristol.ac.uk/Botanic-Garden. *¼m W of Durdham Downs. Located in Stoke Bishop next to Durdham Downs 1m from city centre. After crossing the Downs to Stoke Hill, Stoke Park Rd is 1st on R.* **For NGS: Sun 14 July (10-4.30). Adm £5, chd free. Light refreshments. Hot and cold drinks, sandwiches, salads, cakes and ice cream provided by Chandos Deli at the Botanic Garden.** For other opening times and information, please phone, email or visit garden website. Donation to University of Bristol Botanic Garden.
Exciting contemporary botanic garden with organic flowing network of paths which lead

visitors through collections of Mediterranean flora, rare native, useful plants (incl European and Chinese herbs) and those that illustrate plant evolution. Large floral displays illustrating pollination/flowering plant evolution. Glasshouses, home to giant Amazon waterlily, tropical fruit and medicine plants, orchids, cacti and unique sacred lotus collection. Open at other times by arrangement. Special tours of garden throughout day plus Luke Jerram exhibits. Wheelchair available to borrow from Welcome Lodge. Wheelchair friendly route through garden available upon request, also accessible WCs.

90 VINE HOUSE

Henbury Road, Henbury, Bristol, BS10 7AD. Pippa Atkinson. *2m from M5 J17. From M5 J17 head to Bristol Centre. At 3rd r'about, R to Blaise. L at end of Crow Lane. 1st house on R.* **Sun 3 Feb (1-4). Sun 30 June (1.30-4.30). Home-made teas. Adm £4, chd free. Regret no refreshments available on 3rd February.**

1½ acres of garden behind listed Georgian house. Mature trees, shrubs, herbaceous borders, rock stream and gunnera. Garden originally planted in 1940's for yr-round interest by the Hewer family, and features many unusual plants and trees. Limited wheelchair access, some paths around upper area of garden.

◆ THE WALLED GARDENS OF CANNINGTON

Church Street, Cannington TA5 2HA. (Part of Bridgwater & Taunton College Cannington Campus), 01278 655042, walledgardens@btc.ac.uk, www.canningtonwalledgardens.co.uk. *3m NW of Bridgwater. On A39 Bridgwater-Minehead rd - at 1st r'about in Cannington 2nd exit, through village. War memorial, 1st L into Church Street then 1st L.* **For NGS: Sat 27, Sun 28 Apr, Sat 21, Sun 22 Sept (10-4). Adm £5.95, chd free. Light refreshments.** For other opening times and information, please phone, email or visit garden website.

Within the grounds of a medieval Priory, the Walled Gardens of Cannington are a gem waiting to be discovered! Classic and contemporary features incl the hot herbaceous border, the blue garden, the sub-tropical walk and a Victorian style fernery, amongst others. Botanical glasshouse where arid, sub-tropical and tropical plants can be seen. 2 smaller gardens within the walls (The Bishop's and Southern Hemisphere Gardens) are areas of real tranquillity. Tea Room, Plant Nursery & Gift Shop as well as events throughout the year. So plenty to see and do for all of the family! Gravel paths. Motorised scooter can be borrowed free of charge (only one available).

NPC

91 WATCOMBE

92 Church Road, Winscombe, BS25 1BP. Peter & Ann Owen, 01934 842666, peterowen449@btinternet.com. *12m SW of Bristol, 3m N of Axbridge. 100 yds after yellow signs on A38 turn L, (from S), or R. (from N) into Winscombe Hill. After 1m reach The Square. Watcombe on L after 150yds.* **Sun 28 Apr, Sun 19 May, Thur 6 June (2-5.30). Adm £4, chd free. Home-made cakes and cream teas, gluten-free available.** Visits also by arrangement Apr to June.

¾-acre mature Edwardian garden with colour-themed, informally planted herbaceous borders. Strong framework separating several different areas; pergola with varied wisteria, unusual topiary, box hedging, lime walk, pleached hornbeams, cordon fruit trees, 2 small formal ponds and growing collection of clematis. Many unusual trees and shrubs. Small vegetable plot. Some steps but most areas accessible by wheelchair with minimal assistance.

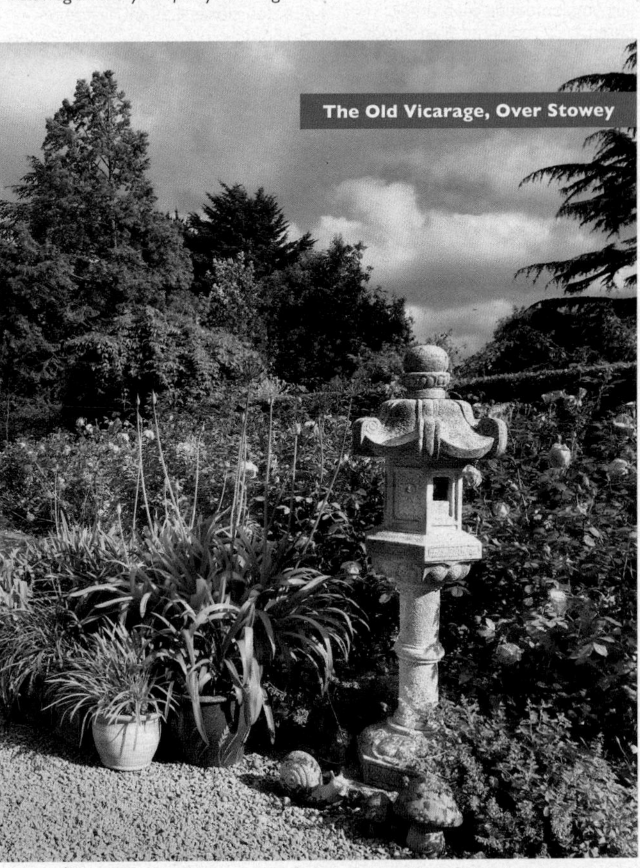
The Old Vicarage, Over Stowey

92 WAVERLEY
Moorland, Bridgwater, TA7 0AT. Ash & Alison Warne, 01278 691058, ashwarne@btinternet.com. *On Somerset Levels, Moorland is 3m from village of Burrowbridge located on A361 twixt Taunton & Street. Turn north off A361 at Burrowbridge signed Moorland - Waverley is opposite church. Park village-hall car-park 300 mtrs past house. Please note no access from Huntworth/ Bridgwater/Jct 24 M5 due to rail bridge renovation Feb-June 2019.* **Wed 22 May, Wed 12 June (11-3.30). Adm £4, chd free. Home-made teas.** Visits also by arrangement May to July for groups of 5 to 30. Any catering considered for arrangement bookings incl cheese & wine evenings.

This ⅓ acre garden is packed with an informal juxtaposition of shrubs, trees, climbers and perennials all complementing each other. Extensively replanted post floods in 2014 the garden demonstrates the resilience of nature in bouncing back after adversity. Collection of 60 roses. Shady areas created under mature trees for acers, hostas and ferns to thrive. Bamboos are a feature. Wildlife friendly. Mostly level paths throughout the garden after negotiating gravel access drive. No slopes.

93 WAYFORD MANOR
Wayford, Crewkerne, TA18 8QG. Wayford Manor. *3m SW of Crewkerne. Turn N off B3165 at Clapton, signed Wayford or S off A30 Chard to Crewkerne rd, signed Wayford.* **Sun 19 May (2-5). Adm £6, chd £3. Home-made teas.**

The mainly Elizabethan manor (not open) mentioned in C17 for its 'fair and pleasant' garden was redesigned by Harold Peto in 1902. Formal terraces with yew hedges and topiary have fine views over W Dorset. Steps down between spring-fed ponds past mature and new plantings of magnolia, rhododendron, maples, cornus and, in season, spring bulbs, cyclamen, giant echium. Primula candelabra, arum lily, gunnera around lower ponds.

94 WELLFIELD BARN
Walcombe Lane, Wells, BA5 3AG. Virginia Nasmyth, 01749 675129. *½m N of Wells. From A39 Bristol to Wells rd turn R at 30 mph sign into Walcombe Lane. Entrance at 1st cottage on R, parking signed.* **Tue 28 May (11.30-4.30). Adm £5, chd free. Light refreshments. Delicious home-made cake.** Visits also by arrangement for groups of up to 30. Adm for By Arrangement visits £6, 1st June to 31st July.

Created over 22 yrs from concrete farmyard into a ½-acre garden, progressively developing. Wonderful views, ha-ha, pond, mixed borders, hydrangea bed, formal sunken garden, grass walks with interesting young and semi-mature trees. Structured design integrates house, lawn and garden with landscape. Featured on BBC Gardeners' World. Moderate slopes in places, some gravel paths. Garden closes 4.30pm, last entry 3.15pm.

95 WESTBROOK HOUSE
West Bradley, BA6 8LS. Keith Anderson & David Mendel, 01458 850604, andersonmendel@aol.com. *4m E of Glastonbury. From A361 at W Pennard follow signs to W Bradley (2m). From A37 at Wraxall Hill follow signs to W Bradley (2m).* **Sat 20 Apr (11-5); Sat 15 June (11-6). Adm £4.50, chd free.** Visits also by arrangement Apr to Sept for groups of 10 to 30. Donation to West Bradley Church.

4 acres comprising 3 distinct gardens with formal layout around house which leads to meadow and orchard with spring bulbs, species roses and lilacs. Planting and layout began 2004 and continues to the present.

96 NEW WILLETT FARM
Willett, Lydeard St. Lawrence, Taunton, TA4 3QB. Mrs Anne White, 01984 667486, acw@willettfarm.co.uk. *10m Taunton, 7m Wiveliscombe, 13m Bridgwater & Minehead. Approx 4½m from junction with B3224 Exmoor rd off A358 Taunton/ Minehead rd. Lone pink cottage on corner of lane to Willett. First farm you come to, parking on R.* **Sat 13 July (10.30-5); Sun 14 July (11-5). Adm £3, chd free. Light refreshments. Self service coffee/tea biscuits/cake.** Visits also by arrangement May to July for groups of up to 10.

Approximately ¾ acre of traditional Victorian style farmhouse garden with small vegetable garden, colourful flower borders, garden rooms and a little woodland corner, overlooking the rolling West Somerset Countryside. Garden is on 2 levels with steps to access higher garden. Always with conservation in mind the hay meadow opposite the farmhouse can also be walked around. Some areas are accessible for wheelchairs but the surfaces make pushing a heavy chair hard work and some paths are quite narrow.

97 WOODLEA BOTTOM
Greyfield Road, High Littleton, Bristol, BS39 6YA. Adrian & Jane Neech. *Follow A39 to High Littleton. Turn into Greyfield Rd, opp Dando's Stores. Garden 400 yds on L. Limited parking available on Greyfield Rd.* **Sat 25, Sun 26 May (10-4). Adm £4, chd free.**

Interesting changes have been made within our garden of rooms with different themes from slate rockery to the new mini stumpery and more, other areas have been redesigned. A balance of naturalised planting and herbaceous borders alongside productive greenhouses and fruit and vegetable areas. Interesting specimen trees and roses, don't forget to look up! Summerhouse and attractive garden pots. Knowledgeable garden owners on hand to talk to, and answer any questions. No dogs please.

GROUP OPENING

98 NEW WRINGTON GARDENS
School Road, Wrington, Bristol, BS40 5NB. 01934 863987. *At top of School Rd, by junction with Ropers Lane, Long Lane and Old Hill. 10m SW of Bristol, midway between A38 at Redhill or Lower Langford and A370 at Congresbury. Beware SatNav may take you to Orchard*

Close. Warfords is opp The Hanging Tree. Car parking in nearby field. **Wed 12, Sun 16 June (2-5.30). Combined adm £5, chd free. Home-made teas at Mathlin Cottage.**

NEW **MATHLIN COTTAGE**
Tony & Sally Harden.

NEW **WARFORDS**
Roger & Susan Vincent.

2 contrasting properties on edge of delightful and historic village. Mathlin Cottage: cottage garden accessed by shallow steps with wonderful views of Mendip Hills. Newly created front garden border with pergola and walkway before entering the back, more cottage-style space full of bee/ butterfly plants. Small pond, greenhouse and salad/soft fruit plot. Large specimen of Paul's Himalayan Musk tumbles over beech hedge which divides flower garden from fruit and vegetable areas. Plenty of seating and places to relax. Warfords: pretty garden remodelled since 2015 and designed to encompass the wide and wonderful backdrop of the Mendip Hills. Plants of interest for all seasons incl alpines in retaining walls, S-facing terrace shaded by tulip tree, sub-tropical species, incl echiums and grapevines. Beyond the greenhouse, with orchids, to sunken gravel vegetable and fruit garden with raised beds.

99 YEO MEADS

High Street, Congresbury, BS49 5JA. Debbie Fortune & Mark Hayward. *150yds along High St from Ship & Castle PH on L. Park in Ship and Castle public car park.* **Sun 9 June (11-4). Adm £4, chd free. Home-made teas.**

1¼ acres, formally laid out in C17 incl 350yr-old Cedar of Lebanon tree which fell in 2007 but survives as a feature, Atlas Blue cedar, 150 yr-old lime, many more with large growths of mistletoe. Lead-lined pond with rill plus Victorian pond. Topiarised golden cypresses set off by darker copper beech behind, octagonal thatched summerhouse. Vegetable garden, orchard, herbaceous borders, rockeries.

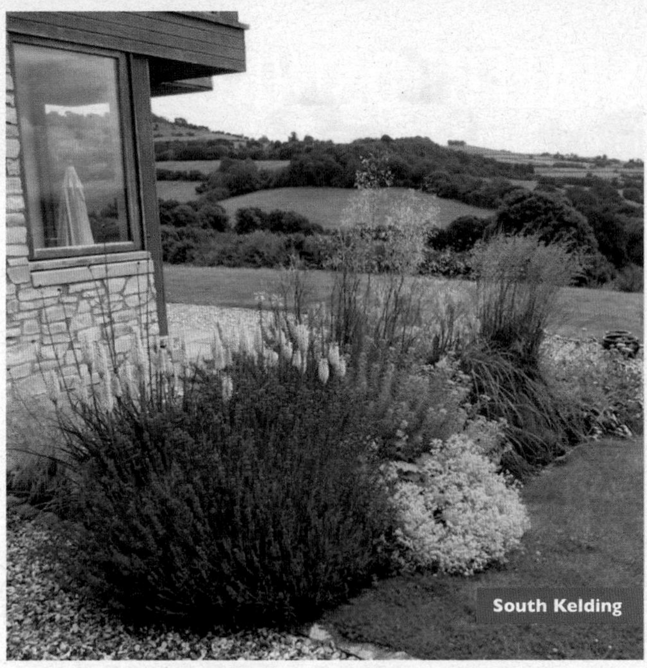

South Kelding

100 ◆ THE YEO VALLEY ORGANIC GARDEN AT HOLT FARM

Bath Road, Blagdon, BS40 7SQ. Mr & Mrs Tim Mead, 01761 461425, visit@yeovalley.co.uk, www.yeovalley.co.uk. *12m S of Bristol. Off A368. Entrance approx ½m outside Blagdon towards Bath, on L, then follow garden signs past dairy.* **For NGS: Sun 28 Apr (2-5). Adm £5, chd free. Home-made teas.** For other opening times and information, please phone, email or visit garden website.

One of only a handful of ornamental gardens that is Soil Association accredited, 6½ acres of contemporary planting, quirky sculptures, bulbs in their thousands, purple palace, glorious meadow and posh vegetable patch. Great views, green ideas. Events, workshops and exhibitions held throughout the year - see website for further details. Level access to café, around garden some grass paths, some uneven bark and gravel paths. Accessibility map available at ticket office.

101 YEWS FARM

East Street, Martock, TA12 6NF. Louise & Fergus Dowding, 01935 822202, fergus.dowding@btinternet.com, www.louisedowding.com. *Turn off main road through village at Market House, onto East St, past PO, garden 150 yards on R, 50m before Nag's Head.* **Sun 30 June (2-6). Adm £7, chd free. Home-made teas. Glass of fine home-made cider to all with a healthy constitution and aged over 18.** Visits also by arrangement May to July.

Theatrical planting in large walled garden. Self seeded Ligusticum lucidum prairie garden. Sculptural planting for height, shape, leaf and texture, espalier apples, excessive cloud pruning. Concrete farmyard garden where hens do the weeding, massive 5 year old 'ecosystem' with hedgehogs. Working organic kitchen garden. Hens, pigs, orchard and active cider barn - the full monty! We grow the Martock broad bean, survivor of a medieval variety of broad bean. Visitors may throw Beauty of Bath apples to the pigs. Child friendly enclosed garden. Mostly wheelchair access.

STAFFORDSHIRE

Birmingham & West Midlands

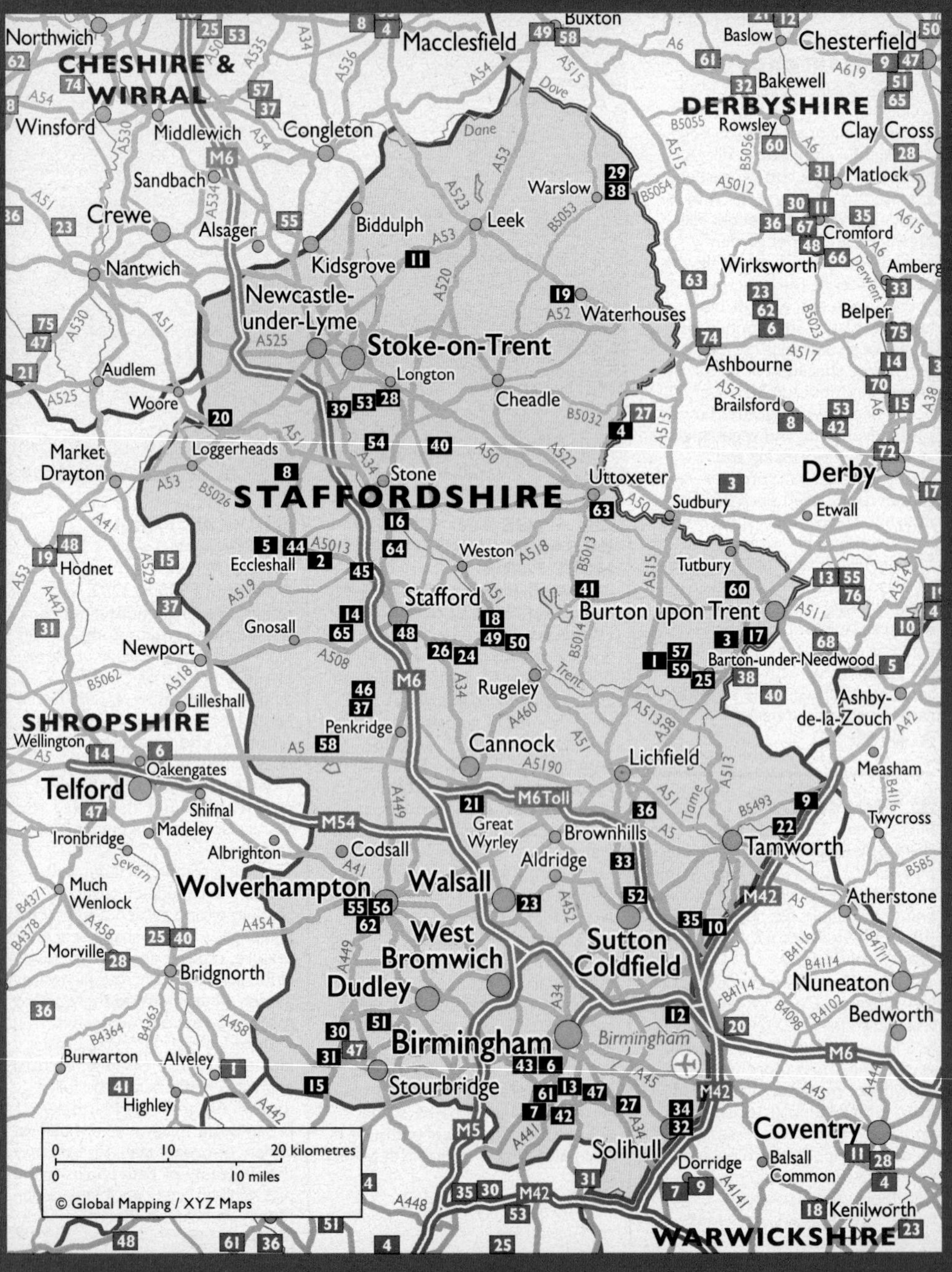

Staffordshire, Birmingham and part of the West Midlands is a landlocked 'county', one of the furthest from the sea in England and Wales.

It is a National Garden Scheme 'county' of surprising contrasts, from the 'Moorlands' in the North East, the 'Woodland Quarter' in the North West, the 'Staffordshire Potteries' and England's 'Second City' in the South East, with much of the rest of the land devoted to agriculture, both dairy and arable.

The garden owners enthusiastically embraced the National Garden Scheme from the very beginning, with seven gardens opening in the inaugural year of 1927, and a further thirteen the following year.

The county is the home of the National Memorial Arboretum, the Cannock Chase Area of Outstanding Natural Beauty and part of the new National Forest.

There are many large country houses and gardens throughout the county with a long history of garden-making and with the input of many of the well known landscape architects.

Today, the majority of National Garden Scheme gardens are privately owned and of modest size. However, a few of the large country house gardens still open their gates for National Garden Scheme visitors.

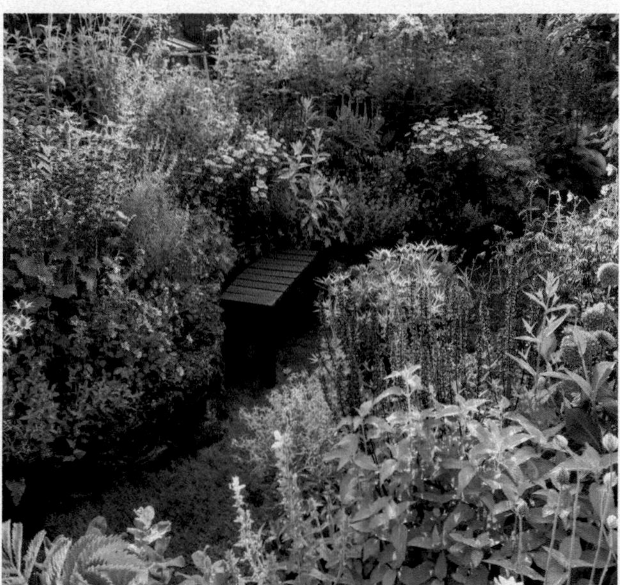

Volunteers

County Organiser
John & Susan Weston
01785 850448
john.weston@ngs.org.uk

County Treasurer
Brian Bailey
01902 424867
brian.bailey@ngs.org.uk

Publicity
Graham & Judy White
01889 563930
graham&judy.white@ngs.org.uk

Booklet Co-ordinator
Peter Longstaff
01785 282582
peter.longstaff@ngs.org.uk

Assistant County Organisers
Jane Cerone
01827 873205
janecerone@btinternet.com

Ken & Joy Sutton
01889 590631
suttonjoy2@gmail.com

Sheila Thacker
01782 791244
metbowers@gmail.com

Left: **Grafton Cottage**

OPENING DATES

All entries subject to change. For latest information check **www.ngs.org.uk**

Map locator numbers are shown to the right of each garden name.

January

Wednesday 16th
◆ The Trentham Estate 53

March

Sunday 24th
The Beeches 4
23 St Johns Road 48

Thursday 28th
◆ The Trentham Estate 53

April

Sunday 7th
The Beeches 4
Millennium Garden 36

Thursday 18th
23 St Johns Road 48

Sunday 21st
'John's Garden' at Ashwood Nurseries 30

Tuesday 30th
NEW The Upper House 54

May

Sunday 5th
Cats Whiskers 13
Keeper's Cottage; Bluebell Wood 31
Yew Tree Cottage 65

Monday 6th
Keeper's Cottage; Bluebell Wood 31

Wednesday 8th
◆ Birmingham Botanical Gardens 6

Saturday 11th
Wild Thyme Cottage 59

Sunday 12th
Whitewood Lodge 57
Wild Thyme Cottage 59

Friday 17th
23 St Johns Road 48

Saturday 18th
NEW Chestnut Lodge 15
Four Seasons 23
Whitewood Lodge 57

Sunday 19th
NEW Chestnut Lodge 15
Dorset House 21
Four Seasons 23
89 Marsh Lane 34
NEW 10 Paget Rise 41
Tanglewood Cottage 50
Whitewood Lodge 57

Wednesday 22nd
The Secret Garden 49

Friday 24th
22 Greenfield Road 26

Saturday 25th
22 Greenfield Road 26

Sunday 26th
The Beeches 4
The Old Dairy House 39

Monday 27th
Bridge House 10
The Old Dairy House 39

June

Sunday 2nd
Coley Cottage 18
The Garth 24
3 Marlows Cottages 33
The Pintles 45
Priory Farm 46
49 The Plantation 51
12 Waterdale 55
19 Waterdale 56

Monday 3rd
◆ Middleton Hall & Gardens 35

Tuesday 4th
◆ Middleton Hall & Gardens 35

Wednesday 5th
High Trees 28
3 Marlows Cottages 33

Friday 7th
Coley Cottage 18
The Secret Garden 49

Sunday 9th
Ashcroft and Claremont 2
Chapel House 14
91 Tower Road 52

Wednesday 12th
Bankcroft Farm 3
◆ The Trentham Estate 53

Friday 14th
22 Greenfield Road 26
23 St Johns Road 48
Tanglewood Cottage 50

Saturday 15th
Colour Mill 19

Sunday 16th
Coley Cottage 18
The Old Vicarage 40
The Secret Garden 49
Wild Wood Lodge 60

Wednesday 19th
Bankcroft Farm 3
5 East View Cottages 22

Friday 21st
Yarlet House 64

Saturday 22nd
Hall Green Gardens 27

Sunday 23rd
The Beeches 4
◆ Castle Bromwich Hall Gardens 12
5 East View Cottages 22
Hall Green Gardens 27
2 Woodland Crescent 62

Wednesday 26th
Bankcroft Farm 3

Saturday 29th
Birch Trees 5

Sunday 30th
Birch Trees 5
Brooklyn 11
5 East View Cottages 22
The Garth 24
Grafton Cottage 25
Marie Curie Hospice Garden 32
Millennium Garden 36
Pereira Road Gardens 43
12 Waterdale 55
19 Waterdale 56

July

Thursday 4th
Yew Tree Cottage 65

Friday 5th
22 Greenfield Road 26

Sunday 7th
21 Alexandra Drive 1
Bournville Village 7
Mitton Manor 37
49 The Plantation 51

Thursday 11th
Yew Tree Cottage 65

Friday 12th
The Bowers 8

Sunday 14th
21 Alexandra Drive 1
Grafton Cottage 25
3 Marlows Cottages 33
2 Woodland Crescent 62

Wednesday 17th
3 Marlows Cottages 33

Thursday 18th
Yew Tree Cottage 65

Saturday 20th
Pershall Farm Cottage 44

Sunday 21st
Breakmills 9
Holmefield 29
Newfields Farm 38
Pershall Farm Cottage 44
56 St Agnes Road 47
Yew Tree Cottage 65

Wednesday 24th
The Secret Garden 49

Sunday 28th
The Beeches 4
Grafton Cottage 25
The Wickets 58

August

Sunday 4th
Grafton Cottage 25

Wednesday 7th
Coley Cottage 18

Thursday 8th
Church Cottage 16

Saturday 10th
Woodbrooke Quaker Study Centre 61

Sunday 11th
Whitewood Lodge 57
Wild Wood Lodge 60

Sunday 18th
NEW 97 Clays Lane 17
Whitewood Lodge 57

Thursday 22nd
Colour Mill 19
The Wickets 58

Sunday 25th
The Wickets 58

September

Sunday 1st
The Beeches 4

Sunday 15th
Bridge House 10

October

Saturday 19th
◆ Dorothy Clive Garden 20

Sunday 20th
◆ Dorothy Clive Garden 20

November

Saturday 2nd
Wild Thyme Cottage 59

Sunday 3rd
Wild Thyme Cottage 59

February 2020

Sunday 16th
5 East View Cottages 22

By Arrangement

Arrange a personalised garden visit with your club, or group of friends, on a date to suit you. See individual garden entries for full details.

The Beeches 4
Birch Trees 5
The Bowers 8
Bridge House 10
NEW Chestnut Lodge 15
Church Cottage 16
Coley Cottage 18
Colour Mill 19
5 East View Cottages 22
36 Ferndale Road, Hall Green Gardens 27
The Garth 24
Grafton Cottage 25
22 Greenfield Road 26
Holmefield 29
Keeper's Cottage; Bluebell Wood 31
Newfields Farm 38
Paul's Oasis of Calm 42
Pershall Farm Cottage 44
The Pintles 45
120 Russell Road, Hall Green Gardens 27
23 St Johns Road 48
The Secret Garden 49
Tanglewood Cottage 50
19 Waterdale 56
Whitewood Lodge 57
The Wickets 58
Wild Thyme Cottage 59
Wild Wood Lodge 60
Woodbrooke Quaker Study Centre 61
2 Woodland Crescent 62
Woodleighton Grove, Karibu Garden 63
Yew Tree Cottage 65

THE GARDENS

1 21 ALEXANDRA DRIVE

Yoxall, Burton-On-Trent, DE13 8PL. Mr & Mrs Paul Shum. *9m SW of Burton On Trent. Located on A515. Easily accessible from A38 at Lichfield or Burton On Trent, can also be accessed via the A50 at Sudbury.* **Sun 7, Sun 14 July (11-5). Adm £3.50, chd free. Cream teas.**
A plant lovers dream, full of colour and perfume. Every inch packed with wide varieties of roses, clematis, sanguisorba, lilies and thalictrum between many other different plants. Also featuring wooden arches and large Indian sandstone patio. A hidden gem-the more you look, the more you will find. Slightly sloping grassed area.

GROUP OPENING

2 ASHCROFT AND CLAREMONT

Eccleshall, ST21 6JP. *7m W of Stafford. J14 M6. At Eccleshall end of A5013 the garden is 100 metres before junction with A519. On street parking nearby. Note: Some Satnavs give wrong directions.* **Sun 9 June (2-5). Combined adm £4.50, chd free. Home-made teas at Ashcroft.**

ASHCROFT
Peter & Gillian Bertram.

26 CLAREMONT ROAD
Maria Edwards.

Weeping limes hide Ashcroft, a 1- acre garden of topiary and green tranquillity, rooms flow seamlessly around the Edwardian house. Covered courtyard with lizard water feature, sunken herb bed, kitchen garden, greenhouse, wildlife boundaries home to five hedgehogs increasing yearly. Deep shade border, woodland area and ruin with stone carvings and stained glass sculpture. Claremont is a master class in clipped perfection. An artist with an artist's eye has blurred the boundaries of this small Italianate influenced garden. Overlooking the aviary, a stone lion surveys the large pots and boarders of vibrant planting, completing the Feng-Shui design of this beautiful all seasons garden. Tickets, teas and plants available at Ashcroft. Wheelchair access at Ashcroft only.

3 BANKCROFT FARM

Tatenhill, Burton-on-Trent, DE13 9SA. Mrs Penelope Adkins. *2m SW of Burton-on-Trent. 2m NW of Burton upon Trent take Tatenhill Rd off A38 on Burton/Branson flyover, 1m 1st house on L after village sign. Parking on farm.* **Wed 12, Wed 19, Wed 26 June (2-5). Adm £3, chd free.**
Lose yourself for an afternoon in our 1½-acre organic country garden. Arbour, gazebo and many other seating areas to view ponds and herbaceous borders, backed with shrubs and trees with emphasis on structure, foliage and colour. Productive fruit and vegetable gardens, wildlife areas and adjoining 12 acre native woodland walk. Picnics welcome. Gravel paths.

Your visits help change lives - your generosity has supported unpaid carers through donations to Carers Trust totalling over £3.9 million since 1996

4 THE BEECHES

Mill Street, Rocester, ST14 5JX. Ken & Joy Sutton, 01889 590631, suttonjoy2@gmail.com. *5m N of Uttoxeter. On B5030 from Uttoxeter turn R at 2nd r'about into village by JCB factory. At Red Lion Pub & mini r'about take rd signed Mill Street. Garden 250 yds on R. Parking at JCB academy Sunday's only.* **Sun 24 Mar, Sun 7 Apr (11-4). Tea. Sun 26 May, Sun 23 June, Sun 28 July, Sun 1 Sept (1.30-5). Home-made teas. Adm £4, chd free.** Visits also by arrangement May to Aug for groups of 20+. Minimum charge £80 if less than 20.

A stunning plant lover's garden of ⅔ acre with countryside views, box garden, shrubs, rhododendrons and azaleas, vibrant colour-themed herbaceous borders, scented roses, clematis and climbing plants, fruit trees, pools, late flowering perennials, vegetable and soft fruit garden. Perennials cut back and shrubs pruned to reveal an under planting of spring jewels from bulbs, hellebores and early perennials (March opening). Partial wheelchair access.

5 BIRCH TREES

Copmere End, Eccleshall, ST21 6HH. Susan & John Weston, 01785 850448, john.weston@ngs.org.uk. *1½m W of Eccleshall. On B5026, turn at junction signed Copmere End. After ½m straight across Xrds by Star Inn.* **Sat 29, Sun 30 June (1.30-5). Adm £4, chd free. Home-made teas.** Visits also by arrangement June & July for groups of 10 to 30.

Surprising ½ acre SW-facing sun trap hidden from the road which takes advantage of the 'borrowed landscape' of the surrounding countryside. Take time to explore the pathways between the island beds which contain many unusual herbaceous plants, grasses, bamboos and shrubs; also vegetable patch, stump bed, alpine house, orchard and water features.

6 ◆ BIRMINGHAM BOTANICAL GARDENS

Westbourne Road, Edgbaston, B15 3TR. Birmingham Botanical & Horticultural Society, 0121 454 1860, admin@birminghambotanicalgardens.org.uk, www.birminghambotanicalgardens.org.uk. *1½m SW of the centre of Birmingham. From J6 M6 take A38(M) to city centre. Follow underpasses signed Birmingham West to A456. At Fiveways island turn L onto B4217 (Calthorpe Rd) signed Botanical Gardens.* **For NGS: Wed 8 May (10-6). Adm £7.50, chd free. Light snacks & refreshments in Terrace Pavilion tearoom. For other opening times and information, please phone, email or visit garden website.**

Extensive botanical garden set in a green urban environment with a comprehensive collection of plants from throughout the world growing in the glasshouses and outside. Four stunning glasshouses take you from tropical rainforest to arid desert. Fifteen acres of beautiful landscaped gardens. Roses, alpines, perennials, rare trees and shrubs. Treetops Playground, Gallery, Gift Shop. Gardens open every day of the year except Christmas Day and Boxing Day.

GROUP OPENING

7 BOURNVILLE VILLAGE

Birmingham, B30 1QY. Bournville Vilage Trust, www.bvt.org.uk. *Gardens spread across 1,000 acre estate. Walks of up to 30 mins between some. Map supplied on day.* **Sun 7 July (10-5). Combined adm £7, chd free. Home-made teas at various locations. Light meals, additional parking & comfort facilities: Wyevale Garden Centre, B30 2AE; Rowheath Pavilion, B30 1HH; Weoley Hill Village Hall, B29 4AA.**

103 BOURNVILLE LANE
B30 1LH. Mrs Jennifer Duffy.

NEW **52 ELM ROAD**
Mr & Mrs Jackie Twigg.

82 HAY GREEN LANE
B30 1UP. Mr Tony Walpole & Mrs Elsie Wheeler.

NEW **21 HIGH HEATH CLOSE**
Dr Faint & Ms Dorward.

NEW **11 KESTREL GROVE**
Mr Julian Stanton.

32 KNIGHTON ROAD
B31 2EH. Mrs Anne Ellis & Mr Lawrence Newman.

40 MIDDLE PARK ROAD
B29 4BJ. Ms Anna De Ville and Mr Chris Elsom.

63 WITHERFORD WAY
Mr Nigel Wood & Mr Vincent Griffith.

Bournville Village is showcasing 8 gardens - 3 of which are new and with the return of the very popular 63 Witherford Way. Bournville is famous for it's large gardens, outstanding open spaces and of course it's chocolate factory! Free information sheet/map available on the day. Gardens spread across the 1,000 acre estate, with walks of up to 30 minutes between sites. For those with a disability, full details of access are available on the NGS website. Visitors with particular concerns with regards to access are welcome to call Bournville Village Trust on 0300 333 6540 or email: CommunityAdmin@bvt.org.uk. Music and singing available across a number of sites. Please check on the day.

8 THE BOWERS

Church Lane, Standon, Eccleshall, ST21 6RW. Maurice & Sheila Thacker, 01782 791244, metbowers@gmail.com. *5m N of Eccleshall. Take A519 & at Cotes Heath turn L signed Standon. After 1m turn R at Xrds by church, into Church Lane ½m on L.* **Fri 12 July (1-4). Adm £3.50, chd free. Home-made teas.** Visits also by arrangement in July for groups of 10+.

A cottage style garden set in the countryside. Colour themed borders contain many herbaceous plants and over 150 clematis climbing up obelisks and arches bringing colour and height. Plenty of interest for the plants person. Some gravel paths may prove difficult.

9 BREAKMILLS

Hames Lane, Newton Regis, Tamworth, B79 0NH. Mr Paul Horobin. *Approx 5m N of Tamworth & 3m S of M42 J11. Signed from B5493, Hames Ln is a single track lane nr the Queens Head Pub. Disabled parking at the house, other visitors please follow parking signs or park in village centre.* **Sun 21 July (12-5.30). Adm £4, chd free. Home-made teas.**

Just under 2 acres of garden featuring small tropical area, island beds, shale area for grasses. Pond, man made stream, vegetable patch and mature trees. Originally a paddock area, trees planted some 15-20 yrs ago but garden really developed over the last 5 yrs and still a work in progress. Recently planted small Cypress Avenue. Lots of seating areas to enjoy both the fun aspects of our garden and the surrounding countryside. Larger grassed area may be difficult for wheelchairs on very wet days but access to long drive and eating area in all conditions.

10 BRIDGE HOUSE

Dog Lane, Bodymoor Heath, B76 9JD. Mr & Mrs J Cerone, 01827 873205, janecerone@btinternet.com. *5m S of Tamworth. From A446 at Belfry Island take A4091 to Tamworth, after 1m turn R onto Bodymoor Heath Lane & continue 1m into village, parking in field opp garden.* **Mon 27 May, Sun 15 Sept (2-5). Adm £4, chd free. Home-made teas. Visits also by arrangement May to Sept for groups of 10 to 30.**

1 acre garden surrounding converted public house. Divided into smaller areas with a mix of shrub borders, azalea and fuchsia, herbaceous and bedding, orchard, kitchen garden with large greenhouse. Pergola walk, formal fish pool, pond, bog garden and lawns. Kingsbury Water Park and RSPB Middleton Lakes Reserve located within a mile.

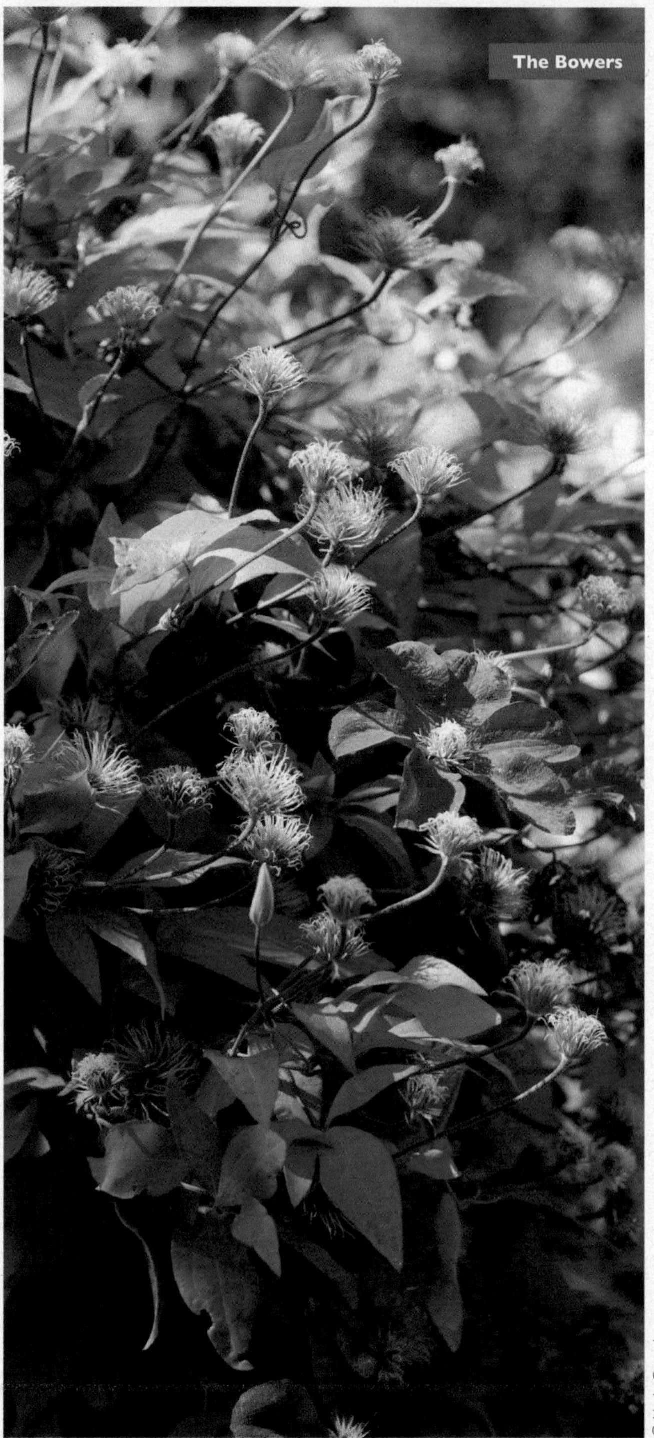

The Bowers

© Linda Greening

11 BROOKLYN

Gratton Lane, Endon, Stoke-on-Trent, ST9 9AA. Janet & Steve Howell. *4m W of Leek. 6m from Stoke-on-Trent on A53 turn at Black Horse Pub into centre of village, R into Gratton Lane 1st house on R. Parking signed in village.* **Sun 30 June (12-5). Adm £3.50, chd free. Cream teas.**

A cottage garden in the picturesque old village of Endon. Pretty front garden overflows with roses, geraniums and astrantia, box surrounds a central sundial. Rear garden features shady area with hostas and ferns, small waterfall and pond. Steps lead to rear lawn, large well stocked borders and summerhouse. Several seating areas with village and rural views. Enjoy tea and cake in the potting shed. Traditional cottage garden in village location.

12 ◆ CASTLE BROMWICH HALL GARDENS

Chester Road, Castle Bromwich, Birmingham, B36 9BT. Castle Bromwich Hall & Gardens Trust, 0121 749 4100, admin@cbhgt.org.uk, www.castlebromwichhallgardens.org.uk. *4m East of Birmingham centre. 1m J5 M6 (exit N only).* **For NGS: Sun 23 June (12.30-4.30). Adm by donation. Home-made teas.** For other opening times and information, please phone, email or visit garden website.

10 acres of restored C17/18 walled gardens attached to a Jacobean manor (now a hotel) just minutes from J5 of M6. Formal yew parterres, wilderness walks, summerhouses, holly maze, espaliered fruit and wild areas. We are opening the Gardens for the Great Get Together (inspired by Jo Cox) #moreincommon. Hopefully people from our wider neighbouring communities will be using the garden and enjoying tea time on the lawn. We will be inviting the community to bring and share food on the day. Paths are either lawn or rough hoggin - sometimes on a slope. Most areas generally accessible, rough areas outside the walls difficult when wet.

13 CATS WHISKERS

42 Amesbury Rd, Moseley, Birmingham, B13 8LE. Dr Alfred & Mrs Michele White. *Opp back of Moseley Hall Hospital. Past Edgbaston Cricket ground straight on at r'about & up Salisbury Rd. Amesbury Rd, 1st on R.* **Sun 5 May (1.30-5). Adm £3.50, chd free. Wine.**

A plantsman's garden developed over the last 38 years but which has kept its 1923 landscape. The front garden whilst not particularly large is full of interesting trees and shrubs; the rear garden is on 3 levels with steps leading to a small terrace and further steps to the main space. At the end of the garden is a pergola leading to the vegetable garden and greenhouse. Two flights of steps in back garden.

14 CHAPEL HOUSE

Coton Clanford, Stafford, ST18 9PE. Mr Richard Clamp. *2m W of J14 M6. From M6 J14 take A5013 to Eccleshall, in 1½m L onto B5405 to Woodseaves, in ¼m L to Seighford. After 1m 3rd L onto Bunns Bank/Clanford Lane. Continue for 1m.* **Sun 9 June (11-4). Adm £4, chd free. Home-made teas.**

Mature country garden in rural location, with 3 distinct areas. Multiple boarders bring colour and foliage in late Spring in the formal garden. The vegetable and fruit garden provides ample produce and feature a small herb bed; while a woodland area creates a natural habitat for wildlife, incl a pond. A number of seating areas around the garden provide quiet spots to enjoy the tranquillity.

15 NEW CHESTNUT LODGE

Dark Lane, Kinver, DY7 6JA. Mrs Carol Westwood, 01384 872 128, kinver5@icloud.com. *Kinver. At SE end of High St at junction with Mill Ln turn into Church Hill, first L to Dark Ln. Park with consideration in Dark Ln.* **Sat 18, Sun 19 May (1-6). Adm £3.50, chd free. Home-made teas.** Visits also by arrangement May to Sept for groups of 10+.

½ acre garden on 3 levels with mature trees, roses, shrubs & folly (Gardener's Chapel). Gradual steps to water feature, seating & Bower

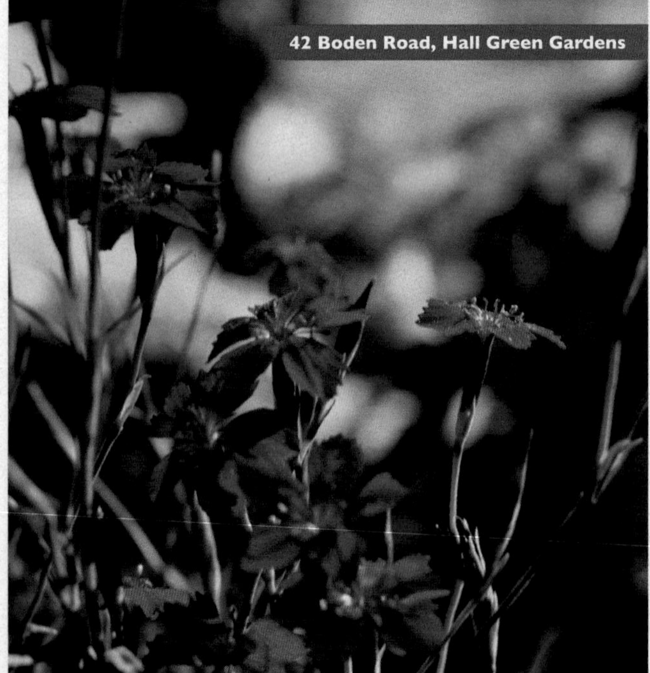

42 Boden Road, Hall Green Gardens

on 2nd level. Steep steps to river views & cave with surprise features on 3rd level.

16 CHURCH COTTAGE

Aston, Stone, ST15 0BJ. Andrew & Anne Worrall, 01785 815239, acworrall@aol.com. *1m S of Stone, Staffordshire. N side of St Saviour's Church, Aston. Go S 150 metres on A34 after junction with A51. Turn L at Aston Village Hall. 200 metres down lane into churchyard for parking.* **Thur 8 Aug (12-4.30). Adm £3.50, chd free.** Visits also by arrangement May to Aug for groups of 5 to 30.

An acre of cottage garden with large pond, waterfall and stream. More than 60 trees, small orchard and wild flowers. Dahlias by award-winning grower Dave Bond. Views across the R Trent. Quiet seating.

17 NEW 97 CLAYS LANE

Branston, Burton-On-Trent, DE14 3HT. Mrs Jan Wood. *From A38 Lichfield or Derby, take Branston exit (A5121) into Branston village. Clays Ln is opp the church & Vicarage Restaurant. 97 is a bungalow on the L side.* **Sun 18 Aug (11-5). Adm £4, chd free. Light refreshments.**

'If you go down to the Wood's today be sure of a big surprise!' A garden of rooms, each themed with its own personality, with tantalising glimpses from one into the next. Mature trees, shrubs, tall hedging, make it a haven for wildlife. Bamboo, grasses, topiary, summer bedding, & over 20 mini-landscapes (created by me), strategically displayed, some for sale, planter-chairs of alpines & succulents.

18 COLEY COTTAGE

Coley Lane, Little Haywood, Stafford, ST18 0UU. Yvonne Branson, 01889 882715, yvonnebranson@outlook.com. *5m SE of Stafford. A51 from Rugeley or Weston signed Little Haywood. ½m from Seven Springs. A513 Coley Lane from Red Lion Pub past Back Lane, 100yds on L opp red post box.* **Sun 2, Fri 7, Sun 16 June, Wed 7 Aug (11-4.30). Adm £2.50, chd free. Home-made teas in the garden and in conservatory.** Visits also by arrangement June to Aug for groups of 5+.

A plant lover's cottage garden, full of subtle colours and perfume, every inch packed with plants. Clematis and old roses covering arches, many hostas and agapanthus, a wildlife pool, all designed to attract birds and butterflies. This garden has now matured and I concentrate on the care of the wildlife it attracts.

19 COLOUR MILL

Winkhill, Leek, ST13 7PR. Bob & Jackie Pakes, 01538 308680, jackie.pakes@icloud.com, www.colourmillbandb.co.uk. *7m E of Leek. Follow A523 from either Leek or Ashbourne, look for NGS signs on the side of the main rd which will direct you down to Colour Mill.* **Sat 15 June, Thur 22 Aug (1.30-5). Adm £3.50, chd free. Home-made teas.** Visits also by arrangement Apr to Oct.

1½ acre S-facing garden, created in the shadow of a former iron foundry, set beside the delightful R Hamps. Informal planting in a variety of rooms surrounded by beautiful 7ft beech hedges. Large organic vegetable patch complete with greenhouse and polytunnel. Maturing trees provide shade for the interesting seating areas. River walk through woodland and willows. Herbaceous borders.

20 ◆ DOROTHY CLIVE GARDEN

Willoughbridge, Market Drayton, TF9 4EU. Willoughbridge Garden Trust, 01630 647237, info@dorothyclivegarden.co.uk, www.dorothyclivegarden.co.uk. *3m SE of Bridgemere Garden World. From M6 J15 take A53 W bound, then A51 N bound midway between Nantwich & Stone, near Woore.* **For NGS: Sat 19, Sun 20 Oct (10-4). Adm £4, chd £2. Light refreshments in tea rooms.** For other opening times and information, please phone, email or visit garden website.

12 informal acres, incl superb woodland garden, alpine scree, gravel garden, fine collection of trees and spectacular flower borders. Renowned in May when woodland quarry is brilliant with rhododendrons. Waterfall and woodland planting. Laburnum Arch in June. Creative planting has produced stunning summer borders. Large Glasshouse. Spectacular autumn colour. Much to see, whatever the season. The Dorothy Clive Tea Rooms will be open throughout the weekend during winter for refreshments, lunch and afternoon tea. Open all week in summer. Plant sales, Gift room Picnic area and children's play area for a wide age range. Wheelchairs (inc. electric) are available to book through the tea rooms . Disabled parking is available. Toilets on both upper and lower car parks.

21 DORSET HOUSE

68 Station Street, Cheslyn Hay, WS6 7EE. David Blundell. *2m SE of Cannock J11 M6 A462 towards Willenhall. L at island. At next island R into 1-way system (Low St), at T junction L into Station St. A5 Bridgetown L to island, L Coppice St. R into Station St.* **Sun 19 May (11-5). Adm £3, chd free. Home-made teas.**

An inspirational ½-acre garden with country cottage planting at its best. Unusual rhododendrons, acers, shrubs and perennials planted in mixed borders. Clematis-covered arches and hidden corners with water features all come together to create a haven of peace and tranquillity. We are opening for the last time in Memory of Mary (the gardener) who passed away, 16th August 2018.

Your visits help change lives – we are Hospice UK's largest charitable funder donating more than £5 million to support hospices in local communities since 1996

22 5 EAST VIEW COTTAGES

School Lane, Shuttington, nr Tamworth, B79 0DX. Cathy Lyon-Green, 01827 892244, cathyatcorrabhan@hotmail.com, www.ramblinginthegarden.wordpress.com. *2m NE of Tamworth. From Tamworth, Amington Rd or Ashby Rd to Shuttington. From M42 J11, B5493 for Seckington & Tamworth; signed L turn to Shuttington. Pink house nr top of School Lane. Parking signed, disabled at house.* **Wed 19 June (1-4); Sun 23, Sun 30 June (1-5). Adm £4, chd free. Home-made teas. 2020: Sun 16 Feb.** Visits also by arrangement June & July. Min charge £60 (excl teas) if less than 15. Groups by appt also in Feb 2020.

Deceptive & quirky plantlover's garden, full of surprises. Informally planted themed borders, cutting beds, woodland, woodland edge borders, shrub border, stream, water features, sitooterie, folly & many artefacts. Roses, clematis, perennials, potted hostas. Snowdrops & witch hazels in Feb. Benches & seating areas to contemplate garden & birdlife or enjoy homemade cake. "A wonderful hour's wander". February 2020 opening price incl tea and cake.

23 FOUR SEASONS

26 Buchanan Road, Walsall, WS4 2EN. Marie & Tony Newton, www.fourseasonsgarden.co.uk. *Adjacent to Walsall Arboretum. From Ring Rd A4148 nr Walsall town centre. At large junction take A461 to Lichfield. At 1st island 3rd exit Buchanan Ave, fork R into Buchanan Rd.* **Sat 18, Sun 19 May (10-5). Adm £4, chd free. Tea.**

Stunning in all seasons. Suburban, S-facing ¼ acre, gently sloping to arboretum. 130 acers, 450 azaleas, bulbs, hellebores, camellias, perennials, begonias, bright conifers, topiary and shrubs. Autumn colours, bark and berries. Semi-formal, oriental, woodland-like areas and jungle. Themes incl contrast of red, blue and yellow. Pagoda, bridges, water features, stone ornaments. Some steps. WC. Please note: access into the garden is down 10 steps.

24 THE GARTH

2 Broc Hill Way, Milford, Stafford, ST17 0UB. David & Anita Wright, 01785 661182, anitawright1@yahoo.co.uk, www.anitawright.co.uk. *4½ m SE of Stafford. A513 Stafford to Rugeley rd; at Barley Mow turn R (S) to Brocton; L after ½ m.* **Sun 2, Sun 30 June (2-6). Adm £3, chd free. Cream teas.** Visits also by arrangement May to Sept for groups of 20+.

½ acre garden of many levels on Cannock Chase AONB. Acid soil loving plants. Series of small gardens, water features, raised beds. Rare trees, island beds of unusual shrubs and perennials, many varieties of hosta and ferns. Varied and colourful foliage, summerhouse, arbours and quiet seating to enjoy the garden. Ancient sandstone caves.

25 GRAFTON COTTAGE

Barton-under-Needwood, DE13 8AL. Margaret & Peter Hargreaves, 01283 713639, marpeter1@btinternet.com. *6m N of Lichfield. Leave A38 for Catholme S of Barton, follow sign to Barton Green, L at Royal Oak, ¼ m.* **Sun 30 June, Sun 14, Sun 28 July, Sun 4 Aug (11.30-5). Adm £4, chd free. Home-made teas.** Visits also by arrangement June to Aug for groups of 10+. Minimum admission £80, if less than 20 people. Donation to Alzheimer's Research Trust.

A visitor commented 'we waited 3 years to visit and it was well worth it, fabulous colour themed borders full of bees'. Admired over 25 years. Unusual herbaceous plants and perfume from old fashioned Roses, Sweet peas, dianthus, phlox and lilies. Particular interests are viticella clematis, salvias and violas. Cottage garden annuals, use of foliage plants and pelargonium, Parterre, brook, amphitheatre.

Your visits help change lives – your generosity helps Marie Curie fund nurses to care for people night and day in their homes, with donations of more than £8.8 million

26 22 GREENFIELD ROAD

Stafford, ST17 0PU. Alison & Peter Jordan, 01785 660819, alison.jordan2@btinternet.com. *3m S of Stafford. Follow the A34 out of Stafford towards Cannock. 2nd L onto Overhill Rd. 1st R into Greenfield Rd.* **Evening opening Fri 24 May (6.30-9). Adm £5, chd free. Wine. Sat 25 May (11.30-4.30). Adm £3, chd free. Cream teas. Evening opening Fri 14 June, Fri 5 July (6.30-9). Adm £5, chd free. Wine.** Visits also by arrangement May to Aug for groups of 5 to 20.

Suburban garden created in the last 7 years, working towards all year round interest. In spring interesting bulbs, in May. stunning azaleas and rhododendrons. June onward; interesting perennials and grasses. A garden that shows being diagnosed with Parkinson's needn't stop you creating a peaceful place to sit, ponder and enjoy. Flat garden but with some gravelled areas.

GROUP OPENING

27 HALL GREEN GARDENS

Hall Green, Birmingham, B28 8SQ. *Off A34, 3m city centre, 6m from M42 J4. From CIty Centre start at 120 Russell Rd B28 8SQ Hall Green. From M42 start at 638 Shirley Rd B28 9LB Hall Green.* **Sat 22, Sun 23 June (1-5.30). Combined adm £5, chd free. Home-made teas at 111 Southam Rd.**

42 BODEN ROAD
Mrs Helen Lycett.

36 FERNDALE ROAD
Mrs E A Nicholson, 0121 777 4921.
Visits also by arrangement Apr to Sept for groups of up to 30. Teas included in admission price.

63 GREEN ROAD
Mr & Mrs A Wilkes.
Visits also by arrangement Apr to July.

120 RUSSELL ROAD
Mr David Worthington, 0121 624 7906, hildave@hotmail.com.

Visits also by arrangement Apr to July for groups of up to 30.

NEW **638 SHIRLEY ROAD**
Dr. and Mrs. M. Leigh.

87 SOUTHAM ROAD
Mrs Sarah Moss.

111 SOUTHAM ROAD
Ms Val Townend & Mr Ian Bate.

A group of diverse suburban gardens. Boden Rd: Large restful garden, mature trees, cottage borders, seating areas and small vegetable area. Ferndale Rd: Florist's large suburban garden, ponds and waterfalls, and fruit garden. Green Rd: Eccentric's north facing wildlife friendly garden. Russell Rd: Plantsman's garden, formal raised pond and hosta collection and unusual perennials, container planting. 87 Southam Rd: Mature garden with deep, sunny herbaceous borders. 111 Southam Rd: Mature garden with well defined areas incl ponds, white garden, rescue hens and a majestic cedar. Shirley Rd: Large young garden with herbaceous borders, vegetables and greenhouses. Some gardens have limited wheelchair access. Telephone for more information or consult the NGS website.

28 HIGH TREES

Drubbery Lane, nr Longton Park, Stoke-on-Trent, ST3 4BA. Peter & Pat Teggin. *5m S of Stoke-on-Trent. Off A5035, midway between Trentham Gardens & Longton. Opp Longton Park.* **Wed 5 June (1-4). Adm £3.50, chd free. Cream Teas.**

A delightful, secluded, inspirational garden. Intensively planted mixed herbaceous borders with bulbs in spring, trillium, climbing roses and clematis with an emphasis on scent and colour combinations. Spires, flats and fluffs interwoven with structure planting and focal points. Planted for year round interest with many unusual plants. Delicious cakes. W.C. And two minutes from a Victorian park.

63 Witherford Way, Bourneville Village

Ashcroft, Ashcroft and Claremont

29 HOLMEFIELD

Sheen, Buxton, SK17 0HW. Connie Chafer & Sean Whittaker, 01298 687066, conniechafer@yahoo.co.uk. *Approx 10m S of Buxton. A515 Buxton/ Ashboune rd. Take B5054 through Hartington after approx 2m take 1st R signed Sheen & Longnor.* **Sun 21 July (1-5). Combined adm with Newfields Farm £6, chd free. Home-made teas.** Visits also by arrangement July & Aug for groups of 10 to 30.

Young cottage garden nestled in the tranquillity of the Peak District National Park. Large sweeping borders filled with perennials, grasses, shrubs and trees provide plenty of interest, colour and texture. Seating placed around the garden gives ample chance to rest, contemplate the garden and drink in the stunning countryside.

30 'JOHN'S GARDEN' AT ASHWOOD NURSERIES

Ashwood Lower Lane, Ashwood, nr Kingswinford, DY6 0AE. John Massey, www.ashwoodnurseries.com. *5m S of Wolverhampton. 1m past Wall Heath on A449 turn R to Ashwood along Doctor's Lane. At T-junction turn L. Park at Ashwood Nurseries.* **Sun 21 Apr (10-4). Adm £5, chd free.**

A stunning private garden adjacent to Ashwood Nurseries, it has a huge plant collection and many innovative design features in a beautiful canal-side setting. There are informal beds, woodland dells, a stunning rock garden, a unique ruin garden, an Anemone pavonina meadow and wildlife meadow. Fine displays of bulbs and Spring-flowering plants and a notable collection of Malus and Amelanchier. Tea Room, Garden Centre and Gift Shop at adjacent Ashwood Nurseries. Coaches are by appointment only. Disabled access difficult if very wet.

♿ ✿ 🚌 NPC ☕

31 KEEPER'S COTTAGE; BLUEBELL WOOD

24 Greensforge Lane, Stourton, Stourbridge, DY7 5BB. Peter & Jenny Brookes, 07974 454503, peter@brookesmedia.com. *2m NW of Stourbridge. At junction of A449 & A458 at Stourton, take Bridgnorth Rd (A458) westward, after ½m turn R into Greensforge Ln. Keeper's Cottage ½m on R.* **Sun 5, Mon 6 May (11-4). Adm £4, chd free. Home-made teas.** Visits also by arrangement in May for groups of 5 to 10.

This stunning bluebell wood adorns the banks of a river deep in the South Staffordshire countryside, yet only a few miles from the conurbation. In May, the bluebells form a beautiful carpet, sweeping through the natural woodland and down to the river, the site of ancient nail making. It is a quintessentially English landscape which can only be glimpsed for a few short weeks of the year. The woods contain steep pathways.

🐕 ☕

32 MARIE CURIE HOSPICE GARDEN

Marsh Lane, Solihull, B91 2PQ. Mrs Do Connolly, www.mariecurie.org.uk/westmidlands. *Close to J5 M42 to E of Solihull Town Centre. M42 J5, travel towards Solihull on A41. Take slip rd toward Solihull to join B4025 & after island take 1st R onto Marsh Lane. Hospice is on R. Limited onsite parking - blue badge holders only.* **Sun 30 June (11-4). Adm £3.50, chd free. Home-made teas plus light refreshments at the hospice bistro.**

The gardens incl two large, formally laid out patients' gardens incl a ball fountain water feature and large rose/clematis arches, indoor courtyards, a vegetable plot, a long border adjoining the car park and a beautiful wildlife and pond area. The volunteer gardening team hope that the gardens provide a peaceful and comforting place for patients, their visitors and staff.

33 3 MARLOWS COTTAGES

Little Hay Lane, Little Hay, WS14 0QD. Phyllis Davies. *4m S of Lichfield. Take A5127, Birmingham Rd. Turn L at Park Lane (opp Tesco Express) then R at T junction into Little Hay Lane, ½m on L.* **Sun 2, Wed 5 June, Sun 14, Wed 17 July (11-4). Adm £3.50, chd free. Home-made teas.**

Long, narrow, gently sloping cottage style garden with borders and beds containing abundant herbaceous perennials and shrubs leading to vegetable patch.

34 89 MARSH LANE

Solihull, B91 2PE. Mrs Gail Wyldes. *½m from Solihull town centre. A41 from M42 J5. Turn sharp L at 1st T-lights. Garden on R. Parking 400 metres further along Marsh Ln at Solihull Cricket Club by mini r'about & Marie Curie car park further along.* **Sun 19 May (2-5). Adm £3.50, chd free. Home-made teas.**

Suburban Oasis. Trees, shrubs and herbaceous planting for all year interest with emphasis on leaf shape and structure. Wildlife pond, bog garden, water features, african style gazebo, gravel gardens, shady places and sunny seating areas. Patio with pergola and raised beds. Hostas and ferns abound. The garden is continually evolving with new plants and features. Wheelchair access - small step from patio to the main back garden and paths may be a little narrow.

35 ◆ MIDDLETON HALL & GARDENS

Middleton, Tamworth, B78 2AE. Middleton Hall Trust, 01827 283095, enquiries@middleton-hall.co.uk, www.middleton-hall.co.uk. *4m S of Tamworth, 2m N of J9 M42. On A4091 between The Belfry & Drayton Manor.* **For NGS: Mon 3, Tue 4 June (11-4). Adm £6, chd free. Light refreshments in our Courtyard Centre. For other opening times and information, please phone, email or visit garden website.**

Our formal gardens form part of the 42 estate of the Grade II* Middleton Hall, the seventeenth-century home of naturalists Francis Willughby and John Ray. The formal gardens are made up of a Walled Garden, lawns and an orchard. The Walled gardens contain a variety of herbaceous and seasonal planting with specimen plants that have a botanical and/or historical significance to our site. Bake 180 Coffee Shop will also be open serving lunches and other light refreshments. Wheelchair access - Walled Garden paths are paved, Glade and Orchard paths are grass. No access to 1st floor of the Hall and Nature Trail.

36 MILLENNIUM GARDEN

London Road, Lichfield, WS14 9RB. Carol Cooper. *1m S of Lichfield. Off A38 along A5206 towards Lichfield ¼m past A38 island towards Lichfield. Park in field on L. Yellow signs on field gate.* **Sun 7 Apr, Sun 30 June (1-5). Adm £3.50, chd free. Home-made teas.**

2-acre garden with mixed spring bulbs in the woodland garden and host of golden daffodils fade slowly into the summer borders in this English country garden. Designed with a naturalistic edge and with the environment in mind. A relaxed approach creates a garden of quiet sanctuary with the millennium bridge sitting comfortably, with its surroundings of lush planting and mature trees. Well stocked borders give shots of colour to lift the spirit and the air fills with the scent of wisterias and climbing roses. A stress free environment awaits you at the Millennium Garden. Park in field then footpath round garden. Uneven surfaces.

37 MITTON MANOR

Mitton, Penkridge, Stafford, ST19 5QW. Mrs E A Gooch, www.mittonmanor.co.uk. *2m W of Penkridge. Property is on Whiston Rd. Parking in field before house. No parking for coaches.* **Sun 7 July (11.30-4.30). Adm £7.50, chd free. Cream teas.**

This 7-acre country garden was started in 2001 and has been developed from an overgrown wilderness. The garden surrounds a Victorian manor (not open) and contains rooms of different styles, formal box/topiary, prairie planting and natural woodland bordered by a stream. Stunning vistas, water features and sculpture. New potager started in 2018. Many levels, narrow and gravel paths.

38 NEWFIELDS FARM

Sheen, Buxton, SK17 0HW. Mr & Mrs John and Margaret Gould, 01298 687085. *Approx 10m S of Buxton. A515 from Buxton/Ashboune Rd .Take B5054 through Hartington after Approx 2m take 1st R signed Sheen/Longnor.* **Sun 21 July (1-5). Combined adm with Holmefield £6, chd free. Home-made teas. Visits also by arrangement July & Aug for groups of 10 to 30.**

Medium size garden in the surrounds of the Peak District National Park. Large borders filled with a riot of colour and harbouring surprises at every turn. A treasure trove of beautiful trees, shrubs, plants and grasses with vistas out over the countryside beyond.

39 THE OLD DAIRY HOUSE

Trentham Park, Stoke-on-Trent, ST4 8AE. Philip & Michelle Moore. *S edge of Stoke-on-Trent. Next to Trentham Gardens. Off Whitmore Rd. Please follow NGS signs or signs for Trentham Park Golf Club. Parking in church car park.* **Sun 26 May (12.30-4.30); Mon 27 May (12-4.30). Adm £3, chd free. Home-made teas.**

Grade 2 listed house (not open) designed by Sir Charles Barry forms backdrop to this 2-acre garden in parkland setting. Shaded area for rhododendrons, azaleas plus expanding hosta and fern collection. Mature trees, 'cottage garden' and long borders. Narrow brick paths in vegetable plot. Large courtyard area for teas. Wheelchair access - some gravel paths but lawns are an option.

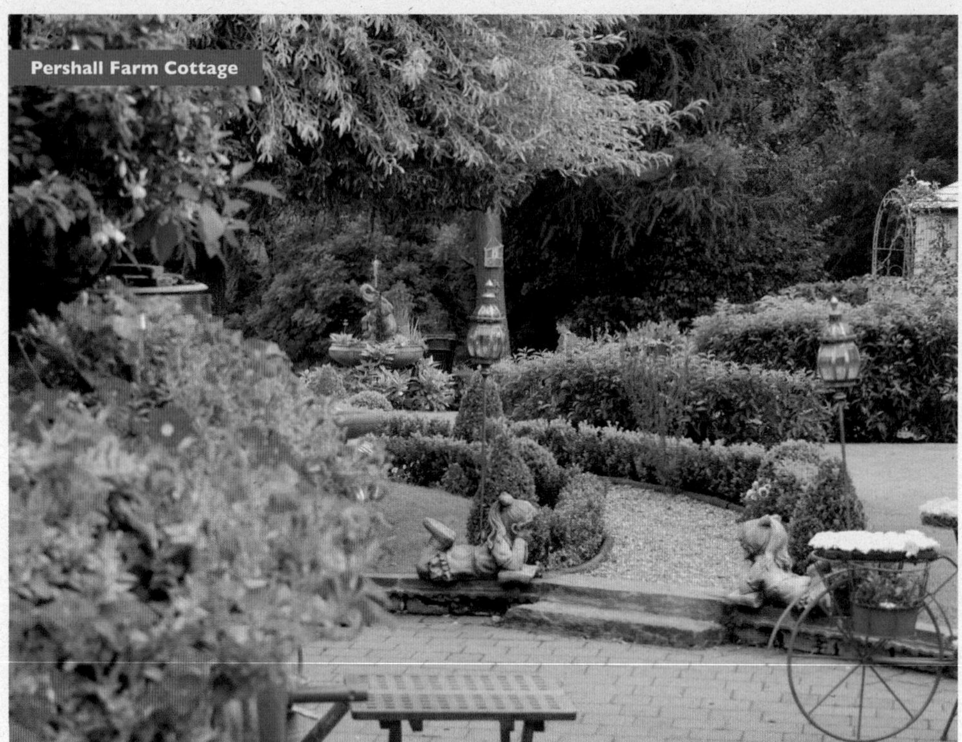
Pershall Farm Cottage

40 THE OLD VICARAGE

Fulford, nr Stone, ST11 9QS. Mike & Cherry Dodson. *4m N of Stone. From Stone A520 (Leek). 1m R turn to Spot Acre & Fulford, turn L down Post Office Terrace, past village green/Pub towards church. Parking signed on L.* **Sun 16 June (1-5). Adm £4. Home-made teas.**

1½ acres of formal sloping garden around Victorian house. Sit on the terrace or in the summerhouse to enjoy home-made cakes and tea amongst mature trees, relaxed herbaceous borders, roses and a small pond. Move to the organic vegetable garden with raised beds, fruit cage and very big compost heaps! In complete contrast, easy walk around the natural setting of a two-acre reclaimed lake planted with native species designed to attract wildlife. Waterfall, jetty, fishing hut, acer and fern glade plus young arboretum provide more interest. Children will enjoy meeting the chickens and horses. Wheelchair access to most areas.

41 NEW 10 PAGET RISE

Paget Rise, Abbots Bromley, Rugeley, WS15 3EF. Mr Arthur Tindle. *4m W of Rugeley 6m S of Uttoxeter and 12m N of Lichfield. From Rugeley: B5013 E. At T junc turn R on B5014. From Uttoxeter take the B5013 S then B5014. From Lichfield take A515 N then turn L on B5234. In Abbots Bromley follow NGS yellow signs.* **Sun 19 May (11-5). Adm £3, chd free. Light refreshments.**

This small 2 level garden has a strong Japanese influence. Evergreens and a wide range of flowering shrubs. Many bonsai-style Acer trees in shallow bowls occupy a central gravel area with stepping stones. The rear of the garden has a woodland feel with a fairy dell under the pine tree. A little gem of a garden! Arthur hopes visitors will be inspired to take away ideas to use in their own garden. Arthur is a watercolour artist & will be displaying a selection of his paintings for sale.

42 PAUL'S OASIS OF CALM

18 Kings Close, Kings Heath, Birmingham, B14 6TP. Mr Paul Doogan, 0121 444 6943, gardengreen18@hotmail.co.uk. *4m from city centre. 5m from M42 J4. Take A345 to Kings Heath High St then B4122 Vicarage Rd. Turn L onto Kings Rd then R to Kings Close.* **Visits by arrangement May to Aug for groups of up to 20. Adm £2.50, chd free. Tea.**

Garden cultivated from nothing into a little oasis. Measuring 18ft x 70ft. It's small but packed with interesting and unusual plants, water features and 7 seating areas. It's my piece of heaven.

GROUP OPENING

43 PEREIRA ROAD GARDENS

Harborne, Birmingham, B17 9JN. *Between Gillhurst Rd & Margaret Grove, ¼m from Hagley Rd or ½m from Harborne High St.* **Sun 30 June (2-5). Combined adm £3, chd free. Home-made teas at Pereira Road allotments, accessed via driveway between 31 and 33 Pereira Road or through 55 Pereira Road.**

14 PEREIRA ROAD
Mike Foster.

50 PEREIRA ROAD
Peg Peil.

55 PEREIRA ROAD
Emma Davies & Martin Commander.

Group of 3 different urban gardens. No.14 a well established suburban garden with mixed herbaceous and shrub borders. Wildlife-friendly with 2 ponds and wild flower area. Ongoing alterations provide new areas of interest each year. No. 50 is a plantaholic's paradise with over 1000 varieties, many rare, incl fruits, vegetables, herbs, grasses and large bed of plants with African connections. Over 100 varieties on sale - see how they grow. No. 55 is a sloping garden, incl gravelled beds with mixed planting, grasses and a pond. All gardens have steps.Free admission to Harborne Nature Reserve and Pereira Road allotments incl.

44 PERSHALL FARM COTTAGE

Pershall, Eccleshall, ST21 6NE. Wendy Johnson, 01785850023, wendy22.johnson@btinternet.com. *1m W of Eccleshall. From Eccleshall Xrds, take High St towards Loggerheads (B5026). In 1m turn L into Pershall.* **Sat 20, Sun 21 July (1-5). Adm £3, chd free. Cream teas.** Visits also by arrangement July & Aug for groups of 10 to 20.
South facing country garden designed for entertaining with herbaceous borders and water feature. Low hedge takes full advantage of the borrowed agricultural landscape of the Sow River valley with distant view of Eccleshall Church tower. Some gravel so assistance will be need with wheelchairs.

45 THE PINTLES

18 Newport Road, Great Bridgeford, Stafford, ST18 9PR. Peter & Leslie Longstaff, 01785 282582, peter.longstaff@ngs.org.uk. *From J14 M6 take A5013 towards Eccleshall, in Great Bridgeford turn L onto B5405 after 600 metres turn L onto Great Bridgeford Village Hall car park The Pintles is opp the hall main doors.* **Sun 2 June (1.30-5). Adm £3.50, chd free. Home-made teas.** Visits also by arrangement in June for groups of 10 to 30.
Located in the village of Great Bridgeford this traditional semi-detached house has a medium sized wildlife friendly garden designed to appeal to many interests. There are two greenhouses, 100s of cacti and succulents, vegetable and fruit plot, wildlife pond, weather station and hidden woodland shady garden. Plenty of outside seating to enjoy the home made cakes and refreshments. Steps or small ramp into main garden.

46 PRIORY FARM

Mitton Road, Bradley, Stafford, ST18 9ED. Debbie Farmer. *3½m W Penkridge. At Texaco island on A449 in Penkridge take Bungham Ln. Continue for 2½m past Swan & Whiston Hall to Mitton. Turn R to Bradley, continue 1m to Priory Farm on L.* **Sun 2 June (11-4). Adm £4, chd free. Home-made teas. BBQ subject to availability.**
A warm welcome awaits you at Priory Farm. Stroll around the lake. See the recently completed stumpery. Explore the 12 acres of grounds with shrubs, herbaceous planting & dell. Indulge in the sumptuous home baked cakes and delicious BBQ. Come see the birds of prey, Aerial lift, Traction Engine rides & Model boats on the lake (weather permitting). Truly a hidden gem.

47 56 ST AGNES ROAD

Moseley, Birmingham, B13 9PN. Michael & Alison Cullen. *3m from city centre. From Moseley T-lights take St Mary's Row which becomes Wake Green Rd. After ½m turn R into St Agnes Rd and L at the church. Number 56 is approx 200 metres on L.* **Sun 21 July (1-5.30). Adm £3, chd free. Home-made teas.**
Immaculately maintained, medium-sized, urban garden with curving borders surrounding a formal lawn punctuated with delicate acers and contemporary sculpture. Seating by a Victorian-style fish pond with a fountain and waterfall offers a peaceful setting to enjoy the tranquillity of this elegant garden.

48 23 ST JOHNS ROAD

Rowley Park, Stafford, ST17 9AS. Fiona Horwath, 07908 918181, fiona_horwath@yahoo.co.uk. *½m S of Stafford Town Centre. Just a few mins from J13 M6, towards Stafford. After approx 2m turn L into St. John's Rd after bus-stop.* **Sun 24 Mar, Thur 18 Apr (2-5). Adm £4, chd free. Home-made teas. Evening opening Fri 17 May (6.30-9). Adm £6, chd free. Wine. Fri 14 June (2-5). Adm £4, chd free. Home-made teas. Refreshments incl in adm Friday 17 May.** Visits also by arrangement Mar to July for groups of 20+.
Pass through the black and white gate of this Victorian house into a part-walled gardener's haven. Bulbs and shady woodlanders in Spring and masses of herbaceous plants and climbers. Sit and enjoy home-made cakes by the pond or Victorian-style greenhouse. Gardener is keen Hardy Plant Society member and sows far too many seeds, so always something good for sale! Our new outdoor kitchen is great for refreshments! The waterlily wildlife pond remains - with the greenhouses - the beating heart of the garden. A growing interest in alpines is leading to a proliferation of troughs. Whilst ferns, the quiet green stars of shady areas are also increasing in number!

Your visits help change lives – we are the largest single funder of the Queen's Nursing Institute

49 THE SECRET GARDEN

3 Banktop Cottages, Little Haywood, ST18 0UL. Derek Higgott & David Aston, 01889 883473, poshanddeks@gmail.com. *5m SE of Stafford. A51 from Rugeley or Weston signed Little Haywood A513 Stafford Coley Ln, Back Ln R into Coley Gr. Entrance 50 metres on L.* **Wed 22 May, Fri 7, Sun 16 June, Wed 24 July (11-4). Adm £4, chd free. Home-made teas. Cream teas. Visits also by arrangement May to Aug for groups of 10+.**

Wander past the other cottage gardens and through the evergreen arch and there before you is a fantasy for the eyes and soul. Stunning garden approx ½ acre, created over the last 30yrs. Strong colour theme of trees and shrubs, underplanted with perennials, 1000 bulbs and laced with clematis; other features incl water, laburnum and rose tunnel and unique buildings. Is this the jewel in the crown? Raised gazebo with wonderful views over untouched meadows and Cannock Chase. Wheelchair access - some slopes.

We help ordinary people open the gates to their extraordinary private gardens to raise impressive amounts of money through admissions, teas and slices of cake!

50 TANGLEWOOD COTTAGE

Crossheads, Colwich, Stafford, ST18 0UG. Dennis & Helen Wood, 01889 882857, shuvitdog@gmail.com. *5m SE of Stafford. A51 Rugeley/Weston R into Colwich. Church on L school on R, under bridge R into Crossheads Ln follow railway approx ¼m (it does lead somewhere). Parking signed on grass opp Brick Kiln Cottage.* **Sun 19 May (10.30-3). Adm £3, chd free. Home-made teas. Evening opening Fri 14 June (7-9.30). Adm £5, chd free. Wine. Visits also by arrangement May to Sept for groups of 20+.**

A country cottage garden incl koi carp pool, vegetables, fruit and an array of wonderful perennials. Meander through the different areas, enjoying sights, sounds and fragrances. Many seats to absorb the atmosphere including the courtyard to enjoy Helen's home-made fayre - cakes and meals. Year on year people spend many hours relaxing with us and don't forget Charlie the parrot. Art/jewellery/crafts/book sales. Annual HPS Plant fair usually on same weekend. Wine evening incl a glass of wine and canapés. Lots of gravel paths, some steps, people with walking sticks seem to manage quite well.

51 49 THE PLANTATION

Pensnett, Brierley Hill, DY5 4RT. Dave & Kath Baker. *From Russells Hall Hospital, take Pensnett High St (A4101) to Kingswinford. After 1½m turn L into The Plantation. Please park with consideration.* **Sun 2 June, Sun 7 July (11-4). Adm £3, chd free. Tea.**

Small suburban garden 60 ft x 30 ft with lots of roses, hemerocallis, well stocked borders and fruit trees. Greenhouse with tomatoes, cucumbers and grape vine. Productive vegetable garden.

52 91 TOWER ROAD

Four Oaks, Sutton Coldfield, B75 5EQ. Heather & Gary Hawkins. *3m N Sutton Coldfield. From A5127 at Mere Green island, turn onto Mere Green Rd towards Sainsburys, L at St James Church, L again onto Tower Rd.* **Sun 9 June (1.30-5.30). Adm £3, chd free. Home-made teas.**

163ft S-facing garden with sweeping borders and island beds planted with an eclectic mix of shrubs and perennials. Please enjoy your tour of our garden and discover our greenhouse, fishpond, cast iron water feature and a hiding Griffin statue. A vast array of home made cakes will tempt you during your visit. The ideal setting for sunbathing, children's hide and seek and lively garden parties. Large selection of home-made cream teas to eat in the garden or take away. Plant sale on front drive for garden visitors and passers by. More than just an Open Garden, we like to think of it as a garden party! There are 2 steps up into the garage and 2 steps down to the garden, which is then completely flat.

53 ◆ THE TRENTHAM ESTATE

Stone Road, Stoke-on-Trent, ST4 8JG. St Modwen Properties Plc, 01782 646646, enquiry@trentham.co.uk, www.trentham.co.uk. *M6 J15. Well signed on r'about, A34 with A5035.* **For NGS: Wed 16 Jan (10-11am); Thur 28 March (10-12). Adm £6.30, chd free. Evening Opening Wed 12 June (5.30 - 7.30). Adm T.B.A. Light refreshments in the garden.**

For other opening times and information, please phone, email or visit garden website.

Trentham Gardens has undergone a major programme of restoration which has both revealed the historic landscape designed by Capability Brown and is replenishing this with vast new contemporary plantings of annuals, perennials, trees and shrubs. NGS Special Openings with Trenthams' Garden Team Manager, Carol Adam and Garden Team members Mark Porter and Richard Hilton, will provide a tour at 10am on 16 Jan and 28 March, and at 5.30pm 12 June. Cost of the tour incl in adm.

54 NEW THE UPPER HOUSE

The Green, Barlaston, Stoke-On-Trent, ST12 9AE. Mr Paul Williams, 01782 373790, enquiries@theupperhouse.com, www.theupperhouse.com. *The grounds of The Upper House Hotel. From the A34 enter Barlaston and*

cross the canal and railway before turning right on The Green. **Tue 30 Apr (10-5). Adm by donation. Light refreshments.**
The gardens at The Upper House were originally created for Francis Wedgwood, the grandson of Josiah, when the house was built around 1850. The house was built to enable the Wedgwood family to escape the pollution of the potteries. The gardens benefit from far ranging views over the Trent valley and are split into distinct areas comprising of woodland, formal gardens and hay meadow. The woodland has a carpet of bluebells at this time of year, if the weather obliges. The Japanese and marriage gardens come into their own as well. Our restaurant can provide more substantial refreshment such as lunch and afternoon teas if required. Please book in advance. Wheelchair access to the bluebell wood and Japanese garden could prove difficult.

55 12 WATERDALE

Compton, Wolverhampton, WV3 9DY. Mr & Mrs Colin Bennett. *1½m W of Wolverhampton city centre. From Wolverhampton Ring Rd take A454 towards Bridgnorth for 1m. Waterdale is on the L off A454 Compton Rd West.* **Sun 2, Sun 30 June (12-5.30). Combined adm with 19 Waterdale £5, chd free. Home-made teas at 19 Waterdale.**
A riot of colour welcomes visitors to this quintessentially English garden. The wide central circular bed and side borders overflow with classic summer flowers, incl the tall spires of delphiniums, lupins, irises, campanula, poppies and roses. Clematis tumble over the edge of the decked terrace, where visitors can sit among pots of begonias and geraniums to admire the view over the garden.

56 19 WATERDALE

Compton, Wolverhampton, WV3 9DY. Anne & Brian Bailey, 01902 424867, m.bailey1234@btinternet.com. *1½m W of Wolverhampton city centre. From Wolverhampton Ring Rd take A454 towards Bridgnorth for 1m. Waterdale is on L off A454 Compton Rd West.* **Sun 2, Sun 30 June (12-5.30). Combined adm with 12 Waterdale £5, chd free. Home-made teas.** Visits also by arrangement June & July for groups of 10 to 30.
A romantic garden of surprises, which gradually reveals itself on a journey through deep, lush planting, full of unusual plants. From the sunny, flower filled terrace, a ruined folly emerges from a luxuriant fernery and leads into an oriental garden, complete with tea house. Towering bamboos hide the way to the gothic summerhouse and mysterious shell grotto. Find us on Facebook at 'Garden of Surprises'.

57 WHITEWOOD LODGE

Sich Lane, Yoxall, Burton-On-Trent, DE13 8NS. Mr & Mrs Michael & Victoria Riley, 01543 472262, vicki-riley@hotmail.com. *From A38 Lichfield or Derby. Exit for Barton under Needwood, straight through village in direction of Yoxall. After Little India on R go straight for 2m. Sich Lane 1st R. 1m down lane to Lodge.* **Sun 12, Sat 18, Sun 19 May, Sun 11, Sun 18 Aug (12-4.30). Adm £4, chd free. Cream teas.** Visits also by arrangement May to Aug.
With panoramic views of stunning Staffordshire countryside, this garden offers a collection of various mature shrubs and flowers. Incl hanging baskets and unusual planters with all their spectacular colours, hosta and rose beds, a large pond filled with carp, a Peter Rabbit vegetable and herb garden, a mediterranean patio, wandering peacocks and a tearoom serving Peggy Porschen recipe cakes. Full disabled access to tearoom and WC. Most of paths have free access for wheelchairs.

Wild Wood Lodge

58 THE WICKETS

47 Long Street, Wheaton Aston, ST19 9NF. Tony & Kate Bennett, 01785 840233, ajtonyb@talktalk.net. *8m W of Cannock, 10m N of Wolverhampton, 10m E of Telford. M6 J12 W towards Telford on A5; 3m R signed Stretton; 150yds L signed Wheaton Aston; 2m L; over canal, garden on R or at Bradford Arms on A5 follow signs.* **Sun 28 July, Thur 22, Sun 25 Aug (1.30-5). Adm £3.50, chd free. Home-made teas.** Visits also by arrangement July & Aug.

There's a delight around every corner and lots of quirky features in this most innovative garden. Its themed areas incl a fernery, grasses bed, hidden gothic garden, succulent theatre, cottage garden beds and even a cricket match! It will certainly give you ideas for your own garden as you sit and have tea and cake. Afterwards, walk by the canal and enjoy the beautiful surrounding countryside. Wheelchair access - two single steps in garden and 2 gravel paths.

59 WILD THYME COTTAGE

Woodhouses, Barton Under Needwood, Burton-On-Trent, DE13 8BS. Ray & Michele Blundell, 01283 711443, wildthymecottage@btinternet.com. *B5016 Midway between villages of Barton & Yoxall. From A38 through Barton Village B5016 towards Yoxall. Or from A513 at Yoxall centre take Town Hill sign for Barton. Garden is at Woodhouses, approx 2m from either village.* **Sat 11, Sun 12 May, Sat 2, Sun 3 Nov (11-5). Adm £4, chd free. Light refreshments.** Visits also by arrangement May to Nov for groups of 20 to 30.

The garden surrounds a self built timber frame house now 20 years old and extends to ⅓ acre. There is a collection of over 120 Japanese Maples with white bark Birch and rare trees, shrubs and herbaceous perennials. Large beds of Ornamental grasses & late flowering perennials. Growers of Zantedeschia (Arum Lily's). Plants sales. Emphasis is on successive interest throughout the year. Newly constructed Lychgate entrance. Ornamental grasses. Rare trees and shrubs. Partial wheelchair access on gravel and grass.

60 WILD WOOD LODGE

Bushton Lane, Anslow, Burton-On-Trent, DE13 9QL. Richard & Dorothy Ward, 01283 812100, poplarsfarm@breathe.com. *Bushton Lane is signed in centre of village. Wild Wood Lodge is ¼ m down Bushton Lane.* **Sun 16 June, Sun 11 Aug (1.30-5). Adm £3.50, chd free. Home-made teas.** Visits also by arrangement June to Aug.

Covering approx 2 acre it consists of a productive orchard with apples,pears and plums. A Soft Fruit Garden with Raspberries and Strawberries etc., a wide selection of vegetables on raised beds, colourful herbaceous borders, shrubs, ornamental trees, wild life pond and fishing lake. The Garden was overall winner in the Burton and District Agricultural Societies Farm Garden Competition 2017. Level garden, wide paths.

High Trees

61 WOODBROOKE QUAKER STUDY CENTRE

1046 Bristol Road, Selly Oak, B29 6LJ. Woodbrooke Quaker Study Centre, 0121 472 5171, enquiries@woodbrooke.org.uk, www.woodbrooke.org.uk. *6m SW of Birmingham. On A38 Bristol Rd, S of Selly Oak, opp Witherford Way.* **Sat 10 Aug (11-3). Adm £5, chd free. Light refreshments. Visits also by arrangement for groups of 5+.**

George Cadbury's former home, which incl a lake, wild area, herbaceous borders, herb garden and a walled garden, the whole area extending to 10 acres. Very fine variety of trees. Our Head Gardener and other staff will be on hand to help visitors to identify the key garden features and make the most of their visit. Garden tours and short talks will be available. Freshly baked cakes and hot drinks will be available to purchase all day. Some paths may be unsuitable for wheelchair access depending on the weather.

62 2 WOODLAND CRESCENT

Finchfield, Wolverhampton, WV3 8AS. Mr & Mrs Parker, 01902 332392, alisonparker1960@hotmail.co.uk. *2m SW of Wolverhampton City centre. From Inner Ring Rd take A41 W to Tettenhall. At junction with A459 turn L onto Merridale Rd. Straight over Bradwell Xrds then R onto Trysull Rd. 3rd R onto Coppice Rd & 1st R onto Woodland Crescent.* **Sun 23 June, Sun 14 July (11.30-4.30). Adm £3, chd free. Home-made teas. Visits also by arrangement June & July for groups of 5 to 30.**

A semi-detached townhouse garden 120 x 25 ft, every inch packed with perennials, trees, acers, shrubs, roses, hostas and clematis. Wildlife pond and nesting boxes to attract birds. Productive vegetable and fruit garden. Informal style but clipped box and topiary animals add some formality.

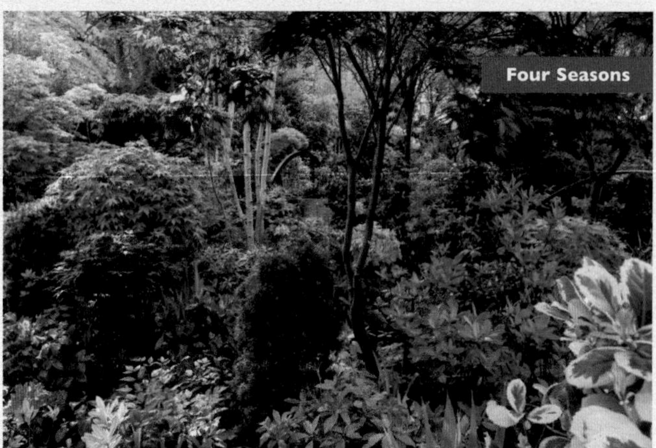

Four Seasons

© Bennet Smith

63 WOODLEIGHTON GROVE, KARIBU GARDEN

9 Woodleighton Grove, Uttoxeter, ST14 8BX. Graham & Judy White, 01889 563930, graham&judy.white@ngs.org.uk. *Take B5017 Marchington Rd from Town Centre. Go over Bridge, 1st exit at r'about, then 3rd exit at next r'about into Highwood Rd, After ¼m turn R then 1st L.* **Visits by arrangement June & July. Prepaid ticketed openings on selected dates, call owner 01889563930 to book. Adm £8, chd free. Price incl refreshments.**

A tranquil & intriguing garden. Unique landscaping & design features incl a Giant Insect Hotel; Bell Tower; Folly; Dovecote; Boardwalk; Stumpery; Archways; Natural Stream; Bridges & Waterfall. Various collections of Plants & Artefacts incl 400 cacti, succulents, sempervivum & jovibaba plus 250 old gardening & farming hand tools. Pre-booking essential for Ticketed Opening Days – please contact the garden owner.

64 YARLET HOUSE

Yarlet, Stafford, ST18 9SD. Mr & Mrs Nikolas Tarling. *2m S of Stone. Take A34 from Stone towards Stafford, turn L into Yarlet School & L again into car park.* **Fri 21 June (10-1.30). Adm £4, chd free. Home-made teas. Donation to Staffordshire Wildlife Trust.**

4 acre garden with extensive lawns, walks, lengthy herbaceous borders and traditional Victorian box hedge. Water gardens with fountain and rare lilies. Sweeping views across Trent Valley to Sandon. Victorian School Chapel. 9 hole putting course. Boules pitch. Yarlet School Art Display. Gravel paths.

65 YEW TREE COTTAGE

Podmores Corner, Long Lane, White Cross, Haughton, ST18 9JR. Clive & Ruth Plant, 07591 886925, pottyplantz@aol.com. *4m W of Stafford. Take A518 W Haughton, turn R Station Rd (signed Ranton) 1m, then turn R at Xrds ¼m on R.* **Sun 5 May (2-5); Thur 4, Thur 11, Thur 18 July (11-4); Sun 21 July (2-5). Adm £3.50, chd free. Home-made teas. Visits also by arrangement May to July for groups of 10+.**

Hardy Plant Society member's garden brimming with unusual plants. All-yr-round interest incl Meconopsis, Trillium, and Arisaema. National Collection Dierama featured on BBC Gardeners World flowering in first half July. ½-acre incl gravel, borders, vegetables and plant sales area. Covered vinery to take tea in if the weather is unkind, and seats in the garden for lingering on sunny days. Partial wheelchair access - level access, grass and paved paths, some narrow and some gravel.

NPC

SUFFOLK

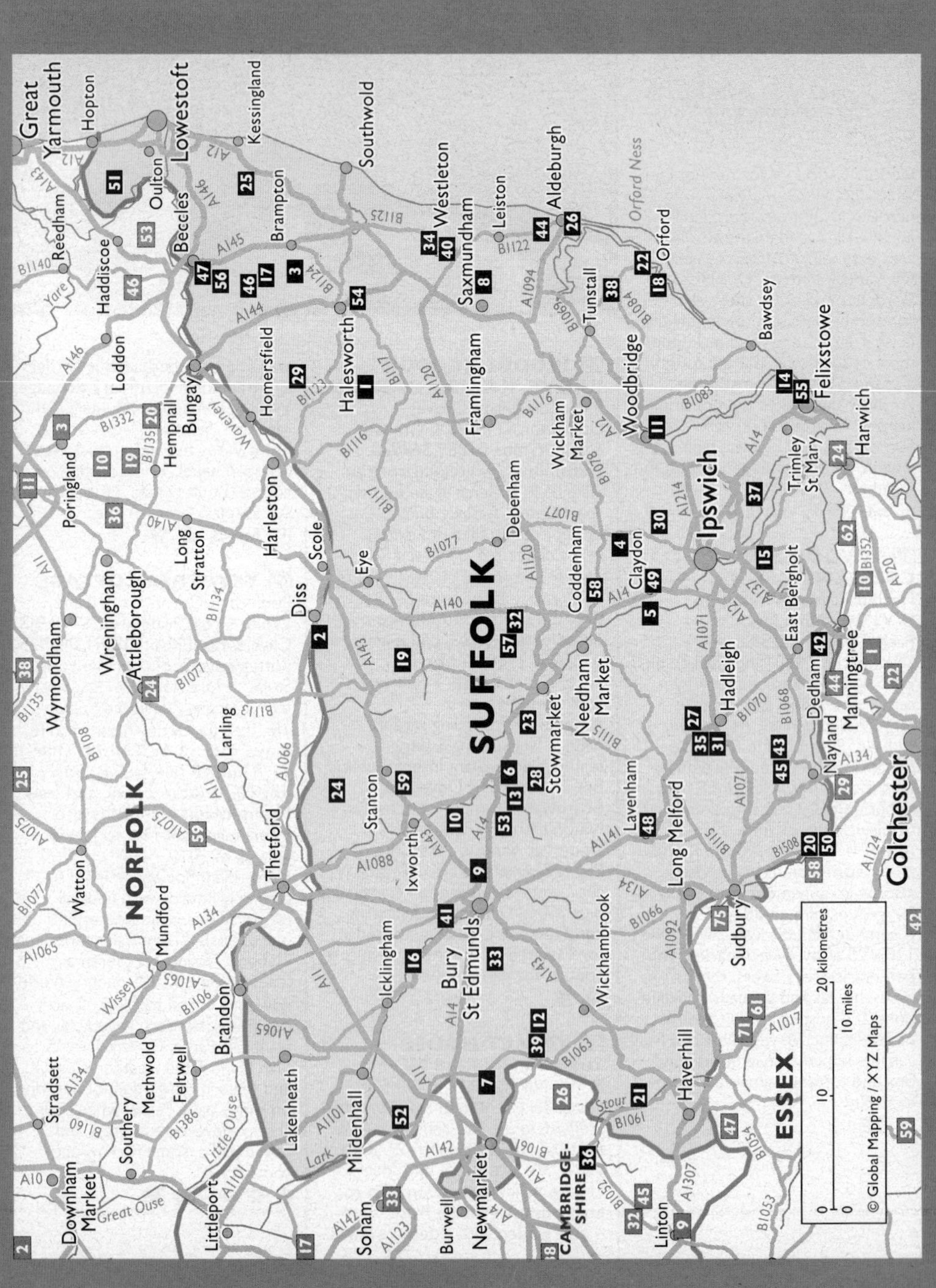
SUFFOLK
NORFOLK
ESSEX
CAMBRIDGE-SHIRE
Great Yarmouth
Hopton
Lowestoft
Kessingland
Southwold
Westleton
Leiston
Aldeburgh
Orford Ness
Orford
Saxmundham
Tunstall
Bawdsey
Felixstowe
Harwich
Oulton
Beccles
Brampton
Reedham
Haddiscoe
Loddon
Bungay
Homersfield
Halesworth
Framlingham
Woodbridge
Wickham Market
Ipswich
Trimley St Mary
Poringland
Hempnall
Harleston
Debenham
Claydon
Coddenham
East Bergholt
Wreningham
Long Stratton
Scole
Eye
Diss
Wymondham
Attleborough
Needham Market
Stowmarket
Hadleigh
Dedham
Manningtree
Nayland
Colchester
Larling
Stanton
Lavenham
Ixworth
Long Melford
Watton
Thetford
Bury St Edmunds
Sudbury
Mundford
Icklingham
Wickhambrook
Brandon
Haverhill
Methwold
Feltwell
Lakenheath
Mildenhall
Stradsett
Southery
Downham Market
Littleport
Soham
Burwell
Newmarket
Linton
Great Ouse
Little Ouse
Lark
Wissey
Waveney
Yare
Stour
0 10 20 kilometres
0 10 miles
© Global Mapping / XYZ Maps

Suffolk has so much to offer – from charming coastal villages, ancient woodlands and picturesque valleys – there is a landscape to suit all tastes.

Keen walkers and cyclists will enjoy Suffolk's low-lying, gentle countryside, where fields of farm animals and crops reflect the county's agricultural roots.

Stretching north from Felixstowe, the county has miles of Heritage Coast set in an Area of Outstanding Natural Beauty. The Suffolk coast was the inspiration for composer Benjamin Britten's celebrated work, and it is easy to see why.

To the west and north of the county are The Brecks, a striking canvas of pine forest and open heathland, famous for its chalky and sandy soils – and one of the most important wildlife areas in Britain.

A variety of gardens to please everyone open for Suffolk NGS, so come along on an open day and enjoy the double benefit of a beautiful setting and supporting wonderful charities.

Volunteers

County Organiser
Jenny Reeve
01638 715289
jenny.reeve@ngs.org.uk

County Treasurer
David Reeve
01638 715289
dreeve43@gmail.com

Publicity
Jenny Reeve
(as above)

Booklet Co-ordinator
Michael Cole
01473 272920
michael.m.d.cole@btinternet.com

Assistant County Organisers
Frances Boscawen
01728 638768
francesboscawen@gmail.com

Yvonne Leonard
01638 712742
yj.leonard@btinternet.com

Marie-Anne Mackenzie
01728 831155
marieanne_mackenzie@yahoo.co.uk

Wendy Parkes
01473 785504
wendyparkes@live.com

Barbara Segall
01787 312046
barbara@bsegall.com

Peter Simpson
01787 249845
bergholt2002@btopenworld.com

Adrian Simpson-James
01502 710555
adriansimpsonjames@gmail.com

Left: **Bridges**

OPENING DATES

All entries subject to change. For latest information check **www.ngs.org.uk**

Map locator numbers are shown to the right of each garden name.

February

Snowdrop Festival

Sunday 17th
◆ Blakenham Woodland Garden 5
Gable House 17

Sunday 24th
The Laburnums 29

March

Sunday 17th
Woodwards 58

April

Sunday 7th
Great Thurlow Hall 21
◆ The Place for Plants, East Bergholt Place Garden 42

Sunday 21st
Woodwards 58

Sunday 28th
◆ Blakenham Woodland Garden 5
Cattishall Farmhouse 9
◆ The Place for Plants, East Bergholt Place Garden 42

May

Sunday 5th
Mulberry House, Westleton 34
Rosedale 50
Trinity House 53

Sunday 12th
Drinkstone Park 13
Street Farm 52
Woodwards 58

Sunday 19th
NEW Bridges 6
Cumberland House 11
◆ Fullers Mill Garden 16
The Priory 45

Sunday 26th
Appleacre 1
Freston House 15
Holm House 28

June

Saturday 1st
◆ Wyken Hall 59

Sunday 2nd
Berghersh Place 4
NEW 246 Ferry Road 14
Great Thurlow Hall 21
NEW Hallcroft House 23
NEW Lillesley Barn 31
NEW Old Gardens 35
Wenhaston Grange 54
41 Westmorland Road 55
Wood Farm, Gipping 57
◆ Wyken Hall 59

Sunday 9th
Drinkstone Park 13
Orford Gardens 38
Ousden House 39
◆ Somerleyton Hall Gardens 51

Sunday 16th
NEW Becks End Farm 3
Gedgrave Hall 18
Green Lane House 22
NEW The Rooks 49

Saturday 22nd
Larks' Hill 30

Sunday 23rd
Great Bevills 20
NEW Hillside 27
5 Parklands Green 41

Sunday 30th
Priors Oak 44

July

Saturday 6th
White House Farm 56

Sunday 7th
Batteleys Cottage 2
NEW Moat Farm 32

Sunday 14th
Redisham Hall 46
5 Ringsfield Road 47
Woodwards 58

Sunday 21st
Paget House 40

Tuesday 30th
Woodwards 58

August

Saturday 3rd
Gislingham Gardens 19

Sunday 4th
Gislingham Gardens 19
Rosedale 50

Sunday 11th
River Cottage 48

Tuesday 13th
Woodwards 58

Sunday 18th
Henstead Exotic Garden 25

Sunday 25th
Woodwards 58

September

Sunday 1st
NEW Bridges 6

Sunday 8th
11 Brookside 7
By the Crossways 8

Saturday 14th
The Old Rectory 36

Sunday 15th
Heron House 26
The Old Rectory 36
NEW The Old Rectory 37

October

Sunday 6th
◆ Fullers Mill Garden 16
◆ The Place for Plants, East Bergholt Place Garden 42

By Arrangement

Arrange a personalised garden visit with your club, or group of friends, on a date to suit you. See individual garden entries for full details.

By the Crossways 8
Church Cottage 10
Dip-on-the-Hill 12
Drinkstone Park 13
NEW 246 Ferry Road 14
Gable House 17
Helyg 24
Henstead Exotic Garden 25
Heron House 26
Holm House 28
Ivy Chimneys, Gislingham Gardens 19
Larks' Hill 30
NEW Lillesley Barn 31
Moat House 33
NEW Old Gardens 35
NEW The Old Rectory 37
Paget House 40
5 Parklands Green 41
Polstead Mill 43
Priors Oak 44
Redisham Hall 46
41 Westmorland Road 55
White House Farm 56
Wood Farm, Gipping 57
Woodwards 58

Hallcroft House

THE GARDENS

Old Gardens

1 APPLEACRE

Bell Green, Cratfield, Halesworth, IP19 0DH. Mr & Mrs Tim & Naomi Shaw. *7m W of Halesworth. B1123 to Harleston. At Linstead Parva, turn L up Godfrey's Hill. After approx 1m turn R onto Mary's Lane & follow NGS signs. 50 metres W of the Poacher pub. Now closed, but sign still there.* **Sun 26 May (11-5). Adm £3.50, chd free. Home-made teas.**

A country garden covering an acre that has evolved over forty years. A garden full of secrets waiting to be revealed, with open vistas over the Suffolk countryside. Explore a variety of large herbaceous borders, box topiary, mature trees, lily pond, greenhouse, lawns, vegetable garden and wildlife area. Partial wheelchair access, but caution needed in some areas.

2 BATTELEYS COTTAGE

The Ling, Wortham, Diss, IP22 1ST. Mr & Mrs Andy & Linda Simpson. *3m W of Diss. Turn signed from A143 Diss/Bury Rd at Wortham. By Church turn R at T-junction. At top of hill turn L. Go down hill & round sharp L corner.* **Sun 7 July (11.30-5.30). Adm £5, chd free. Home-made teas and light refreshments.**

A varied one acre garden planted for abundance in all seasons. Formality and informality, a mix of winding bark paths, light and shade, secluded spots to sit, new vistas at every turn. Fitting into its rural setting, it supports a wealth of bird life. There is a diversity of planting in densely planted borders as well as pots, sculptures, meadow, ponds, stream and vegetable areas to inspire you. Wheelchair access to most parts of the garden, gravel, grass and bark paths.

3 NEW BECKS END FARM

School Road, Westhall, Halesworth, IP19 8QZ. Mr & Mrs John & Marjorie Milbank. *E of Halesworth on A144 between Halesworth & Bungay. From Halesworth turn R at the Spexhall Xrds. Continue along & take 3rd turning L. Becks End Farm is the first house on L.* **Sun 16 June (11-5). Adm £4, chd free. Home-made teas.**

Set in one and a half acres comprising lawns, trees, hard landscaping, wide herbaceous flower borders, orchard, natural pond, vegetable garden and central pole fruit cage. Pleached Hornbeam hedges screen the paddock and stable block. The garden surrounds an old Victorian School house on the edge of the village and has been designed and developed since 2007 when acquired by the present owners. No wheelchair access because of steps.

4 BERGHERSH PLACE

Ashbocking Road, Witnesham, Ipswich, IP6 9EZ. Mr & Mrs T C Parkes. *Farm entrance on bend of B1077 N of Witnesham village. Approx 1m S of Ashbocking Xrds. Concrete drive entrance on sharp bend so please drive slowly. Turn in between North Lodge & Berghersh House.* **Sun 2 June (12-5). Adm £4, chd free. Home-made teas.**

Peaceful walled and hedged gardens surround elegant Regency house (not open) among fields above the Fynn Valley. Circular walk from the farm buildings, around house with lawns and mature trees to a pretty view of the valley. Mound, ponds, bog area and orchard paddock. Informal family garden with shrub and perennial beds. Garden created over last 20 years by current owner. Parking for elderly and disabled at end of farmyard close to family garden. Most areas are accessible to disabled visitors.

5 ◆ BLAKENHAM WOODLAND GARDEN

Little Blakenham, Ipswich, IP8 4LZ. M Blakenham, 07760 342131, www.blakenhamwoodlandgarden.org.uk. *4m NW of Ipswich. Follow signs at Little Blakenham, 1m off B1113 or go to Blakenham Woodland Garden web-site.* **For NGS: Sun 17 Feb, Sun 28 Apr (10-4). Adm £4, chd £2. Home-made teas. Tea, coffee, home-made cakes & plant sales are available on NGS days only. For other opening times and information, please phone or visit garden website.**

Beautiful 6 acre woodland garden with variety of rare trees and shrubs, Chinese rocks and landscape sculpture. Lovely in spring with snowdrops, daffodils, camellias, magnolias and bluebells followed by roses in early summer. Woodland Garden open from 1 March to 31 July. Donations to NGS on NGS days. For groups of ten or more on other days ring 07789 268552 for special arrangements.

6 NEW BRIDGES

The Street, Woolpit, Bury St. Edmunds, IP30 9SA. Mr Stanley Bates & Mr Michael Elles. *Through green coach gates marked Deliveries. From A14 take slip rd to Woolpit, follow signs to centre of village, road curves to R. Bridges is on L & covered in Wisteria & opp Co-op.* **Sun 19 May, Sun 1 Sept (11-5). Adm £5, chd free. Tea.**

C15 Grade 11 terraced house in the centre of a C12 Suffolk village with walled garden to the rear of the property. Additional land was acquired 20 years ago, and this garden was developed into formal and informal planting. The main formal feature is the Shakespeare Garden featuring the bust of Shakespeare, and the 'Umbrello' a recently constructed pavillion in an Italianate design. Statue of Shakespeare, The Umbrello, various surprises for children of all ages. Two public houses The Swan and The Bull in village open for lunch. Not suitable for wheelchairs.

7 11 BROOKSIDE

Moulton, Newmarket, CB8 8SG. Elizabeth Goodrich & Peter Mavroghenis. *Near the Packhorse Bridge & Pub. 3m due E of Newmarket on B1085.* **Sun 8 Sept (2-5). Adm £4, chd free. Light refreshments.**

1½ acres over 4 levels. Traditional hedges, mature trees and roses at the front while rear garden landscaped in contemporary style. Lower terrace with water feature and fig trees. Terraced beds with ornamental grasses, knot garden, hosta courtyard. Metal retaining wall to former paddock, many specimen trees, apple espalier bordered greenhouse with kitchen garden, apples and vines.

8 BY THE CROSSWAYS

Kelsale, Saxmundham, IP17 2PL. Mr & Mrs William Kendall, miranda@bythecrossways.co.uk. *2m NE of Saxmundham, just off Clayhills Rd. ½m N of town centre, turn R to Theberton on Clayhills Rd. After 1½m, 1st L to Kelsale, then turn L immed after white cottage.* **Sun 8 Sept (11-4). Adm £5, chd free. Home-made teas. We also offer soft drinks, tea and coffee. Visits also by arrangement Apr to Sept for groups of up to 10.**

3 acre wildlife garden designed as a garden within an organic farm, where wilderness areas lie next to productive beds. Large semi-walled vegetable and cutting garden, a spectacular crinkle-crankle wall. Extensive perennial planting, grasses and wild areas. Set around the owner's Edwardian family home built by suffragist ancestor. The garden is mostly flat, with paved or gravel pathways around the main house, a few low steps and extensive grass paths and lawns.

9 CATTISHALL FARMHOUSE

Cattishall, Great Barton, Bury St. Edmunds, IP31 2QT. Mrs J Mayer, 07738 936496, joannamayer42@googlemail.com. *3m NE of Bury St Edmunds. Approach Great Barton from Bury on A143 take 1st R turn to church. If travelling towards Bury take last L turn to church as you leave the village. At church bear R & follow lane to Farmhouse on R.* **Sun 28 Apr (1-5). Adm £4, chd free. Home-made teas.**

Approx 2 acre farmhouse garden enclosed by a flint wall and mature beech hedge laid mainly to lawns with both formal and informal planting and large herbaceous border. There is an abundance of roses, small wildlife pond and recently developed kitchen garden incl a wild flower area and fruit cages. Chickens, bees and a boisterous Labrador also live here. Generally flat with some gravel paths. The occasional small step.

10 CHURCH COTTAGE

Church Lane, Troston, Bury St Edmunds, IP31 1EX. Graeme & Marysa Norris, 07855 284816, marysanorris@gmail.com. *5m NE of Bury St Edmunds. From the A143 turn at the Bunbury Arms, signed Troston & Gt Livermere. Follow the rd through Gt Livermere, signed to Troston.* **Visits by arrangement June to Sept for groups of up to 20. Early evening openings and Refreshments by arrangement. Adm £4.50, chd free.**

A ¾ acre garden, of several different themes. A yew allee, mixed borders including grasses, roses and perennials, an informal pond and a 'New Wave Perennial' open border. Also a small area of woodland plants, young trees and shrubs, a gravel garden and a productive kitchen garden with raised beds, including one for alpine plants and a greenhouse. Church Cottage is opposite St Mary's Church, famous for its medieval wall paintings. Uneven and gravel paths, steps and level changes.

11 CUMBERLAND HOUSE

17 Cumberland Street, Woodbridge, IP12 4AH. John & Lindi Carrington. *Town centre; 6 min walk from station car park (parking charge) via Quay St. Exit A12 at r'about southern end of Woodbridge Bypass onto B1438 (Ipswich Rd) towards Woodbridge town centre. Follow signs to station car park IP12 4AJ 1½m. Blue badge parking only in Cumberland St.* **Sun 19 May (11-4). Adm £4, chd free. Home-made teas.**

This large south facing walled garden to the rear of Grade 2* listed Cumberland House (not open) is well hidden in the town centre conservation area. Mature specimen trees (including Arbutus, Japanese cherries, Mulberry, Judas tree) and established flowering shrubs provide shady planting areas in contrast to the new drought tolerant planting schemes. A flower arranger's garden. The garden has sloping uneven paths and changes of level.

12 DIP-ON-THE-HILL

Ousden, Newmarket, CB8 8TW. Geoffrey & Christine Ingham, 01638 500329, gki1000@cam.ac.uk. *5m E of Newmarket; 7m W of Bury St Edmunds. From Newmarket: 1m from junction of B1063 & B1085. From Bury St Edmunds follow signs for Hargrave. Parking at village hall. Follow NGS sign at the end of the lane.* **Visits by arrangement June to Sept for groups of up to 20. Adm £4.50, chd free. Home-made teas.**

Approx one acre in a dip on a S-facing hill based on a wide range of architectural/sculptural evergreen trees, shrubs and groundcover: pines; grove of Phillyrea latifolia; 'cloud pruned' hedges; palms; large bamboo; ferns; range of kniphofia and croscosmia. Visitors may wish to make an appointment when visiting gardens nearby. No wheelchair access. No dogs.

13 DRINKSTONE PARK

Park Road, Drinkstone, Bury St. Edmunds, IP30 9ST. Michael & Christine Lambert, 01359 272513, chris@drinkstonepark.co.uk, www.drinkstonepark.co.uk. *6m from Bury St Edmunds. E on A14 J46 turn L and the R for Drinkstone. W on A14 J46 turn R for Drinkstone. Turn into Park Rd. We are not in the village. Park Rd is parallel to the rd that runs through the village.* **Sun 12 May, Sun 9 June (1-5.30). Adm £4.50, chd free. Home-made teas.** Visits also by arrangement May to July.

Three acre garden with wildlife and ornamental ponds, herbaceous borders, roses, orchard, woodland and wildlife area, productive vegetable plot with poly tunnel and greenhouses. The garden also boasts an original Ha Ha with views across the Suffolk landscape. 'Our Folly' is a sunken garden created from part of the unearthed cellars of an old mansion demolished in 1950 now planted with ferns. Some gravel paths.

14 NEW 246 FERRY ROAD

Felixstowe, IP11 9RU. Mrs Sally Gallant, 01394 276336, sallyjag@hotmail.co.uk. *At Felixstowe Golf Club you will find Ferry Rd opposite, travel up Ferry Rd & house is 4th on R.* **Sun 2 June (11-5). Combined adm with 41 Westmorland Road £5, chd free. Home-made teas. At 41 Westmorland Road.** Visits also by arrangement Apr to Oct for groups of up to 20.

Newly established garden which attempts to give year round colour and interest, places to sit and ponder. Various walkways lead you around this secluded coastal garden, moments from the sea. Some mature trees, and attractive hedging, shady walkway and wooden boardwalk, herbaceous borders and Japanese themed feature. Sunny sheltered sitting areas. Not suitable for wheelchair users due to steps. Well behaved dogs on a lead.

15 FRESTON HOUSE

The Street, Freston, Ipswich, IP9 1AF. Mr & Mrs Andrew & Judith Whittle, www.frestonhouse.co.uk. *Go under the Orwell Bridge from Ipswich towards Holbrook. At the junction for Holbrook & Woolverstone, turn sharp R signed Freston. After 300m, turn L into a no through road.* **Sun 26 May (12-5). Adm £5, chd free. Light refreshments.**

20-acre garden and large Georgian rectory set in parkland, planted from 2006 onwards by the current owners. Individual colour-themed, roomed gardens, cottage garden and formal long borders with mass plantings of hundreds of shrubs and perennials. A one-acre kitchen garden, wildlife pond, winter garden, gravel garden and woodlands with over 1,000 varieties of hostas and other shade-loving plants. One of the largest collections of hostas in the country. Several roomed, coloured-themed gardens, large winter garden. Some gravel paths.

We open the gates to the nation's best gardens, offering a relaxing, memorable and affordable day out. A perfect experience to share with friends and family.

16 ◆ FULLERS MILL GARDEN

West Stow, IP28 6HD. Perennial, 01284 728888, fullersmillgarden@perennial.org.uk, www.fullersmillgarden.org.uk. *6m NW of Bury St Edmunds. Turn off A1101 Bury to Mildenhall Rd, signed West Stow Country Park, go past Country Park continue for ¼ m, garden entrance on R. Sign at entrance.* **For NGS: Sun 19 May, Sun 6 Oct (11-5). Adm £4.50, chd free. Home-made teas.** For other opening times and information, please phone, email or visit garden website.

An enchanting 7 acre garden on the banks of the river Lark. A beautiful site with light dappled woodland and a plantsman's paradise of rare and unusual shrubs, perennials and marginals planted with great natural charm. Euphorbias and lilies are a particular feature with the late flowering colchicums, including many rare varieties, being of great interest in Autumn. Tea, coffee and soft drinks. Home-made cakes. Partial wheelchair access around garden.

17 GABLE HOUSE

Halesworth Road, Redisham, Beccles, NR34 8NE. John & Brenda Foster, 01502 575298, gablehouse@btinternet.com. *5m S of Beccles. Signed from A12 at Blythburgh and A144 Bungay/ Halesworth Rd.* **Sun 17 Feb (11-4.30). Adm £4.50, chd free. Home-made teas. Warming soups available in February.** Visits also by arrangement Feb to Aug for groups of 10+. Donation to St Peter's Church, Redisham.

We have a large collection of snowdrops, cyclamen, hellebores and other flowering plants for the Snowdrop Day in February. Many bulbs and plants will be for sale. Hot soup and home made teas available. Greenhouses contain rare bulbs and tender plants. Featured in Suffolk magazine and East Anglian Daily Times. A one acre garden with lawns and scree with water feature. We have a wide range of unusual trees, shrubs, perennials and bulbs collected over the last fifty years.

18 GEDGRAVE HALL

Gedgrave, Orford, Woodbridge, IP12 2BX. Edward & Clare Greenwell. *In Orford, turn R, past Crown & Castle pub, past Castle, then 1st R, signed Gedgrave Rd. Gedgrave Hall is 1¼m at the end of the rd on R after farm buildings.* **Sun 16 June (1.30-5). Combined adm with Green Lane House £5, chd free. Home-made teas.**
There was no garden at Gedgrave until 1977. Instead, there was a grass bank and a wartime Nissen hut. With no shelter the views were terrific, but so was the wind. We built brick walls and planted quite extensive yew hedges creating a number of 'rooms' in the garden. A mound was created in 2012. The soil is almost pure sand and dries out every year at some point in the summer. Typical English garden, yew hedges, walled garden, cutting garden, vegetable garden, newly planted rose garden. Mound designed by George Carter with views of sea and Orford. Wheelchair access, parking in adjoining field.

GROUP OPENING

19 GISLINGHAM GARDENS

Mill Street, Gislingham, IP23 8JT. *4m W of Eye. Gislingham 2½m W of A140. 9m N of Stowmarket, 8m S of Diss. Disabled parking at Ivy Chimneys. Parking limited to disabled parking at Chapel Farm Close.* **Sat 3, Sun 4 Aug (11-4.30). Combined adm £4, chd free. Light refreshments at Ivy Chimneys.**

12 CHAPEL FARM CLOSE
Ross Harrison.

IVY CHIMNEYS
Iris & Alan Stanley, 01379 788737.
Visits also by arrangement June to Sept for groups of up to 30.

2 varied gardens in a picturesque village with a number of Suffolk timbered houses. Ivy Chimneys is planted for yr round interest with ornamental trees, some topiary, exotic borders and fishpond set in an area of Japanese style. Wisteria draped pergola supports a productive vine. Also a separate ornamental vegetable garden. New for 2014 fruit trees in the front garden. New 12 Chapel Farm Close is a tiny garden, exquisitely planted and an absolute riot of colour. Despite the garden's size, the owner has planted a Catalpa, a Cornus Florida Rubra and many unusual plants. It is a fine example of what can be achieved in a small space. Partial wheelchair access.

20 GREAT BEVILLS

Sudbury Road, Bures, CO8 5JW. Mr & Mrs G T C Probert. *4m S of Sudbury. Just N of Bures on the Sudbury rd B1508.* **Sun 23 June (2-5.30). Adm £4, chd free. Home-made teas.**
Overlooking the Stour Valley the gardens surrounding an Elizabethan manor house are formal and Italianate in style with Irish yews and mature specimen trees. Terraces, borders, ponds and woodland walks. A short drive away from Bevills visitors may wish to also see the C13 St Stephen's Chapel with wonderful views of the Old Bures Dragon recently re-created by the owner. Woodland walks give lovely views over the Stour Valley. Gravel paths.

21 GREAT THURLOW HALL

Great Thurlow, Haverhill, CB9 7LF. Mr George Vestey. *12m S of Bury St Edmunds, 4m N of Haverhill. Great Thurlow village on B1061 from Newmarket; 3½m N of junction with A143 Haverhill/Bury St Edmunds rd.* **Sun 7 Apr, Sun 2 June (2-5). Adm £5, chd free. Home-made teas. Teas and home-made cakes are available in the Church.**
13 acres of beautiful gardens set around the River Stour, the banks of which are adorned with stunning displays of daffodil and narcissi together with blossoming trees in spring. Herbaceous borders, rose garden and extensive shrub borders come alive with colour from late spring onwards, there is also a large walled kitchen garden and arboretum.

22 GREEN LANE HOUSE

Castle Green, Orford, Woodbridge, IP12 2NF. Mr & Mrs Michael Flint. *SatNav IP12 2NG. Go past the Crown & Castle pub & Orford Castle, turn R into Gedgrave Rd. 200 yds along the rd on R there is a field gate. Parking is in field. The drive next to it leads to the garden.* **Sun 16 June (1.30-5). Combined adm with Gedgrave Hall £5, chd free.**
A half acre garden created in 1995 with views over Orfordness. A terrace with perennials and formal croquet lawn gives way to fruit trees in rough grass and large borders of shrubs including a good display of hostas. Colourful pots of summer annuals on terrace. Vegetable area and conservatory. The garden has superb views over Orford Castle and over the R Ore to Orfordness and out to sea. Cars conveying wheelchair visitors can park at the top of the drive near the house.

23 NEW HALLCROFT HOUSE

Harleston, Stowmarket, IP14 3JQ. T Wilkinson & M Bailey. *2.5m NW of Stowmarket. Entrance off Haughley Road, N of Harleston village, next to Harleston Hall.* **Sun 2 June (2-5). Adm £5, chd free. Home-made teas.**
1-acre garden with distinct areas of interest. Lavender walk, 90-foot double herbaceous borders, purple border, circular lawn, specimen trees and shrubs, wildflower garden, large pond, kitchen garden. Lower garden (reached by steps) with parterre and fountain, shrub border, wall-trained fruit trees, S-facing terrace with numerous pots; white garden with lawn, mixed borders and specimen trees. Partial wheelchair access.

24 HELYG

Thetford Road, Coney Weston, Bury St. Edmunds, IP31 1DN. Jackie & Briant Smith, 01359 220106, briant.broadsspirituality@gmail.com. *From Barningham Xrds/shop turn off the B1111 towards Coney Weston & Knettishall Country Park. Helyg will be found on the L behind some large willow trees after approx 1m.* **Visits by arrangement Apr to Sept for groups of 10 to 20. Adm to incl home-made teas. Adm £7, chd free.**

Just under half an acre of garden being developed for ease of maintenance and including new features each year. This relaxing garden, with many secluded seating areas, includes a woodland walk, raised flower beds, rose beds, large vegetable plot, small orchard, chickens, wildlife area, ponds and water features. Most of the garden is wheelchair accessible with a variety of surfaces including concrete slab, gravel and wood-chip paths.

25 HENSTEAD EXOTIC GARDEN

Church Road, Henstead, Beccles, NR34 7LD. Andrew Brogan, 01502 743006, andrew.hensteadexoticgarden@hotmail.co.uk, www.hensteadexoticgarden.co.uk. *Equal distance between Beccles, Southwold & Lowestoft approx 5m. 1m from A12 turning after Wrentham (signed Henstead) very close to B1127.* **Sun 18 Aug (1-5). Adm £4, chd £1. Home-made teas.** Visits also by arrangement July to Sept.

2 acre exotic garden featuring 100 large palms, 20+ bananas and 200 bamboo plants. 2 streams, 20ft tiered walkway leading to Thai style wooden covered pavilion. Mediterranean and jungle plants around 3 large ponds with fish. winner Britains best garden 2015 on itv as voted by Alan Titchmarsh.

26 HERON HOUSE

Aldeburgh, IP15 5EP. Mr & Mrs Jonathan Hale, 01728 452200, jonathanrhhale@aol.com. *At the southeastern junction of Priors Hill Rd & Park Rd. Last house on Priors Hill Rd on south side, at the junction where it rejoins Park Rd.* **Sun 15 Sept (2-5). Adm £5, chd free. Tea.** Visits also by arrangement Apr to Oct for groups of up to 30.

2 acres with views over coastline, river and marshes. Unusual trees, herbaceous beds, shrubs and ponds with waterfall in large rock garden, stream and bog garden. Interesting attempts to grow half hardy plants in the coastal micro-climate. Partial wheelchair access.

27 NEW HILLSIDE

Union Hill, Semer, Ipswich, IP7 6HN. Mr & Mrs Neil Mordey. *Car park through field gate off A1141.* **Sun 23 June (11-5). Adm £4, chd free. Home-made teas.**

This new garden in its historic setting has sweeping lawns running down to a spring fed carp pond. The formal garden has island beds of mixed planting for a long season of interest. The wild area of meadow has been landscaped with extensive tree planting to complement the existing woodland. There is also a small walled kitchen garden. Most areas are accessible although the fruit and veg garden is accessed over a deep gravel drive.

28 HOLM HOUSE

Garden House Lane, Drinkstone, Bury St. Edmunds, IP30 9FJ. Mrs Rebecca Shelley, Rebecca.shelley@hotmail.co.uk. *7m SE of Bury St Edmunds. Coming from the E exit A14 at J47, from the W J46. Follow signs to Drinkstone, then Drinkstone Green. Turn into Rattlesden Road & look for Garden House Lane. Then it is first house on L.* **Sun 26 May (11-5). Adm £5, chd free. Home-made teas.** Visits also by arrangement May to Sept for groups of 10+.

Around 10 acres, including: orchard and lawns with mature trees and clipped Holm Oaks; formal garden with topiary, parterre and borders; rose garden; woodland walk with hellebores, camellias, rhododendrons and bulbs; new lake, woodland planting and wild flower meadow; cut flower garden with greenhouse; large kitchen garden with impressive greenhouse; Mediterranean courtyard with mature olive tree. Much of the garden is wheelchair accessible, but not the kitchen garden.

29 THE LABURNUMS

The Street, St James South Elmham, Halesworth, IP19 0HN. Mrs Jane Bastow. *6m W of Halesworth, 7m E of Harleston & 6m S of Bungay. Parking at nearby village hall. For disabled parking please phone to arrange. Yellow signs from 8miles out in all directions.* **Sun 24 Feb (10-4). Adm £4.50, chd free. Light refreshments. Hot/Cold drinks,variety of home-made cakes and hot soup with crusty bread. Gluten free will be available.**

Our first year for Snowdrops,joining our beautiful Hellebores and other flowering plants and shrubs. Over the last three years around 20,0000 Snowdrops have been added to the garden. The herbaceous beds and borders are always being added to by the 'plantaholic' owner. A garden for wildlife with a large variety of birds and creatures. A haven to relax in and enjoy nature in all forms. Plant stall with a variety of plants and bulbs. Newly restored pond and sunken garden. Thousands of Snowdrops complementing the Hellebores and other plants. Conservatory packed with tender plants. Large glasshouse. Gravel drive. Partial wheelchair access to front garden. Steps to sunken garden. Concrete path in back garden.

30 LARKS' HILL

Clopton Road, Tuddenham St Martin, IP6 9BY. Mr John Lambert, 01473 785248, jrlambert@talktalk.net. *3m NE of Ipswich. From Ipswich take B1077, go through village, take the Clopton Rd to the L, after 300 metres at the brow of the hill you will see the house. Follow the car parking signs.* **Sat 22 June (1.30-5). Adm £5, chd free. Home-made teas. Our Big Shed Café can comfortably seat thirty or so and there is additional seating outside. Sit and talk and plan what to do next.** Visits also by arrangement Apr to Aug for groups of 10+.

The gardens of eight acres comprise woodland, a newly-planted conifer garden, and formal areas, and fall away from the house to the valley floor. A hill within a garden and in Suffolk at that! Hilly garden with a modern castle keep with an interesting and beautiful site overlooking the gentle Fynn valley and the village beyond. A fossil of a limb bone from a Pliosaur that lived at least sixty million years ago was found in the garden in 2013. The discovery was reported in the national press but its importance has been recognised world-wide. A booklet is available to purchase giving all the details.

31 NEW LILLESLEY BARN

The Street, Kersey, Ipswich, IP7 6ED. Mrs Bridget Allen, 07939 866873, bridgetinkerseybarn@gmail.com. *In village of Kersey, 2m NW Hadleigh. Driveway is 200 metres above 'The Bell' pub. Lillesley Barn is situated behind 'The Ancient Houses'.* **Sun 2 June (11-5). Combined adm with Old Gardens £5, chd free. Home-made teas. Meals available at The Bell Inn.** Visits also by arrangement May to Sept for groups of up to 20.

Dry gravel garden (inspired by the Beth Chatto Garden) including variety of mediterranean plants, ornamental grasses, herbs and collection of succulents. Large herbaceous border, rose arbours and small orchard with poultry. Golden willow hedge and fruit trees. The garden contains various species of birch, elder, amelanchier and willow. All within an acre of garden bordered on two sides by fields. Not suitable for Wheelchair access due to gravel, uneven ground and a slope.

32 NEW MOAT FARM

Middlewood Green, Stowmarket, IP14 5HG. Mr David Wicks, www.moatfarm.website. *Do not follow the signs into Moat Farm. Parking is in a field on the other side of the road. Access is across the road, through the orchard and over the bridge into the gardens.* **Sun 7 July (11-5). Adm £4, chd free. Home-made teas. WIne by the glass, beer, cider etc will be on sale.**

Nearly an acre of hedged enclosures surrounded on 3 sides by a moat with a bridge into a large orchard. Twin herbaceous borders, winter walk, minimalist pool, croquet lawn, mature trees, secret garden, rose path, grasses, hosta and fern beds, autumn circle. Hard paved paths provide access to most of the garden. Wheelchair users park inside the moat alongside the house.

33 MOAT HOUSE

Little Saxham, Bury St. Edmunds, IP29 5LE. Mr & Mrs Richard Mason, 01284 810941, rnm333@live.com. *2m SW of Bury St Edmunds. Leave A14 at J42 – leave r'about towards Westley. Through Westley Village, at Xrds R towards Barrow/Saxham. After 1.3m turn L down track. (follow signs).* **Visits by arrangement May to Sept for groups of 20+. Ample parking for cars or coaches. Adm £9, chd free. Home-made teas. Suzanne's home made cakes are renowned. Always a warm welcome at Moat House.**

Set in a 2 acre historic and partially moated site. This tranquil mature garden has been developed over 20yrs. Bordered by mature trees the garden is in various sections incl a sunken garden, rose and clematis arbours, herbaceous borders with hydrangeas and alliums surrounded by box hedging, small arboretum. A Hartley Botanic greenhouse erected and new partere created in 2017.

34 MULBERRY HOUSE, WESTLETON

Darsham Road, Westleton, IP17 3AH. Barbara Buckley & Hillas Smith. *Westleton village is approx. 2m off A12 turnoff at Yoxford heading toward the sea. It is well signed. Please park around the village & green as there is no parking at the house.* **Sun 5 May (12-4.30). Adm £4, chd free. Home-made teas.**

This garden is in its third year . The contemporary house in the centre of a traditional Suffolk village sits in a great space. We want to create a garden to do the architecture, the landscape and the village setting justice. It is a contemporary garden with a traditional cottage garden twist designed to be viewed as much from inside the house as from any point in the garden. Two pubs in the village do lunches, The White Horse and The Crown. Most of the garden is wheelchair accessible, there are some gravel paths but no steps. I am sorry there is no disabled parking at the property.

35 NEW OLD GARDENS

The Street, Kersey, Ipswich, IP7 6ED. Mr & Mrs David Anderson, 01473 828044, davidanderson6@btconnect.com. *10m W of Ipswich. 100 metres from The Bell Inn on the same side of the road.* **Sun 2 June (11-5). Combined adm with Lillesley Barn £5, chd free. Home-made teas at Lillesley Barn, Kersey. Meals available at The Bell Inn and car parking 100 metres away.** Visits also by arrangement May to Sept for groups of up to 20.

Entered from The Street, a natural garden with wild flowers under a copper beech tree. To the rear, a formal garden designed by Cherry Sandford with a sculpture by David Harbour.

36 THE OLD RECTORY

Hall Lane, Brinkley, CB8 0SB. Mr & Mrs Mark Coley. *Hall Lane is a turning off Brinkley High St. At the end of Hall Lane, white gates on the R.* **Sat 14, Sun 15 Sept (1.30-5.30). Adm £4, chd free. Home-made teas in Brinkley Village Hall.**

Two acre garden started in 1973. Interesting trees showing autumn colour planted to supplement beech, yew and chestnut already there. Mixed Herbaceous borders designed for late season interest with dahlias, michaelmas daisies, japanese anemones and hydrangea. Spectacular display of cyclamen hederifolium. Tradtional Potager with box hedges. A small woodland area is still being developed. Limited wheelchair access.

37 NEW THE OLD RECTORY

Nacton, Ipswich, IP10 0HY. Mrs Elizabeth & Mr James Wellesley Wesley, 01473 659673, tizyww@gmail.com. *The garden is down road to Nacton from first A14 turn off after Orwell bridge going N/E. Parking on Church Rd opp Old Rectory driveway. This will be signed.* **Sun 15 Sept (11-5). Adm £4.50, chd free. Home-made teas.** Visits also by arrangement Apr to Oct for groups of up to 10.

Just under 2 acres of garden divided into areas for different seasons: herbaceous borders with trees for Winter interest, herb/picking garden, rose garden. Light soil so many self sown flowers. Damp area with emphasis on foliage (Rheum, Darmera, Rodgersia, Hellebores). Most recently a terrace to West side of the house, all still developing after 28 years, with more projects in the pipeline. The Ship Inn is 2m up road in Levington and does good pub lunches. Lovely walks on the Orwell Estuary with extensive bird life especially at low tide. Nacton is very accessible from Ipswich and surrounding areas. Most areas are accessible for disabled visitors, however several grassy slopes and various different levels so some energy needed to get everywhere!

GROUP OPENING

38 ORFORD GARDENS

High Street, Orford, Woodbridge, IP12 2NW. *8m from Woodbridge. Take the B1084 from Woodbridge & follow NGS signs to Orford. These will direct you to the Old Rectory. From the Old Rectory, follow signs down Rectory Road to Brundish Lodge & Wayside.* **Sun 9 June (2-5). Combined adm £5, chd free. Home-made teas at Brundish Lodge.**

BRUNDISH LODGE
Mrs Elizabeth Spinney.
D

THE OLD RECTORY
Mr & Mrs Timothy Fargher.

WAYSIDE
Geoffrey & Anne Smeed.

Orford is a very attractive village with an historic castle and church. It also has excellent pubs and restaurants. Brundish Lodge is a garden of about one third of an acre and was completely redesigned, reconstructed and replanted in 2005. It has beds which are a mixture of shrubs, herbaceous plants and grasses grouped around a central lawn. The Old Rectory garden is a 4-5 acre layout of mixed borders, shrubbery walks, fountain courtyard, C19 conservatory, vegetable garden largely as laid out by Lanning Roper in the late 1960's with modifications by Mark Rumary (1980), the vagaries of nature and the current owners. Wayside is a village garden of ¼ acre with a mixture of shrubs and perennials chosen to cope with light, dry soil and cold east winds.

39 OUSDEN HOUSE

Ousden, Newmarket, CB8 8TN. Mr & Mrs Alastair Robinson. *Newmarket 6m, Bury St Edmunds 8m. Ousden House stands at the west end of the village next to the Church.* **Sun 9 June (2-5.30). Adm £6, chd free. Home-made teas.**
A large spectacular garden with fine views over the surrounding country. Herbaceous borders, rose garden and lawns leading to Spring woodland, and lake. Additional special features include a long double crinkle-crankle yew hedge leading from the clock tower and a moat garden densely planted with hellebores, flowering shrubs and moisture loving plants. Tea is served in the house or the courtyard. Extensive garden on various levels not suitable for wheelchairs or people who find difficulty in walking.

40 PAGET HOUSE

Back Road, Middleton, Saxmundham, IP17 3NY. Julian & Fiona Cusack, 01728 649060, julian.cusack@btinternet.com. *From A12 at Yoxford take B1122 towards Leiston. Turn L after 1.2m at Middleton Moor. After 1m enter Middleton village & drive straight ahead into Back Road.* **Sun 21 July (10.30-5). Adm £4, chd free. Tea.** Visits also by arrangement Apr to Aug for groups of up to 30.
The garden, started in 2012, is a wildlife friendly garden with formal planting, an orchard, a vegetable plot and areas of woodland. There are laid hedges, a pond supporting amphibians and dragonflies, a wild flower meadow and an abstract garden sculpture by local artist Paul Richardson. We record over 40 bird species each year and a good showing of butterflies and wild flowers including orchids. Gravel drive and mown paths.

41 5 PARKLANDS GREEN

Fornham St Genevieve, Bury St. Edmunds, IP28 6UH. Mrs Jane Newton, newton.jane@talktalk.net. *2m Northwest of Bury St Edmunds off B1106. Plenty of parking on the green.* **Sun 23 June (11-4). Adm £4, chd free. Home-made teas.** Visits also by arrangement Apr to Sept.
1½ acres of gardens developed since the 1980s for all year interest. There are mature and unusual trees and shrubs and riotous herbaceous borders. Explore the maze of paths to find 4 informal ponds, a tree house, the sunken garden, greenhouses and woodland walks. Partial wheelchair access only.

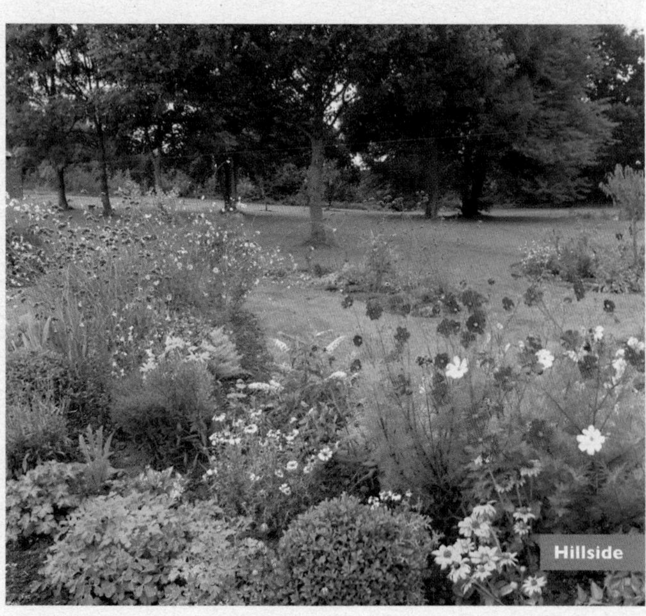

Hillside

42 ◆ THE PLACE FOR PLANTS, EAST BERGHOLT PLACE GARDEN

East Bergholt, CO7 6UP. Mr & Mrs Rupert Eley, 01206 299224, sales@placeforplants.co.uk, www.placeforplants.co.uk. *2m E of A12, 7m S of Ipswich. On B1070 towards Manningtree, 2m E of A12. Situated on the edge of East Bergholt.* **For NGS: Sun 7, Sun 28 Apr (2-5). Adm £7, chd free. Sun 6 Oct (1-4). Adm £6, chd free. Home-made teas.** For other opening times and information, please phone, email or visit garden website.

20-acre garden originally laid out at the turn of the last century by the present owner's great grandfather. Full of many fine trees and shrubs, many seldom seen in East Anglia. A fine collection of camellias, magnolias and rhododendrons, topiary, and the National Collection of deciduous Euonymus. Partial Wheelchair access in dry conditions - it is advisable to telephone before visiting.

♿ ✿ 🚌 NPC ☕

43 POLSTEAD MILL

Mill Lane, Polstead, Colchester, CO6 5AB. Mrs Lucinda Bartlett, 07711 720418, lucyofleisure@hotmail.com. *Between Stoke by Nayland & Polstead on the R Box. From Stoke by Nayland take rd to Polstead - Mill Lane is 1st on L & Polstead Mill is 1st house on R.* **Visits by arrangement May to Sept for groups of 10+. Adm £6.50, chd free. Cream teas. A range of refreshments available from coffee and biscuits to full cream teas and even light lunches..**

The garden has been developed since 2002, it has formal and informal areas, a wild flower meadow and a large productive kitchen garden. The R Box runs through the garden and there is a mill pond, which gives opportunity for damp gardening, while much of the rest of the garden is arid and is planted to minimise the need for watering. Partial wheelchair access.

♿ ✿ ☕

44 PRIORS OAK

Leiston Road, Aldeburgh, IP15 5QE. Mrs Trudie Willis, 01728 452580, trudie.willis@dinkum.free-online.co.uk, www.sites.google.com/site/priorsoakbutterflygarden. *1m N of Aldeburgh on B1122. Garden on L opp RSPB Reserve.* **Sun 30 June (2-6). Adm £5, chd free. Light refreshments. tea and cake.** Visits also by arrangement May to Sept for groups of up to 10.

10-acre wildlife and butterfly garden. Ornamental salad and vegetable gardens with companion planting. Herbaceous borders, ferns and Mediterranean plants. Pond and wild flower acid grassland with a small wood. Skirting the wood are 100 buddleia in excess of 30 varieties forming a perfumed tunnel. Very tranquil and fragrant garden with grass paths and yearly interest. Rich in animal and bird life. Specialist butterfly garden, as seen in SAGA magazine,and Horticulture in USA, renovated railway carriages, tortoise breeding, donkeys, wildlife walks. Coaches or private visits by arrangement only.

♿ ✿ ☕

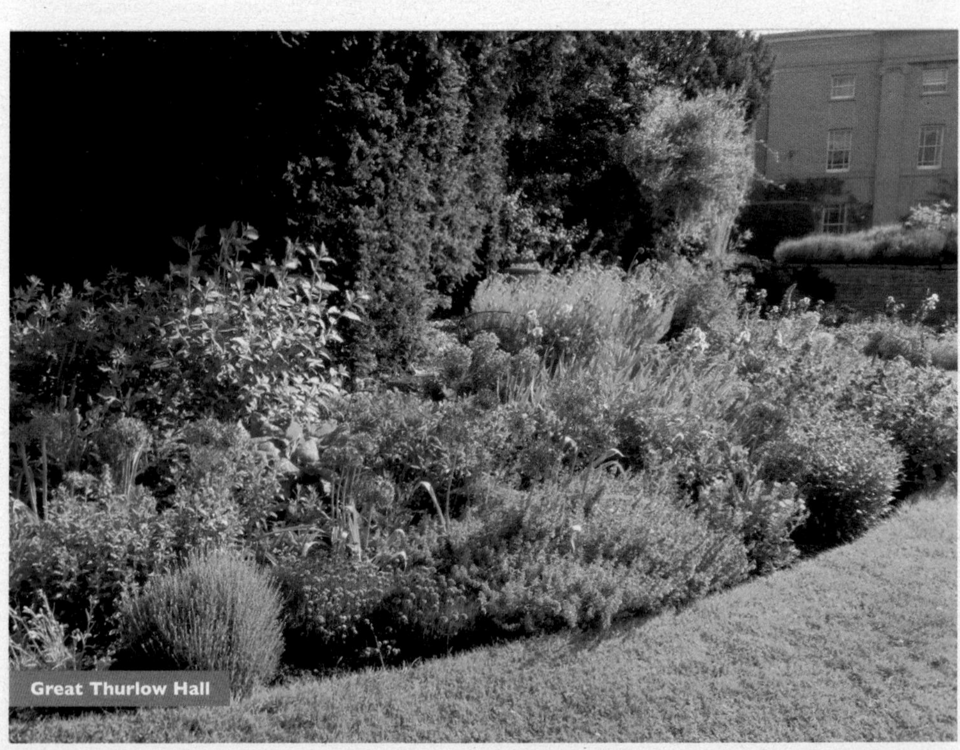
Great Thurlow Hall

45 THE PRIORY

Stoke by Nayland, Colchester, CO6 4RL. Mrs H F A Engleheart. *5m SW of Hadleigh. Entrance on B1068 to Sudbury (NW of Stoke by Nayland).* **Sun 19 May (2-5). Adm £5, chd free. Home-made teas.**

Interesting 9 acre garden with fine views over Constable countryside; lawns sloping down to small lakes and water garden; fine trees, rhododendrons and azaleas; walled garden; mixed borders and ornamental greenhouse. Wide variety of plants. Wheelchair access over most of garden, some steps.

Moat Farm

46 REDISHAM HALL

Redisham Rd, Redisham, nr Beccles, NR34 8LZ. The Palgrave Brown Family, 01502 575894, sarah.hammond7@hotmail.co.uk. *5m S of Beccles. From A145, turn W on to Ringsfield-Bungay rd. Beccles, Halesworth or Bungay, all within 5m.* **Sun 14 July (2-6). Adm £5, chd free. Home-made teas.** Visits also by arrangement June to Aug for groups of 10+.

C18 Georgian house (not open). 5-acre garden set in 400 acres parkland and woods. Incl 2-acre walled kitchen garden (in full production) with peach house, vinery and glasshouses. Lawns, herbaceous borders, shrubberies, ponds and mature trees. Sorry No Dogs. Redisham Hall has been opening it's gardens for the NGS for over 50 yrs. The garden has lots of gravel paths and there are lawned slopes. Wheelchair access is possible with assistance. Parking is on uneven parkland.

47 5 RINGSFIELD ROAD

Beccles, NR34 9PQ. Jan & Mark Oakley. *Next to Sir John Leman High School, Beccles. Signed from Beccles town centre & the Bungay Rd/London Rd T-lights.* **Sun 14 July (11-5). Adm £4, chd free. Home-made teas.**

Stepping around the side of this lovely Arts and Crafts home, you'll discover an acre of gorgeous colour themed garden. The herbaceous beds and borders harmonise beautifully, with sumptuous purples, cool pastels and hot scarlet collections. As you wander through the garden you'll find fun topiary and some fine specimen trees. Please park next door at Sir John Leman High School NR34 9PG. Disabled parking and level access to the rear of the property in Ashmans Road.

48 RIVER COTTAGE

Lower Road, Lavenham, Sudbury, CO10 9QJ. Mr & Mrs Geoff Heald. *It is best to park your car in the Village Square & walk down Prentice Street which can be found by walking past The Angel & The Great House. Proceed to the bottom then turn R on Lower Rd.* **Sun 11 Aug (11-5). Adm £5, chd free. A selection of home-made cakes, teas and coffees.**

A tranquil plantsman's garden with a 400ft river frontage ending with a hydrangea walk with many newly planted hostas, dahlias, lilies,roses, clematis, ivies and grasses.The newly created woodland garden has many rare plants including Paris Arisaemas. Look out for a Spotty Dotty and a giant Amorphophallus. The owners are always looking for new and unusual plants to delight visitors. There will be a wheelchair route clearly signed for use in dry weather.

49 NEW THE ROOKS

Old Paper Mill Lane, Claydon, Ipswich, IP6 0AL. Mrs Marilyn Gillard. *Off A14 at J52. From r'about turn in Claydon & take first available R, into Old Ipswich Rd where parking is available. The Rooks is 200m, first house in Old Paper Mill Lane with thatched roof.* **Sun 16 June (11-4). Adm £4, chd free. Light refreshments. Tea, various homemade cakes.**

The garden surrounds a thatched cottage built c1600. The garden has been divided into rooms to give different feelings of interest, with seating in most areas. There are two ponds, mixed borders, trees, statues and features. Not suitable for wheelchairs because of slopes and steps.

50 ROSEDALE

40 Colchester Road, Bures, CO8 5AE. Mr & Mrs Colin Lorking. *6m SE of Sudbury. From Colchester take B1508. After 10m garden on L as you enter the village, from Sudbury B1508 after 5m garden on R.* **Sun 5 May, Sun 4 Aug (12-5). Adm £3, chd free. Home-made teas.**

Approx one-third of an acre plantsman's garden developed over the last 24 years, containing many unusual plants, herbaceous borders and pond. For the May opening see a super collection of peonies and for the July opening a stunning collection of approx 60 Agapanthus in full flower.

51 ◆ SOMERLEYTON HALL GARDENS

Somerleyton, NR32 5QQ. Lord Somerleyton, 01502 734901, info@somerleyton.co.uk, www.somerleyton.co.uk. *5m NW of Lowestoft. From Norwich (30mins) - on the B1074, 7m SE of Great Yarmouth (A143). Coaches should follow signs to the rear west gate entrance.* **For NGS: Sun 9 June (10-5). Adm £6.95, chd £4.90. Light refreshments in Cafe.** For other opening times and information, please phone, email or visit garden website.

12½ acres of beautiful gardens contain a wide variety of magnificent specimen trees, shrubs, borders and plants providing colour and interest throughout the yr. Sweeping lawns and formal gardens combine with majestic statuary and original Victorian ornamentation. Highlights incl the Paxton glasshouses, pergola, walled garden and famous yew hedge maze. House and gardens remodelled in 1840s by Sir Morton Peto. House created in Anglo-Italian style with lavish architectural features and fine state rooms. All areas of the gardens are accessible, path surfaces are gravel and can be a little difficult after heavy rain. Wheelchairs available on request.

52 STREET FARM

North Street, Freckenham, IP28 8HY. David & Clodagh Dugdale. *3m W of Mildenhall. From Newmarket, follow signs to Snailwell, & Chippenham & then onto Freckenham.* **Sun 12 May (11-5). Adm £4, chd free. Light refreshments.**

Approx 1 acre of landscaped garden, with several mature trees. The garden includes a water cascade, pond with island and a number of bridges. Formal rose garden, rose pergola and hornbeam walk. Gravel paths with steps and slopes.

53 TRINITY HOUSE

Rectory Gardens, Beyton, Bury St. Edmunds, IP30 9UZ. Barbara & Graham Jones. *6m E of Bury St Edmunds. From West A14 exit J46 then R at Green, L at White Horse into Church Rd. After ½m park at church on L & follow signs for garden. From East J46 follow rd to White Horse then as above.* **Sun 5 May (12-5). Adm £3.50, chd free. Light refreshments in Church Hall adjacent to Car Park.**

Peaceful village garden surrounded by mature trees. Meandering paths wind around beds of hydrangea, ferns and not-often seen perennials, along with several unusual trees. Fruiting Kiwi vine and climbing hydrangeas adorn the house walls. Tucked away 'frog' pond. Summerhouse, conservatory with exotic plants, and many seating areas offer vistas over the garden. Summerhouse, greenhouse and conservatory with exotic plants. Several seating areas offer vistas over the garden. A fruiting Kiwi and climbing hydrangea adorn the house walls. Entrance to garden from car-park a little uneven. Access also available through Rectory Gardens, follow signs, but care needed as no path on road.

Your visits help change lives – since 1927, we've donated £55 million to nursing and caring charities

54 WENHASTON GRANGE

Wenhaston, Halesworth, IP19 9HJ. Mr & Mrs Bill Barlow. *Turn SW from A144 between Bramfield & Halesworth. Take the single track rd (signed Walpole 2) Wenhaston Grange is approx ½m, at the bottom of the hill on L.* **Sun 2 June (11-4). Adm £5, chd free. Home-made teas.**

Over 3 acres of varied gardens on a long established site which has been extensively landscaped and enhanced over the last 15 yrs. Long herbaceous borders, old established trees and a series of garden rooms created by beech hedges. Levels and sight lines have been carefully planned. The garden is on a number of levels, with steps so wheelchair access would be difficult.

55 41 WESTMORLAND ROAD

Felixstowe, IP11 9TJ. Mr & Mrs Mick & Diane Elmes, 01394 284647, dianeelmes0@gmail.com. *Enter Felixstowe on A154. At r'about take 1st exit then turn R into Beatrice Avenue. L to High Road East. Proceed to Clifflands Car Park & turn L. Follow signs No. 41 is on the corner of Wrens Park.* **Sun 2 June (11-5). Combined adm with 246 Ferry Road £5, chd free. Light refreshments. Cakes and savouries with a selection of drinks at 41 Westmorland Road.** Visits also by arrangement Feb to Oct for groups of up to 20. Adm incls teas.

We moved into this house in 2009 since when we have recovered the garden by taking down 21 leylandii trees and various other dead trees. It is now a perennial garden(over 400 different types of perennial plants) with interesting and eclectic features. All main areas wheelchair accessible.

56 WHITE HOUSE FARM

Ringsfield, Beccles, NR34 8JU. Jan Barlow, (gardener) 07780 901233, coppertops707@aol.com. *2m SW of Beccles. From Beccles take B1062 to Bungay, after 1¼ turn L signed Ringsfield. Continue for approx 1m. Parking opp church. Garden 300yds on L.* **Sat 6 July (10-4.30). Adm £4, chd free. Light refreshments. Cakes and savoury flans.** Visits also by arrangement Apr to Sept for groups of 10 to 30.

Tranquil park-type garden approx 30 acres, bordered by farmland and with fine views. Comprising formal areas, copses, natural pond, woodland walk, vegetable garden and orchard. Picnickers welcome. NB The pond and beck are unfenced. Partial wheelchair access to the areas around the house.

57 WOOD FARM, GIPPING

Back Lane, Gipping, Stowmarket, IP14 4RN. Mr & Mrs R Shelley, 07809 503019, els@maritimecargo.com. *From A14 take A1120 to Stowupland, Turn L opp Petrol Station, Turn R at T-junction, follow for approx 1m turn L at Walnut Tree Farm, then imm R & follow for 1m along country lane. Wood Farm is on L.* **Sun 2 June (1-4.30). Adm £4.50, chd free. Home-made teas. Large Party Barn with Facilities.** Visits also by arrangement May & June for groups of 10+. Groups welcomed and Home-Made Teas provided.

Wood Farm is an old farm with ponds, orchards and a magnificent 8 acre wild flower meadow (with mown paths) bordered with traditional hedging, trees and woodland. The large cottage garden was created in 2011 with a number of beds planted with flowers, vegetables and topiary. Wildlife is very much encouraged in all parts of the garden (particularly bees and butterflies). In June 2018 used by an International Fashion Brand as their A/W18 Photo Shoot. Partial wheelchair access.

58 WOODWARDS

Blacksmiths Lane, Coddenham, Ipswich, IP6 9TX. Marion & Richard Kenward, 01449 760639, richardwoodwards@btinternet.com. *7m N of Ipswich. From A14 turn onto A140, after ¼m take B1078 towards Wickham Market, Coddenham is on route. Coaches please use postcode IP6 9PS. Ample parking for coaches.* **Sun 17 Mar, Sun 21 Apr, Sun 12 May, Sun 14, Tue 30 July, Tue 13, Sun 25 Aug (10.30-5). Adm £3.50, chd free. Home-made teas.** Visits also by arrangement Mar to Aug. Adm incls home-made tea.

Award winning S facing gently sloping garden of 1½ acres, overlooking the rolling Suffolk countryside. Designed and maintained by owners for yr-round colour and interest, lots of island beds, well stocked with 1000s of bulbs, shrubs and perennials, vegetable plot, display of 100+ hanging baskets for spring and summer. Well kept lawns, with large mature trees. More than 25000 bulbs have been planted over the last 3yrs for our spring display. Teas in aid of St. Mary's Church, Coddenham.

59 ◆ WYKEN HALL

Stanton, IP31 2DW. Sir Kenneth & Lady Carlisle, 01359 250262, kenneth.carlisle@wykenvineyards.co.uk, www.wykenvineyards.co.uk. *9m NE of Bury St Edmunds. Along A143. Follow signs to Wyken Vineyards on A143 between Ixworth & Stanton.* **For NGS: Sat 1, Sun 2 June (10-6). Adm £5, chd free.** For other opening times and information, please phone, email or visit garden website.

4-acres around the old manor with many interesting flowers and shrubs. The gardens include knot and herb gardens, old-fashioned rose garden, kitchen and wild garden, nuttery, pond, gazebo and maze; herbaceous borders and old orchard. Woodland walk, vineyard nearby. Restaurant (booking 01359 250287.) and shop. Vineyard. Farmers' Market Sat 9 - 1.

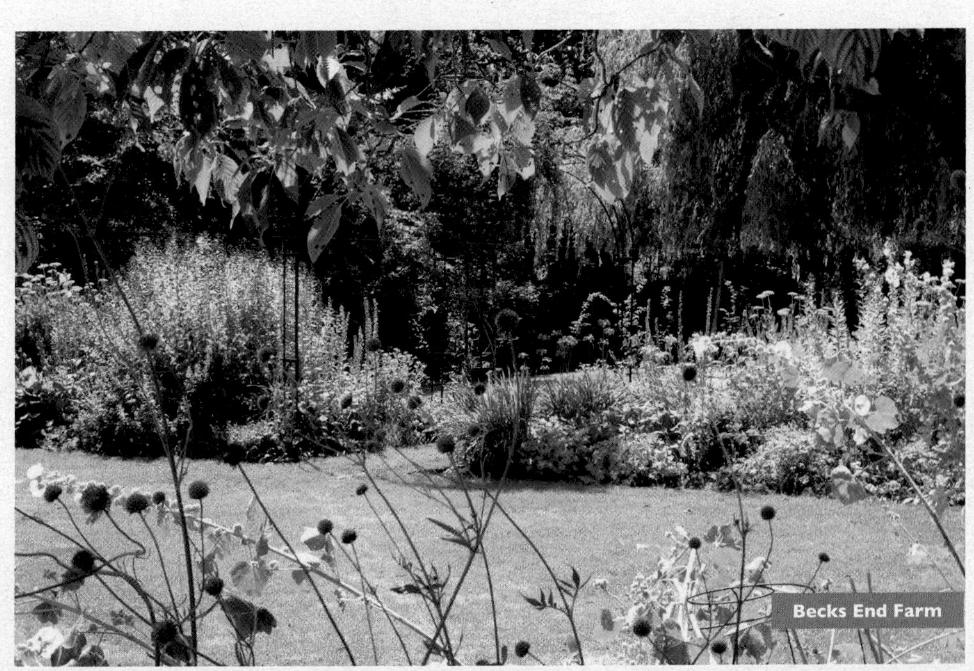

Becks End Farm

SURREY

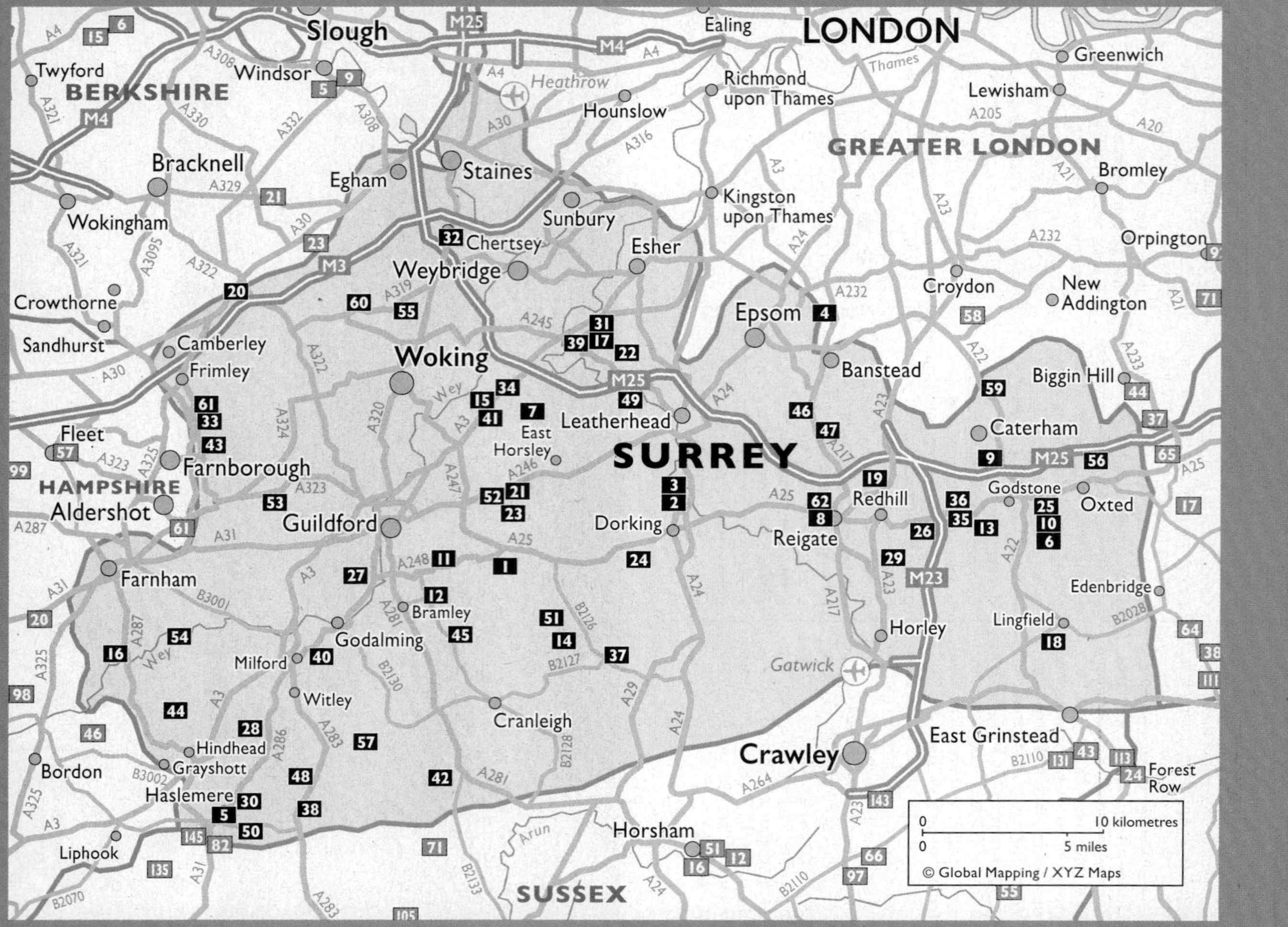

LONDON
GREATER LONDON
SURREY
BERKSHIRE
HAMPSHIRE
SUSSEX
Slough
Ealing
Greenwich
Twyford
Windsor
Heathrow
Richmond upon Thames
Lewisham
Hounslow
Bracknell
Staines
Egham
Bromley
Wokingham
Sunbury
Kingston upon Thames
Chertsey
Esher
Orpington
Weybridge
Croydon
New Addington
Crowthorne
Epsom
Sandhurst
Camberley
Woking
Banstead
Frimley
Biggin Hill
Leatherhead
Fleet
East Horsley
Caterham
Farnborough
Godstone
Redhill
Oxted
Aldershot
Guildford
Dorking
Reigate
Farnham
Edenbridge
Bramley
Godalming
Lingfield
Horley
Milford
Gatwick
Witley
Cranleigh
East Grinstead
Hindhead
Crawley
Bordon
Grayshott
Forest Row
Haslemere
Horsham
Liphook
Thames
Wey
Arun
0 10 kilometres
0 5 miles
© Global Mapping / XYZ Maps

As a designated Area of Outstanding Natural Beauty, it's no surprise that Surrey has a wealth of gardens on offer.

With its historic market towns, lush meadows and scenic rivers, Surrey provides the ideal escape from the bustle of nearby London.

Set against the rolling chalk uplands of the unspoilt North Downs, the county prides itself on extensive country estates with historic houses and ancient manors. Visitors are inspired by the breathtaking panorama from Polesden Lacey, lakeside views at The Old Croft or timeless terraces at Albury Park.

Surrey is the heartland of the NGS at Hatchlands Park and the RHS at Wisley, both promoting a precious interest in horticulture. Surrey celebrates a landscape coaxed into wonderful vistas by great gardeners such as John Evelyn, Capability Brown and Gertrude Jekyll.

With many eclectic gardens to visit, there's certainly plenty to treasure in Surrey.

Below: Ashcombe

Volunteers

County Organiser

Margaret Arnott
01372 842459
margaret.arnott@ngs.org

County Treasurer

Nigel Brandon
020 8643 8686
nbrandon@ngs.org.uk

Booklet Co-ordinator

Annabel Alford-Warren
01483 203330
annabel.alford-warren@ngs.org.uk

Publicity and Advertising

Annabel Alford-Warren
(As above)

Social Media

Laura Mouratsing
07792 607956
lmouratsing@ngs.org.uk

Assistant County Organisers

Anne Barnes
01306 730196
spurfold@btinternet.com

Jan Brandon
020 8643 8686
janmbrandon@outlook.com

Barbara Brooks
01428 687767
barbarabrooks@btinternet.com

Penny Drew
01252 792909
penelopedrew@yahoo.co.uk

Di Grose
01883 742983
di.grose@btinternet.com

Annie Keighley
01252 838660
annie.keighley12@btinternet.com

Caroline Shuldham
01932 596960
c.m.shuldham@btinternet.com

Jean Thompson
01483 425633
norney.wood@btinternet.com

OPENING DATES

All entries subject to change. For latest information check **www.ngs.org.uk**

Extended openings are shown at the beginning of the month.

Map locator numbers are shown to the right of each garden name.

February

Snowdrop Festival

Sunday 10th
◆ Gatton Park 19

Tuesday 12th
NEW ◆ The Sculpture Park 44

March

Sunday 17th
Albury Park 1

Sunday 24th
◆ Vann 57

Monday 25th
◆ Vann 57

Tuesday 26th
◆ Vann 57

April

Sunday 7th
Caxton House 8

Sunday 14th
The Chalet 9
Coverwood Lakes 14
◆ Vann 57

Monday 15th
◆ Vann 57

Tuesday 16th
◆ Vann 57

Wednesday 17th
◆ Dunsborough Park 15
◆ Vann 57

Sunday 21st
The Chalet 9
Shieling 47

Monday 22nd
Coverwood Lakes 14
Timber Hill 55

Saturday 27th
Springwood House 50
NEW 11 West Hill 58

Sunday 28th
◆ Hatchlands Park 21
41 Shelvers Way 46
Springwood House 50
NEW 11 West Hill 58

May

Every Sunday to Thursday
◆ Loseley Park 27

Sunday 5th
Coverwood Lakes 14
The Garth Pleasure Grounds 18
The Therapy Garden 53

Monday 6th
◆ Vann 57

Tuesday 7th
◆ Vann 57

Wednesday 8th
◆ Vann 57

Thursday 9th
◆ Vann 57

Friday 10th
◆ Ramster 38
◆ Vann 57

Saturday 11th
Hall Grove School 20
◆ Vann 57

Sunday 12th
Coverwood Lakes 14
The Garth Pleasure Grounds 18
Roe Deer Farm 40
◆ Vann 57
Westways Farm 60

Sunday 19th
Chilworth Manor 11
Spurfold 51
◆ Titsey Place Gardens 56

Monday 20th
Chauffeur's Flat 10

Tuesday 21st
Chauffeur's Flat 10

Wednesday 22nd
Chauffeur's Flat 10

Thursday 23rd
Chauffeur's Flat 10

Friday 24th
Chauffeur's Flat 10

Saturday 25th
Chauffeur's Flat 10

Sunday 26th
Chauffeur's Flat 10
Shieling 47
57 Westhall Road 59

Monday 27th
Fairmile Lea 17
Moleshill House 31
57 Westhall Road 59

June

Every Sunday to Thursday
◆ Loseley Park 27

Sunday 2nd
High Clandon Estate Vineyard 23
Monks Lantern 32

Saturday 8th
◆ Dunsborough Park 15
7 Rose Lane 41

Sunday 9th
Lower House 28
The Old Rectory 36

Monday 10th
NEW ◆ The Sculpture Park 44

Tuesday 11th
Oakleigh 33

Saturday 15th
The Bothy 6
Little Court House 25
57 Westhall Road 59

Sunday 16th
The Bothy 6
2 Chinthurst Lodge 12
Little Court House 25
Moleshill House 31
◆ Titsey Place Gardens 56
57 Westhall Road 59

Monday 17th
The Bothy 6

Tuesday 18th
The Bothy 6

Wednesday 19th
The Bothy 6
2 Chinthurst Lodge 12

Thursday 20th
The Bothy 6

Friday 21st
NEW Ashcombe 2
Ashleigh Grange 3
The Bothy 6

Saturday 22nd
Little Priory 26
NEW Sleepy Hollow 48

Sunday 23rd
NEW Ashcombe 2
Ashleigh Grange 3
Little Priory 26
NEW Macmillan Cancer Support Centre 29
The Manor House 30
◆ Vann 57

Monday 24th
Chauffeur's Flat 10

Tuesday 25th
Chauffeur's Flat 10

Wednesday 26th
NEW Ashcombe 2
Ashleigh Grange 3
Chauffeur's Flat 10

Thursday 27th
Chauffeur's Flat 10

Friday 28th
Chauffeur's Flat 10

Saturday 29th
Chauffeur's Flat 10

Sunday 30th
Chauffeur's Flat 10

July

Every Sunday to Thursday
◆ Loseley Park 27

Saturday 6th
15 The Avenue 4
Bardsey 5
Woodbury Cottage 62

Sunday 7th
Bardsey 5
Woodbury Cottage 62

Sunday 21st
◆ Titsey Place Gardens 56

Saturday 27th
Earleywood 16

Sunday 28th
Earleywood 16

August

Saturday 10th
69 Salisbury Grove 43

Sunday 11th
41 Shelvers Way 46

Sunday 18th
Pratsham Grange 37
◆ Titsey Place Gardens 56

Saturday 31st
Coldharbour House 13

September

Sunday 1st
Coldharbour House 13
The Therapy Garden 53

Saturday 7th
Woodbury Cottage 62

Sunday 8th
◆ Dunsborough Park 15
Moleshill House 31
NEW Randalls Allotments 39
Woodbury Cottage 62

Sunday 15th
Hill Farm 24

October

Sunday 6th
Albury Park 1

Sunday 13th
Coverwood Lakes 14

By Arrangement

Arrange a personalised garden visit with your club, or group of friends, on a date to suit you. See individual garden entries for full details.

Ashleigh Grange 3
15 The Avenue 4
Bardsey 5
Bridge End Cottage 7
Caxton House 8
2 Chinthurst Lodge 12
Coldharbour House 13
Coverwood Lakes 14
The Garth Pleasure Grounds 18
Heathside 22
Moleshill House 31
Monks Lantern 32
NEW Ockham Mill 34
Odstock 35
The Old Rectory 36
Pratsham Grange 37
Saffron Gate 42
69 Salisbury Grove 43
Shamley Wood Estate 45
41 Shelvers Way 46
Shieling 47
NEW 2 Slyfield Farm Cottages 49
Spurfold 51
Stuart Cottage 52
Tilford Cottage 54
Timber Hill 55
Westways Farm 60
Wildwood 61
Woodbury Cottage 62

THE GARDENS

1 ALBURY PARK

Albury, GU5 9BH. Trustees of Albury Estate. *5m SE of Guildford. From A25 take A248 towards Albury for ¼ m, then up New Rd, entrance to Albury Park immed on L.* **Sun 17 Mar, Sun 6 Oct (2-5). Adm £4.50, chd free. Home-made teas.**

14 acre pleasure grounds laid out in 1670s by John Evelyn for Henry Howard, later 6th Duke of Norfolk. ¼ m terraces, fine collection of trees, lake and river. Gravel path and slight slope.

2 NEW ASHCOMBE

Chapel Lane, Westhumble, Dorking, RH5 6AY. Vivienne & David Murch. *From A24 at Boxhill/ Burford Bridge follow signs to Westhumble. Through village & L up drive by ruined chapel (1m from A24).* **Evening opening Fri 21 June (6-8.30). Combined adm with Ashleigh Grange £8, chd free. Sun 23, Wed 26 June (1-5). Combined adm with Ashleigh Grange £6, chd free. Wine and Pimms available.**

Plantaholics 1½ acre wild life friendly sloping garden on chalk and flint. Enclosed 3rd of acre with large borders of roses, delphiniums & clematis. Amphibian pond. Secluded decking and Patio area with colourful acers and views over garden & Boxhill. Gravel bed of salvia and day lilies. House surrounded by banked flower beds and lawn leading to bee and butterfly garden. Gravel paths, steps and a sloping site.

3 ASHLEIGH GRANGE

off Chapel Lane, Westhumble, RH5 6AY. Clive & Angela Gilchrist, 01306 884613, ar.gilchrist@btinternet.com. *2m N of Dorking. From A24 at Boxhill/ Burford Bridge follow signs to Westhumble. Through village & L up drive by ruined chapel (1m from A24).* **Evening opening Fri 21 June (6-8.30). Combined adm with Ashcombe £8, chd free. Wine. Sun 23, Wed 26 June (1-5). Combined adm with Ashcombe £6, chd free. Home-made teas.** Visits also by arrangement May to July. Sorry, no access for coaches. Donation to Barnardo's.

Plant lover's chalk garden on 3½ acre sloping site in charming rural setting with delightful views. Many areas of interest incl rockery and water feature, raised ericaceous bed, prairie style bank, foliage plants, woodland walk, fernery and folly. Large mixed herbaceous and shrub borders planted for dry alkaline soil and widespread interest.

4 15 THE AVENUE

Cheam, Sutton, SM2 7QA. Jan & Nigel Brandon, 020 8643 8686, janmbrandon@outlook.com. *1m SW of Sutton. By car; exit A217 onto Northey Av, 2nd R into The Avenue. By train; 10 mins walk from Cheam station. By bus; use 470.* **Evening opening Sat 6 July (4-9). Adm £8, chd £3. Wine.** Visits also by arrangement May to Aug for groups of 10 to 30.

A contemporary garden designed by RHS Chelsea Gold Medal Winner, Marcus Barnett. Four levels divided into rooms by beech hedging and columns; formal entertaining area, contemporary outdoor room, lawn and wildflower meadow. Over 100 hostas hug the house. Silver birch, cloud pruned box, ferns, grasses, tall bearded irises, contemporary sculptures. Light refreshments are included in the entry fee. Partial wheelchair access, terraced with steps; sloping path provides view of whole garden but not all accessible.

5 BARDSEY

11 Derby Road, Haslemere, GU27 1BS. Maggie & David Boyd, 01428 652283, maggie.boyd@live.co.uk, www.bardseygarden.co.uk. *¼m N of Haslemere station. Turn off B2131 (which links A287 to A286 through town) 400yds W of station into Weydown Rd, 3rd R into Derby Rd, garden 400yds on R.* **Sat 6, Sun 7 July (1-5). Adm £5, chd free. Home-made teas.** Visits also by arrangement June & July for groups of 10+.

Unexpected 2 acre garden in the heart of Haslemere. Several distinct areas containing scent, colour, texture and movement. Stunning pictorial meadow within an ilex crenata parterre. Prairie planted border provides a modern twist. Large productive fruit and vegetable garden. Natural ponds and bog gardens. Several unusual sculptures. Bee hive and bug hotel. Ducks and chickens supply the eggs for cakes. Classic MGs on parade. Home-made produce stall. Glass sculptures by Wendy Stafford for sale. First third of garden level, other two thirds sloping.

6 THE BOTHY

Tandridge Court, Tandridge Lane, Oxted, RH8 9NJ. Diane & John Hammond, 07785612478, dhammo@hotmail.co.uk. *5 mins from J6 of M25, towards Oxted. From N, at r'about on A25 between A22 & Oxted go S to Tandridge after ¼m follow signs. From S, N up Tandridge Ln from Ray Ln, on exiting Tandridge follow signs. Do not use Jackass Ln from A25.* **Sat 15, Sun 16, Mon 17, Tue 18, Wed 19, Thur 20, Fri 21 June (11-4). Adm £5, chd free. Afternoon teas served at Little Court House (also open) on 15th & 16th June only. Cold drinks & ice creams on weekdays at The Bothy.**

A 1½ acre hillside garden on 5 levels. Accessed by steps and slopes, creating varying views, with specimen trees, incl a Sequoia, Acers and Banana. Explore wild banks, perennial beds, woodland and relaxing areas along with a productive kitchen garden with raised beds, fruit trees, fruit cage and large greenhouse. Each level contains either water features, garden artwork, chickens and more. The garden entrance is down a number of steps and on different levels and therefore it is unsuitable for people with mobility issues.

7 BRIDGE END COTTAGE

Ockham Lane, Ockham, GU23 6NR. Clare & Peter Bevan, 01483 479963, c.fowler@ucl.ac.uk. *Nr RHS Gardens, Wisley. At Wisley r'about turn L onto B2039 to Ockham/Horsley. After ½m turn L into Ockham Lane. House ½m on R. From Cobham go to Blackswan Xrds.* **Visits by arrangement May & June for groups of 10 to 30. Adm £5, chd free. Home-made teas in the garden room.**

A two acre country garden with different areas of interest, incl perennial borders, mature trees, pond and streams, small herb parterre, fruit trees and a vegetable patch. An adjacent two acre field was sown with perennial wild flower seed in May 2013 and has flowered well in June. In recent years the flowering in July has become more varied. Partial wheelchair access.

8 CAXTON HOUSE

67 West Street, Reigate, RH2 9DA. Bob Bushby, 01737 243158 / 07836201740, Bob.bushby@sky.com. *On A25 towards Dorking, approx ¼m W of Reigate. Parking on Rd or past Black Horse PH on Flanchford Rd.* **Sun 7 Apr (2-5). Adm £5, chd free. Cream teas.** Visits also by arrangement Apr to Sept for groups of 10+. Coach parking on drive.

Lovely large spring garden with Arboretum, 2 well stocked ponds, large collection of hellebores and spring flowers. Pots planted with colourful displays. Interesting plants. Small Gothic folly built by owner. Herbaceous borders with grasses, perennials, spring bulbs, and parterre. New bed with wild daffodils and prairie style planting in summer. Antique dog cart completes the picture. 7 acres. Wheelchair access to most parts of the garden.

9 THE CHALET

Tupwood Lane, Caterham, CR3 6ET. Miss Lesley Manning & Mr David Gold. *½m N of M25 J6. Exit J6 off M25 onto A22 to N. After ½m take sharp 1st L, or follow signs from Caterham. Ample free parking. Disabled access via top gate in Tupwood Lane.* **Sun 14, Sun 21 Apr (11-4.30). Adm £5, chd free. Home-made teas.** Donation to St Catherine's Hospice.

A true festival of Spring at The Chalet in 55 acres of stunning grounds with carpets of daffodils. Ornamental ponds with beautiful Koi fish, ancient woodlands and planted terraces. A variety of wildlife incl a badger sett. See Classic cars, Owls Out and About, take the woodland trail and enjoy all-day entertainment. Lots of fun for the children. David and Lesley will be there on both days. On view, a limited edition Blue Train Bentley, a Phantom Rolls Royce and a helicopter plus the oldest FA Cup and other trophies. Toilet facilities available. Partial wheelchair access, some steep slopes. 3 large unfenced ponds.

10 CHAUFFEUR'S FLAT

Tandridge Lane, Tandridge, RH8 9NJ. Mr & Mrs Richins. *2m E of Godstone. 2m W of Oxted. Turn off A25 at r'about for Tandridge. Take 2nd drive on L past church. Follow arrows to circular courtyard. Do not use Jackass Ln even if your SatNav tells you to do so.* **Mon 20, Tue 21, Wed 22, Thur 23, Fri 24, Sat 25, Sun 26 May, Mon 24, Tue 25, Wed 26, Thur 27, Fri 28, Sat 29, Sun 30 June (10-5). Adm £5, chd free. Home-made teas (Sats & Suns only).**

Enter a 1½ acre tapestry of magical secret gardens with magnificent views. Touching the senses, all sure footed visitors may explore the many surprises on this constantly evolving exuberant escape from reality. Imaginative use of recycled materials creates an inspired variety of ideas, while wild and specimen plants reveal an ecological haven.

11 CHILWORTH MANOR

Halfpenny Lane, Chilworth, Guildford, GU4 8NN. Mia & Graham Wrigley, www.chilworthmanorsurrey.com. *3½ m SE of Guildford. From centre of Chilworth village turn into Blacksmith Lane. 1st drive on R on Halfpenny Lane.* **Sun 19 May (11-5). Adm £6, chd free. Home-made teas.**

The grounds of the C17 Chilworth Manor, create a wonderful tapestry: a jewel of an C18 terraced walled garden, topiary, herbaceous borders, sculptures, mature trees and stew ponds that date back a 1000 years. A fabulous, peaceful garden for all the family to wander and explore or just to relax and enjoy! Perhaps our many visitors describe it best: "Magical", "a sheer delight', 'elegant and tranquil", "a little piece of heaven", "spiffing!". Garden and Tree Walks at 12 noon, 1.30pm, 2.30pm and 4pm. Tasting of Chilworth Manor Rose Wine throughout the day.

12 2 CHINTHURST LODGE

Wonersh Common, Wonersh, Guildford, GU5 0PR. Mr & Mrs M R Goodridge, 01483 535108, michaelgoodridge@ymail.com. *4m S of Guildford. From A281 at Shalford turn E onto B2128 towards Wonersh. Just after Waverley sign, before village, garden on R, via stable entrance opposite Little Tangley.* **Sun 16, Wed 19 June (11-5). Adm £5, chd free. Home-made teas.** **Visits also by arrangement May to July for groups of 10+.**

One acre yr-round enthusiast's atmospheric garden, divided into rooms. Herbaceous borders, dramatic white garden, specimen trees and shrubs, gravel garden with water feature, small kitchen garden, fruit cage, two wells, ornamental ponds, herb parterre and millennium parterre garden. Some gravel paths, which can be avoided.

13 COLDHARBOUR HOUSE

Coldharbour Lane, Bletchingley, Redhill, RH1 4NA. Mr Tony Elias, 01883 742685, eliastony@hotmail.com. *Coldharbour Lane off Rabies Heath Rd ½ m from A25 at Bletchingley & 0.9m from Tilburstow Hill Rd. Park in field & walk down to house.* **Sat 31 Aug, Sun 1 Sept (1-5). Adm £5, chd free. Home-made teas.** **Visits also by arrangement Apr to Oct for groups of 10+. Wine can be served as an alternative to teas.**

This 1½ acre garden offers breathtaking views to the South Downs. Originally planted in the 1920's, it has since been adapted and enhanced. Several mature trees and shrubs incl a copper beech, a Canadian maple, magnolias, azaleas, rhododendrons, camellias, wisterias, berberis georgeii, vitex agnus-castus, fuschias, hibiscus, potentillas, mahonias, a fig tree and a walnut tree.

14 COVERWOOD LAKES

Peaslake Road, Ewhurst, GU6 7NT. The Metson Family, 01306 731101, farm@coverwoodlakes.co.uk, www.coverwoodlakes.co.uk. *7m SW of Dorking. From A25 follow signs for Peaslake; garden ½ m beyond Peaslake on Ewhurst rd.* **Sun 14, Mon 22 Apr, Sun 5, Sun 12 May, Sun 13 Oct (11-5). Adm £6, chd free. Light refreshments.** **Visits also by arrangement for groups of 20+.**

14 acre landscaped garden in stunning position high in the Surrey Hills with 4 lakes and bog garden. Extensive rhododendrons, azaleas and fine trees. 3½ acre lakeside arboretum. Marked trail through the 180 acre working farm with Hereford cows and calves, sheep and horses, extensive views of the surrounding hills. Light refreshments, incl home produced beef burgers, gourmet coffee and home-made cakes.

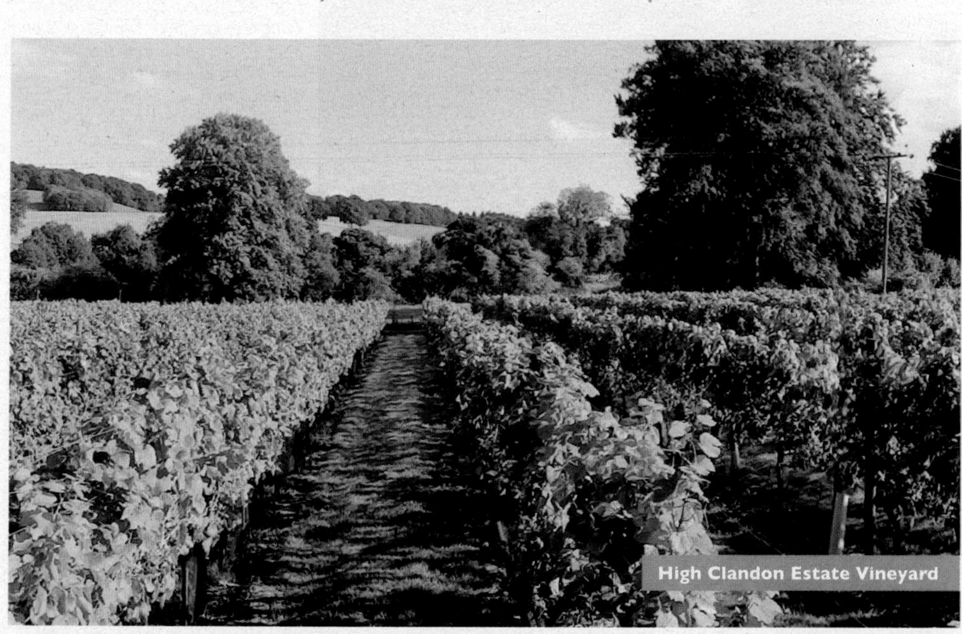

High Clandon Estate Vineyard

15 ◆ DUNSBOROUGH PARK

Ripley, GU23 6AL. Baron & Baroness Sweerts de Landas Wyborgh, 01483 225366, office@sweerts.com, www.dunsboroughpark.com. *6m NE of Guildford. Entrance across Ripley Green via The Milkway past cricket green on R & playground on L, round corner to double brown wooden gates.* **For NGS: Wed 17 Apr (2-6); Sat 8 June (12-4); Sun 8 Sept (2-6). Adm £7, chd free. Home-made teas.** **For other opening times and information, please phone, email or visit garden website.**

6 acres of garden redesigned by Penelope Hobhouse and Rupert Golby – a box parterre showcase for Dahlias. Series of garden rooms; lush herbaceous borders/standard wisteria; 70ft Gingko hedge; Rose Walk; Secret Garden & ancient Mulberry tree; Italian Garden & stone pine; potager; Water Garden with folly bridge. April: Spectacular tulip displays in meadow/Penelope Hobhouse borders/'hot' border/ Peacock Gate. May: peonies and wisteria. June: Roses. Sept: 40+ Dahlia varieties. Produce for sale if available. Cobbled courtyard on entrance. Afterwards gravel paths and grass.

♿ ✽ 🚌 ☕

16 EARLEYWOOD

Hamlash Lane, Frensham, Farnham, GU10 3AT. Mrs Penny Drew. *3m S of Farnham just off A287. From A31 Farnham take A287 to Frensham. R Ist turn passed Edgeborough School. From A3, N on A287 to Frensham. Parking available, More House School Lower Car Park top of Hamlash Lane.* **Sat 27, Sun 28 July (11-5). Adm £5, chd free. Home-made teas.**

Award winning, ½ acre garden with colourful shrubberies, unusual trees and mixed borders throughout. Summer flowering shrubs, particularly hydrangeas and hardy hibiscus, together with herbaceous perennials in colour themed borders and shade loving plants under the trees. Productive greenhouse and small pond. John Negus, well known horticulturalist, gardening writer and broadcaster will be in the garden to answer gardening questions during the weekend. Also demonstration of lavender weaving and craft items for sale. Disabled drop off at front gate, short gravel drive then level lawns throughout.

♿ ✽ ☕

17 FAIRMILE LEA

Portsmouth Road, Cobham, KT11 1BG. Steven Kay. *2m NE of Cobham. On Cobham to Esher rd. Access by lane adjacent to Moleshill House & car park for Fairmile Common woods.* **Mon 27 May (2-5). Combined adm with Moleshill House £6.50, chd free. Home-made teas.**

Large Victorian sunken garden fringed by rose beds and lavender with a pond in the centre. An old acacia tree stands in the midst of the lawn. Interesting planting on a large mound camouflages an old underground air raid shelter. Caged vegetable garden. Formality adjacent to wilderness.

🐕 ☕

18 THE GARTH PLEASURE GROUNDS

Newchapel Road, Lingfield, RH7 6BJ. Mr Sherlock & Mrs Stanley, ab_post@yahoo.com, , www.oldworkhouse.webs.com. *From A22 take B2028 by Mormon Temple to Lingfield. The Garth is on L after 1½m, opp Barge Tiles. Parking: Gun Pit Rd & limited space for disabled at Barge Tiles.* **Sun 5, Sun 12 May (1-5). Adm £5, chd free. Home-made teas.** **Visits also by arrangement May to July for groups of 10 to 30. Please state NGS when booking.**

Mature 9 acre Pleasure Grounds created by Walter Godfrey in 1919 present an idyllic setting surrounding the former parish workhouse refurbished in Edwardian style. The formal gardens, enchanting nuttery, a spinney with many mature trees and a pond attract wildlife. Wonderful bluebells in spring. The woodland gardens and beautiful borders full of colour and fragrance for year round pleasure. Many areas of interest incl pond, woodland garden, formal gardens, spinney w/ large specimen plants incl 500yr old oak, many architectural features designed by Walter H Godfrey.

Westways Farm

© Leigh Clapp

Open 6 May-11 May for Historic Houses Association. We need clarification when booking - HHA or NGS. Partial wheelchair access in woodland, iris and secret gardens.

19 ◆ GATTON PARK

Rocky Lane, Reigate, RH2 0TW. Royal Alexandra & Albert School, 01737 649068, events@gatton-park.org.uk, www.gattonpark.com. *3m NE of Reigate. 5 mins from M25 J8 (A217) or from top of Reigate Hill, over M25 then follow sign to Merstham. Entrance off Rocky Lane accessible from Gatton Bottom or A23 Merstham.* **For NGS: Sun 10 Feb (11-4). Adm £5, chd free. Light refreshments in Gatton Hall. Soup and roll lunch and locally baked cake.** For other opening times and information, please phone, email or visit garden website.

Historic 260-acre estate in the Surrey Hills AONB. 'Capability' Brown parkland with ancient oaks. Discover the Japanese garden, Victorian parterre and breathtaking views over the lake. Seasonal highlights incl displays of snowdrops and aconites in February. Ongoing restoration projects by the Gatton Trust. Bird hide open to see herons nesting. Free guided tours and activities for children.

20 HALL GROVE SCHOOL

London Road (A30), Bagshot, GU19 5HZ. Mr & Mrs A R Graham, www.hallgrove.co.uk. *6m SW of Egham. M3 J3, follow A322 1m until sign for Sunningdale A30, 1m E of Bagshot, opp Longacres garden centre, entrance at footbridge. Ample car parking.* **Sat 11 May (2-4.30). Adm by donation. Home-made teas.**

Formerly a small Georgian country estate, now a co-educational preparatory school. Grade II listed house (not open). Mature parkland with specimen trees. Historical features incl ice house, old walled garden under restoration, lake, woodland walks, rhododendrons and azaleas. Live music at 3pm.

21 ◆ HATCHLANDS PARK

East Clandon, Guildford, GU4 7RT. National Trust, 01483 222482, hatchlands@nationaltrust.org.uk, www.nationaltrust.org.uk/hatchlands-park. *4m E of Guildford. Follow brown signs to Hatchlands Park (NT).* **For NGS: Sun 28 Apr (10-5). Adm £7.50, chd £3.75. Light refreshments.** For other opening times and information, please phone, email or visit garden website.

Garden and park designed by Repton in 1800. Follow one of the park walks to the stunning bluebell wood in spring (2.5km/1.7m round walk over rough and sometimes muddy ground). In autumn enjoy the changing colours on the long walk. Partial wheelchair access to parkland, rough, undulating terrain, grass and gravel paths, dirt tracks, cobbled courtyard. Tramper booking essential.

22 HEATHSIDE

10 Links Green Way, Cobham, KT11 2QH. Miss Margaret Arnott & Mr Terry Bartholomew, 01372 842459, margaret.arnott@ngs.org.uk. *1½m E of Cobham. Through Cobham A245, 4th L after Esso garage into Fairmile Lane. Straight on into Water Lane. Links Green Way 3rd turning on L.* **Visits by arrangement July & Aug for groups of 10+.**

⅓ acre terraced, plants persons garden, designed for yr-round interest. Gorgeous plants all set off by harmonious landscaping. Urns and obelisks aid the display. Two ponds and five water features add tranquil sound. Many topiary shapes add formality. Stunning colour combinations excite. Beautiful Griffin glasshouse housing the exotic. Many inspirational ideas. Situated 5 miles from RHS Wisley.

Your visits help change lives - your generosity has supported unpaid carers through donations to Carers Trust totalling over £3.9 million since 1996

23 HIGH CLANDON ESTATE VINEYARD

High Clandon, East Clandon, GU4 7RP. Mrs Sibylla Tindale, www.highclandon.co.uk. *A3 Wisley junction, L for Ockham/Horsley for 2m to A246. R for Guildford for 2m, then 100yds past landmark Hatchlands NT, turn L into Blakes Lane straight up through gates High Clandon to vineyard entrance. Extensive parking in our woodland area.* **Sun 2 June (11-4). Adm £6, chd free. Home-made teas on lawns of High Clandon Estate Vineyard.**

Vistas, gardens, sculptures, vineyard in beautiful Surrey Hills AONB. 6 acres. Panoramic views to London, water features, Japanese garden, wildflower meadow, truffière, apiary, vineyard with Gold-award vintaged English sparkling wine, High Clandon Cuvée. Twice-over winner Cellar Door of Year 2017-2019. Over 150 sculptures in Vineyard exhibition, percentage of sales to Cherry Trees charity. Atmospheric Glass Barn used for wine tastings and art exhibitions. Sparkling wine tasting available at extra charge of £6 per glass. Also available by the bottle.

24 HILL FARM

Logmore Lane, Westcott, Dorking, RH4 3JY. Helen Thomas. *1m W of Dorking. Parking on Westcott Heath just past Church. Entry to garden just opp.* **Sun 15 Sept (11.30-4.30). Adm £5, chd free. Home-made teas.**

1¾ acre set in the magnificent Surrey Hills landscape. The garden has a wealth of different natural habitats to encourage wildlife, and planting areas which come alive through the different seasons. A wildlife pond, woodland walk, a tapestry of heathers and glorious late summer grasses and perennials. A garden to be enjoyed by all and recently featured in RHS magazine. Everyone welcome. Pond dipping for children. Details of the history of the property and lime kiln are available. Sloping garden, most areas are accessible to wheelchair users. Most paths are grass so care needed if very wet.

D

25 LITTLE COURT HOUSE

Jackass Lane, Tandridge, Oxted, RH8 9NH. Jane and Graham King. *2m from J6 on M25. Head S on A22 from J6, L onto A25 towards Oxted, at mini-r'about R onto Tandridge Ln, 1st R onto Jackass Ln. Do not enter Jackass Ln from A25. Shared parking with The Bothy.* **Sat 15, Sun 16 June (12-5). Adm £5, chd free. Home-made teas in adjacent courtyard. Also open The Bothy.**

¾ acre garden created from scratch in beautiful country setting. Small courtyard style front garden, gate through to charming terraced rear garden with lawn, herbaceous borders, wisteria and rose covered pergola, archway through to wider area of garden and further to kitchen garden with greenhouse, fruit trees, raised cutting and veg beds.

26 LITTLE PRIORY

Sandy Lane, South Nutfield, RH1 4EJ. Liz and Richard Ramsay. *1½m E of Redhill. From Nutfield, on A25, turn into Mid St, following sign for South Nutfield. 1st R into Sandy Lane. Follow signs to parking on R, approx ½m.* **Evening opening Sat 22 June (4-8). Adm £6.50, chd free. Wine. Sun 23 June (11-5). Adm £5, chd free. Also open Macmillan Cancer Support Centre East Surrey Hospital. Light lunches & teas on Sun 23rd.**

Explore a 5 acre country garden where old blends with new. Wander the flower garden; lose yourself in the old orchard meadow; discover cherries and kiwi fruit in the greenhouse of the Victorian kitchen garden; relax beside the large pond, and be inspired by the views. (Also opening Sun with Macmillan Cancer Centre Garden, East Surrey Hospital 10 mins away: an oasis of calm and flowering beauty). Partial wheelchair access.

27 ◆ LOSELEY PARK

Guildford, GU3 1HS. Mr & Mrs A G More-Molyneux, 01483 304440/405112, pa@loseleypark.co.uk, www.loseleypark.co.uk. *4m SW of Guildford. For SatNav please use GU3 1HS Stakescorner Lane Please note: opens May- end of July.* **For NGS: Every Sun to Thur 1 May to 31 July (11-5). Adm £7.50, chd free. Tea.** For other opening times and information, please phone, email or visit garden website.

Delightful 2½ acre walled garden. Award winning rose garden (over 1,000 bushes, mainly old fashioned varieties), extensive herb garden, fruit/flower garden, white garden with fountain, and spectacular organic vegetable garden. Magnificent vine walk, herbaceous borders, moat walk, ancient wisteria and mulberry trees. Refreshments available.

28 LOWER HOUSE

Bowlhead Green, Godalming, GU8 6NW. Mrs Georgina Harvey. *1m from A3 leaving at Thursley/ Bowlhead Green junction. Follow Bowlhead Green signs. Using A286 leave at Brook (6m from Haslemere & 3m from Milford). Follow NGS signs for approx 2m. Field Parking.* **Sun 9 June (11-5). Adm £6, chd free. Home-made teas.**

A mature country garden using trees and shrubs layered above ground cover and low hedges give interest and depth of views by mixing evergreens and deciduous plants with barks, berries and shapes. Roses abound to give colour and a topiary parterre planted with a variety of only white roses gives formality and structure, along with a standard Ballerina rose and Hidcote lavender walk. Also incl a comprehensive kitchen garden of orchard, vegetables and greenhouses. Alternative routes avoiding steps for wheelchairs users, although some paths could be narrow.

Lower House

© Leigh Clapp

29 NEW MACMILLAN CANCER SUPPORT CENTRE

East Surrey Hospital, Canada Avenue, Redhill, RH1 5RH. East Surrey Macmillan Cancer Support Centre. *Front and back garden at the Macmillan Support Centre. Follow signs for East Surrey Hospital. Drive past main hospital entrance; Centre is opp E Entrance. Follow parking signs.* **Sun 23 June (11-4).**

Adm £2.50, chd free. Home-made teas. Also open Little Priory.
The new Macmillan Cancer Support Centre offers holistic support to people affected by cancer. The two small gardens surrounding the state of art Centre provide a peaceful haven to visitors. The thoughtful planting ensures there is interest in the garden throughout the year and offers a therapeutic retreat away from the hospital environment. Also opening with Little Priory, 10 mins away.

30 THE MANOR HOUSE

Three Gates Lane, Haslemere, GU27 2ES. Mr & Mrs Gerard Ralfe. *NE of Haslemere. From Haslemere centre take A286 towards Milford. Turn R after Museum into Three Gates Lane. At T-Junction turn R into Holdfast Lane. Car park on R.* **Sun 23 June (12-5). Adm £5, chd free. Home-made teas.**
Described by Country Life as 'The hanging gardens of Haslemere', The Manor House gardens are in a valley of the Surrey Hills. One of Surrey's inaugural NGS gardens, fine views, 6 acres, water gardens.

31 MOLESHILL HOUSE

The Fairmile, Cobham, KT11 1BG. Penny Snell, pennysnellflowers@btinternet.com, , www.pennysnellflowers.co.uk. *2m NE of Cobham. On A307 Esher to Cobham Rd next to free car park by A3 bridge, at entrance to Waterford Close.* **Mon 27 May (2-5). Combined adm with Fairmile Lea £6.50, chd free. Sun 16 June (2-5). Adm £5, chd free. Sun 8 Sept (2-5). Adm £5, chd free. Also open Randalls Allotments. Visits also by arrangement May to Sept for groups of 10+.**
Romantic garden. Short woodland path leads from dovecote to beehives. Informal planting contrasts with formal topiary box and garlanded cisterns. Colourful courtyard and pots, conservatory, pond with fountain, bog garden. Pleached avenue, circular gravel garden replacing most of the lawn. Gipsy caravan garden, green wall and stumpery. New espaliered crab apples. Chickens. Music at Moleshill House, teas at Fairmile Lea. Garden 5 mins from Claremont Landscape Garden, Painshill Park and Wisley, also adjacent to excellent dog walking woods.

32 MONKS LANTERN

Ruxbury Road, Chertsey, KT16 9NH. Mr & Mrs J Granell, 01932 569578, janicegranell@hotmail.com. *1m NW from Chertsey. M25 J11, signed A320/Woking. R'about 2nd exit A320/Staines, straight over next r'about. L onto Holloway Hill, R Hardwick Lane. ½m, R over motorway bridge, on Almners then Ruxbury Rd.* **Sun 2 June (1-5). Adm £4.50, chd free. Wine. Light refreshments. Visits also by arrangement May to Sept for groups of up to 20.**
A delightful garden with borders arranged with colour in mind: silvers and white, olive trees, nicotiana and senecio blend together. Large rockery and an informal pond. A weeping silver birch leads to the oranges and yellows of a tropical bed, with large bottle brush, hardy palms and fatsia japonica. There is a display of hostas, cytisus battandieri and a selection of grasses in an island bed. Aviary with small finches. Workshop with handmade guitars,and paintings. Pond with ornamental ducks and fish. Music. Wheelchairs are welcome and we reserve a couple of parking spaces at the entrance to the garden, as the gravel drive is not easy for wheelchairs.

33 OAKLEIGH

22 The Hatches, Frimley Green, GU16 6HE. Angela O'Connell. *Frimley Green. 100 metres from village green. On street parking.* **Tue 11 June (1.30-5). Adm £4, chd free. Home-made teas at Wildwood, a neighbouring garden, 100m away.**
A magical long garden with a few surprises. There are plenty of colours and textures with a great variety of different plants. Wander past the long borders and under a rose arch and you will find the garden opens up to two large colour themed mixed beds. The style is naturalistic with just a hint of elegance. Fruit and vegetables grow by the summerhouse and pots adorn the top patio. The garden is mostly level but the side alley is narrow and there are two steps up onto the lawn.

34 NEW OCKHAM MILL

Mill Lane, Ripley, GU23 6QT. Tina, tffou0@gmail.com. *Off Ockham roundabout on A-3 (nr RHS Wisley), down a single-track rd. Parking limited to 5 cars; no coach access. Detailed directions provided at booking.* **Visits by arrangement in June for groups of 5 to 20. Garden may be available in late May. Last available date 21 June. Adm £4, chd free. Home-made teas.**
Working water mill on stream- 2 acre water garden, lake, 5 islands, bridges & gazebo. Herbaceous & shrub borders (gunnera, persicaria) follow natural contours. Summerhouse by perennial bed with roses, grasses, salvia. Mature trees on C13 dam, underplanted with hydrangeas, rhodos & shade-loving plants (hosta, heuchera, ferns). Garden designed by owners and I. Neville. Partial wheelchair access.

35 ODSTOCK

Castle Square, Bletchingley, RH1 4LB. Averil & John Trott, 01883 743100. *3m W of Godstone. Just S of A25 in Bletchingley. At top of village nr Red Lion PH. For ramblers we are on the Greensand Way footpath.* **Visits by arrangement May to Sept for groups of 10+. Adm £5, chd free. Home-made teas available by prior arrangement.**
⅔ acre plantsman's garden maintained by owners and developed for yr-round interest. Special interest in grasses, climbers and dahlias. A no dig, low maintenance vegetable garden. Short gravel drive. Main lawn suitable for wheelchairs but some paths may be too narrow.

36 THE OLD RECTORY

Sandy Lane, Brewer Street, Bletchingley, RH1 4QW. Mr & Mrs A Procter, 01883 743388 or 07515 394506, trudie.y.procter@googlemail.com. *Top of village nr Red Lion PH, turn R into Little Common Lane then R Cross Rd into Sandy Lane. Parking nr house, disabled parking in courtyard.* **Sun 9 June (11-4). Adm £5, chd free. Home-made teas. Visits also by arrangement Apr to Sept for groups of 10 to 30.**

Georgian Manor House (not open). Quintessential Italianate topiary garden, statuary, box parterres, courtyard with columns, water features, antique terracotta pots. Much of the 4 acre garden is the subject of ongoing reclamation. This incl the ancient moat, woodland with fine specimen trees, one of the largest Tulip trees in the country, a rill, sunken and exotic garden. Gravel paths.

37 PRATSHAM GRANGE

Tanhurst Lane, Holmbury St Mary, RH5 6LZ. Alan & Felicity Comber, 01306 621116, alancomber@aol.com. *12m SE of Guildford, 8m SW of Dorking. From A25 take B2126. After 4m turn L into Tanhurst Lane. From A29 take B2126. Before Forest Green turn R on B2126 then 1st R to Tanhurst Lane.* **Sun 18 Aug (1-5). Adm £5, chd free. Home-made teas. Visits also by arrangement June to Aug for groups of 10+.**

5 acre garden overlooked by Holmbury Hill and Leith Hill. Features incl 2 ponds joined by cascading stream, extensive scented rose and blue hydrangea beds. Also herbaceous borders, cutting flower garden, white and yellow beds. South garden replanted over last 4 years. Some steps, slopes and gravel paths. Deep ponds.

38 ◆ RAMSTER

Chiddingfold, Surrey, GU8 4SN. Mr & Mrs Paul Gunn, 01428 654167, office@ramsterhall.com, www.ramsterevents.com. *Ramster is on A283 1½m S of Chiddingfold, large iron gates on R, the entrance is signed from the road.* **For NGS: Fri 10 May (10-5). Adm £7.50, chd free. Light refreshments in the tea house. For other opening times and information, please phone, email or visit garden website.**

A stunning, mature woodland garden set in over 20 acres, famous for its rhododendron and azalea collection and its carpets of bluebells in Spring. Enjoy a peaceful wander down the grass paths and woodland walk, explore the bog garden with its stepping stones, or relax in the tranquil enclosed tennis court garden. The tea house, found by the entrance to the garden, serves sandwiches, cakes and drinks, and is open every day while the garden is open. The teahouse is wheelchair accessible, some paths in the garden are suitable for wheelchairs.

39 NEW RANDALLS ALLOTMENTS

Old Nursery Lane, Cobham, KT11 1BY. Elmbridge Borough Council, www.cobhamgardenclub.com. *Randalls Allotments, Old Nurseries Lane Cobham Surrey. 1.2m from Moleshill House going towards Cobham, off the A307 Esher to Cobham Rd, on the RHS opp Sheargold Pianos & behind Premier Service Station. Entrance is ½ way down.* **Sun 8 Sept (2-5). Adm £3.50, chd free. Home-made teas. Also open Moleshill House.**

Well presented allotments in Cobham, growing unusual vegetables, fruit & salad items from different countries. Guided tours are available by the knowledgeable owners of the plots. Green Fingers Garden Shop on site. If you have ever thought about ' Growing Your Own ' this will inspire you. The Greenfingers Shop will be open for visitors as a special opportunity, offering plants, garden sundries, composts etc. We will also have local honey for sale. There is wheelchair access, but some areas are uneven and will need careful attention.

40 ROE DEER FARM

Portsmouth Road, Godalming, GU7 2JT. Lucy & Justin Gurney. *Godalming/Milford border next to Squire's Garden Centre (GU8 5HL). Please drive through Squire's garden centre car park towards the 'Pick your own'. Turn R & enter through back gate. No entrance from main road.* **Sun 12 May (11-5). Adm £6, chd free. Home-made teas.**

A diverse and varied 17 acre garden incl mature woodlands has been created over the past 10yrs by the present owners. Views through to the parkland setting can be seen from many of the formal and informal areas creating a garden full of interest throughout the seasons. Lawn terraces lead you to naturally planted woodland walks, a kitchen garden, dingly-dell and a pirate ship! Families welcome and children are invited to board the pirate ship and see the ducks and chickens. Please be aware of open water features and swimming pool. Level access for wheelchairs and buggies. Some gravel paths and woodland paths may become difficult to traverse after rain.

41 7 ROSE LANE

Ripley, Woking, GU23 6NE. Mindi McLean, 01483 223200, info@broadwaybarn.com, www.broadwaybarn.com. *Just off Ripley High St on Rose Lane, 3rd house on L next to shoe repair shop.* **Sat 8 June (10-4). Adm £3.50, chd free. Cream teas.**

7 Rose Lane is a small but perfectly formed village centre garden behind an historic listed cottage. It has 3 rooms - a traditional perennial flower garden laid to lawn; a vegetable and fruit garden with Agriframe orchard and a working garden with greenhouse, compost bins and shed. It is a perfect example of how to make the most of a cottage garden. Monthly Ripley Farmers Market and Grapes and Grain Drinks Festival held on 8 June (10am-4pm).

42 SAFFRON GATE

Tickners Heath, Alfold, Cranleigh, GU6 8HU. Mr & Mrs D Gibbison, 01483 200219, clematis@talk21.com. *Between Alfold & Dunsfold. A281 between Guildford & Horsham approx 8m turn at Alfold crossways follow signs for Dunsfold. Do not turn at A281*

T-lights for Dunsfold (wrong road). **Visits by arrangement May to July for groups of 10+. Plenty of parking. Adm £6, chd free. Home-made teas.**
This garden is a plant lovers paradise, colour for most of the year, many unusual plants and a plethora of clematis of all shapes and sizes as featured in the RHS garden magazine. A new bed with scented roses has been added. Arbor with many varieties of climbers. A productive vegetable garden. Garden was subject of a lecture given at Great Dixter. Disabled drop off point.

43 69 SALISBURY GROVE

Mytchett, Camberley, GU16 6DA. Juliette Derwent, 07702 241921, juliette@mycraftedgarden.co.uk, www.mycraftedgarden.co.uk. *At double r'bout in Mytchett, follow signs for Basingstoke Canal Centre, turn L into Salisbury Grove. From Brookwood/ Pirbright, go past Canal Centre, over bridge, turn R before double r'about.* **Sat 10 Aug (12-5). Adm £3, chd free. Home-made teas. Visits also by arrangement June to Sept for groups of up to 20.**
On the Surrey/Hampshire/Berkshire border, My Crafted Garden is a small garden with a difference. Full of garden art/crafts/sculptures and terracotta/glazed pots, there is so much to see! A garden would not be a garden without the plants and My Crafted Garden specialises in acers and grasses, amongst others. There is also a bus shelter (yes really!) and a fish pond. Garden decorations are for sale. Close to Mytchett Canal Centre & Canalside Walks. Partial Wheelchair access possible but not easy due to one small step and gravel paths.

Timber Hill

© Leigh Clapp

The Bothy

© Leigh Clapp

44 NEW ◆ THE SCULPTURE PARK

Tilford Road, Churt, Farnham, GU10 2LH. Eddie Powell, 01428 605453, sian@thesculpturepark.com, www.thesculpturepark.com. *Corner of Jumps and Tilford Rd, Churt. Look out for Bell & The Dragon pub as we are directly opp here. You can use our car park or the pub where refreshments are available.* **For NGS: Tue 12 Feb, Mon 10 June (10-5). Adm £5, chd £3.**

For other opening times and information, please phone, email or visit garden website.

This garden sculpture exhibition is set within an enchanting arboretum and wildlife inhabited water garden. You should set aside between two and four hours for your visit as there are two miles of trail within 10 acres. Our displays evolve and diversify as the seasons pass, with vivid and lush colours of the rhododendrons in May and June to the enchanting frost in the depths of winter. Around ⅓ of The Sculpture Park is accessible to wheelchairs. Disabled toilets are available.

45 SHAMLEY WOOD ESTATE

Woodhill Lane, Shamley Green, Guildford, GU5 0SP. Mrs Claire Merriman, 07595 693132, claire@merriman.co.uk. *5m (15 mins) S of Guildford in village of Shamley Green. Entrance is approx ¼m up Woodhill Lane from centre of Shamley Green.* **Visits by arrangement Mar to Sept for groups of 10+. Adm by donation. Cream teas. Home-made teas incl gluten free options.**

A relative newcomer, this garden is worth visiting just for the setting! Sitting high on the North Downs, the garden enjoys beautiful views of the South Downs and is approached through a 10 acre deer park. Set within approximately 3 acres, there is a large pond and established rose garden. More recent additions incl a stream, fire pits, dry garden, heather, vegetable garden and woodland walk. Most of garden accessible by wheelchair. Large ground level WC but step up to access area.

46 41 SHELVERS WAY

Tadworth, KT20 5QJ. Keith & Elizabeth Lewis, 01737 210707, kandelewis@ntlworld.com. *6m S of Sutton off A217. 1st turning on R after Burgh Heath T-lights heading S on A217. 400yds down Shelvers Way on L.* **Sun 28 Apr, Sun 11 Aug (2-5.30). Adm £5, chd free. Home-made teas. Visits also by arrangement Apr to Aug for groups of 10+.**

Visitors say 'one of the most colourful gardens in Surrey'. In spring, a myriad of small bulbs with specialist daffodils and many pots of colourful tulips. Choice perennials follow, with rhododendrons and azaleas. Cobbles and shingle support grasses and self sown plants with a bubble fountain. Annuals, phlox and herbaceous plants ensure colour well into September. A garden for all seasons.

47 SHIELING

The Warren, Kingswood, Tadworth, KT20 6PQ. Drs Sarah & Robin Wilson, 01737 833370, sarahwilson@doctors.org.uk. *Kingswood Warren Estate. Off A217, gated entrance just before church on S-bound side of dual carriageway after Tadworth r'about . ¾ m walk from Station. Parking on The Warren or by church on A217.* **Sun 21 Apr (2-4). Home-made teas. Sun 26 May (11-4). Adm £5, chd free.** Visits also by arrangement Apr to June for groups of 10+.

One acre garden restored to its original 1920s design. Formal front garden with island beds and shrub border. Unusual large rock garden and mixed borders with collection of beautiful slug free hostas and uncommon perennials. The rest is a woodland garden with acid loving plants and some old and interesting trees and shrubs. Plant list provided for visitors. Lots for children to do with swing, slide, sandpit and Wendy house in woodland glade. Gravel drive and some narrow paths in back garden. Otherwise grass and paths easy for wheelchairs.

48 NEW SLEEPY HOLLOW

Pook Hill, Chiddingfold, Godalming, GU8 4XR. Mrs Susannah Money. *Exit A3 at Milford, follow A283 towards Petworth for 3m, R into Combe Ln. Proceed 1½ miles then R into Prestwick Ln, bear L into Pook Hill.* **Sat 22 June (11-5). Adm £5, chd free. Home-made teas.**

Wander around the formal gardens which incl a knot garden with box hedges, a vegetable garden and greenhouse and a stunning cutting garden. Take a stroll through light woodland along a meandering stream. Incl three paddocks, the garden is just over 15 acres. Enjoy tea on our relaxing terrace looking out over the extensive lawn and summer beds.

49 NEW 2 SLYFIELD FARM COTTAGES

Cobham Road, Stoke D'Abernon, Cobham, KT11 3QH. Mr & Mrs Chrissie & Clive Shaw, 01932 863460, chrissieanneshaw@yahoo.co.uk. *2½M SE of Cobham. Take A245 from Cobham towards Fetcham go over M25 and we are 0.2M (325m) on L up a small farm drive & immediately R.* **Visits by arrangement Apr to June for groups of 5 to 20. Adm £4, chd free. Home-made teas.**

Our tranquil cottage garden has been planted for all year round interest using a tapestry of foliage textures as well as flowers, some of them rare & unusual, lots of them scented. It's planned with nature in mind with plenty of nectar & pollen plants for the bees, butterflies, moths & bats that visit here. Birds also play a big part in the garden with fruit & berry plants for them.

50 SPRINGWOOD HOUSE

85 Petworth Road, Haslemere, GU27 3AX. Mr & Mrs Ian Bateson. *1m E of Haslemere. Entrance to property is almost opp junction of Holdfast Lane with Petworth Rd. Postcode for SatNav brings you approx 300yds W entrance.* **Sat 27, Sun 28 Apr (11-4). Adm £5, chd free. Home-made teas.**

Wooded walkway with large amount of native bluebells at the end of April, and 24 small wooden bridges following spring-fed stream. 3 large ponds with further bridges set in parkland type garden, waterfalls connecting the ponds which contain fish and also three small islands. Two large fields with walkways round the perimeter and an orchard. Bridge walkway is narrow and bare earth, step of 2-3 inches at each bridge. At end of walk there is a steep path, return if necessary.

51 SPURFOLD

Radnor Road, Peaslake, Guildford, GU5 9SZ. Mr & Mrs A Barnes, 01306 730196, spurfold@btinternet.com. *8m SE of Guildford. A25 to Shere then through to Peaslake. Pass Village stores & L up Radnor Rd.* **Sun 19 May (11-5.30). Adm £6, chd free.** Visits also by arrangement May to July for groups of 10+. Refreshments can be negotiated for evening and daytime visits.

2½ acres, large herbaceous and shrub borders, formal pond with Cambodian Buddha head, sunken gravel garden with topiary box and water feature, terraces, beautiful lawns, mature rhododendrons and azaleas, woodland paths, and gazebos. Garden contains a collection of Indian elephants and other objets d'art. Topiary garden created 2010 and new formal lawn area created in 2012.

52 STUART COTTAGE

Ripley Road, East Clandon, GU4 7SF. John & Gayle Leader, 01483 222689, gayle@stuartcottage.com, www.stuartcottage.com. *4m E of Guildford. Off A246 or from A3 through Ripley until r'about, turn L & cont through West Clandon until T-lights, then L onto A246. East Clandon 1st L.* **Visits by arrangement June to Sept for groups of 20+. Home-made teas. Suitable refreshments by arrangement for groups.**

Walk in to this tranquil partly walled ½ acre garden to find an oasis of calm. Beds grouped around the central fountain offer floral continuity through the seasons with soft harmonious planting supported by good structure with topiary, a rose/clematis walk and wisteria walk. Outside the wall is the late border with its vibrant colours and fun planting. A small orchard and decorative organic kitchen garden with central iron structure supporting apple trees.

53 THE THERAPY GARDEN

Manor Fruit Farm, Glaziers Lane, Normandy, Guildford, GU3 2DT. The Centre Manager, www.thetherapygarden.org. *SW of Guildford. Take A323 travelling from Guildford towards Aldershot, turn L into Glaziers Ln in centre of Normandy village opp War Memorial. The Therapy Garden is 200yds on L.* **Sun 5 May, Sun 1 Sept (11-4). Adm £5, chd free. Light refreshments.**

The Therapy Garden is a horticulture and education charity that uses gardening to generate positive change for those living with mental health challenges. This will be our 3rd year of opening and the garden is developing fast. Come and see our new 'Living Shelter' and refreshed sensory garden, together with the ongoing regeneration of our new land. The Therapy Garden is a registered charity that provides social and therapeutic horticulture to different groups in the local community. We are a working garden full of innovation. Light lunches, barbecue, salads and sandwiches, teas, coffees and cakes all available. Paved pathways throughout the garden, many with substantial handrails.

54 TILFORD COTTAGE

Tilford Road, Tilford, GU10 2BX. Mr & Mrs R Burn, 01252 795423 or 07712 142728, rodneyburn@outlook.com, www.tilfordcottagegarden.co.uk. *3m SE of Farnham. From Farnham station along Tilford Rd. Tilford Cottage opp Tilford House. Parking by village green.* **Visits by arrangement Apr to Sept for groups of 10+. Adm £6, chd free.**

Artist's garden designed to surprise, delight and amuse. Formal planting, herb and knot garden. Numerous examples of topiary combine beautifully with the wild flower river walk. Japanese and water gardens, hosta beds, rose, apple and willow arches, treehouse and fairy grotto all continue the playful quality especially enjoyed by children. Local pub within walking distance. Art Exhibition. Holistic Treatment Centre. Partial wheelchair access. Some gravel paths and steep slopes.

55 TIMBER HILL

Chertsey Road, Chobham, GU24 8JF. Nick & Lavinia Sealy, 01932 873875, nicksealy@chobham.net, www.timberhillgarden.co.uk. *4m N of Woking. 2½m E of Chobham & ⅓m E of Fairoaks aerodrome on A319 (N side). 1¼m W of Ottershaw, J11 M25.* **Mon 22 Apr (11-4.30). Adm £6, chd free. Home-made teas/refreshments served in beautiful old Surrey Barn.** Visits also by arrangement Jan to Nov for groups of 10+. Price based on numbers, refreshments, talk/tour. Gardening Groups welcome.

Beautifully kept 15 acre woodland garden. Views to North Downs. A garden for all seasons. Winter- witch hazel, honeysuckle, snowdrop drifts, aconites, crocus, camellia sasanqua. Spring- narcissi, daffodils, more camellias (over 200), camassias, magnolias, cherry blossom. May-bluebells, azaleas, rhododendrons. June- Old roses; Rambling Rector & Kiftsgate. Autumn- glorious colour from maples. Nature & wildlife trails for adults & children. For other information, pop up openings & events, see Timber Hill website or please telephone.

56 ◆ TITSEY PLACE GARDENS

Titsey, Oxted, RH8 0SA. The Trustees of the Titsey Foundation, 01273 715356, titsey@struttandparker.com, www.titsey.org. *3m N of Oxted. A25 between Oxted & Westerham. Follow brown heritage signs to Titsey Estate from A25 at Limpsfield or see website for directions.* **For NGS: Sun 19 May, Sun 16 June, Sun 21 July, Sun 18 Aug (1-5). Adm £5, chd £1.** For other opening times and information, please phone, email or visit garden website.

One of the largest surviving historic estates in Surrey. Magnificent ancestral home and gardens of the Gresham family since 1534. Walled kitchen garden restored early 1990s. Golden Jubilee rose garden. Etruscan summer house adjoining picturesque lakes and fountains. 15 acres of formal and informal gardens in an idyllic setting within the M25. Tearooms with delicious home-made teas served between 12:30-5:00 on open days. Last admissions to gardens at 4pm. Dogs allowed in picnic area, car park and woodland walks. Disabled car park alongside tearooms.

57 ◆ VANN

Hambledon, GU8 4EF. Mrs M Caroe, 01428 683413, vann@caroe.com, www.vanngarden.co.uk. *6m S of Godalming. A283 to Lane End, Hambledon. On NGS days only, follow yellow Vann signs for 2m.*

Woodbury Cottage

© Leigh Clapp

Please park in the field, not in the road. At other times follow the website instructions. **For NGS: Sun 24, Mon 25, Tue 26 Mar, Sun 14, Mon 15, Tue 16, Wed 17 Apr (10-5.30). Mon 6 May (2-6). Tue 7, Wed 8, Thur 9, Fri 10, Sat 11, Sun 12 May, Sun 23 June (10-5.30). Adm £7, chd free. N.B. Home-made teas Mon 6 May only. Group meals/refreshments by arrangement.** For other opening times and information, please phone, email or visit garden website.

5 acre English Heritage registered garden surrounding Tudor and William and Mary house (not open) with Arts and Crafts additions by W D Caröe incl a Bargate stone pergola. At the front, brick paved original cottage garden; to the rear, newly dredged lake, yew walk with rill and Gertrude Jekyll water garden. Snowdrops and hellebores, spring bulbs, spectacular Fritillaria in Feb/March. Island beds, crinkle crankle wall, orchard with wild flowers. Vegetable garden. Gertrude Jekyll water garden and spring bulbs. Also open by appointment for individuals or groups. Water garden paths not suitable for wheelchairs, but many others are. Please ring prior to visit to request disabled parking.

♿ ✿ 🚌 ☕

58 NEW 11 WEST HILL

Sanderstead, CR2 0SB. Rachel and Edward Parsons. *M25, J6, A22, 2.9m r'about 4th exit to Succombs Hill, R to Westhall Rd, at r'about 2nd exit to Limpsfield Rd, r'about 2nd exit on Sanderstead Hill 0.9m a sharp R to West Hill, plse park on West Hill.* **Sat 27, Sun 28 Apr (2-5). Adm £5, chd free. Home-made teas.** Donation to British Hen Welfare Trust.

A hidden gem tucked away... a beautiful country cottage style garden set in ½ acre, designed by Sam Aldridge of Eden Restored. The garden flows through pathways, lawn, vegetable and play areas. Flower beds showcase outstanding tulips, informal seating areas throughout the garden allows you to absorb the wonderful garden, whilst observing our chickens and rabbits!

♿ ☕

59 57 WESTHALL ROAD

Warlingham, CR6 9BG. Robert & Wendy Baston. *3m N of M25. M25, J6, A22 London, at Whyteleafe r'about, take 3rd R, under railway bridge, turn immed R into Westhall Rd.* **Sun 26, Mon 27 May, Sat 15, Sun 16 June (2-5). Adm £4. Home-made teas. Free top ups on tea and coffee.** Donation to Warlingham Methodist Church.

Reward for the sure footed – many steps to 3 levels! Swathes of tulips and alliums. Mature kiwi and grape vines. Mixed borders. Raised vegetable beds. Box, bay, cork oak and yew topiaries. Amphitheatre of potted plants on lower steps. Stunning views of Caterham and Whyteleafe from top garden. Olive tree floating on a circular 'pond' of white flowers. Flint walls, water spilling onto pebbles in secluded lush setting, vegetable borders, summerhouse, large trampoline for children, apple tree with child swing, gravel garden (new).

🐕 ✿ ☕

60 WESTWAYS FARM

Gracious Pond Road, Chobham, GU24 8HH. Paul & Nicky Biddle, 01276 856163, nicolabiddle@rocketmail.com. *4m N of Woking. From Chobham Church proceed over r'about towards Sunningdale, 1st Xrds R into Red Lion Rd to junction with Mincing Lane.* **Sun 12 May (11-5). Adm £4, chd free. Home-made teas.** Visits also by arrangement Apr to June for groups of 10+. Good parking for cars/coach.

6 acre garden surrounded by woodlands planted in 1930s with mature and some rare rhododendrons, azaleas, camellias and magnolias, underplanted with bluebells, lilies and dogwood; extensive lawns and sunken pond garden. Working stables and sandschool. Lovely Queen Anne House (not open) covered with listed *Magnolia grandiflora*. Victorian design glasshouse. New planting round garden room.

♿ 🐕 ✿ 🚌 ☕

61 WILDWOOD

34 The Hatches, Frimley Green, Camberley, GU16 6HE. Annie Keighley, 01252 838660, annie.keighley12@btinternet.com. *3m S of Camberley. M3 J4 follow A325 to Frimley Centre, towards Frimley Green for 1m. Turn R by the green, R into The Hatches for on street parking.* **Visits by arrangement June to Aug for groups of 5 to 20. Adm £4, chd free. Home-made teas.**

Visitors love the hidden surprises in this romantic cottage garden with tumbling roses, topiary and towering magnolia grandiflora. Holly hedges hide a secret haven with wildlife pond, dell, fernery and shaded loggia. Quirky organic potager with raised beds, fruit trees, tadpole nursery, greenhouses and composting areas. Surrey Wildlife Trust winner - Large Private Garden category. Organic/wildlife gardening introduction by owner. Gravel drive and paths. Care needed by pond.

🚌 ☕

62 WOODBURY COTTAGE

Colley Lane, Reigate, RH2 9JJ. Shirley & Bob Stoneley, 01737 244235. *1m W of Reigate. M25 J8, A217 (Reigate). Immed before level crossing turn R into Somers Rd, cont as Manor Rd. At end turn R into Coppice Ln & follow signs to car park. Do not come up Colley Ln from A25.* **Sat 6, Sun 7 July, Sat 7, Sun 8 Sept (1-5). Adm £4, chd free. Home-made teas.** Visits also by arrangement July to Oct for groups of 10 to 20.

Cottage garden just under ¼ acre. It is stepped on a slope, enhanced by its setting under Colley Hill and the North Downs. We grow a colourful diversity of plants incl perennials, annuals and tender ones. A particular feature throughout the garden is the use of groups of pots containing unusual and interesting plants. The garden is colour themed and is still rich and vibrant in September.

✿ ☕

SUSSEX

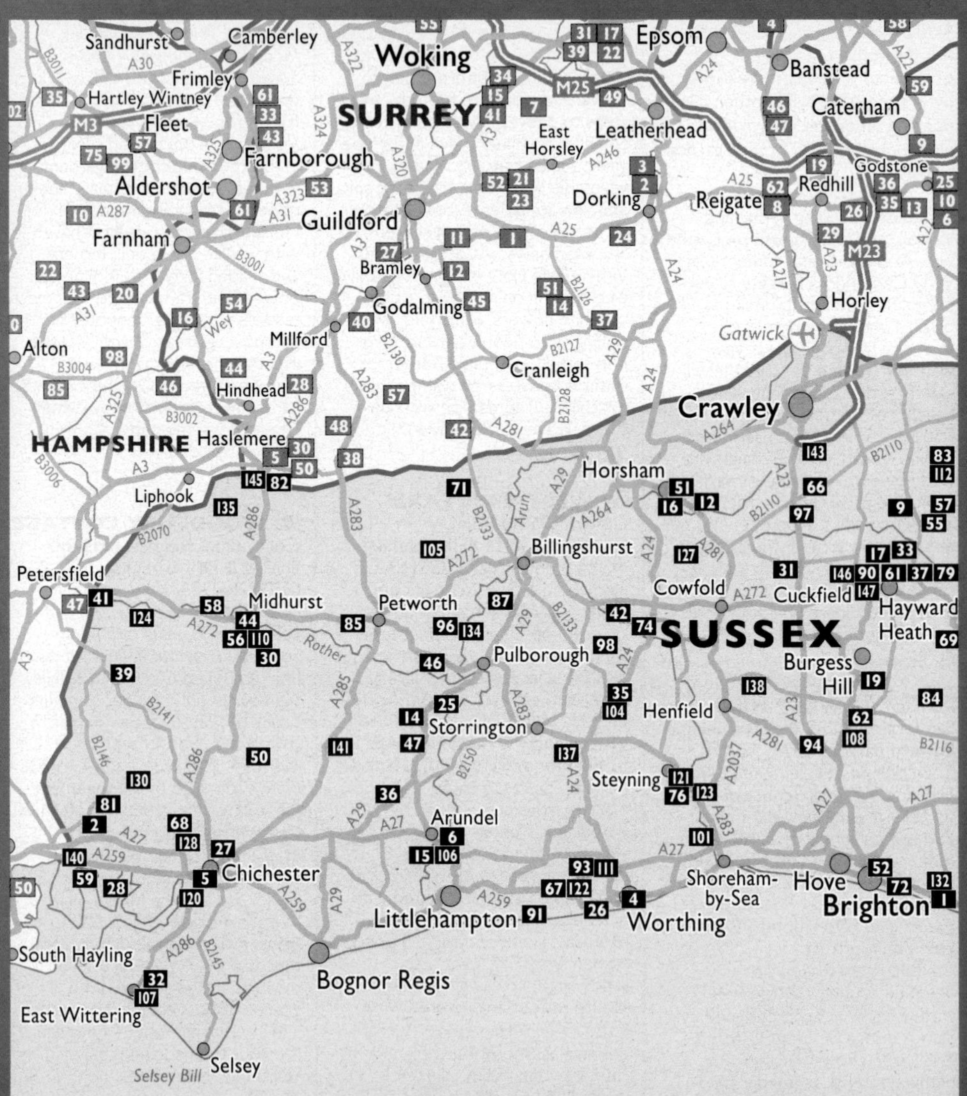
SURREY
HAMPSHIRE
SUSSEX
Woking
Epsom
Banstead
Caterham
Godstone
Redhill
Reigate
Leatherhead
East Horsley
Dorking
Guildford
Farnborough
Aldershot
Farnham
Fleet
Frimley
Camberley
Sandhurst
Hartley Wintney
Bramley
Godalming
Millford
Cranleigh
Horley
Gatwick
Crawley
Alton
Hindhead
Haslemere
Liphook
Horsham
Billingshurst
Cowfold
Cuckfield
Hayward Heath
Burgess Hill
Petersfield
Midhurst
Petworth
Pulborough
Henfield
Storrington
Steyning
Arundel
Chichester
Littlehampton
Worthing
Shoreham-by-Sea
Hove
Brighton
Bognor Regis
South Hayling
East Wittering
Selsey
Selsey Bill
Wey
Rother
Arun

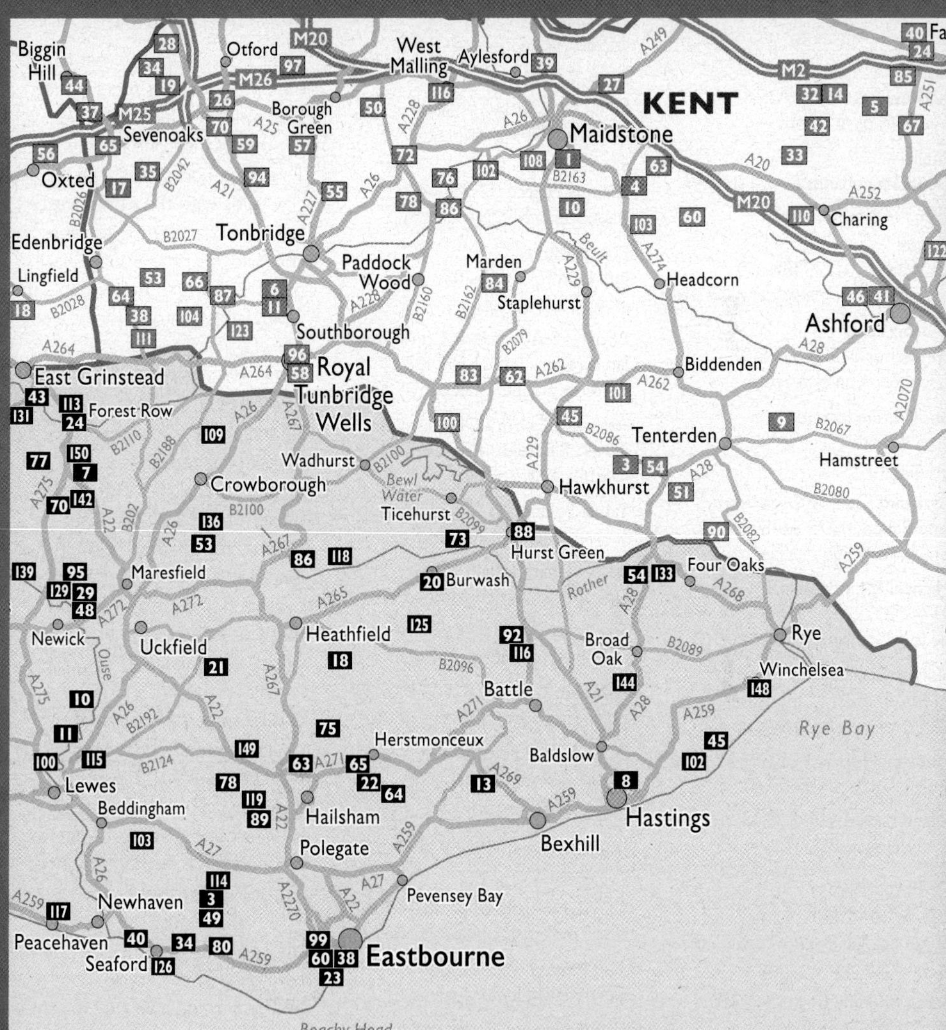
KENT
Biggin Hill
Otford
West Malling
Aylesford
Maidstone
Sevenoaks
Borough Green
Oxted
Charing
Edenbridge
Tonbridge
Paddock Wood
Marden
Lingfield
Staplehurst
Headcorn
Ashford
Southborough
East Grinstead
Royal Tunbridge Wells
Biddenden
Forest Row
Tenterden
Hamstreet
Wadhurst
Crowborough
Bewl Water
Ticehurst
Hawkhurst
Hurst Green
Four Oaks
Maresfield
Burwash
Rother
Newick
Uckfield
Heathfield
Broad Oak
Rye
Ouse
Winchelsea
Battle
Rye Bay
Herstmonceux
Baldslow
Lewes
Beddingham
Hailsham
Hastings
Bexhill
Polegate
Pevensey Bay
Newhaven
Peacehaven
Seaford
Eastbourne
Beachy Head
0 10 kilometres
0 5 miles
© Global Mapping / XYZ Maps

East & Mid Sussex Volunteers

County Organiser, Booklet & Advertising Co-ordinator
Irene Eltringham-Willson
01323 833770
irene.willson@btinternet.com

County Treasurer
Andrew Ratcliffe 01435 873310
anratcliffe@gmail.com

Publicity
Geoff Stonebanks 01323 899296
ngseastsussex@gmail.com

Twitter
Liz Warner 01273 586050
liz@elizabethwarnergardendesign.com

Photographer
Liz Seeber 01323 639478
lizseeber@btinternet.com

Booklet Distributor
Liz Warner
(as above)

Assistant County Organisers
Jane Baker 01273 842805
jane.baker47@btinternet.com

Michael & Linda Belton
01797 252984
belton.northiam@gmail.com

Shirley Carman-Martin
01444 473520
shirleycarmanmartin@gmail.com

Linda Field 01323 720179
lindafield3@gmail.com

Diane Gould 01825 750300
lavenderdgould@gmail.com

Aideen Jones 01323 899452
sweetpeasa52@gmail.com

Susan Laing 01444 892500
splaing@btinternet.com

Sarah Ratcliffe 01435 873310
sallyrat@btinternet.com

Geoff Stonebanks (as above)

Liz Warner (as above)

David Wright 01435 883149
david.wright101@btinternet.com

West Sussex Volunteers

County Organiser
Patty Christie 01730 813323
sussexwestngs@gmail.com

County Treasurer
Liz Collison 01903 719245
liz.collison@ngs.org.uk

Publicity
Philip Duly 01428 661089
philipduly@tiscali.co.uk

Social Media
Claudia Pearce 07985 648216
claudiapearce17@gmail.com

Photographer
Judi Lion 07810 317057
judilion.ngs@gmail.com

Booklet & Advertising Co-ordinator
Ian Gregory 01903 892433
id.gregory@btinternet.com

Assistant County Organisers
Teresa Barttelot 01798 865690
tbarttelot@gmail.com

Sanda Belcher 01428 723259
sandambelcher@gmail.com

Lesley Chamberlain 07950 105966
chamberlain_lesley@hotmail.com

Sue Foley 01243 814452
suefoley@mac.com

Elizabeth Gregory 01903 892433
elizabethgregory1@btinternet.com

Peter & Terri Lefevre 01403 256002
teresalefevre@outlook.com

Judi Lion (as above)

Jane Lywood 07852 684488
jmlywood@aol.com

Carrie McArdle 01403 820272
carrie.mcardle@btinternet.com

Ann Moss 01243 370048
ann.moss8@btinternet.com

Claudia Pearce (as above)

Fiona Phillips 01273 462285
fiona.h.phillips@btinternet.com

Susan Pinder 01403 820430
nasus.rednip@gmail.com

Diane Rose 07789 565094
dirose8@me.com

Sussex is a vast county with two county teams, one covering East and Mid Sussex and the other covering West Sussex.

Over 80 miles from west to east, Sussex spans the southern side of the Weald from the exposed sandstone heights of Ashdown Forest, past the broad clay vales with their heavy yet fertile soils and the imposing chalk ridge of the South Downs National Park, to the equable if windy coastal strip.

Away from the chalk, Sussex is a county with a largely wooded landscape with imposing oaks, narrow hedged lanes and picturesque villages. The county offers much variety and our gardens reflect this. There is something for absolutely everyone and we feel sure that you will enjoy your garden visiting experience - from rolling acres of parkland, country and town gardens, to small courtyards and village trails. See the results of the owner's attempts to cope with the various conditions, discover new plants and talk with the owners about their successes.

Many of our gardens are open by arrangement, so do not be afraid to book a visit or organise a visit with your local gardening or U3A group.

Should you need advice, please e-mail ngseastsussex@gmail.com for anything relating to East and Mid Sussex or sussexwestngs@gmail.com for anything in West Sussex.

OPENING DATES

All entries subject to change. For latest information check **www.ngs.org.uk**

Map locator numbers are shown to the right of each garden name.

February

Snowdrop Festival

By Arrangement
Pembury House 108
5 Whitemans Close 147

Sunday 3rd
◆ Highdown Gardens 67

Sunday 10th
Manor of Dean 85
Sandhill Farm House 124

Sunday 17th
The Old Vicarage 104

Saturday 23rd
NEW Coign Cottage 30

March

Friday 8th
The Garden House 52

Sunday 24th
◆ King John's Lodge 73
Manor of Dean 85
The Old Vicarage 104

Saturday 30th
Butlers Farmhouse 22

Sunday 31st
Butlers Farmhouse 22

April

Saturday 13th
Rymans 120
Sandhill Farm House 124

Sunday 14th
Newtimber Place 94
Penns in the Rocks 109
Sandhill Farm House 124

Tuesday 16th
Bignor Park 14

Friday 19th
◆ Great Dixter House, Gardens & Nurseries 54

Saturday 20th
Winchelsea's Secret Gardens 148

Monday 22nd
The Old Vicarage 104

Wednesday 24th
Fittleworth House 46

Saturday 27th
Banks Farm 10
Down Place 39
The Garden House 52

Sunday 28th
Banks Farm 10
◆ Clinton Lodge 29
Down Place 39
The Garden House 52
Manor of Dean 85
Offham House 100

May

Wednesday 1st
Fittleworth House 46

Thursday 2nd
Fairlight End 45

Saturday 4th
◆ King John's Lodge 73

Sunday 5th
Hammerwood House 58
◆ King John's Lodge 73
Stanley Farm 135

Monday 6th
Copyhold Hollow 33

Wednesday 8th
Fittleworth House 46
◆ Sheffield Park and Garden 129

Friday 10th
96 Ashford Road 8

Saturday 11th
Blue Jays 16
Cookscroft 32
Ham Cottage 57
Holly House 70
Springs Hanger 134
Stone Cross House 136

Sunday 12th
Blue Jays 16
Champs Hill 25
Ham Cottage 57
Hammerwood House 58
Holly House 70
Legsheath Farm 77
Mountfield Court 92
Penns in the Rocks 109
Stone Cross House 136

Tuesday 14th
Bignor Park 14
NEW Riverhall House 116

Wednesday 15th
Balcombe Gardens 9
Cookscroft 32
Fittleworth House 46

Friday 17th
Caxton Manor 24
2 Quarry Cottages 113

Saturday 18th
96 Ashford Road 8
51 Carlisle Road 23
Caxton Manor 24
Harlands Gardens 61
2 Quarry Cottages 113

Sunday 19th
The Beeches 11
51 Carlisle Road 23
Great Lywood Farmhouse 55
Harlands Gardens 61
The Old Vicarage 104
Seaford Gardens 126
Shepherds Cottage 130

Monday 20th
Shepherds Cottage 130

Wednesday 22nd
The Walled Garden at Tilgate Park 143

Thursday 23rd
The Walled Garden at Tilgate Park 143

Friday 24th
Great Lywood Farmhouse 55

Saturday 25th
96 Ashford Road 8
54 Elmleigh 44
◆ The Priest House 112

Sunday 26th
Bexhill-on-Sea Trail 13
54 Elmleigh 44
Foxglove Cottage 51
The Moongate Garden 91
Peelers Retreat 106
Sienna Wood 131
Upwaltham Barns 141

Monday 27th
Copyhold Hollow 33
54 Elmleigh 44
Great Lywood Farmhouse 55
Upwaltham Barns 141

Wednesday 29th
◆ Highdown Gardens 67

June

Saturday 1st
12 Ainsworth Avenue 1
NEW Holford Manor 69
◆ King John's Lodge 73
Lordington House 81
Lowder Mill 82
Skyscape 132
Waterworks & Friends 144

Sunday 2nd
12 Ainsworth Avenue 1
Guillards Oak Gardens 56
◆ King John's Lodge 73
Lordington House 81
Lowder Mill 82
Mill Hall Farm 90
Offham House 100
Skyscape 132

Thursday 6th
Chidmere Gardens 28
NEW Kemp Town Enclosures: South Garden 72

Friday 7th
1 Pest Cottage 110

Saturday 8th
NEW Bushbury 21
Channel View 26
54 Elmleigh 44
Oaklands Farm 98
Old Vicarage 103

Sunday 9th
NEW Bushbury 21
Channel View 26
Dale Park House 36
Dittons End 38
54 Elmleigh 44
Fairlight End 45
Hardwycke 60
NEW Hassocks Village Garden Trail 62
Herstmonceux Parish Trail 65
◆ High Beeches Woodland and Water Garden 66

1 Pest Cottage 110
NEW St Barnabas House Hospice 122
Sennicotts 128
Town Place 139

Monday 10th
Channel View 26
◆ Clinton Lodge 29
Sennicotts 128

Wednesday 12th
Fittleworth House 46
4 Hillside Cottages 68
Rolfs Farm 118

Thursday 13th
Town Place 139

Saturday 15th
Balcombe Gardens 9
Cookscroft 32
Durford Abbey Barn 41
◆ Herstmonceux Castle Gardens and Grounds 64
Mayfield Gardens 86
Rymans 120
Winchelsea's Secret Gardens 148

Sunday 16th
Down Place 39
Durford Abbey Barn 41
Mayfield Gardens 86
Meadow Farm 87
The Old Vicarage 104
33 Peerley Road 107
Ringmer Park 115
Rymans 120
NEW St Barnabas House Hospice 122
Seaford Gardens 126

Monday 17th
Down Place 39
Sennicotts 128

Tuesday 18th
◆ Alfriston Clergy House 3
NEW Quince Cottage 114

Wednesday 19th
Cupani Garden 34
Fittleworth House 46
Rolfs Farm 118

Thursday 20th
Town Place 139

Friday 21st
NEW The Garden House, Crowborough 53
Parsonage Farm 105

Saturday 22nd
54 Elmleigh 44
NEW The Garden House, Crowborough 53
North Hall 95

Sunday 23rd
Ambrose Place Back Gardens 4
Ashdown Park Hotel 7
Bexhill-on-Sea Trail 13
54 Elmleigh 44
NEW Holford Manor 69
North Hall 95
Sedgwick Park House 127
Town Place 139

Monday 24th
◆ Clinton Lodge 29
Sennicotts 128

Tuesday 25th
Driftwood 40

Wednesday 26th
◆ The Apuldram Centre 5

Thursday 27th
◆ The Apuldram Centre 5

Friday 28th
◆ St Mary's House Gardens 123

Saturday 29th
Burwash Hidden Gardens 20
Foxglove Cottage 51
◆ St Mary's House Gardens 123

Sunday 30th
Cupani Garden 34
North Springs 96
Town Place 139
NEW Tuppenny Barn 140

July

Wednesday 3rd
◆ The Apuldram Centre 5

Thursday 4th
◆ The Apuldram Centre 5

Saturday 6th
54 Elmleigh 44
Luctons 83
NEW 49 New Road 93
◆ The Priest House 112

Sunday 7th
NEW Chanterelle 27
54 Elmleigh 44
Hellingly Parish Trail 63
Luctons 83
Town Place 139

Tuesday 9th
Driftwood 40
Luctons 83

Wednesday 10th
◆ The Apuldram Centre 5
Fittleworth House 46
Wych Warren House 150

Thursday 11th
◆ The Apuldram Centre 5

Friday 12th
Cupani Garden 34

Saturday 13th
Fletching Secret Gardens 48

Monday 15th
Cupani Garden 34

Wednesday 17th
◆ The Apuldram Centre 5
Fittleworth House 46
Oaklands Farm 98
The Walled Garden at Tilgate Park 143

Thursday 18th
◆ The Apuldram Centre 5
The Walled Garden at Tilgate Park 143

Saturday 20th
The Beeches 11
54 Elmleigh 44
NEW 49 New Road 93
NEW Rodmell & Peacehaven Trail 117

Sunday 21st
The Beeches 11
East Grinstead Town Gardens 43
54 Elmleigh 44
The Folly 50
4 Hillside Cottages 68
NEW Rodmell & Peacehaven Trail 117

Wednesday 24th
Burgess Hill NGS Gardens 19

Thursday 25th
Cupani Garden 34

Saturday 27th
The Moongate Garden 91

Sunday 28th
The Moongate Garden 91

August

Saturday 3rd
54 Elmleigh 44

Sunday 4th
54 Elmleigh 44

Monday 5th
◆ Clinton Lodge 29

Wednesday 7th
◆ Merriments Gardens 88

Saturday 10th
Butlers Farmhouse 22
Follers Manor 49

Sunday 11th
Butlers Farmhouse 22
Champs Hill 25
Follers Manor 49

Wednesday 14th
Fittleworth House 46

Saturday 17th
Holly House 70
Limekiln Farm 78
NEW 49 New Road 93

Sunday 18th
The Folly 50
Holly House 70
Limekiln Farm 78
Malthouse Farm 84

Wednesday 21st
Fittleworth House 46
Malthouse Farm 84

Saturday 24th
4 Ben's Acre 12

Monday 26th
Durrance Manor 42
Lindfield Jungle 79
The Old Vicarage 104
5 Whitemans Close 147

Saturday 31st
NEW 49 New Road 93

September

Sunday 1st
Jacaranda 71

Thursday 5th
Chidmere Gardens 28

Sunday 8th
Parsonage Farm 105
◆ Sussex Prairies 138

Wednesday 11th
NEW Knightsbridge House 75

Thursday 12th
◆ Sarah Raven's Cutting Garden 125

Saturday 14th
NEW Knightsbridge House 75
Rymans 120
South Grange 133

Sunday 15th
The Moongate Garden 91
Peelers Retreat 106
South Grange 133

Tuesday 17th
Vachery Forest Garden 142

Sunday 22nd
◆ High Beeches Woodland and Water Garden 66
◆ King John's Lodge 73
◆ Nymans 97

Saturday 28th
Sandhill Farm House 124

Sunday 29th
Bignor Park 14
Sandhill Farm House 124

Monday 30th
◆ Borde Hill Garden 17

October

Sunday 6th
Peelers Retreat 106
NEW Tuppenny Barn 140

Sunday 13th
The Old Vicarage 104

By Arrangement

Arrange a personalised garden visit with your club, or group of friends, on a date to suit you. See individual garden entries for full details.

Aldsworth House 2
The Beeches 11
4 Ben's Acre 12
4 Birch Close 15
Blue Jays 16
NEW Boxworth, Rodmell & Peacehaven Trail 117
Brightling Down Farm 18
Butlers Farmhouse 22
Champs Hill 25
Channel View 26
Colwood House 31
Cookscroft 32
Copyhold Hollow 33
NEW Cosy Cottage, Seaford Gardens 126
Cupani Garden 34
Dachs 35
Dale Park House 36
47 Denmans Lane 37
Dittons End 38
Down Place 39
Driftwood 40
Durrance Manor 42
54 Elmleigh 44
Fairlight End 45
Fittleworth House 46
Five Oaks Cottage 47
The Folly 50
Foxglove Cottage 51
The Garden House 52
Garden House, 49 Guillards Oak, Guillards Oak Gardens 56
NEW The Garden House, Crowborough 53
Great Lywood Farmhouse 55
Ham Cottage 57
Harbourside 59
Hardwycke 60
4 Hillside Cottages 68
NEW Holford Manor 69
Holly House 70
Jacaranda 71
Laroche, 43 Coombe Drove 76
Legsheath Farm 77
Lindfield Jungle 79
The Long House 80
Lordington House 81
Luctons 83
Malthouse Farm 84
Manor of Dean 85
Mill Hall Farm 90
The Moongate Garden 91
NEW 49 New Road 93
North Hall 95
Oaklands Farm 98
Ocklynge Manor 99
Old Erringham Cottage 101
The Old Vicarage 104
Parsonage Farm 105
Peelers Retreat 106
33 Peerley Road 107
Pembury House 108
Penns in the Rocks 109
6 Plantation Rise 111
1 Rose Cottage 119
Rymans 120
Saffrons 121
Sandhill Farm House 124
Sedgwick Park House 127
Shepherds Cottage 130
Sienna Wood 131
South Grange 133
Springs Hanger 134
Sullington Old Rectory 137
30 Sycamore Drive, Burgess Hill NGS Gardens 19
NEW Tor Cottage, Rodmell & Peacehaven Trail 117
Town Place 139
46 Westup Farm Cottages, Balcombe Gardens 9
Whitehanger 145
NEW 3 Whitemans Close 146
5 Whitemans Close 147
Winterfield, Balcombe Gardens 9
2 Woodside 149

Great Lywood Farmhouse

© Leigh Clapp

THE GARDENS

1 12 AINSWORTH AVENUE

Ovingdean, Brighton, BN2 7BG. Jane & Chris Curtis. *From Brighton take A259 coast road E, passing Roedean School on L. Take 1st L at the r'about into Greenways & 2nd R into Ainsworth Ave. No 12 on R.* **Sat 1, Sun 2 June (1-5). Combined adm with Skyscape £4, chd free. Tea & cake at Skyscape.**

A small (36ft x 46ft at back and 36ft x 36ft at front) coastal garden begun in 2014 and still developing. Pergola, arches and arbor strategically positioned to provide privacy and a choice of places to sit with different aspects, even a glimpse of the sea. Mixed planting, mostly new but several mature trees, incl a large walnut that creates a focal point.

2 ALDSWORTH HOUSE

Emsworth Common Road, Aldsworth, PO10 8QT. Tom & Sarah Williams, darmady1@btinternet.com. *6m W of Chichester. From Havant follow signs to Stansted House until Emsworth Common Rd, stay on this road until Aldsworth. From Chichester B2178/B2146 follow road through Funtington to Aldsworth.* **Visits by arrangement Feb to May for groups of 10+. Adm £5, chd free. Drinks & biscuits.**

6 acre tranquil garden being adapted to modern needs by plantaholic owners with enthusiastic help from two terriers. Unusual trees, shrubs, perennials, ancient apple trees, magnolias, roses and peonies. Beautiful views over National Park. Carpets of spring bulbs including snowdrops, crocuses, daffodils, bluebells and fritillaries. Two arboretums, two gravel gardens and mixed borders. Short DVD showing the garden and family in the 1930s. Gravel and slope areas a little difficult, but the majority of the garden is flat.

3 ◆ ALFRISTON CLERGY HOUSE

Alfriston, BN26 5TL. National Trust, 01323 871961, alfriston@nationaltrust.org.uk, www.nationaltrust.org.uk/alfriston. *4m NE of Seaford. Just E of B2108, in Alfriston village, adjoining The Tye & St Andrew's Church.* **For NGS: Tue 18 June (10.30-4.30). Adm £6, chd £3. Also open Quince Cottage.** For other opening times and information, please phone, email or visit garden website.

Enjoy the scent of roses; admire the vegetable garden and orchard in a tranquil setting with views across the River Cuckmere. Visit this C14 thatched Wealden hall house, the first building to be acquired by the NT in 1896. Our gardener will be available to talk to you about the garden. Partial wheelchair access.

GROUP OPENING

4 AMBROSE PLACE BACK GARDENS

Richmond Road, Worthing, BN11 1PZ. *Worthing Town Centre. Entry points: Ambrose Villa, corner Portland Rd & Richmond Rd; No 4 Ambrose Place (opp Worthing Library).* **Sun 23 June (10.30-4.30). Combined adm £6, chd free. Home-made teas & cakes at Ambrose Villa & 5 Ambrose Place. Please note all gardens closed 1-2pm.**

3 AMBROSE PLACE
Michael & Claire Victory.

4 AMBROSE PLACE
Graham Heald & Charlotte Tangye.

5 AMBROSE PLACE
Sue Owen.

8 AMBROSE PLACE
Steve & Claire Hughes.

9 AMBROSE PLACE
Anna Irvine.

10 AMBROSE PLACE
Marie Pringle.

11 AMBROSE PLACE
Stephen & Carolyn Bailey.

12 AMBROSE PLACE
Peter May.

13 AMBROSE PLACE
Malcolm & Hilary Leeves.

14 AMBROSE PLACE
Andrew & Kristen Dryden.

AMBROSE VILLA
Mark & Christine Potter.

The highly acclaimed hidden back gardens of Ambrose Place have been described as a horticultural phenomenon and for 2019, 11 gardens will be open for visitors. Behind a classic Regency terrace, itself the architectural jewel of Worthing, the gardens have a rich panoply of styles, plantings and layouts, drawing inspiration from such exotic diversity as Morocco, Provence and the Alhambra, to the more traditional sources of the English cottage and Victorian gardens. All within the typically limited space of a terrace. A variety of imaginative water features add to the charm and attraction for all gardeners and prove that small can be beautiful. Do come and enjoy our special spaces.

5 ◆ THE APULDRAM CENTRE

Appledram Lane South, Apuldram, Chichester, PO20 7PE. 01243 783370, info@apuldram.org, www.apuldram.org. *1m S of A27. Follow A259 Fishbourne & turn into Appledram Lane South.* **For NGS: Weds & Thurs 26, 27 June; 3, 4, 10, 11, 17, 18 July (10-3). Adm £4, chd free. Light refreshments.** For other opening times and information, please phone, email or visit garden website.

Award-winning wildlife and sensory garden. Winding pathway sensitively planted with bee loving plants, all grown from seed, which leads to a tranquil pond and garden. Full of surprises, this garden encompasses many interesting features incl sculptures and other art works created by our adult trainees with learning difficulties. Teas, coffees, light lunches and home-made cakes served in the café until 4pm. Local produce incl home-made apple juice, local honey and a large selection of bedding plants and perennials for sale. Wheelchair access throughout sensory garden. Restricted access to working greenhouses and vegetable plots.

6 ◆ ARUNDEL CASTLE & GARDENS - THE COLLECTOR EARL'S GARDEN

Arundel, BN18 9AB. Arundel Castle Trustees Ltd, 01903 882173, visits@arundelcastle.org, www.arundelcastle.org. *In the centre of Arundel, N of A27.* For opening times and information, please phone, email or visit garden website.

Ancient castle. Family home of the Duke of Norfolk. 40 acres of grounds and gardens. The Collector Earl's Garden with hot subtropical borders and wild flowers. English herbaceous borders. Stumpery. Wild flower garden, two Victorian glasshouses with exotic fruit and vegetables. Walled flower and organic kitchen gardens. C14 Fitzalan Chapel white garden.

7 ASHDOWN PARK HOTEL

Wych Cross, East Grinstead, RH18 5JR. Mr Kevin Sweet, 01342 824988, reservations@ashdownpark.co.uk, www.elitehotels.co.uk. *6m S of East Grinstead. Turn off A22 at Wych Cross T-lights.* **Sun 23 June (1-5). Adm £5, chd free. Light refreshments.**

186 acres of parkland, grounds and gardens surrounding Ashdown Park Hotel. Our Secret Garden is well worth a visit with many new plantings. Large number of deer roam the estate and can often be seen during the day. Enjoy and explore the woodland paths, quiet areas and views. Some gravel paths and uneven ground with steps.

8 96 ASHFORD ROAD

Hastings, TN34 2HZ. Lynda & Andrew Hayler. *From A21 (Sedlescombe Rd N) towards Hastings, take 1st exit on r'about A2101, then 3rd on L (approx 1m).* **Fri 10, Sat 18, Sat 25 May (1-5). Adm £3, chd free.**

Small (100ft x 52ft) Japanese inspired front and back garden. Full of interesting planting with many acers, azaleas and bamboos. Over 100 different hostas, many miniature. Lower garden with greenhouse and raised beds. Also an attractive Japanese Tea House.

St Barnabas House Hospice

GROUP OPENING

9 BALCOMBE GARDENS

Follow B2036 N from Cuckfield for 3m. ¼m N of Balcombe Station, turn L immed before Balcombe Primary School (signed) for ¾m. From N, take J10A from M23 & follow S for 2½m. **Wed 15 May, Sat 15 June (12-5). Combined adm £6, chd free. Light refreshments at Stumlet.**

STUMLET
Oldlands Avenue, RH17 6LW. Max & Nicola Preston Bell.

46 WESTUP FARM COTTAGES
London Road, RH17 6JJ. Chris Cornwell, 01444 811891, chris.westup@btinternet.com. **Visits also by arrangement Apr to Sept. Minimum £10.**

WINTERFIELD
Oldlands Avenue, RH17 6LP. Sue & Sarah Howe, 01444 811380, sarahjhowe_uk@yahoo.co.uk. **Visits also by arrangement May to July for groups of 4+.**

Balcombe is in a designated AONB. Traceable back to the Saxons, the village contains 55 listed buildings incl C15 parish church of St Mary's. Nearby is the famous Ouse Valley Viaduct, ancient woodlands, lake, millpond and reservoir. Within this setting there are three quite different gardens that will appeal to plant lovers. They are full of variety and interest. No 46 is a classic cottage garden with borders, trees, shrubs, vegetables and a new herb garden amidst the countryside of the High Weald. In the village, Winterfield is a country garden packed with uncommon shrubs and trees, and a wildlife area. Whereas nearby Stumlet is a garden changing from being a space for boys to play, to becoming a peaceful area with places to sit and calming views, plus a vegetable garden. Wheelchair access at Winterfield and Stumlet.

10 BANKS FARM
Boast Lane, Barcombe, Lewes, BN8 5DY. Nick & Lucy Addyman. *From Barcombe Cross follow signs to Spithurst & Newick. 1st road on R into Boast Lane towards the Anchor Pub. At sharp bend carry on into Banks Farm.* **Sat 27, Sun 28 Apr (11-5). Adm £5, chd free. Tea.**
9 acre garden set in rural countryside. Extensive lawns and shrub beds merge with the more naturalistic woodland garden set around the lake. An orchard, vegetable garden, ponds and a wide variety of plant species add to an interesting and very tranquil garden. Wheelchair access to the lower part of the garden with sloping grass paths, which may be difficult.

11 THE BEECHES
Church Road, Barcombe, Lewes, BN8 5TS. Sandy Coppen, 01273 401339, sand@thebeechesbarcombe.com, www.thebeechesbarcombe.com. *From Lewes, A26 towards Uckfield for 3m, turn L signed Barcombe. Follow road for 1½m, turn L signed Hamsey & Church. Follow road for approx ½m & parking on the R in a field.* **Sun 19 May, Sat 20, Sun 21 July (2-5). Adm £6, chd free. Home-made teas.** Visits also by arrangement June to Aug for groups of 10 to 20.
C18 walled garden with cut flowers, vegetables, salads and fruit. Separate orchard and rose garden. Herbaceous borders and hot border. There are two ponds, one with a willow house. Extensive lawns and a C18 barn. A hazel walk is being developed and a short woodland walk. An old ditch has been made into a flowing stream with gunnera, ferns, hostas and a few flowers. Wheelchair access without steps, but some ground is a little bumpy.

12 4 BEN'S ACRE
Horsham, RH13 6LW. Pauline Clark, 01403 266912, brian.clark8850@yahoo.co.uk. *E of Horsham. A281 via Cowfold, after Hilliers Garden Centre, turn R by Tesco, St Leonards Rd-Comptons Lane. 5th R Heron Way at r'about, 2nd L Glebe Crescent, 1st L Ben's Acre. From N A264-B2195, 1st exit Comptons Lane.* **Sat 24 Aug (1-5). Adm £4.50, chd free. Home-made teas.** Visits also by arrangement June to Aug for groups of 10 to 30. Garden groups & clubs most welcome.
Described as inspirational, a visual delight on different levels featuring ponds, rockery, summerhouse, arbours, topiary and succulent all interspersed with colourful containers and statuettes. An oasis of colour, texture and harmony with roses, flowering shrubs, perennials and clematis. See what a diverse space can be created on a small scale with surprises at every turn. Seating throughout the garden and a large selection of delicious home-made cakes and tea served from trays in teapots with cosies and fine China. Just 15 mins from NT Nymans and the recently reopened Leonardslee, this is a garden not to be missed! Visit us on YouTube Pauline & Brian's Sussex Garden.

GROUP OPENING

13 BEXHILL-ON-SEA TRAIL
Bexhill & Little Common. Follow individual NGS signs to gardens from main roads. 3 gardens open in May & 4 gardens open in June. Tickets & maps at all gardens. **Sun 26 May (11-4). Combined adm £4, chd free. Sun 23 June (11-5). Combined adm £5, chd free. Home-made teas at Westlands (May) & BLODS Hall (June).**

1 ASHCOMBE DRIVE
TN39 3UJ. Richard & Liz Chown.
Open on Sun 26 May

89 COODEN DRIVE
TN39 3AN. Carole & Ian Woodland.
Open on Sun 26 May

NEW **147 DORSET ROAD**
TN40 2HU. Anita Jones.
Open on Sun 23 June

GARDEN FLAT 1
Elm Tree House, TN40 2FQ. Linda Exley.
Open on Sun 23 June

NEW **WESTLANDS**
36 Collington Avenue, TN39 3NE. Madeleine Gilbart & David Harding.
Open on Sun 26 May

NEW **24 WINSTON DRIVE**
TN39 3RP. Keith & Eileen Osborne.
Open on Sun 23 June

26 WINSTON DRIVE
TN39 3RP. Ron & Clare Brazier.
Open on Sun 23 June

3 gardens will open on 26 May; the spring garden at Westlands (New) with mature shrubs in the front and a large walled rear garden with shrubs, trees, lawn, fruit and vegetables. 89 Cooden Drive is an established plant lover's garden with a wide variety of herbaceous plants, shrubs and trees, many from the southern hemisphere. 1 Ashcombe Drive is a delightful garden full of unusual plants. On the 23 June, 4 gardens will open; 147 Dorset Road (New), a sunny tropical style garden with raised patio and pond. 5 Hastings Road, pretty cottage style with climbing plants and pergola. 24 Winston Drive (New), traditional garden with lawns, herbaceous planting, roses and colour provided in pots, plus an arbour and other seating areas. 26 Winston Drive with sweeping borders, 275 species of shrubs, trees and perennials, topiary balls and structural planting. Home-made teas at Westlands in May only. The tea venue in June is at BLODS Hall, situated in the beautiful public garden at Manor Barn, De La Warr Road, TN40 2JA, which is free to visit and has good parking. Full and partial access to some gardens, but no wheelchair access to 89 Cooden Drive & Westlands.

14 BIGNOR PARK
Pulborough, RH20 1HG. The Mersey Family, www.bignorpark.co.uk. *5m S of Petworth & Pulborough. Well signed from B2138. Nearest villages Sutton, Bignor & West Burton. Approach from the E, directions & map available on website.* **Tue 16 Apr, Tue 14 May, Sun 29 Sept (2-5). Adm £5, chd free. Home-made teas.**

11 acres of peaceful garden to explore with magnificent views of the South Downs. Interesting trees, shrubs, wild flower areas, with swathes of daffodils in spring. The walled flower garden has been replanted with herbaceous borders. Temple, Greek loggia, Zen pond and unusual sculptures. Former home of romantic poet Charlotte Smith, whose sonnets were inspired by Bignor Park. Spectacular Cedars of Lebanon and rare Lucombe Oak. Wheelchair access to shrubbery and croquet lawn, gravel paths in rest of garden and steps in stables quadrangle.

15 4 BIRCH CLOSE

Arundel, BN18 9HN. Elizabeth & Mike Gammon, 01903 882722, e.gammon@talktalk.net. *1m S of Arundel. From A27 & A284 r'about at W end of Arundel take Ford Rd. Immed turn R & follow Torton Hill Rd to Dalloway Rd (straight on), Birch Close on L after bend.* **Visits by arrangement Apr & May for groups of 10 to 30. Adm £3.50, chd free. Light refreshments on request.**

⅓ acre of woodland garden on edge of Arundel. Wide range of mature trees and shrubs with many hardy perennials. Emphasis on extensive selection of spring flowers and clematis (over 100 incl 12 montana). All in a tranquil setting with secluded corners, meandering paths and plenty of seating. Partial wheelchair access to approx half of garden.

16 BLUE JAYS

Chesworth Close, Horsham, RH13 5AL. Stella & Mike Schofield, 01403 251065. *5 mins walk SE of St Mary's Church, Horsham. From A281 (East St) L down Denne Rd, L to Chesworth Lane, R to Chesworth Close. Garden at end of close. 4 disabled spaces, other parking in local streets & Denne Rd car park.* **Sat 11, Sun 12 May (12.30-5). Adm £4, chd free. Home-made teas.** Visits also by arrangement Apr to July for groups of 10+. Refreshments on request. Donation to The Badger Trust.

Wooded 1 acre garden with rhododendrons, camellias and azaleas. Candelabra primulas and ferns edge the River Arun. Primroses and spring bulbs border woodland path and stream. Cordylines, gunneras, flower beds, a pond, a fountain and formal rose garden set in open lawns. Arch leads to a vegetable plot and orchard bounded by the river. Large WW2 pill box in the orchard; visits inside with short talk are available. Wheelchair access to most areas.

17 ◆ BORDE HILL GARDEN

Borde Hill Lane, Haywards Heath, RH16 1XP. Borde Hill Garden Ltd, 01444 450326, info@bordehill.co.uk, www.bordehill.co.uk. *1½m N of Haywards Heath. 20 mins N of Brighton, or S of Gatwick on A23 taking exit 10a via Balcombe.* **For NGS: Mon 30 Sept (10-5). Adm £9.50, chd £6.35. Light refreshments.** For other opening times and information, please phone, email or visit garden website.

Rare plants and stunning landscapes make Borde Hill Garden the perfect day out for horticultural enthusiasts, families and those who love beautiful countryside. Enjoy tranquil outdoor rooms, woodland walks, playgrounds, picnic areas, home-cooked food and events throughout the season. Wheelchair access to 17 acres of formal garden. Dogs welcome on leads.

18 BRIGHTLING DOWN FARM

Observatory Road, Dallington, TN21 9LN. Val & Pete Stephens, 07770 807060 / 01424 838888, valstephens@icloud.com. *1m from Woods Corner. At Swan Pub at Woods Corner, take road opp signed Brightling. Take 1st L signed Burwash & almost immed, turn into 1st driveway on L.* **Visits by arrangement for groups of 10 to 30, on Thurs 13, Fri 14 June & Thurs 19, Fri 20 Sept only. Adm £10, chd free. Home-made teas included.**

The garden has several different areas incl a Zen garden, water garden, walled vegetable garden with two large greenhouses, herb garden, herbaceous borders and a new woodland walk. The garden makes clever use of grasses and is set amongst woodland with stunning countryside views. Winner of the Society of Garden Designers award. Most areas can be accessed with the use of temporary ramps.

GROUP OPENING

19 BURGESS HILL NGS GARDENS

10m N of Brighton, off B2113. Good walkers can reach 20 The Ridings first by walking from train station. Bus stops in area. Tickets & maps from any garden. **Wed 24 July (1-5). Combined adm £6, chd free. Home-made teas at 14 Barnside Avenue.**

14 BARNSIDE AVENUE
RH15 0JU. Brian & Sue Knight.

NEW **20 THE RIDINGS**
RH15 0LW. Rachelle & Malcolm Russell.

9 SYCAMORE DRIVE
RH15 0GG. Peter Machin & Martin Savage.

30 SYCAMORE DRIVE
RH15 0GH. John Smith & Kieran O'Regan, 01444 871888, jsarastroo@aol.com.
Visits also by arrangement June to Sept for groups of 5 to 10.

59 SYCAMORE DRIVE
RH15 0GG. Steve & Debby Gill.

This diverse group of five gardens is a mixture of established and small new gardens. Three of the group are a great example of what can be achieved over a 10 yr period from a blank canvas in a new development (Sycamore Drive), while close by is 14 Barnside Avenue, a wisteria clad house (pruning advice given) with a more mature garden with family lawn and borders, likewise 20 The Ridings is a mature garden with productive outside grapevine (pruning advice given). Many useful ideas for people living in new build properties with small gardens and heavy clay soil. Partial wheelchair access to some gardens.

GROUP OPENING

20 BURWASH HIDDEN GARDENS

Burwash, TN19 7EN. www.burwashopengardens.org.uk. *In Burwash village on A265. Burwash is 3m W of junction with A21 at Hurst Green; 6m E of Heathfield. Follow signs for parking from High St. Tickets & maps at all gardens.* **Sat 29 June (2-5.30). Combined adm £6, chd free. Home-made teas in Swan Meadow Sports Pavilion, Ham Lane.**

BOWZELL
Shirley Viney.

BRAMDEAN
Fiona Barkley.

LINDEN COTTAGE
Philip & Anne Cutler.

LONGSTAFFES
Dorothy & Paul Bysouth.

MANDALAY
David & Vivienne Wright.

MOUNT HOUSE
Richard & Lynda Maude-Roxby.

3 PROSPECT COTTAGES
Mary Clarke.

Come and have your photo taken with Rudyard Kipling! Well obviously not the author himself, but you can join our most famous resident for a selfie on his new life size bronze sculpture in the centre of the village. Admire our collection of hidden gardens, many behind centuries old period houses, here in the heart of the High Weald AONB. The seven gardens vary in design, style and planting, and range in size from small cottage gardens to three acres. Located on and around the picturesque High Street, all are within a level and easy walking distance of each other. Restricted wheelchair access to rear gardens as mainly terraced properties.

21 NEW BUSHBURY

Bushbury Lane, Blackboys, Uckfield, TN22 5JE. Scott McLean & Victoria Brocklebank. *4m SE of Uckfield. From B2192 turn S, 1m S of the Blackboys Inn turn L onto Bushbury Lane. After RH-bend parking in field on the L, past house.* **Sat 8, Sun 9 June (1-5). Adm £5, chd free. Home-made teas.**
3 acre rural garden created from scratch by the owners over the past 6 yrs. This is a young garden, laid out in a formal style with garden rooms, many newly planted or still being developed. Highlights incl formal rose gardens, herbaceous borders, vegetable garden, orchard, pond and mature trees.

22 BUTLERS FARMHOUSE

Butlers Lane, Herstmonceux, BN27 1QH. Irene Eltringham-Willson, 01323 833770, irene.willson@btinternet.com, www.butlersfarmhouse.co.uk. *3m E of Hailsham. Take A271 from Hailsham, go through village of Herstmonceux, turn R signed Church Rd then approx 1m turn R. Do not use SatNav!* **Sat 30, Sun 31 Mar (2-5). Adm £3.50, chd free. Sat 10, Sun 11 Aug (2-5). Adm £6, chd free. Home-made teas. Jazz in the garden in Aug. Visits also by arrangement Mar to Oct. Refreshments on request.**
Lovely rural setting for 1 acre garden surrounding C16 farmhouse with views of South Downs. Pretty in spring with daffodils, hellebores and primroses. Mainly herbaceous with rainbow border, small pond and Cornish inspired beach corners. Restored to former glory, as shown in old photographs, but with a few quirky twists such as a poison garden, secret jungle garden and some naturalistic areas. Relax and listen to live jazz in the garden in Aug. Most of garden accessible by wheelchair.

23 51 CARLISLE ROAD

Eastbourne, BN21 4JR. Mr & Mrs N Fraser-Gausden. *200yds inland from seafront (Wish Tower), close to Congress Theatre.* **Sat 18, Sun 19 May (2-5). Adm £3, chd free. Home-made teas.**
Small walled, s-facing garden (82ft x 80ft) with mixed beds intersected by stone paths and incl small pool. Profuse and diverse planting. Wide selection of shrubs, old roses, herbaceous plants and perennials mingle with specimen trees and climbers. Constantly revised planting to maintain the magical and secluded atmosphere.

24 CAXTON MANOR

Wall Hill, Forest Row, RH18 5EG. Adele & Jules Speelman. *1m N of Forest Row, 2m S of East Grinstead. From A22 take turning to Ashurstwood, entrance on L after ⅓m, or 1m on R from N.* **Fri 17, Sat 18 May (2-5). Adm £5, chd free. Home-made teas. Donation to St Catherine's Hospice, Crawley.**
Delightful 5 acre Japanese inspired gardens planted with mature rhododendrons, azaleas and acers surrounding large pond with boathouse, massive rockery and waterfall, beneath the home of the late Sir Archibald McIndoe (house not open). Japanese tea house and Japanese style courtyard. **Also open 2 Quarry Cottages (separate admission).**

25 CHAMPS HILL

Waltham Park Road, Coldwaltham, Pulborough, RH20 1LY. Mr & Mrs David Bowerman, 01798 831205, mary@thebct.org.uk, www.thebct.org.uk. *3m S of Pulborough. On A29 turn R to Fittleworth into Waltham Park Rd, garden 400 metres on R.* **Sun 12 May, Sun 11 Aug (2-5). Adm £5, chd free. Tea. Visits also by arrangement Apr to Sept for groups of 10+.**
A natural landscape, the garden has been developed around three disused sand quarries, with far-reaching views across the Amberley Wildbrooks to the South Downs. A woodland walk in spring, leads you past beautiful sculptures against a backdrop of colourful rhododendrons and azaleas. In summer the garden is a colourful tapestry of heathers, which are renowned for their abundance and variety.

26 CHANNEL VIEW

52 Brook Barn Way, Goring-by-Sea, Worthing, BN12 4DW. Jennie & Trevor Rollings, 01903 242431, tjrollings@gmail.com. *1m W of Worthing, near seafront. Turn S off A259 into Parklands Ave, L at T-junction into Alinora Crescent. Brook Barn Way is immed on L.* **Sat 8, Sun 9, Mon 10 June (2-5). Adm £5, chd free. Home-made teas.** Visits also by arrangement May & June for groups of 10 to 30.

A seaside Tudor cottage garden, cleverly blending the traditional, antipodean and subtropical with dense planting, secret rooms and intriguing sight-lines. Sunny patios, insect friendly flowers and unusual structures supporting over a hundred roses, clematis and other climbers, as well as brick and flint paths inlaid with thundereggs, radiating from a wildlife pond in the heart of the garden. Numerous planted hanging baskets and containers, sinuous beds packed with flowers and foliage, with underplanting to ensure a 3D experience. Lots of unusual plants for sale. Limited wheelchair access.

27 NEW CHANTERELLE

The Lane, Chichester, PO19 5PY. Mrs Julia Farwell. *Turn off the A286 into The Avenue, then turn R into The Lane. House on corner of The Avenue & The Lane.* **Sun 7 July (2-5). Adm £4.50, chd free. Home-made teas.**

Mature, well maintained town garden cleverly designed in different areas for yr-round interest. Developed by the present owner over a period of 16 yrs. Wrap around garden with ornamental shrubs, with a wide variety of interesting species. Perennial planting, rhododendrons, azaleas, actinidia, crinodendron, camellias, large magnolia tree and a water feature.

Your visits help change lives - your generosity helps Marie Curie fund nurses to care for people night and day in their homes, with donations of more than £8.8 million

47 Denmans Lane

© Leigh Clapp

Durrance Manor

© Judi Lion

28 CHIDMERE GARDENS

Chidham Lane, Chidham, Chichester, PO18 8TD. Jackie & David Russell, www.chidmerefarm.com. *6m W of Chichester on A259. Turn into Chidham Lane, continue until a RH-bend, followed by a 2nd RH-bend. Chidmere Gardens is on the L immed after the large village pond.* **Thur 6 June (2-5); Thur 5 Sept (2-4.30). Adm £5, chd free. Home-made teas.**

Wisteria clad C15 house (not open) surrounded by yew and hornbeam hedges situated next to Chidmere pond; a natural wildlife preserve approx 5 acres. Garden incl formal rose garden, well stocked herbaceous borders, contemporary borders and 8 acres of orchards with wide selection of heritage and modern varieties of apples, pears and plums. Partial wheelchair access.

29 ◆ CLINTON LODGE

Fletching, TN22 3ST. Lady Collum, 01825 722952, garden@clintonlodge.com, www.clintonlodgegardens.co.uk. *4m NW of Uckfield. Clinton Lodge is situated in Fletching High St, N of Rose & Crown Pub. Off road parking provided. It is important visitors do not park in street. Parking available from 1pm.* **For NGS: Sun 28 Apr, Mon 10, Mon 24 June, Mon 5 Aug (2-5.30). Adm £6, chd free. Home-made teas.** For other opening times and information, please phone, email or visit garden website. Donation to local charities.

6 acre formal and romantic garden overlooking parkland with old roses, William Pye water feature, double white and blue herbaceous borders, yew hedges, pleached lime walks, copy of C17 scented herb garden, Medieval style potager, vine and rose allée, wild flower garden. Canal garden, small knot garden, shady glade and orchard. Caroline and Georgian house (not open).

30 NEW COIGN COTTAGE

Church Road, West Lavington, Midhurst, GU29 0EH. Stephanie Jenkins. *From Spreadeagle Hotel, passing pond on R, turn L into Selham Rd. Church Rd is the 1st turning on R. Coign Cottage is 3rd house on L. Limited parking at Coign Cottage & no parking on Church Rd.*

Sat 23 Feb (10.30-4). Adm £4, chd free. Light refreshments. Due to limited parking, pre-booking essential, please phone 07766 407524.
Snowdrops and hellebores should be at their best at the end of February, depending of course on the vagaries of the (British) weather. It is a country garden, just over 1 acre, which has been created and developed over the last 9 yrs. Tidy but not manicured and there are always several projects underway, most recently a new patio installed at the rear of the house.

31 COLWOOD HOUSE

Cuckfield Lane, Warninglid, RH17 5SP. Mrs Rosy Brenan, 01444 461352. *6m W of Haywards Heath, 6m SE of Horsham. Entrance on B2115 (Cuckfield Lane). From E, N & S, turn W off A23 towards Warninglid for ¾m. From W come through Warninglid village.* **Visits by arrangement Apr to Sept for groups of 5+. Adm £5. Tea.** Donation to Seaforth Hall.
12 acres of garden with mature and specimen trees from the late 1800s, lawns and woodland edge. Formal parterre, rose and herb gardens. 100ft terrace and herbaceous border overlooking flower rimmed croquet lawn. Cut turf labyrinth and forsythia tunnel. Water features, statues and gazebos. Pets' cemetery. Giant chessboard. Lake with island and temple. The garden has gravel paths and some slopes.

32 COOKSCROFT

Bookers Lane, Earnley, Chichester, PO20 7JG. Mr & Mrs J Williams, 01243 513671, williams.cookscroft330@btinternet.com, www.cookscroft.co.uk. *6m S of Chichester. At end of Birdham Straight A286 from Chichester, take L fork to East Wittering B2198. 1m before sharp bend, turn L into Bookers Lane, 2nd house on L. Parking available.* **Sat 11, Wed 15 May (11-4). Light refreshments. Evening opening Sat 15 June (5-9). Wine. Adm £5, chd free.** Visits also by arrangement May to July for groups of up to 30.
A garden for all seasons which delights the visitor. Started in 1988, it features cottage, woodland and Japanese style gardens, water features and borders of perennials with a particular emphasis on southern hemisphere plants. Unusual plants for the plantsman to enjoy, many grown from seed. The differing styles of the garden flow together making it easy to wander anywhere. The garden has grass paths and unfenced ponds.

33 COPYHOLD HOLLOW

Copyhold Lane, Borde Hill, Haywards Heath, RH16 1XU. Frances Druce, 01444 413265, ngs@copyholdhollow.co.uk, www.copyholdhollow.co.uk. *2m N of Haywards Heath. Follow signs for Borde Hill Gardens. With Borde Hill Gardens on L over brow of hill, take 1st R signed Ardingly. Garden ½m. If the drive is full, please park in the lane.* **Mon 6, Mon 27 May (12-4). Adm £4, chd free. Home-made teas.** Visits also by arrangement May & June.
A different NGS experience in 2 n-facing acres. The cottage garden surrounding C16 house (not open) gives way to steep slopes up to woodland garden, a challenge to both visitor and gardener. Species primulas a particular interest of the owner. Stumpery, dizzy crow's nest viewing platform. Not a manicured plot, but with a relaxed attitude to gardening, an inspiration to visitors. Partial wheelchair access.

34 CUPANI GARDEN

8 Sandgate Close, Seaford, BN25 3LL. Dr D Jones & Ms A Jones OBE, 01323 899452, sweetpeasa52@gmail.com, www.cupanigarden.com. *From A259 follow signs to Alfriston, E of Seaford. Turn R into Hillside Ave, L into Hastings Ave, R into Deal Close & R into Sandgate Close. Bus route 12A from Brighton & Eastbourne to Hillside Ave. A walk down narrow pathway (twitten) & garden on R. No parking in Sandgate Close.* **Wed 19, Sun 30 June, Fri 12, Mon 15, Thur 25 July (12-5). Adm £4.50, chd free. Light refreshments.** Visits also by arrangement May to July for groups of 5 to 20. Talk by owners & handout. Various refreshment options.
Cupani is a tranquil haven with a delightful mix of trees, shrubs and perennial borders in different themed beds. Courtyard garden, gazebo, summerhouse, water features, sweet pea obelisks, huge range of plants. Plenty of places to sit and enjoy, either in the shade or under cover. New projects underway to provide variety for visitors. See TripAdvisor reviews. Delicious afternoon tea and a good range of lunches, see menu on our website. Phone in advance to pre-book lunch and/or any dietary requirements. Plants, jams, and china for sale. Although mostly flat, the garden is not suitable for wheelchairs. Steps to courtyard and steep steps to WC.

35 DACHS

Spear Hill, Ashington, RH20 3BA. Bruce Wallace, 01903 892466, wallacebuk@aol.com. *Approx 6m N of Worthing. From A24 at Ashington onto B2133 Billingshurst Rd, R into Spear Hill. We are the 1st house, garden runs along Billingshurst Rd. Do not go up Spear Hill as we are at the bottom.* **Visits by arrangement Apr to Aug for groups of 10+. Adm £4.50, chd free.**
A waterlogged field turned into a beautiful garden of about 2 acres incl white garden, bog area and stream. Over 250 varieties of daffodil and narcissus, with more added each year. AGM varieties for sale. Free gifts for children to encourage them to grow things and a number of plants for sale at economical prices. Disabled parking by house on tarmac drive and access to the rear patio by ramp. No steps.

Your visits help change lives – we are the largest single funder of the Queen's Nursing Institute

36 DALE PARK HOUSE

Madehurst, Arundel, BN18 0NP. Robert & Jane Green, 01243 814260, robertgreen@farming.co.uk. *4m W of Arundel. Take A27 E from Chichester or W from Arundel, then A29 (London) for 2m, turn L to Madehurst & follow red arrows.* **Sun 9 June (2-5). Adm £4.50, chd free. Home-made teas.** Visits also by arrangement May to July for groups of 10+.

Set in parkland, enjoying magnificent views to the sea. Come and relax in the large walled garden which features an impressive 200ft herbaceous border. There is also a sunken gravel garden, mixed borders, a small rose garden, dreamy rose and clematis arches, interesting collection of hostas, foliage plants and shrubs, an orchard and kitchen garden. Wheelchair access not easy.

37 47 DENMANS LANE

Lindfield, Haywards Heath, RH16 2JN. Sue & Jim Stockwell, 01444 459363, jamesastockwell@aol.com, www.lindfield-gardens.co.uk/47denmans-lane. *Approx 1½m NE of Haywards Heath town centre. From Haywards Heath train station follow B2028 signed Lindfield & Ardingly for 1m. At T-lights turn L into Hickmans Lane, then after 100 metres take 1st R into Denmans Lane.* **Visits by arrangement Mar to Sept for groups of 10+. Adm £8, chd free. Home-made teas incl. Wine & canapés option for pm visits only. Visit can be combined with Lindfield Jungle.**

This beautiful and tranquil 1 acre garden was described by Sussex Life as a 'Garden Where Plants Star'. Created by the owners, Sue and Jim Stockwell, over the past 20 yrs it is planted for interest throughout the yr. Spring bulbs are followed by azaleas, rhododendrons, alliums, roses and herbaceous perennials. The garden also incl ponds, vegetable and fruit gardens. NB: Deep water. Most of the garden accessible by wheelchair, but some steep slopes.

38 DITTONS END

Southfields Road, Eastbourne, BN21 1BZ. Mrs Frances Hodkinson, 01323 647163. *Town centre, ⅓m from train station. Off A259 in Southfields Rd. House directly opp Dittons Rd. 3 doors from NGS open garden Hardwycke.* **Sun 9 June (11-5). Combined adm with Hardwycke £5, chd free. Home-made teas at Hardwycke.** Visits also by arrangement May to Sept for groups of 10 to 20.

Lovely well maintained, small town garden. At the back, a very pretty garden (35ft x 20ft) with small lawn area, patio surrounded by a selection of pots and packed borders with lots of colour. In the front a compact lawn with colourful borders (25ft x 18ft).

39 DOWN PLACE

South Harting, Petersfield, GU31 5PN. Mr & Mrs D M Thistleton-Smith, 01730 825374, selina@downplace.co.uk. *1m SE of South Harting. B2141 to Chichester, turn L down unmarked lane below top of hill.* **Sat 27, Sun 28 Apr, Sun 16, Mon 17 June (2-6). Adm £4.50, chd free. Home-made & cream teas.** Visits also by arrangement Apr to July for groups of 10+. Donation to The Friends of Harting Church.

7 acre hillside, chalk garden on the north side of the South Downs with fine views of surrounding countryside. Extensive herbaceous, shrub and rose borders on different levels merging into natural wild flower meadow renowned for its collection of native orchids. Fully stocked vegetable garden and greenhouses. Spring flowers and blossom. Substantial top terrace and borders accessible to wheelchairs.

40 DRIFTWOOD

4 Marine Drive, Bishopstone, Seaford, BN25 2RS. Geoff Stonebanks & Mark Glassman, 01323 899296, geoffstonebanks@gmail.com, www.driftwoodbysea.co.uk. *A259 between Seaford & Newhaven. Turn L into Marine Drive from Bishopstone Rd, 2nd on R. Only park same side as house please, not on bend beyond the drive.* **Tue 25 June, Tue 9 July (11-5). Adm £6, chd free. Light refreshments.** Visits also by arrangement June & July for groups of up to 20. Tour and talk included. Refreshments can be ordered.

A small garden by the sea, full of character, with inspired planting and design, said Monty Don in his introduction to Driftwood on BBC 2 Gardeners' World. Sunday Telegraph said Geoff's enthusiasm is catching, he and his amazing garden deserve every visitor that makes their way up his enchanting garden path. Coast Magazine said Geoff's baking is almost as big a draw as his inventive plantsmanship. A real must see garden say many TripAdvisor visitors - awarded

Town Place

Certificate of Excellence 2018 for over 88, 5-star reviews. Large selection of home-made cakes and savoury items available, all served on vintage china, on trays, in the garden. Steep drive, narrow paths and many levels with steps. Help readily available on-site or call ahead before visit.

41 DURFORD ABBEY BARN

Petersfield, GU31 5AU. Mr & Mrs Lund. *3m from Petersfield. Situated on the S side of A272 between Petersfield & Rogate, 1m from the junction with B2072. Limited parking by house.* **Sat 15, Sun 16 June (2-5.30). Adm £4, chd free. Home-made teas.**
With lovely views across open countryside to the South Downs, this 1 acre garden is set around a converted barn in the National Park. It has distinct levels and areas incl cottage garden with roses and herbaceous borders, a natural pond, shady vine covered pergola, productive vegetable terrace, lawns and shrubberies, prairie border, and seating placed to enjoy the surroundings. Partial wheelchair access as some areas have quite steep grass slopes to negotiate.

42 DURRANCE MANOR

Smithers Hill Lane, Shipley, RH13 8PE. Gordon & Joan Lindsay, 01403 741577, galindsay@gmail.com. *7m SW of Horsham. A24 to A272 (S from Horsham, N from Worthing), turn W towards Billingshurst. Approx 1¾m, 2nd L Smithers Hill Lane signed to Countryman Pub. Garden 2nd on L.* **Mon 26 Aug (12-6). Adm £6, chd free. Home-made teas.** Visits also by arrangement Apr to Oct.
This 2 acre garden surrounding a Medieval hall house (not open) with Horsham stone roof, enjoys uninterrupted views over a ha-ha of the South Downs and Chanctonbury Ring. There are many different gardens here, Japanese inspired gardens, a large pond, wild flower meadow and orchard, colourful long borders, hosta walk, and vegetable garden. There is a Monet style bridge over a pond with waterlilies.

GROUP OPENING

43 EAST GRINSTEAD TOWN GARDENS

East Grinstead, RH19 4DD. *7m E of Crawley on A264 & 14m N of Uckfield on A22. Tickets & maps at each garden. Parking at The Meads Primary School (RH19 4DD) for 4 of the gardens.* **Sun 21 July (1-5). Combined adm £6, chd free. Home-made teas at 16 Musgrave Avenue.**

27 MILL WAY
RH19 4DD. Jeff Dyson.

29 MILL WAY
RH19 4DD. Dee & Richard Doyle.

16 MUSGRAVE AVENUE
RH19 4BS. Carole & Bob Farmer.

NEW **7 NIGHTINGALE CLOSE**
RH19 4DD. Gail & Andy Peel.

NEW **TWYFORD, 35 DORSET AVENUE**
RH19 2AB. Norman & Julie Mockford.

Gardens to lift the spirits and make you smile! Three of these gardens are past winners of East Grinstead in Bloom Best Front Garden. The back gardens have quite different styles. The gardens are established, displaying a mix of planting incl shrubs, perennials and annuals, tubs and baskets. The enthusiastic owners are keen propagators, growing from seed, cuttings and plugs, sharing their surplus plants. 16 Musgrave Avenue has a thriving vegetable garden. The two new gardens have softer, relaxed planting with areas under development. 7 Nightingale Close is on heavy clay in a frost pocket going down to a stream (no access), plus a potager and collection of bonsai. 35 Dorset Avenue has an eclectic mix of garden rooms. Plenty of advice available at each garden and plants for sale at several gardens. The Town Council hanging baskets and planting are not to be missed. For steam train fans, the Bluebell Railway starts nearby. Partial wheelchair access at some gardens.

44 54 ELMLEIGH

Midhurst, GU29 9HA. Wendy Liddle, 07796 562275, wendyliddle@btconnect.com. *¼m W of Midhurst off A272. Reserved disabled parking at the top of the drive, please phone on arrival for assistance.* **Sat 25, Sun 26, Mon 27 May; Sats & Suns 8, 9, 22, 23 June; 6, 7, 20, 21 July; 3, 4 Aug (10-5). Adm £3.50, chd free. Home-made teas & cream teas.** Visits also by arrangement May to Aug for groups of 10 to 30.
⅓ acre property with terraced front garden, leading to a heavily planted rear garden with majestic 100 yr old Black Pines. Shrubs, perennials, packed with interest around every corner, providing all season colours. Many raised beds, numerous sculptures, vegetables in boxes, a greenhouse, pond, and hedgehogs in residence. Child friendly. Come and enjoy the peace and tranquillity in this award-winning garden, our little bit of heaven. Not suitable for electric buggies.

45 FAIRLIGHT END

Pett Road, Pett, Hastings, TN35 4HB. Chris & Robin Hutt, 07774 863750, chrishutt@fairlightend.co.uk, www.fairlightend.co.uk. *4m E of Hastings. From Hastings take A259 to Rye. At White Hart Beefeater turn R into Friars Hill. Descend into Pett village. Park in village hall car park, opp house.* **Thur 2 May (2-5); Sun 9 June (11-5). Adm £5, chd free. Home-made teas.** Visits also by arrangement May to Sept for groups of 10+. Donation to Pett Village Hall.
Gardens Illustrated, June 2016, said 'The 18th century house is at the highest point in the garden with views down the slope over abundant borders and velvety lawns that are punctuated by clusters of specimen trees and shrubs. Beyond and below are the wild flower meadows and the ponds with a backdrop of the gloriously unspoilt Wealden landscape'. Steep paths, gravelled areas, unfenced ponds.

D

46 FITTLEWORTH HOUSE

Bedham Lane, Fittleworth, Pulborough, RH20 1JH. Edward & Isabel Braham, 01798 865074, marksaunders66.com@gmail.com, www.racingandgreen.com. *2m E, SE of Petworth. Midway between Petworth & Pulborough on the A283 in Fittleworth, turn into lane by sharp bend signed Bedham. Garden is 50yds along on the L.* **Weds 24 Apr; 1, 8, 15 May; 12, 19 June; 10, 17 July; 14, 21 Aug (2-5). Adm £5, chd free. Home-made teas.** Visits also by arrangement May to Aug for groups of 10+.

3 acre tranquil, romantic country garden featuring working walled kitchen garden growing a wide range of fruit, vegetables and flowers. Large glasshouse and old potting shed, mixed flower borders, rose beds, rhododendrons and lawns. Magnificent 112ft tall Cedar overlooks wisteria covered Grade II listed Georgian house (not open). Wildlife pond, wild garden, long grass areas and spring bulbs. The garden sits on a gentle slope but is accessible for wheelchairs and buggies. Non-disabled WC.

47 FIVE OAKS COTTAGE

Petworth, RH20 1HD. Jean & Steve Jackman, 07939 272443, jeanjackman@hotmail.com. *5m S of Pulborough. SatNav does not work! To ensure best route, we will provide printed directions at the time of booking.* **Visits by arrangement in July for groups of up to 30. Adm £5, chd free. Happy to do tea & cakes or wine & nibbles.**

An acre of delicate jungle surrounding an Arts and Crafts style cottage (not open), with stunning views of the South Downs. Our unconventional garden is designed to encourage maximum wildlife, with a knapweed and hogweed meadow on clay attracting clouds of butterflies in July, plus two small ponds and lots of seating. An award-winning, organic garden with a magical atmosphere. Open in July, flexible on dates and time, please call or email us now to arrange.

GROUP OPENING

48 FLETCHING SECRET GARDENS

High Street, Fletching, Uckfield, TN22 3SS. *4m NW of Uckfield. Follow signs to Church Farm, Church St, TN22 3SP for parking. For Holmesdale Oast park on Bell Lane, TN22 3YB, approx ½m N from the High St (take R at junction into Bell Lane, continue ½m).* **Sat 13 July (12-5). Combined adm £6, chd free. Home-made teas at 4 Corner Cottages.**

4 CORNER COTTAGES
Mrs Jackie Pateman.

HOLMESDALE OAST
Susanna Martin.

STONES
Belinda & David Croft.

4 WHITES COTTAGES
Philip & Joy Burchell.

In the heart of the picturesque village of Fletching, near the historic church are three small, welcoming cottage style gardens, each with their own character. 4 Corner Cottages where home-made teas will be served, is a small restful garden, tucked behind the High St with a pond, small white border and more. Stunning views across farmland to Sheffield Park. The garden at Stones is packed with interest in a relatively small space. Colourful hanging baskets and pots, vegetable plot, fruiting kiwi climber, cardoon bed and mistletoe. The edge of the garden is wild to provide habitat for birds and wildlife. 4 Whites Cottages has much packed into it, incl soft fruit, cottage flowers, shrubs and herbs, plus an observatory. Holmesdale Oast is a pleasant surprise. Situated out of main village, down a track, this cottage garden with a difference has a deep restored Oast pond, and a sandstone restored bridge which is not to be missed. Partial wheelchair access to some parts of the gardens.

49 FOLLERS MANOR

White Way, Alfriston, BN26 5TT. Geoff & Anne Shaw, www.followersmanor.co.uk. *½m S of Alfriston. From Alfriston uphill towards Seaford. Park on L in paddock before garden. Garden next door to old Alfriston Youth Hostel, immed before road narrows. Visitors with walking difficulties drop at gate.* **Sat 10, Sun 11 Aug (12-5). Adm £7, chd free. Home-made teas.**

Contemporary garden designed by Ian Kitson attached to C17 listed historic farmhouse. Entrance courtyard, sunken garden, herbaceous displays, wildlife pond, wild flower meadows, woodland area and beautiful views of the South Downs. Winner of Sussex Heritage Trust Award and three awards from the Society of Garden Designers; Best Medium Residential Garden, Hard Landscaping and, most prestigious, the Judges Award. New for 2019, a newly designed area of the garden by original designer Ian Kitson. Please No Dogs.

50 THE FOLLY

Charlton, Chichester, PO18 0HU. Joan Burnett & David Ward, 07711 080851, jkburnett@hotmail.co.uk, www.thefollycharlton.com. *7m N of Chichester & S of Midhurst off A286 at Singleton, follow signs to Charlton. Follow NGS parking signs. No parking in lane, drop off only. Parking near pub 'Fox Goes Free'.* **Sun 21 July, Sun 18 Aug (2-5). Adm £4, chd free. Home-made teas.** Visits also by arrangement June to Sept for groups of 10 to 30.

Colourful cottage garden surrounding a C16 period house (not open), set in pretty downland village of Charlton, close to Levin Down Nature Reserve. Herbaceous borders well stocked with a wide range of plants. Variety of perennials, grasses, annuals and shrubs to provide long season of colour and interest. Old well. Busy bees. Partial wheelchair access. Steps from patio to lawn. No dogs.

© Leigh Clapp

51 FOXGLOVE COTTAGE

29 Orchard Road, Horsham, RH13 5NF. Peter & Terri Lefevre, 01403 256002, teresalefevre@outlook.com. *From Horsham station, over bridge, at r'about 3rd exit (signed Crawley), 1st R Stirling Way, at end turn L, 1st R Orchard Rd. From A281, take Clarence Rd, at end turn R, at end turn L. Street parking.* **Sun 26 May, Sat 29 June (1-5). Adm £4.50, chd free. Home-made teas. Gluten & dairy free cake available.** Visits also by arrangement in June for groups of 10+.

Unusual 150ft x 50ft plantaholic's garden, full of containers, quirky vintage finds and gardenalia. No lawn but gravel and bark paths dissect the sun and shade borders stuffed full of colourful planting. A beach inspired summerhouse and deck are flanked by a water feature and gravel area. The end of the garden is dedicated to propagation, cut flowers and fruit growing. Members of the Hardy Plant Society. Plenty of seating areas. New planting schemes and water feature for 2019.

52 THE GARDEN HOUSE

5 Warleigh Road, Brighton, BN1 4NT. Bridgette Saunders & Graham Lee, 07729 037182, contact@gardenhousebrighton.co.uk, www.gardenhousebrighton.co.uk. *1½m N of Brighton Pier. The Garden House can be found 1½m N of seafront, 1st L off Ditching Rd, past T-lights. Paid street parking available. London Road Station is a short walk away & buses 46 & 26 stop nearby.* **Fri 8 Mar (11.30-3.30); Sat 27, Sun 28 Apr (11.30-4.30). Adm £5, chd free. Hot soup & bread, mulled cider, tea & coffee (Mar). Home-made teas (Apr).** Visits also by arrangement Mar to Aug for groups of 10 to 30.

Tucked away in the heart of the city, this really is a secret garden, in Victorian times a market garden. Organically grown fruit, vegetables, cut flowers, roses, shrubs and trees give yr-round interest, making this a peaceful oasis in the midst of a bustling city. Most of the plants have been propagated on-site. It is hoped that the garden will inspire experienced and beginner gardeners alike. Garden produce and plants for sale.

53 NEW THE GARDEN HOUSE, CROWBOROUGH

Burnt Oak Road, Burnt Oak, Nr Crowborough, TN6 3SD. Mrs Jane Smith, 01892 654301, janemanchoo@btinternet.com. *From Crowborough town centre, turn into Croft Rd & continue into Whitehill Rd. At end of road, go straight across r'about into Alice Bright Lane, continue on to Burnt Oak Rd. House is ¾m on L.* **Fri 21, Sat 22 June (1-5). Adm £5, chd free. Home-made teas.** Visits also by arrangement June to Sept for groups of 10 to 30.

3 acre garden set in rural countryside, designed by award-winning Juliet Sergeant. The garden is divided into different rooms starting at the front with fun topiary, large trees and a wildflower meadow, leading to the white courtyard, formal rose garden, feature flower beds, rhododendron walk, and veggies. Mature trees and hedges and clever sculptures makes for interesting surprises. Water features both formal and for wildlife, quiet places to sit and enjoy the seasons and colours.

54 ◆ GREAT DIXTER HOUSE, GARDENS & NURSERIES

Northiam, TN31 6PH. Great Dixter Charitable Trust, 01797 253107, linda@greatdixter.co.uk, www.greatdixter.co.uk. *8m N of Rye. Off A28 in Northiam, follow brown signs.* **For NGS: Fri 19 Apr (2-5). Adm £10, chd free.** For other opening times and information, please phone, email or visit garden website.

Designed by Edwin Lutyens and Nathaniel Lloyd. Christopher Lloyd made the garden one of the most experimental and constantly changing gardens of our time, a tradition now being carried on by Fergus Garrett. Clipped topiary, wild flower meadows, the famous long border, pot displays, exotic garden and more. Spring bulb displays are of particular note. Ask at gate for details of disabled access.

55 GREAT LYWOOD FARMHOUSE

Lindfield Road, Ardingly, RH17 6SW. Richard & Susan Laing, 01444 892500, splaing@btinternet.com. *2½m N of Haywards Heath. Between Lindfield & Ardingly on B2028. From Lindfield, after approx 2m turn L down signed paved track. 1st house on R, car park beyond house.* **Sun 19, Fri 24, Mon 27 May (2-6). Adm £6, chd free. Home-made teas.** Visits also by arrangement May & June for groups of 10 to 30.

Approx 1½ acre garden surrounding C17 Sussex farmhouse (not open). The extensive but accessible and gentle terracing provides immediate views of many different aspects of the garden and distant views towards the South Downs. There are garden seats on every level making this a garden in which to rest and enjoy the countryside. Wheelchair access possible, some slopes and short grass.

GROUP OPENING

56 GUILLARDS OAK GARDENS

Guillards Oak, Midhurst, GU29 9JZ. *Leave Midhurst on the A272 towards Petersfield. Guillards Oak is the wide opening on the L, halfway up the hill before the pelican crossing. Purchase tickets from Garden House, 49 Guillards Oak.* **Sun 2 June (2-5). Combined adm £5, chd free. Home-made teas at Garden House, 49 Guillards Oak.**

GARDEN HOUSE, 49 GUILLARDS OAK

Mr & Mrs David Christie, 01730 813323, pattychristie49@gmail.com. **Visits also by arrangement May to July for groups of 5 to 20.**

14 GUILLARDS OAK

Mrs Jill Emery.

Two very different gardens on the same road in the old market town of Midhurst. 14 Guillards Oak owned by a plants woman, crammed with many interesting and colourful plants, greenhouse and lots of pots. The garden is on several levels, accessed by steps so is not suitable for wheelchair access. Garden House, 49 Guillards Oak is one third of the original house. The ¼ acre garden has a formal design, but is very informally planted by a real plantaholic and is always being developed. The garden incl a parterre with clematis, roses and trained fruit on arches, greenhouse, fruit cage, wendy house and bug palace. All connected by a small woodland walk under a huge Swamp Cypress, Banksia rose and Trachelospermum climbing up the house. There are two shallow steps from the road onto the patio, and three down onto the lawn.

57 HAM COTTAGE

Hammingden Lane, Highbrook, Ardingly, RH17 6SR. Peter & Andrea Browne, 01444 892746, aegbrowne@btinternet.com, hamcottage.com. *5m N of Haywards Heath. On B2028 1m S of Ardingly turn into Burstow Hill Lane signed to Highbrook, then follow NGS signs.* **Sat 11, Sun 12 May (2-5). Adm £5, chd free. Home-made teas.** Visits also by arrangement May to Sept for groups of up to 30.

8 acre garden created from agricultural land during the last 30 yrs by the present owners. The garden is now well established with yr-round colour bursting from the many borders, large bog garden and winter garden. A gentle stream flows down over waterfalls into a bluebell carpeted wood. Above the arboretum there is an amphitheatre within an old sandstone quarry.

58 HAMMERWOOD HOUSE

Iping, Midhurst, GU29 0PF. Mr & Mrs M Lakin. *3m W of Midhurst. Take A272 from Midhurst, approx 2m outside Midhurst turn R for Iping. From A3 leave for Liphook, follow B2070, turn L for Milland & Iping.* **Sun 5, Sun 12 May (1.30-5). Adm £5, chd free. Home-made teas.** Donation to Iping Church.

Large s-facing garden with lots of mature shrubs incl camellias, rhododendrons and azaleas. An arboretum with a variety of flowering and fruit trees. The old yew and beech hedges give a certain amount of formality to this traditional English garden. Tea on the terrace is a must with the most beautiful view of the South Downs. For the more energetic there is a woodland walk. Partial wheelchair access as garden is set on a slope.

59 HARBOURSIDE

Prinsted Lane, Prinsted, Southbourne, PO10 8HS. Ann Moss, 01243 370048, ann.moss8@btinternet.com. *6m W of Chichester, 1m E of Emsworth, off A259. Chinese restaurant on corner of Prinsted Lane & A259, follow lane until forced to the R. Past scout hut & car park on R. House next door with old boat in front garden. House sign on old buoy on post.* **Visits by arrangement for groups of 10 to 30. Adm £4.50, chd free. Light refreshments.**

Award-winning coastal garden takes you on a journey through garden styles from around the world. Visit France, Holland, New Zealand and Japan. View and enjoy tree ferns, topiary, shady area, secret woodland parlour, potager, containers, unusual shrubs and plants, silver birch walk, herbaceous borders, art and crafts, seaside garden, blue and white area. A garden with yr-round colour and interest. Plants for sale. Wheelchair access to most of the garden, after 10ft of gravel at entrance.

60 HARDWYCKE

Southfields Road, Eastbourne, BN21 1BZ. Lois Machin, 01323 729391, loisandpeter@yahoo.co.uk. *Centre of Eastbourne, Upperton. A259 towards Eastbourne, Southfields Rd on R just before junction with A2270 (Upperton Rd). Limited parking, public car park (pay) in Southfields Rd.* **Sun 9 June (11-5). Combined adm with Dittons End £5, chd free. Home-made teas.** Visits also by arrangement Apr to Sept for groups of 10 to 20.

Delightful s-facing town garden mainly of chalky soil, with many usual and unusual plants and small new summerhouse. Smart front garden with sunken patio. Wide selection of shrubs including 50 types of clematis. Square garden at rear 70ft x 50ft. Wheelchair access with care, two slight steps to rear garden.

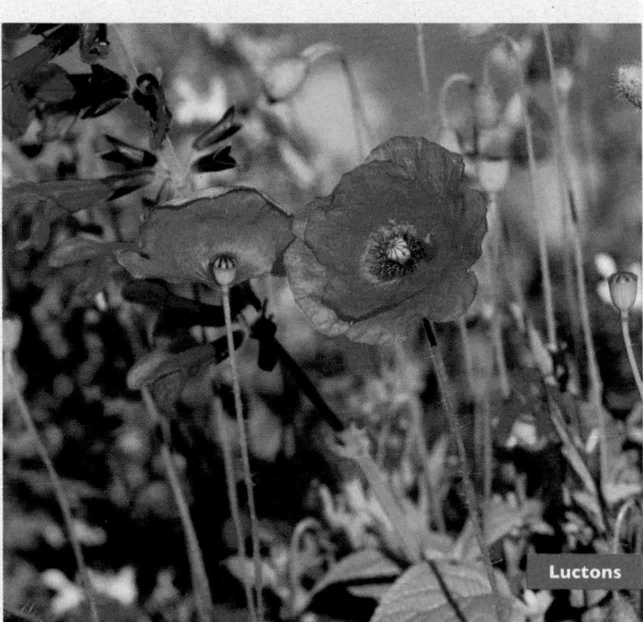

Luctons

Manor of Dean

© Judi Lion

GROUP OPENING

61 HARLANDS GARDENS

Penland Road, Haywards Heath, RH16 1PH. *Follow the yellow signs from Balcombe Rd or Milton Rd & Bannister Way (Sainsbury's). Bus stop on Bannister Way (Route 30, 31, 39 & 80). Gardens within 5 min easy walk from train station & bus stop.* **Sat 18, Sun 19 May (1-5). Combined adm £5, chd free. Home-made teas at 55 Penland Road.**

52 PENLAND ROAD
Karen & Marcel van den Dolder.

55 PENLAND ROAD
Steve & Lisa Williams.

5 SUGWORTH CLOSE
Lucy & Brian McCully.

27 TURNERS MILL ROAD
Sam & Derek Swanson.

Building on the success of 2018, we are thrilled to re-open our eclectic mix of town gardens designed, built and maintained by busy people who love and enjoy their gardens. We comprise awkward shapes and differing gradients, designed with relaxation and socialisation in mind. Our gardens offer rich cottage-style planting schemes, varied ponds, delightful courtyards, practical kitchen gardens and habitats for wildlife. Look out for interesting pots and carnivorous plants. Please check our Facebook page 'Harlands Gardens' for updated information about the weekend. Adjacent woodland provides beautiful walks (maybe muddy) to extend your visit. Roadside parking is readily available. Park once to visit all gardens. Plants sale at 52 Penland Road. The nearby quaintly English villages of Cuckfield and Lindfield are worthy of a visit. Partial wheelchair access to all gardens.

GROUP OPENING

62 NEW HASSOCKS VILLAGE GARDEN TRAIL

Hassocks, BN6 8EY. *6m N of Brighton, off A273. Gardens are E of Stonepound Xrds & 2m W of Ditchling N & S B2116. Trail can be walked. Hassocks train station nearby. Park on road or in car parks. No parking in Parklands Rd.* **Sun 9 June (1-5). Combined adm £6, chd free. Home-made teas at United Reformed Church (1.15-5).**

NEW **13 CHANCELLORS PARK**
Steve Richards & Pierre Voegeli.

NEW **2 OCKLEY LANE**
Simon & Judith Amey.

NEW **PARKLANDS ROAD ALLOTMENTS**
Tony Copeland & Jeannie Brooker.

The two gardens on this trail are quite different but each have a wide range of unusual plants and shrubs. One is well established, the other looks established but is relatively new. Excellent examples of use of space to incl seating places, winding paths and wonderful selections of plants. The 55 allotments are not to be missed, where a wide range of classic vegetables, plus some exotic vegetables grow. The allotmenteers will show you their plots and answer questions. There are spectacular views across the Downs and up to Jack and Jill Windmills, and an ancient woodland lies along the north side of the allotments. One of the few remaining chalk streams, the Herring Stream, flows through the village, where flash floods have occurred. Whilst on the trail, you can visit the rain gardens in Adastra Park, BN6 8QH that shows how house holders can reduce flash flooding by holding back rain water. WC also available. Dogs permitted at allotments only.

GROUP OPENING

63 HELLINGLY PARISH TRAIL

Gardens are close by, although Brook Cottage is 500 metres from Priors Grange. Parking in the field opp Brook Cottage, otherwise park in the roads & lanes around church. Follow yellow signs. **Sun 7 July (12.30-4.30). Combined adm £4, chd free. Ploughman's lunches & afternoon tea at Brook Cottage.**

BROADVIEW
BN27 4EX. Gill Riches.

NEW **BROOK COTTAGE**
BN27 4HD. Dr Colin Tourle MBE & Mrs Jane Tourle.

PRIORS GRANGE
BN27 4EZ. Sylvia Stephens.

Two examples of delightful cottage gardens, one of which wraps around a Grade II listed house (not open). The third garden is a green oasis of mature shrubs and trees surrounded by water (children must be supervised at all times) and is the lunch and tea venue for the trail. The village and its Grade I listed church which has the oldest circ in England, can be reached on the 51 bus from Eastbourne, and the Cuckoo Cycle Trail is nearby.

64 ◆ HERSTMONCEUX CASTLE GARDENS AND GROUNDS

Herstmonceux, Hailsham, BN27 1RN. Bader International Study Centre, Queen's University (Canada), 01323 833816, c_harber@bisc.queensu.ac.uk, www.herstmonceux-castle.com. *Located between Herstmonceux & Pevensey on the Wartling Rd. From Herstmonceux take A271 to Bexhill, 2nd R signed Castle. Do not use SatNav.* **For NGS: Sat 15 June (10-6). Adm £6, chd free. Cream teas & light lunches in Chestnuts Tearoom. For other opening times and information, please phone, email or visit garden website.**
Herstmonceux is renowned for its magnificent moated castle set in beautiful parkland and superb Elizabethan walled gardens, leading to delightful discoveries such as our rhododendron, rose and herb gardens and onto our woodland trails. Take a slow stroll past the lily covered lakes to the 1930s folly and admire the sheer magnificence of the castle. The Gardens and Grounds first opened for the NGS in 1927. Partial wheelchair access to formal gardens.

We help ordinary people open the gates to their extraordinary private gardens to raise impressive amounts of money through admissions, teas and slices of cake!

GROUP OPENING

65 HERSTMONCEUX PARISH TRAIL

4m NE of Hailsham. Tickets & map available at any garden except Lime Cross Nursery. Please note this is not a walking trail. **Sun 9 June (12-5). Combined adm £6, chd free. Teas & BBQ lunch at The Windmill.**

THE ALLOTMENTS, STUNTS GREEN
BN27 4PP. Nicola Beart.

COWBEECH HOUSE
BN27 4JF. Mr Anthony Hepburn.

1 ELM COTTAGES
BN27 4RT. Audrey Jarrett.

LIME CROSS NURSERY PINETUM
BN27 4RS. Vicky & Helen Tate, www.limecross.co.uk.

NEW **MERRIE HARRIERS BARN**
BN27 4JQ. Lee Henderson.

THE WINDMILL
BN27 4RT. Windmill Hill Windmill Trust.

Five gardens and a historic windmill will open as part of the Herstmonceux Parish Trail. Cowbeech House, a place to linger, has an exciting range of water features and sculpture in the garden, dating back to 1731. Vintage car collection available to view. Merrie Harries Barn (New), is a garden with sweeping lawn and open countryside beyond. Colourful herbaceous planting and a large pond with places to sit and enjoy the view, this is a developing garden that 4 yrs ago was agricultural land. The Allotments comprise 54 allotments growing a huge variety of traditional and unusual crops. Lime Cross Nursery is an award-winning Pinetum with an interesting Ood House and lake in the grounds. A short stroll or drive into Windmill Hill brings you to 1 Elm Cottages, a stunning cottage garden packed full of edible and flowering plants you cannot afford to miss. The Windmill, is a restored historic Mill and will be the venue for teas and a lovely BBQ lunch.

66 ◆ HIGH BEECHES WOODLAND AND WATER GARDEN

High Beeches Lane, Handcross, Haywards Heath, RH17 6HQ. High Beeches Gardens Conservation Trust, 01444 400589, gardens@highbeeches.com, www.highbeeches.com. *5m NW of Cuckfield. On B2110, 1m E of A23 at Handcross.* **For NGS: Sun 9 June, Sun 22 Sept (1-5). Adm £8.50, chd £2.** For other opening times and information, please phone, email or visit garden website.

25 acres of enchanting landscaped woodland and water gardens with spring daffodils, bluebells and azalea walks, many rare and beautiful plants, an ancient wild flower meadow and glorious autumn colours. Picnic area. National Collection of Stewartias.

NPC

67 ◆ HIGHDOWN GARDENS

33 Highdown Rise, Littlehampton Road, Goring-by-Sea, Worthing, BN12 6FB. Worthing Borough Council, 01903 501054, highdown.gardens@adur-worthing.gov.uk, www.highdowngardens.co.uk. *3m W of Worthing. Off the A259 approx 1m from Goring-by-Sea Train Station.* **For NGS: Sun 3 Feb (10-4); Wed 29 May (10-6). Adm by donation.** For other opening times and information, please phone, email or visit garden website.

We are delighted to again offer our popular spring bulb guided tours by the Head Gardener on Sun 3 Feb, for £2.50 at 11am, 12pm, 1pm, 2pm and 3pm. Created by Sir Frederick Stern and situated on downland countryside in a chalk pit, Highdown features a wide collection of plants, with many raised from seed brought from China by great collectors like Wilson, Farrer and Kingdon-Ward. In spring and early summer a colourful succession of bulbs such as snowdrops, crocus, anemones and daffodils are followed by paeonies and bearded iris. Partial wheelchair access to hillside garden with mainly grass paths.

NPC

68 4 HILLSIDE COTTAGES

Downs Road, West Stoke, Chichester, PO18 9BL. Heather & Chris Lock, 01243 574802, chlock@btinternet.com. *3m NW of Chichester. From A286 at Lavant, head W for 1½m, nr Kingley Vale.* **Wed 12 June (11-4); Sun 21 July (2-5). Adm £4, chd free. Home-made teas.** Visits also by arrangement June & July.

Garden 120ft x 27ft in a rural setting, densely planted with mixed borders and shrubs. Large collection of roses, mainly New English shrub roses; walls, fences and arches covered with mid and late season clematis; baskets overflowing with fuchsias. A profusion of colour and scent in a well maintained small garden.

69 NEW HOLFORD MANOR

Holford Manor Lane, North Chailey, Lewes, BN8 4DU. Martyn Price, 01444 471714, martyn@holfordmanor.com. *4½m SE of Haywards Heath. SE From Scaynes Hill on A272, after 1¼m turn R onto Holford Manor Lane.* **Sat 1, Sun 23 June (11-4). Adm £6, chd free. Home-made teas.** Visits also by arrangement May to Sept for groups of 10+.

5 acre garden for all seasons, surrounding a C16 Manor (not open) with far reaching views over the ha-ha to open fields with rare breed sheep and geese. Designed and laid out by the current owners with extensive herbaceous borders, iris beds, and formal parterre rose garden. Garden rooms incl a secret Chinese garden, tropical beds and wildflower meadow. Ornamental pond with water lilies and 2 acre lake walk. Brick or gravel paths give access to most of the garden.

70 HOLLY HOUSE

Beaconsfield Road, Chelwood Gate, Haywards Heath, RH17 7LF. Mrs Deirdre Birchell, 01825 740484, db@hollyhousebnb.co.uk, www.hollyhousebnb.co.uk. *7m E of Haywards Heath. From Nutley village on A22 turn off at Hathi Restaurant signed Chelwood Gate 2m. Chelwood Gate Village Hall on R, Holly House is opp.* **Sat 11, Sun 12 May, Sat 17, Sun 18 Aug (2-5). Adm £5, chd free. Home-made teas.** Visits also by arrangement May to Sept for groups of up to 30.

An acre of English garden providing views and cameos of plants and trees round every corner with many different areas giving constant interest. A fish pond and a wildlife pond beside a grassy area with many shrubs and flower beds. Among the trees and winding paths there is a cottage garden which is a profusion of colour and peace. Exhibition of paintings and cards by owner. Garden accessible by wheelchair in good weather, but it is not easy.

71 JACARANDA

Chalk Road, Ifold, RH14 0UE. Brian & Barbara McNulty, 01403 751532, bmcn0409@icloud.com. *1m S of Loxwood. From A272/A281 take B2133 (Loxwood). ½m S of Loxwood take Plaistow Rd, then 3rd R into Chalk Rd. Follow signs for parking & garden. Wheelchair users can park in driveway.* **Sun 1 Sept (2-5). Adm £4, chd free. Home-made teas.** Visits also by arrangement Apr to Oct for groups of up to 20.

A plant lover's garden which has slowly evolved over the past 20 yrs. Curved borders take you on a journey around the garden where you will find trees with interesting bark, many unusual shrubs and several hosta displays. Perennials, roses, climbers and bulbs make this a garden for all seasons. In the vegetable area there is a large raised bed, a greenhouse and a hanging potting bench.

72 NEW KEMP TOWN ENCLOSURES: SOUTH GARDEN

Lewes Crescent, Brighton, BN2 1FH. Kemp Town Enclosures Ltd, kte.org.uk. *On S coast, 1m E of Brighton Palace Pier, ½m W of Brighton Marina. 2m from Brighton station bus no 7, stop St Mary's Hall. M23/A23 to Brighton Palace Pier; L on A259. 5m S A27 on B2123, R on A259. No refreshments, coffee shops nearby.* **Thur 6 June (12-5). Adm £7.50. Tours every 30 mins from 12pm to 3.30pm (2 groups of 15 per tour) included. Pre-booking essential, please visit www.ngs.org.uk for information & booking.** Unique historic Grade II listed Regency private town garden in a spectacular seaside location. Enduring strong salty winds and thin chalk soil, the garden balances naturalistic planting and a more ordered look, relaxed not manicured. With several distinctive areas, this wonderful 5 acre garden combines open lawns, winding paths, trees, herbaceous and shrub borders and a shaded woodland garden. Designed by Henry Phillips in 1820s, the garden was a central feature of the Regency Development of the Kemp Town Estate. Queen Victoria and Edward VII walked in these gardens. Lewis Carroll visited many times and the garden tunnel is said to have inspired the rabbit hole in 'Alice in Wonderland'. Ramped gate entry. Gravel winding paths give access to most of the garden. There are relatively steep slopes on main lawn and in the garden tunnel.

73 ◆ KING JOHN'S LODGE

Sheepstreet Lane, Etchingham, TN19 7AZ. Jill Cunningham, 01580 819220, harry@kingjohnsnursery.co.uk, www.kingjohnsnursery.co.uk. *2m W of Hurst Green. Off A265 near Etchingham. From Burwash turn L before Etchingham Church, from Hurst Green turn R after church, into Church Lane, which leads into Sheepstreet Lane after ½m, then L after 1m.* **For NGS: Sun 24 Mar, Sat 4, Sun 5 May, Sat 1, Sun 2 June, Sun 22 Sept (11-4). Adm £5, chd free. Home-made teas & lunches in the tearoom of King John's Nursery.** For other opening times and information, please phone, email or visit garden website.

4 acre romantic garden for all seasons. An ongoing family project since 1987. From the eclectic shop, nursery and tearoom, stroll past wildlife pond through orchard with bulbs, meadow, rose walk, and fruit according to the season. Historic house (not open) has broad lawn, fountain, herbaceous border, pond, and ha-ha. Explore secret woodland with renovated pond, and admire majestic trees and 4 acre meadows. Small children's soft play. Garden is mainly flat. Stepped areas can usually be accessed from other areas. Disabled WC.

75 NEW KNIGHTSBRIDGE HOUSE

Grove Hill, Hellingly, Hailsham, BN27 4HH. Andrew & Karty Watson, 07879 407408. *3m N of Hailsham, 2m S of Horam. From A22 at Boship r'about take A271, at 1st set of T-lights turn L into Park Rd & drive for 2m, garden on R.* **Wed 11, Sat 14 Sept (11-5). Adm £5, chd free. Home-made teas.** Mature landscaped garden set in 5 acres of tranquil countryside surrounding Georgian house (not open). Several garden rooms, spectacular herbaceous borders planted in contemporary style in traditional setting. Lots of late season colour with grasses and some magnificent specimen trees; also partly walled garden. Wheelchair access to most of garden, gravel paths.

76 LAROCHE, 43 COOMBE DROVE

Bramber, Steyning, BN44 3PW. Lynne Broome, 01903 814170, lynnecbroome@gmail.com. *From Bramber Castle r'about, take Clays Hill signed Steyning, turn 2nd L into Maudlin Lane, after 100 metres, turn R into Coombe Drove. Garden at top of road.* **Visits by arrangement from 14 Feb to end of March & in June for groups of 10 to 30. If group is smaller, you can join another group. Adm £4, chd free. Home-made teas.**

⅓ acre garden situated on lower slope of the South Downs. Very wide variety of plants, many unusual. Portland stone terracing, with a small but steep woodland path with many snowdrops, hellebores, aconites and cyclamen in spring. In summer the garden bursts into colour with a white bed, hot bed, an array of containers, hanging baskets and a beautiful pergola covered in roses and clematis. Due to steep slope and steps, wheelchair access only to lower lawn.

77 LEGSHEATH FARM

Legsheath Lane, nr Forest Row, RH19 4JN. Mr & Mrs M Neal, legsheath@btinternet.com. *4m S of East Grinstead. 2m W of Forest Row, 1m S of Weirwood Reservoir.* **Sun 12 May (1.30-4). Adm £5, chd free. Home-made teas.** Visits also by arrangement May to Sept for groups of 20+. Donation to Holy Trinity Church, Forest Row. Legsheath was first mentioned in Duchy of Lancaster records in 1545. It was associated with the role of Master of the Ashdown Forest. Set high in the Weald, it has far reaching views of East Grinstead and Weirwood Reservoir. The garden covers 11 acres with a spring fed stream feeding ponds. There is a magnificent davidia, rare shrubs, embothrium, many different varieties of meconopsis, abutilons.

We open the gates to the nation's best gardens, offering a relaxing, memorable and affordable day out. A perfect experience to share with friends and family.

78 LIMEKILN FARM

Chalvington Road, Chalvington, Hailsham, BN27 3TA. Dr J Hester & Mr M Royle. *10m N of Eastbourne. Nr Hailsham. Turn S off A22 at Golden Cross & follow the Chalvington Rd for 1m. The entrance has white gates on the LH-side. Disabled parking space close to the house, other parking 100 metres further along road.* **Sat 17, Sun 18 Aug (2-5). Adm £5, chd free. Home-made teas in the Oast House.**

The garden was designed in the 1930s when the house was owned by Charles Stewart Taylor, MP for Eastbourne. It has not changed in basic layout since then. The planting aims to reflect the age of the C17 property (not open) and original garden design. The house and garden are mentioned in Virginia Woolf's diaries of 1929, depicting a particular charm and peace that still exists today. Flint walls enclose the main lawn, herbaceous borders and rose garden. Nepeta lined courtyard, Physic garden, informal pond, and specimen trees including a very ancient oak.

79 LINDFIELD JUNGLE

16 Newton Road, Lindfield, Haywards Heath, RH16 2ND. Tim Richardson & Clare Wilson, 01444 484132, info@lindfieldjungle.co.uk, www.lindfieldjungle.co.uk. *Approx 1½m NE of Haywards Heath town centre. Take B2028 signed Lindfield into the village. Turn R onto Lewes Rd, turn L onto Chaloner Rd & turn R into Chaloner Close. Garden is located at the far end, please use postcode RH16 2NH.* **Mon 26 Aug (1-5). Combined adm with 5 Whitemans Close £6, chd free. Home-made teas at 5 Whitemans Close.** Visits also by arrangement June to Sept for groups of up to 10. Visit can be combined with 47 Denmans Lane.

A surprising, intimate garden, approx 17 metres x 8 metres. Transformed since 1999 into an atmospheric jungle oasis planted for tropical effect. Lush and exuberant with emphasis on foliage and hot colours that develop through the seasons. From the planter's terrace enjoy the winding path through lillies, cannas, ginger and bamboo, to the tranquil sundowner's deck over hidden pools. Join Tim & Clare for tiffin and celebrate with them coming 2nd in the Gardener's World magazine Garden of the Year competition 2018!

80 THE LONG HOUSE

The Lane, Westdean, Nr Seaford, BN25 4AL. Robin & Rosie Lloyd, 01323 870432, rosiemlloyd@gmail.com, www.thelonghousegarden.co.uk. *3m E of Seaford, 6m W of Eastbourne. From A27 follow signs to Alfriston then Litlington, Westdean 1m on L. From A259 at Exceat, L on Litlington Rd, ¼m on R. Free parking in the village.* **Visits by arrangement May to July for groups of 10+. Owners on hand to guide & answer questions. Tea, coffee & cake included. Adm £10, chd free.**

The Long House's 1 acre garden has become a favourite for private group visits, being compared for romance, atmosphere and cottage garden planting to Great Dixter and Sissinghurst. Lavenders, hollyhocks, roses, a wild flower meadow, a long perennial border, water folly and pond are just some of the features, and everyone says Rosie's home-made cakes are second to none. Situated on the South Downs Way in the SDNP. Gravel forecourt at entrance, some slopes and steps.

81 LORDINGTON HOUSE

Lordington, Chichester, PO18 9DX. Mr & Mrs John Hamilton, 01243 375862, hamiltonjanda@btinternet.com. *7m W of Chichester. On W side of B2146, ½m S of Walderton, 6m S of South Harting. Enter through white railings.* **Sat 1, Sun 2 June (1.30-4.30). Adm £5, chd free. Home-made teas.** Visits also by arrangement in June for groups of up to 30.

Early C17 house (not open) and walled gardens in SDNP. Clipped yew and box, lawns, borders and fine views. Vegetables, fruit and poultry in kitchen garden. Carpet of daffodils in spring. Over 100 roses planted since 2008. Various trees both mature and young. Lime avenue planted in 1973 to replace elms. Overlooks Ems valley, farmland and wooded slopes of South Downs, all in AONB. Wheelchair access is possible but challenging with gravel paths, uneven paving and slopes.

82 LOWDER MILL

Bell Vale Lane, Fernhurst, Haslemere, GU27 3DJ. Anne & John Denning, 01428 644822, anne@denningconsultancy.co.uk, www.lowdermill.com. *1½m S of Haslemere. Follow A286 out of Midhurst towards Haslemere, through Fernhurst & take 2nd R after Kingsley Green into Bell Vale Lane. Lowder Mill is approx ½m on R.* **Sat 1 June (11-5.30); Sun 2 June (10.30-5.30). Adm £4.50, chd £2. Home-made tea & cake served overlooking the lake.**

C17 mill house and former mill set in 3 acre garden. The garden has been restored with the help of Bunny Guinness. Interesting assortment of container planting, forming a stunning courtyard between house and mill. Streams, waterfalls, innovative and quirky container planting around the potting shed and restored greenhouse. Raised vegetable garden. Rare breed chickens and ducks, as well as resident kingfishers. Extensive plant stall, mainly home propagated.

83 LUCTONS

North Lane, West Hoathly, East Grinstead, RH19 4PP. Drs Hans & Ingrid Sethi, 01342 810085, ingrid@sethis.co.uk. *4m SW of East Grinstead, 6m E of Crawley. Off minor road between Turners Hill & Forest Row. Nr Church, Cat Inn & Priest House. Car parks in village.* **Sat 6 July (1-5), also open The Priest House. Sun 7, Tue 9 July (1-5). Adm £5, chd free. Home-made teas.** Visits also by arrangement Mar to Sept for groups of 10 to 30.

A 2 acre Gertrude Jekyll style garden with box parterre, topiary, acclaimed herbaceous borders, swathes of spotted orchids, wild flower orchard, pond, chickens, greenhouses, large vegetable and fruit garden, croquet lawn, revamped herb garden, and a huge variety of plants, especially salvias. Admired by overseas garden tour visitors, and cared for lovingly by the Indian owner, a partition refugee.

84 MALTHOUSE FARM

Streat Lane, Streat, Hassocks, BN6 8SA. Richard & Helen Keys, 01273 890356, helen.k.keys@btinternet.com. *2m SE of Burgess Hill. From r'about between B2113 & B2112 take Folders Lane & Middleton Common Lane E (away from Burgess Hill); after 1m, R into Streat Lane, garden is ½m on R. Parking on grass verge.* **Sun 18, Wed 21 Aug (2-5.30). Adm £5, chd free. Home-made teas.** Visits also by arrangement Apr to Sept for groups of 10+.

Rural 5 acre garden with stunning views to South Downs. Garden divided into separate rooms; box parterre and borders with glass sculpture, herbaceous and shrub borders, mixed border for seasonal colour and kitchen garden. Orchard leading to partitioned areas with grass walks, snail mound, birch maze and willow tunnel. Wildlife farm pond with planted surround. Stunning views to the South Downs. Wheelchair access possible, although some steps. Caution if wet as much access is across grass.

85 MANOR OF DEAN

Tillington, Petworth, GU28 9AP. Mr & Mrs James Mitford, 07887 992349, emma@mitford.uk.com. *3m W of Petworth. From Petworth towards Midhurst on A272, pass Tillington & turn R onto Dean Lane following NGS signs. From Midhurst on A272 towards Petworth past Halfway Bridge, turn L following NGS signs.* **Sun 10 Feb (2-4); Sun 24 Mar, Sun 28 Apr (2-5). Adm £4.50, chd free. Home-made teas.** Visits also by arrangement Feb to June for groups of 20+. School term time dates only.

Traditional English garden, approx 3 acres with herbaceous borders, a variety of early flowering bulbs, snowdrops, spring bulbs, grass walks and grass steps. Walled kitchen garden with fruit, vegetables and cutting flowers. Lawns, rose garden and informal areas with views of the South Downs. Garden under a long-term programme of improvements. Garden on many levels with old steps and paths making it unsuitable for buggies or wheelchairs.

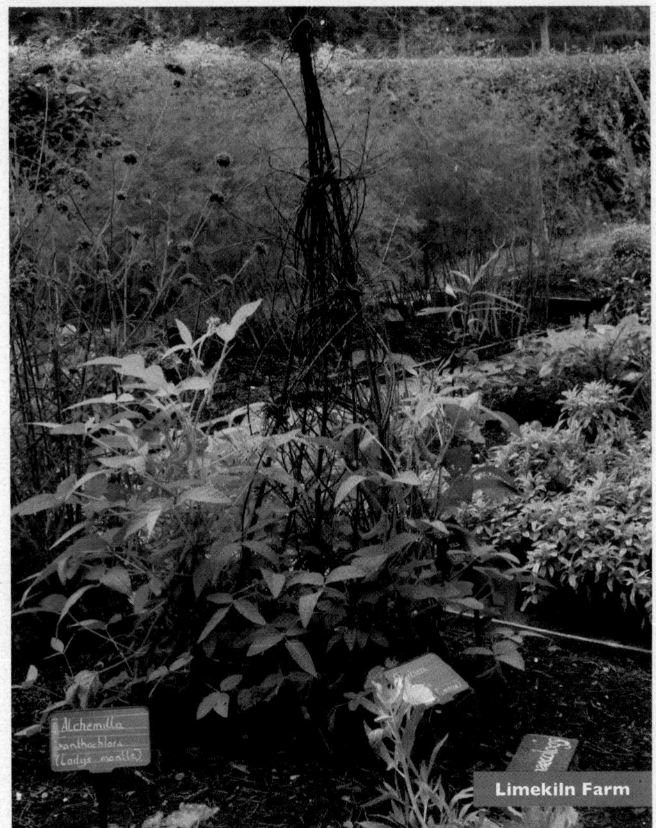

Limekiln Farm

GROUP OPENING

86 MAYFIELD GARDENS

Mayfield, TN20 6AB. *10m S of Tunbridge Wells. Turn off A267 into Mayfield. Parking is available in the village & field parking at Hoopers Farm, TN20 6BD. A detailed map will be available at each of the gardens.* **Sat 15, Sun 16 June (1-5). Combined adm £7, chd free. Home-made teas at Hoopers Farm & The Oast.**

HOOPERS FARM
Andrew & Sarah Ratcliffe.

MAY COTTAGE
M Prall.

MULBERRY
M Vernon.

OAKCROFT
Nick & Jennifer Smith.

THE OAST
Mike & Tessa Crowe.

SHALDON
William & Phyllida de Salis.

SOUTH STREET PLOTS
Val Buddle.

Mayfield is a beautiful Wealden village with tearooms, an old pub and many interesting historical connections. The gardens to visit are all within walking distance of the village centre. They vary in size and style, including colour themed courtyard and cottage garden planting, wildlife meadows and fruit and vegetable plots. There are far reaching, panoramic views over the beautiful High Weald. Partial wheelchair access to some gardens; see leaflet on the day for details.

Cookscroft

© Judi Lion

87 MEADOW FARM

Blackgate Lane, Pulborough, RH20 1DF. Charles & Vanessa Langdale. *5m N of Pulborough. From Pulborough take A29 N. Just outside Pulborough L into Blackgate Lane signed to Toat. Continue on road for 1½m. At sign for Scrase Farms keep going straight. Look out for parking signs on R.* **Sun 16 June (2.30-5.30). Adm £4, chd free. Home-made teas.**

Approx 1 acre garden built from scratch over the last 11 yrs; designed and planted by current owners. New green and white courtyard garden for 2019. Colour themed beds, including double borders with a formal pond.

A pleached hornbeam avenue taking the eye out to the Sussex countryside. A walled garden providing fruit, cut flowers and vegetables. Extensive orchard with bees and a hazelnut walk. Unfortunately, no wheelchair access due to gravel drive, paths and uneven ground.

88 ◆ MERRIMENTS GARDENS

Hawkhurst Road, Hurst Green, TN19 7RA. Lucy Cross, 01580 860666, bookings@merriments.co.uk, www.merriments.co.uk. *Off A21, 1m N of Hurst Green. On A229 Hawkhurst Rd. Situated between Hurst Green & Hawkhurst 300yds on R from A21/A229 junction.* **For NGS: Wed 7 Aug (9.30-5). Adm £8, chd free. For other opening times and information, please phone, email or visit garden website.**

Our beautiful 4 acre garden with colour themed borders is set amongst the rolling countryside of East Sussex. Seamlessly blending, its large borders of inspiring planting evolve through the seasons from spring pastels to the fiery autumn hues of the many trees, all on a gently sloping s-facing site with good parking and easy access. There are a number of benches in the garden to allow visitors to enjoy the atmosphere of this special ever-evolving garden. There are many unusual plants most of which are sold in the plant centre; there is also a great shop and restaurant serving home-made lunches and teas. Wheelchairs available from the shop. Dogs are welcome on leads.

89 ◆ MICHELHAM PRIORY

Upper Dicker, Hailsham, BN27 3QS. Sussex Archaeological Society, 01323 844224, propertymich@sussexpast.co.uk, www.sussexpast.co.uk. *3m W of Hailsham. A22 N from Eastbourne, exit L to Arlington Rd W. 1⅙m turn R, Priory on R after approx 300yds.* **For opening times and information, please phone, email or visit garden website.**

The stunning 7 acre gardens at Michelham Priory (open to the public) are enclosed by England's longest water-filled moat, which teams with wildlife and indigenous waterlilies. Cloister and Physic gardens weave together features of medieval gardening. Over 40 yrs of developments have created a variety of features incl herbaceous borders, orchard, kitchen garden and tree lined Moat Walk. The gardens have 80,000 daffodils that create a blaze of colour from early spring onwards.

90 MILL HALL FARM

Whitemans Green, Cuckfield, Haywards Heath, RH17 5HX. Kate & Jonathan Berry, 01444 455986, katehod@gmail.com. *2½m E of A23, junction with B2115. Driveway on N-side B2115 at W-end of Burrell Cottages. Parking in paddock on R at top of drive.* **Sun 2 June (12.30-5.30). Adm £5, chd free. Home-made teas. Visits also by arrangement May to July.**

2½ acre garden. Planting began March 2012. N-facing long view sloping down to pond with lilies, irises, sanguisorba. Long border with young trees and herbaceous plants incl cercidiphyllum, catalpa aurea, Metasequoia Gold Rush, cornus, acers, pulmonarias, daylilies, phlox, penstemon and brunnera, climbing roses, clematis and also a fruit and vegetable garden. Victorian underground water cistern. Plants for sale. Garden is generally bumpy with sloping lawn. Deep pond. No wheelchair access to WC.

91 THE MOONGATE GARDEN

6 Elm Avenue, East Preston, Littlehampton, BN16 1HJ. Helen & Derek Harnden, 07870 324654, derek@shiningmylight.plus.com. *Over railway crossing from A259, continue straight onto Golden Ave. Turn R into Elm Ave, within 110 metres.* **Sun 26 May, Sat 27, Sun 28 July, Sun 15 Sept (12-4). Adm £5, chd free. Home-made teas.** Visits also by arrangement May to Sept for groups of 20+. If your group is smaller, please ask to join another.

A main feature is the stunning Purbeck stone wall with a moongate opening bisecting the garden, creating 2 distinct halves. Other features incl circular lawns, a Hobbit house, vertical planting, fern-stumpery, 2 ponds with a contemporary stainless steel waterfall, Japanese area, vegetables and fruit cage. A haze of purple alliums in May, followed by verbena and persicarias in summer. Unusual grasses and cosmos carry the garden into autumn. Wheelchair access through large gate on left side of house, with direct access to garden on flat paving.

92 MOUNTFIELD COURT

Robertsbridge, TN32 5JP. Mr & Mrs Simon Fraser. *3m N of Battle. On A21 London-Hastings; ½m NW from Johns Cross.* **Sun 12 May (2-5). Adm £5, chd free. Home-made teas.**

3 acre wild woodland garden; bluebell lined walkways through exceptional rhododendrons, azaleas, camellias, and other flowering shrubs; fine trees and outstanding views. Stunning paved herb garden. Recently restored unique C18 walled garden.

93 NEW 49 NEW ROAD

Durrington, Worthing, BN13 3JG. Ian & Wendy Nicholson, 07881 922312, wendy@housecoach.co.uk. *3m NW of Worthing. From A27 at Worthing turn off into Durrington Hill, take the 3rd turning on the R into New Rd. Number 49 is on the corner of New Rd & Arun Crescent.* **Sat 6, Sat 20 July, Sat 17, Sat 31 Aug (10-4). Adm £4, chd free. Home-made teas.** Visits also by arrangement June to Sept for groups of up to 20.

Contemporary town garden in its infancy, but ready to be shared! The resourceful owners have carved out a series of garden rooms to create paradise on a shoestring. Ingenious use is made of upcycled materials and gifted plants give the borders a colourful and eclectic feel. The veranda has the best vantage point. The dining area is flanked by a generously proportioned fish pond and sun deck. A slatted screen with moongate opening separates the fire pit seating area from the rest and here, entertaining is key! Partial wheelchair access, some gravel and small variations on levels. Dogs on leads welcome.

94 NEWTIMBER PLACE

Newtimber, BN6 9BU. Mr & Mrs Andrew Clay, 01273 833104, andy@newtimberholidaycottages.co.uk, www.newtimberplace.co.uk. *7m N of Brighton. From A23 take A281 towards Henfield. Turn R at small Xrds signed Newtimber in approx ½m. Go down Church Lane, garden is on L at end of lane.* **Sun 14 Apr (2-5.30). Adm £5, chd free. Home-made teas.**

Beautiful C17 moated house (not open). Gardens and woods full of bulbs and wild flowers in spring. Herbaceous border and lawns. Moat flanked by water plants. Mature trees, wild garden, ducks, chickens and fish. Wheelchair access across lawn to parts of garden, tearoom and WC.

95 NORTH HALL

North Hall Lane, Sheffield Green, Uckfield, TN22 3SA. Celia & Les Everard, 01825 791103, indigodogs@yahoo.co.uk. *1½m NW of Fletching village. 6m N of Uckfield. From A272 turn N at Piltdown or N Chailey. From A275 turn E at Sheffield Green into North Hall Lane.* **Sat 22, Sun 23 June (2-5.30). Adm £4.50, chd free. Home-made teas.** Visits also by arrangement Apr to June for groups of 10+.

A quintessential cottage garden surrounding a C16 house (not open) planted to please the senses. Owner maintained, planting is dense and varied in an informal fusion of soft colours complimented by beautiful shade loving foliage. Flowing themed island beds and a moated terrace add to many other cottage garden features. Wildlife and self-seeding encouraged. Homegrown plants and scrumptious teas.

96 NORTH SPRINGS

Bedham, nr Fittleworth, RH20 1JP. Mr & Mrs R Haythornthwaite. *Between Fittleworth & Wisborough Green. From Wisborough Green take A272 towards Petworth. Turn L into Fittleworth Rd signed Coldharbour & proceed 1½m. From Fittleworth take Bedham Lane off A283 & proceed for approx 3m NE. Limited parking.* **Sun 30 June (1-6). Adm £4.50, chd free. Home-made teas.**

Hillside garden with beautiful views surrounded by mixed woodland. Focus on structure with a wide range of mature trees and shrubs. Stream, pond and bog area. Abundance of roses, clematis, hostas, rhododendrons and azaleas.

97 ◆ NYMANS

Staplefield Road, Handcross, RH17 6EB. National Trust, 01444 405250, nymans@nationaltrust.org.uk, www.nationaltrust.org.uk/nymans. *4m S of Crawley. On B2114 at Handcross signed off M23/A23 London-Brighton road. Metrobus 271 & 273 stop nearby.* **For NGS: Sun 22 Sept (10-5). Adm £13.23, chd £6.62. Light refreshments.** For other opening times and information, please phone, email or visit garden website.

One of the National Trust's premier gardens with rare and unusual plant collections of national significance. In autumn dramatic shows of native tree colour can be seen in the adjoining woodland, where there are opportunities to spot wildlife. The comfortable yet elegant house, a partial ruin, reflects the personalities of the creative Messel family. Some level pathways. See full access statement on the Nymans website.

NPC

98 OAKLANDS FARM

Hooklands Lane, Shipley, Horsham, RH13 8PX. Zsa & Stephen Roggendorff, 01403 741270, zedrog@roggendorff.co.uk. *S of A272, R at Countryman Pub, follow yellow signs. Or N of A24 Ashington. Head along Billingshurst Rd, take 1st R signed Shipley, garden 2m up lane, S of Shipley village.* **Sat 8 June, Wed 17 July (11-5.30). Adm £5, chd free.** Visits also by arrangement Apr to Sept for groups of 5 to 20.

Country garden designed by Nigel Philips. Approached from a small lane, along an oak lined drive leading to the house and farm. The drive opens out to an enclosed courtyard with pleached hornbeam and yew. The herbaceous borders are filled with summer colours. Small orchard beyond the tennis court and wild meadow area with views into the fields. Vegetable garden with raised beds and greenhouse. Gravel and brick paths, large lawn area and grassy paths.

99 OCKLYNGE MANOR

Mill Road, Eastbourne, BN21 2PG. Wendy & David Dugdill, 01323 734121, ocklyngemanor@hotmail.com, www.ocklyngemanor.co.uk. *Close to Eastbourne District General Hospital. Take A22 (Willingdon Rd) towards Old Town, turn L into Mill Rd just before parade of shops.* **Visits by arrangement May to Aug for groups of 5 to 10. Adm £6, chd free.**

A welcome return to the NGS for this hidden oasis behind an ancient, flint wall. Informal and tranquil, ½ acre chalk garden with sunny and shaded places to sit. Use of architectural and unusual trees. Rhododendrons, azaleas and acers in raised beds. Garden evolved over 20 yrs, maintained by owners. Georgian house (not open), former home of Mabel Lucie Attwell. Short gravel path before entering garden. Brick path around perimeter.

100 OFFHAM HOUSE

The Street, Offham, Lewes, BN7 3QE. Mr S Goodman and Mr & Mrs P Carminger. *2m N of Lewes on A275. Offham House is on the main road (A275) through Offham between the filling station & the Blacksmiths Arms.* **Sun 28 Apr, Sun 2 June (1-5). Adm £5, chd free. Tea & home-made cake.**

Romantic garden with fountains, flowering trees, arboretum, double herbaceous border and long peony bed. 1676 Queen Anne house (not open) with well knapped flint facade. Herb garden and walled kitchen garden with glasshouses, coldframes, chickens, guinea fowl, sheep and ducks. Large selection of pelargoniums for sale.

101 OLD ERRINGHAM COTTAGE

Steyning Road, Shoreham-By-Sea, BN43 5FD. Fiona & Martin Phillips, 01273 462285, fiona.h.phillips@btinternet.com. *2m N of Shoreham by Sea. From A27 Shoreham flyover take A283 towards Steyning. Take 2nd R into private lane. Follow sharp LH-bend at top, house on L.* **Visits by arrangement from end of May & June for groups of 10 to 30. If group is smaller, ask to join another group. Adm £5, chd free.**

Plantsman's garden set high on the South Downs with panoramic views overlooking the Adur valley. 1⅓ acres with flower meadow, stream bed and ponds, formal and informal planting areas with over 600 varieties of plants. Very productive fruit and vegetable garden with glasshouses. Many plants grown from seed and coastal climate gives success with tender plants. Part of house dates from 1480 (not open).

103 OLD VICARAGE

The Street, Firle, Lewes, BN8 6NR. Mr & Mrs Charlie Bridge. *Off A27 5m E of Lewes. Signed from main road.* **Sat 8 June (1-4). Adm £5, chd free. Cream teas.**

Garden originally designed by Lanning Roper in the 1960s. 4 acre garden with lots of different rooms, set around a Regency vicarage (not open) with wonderful Downland views. Features a walled garden with vegetable parterre and flower borders, wild flower meadow, pond, pleached limes and over 100 roses. Partial wheelchair access as some areas may be difficult.

104 THE OLD VICARAGE

The Street, Washington, RH20 4AS. Sir Peter & Lady Walters, 07766 761926, meryl.walters@me.com. *2½ m E of Storrington, 4m W of Steyning. From Washington r'about on A24 take A283 to Steyning. 500yds R to Washington. Pass Frankland Arms, R to St Mary's Church.* **Sun 17 Feb, Sun 24 Mar (10.30-4); Mon 22 Apr, Sun 19 May, Sun 16 June, Mon 26 Aug, Sun 13 Oct (10.30-4.30). Adm £6, chd free. Home-made teas. Gluten free cakes & biscuits.** Visits also by arrangement Mar to Oct for groups of 10 to 30.

Gardens of 3½ acres set around 1832 Regency house (not open). The front, formally laid out with topiary, wide lawn, mixed border, and contemporary water sculpture. The rear, features new and mature trees from C19, herbaceous borders, water garden and stunning uninterrupted views of the North Downs. Also Japanese garden with waterfall and pond, a large copse, stream, treehouse and stumpery. 2000 tulips have been planted for spring as well as 10,000 mixed bulbs in the meadow area. New for 2019 an Italianate gazebo with green oak columns and lead roof. Wheelchair access to the front garden, but the rear garden is on a slope.

105 PARSONAGE FARM

Kirdford, RH14 0NH. David & Victoria Thomas, 01403 820295, davidandvictoria.thomas@gmail.com. *5m NE of Petworth. From centre of Kirdford (before church) turn R through village towards Balls Cross, past Foresters Pub on R. Entrance on L, just past R turn to Plaistow. For SatNav use RH14 0NG.* **Fri 21 June, Sun 8 Sept (2-6). Adm £6, chd free. Home-made teas.** Visits also by arrangement Apr to Nov.

Major garden in beautiful setting developed over 20 yrs with fruit theme and many unusual plants. Formally laid out on grand scale with long vistas; C18 walled garden with borders in apricot, orange, scarlet and crimson; topiary walk; pleached lime allée; tulip tree avenue; rose borders; large vegetable garden with trained fruit; turf amphitheatre; lake; informal autumn shrubbery and jungle walk.

106 PEELERS RETREAT

70 Ford Road, Arundel, BN18 9EX. Tony & Lizzie Gilks, 01903 884981, timespan70@tiscali.co.uk, www.peelersretreat.co.uk. *1m S of Arundel. At Chichester r'about take exit to Ford & Bognor Regis onto Ford Rd. We are situated close to Maxwell Rd, Arundel.* **Sun 26 May, Sun 15 Sept, Sun 6 Oct (2-5). Adm £4, chd free. Home-made teas.** Visits also by arrangement Apr to Oct for groups of up to 30. New option for group visits 2019, an amusing talk 'You Reap What You Sow' about our NGS journey, followed by afternoon tea.

A stunning garden filled with imaginative woodland sculptures, natural features and a flare for the unusual. This inspirational space is a delight in which to sit and relax, enjoying a truly delicious home-made tea. Set around interlocking beds packed with colour and scent, gently shaded by specimen trees, tinkling water from a pebbled stream and raised fish pond. Sun 6 Oct we will open for a pre-Christmas afternoon, serving mulled wine with gifts and decorations for sale. Restricted wheelchair access due to narrow side entrance, regret no motorised wheelchairs.

107 33 PEERLEY ROAD

East Wittering, PO20 8PD. Paul & Trudi Harrison, 01243 673215, stixandme@aol.com. *7m S of Chichester. From A286 take B2198 to Bracklesham. Turn R into Stocks Lane, L at Royal British Legion into Legion Way. Follow road round to Peerley Rd. No 33 is halfway along.* **Sun 16 June (12-4). Adm £2.50, chd free.** Visits also by arrangement May to Oct for groups of up to 20.

Small seaside garden 65ft x 32ft, 110yds from the sea. Packed full of ideas and interesting plants using every inch of space to create rooms and places for adults and children to play. A must for any suburban gardener. Specialising in unusual plants that grow well in seaside conditions with advice on coastal gardening.

✻

108 PEMBURY HOUSE

Ditchling Road, Clayton, BN6 9PH. Nick & Jane Baker, 01273 842805, pemburyjane@btinternet.com, www.pemburyhouse.co.uk. *6m N of Brighton, off A23. On B2112, 110yds from A273. Parking for groups at house. Please car share. Overflow parking at village green, BN6 9PJ; then enter by Cinder Track & back gate. Good public transport service.* **Visits by arrangement for groups of up to 30, Mon-Fri 11-27 Feb & 7-15 Mar (am only). Individuals welcome to book. Adm £9, chd free. Home-made teas incl. No concessions.**

Depending on the vagaries of the season, hellebores and snowdrops are at their best in Feb and March. It is a country garden, tidy but not manicured. Work always in progress on new areas. Winding paths give a choice of walks through 2 acres of owner maintained garden, which is in and enjoys views of the SDNP. Wellies, macs and winter woolies advised. A German visitor observed 'this is the perfect woodland garden'.

109 PENNS IN THE ROCKS

Groombridge, Tunbridge Wells, TN3 9PA. Mr & Mrs Hugh Gibson, 01892 864244, www.pennsintherocks.co.uk. *7m SW of Tunbridge Wells. On B2188 Groombridge to Crowborough road, just S of Xrd to Withyham. For SatNav use TN6 1UX which takes you to the white drive gates, through which you should enter the property.* **Sun 14 Apr, Sun 12 May (2-6). Adm £6, chd free. Home-made teas.** Visits also by arrangement Feb to July for groups of 10+.

Large garden with spectacular outcrop of rocks, 140 million yrs old. Lake, C18 temple and woods. Daffodils, bluebells, azaleas, magnolias and tulips. Old walled garden with herbaceous borders, roses and shrubs. Stone sculptures by Richard Strachey. Part C18 house (not open) once owned by William Penn of Pennsylvania. Restricted wheelchair access. No disabled WC. Dogs on lead in park only.

♿ ✻

Ringmer Park

110 1 PEST COTTAGE

Carron Lane, Midhurst, GU29 9LF. Jennifer Lewin. *W edge of Midhurst behind Carron Lane Cemetery. Free parking at recreation ground at top of Carron Lane. Short walk on woodland track to garden, please follow signs.* **Evening opening Fri 7 June (4-7). Sun 9 June (2-6). Adm £4, chd free. Light refreshments.**

This edge of woodland, architects' studio garden of approx ¾ acre sits on a sloping sandy site. Designed to support wildlife and bio-diversity, a series of outdoor living spaces, connected with informal paths through lightly managed areas, creates a charming secret world tucked into the surrounding common land. The garden spaces have made a very small house (not open) into a hospitable family home. Exhibition of Architects projects. Track access and sloping site makes the garden unsuitable for wheelchairs or restricted mobility.

111 6 PLANTATION RISE

Worthing, BN13 2AH. Nigel & Trixie Hall, 01903 262206, trixiehall@btinternet.com. *2m from seafront on outskirts of Worthing. A24 meets A27 at Offington r'about. Turn into Offington Lane, 1st R into The Plantation, 1st R again into Plantation Rise.* **Visits by arrangement Mar to Sept for groups of 5 to 20. Adm £5, chd free. Home-made teas included.**

Clever use is made of evergreen shrubs, azaleas, rhododendrons and acers enclosing our 70' x 80' garden, enhancing the flower decked pergolas, folly and summerhouse, which overlooks the pond. Planting incl 9 Tristus silver birches, which are semi pendula, plus a lovely combination of primroses, anemones and daffodils in spring and a profusion of roses, clematis and perennials in summer. The garden has some steps. WC available on request.

112 ◆ THE PRIEST HOUSE

North Lane, West Hoathly, RH19 4PP. Sussex Archaeological Society, 01342 810479, priest@sussexpast.co.uk, www.sussexpast.co.uk. *4m SW of East Grinstead. Turn E to West Hoathly, 1m S of Turners Hill at Selsfield Common junction on B2028. 2m S turn R into North Lane, garden ¼ m straight on.* **For NGS: Sat 25 May (10.30-5.30). Sat 6 July (10.30-5.30), also open Luctons. Adm £2, chd free. Home-made teas. For other opening times and information, please phone, email or visit garden website.**

C15 timber-framed farmhouse with cottage garden on acid clay. Large collection of culinary and medicinal herbs in a small formal garden and mixed with perennials and shrubs in exuberant borders. Long established yew topiary, box hedges and espalier apple trees provide structural elements. Traditional fernery and stumpery, recently enlarged with a small secluded shrubbery and gravel garden. Be sure to visit the fascinating Priest House Museum, adm £1 for NGS visitors.

113 2 QUARRY COTTAGES

Wall Hill Road, Ashurst Wood, East Grinstead, RH19 3TQ. Mrs Hazel Anne Archibald. *1m S of East Grinstead. From N turn L off A22 from East Grinstead, garden adjoining John Pears Memorial Ground. From S turn R off A22 from Forest Row, garden on R at top of hill.* **Fri 17, Sat 18 May (2-5). Adm £3.50, chd free. Home-made teas.**

Peaceful little garden that has evolved over 40 yrs by present owners. A natural sandstone outcrop hangs over an ornamental pond; mixed borders of perennials and shrubs with specimen trees. Many seating areas tucked into corners. Highly productive vegetable plot. Terrace round house. Florist and gift shop in barn. **Also open Caxton Manor (separate admission).**

114 NEW QUINCE COTTAGE

Sloe Lane, Alfriston, Polegate, BN26 5UT. Aileen Rhodes. *4½ m NE of Seaford, just N of Alfriston village. Sloe Lane junction between High St & North St, adjacent to Denes car park & opp Willows car park. No parking on-site. Follow yellow signs.* **Tue 18 June (10.30-4.30). Adm £3, chd free. Home-made teas. Also open Alfriston Clergy House.**

Award-winning BBC Surrey/Sussex Digit Garden. Listed Georgian cottage (not open) with s-facing flint walled gardens. The main garden (9 metres x 35 metres) with views towards Windover Hill and Lullington Church has raised vegetable beds, naturalistic herbaceous border, dwarf quince tree, cordon fruit espaliered plum, fan trained fig, clematis, soft fruit and vines. The front garden (10 metre sq) features angustifolia and intermedia lavenders and old roses.

115 RINGMER PARK

Uckfield Road, Ringmer, Lewes, BN8 5RW. Deborah & Michael Bedford, www.ringmerpark.com. *On A26 Lewes to Uckfield road. 1½ m NE of Lewes, 5m S of Uckfield.* **Sun 16 June (2-5). Adm £5, chd free. Home-made teas.**

A welcome return to the NGS for this wonderful garden with its beautiful roses. The garden at Ringmer Park has been developed over the last 33 yrs as the owner's interpretation of a classic English country house garden. It extends over nearly 8 acres and comprises 15 carefully differentiated individual gardens and borders which are presented to optimise the setting of the house (not open), close to the South Downs.

116 NEW RIVERHALL HOUSE

Mountfield, Robertsbridge, TN32 5LY. Sylvia Brady. *3m N of Battle. From Battle on A2100 take 1st turning L, 200yds after level crossing. From A21 John's Cross take A2100 to Battle, after 600yds take 2nd R into Solomon's Lane.* **Tue 14 May (11-3). Adm £5, chd free. Light refreshments.**

A C16 cottage (not open) surrounded by a new and evolving garden for all seasons with an eclectic mix of garden sculptures and something around every corner. Planted with wildlife in mind. The River Line divides the garden, and cross the poohsticks bridge to meet the friendly sheep. Tea, coffee, squash (free to children) and biscuits will be available in the conservatory. Garden is quite uneven for wheelchairs, but otherwise accessible.

GROUP OPENING

117 NEW RODMELL & PEACEHAVEN TRAIL

Two gardens are in Peacehaven & one garden is 6m away in Rodmell. All gardens will be clearly signed from the A259 for Peacehaven & from the C7 for Rodmell. Please note a car is needed for this trail. **Sat 20, Sun 21 July (12-5). Combined adm £5, chd free. Home-made teas.**

NEW BOXWORTH
21 Tor Road, Peacehaven, BN10 7SX. Gerard Rooney & Duncan Ward, 07719 318452, info@boxworthflowers.com, www.boxworthflowers.com. **Visits also by arrangement in Aug for groups of up to 20. Sundays 1pm-4pm only.**

NEW PLACE HOUSE
The Street, Rodmell, BN7 3HF. Marcy & John Heywood.

NEW TOR COTTAGE
8 Tor Road, Peacehaven, BN10 7SX. Julie & Ron Basham, 01273 582598, artypantsjmm@yahoo.com. **Visits also by arrangement May to Aug for groups of up to 10.**

All 3 gardens are new to NGS this year. Boxworth is a new seaside garden developed over the last 5 yrs. Packed full of ideas and colour, perennial border, dahlias and shade area. Displays of floral art and a distant sea view. Tor Cottage is a mature garden with trees, perennial planting, koi pond, vegetable patch and rockeries. Place House is C18 flint house (not open) with 3 acres of garden and meadow, set in the heart of the small village of Rodmell. Nestled among mature ash, sycamore and oak trees, it looks out over farmland with wide vistas. Informal herbaceous flower and shrub beds encircle the house while further away a grove of beech and birch trees, under planted with long grasses, gives way to hawthorn and viburnum. Refreshments available at each garden, with cold drinks and ice-cream at Tor Cottage. Boxworth has a flower arranging studio and Tor Cottage has an artist's studio. Plants for sale. Wheelchair access at Place House only.

118 ROLFS FARM

Witherenden Road, Mayfield, TN20 6RP. Kate Langdon. *2m E of Mayfield (approx 5 mins). On Witherenden Rd, we are ½m from Mayfield end of road. Do not follow SatNav to postcode. Long, narrow, uneven driveway downhill through woods.* **Wed 12, Wed 19 June (10-4). Adm £5, chd free. Light refreshments.**

Very different from the usual NGS garden! Large wildlife friendly garden (no boundary fences to encourage visiting wildlife) with wildflower meadows, hazel trees, and clipped box hedging. Large orchard next to the garden. Tom Stuart-Smith designed modern meadow garden. Two ponds, small vegetable garden, and informal, naturalistic planting throughout. Uneven grass paths, sensible shoes please. Sorry, no wheelchair access as steep uneven driveway, and many steps in garden.

119 1 ROSE COTTAGE

Chalvington Road, Golden Cross, Nr Hailsham, BN27 3SS. Chris & Jackie Burgess, 01825 872753, burgess.clan24@gmail.com, www.rosecottagegarden.co.uk. *Approx 11m N of Eastbourne. Travelling N on the A22, turn L into Chalvington Rd immed S of Golden Cross Pub. Our property is the 1st on the R, approx 100yds after leaving the A22.* **Visits by arrangement May to Aug. Home-made teas.**

A cottage garden with densely planted borders. A wide range of cottage garden plants give yr-round interest. These are viewed as you walk along meandering paths with several secluded seating areas. Fruit cage, large productive greenhouse and several raised 'no dig' vegetable beds add interest. Pots of tea and home-made cakes served on pretty china with delightful tablecloths. No wheelchair access.

120 RYMANS

Apuldram, Chichester, PO20 7EG. Mrs Michael Gayford, 01243 783147, suzanna.gayford@btinternet.com. *1m S of Chichester. Take Witterings Rd, at 1½m SW turn R signed Dell Quay. Turn 1st R, garden ½m on L.* **Sat 13 Apr, Sat 15, Sun 16 June, Sat 14 Sept (2-5). Adm £6, chd free. Home-made teas. Visits also by arrangement Apr to Sept for groups of 10+.**

Walled and other gardens surrounding lovely C15 stone house (not open); bulbs, flowering shrubs, roses, ponds, and potager. Many unusual and rare trees and shrubs. In late spring the wisterias are spectacular. The heady scent of hybrid musk roses fills the walled garden in June. In late summer the garden is ablaze with dahlias, sedums, late roses, sages and Japanese anemones. No wheelchair access.

121 SAFFRONS

Holland Road, Steyning, BN44 3GJ. Tim Melton & Bernardean Carey, 01903 810082, tim.melton@btinternet.com. *6m NE of Worthing. Exit r'about on A283 at S end of Steyning bypass into Clays Hill Rd. 1st R into Goring Rd, 4th L into Holland Rd. Park in Goring Rd & Holland Rd.* **Visits by arrangement June & July for groups of 10 to 30. If your group is smaller, ask if you can join another group. Adm £5, chd free. Home-made teas.**

An artist's garden of textural contrasts and complementary colors. Well-furnished late summer flower beds of shrubby salvias, eryngiums, agapanthus, dahlias and lilies. The broad lawn is surrounded by borders with maples, rhododendrons, hydrangeas and mature trees interspersed with ferns and grasses. A large fruit cage and vegetable beds comprise the productive area of the garden. Plant sale. Wheelchair access difficult in very wet conditions.

122 NEW ST BARNABAS HOUSE HOSPICE

2 Titnore Lane, Goring-By-Sea, Worthing, BN12 6NZ. *W of Worthing & just N of the r'about between the A259 & the A2032. Titnore Lane can be accessed via the A27 from the N, the A259 from the W (Littlehampton) or the A2032 from the E (Worthing).* **Sun 9, Sun 16 June (2-4.30). Adm £4, chd free. Light refreshments in onsite coffee shop.**

Our grounds have a central courtyard garden like an exotic atrium with seating, water features and abundant foliage from tree ferns, magnolias and katsura trees. Outside there is a large pond with fountain-aerator, adding tranquillity with the sound of running water. There is also a lavender maze, meadow and areas depicting roundhouses which were part of a settlement dating back to 800BC. Good access to the site, central courtyard, main surrounding gardens and car park. Pond area paths can be affected by heavy rain.

123 ♦ ST MARY'S HOUSE GARDENS

Bramber, BN44 3WE. Roger Linton & Peter Thorogood, 01903 816205, info@stmarysbramber.co.uk, www.stmarysbramber.co.uk. *1m E of Steyning. 10m NW of Brighton in Bramber village off A283.* **For NGS: Fri 28, Sat 29 June (2-5). Adm £6, chd free. Tea.** For other opening times and information, please phone, email or visit garden website.

5 acres incl formal topiary, large prehistoric *Ginkgo biloba*, and magnificent *Magnolia grandiflora* around enchanting timber-framed Medieval house (not open for NGS). Victorian 'Secret Gardens' incl splendid 140ft fruit wall with pineapple pits, Rural Museum, Terracotta Garden, Jubilee Rose Garden, King's Garden and circular Poetry Garden. Woodland walk and Landscape Water Garden. In the heart of the SDNP. Level paths throughout.

124 SANDHILL FARM HOUSE

Nyewood Road, Rogate, Petersfield, GU31 5HU. Rosemary Alexander, 07551 777873, rosemary@englishgardeningschool.co.uk, www.rosemaryalexander.co.uk. *4m SE of Petersfield. From A272 Xrds in Rogate take road S signed Nyewood & Harting. Follow road for approx 1m over small bridge. Sandhill Farm House on R, over cattle grid.* **Sun 10 Feb (12-4); Sat 13, Sun 14 Apr, Sat 28, Sun 29 Sept (2-5). Adm £5, chd free. Hot chocolate served on Sun 10 Feb. Home-made teas in Apr & Sept.** Visits also by arrangement Feb to Oct for groups of 10+.

Front and rear gardens broken up into garden rooms incl small kitchen garden. Front garden incl small woodland area, White garden, large leaf border and terraced area. Rear garden has mirror borders, small decorative vegetable garden, red border and grasses border. Home of author and principal of The English Gardening School. The garden has gravel paths and a few steps not easily negotiated in a wheelchair.

125 ♦ SARAH RAVEN'S CUTTING GARDEN

Perch Hill Farm, Willingford Lane, Robertsbridge, Brightling, TN32 5HP. Sarah Raven, 01424 838000, school@thecuttinggarden.com, www.sarahraven.com. *7m SW of Hurst Green. From Burwash turn off A265 by church & memorial, follow road for 3m. From Woods Corner take road opp Swan Inn, take 1st L, go uphill & take 1st L again. Parking is in a field (uneven ground possible).* **For NGS: Thur 12 Sept (9.30-4). Adm £7.50, chd free. Tea, coffee & cake served all day. Lunch available from 12.15.** For other opening times and information, please phone, email or visit garden website.

Sarah's inspirational, productive 2 acre working garden with different garden rooms including large cut flower garden, vegetable and fruit garden, salads and herbs area, plus two ornamental gardens. We have some steps and gravel paths so wheelchair access is difficult in these areas.

GROUP OPENING

126 SEAFORD GARDENS

Tickets & maps available at each garden. 4 gardens open on 19 May & 5 gardens open on 16 June. All signed from the A259. 12a bus route goes to Seaford. Please note: this is not a walking trail. **Sun 19 May (12-5). Combined adm £5, chd free. Sun 16 June (12-5). Combined adm £6, chd free. Home-made teas.**

2 BARONS CLOSE
BN25 2TY. Diane Hicks.
Open on Sun 16 June

34 CHYNGTON ROAD
BN25 4HP. Dr Maggie Wearmouth & Richard Morland.
Open on Sun 19 May

NEW **COSY COTTAGE**
69 Firle Road, BN25 2JA. Ernie & Carol Arnold, 07763 196343, ernie.whitecrane@gmail.com.
Open on all dates
Visits also by arrangement Apr to Sept.

HIGH TREES
83 Firle Road, BN25 2JA. Tony & Sue Luckin.
Open on Sun 16 June

LAVENDER COTTAGE
69 Steyne Road, BN25 1QH. Christina & Steve Machan.
Open on all dates

NEW **SEAFORD ALLOTMENTS**
Sutton Drove, BN25 3NQ. Peter Sudell.
Open on Sun 16 June

SEAFORD COMMUNITY GARDEN
East Street, BN25 1AD. www.seaford-sussex.co.uk/scg/.
Open on Sun 19 May

Seaford Gardens will open twice in 2019. On 19 May, 4 gardens will open. 34 Chyngton Road is divided into garden rooms with pastels, hot beds, a small meadow, Japanese inspired courtyard and a prairie. Cosy Cottage (New) is a large cottage garden over 3 levels with ponds, flowers, vegetables, shrubs and a Tai Chi Temple. Lavender Cottage is a flint walled garden with a coastal and kitchen garden, terraced bank and views of Seaford Head from the balcony. Seaford Community Garden provides an interesting space for members of the community to come together and share a gardening experience. On 16 June, 5 gardens will open including Cosy Cottage and Lavender Cottage who opened in May. 2 Barons Close is a riot of colour with beautiful roses weaving in, out, and over fences. Mature shrubs frame the garden. High Trees is a beautiful garden with plants, ferns and grasses, plus a woodland garden. Seaford Allotments (New) is a site of 189 well maintained plots with a wildlife area, a dye bed and a compost WC. Home-made teas at 2 Barons Close, Cosy Cottage, Lavender Cottage and High Trees. Wheelchair access to Community Garden and partial access to 34 Chyngton Road.

127 SEDGWICK PARK HOUSE

Sedgwick Park, Horsham, RH13 6QQ. Clare Davison, 01403 734930, clare@sedgwickpark.com, www.sedgwickpark.co.uk. *1m S of Horsham off A281. A281 towards Cowfold, Hillier Garden Center on R, then 1st R into Sedgwick Lane. At end of lane enter N gates of Sedgwick Park or W gate via Broadwater Lane, from Copsale or Southwater off A24.* **Sun 23 June (12-5). Adm £6, chd free. Home-made teas. Visits also by arrangement May to Sept for tours of house & gardens.**

Parkland, meadows and woodland. Formal gardens by Harold Peto featuring 20 interlinking ponds, impressive water garden known as The White Sea. Large Horsham stone terraces and lawns look out onto clipped yew hedging and specimen trees. Well stocked herbaceous borders, set in the grounds of Grade II listed Ernest George Mansion. One of the finest views of the South Downs, Chanctonbury Ring and Lancing Chapel. Turf labyrinth and organic vegetable garden. Garden has uneven paving, slippery when wet; unfenced ponds and swimming pool.

128 SENNICOTTS

West Broyle, Chichester, PO18 9AJ. Mr & Mrs James Rank, www.sennicotts.com. *2m NW of Chichester. White gates diagonally opp & W of the junction between Salthill Rd & the B2178.* **Sun 9 June (10-5). Home-made teas. Mon 10, Mon 17, Mon 24 June (9-4). Light refreshments. Adm £4, chd free.**

Historic gardens set around a Regency villa (not open) with views across mature Sussex parkland to the South Downs. Working walled kitchen and cutting garden where refreshments will be available. Lots of space for children and a warm welcome for all.

129 ◆ SHEFFIELD PARK AND GARDEN

Uckfield, TN22 3QX. National Trust, 01825 790231, sheffieldpark@nationaltrust.org.uk, www.nationaltrust.org.uk/sheffieldpark. *10m S of East Grinstead. 5m NW of Uckfield; E of A275.* **For NGS: Wed 8 May (10-5). Adm £11, chd £5.50. Light refreshments in Coach House Tearoom. For other opening times and information, please phone, email or visit garden website.**

Magnificent 120 acres (40 hectares) landscaped garden laid out in C18 by Capability Brown and Humphry Repton. Further development in early years of this century by its owner Arthur G Soames. Centrepiece is original lakes with many rare trees and shrubs. Beautiful at all times of the year, but noted for its spring and autumn colours. National Collection of Ghent azaleas. Natural play trail for families on South Park. Large number of Champion Trees, 87 in total. Garden largely accessible for wheelchairs, please call for information.

NPC

Saffrons

130 SHEPHERDS COTTAGE

Milberry Lane, Stoughton, Chichester, PO18 9JJ. Jackie & Alan Sherling, 07795 388047, milberrylane@gmail.com. *9⅙m NW Chichester. Off B2146, next village after Walderton. Cottage is near telephone box & beside St Mary's Church. No parking in lane beside house.* **Sun 19, Mon 20 May (2-5). Adm £5, chd free. Home-made teas.** Visits also by arrangement May to Sept for groups of 10 to 30.

A compact terraced garden using the borrowed landscape of Kingley Vale in the South Downs. The s-facing flint stone cottage (not open) is surrounded by a Purbeck stone terrace with lush planting schemes. The upper beds are planted with a profusion of tulips, alliums, roses, verbascum and lilies. A small orchard (under-planted with meadow), lawns, yew hedges, ilex balls and drifts of wind grass provide structure and yr-round interest. Many novel design ideas for a small garden. Ample seating throughout the garden to enjoy the views. Lunches and WC at the Hare & Hound Pub, a 5 min walk away. Not suitable for wheelchairs or people with mobility issues.

131 SIENNA WOOD

Coombe Hill Road, East Grinstead, RH19 4LY. Belinda & Brian Quarendon, 07970 707015, Belinda222@hotmail.com. *1m W of East Grinstead, off B2110 East Grinstead to Turners Hill. Garden is ½m down Coombe Hill Rd on L.* **Sun 26 May (1-5). Adm £5, chd free. Home-made teas.** Visits also by arrangement Mar to Oct for groups of 5+.

Explore our beautiful 3½ acre garden, picturesque lakeside walk and 6 acre ancient woodland behind. Start at the herbaceous borders surrounding the croquet lawn, through the formal rose garden to the lawns and summer borders; then down through the arboretum to the lake and back past the exotic border, orchard and vegetable garden. Many unusual trees and shrubs. Child friendly with children's nature trail, treehouse and play area. Possible sighting of wild deer including white deer. Partial wheelchair access to many parts of the garden.

132 SKYSCAPE

46 Ainsworth Avenue, Ovingdean, Brighton, BN2 7BG. Lorna & John Davies. *From Brighton take A259 coast road E, passing Roedean School on L. Take 1st L at the r'about into Greenways & 2nd R into Ainsworth Ave, Skyscape at the top on R.* **Sat 1, Sun 2 June (1-5). Combined adm with 12 Ainsworth Avenue £4, chd free. Tea & cake served on the patio.**

250ft s-facing rear garden on a sloping site with fantastic views of South Downs and sea. Garden created by owners over past 6 yrs. New orchard, flower beds and planting with bees in mind. Full access to site via purpose built sloping path.

133 SOUTH GRANGE

Quickbourne Lane, Northiam, Rye, TN31 6QY. Linda & Michael Belton, 01797 252984, belton.northiam@gmail.com. *Between A268 & A28, approx ½m E of Northiam. From Northiam centre follow Beales Lane into Quickbourne Lane, or Quickbourne Lane leaves A286 approx ½m S of A28 & A286 junction. Disabled parking at front of house.* **Sat 14, Sun 15 Sept (11-5). Adm £5, chd free. Home-made teas. Light lunches made to order.** Visits also by arrangement Apr to Oct.

Hardy Plant Society members' garden with a wide variety of trees, shrubs, perennials and pots arranged into a complex garden display for yr-round colour and interest. Raised vegetable beds, wildlife pond, orchard with rose arbour, soft fruit cage and living gazebo. House roof runoff diverted to storage and pond. Small area of wildwood. We hope Sept opening will show late season colour. We try to maintain nectar and pollen supplies and varied habitats for most of the creatures that we share the garden with, hoping that this variety will keep the garden in good heart. Home propagated plants for sale. Hard paths through much of the garden, but steps up to patio and WC.

134 SPRINGS HANGER

Bedham Lane, Bedham, Pulborough, RH20 1JP. Mr & Mrs I Anderson, 07539 773164, janegog@hotmail.co.uk. *Situated between Wisborough Green & Fittleworth. Limited parking.* **Sat 11 May (10-4.30). Adm £10. Due to limited numbers, pre-booking is essential. Open for guided tours only. Approx 2½ hr guided tour at 10am or 2.30pm, incl home-made teas.** Visits also by arrangement in May for groups of 5 to 10. If your group is smaller, do ask to join another group.

Mainly woodland in nature with azaleas, magnolias, rhododendrons and a variety of other unusual trees and shrubs underplanted. This is a sloping garden of approx 7 acres, planted from 1994 and still developing. Herbaceous border, vegetable garden, glasshouse, exotic and other areas of informal planting. Very fine views to the south and east. This garden is for the sure-footed plantsman, capable of steps and slopes.

135 STANLEY FARM

Highfield Lane, Liphook, GU30 7LW. Bill & Emma Mills. *For SatNav please use GU30 7LN, which takes you to Highfield Lane & then follow NGS signs. Track to Stanley Farm is 1m.* **Sun 5 May (12-5). Adm £5, chd free. Home-made teas.**

1 acre garden created over the last 15 yrs around an old West Sussex farmhouse (not open), sitting in the midst of its own fields and woods. The formal garden incl a kitchen garden with heated glasshouse, orchard, espaliered wall trained fruit, lawn with ha-ha, and cutting garden. A motley assortment of animals incl sheep, donkeys, chickens, ducks and geese. Bluebells flourish in the woods, so feel free to bring dogs and a picnic, and take a walk after visiting the gardens. Tea and cakes served in the courtyard. Wheelchair access via a ramp to view main part of the garden. Difficult access to woods due to muddy, uneven ground.

136 STONE CROSS HOUSE

Alice Bright Lane, Crowborough, TN6 3SH. Mr & Mrs D A Tate. *1½m S of Crowborough Cross. At Crowborough T-lights (A26) turn S into High St & shortly R onto Croft Rd. Over 3 mini-r'abouts to Alice Bright Lane. Garden on L at next Xrds.* **Sat 11, Sun 12 May (2-5). Adm £5, chd free. Home-made teas.**

Beautiful 9 acre country property (not open) with gardens containing a delightful array of azaleas, acers, rhododendrons and camellias, interplanted with an abundance of spring bulbs. The very pretty cottage garden has interesting examples of topiary and unusual plants. Jacob sheep graze the surrounding pastures. Mainly flat and no steps. Gravel drive. No WC available.

137 SULLINGTON OLD RECTORY

Sullington Lane, Storrington, Pulborough, RH20 4AE. Oliver & Mala Haarmann. Mark Dixon, Head Gardener, 07749 394012, mark@sullingtonoldrectory.com. *Traveling S on A24 take 3rd exit on Washington r'about. Proceed to Xrds on A283 for Sullington Lane & Water Lane. Take L onto Sullington Lane & garden located at the top.* **Visits by arrangement in July for groups of up to 30. Limited dates only. If group is smaller, ask to join another. Adm £12, chd free. Tour with Head Gardener at 10.30am or 2pm & home-made teas included.**

With a backdrop of stunning views of the South Downs, the naturalistic style of this country garden sits well into the surrounding landscape. Many areas to enjoy incl potager, orchard, herb garden, pleached lime walk, perennial borders and moist meadow. With a strong framework of established trees and shrubs, new plantings and areas under development. Wheelchair access to most areas.

138 ◆ SUSSEX PRAIRIES

Morlands Farm, Wheatsheaf Road (B2116), Henfield, BN5 9AT. Paul & Pauline McBride, 01273 495902, morlandsfarm@btinternet.com, www.sussexprairies.co.uk. *2m NE of Henfield on B2116 Wheatsheaf Rd (also known as Albourne Rd). Follow Brown Tourist signs indicating Sussex Prairie Garden.* **For NGS: Sun 8 Sept (11-5). Adm £8, chd free. Home-made teas.** For other opening times and information, please phone, email or visit garden website.

Exciting prairie garden of approx 8 acres planted in the naturalistic style using 60,000 plants and over 1,600 different varieties. A colourful garden featuring a huge variety of unusual ornamental grasses. Expect layers of colour, texture and architectural splendour. Surrounded by mature oak trees with views of Chanctonbury Ring and Devil's Dyke on the South Downs. Permanent sculpture collection and exhibited sculpture throughout the season. Rare breed sheep and pigs. New tropical entrance garden planted in 2018. Woodchip pathway at entrance. Soft woodchip paths in borders not accessible, but flat garden for wheelchairs and mobility scooters. Disabled WC.

139 TOWN PLACE

Ketches Lane, Freshfield, Sheffield Park, RH17 7NR. Anthony & Maggie McGrath, 01825 790221, mcgrathsussex@hotmail.com, www.townplacegarden.org.uk. *5m E of Haywards Heath. From A275 turn W at Sheffield Green into Ketches Lane for Lindfield. 1¾m on L.* **Sun 9, Thur 13, Thur 20, Sun 23, Sun 30 June, Sun 7 July (2-6). Adm £6, chd free. Cream teas.** Visits also by arrangement June & July for groups of 20+. No refreshments.

A stunning 3 acre garden with a growing international reputation for the quality of its design, planting and gardening. Set round a C17 Sussex farmhouse (not open), the garden has over 600 roses, herbaceous borders, herb garden, topiary inspired by the sculptures of Henry Moore, ornamental grasses, an 800 yr old oak, potager, and a unique ruined Priory Church and Cloisters in hornbeam. There are steps in the garden, but all areas can be viewed from a wheelchair.

140 NEW TUPPENNY BARN

Main Road, Southbourne, PO10 8EZ. Maggie Haynes, tuppennybarn.co.uk. *6m W of Chichester, 1m E of Emsworth. On Main Rd A259, corner of Tuppenny Lane. Disabled parking.* **Sun 30 June (11-4); Sun 6 Oct (2-5). Adm £4, chd free. Cream teas. Food intolerances & allergies catered for.**

An iconic, organic smallholding used as an outdoor classroom to teach children about the environment, sustainability and healthy food. 2½ acres packed with a wildlife pond, orchard with heritage top fruit varieties, two solar polytunnels, fruit cages, raised vegetables, herbs, and cut flower garden. Willow provides natural arches and wind breaks. Bug hotel and beehives support vital pollinators. Children's activities, apple education and talks. Come and visit on 30 June for Soft Fruit Season Open Day and on 6 Oct for Apple Open Afternoon! Most of the grounds are accessible for wheelchairs, but there are undulated areas that are more difficult.

NPC

141 UPWALTHAM BARNS

Upwaltham, GU28 0LX. Roger & Sue Kearsey. *6m S of Petworth. 6m N of Chichester on A285.* **Sun 26, Mon 27 May (1.30-5.30). Adm £4.50, chd free. Home-made teas.** Donation to St Mary's Church.

Unique farm setting transformed into a garden of many rooms. Entrance is a tapestry of perennial planting to set off C17 flint barns. At the rear is a walled, terraced garden redeveloped and planted with an abundance of unusual plants, we are always adding something new. Beautiful inner courtyard and seating area for tea, coffee and great home-made cakes. Extensive vegetable garden. Roam at leisure, relax and enjoy. Features incl lovely views of the South Downs and a C12 Shepherds Church (open to visitors). Partial wheelchair access with some gravel paths.

142 VACHERY FOREST GARDEN

Wych Cross, TN22 3HR. Conservators of Ashdown Forest, 01342 823583, conservators@ashdownforest.org, www.ashdownforest.org. ⅔m *W of A22 between Wych Cross & Nutley. Park 1½m S of Wych Cross on A22 at Trees Car Park. Access along rides, across heath & down steepish bridleway. Round trip 2½m, no facilities.* **Tue 17 Sept (10.30-4). Adm £5, chd free.**

The Vachery Garden, a hidden gem of Ashdown Forest is being part restored. It comprises a string of lakes, sluices and weirs with a Folly Bridge; a gorge of Cheddar Gorge limestone landscaped by Gavin Jones in 1925; and fine stands of rhododendrons, native and introduced trees. Guided tours at 10.30am and 2pm, starting from Trees Car Park on A22. Circular walk, approx 2 hrs over steep and rugged terrain, will only take place weather permitting, please phone on the day by 9am for confirmation or check website. Pre-booking is essential, please phone or email by Wed 11 Sept.

143 THE WALLED GARDEN AT TILGATE PARK

Tilgate Drive, Tilgate, Crawley, RH10 5PQ. Nick Hagon, www.friendsoftilgatepark.co.uk. *SE Crawley. Leave M23 at J11. From r'about follow A23 Brighton Rd for short distance. At T-lights turn R at sign to Tilgate Park onto Tilgate Drive. Follow signs in Park for parking incl disabled parking.* **Evening opening Wed 22, Thur 23 May, Wed 17, Thur 18 July (6.30-9). Adm £7, accompanied children under 16 free. No concessions. Cash only. Home-made teas included.**

There is much more to know about the award-winning Tilgate Park than is realised on a family visit. Why not join a tour with Park Manager, Nick Hagon to discover more about this special environment? In spring learn about the azaleas, camellias, primulas and rhododendrons, and in July the walled garden and the specimen trees planted centuries ago. Talk and tour begins at 7pm, near the Walled Garden. Coaches must book in advance, please phone 01293 521168. Wheelchair access within the walled garden.

GROUP OPENING

144 WATERWORKS & FRIENDS

Broad Oak & Brede, TN31 6HG. *Waterworks Cots Brede, off A28 by church & opp Red Lion Pub, ¾m at end of lane. Sculdown on B2089 Chitcombe Rd, W off A28 at Broad Oak Xrds. Start at either garden, directions will be provided. Please note a car is needed for this trail.* **Sat 1 June (10.30-4). Combined adm £5, chd free. Light refreshments at Sculdown.**

SCULDOWN
TN31 6EX. Mrs Christine Buckland.

4 WATERWORKS COTTAGES
TN31 6HG. Mrs Kristina Clode, www.kristinaclodegardendesign.co.uk.

An opportunity to visit 2 unique gardens and discover the Brede Steam Giants 35ft Edwardian water pumping engines and Grade II listed pump house located behind 4 Waterworks Cottages. Garden designer Kristina Clode has created her wildlife friendly garden at 4 Waterworks Cottages over the last 9 yrs. Delightful perennial wildflower meadow, pond, wisteria covered pergola and mixed borders packed full of unusual specimens with yr-round interest and colour. Sculdown's garden is dominated by a very large wildlife pond formed as a result of iron-ore mining over 100 yrs ago. The stunning traditional cottage (not open) provides a superb backdrop for several colourful herbaceous borders and poplar trees. Plants for sale at 4 Waterworks Cottages. At Brede Steam Giants, WC available, but regret no disabled facilities and assistance dogs only (free entry, donations encouraged). Wheelchair access at Sculdown (please park in the flat area at the top of field) and in the front garden of 4 Waterworks Cottages only.

145 WHITEHANGER

Marley Lane, Haslemere, GU27 3PY. David & Lynn Paynter, 07774 010901, l.paynter@btopenworld.com. *3m S of Haslemere. Take the A286 Midhurst road from Haslemere & after approx 2m turn R into Marley Lane (opp Hatch Lane). After 1m turn into drive shared with Rosemary Park Nursing Home.* **Visits by arrangement June to Sept for groups of 10 to 30. Refreshments incl tea & cake (day), wine (eve).**

Set in 6 acres on the edge of the SDNP surrounded by NT woodland, this rural garden was started in 2012 when a new Huf house was built on a derelict site. Now there are lawned areas with beds of perennials, a serenity pool with Koi carp, a wild flower meadow, a Japanese garden, a sculpture garden, a woodland walk and a large rockery.

146 NEW 3 WHITEMANS CLOSE

Cuckfield, Haywards Heath, RH17 5DE. David & Christine Hart, 01444 473520, shirleycarmanmartin@gmail.com. *1m N of Cuckfield. On B2036 signed Balcombe, Whitemans Close is 250yds from r'about on LH-side. Park on road, no parking in Whitemans Close. Buses stop at Whitemans Green, where there is also a large car park.* **Visits by arrangement June & July for groups of up to 20. Combined visit with 5 Whitemans Close only. Adm £8, chd free.**

A new garden recently planted with some very special perennials, grasses, shrubs and trees. The small back garden has been a challenge! The plantaholic owner has packed every square inch with real gems and then more, likewise the front area with its treasures. The enthusiastic owner will explain her planting ideas. A garden to follow from its newness now, to becoming established in the future.

147 5 WHITEMANS CLOSE

Cuckfield, Haywards Heath, RH17 5DE. Shirley Carman-Martin, 01444 473520, shirleycarmanmartin@gmail.com. *1m N of Cuckfield. On B2036 signed Balcombe, Whitemans Close is 250yds from r'about on LH-side. Park on road, no parking in Whitemans Close. Buses stop at Whitemans Green, where there is also a large car park.* **Mon 26 Aug (1-5). Combined adm with Lindfield Jungle £6, chd free. Home-made teas.** Visits also by arrangement for groups of up to 20. Snowdrop visits on 15 & 18 Feb. In June & July combined visit with 3 Whitemans Close.

A garden visit for snowdrop and plant lovers. Individuals welcome to pre-book. A relatively small cottage garden packed full of exciting and unusual plants, plus a large snowdrop collection. Flower beds overflow with gorgeous plants in colour schemed borders, small but productive vegetable garden, collection of echeveria and sempervivum and half hardy plants too. A plantsman's garden not to miss.

GROUP OPENING

148 WINCHELSEA'S SECRET GARDENS

Winchelsea, TN36 4EJ. *2m W of Rye, 8m E of Hastings. Purchase ticket for all gardens at first garden visited; a map will be provided showing gardens & location of teas.* **Sat 20 Apr (1-5.30); Sat 15 June (11-5). Combined adm £6, chd free. Home-made teas at Winchelsea New Hall.**

ALARDS PLAT
Richard & Cynthia Feast.
Open on Sat 15 June

THE ARMOURY
Mr & Mrs A Jasper.
Open on all dates

BACKFIELDS END
Sandra & Peter Mackenzie Smith.
Open on Sat 15 June

CLEVELAND HOUSE
Mr & Mrs J Jempson.
Open on Sat 15 June

CLEVELAND PLACE
Sally & Graham Rhodda.
Open on all dates

NEW **EVENS**
Judith & James Payne.
Open on Sat 15 June

KING'S LEAP
Philip Kent.
Open on all dates

LOOKOUT COTTAGE
Mary & Roger Tidyman.
Open on Sat 15 June

MAGAZINE HOUSE
Susan Stradling.
Open on Sat 15 June

PERITEAU HOUSE
Dr & Mrs Lawrence Youlten.
Open on all dates

RYE VIEW
Howard Norton & David Page.
Open on all dates

THE WELL HOUSE
Alice Kenyon.
Open on Sat 20 Apr

Many styles, large and small, secret walled gardens, spring bulbs, herbaceous borders and more, in the beautiful setting of the Cinque Port of Winchelsea. Explore the town with its magnificent church and famous medieval merchants' cellars. Guided tours of cellars, booking essential 07596 182874. Information at winchelsea.com and winchelseachurch.co.uk. For enquiries, or if you are bringing a coach please contact david@ryeview.net, 01797 226524. Wheelchair access to four gardens in April and eight in June; see map provided on the day for details.

149 2 WOODSIDE

Lewes Road, Laughton, Lewes, BN8 6BL. Dick & Kathy Boland, 01323 811507, kathy.boland01@btinternet.com. *Approx 6m E of Lewes on B2124. In Laughton village 300yds E of Roebuck Pub.* **Visits by arrangement June & July for groups of up to 20.**

The garden was designed for summer living by its retired owners. It is approx ⅓ acre and comprises a herb garden, a rockery and pond with fish, lawn and herbaceous borders, a small stream and wildlife pond, fruit trees, fruit cage, rose garden and vegetables in raised beds. A shaded area is being developed in a less formal setting among trees, planted with shade loving plants. The garden is not suitable for wheelchairs.

150 WYCH WARREN HOUSE

Wych Warren, Forest Row, RH18 5LF. Colin King & Mary Franck. *1m S of Forest Row. Proceed S on A22, track turning on L, 100 metres past 45mph warning triangle sign. Or 1m N of Wych Cross T-lights track turning on R. Go 400 metres across golf course till the end.* **Evening opening Wed 10 July (5-9). Adm £4, chd free. Wine.**

6 acre garden in Ashdown Forest, AONB, much of it mixed woodland. Perimeter walk around property (not open). Delightful and tranquil setting with various aspects of interest, as works in progress incl a large pond, bog garden, Mediterranean and exotic garden and mixed herbaceous borders. Fine specimen trees and shrubs, rhododendrons and azaleas, lovely stonework. Much to please the eye! From the terrace beautiful views and refreshments available. Partial wheelchair access by tarmac track to the kitchen side gate.

Your visits help change lives – since 1927, we've donated £55 million to nursing and caring charities

WARWICKSHIRE

For Birmingham & West Midlands see Staffordshire

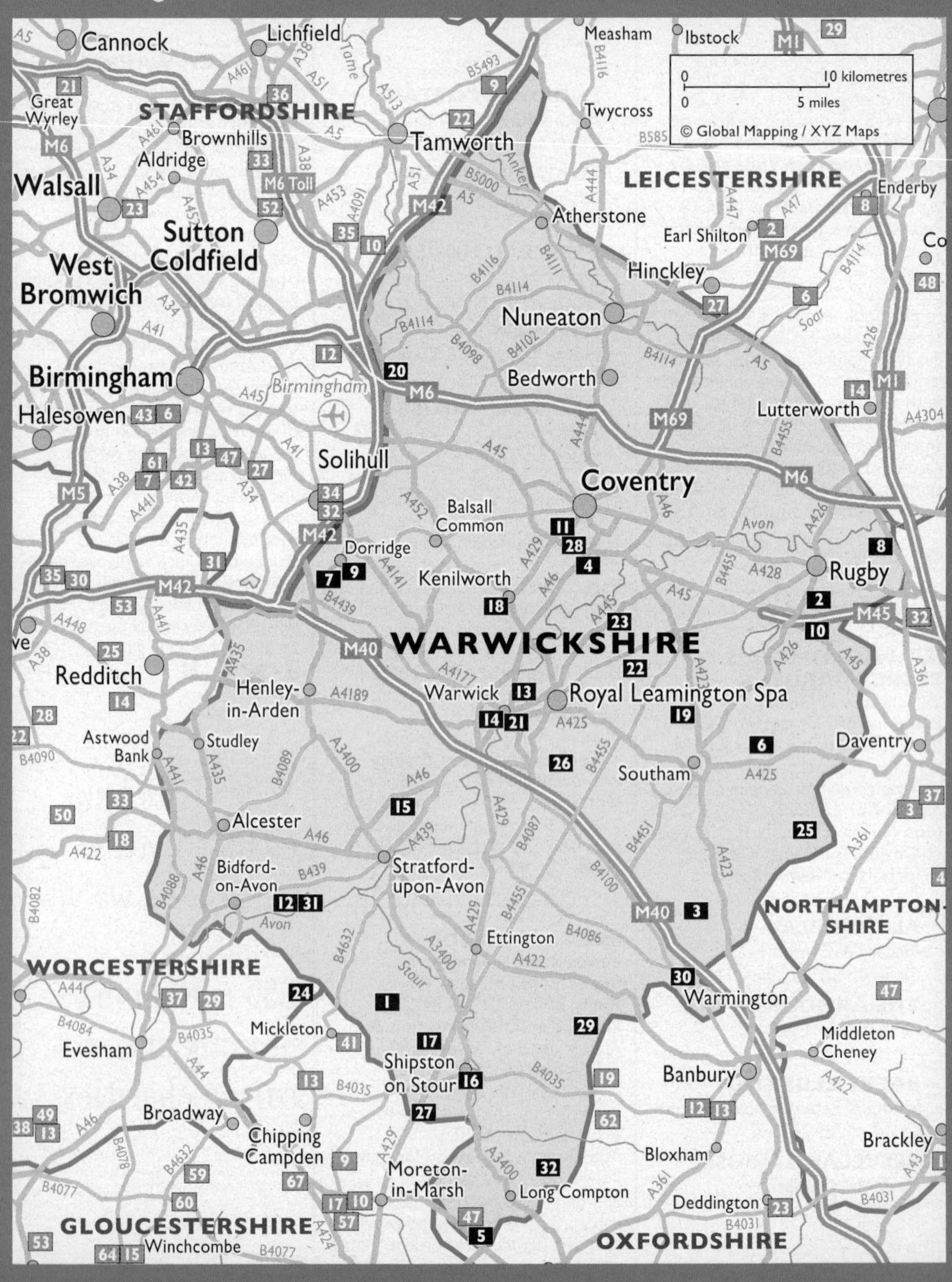

This county – say 'Worrick-sher' – is a landlocked county, with a small capital town, a fashionable spa and plenty of quintessentially English villages.

There are also many welcoming Tudor beams and pretty stone 'foodie' pubs, and many varieties of plants and trees, depending on the soil type, all year round. Undulating countryside takes you from the edge of the Cotswolds in the south to the Evesham Vale in the west, up to the hillside of Atherstone in the north and on to Rugby and the farming land of the east. The gardens of Warwickshire are as varied as its landscape; gardens of every shape and size welcome visitors in aid of the National Garden Scheme.

Today, Warwickshire has a new theme for a new century – Tourism. Inspired by our old poacher William Shakespeare at Stratford-upon-Avon, the Bard's fans flock to Warwickshire from all over the world to delight in theatre, history and castles. But Warwickshire's gardens are also well worth a visit, being wonderfully varied in size and style, and all lovingly-looked after by very generous owners.

So next time you are visiting Warwickshire be sure to bring your Garden Visitor's Handbook with you, and enjoy the wonderful gardens our county has to offer!

Volunteers

County Organiser
Liz Watson
01926 512307
liz.watson@ngs.org.uk

County Treasurer
Dee Broquard
07773 568317
dee@ngs.org.uk

Publicity
Lily Farrah
07545 560298
lily.farrah@ngs.org.uk

Social Media
Fiona Anderson
07754 943277
fionajanderson29@gmail.com

Sal Renwick
01564 770215
sal.renwick@blueyonder.co.uk

Booklet Advertising
Dee Broquard
(as above)

Booklet Co-ordinator
Hugh Thomas
01926 423063
hughthomas1203@gmail.com

Assistant County Organisers
Elspeth Napier
01608 666278
elspethmjn@gmail.com

Jane Redshaw
07803 234627
janer.redshaw@gmail.com

David Ruffell
01926 316456
de.ruffell@btinternet.com

Wendi Bowron Weller
01789 720803
wendibowz@googlemail.com

Left: **Lantern House, Warmington Gardens**

OPENING DATES

All entries subject to change. For latest information check **www.ngs.org.uk**

Extended openings are shown at the beginning of the month.

Map locator numbers are shown to the right of each garden name.

February

Snowdrop Festival

Saturday 16th
Elm Close 12
◆ Hill Close Gardens 14

Sunday 17th
Elm Close 12

April

Every Saturday and Sunday from Saturday 13th
◆ Bridge Nursery 6

Sunday 14th
Stretton-on-Fosse Gardens 27

Sunday 21st
Broadacre 7

Monday 22nd
◆ Bridge Nursery 6

Sunday 28th
NEW Blacksmiths Cottage 5

May

Every Saturday and Sunday
◆ Bridge Nursery 6

Monday 6th
◆ Bridge Nursery 6
Earlsdon Gardens 11

Saturday 25th
Ilmington Gardens 17

Sunday 26th
Ilmington Gardens 17
Pebworth Gardens 24

Monday 27th
◆ Bridge Nursery 6
Pebworth Gardens 24

June

Every Saturday and Sunday
◆ Bridge Nursery 6

Saturday 1st
Tysoe Gardens 29

Sunday 2nd
Maxstoke Castle 20
Tysoe Gardens 29
Warmington Gardens 30

Sunday 9th
Styvechale Gardens 28

Saturday 15th
NEW Long Itchington Village Gardens 19

Sunday 16th
Honington Gardens 16
Kenilworth Gardens 18
NEW Long Itchington Village Gardens 19
Whichford & Ascott Gardens 32

Sunday 23rd
Dorridge Gardens 9

Saturday 29th
Welford-on-Avon Gardens 31

Sunday 30th
Welford-on-Avon Gardens 31

July

Every Saturday and Sunday
◆ Bridge Nursery 6

Tuesday 2nd
NEW Dunchurch Park Hotel 10

Sunday 7th
Avon Dassett Gardens 3

Saturday 20th
Guy's Cliffe Walled Garden 13

Sunday 21st
◆ Avondale Nursery 4

Sunday 28th
NEW Dunchurch Park Hotel 10

August

Every Saturday and Sunday
◆ Bridge Nursery 6

Saturday 3rd
NEW Anya Court Care Home 2

Sunday 4th
NEW Anya Court Care Home 2

Sunday 18th
◆ Avondale Nursery 4

Monday 26th
◆ Bridge Nursery 6

Saturday 31st
NEW Squab Hall Farm 26

September

Every Saturday and Sunday to Sunday 22nd
◆ Bridge Nursery 6

Sunday 1st
NEW Squab Hall Farm 26
Stretton-on-Fosse Gardens 27

Saturday 7th
◆ Hill Close Gardens 14
NEW Squab Hall Farm 26

Sunday 8th
NEW Squab Hall Farm 26

Saturday 14th
NEW Squab Hall Farm 26

Sunday 15th
NEW Squab Hall Farm 26

By Arrangement

Arrange a personalised garden visit with your club, or group of friends, on a date to suit you. See individual garden entries for full details.

Admington Hall 1
10 Avon Carrow, Avon Dassett Gardens 3
Broadacre 7
Clifton Hall Farm 8
Court House, Stretton-on-Fosse Gardens 27
16 Delaware Road, Styvechale Gardens 28
Elm Close 12
Fieldgate, Kenilworth Gardens 18
The Hill Cottage 15
2 The Hiron, Styvechale Gardens 28
Honington Glebe, Honington Gardens 16
NEW 19 Leigh Crescent, Long Itchington Village Gardens 19
The Motte 22
NEW Oak House 23
Priors Marston Manor 25
1 Siddeley Avenue, Kenilworth Gardens 18

164 Baginton Road, Styvechale Gardens

THE GARDENS

1 ADMINGTON HALL

Admington, Shipston-on-Stour, CV36 4JN. Mark & Antonia Davies, 01789 450279, adhall@admington.com. *6m NW of Shipston-on-Stour. From Ilmington, follow signs to Admington. Approx 2m, turn R to Admington by Polo Ground. Continue for 1m.* **Visits by arrangement May to Sept. Adm £7.50. Home-made teas.**

A continually evolving 10 acre garden with an established structure of innovative planning and planting. An extensive collection of fine and mature specimen trees provide the essential core structure to this traditional country garden. Features incl a lush broad lawn, orchard, water garden, large walled garden, wild flower meadows and extensive modern topiary. This is a garden in motion. Wheelchair access to most parts of garden, albeit some routes will take slightly longer.

2 NEW ANYA COURT CARE HOME

286 Dunchurch Road, Rugby, CV22 6JA. Karen Handley. *Opp Sainsbury's on the Dunchurch Rd. If our car park is busy please use their car park as an alternative. Please go to Anya Court reception, who will guide you to garden.* **Sat 3, Sun 4 Aug (2-5). Adm £5, chd free. Home-made teas.**

A large landscaped garden with an abundance of trees giving the feel of a woodland walk. As you follow the paths around towards the chicken coop there is a raised fish pond, which leads to our residents garden club with raised vegetable beds. The garden also incl a boules court with café patio area to enjoy a cup of tea and home-made cake, whilst appreciating the plants and the wildlife.

GROUP OPENING

3 AVON DASSETT GARDENS

Southam, CV47 2AE. *7m N of Banbury. From M40 J12 turn L & L again onto the B4100, following signs to Herb Centre & Gaydon. Take 2nd L into village (signed). Park in village & at cemetery car park at the top of the hill.* **Sun 7 July (2-6). Combined adm £7, chd free. Home-made teas at The Coach House.**

10 AVON CARROW
Anna Prosser, annaatthecarrow@btopenworld.com.
Visits also by arrangement Apr to Aug for groups of 5 to 30. Combined visit with two neighbours' gardens & a brief history of main house.

11 AVON CARROW
Mick & Avis Forbes.

THE COACH HOUSE
Diana & Peter Biddlestone.

THE EAST WING, AVON CARROW
Christine Fisher & Terry Gladwin.

HILL TOP FARM
Mr D Hicks.

THE NEW RECTORY
Mrs Victoria Pick.

OLD MILL COTTAGE
Mike & Jill Lewis.

THE OLD RECTORY
Lily Hope-Frost.

POPPY COTTAGE
Bob & Audrey Butler.

NEW **THE SNUG**
Mrs Deb Watts.

THE THATCHES
Trevor & Michele Gill.

Pretty Hornton stone village sheltering in the lee of the Burton Dassett hills, well wooded with parkland setting and The Old Rectory mentioned in Domesday Book. Wide variety of gardens including kitchen gardens, cottage, gravel and tropical gardens. Range of plants incl alpines, herbaceous, perennials, roses, climbers and shrubs. The gardens are along the main road through the village which is up a relatively steep hill. For 2019, there may be a shuttle available, please see website closer to our opening for updated information. Features incl book sale, plant sales, tombola and historic church open. Wheelchair access to most gardens.

4 ◆ AVONDALE NURSERY

at Russell's Nursery, Mill Hill, Baginton, CV8 3AG. Mr Brian Ellis, 02476 673662, enquiries@avondalenursery.co.uk, www.avondalenursery.co.uk. *3m S of Coventry. At junction of A45 & A46 take slip road to Baginton, 1st L to Mill Hill, opp Old Mill Inn.* **For NGS: Sun 21 July, Sun 18 Aug (11-4). Adm £3, chd free. Light refreshments in Potting Shed Cafe at Russell's Nursery.**
For other opening times and information, please phone, email or visit garden website.

Vast array of flowers and ornamental grasses, incl National Collections of *Anemone nemorosa*, *Sanguisorba* and *Aster novae-angliae*. Choc-a-bloc with plants, our Library Garden is a well labelled reference book illustrating the unusual, exciting and even some long-lost treasures. Adjacent nursery is a plantaholic's delight! Big collections of *Helenium, Crocosmia, Agapanthus, Sanguisorba* and ornamental grasses, and the garden will be looking at its best in July and August!

NPC

5 NEW BLACKSMITHS COTTAGE

Little Compton, Moreton-In-Marsh, GL56 0SE. Mrs Andrew Lukas. *Garden entrance is opp the village hall car park. Please park at village hall or in Reed College car park nearby.* **Sun 28 Apr (2-5). Adm £5, chd free. Home-made teas at village hall.**

This walled garden has been created in the last 4 yrs. The planting is for all seasons with many fine and unusual trees, shrubs, plants and bulbs set around a large lawn with a beautiful Aqualens fountain at its centre. In April tulips bring the beds alive. There is a productive vegetable garden, greenhouse and summerhouse. All designed and made by the owners to create a sense of magic. No wheelchair access.

6 ◆ BRIDGE NURSERY

Tomlow Road, Napton, Southam, CV47 8HX. Christine Dakin & Philip Martino, 01926 812737, chris.dakin25@yahoo.com, www.bridge-nursery.co.uk. *3m E of Southam. Brown tourist sign at Napton Xrds on A425 Southam to Daventry road.* **For NGS: Every Sat and Sun 13 Apr to 22 Sept (10-4). Mons 22 Apr; 6, 27 May; 26 Aug (10-4). Adm £3, chd free.** For other opening times and information, please phone, email or visit garden website.

Clay soil? Don't despair. Here is a garden full of an exciting range of plants which thrive in hostile conditions. Grass paths lead you round borders filled with many unusual plants. Features incl a pond and a bamboo grove complete with panda! A peaceful haven for wildlife and visitors. Christine and Philip will gladly provide tea or coffee and biscuits on request. Visits also by arrangement, groups welcome, all proceeds to the NGS.

7 BROADACRE

Grange Road, Dorridge, Solihull, B93 8QA. John Woolman, 07818 082885, jw234567@gmail.com, www.broadacregarden.org. *Approx 3m SE of Solihull. On B4101 opp Railway Pub. Plenty of parking available.* **Sun 21 Apr (2-6). Adm £5, chd free. Home-made teas.** Visits also by arrangement.

Broadacre is a semi-wild garden, managed organically. Attractively landscaped with pools, lawns and trees, beehives, and adjoining stream and wild flower meadows. Bring stout footwear to follow the nature trail. Dorridge Cricket Club is on-site (the bar will be open). Lovely venue for a picnic. Dogs and children are welcome. Excellent country pub, The Railway at the bottom of the drive.

8 CLIFTON HALL FARM

Lilbourne Road, Clifton-upon-Dunsmore, Rugby, CV23 0BB. Robert & Jenny Spencer, 07717 650837, Jenny.ruth.spencer@gmail.com. *2m E of Rugby. From Clifton Church take Lilbourne Rd out of village. 1st farm on R, just past the 30mph limit.* **Visits by arrangement for groups of 5 to 30. Adm £5, chd free. Home-made teas.**

A feast of flowers down on the farm. A garden blossoming with emerald lawns and billowing borders. Silvery foliage, pond, waving grasses and 'pop' plants all there for a yr-round display. The different garden areas incl a jungle area, pool area with a bridge across, and small arboretum, together with a display of old farm machinery, providing a variety of interest. Farm walk included on request. A few gravel areas.

GROUP OPENING

9 DORRIDGE GARDENS

Blue Lake Road, Dorridge, Solihull, B93 8BH. *E of M40 & S of M42. Approx 4m S of Solihull. Parking in Hansell Drive, Blue Lake Rd, Rodborough Rd, & in a paddock at Coppice Wood Farm.* **Sun 23 June (2-5.30). Combined adm £6, chd free. Home-made teas at 75 Blue Lake Road.**

75 BLUE LAKE ROAD
Sal & Peter Renwick.

NEW **COPPICE WOOD FARM**
Mrs Teresa Morse.

NEW **10 HANSELL DRIVE**
Rosemary Harris.

NEW **6 RODBOROUGH ROAD**
Beryl & Peter Harrison.

NEW **14 WYKEN CLOSE**
Carolyn Travis.

Come and enjoy five lovely gardens in Dorridge with very different character and style. Coppice Wood Farm is a peaceful, informal garden, set in well-tended lawns with lovely views over pastureland. Watch out for the hens! At 10 Hansell Drive, you'll find a stunning garden, created by the owners over the last 31 yrs. A haven for wildlife with art work, driftwood and seaside finds. At 6 Rodborough Road, a ¼ acre garden with a wide range of plants incl flowering evergreen shrubs, acers, roses and herbaceous perennials in a relaxed mingled style. At 14 Wyken Close, enjoy a pocket sized pleasure, a real plant lover's garden, incl different planting areas for wildlife, vegetables and beautiful cottage garden flowers. 75 Blue Lake Road is a lovely ½ acre garden, laid out with lawns, hedges, topiary and deep herbaceous borders. Paths lead to secret corners, incl a gazebo by a large pond, a wonderful spot to sit quietly and look for wildlife, incl newts, water boatmen and the occasional toad! Sloping ground and steps in all gardens.

10 NEW DUNCHURCH PARK HOTEL

Rugby Road, Dunchurch, Rugby, CV22 6QW. Dunchurch Park Hotel, 01788 810656, reservations@dunchurch.co.uk, www.dunchurch.co.uk. *Just S of Rugby on the A426 & just N of the A45/M45 J1.* **Tue 2, Sun 28 July (10-5). Adm £4, chd free. Light refreshments. Tue 2 July incl an indoor Bonhams Valuation Day (11-2), suggested donation £2 per item, proceeds to NGS.**

Dunchurch Park Hotel is set in beautiful Grade II* listed grounds and gardens, a perfect setting in which to relax and unwind. The gardens were designed by the famous Victorian landscape architect, Thomas Mawson and remain one of the best examples of his work today. Bar 1823 will be offering a selection of refreshments on the day which can be enjoyed in the bar itself or on our terrace overlooking the gardens. Partial wheelchair access to some areas of the grounds.

GROUP OPENING

11 EARLSDON GARDENS

Coventry, CV5 6FS. *Turn towards Coventry at A45 & A429 T-lights. Take 3rd L into Beechwood Ave, continue ½m to St Barbara's Church at Xrds with Rochester Rd. Maps & tickets at St Barbara's Church Hall.* **Mon 6 May (11-4). Combined adm £4, chd free. Light refreshments at St Barbara's Church Hall.**

43 ARMORIAL ROAD
Gary & Jane Flanagan.

3 BATES ROAD
Victor Keene MBE.

NEW **28 CLARENDON STREET**
Ruth & Symon Whitehouse.

27 HARTINGTON CRESCENT
David & Judith Bogle.

40 HARTINGTON CRESCENT
Viv & George Buss.

114 HARTINGTON CRESCENT
Liz Campbell & Denis Crowley.

40 RANULF CROFT
Spencer & Sue Swain.

NEW **15 ROCHESTER ROAD**
Professor Jane Hutton.

54 SALISBURY AVENUE
Pam Moffit.

2 SHAFTESBURY ROAD
Ann Thomson & Bruce Walker.

23 SPENCER AVENUE
Susan & Keith Darwood.

27 SPENCER AVENUE
Helene Devane.

Varied selection of town gardens from small to more formal with interest for all tastes incl a mature garden with deep borders bursting with spring colour; a large garden with extensive lawns and an array of rhododendrons, azaleas and large mature trees; densely planted town garden with sheltered patio area and wilder woodland; and a surprisingly large garden offering interest to all ages! There is also a pretty garden set on several levels with hidden aspect; a large peaceful garden with water features and vegetable plot; a large mature garden in peaceful surroundings; and a plantaholic's garden with a large variety of plants, clematis and small trees.

12 ELM CLOSE

Welford-on-Avon, CV37 8PT. Eric & Glenis Dyer, 01789 750793, glenisdyer@gmail.com. *5m SW of Stratford, off B4390. Elm Close is between Welford Garage & The Bell Inn, roadside parking.* **Sat 16, Sun 17 Feb (11-3.30). Adm £4, chd free. Opening with Welford-on-Avon Gardens on Sat 29, Sun 30 June.** Visits also by arrangement Feb to Sept for groups of 10 to 30.
Drifts of snowdrops, aconites, erythroniums and hellebores in spring are followed by species peonies, sumptuous tree peonies, herbaceous peonies and delphiniums. Colourful Japanese maples, daphnes and cornus are underplanted with hostas, heucheras and brunneras. Then agapanthus, salvias and hydrangeas extend the seasons, with hundreds of clematis providing yr-round colour. Gravel front drive slightly sloping, garden mainly flat.

13 GUY'S CLIFFE WALLED GARDEN

Coventry Road, Guy's Cliffe, Warwick, CV34 5FJ.
Sarah Ridgeway, www.guyscliffewalledgarden.org.uk.
Behind Hintons Nursery in Guy's Cliffe. Guy's Cliffe is on the A429, between North Warwick & Leek Wootton. **Sat 20 July (10-3.30). Adm £3, chd free. Home-made teas.**
A Grade II listed garden of special historic interest, having been the kitchen garden for Guy's Cliffe House. The garden dates back to the mid-1700s. Restoration work started 5 yrs ago; using plans from the early C19, the garden layout has already been reinstated and the beds, once more, planted with fruit, flowers and vegetables incl many heritage varieties. Glasshouses awaiting restoration. Original C18 walls. Exhibition of artefacts discovered during restoration.

14 ◆ HILL CLOSE GARDENS

Bread and Meat Close, Warwick, CV34 6HF. Hill Close Gardens Trust, 01926 493339, centremanager@hcgt.org.uk, www.hillclosegardens.com. *Town centre. Follow signs to Warwick racecourse. Entry from Friars St onto Bread and Meat Close. Car park by entrance next to racecourse. 2 hrs free parking. Disabled parking outside the gates.* **For NGS: Sat 16 Feb (11-4); Sat 7 Sept (11-5). Adm £4.50, chd £1. Home-made teas in Visitor Centre. Gluten free options.** For other opening times and information, please phone, email or visit garden website.
Restored Grade II* Victorian leisure gardens comprising 16 individual hedged gardens, 8 brick summerhouses. Herbaceous borders, heritage apple and pear trees, C19 daffodils, over 100 varieties of snowdrops, many varieties of asters and chrysanthemums. Heritage vegetables. Plant Heritage border, auricula theatre, and Victorian style glasshouse. Children's garden. Wheelchair available, please phone to book in advance.

NPC

15 THE HILL COTTAGE

Kings Lane, Snitterfield, Stratford-upon-Avon, CV37 0QA. Gillie & Paul Waldron, 07895 369387, info@thehillcottage.co.uk, www.thehillcottage.co.uk. *5 mins from M40 J15. From village, up White Horse Hill, R at T-junction, R into Kings Lane, 2nd house on L. From M40 J15 take A46 to Stratford, 1m take 2nd exit at r'about, ½m R into Kings Lane, over A46 1st R, 2nd house on L.* **Visits by arrangement Apr to Sept for groups of 5 to 20. Adm £5, chd free. Home-made teas £3 per person.**
High on a ridge overlooking orchards and golf course with fabulous views to distant hills, this extensive garden, full of surprises, offers varied planting areas; open, sunny gravel with exotic specimens; cool, shady woodland with relaxed perennial groups; romantic greenoak pond garden with stone summerhouse; pool with newts and dragonflies. Bluebell wood best in late April. Gazebo, pergolas, lavender walk, lilies, clematis, and too many pots to count! New glasshouse and vegetable garden for 2019. Extensive views across rural Warwickshire. Not suitable for wheelchairs or scooters as many steps and slopes.

Your visits help change lives – we've donated over £16.7 million to Macmillan Cancer Support since 1984

GROUP OPENING

16 HONINGTON GARDENS

Shipston-on-Stour, CV36 5AA. *1½m N of Shipston-on-Stour. Take A3400 towards Stratford-upon-Avon, then turn R signed Honington.* **Sun 16 June (2-5.30). Combined adm £6, chd free. Home-made teas.**

HONINGTON GLEBE
Mr & Mrs J C Orchard, John@johnorchard.co.uk. **Visits also by arrangement May & June for groups of 10+.**

HONINGTON HALL
B H E Wiggin.

MALT HOUSE RISE
Mr P Weston.

THE MALTHOUSE
Mr & Mrs R Hunt.

THE OLD COTTAGE
Liz Davenport.

THE OLD HOUSE
Mr & Mrs I F Beaumont.

ORCHARD HOUSE
Mr & Mrs Monnington.

SHOEMAKERS COTTAGE
Christopher & Anne Jordan.

C17 village, recorded in Domesday, entered by old toll gate.
Ornamental stone bridge over the River Stour and interesting church with C13 tower and late C17 nave after Wren. Eight super gardens. 2 acre plantsman's garden consisting of rooms planted informally with yr-round interest in contrasting foliage and texture, lily pool and parterre. Extensive lawns and fine mature trees with river and garden monuments. Secluded walled cottage garden with roses, and a structured cottage garden formally laid out with box hedging and small fountain. Small, developing garden created by the owners with informal mixed beds and borders. Wheelchair access to most gardens.

GROUP OPENING

17 ILMINGTON GARDENS

Ilmington, CV36 4LA.
01608 682230. *8m S of Stratford-upon-Avon. 8m N of Moreton-in-Marsh. 4m NW of Shipston-on-Stour off A3400. 3m NE of Chipping Campden.* **Sat 25, Sun 26 May (1-5). Combined adm £7, chd free.** Donation to Shipston Home Nursing.

THE BEVINGTONS
Mr & Mrs N Tustain.

CHERRY ORCHARD
Mr Angus Chambers.

COMPTON SCORPION FARM
Mrs Karlsen.

FOXCOTE HILL
Mr & Mrs Michael Dingley.

FROG ORCHARD
Mr & Mrs Jeremy Snowden.

GRUMP COTTAGE
Mr & Mrs Martin Underwood.

ILMINGTON MANOR
Mr Martin Taylor.

RAVENSCROFT
Mr & Mrs Clasper.

STUDIO COTTAGE
Sarah Hobson.

7 WILKINS WAY
Mr & Mrs Steve & Pam Routly.

Ilmington is an ancient hillside Cotswold village 2m from the Fosse Way with two good pubs and splendid teas at the village hall. Buy your ticket at Ilmington Manor (next to the Red Lion Pub); wander the 3 acre gardens with fish pond. Then walk to the upper green behind the village hall to Foxcote Hill's large gardens then tiny Grump Cottage's small stone terraced suntrap.
Up Grump St to Ravenscroft's large sculpture filled sloping vistas commanding the hilltop. Walk to nearby Frog Lane, view cottage gardens of Cherry Orchard, Frog Orchard, and Studio Cottage. Then to the Bevingtons many-chambered cottage garden at the bottom of Vallenders Lane near the church and manor ponds. Also visit the delightful newly planted cottage garden of 7 Wilkins Way, on the Armscote Rd on the northeastern fringe of the village and Compton Scorpion Farmhouse's magic garden a mile way. The Ilmington Morris Men performing round the village on Sun 26 May only.

Guy's Cliffe Walled Garden

GROUP OPENING

18 KENILWORTH GARDENS

Kenilworth, CV8 1BT. *Fieldgate Lane, off A452. Tickets & maps available at most gardens. Parking available at Abbey Fields. Street parking on Fieldgate Lane (limited), Siddley Avenue & Beehive Hill.* **Sun 16 June (12-5). Combined adm £7, chd free. Home-made teas at St Nicholas Parochial Hall from 1pm.**

BEEHIVE HILL ALLOTMENTS
Kenilworth Allotment Association.

FIELDGATE
Liz & Bob Watson, 01926 512307, liz.watson@ngs.org.uk
Visits also by arrangement May to Sept for groups of 5 to 30. Adm £4, chd free.

14C FIELDGATE LANE
Mrs Sandra Aulton.

7 FIELDGATE LAWN
Simon Cockell.

NEW **THE HOLLIES**
Mr Neil Darnell.

NEW **LADBROKE HOUSE**
Alan & Debra Green.

OAKWOOD HOUSE
Mrs Jan Kenyon.

NEW **PURLIEU GATE COTTAGE**
John & Alix Dearing.

NEW **2 ST NICHOLAS AVENUE**
Mr Ian Roberts.

ST NICHOLAS PAROCHIAL HALL
St Nicholas Church.

1 SIDDELEY AVENUE
Clare Wightman, siddeley1@sky.com.
Visits also by arrangement May to Aug for groups of 5 to 10.

THE STABLES, 3 FIELDGATE LAWN
Gerry Rutter.

Kenilworth was historically a very important town in Warwickshire. It has one of England's best castle ruins and plenty of pubs and good restaurants. This year we welcome four new gardens to the group making twelve gardens in all, providing great variety. There are small and large gardens, formal, contemporary and cottage styles with trees, shrubs, herbaceous borders, ponds and more intimate, wildlife friendly areas, plus plenty of vegetables at the allotments. Many of the gardens have won Gold in the Kenilworth in Bloom garden competition. Partial wheelchair access to most of the gardens.

GROUP OPENING

19 NEW LONG ITCHINGTON VILLAGE GARDENS

Long Itchington, near Southam, CV47 9PD. *2½ m N of Southam on A423 between Coventry & Banbury, next to Grand Union Canal. Leamington 6m W, also access by A426 from Rugby & A425 from Daventry. Car parks signed at all entries to village.* **Sat 15, Sun 16 June (12-5). Combined adm £7, chd free. Home-made teas in Holy Trinity Church, Church Road.**

NEW **BAKEHOUSE COURT**
Martyn & Erica Smith.

NEW **1 BRAKELEY COTTAGES**
Andy & Sue Jack.

NEW **CHERRYWOOD**
Andy & Rosie Skilbeck.

NEW **38 DALE CLOSE**
Simon & Jeni Neale.

NEW **IFFLEY LODGE**
John Glare.

NEW **19 LEIGH CRESCENT**
Tony & Linda Shorthouse, 01926 817192, Tonyshorthouse19@gmail.com.
Visits also by arrangement June to Dec for groups of 5-10.

NEW **MEADOW COTTAGE**
Charlotte Griffin.

NEW **3 ODINGSELL DRIVE**
Adrienne & Steve Mitchell.

NEW **20 ODINGSELL DRIVE**
Jean & Gerry Bailey.

NEW **8 ORCHARD WAY**
Colin & Val Martin.

SANDY ACRE
David & Janis Tait.

NEW **8 THE SQUARE**
George & Janet Powell.

NEW **THORN VILLA**
Barbara Atkins.

NEW **THE WILLOWS**
Simon & Charlotte Collyer.

Opening its gardens for the first time in 2019, Long Itchington is a large village in south Warwickshire next to the Grand Union Canal. It features a network of waymarked paths and several historic buildings including a half-timbered Tudor house where Queen Elizabeth I once stayed, a C15 Manor House and a C12/C13 church. It also boasts the biggest village pond in Warwickshire, and next to the village green, six pubs, a Co-op and a public park and playing field with children's playground, picnic area and a wildflower meadow. Fourteen different gardens of all types are featured including gravel, tropical, vegetable, cottage and contemporary. These range in size from a small courtyard garden to an extensive landscaped garden with panoramic countryside views. Refreshments and plant sale at Holy Trinity Church. Maps of the village showing all open gardens available at the main car parks and church.

20 MAXSTOKE CASTLE

Coleshill, B46 2RD. G M Fetherston-Dilke. *2½ m E of Coleshill. E of Birmingham, on B4114. Take R turn down Castle Lane, Castle drive 1¼ m on R.* **Sun 2 June (11-5). Adm £7.50, chd £5. Light refreshments.**
Approx 5 acres of garden and grounds with herbaceous, shrubs and trees in the immediate surroundings of this C14 moated castle. No wheelchair access to house.

21 ◆ THE MILL GARDEN

55 Mill Street, Warwick, CV34 4HB. Julia (née Measures) Russell & David Russell, www. visitwarwick.co.uk/placeofinterest/ the-mill-garden. *Off A425 beside old castle gate, at the bottom of Mill St. Disabled parking & drop off only, use nearby St Nicholas car park.* **For opening times and information, please visit garden website.**

This garden lies in a magical setting on the banks of the River Avon, beneath the walls of Warwick Castle. Winding paths lead round every corner to dramatic views of the castle and ruined Medieval bridge. This informal cottage garden is a profusion of plants, shrubs and trees. Beautiful all year. In 2018 the garden won Gold in the Warwick in Bloom competition for 'Best Garden Open to the Public' and was awarded Certificate of Excellence from Trip Advisor. Open daily 1st April to 31st October 9am-6pm. Partial wheelchair access. Not suitable for electric wheelchairs or large pushchairs. Sorry no dogs.

22 THE MOTTE

School Lane, Hunningham, Leamington Spa, CV33 9DS. Margaret & Peter Green, 01926 632903, margaretegreen100@gmail.com. *5m E of Leamington Spa. 1m NW off B4455 (Fosse Way) at Hunningham Hill Xrds.* **Visits by arrangement May to Aug for groups of up to 20. Adm £4, chd free. Home-made teas by prior request.**

Plant lover's garden of about ⅓ acre, well stocked with unusual trees, shrubs and herbaceous plants. Set in the quiet village of Hunningham with views over the River Leam and surrounding countryside. The garden has been developed over the last 16yrs and incl woodland, exotic and herbaceous borders, raised alpine bed, troughs, pots, wildlife pond, fruit and vegetable plot. Plant-filled conservatory. Wheelchair access to front and upper rear garden.

23 NEW OAK HOUSE

Waverley Edge, Bubbenhall, Coventry, CV8 3LW. Helena Grant, 07731 419685, helena.grant@btinternet.com. *15 mins from Leamington Spa via the Oxford Rd/A423 & the Leamington Rd/A445 & the A46. Spaces for 4 cars only.* **Visits by arrangement Mar to Oct. Due to parking limitations, we can accommodate groups up to 15 max. Adm £5, chd free. Tea & cake £3 per person.**

Tucked away next to Waverley Woods, Oak House has a small walled garden that has been landscaped and extended over 27 yrs. The garden is split on 2 levels with 7 seating areas in sun and shade, allowing relaxed appreciation of every aspect of the garden, with peaceful places to sit, ponder and enjoy. A focal point is the large terracotta urn, over 60 yrs old, which delivers horizontal interest and the summerhouse and arbour face each other diagonally across the garden. The curved borders have a wide range of planting creating distinct areas which surround a circular lawn. There are over 80 different plant varieties giving yr-round interest and a haven for birds and other wildlife. Wheelchair access on level path which runs round the house.

Your visits help change lives – your generosity has supported unpaid carers through donations to Carers Trust totalling over £3.9 million since 1996

GROUP OPENING

24 PEBWORTH GARDENS

Stratford-upon-Avon, CV37 8XZ. www.pebworth.org/ngs-open-gardens. *7m SW of Stratford-upon-Avon. On B439 at Bidford turn S towards Honeybourne, at 3m turn L at Xrds Stratford A4390, A3400 to Waitrose, to B4362 Camden Rd, R Station Rd, R at T-junction, then L to Long Marston Rd. Follow signs for Village Hall.* **Sun 26, Mon 27 May (1-5.30). Combined adm £8, chd free. Home-made teas at Pebworth Village Hall (no lunches available).**

BANK HOUSE
Clive & Caroline Warren.

NEW **FAR VIEW**
Mr & Mrs Adrian Carus.

FELLY LODGE
Maz & Barrie Clatworthy.

IVYBANK
Mr & Mrs R Davis.
NPC

THE KNOLL
Mr & Mrs K Wood.

MAPLE BARN
Richard & Wendi Weller.

MEON COTTAGE
David & Sally Donnison.

OAK HOUSE
Sue & Oz Jordan.

NEW **THE OLD BARN**
Kevin & Tracey Morley.

PETTIFER HOUSE
Mr & Mrs Michael Veal.

4 WESLEY GARDENS
Anne & Mike Johnson.

Pebworth is a delightful village with thatched cottages and properties young and old. There are a variety of garden styles from cottage gardens to modern, walled and terraced gardens. Pebworth is topped by St Peter's Church, which has a large ring of ten bells, unusual for a small rural church. This year we have 11 gardens opening, with scrumptious tea and cakes provided by the Pebworth WI in the village hall. Please ask for the ramp for wheelchair access to village hall. Wheelchair access is limited in some gardens. Guide and Assistance dogs welcome.

25 PRIORS MARSTON MANOR

The Green, Priors Marston, CV47 7RH. Dr & Mrs Mark Cecil, 07934 440949, whewitt15@yahoo.co.uk. *8m SW of Daventry. Off A361 between Daventry & Banbury at Charwelton. Follow sign to Priors Marston approx 2m. Arrive at T-junction with war memorial on R. Manor on L.* **Visits by arrangement June to Sept. Mon-Thurs only (excl BH). Teas for group bookings only. Adm £6, chd free.**

Arrive in Priors Marston village and explore the manor gardens. Greatly enhanced by present owners to relate back to a Georgian manor garden and pleasure grounds. Wonderful walled kitchen garden provides seasonal produce and cut flowers for the house. Herbaceous flower beds and a sunken terrace with water feature by William Pye. Lawns lead down to the lake around which you can walk amongst the trees and wildlife, with stunning views up to the house and garden aviary. Sculpture on display. Partial wheelchair access.

26 NEW SQUAB HALL FARM

Harbury Lane, Bishops Tachbrook, Leamington Spa, CV33 9QB. Mrs Bec Evans. *10 mins from J13/14 M40. From the Tachbrook Rd/ Harbury Lane junction, head towards Harbury on the Harbury Lane, 300 metres past the entrance to Mallory Court Hotel on the same side of the road.* **Sat 31 Aug, Sun 1, Sat 7, Sun 8, Sat 14, Sun 15 Sept (11-4.30). Adm £5, chd free. Home-made teas.**

My garden is an expression of gratitude hidden from view by its natural surroundings. Discover its secret and you will be warmly welcomed. You will also be able to visit Marilyn's Gallery which sits within the grounds. Very short pathway with loose pea gravel.

♿ ☕

GROUP OPENING

27 STRETTON-ON-FOSSE GARDENS

Stretton on Fosse, GL56 9SD. *Off A429 between Moreton-in-Marsh & Shipston-on-Stour. Two gardens in the centre of the village. Court House is next to the church, Old Beams a few doors away.* **Sun 14 Apr, Sun 1 Sept (2-5.30). Combined adm £6.50, chd free. Home-made teas at Court House.**

COURT HOUSE
Christopher White, 01608 663811, mum@star.co.uk. **Visits also by arrangement Feb to Sept for groups of 10+.**

OLD BEAMS
Mrs Hilary Fossey.

Court House is a continually evolving, 4 acre garden with yr-round interest and colour. Extensive and varied spring bulbs. Herbaceous borders, fernery, recently redesigned and restored walled kitchen garden. Rose garden, winter garden, pond area and paddocks which are gradually being established with wild flowers. Old Beams is a walled cottage garden on a slope with traditional cottage garden plants, small lawn, rockery, fruit cage and vegetable garden.

GROUP OPENING

28 STYVECHALE GARDENS

Baginton Road, Coventry, CV3 6FP. *The gardens are located on the s-side of Coventry close to A45. Tickets & map available on the day from West Orchard United Reformed Church, The Chesils, CV3 6FP. Advance tickets available from suepountney@btinternet.com.* **Sun 9 June (11-5). Combined adm £5, chd free. Light refreshments throughout the day & hot bacon or sausage batches from 11-2.** Donation to Coventry Myton Hospice.

11 BAGINTON ROAD
Ken & Pauline Bond.

164 BAGINTON ROAD
Fran & Jeff Gaught.

16 DELAWARE ROAD
Val & Roy Howells, 02476 419485, valshouse@hotmail.co.uk. **Visits also by arrangement May to Sept for groups of 10 to 30. Combined visit with 2 The Hiron.**

NEW 6 HANDCROSS GROVE
Mary & John Murphy.

2 THE HIRON
Sue & Graham Pountney, 02476 502044, Suepountney@btinternet.com. **Visits also by arrangement May to Sept for groups of 10 to 30. Combined visit with 16 Delaware Road.**

177 LEAMINGTON ROAD
Barry & Ann Suddens.

NEW 27 RODYARD WAY
Jon & Karen Venables.
D

A collection of lovely, mature, suburban gardens, each one different in style and size. Come and enjoy the imaginatively planted herbaceous borders, spectacular roses, water features, fruit and vegetable patches, cottage garden planting and shady areas, something for everyone and plenty of ideas for you to take home. Relax in the gardens and enjoy the warm, friendly welcome you will receive from us all. There will be refreshments available, including hot bacon or sausage batches at lunchtime, and plants for sale in some of the gardens. Several other gardens will be open on the day, including one devoted to memorabilia from the age of steam railway. The gardens open include the winner of the 2017 Daily Mail National Garden Competition and two being featured in Garden News in 2019.

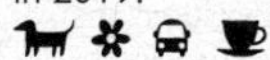

GROUP OPENING

29 TYSOE GARDENS

Middle and Upper Tysoe, Warwick, CV35 0SE. *W of A422, N of Banbury (9m). E of A3400 & Shipston-on-Stour (4m). N of A4035 & Brailes (3m). Parking on the recreation ground CV35 0SE. Entrance tickets & maps at the village hall. Free bus.* **Sat 1, Sun 2 June (2-6). Combined adm £6, chd free. Home-made teas in Tysoe Village Hall & cold drinks at Garden Cottage.**

NEW **5 AVON AVENUE**
Penny & Rob Varley.

DINSDALE HOUSE
Julia & David Sewell.

GARDEN COTTAGE & WALLED KITCHEN GARDEN
Sue & Mike Sanderson, www.twkg.co.uk.

IVYDALE
Sam & Malcolm Littlewood.

7 JEFFS CLOSE
Emma & Tom Moffatt.

KERNEL COTTAGE
Christine Duke.

LAUREL HOUSE
Damaris & Michael Appleton.

THE OLD POLICE HOUSE
Bridget & Digby Norton.

THE WILLOWS
Alan & Ethel Birkbeck.

Tysoe, an original Hornton stone village divided into three parts. The gardens making up this group in Middle and Upper Tysoe are diverse in character of house, planting, size and style. As we are opening on the very first two days of June the variety of flora will be very weather dependent! With this prospect in mind we suspect that our visitors will be as surprised and delighted as us, to discover exactly which plants have made it through the winter on time for our opening and which ones are being rather idle about putting their heads above the parapet so early in the summer. However, we can be sure that Tysoe will always offer a happy atmosphere, some glorious gardens, a good walk round the village or, if you prefer, a free bus ride and a jolly good tea made by the large band of WI bakers and other cooking enthusiasts living in the village. A warm welcome awaits you in this buzzy, energetic, friendly village and gardening community. Come and check us out! Partial wheelchair access.

GROUP OPENING

30 WARMINGTON GARDENS

Banbury, OX17 1BU. *5m NW of Banbury. Take B4100 N from Banbury, after 5m turn R across short dual carriageway into Warmington. From N take J12 off M40 onto B4100.* **Sun 2 June (1-5). Combined adm £6, chd free. Light refreshments at village hall.**

2 CHAPEL STREET
c/o Mark Broadbent, Group Coordinator.

3 COURT CLOSE
Mr & Mrs C J Crocker.

GOURDON
Jenny Deeming.

GREENWAYS
Mark Broadbent.

LANTERN HOUSE
Peter & Tessa Harborne.

THE MANOR HOUSE
Mr & Mrs G Lewis.

THE ORCHARD
Mike Cable.

SPRINGFIELD HOUSE
Jenny & Roger Handscombe, 01295 690286, jehandscombe@btinternet.com.

UNDEREDGE
Alison & Nick Jackson.

1 THE WHEELWRIGHTS
Ms E Bunn.

Warmington is a charming historic village, mentioned in the Doomsday Book, situated at the north-east edge of the Cotswolds in a designated AONB. There is a large village green with a pond overlooked by an Elizabethan Manor House. There are other historic buildings including St Michael's Church, The Plough Inn and Springfield House all dating from the C16 or before. There is a mixed and varied selection of gardens to enjoy during your visit to Warmington. These include the formal knot gardens and topiary of The Manor House, cottage and courtyard gardens, terraced gardens on the slopes of Warmington Hill and orchards containing local varieties of apple trees. Some gardens will be selling home-grown plants. WC at village hall, along with delicious home-made cakes, and hot and cold drinks. Warmington is on a hill with many steps and gravel driveways which could be difficult for wheelchair access.

Ilmington Manor, Ilmington Gardens

Fieldgate, Kenilworth Gardens

GROUP OPENING

31 WELFORD-ON-AVON GARDENS

Welford-on-Avon, CV37 8PT. *5m SW of Stratford-upon-Avon. Off B439 towards Bidford-on-Avon from Stratford upon Avon.* **Sat 29, Sun 30 June (1-5). Combined adm £5, chd free. Light refreshments in Village Memorial Hall.**

ASH COTTAGE
Peter & Sue Hook.

ELM CLOSE
Eric & Glenis Dyer.
(See separate entry)

6 QUINEYS LEYS
Gordon & Penny Whitehurst.

NEW **16 QUINEYS LEYS**
Reeve & Charlotte Carter.

NEW **5 WILLOWBANK**
Mrs Jane Badcock.

Welford-on-Avon has a superb position on the river with serene swans, dabbling ducks and resident herons. It also has a beautiful C12 church and a selection of pubs serving great food. There are many different house styles and an abundance of beautiful cottages with thatched roofs, some dating from C17. The village has chocolate-box charisma! Welford also has many keen gardeners. The gardens that open for the NGS range from small to large, from established to newly designed and planted, and include some with fruit and vegetable plots.

GROUP OPENING

32 WHICHFORD & ASCOTT GARDENS

Whichford & Ascott, Shipston-on-Stour, CV36 5PG. *6m SE of Shipston-on-Stour. For parking please use CV36 5PG. We have a large car park.* **Sun 16 June (1.30-5.30). Combined adm £6, chd free. Home-made teas at Knight's Place.**

ASCOTT LODGE
Charlotte Copley.

BELMONT HOUSE
Robert & Yoko Ward.

KNIGHT'S PLACE
Mrs D Atkins.

NEW **MULBERRY HOUSE**
Mr Richard Thomas.

THE OLD RECTORY
Peter & Caroline O'Kane.

PLUM TREE COTTAGE
Janet Knight.

WHICHFORD HILL HOUSE
Mr & Mrs John Melvin.

THE WHICHFORD POTTERY
Jim & Dominique Keeling, www.whichfordpottery.com.

The gardens in this group reflect many different styles. The two villages are in an AONB, nestled within a dramatic landscape of hills, pasture and woodland, which is used to picturesque effect by the garden owners. Fine lawns, mature shrub planting and much interest to plantsmen provide a peaceful visit to a series of beautiful gardens. Many incorporate the inventive use of natural springs, forming ponds, pools and other water features. Classic cottage gardens contrast with larger and more classical gardens which adopt variations on the traditional English garden of herbaceous borders, climbing roses, yew hedges and walled enclosures. Partial wheelchair access as some gardens are on sloping sites.

WILTSHIRE

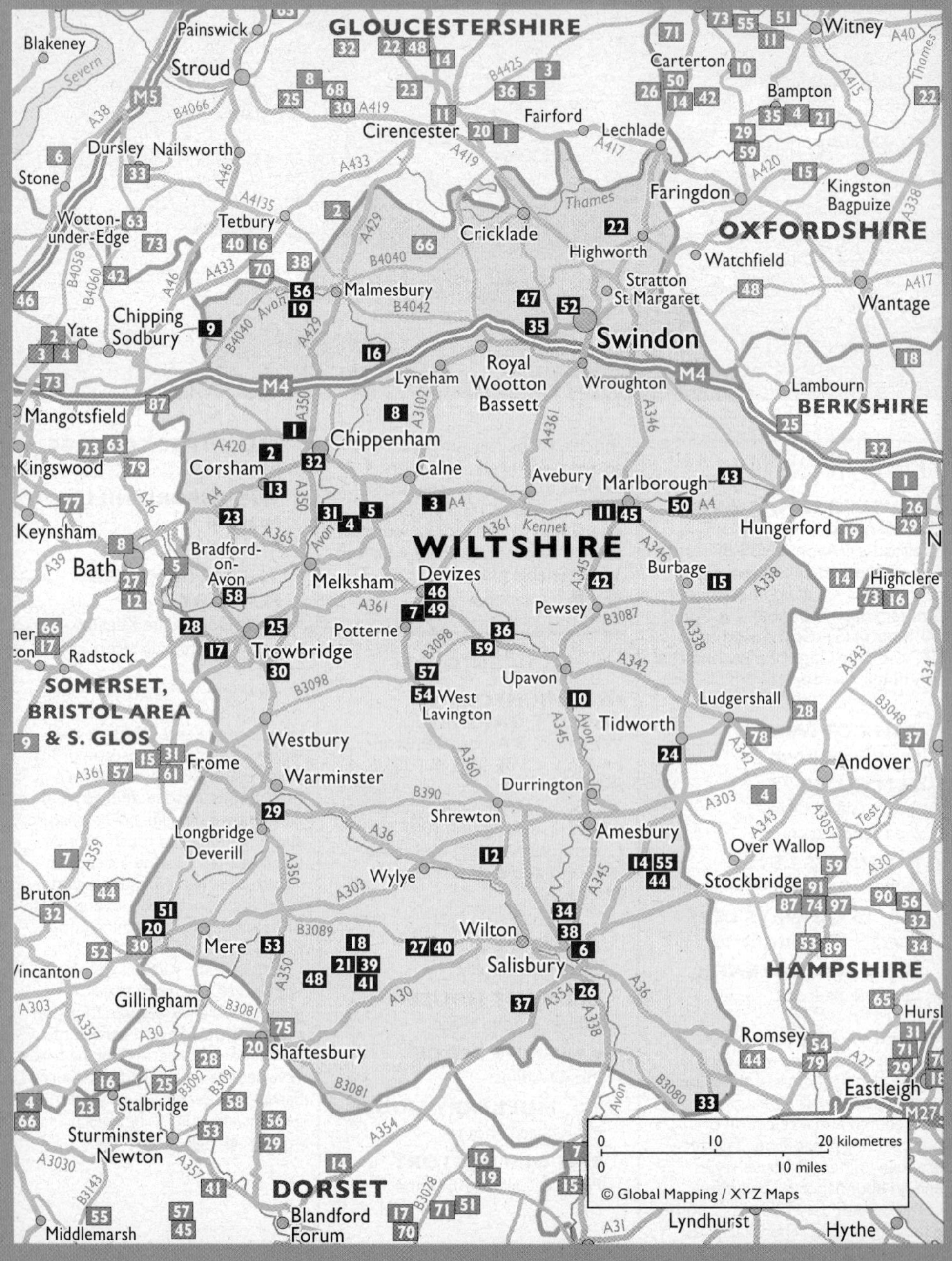
GLOUCESTERSHIRE
OXFORDSHIRE
BERKSHIRE
WILTSHIRE
SOMERSET, BRISTOL AREA & S. GLOS
HAMPSHIRE
DORSET
Blakeney
Painswick
Stroud
Witney
Carterton
Bampton
Fairford
Lechlade
Cirencester
Dursley
Nailsworth
Stone
Wotton-under-Edge
Tetbury
Cricklade
Highworth
Faringdon
Kingston Bagpuize
Watchfield
Stratton St Margaret
Wantage
Malmesbury
Chipping Sodbury
Yate
Swindon
Royal Wootton Bassett
Lyneham
Wroughton
Lambourn
Mangotsfield
Chippenham
Kingswood
Corsham
Calne
Avebury
Marlborough
Hungerford
Keynsham
Bath
Bradford-on-Avon
Melksham
Devizes
Burbage
Highclere
Pewsey
Potterne
Trowbridge
Radstock
Upavon
West Lavington
Ludgershall
Tidworth
Westbury
Frome
Warminster
Andover
Durrington
Shrewton
Amesbury
Longbridge Deverill
Over Wallop
Stockbridge
Wylye
Bruton
Wilton
Mere
Salisbury
Vincanton
Gillingham
Romsey
Shaftesbury
Eastleigh
Stalbridge
Sturminster Newton
Blandford Forum
Middlemarsh
Lyndhurst
Hythe
Severn
Thames
Avon
Kennet
Test
M5
M4
M27
0 10 20 kilometres
0 10 miles
© Global Mapping / XYZ Maps

Wiltshire, a predominantly rural county, covers 1,346 square miles and has a rich diversity of landscapes, including downland, wooded river valleys and Salisbury Plain.

Chalk lies under two-thirds of the county, with limestone to the north, which includes part of the Cotswolds Area of Outstanding Natural Beauty. The county's gardens reflect its rich history and wide variety of environments.

Gardens opening for the National Garden Scheme include the celebrated landscape garden of Stourhead and large privately owned gems such as Broadleas, Oare House and Cadenham Manor, and more modest properties that are lovingly maintained by the owners, such as Crofton Lock House and North Cottage.

The season opens with the snowdrops at Westcroft and continues with fine spring gardens like Fonthill House and Job's Mill.

A wide selection of gardens, large and small, are at their peak in the summer. There are also town gardens, a village opening at Hannington, allotments, manor houses and a garden to Help The Heroes. There is something to delight the senses from January to September.

Volunteers

County Organiser
Annabel Dallas
01672 520266
annabel.dallas@btinternet.com

Amelia Tester
amelia@mememe.plus.com

County Treasurer
Sean Magee
01666 880009
spbmagee@gmail.com

Publicity & Booklet Co-ordinator
Tricia Duncan
01672 810443
tricia@windward.biz

Social Media
Marian Jones
01249 657400
marian.jones@ngs.org.uk

Assistant County Organiser
Suzie Breakwell
01985 850297
suzievb@me.com

Sarah Coate
01722 782365
sarahpcoate@gmail.com

Jo Hankey
01722 742472
rbhankey@gmail.com

Tracey Mosley
01249 782515
traceyemosley1@gmail.com

Diana Robertson
01672 810515
didyrob@gmail.com

Left: Pear Cottage

OPENING DATES

All entries subject to change. For latest information check **www.ngs.org.uk**

Map locator numbers are shown to the right of each garden name.

January

Thursday 17th
Westcroft 55

Thursday 24th
Westcroft 55

Thursday 31st
Westcroft 55

February

Snowdrop Festival

Thursday 7th
Westcroft 55

Friday 8th
Westcroft 55

Thursday 14th
Westcroft 55

Friday 15th
Westcroft 55

Sunday 17th
Westcroft 55

Thursday 21st
Westcroft 55

Saturday 23rd
◆ Lacock Abbey Gardens 31
Westcroft 55

Sunday 24th
Westcroft 55

Thursday 28th
Westcroft 55

March

Thursday 7th
Westcroft 55

Sunday 17th
Fonthill House 18

Sunday 24th
Broadleas House Gardens 7

April

Sunday 7th
◆ Stourhead Garden 51

Saturday 13th
Job's Mill 29

Sunday 14th
Foxley Manor 19

Wednesday 24th
Hazelbury Manor Gardens 23

Friday 26th
◆ Bowood Woodland Gardens 5

Saturday 27th
Allington Grange 1
◆ Iford Manor 28

Sunday 28th
Allington Grange 1
◆ Corsham Court 13
Cottage in the Trees 14
Oare House 42

May

Wednesday 1st
NEW Blackland House 3

Sunday 5th
NEW Stitchcombe House 50
◆ Waterdale House 53

Sunday 12th
◆ Corsham Court 13

Wednesday 15th
Bowden Park 4

Sunday 19th
Broadleas House Gardens 7
The Old Mill 43
◆ Twigs Community Garden 52

Thursday 23rd
Windmill Cottage 57

Friday 24th
Windmill Cottage 57

Saturday 25th
Job's Mill 29

Sunday 26th
Cottage in the Trees 14
Little Durnford Manor 34

Monday 27th
NEW Manor Farm House 36

Wednesday 29th
NEW Woolley Grange Hotel 58

Thursday 30th
NEW Woolley Grange Hotel 58

Friday 31st
NEW Woolley Grange Hotel 58

June

Sunday 2nd
Hazelbury Manor Gardens 23
Hyde's House 27
Purton House 47

Thursday 6th
Cadenham Manor 8
Windmill Cottage 57

Friday 7th
Windmill Cottage 57

Saturday 8th
Crofton Lock House 15
West Lavington Manor 54

Sunday 9th
Chisenbury Priory 10
Cottage in the Trees 14
Crofton Lock House 15
Landford Village Gardens 33
◆ Lydiard Park Walled Garden 35
Mawarden Court 38
North Cottage 41
The Old Rectory, Boscombe 44

Sunday 16th
Dauntsey Gardens 16

Sunday 23rd
Broadleas House Gardens 7
NEW Gold Hill 21
Hannington Village Gardens 22
NEW Hilperton House 25
NEW The Meadows 39

Thursday 27th
Whatley Manor 56

Sunday 30th
Braemar Lodge 6
Duck Pond Barn 17
NEW Help for Heroes 24
Mitre Cottage 40
North Cottage 41
Oare House 42
Pear Cottage 46
1 Southview 49

July

Thursday 4th
Windmill Cottage 57

Friday 5th
Windmill Cottage 57

Sunday 7th
Cherry Orchard Barn 9

Sunday 14th
Broadleas House Gardens 7

Sunday 21st
130 Ladyfield Road & Allotments 32
◆ Twigs Community Garden 52

Sunday 28th
NEW The Coach House 11
NEW Peacock Cottage 45

August

Sunday 4th
The Old Mill 43

Sunday 11th
NEW Gasper Cottage 20

Sunday 18th
Broadleas House Gardens 7

September

Thursday 5th
Pythouse Kitchen Garden 48

Sunday 15th
Horatio's Garden 26

Wednesday 25th
Hazelbury Manor Gardens 23

February 2020

Saturday 22nd
◆ Lacock Abbey Gardens 31

By Arrangement

Arrange a personalised garden visit with your club, or group of friends, on a date to suit you. See individual garden entries for full details.

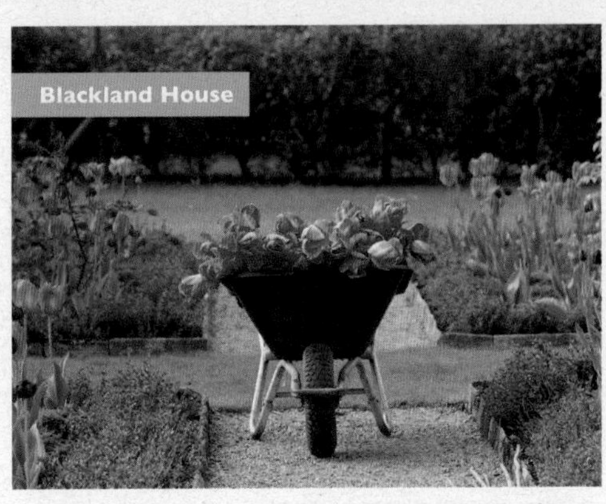

THE GARDENS

1 ALLINGTON GRANGE

Allington, Chippenham, SN14 6LW. Mrs Rhyddian Roper, www.allingtongrange.com. *2m W of Chippenham. Take A420 W from Chippenham. 1st R signed Allington Village, entrance 1m up lane on L.* **Sat 27, Sun 28 Apr (2-5). Adm £5, chd free. Home-made teas.** Informal country garden of approx 1½ acres, around C17 farmhouse (not open) with yr-round interest and a diverse range of plants. Many early spring bulbs. Mixed and herbaceous borders, colour themed; white garden with water fountain. Pergola lined with clematis and roses. Walled potager. Small orchard with chickens. Wildlife pond with natural planting. Mainly level with ramp into potager. Dogs on leads.

2 BIDDESTONE MANOR

Chippenham Lane, Biddestone, SN14 7DJ. Rosie Harris, Head Gardener, 01249 713211. *5m W of Chippenham. On A4 between Chippenham & Corsham turn N. From A420, 5m W of Chippenham, turn S.* **Visits by arrangement Apr to June for groups of 10+, weekdays afternoon or evenings. Adm £10, chd free.** A Cotswold stone C17 manor house, not open, with 5 acres of garden to enjoy. Lake, ponds and streams, arboretum, vegetable and cutting gardens. Formal front garden and natural plantings for wildlife around watersides. Refreshments as requested on booking. Guided walks with Rosie Harris. Wheelchair access to most parts, a few steps, help always available.

3 NEW BLACKLAND HOUSE

Quemerford, Calne, SN11 8UQ. Polly & Edward Nicholson, www.bayntunflowers.co.uk. *Just off A4 heading E as you leave Calne towards Marlborough.* **Wed 1 May (2-5). Adm £10, chd free. Home-made teas incl in admission.** Donation to Dorothy House Hospice.
A wonderfully varied 4½ acre garden adjacent to River Marden. (House not open). Formal walled productive and cutting garden, traditional glasshouses, rose garden and wide herbaceous borders. Interesting topiary, trained fruit trees and specialist displays of historic tulips and unusual spring bulbs. Hand-tied bunches of flowers for sale. Partial wheelchair access, grass and cobbles.

4 BOWDEN PARK

Lacock, Chippenham, SN15 2PP. Bowden Park Estate. *10 mins from Chippenham. Entrance via Top Lodge at top of Bowden Hill, between A342 at Sandy Lane and A350 in Lacock.* **Wed 15 May (11-4). Adm £5, chd free. Light refreshments.**
22 acre private garden within surrounding parkland. Pleasure garden, water garden, working kitchen garden with formal lawns and grotto. Rhododendrons and azaleas in flower.

5 ◆ BOWOOD WOODLAND GARDENS

Calne, SN11 9PG. The Marquis of Lansdowne, 01249 812102, reception@bowood.org, www.bowood.org. *3½m SE of Chippenham. Located off J17 M4 nr Bath & Chippenham. Entrance off A342 between Sandy Lane & Derry Hill Villages. Follow brown tourist signs. For SatNav please use SN11 9PG.* **For NGS: Fri 26 Apr (11-6). Adm £7, chd free. For other opening times and information, please phone, email or visit garden website.**
This 60 acre woodland garden of azaleas, magnolias, rhododendrons and bluebells is one of the most exciting of its type in the country. From the individual flowers to the breathtaking sweep of colour formed by hundreds of shrubs, this is a garden not to be missed. The Woodland Gardens are located 2m from Bowood House and Garden.

Your visits help change lives – we are the largest single funder of the Queen's Nursing Institute

6 BRAEMAR LODGE

18-20 Stratford Road, Salisbury, SP1 3JH. Charles Hubberstey, www.braemarlodgecare.co.uk. *A345 off Salisbury ring rd, Stratford Rd 2nd L, garden 300 yards on L.* **Sun 30 June (1.30-5). Adm £3.50, chd free. Home-made teas. Donations welcome!**

Vibrant and colourful nursing home garden tucked all around the building. Paths lead through butterfly walk, down past our small orchard, along woodland walk, to main courtyard garden of roses, clematis and perennials. Plenty of seating with tea house by rose garden. All main garden areas are accessible, sloping, rolled gravel path to garden.

7 BROADLEAS HOUSE GARDENS

Devizes, SN10 5JQ. Mr & Mrs Cardiff, 07884 340103, broadbridge_jon@hotmail.com. *1m S of Devizes. From Hartmoor Rd turn L into Broadleas Park, follow rd for 350 metres then turn R into estate. Please note, there is no access from A360 Potterne Rd.* **Suns 24 Mar; 19 May; 23 June; 14 July; 18 Aug (2-5). Adm £5, chd free. Home-made teas. Visits also by arrangement Mar to Sept for groups of 10+.**

6 acre garden of hedges, herbaceous borders, rose arches, bee garden and orchard stuffed with good plants. Well stocked kitchen and herb gardens. Mature collection of specimen trees incl magnolia, handkerchief, redwood, dogwood. Overlooked by the house and arranged above the small valley garden which is crowded with magnolias, camellias, rhododendrons, azaleas, cornus and hydrangeas. Wheelchair access to upper garden only, some gravel and narrow grass paths.

8 CADENHAM MANOR

Foxham, Chippenham, SN15 4NH. Victoria & Martin Nye. *B4069 from Chippenham or M4 J17 through Sutton Benger, turn R in Christian Malford and L in Foxham. From A3102 turn L from Calne or R from Lyneham (NW) at Xrds between Hilmarton and Goatacre.* **Thur 6 June (2-5.30). Adm £10, chd free. Pre-booking essential, please visit www.ngs.org.uk for information & booking. Home-made teas.**

The glorious 4 acre garden comprises a series of rooms around a listed manor and dovecote. Divided by yew hedges and moats, the rooms are furnished with specimen trees, mixed borders, plus fountains and statues to focus the eye. Vegetable garden, herb garden and water garden in old canal. June's highlights are a spectacular range of old roses and the peony walk.

9 CHERRY ORCHARD BARN

Luckington, SN14 6NZ. Paul Fletcher & Tim Guard. *Cherry Orchard Barn is ¾ m before the centre of SN14 6NZ, at a T junction. Passing the Barn is ill-advised, as turning rapidly becomes difficult.* **Sun 7 July (1.30-5). Adm £5, chd £2. Home-made teas.**

A charming 1 acre garden created over the past 5 yrs from the corner of a field, with open views of surrounding countryside. Containing 7 rooms, 3 of which are densely planted with herbaceous perennials, each with individual identities and colour themes. The garden is described by visitors as a haven of tranquillity. Largely level access to all areas of the garden. Some gravel paths.

10 CHISENBURY PRIORY

East Chisenbury, SN9 6AQ. Mr & Mrs John Manser, peterjohnmanser@yahoo.com. *3m SW of Pewsey. Turn E from A345 at Enford then N to E Chisenbury, main gates 1m on R.* **Sun 9 June (2-6). Adm £5, chd free. Home-made teas. Visits also by arrangement.**

Medieval Priory with Queen Anne face and early C17 rear (not open) in middle of 5 acre garden on chalk. Mature garden with fine trees within clump and flint walls, herbaceous borders, shrubs, roses. Moisture loving plants along mill leat, carp pond, orchard and wild garden, many unusual plants.

11 NEW THE COACH HOUSE

Bridge Street, Manton, Marlborough, SN8 4HR. Anna Marsden. *Travelling W out of Marlborough on A4 turn L after 1m to Manton village. Garden is 50 metres from A4 by telegraph pole on R. For parking continue into village and follow signs.* **Sun 28 July (2-5). Combined adm with Peacock Cottage £7, chd free. Home-made teas.**

½ - acre country garden surrounding C18 barn, comprising herbaceous border, mixed colour themed beds, pond garden and small veg/soft fruit patch. Informal lawns and mature trees provide a relaxed setting for garden art and wild flowers. C18 well used to water garden. ¾ of garden has disabled access on grass and gravel paths. Dogs on leads welcome. Plants at Peacock Cottage.

12 COCKSPUR THORNS

Berwick St James, Salisbury, SP3 4TS. Stephen & Ailsa Bush, 01722 790445, stephenjdbush@gmail.com. *8m NW of Salisbury. 1m S of A303, on B3083 at S end of village of Berwick St James.* **Visits by arrangement May to Aug for groups of 10 to 20. Weekdays preferred. Adm £5, chd free. Home-made teas.**

2¼ acre garden, completely redesigned 19 yrs ago and developments since, featuring roses (particularly colourful in June), herbaceous border, shrubbery, small walled kitchen garden, secret pond garden, mature and new unusual small trees, fruit trees and areas of wild flowers. Beech, yew and thuja hedgings planted to divide the garden. Small number of vines planted during early 2016.

13 ◆ CORSHAM COURT

Corsham, SN13 0BZ. Lord Methuen, 01249 701610, staterooms@corsham-court.co.uk, www.corsham-court.co.uk. *4m W of Chippenham. Signed off A4 at Corsham.* **For NGS: Sun 28 Apr, Sun 12 May (2-5.30). Adm £10, chd £5. For other opening times and information, please phone, email or visit garden website.**

Park and gardens laid out by Capability Brown and Repton.

Large lawns with fine specimens of ornamental trees surround the Elizabethan mansion. C18 bath house hidden in the grounds. Spring bulbs, beautiful lily pond with Indian bean trees, young arboretum and stunning collection of magnolias. Wheelchair (not motorised) access to house, gravel paths in garden.

♿

14 COTTAGE IN THE TREES

Tidworth Rd, Boscombe Village, nr Salisbury, SP4 0AD. Karen & Richard Robertson, 01980 610921, robertson909@btinternet.com. *7m N of Salisbury. Turn L off A338 just before Social Club. Continue past church, turn R after bridge to Queen Manor, cottage 150yds on R.* **Sun 28 Apr, Sun 26 May (1.30-5). Adm £3.50, chd free. Sun 9 June (1.30-5). Combined adm with The Old Rectory, Boscombe £6, chd free. Home-made teas.** Visits also by arrangement Mar to Sept for groups of 10+.

Enchanting ½ acre cottage garden, immaculately planted with water feature, raised vegetable beds, small wildlife pond and gravel garden. Spring bulbs, hellebores and pulmonarias give a welcome start to the season, with pots and baskets, roses and clematis. Mixed borders of herbaceous plants, dahlias, grasses and shrubs giving all-yr interest.

15 CROFTON LOCK HOUSE

Crofton, Great Bedwyn, Marlborough, SN8 3DW. Michael & Jenny Trussell. *Lock 62, K&A Canal, Crofton, 1m W of Great Bedwyn. 4m W of Hungerford. Follow brown signs to Crofton Beam Engines, then NGS arrows. Garden 8 - 10 mins walk along towpath. See map on NGS website.* **Sat 8, Sun 9 June (1.30-5.30). Adm £3.50, chd free. Home-made teas.** Donation to Wiltshire Air Ambulance.

¾ acre garden in idyllic setting around 200 yr old, off grid lock keeper's cottage. Garden comprises herbaceous beds designed with a painter's eye to provide riotous colour, sculptural form, and an abundance of wildlife from spring to autumn; at rear a small orchard, collection of apple and soft fruit trees, raised vegetable beds, artists' studio (open) and restored privy. Featured in Amateur Gardening Magazine and on BBC Radio Wiltshire. There is no access by car. Wheelchairs have to be pushed along the tow path.

♿

GROUP OPENING

16 DAUNTSEY GARDENS

Church Lane, Dauntsey, Malmesbury, SN15 4HW. *5m SE of Malmesbury. Approach via Dauntsey Rd from Gt Somerford, 1¼m from Volunteer Inn Great Somerford.* **Sun 16 June (1-5). Combined adm £7.50, chd free. Home-made teas at Idover House.**

THE COACH HOUSE
Col & Mrs J Seddon-Brown.

DAUNTSEY PARK
Mr & Mrs Giovanni Amati, 01249 721777, enquiries@dauntseyparkhouse.co.uk.

THE GARDEN COTTAGE
Miss Ann Sturgis.

IDOVER HOUSE
Mr & Mrs Christopher Jerram.

THE OLD COACH HOUSE
Tony & Janette Yates.

THE OLD POND HOUSE
Mr & Mrs Stephen Love.

This group of 6 gardens, centred around the historic Dauntsey Park Estate, ranges from the Classical C18 country house setting of Dauntsey Park, with spacious lawns, old trees and views over the River Avon, to mature country house gardens and traditional walled gardens. Enjoy the formal rose garden in pink and white, old fashioned borders and duck ponds at Idover House, and the quiet seclusion of The Coach House with its thyme terrace and gazebos, climbing roses and clematis. Here, mop-headed pruned crataegus prunifolia line the drive. The Garden Cottage has a traditional walled kitchen garden with organic vegetables, apple orchard, woodland walk and yew topiary. Meanwhile the 2 acres at The Old Pond House are both clipped and unclipped! Large pond with lilies and fat carp, and look out for the giraffe and turtle. The Old Coach House is a small garden with perennial plants, shrubs and climbers.

♿

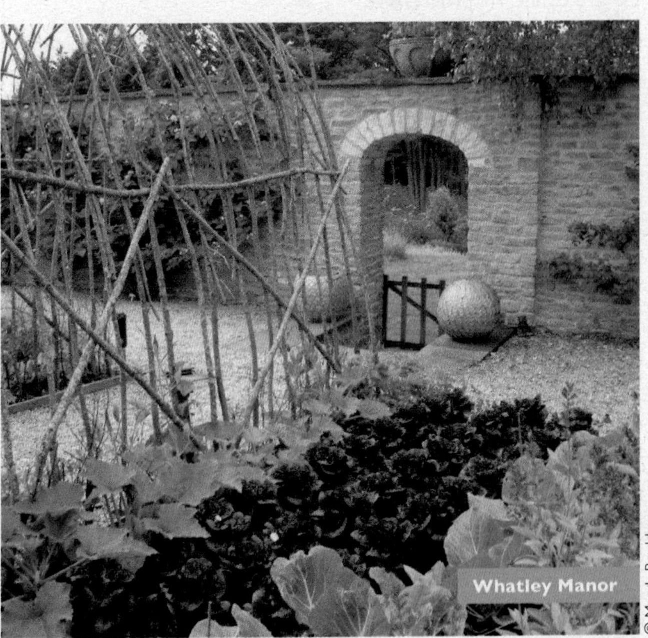

Whatley Manor

© Mandy Bradshaw

17 DUCK POND BARN

Church Lane, Wingfield, Trowbridge, BA14 9LW. Janet & Marc Berlin, 01225 777764, janet@berlinfamily.co.uk. *On B3109 from Frome to Bradford on Avon, turn opp Poplars PH into Church Lane. Duck Pond Barn is at end of lane. Big field for parking.* **Sun 30 June (2-5). Adm £4, chd free. Light refreshments.** Visits also by arrangement May to Aug.
Garden of 1.6 acres with large duck pond, lawns, ericaceous beds, orchard, vegetable garden, big greenhouse, spinney and wild area of grass and trees. Large dry stone wall topped with flower beds with rose arbour. New addition of 3 ponds linked by a rill in flower garden and large pergola in orchard. Set in farmland and mainly flat. Coach parties please ring in advance for catering purposes.

18 FONTHILL HOUSE

Tisbury, SP3 5SA. The Lord Margadale of Islay, www.fonthill.co.uk/gardens. *13m W of Salisbury. Via B3089 in Fonthill Bishop. 3m N of Tisbury.* **Sun 17 Mar (12-5). Adm £6, chd free. Light refreshments. Sandwiches, quiches and cakes, soft drinks, tea and coffee. All proceeds to NGS.** Visits also by arrangement.
Large woodland garden. Daffodils, rhododendrons, azaleas, shrubs, bulbs; magnificent views; formal gardens. The gardens have been extensively redeveloped under the direction of Tania Compton and Marie-Louise Agius. The formal gardens are being continuously improved with new designs, exciting trees, shrubs and plants. Beckford Bottle Shop will have a stall selling wine. Partial wheelchair access.

19 FOXLEY MANOR

Foxley, Malmesbury, SN16 0JJ. Richard & Louisa Turnor. *2m W of Malmesbury. 10 mins from J17 on M4. Turn towards Malmesbury/ Cirencester, then towards Norton and follow signs for the Vine Tree, yellow signs from here.* **Sun 14 Apr (11-5). Adm £5, chd free. Home-made teas.**
Yew hedges divide lawns, borders, rose garden, lily pond and a newer wild area with a natural swimming pond shaded by a Liriodendron. Views through large Turkey Oaks to farmland beyond. Small courtyard gravel garden. Sculptures are sited throughout the gardens. Regret steps and gravel paths make this unsuitable for wheelchairs.

20 NEW GASPER COTTAGE

Gasper Street, Gasper Stourton, Warminster, BA12 6PY. Bella Hoare & Johnnie Gallop. *Near Stourhead Gardens, 4m from Mere, off A303. Turn off A303 at B3092 Mere. Follow Stourhead signs. Go through Stourton. After 1m, turn R after phone box, signed Gasper. House 2nd on R going up hill. Parking past house on L, in field.* **Sun 11 Aug (10.30-5). Adm £5, chd free. Home-made teas.**
1½ acre garden, with views to glorious countryside. Luxurious planting of dahlias, grasses, asters, cardoons and more, incl new perennial planting. Orchard with wildlife pond. Artist studio surrounded by colour balanced planting with formal pond. Pergola with herb terrace. Several seating areas. Garden model railway. 1 step into studio garden, 3 steps to access garden by house. Orchard accessible if not too wet.

21 NEW GOLD HILL

Hindon Lane, Tisbury, Salisbury, SP3 6PZ. Anne Ralphs. *On Hindon Lane, 500 yds up on R from top of Tisbury High street. From Hindon, on L 500yds after road narrows. Parking in field behind The Meadows.* **Sun 23 June (2-5.30). Combined adm with The Meadows £6, chd free. Home-made teas.**
Overlooking the Nadder Valley the house and garden, which are Arts and Crafts inspired, were created on a 1.2-acre derelict builder's yard and field between 2015 and 2017. Formal garden with mixed shrub and perennial planting giving interest throughout the year. Sunken garden, rose garden, fruit trees, walled garden, pond and fountain, parterre beds. Anne Keenan, Landscape Architect and Garden Designer, who designed the garden, will be available to answer any questions on the open day. Regret not suitable for wheelchairs.

GROUP OPENING

22 HANNINGTON VILLAGE GARDENS

Hannington, Swindon, SN6 7RP. *Off B4019 Blunsdon to Highworth Rd by the Freke Arms. Park behind the Jolly Tar PH, tickets from Quarry Bank, 14 Queens Road.* **Sun 23 June (11-5.30). Combined adm £5, chd free. Home-made teas in Hannington Village Hall. Profits in aid of Village Hall.**

BUTLER'S COTTAGE
Mr & Mrs John & Karen Mayell.

NEW **CHESTNUT VILLA**
David Cornish.

GLEBE HOUSE
Charlie & Tory Barne.

HANNINGTON HALL
Guillaume Molhant-Proost.

LUSHILL HOUSE
John & Sasha Kennedy.

QUARRY BANK
Paul Minter & Michael Weldon.

NEW **22 QUEENS ROAD**
Jan & Pete Willis.

ROSE COTTAGE
Mr & Mrs Keith & Ruth Scholes.

Hannington has a dramatic hilltop position and the views into and out of the village resulted in it being made a very large conservation area. The C12 church stands apart from the settlement which has a Jacobean Manor House and many other listed buildings. Large and small gardens in a variety of styles. Many of the gardens follow the brow of the hill and afford stunning views of the upper Thames Valley and the surrounding farm land which is crossed by footpaths and bridleways. Limited wheelchair access as many gardens are on steep hills and feature steps.

23 HAZELBURY MANOR GARDENS

Wadswick, Box, Corsham, SN13 8HX. Mr L Lacroix. *5m SW of Chippenham, 5m NE of Bath. From A4 at Box, A365 to Melksham, at Five Ways junction L onto B3109 towards Corsham; 1st L in ¼ m, drive immed on R.* **Wed 24 Apr (10-4); Sun 2 June**

(1-5); Wed 25 Sept (10-4). Adm £5, chd free. Home-made teas. The C15 Manor house comes into view as you descend along the drive and into the Grade II landscaped Edwardian gardens. The extensive plantings that surround the house are undergoing considerable redevelopment by the owners and their Head Gardener. A wide range of organic horticulture is practiced in 8 acres of relaxed yet playful gardens. Regret much of garden inaccessible to wheelchair users.

24 NEW HELP FOR HEROES

Tedworth House Recovery Centre, Arcot Road, Tidworth, SP9 7AJ. Help for Heroes, www.helpforheroes.org.uk. *Tedworth House Recovery Centre is located off the A338 just S of Tidworth and 3m N of A303.* **Sun 30 June (1-4). Adm £5, chd free. Home-made teas. Refreshments made by volunteers with donations to Help for Heroes.** Help for Heroes run Tedworth House Recovery Centre to provide Recovery and Rehabilitation for wounded, injured and sick service personnel, Veterans and their families. The grounds include a fruit and vegetable garden which is used as a therapeutic gardening space for horticultural activities and further woodlands with an Iron-Age style roundhouse where Veterans can learn woodworking skills.

25 NEW HILPERTON HOUSE

The Knap, Hilperton, Trowbridge, BA14 7RJ. Chris & Ros Brown, candros@blueyonder.co.uk *1½m NE of Trowbridge. Follow A361 towards Trowbridge and turn R at r'about signed Hilperton. House is next door to St Michael's Church in the Knapp off Church St.* **Sun 23 June (2-6). Adm £5, chd free. Home-made teas.** Visits also by arrangement June & July for groups of 20 to 30. 3 weeks notice required.
2½ acres well stocked borders, small stream leading to large pond with fish, water lilies, waterfall and fountain. Fine mature trees incl unusual specimens. Walled fruit and vegetable garden, small woodland area. Rose walk with roses and clematis. Interesting wood carvings, mainly teak. 160yr old vine in conservatory of Grade II listed house, circa 1705 (not open). Activity sheets for children. Some gravel and lawns. Conservatory not wheelchair accessible. Path from front gate has uneven paving but can be bypassed on lawn.

26 HORATIO'S GARDEN

Duke of Cornwall Spinal Treatment Centre, Salisbury Hospital NHS Foundation Trust, Odstock Road, Salisbury, SP2 8BJ. Horatio's Garden Charity, www.horatiosgarden.org.uk. *1m from centre of Salisbury. Please park in car park 8 or 10.* **Sun 15 Sept (1-4). Adm £5, chd free. Tea and delicious cakes - made by Horatio's Garden volunteers - will be served in the Garden Room.** Donation to Horatio's Garden.
Award winning hospital garden which opened in Sept 2012 and was designed by Cleve West for patients with spinal cord injury at the Duke of Cornwall Spinal Treatment Centre. Built from donations given in memory of Horatio Chapple who was a volunteer at the centre in his school holidays. Low limestone walls, which represent the form of the spine, divide densely planted beds and double as seating. Everything in the garden has been designed to benefit patients during their long stays in hospital. Garden is run by Head Gardener and team of volunteers. At 3pm there will be a talk about therapeutic gardens by Charity Chair Dr Olivia Chapple & Head Gardener, Stephen Hackett. 3 Society of Garden Designers Awards 2015 and Bali Award 2014. Cleve West has 8 RHS gold medals, incl Best in Show at Chelsea Flower Show in 2011 and 2012. Fully accessible to wheelchairs.

D

27 HYDE'S HOUSE

Dinton, SP3 5HH. Mr George Cruddas. *9m W of Salisbury. Off B3089 nr Dinton Church on St Mary's Rd.* **Sun 2 June (2-5). Adm £6, chd free. Home-made teas at Thatched Old School Room with outside tea tables.**
3 acres of wild and formal garden in beautiful situation with series of hedged garden rooms. Numerous shrubs, flowers and borders, all allowing tolerated wild flowers and preferred weeds, while others creep in. Large walled kitchen garden, herb garden and C13 dovecote (open). Charming C16/18 Grade I listed house (not open), with lovely courtyard. Every year varies. Free walks around park and lake. Steps, slopes, gravel paths and driveway.

28 ◆ IFORD MANOR

Bradford-on-Avon, BA15 2BA. Mr Cartwright-Hignett, 01225 863146, info@ifordmanor.co.uk, www.ifordmanor.co.uk. *7m S of Bath. Off A36, brown tourist sign to Iford 1m. Or from Bradford-on-Avon or Trowbridge via Lower Westwood Village (brown signs). Campervans should call ahead for directions avoiding narrow lanes.* **For NGS: Sat 27 Apr (11-4). Adm £6, chd £5.20. Cream teas. Please see website for details.** For other opening times and information, please phone, email or visit garden website.
Romantic, award-winning, Grade I listed Italianate garden famous for its tranquil beauty and unique design. Home to Edwardian architect and designer Harold Peto 1899-1933. The garden is characterised by steep steps, terraces, sculpture and magnificent rural views. Narrow, twisting paths lead you on in anticipation of the next delight. (House not open). Last garden entry at 3.30pm.

Your visits help change lives – we are Hospice UK's largest charitable funder donating more than £5 million to support hospices in local communities since 1996

29 JOB'S MILL

Five Ash Lane, Crockerton, Warminster, BA12 8BB. Lady Silvy McQuiston. *1½m S of Warminster. Down lane E of A350, S of A36 r'about.* **Sat 13 Apr (2-5); Sat 25 May (2-5.30). Adm £4.50, chd free. Home-made teas.**

Delightful 5 acre garden through which River Wylye flows. Laid out on many levels surrounding old converted water mill. Water garden, herbaceous border, vegetable garden, orchard, riverside and woodland walks and secret garden. Grass terraces designed by Russell Page. Bulbs and erythronium in the spring and perhaps the tallest growing wisteria?

30 NEW KETTLE FARM COTTAGE

Kettle Lane, West Ashton, Trowbridge, BA14 6AW. Tim & Jenny Woodall, 01225 753474, trwwoodall@outlook.com. *Kettle Lane is halfway between West Ashton traffic lights and Yarnbrook roundabout on south side of A350. Garden ½m down end of lane.* **Visits by arrangement May to Oct for groups of up to 10. Adm £3.50, chd free. Home-made teas. Light refreshments incl tea, coffee and/or wine.**

Previously of Priory House, Bradford on Avon, the garden of which was on Gardeners World, September 2017, we have now created a new cottage garden, full of colour and style, flowering from May to Oct. Bring a loved one/ friend to see the garden and have some refreshment. One or two steps.

31 ◆ LACOCK ABBEY GARDENS

High Street, Lacock, Chippenham, SN15 2LG. National Trust, 01249 730459, lacockabbey@nationaltrust.org.uk, www.nationaltrust.org.uk/lacock. *3m S of Chippenham. Off A350. Follow NT signs. Use public car park (parking fee).* **For NGS: Sat 23 Feb (10.30-5.30). Adm £6, chd £3. Light refreshments in courtyard tea room. Several pubs and tea rooms in village. 2020: Sat 22 Feb.** For other opening times and information, please phone, email or visit garden website.

Woodland garden with carpets of aconites, snowdrops, crocuses and daffodils. Botanic garden with greenhouse, medieval cloisters and magnificent trees. Mostly level site, some gravel paths.

32 130 LADYFIELD ROAD & ALLOTMENTS

Ladyfield Road, Chippenham, SN14 0AP. Philip & Pat Canter and Chippenham Town Council. *1m SW of Chippenham. Between A4 Bath and A420 Bristol rds. Signed off B4528 Hungerdown Lane which runs between A4 & A420.* **Sun 21 July (1.30-5.30). Adm £4, chd free. Home-made teas. Light refreshments.**

Very pretty small garden with more than 40 clematis, climbing roses and small fish pond. Curved neat edges packed with colourful herbaceous plants and small trees. 2 patio areas with lush lawn, pagoda and garden arbour. Also Hungerdown Allotments, 15 allotments owned by Chippenham Town Council. Wheelchair access to main path in garden and to allotments on main drive only.

GROUP OPENING

33 LANDFORD VILLAGE GARDENS

Landford, Salisbury, SP5 2AX. *Landford is off A36 between Salisbury and Southampton. From S leave M27 at J2 onto A36. From S/N A36 turn into Landford and through village. At Xrds take Forest Rd. Parking on L.* **Sun 9 June (1-6). Combined adm £6, chd free. Home-made teas at Bentley, Whitehorn Drive.**

BENTLEY
Jacky Lumby.

COVE COTTAGE
Mrs Gina Dearden.

FOREST COTTAGE
Norah Dunn.

THE GATEHOUSE
Mrs Jackie Beatham.

5 WHITEHORN DRIVE
Jackie & Barry Candler.

Landford is a small village set in the northern New Forest, famous for the beauty of its beech and oak trees and freeroaming livestock. The 5 gardens range in size, planting conditions and setting. 3 are in the village, adjacent to Nomansland with its green grazed by New Forest ponies. The Gatehouse has formal herbaceous borders with exuberant planting and colour schemes in mixed herbaceous borders, looking out over paddocks to the forest. Bentley is a small garden, a green oasis containing a wide range of plants and raised vegetable borders. 5 Whitehorn Drive is a damp garden with lush colour and surprises in planting. A short distance away in the forest itself are Forest Cottage, a naturalistic garden with hidden delights around each corner, incl field of wild orchids, and next door Cove Cottage, a mature garden showing a digital screening of the wildlife found in both gardens yr round, which may be of special interest to children.

34 LITTLE DURNFORD MANOR

Little Durnford, Salisbury, SP4 6AH. The Earl & Countess of Chichester. *3m N of Salisbury. Just N beyond Stratford-sub-Castle. Remain to E of R Avon at road junction at Stratford Bridge and continue towards Salterton for ½m heading N. Entrance on L just past Little Durnford sign.* **Sun 26 May (2-5). Adm £4, chd free. Home-made teas in cricket pavilion within grounds.**

Extensive lawns with cedars, walled gardens, fruit trees, large vegetable garden, small knot and herb gardens. Terraces, borders, sunken garden, water garden, lake with islands, river walks, labyrinth walk. Little Durnford Manor is a substantial grade II listed, C18 private country residence (not open) built of an attractive mix of Chilmark stone and flint. Camels, alpacas, llama, pigs, pygmy goats, donkeys and sheep are all grazing next to the gardens. Gravel paths, some narrow. Steep slope and some steps.

35 ◆ LYDIARD PARK WALLED GARDEN

Lydiard Tregoze, Swindon, SN5 3PA. Swindon Borough Council, 01793 466664, lydiardpark@swindon.gov.uk, www.lydiardpark.org.uk. *3m W Swindon, 1m from J16 M4. Follow brown signs from W Swindon.* **For NGS: Sun 9 June (11-4). Adm £3, chd £2. Light refreshments in Coach House Tea Rooms.** For other opening times and information, please phone, email or visit garden website.

Beautiful ornamental C18 walled garden. Trimmed shrubs alternating with individually planted flowers and bulbs incl rare daffodils and tulips, sweet peas, annuals and wall-trained fruit trees. Unique features incl well and sundial. Wide level paths, no steps.

36 NEW MANOR FARM HOUSE

Manor Farm Lane, Patney, Devizes, SN10 3RB. Mr & Mrs Mark Alsop. *Between Pewsey and Devizes. Take 3rd entrance on L going up Manor Farm Lane from village green. Parking available in paddock.* **Mon 27 May (2-5). Adm £5, chd free. Home-made teas. Refreshments in aid of The Wiltshire Bobby Van Trust.**

2-acre plantsman's garden designed in 1980s and updated by us over the past 7 yrs. Lawned areas with borders surrounded by yew hedging, large border by tennis court, formal vegetable garden with buxus parterres and meadow with spring bulbs, box mound and new moist plants garden. Limited wheelchair access due to upward slope and gravel paths. No toilets.

37 MANOR HOUSE, STRATFORD TONY

Stratford Tony, Salisbury, SP5 4AT. Mr & Mrs Hugh Cookson, 01722 718496, lucindacookson@stratfordtony.co.uk, www.stratfordtony.co.uk. *4m SW of Salisbury. Take minor rd W off A354 at Coombe Bissett. Garden on S after 1m. Or take minor rd off A3094 from Wilton signed Stratford Tony and racecourse.* **Visits by arrangement May to Aug for groups of up to 30. Adm £5, chd free. Refreshments by arrangement.**

Varied 4 acre garden with all yr interest. Formal and informal areas. Small lake fed from R Ebble. Pergola-covered vegetable garden, parterre garden, orchard, shrubberies, roses, specimen trees, waterside planting, winter colour and structure, many original contemporary features and places to sit and enjoy the downland views. 2019 the herbaceous beds are undergoing renovation. Some gravel.

38 MAWARDEN COURT

Stratford Road, Stratford Sub Castle, SP1 3LL. Alastair & Natasha McBain. *2m WNW Salisbury. A345 from Salisbury, L at T-lights, opp St Lawrence Church.* **Sun 9 June (2-5.30). Adm £5, chd free. Home-made teas in pool pavilion.** Donation to Friends of St Lawrence.

Mixed herbaceous and rose garden set around C17 house (not open). Pergola walk down through white beam avenue to River Avon and pond pontoon with walk through poplar wood and along river.

39 NEW THE MEADOWS

Hindon Lane, Tisbury, Salisbury, SP3 6PZ. Liz Curzen. *On R on Hindon Lane 600 yds beyond top of Tisbury High Street. From Hindon on L 500 yds from where road narrows. Parking in field.* **Sun 23 June (2-5.30). Combined adm with Gold Hill £6, chd free. Home-made teas at Gold Hill, a short distance across the meadow.**

Large island beds filled with perennials, shrubs, grasses and specimen trees, surrounded by lawns. Garden statues strategically placed, adding to the charm. The garden leads down to fields with wonderful views across R Nadder. Not suitable for wheelchairs.

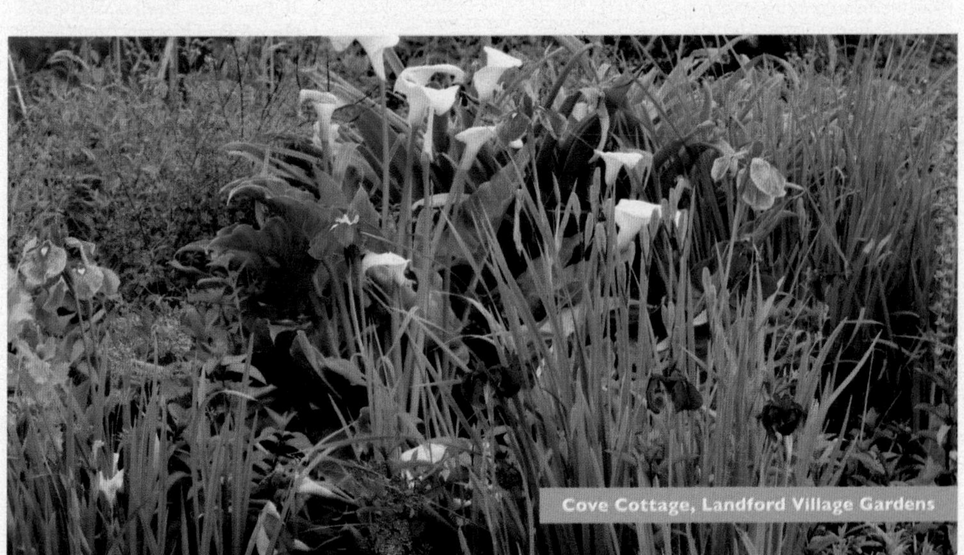

Cove Cottage, Landford Village Gardens

40 MITRE COTTAGE

Snow Hill, Dinton, SP3 5HN. Mrs Beck. *9m W of Salisbury. From B3089 turn up Snowhill by shop. From Wylye bear L at fork by church.* **Sun 30 June (2-6). Adm £5, chd free.**

'Mitre cottage exemplifies what can be achieved in ¾ of an acre without looking contrived or over designed. Well chosen and often unusual plants are balanced at this time of the year by effusive plantings of old fashioned roses and perennials. Set on a slight hillside, paths lead enticingly from one area to another.' Daily Telegraph July 2016. A water feature is a recent addition to the garden.

41 NORTH COTTAGE

Tisbury Row, Tisbury, SP3 6RZ. Jacqueline & Robert Baker, 01747 870019, baker_jaci@yahoo.co.uk. *12m W of Salisbury. From A30 turn N through Ansty, L at T-junction, towards Tisbury. From Tisbury take Ansty road. Car park entrance nr junction signed Tisbury Row.* **Sun 9, Sun 30 June (11.30-5). Adm £4, chd free. Home-made teas. Home-made light lunches.**

On leaving car park, walk past vegetables and through wild flowers to reach house and gardens. Although small there is much variety to find. Garden is divided with lots to explore as each part differs in style and feel. From the intimacy of the garden go out to see the orchard, find the ponds, walk the coppice wood and see the rest of the smallholding. Ceramics, wooden furniture and handicrafts all made by garden owners, including creations from their own sheep's wool for sale. Exciting metal work sculpture exhibition. Large variety of plants for sale.

42 OARE HOUSE

Rudge Lane, Oare, nr Pewsey, SN8 4JQ. Sir Henry Keswick. *2m N of Pewsey. On Marlborough Rd (A345).* **Sun 28 Apr, Sun 30 June (2-6). Adm £6, chd free. Home-made teas.** Donation to The Order of St John.

1740s mansion house later extended by Clough Williams Ellis in 1920s (not open). The formal gardens originally created around the house have been developed over the years to create a wonderful garden full of many unusual plants. Current owner is very passionate and has developed a fine collection of rarities. Garden is undergoing a renaissance but still maintains split compartments each with its own individual charm; traditional walled garden with fine herbaceous borders, vegetable areas, trained fruit, roses and grand mixed borders surrounding formal lawns. The Magnolia garden is wonderful in spring with some trees dating from 1920s, together with strong bulb plantings. Large arboretum and woodland with many unusual and champion trees. In spring and summer there is always something of interest, with the glorious Pewsey Vale as a backdrop. Partial wheelchair access.

43 THE OLD MILL

Ramsbury, SN8 2PN. Annabel & James Dallas. *8m NE of Marlborough. From Marlborough head to Ramsbury. At The Bell PH follow sign to Hungerford. Garden behind yew hedge on R 100yds beyond The Bell.* **Sun 19 May, Sun 4 Aug (2-5). Adm £5.50, chd free. Tea.**

Water running through a multitude of channels no longer drives the mill but provides a backdrop for whimsical garden of pollarded limes and naturalistic planting. Paths meander by streams and over small bridges. Vistas give dramatic views of downs beyond. Potager style kitchen garden and separate cutting garden provide a more formal contrast to the relaxed style elsewhere. Limited wheelchair access as gravel paths and bridges and very soft ground in places.

44 THE OLD RECTORY, BOSCOMBE

Tidworth Road, Boscombe, Salisbury, SP4 0AB. Helen & Peter Sheridan, helen.sheridan@uwclub.net. *7m N of Salisbury on A338. From Salisbury, 2nd L turning after Earl of Normanton PH, just S of Boscombe Social Club and Black Barn.* **Sun 9 June (1.30-5). Combined adm with Cottage in the Trees £6, chd free. Home-made teas.** Visits also by arrangement May & June for groups of 10+.

The elegant gardens of this period property feature a traditional walled garden with herbaceous borders and vegetable beds, contrasting with a parkland of sweeping lawns, mature trees and flowering shrubs. Wheelchair access, though ground may be soft after rain. Gravel paths.

45 NEW PEACOCK COTTAGE

Preshute Lane, Manton, Marlborough, SN8 4HQ. Ian & Clare Maurice. *1m to W of Marlborough along A4, turn L at Manton Village sign. Pass signs to partner garden and follow Car Park signs. If arriving through Manton village turn R by pub.* **Sun 28 July (2-5). Combined adm with The Coach House £7, chd free.**

Set in rural surroundings, this expertly tended, undulating garden, sweeps up from the rear of the house and comprises herbaceous and mixed borders, parterre and exotic bed. Created in 1966 when 2 cottages and their gardens combined, and has been developed considerably over last 15yrs. Disabled parking and access is to the rear of the garden - enquire at Car Park. Wheelchair access is via lawns and grass paths.

46 PEAR COTTAGE

28 Pans Lane, Devizes, SN10 5AF. Mary & Paul Morgan. *From Devizes Mkt Pl go S (Long St). At r'about go L (Southbroom) & R at r'about - Pans Ln. Park in road or roads nearby (easier nr 1 Southview, Wick Lane, SN10 5DR, 5 minutes walk away).* **Sun 30 June (2-5). Combined adm with 1 Southview £6, chd free. Home-made teas.**

'Jewel of a small garden' with interest all yr. Spiral parterres, with alpines, perennials, peonies in the front. Vibrant exotic patio at back, steps up to topiary, roses, grasses, clematis, herbs, trained fruit. Timber greenhouse. Beyond is a wild garden with trees, perennials, alliums, willow arbour and pond with amphibians and dragonflies. Featured in Amateur Gardening and on BBC Radio Wilts. Wheelchair access to front garden and rear patio only.

47 PURTON HOUSE

Church End, Purton, Swindon, SN5 4EB. Mrs Myf Barker. *Turn off Purton High St towards St Mary Church into Church St. At tithe barn L into Church End, after about 300 metres car park on R opp Purton Organics sign (shop open).* **Sun 2 June (10-4.30). Adm £5, chd free. Cream teas.**

This is something different. A large organically managed garden with beautiful specimen trees and Georgian house. Used as wedding venue. The huge ancient plane tree by the lake (formerly monastic carp ponds) is home to a fairy garden. Walled garden with many old varieties of fruit trees, soft fruit and vegetables. NB some weeds as garden is in mid restoration. Interesting sculptures, dove cote, boat house, Italian style garden, fernery, large ancient carp pond, huge plane tree along with many other interesting specimen trees. Possible wheelchair access to lawn areas although some rough ground.

48 PYTHOUSE KITCHEN GARDEN

West Hatch, Tisbury, SP3 6PA. Mr Piers Milburn, 01747 870444, info@pythousekitchengarden.co.uk, www.pythousekitchengarden.co.uk. *A350 S of E Knoyle, follow brown signs to Walled Garden approx 3m. From Tisbury take Newtown road past church, stay on it 2½ m, garden on R. Check map on www.pythousekitchengarden.co.uk.* **Thur 5 Sept (10-5). Adm £4.50, chd free. Light refreshments.** **Visits also by arrangement Apr to Oct. Groups welcome.**

3 acres of working kitchen garden, in largely continuous use since C18, with fruit-lined walls and gnarled apple trees leading down to an orchard, via ravishing, rosa rugosa-edged, beds of flowers, soft fruit, vegetables and beehives. A restaurant now occupies the old potting shed and conservatory, with terraces for tea on open days. Abundant herbs, kiwis and apricots, as well as the deliciously scented 1920s HT rose, Mrs Oakley Fisher, growing by the kitchen door. Restaurant opens 10am for delicious home-made food at coffee, lunch and teatime, served both inside and out on terrace, open until 5pm on open days. Grass paths across slope.

49 1 SOUTHVIEW

Wick Lane, Devizes, SN10 5DR. Teresa Garraud. *From Devizes Mkt Pl go S (Long St). At r'about go L (Southbroom) and R at r'about - Pans Lane, continue over bridge turn R at r'about (Wick Ln). Gdn on R. Park in road or roads nearby.* **Sun 30 June (2-5). Combined adm with Pear Cottage £6, chd free. Home-made teas.**

An atmospheric small town garden that leads you through many different, fascinating areas as it seems to go on and on. A plantswoman's garden with mature topiary and trees including acers and a Cercis canadensis setting off colourful shrub/herbaceous borders. A multitude of large pots on the patio. Featured in Amateur Gardening and BBC Radio Wiltshire. Home-made teas available both here and at Pear Cottage.

50 NEW STITCHCOMBE HOUSE

Stitchcombe, Marlborough, SN8 2EU. Marianne & Bob Benton. *Signed off A4 between Hungerford and Marlborough.* **Sun 5 May (2-5.30). Adm £5, chd free. Home-made teas.**

Garden created in 2009 with brick and flint walls, parterre, box maze, wild flower patch, rill and water feature, beech hedges, far reaching views westward. Tulips in beds and containers. Look out for the parrot that flies free in the garden and whistles at visitors!

51 ◆ STOURHEAD GARDEN

Stourton, Warminster, BA12 6QD. National Trust, 01747 841152, stourhead@nationaltrust.org.uk, www.nationaltrust.org.uk/stourhead. *3m NW of Mere on B3092. Follow NT signs, the property is very well signed from all main roads incl A303.* **For NGS: Sun 7 Apr (9-6). Adm £19.50, chd £9.70. Admission incl house and garden.** **For other opening times and information, please phone, email or visit garden website.**

One of the earliest and greatest landscape gardens in the world, creation of banker Henry Hoare in 1740s on his return from the Grand Tour, inspired by paintings of Claude and Poussin. Planted with rare trees, rhododendrons and azaleas over last 250yrs. Wheelchair access, buggy available.

Wudston House

Pythouse Kitchen Garden

52 ◆ TWIGS COMMUNITY GARDEN

Manor Garden Centre, Cheney Manor, Swindon, SN2 2QJ. TWIGS, 01793 523294, twigs.reception@gmail.com, www.twigscommunitygardens.org.uk. *From Gt Western Way, under Bruce St Bridges onto Rodbourne Rd. 1st L at r'about, Cheney Manor Industrial Est. Through estate, 2nd exit at r'about. Opp Pitch & Putt. Signs on R to Manor Garden Centre.* **For NGS: Sun 19 May, Sun 21 July (1-5). Adm £3, chd free. Home-made teas. Excellent hot and cold lunches available at Olive Tree café within Manor Garden centre adj to Twigs.** For other opening times and information, please phone, email or visit garden website.

Delightful 2 acre community garden, created and maintained by volunteers. Features incl 7 individual display gardens, ornamental pond, plant nursery, Iron Age round house, artwork, fitness trail, separate kitchen garden site, Swindon beekeepers and the haven, overflowing with wild flowers. Featured in Garden Answers & Wiltshire Life magazine and on Great British Gardens website. In Top 100 Attractions in SW England. Most areas wheelchair accessible. Disabled WC.

53 ◆ WATERDALE HOUSE

East Knoyle, SP3 6BL. Mr & Mrs Julian Seymour, 01747 830262. *8m S of Warminster. N of East Knoyle, garden signed from A350. Do not use SatNav.* **For NGS: Sun 5 May (2-6). Adm £5, chd free. Home-made teas.** For other opening times and information, please phone.

In the event of inclement weather, before visiting, please check www.ngs.org.uk/find-a-garden/cancelled-openings/. 4 acre mature woodland garden with rhododendrons, azaleas, camellias, maples, magnolias, ornamental water, bog garden, herbaceous borders. Bluebell walk. Shrub border created by storm damage, mixed with agapanthus and half hardy salvias. Difficult surfaces, sensible footwear essential, parts of garden very wet. Please keep to raked and marked paths in woodland. Partial wheelchair access.

54 WEST LAVINGTON MANOR

1 Church Street, West Lavington, SN10 4LA. Andrew Doman, andrewdoman01@gmail.com. *6m S of Devizes, on A360. House opp White St, where parking is available.* **Sat 8 June (11-6). Adm £10, chd free. Home-made teas and lunch provided by West Lavington Youth Club.** Visits also by arrangement Jan to Dec. Donation to West Lavington Youth Club.

5 acre walled garden first established in C17 by John Danvers who brought Italianate gardens to the UK. Herbaceous border, redeveloped Japanese garden, rose garden, orchard and arboretum with some outstanding specimen trees all centred around a trout stream and duck pond. White Birch grove and walk along southern bank of the stream. Picnics welcome. Only limited areas of garden accessible by wheelchair.

55 WESTCROFT

Boscombe Village, nr. Salisbury, SP4 0AB. Lyn Miles, 01980 610877, lynmiles@icloud.com, www.westcroftgarden.co.uk. *7m N/E Salisbury. On A338 from Salisbury, just past Boscombe & District Social Club, park here or in field opp house, signed on day. Disabled parking only on drive.* **Thurs 17, 24, 31 Jan; 7 Feb (11-4); Fri 8 Feb (1-4); Thur 14 Feb (11-4); Fri 15 Feb (1-4); Sun 17, Thur 21, Sat 23, Sun 24, Thur 28 Feb, Thur 7 Mar (11-4). Adm £3, chd free. Home-made soups, scrummy teas.** Visits also by arrangement Jan to Mar for groups of 20+ on weekdays only except Thursdays.

Whilst overflowing with roses in June, in Jan and Feb the bones of this ⅔ acre galanthophile's garden on chalk are on show. Brick and flint walls, terraces, rustic arches, gates and pond add character. Drifts of snowdrops carpet the floor whilst throughout is a growing collection of nearly 400 named varieties. Many hellebores, pulmonarias, grasses and seedheads add interest. Snowdrops (weather dependent) and snowdrop sundries for sale, greetings cards, mugs, bags, serviettes etc. Wheelchair access is limited to lower levels.

56 WHATLEY MANOR

Twatley, Malmesbury, SN16 0RB. Christian & Alix Landolt, 01666 822888, reservations@whatleymanor.com, www.whatleymanor.com. *4m W of Malmesbury. From A429 at Malmesbury take B4040 signed Sherston. Manor 2m on L.* **Thur 27 June (2-7). Adm £5, chd free. Light refreshments. Tea, coffee and home-made cake in The Loggia Garden. Hotel also open for lunch and full afternoon tea.**

12 acres of English country gardens with 26 distinct rooms each with a strong theme based on colour, scent or style. Original 1920s plan inspired the design and combines classic style with more contemporary touches; incl specially commissioned sculpture. Dogs must be on a lead at all times.

57 WINDMILL COTTAGE

Kings Road, Market Lavington, SN10 4QB. Rupert & Gill Wade, 01380 813527. *5m S of Devizes. Turn E off A360 1m N of West Lavington, 2m S of Potterne. At top of hill turn L into Kings Rd, L into Windmill Lane after 200yds. Limited parking on site, ample parking nearby.* **Thur 23, Fri 24 May, Thur 6, Fri 7 June, Thur 4, Fri 5 July (2-5). Adm £4, chd free. Home-made teas.** Visits also by arrangement May to July. Please phone first. Conducted tours for small groups only.

1 acre cottage style, wildlife friendly garden on greensand. Mixed beds and borders with long season of interest. Roses on pagoda, large vegetable patch for kitchen and exhibition at local shows, greenhouse, polytunnel and fruit cage. Whole garden virtually pesticide free for last 20 yrs. Small bog garden by wildlife pond. Secret glade with prairie. Grandchildren's little wood. Majority of garden accessible. Some soft and gravel paths.

58 NEW WOOLLEY GRANGE HOTEL

Woolley Green, Bradford-on-Avon, BA15 1TX. 01225 864705, info@woolleygrangehotel.co.uk, www.woolleygrangehotel.co.uk. *1m NE of Bradford-on-Avon. Just off B3105 at Woolley Green.* **Wed 29, Thur 30, Fri 31 May (10-4). Adm £5, chd free. Cream teas in garden on open days.** Visits also by arrangement May to Sept for groups of 10 to 30.

Beautiful 14 acre garden with mixed borders, pond, orchard and wildlife garden. The Victorian walled garden has been restored and is fully productive, and a gang of Indian runner ducks roam free keeping the slugs at bay. Lots to do for the children incl White Witch's House and Woolley Sheep Trail. All set against the stunning backdrop of this Jacobean manor house hotel. Lots of play areas for children. Garden staff available for help & advice. Walled Garden produce is grown for the hotel restaurant, open to the public for lunches, teas and evening meals. Several steps around the gardens, but walled garden is accessible to wheelchairs.

59 WUDSTON HOUSE

High Street, Wedhampton, Devizes, SN10 3QE. David Morrison, djm@piml.co.uk. *Wedhampton lies on N side of A342 approx 4m E of Devizes. House is set back on E side of village street at end of drive with beech hedge on either side.* **Visits by arrangement June to Sept for groups of 10+. Refreshments can be arranged as required for visiting groups.**

The garden of Wudston House was started in 2010 following completion of the house. It consists, inter alia, of formal gardens round the house, a perennial meadow, pinetum and an arboretum. Nick Macer and James Hitchmough, who has pioneered the concept of perennial meadows, have been extensively involved in aspects of the garden, which is still developing. Partial wheelchair access.

Your visits help change lives – your generosity helps Marie Curie fund nurses to care for people night and day in their homes, with donations of more than £8.8 million

WORCESTERSHIRE

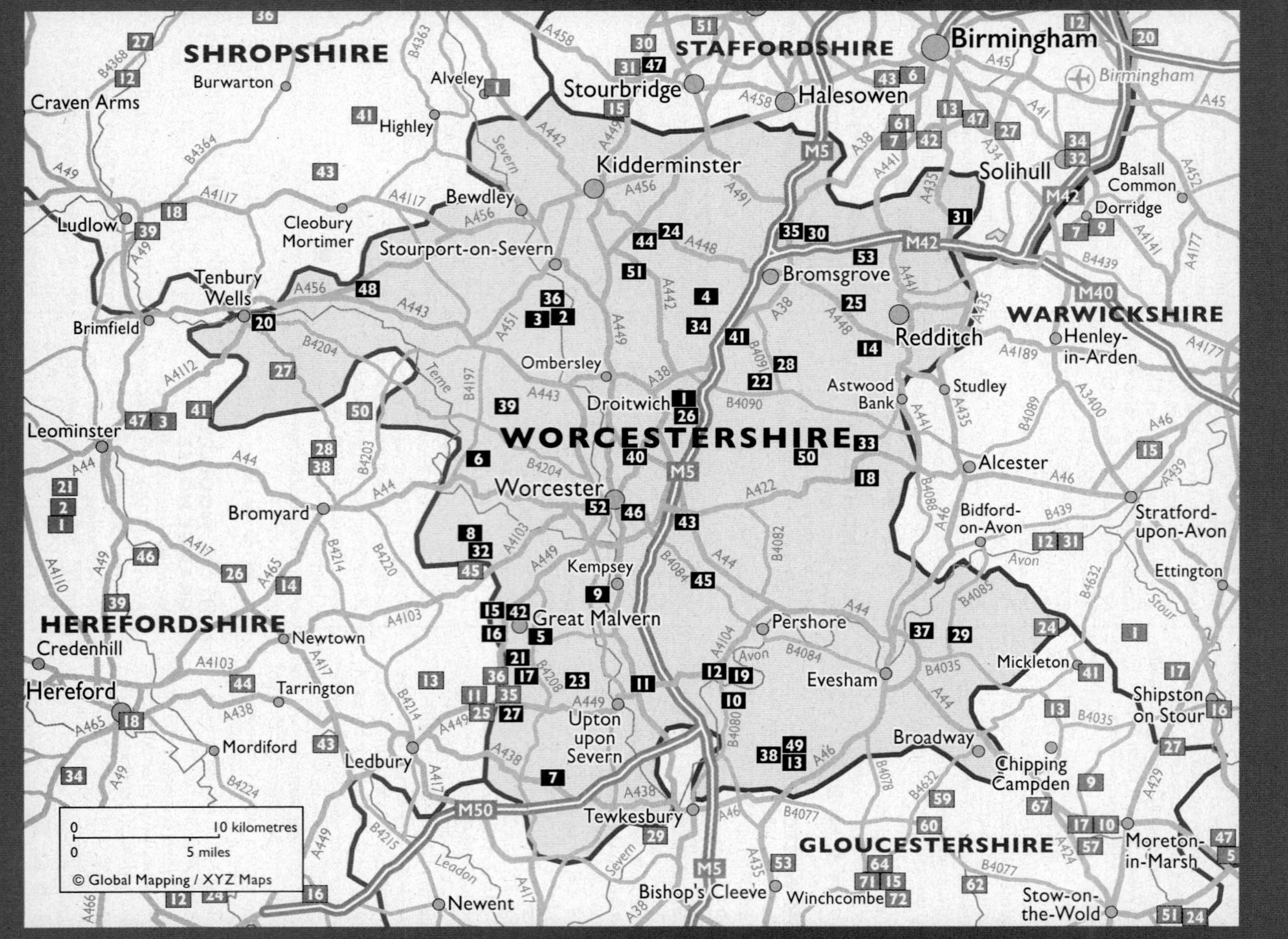

Worcestershire has something to suit every taste, and the same applies to its gardens.

From the magnificent Malvern Hills, the inspiration for Edward Elgar, to the fruit orchards of Evesham which produce wonderful blossom trails in the spring, and from the historic city of Worcester, with its 11th century cathedral and links to the Civil War, to the numerous villages and hamlets that are scattered throughout the county, there is so much to enjoy in this historic county.

Worcestershire is blessed with gardens created by celebrated gardeners such as Capability Brown to ordinary amateur gardeners, and the county can boast properties with grounds of many acres to small back gardens of less than half an acre, but all have something special to offer.

There are gardens with significant historical interest and some with magnificent views and a few that are not what you might consider to be a "typical" National Garden Scheme garden! We also have a number of budding artists within the Scheme, and a few display their works of art on garden open days.

Worcestershire's garden owners guarantee visitors beautiful gardens, some real surprises and a warm welcome.

Volunteers

County Organiser
David Morgan
01214 453595
meandi@btinternet.com

County Treasurer
Lynn Glaze
01386 751924
lynnglaze@cmail.co.uk

Publicity
Pamela Thompson
01886 888295
peartree.pam@gmail.com

Social Media
Brian Skeys
01684 311297
brian.skeys@ngs.org.uk

Advertising & Booklet Co-ordinator
Alan Nokes
01214 455520
alan.nokes@ngs.org.uk

Assistant County Organisers
Brian Bradford
07816 867137
brianbradford101@outlook.com

Philippa Lowe
01684 891340
p.a.lowe140@btinternet.com

Stephanie & Chris Miall
0121 445 2038
stephaniemiall@hotmail.com

Hugh Thomas
07723 347840
hughthomas29ml@aol.com

Left: **Wharf House**

OPENING DATES

All entries subject to change. For latest information check **www.ngs.org.uk**

Map locator numbers are shown to the right of each garden name.

February

Snowdrop Festival

Sunday 17th
Brockamin 9

March

Friday 15th
◆ Little Malvern Court 27

Friday 22nd
◆ Little Malvern Court 27

Sunday 24th
Brockamin 9

Friday 29th
◆ Little Malvern Court 27

April

Saturday 6th
◆ Whitlenge Gardens 51

Sunday 7th
Bylane 11
◆ Whitlenge Gardens 51

Friday 12th
◆ Spetchley Park Gardens 43

Sunday 14th
White Cottage & Nursery 50

Sunday 21st
24 Alexander Avenue 1

Saturday 27th
NEW Millbrook Lodge 32
The River School 40
The Walled Garden 46

Sunday 28th
Hiraeth 26
NEW Millbrook Lodge 32

May

Wednesday 1st
The Walled Garden 46

Saturday 4th
Hewell Grange 25
New House Farm 34

Sunday 5th
1 Church Cottage 12
Hewell Grange 25
New House Farm 34

Monday 6th
1 Church Cottage 12
◆ Little Malvern Court 27

Saturday 11th
Oak Tree House 35

Sunday 12th
White Cottage & Nursery 50

Sunday 19th
Bylane 11

Sunday 26th
1 Church Cottage 12
3 Oakhampton Road 36
Pear Tree Cottage 39
Whitcombe House 49
White Cottage & Nursery 50
68 Windsor Avenue 52

Monday 27th
1 Church Cottage 12
Rothbury 42
White Cottage & Nursery 50
68 Windsor Avenue 52

Tuesday 28th
Hanley Swan NGS Gardens 23

June

Saturday 1st
Eckington Gardens 19

Sunday 2nd
24 Alexander Avenue 1
Eckington Gardens 19

Saturday 8th
The Barton 6
◆ Hanbury Hall & Gardens 22
Wharf House 48

Sunday 9th
The Barton 6
Birtsmorton Court 7
◆ Hanbury Hall & Gardens 22
Hiraeth 26
Wharf House 48

Saturday 15th
Long Hyde House 29

Sunday 16th
Long Hyde House 29
White Cottage & Nursery 50

Monday 17th
Hanley Swan NGS Gardens 23

Saturday 22nd
Astley Country Gardens 2
Eckington Gardens 19
◆ Whitlenge Gardens 51

Sunday 23rd
Astley Country Gardens 2
Cowleigh Lodge 15
Rothbury 42
Whitcombe House 49
◆ Whitlenge Gardens 51

Saturday 29th
24 Croft Bank 16
◆ Harvington Hall 24
The Lodge 28

Sunday 30th
24 Croft Bank 16
◆ Harvington Hall 24
The Lodge 28
3 Oakhampton Road 36
White Cottage & Nursery 50
Withybed Green 53

July

Friday 5th
◆ Spetchley Park Gardens 43

Sunday 7th
NEW The Folly 21

Sunday 14th
Bylane 11

Saturday 20th
Westacres 47

Sunday 21st
Marlbrook Gardens 30
3 Oakhampton Road 36
Rothbury 42
Westacres 47
White Cottage & Nursery 50

Sunday 28th
24 Alexander Avenue 1
Astley Towne House 3

The Dell House

August

Saturday 3rd
Offenham Gardens 37
The River School 40

Sunday 4th
Hiraeth 26
Offenham Gardens 37

Saturday 10th
The Cottage, 3 Crumpfields Lane 14

Sunday 11th
Bridges Stone Mill 8
The Cottage, 3 Crumpfields Lane 14

Sunday 18th
Cowleigh Lodge 15

Sunday 25th
Astley Towne House 3
1 Church Cottage 12
3 Oakhampton Road 36
Pear Tree Cottage 39

Monday 26th
Astley Towne House 3
1 Church Cottage 12
3 Oakhampton Road 36

Saturday 31st
Morton Hall Gardens 33

September

Saturday 7th
New House Farm 34

Sunday 8th
NEW The Folly 21
New House Farm 34

Saturday 14th
◆ Whitlenge Gardens 51

Sunday 15th
◆ Whitlenge Gardens 51

Sunday 22nd
Brockamin 9

By Arrangement

Arrange a personalised garden visit with your club, or group of friends, on a date to suit you. See individual garden entries for full details.

24 Alexander Avenue 1
Badge Court 4
Barnard's Green House 5
The Barton 6
Brockamin 9
Brook House 10
1 Church Cottage 12
Conderton Manor 13
The Cottage, 3 Crumpfields Lane 14
Cowleigh Lodge 15
24 Croft Bank 16
The Dell House 17
6 Dingle End 18
Eckington Gardens 19
Farlands 20
NEW The Folly 21
Hilltop Farm, Eckington Gardens 19
Hiraeth 26
The Lodge 28
Long Hyde House 29
Mantoft, Eckington Gardens 19
74 Meadow Road 31
NEW Millbrook Lodge 32
New House Farm 34
Oak Tree House 35
Overbury Court 38
Pear Tree Cottage 39
The River School 40
The Tynings 45
Westacres 47
Whitcombe House 49
White Cottage & Nursery 50
68 Windsor Avenue 52
19 Winnington Gardens, Hanley Swan NGS Gardens 23

THE GARDENS

1 24 ALEXANDER AVENUE

Droitwich Spa, WR9 8NH. Malley & David Terry, 01905 774907, terrydroit@aol.com. *1m S of Droitwich. Droitwich Spa towards Worcester A38. Or from M5 J6 to Droitwich Town centre.* **Sun 21 Apr, Sun 2 June, Sun 28 July (2-5). Adm £3.50, chd free.** Visits also by arrangement Apr to Sept. Coffee and afternoon tea by arrangement only (not available on open days).

Beautifully designed, now with mature plantings and giving feeling of space and tranquillity, many varieties of clematis growing through shrubs and high hedges. Borders with rare plants and shrubs. Sweeping curves of lawns and paths to woodland area with shade-loving plants. Drought-tolerant plants in S-facing gravel front garden. Alpine filled troughs. April spring bulbs including good variety of snowdrops, erythroniums, specie tulips and alpines, July/August clematis, colourful mixed shrub and herbaceous borders. Partial wheelchair access.

♿ 🚌

Brockamin

GROUP OPENING

2 ASTLEY COUNTRY GARDENS

Longmore Hill Farmhouse, Group Co-ordinator Roger Russell, Astley, Stourport-on-Severn, DY13 0SG. *3m SW of Stourport-on-Severn. Register at Village Hall to receive map. Situated off B4196 - accessed via Ridleys Cross in centre of Astley (DY13 0RE). Car parking available at each venue.* **Sat 22, Sun 23 June (1-6). Combined adm £6, chd free. Home-made teas at Astley Towne House and Longmore Hill Farmhouse.**

ASTLEY TOWNE HOUSE
Tim & Lesley Smith.
(See separate entry)

NEW **HOME WOODS**
Mr & Mrs Keith & Joyce Harris.

LITTLE LARFORD
Lin & Derek Walker.

LITTLE YARHAMPTON
Skene & Petrena Walley.

LONGMORE HILL FARMHOUSE
Roger & Christine Russell.

THE WHITE HOUSE
Tony & Linda Tidmarsh.

THE WHITE HOUSE
John & Joanna Daniels, www.talesfromacountrygarden.wordpress.com.

WOOD FARM
Mr & Mrs W Yarnold.

A wonderful range of 8 country gardens of great variety, in picturesque, peaceful and colourful settings. These incl the garden of a Grade II listed half timbered house with sub tropical planting, stumpery with tree ferns and woodland temple, underground grotto and water features; classical style garden with a variety of features celebrating events in the owner's family; ½ acre garden with mixed borders and large paddock with specimen trees; a Grade II listed C16 farmhouse garden with herbaceous borders, small feature courtyard leading to a part-walled terrace and lily pond; thatched cottage surrounded by mixed borders, bedding displays and woodland; spacious garden with beautiful views and a lake in a secluded valley with an arboretum; farmhouse garden with stream and bog garden, mixed borders and pathways through shrubs and woodland; country bungalow with choice plants in a cottage style garden and wildlife pools. Wheelchair or partial wheelchair access in 5 of the gardens only. See individual gardens for details.

3 ASTLEY TOWNE HOUSE

Astley, DY13 0RH. Tim & Lesley Smith, www.astleytownehousesubtropicalgarden.co.uk. *3m W of Stourport-on-Severn. On B4196 Worcester to Bewdley Road.* **Sun 28 July, Sun 25, Mon 26 Aug (12.30-4.30). Adm £5, chd free. Home-made teas. Opening with Astley Country Gardens on Sat 22, Sun 23 June.**

2½ acres garden of a Grade II listed timber building (not open) incl sub-tropical planting. Stumpery garden with tree ferns and woodland temple. Mediterranean garden, tree house, revolving summerhouse and underground grotto with shell mosaics and water features. In addition there is 'Mr McGregor's' vegetable garden.

We help ordinary people open the gates to their extraordinary private gardens to raise impressive amounts of money through admissions, teas and slices of cake!

4 BADGE COURT

Purshull Green Lane, Elmbridge, Droitwich, WR9 0NJ. Stuart & Diana Glendenning, 01299 851216, dianaglendenning1@gmail.com. *5m N of Droitwich Spa. 2½m from J5 M5. Turn off A38 at Wychbold down side of the Swan Inn. Turn R into Berry Lane. Take next L into Cooksey Green Lane. Turn R into Purshull Green Lane. Garden is on L.* **Visits by arrangement May to July for groups of 10 to 30. Weekdays only outside school hours. Adm £5, chd free.**

Tudor house (not open) set in over 2 acres of garden which includes a large pool, aquaponic fish tanks, topiary garden, rockery, orchard (with 16 varieties of apple trees) formal lawns and borders, large vegetable garden with soft fruits, aviary, greenhouses and terrace where teas are served. Also within the curtilage is the Garden House with cottage garden.

5 BARNARD'S GREEN HOUSE

Hastings Pool, Poolbrook Road, Malvern, WR14 3NQ. Mrs Sue Nicholls, 01684 574446. *1m E of Malvern. At junction of B4211 & B4208.* **Visits by arrangement Apr to Sept for groups of up to 20. Adm £4, chd free. Light refreshments by prior arrangement possible (depending on numbers)..**

With a magnificent backdrop of the Malvern Hills, this 1½ acre old-fashioned garden is a plantsman's paradise. The main feature is a magnificent cedar. 3 herbaceous and 2 shrub borders, rose garden, red and white and yellow borders, an evergreen and hydrangea bed, 2 rockeries, pond, sculptures and vegetable garden. Good garden colour throughout the year. Was the home of Charles Hastings - founder of the British Medical Association (1794-1866). Dogs on leads.

6 THE BARTON

Berrow Green, Martley, WR6 6PL. David & Vanessa Piggott, 01886 822148, v.piggott@btinternet.com. *1m S of Martley. On B4197 between Martley & A44 at Knightwick, corner of lane to Broadheath. Parking at Admiral Rodney Pub opp.* **Sat 8, Sun 9 June (1-5). Adm £4, chd free. Home-made**

teas. waiter/waitress service if required. Visits also by arrangement June & July for groups of 5+. Parking at Admiral Rodney Pub opposite.
This ½ acre cottagey garden full of colour and texture contains unusual shrubs and billowing herbaceous planting. Paths wind through colour-themed gardens, gravel and grass beds. Roses, clematis and unusual climbers decorate pergolas and trellises. Terracotta-decorated walls enclose a vegetable plot and new tender bed. Visitors comments 'Best private garden I've seen.' ' So unusual and beautiful'. Book sale.

7 BIRTSMORTON COURT

Birtsmorton, nr Malvern, WR13 6JS. Mr & Mrs N G K Dawes. *7m E of Ledbury. Off A438 Ledbury/Tewkesbury rd.* **Sun 9 June (2-5.30). Adm £6, chd free. Home-made teas provided by Castlemorton School.**
10 acre garden surrounding beautiful medieval moated manor house (not open). White garden, built and planted in 1997 surrounded on all sides by old topiary. Potager, vegetable garden and working greenhouses, all beautifully maintained. Rare double working moat and waterways including Westminster Pool laid down in Henry VII's reign to mark the consecration of the knave of Westminster Abbey. Ancient yew tree under which Cardinal Wolsey reputedly slept in the legend of the Shadow of the Ragged Stone. No dogs.

8 BRIDGES STONE MILL

Alfrick Pound, WR6 5HR. Sir Michael & Lady Perry. *6m NW of Malvern. A4103 from Worcester to Bransford r'about, then Suckley Rd for 3m to Alfrick Pound.* **Sun 11 Aug (2-5.30). Adm £6, chd free. Home-made teas.**
Once a cherry orchard adjoining the mainly C19 flour mill, this is now a 2½ acre all-year-round garden laid out with trees, shrubs, mixed beds and borders. The garden is bounded by a stretch of Leigh Brook (an SSSI), from which the mill's own weir feeds a mill leat and small lake. A newly completed traditional Japanese garden completes the scene. Wheelchair access by car to courtyard.

24 Alexander Avenue

9 BROCKAMIN

Old Hills, Callow End, Worcester, WR2 4TQ. Margaret Stone, 01905 830370, stone.brockamin@btinternet.com. *5m S of Worcester. ½m S of Callow End on the B4424, on an unfenced bend, turn R into the car-park signed Old Hills. Walk towards the houses keeping R.* **Sun 17 Feb (11-4); Sun 24 Mar (2-5); Sun 22 Sept (2-4). Adm £4, chd free. Teas with home-made cakes from Malvern Country Markets.** Visits also by arrangement Feb to Oct for groups of 10+.

Unlike many NGS gardens this is a plant specialist's 1½ acre informal working garden, parts of which are used for plant production rather than for show. Situated next to common land. Mixed borders with wide variety of hardy perennials where plants are allowed to self seed. Includes Plant Heritage National Collections of Symphyotrichum (Aster) novae-angliae and some Hardy Geraniums. Open for snowdrops in Feb, daffodils in March and asters in September. Good collection of Pulmonarias. Seasonal pond/ bog garden and kitchen garden. An access path reaches a large part of the garden.

NPC

10 BROOK HOUSE

Manor Road, Eckington, WR10 3BH. George & Lynn Glaze, 01386 751924, lynnglaze@cmail.co.uk. *At war memorial in centre of village, take Hammock Rd, then second L into Manor Rd, follow round S bend, on R with name plaque on dry stone wall.* **Visits by arrangement Apr to Sept for groups of 10+. Tea/ cakes or alternative if evening visit, can be arranged. Adm £3, chd free.**

1 acre - back garden is cottage garden, lawned with herbaceous perennial planting, large pond with koi carp, surrounded by alpine rockery, small vegetable patch - front garden lawned with different trees and herbaceous borders. Large open garden with traditional planting. tarmac drive, paths, leading to lawned rear garden - flat but without formal paths - happy for wheelchairs to have access to lawn when weather allows.

11 BYLANE

Worcester Road, Earls Croome, WR8 9DA. Shirley & Fred Bloxsome. *1m N of Upton on Severn turning. On main A38 directly past Earls Croome Garden Centre, signed Bridle Way turn down bridle way to park.* **Sun 7 Apr, Sun 19 May, Sun 14 July (1-5). Adm £3.50, chd free. Light refreshments.**

Herbaceous garden, paddock with wildlife pond, vegetable garden, and chickens, woodland walk with mature trees and wild flowers, approximately 2 acres in all. Plenty of seating areas and shelter if needed, very quiet and secluded. Children welcome.

12 1 CHURCH COTTAGE

Church Road, Defford, Worcester, WR8 9BJ. John Taylor & Ann Sheppard, 01386 750863, ann98sheppard@btinternet.com. *3m SW of Pershore. A4104 Pershore to Upton rd, turn into Harpley Rd, Defford, black & white cottage at side of church. Parking in village hall car park.* **Sun 5, Mon 6, Sun 26, Mon 27 May, Sun 25, Mon 26 Aug (11-5). Adm £3.50, chd free. Home-made teas.** Visits also by arrangement May to Aug for groups of 10 to 30.

True countryman's ⅓ acre garden. Interesting layout. Japanese - style feature with 'dragons den'. Specimen trees; water features; perennial garden, vegetable garden; poultry and cider making, small stream side bog garden. New features in progress. Wheelchair access to most areas.

13 CONDERTON MANOR

Conderton, nr Tewkesbury, GL20 7PR. Mr & Mrs W Carr, 01386 725389, carrs@conderton.com. *5½m NE of Tewkesbury. From M5 - A46 to Beckford - L for Overbury/Conderton. From Tewkesbury B4079 to Bredon - then follow signs to Overbury. Conderton from B4077 follow A46 directions from Teddington r'about.* **Visits by arrangement Apr to Nov for groups of up to 30. Light refreshments. Coffee and biscuits in the morning. Tea and biscuits/cakes in the afternoon Wine and snacks in the evening..**

7 acre garden with magnificent views of Cotswolds. Flowering cherries and bulbs in spring. Formal terrace with clipped box parterre; huge rose and clematis arches, mixed borders of roses and herbaceous plants, bog bank and quarry garden.

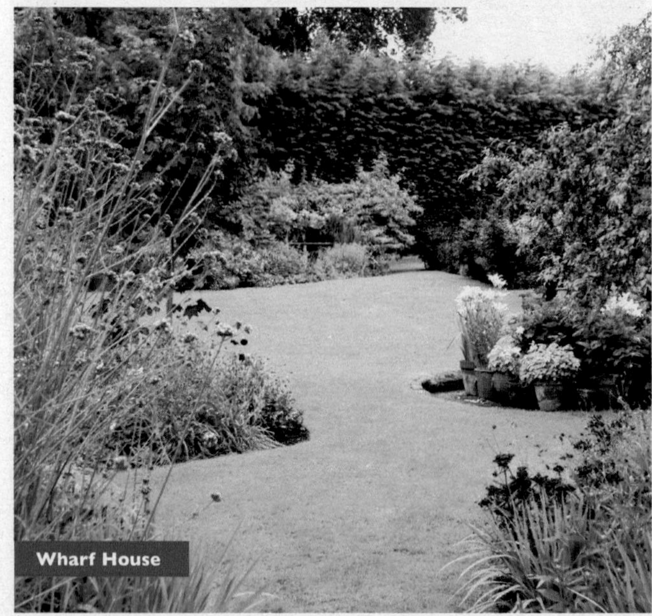

Wharf House

Many unusual trees and shrubs make this a garden to visit at all seasons. Visitors are particularly encouraged to come in spring and autumn when the trees are at their best. This is a garden/small arboretum of particular interest for tree lovers. The views towards the Cotswolds are spectacular and it provides a peaceful walk of about an hour. Some gravel paths and steps - no disabled WC.

14 THE COTTAGE, 3 CRUMPFIELDS LANE

Webheath, Redditch, B97 5PN. Victor Johnson, pjohnson889@btinternet.com. *From A448 through Redditch take slip rds signed to Headless Cross, at r'about take 3rd exit then follow NGS signs.* **Sat 10 Aug (10.30-4.30); Sun 11 Aug (11-4). Adm £5, chd free. Home-made teas. Tea/coffee, cakes and soft drinks.** Visits also by arrangement July & Aug for groups of up to 20.
Established in 2012/13 a 1½ - acre garden landscaped to provide 5 rooms on 4 levels stepped into a hillside. From the 2nd level are stunning views over Vale of Evesham. 2 water features, (1 in a cave) and places to sit and enjoy the wildlife. Wonderland can be found in meadow area of wild flowers. Most paths and steps have a handrail. Partial wheelchair access to levels 2 and 3 are accessible with able body escort (help available).

15 COWLEIGH LODGE

16 Cowleigh Bank, Malvern, WR14 1QP. Jane & Mic Schuster, 01684 439054, dalyan@hotmail.co.uk. *7m SW from Worcester, on the slopes of the Malvern Hills. From Worcester or Ledbury follow the A449 to Link Top. Take North Malvern Rd (behind Holy Trinity church), follow yellow signs. From Hereford take B4219 after Storridge church, follow yellow signs.* **Sun 23 June, Sun 18 Aug (11-5). Adm £4.50, chd free. Home-made teas.** Visits also by arrangement June to Aug for groups of 10 to 30.
The garden on the slopes of the Malvern Hills has been described as 'quirky'! Formal rose garden, grass beds, bamboo walk, colour themed beds, nature path leading to a pond. Large vegetable plot and orchard with views overlooking the Severn Valley. Explore the poly tunnel and then relax with a cuppa and slice of homemade cake. Kids quiz sheet with goody bag for all returned sheets. This is the fifth year of opening of a developing and expanding garden - visitors from previous years will be able to see the difference! Lots of added interest with staddle stones, troughs, signs and other interesting artefacts. Slopes and steps throughout the garden. WC and refreshments.

16 24 CROFT BANK

Malvern, WR14 4DU. Andy & Cathy Adams, 01684 899405, andrewadams2005@yahoo.co.uk. *From Worcester on A449 to Gt Malvern. R onto B4232 signed Bromyard & West Malvern. Continue approx 1½m. Turn R at Elim College Conference centre onto Croft Bank. No 24 is on R.* **Sat 29, Sun 30 June (11-5). Adm £3.50, chd free. Home-made teas.** Visits also by arrangement May to Aug for groups of up to 30.
This half acre garden enjoys wonderful far reaching south and westerly views from high on the Malvern Hills. It continues to evolve with new projects each year. There are colourful flower borders for all seasons, vegetable beds, a small woodland area and bog garden as well as a studio containing artwork inspired by its surroundings. There are places to sit in sun, shade and shelter. This years new garden feature is a stone, timber and brick built gazebo, which provides shelter and a fire in winter. Sloping areas and woodland walk not suitable for wheelchairs. Some steps.

We open the gates to the nation's best gardens, offering a relaxing, memorable and affordable day out. A perfect experience to share with friends and family.

17 THE DELL HOUSE

2 Green Lane, Malvern Wells, WR14 4HU. Kevin & Elizabeth Rolph, 01684 564448, stay@thedellhouse.co.uk, www.thedellhouse.co.uk. *2m S of Great Malvern. Behind former church on corner of Wells Rd & Green Lane just north of petrol station on A449 Wells Rd. Beware satnavs & Google get incorrect location from postcode.* **Visits by arrangement Mar to Nov for groups of up to 20. Short notice visits possible. Adm £4, chd free. Light refreshments.**
Two acre wooded hillside garden of the 1820s former rectory, now a B&B. In the latter stages of recovery by new owners. Peaceful and natural, the garden contains many magnificent specimen trees including a Wellingtonia Redwood. Informal in style with meandering bark paths, historic garden buildings, garden railway and a paved terrace with outstanding views. Several spectacular tree carvings by Steve Elsby, and other sculptures by various artists. Wheelchair access limited but good views from the terrace. Parking is on gravel. Sloping bark paths, some quite steep.

18 6 DINGLE END

Inkberrow, Worcester, WR7 4EY. Mr & Mrs Glenn & Gabriel Allison, 01386 792039. *12m E of Worcester. A422 from Worcester. At the 30 sign in Inkberrow turn R down Appletree Lane then 1st L up Pepper St. Dingle End is 4th on R of Pepper St. Limited parking in Dingle End but street parking on Pepper St.* **Visits by arrangement Apr to Sept. Minimum 6 Maximum 26. Adm £3, chd free. Home-made teas. Soup and sandwiches if required and arranged in advance..**
Over 1 acre garden with formal area close to the house opening into a flat area featuring a large pond, stream and weir with apple orchard and woodland area. Large vegetable garden incl an interesting variety of fruits. Garden designed for wildlife and attractive to birds on account of water and trees. Refreshments for pre arranged groups can be tailored by arrangement e.g. soup and sandwiches, tea and cakes etc. Wheelchair access - slopes alongside every terrace.

GROUP OPENING

19 ECKINGTON GARDENS

Hilltop, Nafford Road, Eckington, WR10 3DH. Group Coordinator Richard Bateman, 01386 750667, richard.bateman111@btinternet.com. *2 gardens - 1 in Nafford Rd the other in Upper End. A4104 Pershore to Upton & Defford, L turn B4080 to Eckington. In centre, by war memorial turn L into New Road (becomes Nafford Road).* **Sat 1, Sun 2 June (11-5). Light refreshments at Mantoft. Evening opening Sat 22 June (6-9). Wine at Mantoft. Combined adm £5, chd free. Tea/coffee and cake or wine available on Sat/ Sun June 1st/2nd. Canapes/wine available on request on evening opening (not incl. in adm).** Visits also by arrangement May to Sept for groups of 10+.

HILLTOP FARM

Richard & Margaret Bateman, 01386 750667, richard.bateman111@btinternet.com. **Visits also by arrangement May to Sept for groups of 10+.**

MANTOFT

Mr & Mrs M J Tupper, 01386 750667. **Visits also by arrangement May to Sept for groups of 10+.**

2 very diverse gardens set in/ close to lovely village of Eckington. Hilltop - 1 acre garden designed by owners from a field 35yrs ago, with sunken garden/pond, rose garden, herbaceous borders, interesting topiary incl. cloud pruning and formal hedging designed to reduce the affect of wind and having 'windows' linking to extensive views over the beautiful Worcestershire countryside. Sculptures made by owner. Vegetable yurt (added 2018) has been successful in allowing pollination and preventing damage to young plants from pigeons, rabbits, butterflies and deer. Mantoft (formerly The Croft) - Wonderful ancient thatched cottage with 1½ acres of magical gardens. Fish pond with ghost koi, Cotswold and red brick walls, large topiary, treehouse with seating, summer house and dovecote, pathways, vistas and stone statues, urns and herbaceous borders. Recently featured in Cotswold Life - should not be missed. Some wheelchair access issues.

20 FARLANDS

Kyrewood, Tenbury Wells, WR15 8SG. Alan & Frances Eachus, 01584 810288, frances.eachus@btinternet.com. *½m E of Tenbury Wells on B4204. Approaching from Tenbury slow down when you reach the 40mph sign at Kyrewood. The rd bends sharply to the L & the garden entrance is on R through the open timber gates.* **Visits by arrangement in Aug for groups of up to 20. Adm £5, chd free. Home-made teas.** Beech and hornbeam hedges divide the one acre garden into separate compartments all linked by a central hedged pathway. There is a mature Atlantic cedar at the centre of the garden but the most striking features are the extensive drifts of herbaceous perennials planted around a naturalised pond and through the kitchen garden. Vegetable garden in a series of raised beds.

21 NEW THE FOLLY

87 Wells Road, Malvern, WR14 4PB. David & Lesley Robbins, 01684 567253, lesleycmedley@btinternet.com. *1½m S of Great Malvern & 9m S of Worcester. Approx 8m from M5 via J7 or J8 exits. Situated in Malvern Wells on A449, 0.7m N of B4209 and 0.2m S of Malvern Common. Parking off A449 0.25m N on lay-by or side road, or in 0.1m N turn E on Peachfield Road which runs by Malvern Common.* **Sun 7 July, Sun 8 Sept (1.30-5.30). Adm £4, chd free. Home-made teas. Tea, coffee and home baking available.** Visits also by arrangement June to Sept for groups of 10 to 20. August excluded. Smaller group size can be discussed.

Steeply sloping garden on Malvern Hills with views over Severn Vale. 3 levels accessed by steps, paved/ gravel paths and ramps. Potager and greenhouse, courtyard, formal terrace and lawn, pergola, mature cedars, ornaments and sculpture in landscaped beds and borders. Climbers, small trees, shrubs, hostas, grasses and ferns, with new areas developing. Seating on each level. Gravel and rockery gardens, small cottage garden, stumpery and shrubbery linked by winding paths with an intimate atmosphere as views are concealed and revealed.

22 ◆ HANBURY HALL & GARDENS

School Road, Hanbury, Droitwich, WR9 7EA. National Trust, 01527 821214, hanburyhall@nationaltrust.org.uk, www.nationaltrust.org.uk/hanburyhall. *4m E of Droitwich. From M5 exit 5 follow A38 to Droitwich; from Droitwich 4m along B4090.* **For NGS: Sat 8, Sun 9 June (9-5). Adm £9, chd £4.50. Light refreshments in the Servants Hall Tea-room. NB Adm quoted are for gardens and park. For whole site Adm £13.40 chd £6.70.** For other opening times and information, please phone, email or visit garden website.

The early eighteenth century gardens and park at Hanbury Hall are a rare example of the work of Royal Designer, George London. The pre-eminent Gardener of his time, his creations provided soothing, order in a chaotic world and initiated the later English Landscape Movement. Servants Hall Tea-Room - hot lunches, tea and cake. Stableyard Cafe for take away snacks and drinks. Chambers Tea-Room for traditional afternoon tea. Buggy available to bring visitors from the car park to the front of the property and wheelchairs are available to borrow from the house.

GROUP OPENING

23 HANLEY SWAN NGS GARDENS

Hanley Swan, Worcester, WR8 0DJ. Group Co-ordinator Brian Skeys. *5m E of Malvern, 3m NW of Upton upon Severn, 9m S of Worcester & M5. From Worcester/ Callow End take B4424 to Hanley Castle then turn R. From Upton upon Severn B4211 to Hanley Castle turn L. From Malvern/Ledbury from A449 take B4209. Signed from village Xrds.* **Tue 28 May, Mon 17 June (11-3). Combined adm £6, chd free. Home-made teas at 19 Winnington Gardens.**

NEW **ORCHARD HOUSE**
Mr & Mrs George & Rachel Salmon.

19 WINNINGTON GARDENS
Brian & Irene Skeys, 01684311297, brimfields@icloud.com.
Visits also by arrangement June to Sept for groups of up to 30.

YEW TREE COTTAGE
Mr & Mrs David & Margaret Read.

3 gardens different in style in Hanley Swan. Orchard House, a one acre garden created from a field just eight years ago. Formal herbaceous beds, a small orchard with an old thorn perry pear, vegetable garden, meadow, dry garden, wild area, home to chickens and bees. Plenty of space and seats from which to admire the view to the Malvern Hills. Yew Tree is a C17 black and white cottage, (not open) and well, within a cottage garden, with field views at rear. A raised bed with penstemon, dahlias, mixed borders. Rose trellis and specimen trees mark the boundaries. At the rear up three steps, there are raised, vegetable beds, greenhouse, soft fruit. 19 Winnington Gardens is a wildlife friendly garden of rooms. Mixed borders planted for year round colour enclosed with climbing roses, a small oriental garden, white and green garden,fruit trees, raised herb bed with a special standard gooseberry bush, a display of wildlife photos taken in the garden and a collection of vintage garden tools. Entrance tickets from Orchard House & 19 Winnington Gardens. Access too narrow for wheelchairs and mobility scooters at 19 Winnington Gardens. One with access and one partial access with gravel paths.

24 ◆ HARVINGTON HALL
Harvington, Kidderminster, DY10 4LR. The Roman Catholic Archdiocese of Birmingham, 01562 777846, harvingtonhall@btconnect.com, www.harvingtonhall.com. *3m SE of Kidderminster. ½m E of A450 Birmingham to Worcester Rd & approx ½m N of A448 from Kidderminster to Bromsgrove.* **For NGS: Sat 29, Sun 30 June (11.30-4). Adm £3.50, chd £1.50. Light refreshments at Harvington Hall.** For other opening times and information, please phone, email or visit garden website.
Romantic Elizabethan moated manor house with charming walled gardens and a small Elizabethan-style herb garden, all tended by volunteers. Tours of the Hall, which contain secret hiding places and rare wall paintings, are also available. Visitor Centre, Tea Room serving light lunches, homemade cakes, and hot and cold beverages, shop and WC. Wheelchair access to gardens and ground floor of Malt House Visitor Centre.

25 HEWELL GRANGE
Hewell Lane, Tardebigge, Redditch, B97 6QS. HMP Hewell. *2m NW of Redditch. HMP Hewell is situated on B4096. For SatNav use B97 6QQ. Follow NGS signs to Grange . Visitors must book in advance via email (address below). This is a prison with booking and security procedures to be followed.* **Sat 4, Sun 5 May (9-3.30). Adm £5, chd free. Home-made teas. Visitors must be pre booked by email to roy.jones01@hmps.gsi.gov.uk before arrival. No booking will result in no entry as this is a working prison.**
C18 landscape park and lake by Lancelot Brown, modified c1812 by Humphery Repton. Blubells, lake and Repton bridge, formal garden, water tower, rock garden and mature woodland. This is Not a flower garden. Visitors will be escorted in small groups. Tour may be over 60 mins and visitors must be able to walk for this length of time. Uneven surfaces so sensible walking footwear is essential. Lakeside walk and bluebell walk a chance to see a historic garden not normally open to the public. Please Note - All visits have to have been booked prior to date for security reasons. There is no wheelchair access to the Gardens.

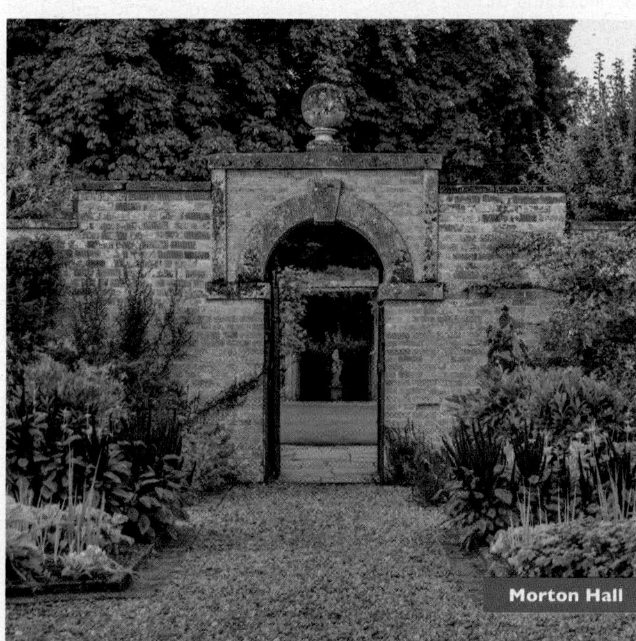
Morton Hall

26 HIRAETH

30 Showell Road, Droitwich, WR9 8UY. Sue & John Fletcher, 07752 717243 or 01905 778390, sueandjohn99@yahoo.com. *1m S of Droitwich. On The Ridings estate. Turn off A38 r'about into Addyes Way, 2nd R into Showell Rd, 500yds on R. Follow the yellow signs!* **Sun 28 Apr, Sun 9 June, Sun 4 Aug (2-5). Adm £3.50, chd free. Home-made teas.** Visits also by arrangement May to Aug for groups of 10 to 30.

Third acre gardens, front, rear contain many plant species, cottage, herbaceous, hostas, ferns, acer trees, 300yr old Olive Tree, pool, waterfall, oak sculptures, metal animals etc inc giraffes, elephant, birds. New patio this year, rear lawn removed, but still an oasis of colours in a garden not to be missed described by visitor as 'A haven on the way to Heaven'. Excellent tea, coffee, cold drinks, home-made cakes and scones served with china cups, saucers, plates, tea-pots and coffee-pots - silver service! Partial wheelchair access.

27 ◆ LITTLE MALVERN COURT

Little Malvern, WR14 4JN. Mrs T M Berington, 01684 892988, littlemalverncourt@hotmail.com, www.littlemalverncourt.co.uk. *3m S of Malvern. On A4104 S of junction with A449.* **For NGS: Fri 15, Fri 22, Fri 29 Mar (2-5.30). Adm £6, chd £2. Tea. Mon 6 May (2-5.30). Adm £8, chd £2. Home-made teas. Tea & biscuits available in March. Homemade teas available on May Bank Holiday.** For other opening times and information, please phone, email or visit garden website.

10 acres attached to former Benedictine Priory, magnificent views over Severn valley. Garden rooms and terrace around house designed and planted in early 1980s; chain of lakes; wide variety of spring bulbs, flowering trees and shrubs. Notable collection of old-fashioned roses. Topiary hedge and fine trees. The May Bank Holiday - Flower Festival in the Priory Church. Partial wheelchair access.

28 THE LODGE

off Holmes Lane, Dodderhill Common, Hanbury, Bromsgrove, B60 4AU. Mark & Lesley Jackson, 07595 085745, mnljack@aol.com. *1m N of Hanbury Village. 3½m E from M5 J5, on A38 at the Hanbury Turn Xrds, take A4091 S towards Hanbury. After 2½m turn L into Holmes Lane, then IMMEDIATE L again into dirt track. Car Park (Worcs Woodland Trust) on L.* **Sat 29, Sun 30 June (11-4). Adm £4, chd free. Cream teas. Tea, coffee, soft drinks, cream teas and home made cakes served 11am - 4pm.** Visits also by arrangement July & Aug for groups of 10+.

A one and half acre garden attached to a part c16 black and white house (not open) with 3 lawned areas, traditional greenhouse, various beds plus stunning views from Dodderhill Common over the North Worcestershire countryside. Small display of classic cars plus other cars of interest. Garden is wheelchair accessible, disabled parking within grounds, toilets not wheelchair accessible No dogs.

29 LONG HYDE HOUSE

Long Hyde Road, South Littleton, Evesham, WR11 8TH. David & Linda Lamb, 01386 834697, davidlamb1943@gmail.com. *From the Badsey r'about on A46, follow B4035 towards Bretforton, then L on B4085 to The Littletons approx 1.7m. L onto Long Hyde Rd. Garden on L opp playing field.* **Sat 15, Sun 16 June (2-5). Adm £5, chd free. Cream teas.** Visits also by arrangement June & July for groups of up to 30. Parking available for a coach.

Beautiful 1 acre traditional garden in Vale of Evesham with stunning views of Cotswolds. Formal rose garden, clipped box hedging, herb garden with 2 ponds, large vegetable area, extensive borders, giant chess set with dark planting , lavender bed, and variety of baskets and tubs. Honey locust tree dominates main lawn, raised patios and seating areas. Wide paths and disabled parking.

GROUP OPENING

30 MARLBROOK GARDENS

Braces Lane, Marlbrook, Bromsgrove, B60 1DY. Group Co-ordinator David Morgan. *2m N of Bromsgrove. 1m N of M42 J1, follow B4096 signed Rednal, turn L at Xrds into Braces Lane. 1m S of M5 J4, follow A38 signed Bromsgrove, turn L at T-lights into Braces Lane. Parking available.* **Sun 21 July (1.30-5.30). Combined adm £5, chd free. Home-made teas. Refreshments in both gardens.**

OAK TREE HOUSE
Di & Dave Morgan.
(See separate entry)

SARANACRIS
John & Janet Morgan.

2 unique and stunning gardens with contrasting styles, Saranacris steeply sloping garden designed and built by owners where frogs stand guard over a plethora of luxuriant hostas and riotous colours dance merrily through jungle planting amidst rare and unusual plants. Streams tinkle over glittering waterfalls and koi swim lazily in sunny ponds. Ascend the spiral stairs and view all from the roof terrace and conservatory on high. Oak Tree House a plantswoman's cottage garden with views over open fields. Past the twisted rail, through the arch leads to a garden packed full of shrubs and herbaceous planting with grass paths weaving in and out. Both gardens overflowing with plants for sun and shade, also ponds, water features, patios, artifacts and sculptures. Recognised for excellence, with many articles over the years in national papers/gardening magazines. Continually evolving, many repeat visitors enjoy sharing with us their new discoveries. Art display at Oak Tree House by garden owners. New for 2019: Wynn's patch - part of garden next door to Oak Tree House being maintained on behalf of the owner. Garden Quiz for children.

31 74 MEADOW ROAD

Wythall, B47 6EQ. Joe Manchester, 01564 829589, joe@cogentscreenprint.co.uk. *4m E of Alvechurch. 2m N from J3 M42. On A435 at Becketts Farm r'about take rd signed Earlswood/Solihull. Approx 250 metres turn L into School Drive, then L into Meadow Rd.* **Visits by arrangement May to Aug. Adm £3.50, chd free. Home-made teas.**

Has been described one of the most unusual urban garden dedicated to woodland, shade-loving plants. 'Expect the unexpected' in a few tropical and foreign species. Meander through the garden under the majestic pine, eucalyptus and silver birch. Sit and enjoy the peaceful surroundings and see how many different ferns and hostas you can find. As seen on BBC Gardeners' World.

32 NEW MILLBROOK LODGE

Millham Lane, Alfrick, Worcester, WR6 5HS. Andrea & Doug Bright, andreabright@hotmail.co.uk. *11m from M5 J7. A4103 from Worcester to Bransford r'about, then Suckley Rd for 3m to Alfrick Pound to find car park on L for Nature Reserve* **Sat 27, Sun 28 Apr (11-5). Adm £5, chd free. Home-made teas. Light refreshments, Tea/ coffee, homemade cakes and homemade soup.** Visits also by arrangement Apr to June for groups of 10+.

A 3½ acre garden and woodland developed by current owners over 22 years. Large informal flowerbeds planted for all year round interest, contains camellias, magnolias and acers. Spring flowering bulbs through to asters and dahlias. Pond with stream and bog garden. Fruit and vegetable garden and gravel garden. Situated in an area of outstanding natural beauty and opposite a nature reserve. Slopes and grass/woodland paths.

33 MORTON HALL GARDENS

Morton Hall Lane, Holberrow Green, Redditch, B96 6SJ. Mrs A Olivieri, www.mortonhallgardens.co.uk. *In the centre of Holberrow Green, at a wooden bench around a tree, turn up Morton Hall Lane. Follow the NGS signs to the gate opposite Morton Hall Farm.* **Sat 31 Aug (10-4). Adm £9, chd free. Light refreshments. (refreshments are new for 2019).**

One of Worcestershire's best kept secrets. Perched atop an escarpment with breath taking views, hidden behind a tall hedge, lies a unique garden of outstanding beauty. A garden for all seasons, it features one of the country's largest fritillary spring meadows, sumptuous herbaceous summer borders, a striking potager, a majestic woodland rockery and an elegant Japanese Stroll Garden with tea house. For other garden openings please see website.

34 NEW HOUSE FARM

Elmbridge Lane, Elmbridge, WR9 0DA. Charles & Carlo Caddick, 01299 851249, Carlocaddick@hotmail.com. *2½ m N of Droitwich Spa. A442 from Droitwich to Cutnall Green. Take lane opp Chequers Pub. Go 1m to T-junction. L towards Elmbridge Green/Elmbridge (past church & hall). At T-junction go R into Elmbridge Lane, garden on L.* **Sat 4, Sun 5 May, Sat 7, Sun 8 Sept (2-4.30). Adm £4.50, chd free. Home-made teas.** Visits also by arrangement May to Sept.

This charming one acre garden surrounding an early C19 farm house (not open) has a wealth of rare trees and shrubs under planted with unusual bulbs and herbaceous plants. Special features are the topiary and perry wheel, natural pond, dry garden, rose garden, and small courtyard retreat. Exotics for sun and shade. Plants for sale in aid of Alzheimer's. Limited wheelchair access due to steps.

68 Windsor Avenue

35 OAK TREE HOUSE

504 Birmingham Road, Marlbrook, Bromsgrove, B61 0HS. Di & Dave Morgan, 0121 445 3595, meandi@btinternet.com. *On A38 midway between M42 J1 & M5 J4. When open individually park in old A38 - R fork 250 yds N of garden or small area in front of Marlbrook Pub car park 200 yds S.* **Evening opening Sat 11 May (5-9). Adm £4.50, chd free. Wine. Opening with Marlbrook Gardens on Sun 21 July.** Visits also by arrangement May to Aug for groups of 10+.

Plantswoman's cottage garden overflowing with plants, pots and interesting artifacts. Secluded patio with plants and shrubs for Spring, small pond and waterfall. Plenty of seating, separate wildlife pond, water features, alpine area, rear open vista. Scented plants, hostas, dahlias and lilies. Conservatory with art by owners. Visitor HS said: "Such a wonderful peaceful oasis". New for 2019: 'Wynn's Patch' - part of next door's garden being maintained on behalf of the owner. Oak Tree House open as single garden by arrangement May to August.

36 3 OAKHAMPTON ROAD

Stourport-On-Severn, DY13 0NR. Sandra & David Traynor. *Between Astley Cross & Kings Arms Public Houses. From Stourport take A451 Dunley Rd towards Worcester. 1600 yds turn L into Pearl Lane. 4th R into Red House Rd, past the Kings Arms Pub, and next L to Oakhampton Rd. Extra parking at Kings Arms Pub.* **Sun 26 May, Sun 30 June, Sun 21 July, Sun 25, Mon 26 Aug (11-5.30). Adm £3.50, chd free. Light refreshments.**

Beginning in March 2016 our plan was to put together a garden with a decidedly tropical feel to include palms from around the world, with tree ferns, bananas and as many other strange and unusual plants from warmer climes that would normally be considered difficult to grow here, as well as a pond and small waterfall. Not a large garden but you'll be surprised what can be done with a small space! Some narrow paths.

GROUP OPENING

37 OFFENHAM GARDENS

Main Street, Offenham, WR11 8QD. *Approaching Offenham on B4510 from Evesham, L into village signed Offenham & ferry ¾m. Follow road round into village. Park in Village Hall car park opp Church. Walk to gardens from car park.* **Sat 3, Sun 4 Aug (11-5). Combined adm £5, chd free. Light refreshments. Light savoury snacks around lunch time, home made teas, strawberries & cream and ice-creams.**

NEW **BROADWAY VIEW**
Brett Pillinger.

DECHMONT
Angela & Paul Gash.

FORGE HOUSE
Mr & Mrs Rob & Maggie Watts.

LANGDALE
Sheila & Adrian James, www.adrianjames.org.uk.

NEW **ROSELEA**
Mike & Linda Ansell.

WILLOWAY
Stephen & Linda Pitts.

Offenham is a picturesque village in the heart of the Vale of Evesham, with thatched cottages and traditional maypole. Six gardens of diverse styles from plantsman to exotic. Broadway View has a formal front garden. In the rear courtyard garden peaceful water features together with lush big leaf plants, olives and lemon trees make for a very tranquil space. With a mature walnut tree Dechmont features box topiary, conifers, shrubs and acers, colour from bulbs, perennials, annuals, clematis and roses set within curved borders. Forge House is a newly created garden with exciting tropical exotics set amongst more traditional plants. Langdale is a plant lover's garden designed for all year round interest. Surrounding a tranquil rill are garden rooms in a variety of styles with many unusual plants. Roselea is a lovely new garden with added interest of an aviary, some sheep and goats in the smallholding to the rear of the garden, and a good size vegetable and fruit garden. At Willoway, a corridor of Hostas leads to a lush carpet of lawn, then to an oriental area containing 2 well stocked ponds, waterfalls, many varieties of Acer and Hydrangea. Interesting plants for sale.

38 OVERBURY COURT

Overbury, GL20 7NP. Sir Bruce & Lady Bossom, 01386 725111(office), pa@overburyenterprises.co.uk. *5m NE of Tewkesbury. Village signed off A46. Turn off village rd beside the church. Park by the gates & walk up the drive.* **Visits by arrangement Mar to Oct for groups of 10+. No refreshments available on site. Adm £4.50, chd free.**

Georgian house 1740 (not open); landscaped garden of same date with stream and pools; daffodil bank and grotto. Plane trees, yew hedges; shrubs; cut flowers; coloured foliage; gold and silver, shrub rose borders. Norman church adjoins garden. Close to Whitcombe and Conderton Manor. Some slopes, while all the garden can be viewed, parts are not accessible to wheelchairs.

39 PEAR TREE COTTAGE

Witton Hill, Wichenford, Worcester, WR6 6YX. Pamela & Alistair Thompson, 01886 888295, peartree.pam@gmail.com, www.peartreecottage.me. *13m NW of Worcester & 2m NE of Martley. From Martley, take B4197. Turn R into Horn Lane then take 2nd L signed Witton Hill. Keep L & Pear Tree Cottage is on R at top of hill.* **Sun 26 May (2-6). Evening opening Sun 25 Aug (4-10). Adm £5, chd free. Home-made teas. Sun 25 August wine served after 6pm.** Visits also by arrangement May to Sept. With notice, evening visits with wine can be arranged.

A Grade II listed black and white cottage (not open) SW-facing gardens and far reaching views across orchards to Abberley Clock Tower. The ¾ acre gardens comprise of gently sloping lawns with mixed and woodland borders, shade and plenty of strategically placed seating. The garden exudes a quirky and humorous character with the odd surprise and even includes a Shed of the Year Runner Up 2017! 'Garden by Twilight' evenings are very popular. Trees, shrubs and sculptures are softly uplit and the garden is filled with 100's of candles and nightlights (weather permitting!) Visitors are invited to listen to the owls and watch the bats whilst enjoying a glass of wine. Partial wheelchair access.

40 THE RIVER SCHOOL

Oakfield House, Droitwich Road, Worcester, WR3 7ST. Christian Education Trust-Worcester, 01905 451309, lacerta@btinternet.com, www.riverschool.co.uk. *2.4m N of Worcester City Centre on A38 towards Droitwich. At J6 M5, take A449 signed for Kidderminster, turn off at 1st turning marked for Blackpole. Turn R to Fernhill Heath & at T-junction with A38 turn L. The school is ½m on R.* **Sat 27 Apr, Sat 3 Aug (10.30-3.30). Adm £5, chd free. Light refreshments in the Lewis Room near garden entrance. Teas. coffees, cold drinks, cakes and savouries.** Visits also by arrangement Mar to Oct for groups of 10 to 30. Outside school hours.

Worcester's lost garden. A Horticultural College garden being brought back to life. For 35 years after WW2 it was known as Oakfield Teacher Training College for Horticulture. With its reputation visitors came from 58 countries & at least 8 other Horticultural Colleges were founded by people inspired by it. The estate features many less common shrubs and trees as well as a forest school pond area. These are working school grounds being recovered mainly by volunteers, with children encouraged to garden in term time. A historically important but not traditional NGS garden! No dogs allowed.

41 ◆ RIVERSIDE GARDENS AT WEBBS

Wychbold, Droitwich, WR9 0DG. Webbs of Wychbold, 01527 860000, www.webbsdirect.co.uk. *2m N of Droitwich Spa. 1m N of M5 J5 on A38. Follow tourism signs from M5.* For opening times and information, please phone or visit garden website.

2½ acres. Themed gardens incl Colour spectrum, tropical and dry garden, Rose garden, vegetable garden area, seaside garden, bamboozelum and self sufficient Garden. New Wave gardens opened 2004 includes natural seasonal interest with grasses and perennials. This area is also home to beehives which produce honey for our own food hall. The New Wave Garden was slightly changed over 2014 to become more of a natural wildlife area. There are willow wigwams made for children to play in. This area now incl a bird hide and new in 2016 the Hobbit house. Open all yr except Christmas, Boxing Day and Easter Sun. Our New Wave Gardens area has grass paths which are underlaid with mesh so people with heavy duty wheelchairs can be taken around.

42 ROTHBURY

5 St Peters Road, North Malvern, WR14 1QS. John Bryson, Philippa Lowe & David. *7m W of M5 J7 (Worcester). Turn off A449 Worcester to Ledbury Rd at B4503, signed Leigh Sinton. Almost immed take the middle rd (Hornyold Rd). St Peter's Rd is ¼m uphill, 2nd R.* **Mon 27 May (8.30-5); Sun 23 June, Sun 21 July (11-5). Adm £3.50, chd free. Light refreshments. Fresh coffee, pots of tea, filled rolls, homemade cakes, cream teas. Gluten free cake and rolls available. Continental breakfast on 27 May.**

Set on slopes of Malvern Hills, ⅓ acre plant-lovers' garden surrounding Arts and Crafts house (not open), created by owners since 1999. Herbaceous borders, rockery, wildlife pond, vegetables, small orchard, containers. Magnificent Eucryphia glutinosa in July. A series of hand-excavated terraces accessed by sloping paths and steps. Views and seats. www.facebook.com/rotherbury/ngs. Partial wheelchair access. One very low step at entry, one standard step to main lawn and one to WC. Decking slope to top lawn.

43 ◆ SPETCHLEY PARK GARDENS

Spetchley, Worcester, WR5 1RS. Mr Henry Berkeley, 01905 345106, enquiries@spetchleygardens.co.uk, www.spetchleygardens.co.uk. *2m E of Worcester. On A44, follow brown signs.* **For NGS: Fri 12 Apr, Fri 5 July (10.30-6). Adm £8, chd £2.50. Light refreshments.** For other opening times and information, please phone, email or visit garden website.

Surrounded by glorious countryside lays one of Britain's best-kept secrets. Spetchley is a garden for all tastes and ages, containing one of the biggest private collections of plant varieties outside the major botanical gardens and weaving a magical trail for younger visitors. Spetchley is not a formal paradise of neatly manicured lawns or beds but rather a wondrous display of plants, shrubs and trees woven into a garden of many rooms and vistas. Plant sales, gift shop and tea room. Annual Specialist Plant Fair will be held on Sun 28 April 2019. Gravel paths.

44 ◆ STONE HOUSE COTTAGE GARDENS

Church Lane, Stone, DY10 4BG. Louisa Arbuthnott, 07817 921146, louisa@shcn.co.uk, www.shcn.co.uk. *2m SE of Kidderminster. Via A448 towards Bromsgrove, next to church, turn up drive.* For opening times and information, please phone, email or visit garden website.

A beautiful and romantic walled garden adorned with unusual brick follies. This acclaimed garden is exuberantly planted and holds one of the largest collections of rare plants in the country. It acts as a shop window for the adjoining nursery. Open Wed to Sat late March to early Sept 10-5. Partial wheelchair access.

Your visits help change lives – since 1927, we've donated £55 million to nursing and caring charities

45 THE TYNINGS

Church Lane, Stoulton, Worcester, WR7 4RE. John & Leslie Bryant, 01905 840189, johnlesbryant@btinternet.com. *5m S of Worcester; 3m N of Pershore. On the B4084 between M5 J7 & Pershore. The Tynings lies beyond the church at the extreme end of Church Lane. Ample parking.* **Visits by arrangement June to Sept. Adm £4, chd free. Light refreshments.**

Acclaimed plantsman's ½-acre garden, generously planted with a large selection of rare trees and shrubs. Features incl specialist collection of lilies, many unusual climbers and rare ferns. The colour continues into late summer with cannas, dahlias, berberis, euonymus and tree colour. Surprises around every corner. Lovely views of adjacent Norman Church and surrounding countryside. Plants labelled and plant lists available.

46 THE WALLED GARDEN

6 Rose Terrace, off Fort Royal Hill, Worcester, WR5 1BU. William & Julia Scott. *Close to the City centre. ½m from Cathedral. Via Fort Royal Hill, off London Rd (A44). Park on 1st section of Rose Terrace & walk the last 20yds down track.* **Sat 27 Apr, Wed 1 May (1-5). Adm £4, chd free. Tea.**

This C19 Walled Kitchen Garden, reawakened in 1995 is a peaceful oasis near the centre of Worcester. A tapestry of culinary and medicinal herbs, fruit of all sorts including medlar, mulberry and quince, vegetables and flowers are all grown organically. History is at the centre of the rescue and evolution of this enclosed garden. Featured in Kitchen Garden magazine.

47 WESTACRES

Wolverhampton Road, Prestwood, Stourbridge, DY7 5AN. Mrs Joyce Williams, 01384 877496, Koijoy62@yahoo.co.uk. *3m W of Stourbridge. A449 in between Wall Heath (2m) & Kidderminster (6m). Ample parking Prestwood Nurseries (next door).* **Sat 20, Sun 21 July (11-4). Adm £4, chd free. Light refreshments.** Visits also by arrangement June to Sept.

¾-acre plant collector's garden with unusual plants and many different varieties of acers, hostas, shrubs. Woodland walk, large koi pool. Covered tea area with home-made cakes. Come and see for yourselves, you won't be disappointed. Described by a visitor in the visitors book as 'A garden which we all wished we could have, at least once in our lifetime'. Garden is flat. Disabled parking.

48 WHARF HOUSE

Newnham Bridge, Tenbury Wells, WR15 8NY. Gareth Compton & Matthew Bartlett, www.wharfhousegardener.blog. *Off the A456 in hamlet of Broombank, between Mamble & Newnham Bridge. Garden signed. Do not rely on SatNav.* **Sat 8, Sun 9 June (12-5). Adm £5, chd free. Home-made teas.**

A 2 acre country garden, set around an C18 house and out-buildings (not open). Mixed herbaceous borders with some colour theming: White Garden; Bright Garden; Spring Garden; long double borders; courtyards; stream; vegetable garden. The garden is on several levels, with limited wheelchair access and some uneven paths. Parking 400 yards from garden. Limited disabled parking at house.

49 WHITCOMBE HOUSE

Overbury, Tewkesbury, GL20 7NZ. Faith & Anthony Hallett, 01386 725206, faith.hallett1@gmail.com. *9m S of Evesham, 5m NE Tewkesbury. Leave A46 at Beckford to Overbury (2m). Or B4080 from Tewkesbury through Bredon/Kemerton (5m). Or small lane signed Overbury at r'about junction A46, A435 & B4077. Approx 5m from J9 M5.* **Sun 26 May, Sun 23 June (2-5). Adm £4, chd free. Wine. Rose wine, Elderflower and Chilled Sparkling Water.** Visits also by arrangement Apr to Aug. Teas can be arranged for group visits with prior notice.

A classical English cottage garden, set in the beautiful Cotswold village

Millbrook Lodge

of Overbury. Long borders of herbaceous, climbers and shrubs, surrounded by stone walls and including a stream, banked with primula, astilbe and geranium. Pastel colours merge with cool and hot planting beneath a canopy of acer, Catalpa and beech. Yew hedges and a vegetable parterre adjoin the plantstall and Greenhouse.

50 WHITE COTTAGE & NURSERY

Earls Common Road, Stock Green, Inkberrow, B96 6SZ. Mr & Mrs S M Bates, 01386 792414, smandjbates@aol.com, whitecottage.garden. *2m W of Inkberrow, 2m E of Upton Snodsbury. A422 Worcester to Alcester, turn at sign for Stock Green by Red Hart Pub, 1½m to T-junction, turn L 500 yds on the L.* **Sun 14 Apr, Sun 12, Sun 26, Mon 27 May, Sun 16, Sun 30 June, Sun 21 July (11-4.30). Adm £4, chd free.** Visits also by arrangement Apr to Sept. Groups and individuals welcome.

2 acre garden with large herbaceous and shrub borders, island beds, stream and bog area. Spring meadow with 1000's of snakes head fritillaries. Formal area with lily pond and circular rose garden. Alpine rockery and new fern area. Large collection of interesting trees incl Nyssa Sylvatica, Parrotia persica, and Acer 'October Glory' for magnificent Autumn colour and many others. Nursery and Garden open most Thursdays from 10.30-5pm please check. For other opening times and information please phone, email or visit garden website and Facebook. Wheelchair access.

51 ◆ WHITLENGE GARDENS

Whitlenge Lane, Hartlebury, DY10 4HD. Mr & Mrs K J Southall, 01299 250720, keith.southall@creativelandscapes.co.uk, www.whitlenge.co.uk. *5m S of Kidderminster, on A442. A449 Kidderminster to Worcester L at T-lights, A442 signed Droitwich, over island, ¼m, 1st R into Whitlenge Lane. Follow brown signs.* **For NGS: Sat 6, Sun 7 Apr, Sat 22, Sun 23 June, Sat 14, Sun 15 Sept (10-5). Adm £3.50, chd £2. Light refreshments in the adacent Tea rooms.** For other opening times and information, please phone, email or visit garden website.

3 acre show garden of a professional designer incorporating a large variety of trees, shrubs etc. features include a Twisted brick pillar pergola, Moongate as featured on TV, waterfalls, ponds and streams. Mystic features of the Green Man, 'Sword in the Stone' and cave fernery. Walk the turf labyrinth and take refreshments in The Garden 'Design Studio' tearoom. 2½ metre high circular reclaim brickwork with solid Oak Moongate and 4 cascading waterfalls, deck walk through giant Gunnera leaves, herb gardens, 400 sq metre grass labyrinth, 'Garden of Thyme/time' plus children's play/pet corner. Locally sourced home-made food in tearoom, extensive plant nursery. mix of hard pathways, gravel pathways and lawn,.

52 68 WINDSOR AVENUE

St.Johns, Worcester, WR2 5NB. Roger & Barbara Parker, 01905 428723, robarpark@googlemail.com. *W area of Worcester, W side of R Severn. Off the A44 to Bromyard. Into Comer Rd, 3rd L Into Laugherne Rd, 3rd L into Windsor Ave, at bottom in Cul-de-sac. Limited parking, please park courteously on road sides, car share if possible.* **Sun 26, Mon 27 May (1-5). Adm £4.50, chd free. Light refreshments. Tea, Coffee and Cake , Soft drinks also available.** Visits also by arrangement May & June for groups of 10 to 30.

Almost one acre garden divided into three areas, situated behind a 1930's semi detached house in a cul-de-sac. Visitors are amazed and comment on size of garden and the tranquility! The garden includes bog gardens, flower beds, 'oriental' area, vegetable patch, five greenhouses and a Koi pond plus three other ponds each in very different styles. We also have Ornamental Pheasants and other birds! Gravel paths are everywhere.

GROUP OPENING

53 WITHYBED GREEN

Front Cottages, Withybed Green, Alvechurch, B48 7RJ. *3m N of Redditch, 11m SW of Birmingham. 6mins from J2 of M42. From Alvechurch centre take Tanyard Lane or Bear Hill. Follow NGS signs along Snake Lane & Withybed Lane. Rail Alvechurch Stn then a 10 minute walk up the canal towpath.* **Sun 30 June (1-6). Combined adm £5, chd free. Home-made teas at 'The New Smithy' next to the Crown public house. Hot and cold drinks. Homemade cakes.**

5 FORWARD COTTAGES
Mary Green.

NEW **1 FRONT COTTAGES**
Mr & Mrs John & Janice Barnett.

2 FRONT COTTAGES
Clive & Ann Southern.

6 FRONT COTTAGES
Mr & Mrs Horne.

THE MOUSEHOLE
Lucy Hastie.

NEW **1 REAR COTTAGES**
Mr & Mrs David & Serena Saunders.

6 REAR COTTAGES
Amelda Brown and John Adams.

SELVAS COTTAGE
Mr & Mrs J L Plewes.

Withybed Green is a small secret hamlet to the west of Alvechurch set between semi wooded hillsides and the Birmingham and Worcester canal. With eight varied gardens opening (two new this year) the gardens include one that is at the start of their horticultural journey through to a mature woodland garden with a streamside walk. There is also a rose garden that has featured on TV, a small wild garden and a range of terrace cottage gardens. Withybed Green is compact and in a charming environment and you can easily walk round all eight gardens. Refreshments will be hosted at the New Smithy. The houses and cottages mostly date from C19, built for farm workers, nail makers, canal and railway builders. Withybed Green has its own canal-side public house, The Crown. Only 3 gardens are suitable for wheelchair access.

YORKSHIRE

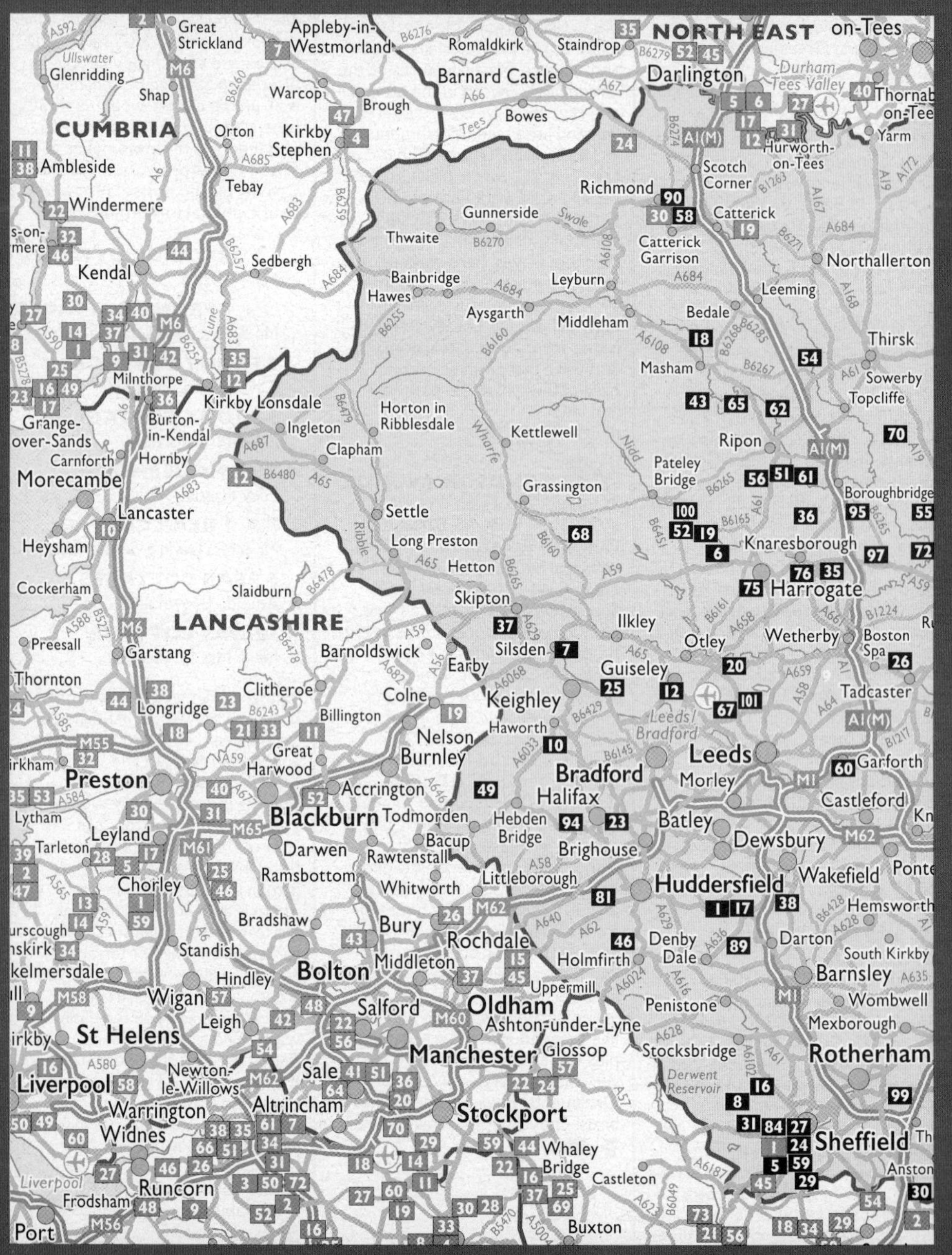
NORTH EAST
CUMBRIA
LANCASHIRE
Great Strickland
Appleby-in-Westmorland
Romaldkirk
Staindrop
Darlington
Glenridding
Shap
Warcop
Brough
Barnard Castle
Bowes
Durham Tees Valley
Thornaby-on-Tees
Yarm
Orton
Kirkby Stephen
Hurworth-on-Tees
Ambleside
Tebay
Scotch Corner
Windermere
Richmond
Gunnerside
Catterick
Thwaite
Catterick Garrison
Northallerton
Kendal
Sedbergh
Bainbridge
Hawes
Leyburn
Leeming
Aysgarth
Middleham
Bedale
Thirsk
Milnthorpe
Masham
Sowerby
Kirkby Lonsdale
Topcliffe
Grange-over-Sands
Burton-in-Kendal
Ingleton
Horton in Ribblesdale
Kettlewell
Ripon
Carnforth
Hornby
Clapham
Pateley Bridge
Morecambe
Grassington
Boroughbridge
Lancaster
Settle
Heysham
Long Preston
Knaresborough
Hetton
Harrogate
Cockerham
Slaidburn
Skipton
Ilkley
Wetherby
Preesall
Garstang
Barnoldswick
Silsden
Otley
Boston Spa
Earby
Guiseley
Thornton
Clitheroe
Colne
Keighley
Tadcaster
Longridge
Billington
Haworth
Leeds/Bradford
Nelson
Great Harwood
Burnley
Leeds
Garforth
Preston
Bradford
Morley
Accrington
Halifax
Lytham
Blackburn
Todmorden
Hebden Bridge
Batley
Castleford
Leyland
Dewsbury
Tarleton
Darwen
Bacup
Rawtenstall
Brighouse
Wakefield
Chorley
Ramsbottom
Whitworth
Littleborough
Huddersfield
Hemsworth
Bradshaw
Bury
Rochdale
Denby Dale
Darton
Standish
Holmfirth
South Kirkby
Bolton
Middleton
Barnsley
Hindley
Uppermill
Wigan
Penistone
Wombwell
Salford
Oldham
Leigh
Ashton-under-Lyne
Mexborough
St Helens
Manchester
Glossop
Stocksbridge
Rotherham
Newton-le-Willows
Sale
Liverpool
Derwent Reservoir
Warrington
Altrincham
Stockport
Widnes
Sheffield
Whaley Bridge
Castleton
Anston
Runcorn
Frodsham
Buxton
Preston
Swale
Tees
Wharfe
Nidd
Ribble
Lune
Ullswater

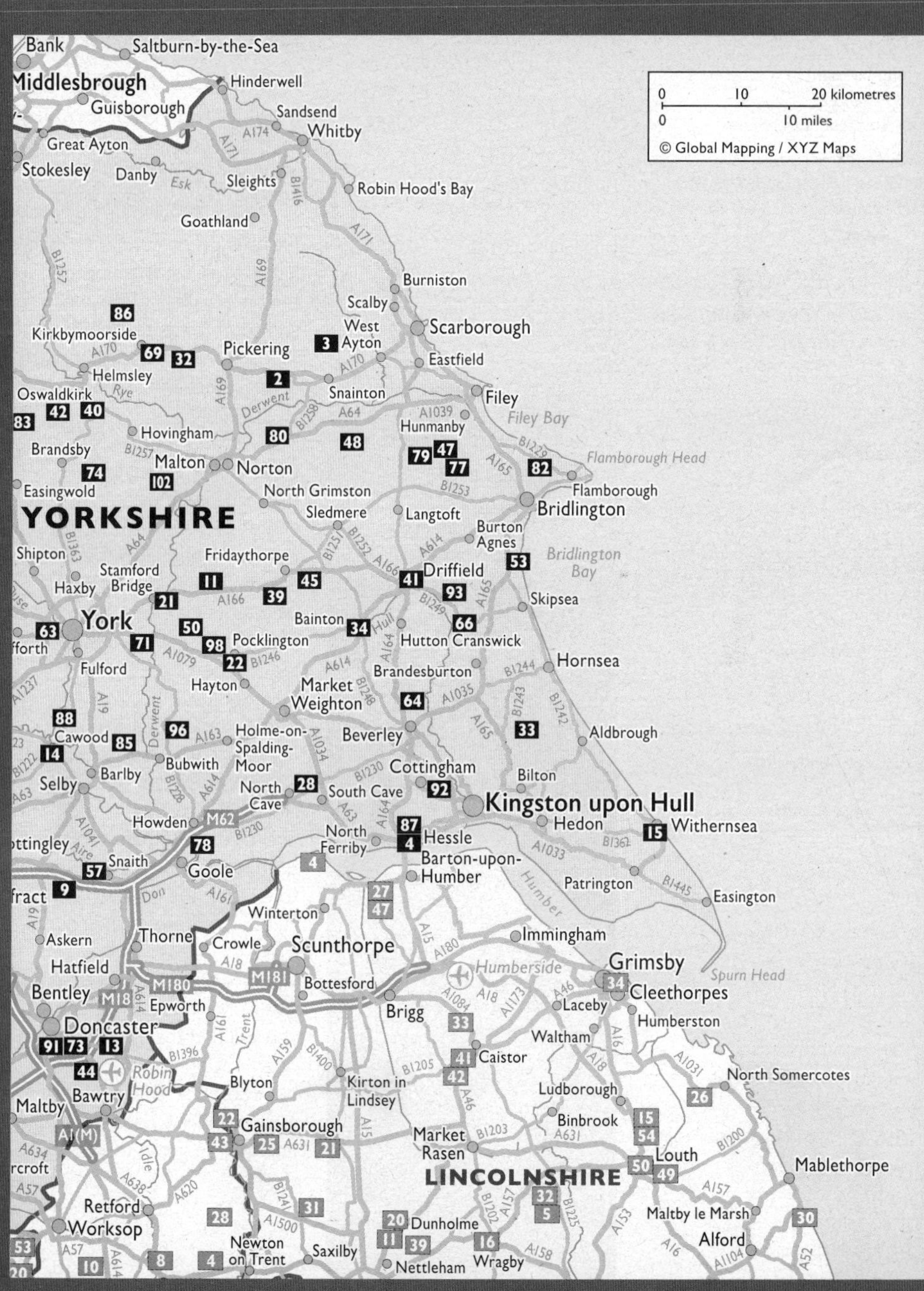
0 10 20 kilometres
0 10 miles
© Global Mapping / XYZ Maps
YORKSHIRE
LINCOLNSHIRE
Middlesbrough
Saltburn-by-the-Sea
Guisborough
Whitby
Robin Hood's Bay
Scarborough
Pickering
Filey
Filey Bay
Flamborough Head
Flamborough
Bridlington
Bridlington Bay
Malton
Norton
York
Driffield
Hornsea
Beverley
Kingston upon Hull
Hedon
Withernsea
Goole
Scunthorpe
Grimsby
Cleethorpes
Spurn Head
Doncaster
Gainsborough
Louth
Mablethorpe
Worksop
Retford
Market Rasen
Alford

Volunteers

County Organisers

East Yorks
Helen Marsden
01430 860222
jerryhelen@btinternet.com

North Yorks – Cleveland, Hambleton, Richmond, Rydale & Scarborough
Hugh Norton
01653 628604
hughnorton0@gmail.com

South & West Yorks & North Yorks – Craven, Harrogate, Selby & York
Veronica Brook
01423 340875
veronica.brook@ngs.org.uk

County Treasurer
Angela Pugh
01423 330456
amjopugh@clannet.co.uk

Publicity & Social Media
Jane Cooper 01484 604232
jane.cooper@ngs.org.uk

Booklet Advertising
John Plant
01347 888125
plantjohnsgarden@btinternet.com

By Arrangement Visits
Penny Phillips
01937 834970
penny.phillips@ngs.org.uk

Clubs & Societies
Penny Phillips (as above)

Assistant County Organisers

East Yorks
Ian & Linda McGowan
01482 896492
adnil_magoo@yahoo.com

Hazel Rowe 01430 861439
hrowe@uwclub.net

Natalie Verow 01759 368444
natalieverow@aol.com

North Yorks
Gillian Mellor 01723 891636
gill.mellor234@gmail.com

Judi Smith 01845 567518
judiandsteve@outlook.com

West & South Yorks
Deborah Bigley 01423 330727
debsandbobbigley@btinternet.com

Felicity Bowring 01729 823551
f.bowring@gmail.com

Rosie Hamlin 01302 535135
rosiehamlin@aol.com

Jane Hudson 01924 840980
janehudson42@btinternet.com

Chris & Fiona Royffe
01937 530306
plantsbydesign@btinternet.com

Elizabeth & David Smith
01484 644320
elizabethrfsmith@btinternet.com

Bridget Marshall BEM
01423 330474
biddymarshall@btinternet.com

Yorkshire, England's largest county, stretches from the Pennines in the west to the rugged coast and sandy beaches of the east: a rural landscape of moors, dales, vales and rolling wolds.

Nestling on riverbanks lie many historic market towns, and in the deep valleys of the west and south others retain their 19th century industrial heritage of coal, steel and textiles.

The wealth generated by these industries supported the many great estates, houses and gardens throughout the county. From Hull in the east, a complex network of canals weaves its way across the county, connecting cities to the sea and beyond.

The Victorian spa town of Harrogate with the RHS garden at Harlow Carr, or the historic city of York with a minster encircled by Roman walls, are both ideal centres from which to explore the gardens and cultural heritage of the county.

We look forward to welcoming you to our private gardens – you will find that many of them open not only on a specific day, but also 'by arrangement' for groups and individuals - we can help you to get in touch.

Left: **Rewela Cottage**

OPENING DATES

All entries subject to change. For latest information check **www.ngs.org.uk**

Extended openings are shown at the beginning of the month.

Map locator numbers are shown to the right of each garden name.

February

Snowdrop Festival

Sunday 24th
72 Church Street 16
Devonshire Mill 22

March

Sunday 17th
Fawley House 28

Saturday 30th
Primrose Bank Garden and Nursery 71

Sunday 31st
Primrose Bank Garden and Nursery 71

April

Sunday 7th
Clifton Castle 18
Goldsborough Hall 35

Saturday 27th
NEW 249 Barnsley Road 1

Sunday 28th
NEW 249 Barnsley Road 1
The Circles Garden 17
Fawley House 28
Friars Hill 32

May

Sunday 5th
Highfield Cottage 41
◆ RHS Garden Harlow Carr 75

Monday 6th
Whixley Gardens 97

Wednesday 8th
Well House 95
Whixley Gardens 97

Sunday 12th
◆ Jackson's Wold 48
Low Hall 52
Scape Lodge 81
◆ Stillingfleet Lodge 88
Warley House Garden 94
Woodlands Cottage 100

Wednesday 15th
Warley House Garden 94

Thursday 16th
NEW Cantley Hall 13

Sunday 19th
Barnville 2
Millrace Garden 60
Rustic Cottage 79

Monday 20th
Himalayan Garden & Sculpture Park 43

Wednesday 22nd
Land Farm 49

Saturday 25th
The Red House 73
Tamarind 91

Sunday 26th
Beacon Garth 4
NEW Bramblewood Cottage 8
Creskeld Hall 20
Highfield Cottage 41
115 Millhouses Lane 59
Penny Piece Cottages 69
The Red House 73
Rewela Cottage 74
Rosemary Cottage 78
1 School Lane 82
113 Southfield 87
Tamarind 91

Monday 27th
Bridge Farm House 9

June

Saturday 1st
NEW The Grange 36
Hunmanby Grange 47
Old Sleningford Hall 65

Sunday 2nd
Brookfield 10
Fernleigh 29
NEW The Grange 36
Hunmanby Grange 47
◆ Norton Conyers 62
Old Sleningford Hall 65
◆ The Yorkshire Arboretum 102

Wednesday 5th
Sleightholmedale Lodge 86

Thursday 6th
Skipwith Hall 85

Friday 7th
◆ Shandy Hall Gardens 83

Saturday 8th
Linden Lodge 50

Sunday 9th
Clifton Castle 18
Linden Lodge 50
The Orchard 67
Scape Lodge 81
NEW White Wynn 96
Whixley Gardens 97

Friday 14th
Holmfield 45
NEW Markenfield Hall 56

Sunday 16th
NEW Bramblewood Cottage 8
◆ Dove Cottage Nursery Garden 23
Glaramara 33
Holmfield 45
Midendale 57
The Ridings 77
Rustic Cottage 79
Willow Cottage 98

Saturday 22nd
NEW Winthrop Gardens 99

Sunday 23rd
Birstwith Hall 6
3 Embankment Road 27
◆ Jackson's Wold 48
NEW Ridgefield Cottage & Nursery 76
NEW Tythe Farm House 93
NEW Winthrop Gardens 99

Wednesday 26th
Bramble Croft 7
NEW East Morton Gardens 25

Friday 28th
34 Dover Road 24
◆ Shandy Hall Gardens 83

Sunday 30th
Bugthorpe Gardens 11
72 Church Street 16
Daneswell House 21
34 Dover Road 24
Fernleigh 29
Havoc Hall 40
2 Hollin Close 44
NEW Low Stonehills Farm 53
Millgate House 58
The Old Vicarage 66

July

Wednesday 3rd
Brookfield 10
Land Farm 49
◆ Parcevall Hall Gardens 68

Saturday 6th
Sue Proctor Plants Nursery Garden 89

Sunday 7th
Honey Head 46
Millgate House 58
Primrose Bank Garden and Nursery 71
The Priory, Nun Monkton 72
Sue Proctor Plants Nursery Garden 89

Wednesday 10th
The Grange 37

Saturday 13th
NEW 249 Barnsley Road 1
Cawood Gardens 14

Sunday 14th
NEW 249 Barnsley Road 1
Cawood Gardens 14
NEW The Manor House 54
The Nursery 63
NEW Sheffield Gardens 84
NEW 23 The Paddock 92

Wednesday 17th
The Nursery 63

Saturday 20th
NEW Freeman Biodynamic Garden 31

Sunday 21st
Cow Close Cottage 19
◆ Dove Cottage Nursery Garden 23
East Wing, Newton Kyme Hall 26

Goldsborough Hall 35

Sunday 28th

Fernleigh 29
Littlethorpe Gardens 51
Rewela Cottage 74

Wednesday 31st

Land Farm 49

August

Sunday 4th

NEW Bramblewood Cottage 8
14 Chellsway 15

Wednesday 7th

The Grange 37

Sunday 11th

Sleightholmedale Lodge 86

Sunday 18th

◆ Dove Cottage Nursery Garden 23
NEW Great Cliff Exotic Garden 38

Sunday 25th

Fernleigh 29
Highfield Cottage 41
Pilmoor Cottages 70

Saturday 31st

Hillside 42

September

Sunday 1st

Bramble Croft 7
Hillside 42

Thursday 12th

The Priory, Nun Monkton 72

Sunday 15th

◆ Stillingfleet Lodge 88

By Arrangement

Arrange a personalised garden visit with your club or group of friends, on a date to suit you. See individual garden entries for full details.

Barnville 2
Basin Howe Farm 3
90 Bents Road 5
Birstwith Hall 6
Bramble Croft 7
NEW Bramblewood Cottage 8
Bridge Farm House 9
Brookfield 10
Butterfield Heights 12
Cawood Gardens 14
72 Church Street 16
3 Church Walk, Bugthorpe Gardens 11
Cobble Cottage, Whixley Gardens 97
Cow Close Cottage 19
Daneswell House 21
34 Dover Road 24
Fawley House 28
Fernleigh 29
Firvale Allotment Garden 30
Friars Hill 32
Glencoe House 34
The Grange 37
NEW Great Cliff Exotic Garden 38
Greencroft, Littlethorpe Gardens 51
Greenwick Farm 39
Havoc Hall 40
Highfield Cottage 41
Hillside 42
Holmfield 45
Hunmanby Grange 47
Linden Lodge 50
Low Hall 52
NEW Low Stonehills Farm 53
The Manor House 55
NEW The Manor House 54
NEW Markenfield Hall 56
The Nursery 63
NEW The Old Rectory 64
The Old Vicarage, Whixley Gardens 97
The Orchard 67
Pilmoor Cottages 70
Primrose Bank Garden and Nursery 71
Rewela Cottage 74
The Ridings 77
Rustic Cottage 79
Scape Lodge 81
1 School Lane 82
Skipwith Hall 85
Sue Proctor Plants Nursery Garden 89
Swale Cottage 90
NEW Tythe Farm House 93
Warley House Garden 94
Willow Cottage 98
Woodlands Cottage 100

90 Bents Road

THE GARDENS

1 NEW 249 BARNSLEY ROAD

Flockton, Wakefield, WF4 4AL. Nigel & Anne Marie Booth. *Located on A637 Barnsley Road. M1 J38 or 39 follow the signs for Huddersfield. Park on Manor House Road. (WF4 4AL for sat Nav).* **Sat 27, Sun 28 Apr, Sat 13, Sun 14 July (1-5). Adm £3, chd free. Home-made teas.**

An elevated garden with fantastic panoramic views. ⅓ acre south facing garden packed with an abundance of spring colour, created from 1000's of bulbs, perennials, shrubs and trees. Make a return visit in the summer to view the transformation, displaying up to 60 hanging baskets and over 150 pots, creating the 'wow factor' garden. Many seating areas. Limited wheelchair access.

2 BARNVILLE

Wilton, Nr Pickering, YO18 7LE. Bill & Liz Craven, 07867 503242, lizcraven40@gmail.com. *4m E of Pickering. On main A170, travelling from Pickering towards Scarborough, enter village of Wilton. Turn R. House on L in 200yrds.* **Sun 19 May (12-5). Adm £4, chd free. Home-made teas.** Visits also by arrangement Apr to Sept for groups of 10+. Please book early to help us accommodate the date you require.

Over an acre of hidden gardens on edge of North York Moors. Unusual plants make a true all season garden. In Spring, magnolia, camellia and azalea shelter naturalised bulbs, trillium and erythronium. Summer's cool green foliage highlights allium, agapanthus and turk's cap lilies. Autumn brings blazing colour, acers, rowan and unusual birches underplanted with carpets of cyclamen and autumn crocus. Scrumptious home baked cakes and cream teas, included in the Private Tour adm, Proceeds from plant sales to our favourite charity Greyhound Gap. Lower garden unsuitable for wheelchairs in wet, but level stone paths in upper gardens. Access to sunken garden via steps - can be viewed from above.

3 BASIN HOWE FARM

Cockmoor Road, Sawdon, Scarborough, YO13 9EG. Richard & Heather Mullin, 01723 850180, heather@basinhowefarm.co.uk, www.basinhowefarm.co.uk. *Turn off A170 between Scarborough & Pickering at Brompton by Sawdon follow sign to Sawdon. Basin Howe Farm 1½m above Sawdon village on the L.* **Visits by arrangement May to Aug for groups of up to 30. Adm £5, chd free. Home-made teas.**

3 acres of gardens with a lovely atmosphere. featuring a box parterre with seasonal planting, gravel garden with dragon sculpture, koi pond, herbaceous borders, wildlife pond and elevated viewing deck with Pod summer house and a number of sculptures. Orchard and woodland, ferns, lawns and shrubs. Paved seating areas but gravel paths. Basin Howe has a Bronze Age Burial Mound, maintained by owners. Wheelchair Access is possible to most areas but a helper is required. Access is via gravel paths and grass.

4 BEACON GARTH

Redcliff Road, Hessle, Hull, HU13 0HA. Ivor & June Innes. *4½m W of Hull. Follow signs for Hessle Foreshore. Parking available in foreshore car park followed by a short walk up Cliff Rd. Enter the garden through the double gates on Redcliff Rd.* **Sun 26 May (12-5.30). Combined adm with 113 Southfield £6, chd free. Home-made teas.**

Edwardian, Arts and Crafts house (mentioned in Pevsner's Guide to Hull) and S-facing garden set in 3½ acres, in an elevated position overlooking the Humber. Stunning sunken rock garden with bulbs and specimen trees, hostas and ferns. Mature trees, large lawns and herbaceous borders. Gravel paths, haha, box hedges and topiary. Child friendly; children's play area. Teas served in main hallway of house. Partial wheelchair access.

5 90 BENTS ROAD

Bents Green, Sheffield, S11 9RL. Mrs Hilary Hutson, 011422 58570, h.hutson@paradiseregained.net. *3m SW of Sheffield. From Moore St r'about in Sheffield Centre (nr Waitrose), follow A625. After approx 3m turn R on to Bents Rd.* **Visits by arrangement July & Aug for groups of up to 30. Adm £3, chd free. Light refreshments.**

Plantswoman's NE facing garden. Patio with alpine troughs for year-round interest, plus pots of colourful tropical plants in summer. Mixed borders surround a lawn, which leads to mature trees underplanted with shade-loving plants at end of garden. Many unusual and borderline-hardy species. Front garden peaks in summer with hot-coloured blooms. Front garden and patio flat and accessible. Remainder of back garden accessed via 6 steps (with handrail), so unsuitable for wheelchairs.

6 BIRSTWITH HALL

High Birstwith, Harrogate, HG3 2JW. Sir James & Lady Aykroyd, 01423 770250, ladya@birstwithhall.co.uk. *5m NW of Harrogate. Between Hampsthwaite & Birstwith villages, close to A59 Harrogate/Skipton Rd.* **Sun 23 June (2-5). Adm £5, chd free. Home-made teas. Visits also by arrangement. Small coaches welcome.**

Large 4 acre garden nestling in secluded Yorkshire dale with formal garden and ornamental orchard, extensive lawns, picturesque stream, large pond and Victorian greenhouse. Also home-made teas and refreshments for large groups.

Your visits help change lives – we've donated over £16.7 million to Macmillan Cancer Support since 1984

7 BRAMBLE CROFT

Howden Road, Silsden, Keighley, BD20 0JB. Debbi Wilson, 01535 658032, deb2711@googlemail.com. *Next to Springbank Nursing Home, please park in Howden Rd. Steep access.* **Wed 26 June, Sun 1 Sept (11-4). Adm £3.50, chd free. Light lunches, cakes and hot drinks** **Visits also by arrangement May to Sept for groups of 10+.**

Bramble Croft's small hidden hillside artist's garden full of colour, texture and newly developed borders includes perennials, ferns, climbers, grasses, topiary and sculptures, lies on the edge of Silsden village. Wildlife encouraged with pond, bird and insect boxes. Original paintings are on show and for sale in the new tranquil garden room. Terrace and outdoor covered dining patio. Seating available. WC. No dogs please as we have our own.

8 NEW BRAMBLEWOOD COTTAGE

Old Coach Road, Bradfield, Sheffield, S6 6HX. Nigel Dunnett, 0114 2851688, n.dunnett@sheffield.ac.uk. *6m from Sheffield City centre. Follow Loxley Road (B6077) turn L onto New Road just before Damflask reservoir. Follow alongside reservoir until Old Coach Road.* **Sun 26 May, Sun 16 June, Sun 4 Aug (2-7). Adm £5, chd free. Home-made teas. Opening with Sheffield Gardens on Sun 14 July. Visits also by arrangement May to Sept for groups of 10+.**

Garden of one acre, with extensive areas of naturalistic perennial planting, and large-scale log-pile sculptures. A wide range of different types of designed annual and perennial meadows; a Bluebell woodland; Sand Garden; Swedish Garden, and unusual annuals. A front garden pool, rain gardens and bioswales. Pennine views. Featured in Gardens Illustrated July 2019. Signed copies of books by Nigel Dunnett available. The garden is an experimental working environment for the owner, testing out different methods of planting and combinations that might be used more widely. No wheelchair access possible.

9 BRIDGE FARM HOUSE

Long Lane, Great Heck, Selby, DN14 0BE. Barbara & Richard Ferrari, 01977 661277, barbaraferrari@mypostoffice.co.uk. *6m S of Selby, 3m E M62 J34. At M62 J34 take A19 to Selby, at r'about turn E towards Snaith on A645. After level crossing turn R at T-lights, L at T-junction onto Main St, past Church, to T-junction, cross to car park.* **Mon 27 May (12-4). Adm £4, chd free. Visits also by arrangement Feb & Sept only.**

2 acre garden divided by hedges into separate areas planted with unusual and interesting plants. All yr interest starts with hellebores, winter shrubs and over 150 named snowdrops. Long double mixed borders; bog, gravel garden, interesting trees. Hens; compost heaps and wildlife areas. Wheelchair access easiest by front gate, please ask.

10 BROOKFIELD

Jew Lane, Oxenhope, Keighley, BD22 9HS. Mrs R L Belsey, 01535 643070. *5m SW of Keighley. From Keighley take A629 (Halifax) Fork R A6033 towards Haworth & Oxenhope turn L at Xrds into village. Turn R (Jew Lane) at bottom of hill.* **Sun 2 June, Wed 3 July (1-5.30). Adm £4, chd free. Home-made teas. Visits also by arrangement May to Aug for groups of 20 to 30.**

An intimate 1 acre garden with steps and paths leading down to a large pond with an island, mallards, wild geese and greylags. Many varieties of Primula, candelabra and florindae and Dactylorrhiza majalis which have seeded into the lower lawn around a small pond with stream; azaleas and rhododendrons. Unusual trees and shrubs in a series of island beds, screes, greenhouse and conservatory. 'Round and Round the Garden' children's quiz.

GROUP OPENING

11 BUGTHORPE GARDENS

Bugthorpe, York, YO41 1QG. *Bugthorpe. 4m E of Stamford Bridge, A166, village of Bugthorpe.* **Sun 30 June (10-4). Combined adm £6, chd free. Light refreshments. Also open Daneswell House.**

3 CHURCH WALK

Barrie Creaser & David Fielding, 01759 368152, barriecreaser@gmail.com. Visits also by arrangement for groups of up to 20.

THE OLD RECTORY

Dr & Mrs P W Verow.

Two contrasting gardens situated in the small village of Bugthorpe. Barrie Creaser & David Fielding, 3 Church Walk: a garden created in 2000, surprisingly mature, with mixed borders and trees, water feature and pond. Raised vegetable garden and greenhouse. The lawn leads onto a paddock with views of open countryside. Dr & Mrs P W Verow, The Old Rectory: ¾ acre country garden with views of the Yorkshire Wolds. Mixed borders, ponds, terrace, summerhouse, courtyard and many mature trees. Raised vegetable beds.

12 BUTTERFIELD HEIGHTS

4 Park Crescent, Guiseley, Leeds, LS20 8EL. Vicky Harris, 07852163733, vickyharris1951@gmail.com. *11m NW of Leeds. From Guiseley A65 (Otley-Leeds) A6038 towards Shipley (Bradford Rd). Park Crescent ½m on L. Park on Bradford Rd.* **Visits by arrangement July to Sept for groups of 10+. Adm £5, chd free. Cream teas.**

Garden completely restored over 21 years but retaining and enhancing the original 1930's landscaping. Mixed planting of unusual shrubs, perennials and mature trees now undergoing further transitions as the owners try to reduce their garden workload. Statuesque planting creates a riot of colour while topiary features and tall perennials add to the character of the garden at the height of summer. Tree carving and Fairy Post Office (with gifts). Garden on three levels with some steep steps and gravel paths.

13 NEW CANTLEY HALL

School Lane, Old Cantley, Doncaster, DN3 3QG. Lord & Lady Kirkham. *Information for directions and fully guided tour will be sent out with the tickets (limited).* **Thur 16 May (10-4). Adm £75,**

chd free. Pre-booking essential, please visit www.ngs.org.uk for information & booking. Adm includes morning coffee, afternoon tea at the Hall and lunch at Walkers Nurseries, Blaxton DN9 3BA.
A garden to delight the senses in a parkland setting surrounding a Georgian house (not open), extensively restored and replanted over 25 years by Lord and Lady Kirkham and their gardening team led by Ian Fretwell. Parterre with roses and walled flower gardens all lead to light woodland with fine mature trees and shrubs underplanted with spring bulbs. The paths eventually culminate at a two acre fully operational walled vegetable, fruit and cut flower garden with central pool and double herbaceous borders, restored glass houses, potting shed, fruit store, melon house and heated wall. An arboretum with many rarely seen species of pine and conifer, Victorian fernery with grotto.

GROUP OPENING

14 CAWOOD GARDENS

Cawood, nr Selby, YO8 3UG. 01757 268571, dave-judyjones@hotmail.co.uk. *On B1223 5m N of Selby & 7m SE of Tadcaster. Between York & A1 on B1222. Village maps given at all gardens.* **Sat 13, Sun 14 July (12-5). Combined adm £6, chd free. Home-made teas at 9 Anson Grove & 21 Great Close.** Visits also by arrangement June & July.

9 ANSON GROVE
Tony & Brenda Finnigan, 01757 268888, beeart@ansongrove.co.uk.

21 GREAT CLOSE
David & Judy Jones, 01757 268571, dave-judyjones@hotmail.co.uk.

THE PIGEONCOTE
Maria Parks & Angela Darlington, 01757 268661, mariaparks@gmail.com.

These three contrasting gardens in an attractive historic village are linked by a pretty riverside walk to the C11 church and Memorial garden and across the Castle Garth to the remains of Cawood Castle. 9 Anson Grove is a small garden with tranquil pools and secluded sitting places. Narrow winding paths and raised areas give views over oriental-style pagoda, bridge and Zen garden. 21 Great Close is a flower arranger's garden, designed and built by the owners. Interesting trees and shrubs combine with herbaceous borders incl many grasses. Two ponds are joined by a stream, winding paths take you to the vegetable garden and summerhouse, then back to the colourful terrace for views across the garden and countryside beyond. The small walled garden, Pigeoncote at 2 Wistowgate is surrounded by historic C17 buildings. A balanced design of formal box hedging, cottage garden planting and creative use of grasses. Angled brick pathways lead to shaded seating areas with all day sunny views. Crafts and paintings on sale at 9 Anson Grove. Wheelchair access limited at 9 Anson Grove and 21 Great Close.

15 14 CHELLSWAY

Chellsway, Withernsea, HU19 2EN. Neil & Caroline Ziemski. *15m E of Hull. Enter Withernsea on A1033, turn L onto B1362, 2nd L onto Carrs Meadow, L onto Beaconsfield R onto Chellsway.* **Sun 4 Aug (12-5). Adm £3, chd free. Home-made teas.**
Jungle garden with grass and gravel paths surrounded by hardy and tender plants. Collection of bamboo, bananas, gingers, palms, succulents and other exotic plants, combine to create a tropical effect rarely seen on the Yorkshire coast. An authentic jungle hut and various seating areas allow the visitor to see different aspects of the garden. Small pond and rockery area to see.

16 72 CHURCH STREET

Oughtibridge, Sheffield, S35 0FW. Linda & Peter Stewart, 011428 63847, lindaandpeter@thestewarthouse.me.uk. *6m N of Sheffield. M1 (J36) A61 (Sheffield). Turn R at Norfolk Arms pub. In Oughtibridge follow one-way system turning L immed after zebra crossing.* **Sun 24 Feb (11-2.30); Sun 30 June (11-4). Adm £3.50, chd free. Home-made teas.** Visits also by arrangement Feb to Sept.
Hidden from the busy street is our peaceful country garden with naturalistic planting leading down to Coumes Brook and backed by native woodland. In February the garden bursts into life with a stunning display of snowdrops. The garden railway next door will be open to garden visitors on 30th June.

17 THE CIRCLES GARDEN

8 Stocksmoor Road, Midgley, nr Wakefield, WF4 4JQ. Joan Gaunt. *Equidistant from Huddersfield, Wakefield & Barnsley, W of M1. Turn off A637 in Midgley at the Black Bull Pub (sharp bend) onto B6117 (Stocksmoor Rd). Please park on L adjacent to houses.* **Sun 28 Apr (1.30-4.30). Adm £4, chd free. Home-made teas.**
An organic and self-sustaining plantswoman's ½ acre garden on gently sloping site overlooking fields, woods and nature reserve opposite. Designed and maintained by owner. Herbaceous, bulb and shrub plantings linked by grass and gravel paths, woodland area with mature trees, meadows, fernery, greenhouse, fruit trees, viewing terrace with pots. About 100 hellebores grown from my seed. In Amateur gardening July 2018. Hellebore, South African plants, hollies, and small bulbs are particular interests.

18 CLIFTON CASTLE

Ripon, HG4 4AB. Lord & Lady Downshire. *2m N of Masham. On rd to Newton-le-Willows & Richmond. Gates on L next to red telephone box.* **Sun 7 Apr, Sun 9 June (2-5). Adm £5, chd free. Home-made teas.**
Fine views, river walks, wooded pleasure grounds with bridges and follies. Cascades, wild flower meadow and C19 walled kitchen garden. Gravel paths and steep slopes to river.

19 COW CLOSE COTTAGE

Stripe Lane, Hartwith, Harrogate, HG3 3EY. William Moore & John Wilson, 01423 779813, cowclose1@btinternet.com. *8m NW of Harrogate. From A61 (Harrogate-Ripon) at Ripley take B6165 to Pateley Bridge. 2m beyond Burnt Yates turn R, signed Hartwith/ Brimham Rocks onto Stripe Lane. Parking available.* **Sun 21 July (10.30-4.30). Adm £4, chd free. Home-made teas.** Visits also by arrangement in July for groups of 10+.

⅔ acre country garden on sloping site with stream and far reaching views. Large borders with drifts of interesting, well-chosen, later flowering summer perennials and some grasses contrasting with woodland shade and streamside plantings. Gravel path leading to vegetable area. Courtyard area, terrace and seating with views of the garden. Orchard and ha-ha with steps leading to wild flower meadow. The lower part of the garden can be accessed via the orchard.

20 CRESKELD HALL

Creskeld Lane, Arthington, Leeds, LS21 1NT. J & C Stoddart-Scott. *5m E of Otley. Off A659 between Pool & Harewood.* **Sun 26 May (12-5). Adm £5, chd free. Home-made teas.**

Historic picturesque 3½ acre Wharfedale garden with beech avenue, mature rhododendrons and azaleas. Gravel path from terrace leads to attractive water garden with canals set amongst woodland plantings. Walled kitchen garden and flower garden. Specialist nurseries.

21 DANESWELL HOUSE

35 Main Street, Stamford Bridge, YO41 1AD. Brian & Pauline Clayton, 01759 371446, Pauline-clayton44@outlook.com. *7m E of York. On A166 at the E end of the village. Garden on your L as you leave the village towards Bridlington.* **Sun 30 June (10-4). Adm £4, chd free. Home-made teas. Also open Bugthorpe Gardens.** Visits also by arrangement.

A ¾ acre secluded garden that sweeps down to the R Derwent. It has tiered terraces, ponds, including a new pond with bridge, water feature, shrubs, borders. New feature is a copy of the Yorkshire garden as seen at Chelsea Flower Show 2018. The garden attracts abundant wildlife. Teas are served at the top of the garden. This is a sloping garden down to river, however access is possible with care.

22 DEVONSHIRE MILL

Canal Lane, Pocklington, York, YO42 1NN. Sue & Chris Bond, 01759 302147, chris.bond.dm@btinternet.com, www.devonshiremill.co.uk. *1m S of Pocklington. Canal Lane, off A1079 at The Wellington Oak Pub.* **Sun 24 Feb (11-5). Adm £4, chd free. Home-made teas.**

Drifts of double snowdrops, hellebores and ferns surround the historic grade II listed water mill. Explore the two acre garden with mill stream, orchards, woodland, herbaceous borders, hen run and greenhouses. The old mill pond is now a vegetable garden with raised beds and polytunnel. Over the past twenty years the owners have developed the garden on organic principles to encourage wildlife.

23 ◆ DOVE COTTAGE NURSERY GARDEN

Shibden Hall Road, nr Halifax, HX3 9XA. Kim & Stephen Rogers, 01422 203553, info@dovecottagenursery.co.uk, www.dovecottagenursery.co.uk.

Linden Lodge

1m E Halifax. From Halifax take A58 turn L signed Claremount, cont over bridge, cont ½m. J26 M62- A58 Halifax. Drive 4m. L turn at Paw Prints pet store down Tanhouse Hill, cont ½m. **For NGS: Sun 16 June, Sun 21 July, Sun 18 Aug (10-4). Adm £4, chd free. Home-made teas.** For other opening times and information, please phone, email or visit garden website.

North facing, ⅓ acre sloping garden with rural views. A beautiful mix of summer flowering perennials and grasses. Winding paths and comfortable benches. Garden open Thurs to Sat June to Sept. Plants for sale in nursery. Wildlife friendly.

24 34 DOVER ROAD

Hunters Bar, Sheffield, S11 8RH. Marian Simpson, 07957 536248, marian@mjsimpson.plus.com. *1½m SW of city centre. From A61 (ring rd) A625 Moore St/Ecclesall Rd for approx 1m. Dover Rd on R.* **Evening opening Fri 28 June (6.30-8.30). Wine. Sun 30 June (10-4). Home-made teas. Adm £3.50, chd free. please tel: 0114 2661573 for evening opening tickets, Friday 28 June.** Visits also by arrangement May to Aug for groups of 10+.

Colourful, small town garden packed with interest and drama, combining formality with exotic exuberance. Attractive alpine area replacing old driveway, many interesting containers and well-stocked borders. Conservatory, seating areas and lawns complement unusual plants and planting combinations. Sage Sheffield Greenfingers Question Time Panellist, Radio Sheffield.

GROUP OPENING

25 NEW EAST MORTON GARDENS

Dimples Lane, East Morton, Keighley, BD20 5SU. *Between Keighley & Bingley. From A650 Keighley r'about take B6265 towards Bingley & East Riddlesden Hall NT. Turn L to East Morton.* **Wed 26 June (11-5). Combined adm £4, chd free. Light refreshments at Busfeild Arms pub, opp Dimples Lane.**

NEW CLIFF HOUSE
Pauline Horne.

NEW 24 DIMPLES LANE
Margaret Irving.

Two small south facing village gardens overlooking a wooded valley and Airedale. Cliff House cottage garden is on three levels with colourful mixed herbaceous and shrub borders, pots, terrace and several seating areas and new gazebo. The garden is approached by a steep Yorkshire stone sett driveway. Almost adjacent is 24 Dimples Lane which is densely planted for seasonal colour; shaped and pruned trees, shrubs and a variety of topiaried evergreens giving structure. The garden is completely enclosed by clipped mixed hedging. A small stumpery, structures and a clever use of vistas, raised beds and small spaces make this garden feel much larger than it is. The garden studio has a sedum roof. Art Exhibition. Not suitable for wheelchairs.

26 EAST WING, NEWTON KYME HALL

Croft Lane, Newton Kyme, nr Boston Spa, LS24 9LR. Fiona & Chris Royffe, www.plantsbydesign.info. *2m from Tadcaster or Boston Spa. Follow directions for Newton Kyme Village from A659.* **Sun 21 July (11-5). Adm £4, chd free. Home-made teas.**

Small owner designed contemporary garden in dramatic setting creating a unique sense of place. Views of medieval ruins of Kyme Castle, St Andrews Church and C18 Fairfax family home Newton Kyme Hall (not open). Sculptural beech and yew hedges enclose spaces for features such as herb and cutting gardens, lawns and small meadow. Includes exhibition of garden design.

27 3 EMBANKMENT ROAD

Broomhill, Sheffield, S10 1EZ. Charlotte Cummins. *1½m W of city centre, 7½m from J33 M1. A61 ring rd follow A57 to Manchester. In Broomhill turn R onto Crookes Rd, 1st R on to Crookesmoor Rd. Embankment Rd is 2nd on L.* **Sun 23 June (10-4). Adm £3.50, chd free. Light refreshments.**

Compact city garden. Cottage styled planting, with well stocked borders of interesting and carefully selected herbaceous perennials. Patio with steps leading to elevated lawn, raised vegetable beds and garden. Clipped box, Hostas and Lavender bed with Alliums in the front garden. Collections of Astrantias, Ferns, Heucheras and over 100 different varieties of Hostas. Home grown plants for sale.

28 FAWLEY HOUSE

7 Nordham, North Cave, nr Brough, Hull, HU15 2LT. Mr & Mrs T Martin, 01430 422266, louisem200@hotmail.co.uk, www.nordhamcottages.co.uk. *15m W of Hull. L at J38 on M62E. L at '30' & signs: Wetlands & Polo. At L bend, R into Nordham. Fawley's on RHS. Car park further ahead. From Beverley, B1230 to N Cave. R after church. Over bridge. Car park ahead.* **Sun 17 Mar, Sun 28 Apr (12-5). Adm £5, chd free. Home-made teas. Refreshments in the stone cottage with log fires in March and also in April if necessary! ART EXHIBITION.** Visits also by arrangement Feb to June for groups of 10+. £8 incl tea. Coaches park at road end, near salt box as nowhere to turn.

Tiered, 2½ acre garden with lawns, mature trees, formal hedging and gravel pathways. Lavender beds, mixed shrub/herbaceous borders, and hot double herbaceous borders. Apple espaliers, pears, soft fruit, produce and herb gardens. Terrace with pergola and vines. Sunken garden with white border. Woodland with naturalistic planting and spring bulbs. Quaker well, stream and spring area with 3 bridges, ferns and hellebores near mill stream. Beautiful snowdrops and aconites early in year. Treasure Hunt for children. Self catering accommodation at Nordham Cottages see website. Partial wheelchair access to top of garden and terrace on pea gravel. Sloping paths thereafter.

29 FERNLEIGH

9 Meadowhead Avenue, Meadowhead, Sheffield, S8 7RT. Mr & Mrs C Littlewood, 01142 747234, littlewoodchristine@gmail.com. *4m S of Sheffield city centre. From Sheffield city centre. A61, A6102, B6054 r'about, exit B6054. 1st R Greenhill Ave, 2nd R. From M1 J33, A630 to A6102, then as above.* **Sun 2, Sun 30 June, Sun 28 July, Sun 25 Aug (11-5). Adm £3.50, chd free. Light refreshments. Home-made cakes.** Visits also by arrangement Apr to Sept for groups of 10 to 30.

Plantswoman's ⅓ acre cottage style garden. Large variety of unusual plants set in differently planted sections to provide all-yr interest. Seating areas to view different aspects of garden. Auricula theatre, patio, gazebo and greenhouse. Miniature log cabin with living roof and cobbled area with unusual plants in pots. Sempervivum, alpine displays and wildlife 'hotel'. Wide selection of home grown plants for sale. Animal Search for children.

ALLOTMENTS

30 FIRVALE ALLOTMENT GARDEN

Winney Hill, Harthill, nr Worksop, S26 7YN. Don & Dot Witton, 01909 771366, donshardyeuphorbias@btopenworld.com, www.euphorbias.co.uk. *12m SE of Sheffield, 6m W of Worksop. M1 J31 A57 to Worksop. Turn R to Harthill. Allotments at S end of village, 26 Casson Drive at N end on Northlands Estate.* **Visits by arrangement Mar to July. Adm £3, chd free. Home-made teas at 26 Casson Drive Harthill (S26 7WA).**

Large allotment containing 13 island beds displaying 500+ herbaceous perennials incl the National Collection of hardy Euphorbias with over 100 varieties flowering between March and October. Organic vegetable garden. Refreshments, WC, plant sales at 26 Casson Drive – small garden with mixed borders, shade and seaside garden.

NPC

31 NEW FREEMAN BIODYNAMIC GARDEN

Riggs High Road, Stannington, Sheffield, S6 6DA. Peter van Vliet. *5¾m W from Sheffield city centre. Follow signs for Glossop A57, at Rivelin Valley Rd junction take B6076 for Stannington & Dungworth, to Riggs High Road, entrance on L at top of hill.* **Sat 20 July (10-2). Adm £3, chd free. Light refreshments.**

1½ acres of intensive and diversified market garden including field and indoor vegetables, cut flowers, herbs, top and soft fruit on south facing hillside with stunning views, using organic/biodynamic methods and providing therapy and education for young people with learning difficulties. 4 acres of 25 yr old mixed woodland providing sheltered area devoted to green wood turning, composting leaves, woodchips and other organic vegetable waste.

32 FRIARS HILL

Sinnington, YO62 6SL. Mr & Mrs C J Baldwin, 01751 432179, friars.hill@abelgratis.co.uk. *4m W of Pickering. On A170.* **Sun 28 Apr (1-5). Adm £4, chd free.** Visits also by arrangement Mar to July.

Plantswoman's 1¾ acre garden containing over 2500 varieties of perennials and bulbs, with yr-round colour. Early interest with hellebores, bulbs and woodland plants. Herbaceous beds. Hostas, delphiniums, old roses and stone troughs. Excellent Autumn colour.

33 GLARAMARA

Lambwath Lane, New Ellerby, Hull, HU11 5BT. Pam & Giles Hufford. *From Hull, leave A165 just before Skirlaugh, turn R onto Mulberry Lane. After 1½m, turn L on to Lambwath Lane. Glaramara is 200yds on L.* **Sun 16 June (10.30-4). Adm £3, chd free. Home-made teas.**

Wildlife haven on the highest point of the Holderness Plain. Steps leading to patio, lawn with borders and small pond. Archway to henhouse and willow windbreaks surrounded by too many trees and plants to list. Twisting pathways to the sleep house and secret garden. Small wooded area with gate leading to greenhouse, apiary, mixed fruit and vegetable plots with specimen trees.

34 GLENCOE HOUSE

Main Street, Bainton, Driffield, YO25 9NE. Liz Dewsbury, 01377 217592, efdewsbury@gmail.com. *6m SW of Driffield on A614. 10m N of Beverley on B1248 Malton Rd. The house is on the W side of A614 in centre of the village. Parking is around village or in lay-by 280m N of house towards the Bainton r'about.* **Visits by arrangement May to July. Adm £4, chd free. Home-made teas. Full afternoon teas can be pre booked for groups of 4 to 10 people.**

3 acres of garden developed over 41 years. Extensively planted with trees, shrubs, roses, clematis and perennials, the cottage garden next to the house adjoins a mown field planted with specimen trees and an orchard. Furthest from the house, a naturalistic planting of native and unusual trees and a large wildlife pond have been established. There is also a kitchen garden and greenhouse. Wheelchair access to paved area in cottage garden but difficult elsewhere.

35 GOLDSBOROUGH HALL

Church Street, Goldsborough, HG5 8NR. Mr & Mrs M Oglesby, 01423 867321, info@goldsboroughhall.com, www.goldsboroughhall.com. *2m SE of Knaresborough. 3m W of A1M. Off A59 (York-Harrogate) carpark 300yds past pub on R.* **Sun 7 Apr (12-4); Sun 21 July (12-5). Adm £5, chd free. Light lunches, cream teas, sandwiches and cakes.** Donation to St Mary's Church.

Previously opened for NGS from 1928-30 and now beautifully restored by present owners (re-opened in 2010). 12 acre garden and formal landscaped grounds in parkland setting and Grade II*, C17 house, former residence of the late HRH Princess Mary, daughter of George V and Queen Mary. Gertrude Jekyll inspired replanted 120ft double herbaceous borders and rose garden. Quarter-mile Lime Tree Walk planted by royalty in the 1920s, orchard, redesigned kitchen garden and a flower border featuring 'Yorkshire Princess' rose, named after Princess Mary. Gravel paths and some steep slopes.

36 NEW THE GRANGE

Wath Lane, Copgrove, Harrogate, HG3 3TA. Peter & Maggie Edwards. *10m N of Harrogate. Between Burton Leonard & Staveley, 200yds E of Copgrove Church, next to business park where parking is available.* **Sat 1, Sun 2 June (11-5). Adm £4, chd free. Light refreshments.**

Mature 1 acre gardens created by the present owners over the last 30 years. Special features include an extended laburnum arch, a pleached Liquidamber hedge and a rose pergola leading to a formal lily pond. Planting includes conifer and heather beds, specimen trees and mixed shrub and herbaceous borders, a greenhouse and a raised Alpine bed and gravel paths. Teas in aid of Copgrove Church. Paths around the pond are narrow.

37 THE GRANGE

Carla Beck Lane, Carleton in Craven, Skipton, BD23 3BU. Mr & Mrs R N Wooler, 07740 639135, margaret.wooler@hotmail.com. *1½m SW of Skipton. Turn off A56 (Skipton-Clitheroe) into Carleton. Keep L at Swan Pub, continue to end of village then turn R into Carla Beck Lane.* **Wed 10 July, Wed 7 Aug (12-4.30). Adm £5, chd free. Cream teas. Visits also by arrangement July & Aug for groups of 30+. Garden Tour and Refreshments. Donation to Sue Ryder Care Manorlands Hospice.**

Over 4 acres set in the grounds of Victorian house (not open) with mature trees and panoramic views towards The Gateway to the Dales. The garden has been restored by the owners over the last 2 decades with many areas of interest being added to the original footprint. Bountiful herbaceous borders with many unusual species, rose walk, parterre, mini-meadows and water features. Large greenhouse and raised vegetable beds. Oak seating placed throughout the garden invites quiet contemplation - a place to 'lift the spirit'. Gravel paths and steps.

38 NEW GREAT CLIFF EXOTIC GARDEN

5 Cliff Drive, Crigglestone, Wakefield, WF4 3EN. Kristofer Swaine, yorkshirekris@hotmail.co.uk, , www.facebook.com/yorkshirekris. *1m from J39 M1 motorway. From M1 (J39) take A636 towards Denby Dale, past Cedar Court Hotel then L at British Oak pub onto Blacker Lane. Parking on Cliff Road motorway bridge.* **Sun 18 Aug (1-5). Adm £3.50, chd free. Visits also by arrangement July to Oct for groups of 10 to 20.**

An exotic garden on a long narrow plot. Possibly the largest collection of palm species planted out in Northern England including a large Chilean Wine Palm. Colourful exotic borders with Zinnias, Cannas, Ensete, Bananas, Tree ferns, Agaves, Aloes, Colocasias and bamboos. Jungle hut, winding paths, pond that traverses the full width of the garden and vegetable plot. Unsuitable for wheelchairs.

39 GREENWICK FARM

Huggate, York, YO42 1YR. Fran & Owen Pearson, 01377 288122, greenwickfarm@hotmail.com. *2m W of Huggate. From York on A166, turn R 1m after Garrowby Hill, at brown sign for picnic area & scenic route. White wind turbine on drive.* **Visits by arrangement July & Aug. Adm £6.50 incls Home-made teas. Tea tables in conservatory and outside.**

1 acre woodland garden created in 2010 from disused area of the fam. Set in a large dell with mature trees. Paths up the hillside through borders lead to terrace and Hydrangeas. Many seating areas with spectacular views across wooded valley and the Wolds. Stumpery and hot border. Mixed borders. New summerhouse, water feature and brushed steel sculpture. Described by guests as a graceful and tranquil garden. Access for wheelchairs difficult, but good view of garden from hard standing outside house/tea area.

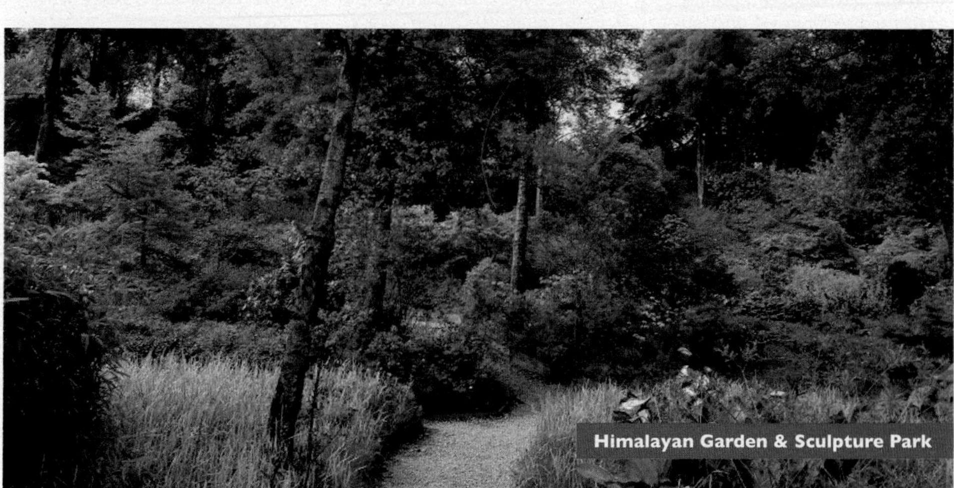

Himalayan Garden & Sculpture Park

40 HAVOC HALL

York Rd, Oswaldkirk, York, YO62 5XY. David & Maggie Lis, 01439 788846, Davidglis@me.com, www.havochall.co.uk. *21m N of York. On B1363, 1st house on R as you enter Oswaldkirk from S & last house on L as you leave village from N.* **Sun 30 June (1-5). Adm £5.50, chd free. Home-made teas.** Visits also by arrangement.

Started in 2009, comprising 8 areas incl knot, herbaceous, mixed shrub and flower gardens, courtyard, vegetable area and orchard, woodland walk and large lawned area with hornbeam trees and hedging. To the S is a 2 acre wild flower meadow and small lake. Extensive collection of roses, herbaceous perennials and grasses. See website for other opening times. Some steps but these can be avoided.

41 HIGHFIELD COTTAGE

North Street, Driffield, YO25 6AS. Debbie Simpson, 01377 256562, debbie@simpsonhighfield.karoo.co.uk. *30m E of York, 29m E of M62. Exit at A614/A166 r'about onto York Rd into Driffield. Carry straight until you reach the park with the Indian takeaway opp. the park. Highfield Cottage is the white detached house next to this.* **Sun 5, Sun 26 May, Sun 25 Aug (10.30-3.30). Adm £4, chd free.** Visits also by arrangement Apr to Sept.

A ¾ acre suburban garden bordered by mature trees and stream. Structure is provided by numerous yew and box topiary, a pergola and sculptures. Constantly evolving, the garden has something for everyone; lawns with island beds, mixed shrubs, fruit trees and herbaceous borders. The garden has been described as 'magical' and a 'hidden gem' by NGS visitors. The garden is not suited to wheelchairs and access is uneven.

42 HILLSIDE

West End, Ampleforth, York, YO62 4DY. Sue Shepherd & Jon Borgia, 01439 788993, sue@sueandjon.net. *West End of Ampleforth village, 4m S of Helmsley. From A19, follow brown sign to Byland Abbey & continue to Ampleforth. From A170 take B1257 to Malton, after 1m turn R to Ampleforth. Roadside parking only. Please be considerate.* **Sat 31 Aug, Sun 1 Sept (10.30-4.30). Adm £4, chd free. Light refreshments.** Visits also by arrangement June to Oct for groups of 10 to 30.

Half acre garden on a south facing slope, and half acre field. The design is evolving, based on informal planting and a wildlife friendly approach. Woodland and meadow areas. Ponds and boggy areas. Lawn rising up to summer house and deck with fine views of the Coxwold - Gilling Gap. Fruit trees and kitchen garden. Wild garden in field. All year round interest with an emphasis on autumn colour.

43 HIMALAYAN GARDEN & SCULPTURE PARK

The Hutts, Hutts Lane, Grewelthorpe, Ripon, HG4 3DA. Mr & Mrs Peter Roberts, www.himalayangarden.com. *5m NW of Ripon. From N: A1(M) J51 A684 (Bedale) then B6268 (Masham). From S: A1M J50 (Ripon) then A6108 (Masham) after North Stainley turn L (Mickley & Grewelthorpe). Follow garden signs.* **Evening opening Mon 20 May (4-8.30). Adm £9, chd £2.**

Winner of Yorkshire in Bloom Tourist Attractions Award 2018. 40 acres of garden inspired by the Himalayas. Considered home to the North's largest collection of rhododendrons, azaleas and magnolias. There are nearly 20,000 plants including some 1,400 rhododendron varieties, 250 azalea varieties and 150 different magnolias; and a newly planted 20-acre arboretum. 70 Contemporary Sculptures, Himalayan Shelter, Lakeside Pagoda, Thatched Summer House, Buddha Garden, Norse Shelter, Contemplation Circle and three lakes. Limited Wheelchair Access.

44 2 HOLLIN CLOSE

Rossington, nr Doncaster, DN11 0XX. Mr & Mrs Hann. *5m S of Doncaster. At J3 on M18 take A6182 signed Airport. At r'about, A638 signed Bawtry turn R (Littleworth Lane) 5m N of Bawtry after T-lights signed Airport take next L (Littleworth Lane) Hollin Close is 2nd R.* **Sun 30 June (11-5). Adm £3, chd free. Home-made teas.**

⅓ acre terraced garden designed and maintained by owners with four themes on three levels. Cottage style herbaceous planting surrounds a circular lawn alongside a tranquil oriental garden. Steps lead to the greenhouse and Mediterranean gravel garden with sun-loving plants for bees and butterflies. Below lies a wildlife friendly small woodland glade with bug hotel, stumpery, fruit and ferns. 3 times winner of Doncaster in Bloom Best Private Residents Garden.

45 HOLMFIELD

Fridaythorpe, YO25 9RZ. Susan & Robert Nichols, 01377 236627, susan@wiresculptures.net. *9m W of Driffield. From York A166 through Fridaythorpe. 1m turn R signed Holmfield. 1st house on lane.* **Evening opening Fri 14 June (5.30-8.30). Adm £6, chd free. Wine. Sun 16 June (12-5). Adm £4.50, chd free. Home-made teas. Also open Rustic Cottage and The Ridings.** Visits also by arrangement May to July for groups of 10+.

Informal 2 acre country garden on gentle S-facing slope. Developed from a field over last 28yrs. Large mixed borders, bespoke octagonal gazebo, family friendly garden with 'Hobbit House', sunken trampoline, large lawn, tennis court, hidden paths for hide and seek. Productive fruit cage, vegetable and cut flower area. Collection of Phlomis. Display of wire sculptures. Bee friendly planting. Some gravel areas, sloping lawns. Wheelchair access possible with help.

46 HONEY HEAD

Wood Nook, Meltham, Holmfirth, HD9 4DU. Susan & Andrew Brass. *6m S of Huddersfield. Turn from A616 to Honley, through village then follow Meltham rd for 1m, turn L on Wood Nook Lane.* **Sun 7 July (10-4). Adm £4, chd free. Home-made teas.**

Set high on a Pennine hillside with panoramic views, Honey Head aspires to provide year round interest whilst attempting to be self sufficient in fruit, vegetables, cut flowers and plants. Formal gardens with interconnecting ponds lead to extensive kitchen gardens with greenhouses complemented by areas planted to encourage

The Manor House, Tollerton

wildlife. Weather permitting we will have "The Saxpots" playing an assortment of music, a local ensemble who are keen to support our event.

47 HUNMANBY GRANGE
Wold Newton, Driffield, YO25 3HS. Tom & Gill Mellor, 01723 891636, gill.mellor234@gmail.com. *12½m SE of Scarborough. Hunmanby Grange home of Wold Top Brewery, between Wold Newton & Hunmanby on rd from Burton Fleming to Fordon.* **Sat 1, Sun 2 June (11-5). Adm £5, chd free. Light refreshments in Wold Top Brewery bar area. Field and Forage will also be catering in courtyard.** Visits also by arrangement June & July for groups of 10+. Please contact Wold Top Brewery 017238 92222 for details.

Hunmanby Grange sits high on the Yorkshire Wolds where the power of the wind and the shallow chalk wolds soils have dictated the garden design .A series of gardens surround the house giving scope for changes in design and planting. In the Brewery courtyard is the water feature from The Welcome to Yorkshire Chelsea Garden - The Brewers Yard. The Wold Top Brewery will also be open. Children are very welcome in the garden. There is plenty of space in the woodland with mown and bark paths for exploration, garden games are stored in the tennis house and picnics are welcome in this area too. Steps can be avoided by using grass paths and lawns. Pond garden not completely accessible to wheelchairs but can be viewed from gateway.

48 ◆ JACKSON'S WOLD
Sherburn, Malton, YO17 8QJ. Mr & Mrs Richard Cundall, 07966 531995, jacksonswoldgarden@gmail.com, www.jacksonswoldgarden.com. *11m E of Malton, 10m SW of Scarborough. Signs only from A64. A64 Eastbound to Scarborough. R at T-lights in Sherburn, take the Weaverthorpe rd, after 100 metres R fork to Helperthorpe & Luttons. 1m to top of hill, turn L at garden sign.* **For NGS: Sun 12 May, Sun 23 June (1-5). Adm £4, chd free. Home-made teas.** For other opening times and information, please phone, email or visit garden website.

2 acre garden with stunning views of the Vale of Pickering. Walled garden with mixed borders, numerous old shrub roses underplanted with unusual perennials. Woodland paths lead to further shrub and perennial borders. Lime avenue with wild flower meadow. Traditional vegetable garden with roses, flowers and framed by a Victorian greenhouse. Adjoining nursery. Tours by appointment.

49 LAND FARM
Edge Lane, Colden, Hebden Bridge, HX7 7PJ. Mr J Williams. *8m W of Halifax. At Hebden Bridge (A646) after 2 sets of T-lights take turning circle to Heptonstall & Colden. After 2¾m in Colden village turn R at Edge Lane 'no through rd'. In ¾m turn L down lane.* **Wed 22 May, Wed 3, Wed 31 July (10-5). Adm £5.50, chd free. Home-made teas.**

An intriguing 6 acre upland garden within a sheltered valley, created entirely by the present owner over a period of 40 years. In that time the valley has been planted with 20,000 trees by friends, neighbours and myself, which has encouraged a habitat rich in bird and wildlife. Within the garden, vistas have been created around thought provoking sculpture. Meconopsis and cardiocrimum lilies. Latest addition is a half-acre highly individual moss garden. Partial wheelchair access, please telephone 01422 842260.

50 LINDEN LODGE

Newbridge Lane, nr Wilberfoss, York, YO41 5RB. Robert Scott & Jarrod Marsden, 07900 003538, rdsjsm@gmail.com. *10m E of York. From York on the A1079, ignore signs for Wilberfoss, take next turning signed Bolton village, after 1m at the Xrds, turn L onto Newbridge Lane, Linden Lodge is on R in 200m.* **Sat 8, Sun 9 June (12-5). Adm £4.50, chd free. Light refreshments. All garden openings, light lunches, cakes & cream teas are served.** Visits also by arrangement in June for groups of 20+.

6 acres in all. 1 acre garden, owner designed and constructed since 2000. Gravel paths edged with brick or lavender, many borders with unusual mixed herbaceous perennials, shrubs and feature trees. A wildlife pond, summer house, kitchen garden, glasshouse. Orchard and woodland area. Formal garden with pond and water feature. 5 acres of developing meadow, trees, pathways, hens and Shetland sheep. Plant sales. Gravel paths and shallow steps.

GROUP OPENING

51 LITTLETHORPE GARDENS

Pottery Lane, Ripon, HG4 3LS. *1½m SE of Ripon. Off A61 bypass follow signs to Littlethorpe. Turn R at church. From Bishop Monkton follow signs to Ripon (Knaresborough Rd), turn R to Littlethorpe.* **Sun 28 July (1-5). Combined adm £6, chd free. Home-made teas at Greencroft.**

GREENCROFT
David & Sally Walden, 01765 602487, s-walden@outlook.com.
Visits also by arrangement July & Aug for groups of 20+. Refreshments available.

LITTLETHORPE HOUSE
Mr & Mrs James Hare.

Littlethorpe is a small village characterised by houses interspersed with fields close to Ripon. The gardens are at least half a mile apart and there is a car park at each garden. Greencroft is a one acre informal garden made by the owners. Special ornamental features incl gazebo, temple pavilions, formal pool, stone wall with mullions, and gate to rose pergola leading to a cascade water feature. Long herbaceous borders packed with colourful late flowering perennials, annuals and exotics culminate in circular garden with views through to large wildlife pond and surrounding countryside. Littlethorpe House has expansive lawns, topiary and clipped yews hedges and large borders for mixed herbaceous, roses and shrubs.

52 LOW HALL

Dacre Banks, Nidderdale, HG3 4AA. Mrs P A Holliday, 01423 780230, 1pamelaholliday@gmail.com. *10m NW of Harrogate. On B6451 between Dacre Banks & Darley.* **Sun 12 May (1-5). Adm £4.50, chd free. Home-made teas. Also open Woodlands Cottage.** Visits also by arrangement May to Sept. Small groups of 3 or 4 and large groups up to 50. Teas by prior arrangement.

Romantic walled garden set on differing levels designed to complement historic C17 family home (not open). Spring bulbs, rhododendrons; azaleas round tranquil water garden. Asymmetric rose pergola underplanted with auriculas and lithodora links orchard to the garden. Extensive herbaceous borders, shrubs and climbing roses give later interest. Bluebell woods and lovely countryside of the farm all round overlooking the R Nidd. 80% of garden can be seen from a wheelchair but access involves three stone steps.

53 NEW LOW STONEHILLS FARM

Fraisthorpe, Bridlington, YO15 3QR. Jackie Riby, 07751257420, jackieriby@hotmail.com. *On main A165, 4m S of Bridlington. ½m from Fraisthorpe village on opposite side of the main rd.* **Sun 30 June (11-4). Adm £4.50, chd free. Light refreshments. Also open The Old Vicarage.** Visits also by arrangement June to Aug.

This exposed garden 1mile from the coast has mixed beds and borders creating a cottage garden feel, with a large herbaceous planting to the East side. Over the hedge is a natural filled pond with soft fruit area. A meandering path around a large ash tree under which is planted to suit shade and wildlife. Veg garden to the West leads onto a 6 yr old orchard with rare breed Poultry. The garden is developing for the benefit of my family and to encourage wildlife and insects to be part of it.

54 NEW THE MANOR HOUSE

Holme-On-Swale, Thirsk, YO7 4JE. Mr & Mrs Steve & Judi Smith, 01845 567518, judiandsteve@outlook.com. *7m S/W from Thirsk. From A1 J50 onto A6055 N, onto B6267 E from Ripon/Thirsk A61 onto B6267.* **Sun 14 July (1-5). Adm £4.50, chd free. Home-made teas. Variety of home baked refreshments and drinks.** Visits also by arrangement Feb to Sept for groups of up to 30. Limited parking, group organiser please contact owners for details.

Almost two acres of mature, well established gardens with level lawns, a variety of specimen trees and shrubs, magnolias, rhododendrons, camellias. Sweeping herbaceous beds with many seasonal bulbs, and perrenial planting, peonies, roses, rambling clematis. Restored walled kitchen garden with vegetables, herbs and fruit, greenhouse and potting shed, newly planted orchard and woody wild areas. Access by gravelled path onto large level lawns.

55 THE MANOR HOUSE

Main Street, Tollerton, York, YO61 1QQ. Dr Weland & Audrey Stone, 01347 838454, weland.stone@btinternet.com. *10m N of York off A19. Turn up Main Street from village green. House is 200 yards on R.* **Visits by arrangement May to Sept for groups of up to 20. Adm £5, chd free. Light refreshments.**

An acre in village centre, developed over 45 years. Outbuildings and barn of old brick are covered with climbers. Various mixed borders, shrub rose and geranium bed, smaller areas of Hostas and Heathers. Vegetable bed behind yew hedge. Shaded front garden mainly for spring, Rear lawn dominated by fine Genista aetnensis in July. Tarmac drive and lawns.

56 NEW MARKENFIELD HALL

Ripon, HG4 3AD. Lady Deirdre & Mr Ian Curteis, 01765 692303, info@markenfield.com, www.markenfield.com. *3m S of Ripon. A61 between Ripon & Ripley. Turning between two low stone gateposts. Beware Sat-Navs.* **Fri 14 June (2-5). Adm £6, chd free. Home-made teas. Visits also by arrangement May to Sept for groups of 10 to 20. Can be combined with a tour of the Hall.**
The work of the Hall's owner Lady Deirdre Curteis and Giles Gilbey. Mature planting combines with newly-designed areas, where walls with espaliered apricots and figs are foregrounded by a mix of hardy perennials. The final phase of restoration started in 2017 when the Farmhouse-wing's garden was re-planted to eventually blend seamlessly with the Hall's main East Border. The gardens surround Markenfield Hall - a moated, medieval manor house, and one of the oldest, continuously inhabited houses in the country. Limited wheelchair access.

57 MIDENDALE

76 Main Street, Gowdall, Goole, DN14 0AE. Mr & Mrs Peter & Pauline Lacy. *M62 J34 take A19 towards Selby approx 1m then R on to A645 towards Goole in approx 4½m turn L to Gowdall. Roadside parking only.* **Sun 16 June (11-4). Adm £4, chd free. Home-made teas.**
2 acre garden built on a disused railway track and started in 2003. Flower, rose and conifer beds, a vegetable garden with raised beds, greenhouse and a herb potager area. An interesting feature is 'Ironhenge' an unusual use of scrap metal. At the bottom of the garden there is a wild flower meadow, orchard, small stumpery and compost area. Plenty of seating around the garden. A variety of plants and topiary plants for sale. Wheelchairs can access most areas of the garden but will require pushing over the gravelled area. WC facilities are available.

58 MILLGATE HOUSE

Millgate, Richmond, DL10 4JN. Tim Culkin & Austin Lynch, 01748 823571, oztim@millgatehouse.demon.co.uk, www.millgatehouse.com. *Centre of Richmond. House located at bottom of Market Place opp Barclays Bank. Just off corner of Market Place. Park in the Market Place no restrictions on Sunday.* **Sun 30 June, Sun 7 July (8-8). Adm £3.50, chd free.**
SE walled town garden overlooking R Swale. Although small, the garden is full of character, enchantingly secluded with plants and shrubs. Foliage plants incl ferns and hostas. Old roses, interesting selection of clematis, small trees and shrubs. RHS associate garden. Immensely stylish, national award-winning garden. Featured in GGG. Gardeners' World. Specialist collections of clematis, ferns, hostas and roses. MANY STEPS AND STEEP SLOPES SLIPPERY SURFACES.

59 115 MILLHOUSES LANE

Sheffield, S7 2HD. Sue & Phil Stockdale. *Approx 4m SW of Sheffield City Centre. Follow A625 Castleton/Dore Road, 4th L after Prince of Wales Pub, 2nd L. OR take A621 Baslow Rd; after Tesco garage take 2nd R, then 1st L.* **Sun 26 May (12.30-4.30). Adm £3.50, chd free. Home-made teas.**
Plantswoman's ⅓ acre south facing level cottage style garden, containing many choice and unusual perennials and bulbs, providing year round colour and interest. Large collection of 50+hostas, roses, peonies and clematis, together with unusual, tender and exotic plants - aeoniums, echeverias, bananas etc. Seating areas throughout the garden. Wide range of home propagated plants for sale.

60 MILLRACE GARDEN

84 Selby Road, Garforth, Leeds, LS25 1LP. Mr & Mrs Carthy, www.millrace-plants.co.uk. *5m E of Leeds. On A63 in Garforth. 1m from M1 J46, 3m from A1.* **Sun 19 May (1-5). Adm £4, chd free. Home-made teas.**
Overlooking a secluded valley, garden incl large herbaceous borders containing over 3000 varieties of perennials, shrubs and trees, many of which are unusual and drought tolerant. Ornamental pond, vegetable garden and walled terraces leading to wild flower meadow, small woodland, bog garden and wildlife lakes. Cuttings opportunity. Art exhibition. Most of the garden is accessible for wheelchairs. Although there are steps in places there is generally an alternative ramp.

61 ◆ NEWBY HALL & GARDENS

Ripon, HG4 5AE. Mr R C Compton, 01423 322583, info@newbyhall.com, www.newbyhall.com. *4m SE of Ripon. (HG4 5AJ for Sat Nav). Follow brown tourist signs from A1(M) or from Ripon town centre.* **For opening times and information, please phone, email or visit garden website.**
40 acres of extensive gardens and woodland laid out in 1920s. Full of rare and beautiful plants. Formal seasonal gardens, stunning double herbaceous borders to R Ure and National Collection of Cornus. Miniature railway and adventure gardens for children. Sculpture exhibition (open June - Sept). Free parking licensed restaurant. Shop and Plant Nursery. Wheelchair map available Disabled parking. Manual and electric wheelchairs available on loan, please call to reserve.

NPC

Your visits help change lives – your generosity has supported unpaid carers through donations to Carers Trust totalling over £3.9 million since 1996

62 ◆ NORTON CONYERS

Wath, Ripon, HG4 5EQ. Sir James & Lady Graham, 01765 640333, info@nortonconyers.org.uk, www.nortonconyers.org.uk. *4m NW of Ripon. Take Melmerby & Wath sign off A61 Ripon-Thirsk. Go through both villages to boundary wall. Signed entry 300 metres on right, follow track to our car park.* **For NGS: Sun 2 June (2-5). Adm £6, chd free. Home-made teas.** For other opening times and information, please phone, email or visit garden website.

Romantic mid C18 walled garden of interest to garden historians. Lawns, herbaceous borders, yew hedges, and Orangery with attractive pond. The garden retains essential features of its original C18th design with sympathetic planting in the English style. There are borders of gold and silver plants, of old fashioned peonies and irises in season. Visitors frequently comment on the tranquil and romantic atmosphere. For House opening dates and times see website. Unusual hardy plants for sale. Most areas wheelchair accessible, gravel paths.

63 THE NURSERY

15 Knapton Lane, Acomb, York, YO26 5PX. Tony Chalcraft & Jane Thurlow, 01904 781691, janeandtonyatthenursery@hotmail.co.uk. *2½m W of York. From A1237 take B1224 direction Acomb. At r'about turn L (Beckfield Ln.), after 150 metres Turn L.* **Sun 14 July (1-5); Wed 17 July (2-7). Adm £3, chd free. Home-made teas.** Visits also by arrangement Apr to Sept for groups of 10+.

Hidden, attractive and productive 1 acre organic garden behind suburban house (not open). Wide range of top and soft fruit with over 100 fruit trees, many in trained form. Many different vegetables grown both outside and under cover incl a large 20m greenhouse. Productive areas interspersed with informal ornamental plantings providing colour and habitat for wildlife. The extensive planting of different forms and varieties of fruit trees make this an interesting garden for groups to visit by appointment at blossom and fruiting times in addition to the main summer openings.

64 NEW THE OLD RECTORY

Arram Road, Leconfield, Beverley, HU17 7NP. David Baxendale, 01964 502037, davidbax@newbax.co.uk. *On entering Arram Rd you will see a double bend sign approx 80yds on L. The entrance to the Old Rectory is by the sign. If you reach the church you have missed it.* **Visits by arrangement Jan to June for groups of up to 10.**

Approx 3 acres of garden and paddock. The garden is particularly attractive from early spring until mid summer. Notable for aconites, snowdrops, crocuses, daffodils and bluebells. Later hostas, irises, lilies and roses. There is a small wildlife pond with all the usual residents incl grass snakes. Well established trees and shrubs, with new trees planted when required.

65 OLD SLENINGFORD HALL

Mickley, nr Ripon, HG4 3JD. Jane & Tom Ramsden. *5m NW of Ripon. Off A6108. After N Stainley turn L, follow signs to Mickley. Gates on R after 1½m opp cottage.* **Sat 1, Sun 2 June (12-4). Adm £5, chd free. Home-made teas.**

A large English country garden and award winning permaculture forest garden. Early C19 house (not open) and garden with original layout; wonderful mature trees, woodland walk and Victorian fernery; romantic lake with islands, watermill, walled kitchen garden; beautiful long herbaceous border, yew and huge beech hedges. Several plant and other stalls. Picnics very welcome. Reasonable wheelchair access to most parts of garden. Disabled WC at Old Sleningford Farm next to the garden.

66 THE OLD VICARAGE

North Frodingham, Driffield, YO25 8JT. Professor Ann Mortimer. *6m E of Driffield on B1249. From Driffield take B1249 E for approx 6m. The church is on L. Garden is opp. Entrance is on T-junction of rd to Emmotland & B1249. From North Frodingham take the B1249 W for ½m.* **Sun 30 June (10.30-5.30). Adm £4.50, chd free. Home-made teas courtesy of the Nafferton Methodists.**

1½ acre plantsman's garden, owner developed over 21 years. Many themed areas e.g. rose garden, jungle, desert, fountain, scented, kitchen gardens, glasshouses. Numerous classical statues, unusual trees and shrubs, 1 large 1 small pond, orchard, nuttery. Children's interest with 'jungle book' and wild animal statues. Neo-Jacobean revival house, built 1837, mentioned in Pevsner (not open). The land now occupied by the house and garden was historically owned by the family of William Wilberforce. Visitors are welcome to pick produce from the fruit cage and kitchen garden. Parking along the B1249 courtesy of the farm opp. Parts of the garden are inaccessible but can be viewed from above.

67 THE ORCHARD

4a Blackwood Rise, Cookridge, Leeds, LS16 7BG. Carol & Michael Abbott, 0113 2676764. *5m N of Leeds centre, 5 minutes from York Gate garden. Off A660 (Leeds-Otley) N of A6120 Ring Rd. Turn L up Otley Old Rd. At top of hill turn L at T-lights (Tinshill Lane). Please park in Tinshill Lane.* **Sun 9 June (12-4.30). Adm £3.50, chd free. Light refreshments. Pop up cafe and cover for inclement weather.** Visits also by arrangement in June for groups of 10+. Visitors by arrangement.

⅓ acre plantswoman's hidden oasis. A wrap around garden of differing levels made by owners using stone found on site, planted for yr-round interest. Extensive rockery, unusual fruit tree arbour, oriental style seating area and Tea House, linked by grass paths, lawns and steps. Mixed perennials, hostas, ferns, shrubs, bulbs and pots amongst paved and pebbled areas. Best in area award Leeds in Bloom.

68 ◆ PARCEVALL HALL GARDENS

Skyreholme, Skipton, BD23 6DE. Walsingham College, 01756 720311, parcevallhall@btconnect.com, www.parcevallhallgardens.co.uk. *9m N of Skipton. Signs from B6160 Bolton Abbey-Burnsall rd or off B6265 Grassington-Pateley Bridge &*

at A59 Bolton Abbey r'about. **For NGS: Wed 3 July (10-5). Adm £7, chd free. Light refreshments.** For other opening times and information, please phone, email or visit garden website.
The only garden open daily in the Yorkshire Dales National Park. 24 acres in Wharfedale sheltered by mixed woodland; terrace garden, rose garden, rock garden, ponds. Mixed borders, spring bulbs, tender shrubs and autumn colour. Tea rooms (contact no. 01756 720630) at the foot of the gardens. There is no wheelchair access in the garden as it is set on a steep hillside with uneven paths.

69 PENNY PIECE COTTAGES

41/43 Piercy End, Kirkbymoorside, York, YO62 6DQ. Mick & Ann Potter. *Follow A170 to Kirkbymoorside at r'about turn up into Kirkby Main St approx 300yds on R. Street parking plus council car park at top of Main St.* **Sun 26 May (11-5). Adm £4, chd free. Home-made teas.**
Hidden away off the main street in Kirkbymoorside is a romantic cottage garden. Now fully matured it offers a sunny circular gravel garden, lawns with island beds planted with mixed shrubs and border perennials. Gravel pathway leads to a brick garden, informal pond, bog garden and colourful herbaceous border. Wildlife pond and pretty wild flower meadow. Lots of places to sit and relax.

70 PILMOOR COTTAGES

Pilmoor, nr Helperby, YO61 2QQ. Wendy & Chris Jakeman, 01845 501848, cnjakeman@aol.com. *20m N of York. From A1M J48. N end B'bridge follow rd towards Easingwold. From A19 follow signs to Hutton Sessay then Helperby. Garden next to mainline railway.* **Sun 25 Aug (12-5). Adm £3.50, chd free. Light refreshments by local WIs.** Visits also by arrangement May to Sept.
A year round garden for rail enthusiasts and garden visitors. A ride on the 71/4' Gauge railway runs through 2 acres of gardens and gives you the opportunity to view the garden from a different perspective. The journey takes you across water, through a little woodland area, past flower filled borders, and through a tunnel behind the rockery and water cascade. 1½ acre wild flower meadow and pond. Clock-golf putting green. Refreshments by two local WIs with donation to NGS

71 PRIMROSE BANK GARDEN AND NURSERY

Dauby Lane, Kexby, York, YO41 5LH. Sue Goodwill & Terry Marran, www.primrosebank.co.uk. *4m E of York. At J of A64 & A1079 take rd signed to Hull, Travel 3m & just as entering Kexby, turn R onto Dauby Lane, signed for Elvington. From the E travel on A1079 towards York. Turn L in Kexby.* **Sat 30, Sun 31 Mar (11-4); Sun 7 July (11-5). Adm £4, chd free. Home-made teas. Includes designated area for dogs.** Visits by arrangement Feb to Sept for groups of 15+ Refreshments on request when booking.
Over an acre of rare and unusual plants, shrubs and trees. Bulbs, Hellebores and flowering shrubs in spring, followed by planting for yr round interest. Courtyard garden, mixed borders, summer house and pond. Lawns, Contemporary Rock Garden, Shade and Woodland garden with pond, stumpery, and shepherds' hut. Poultry and Hebridean sheep. Dogs allowed in car park and designated tables outside the tearoom. Our Eranthis collection has been inspected and we are hoping for creditation for National Collection status. Most areas of the garden are level and are easily accessible for wheelchairs, accessible WC.

72 THE PRIORY, NUN MONKTON

York, YO26 8ES. Mr & Mrs R Harpin. *9m W of York, 12 E of Harrogate. E of A1M J47 off A59 signed Nun Monkton.* **Sun 7 July, Thur 12 Sept (11-5). Adm £5, chd free. Home-made teas.**
Large country garden at the confluence of the rivers Nidd and Ouse surrounding a William and Mary house (not open). Formal rose garden. Old walls support climbers and give a backdrop to long mixed flower borders, mature specimen trees and clipped yew walk leading to informal parkland with beck. Kitchen garden, greenhouse and glasshouse for ornamentals. Adjacent is St Mary's Church with Burne-Jones stained glass window. Gravel paths.

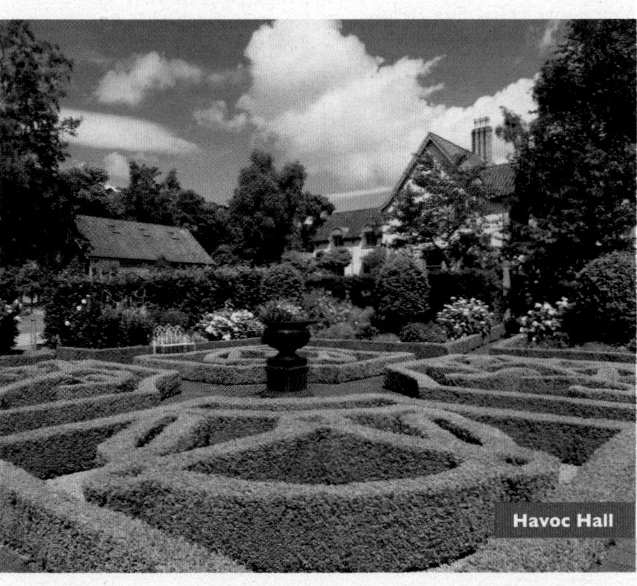
Havoc Hall

73 THE RED HOUSE

17 Whin Hill Road, Bessacarr, Doncaster, DN4 7AF. Rosie Hamlin, www.pyjamagardenersyorks.com. *2m S of Doncaster. A638 South, L at T-lights for B1396, Whin Hill Rd is 2nd R. A638 North, R signed Branton B1396 onto Whin Hill.* **Sat 25, Sun 26 May (1-5). Combined adm with Tamarind £5, chd free. Home-made teas on Sat at Tamarind; Sun at The Red House.**

Mature ⅔ acre garden. Dry shade a challenge but acid loving plants a joy. Fine acers, camellia, daphne, rhodos, skimmia and eucryphia. Alpine Terrace, rockery, mature shrubs, stepping stones through small woodland garden to lawn with modern rotating summerhouse, shrubs and young trees. White border conceals pond, compost and hens. NEW woodland being restored: planting large leaved rhodos.

74 REWELA COTTAGE

Skewsby, YO61 4SG. John Plant & Daphne Ellis, 01347 888125, rewelacottage@gmail.com. *4m N of Sheriff Hutton, 15m N of York. After Sheriff Hutton, towards Terrington, turn L towards Whenby & Brandsby. Turn R just past Whenby to Skewsby. Turn L into village. 400yds on R.* **Sun 26 May (11-5). Home-made teas. Sun 28 July (11-5). Light refreshments. Adm £5, chd free. Great cakes & scones, teas & coffees, soft drinks. Plus BBQ serving 100% Angus Beef-Burgers & Lincolnshire Sausages.** Visits also by arrangement May to July for groups of 20+.

Situated in a lovely quiet country village, a little bit off the beaten track is one of Yorkshire little hidden treasures. Rewela Cottage was designed from a empty paddock, to be as labour saving as possible, using mainly unusual trees and shrubs offering interest all year, using foliage bark and berries, enhancing the well-designed structure. All unusual trees and shrubs have labels giving full descriptions, picture, and any cultivation notes incl propagation. Plant sales are specimens from garden. Many varieties of Heuchera, Heucherella and Tiarellas, Penstemon, Hostas, ferns and herbs for sale. Some gravel paths may be a slight effort for a wheelchair. Plenty of seats. Lovely WC.

75 ◆ RHS GARDEN HARLOW CARR

Crag Lane, Harrogate, HG3 1QB. Royal Horticultural Society, 01423 565418, harlowcarr@rhs.org.uk, www.rhs.org.uk/harlowcarr. *1½m W of Harrogate town centre. On B6162 (Harrogate - Otley).* **For NGS: Sun 5 May (9.30-5). Adm £11.80, chd £5.90. For other opening times and information, please phone, email or visit garden website.**

One of Yorkshire's most relaxing yet inspiring locations! Highlights include spectacular herbaceous borders, streamside garden, alpines, scented and kitchen gardens. Lakeside Gardens, woodland and wild flower meadows. Betty's Cafe Tearooms, gift shop, plant centre and childrens play area incl tree house and log ness monster. Wheelchairs and mobility scooters available, advanced booking recommended.

76 NEW RIDGEFIELD COTTAGE & NURSERY

Forest Moor Road, Knaresborough, HG5 8JP. Tony & Jo Pickering. *Between Knaresborough & Harrogate. From A1(J47) take A59 then A658 towards Harrogate & Bradford over 3 r'abouts. After 1½m turn R (B6163) to Knaresborough & Calcutt. In ¾m turn L opposite Union pub.* **Sun 23 June (11-5). Adm £3.50, chd free. Home-made teas.**

½ acre garden evolved over 20yrs around Victorian mound planted orchard. Rocks and dry stone walling surround island beds . Unusual trees, shrubs and shade loving perennials are planted amongst old apple, damson and plum trees. Small fish pond and raised alpine bed. The plant nursery will be open. Car parking in field. For disabled some flat grass and gravel.

77 THE RIDINGS

South Street, Burton Fleming, Driffield, YO25 3PE. Roy & Ruth Allerston, 01262 470489. *11m NE of Driffield. 11m SW of Scarborough. 7m NW of Bridlington. From Driffield B1249, before Foxholes turn R to Burton Fleming. From Scarborough A165 turn R to Burton Fleming.* **Sun 16 June (1-5). Combined adm with Rustic Cottage £6, chd free. Home-made teas. Also open Holmfield** Visits also by arrangement Apr to July. No WC facilities.

Secluded cottage garden with colour-themed borders surrounding neat lawns. Grass and paved paths lead to formal and informal areas through rose and clematis covered pergolas and arbours. Box hedging defines well stocked borders with roses, herbaceous plants and trees. Seating in sun and shade offer vistas and views. Potager, greenhouse and summerhouse. Terrace with waterfeature and farming bygones. Terrace, tea area and main lawn accessible via ramp.

78 ROSEMARY COTTAGE

163 High Street, Hook, Goole, DN14 5PL. Justine Dixon, www.rosemarycottagehook.co.uk. *Between Goole, Howden & Airmyn, close to M62 J36. Close to M62 J36. Approach Hook from Boothferry Rd r'about 300yds S of Boothferry Bridge. Follow signs for Hook at Xrds turn L. Garden is 550yds on L. Garden entry is from rear through Car park.* **Sun 26 May (12-4). Adm £3.50, chd free. Cream teas. Access to refreshments is by steps.**

Delightful quaint cottage garden - combination of traditional cottage garden theme planting linking the individual garden 'rooms' to a small orchard leading through living willow arch to herbaceous perennial border and onto the edible garden overlooking open fields. Cake stall in aid of St Mary's Ch, Hook. Publicity stalls for Selby Beekeepers, Pricklington Palace Hedgehog Rescue, M &M Sheds selling garden ware and Roanne Nurseries selling plants. Wheelchair access is available to most of the garden (from rear carpark) albeit ground a little uneven, one part of the garden has stepped access.

79 RUSTIC COTTAGE

Front Street, Wold Newton, nr Driffield, YO25 3YQ. Jan Joyce, 01262 470710, janetmjoyce@icloud.com. *13m N of Driffield. From Driffield take B1249 to Foxholes (12m), take R turning signed Wold Newton. Turn L onto Front St, opp village pond, continue up hill, garden on L.* **Sun 19 May (12-4). Adm £3.50, chd free. Sun 16 June (12-4). Combined adm with The Ridings £6, chd free. (June) home-made teas at The Ridings. Single adm £3.50. Also open Holmfield.** Visits also by arrangement for groups of up to 20.

Plantswoman's cottage garden of much interest with many choice and unusual plants. Hellebores and bulbs are treats for colder months. Old-fashioned roses, fragrant perennials, herbs and wild flowers, all grown together provide habitat for birds, bees, butterflies and small mammals. It has been described as 'organised chaos'! The owner's 2nd NGS garden. Small dogs only.

80 ◆ SCAMPSTON WALLED GARDEN

Scampston Hall, Scampston, Malton, YO17 8NG. The Legard Family, 01944 759111, info@scampston.co.uk, www.scampston.co.uk/gardens. *5m E of Malton. ½m N of A64, nr the village of Rillington & signed Scampston only.* **For opening times and information, please phone, email or visit garden website.**

An exciting modern garden designed by Piet Oudolf. The 4-acre walled garden contains a series of hedged enclosures designed to look good throughout the year. The garden contains many unusual species and is a must for any keen plantsman. The Walled Garden is set within the grounds and parkland surrounding Scampston Hall. The Hall opens to visitors for a short period during the summer months. A newly restored Richardson conservatory at the heart of the Walled Garden re-opened as a Heritage and Learning Centre in 2015. The Walled Garden, Cafe and facilities are accessible by wheelchair. Some areas of the Parkland and the first floor of Hall are harder to access.

81 SCAPE LODGE

11 Grand Stand, Scapegoat Hill, Golcar, Huddersfield, HD7 4NQ. Dr & Mrs David Smith, 01484 644320, elizabethrfsmith@btinternet.com. *5m W of Huddersfield. From J23 or 24 M62 follow signs to Rochdale. After Outlane village, 1st L. At top of hill, 2nd L. Parking at Scapegoat Hill Baptist Church (HD7 4NU) or in village. 5 mins walk to garden. 303/304 bus.* **Sun 12 May, Sun 9 June (1.30-4.30). Adm £4, chd free. Home-made teas.** Visits also by arrangement May to Aug. Coach access to village. 5 minutes walk to garden. Donation to Mayor of Kirklees Charity Appeal.

⅓ acre contemporary country garden at 1000ft in the Pennines on a steeply sloping site with far-reaching views. Gravel paths lead between mixed borders on many levels. Colour themed informal planting chosen to sit comfortably in the landscape and give year round interest. Steps lead to terraced kitchen and cutting garden. Gazebo, pond, shade garden, collection of pots and tender plants.

82 1 SCHOOL LANE

Bempton, Bridlington, YO15 1JA. Mr Robert Tyas, rktyas10@gmail.com. *Close to the centre of village. 3m N of Bridlington. From Brid take B1255 toward Flamborough. L at 1st T-lights. Follow Bempton Lane out of residential area then 2nd R onto Bolam Lane. Continue to end and garden is facing.* **Sun 26 May (10-4). Adm £4, chd free. Light refreshments.** Visits also by arrangement May to July for groups of 5 to 30.

A short distance from stunning Bempton Cliffs this village garden provides all year round interest. Beds and borders boast a wide variety of mixed planting to offer a cottage garden feel with many interesting features adding to the overall effect e.g rare plants, alpines in troughs, pots and a unusual crevice rockery, along with a fruiting theme and a growing display of Lewisia. All areas of the garden can be viewed from the wheelchair.

Holmfield

Goldsborough Hall

83 ◆ SHANDY HALL GARDENS

Coxwold, YO61 4AD. The Laurence Sterne Trust, 01347 868465, www.laurencesternetrust.org.uk/shandy-hall-garden.php. *N of York. From A19, 7m from both Easingwold & Thirsk, turn E signed Coxwold.* **For NGS: Evening opening Fri 7, Fri 28 June (6.30-8). Adm £3, chd free.** For other opening times and information, please phone or visit garden website.

Home of C18 author Laurence Sterne. 2 walled gardens, 1 acre of unusual perennials interplanted with tulips and old roses in low walled beds. In old quarry, another acre of trees, shrubs, bulbs, climbers and wild flowers encouraging wildlife, incl. over 430 recorded species of moths. Moth trap, identification and release. Wildlife garden. Wheelchair access to wild garden by arrangement.

GROUP OPENING

84 NEW SHEFFIELD GARDENS

Crookes, Sheffield, S10 1UZ. *Two city centre gardens and one at Bradfield. A map with directions will be supplied on booking.* **Sun 14 July (11-6). Combined adm £10, chd free. Pre-booking essential, please visit www.ngs.org.uk for information & booking. Home-made teas at Bramblewood Cottage and 68 Tasker Road.**

NEW BRAMBLEWOOD COTTAGE
S6 6HX. Nigel Dunnett.
(See separate entry)

NEW 19 FIR STREET
S6 3TG. James Hitchmough.

NEW 68 TASKER ROAD
S10 1UZ. Andy Clayden.

Three inspiring yet individual gardens designed and owned by members of the Landscape Architecture Department, University of Sheffield, who are at the forefront of current ideas in naturalistic planting design, creating sustainable landscapes, and gardening for a changing climate. Their work included the Olympic Park, Pictorial Meadows and has come to be known as 'The Sheffield School' of planting design. Bramblewood Cottage, a one acre garden six miles from Sheffield centre has areas of naturalistic perennial planting, large log-pile sculptures and designed annual and perennial meadows, rain gardens and bioswales. 68 Tasker Road is a family garden using reclaimed materials, managing water through green roofs, ponds and soakaways. 19 Fir Street explores a meadow aesthetic using many plants usually considered tender for a northern city to mantain colour and foliage interest from February to November.

85 SKIPWITH HALL

Skipwith, Selby, YO8 5SQ. Mr & Mrs C D Forbes Adam, rosalind@escrick.com, , www.escrick.com/hall-gardens. *9m S of York, 6m N of Selby. From York A19 Selby, L in Escrick, 4m to Skipwith. From Selby A19 York, R onto A163 to Market Weighton, then L after 2m to Skipwith.* **Thur 6 June (1-4). Adm £5, chd free. Home-made teas.** Visits also by arrangement in June for groups of 10 to 30.

4-acre walled garden of Queen Anne house (not open). Extensive mixed borders and lawns, walled areas by renowned designer Cecil Pinsent. Recreated working kitchen garden with 15' beech hedge, pleached fruit, herb maze and pool. Woodland with specimen trees and shell house. Decorative orchard with espaliered and fan-trained fruit on walls. Italian Garden recently restored. Gravel paths.

86 SLEIGHTHOLMEDALE LODGE

Fadmoor, YO62 7JG. Patrick & Natasha James. *6m NE of Helmsley. Parking can be limited in wet weather. Garden is 1st property in Sleightholmedale, 1m from Fadmoor.* **Wed 5 June, Sun 11 Aug (2-6). Adm £5, chd free. Home-made teas.**
Hillside garden, walled rose garden and herbaceous borders with delphiniums, roses, verbascums in June and July. Views over peaceful valley in N Yorks Moors.

87 113 SOUTHFIELD

Southfield, Hessle, HU13 0ET. Michael & Nancy Baitson. *At r'about where A164 meets A15 go E onto A1105(to Hull). At 1st lights turn R onto Heads Lane. Cross Ferriby Rd at Xrds. Southfield is 2nd L.* **Sun 26 May (12-5.30). Combined adm with Beacon Garth £6, chd free. Tea at Beacon Garth.**
A wrap round garden in ⅓ acre with a surprise at each corner. 2 water features, woodland pathway, unusual shrubs, a variety of Hellebores and Ferns. No lawn! The garden has been developed and maintained since 2003 by current owners. Changes are on going. Plenty of quiet seating areas to appreciate the garden.

88 ◆ STILLINGFLEET LODGE

Stewart Lane, Stillingfleet, York, YO19 6HP. Mr & Mrs J Cook, 01904 728506, vanessa.cook@stillingfleetlodgenurseries.co.uk, www.stillingfleetlodgenurseries.co.uk. *6m S of York. From A19 York-Selby take B1222 towards Sherburn in Elmet. In village turn opp church.* **For NGS: Sun 12 May, Sun 15 Sept (1-5). Adm £5, chd £1. Home-made teas.** For other opening times and information, please phone, email or visit garden website.
Organic, wildlife garden subdivided into smaller gardens, each based on colour theme with emphasis on use of foliage plants. Wild flower meadow and natural pond. 55yd double herbaceous borders. Modern rill garden. Rare breeds of poultry wander freely in garden. Adjacent nursery. Wildlife Day in June. Garden Courses run all summer see website. Art exhibitions in the cafe. Gravel paths and lawn. Ramp to cafe if needed. No disabled WC.

89 SUE PROCTOR PLANTS NURSERY GARDEN

69 Ings Mill Avenue, Clayton West, Huddersfield, HD8 9QG. Sue & Richard Proctor, 01484 866189, hostas@sueproctorplants.co.uk, www.sueproctorplants.co.uk. *9m NE of Holmfirth, 10m SW of Wakefield. Off A636 Wakefield/ Holmfirth. From M1 J39 in Clayton West Village turn L signed Clayton West, High Hoyland, then R signed Kaye's F & N School. Turn 1st R to Ings Mill Avenue.* **Sat 6, Sun 7 July (11-4). Adm £3.50, chd free. Light refreshments. Gluten free available.** Visits also by arrangement Apr to Aug for groups of 10 to 30.
Small, mainly sloping, suburban garden packed full of interest. Summer highlights include over 300 varieties of hostas and close plantings of flowering perennials with some rare and unusual plants. Shaded gravel and rock gardens show off acers, ferns and hostas, especially miniature hostas, the nursery specialism. Many southern hemisphere and half/borderline hardy plants, including gingers, salvias and echiums. A notable feature is our collection of hostas, one of the largest in the North of England, including the smallest miniature hostas, less than 4" in height, to the world's largest 'Empress Wu'. A variety of half-hardy plants, especially climbers, flower throughout the summer. Partial wheelchair access and a graded path to the top of the garden.

90 SWALE COTTAGE

Station Road, Richmond, DL10 4LU. Julie Martin & Dave Dalton, 01748 829452, jmalandplan@btinternet.com. *Richmond town centre. On foot, facing bottom of Market Place, turn L onto Frenchgate, then R onto Station Rd. House 1st on R.* **Visits by arrangement May to Sept for groups of 10+. Adm £5, chd free. Teas and refreshments available in town centre nearby.**
½-acre urban oasis on steep site, with sweeping views and hidden corners. Several enclosed garden rooms on different levels. Mature herbaceous, rose and shrub garden with strong foliage interest. Magnificent yew and cedar. Organic vegetables and soft fruit and pond. Adjacent orchard and paddock with sheep.

91 TAMARIND

2 Whin Hill Road, Bessacarr, Doncaster, DN4 7AE. Ken & Carol Kilvington. *2m S of Doncaster. Through Lakeside, pass Dome on R turn R at Bawtry Rd T-lights, through pedestrian crossing & T-lights then 1st L. A638 - North from Bawtry to Doncaster turn R signed Cantley-Branton (B1396).* **Sat 25 May (1-5). Light refreshments. Sun 26 May (1-5). Combined adm with The Red House £5, chd free. Home-made teas on Sat at Tamarind; Sun at The Red House.. The gardens are within easy walking distance of each other.**
A ⅔ acre garden is level at the front with acers and interesting varied planting. Shaped lawn leads to a steeply terraced rear garden full of colour and differing styles. White border with dovecote and doves; hot border, rose garden, herbaceous, embankment, fern garden and rhododendron garden. Stream with waterfalls, ponds, rockery and bog garden, thatched summerhouse, patio. Steep steps. The front garden and rear lower patio is accessible to wheelchairs, from which most of the rear garden can be viewed. Steps to the rest of the garden.

Your visits help change lives – we are the largest single funder of the Queen's Nursing Institute

92 NEW 23 THE PADDOCK

Cottingham, HU16 4RA. Jill & Keith Stubbs. *From Humber Bridge signs to Beverley - Castle Rd on R past hospital & follow NGS signs. From York/Beverley signs to Humber Bridge - Harland Way on L & follow NGS signs. At the head of a cul-de-sac at the southern end of the village. Parking for disabled next door.* **Sun 14 July (10.30-4.30). Adm £3.50, chd free. Cream teas.**

A secret garden found behind a small mixed frontage. Archway to themed areas within garden created and maintained by current owners - Japanese, Mediterranean, fairy, mixed herbaceous, patios and lawns. Also two differing ponds, ornamental and tree sculptures. Access for disabled only for 23 The Paddock through a connecting gate.

93 NEW TYTHE FARM HOUSE

Carr Lane, Wansford, Driffield, YO25 8NP. Terry & Susanne Hardcastle, 01377 272280, hardcropstores@btconnect.com. *3m E of Driffield, E Yorkshire. Wansford is 3m E of Driffield on B1249. Turn L at mini r'about onto Nafferton Rd. Carr Lane is opposite the Church. Approx 600 yds on R.* **Sun 23 June (10.30-4). Adm £5, chd free. Home-made teas served in the Courtyard garden, weather permitting, or inside the Garden Room. Visits also by arrangement Mar to Sept. Two weeks minimum notice required.**

Terry and Susanne welcome you to their secret garden that extends to ten acres incl deciduous woodlands, orchards, lake, formal courtyard garden, herbaceous and rose garden. Formerly a working farm with traditional buildings now renovated. A planting scheme 25 years ago is now maturing. Excavation of the lake and landscaping projects have created something very special as you will see. The first public opening of our very private garden. We have ample parking space on site and easy access to most areas. An optional short hike through the woods will prepare you for a home made tea in the Courtyard Garden or the Garden Room as the weather dictates. There are a limited number of paved paths and access to many parts of the garden is via level lawns that can become boggy in wet weather.

94 WARLEY HOUSE GARDEN

Stock Lane, Warley, Halifax, HX2 7RU. Dr & Mrs P J Hinton, 01422 831431, warleyhousegardens@yahoo.com, www.warleyhousegardens.com. *2m W of Halifax. Take A646 (towards Burnley) from Halifax centre. Go through large intersection after approx 1m. After further 1m take R turn up Windle Royd Lane. Signs will direct you from here. There is disabled parking on site, but limited to 4/5 vehicles.* **Sun 12, Wed 15 May (1-5). Adm £4, chd free. Home-made teas. A very wide range of home-made cakes available along with tea and coffee. Visits also by arrangement May to July. Min. 4 weeks notice with telephone enquiry at outset.**

Partly walled 2½ acre garden of demolished C18 House, renovated by the present owners. Rocky paths and Japanese style planting lead to lawns and lovely S-facing views. Alpine ravine planted with ferns and fine trees give structure to the woodland area. Drifts of shrubs, herbaceous plantings, wild flowers and heathers maintain constant seasonal interest. This is an historic garden, renovated after total neglect from 1945 to 1995. Spring planting is enhanced by many new rhododendrons and woodland. A lengthy rockery, alpine ravine and the Japanese Garden are areas of special interest. Lots of the garden accessible to wheelchairs. Lawns usually suitable - unless very wet. Disabled access to WCs and tea-room.

95 WELL HOUSE

Grafton, YO51 9QJ. Glen Garnett. *2½m S of Boroughbridge. Turn off B6265 or A168 S of Boroughbridge.* **Wed 8 May (1-5). Single adm £3.50. Combined adm with Whixley Gardens £7, chd free.**

On the outskirts of Grafton village, nestling under a hillside with long views to the White Horse and Hambleton hills, extending to 1½ acres, this garden was begun 38 years ago and is under constant change. A traditional English cottage garden, with herbaceous borders, climbing and rambling roses, and ornamental shrubs with a variety of interesting species. Paths lead to orchard with geese, ducks and chickens.

96 NEW WHITE WYNN

Ellerton, York, YO42 4PN. Cindy & Richard Hutchinson. *½m up Shortacre lane, no through road. From York B1228 through Sutton, turning R towards Howden, NGS signs from here. From Selby A19 north. Turn R along A163 towards Market Weighton. Turn L at Bubwith Xrds follow NGS signs.* **Sun 9 June (2-5). Adm £3.50, chd free. Light refreshments.**

1½ acres developed over 10 years. Front garden and gravel areas. Lawns and patios adjoining 60m long border, wildflower meadow, heather bed, orchard, rose garden with arbour, veg beds, woodland and shade beds. A secret garden contains less usual plantings to give a tropical feel. Wildlife friendly with 2 ponds, blackthorn and damson copses, stored logs provide shelter for hedgehogs and toads. In aid of local church.

GROUP OPENING

97 WHIXLEY GARDENS

York, YO26 8AR. *8m W of York, 8m E of Harrogate, 6m N of Wetherby. 3m E of A1(M) off A59 York-Harrogate. Signed Whixley.* **Mon 6 May (1.30-5). Combined adm £6, chd free. Wed 8 May (1-5). Combined adm with Well House £7, chd free. Sun 9 June (1.30-5). Combined adm £6, chd free. Home-made teas at The Old Vicarage.**

COBBLE COTTAGE

John Hawkridge & Barry Atkinson, 01423 331419, john_barry44@outlook.com. **Visits also by arrangement May to July for groups of 20+.**

THE OLD VICARAGE

Mr & Mrs Roger Marshall, biddymarshall@btinternet.com. **Visits also by arrangement May & June.**

Attractive rural yet accessible village nestling on the edge of the York Plain with beautiful historic church and Queen Anne Hall (not open). The gardens are at opposite ends of the village with good footpaths. A plantsman's and flower arranger's garden at Cobble Cottage has views to the Hambleton Hills. Close to the church, The Old Vicarage, with a ¾-acre walled flower garden, overlooks the old deer park. The walls, house and various structures are festooned with climbers. Gravel and old brick paths lead to hidden seating areas creating the atmosphere of a romantic English garden.

98 WILLOW COTTAGE

Beckside, Barmby Moor, York, YO42 4HA. Mrs Tez McCloskey, 07790 825110 or 07962 225600. *8m E of York just off A1079, 2m from Pocklington. Centre of village on village green. Parking is on Main street. Cut through church yard & turn R onto Beck Side.* **Sun 16 June (10-5). Adm £4, chd free.** Visits also by arrangement in June for groups of up to 20.

An all white garden, north facing, perfectly formed with several seating areas giving time to absorb the garden. A secret garden atmosphere, calm and peaceful. Split into three sections and planted for scent. Patio with raised beds, shade area, and sunny lawn with borders summerhouse and home made greenhouse. Also of interest, pretty beck, village green with wild flower meadow. Wheelchair access. Gravel drive and single step up to lawn.

99 NEW WINTHROP GARDENS

Second Lane, Wickersley, Rotherham, S66 1EE. Wickersley Parish Council, www.winthropgardens.org.uk. *Located off Morthen Rd in Wickersley. From centre Wickersley, big r'about, take B6060/Morthen Rd over 6 speed humps then turn L, by bus stop, down Second Lane off Newhall Ave. On Open Days watch for A board on verge.* **Sat 22, Sun 23 June (10.30-4). Adm £5, chd free. Home-made teas.**

A one-acre community garden, designed for peace and tranquillity with emphasis on colour and scent. Comprising herbaceous border with many varieties of perennials, a rose and wisteria pergola, a Japanese garden with a large rare Robinia 'Lace Lady', and a selection of David Austin roses. Many relatively rare ornamental trees, a bee and butterfly garden plus area of less hardy New Zealand plants. Accessible for wheelchair users, both within the Gardens and access to and within the Tea Rooms, including a wheelchair accessible WC.

100 WOODLANDS COTTAGE

Summerbridge, Harrogate, HG3 4BT. Mr & Mrs Stark, 01423 780765, annstark@btinternet.com, www.woodlandscottagegarden.co.uk. *10m NW of Harrogate. On the B6165 W of Summerbridge.* **Sun 12 May (1-5). Adm £4, chd free. Home-made teas. Also open Low Hall.** Visits also by arrangement May to Aug.

A one acre country garden in Nidderdale, created by its owners and making full use of its setting, which includes natural woodland with wild bluebells and gritstone boulders. There are several gardens within the garden, from a wild flower meadow and woodland rock-garden to a formal herb garden and herbaceous areas; also a productive fruit and vegetable garden. Gravel paths with some slopes.

101 ◆ YORK GATE

Back Church Lane, Adel, Leeds, LS16 8DW. Perennial, 0113 267 8240, yorkgate@perennial.org.uk, www.yorkgate.org.uk. *5m N of Leeds. On A660 from Leeds past Headingley & Weetwood to Adel, turn right at lights a few meters before 'Divino' restaurant then L on to Church Lane. Park in lay-bys with nose out to the road (not sideways).* For opening times and information, please phone, email or visit garden website.

Listed as the '7th best garden to visit in the UK' in The Times 2017. An internationally acclaimed one acre jewel. 14 rooms, reflecting the Arts & Crafts period, linked by delightful vistas. Enjoy home baking in our tea room and browse the gift shop. Owned by Perennial, the charity that looks after horticulturists and their families in times of need. Sun - Thurs 12.30-4.30 £6 adults (U16 free). Gravel paths, some slopes. Tea Room and WC are accessible drop off at the gate.

102 ◆ THE YORKSHIRE ARBORETUM

Castle Howard, York, YO60 7BY. The Castle Howard Arboretum Trust, 01653 648598, visit@yorkshirearboretum.org, www.yorkshirearboretum.org. *15m NE of York. Off A64. Follow signs to Castle Howard then look for Yorkshire Arboretum signs at the obelisk r'about.* **For NGS: Sun 2 June (10-4.30). Adm £7, chd free.** For other opening times and information, please phone, email or visit garden website.

A glorious, 120 acre garden of trees from around the world set in a stunning landscape of parkland, lakes and ponds. Walks and lakeside trails, tours, family activities. We welcome visitors of all ages wanting to enjoy the space, serenity and beauty of this sheltered valley as well as those interested in our extensive collection of trees and shrubs. Internationally renowned collection of trees in a beautiful setting, accompanied by a diversity of wild flowers, birds, insects and other wildlife. Children's playground, cafe and gift shop. Dogs on leads welcome. Not suitable for wheelchairs. Motorised all-terrain buggies are available on loan, please book 24hrs in advance on 01653 648598.

NPC

WALES

Cheshire
& Wirral
North East Wales
Gwynedd &
Anglesey
Shropshire
WALES
Ceredigion
Powys
Herefordshire
Carmarthenshire &
Pembrokeshire
Gwent
Glamorgan
The areas shown on this map are specific to the organisation of The National Gardens Scheme. The Gardens of England, listed by area, precede the Gardens of Wales.
Somerset,
Bristol Area
& S. Glos

CARMARTHENSHIRE & PEMBROKESHIRE

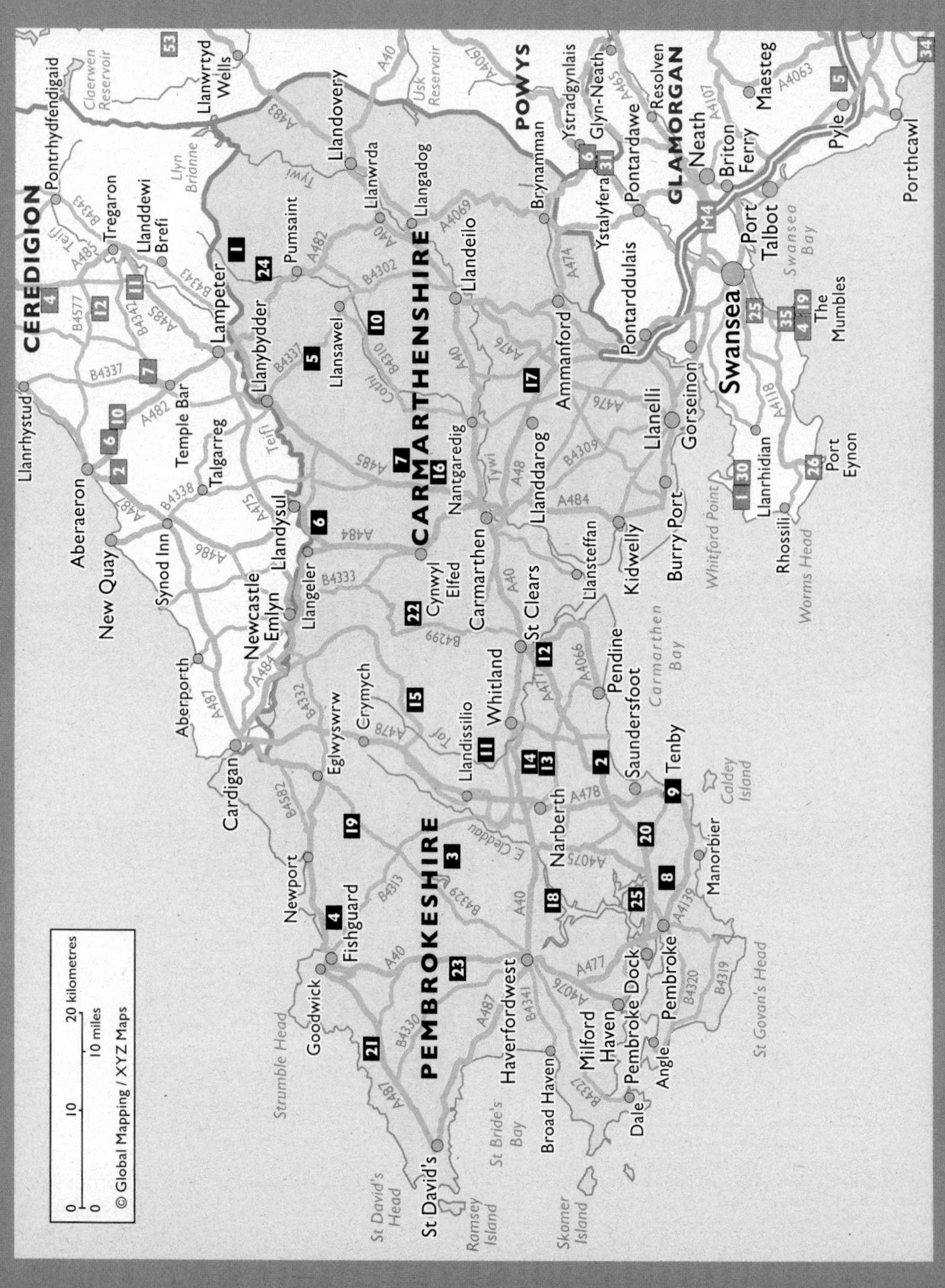

From the rugged Western coast and beaches to the foothills of the Brecon Beacons and Black Mountain, these counties offer gardens as varied as the topography and weather.

The remote and romantic gardens such as Rhyd-y-Groes, Bwlchau Duon and Gelli Uchaf will delight with superb views and borrowed landscape, whilst in gardens such as Greenacres, Llwyngarreg, Panteg and Nantyietau, tender plants flourish. Each of our many gardens has something different to offer the visitor and many now welcome dogs as well as their owners!

Several fascinating gardens have restricted parking areas and so are only open 'By Arrangement'; the owners will be delighted to see you, but please do telephone first to arrange a visit. Most of our gardens also offer teas or light refreshments and what better way to enjoy an afternoon in a garden, where there is no weeding or washing up for you to do! We look forward to welcoming you to our gardens.

Volunteers

County Organisers

Jackie Batty
01437 741115
bathole2000@aol.com

County Treasurer

Christine Blower
01267 253334
cheahnwood@toucansurf.com

Assistant County Organisers

Elena Gilliatt
01558 685321
elenamgilliatt@hotmail.com

Liz and Paul O'Neill
01994 240717
lizpaulfarm@yahoo.co.uk

Ivor Stokes
01558 823233
ivor.t.stokes@btopenworld.com

Brenda Timms
01558 650187
brendatimmsuk@gmail.com

Carmarthenshire Social Media

Mary-Ann Nossent
07985077022
ma@penygarncottage.co.uk

Left: **Panteg**

OPENING DATES

All entries subject to change. For latest information check **www.ngs.org.uk**

Extended openings are shown at the beginning of the month.

Map locator numbers are shown to the right of each garden name.

February

Saturday 23rd
Gelli Uchaf 5

Sunday 24th
Gelli Uchaf 5

April

Sunday 21st
Llwyngarreg 11

May

Sunday 5th
◆ Dyffryn Fernant 4
Treffgarne Hall 23

Saturday 11th
◆ Colby Woodland Garden 2

Sunday 12th
◆ Colby Woodland Garden 2

Sunday 19th
Llwyngarreg 11
◆ Picton Castle & Gardens 18

Monday 27th
The Old Rectory 13

June

Saturday 8th
Rhyd-y-Groes 19

Sunday 9th
◆ Picton Castle & Gardens 18
Rhyd-y-Groes 19

Sunday 16th
Tradewinds 22

Saturday 22nd
Glangwili Lodges 7

Sunday 23rd
Glangwili Lodges 7
◆ Upton Castle Gardens 25

Sunday 30th
Bwlchau Duon 1
Heywood Lane Gardens 9

July

Saturday 6th
Glandwr 6

Sunday 7th
Glandwr 6
Llwyngarreg 11
Pentresite 16

Saturday 20th
Rhyd-y-Groes 19

Sunday 21st
Rhyd-y-Groes 19
Treffgarne Hall 23

Sunday 28th
NEW Greenacre 8

August

Sunday 4th
◆ Dyffryn Fernant 4
Tradewinds 22

Saturday 10th
Rhyd-y-Groes 19

Sunday 11th
Rhyd-y-Groes 19
Ty'r Maes 24

September

Sunday 1st
◆ Dyffryn Fernant 4
Llwyngarreg 11

Sunday 8th
Pentresite 16

Saturday 21st
Pen-y-Garn 17

Sunday 22nd
Pen-y-Garn 17

By Arrangement

Arrange a personalised garden visit with your club, or group of friends, on a date to suit you. See individual garden entries for full details.

Bwlchau Duon 1
Cwm Pibau 3
Gelli Uchaf 5
Glandwr 6
NEW Greenacre 8
Lan Farm 10
Llwyngarreg 11
Nantyietau 12
The Old Rectory 13
Panteg 14
Pencwm 15
Pentresite 16
Pen-y-Garn 17
Rhyd-y-Groes 19
Rosewood 20
Scotsborough House, Heywood Lane Gardens 9
Stable Cottage 21
Treffgarne Hall 23
Ty'r Maes 24

THE GARDENS

1 BWLCHAU DUON

Ffarmers, Llanwrda, Carmarthenshire, SA19 8JJ. Brenda & Allan Timms, 01558 650187, brendatimmsuk@gmail.com. *7m SE Lampeter, 8m NW Llanwrda. From A482 turn to Ffarmers. In Ffarmers, take lane opp Drovers Arms PH. Shortly after caravan site on L there is a very small Xrds, turn L into single track lane & follow NGS arrows.* **Sun 30 June (2-6). Adm £3.50, chd free. Home-made teas.** Visits also by arrangement July & Aug. No access for large coaches.

A 1 acre, ever evolving garden challenge, set in the foothills of the Cambrian Mountains at 1100ft. This is a plantaholics haven where borders are full of many unusual plants and lots of old favourites. There are raised vegetable gardens, a 100ft herbaceous border, recently planted natural bog areas, winding pathways through semi-woodland and magnificent views over the Cothi valley. Rare breed turkeys, chickens, geese and rabbits!

2 ◆ COLBY WOODLAND GARDEN

Amroth, Narberth, Pembrokeshie, SA67 8PP. National Trust, 01834 811885, colby@nationaltrust.org.uk, www.nationaltrust.org.uk. *6m N of Tenby, 5m SE of Narberth. Follow brown tourist signs on coast rd & A477.* **For NGS: Sat 11, Sun 12 May (10-5). Adm £8.40, chd £4.20. Home-made teas in the Bothy Tearoom.** For other opening times and information, please phone, email or visit garden website.

8 acre woodland garden in a secluded valley with fine collection of rhododendrons and azaleas. Wildflower meadow and stream with rope swings and stepping stones for children to explore and play. Ornamental walled garden incl unusual gazebo, designed by Wyn Jones, with internal tromp l'oeil. Incl in the *Register of Historic*

Parks and Gardens: Pembrokeshire. Extensive play area for children incl den building and log climbing. Free family activities incl duck racing, pond dipping, etc. Children under 5, free entry. Full range of refreshments incl lunches. Partial access for wheelchair users.

3 CWM PIBAU

New Moat, Clarbeston Road, Haverfordwest, Pembrokeshire, SA63 4RE. Mrs Duncan Drew, 01437 532454. *10m NE of Haverfordwest. 3m SW of Maenclochog. Off A40, take B4313 to Maenclochog, follow signs to New Moat, past church, then 2nd concealed drive on L, ½m rural drive.* **Visits by arrangement. Adm £3, chd free.**

5 acre woodland garden surrounded by old deciduous woodland and streams. Created in 1978, contains many mature, unusual shrubs and trees from Chile, New Zealand and Europe, set on S-facing hill. More conventional planting nearer house.

4 ◆ DYFFRYN FERNANT

Llanychaer, Fishguard, Pembrokeshire, SA65 9SP. Christina Shand & David Allum, 01348 811282, christina@dyffrynfernant.co.uk, www.dyffrynfernant.co.uk. *3m E of Fishguard, then ½m inland. A487 E 2m from Fishguard turn R towards Llanychaer at garden signs. ½m entrance is on L. Coming from direction of Dinas/Newport Pemb, look for L turn off A487.* **For NGS: Sun 5 May (12-5), also open Treffgarne Hall. Sun 4 Aug, Sun 1 Sept (12-5). Adm £7, chd free. Home-made teas.** **For other opening times and information, please phone, email or visit garden website.**

Many differently planted areas in a 6 acre garden. 'Beautifully conceived small gardens brimming with rich, contemporary planting surround a glowing raspberry-fool coloured house, while a bog garden subtly gives way to a wetland valley floor. The best domestic garden in Wales', Stephen Anderton, The Times. A library for garden visitors incl a wide selection of books on gardening and art. Home-made teas on NGS days and for pre-booked groups. Walks and talks, guided tours available - please see website. Wheelchair access is difficult but please contact us directly to discuss how we can help you to enjoy the garden.

5 GELLI UCHAF

Rhydcymerau, Llandeilo, Carmarthenshire, SA19 7PY. Julian & Fiona Wormald, 01558 685119, thegardenimpressionists@gmail.com, www.thegardenimpressionists.com. *5m SE of Llanybydder. 1m NW of Rhydcymerau. In Rhydcymerau on B4337 turn up Mountain Rd for Llanllwni (by BT phone box). After about 300yds turn R up farm track (uneven surface 10mph max please), cont ½m bearing R up hill at fork in track.* **Parking v. limited, so please phone first even on Open Days. Sat 23, Sun 24 Feb (10.30-5.30). Adm £5, chd free. Home-made teas. Visits also by arrangement in Feb for groups of 10 to 30. See website for 'pop-up' openings at other times.**

Complementing a C17 Longhouse and 11acre smallholding this 1½ acre garden is mainly organic. Trees & shrubs are underplanted with hundreds of thousands of snowdrops (200 cultivars & unique Welsh Snowdrop Collection), crocus, cyclamen, scillas, daffodils & other bulbs. Many different garden areas. Extensive views, Shepherds hut & seats to enjoy them. 6 acres of wildflower meadows, 2 ponds and stream.

6 GLANDWR

Pentrecwrt, Llandysul, Carmarthenshire, SA44 5DA. Mrs Jo Hicks, 01559 363729, leehicks@btinternet.com. *15m N of Carmarthen, 2m S of Llandysul, 7m E of Newcastle Emlyn. On A486. At Pentrecwrt village, take minor rd opp Black Horse PH. After bridge keep L for ¼m. Glandwr is on R.* **Sat 6, Sun 7 July (11-5). Adm £3, chd free. Home-made teas. Visits also by arrangement July to Sept.**

Delightful easily accessed 1 acre cottage garden, bordered by a natural stream. Incl a rockery and colour themed beds. Enter the mature woodland, transformed into an adventurous wander with plenty of shade loving plants, ground cover, interesting trees, shrubs and many surprises.

7 GLANGWILI LODGES

Llanllawddog, Carmarthenshire, SA32 7JE. Chris & Christine Blower. *7m NE of Carmarthen. Take A485 from Carmarthen. ¼m after Gwili Pottery on L in Pontarsais, turn R for Llanllawddog and Brechfa. ½m after Llanllawddog Chapel, rd bears sharply R, Glangwili Lodges 100yds on R.* **Sat 22, Sun 23 June (11-5). Adm £4, chd free. Sweet and savoury refreshments.**

Our 16 acre estate has a one acre enclosed walled garden, with rockeries, water features, flower and shrub beds, a wisteria arbour, maples, magnolias and espalier fruit trees. Areas outside the wall incl one acre of woodland, with stream, an orchard, 2 acre wildlife area and a hedge tunnel containing a diverse collection of trees.There is also a productive vegetable garden and a polytunnel.

8 NEW GREENACRE

Deer Park Lane, Nr Milton, Tenby, Pembrokeshire, SA70 8PR. Andrew and Jill Baxter, 01646651918, jillbax55@btinternet.com. *7m W of Tenby. From A477 at Milton, take turning signposted Lamphey (Stephens Green Lane). Continue to brow of hill then turn R onto Deer Park Lane. Garden ½m along Rd on L.* **Sun 28 July (12.30-6). Adm £4, chd free. Tea. Visits also by arrangement June to Aug for groups of up to 10. Limited parking for no more than 6 cars. Tea must be arranged in advance.**

Plantaholic's garden of around ⅔ acre intensively planted and developed into a lush, colourful, exotic plant packed haven. Shady jungle garden, raised arid bed, scree garden, tender Tropicals in pots, greenhouse with carnivorous plants. Meandering paths leading to lots of different areas; be prepared for surprises around every corner. Uneven paths unsuitable for wheelchairs.

GROUP OPENING

9 HEYWOOD LANE GARDENS

Heywood Lane, Tenby Pembrokeshire, SA70 8BZ. Mrs Shari Argent. *½m W of Tenby. From N (A478) R onto A4218, then R onto Serpentine Rd, R into Heywood Ln. From S (B4318), bear L into Heywood Ln. Entry via Scotsborough House Garden drive. Park next door at Tenby Jnr School.* **Sun 30 June (1-5). Combined adm £5, chd free.**

THE GROVE
Rosemary Rhys Davies.

SCOTSBOROUGH HOUSE
John and Shari Argent, 01834 842 077, shari.argent@gmail.com. **Visits also by arrangement June to Aug for groups of 10+. Scotsborough House Garden only.**

WEST GROVE
Julius Rhys Davies.

Scotsborough House and The Grove were built on land owned by the Mayor, Aldermen and Burgesses of Tenby. This land, known as West Heywood Meadow, was used as a nursery garden where the Tenby Daffodil was first propagated. Scotsborough House Garden, with greenhouse buildings, walls and trees from the early 1900s, has varied planting incl. Blue Atlantic Cedars, beeches, woodland walk, acers, magnolias, many roses, *Hydrangea sargentiana*, an Edwardian grapevine and vegetable garden. The Grove and West Grove were restored to one property by the current owner of the Grove. The Grove Garden consists of land surrounding the original house and contains mature trees, incl. a Monkey Puzzle (*Araucaria*), manicured hedging, sculptures and seating areas in a tranquil setting. West Grove Garden has steep access, fabulous views, mature trees and hidden paths/corners of interest to children. These three gardens, each with styles of their own, are linked by pathways, reflecting their historic connection. Partial wheelchair access.

♿ ✿

Gelli Uchaff

10 LAN FARM

Talley, Llandeilo, Carmarthenshire, SA19 7BQ. Karen & David Thomas, 07930 351483, karenjuliethomas@gmail.com. *10m N of Llandeilo. Talley is on B4302 between Llandeilo & Crugybar. In Talley follow signs to Abbey, passing it on R. Cont on single track lane for 2m. Drive to Lan, ¼m, on L, uneven surface, please take care.* **Visits by arrangement. 15 June - 14 July (9am-4pm). Adm £3.50, chd free. Teas on request when booking.**

Picturesque rural 2 acre SW facing garden oasis 900ft above sea level that has been sympathetically developed to augment the countryside. There are spectacular borrowed views in all directions. Interesting planting with plenty of surprises incl a wildflower meadow, utilisation of old farm buildings, bog and Mediterranean areas. There is also a small lake that attracts a variety of wildlife. A private and romantic garden!

11 LLWYNGARREG

Llanfallteg, Whitland, Carmarthenshire, SA34 0XH. Paul & Liz O'Neill, 01994 240717, lizpaulfarm@yahoo.co.uk, www.llwyngarreg.co.uk. *19m W of Carmarthen. A40 W from Carmarthen, turn R at Llandewi Velfrey, 2½m to Llanfallteg. Go through village, garden ½m further on: 2nd farm on R. Disabled car park in bottom yard on R.* **Sun 21 Apr (1-6). Sun 19 May (1-6), also open Picton Castle & Gardens. Sun 7 July, Sun 1 Sept (1-6). Adm £4.50, chd free. Home-made teas.** Visits also by arrangement Mar to Oct. We welcome visitors most days: Please ring to check to avoid disappointment.

Llwyngarreg continues to develop further, delighting plant lovers with its many rarities incl species Primulas, many bamboos with *Roscoeas*, *Hedychiums* and *Salvias* extending the season through to riotous autumn colour. Trees and rhododendrons have been underplanted with perennials. The sunken garden for tender/exotic gems and gravel terraces with formal pool continues to mature. Springs form a series of linked ponds across the main garden, providing colourful bog gardens. Wildlife ponds, fruit and veg, composting, twig piles, numerous living willow structures, swings, chickens, goldfish. Partial wheelchair access.

12 NANTYIETAU

New Mill Road, St Clears, Carmarthenshire, SA33 4HF. Matt Richards, 01994 231345, mattrichards320@gmail.com. *10m W of Carmarthen. Take the Laugharne turning off A40 then A4066 to Lower St Clears. Take first R after river bridge, continue for ½m along country lane, passing junction to R. Nantyietau is next house on L.* **Visits by arrangement June to Aug. Usually Sundays are best. Adm £5.**

A one acre garden with a surprising and eclectic mix of the unusual and traditional which reflects a passion for plants. Tropical and tender with hardier companions in a cottage exotic mix. Poultry, fish and other pets complete the quirky mix. Polytunnel and outbuildings with exotic and spiky plants squeezed into every corner.

13 THE OLD RECTORY

Lampeter Velfrey, Narberth, Pembrokeshire, SA67 8UH. Jane & Stephen Fletcher, 01834 831444, jane_e_fletcher@hotmail.com. *3m E of Narbeth. The Old Rectory is next to the church in the middle of Lampeter Velfrey. Parking in the church yard car park.* **Mon 27 May (1-5). Adm £3.50, chd free. Home-made teas. Visits also by arrangement May to Aug.**

Historic approx 2 acre garden, sympathetically redesigned and replanted since 2009 and still being restored. Many unique trees, some over 300yrs old, wide variety of planting and several unique, architecturally designed buildings. Formal beds, mature woodland surrounding an old quarry with recently planted terraces and rhododendron bank. Newly planted meadow and orchard.

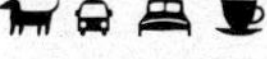

14 PANTEG

Llanddewi Velfrey, Narberth, Pembrokeshire, SA67 8UU. Mr & Mrs D Pryse Lloyd, 01834 860081, d.pryselloyd@btinternet.com. *Situated off main A40 in village of Llanddewi Velfrey. A40 from Carmarthen, after garage take 1st L. At next T-junction turn L. On R gateway with stone gate pillars which is ½m drive to Panteg.* **Visits by arrangement Mar to Sept for groups of 5+. Adm £4, chd free.**

Approached down a woodland drive, this tranquil, S-facing, large garden, surrounding a Georgian house (not open), has been developed since early 1990s. Plantsman's garden set off by lawns on different levels. Walled garden, wisteria covered pergola. Vegetable garden, camellia and azalea bank, wildflower woodland. Many rare shrubs and plants incl, *Embothrium, Eucryphia* and *Hoheria*.

15 PENCWM

Hebron, Whitland, Carmarthenshire, SA34 0JP. Lorna Brown, 01994 419471, lornambrown@hotmail.com. *10m N of Whitland. From A40 take St Clears exit and head N to Llangynin then on to Blaenwaun. Through village, after speed limit signs take 1st L. Over Xrds, 1¼m then 2nd lane on L marked Pencwm.* **Visits by arrangement Feb to Oct for groups of 5 to 30. Adm £4, chd free. Teas on request when booking.**

A secluded garden of about one acre set among large native trees, designed for year round interest and for benefit of wildlife. A wide variety of exotic specimen trees and shrubs incl magnolias, rhododendrons, hydrangeas, bamboos and acers. Drifts of bluebells and other spring bulbs and good autumn colour. Incl boggy area and pond with appropriate planting.

16 PENTRESITE

Rhydargaeau Road, Carmarthen, SA32 7AJ. Gayle & Ron Mounsey, 01267 253928, gayle.mounsey@gmail.com. *4m N of Carmarthen. Take A485 heading N out of Carmarthen, once out of village of Peniel take 1st R to Horeb & cont for 1m. Turn R at NGS sign, 2nd house down lane.* **Sun 7 July, Sun 8 Sept (2-5). Adm £3.50, chd free. Home-made teas. Visits also by arrangement Apr to Oct.**

1¼ acre garden developed over the last 10yrs with extensive lawns, colour filled herbaceous and mixed borders, on several levels. A bog garden and magnificent views of the surrounding countryside. There is now an area planted with trees and gradually being filled with more herbaceous plants,. This garden is south facing and catches the south westerly winds from the sea. Steep in places but possible for wheelchairs.

17 PEN-Y-GARN

Foelgastell, Cefneithin, Llanelli, Carmarthenshire, SA14 7EU. Mary-Ann Nossent & Mike Wood, 07985077022, ma@penygarncottage.co.uk, www.penygarncottage.co.uk. *10m SE Carmarthen. A48 N take 1st L to Foelgastell R at T junction, 300m sharp L, 300m 1st gateway on L. A48 S NBGW turning r'about R to Porthythyd 1st L before T junction. 1m 1st R & 300m on L.* **Sat 21, Sun 22 Sept (11-5). Adm £4, chd free. Home-made teas. Visits also by arrangement July to Sept for groups of up to 10.**

1.3 acres set within a former old limestone quarry, the garden is on several levels with slopes and steps. Sympathetically developed to sit within the landscape, there are 5 distinct areas with a mixture of wild and cultivated plants. A shady area with woodland planting & wild ponds; kitchen garden; terraced borders with shrubs and herbaceous planting; lawns and pond; and a wild garden. This site is a challenge for people who are ambulant disabled as it is on many levels with slopes, steps and narrow paths.

Your visits help change lives – your generosity helps Marie Curie fund nurses to care for people night and day in their homes, with donations of more than £8.8 million

Llwyngarreg

18 ◆ PICTON CASTLE & GARDENS

The Rhos, Haverfordwest, Pembrokeshire, SA62 4AS. Picton Castle Trust, 01437 751326, info@pictoncastle.co.uk, www.pictoncastle.co.uk. *3m E of Haverfordwest. On A40 to Carmarthen, signed off main rd.* **For NGS: Sun 19 May (9-5), also open Llwyngarreg. Sun 9 June (9-5). Adm £8, chd £5. Lunches and teas at Maria's Courtyard Restaurant.** For other opening times and information, please phone, email or visit garden website.

Mature 40 acre woodland garden with unique collection of rhododendrons and azaleas, many bred over decades, producing hybrids of great merit and beauty; rare and tender shrubs and trees incl *Magnolia*, myrtle, *Embothrium* and *Eucryphia*. Wild flowers abound. Walled garden with roses; fernery; herbaceous and climbing plants and large clearly labelled collection of herbs. Exciting art exhibitions and a wide range of seasonal events. Visit Maria's@ Picton - our famous Spanish influenced restaurant. Some woodland walks unsuitable for wheelchair users.

19 RHYD-Y-GROES

Brynberian, Crymych, Pembrokeshire, SA41 3TT. Jennifer & Kevin Matthews, 01239 891363, rhydygroesgardeners@gmail.com. *12m SW of Cardigan. 5m W of Crymych, 16m NE of Haverfordwest, on B4329, ¾m downhill from cattlegrid (from Haverfordwest) & 1m uphill from signpost to Brynberian (from Cardigan).* **Sat 8, Sun 9 June, Sat 20 July (1-5). Sun 21 July (1-5), also open Treffgarne Hall. Sat 10, Sun 11 Aug (1-5). Adm £4.50, chd £1.50. Home-made teas.** Visits also by arrangement May to Aug for groups of 20+. Refreshments by request when booking.

Colourful 4 acre country garden at 200m on exposed NE hillside. Dramatic, extensive views across upland bogs and moorland may be enjoyed from strategically placed seating. Exuberantly and skilfully planted to suit the varied conditions. Formal herbaceous borders, shrubbery, woodland area, bog, ornamental and natural meadow. Diverse plantings show what is possible without chemicals in this challenging environment. Beautiful mollusc proof planting demonstrates what can be achieved without using slug killer, pesticides and fungicides, resulting in a garden that is full of wildlife.

20 ROSEWOOD

Redberth, Nr Tenby, Pembrokeshire, SA70 8SA. Keith Treadaway, 07855 192781 text only, keithatredberth@btinternet.com. *3m WSW of Kilgetty. On W side of village on old A477, now bypassed. Parking in field opp if dry, or on verge by side of rd if wet.* **Visits by arrangement May to July. Light refreshments by request when booking. Adm £3.50, chd free.**

Intimate well maintained ¼ acre garden, cleverly designed in different areas with long season of interest. Abundant colourful mixed plantings with exotic species and a collection of clematis, at its best in summer. There is a pergola with clematis and other climbers, as well as a good selection of Hemerocallis and many other plants. A pond and bog garden were added recently. Partial wheelchair access.

21 STABLE COTTAGE

Rhoslanog Fawr, Mathry, Haverfordwest, Pembrokeshire, SA62 5HG. Mr Michael & Mrs Jane Bayliss, 01348 837712, michaelandjane1954@ michaelandjane.plus.com. *Between Fishguard & St David's. Head W on A487 turn R at Square & Compass sign. ½m, at hairpin take track L. Stable Cottage on L with block paved drive.* **Visits by arrangement May to Sept for groups of up to 20. Limited parking for max. 4/5 cars. Adm £3, chd free. Refreshments available with prior notice.**

Garden extends to approx ⅓ of an acre. It is divided into several smaller garden types, with a seaside garden, small orchard and wildlife area, scented garden, small vegetable/kitchen garden, and two Japanese areas - a stroll garden and courtyard area.

22 TRADEWINDS

Ffynnonwen, Pen-y-Bont, nr Trelech,Carmarthenshire, SA33 6PX. Stuart & Eve Kemp-Gee. *10m NW of Carmarthen. From A40 W of Carmarthen, take B4298 to Meidrim, then R onto B4299 towards Trelech. After 5m turn R at Tradewinds sign.* **Sun 16 June, Sun 4 Aug (11-5). Adm £4, chd free.**

Home-made teas.
This 3 acre plantsman garden is for the gardener who wants to see unusual and rare plants in a tranquil setting. A garden that is good for the senses, whether it is the scents, sounds of the countryside or the visually dazzling displays of vivid colour, plant harmonies coupled with textual contrast. The large herbaceous borders, trees, shrubs, roses and shade borders are in abundance. With natural streams flowing through the garden it is a garden for all seasons whatever the weather. Art studio open.

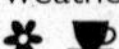

23 TREFFGARNE HALL

Treffgarne, Haverfordwest, Pembrokeshire, SA62 5PJ. Martin & Jackie Batty, 01437 741115, bathole2000@aol.com. *7m N of Haverfordwest, signed off A40. Proceed up through village & follow rd round sharply to L, Hall ¼m further on L.* **Sun 5 May (1-5), also open Dyffryn Fernant. Sun 21 July (1-5), also open Rhyd-y-Groes. Adm £4, chd free. Home-made teas.** **Visits also by arrangement. Teas on request when booking.**
Stunning hilltop location with panoramic views: handsome Grade II listed Georgian house (not open) provides formal backdrop to garden of 4 acres with wide lawns and themed beds. A walled garden, with double rill and pergolas, is planted with a multitude of borderline hardy exotics. Also large scale sculptures, summer broadwalk, meadow patch, gravel garden, heather bed and stumpery. Planted for yr-round interest. The planting schemes are the owner's, and seek to challenge the boundaries of what can be grown in Pembrokeshire.

24 TY'R MAES

Ffarmers, Carmarthenshire, SA19 8JP. John & Helen Brooks, 01558 650541, johnhelen140@gmail.com. *7m SE of Lampeter. 8m NW of Llanwrda. 1½m N of Pumsaint on A482, opp turn to Ffarmers.* **Sun 11 Aug (1.30-5.30). Adm £4, chd free.** **Visits also by arrangement Apr to Oct. Teas on request when booking.**
4 acre garden with splendid views. Herbaceous and shrub beds – formal design, exuberantly informal planting, full of cottage garden favourites and many unusual plants. Woodland garden with over 200 types of tree; wildlife and lily ponds; pergola, gazebos, post and rope arcade covered in climbers. Gloriously colourful from early spring till late autumn. Book, jewellery and craft stalls. Some gravel paths.

25 ♦ UPTON CASTLE GARDENS

Cosheston, Pembroke Dock, Pembroke Dock, SA72 4SE. Prue & Stephen Barlow, 01646 689996, info@uptoncastle.com, www.uptoncastlegardens.com. *4m E of Pembroke Dock. 2m N of A477 between Carew & Pembroke Dock. Follow brown signs to Upton Castle Gardens through Cosheston.* **For NGS: Sun 23 June (10-4.30). Adm £5, chd free. Home-made teas.** **For other opening times and information, please phone, email or visit garden website.**
Privately owned listed historic gardens with an exceptional collection of mature trees and plants extending to over 35 acres. Rare rhododendrons, camellias and magnolias abound. Formal rose garden contains over 150 roses of many varieties and colours. Fully stocked herbaceous borders provide constant interest. Traditional walled, productive kitchen garden. Arboretum with 15 champion trees. Walk on the Wild Side: Woodland walks funded by C.C.W. and Welsh Assembly Government. Medieval chapel as featured on Time Team. Partial wheelchair access.

Dyffryn Fernant

CEREDIGION

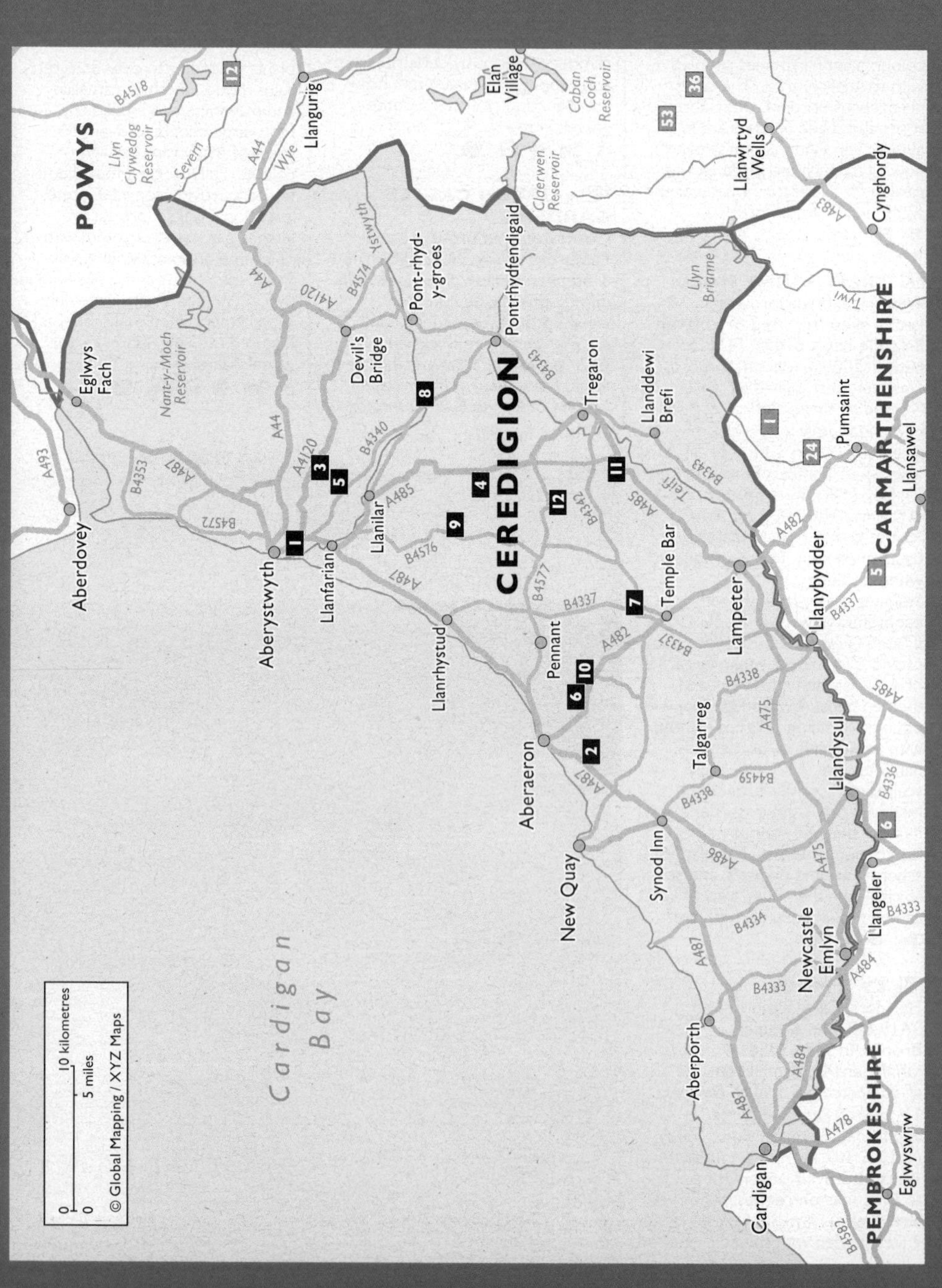
POWYS
CEREDIGION
CARMARTHENSHIRE
PEMBROKESHIRE
Cardigan Bay
Aberdovey
Eglwys Fach
Aberystwyth
Llanfarian
Llanilar
Devil's Bridge
Pont-rhyd-y-groes
Pontrhydfendigaid
Tregaron
Llanddewi Brefi
Llanrhystud
Pennant
Temple Bar
Lampeter
Llanybydder
Aberaeron
Talgarreg
New Quay
Synod Inn
Llandysul
Llangeler
Newcastle Emlyn
Aberporth
Cardigan
Eglwyswrw
Llangurig
Elan Village
Caban Coch Reservoir
Claerwen Reservoir
Llyn Clywedog Reservoir
Nant-y-Moch Reservoir
Llyn Brianne
Llanwrtyd Wells
Cynghordy
Pumsaint
Llansawel
Severn
Wye
Ystwyth
Teifi
Tywi
A44
A487
A493
A4120
A485
A482
A475
A486
A484
A478
A483
B4518
B4574
B4353
B4572
B4340
B4576
B4343
B4342
B4577
B4337
B4338
B4459
B4334
B4333
B4336
B4582
1
2
3
4
5
6
7
8
9
10
11
12
24
36
53
0 5 miles
0 10 kilometres
© Global Mapping / XYZ Maps

Ceredigion is a rural county and the second most sparsely populated in Wales.

Much of the land is elevated, particularly towards the east of the county. There are steep-sided wooded valleys, fast flowing rivers and streams, acres of moorland and a dramatic coastline with some lovely sandy beaches. From everywhere in the county there are breath taking views of the Cambrian Mountains and from almost everywhere views of the sea and glimpses of the stunning Cardigan Bay are visible.

The gardens in Ceredigion reflect this natural beauty and sit comfortably in the rugged scenery. There are some gardens that have been created with great imagination and enterprise from the barren water-soaked moorland, others have sensitively enhanced and embellished steep stony hillsides. Rhododendrons, azaleas and camellias thrive in the acid soil, and from April till June the gardens are awash with their bright jewel-like blossoms.

We have two gardens which are particularly family-friendly; both Bwlch y Geuffordd and Ty Glyn Walled Garden will provide children of all ages with hours of fun and adventure. There are a number of dedicated vegetable growers, you can see the fruits of their labours in the Aberystwyth allotments and Yr Efail. In one small hilly, rock-strewn county, it is surprising how different the gardens are from each other, yet they have one thing in common; they are all created and tended with love, care and imagination.

Volunteers

County Organiser
Pat Causton
01974 272619
pat.causton30@gmail.com

County Treasurer
Steve Yeomans
01974 299370
s.j.yeomans@btinternet.com

Booklet Co-ordinator
Shelagh Yeomans
01974 299370
shelaghyeo@hotmail.com

Assistant County Organiser
Gay Acres
01974 251559
gayacres@aol.com

Below: Bryngwyn

OPENING DATES

All entries subject to change. For latest information check **www.ngs.org.uk**

Map locator numbers are shown to the right of each garden name.

May

Sunday 19th
Bwlch y Geuffordd 5

Sunday 26th
Arnant House 2

Monday 27th
Arnant House 2

June

Saturday 15th
NEW Bryngwyn 3

Thursday 20th
◆ Llanerchaeron 6

Saturday 22nd
NEW Bryngwyn 3

Sunday 23rd
Llanllyr 7

Sunday 30th
Ysgoldy'r Cwrt 12

July

Sunday 21st
Aberystwyth Allotments 1

Sunday 28th
◆ Ty Glyn Walled Garden 10

August

Every Saturday from Saturday 10th
NEW Plas Treflys 9

Saturday 3rd
Penybont 8

Sunday 4th
Penybont 8

By Arrangement

Arrange a personalised garden visit with your club, or group of friends, on a date to suit you. See individual garden entries for full details.

Arnant House 2
Bwlch y Geuffordd Gardens 4
Llanllyr 7
Penybont 8
Yr Efail 11
Ysgoldy'r Cwrt 12

Your visits help change lives – since 1927, we've donated £55 million to nursing and caring charities

Plas Treflys

THE GARDENS

1 ABERYSTWYTH ALLOTMENTS

5th Avenue, Penparcau, Aberystwyth, SY23 1QT. Aberystwyth Town Council. *On S side of R Rheidol on Aberystwyth by-pass. From N or E, take A4120 between Llanbadarn & Penparcau. Cross bridge then take 1st R into Minyddol. Allotments ¼m on R.* **Sun 21 July (1-5). Adm £4, chd free. Home-made teas.**

There are 37 plots in total on 2 sites just a few yards from each other. The allotments are situated in a lovely setting alongside River Rheidol close to Aberystwyth. Wide variety of produce grown, vegetables, soft fruit, top fruit, flowers. Car parking available. For more information contact Brian Heath 01970 617112. Sample tastings from allotment produce. Grass and gravel paths.

2 ARNANT HOUSE

Llwyncelyn, Aberaeron, SA46 0HF. Pam & Ron Maddox, 01545 580083. *On A487, 2m S of Aberaeron. Next to Llwyncelyn Village Hall. Parking in lay-by opp house.* **Sun 26 May (12-5); Mon 27 May (1-5). Adm £4, chd free. Home-made teas.** Visits also by arrangement Apr to Sept.

Garden created 17yrs ago from derelict ground. 1 acre, in Victorian style and divided into rooms and themes. Laburnum arch, wildlife ponds, rotunda and tea house. Wide, long borders full of perennial planting with a good variety of species, numerous statues and oddities to be discovered. Many attractive ornamental shrubs incl acers, magnolias and rhododendrons in May, plus about 50 different types of clematis. Also a good selection of hellebores, primulas and fritillaries. Partial wheelchair access. Garden is level, but help may be needed on gravel paths. Some paths are very narrow.

3 NEW BRYNGWYN

Capel Seion, Aberystwyth, SY23 4EE. Mr & Mrs Sue and Terry Reeves. *On A4120 between the villages of Capel Seion & Pant y Crug.* **Sat 15, Sat 22 June (10.30-4.30). Adm £3.50, chd free. Home-made teas.**

Traditional wildflower rich hay meadows managed for wildlife. As a result of conservation grazing, hedgerow renovation and tree planting, habitat has been restored such that numbers and diversity of wild flowers and wildlife have increased. Pond with associated water loving plants. Meander along mown paths through the meadows. Small orchard containing Welsh heritage apples and pears. Some areas accessible by standard wheelchair. Most paths are sloping mown grass, access at users discretion.

We help ordinary people open the gates to their extraordinary private gardens to raise impressive amounts of money through admissions, teas and slices of cake!

4 BWLCH Y GEUFFORDD GARDENS

Bronant, Aberystwyth, SY23 4JD. Mr & Mrs J Acres, 01974 251559, gayacres@aol.com, bwlch-y-geufforddd-gardens.myfreesites.net. *12m SE of Aberystwyth, 6m NW of Tregaron off A485. Take turning opp Bronant school for 1½m then L up ½m uneven track.* **Visits by arrangement throughout the year. Adm £5, chd £1. Tea. Please ring to confirm and discuss refreshments.**

1000ft high, 3 acre, constantly evolving wildlife garden featuring a lake and several pools. There are a number of themed gardens, incl Mediterranean, cottage garden, woodland, oriental, memorial and jungle. An adventure garden for children, incl pond dipping and treasure hunt. Plenty of seating. Unique garden sculptures and buildings, incl a cave, temple, gazebo, jungle hut and willow den. Children's adventure garden, Musical instruments, Pond dipping, Treasure hunt, Beautiful lake, Temple and labyrinth, Sculptures. Paths are gravel, and there are some steps. There is a shorter route covering the main features, without steps.

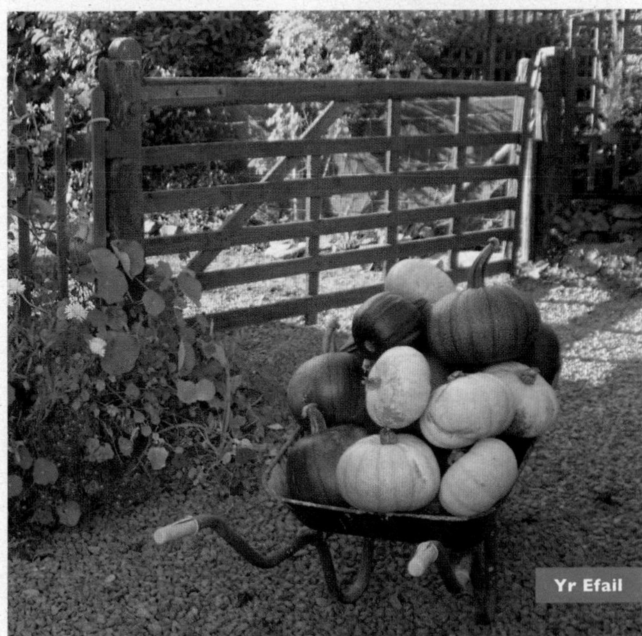

Yr Efail

5 BWLCH Y GEUFFORDD

New Cross, Aberystwyth, SY23 4LY. Manuel & Elaine Grande. *5m SE of Aberystwyth. Off A487, take B4340 to New Cross. Garden on R at bottom of small dip. Parking in lay-bys opp house.* **Sun 19 May (10.30-4.30). Adm £4, chd free. Home-made teas.**

Lovely sloping 1½ acre garden, fine views of Cambrian mountains. Embraces its natural features with different levels, 3 ponds, mixed borders merging into carefully managed informal areas. Banks of rhododendrons, azaleas and bluebells in spring. Full of unusual shade & damp-loving plants, flowering shrubs, mature trees, clematis & climbing roses scrambling up the walls of the old stone buildings. Partial wheelchair access to lower levels around house. Some steps and steep paths further up.

6 ◆ LLANERCHAERON

Ciliau Aeron, Lampeter, SA48 8DG. National Trust, 01545 573029, tim.newby@nationaltrust.org.uk, www.nationaltrust.org.uk. *2½m E of Aberaeron. On A482 Lampeter to Aberaeron. Brown sign to Llanerchaeron gardens from Aberaeron & opp turning off A487.* **For NGS: Evening opening Thur 20 June (6-9). Adm £3.50, chd free. Light refreshments.** **For other opening times and information, please phone, email or visit garden website.**

Llanerchaeron is a small C18 Welsh gentry estate set in the beautiful Dyffryn Aeron. The estate survived virtually unaltered into the 20th Century. 2 extensive restored walled gardens produce home grown vegetables, fruit and herbs for sale. The kitchen garden sits at the core of the estate with a John Nash villa built in 1795 and home farm, all virtually unaltered since its construction. Music, refreshments, plant and produce sales.

7 LLANLLYR

Talsarn, Lampeter, SA48 8QB. Mr & Mrs Robert Gee, 01570 470900, lgllanllyr@aol.com. *6m NW of Lampeter. On B4337 to Llanrhystud. From Lampeter, entrance to garden on L, just before village of Talsarn.* **Sun 23 June (2-6). Adm £4.50, chd free. Home-made teas.** **Visits also by arrangement Apr to Oct.**

Large early C19 garden on site of medieval nunnery, renovated and replanted since 1989. Large pool, bog garden, formal water garden, rose and shrub borders, gravel gardens, laburnum arbour, allegorical labyrinth and mount, all exhibiting fine plantsmanship. Yr-round appeal, interesting and unusual plants. Spectacular rose garden planted with fragrant old fashioned shrub and climbing roses. Specialist Plant Fair by Ceredigion Growers Association.

8 PENYBONT

Llanafan, Aberystwyth, SY23 4BJ. Norman & Brenda Jones, 01974 261737, tobrenorm@gmail.com. *9m SE of Aberystwyth. Ystwyth Valley B4340 from Aberystwyth. Stay on B4340 for 9m via Trawscoed towards Pontrhydfendigaid. Curve R over stone bridge. ¼m up hill, R by row of cream houses.* **Sat 3, Sun 4 Aug (11-5). Adm £4, chd free. Home-made teas.** **Visits also by arrangement May to Aug. Please telephone in advance.**

Penybont in Wild Wales shows what can be achieved from a green field sloping site in just a few years. This exciting garden (about an acre) extended in 2017 is designed to compliment the modern building, its forest backdrop and panoramic views. A chance to see plants at various stages of maturity in full colour from spring through until autumn. The pond has around 50 good sized Orfe and Koi Carp. Original design, Wild Wales location with stunning views of the Ystwyth valley and hill forts. Azaleas, Rhododendrons, Acers, Lavender, Roses, Hydrangeas. Partial wheelchair access only. Sloping ground, gravel paths and lawn.

9 NEW PLAS TREFLYS

Llangwyryfon, Aberystwyth, SY23 4HD. Mrs Pat Causton. *11m SE of Aberystwyth on B4576 between Llangwyryfon and Bethania. From Llangwyryfon, continue on B4576 for 1m, take 2nd turning on R after staggered crossroad. Garden at bottom of track (about ⅓m).* **Every Sat 10 Aug to 31 Aug (12-5). Adm £3.50, chd free. Home-made teas.**

Tranquil 1 acre garden in rural situation with a variety of habitats incorporating lawns, exuberant flower borders, wildlife pond, shaded stream fringed with irises, marsh marigolds and ferns, bog, dry and herb borders, terraced banks. Woodland areas and productive ornamental kitchen garden. Grass and gravel paths, steps and slopes.

10 ◆ TY GLYN WALLED GARDEN

Ciliau Aeron, Lampeter, SA48 8DE. Ty Glyn Davis Trust, 07832970896, gardener@tyglyndavistrust.co.uk, www.tyglyndavistrust.co.uk. *3m SE of Aberaeron. Turn off A482 Aberaeron to Lampeter at Ciliau Aeron signed to Pennant. Entrance 700 metres on L.* **For NGS: Sun 28 July (12-5). Adm £4, chd free. Home-made teas.** **For other opening times and information, please phone, email or visit garden website.**

Secluded walled garden in beautiful woodland setting alongside River Aeron, developed specifically for special needs children. Terraced kitchen garden overlooks herbaceous borders, orchard and ponds with child orientated features and surprises amidst unusual shrubs and perennials. Planted fruit trees selected from former gardener's notebook of C19. Walled Garden, Children's play area. Access paths, lower garden and woodland walk accessible to wheelchairs.

11 YR EFAIL

Llanio Road, Tregaron, SY25 6PU. Mrs Shelagh Yeomans, 01974 299370, shelaghyeo@hotmail.com. *3m SW of Tregaron. A485 from Lampeter. L at Llanio to B4578 or A487 from Aberystwyth, L at Llanfarian (A485) towards Tregaron. At Tyncelyn B4578, 4m on R.* **Visits by arrangement Feb to Oct for groups of up to 30. Please phone or email in advance. Adm £4, chd free. Home-made teas. Refreshments served in conservatory with garden views.**

Savour one of the many quiet

spaces to sit and reflect amongst the informal gardens of relaxed perennial planting, incl a wildlife pond, shaded areas, bog and gravel gardens. Be inspired by the large productive vegetable plots, two polytunnels and greenhouse. Wander along grass paths through the maturing, mostly native, woodland. Enjoy homemade teas incorporating homegrown fruit and veg. Bilingual quiz sheet for children. Garden vegetables for sale. Gravel and grass paths accessible to wheelchairs with pneumatic wheels.

12 YSGOLDY'R CWRT

Llangeitho, Tregaron, SY25 6QJ. Mrs Brenda Woodley, 01974 821542. *1½m N of Llangeitho. Llangeitho, turn L at school signed Penuwch. Garden 1½m on R. From Cross Inn take B4577 past Penuwch Inn, R after brown sculptures in field. Garden ¾m on L.* **Sun 30 June (11-5). Adm £4, chd free. Home-made teas.** Visits also by arrangement May to Aug. Disabled parking next to house.

One acre hillside garden, with 4 natural ponds which are a magnet for wildlife plus a fish pond. Areas of wildflower meadow, bog, dry and woodland gardens. Established rose walk. Rare trees, new large herbaceous beds with ornamental grasses, acer collection, bounded by a mountain stream, with 2 natural cascades and magnificent views. Shade bed with acers and azaleas. Large Iris ensata and Iris laevigata collections in a variety of colours. Steeply sloping ground.

We open the gates to the nation's best gardens, offering a relaxing, memorable and affordable day out. A perfect experience to share with friends and family.

Llanllyr

© Helen Harrison

GLAMORGAN

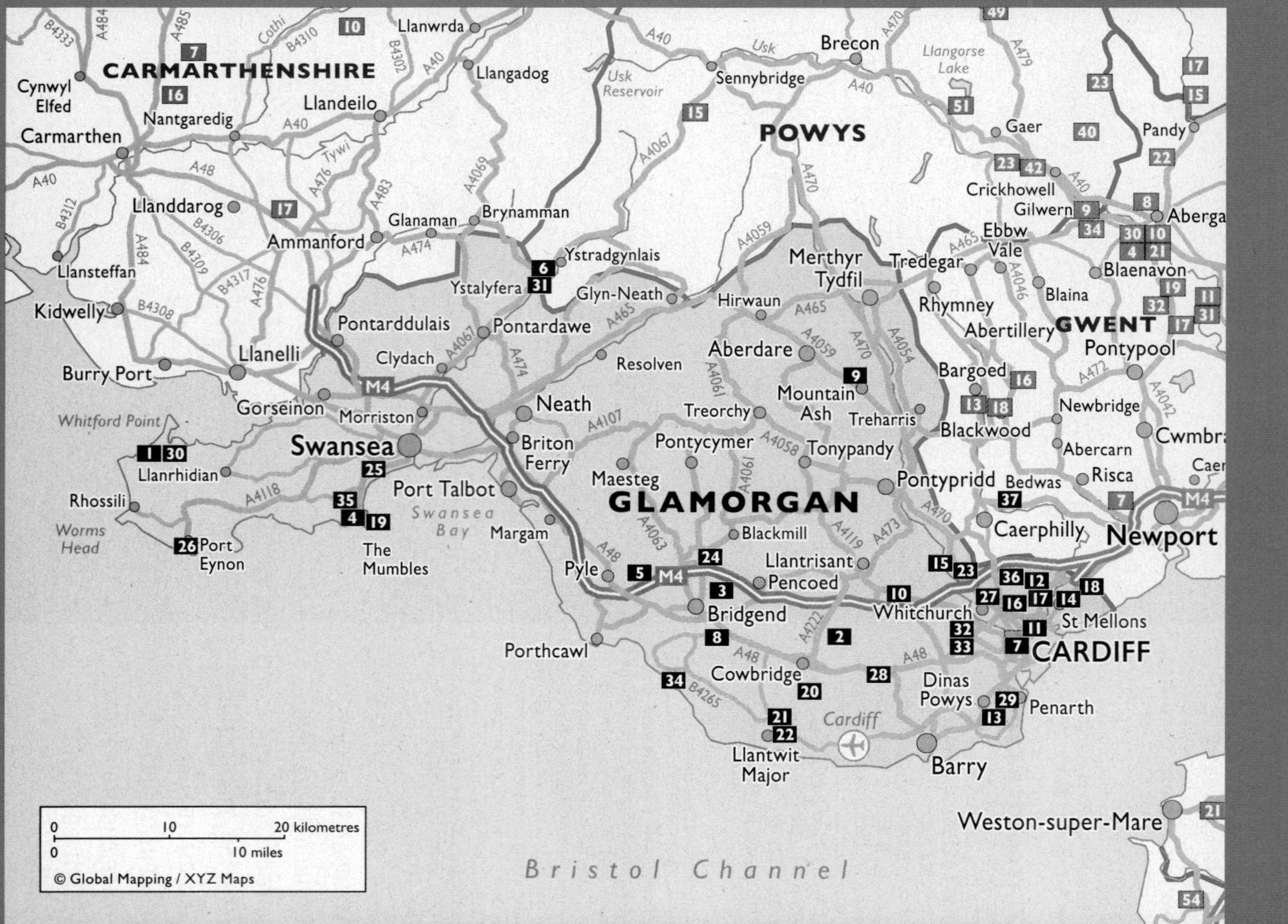
POWYS
GWENT
GLAMORGAN
CARMARTHENSHIRE
CARDIFF
Bristol Channel
Brecon
Sennybridge
Crickhowell
Gilwern
Blaenavon
Pontypool
Cwmbran
Newport
Merthyr Tydfil
Tredegar
Rhymney
Ebbw Vale
Blaina
Abertillery
Bargoed
Blackwood
Newbridge
Abercarn
Risca
Bedwas
Caerphilly
Pontypridd
St Mellons
Whitchurch
Penarth
Dinas Powys
Barry
Weston-super-Mare
Llantrisant
Pencoed
Blackmill
Bridgend
Cowbridge
Llantwit Major
Porthcawl
Pyle
Margam
Port Talbot
Maesteg
Tonypandy
Treharris
Mountain Ash
Aberdare
Hirwaun
Treorchy
Pontycymer
Resolven
Glyn-Neath
Ystradgynlais
Ystalyfera
Pontardawe
Neath
Briton Ferry
Clydach
Morriston
Swansea
Swansea Bay
The Mumbles
Port Eynon
Llanrhidian
Rhossili
Worms Head
Whitford Point
Gorseinon
Llanelli
Burry Port
Kidwelly
Llansteffan
Carmarthen
Cynwyl Elfed
Nantgaredig
Llanddarog
Ammanford
Glanaman
Brynamman
Llandeilo
Llangadog
Llanwrda
Pontarddulais
Pandy
Gaer
Llangorse Lake
Usk Reservoir
Cardiff
0 10 20 kilometres
0 10 miles
© Global Mapping / XYZ Maps

Glamorgan is a large county stretching from the Brecon Beacons in the north to the Bristol Channel in the south, and from the city of Cardiff in the east to the Gower Peninsula in the west. The area has a natural divide where the hills rise from the vale in a clear line of demarcation.

There are gardens opening for the National Garden Scheme throughout the county, and in recent years the number of community openings has greatly increased and have been very successful.

A number of gardens open in villages or suburbs, often within walking distance of each other, providing a very pleasant afternoon for the visitors. Each garden has its own distinct character and the locality is full of hospitality and friendliness.

Gardens range from Mediterranean-style to gardens designed to encourage wildlife. Views from our coastal gardens are truly spectacular.

Our openings start around Easter with a woodland and spring bulbs garden and continue through to mid-September.

So just jump in the car – *Gardens to Visit* book in hand – and head west on the M4. The gardens in Wales are waiting for you!

Below: **Henllys Road**

Volunteers

County Organiser
Rosamund Davies
01656 880048
rosamund.davies@ngs.org.uk

County Treasurer
Trevor Humby
02920 512709
humbyt@cardiff.ac.uk

Publicity & Social Media
Rhian Rees
rhianedrees@gmail.com
07802 438299

Booklet Co-ordinator
Lesley Sherwood
02920 890055
lesleysherwood@btinternet.com

Talks Co-ordinator
Frances Bowyer
02920 892264
frances5860@icloud.com

Health and Gardens Co-ordinator
Miranda Workman
02920 766225
miranda.parsons@talktalk.net

Assistant County Organisers
Sol Blytt Jordens
01792 391676
solinge22@yahoo.co.uk

Ceri Macfarlane
01792 404906
ceri@mikegravenor.plus.com

OPENING DATES

All entries subject to change. For latest information check **www.ngs.org.uk**

Map locator numbers are shown to the right of each garden name.

April

Saturday 27th
Slade 34

Sunday 28th
Slade 34

May

Saturday 18th
◆ Bordervale Plants 2

Sunday 19th
Greenfields 14
110 Heritage Park 18
Llanmaes Gardens 21
19 Slade Gardens 35

Saturday 25th
17 Maes y Draenog 23

Sunday 26th
Llantwit Garden 22
17 Maes y Draenog 23
NEW Plas y Coed 28

June

Saturday 1st
4 Clyngwyn Road 6
Rhos y Bedw 31

Sunday 2nd
4 Clyngwyn Road 6
Rhos y Bedw 31

Tuesday 4th
NEW ◆ Sbectrwm Community Garden 33

Wednesday 5th
NEW ◆ Sbectrwm Community Garden 33

Saturday 8th
◆ Bordervale Plants 2
Cornerstone 7
Gwaelod Village Gardens 15
NEW Sunny Cottage 37

Sunday 9th
Gwaelod Village Gardens 15
NEW Sunny Cottage 37

Saturday 15th
38 South Rise 36

Sunday 16th
Cefn Cribwr Garden Club 5
Creigiau Village Gardens 10
Overton and Port Eynon Gardens 26
38 South Rise 36

Sunday 23rd
Big House Farm 1
Corntown Gardens 8
22 Dan-y-Coed Road 12
The Retreat 30

Saturday 29th
St Peter's Community Garden 32

Sunday 30th
St Peter's Community Garden 32

July

Sunday 7th
◆ Bordervale Plants 2

Saturday 13th
Dinas Powys 13
NEW 164 Redlands Road 29

Sunday 14th
Dinas Powys 13
Maes-y-Wertha Farm 24
50 Pen y Dre 27
NEW 164 Redlands Road 29

Sunday 21st
NEW The Cedars 4

August

Friday 2nd
NEW 11 Castle Meadows 3

Saturday 3rd
NEW 11 Castle Meadows 3

Sunday 4th
7 Cressy Road 11

Monday 26th
◆ Bordervale Plants 2

September

Sunday 8th
NEW 105 Heath Park Avenue 16

Sunday 22nd
NEW 4 Hillcrest 19

By Arrangement

Arrange a personalised garden visit with your club, or group of friends, on a date to suit you. See individual garden entries for full details.

Big House Farm 1
The Cottage 9
7 Cressy Road 11
22 Dan-y-Coed Road 12
NEW 23 Henllys Road 17
Llandough Castle 20
Maggie's Swansea 25
NEW 164 Redlands Road 29

4 Clyngwyn Road

THE GARDENS

1 BIG HOUSE FARM

Llanmadoc, Gower, Swansea, SA3 1DE. Mark & Sheryl Mead, 07831 725753, mark@bighousefarm.net. *15m W of Swansea. M4 J47, L A483 for Swansea, 2nd r'about R, A484 Llanelli 3rd r'about L, B4296 Gowerton T-lights, R B4295, pass Bury Green R to Llanmadoc.* **Sun 23 June (1-5.30). Combined adm with The Retreat £6, chd free. Home-made teas.** Visits also by arrangement June to Aug for groups of 10+.

Multi awarded inspirational garden of around 1 acre at this lovely listed property combines colour form and texture, described by visitors as 'the best I've seen', 'a real gem'. 'better than Chelsea & Gardeners World, should visit'. Large variety of interesting plants and shrubs, with ambient cottage garden feel, Victorian glasshouse with rose garden potager. Beautiful views over sea and country. Located on the Gower Peninsular, Britain's first designated Area of Outstanding Natural Beauty. Majority of garden accessible to wheelchairs.

2 ◆ BORDERVALE PLANTS

Sandy Lane, Ystradowen, Cowbridge, CF71 7SX. Mrs Claire Jenkins, 01446 774036, bordervaleplants@gmail.com, www.bordervale.co.uk. *8m W of Cardiff. 10 mins from M4 or take A4222 from Cowbridge. Turn at Ystradowen postbox, then 3rd L & proceed ½m, follow brown signs. Garden on R. Parking in rd.* **For NGS: Sat 18 May, Sat 8 June, Sun 7 July, Mon 26 Aug (11-4). Adm £3.50, chd free.** For other opening times and information, please phone, email or visit garden website.

Within mature woodland valley (semi-tamed), with stream and bog garden, extensive mixed borders. Children must be supervised. The Nursery specialises in unusual perennials and cottage garden plants. See website for non NGS openings. Coach parties welcome by arrangement. Awarded Silver Gilt Medal (for Unusual Welsh grown trees, shrubs & perennials) RHS Flower Show Cardiff. Wheelchair access to top third of garden as well as Nursery.

3 NEW 11 CASTLE MEADOWS

Coity, Bridgend, CF35 6DA. Mrs Tina & Mr Colin Edmunds. *J36 off M4, follow signs for Bridgend then Coity at the T-lights. Follow yellow signs to cul-de-sac opp Coity Castle. On street parking in village.* **Fri 2, Sat 3 Aug (12-5). Adm £3.50, chd free. Tea.**

Situated in the historic village of Coity with views to the castle, this family garden has an eclectic planting style. The 'stick it there' policy results in a mixture of perennials, roses and climbers which jostle for attention along with annuals, self seeders and pots. The summerhouse and pond add extra interest. A local art group will be exhibiting some of their work. Good wheelchair access to patio area which gives views over the whole garden.

4 NEW THE CEDARS

20A Slade Road, Newton, Swansea, SA3 4UF. Mr & Mrs Ian and Madelene Scott. *Take the A4067 to Oystermouth, turn right at White Rose PH continue along Newton Rd keeping R at fork to T-junction, turn R & 1st R into Slade Rd, follow yellow signs.* **Sun 21 July (2-5). Adm £4, chd free. Home-made teas.**

South facing garden on a sloping site consisting of rooms subdivided by large shrubs and trees.Small kitchen garden with greenhouse. Ornamental pond. Herbaceous perennials,number of fruit trees. It is a garden which affords all year interest with azalea camellias rhododendrons magnolias hydrangeas. Limited number of plants for sale.

Your visits help change lives – we've donated over £16.7 million to Macmillan Cancer Support since 1984

GROUP OPENING

5 CEFN CRIBWR GARDEN CLUB

Cefn Cribwr, Bridgend, CF32 0AP. www.cefncribwrgardeningclub.com. *5m W of Bridgend on B4281.* **Sun 16 June (11-5). Combined adm £5, chd free. Tea.**

6 BEDFORD ROAD
Carole & John Mason.

13 BEDFORD ROAD
Mr John Loveluck.

2 BRYN TERRACE
Alan & Tracy Birch.

CEFN CRIBWR GARDEN CLUB ALLOTMENTS
Cefn Cribwr Garden Club.

CEFN METHODIST CHURCH
Cefn Cribwr Methodist Church.

77 CEFN ROAD
Peter & Veronica Davies & Mr Fai Lee.

25 EAST AVENUE
Mr & Mrs D Colbridge.

15 GREEN MEADOW
Tom & Helen.

6 TAI THORN
Mr Kevin Burnell.

Cefn Cribwr is an old mining village atop a ridge with views to Swansea in the west, Somerset to the south and home to Bedford Park and the Cefn Cribwr Iron Works. The village hall is at the centre with teas, cakes and plants for sale. The allotments are to be found behind the hall. Children, art and relaxation are just some of the themes to be found in the gardens besides the flower beds and vegetables. There are also water features, fish ponds, wildlife ponds, summerhouses and hens adding to the diverse mix. Themed colour borders, roses, greenhouses, recycling, composting and much more. The chapel grounds are peaceful with a meandering woodland trail. There will also be tea, coffee and cakes, craft stalls, games, raffles and a table top sale in the hall. For more information please see our website.

6 4 CLYNGWYN ROAD

Ystalyfera, Swansea, SA9 2AE. Paul Steer, www.artinacorner.blogspot.com. *Follow NGS signs from Rhos y Bedw.* **Sat 1, Sun 2 June (12-5). Combined adm with Rhos y Bedw £4, chd free. Light refreshments.**

The Coal Tip Cloister Garden is a small personal space created in order to help us unwind from our work as nurses. Its main character is enclosure and a sense of rest. It is not a flowery garden but is formed out of shrubs and trees - forming a tapestry of hedging with arches and niches being cut out in order to place seats and sculpture and to produce a visual rhythm. An intimate space designed for rest and contemplation.

7 CORNERSTONE

Charles Street, Cardiff, CF10 2GA. Mrs Lucy King. *The Cornerstone Sensory Garden is just off Queen St, behind Next and M&S and opp St David's Cathedral.* **Sat 8 June (10-4). Adm £3.50, chd free.**

This is a new garden created from scratch in December 2016. It has been designed to facilitate disabled access and the needs of the Blind Gardening Club of Cardiff Institute for the Blind and has been planted with a mixture of plants to create highly visible contrasting colours and also scents. It is truly an inner city garden, providing vibrant colour and gentle scents in the heart of the city. The garden and adjoining buildings are fully accessible for wheelchair users and those with restricted mobility.

Your visits help change lives – your generosity has supported unpaid carers through donations to Carers Trust totalling over £3.9 million since 1996

GROUP OPENING

8 CORNTOWN GARDENS

Corntown, Bridgend, CF35 5BB. *Take B4265 from Bridgend to Ewenny. Take L in Ewenny on B4525 to Corntown follow yellow NGS signs. From A48 take B4525 to Corntown.* **Sun 23 June (11-4). Combined adm £4, chd free. Home-made teas at Y Bwthyn.**

RHOS GELER
Bob Priddle & Marie D Robson.

Y BWTHYN
Mrs Joyce Pegg.

Y Bwythyn has had over 30yrs of hard labour, some guesswork and considerable good luck resulting in a delightful garden. The area at the front of the house is a mixture of hot colour combinations whilst at the rear of this modest sized garden the themes are of a more traditional cottage garden style which incl colour themed borders as well as soft fruit, herbs and vegetables. Rhos Geler's garden has a lavender hedge at the front and subjects to attract butterflies. The main garden area at the back of the house is a long narrow garden that is in a series of themed areas. These incl an herbaceous border, shade loving plants, an Elizabethan style knot garden and a Japanese influenced area. Containers hold a range of subjects incl a collection of sempervivums. As well as the garden, visitors to Rhos Geler are invited to view the owners extensive collections.These incl advertising tins, welsh studio pottery and items connected with the American Cowboy.

9 THE COTTAGE

Cwmpennar, Mountain Ash, CF45 4DB. Helen & Hugh Jones, 01443 472784, hhjones1966@yahoo.co.uk. *18m N of Cardiff. A470 from N or S. Then follow B4059 to Mountain Ash. Follow signs for Cefnpennar then turn R before bus shelter into village of Cwmpennar & to top of lane at end of Middle Row.* **Visits by arrangement May to July for groups of up to 10. Adm £4, chd free. Home-made teas.**

4 acres and 40yrs of amateur muddling have produced what it is hoped is an interesting garden incl bluebell wood, rhododendron and camellia shrubbery, herbaceous borders, rose garden, small arboretum, many uncommon trees and shrubs. Garden slopes NE/SW.

GROUP OPENING

10 CREIGIAU VILLAGE GARDENS

Maes Y Nant, Creigiau, CF15 9EJ. *W of Cardiff (J34 M4). From M4 J34 follow A4119 to T-lights, turn R by Castell Mynach Pub, pass through Groes Faen & turn L to Creigiau. Follow NGS signs.* **Sun 16 June (12-5). Combined adm £5, chd free. Home-made teas at 28 Maes y Nant.**

28 MAES Y NANT
Mike & Lesley Sherwood.

31 MAES Y NANT
Frances Bowyer.

WAUNWYLLT
John Hughes & Richard Shaw.

On the NW side of Cardiff and with easy access from the M4 J34, Creigiau Village Gardens incl three vibrant and innovative gardens. Each quite different, they combine some of the best characteristics of design and planting for modern town gardens with the naturalism of old fashioned cottage gardens. Each has its own forte; the garden at Waunwyllt has been achieved over 7yrs with coloured themed rooms. At 28 Maes y Nant, cottage garden planting reigns. This is in complete contrast to the strong architecture of 31 Maes y Nant, where the design coordinates water, the garden room and planting, incl a small scale prairie. Anyone looking for ideas for a garden in an urban setting will not go away disappointed; enjoy a warm welcome, home-made teas and plant sales.

11 7 CRESSY ROAD

Penylan, Cardiff, CF23 5BE. Victoria Thornton, 02920 311215, penylanhillbilys@hotmail.com. *Penylan Cardiff. Approaching from Wellfield Rd, turn R at the T-lights into Marlborough Rd & Cressy Rd is the 3rd turning on the L. From Newport Rd follow Marlborough Rd to Thomas Court, turn L.* **Sun 4 Aug (2-6). Adm £3, chd free. Home-made teas.** Visits also by arrangement July & Aug for groups of up to 10.

Enjoy a warm welcome at No 7. Small subtropical garden, creating an illusion of a much larger space. Lush tropical planting, alive with colour and texture. With an emphasis on wildlife, nectar rich planting, barrel pond, attracting frogs, dragonflies and damselflies. Silver medal, Cardiff in Bloom 2014.

12 22 DAN-Y-COED ROAD

Cyncoed, Cardiff, CF23 6NA. Alan & Miranda Workman, 029 2076 6225, miranda.parsons@talktalk.net. *Dan y Coed Rd leads off Cyncoed Rd at the top and Rhydypenau Rd at the bottom. No 22 is at the bottom of Dan y Coed Rd. There is street parking and level access to the R of the property.* **Sun 23 June (2-6). Adm £3.50, chd free. Home-made teas.** Visits also by arrangement Apr to Sept for groups of 5+.

A medium sized, much loved garden. Owners share a passion for plants and structure, each yr the lawn gets smaller to allow for the acquisition of new plants and features! Hostas, ferns, Acers and other trees form the central woodland theme as there is a lovely backdrop provided by the Nant Fawr woods. Yr round interest has been created for the owner's and visitor's greater pleasure. There is a wildlife pond, many climbing plants and a greenhouse with a cactus and succulent collection. There is partial wheelchair access to the patio area only (the gravel path at the side makes this difficult, but not impossible).

GROUP OPENING

13 DINAS POWYS

Dinas Powys, CF64 4TL. *Approx 6m SW of Cardiff. Exit M4 at J33, follow A4232 to Leckwith, onto B4267 & follow to Merry Harrier T-lights. Turn R & enter Dinas Powys. Follow yellow NGS signs.* **Sat 13, Sun 14 July (11-5). Combined adm £4, chd free. Home-made teas at all gardens.** Donation to Dinas Powys Voluntary Concern and Dinas Powys Community Library.

1 ASHGROVE
Sara Bentley.

NIGHTINGALE COMMUNITY GARDENS
Keith Hatton.

There are three gardens to visit in this small friendly village, all with something different to offer. The gardens at 1 Ashgrove, has a large variety of different plants and trees in sweeping beds, with many hidden nooks and places to sit. The community garden features lovely displays of vegetable and fruit. Our village church, St Peters, is also opening with displays of flowers, classic cars and other attractions. Delicious home-made teas will be served, incl vegan and gluten free options, at all locations, and there will be plants for sale also. There are many restful and beautiful areas to sit and relax. Good wheelchair access at the community gardens. Partial access elsewhere.

14 GREENFIELDS

Newport Road, St Mellons, Cardiff, CF3 5TW. Roger & Kate Verrier Jones. *4 m NE of Cardiff. SE-side Newport Rd (B4487) on top of hill ¼ m SW of St Mellons village, 200yds NE of St Illtyd's School. Park at Fox & Hounds, Old Hill or Quarry Hall nursing home, please follow yellow signs.* **Sun 19 May (12-5). Combined adm with 110 Heritage Park £4, chd free. Home-made teas.**

¾-acre garden incl a cottage style front garden with herbaceous and wild areas. Pergola, vista to formal pond and beyond, knot garden and water feature. Rear garden open and terraced with topiary, shady areas and views of Bristol Channel leading to parterre style kitchen garden and fruit cage. Sale of plants, teas. Gravel drive & limited wheelchair access to front garden. Good access to rear garden.

110 Heritage Park

GROUP OPENING

15 GWAELOD VILLAGE GARDENS

Main Road, Gwaelod-Y-Garth, Cardiff, CF15 9HJ. Ms Christine Myant. *Located near the A470 Castel Coch/Radyr turn off. Main parking is at the primary school car park.* **Sat 8, Sun 9 June (11-5). Combined adm £4, chd free. Home-made teas.**

THE OLD POST OFFICE
Ms Christine Myant.

PEAR TREE COTTAGE
Yvonne Reid.

Gwaelod y Garth is an old mining village. The two open gardens nestle on the hillside of The Garth Mountain. Both gardens and the village are hidden gems of Cardiff's outer suburbs. Set in a rural setting with views to the valley beyond, the two adjoining gardens offer the visitor much to enjoy. Pear Tree Cottage opened in 2018 to much acclaim. Its large well stocked flower beds are a riot of summer colour. The many seating areas allow the visitor time to sit and soak up the experience. The Old Post Office offers a mature terraced garden. With its cottage garden style of planting and it's many paths and areas of contemplation visitors are able to take full advantage of the views, fragrance and colour.

16 NEW 105 HEATH PARK AVENUE

Heath, Cardiff, CF14 3RG. Mr and Mrs Gambles, beverly_gambles@hotmail.com. *Heath, Cardiff. Approx 1m from University Hospital. From Gabalfa R'about into Birchgrove turn R into Heathwood Rd. At top of Rd turn R at T-lights into Heath Park Ave. Follow NGS signs.* **Sun 8 Sept (12-5). Adm £3.50, chd free. Home-made teas.**
A South facing family garden that has undergone some restructuring in 2018. Perennial borders and plenty of pots surrounding a central lawn give lots of colour throughout the year. A small vegetable plot and greenhouse to grow a variety of plants and vegetables. Small fishpond with lots of frogs and newts.

17 NEW 23 HENLLYS ROAD

Cyncoed, Cardiff, CF23 6NL. Mrs Jill Evans, 07870654205, jilltreenut@uwclub.net. *Turn off Cyncoed Rd, in Cyncoed Village down Bettws y Coed Rd. Take 2nd L onto Llangorse Rd and 2nd R into Henllys Rd. Garden is halfway down on the R.* **Visits by arrangement May to Sept for groups of up to 10. Open only by arrangement to Health groups/local charities. Adm by donation.**
Urban garden with cottage style planting, with some unusual shrubs, perennials, and bulbs, which try to provide all year round colour. When we started on the garden from scratch, in 2011, one criterion was that all of it couldn't be seen at once. As a result, the garden has various seating areas with different aspects incl a summerhouse. The borders are usually full of plants so that very little bare soil is visible. The garden has lawns, a pergola with wisteria, roses and clematis, with garden sculptures and water features. In the Spring the many containers are filled with dozens of varieties of tulips, which are followed by Agapanthus, and Dahlias. Autumn colour is provided by late flowering perennials and shrubs incl Acers, Viburnams, Enkianthus and Cercis. The garden is constantly evolving with new plants and ideas, usually after visiting other gardens and gardening shows! There are some steps and gravel paths but most of the garden can be accessed by wheelchair. Garden entered via side gate on tarmac drive. Paved ramp down to middle of garden & gravel paths elsewhere.

18 110 HERITAGE PARK

St Mellons, Cardiff, CF3 0DS. Sarah Boorman. *Leave A48 at St Mellons junction, take 2nd exit at r'about. Turn R to Willowdene Way & R to Willowbrook Drive. Heritage Park is 1st R. Park outside the cul-de-sac.* **Sun 19 May (12-5). Combined adm with Greenfields £4, chd free. Home-made teas. Gluten free available.**
An unexpected gem within a modern housing estate. Evergreen shrubs, herbaceous borders, box topiary and terracotta pots make for a mix between cottage garden and Italian style. With numerous seating areas and a few quirky surprises this small garden is described by neighbours as a calm oasis.

19 NEW 4 HILLCREST

Langland, Swansea, SA3 4PW. Mr & Mrs Gareth & Penny Cross. *Approach from L, turn at Langland corner on Langland Rd Mumbles; take first L. off Higher Lane; take 3rd L. up Worcester Rd and bungalow faces you at top.* **Sun 22 Sept (1-5). Adm £5, chd free. Tea.**
Redesigned and developed over the last 4 years, our hilltop garden backs onto woodland overlooking Swansea bay and attracts many birds. We have planted large herbaceous borders with mainly perennial plants/shrubs to provide interest and colour through the seasons. We have surrounded a fruit/vegetable area with stepover apple trees and created a wildlife pond.

20 LLANDOUGH CASTLE

Llandough, Cowbridge, CF71 7LR. Mrs Rhian Rees, 07802438299, rhianedrees@gmail.com. *1½m outside Cowbridge. At the T- lights in Cowbridge turn onto the St Athan Rd. Continue then turn R to Llandough. Drive into the village and park in Castle Precinct. Walk up a short lane and into the gardens.* **Visits by arrangement Mar to Sept for groups of up to 30. Please email to book. Adm £5, chd free. Home-made teas.**
Set within castle grounds and with a backdrop of an ancient monument, the 3½ acres of garden incl a contemporary twist on a Victorian kitchen garden with a hint of the Mediterranean, formal lawns and herbaceous beds, a wildlife pond with waterfall and a woodland garden with stumpery and sculpture. Why not plan a visit with friends and family? We can include homemade teas too! Although some of the gardens are flat, areas like the woodland and gravel drive may be difficult for wheelchair access.

GROUP OPENING

21 LLANMAES GARDENS

Llanmaes, Llantwit Major, CF61 2XR. 01446796676, oldfroglands@btinternet.com. *5m S of Cowbridge. At traffic lights on the B4265 turn off towards Llanmaes to Mehefin, Travel to Church House before the Church, and continue down lane to Brown Lion House and on for about 1km to Old Froglands.* **Sun 19 May (12-5). Combined adm £5, chd free. Light refreshments at Old Froglands & Mehefin.**

BROWN LION HOUSE
Mrs Wendy Hewitt-Sayer.
D

CHURCH COTTAGE
Annie Grujic.

MEHEFIN
Mrs Alison Morgan, 01446 793427, bb@mehefin.com, www.mehefin.com.

OLD FROGLANDS
Dorne & David Harris, 07702502950, dorneharris@hotmail.co.uk.

Llanmaes, 1m from Llantwit Major, is a pretty village with attractive village green, stream running through and C13 church. Old Froglands is an historic farmhouse with streams and woodland areas linked by bridges. Ducks swim and chickens roam free. Plantings are varied with interesting foliage. Church Cottage has a pretty garden to the rear, is newly acquired and the owner is still discovering its unknown delights. Mehefin is an enchanting garden with bursts of colour, a huge variety of plants and a wild flower meadow. Brown Lion House is a newly renovated garden with mature trees and shrubs, patios and pathways and a well established fish pond.

Llantwit Garden

22 LLANTWIT GARDEN

21 Monmouth Way, Boverton, Llantwit Major, CF61 2GT. Don & Ann Knight. *At Llanmaes rd T-lights turn onto Eagleswell Rd, next L into Monmouth Way, garden ½ way down on R.* **Sun 26 May (11-5). Adm £4, chd free.**

This is a Japanese style garden with a Zen gate, Torri gate and Japanese lanterns featuring a large collection of Japanese style trees, a pagoda and 3 water features which incl the great Amazon waterfall along with large Buddha's head and new pond.

23 17 MAES Y DRAENOG

Maes Y Draenog, Tongwynlais, Cardiff, CF15 7JL. Mr Derek Price. *N of M4. From S: M4 , J32, take A4054 into village. R at Lewis Arms pub, up Mill Rd. 2nd L into Catherine Drive, park in signed area (no parking in Maesydraenog). Follow signs to 17 Maesydraenog.* **Sat 25, Sun 26 May (12.30-5.30). Adm £4, chd free. Light refreshments.**

A hidden gem of a garden, in the shadow of Castell Coch, fed by a stoned mountain stream. Footbridge invites you to naturalised areas, set against a woodland backdrop. Developed over 10 yrs with a good variety of plants, filling two main borders of herbaceous plants for spring and summer displays. Garden structures, summer house, patios, greenhouse and small veg area with. mountain stream with wooden footbridge, Summer house, greenhouse and good variety of plants in borders around house. Rear of house is set against woodland. Not suitable for young children and partial access for wheelchair users.

24 MAES-Y-WERTHA FARM

Bryncethin, CF32 9YJ. Stella & Tony Leyshon. *3m N of Bridgend. Follow sign for Bryncethin, turn R at Masons Arms. Follow sign for Heol-y-Cyw garden about 1m outside Bryncethin on R.* **Sun 14 July (12-7). Adm £5, chd free. Home-made teas.**

A 3 acre hidden gem outside Bridgend. Entering the garden you find a small Japanese garden fed by a stream, this leads you to informal mixed beds & enclosed herbaceous borders. Ponds & rill are fed by a natural spring. A meadow with large lawns under new planting gives wonderful vistas over surrounding countryside. Mural in the summerhouse by contemporary artist Daniel Llewelyn Hall. His work is represented in the Royal Collection and House of Lords.

25 MAGGIE'S SWANSEA

Singleton Hospital, Sketty Lane, Sketty, Swansea, SA2 8QL. Miss Leanne Jennett, www.maggiescentres.org/swansea. *On the grounds of Singleton Hospital. They are next to the Genetic Building & close to the chemotherapy day unit at the back of the main hospital. Please follow yellow signs.* **Visits by arrangement Mar to Nov. Adm by donation.**
Maggie's Swansea's gardens wrap around the building, and overlook into Swansea Bay. The garden, designed by Kim Wilkie, attracts wildlife, heightening the natural and tranquil feel, and there is also a fully functional allotment. The Centre sits among a small wooded area, and the wings of the design also help to shelter the outside seating areas, meaning that visitors can enjoy sitting out for as much of the year as possible. Decking all the way around the building.

GROUP OPENING

26 OVERTON AND PORT EYNON GARDENS

Overton Lane, Port Eynon, Swansea, SA3 1NR. *16.8m W of Swansea on Gower Peninsula. From Swansea follow A4118 to Port Eynon. Parking in public car park in Port Eynon. Yellow NGS signs showing gardens. Maps of garden locations available.* **Sun 16 June (2-5.30). Combined adm £4.50, chd free. Home-made teas.**

THE BAYS FARM
Sol Blytt Jordens.

6 THE BOARLANDS
Robert & Annette Dyer.

Overton offers breathtaking views of the Gower Peninsula. Port Eynon is the most southerly point on the Gower. Set in the heart of Port Eynon, 6 The Boarlands is a plantman's paradise! A gently sloping garden designed for yr-round interest with shrubs, bulbs and perennials. The Bays Farm is an ever developing garden in spite of a large puppy racing around and digging his own holes! Teas can be enjoyed here with views over the sea. Plants will be for sale here. Many rare and unusual plants. Lovely views over the sea. Partial wheelchair access.

27 50 PEN Y DRE

Rhiwbina, Cardiff, CF14 6EQ. Ann Franklin. *N Cardiff. M4 J32, A470 to Cardiff, 1st L to mini r'about, turn R. At T-lights in village, turn R to Pen-y-Dre.* **Sun 14 July (11-4.30). Adm £3, chd free. Home-made teas.**
Mixed mature borders in cottage garden style with many old favourites incl vegetable plot.

28 NEW PLAS Y COED

Bonvilston, CF5 6TR. Hugh & Gwenda Child. *Plas y Coed is just off the A48 at Bonvilston. Find the Church and you will find us. Parking will be clearly marked at the Reading Rooms.* **Sun 26 May (9.30-6). Adm £5, chd free. Home-made teas.**
The garden at Plas y Coed extends to a couple of acres. It is both whimsical and romantic and a wonderful spot to sit and dream - if only there was time! The field to the rear of the garden is now developing into an arboretum. We have been planting trees since 2006 and continue to do so, which is a source of great pleasure. Most trees have markers with Latin name, common English name and the year of planting. We are now up to 33 and counting. Partial wheelchair access.

29 NEW 164 REDLANDS ROAD

Penarth, CF64 2QR. Mrs Jane Starling, 07526633699, Jane.starling@hotmail.co.uk. *Approx 5m SW of Cardiff. Exit M4 at J33 follow A4232 to Leckwith onto B4267 to Merry Harrier. Turn R & 1st L onto Redlands Rd. Over brow of hill on RHS. Follow NGS yellow signs.* **Sat 13, Sun 14 July (9-6). Adm £4.50, chd free. Home-made teas.** Visits also by arrangement in July.
An unexpected delight when you come through side gate. Such a lot to explore. Explosion of colour in this very large garden. Veg plot, pond, summerhouse and loads of varied planting. Something for everyone, a real treat.

30 THE RETREAT

Llanmadoc, Swansea, SA3 1DE. Richard & Sue McCauley. *15m W of Swansea. M4 J47, L A483 for Swansea, 2nd r'about R, A484 Llanelli 3 r'about L, B4296 Gowerton T-lights, R B4295, pass Burry Green R to Llanmadoc.* **Sun 23 June (1-5.30). Combined adm with Big House Farm £6, chd free.**
Our garden has evolved over many yrs. It now has several distinct areas, varied borders range from cottage style perennial planting, an area of large structured plants, a vegetable garden along with a small orchard in a wildlife friendly area. The garden is also one of a group which has won awards in the Swansea in Bloom competition.

Plas y Coed

Some steps and uneven ground. Partial wheelchair access, gravel path around bungalow to rear terrace.

31 RHOS Y BEDW

4 Pen y Wern Rd, Ystalyfera, Swansea, SA9 2NH. Robert & Helen Davies. *13m N of Swansea. M4 J45 take A4067. Follow signs for Dan yr Ogof caves across 5 r'abouts. After T-lights follow yellow NGS signs. Parking above house on rd off to R.* **Sat 1, Sun 2 June (12-5). Combined adm with 4 Clyngwyn Road £4, chd free. Home-made teas. Gluten free options available.**

A haven of peace and tranquillity with spectacular views, this glorious compact garden with its amazing array of planting areas is constantly evolving. Our diverse planting areas incl cottage, herb, and bog gardens also an array of roses and a knot garden are sure to provide inspiration. A garden with something different around every corner to be savoured slowly, relax and enjoy.

32 ST PETER'S COMMUNITY GARDEN

St Fagans Road, Cardiff, CF5 3DW. St Peter's Church, www.stpeterschurchfairwater.org.uk. *On the St Fagans Road opp Gorse Place. Next Door to Church,. A48 to Culverhousecross r'bout take A48 Cowbridge Rd West to Ely r'bout 1st L. At T-lights go L B4488 to Fairwater Green, follow yellow NGS signs.* **Sat 29, Sun 30 June (10-4). Adm £3.50, chd free. Light refreshments. All day refreshments.**

Secret garden in city suburb. Unusual combination of flower beds, raised vegetable beds and nature reserve, all created by volunteers. Features incl a large natural pond surrounded by wild plants, Welsh heritage apple trees, long herb border and wild flower meadow. This year our major attractions will be our Quiet Garden with a zen feel - water features and monoliths. New Quiet Garden. Craft, book browsing area, Fairtrade wine and chocolate tasting. All day refreshments, mostly home-made, and specialist quality plant sales from various growers in South Wales. Disabled WC available. Most of the Garden wheelchair access friendly.

33 NEW ◆ SBECTRWM COMMUNITY GARDEN

Bwlch Road, Fairwater, Cardiff, CF5 3EF. Mr Ken Bray. *Just off Cowbridge Rd.* **For NGS: Tue 4 June (10-2). Home-made teas. Wed 5 June (10-2). Adm £3, chd free.**

Sbectrum Community Garden is an educational project run by the charity Vision 21, for adults with Additional Learning Needs. It is also open to the local community. The garden features flower borders, mature fig and cherry trees, an espaliered apple tree and a large kiwi. There is a vegetable garden, circular herb garden, wildlife pond, large greenhouse and poly tunnel.

34 SLADE

Southerndown, CF32 0RP. Rosamund & Peter Davies, 01656 880048, ros@sladewoodgarden.plus.com, www.sladeholidaycottages.co.uk. *5m S of Bridgend. M4 J35 Follow A473 to Bridgend. Take B4265 to St. Brides Major. Turn R in St. Brides Major for Southerndown, then follow yellow NGS signs.* **Sat 27, Sun 28 Apr (12-6). Adm £5, chd free. Home-made teas.**

Hidden away Slade garden is an unexpected jewel to discover next to the sea with views overlooking the Bristol Channel. The garden tumbles down a valley protected by a belt of woodland. In front of the house are delightful formal areas a rose and clematis pergola and herbaceous borders. From terraced lawns great sweeps of grass stretch down the hill enlivened by spring bulbs and fritillaries. Heritage Coast wardens will give guided tours of adjacent Dunraven Gardens with slide shows every hour from 2pm. Partial wheelchair access.

35 19 SLADE GARDENS

West Cross, Swansea, SA3 5QP. Norma & Peter Stephen. *5m SW of Swansea. At mini r'about on Mumbles Rd A4067 take 2nd exit (Fairwood Rd), 1st L onto West Cross Lane & follow yellow NGS signs.* **Sun 19 May (2-5). Adm £3, chd free. Light refreshments.**

A very small enclosed front and rear garden, designed to lead you around its informal planting of over 200 species. A garden to sit in! Narrow paths and steps make access difficult for less mobile visitors.

36 38 SOUTH RISE

Lanishen, Cardiff, CF14 0RH. Dr Khalida Hasan. *N of Cardiff, from Llanishen Village Station Rd past Train Stn go R down The Rise or further down onto S Rise directly. Following yellow signs.* **Sat 15, Sun 16 June (11-4). Adm £4, chd free. Home-made teas.**

A relatively new garden backing on to Llanishen Reservoir gradually establishing with something of interest and colour all yr round. Herbaceous borders, vegetables and fruit plants surround central lawn. Wild life friendly; variety of climbers and exotics. In front shrubs and herbaceous borders to a lawn. Stepping stones leading to children's play area and vegetable plot also at the back. Variety of home made cakes and Asian savouries such as samosas, yoghurt and chick peas chat. Wheelchair access to rear from the side of the house.

37 NEW SUNNY COTTAGE

Mountain Road, Bedwas, Caerphilly, CF83 8ES. Mr & Mrs Paul & Carol Edwards. *Head E from Caerphilly to Bedwas on A468. Turn L at T-lights into village onto Church St follow rd up to St Barrwgs Church. Turn R after bridge then 1st l onto Mountain Rd. Follow NGS signs.* **Sat 8, Sun 9 June (11-4). Adm £3.50, chd free. Home-made teas.**

Terraced garden surrounded by wildlife friendly hedges. Hidden areas on the terraces are linked by paths and arches. Each level is very well stocked with a multitude of flowers, shrubs & trees. Something of interest for every season. 2 lawn areas provide a welcome splash of green. One is shaded by 2 mature apple trees. Seating areas to relax and enjoy the vistas can be found on most levels.

GWENT

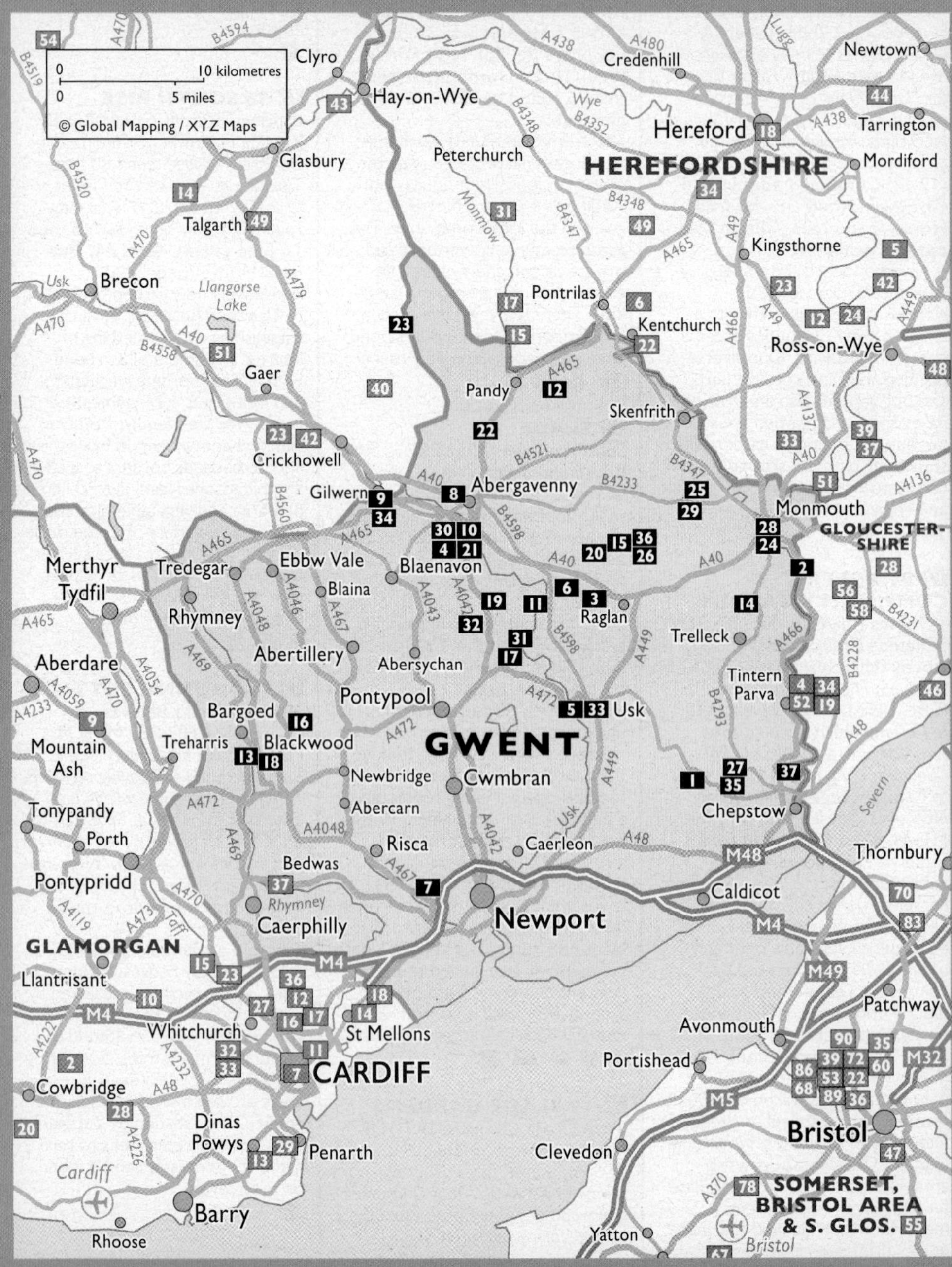
0 10 kilometres
0 5 miles
© Global Mapping / XYZ Maps
HEREFORDSHIRE
GWENT
GLOUCESTER-SHIRE
GLAMORGAN
SOMERSET, BRISTOL AREA & S. GLOS.
Clyro
Hay-on-Wye
Glasbury
Talgarth
Brecon
Llangorse Lake
Gaer
Crickhowell
Gilwern
Credenhill
Hereford
Newtown
Tarrington
Mordiford
Peterchurch
Kingsthorne
Pontrilas
Kentchurch
Ross-on-Wye
Pandy
Skenfrith
Abergavenny
Monmouth
Merthyr Tydfil
Tredegar
Ebbw Vale
Blaina
Blaenavon
Rhymney
Raglan
Trelleck
Aberdare
Abertillery
Abersychan
Tintern Parva
Pontypool
Usk
Bargoed
Blackwood
Treharris
Mountain Ash
Newbridge
Cwmbran
Abercarn
Chepstow
Tonypandy
Porth
Pontypridd
Risca
Bedwas
Caerleon
Thornbury
Caldicot
Caerphilly
Newport
Llantrisant
Whitchurch
St Mellons
Patchway
Avonmouth
CARDIFF
Portishead
Cowbridge
Dinas Powys
Penarth
Bristol
Clevedon
Barry
Rhoose
Yatton
Cardiff
Bristol
Usk
Wye
Lugg
Monnow
Rhymney
Taff
Severn
M4
M48
M49
M5
M32

From the old coal mining villages in the west to the gentle hills and valleys on the east side of the county, from the sea and estuaries in the south to the rugged mountains in the north, Gwent is Wales writ small. It's a county of castles and farms, of country lanes yet very accessible main roads, easily reached from Cardiff, Bristol or Hereford.

Some of our gardens are clustered around the delightful market towns of Monmouth and Abergavenny, many with breathtaking panoramic views. The historic small town of Usk opens around 20 varied gardens over a June weekend. Our Gwent gardens range from small jewels of town gardens to gracious estates, from manicured lawns to hillside gardens that blend into the landscape. But they all have something special, and all have in common the passionate enthusiasm and dedication of their owners. These very generous folk will love to share this passion with you, the visitors. And there will be tea and cake!

Volunteers

County Organiser
Cathy Davies
01291 672625 / 07976 633 743
cathy-davies@btconnect.com

County Treasurer
Ian Mabberley
01873 890219
ian.mabberley@ngs.org.uk

Publicity
Ian Mabberley
(as above)

Social Media
Cherry Taylor
01600 715404
cherry.taylor@dynamicmarkets.co.uk

Assistant County Organiser
Sue Torkington
01873 890045
sue@torkington.myzen.co.uk

Veronica Ruth
01873 859757
vruth@btinternet.com

Jenny Lloyd
01873 880030 / 07850 949 209
jenny.plants@btinternet.com

Booklet Co-Ordinator
Veronica Ruth (as above)

Left: **Woodlands Farm**

OPENING DATES

All entries subject to change. For latest information check **www.ngs.org.uk**

Extended openings are shown at the beginning of the month.

Map locator numbers are shown to the right of each garden name.

March

Sunday 31st
Llanover 19

May

Saturday 4th
Park House 27
Woodhaven 35

Sunday 5th
High House 15
The Old Vicarage 26

Monday 6th
Great Campston 12

Sunday 12th
The Alma 1
High Glanau Manor 14

Saturday 18th
Dan-y-Warren 9
Glebe House 11

Sunday 19th
Dan-y-Warren 9
Glebe House 11

Wednesday 22nd
The Nelson Garden 24

Saturday 25th
Hillcrest 18

Sunday 26th
Hillcrest 18
◆ Nant y Bedd 23
Wenallt Isaf 34

Monday 27th
Hillcrest 18
◆ Nant y Bedd 23

Friday 31st
NEW Cwmgyst 8

June

Sunday 2nd
Castell Cwrt 4
NEW Cwmgyst 8
Middle Ninfa Farm & Bunkhouse 21

Tuesday 4th
Wyndcliffe Court 37

Sunday 9th
Glannant y llan 10
Rockfield Park 28
7 The Cedars 30

Saturday 15th
Longhouse Farm 20
Ty Boda 32

Sunday 16th
Longhouse Farm 20
Ty Boda 32

Friday 21st
Mione 22

Sunday 23rd
NEW Highfield Farm, Star Road 17
Mione 22
NEW Trengrove House 31

Saturday 29th
Castle House 5
Usk Open Gardens 33

Sunday 30th
Castle House 5
Usk Open Gardens 33

July

Friday 5th
NEW Cwmgyst 8
Mione 22

Sunday 7th
NEW Cwmgyst 8
Mione 22

Saturday 13th
14 Gwerthonor Lane 13

Sunday 14th
Clytha Park 6
14 Gwerthonor Lane 13

Sunday 21st
Birch Tree Well 2

Sunday 28th
NEW Highfield Farm, Star Road 17

August

Friday 2nd
NEW Cwmgyst 8

Saturday 3rd
NEW 32/33 High Street 16

Sunday 4th
NEW Cwmgyst 8
NEW 32/33 High Street 16

Sunday 18th
Croesllanfro Farm 7

September

Sunday 1st
NEW Highfield Farm, Star Road 17

Sunday 15th
Old Llangattock Farm 25

October

Sunday 13th
Castell Cwrt 4

By Arrangement

Arrange a personalised garden visit with your club, or group of friends, on a date to suit you. See individual garden entries for full details.

The Alma 1
Birch Tree Well 2
Bryngwyn Manor 3
Castle House 5
Croesllanfro Farm 7
NEW Cwmgyst 8
Dan-y-Warren 9
Glebe House 11
Great Campston 12
NEW Highfield Farm, Star Road 17
Hillcrest 18
Llanover 19
Longhouse Farm 20
Old Llangattock Farm 25
Rockfield Park 28
Sunnyside 29
Woodhaven 35
Woodlands Farm 36
Wyndcliffe Court 37

High Glanau Manor

THE GARDENS

1 THE ALMA

Bully Hole Bottom, Usk Road, Shirenewton, NP16 6SA. Dr Pauline Ruth, 01291 641902, pmruth@hotmail.co.uk. *S-west facing slope overlooking valley. B4235 Usk to Chepstow signposted Bully Hole Bottom. Down hill over bridge up to T junction. Drive straight ahead along track signposted The Alma. Parking in meadow on L.* **Sun 12 May (11-6). Adm £4, chd free. Home-made teas. Visits also by arrangement Mar to June.**

Large and beautiful sheltered SW facing garden, uncommon trees, wisteria, roses and acid loving shrubs. Long border, hot border, productive vegetable garden, old brick outbuildings, fruit cage and vines, wildlife pond, sunset arbour and stream side walk. Drive packed with native daffodils, snowdrops and bluebells in the spring. Wildflower meadow and orchard in development. Sunny terrace for teas. Wheelchair access to level terrace.

2 BIRCH TREE WELL

Upper Ferry Road, Penallt, Monmouth, NP25 4AN. Jill Bourchier, gillian.bourchier@btinternet.com. *4m SW of Monmouth. Approx 1m from Monmouth on B4293, turn L for Penallt & Trelleck. After 2m turn L to Penallt. On entering village turn L at Xrds & follow yellow signs.* **Sun 21 July (2-5.30). Adm £4, chd free. Cream teas. Visits also by arrangement May to Sept for groups of 5 to 30.**

Situated in the heart of the Lower Wye Valley, amongst the ancient habitat of woodland, rocks and streams. These 3 acres are shared with deer, badgers and foxes. A woodland setting with streams and boulders which can be viewed from a lookout tower and a butterfly garden planted with specialist hydrangeas incl many plants to also attract bees and insects. Live music will be played (harp and cello). Children are very welcome (under supervision) with plenty of activities in the form of treasure hunts. Not all areas of garden suitable for wheelchairs but refreshments certainly are!

♿ ✿ ☕

3 BRYNGWYN MANOR

Raglan, NP15 2JH. Peter and Louise Maunder, 01291 691485, louiseviola@live.co.uk. *2m W of Raglan Turn S off B4598 (old A40) Abergavenny-Raglan rd at Croes Bychan. House ¼m up lane* **Visits by arrangement Mar to Oct. Refreshments to be discussed when booking.**

3 acres. Good trees; walled parterre garden; mixed borders; lawns; new shrubbery

♿ 🐕 ☕

4 CASTELL CWRT

Llanelen, Abergavenny, NP7 9LE. Lorna & John McGlynn. *1m S of Abergavenny. From Llanfoist B4629 signed Llanelen. ½m R up single track rd. Approx 500yds past canal, garden entrance 2nd on L. Disabled parking. On combined opening day (June) main parking at Castell Cwrt.* **Sun 2 June (1-5). Combined adm with Middle Ninfa Farm & Bunkhouse £5, chd free. Sun 13 Oct (2-5). Adm £3.50, chd free. Home-made teas.**

Large informal wildlife friendly, family garden on 10 acre small holding with fine views overlooking Abergavenny. Lawns with established trees, shrubs and perennial borders. Soft fruit and vegetable gardens. Woodland and hay meadow walks, chickens and geese, bees, livestock in fields and family pets. Children very welcome, animals to see and space to let off steam. Farm Shop with own produce. Hay meadow in bloom in June, Autumn colour in October. Canal & hill Walking on the doorstep! Some gravel paths.

♿ 🐕 ✿ ☕

5 CASTLE HOUSE

Castle Parade, Usk, NP15 1SD. Mr & Mrs J H L Humphreys, 01291 672563, info@uskcastle.com, www.uskcastle.com. *200yds NE from Usk centre. Access on foot signed to Usk Castle 300yds E from town square, opp Fire Station. Vehicles 400yds (next L) on Castle Parade in Usk.* **Sat 29, Sun 30 June (10-5). Combined adm with Usk Open Gardens £7.50, chd free. Tea in Conservatory or Tithe Barn. Visits also by arrangement May to July for groups of 10 to 30. House also open in May (not Mondays) & BHs,2-5pm; guided tours & refreshment.**

Overlooked by the romantic ruins of Usk Castle which is also open, the gardens were established over 100 years ago, with yew hedges and topiary, long border planted as a pictorial meadow, a croquet lawn and pond. The herb garden has plants that would have been used when the castle was last lived in c.1469. Most areas accessible to wheelchair users.

♿ 🐕 ✿ 🚌 ☕

6 CLYTHA PARK

Abergavenny, NP7 9BW. Jack and Susannah Tenison. *Between Abergavenny (5m) & Raglan (3m). On old A40 signed Clytha at r'abouts either end.* **Sun 14 July (2-5). Adm £5, chd free. Home-made teas.**
Large C18/19 garden around lake with wide lawns and specimen trees, original layout by John Davenport, with C19 arboretum, and H. Avray Tipping influence. Visit the 1790 walled garden and the newly restored greenhouses. Some stalls. Gravel and grass paths.

7 CROESLLANFRO FARM

Groes Road, Rogerstone, Newport, NP10 9GP. Barry & Liz Davies, 01633 894057, lizplants@gmail.com. *3m W of Newport. From M4 J27 take B4591 towards Risca. Take 3rd R, Cefn Walk (also signed 14 Locks Canal Centre). Proceed over bridge, cont ½m to island in middle of rd.* **Sun 18 Aug (1.30-5). Adm £5, chd free. Home-made teas.** **Visits also by arrangement May to Sept.**
Two acres of informal, mass planted perennial borders. Spring and early summer is a tapestry of green concentrating on leaf form and texture. Late summer, early autumn brings the the garden to a finale with an explosion of colour, incl an exotic garden. A barn stands in a large formal courtyard designed on 6 different levels. Children can explore the folly, grotto and try the treasure hunt! Large barn open to the public. Some gravel paths and shallow steps to main area of garden.

8 NEW CWMGYST

Pentre Lane, Abergavenny, NP7 7HE. Matthew and Amie Symes, 07845 942483, amiesymes123@btinternet.com. *Single lane road access. Pass Nevill Hall Hospital on Brecon Rd heading towards Crickhowell. Pass ⅓m Take 1st R turn onto Pentre Rd (concealed entrance). Take 1st L onto Pentre Lane.* **Evening opening Fri 31 May, Sun 2 June, Fri 5, Sun 7 July, Fri 2, Sun 4 Aug (4-8). Adm £5, chd free. Home-made teas.** **Visits also by arrangement May to Sept for groups of up to 20.**
Beautiful and mature secret stone walled garden with a colourful array of perennials, shrubs and shaped trees. Shady corners and lush lawns, with various seating areas to admire each angle. Wonderful views from elevated seating area. Small fish pond and water feature. Very close to Sugar Loaf mountain, with walks and trails. Sugarloaf Vineyard a short walk away. Please advise on arrival if wheelchair access is required.

9 DAN-Y-WARREN

Crickhowell Road, Gilwern, Abergavenny, NP7 0EH. John & Olive Scurr, 01873 830274. *From centre of Gilwern, turn R for Crickhowell & Brecon. Proceed about 1½ miles, entrance is on the R.* **Sat 18, Sun 19 May (2-6). Adm £5, chd free. Home-made teas.** **Visits also by arrangement Feb to July.**
Dan-y-Warren was originally part of the Dan-y-Parc Estate. It borders the River Usk and has large old oaks, a circle of redwoods and other interesting trees. The garden contains a variety of rhododendrons, azaleas, flower borders, an orchard, vegetable beds and a fruit cage. A woodland walk through a dell and newly planted valley goes down to the River Usk. No wheelchair access to woodland walk.

10 GLANNANT Y LLAN

Merthyr Road, Llanfoist, Abergavenny, NP7 9LP. Mr Andrew Kilsby. *To Abergavenny. Follow signs for Llanfoist, in the village turn into village hall car park (sign posted) the garden entrance is direct from car park.* **Sun 9 June (1-5). Combined adm with 7 The Cedars £5, chd free. Light refreshments at Village Hall next to garden.**
A garden with planting mixed in age and style. There are mature trees, the oldest planted as long ago as Victoria's reign. Underplanted in difficult dry shade. Next in age are the generous lawns, one was a tennis court – it now has a cherry tree on the service line. There is a growing collection of climbing roses and clematis now beginning to add impact. The lawns are bordered by herbaceous beds. Wheelchair access is easy from the front gate (100 yds from the car park).

11 GLEBE HOUSE

Llanvair Kilgeddin, Abergavenny, NP7 9BE. Mr & Mrs Murray Kerr, 01873 840422, joanna@amknet.com. *Midway between Abergavenny (5m) & Usk (5m) on B4598.* **Sat 18, Sun 19 May (2-6). Adm £5, chd free. Home-made teas.** **Visits also by arrangement Apr to July.**
Borders bursting with late spring colour including alliums and smyrnium. South facing terrace with wisteria and honeysuckle, decorative veg garden, orchard and wildflower meadow in development. Some topiary and formal hedging in 1½ acre garden set in AONB in Usk valley. Old rectory of St Mary's, Llanfair Kilgeddin which will also be open to view famous Victorian Scraffito Murals. Some gravel and gently sloping lawns.

12 GREAT CAMPSTON

Campston Hill, Pandy, Abergavenny, NP7 8EE. Mr & Mrs C Dunn, 01873 890830, ccdunn@greatcampston.com. *7m NE of Abergavenny. 13m SW of Hereford. 2½m towards Grosmont off A465 at Pandy. Drive on R just before brow of hill. 10m SW of Hereford on A465. Over bridge into Wales, L in Llangua follow rd for 4m. Drive on L.* **Mon 6 May (2-6). Adm £5, chd free. Home-made teas in the garden.** **Visits also by arrangement Mar to Aug for groups of up to 20.**
Pretty 3 acres set in wonderful surroundings with far reaching views, on the edge of the Breacon Beacons National Park. Lots of beautiful spring bulbs, tulips in particular, wide variety of interesting plants and trees, a woodland walk with magnolias, rhododendrons and camellias, stone walls and summerhouse. Set 750ft above sea level on S-facing hillside with spring fed stream feeding pond. All teas are home-made and use freshly made local clotted cream. Wheelchair access to lower section of garden only.

13 14 GWERTHONOR LANE

Gilfach, Bargoed, CF81 8JT. Suzanne & Philip George. *8m N of Caerphilly. A469 to Bargoed, through the T-lights next to school then L filterlane at next T-lights onto Cardiff Rd. First L into Gwerthonor Rd, 4th R into Gwerthonor Lane.* **Sat 13, Sun 14 July (11-6). Adm £3.50, chd free. Light refreshments.**

The garden has a beautiful panoramic view of the Rhymney Valley. A real plantswoman's garden with over 800 varieties of perennials, annuals, bulbs, shrubs and trees. There are numerous rare, unusual and tropical plants combined with traditional and well loved favourites (many available for sale). A pond with a small waterfall adds to the tranquil feel of the garden.

14 HIGH GLANAU MANOR

Lydart, Monmouth, NP25 4AD. Mr & Mrs Hilary Gerrish. *4m SW of Monmouth. Situated on B4293 between Monmouth & Chepstow. Turn R into private rd, ¼m after Craig-y-Dorth turn on B4293.* **Sun 12 May (2-5.30). Adm £6, chd free. Home-made teas.**

Listed Arts and Crafts garden laid out by H Avray Tipping in 1922. Original features incl impressive stone terraces with far reaching views over the Vale of Usk to Blorenge, Skirrid, Sugar Loaf and Brecon Beacons. Pergola, herbaceous borders, Edwardian glasshouse, rhododendrons, azaleas, tulips, orchard with wild flowers. Originally open for the NGS in 1927. Garden guidebook by owner, Helena Gerrish, available to purchase.

15 HIGH HOUSE

Penrhos, NP15 2DJ. Mr & Mrs R Cleeve. *4m N of Raglan. From r'about on A40 at Raglan take exit to Clytha. After 50yds turn R at Llantilio Crossenny. Follow NGS signs, 10mins through lanes.* **Sun 5 May (2-5.30). Combined adm with The Old Vicarage £6, chd free. Home-made teas.**

3 acres of spacious lawns and trees surrounding C16 house (not open) in a beautiful, hidden part of Monmouthshire. South facing terrace and extensive bed of old roses. Swathes of grass with tulips, camassias, wild flowers and far reaching views. Espaliered cherries, pears and scented evergreens in courtyard. Large extended pond, orchard with chickens and ducks, large vegetable garden. Partial wheelchair access, some shallow steps, sloping lawn, gravel courtyard.

16 NEW 32/33 HIGH STREET

Argoed, Blackwood, NP12 0HG. Graeme & Sue Moore. *E into High St, Argoed, from A4048 Blackwood to Tredegar Rd.* **Sat 3, Sun 4 Aug (10-5). Adm £3.50, chd free. Home-made teas.**

An Arts and Crafts garden laid out by the present owners amongst a wide range of hardy flowering plants collected by the previous owner, Angelina Cossey (now gardening in Cornwall), and all now well established. Attractions nearby incl Maes Manor Hotel, with remains of a garden by the celebrated Edwardian garden designer, Thomas H Mawson; and Oakdale, the first garden village in Wales.

17 NEW HIGHFIELD FARM, STAR ROAD

Penperlleni, Pontypool, NP4 0AA. Dr and Mrs Roger and Jenny Lloyd, 01873 880030, jenny.plants@btinternet.com. *4m W of Usk, 6m S of Abergavenny. Turn off the A4042 at the Goytre Arms, over railway bridge, bear L. Garden ½m on R. From Usk off B4598, turn L after Chain bridge, then L at crossroads. Garden 1m on L.* **Sun 23 June, Sun 28 July, Sun 1 Sept (2-5). Adm £4.50, chd free. Home-made teas.** Visits also by arrangement June to Sept for groups of 5+.

What happens when you take a three acre site, an overgrown garden and add in a proper gardener and a plant obsessive? Well, come and see. We'll be three years into the project in 2019 and a new garden is now clearly emerging. It has the classic elements - kitchen garden, small orchard, mixed borders, gravel garden and shrub walk, prairie garden with considered plant choices. Access to almost all garden without steps.

Usk Open Gardens

18 HILLCREST

Waunborfa Road, Cefn Fforest, Blackwood, NP12 3LB. Mr M O'Leary & Mr B Price, 01443 837029, bev.price@mclweb.net. *3m W of Newbridge. Follow A4048 to Blackwood town centre or A469 to Pengam (Glan-y-Nant) T-lights, then NGS signs.* **Sat 25, Sun 26, Mon 27 May (11-6). Adm £4, chd free. Cream teas.** Visits also by arrangement Apr to Oct for groups of up to 30.

A cascade of secluded gardens of distinct character, all within 1½ acres. Magnificent, unusual trees with interesting shrubs and perennials. With choices at every turn, visitors exploring the gardens are well rewarded as hidden delights and surprises are revealed. Well placed seats encourage a relaxed pace to fully appreciate the garden's treasures. Delicious cream teas to be enjoyed. Tulips in April, glorious blooms of the Chilean Firebushes and Handkerchief Tree in May and many trees in their autumnal splendour in October. Lowest parts of garden not accessible to wheelchairs.

19 LLANOVER

nr Abergavenny, NP7 9EF. Mr & Mrs M R Murray, 07753 423635, www.llanovergarden.co.uk. *4m S of Abergavenny, 15m N of Newport, 20m SW Hereford. On A4042 Abergavenny - Cwmbran Rd, in village of Llanover.* **Sun 31 Mar (2-5). Adm £5, chd free. Home-made teas.** Visits also by arrangement Apr to Oct for groups of 20+.

Stunning 15 acre garden laid out in C18. The Rhyd-y-Meirch stream creates sound and movement throughout the garden as it flows into ponds, through the round garden, over cascades and beneath flagstone bridges. Children can run on the lawns, play pooh-sticks along the stream and rills or hide and seek amongst the trees, particularly the numerous early flowering magnolias. The house (not open) is the birthplace of Augusta Waddington, Lady Llanover, C19 patriot, supporter of the Welsh language and traditions. Gwerinyr Gwent will be performing Welsh folk dances during the afternoon in traditional Welsh costume. Lawns, spring bulbs, shrubs and trees. Gravel and grass paths. No disabled WC.

Great Campston

20 LONGHOUSE FARM

Penrhos, Raglan, NP15 2DE. Mr & Mrs M H C Anderson, 01600 780389, m.anderson666@btinternet.com. *Midway between Monmouth & Abergavenny. 4m from Raglan. Off Old Raglan/Abergavenny rd signed Clytha. At Bryngwyn/Great Oak Xrds turn towards Great Oak - follow yellow NGS signs from red phone box down narrow lane.* **Sat 15, Sun 16 June (2-6). Adm £5, chd free. Home-made teas.** Visits also by arrangement June to Sept for groups of 5+.

Hidden 2 acre garden with S-facing terrace, collection of pelargoniums, millrace wall, pond and spacious lawns with extensive views. Colourful and unusual plants in the borders, a malus avenue and a recently revamped productive vegetable garden. A woodland walk is being created with a stream, hidden ponds and massed bluebells in spring.

21 MIDDLE NINFA FARM & BUNKHOUSE

Llanelen, Abergavenny, NP7 9LE. Richard Lewis, 01873 854662, bookings@middleninfa.co.uk, www.middleninfa.co.uk. *2½m SSW Abergavenny. At A465/ B4246 junction, S for Llanfoist, L at mini r'about, B4269 towards Llanelen, ½m R turn up steep lane, over canal. ¾m to Middle Ninfa on R. Main parking at Castel Cwrt.* **Sun 2 June (1-5). Combined adm with Castell Cwrt £5, chd free. Home-made teas at Castel Cwrt.**

Large terraced eco-garden on east slopes of the Blorenge mountain. Vegetable beds, polytunnel, 3 greenhouses, orchard, flower borders, wild flowers. Great views, woodland walks, cascading water and ponds. Paths steep in places, unsuitable for less able. Campsite and small bunkhouse on farm. 5 mins walk uphill to scenic Punchbowl Lake and walks on the Blorenge.

22 MIONE

Old Hereford Road, Llanvihangel Crucorney, Abergavenny, NP7 7LB. Yvonne & John O'Neil. *5m N of Abergavenny. From Abergavenny take*

A465 to Hereford. After 4.8m turn L - signed Pantygelli. Mione is ½m on L. **Fri 21, Sun 23 June, Fri 5, Sun 7 July (10.30-6). Adm £4, chd free. Home-made teas.**
Beautiful garden with a wide variety of established plants, many rare and unusual. Pergola with climbing roses and clematis. Wildlife pond with many newts, insects and frogs. Numerous containers with diverse range of planting. Several seating areas, each with a different atmosphere. Lovely home-made cakes, biscuits and scones to be enjoyed sitting in the garden or pretty summerhouse.

23 ◆ NANT Y BEDD

Grwyne Fawr, Fforest Coal Pit, Abergavenny, NP7 7LY. Sue & Ian Mabberley, 01873 890219, garden@nantybedd.com, www.nantybedd.com. *In Grwyne Fawr valley. From A465 Llanv Crucorney, direction Llanthony, then L to Fforest Coal Pit. At grey telephone box cont for 4½m towards Grwyne Fawr Reservoir.* **For NGS: Sun 26, Mon 27 May (2-6). Adm £5, chd free. Home-made teas. For other opening times and information, please phone, email or visit garden website.**
Blending wild and tame, 6½ acre garden described as 'Absolutely enchanting', 'of the place', 'so imaginative'. Set high in the Black Mountains by the Grwyne Fawr river with places to sit & enjoy the tranquility. An 'amazing mixture and riot of interest' with vegetables and fruit, mature trees and water. 'A lesson in working with the land and listening to what she tells you.' 'Visionary gardening.'. Productive organic vegetable and fruit gardens, stream, forest and river walk, wildflowers, natural swimming pond, tree sculpture, shepherd's hut and eco-features. Ducks, chickens, sheep, pigs, cats. Plants and garden accessories for sale. See www.nantybedd.com for details.

24 THE NELSON GARDEN

Monnow Street, Monmouth, NP25 3EE. Penny Thomas (Leader - Nelson Garden Gardening Group). *Garden accessed via Blestium St. follow yellow NGS signs. Also tourist signs indicating the Nelson Garden.* **Wed 22 May (1.30-5). Adm £4, chd free. Home-made teas.**
This ancient town garden was the site of a real tennis court in C17 and a bowling green by 1718. Roman and Norman remains lie deep beneath the lawn. Admiral Lord Nelson and his entourage took tea here on 19th August 1802. Planting throughout the garden is designed around species that would have been popular in informal gardens of the late C18, early C19.

25 OLD LLANGATTOCK FARM

Llangattock Vibon-Avel, Monmouth, NP25 5NG. Dr Cherry Taylor, 07803 853681. *4m W of Monmouth. Follow B4233 Monmouth to Abergavenny rd, turn R after ~3m, signposted Llangattock. Follow rd for 1m, turning L at the lodge onto dirt track leading to the garden.* **Sun 15 Sept (12-6). Adm £5, chd free. Home-made teas. Visits also by arrangement Mar to Oct for groups of 5 to 20.**
No-dig, organic garden started in late 2015, with unusual plants, plus a large vegetable garden, greenhouses, orchard and field totalling 1¾ acres. No-dig methods have enabled rapid progress. Garden has been used for no-dig courses to demonstrate the method. Far-reaching views of the Blorange, Skirrid and Black Mountains. Steps, slopes, gravel and woodchip paths. By arrangement bookings will incl an explanation of no dig and the development of the garden.

26 THE OLD VICARAGE

Penrhos, Raglan, Usk, NP15 2LE. Mrs Georgina Herrmann. *3m N of Raglan. From A449 take Raglan exit, join A40 & move immed into R lane & turn R across dual carriageway. Follow yellow NGS signs.* **Sun 5 May (2-5.30). Combined adm with High House £6, chd free. Home-made teas at High House.**
Set in the rolling Monmouthshire countryside, the Old Vicarage, a 152yr old (1867) Victorian Gothic house, is surrounded by sweeping lawns with young and mature trees. In addition to traditional and kitchen gardens, there is a parterre with a charming gazebo and a pond area. This gem is not one to be rushed and gets better each year.

27 PARK HOUSE

School Lane, Itton, Chepstow, NP16 6BZ. Professor Bruce & Dr Cynthia Matthews. *From M48 take A466 Tintern. At 2nd r'about turn L B4293 After blue sign Itton turn R Park House is at end of lane. Parking 200m before house. From Devauden B4293 1st L in Itton.* **Sat 4 May (10-5). Combined adm with Woodhaven £6, chd free.**
Approx one acre garden with large vegetable areas and many mature trees, rhododendrons, azaleas, camellias in a woodland setting. Bordering on Chepstow Park Wood. Magnificent views over open country. A few small steps. and irregular paths too narrow for wheelchairs. Disabled parking adjacent to house.

28 ROCKFIELD PARK

Rockfield, Monmouth, NP25 5QB. Mark & Melanie Molyneux, 07803 952027, melmolyneux@yahoo.co.uk. *On arriving in Rockfield village from Monmouth, turn R by phone box. After approx 400yds, church on L. Entrance to Rockfield Park on R, opp church, via private bridge over river.* **Sun 9 June (11-5). Adm £5, chd free. Home-made teas. Visits also by arrangement May & June for groups of up to 30.**
Rockfield Park dates from C17 and is situated in the heart of the Monmouthshire countryside on the banks of the River Monnow. The extensive grounds comprise formal gardens, meadows and orchard, complemented by riverside and woodland walks. Possible to picnic on riverside walks. Main part of gardens can be accessed by wheelchair but not steep garden leading down to river.

29 SUNNYSIDE

The Hendre, Monmouth, NP25 5HQ. Helen & Ralph Fergusson-Kelly, 01600 714928, helen_fk@hotmail.com. *4m W of Monmouth. On B4233 Monmouth to Abergavenny rd.* **Visits by arrangement May to Oct for**

groups of up to 30. Adm £4.50, chd free. Home-made teas.

A sloping ⅓ acre garden on the old Rolls estate. There is much to be enjoyed throughout the year with formal plant and topiary structure. The garden builds to a profusion of colour towards the end of the summer from russet tones of grasses, then bold injections of scarlet, cerise, violet and gold from bulbs, perennials and trees. Quiet seating areas to enjoy views of the Monmouthshire countryside. Some gravel paths.

30 7 THE CEDARS

Llanfoist, Abergavenny, NP7 9LX. Janet Benjamin. *From Abergavenny A4143, signposted Merthyr Llanfoist, at mini r'about take B4246- Llanfoist Blaenavon. Village Hall parking can be found at the 3rd R turn signed Village Hall and Garden Centre.* **Sun 9 June (1-5). Combined adm with Glannant y llan £5, chd free. Light refreshments in Llanfoist Village Hall.**

A garden pairing mature shrubs with herbaceous plants and supported by colourful annuals in pots and baskets. It also has a wild life pond, raised veg beds and a greenhouse. Light refreshments and wonderful cakes served at the adjacent Village Hall where parking is also available. The Cedars is a short walk from the hall and will be sign posted. The garden is open on the same day with Glannant Y Llan also situated in The Cedars as a joint opening. Sloping access road but flat garden suitable for wheelchair access.

31 NEW TRENGROVE HOUSE

Nantyderry, Abergavenny, NP7 9DP. Guin Vaughan and Chris Jofeh. *Approx 4m N of Usk , 6m SE of Abergavenny. From Abergavenny, L off the A4042 after Llanover, signed to Nantyderry. From Usk, B4598 N to Chainbridge, then immediately L after bridge.* **Sun 23 June (1.30-5). Adm £4, chd free. Home-made teas in the garden. Also open Highfield Farm, Star Road.**

Informal 2½ acre country garden developed over 15 yrs along 'right plant, right place' lines. Mixed borders planted for a range of conditions with interesting shrubs, trees, perennials and grasses. The garden is designed to be managed more or less single handed. 1 acre meadow, managed to encourage only naturally occurring species and now supporting many wildflowers and grasses.

32 TY BODA

Upper Llanover, Abergavenny, NP7 9EP. Mike & Mary Shooter. *Off A4042. Follow directions to Upper Llanover (coming from Abergavenny) or Pencroesoped (coming from Cwmbran), narrow lanes. Watch out for signs to Goose & Cuckoo Pub. If you get there, you've past us!* **Sat 15, Sun 16 June (10-5). Adm £5, chd free. Home-made teas.**

A 4 acre hillside garden with stunning views out over the Vale of Usk. Wildlife pond, stream and winding paths through a meadow newly planted with fifteen hundred native trees. Medieval style medicinal herb garden, potager, fernery, orchard, rope swing, stone circle and roses, roses everywhere! Steep slopes and slippery steps, so come prepared! Scrumptious home-made cakes and tea.

GROUP OPENING

33 USK OPEN GARDENS

Twyn Square, Usk, NP15 1BH. 07944 616448, UskOpenGardens@gmail.com, www.uskopengardens.com. *From M4 J24 take A449, proceed 8m N to Usk exit. Free parking signposted in town. Blue badge car parking in main car parks & at Usk Castle. Map of gardens provided with ticket.* **Sat 29, Sun 30 June (10-5). Combined adm with Castle House £7.50, chd free.**

Winner of Wales in Bloom for over 30yrs, Usk is full of hanging baskets and boxes and a wonderful backdrop to around 20 gardens from small cottages packed with colourful and unusual plants to large gardens with brimming herbaceous borders. Romantic garden around the ramparts of Usk Castle. Gardeners' Market with interesting plants. Great day out for all the family with lots of places to eat and drink incl places to picnic. Various cafes, PH and restaurants available for refreshments, plus volunteer groups offering teas and cakes; usually one of the gardens has a pop up Pimms, Prosecco and ice cream bar with a picnic and children's play area by their lake. Gardens allowing well-behaved dogs on leads noted on ticket/map. Usk Castle and School fully accessible but some gardens/areas of gardens are partially wheelchair accessible. Accessibility noted on ticket/map.

34 WENALLT ISAF

Twyn Wenallt, Gilwern, Abergavenny, NP7 0HP. Tim & Debbie Field. *3m W of Abergavenny. Between Abergavenny and Brynmawr. Leave the A465 at Gilwern and follow yellow NGS signs through the village. Sat navs may not be accurate due to recent road changes.* **Sun 26 May (2-5.30). Adm £5, chd free. Home-made teas. Incl gluten free and lactose free cakes.**

A garden of nearly 3 acres designed in sympathy with its surroundings and the challenges of being 650ft up on a N facing hillside. Far reaching views of the magnificent Black Mountains, mature trees, shrubs, borders, productive vegetable garden, small polytunnel, orchard, pigs, chickens, bee hives. Child friendly with plenty of space to run about.

35 WOODHAVEN

Itton, Chepstow, NP16 6BX. Mr & Mrs Kelly, 01291 641219. *Take the B4293 at Chepstow Racecourse r'about at Itton Common triangle, turn L at red telephone box, and then L along the the rd to Shirenewton, Woodhaven is on the L.* **Sat 4 May (10-5). Combined adm with Park House £6, chd free. Home-made teas. Visits also by arrangement May to Sept for groups of 10 to 30. Access by coach is available and parking can be arranged for a coach.**

A modern house built on the site of a former sawmills for the Itton Court Estate. Garden of two-thirds of an acre developed over the last twenty years for all yr round colour and interest. Level front garden and gently sloping rear garden with extensive views over the valley. Lots of seating areas to enjoy the views. Meadow area with bulbs, display of tulips in spring, fruit trees and wild flowers.

36 WOODLANDS FARM

Penrhos, NP15 2LE. Craig Loane & Charles Horsfield, 01600 780203, Woodlandsfarmwales@gmail.com, www.woodlandsfarmwales.com. *3m N of Raglan. From A449 take Raglan exit, join A40 & move immed into R lane & turn R across dual carriageway towards Tregare. Take first L down narrow lane. Follow yellow NGS signs.* **Visits by arrangement Apr to Sept for groups of 10+. Or come to a pop up opening to be published on our and the NGS websites. Adm £5, chd free. Home-made teas in the Pavilion at Woodlands Farm Barns.**

A design led garden that's built to entertain even your reluctant partner. In 2019 there will be a Spring & Summer pop up opening with dates published on the NGS website 2 weeks in advance. The four acres contain rooms & hidden spaces which draw you in. With ponds, viewing platform, hard landscaping, sculptures & more, there's something for all. Weekend pop up openings with wine on Saturday evenings and home-made teas on Sunday afternoon.

NEW 37 WYNDCLIFFE COURT

St Arvans, NP16 6EY. Mr and Mrs Anthony Clay, 07710 138972, jsarahclay@btinternet.com, www.wyndcliffecourt.com. *3m N of Chepstow. Off A466, turn at Wyndcliffe signpost coming from the Chepstow direction.* **Tue 4 June (2-6). Adm £10. Pre-booking essential, please visit www.ngs.org.uk for information and booking. Home-made teas. Visits also by arrangement May to Sept for groups of 10+.**

Exceptional and unaltered garden designed by H. Avray Tipping and Sir Eric Francis in 1922. Arts and Crafts 'Italianate' style. Stone summerhouse, terracing and steps with lily pond. Yew hedging and topiary, sunken garden, rose garden, bowling green and woodland. Walled garden and double tennis court lawn under refurbishment. Rose garden completely replanted to a new design by Sarah Price in 2017. Not suitable for children under 12.

Llanover

© Carole Drake

GWYNEDD & ANGLESEY

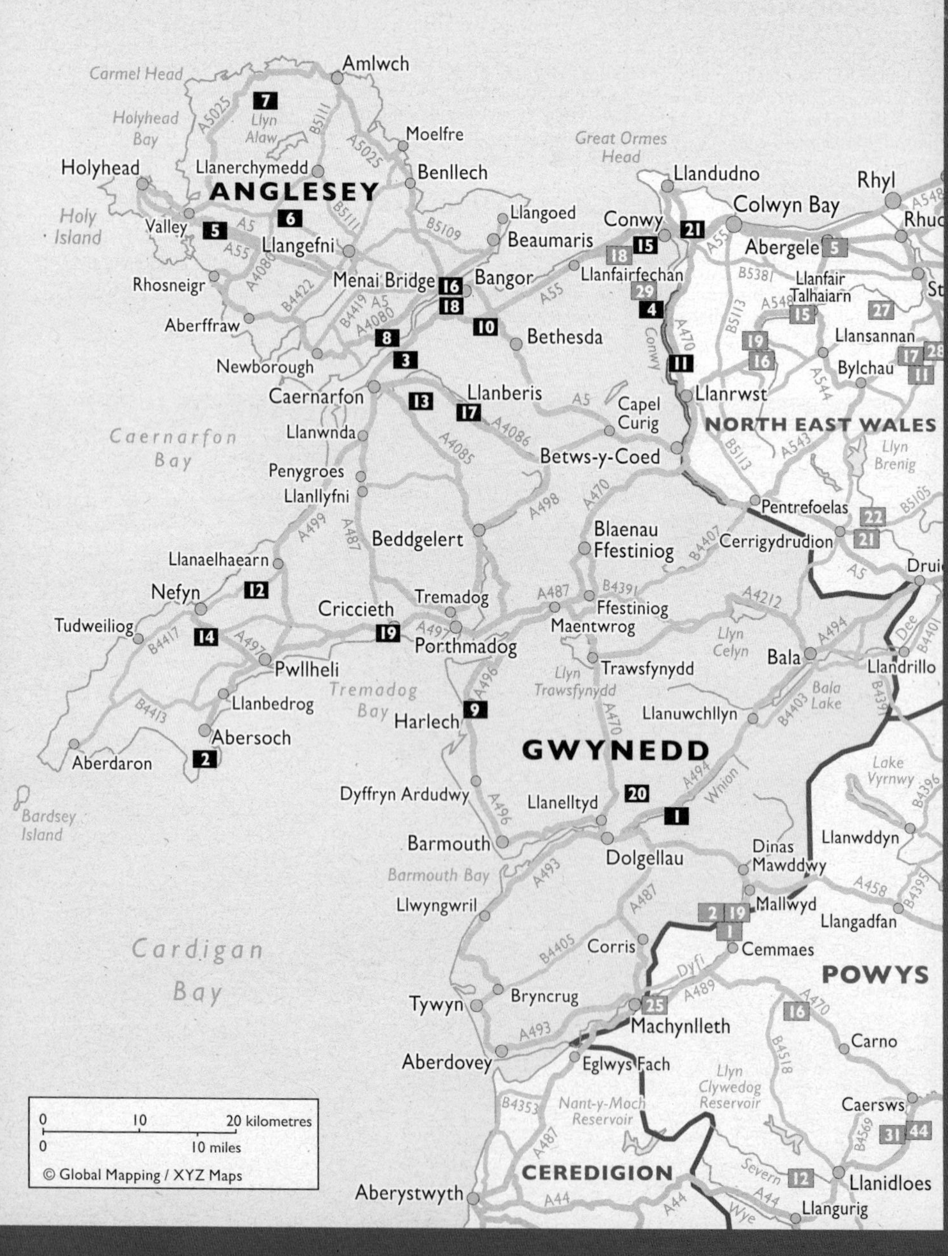

Gwynedd is a county rich in history and outstanding natural beauty. Bordered by the Irish Sea and home to Snowdonia National Park, Gwynedd can boast some of the most impressive landscapes in the UK.

The mountains in Gwynedd are world famous, and have attracted visitors for hundreds of years – the most famous perhaps, was Charles Darwin in 1831. As well as enjoying the tallest peaks in the UK, Gwynedd has fine woodland – from hanging oak forests in the mountains to lush, riverside woods.

Holiday-makers flock to Gwynedd and Anglesey to take advantage of the sandy beaches, and many can enjoy sightings of dolphins and porpoises off the coast.

The gardens of Gwynedd and Anglesey are just as appealing an attraction for visitors. A variety of gardens open for Gwynedd NGS, ranging from Crowrach Isaf a two-acre garden with views of Snowdonia and Cardigan Bay to Ty Capel Ffrwd, a true cottage garden in the Welsh mountains.

So why not escape from the hustle and bustle of everyday life and relax in a beautiful garden? You will be assured of a warm welcome at every garden gate.

Below: Trefaes

Volunteers

Gwynedd & Anglesey County Organiser
Position Vacant – For details please contact hello@ngs.org.uk or 01483 211535

County Treasurer
Nigel Bond
01407 831354
nigel.bond@ngs.org.uk

Assistant County Organisers
Hazel Bond
01407 831354
nigel@cae-newydd.co.uk

Grace Meirion-Jones
01286 831195

Janet Jones
01758 740296
janetcoron@hotmail.co.uk

Delia Lanceley
01286 650517
delia@lanceley.com

OPENING DATES

All entries subject to change. For latest information check **www.ngs.org.uk**

Extended openings are shown at the beginning of the month.

Map locator numbers are shown to the right of each garden name.

April

Every day from Saturday 20th to Sunday 28th
Llyn Rhaeadr 9

Wednesday 24th
Plas Cadnant Hidden Gardens 16

Saturday 27th
Llanidan Hall 8

Sunday 28th
Maenan Hall 11

May

Every day from Sunday 26th
Llyn Rhaeadr 9

Sunday 5th
Llyn Rhaeadr 9

Monday 6th
Llyn Rhaeadr 9

Saturday 18th
Ty Capel Ffrwd 20

Sunday 19th
Bryn Gwern 1
Gilfach 4
Llys-y-Gwynt 10
Ty Capel Ffrwd 20

Sunday 26th
Mynydd Heulog 12
Pant Ifan 13

June

Every day to Sunday 2nd
Llyn Rhaeadr 9

Saturday 1st
◆ Crûg Farm 3

Sunday 2nd
Mynydd Heulog 12
◆ Pensychnant 15

Saturday 22nd
Crowrach Isaf 2
Llanidan Hall 8

Sunday 23rd
Crowrach Isaf 2
Gwyndy Bach 6

Saturday 29th
NEW Pen y Bryn 14
Trefaes 19

Sunday 30th
Llys-y-Gwynt 10
NEW Pen y Bryn 14
Trefaes 19

July

Saturday 6th
Llanidan Hall 8

Sunday 14th
41 Victoria Drive 21

Sunday 21st
◆ Pensychnant 15

Sunday 28th
Bryn Gwern 1
Llanfechell Allotments 7

August

Every day from Sunday 25th
Llyn Rhaeadr 9

Saturday 3rd
Swn-Y-Gwynt 17

Sunday 18th
Maenan Hall 11

September

Sunday 1st
Llyn Rhaeadr 9

Saturday 21st
Treborth Botanic Garden, Bangor University 18

By Arrangement

Arrange a personalised garden visit with your club, or group of friends, on a date to suit you. See individual garden entries for full details.

Bryn Gwern 1
Crowrach Isaf 2
Gilfach 4
Gwaelod Mawr 5
Gwyndy Bach 6
Llanidan Hall 8
Llyn Rhaeadr 9
Llys-y-Gwynt 10
Mynydd Heulog 12
NEW Pen y Bryn 14
Ty Capel Ffrwd 20

Your visits help change lives – we are Hospice UK's largest charitable funder donating more than £5 million to support hospices in local communities since 1996

Plas Cadnant Hidden Gardens

© Val Corbett

THE GARDENS

1 BRYN GWERN

Llanfachreth, Dolgellau, LL40 2DH. H O & P D Nurse, 01341 450 255, antique_pete@btinternet.com. *5m NE of Dolgellau. Do not go to Llanfachreth, stay on Bala road, A 494, 5m from Dolgellau, 14m from Bala.* **Sun 19 May, Sun 28 July (10-5). Adm £4, chd free. Cream teas.** Visits also by arrangement May to Oct.

Sloping 2 acre garden in the hills overlooking Dolgellau with views to Cader Idris, originally wooded but redesigned to enhance its natural features with streams, ponds and imaginative and extensive planting and vibrant colour. The garden is now a haven for wildlife with hedgehogs and 26 species of birds feeding last winter as well as being home to ducks, dogs and cats. Stone mason at work and items for sale or orders taken. Wheelchair access to main area of garden but only when dry. Not suitable for mobility scooters.

2 CROWRACH ISAF

Bwlchtocyn, LL53 7BY. Margaret & Graham Cook, 01758 712860, crowrach_isaf@hotmail.com. *1½m SW of Abersoch. Follow rd through Abersoch & Sarn Bach, L at sign for Bwlchtocyn for ½m until junction & no-through rd - TG Holiday Complex. Turn R, parking 50 metres on R.* **Sat 22, Sun 23 June (1-5). Adm £4, chd free. Cream teas.** Visits also by arrangement May to Sept for groups of 20+.

2 acre plot incl 1 acre fenced against rabbits, developed from 2000, incl island beds, windbreak hedges, vegetable garden, wild flower area and wide range of geraniums, shrubs and herbaceous perennials. Views over Cardigan Bay and Snowdonia. Grass and gravel paths, some gentle slopes. Parking at garden for disabled visitors.

3 ◆ CRÛG FARM

Griffiths Crossing, Caernarfon, LL55 1TU. Mr & Mrs B Wynn-Jones, 01248 670232, sue@crug-farm.co.uk, www.crug-farm.co.uk. *2m NE of Caernarfon. ¼m off main A487 Caernarfon to Bangor rd. Follow signs from r'about.* **For NGS: Sat 1 June (9.30-4.30). Adm £3.50, chd free. Home-made teas.** For other opening times and information, please phone, email or visit garden website.

3 acres; grounds to old country house (not open). Gardens filled with choice, unusual plants collected by the Wynn-Jones. Woodland garden with shade loving plants, many not seen in cultivation before. Walled garden with more wonderful collections growing. Chelsea Gold Medallists and winners of the President's Award among other many prestigious awards. Partial wheelchair access.

4 GILFACH

Rowen, Conwy, LL32 8TS. James & Isoline Greenhalgh, 01492 650216, isolinegreenhalgh@btinternet.com. *4m S of Conwy. At Xrds 100yds E of Rowen S towards Llanrwst, past Rowen School on L, turn up 2nd drive on L.* **Sun 19 May (2-5.30). Adm £3.50, chd free. Home-made teas.** Visits also by arrangement Apr to Aug. Coffee/biscuits(am), tea/cake (pm).

1 acre country garden on S-facing slope with magnificent views of the River Conwy and mountains; set in 35 acres of farm and woodland. Collection of mature shrubs is added to yearly; woodland garden, herbaceous border and small pool. Spectacular panoramic view of the Conwy Valley and the mountain range of the Carneddau. Classic cars. Large coaches can park at bottom of steep drive, disabled visitors can be driven to garden by the owner.

5 GWAELOD MAWR

Caergeiliog, Anglesey, LL65 3YL. Tricia Coates, 01407 740080, patriciacoates36@gmail.com. *6m E of Holyhead. ½m E of Caergeiliog. From A55 J4. r'about 2nd exit signed Caergeiliog. 300yds, Gwaelod Mawr is 1st house on L.* **Visits by arrangement May to Aug. Adm £4, chd free.**

2 acre garden created by owners over 20 yrs with lake, large rock outcrops and palm tree area. Spanish style patio and laburnum arch lead to sunken garden and wooden bridge over lily pond with fountain and waterfall. Peaceful Chinese orientated garden offering contemplation. Separate Koi carp pond. Abundant seating throughout. Mainly flat, with gravel and stone paths, no wheelchair access to sunken lily pond area.

6 GWYNDY BACH

Tynlon, Llandrygarn, LL65 3AJ. Keith & Rosa Andrew, 01407 720651, keithandrew.art@gmail.com. *5m W of Llangefni. From Llangefni take B5109 towards Bodedern, cottage exactly 5m out on L. Postcode good for SatNav.* **Sun 23 June (11-4.30). Adm £3.50, chd free. Home-made teas.** Visits also by arrangement May to July for groups of 5+.

¾ acre artist's garden, set amidst rugged Anglesey landscape. Romantically planted in informal intimate rooms with interesting rare plants and shrubs, box and yew topiary, old roses and Japanese garden with large Koi pond (deep water, children must be supervised). Gravel entrance to garden.

7 LLANFECHELL ALLOTMENTS

Brynddu Road, Llanfechell, Amlwch, LL68 0PU. Mike Harris, Secretary. *5 miles NW of Amlwch, 1 mile S of Cemaes on Anglesey. From Amlwch on A5025 take L just before Cemaes: from Holyhead on A5025 take R just before Cemaes: from Llangefni, take R at Sportsman's Lodge in Rhosgoch then follow NGS signs.* **Sun 28 July (10-4). Adm £3.50, chd free. Teas in café (open 11am-3pm).**

Established just a few years ago and building on initial success, we now have 18 plots with sheds/greenhouses, and grow a variety of vegetables, soft fruit and flowers. The walled garden at Brynddu, the C17 manor house home of Anglesey diarist W Bulkeley also open. Visit Llanfechell church and/or take a short local walk (maps available at the community shop/cafe) to complete your visit. Cafe open 11am to 3pm.

Llanidan Hall

8 LLANIDAN HALL

Brynsiencyn, LL61 6HJ. Mr J W Beverley (Head Gardener), 07759 305085, Work.beverley@btinternet.com. *5m E of Llanfair Pwll. From Llanfair PG follow A4080 towards Brynsiencyn for 4m. After Hooton's farm shop on R take next L, follow lane to gardens.* **Sat 27 Apr, Sat 22 June, Sat 6 July (10-4). Adm £3.50, chd free. Tea. Visits also by arrangement Apr to Aug for groups of 5+. No evening visits. Donation to CAFOD.**

Walled garden of 1¾ acres. Physic and herb gardens, ornamental vegetable garden, herbaceous borders, water features and many varieties of old roses. Sheep, rabbits and hens to see. Children must be kept under supervision. Well behaved dogs on leads welcome. Llanidan Church will be open for viewing. The walled garden will be open early in the season for viewing of the spring bulbs. No plant sale at spring opening. Hard gravel paths, gentle slopes.

9 LLYN RHAEADR

15 Parc Bron-y-Graig, Centre of Harlech, LL46 2SR. Mr D R Hewitt & Miss J Sharp, 01766 780224. *From A496 take B4573 into Harlech, take turning to main car parks S of town, L past overspill car park, garden 75yds on R.* **Daily Sat 20 Apr to Sun 28 Apr (2-5). Sun 5, Mon 6 May (2-5). Daily Sun 26 May to Sun 2 June (2-5). Daily Sun 25 Aug to Sun 1 Sept (2-5). Adm £3.50, chd free. Visits also by arrangement Mar to Oct for groups of up to 30. Donation to W.W.F.**

Landscaped hillside garden blending natural areas with garden plants, shrubs and trees with wildlife, small lake with many species of unusual ducks, fish and wildlife ponds, waterfalls, woodland, gazebos, rockeries, lawns, borders, snowdrops, daffodils, bluebells, ferns, heathers, camellias, azaleas, Rhododendrons, wild flowers. Good paths and seating views of Tremadog Bay, Lleyn Peninsula. Waterfowl collection. Pond fish collection.

10 LLYS-Y-GWYNT

Pentir Road, Llandygai, Bangor, LL57 4BG. Jennifer Rickards & John Evans, 01248 353863. *3m S of Bangor. 300yds from Llandygai r'about at J11, A5 & A55, just off A4244. Follow signs for services (Gwasanaethau). Turn off at no through rd sign, 50yds beyond. Do not use SatNav.* **Sun 19 May, Sun 30 June (11-4). Adm £4, chd free. Home-made teas. Visits also by arrangement. £5 to inc tea/ coffee & biscuits.**

Interesting, harmonious and very varied 2 acre garden incl magnificent views of Snowdonia. An exposed site incl Bronze Age burial cairn. Winding paths and varied levels planted to create shelter, yr-round interest, microclimates and varied rooms. Ponds, waterfall, bridge and other features use local materials and craftspeople. Wildlife encouraged, well organised compost. Good family garden.

11 MAENAN HALL

Maenan, Llanrwst, LL26 0UL. The Hon Mr & Mrs Christopher Mclaren. *2m N of Llanrwst. On E side of A470, ¼m S of Maenan Abbey Hotel.* **Sun 28 Apr, Sun 18 Aug (10.30-4.30). Adm £4, chd free. Light refreshments. Donation to Wales Air Ambulance.**

A superbly beautiful 4 hectares on the slopes of the Conwy Valley, with dramatic views of Snowdonia, set amongst mature hardwoods. Both the upper part, with sweeping lawns, ornamental ponds and retaining walls, and the bluebell carpeted woodland dell contain copious specimen shrubs and trees, many originating at Bodnant. Magnolias, rhododendrons, camellias, pieris, cherries and hydrangeas, amongst many others, make a breathtaking display. Treasure Hunt (£1) on both open days. Upper part of garden accessible but with fairly steep slopes.

12 MYNYDD HEULOG

Llithfaen, Pwllheli, LL53 6PA. Mrs Christine Jackson, 01758 750400, christine.jackson007@btinternet.com. *From A499 take B4417 road at r'about signed Nefyn, approx 3m enter Llithfaen, 1st R turn opp chapel. Follow NGS signs, garden last property on R, limited parking.* **Sun 26 May, Sun 2 June (10.30-3). Adm £3.50, chd free. Cream teas.** Visits also by arrangement. Donation to Dog's Trust.

Mynydd Heulog is an C18 stone cottage set in approx. 1 acre of sloping garden with amazing views over the Lleyn and Cardigan Bay. Gradually being developed over 25 years, the garden is now an eclectic mix of mature trees, shrubs, perennials and exotics. Features incl arches, statues, bridges, summer house and shepherds hut. Large terrace and verandah with views and secret seating areas.

13 PANT IFAN

Ceunant, LLanrug, Caernarfon, LL55 4HX. Mrs Delia Lanceley. *2m E of Caernarfon. From Llanrug take rd opp old PO between Premier Store & Monumental Mason. Straight across at next Xrds. Then 3rd turn on L at Xrds. Pant Ifan 2nd house on L.* **Sun 26 May (11-5). Adm £4, chd free. Home-made teas.**

2 acre mix of formal and wildlife garden set around farmhouse and yard. Herbaceous borders, shrubs, vegetables, fruit, ponds and recently planted woodland. Field walks, sitting areas in the sun or shade. Poultry, ducks, geese, donkeys, horse and two ponies, greenhouses and poly tunnel. Deep water, children must be supervised at all times. Wheelchair users can access yard and teas.

14 NEW PEN Y BRYN

Boduan, Pwllheli, LL53 8UY. Sandra and Stephen Deer, 01758 721436, stevedeer@hotmail.com. *4½m NW of Pwllheli. A497 Pwllheli to Nefyn, in 4m pass lay by & AA box on R. 200yds on take L turn. Signs will be situated approx 300 yards along lane. B4354 from Y Ffor, L at T junction, turn 1st R & follow signs.* **Sat 29, Sun 30 June (11-5). Adm £3.50, chd free. Home-made teas.** Visits also by arrangement Apr to Aug for groups of 5 to 10. Not Saturdays.

A ¾ acre garden with eclectic mix of wildlife & lily ponds, gravel gardens, mixed borders, small orchard, dell & bog garden, new potager garden & fountain, interlaced with meandering gravel paths & brick steps to accommodate the gentle slope. Mature shrubs & trees create secluded, intimate seating areas to enjoy the tranquillity & glimpses of distant views to the coast, Garn Fadryn & Garn Boduan. Partial wheelchair access to part of the garden but only if the ground is dry. Please contact us beforehand and we will do our best to accommodate.

Gilfach

Ty Capel Ffrwd

15 ◆ PENSYCHNANT

Sychnant Pass, Conwy, LL32 8BJ. Pensychnant Foundation; Wardens Julian Thompson & Anne Mynott, 01492 592595, jpt.pensychnant@btinternet.com, www.pensychnant.co.uk. *2½m W of Conwy at top of Sychnant Pass. From Conwy: L into Upper Gate St; after 2½m Pensychnant's Dr signed on R. From Penmaenmawr: fork R, up pass, after walls U turn L into drive.* **For NGS: Sun 2 June, Sun 21 July (10-5). Adm £3.50, chd free. Home-made teas.** For other opening times and information, please phone, email or visit garden website.

Wildlife Garden. Diverse herbaceous cottage garden borders surrounded by mature shrubs, banks of rhododendrons, ancient and Victorian woodlands. 12 acre woodland walks with views of Conwy Mountain and Sychnant. Woodland birds. Picnic tables, archaelogical trail on mountain. A peaceful little gem. Large Victorian Arts and Crafts house (open) with art exhibition. Partial wheelchair access, please phone for advice.

♿ ✿ ☕

16 PLAS CADNANT HIDDEN GARDENS

Cadnant Road, Menai Bridge, LL59 5NH. Mr Anthony Tavernor, 01248 717174, plascadnantgardens@gmail.com, www.plascadnantgardens.co.uk. *½m E of Menai Bridge. Take A545 & leave Menai Bridge heading for Beaumaris, then follow brown tourist information signs.* **Wed 24 Apr (12-5). Adm £7.50, chd £2. Light lunches and refreshments available to purchase all day.** Donation to Wales Air Ambulance; Anglesey Red Squirrel Trust; Menai Bridge Community Heritage Trust.

Early C19 picturesque garden undergoing restoration since 1996. Valley gardens with waterfalls, large ornamental walled garden, woodland and early pit house. Recently created Alpheus water feature and Ceunant (Ravine) which gives visitors a more interesting walk featuring unusual moisture loving Alpines. Restored area following flood damage. New guidebook available. Visitor centre open. Partial wheelchair access to parts of gardens. Some steps, gravel paths, slopes. Access statement available. Accessible Tea Room and WC.

♿ ✿ 🚌 🛏 ☕

17 SWN-Y-GWYNT

High Street, Llanberis, Caernarfon, LL55 4EN. Mr Keith Chadwick. *Foot of Snowdon. Turn off the A4086, follow NGS sign onto Llanberis High St then a green sign for Swn-y-Gwynt with the driveway entrance and private car park.* **Sat 3 Aug (10.30-5). Adm £3.50, chd free. Home-made teas.**

A S-facing terraced garden with dramatic views of Snowdon and surrounding hills. Steep slate steps lead to the garden comprising of a variety of conifers, mature acers, azaleas, rose bed and herbaceous perennial border with a variety of spring bulbs complemented by hellebores and ferns. There is also a secluded small pond area leading onto slate steps towards a Scots pine terraced area. Children must be supervised at all times.

🐕 ✿ ☕

18 TREBORTH BOTANIC GARDEN, BANGOR UNIVERSITY

Treborth, Bangor, LL57 2RQ. Natalie Chivers, treborth.bangor.ac.uk. *On the outskirts of Bangor towards Anglesey. Approach Menai Bridge either from Upper Bangor on A5 or leave A55 J9 & travel towards Bangor for 2m. At Antelope Inn r'bout turn L just before entering Menai Bridge.* **Sat 21 Sept (10-1). Adm £3, chd free. Home-made teas. Guided walks.**

Owned by Bangor University and used as a resource for teaching, research, public education and enjoyment. Treborth comprises planted borders, species rich natural grassland, ponds, arboretum, Chinese garden, ancient woodland, and a rocky shoreline habitat. Six glasshouses provide specialised environments for tropical, temperate, orchid and carnivorous plant collections. Partnered with National Botanic Garden of Wales to champion Welsh horticulture, protect wildlife and extol the virtues of growing plants for food, fun, health and wellbeing. Wheelchair access to some glasshouses and part of the garden. Woodland path is surfaced but most of the borders only accessed over grass.

♿ 🐕 ✿ 🚌 ☕

19 TREFAES

Y Maes, Criccieth, LL52 0AE. Patricia Stephens. *On entering Criccieth High St take the Caernarfon rd. The garden is on the R at the top of the hill looking down on the green with a front hedge. Roadside parking by house & public car park.* **Sat 29, Sun 30 June (2-5). Adm £3, chd free. Light refreshments.**

The garden is on three levels, the bottom level has a lawn with borders, an apple tree and a large display of container pots set on slate chippings and flagstones and a rockery. The centre has a pond, a raised vegetable bed and an island bed. The top has a lawn surrounded by herbaceous borders with trees and shrubs.

20 TY CAPEL FFRWD

Llanfachreth, Dolgellau, LL40 2NR. Revs Mary & George Bolt, 01341 422006, georgebolt34@gmail.com. *4m NE of Dolgellau, 18m SW of Bala. From Dolgellau 4m up hill to Llanfachreth. Turn L at War Memorial. Follow lane ½m to chapel on R. Park & walk down lane past chapel to cottage.* **Sat 18 May (11-5). Sun 19 May (11-5), also open Bryn Gwern. Adm £3.50, chd free. Cream teas. Visits also by arrangement May to Sept for groups of up to 10.**

True cottage garden in Welsh mountains. Azaleas, rhododendrons, acers; large collection of aquilegia. Many different hostas give added strength to spring bulbs and corms. Stream flowing through the garden, 10ft waterfall and on through a small woodland bluebell carpet. For summer visitors there is a continuous show of colour with herbaceous plants, roses, clematis and lilies, incl Cardiocrinum giganteum. Harp will be played in the garden.

21 41 VICTORIA DRIVE

Llandudno Junction, LL31 9PF. Allan and Eirwen Evans. *A55 J18. From Bangor 1st exit, from Colwyn Bay 2nd exit, A546 to Conwy. Next r'about 3rd exit then 1st Left.* **Sun 14 July (2-4). Adm £3, chd free. Home-made teas.**

A very interesting small urban garden, offering so many creative ideas incl growing exhibition sweet peas and dahlias also colourful bedding plants and other shrubs and herbaceous plants. Friendly hosts with a nice tea and cake stall.

Your visits help change lives - your generosity helps Marie Curie fund nurses to care for people night and day in their homes, with donations of more than £8.8 million

41 Victoria Drive

NORTH EAST WALES

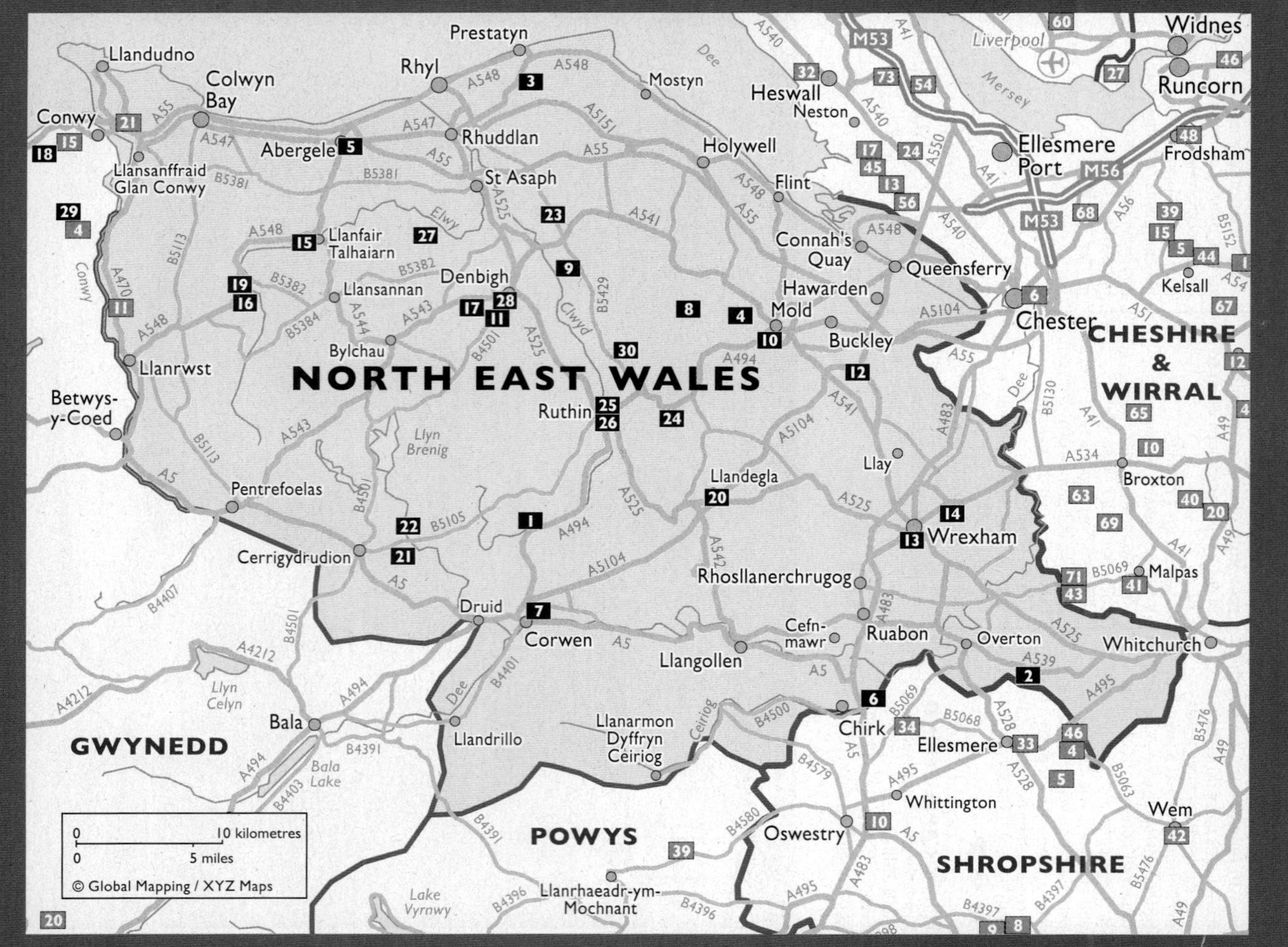

With its diversity of countryside from magnificent hills, seaside vistas and rolling farmland, North East Wales offers a wide range of gardening experiences.

Our gardens offer a wealth of designs and come in all shapes and sizes, ranging from abundant plantsmen's gardens to informal natural hillside planting. Visitors will have something to see from the frost-filled days of February through till the magnificent colourful days of autumn.

The majority of our gardens are within easy reach of North West England, and being a popular tourist destination make an excellent day out for all the family.

Come and enjoy the beauty and the variety of the gardens of North East Wales with the added bonus of a delicious cup of tea and a slice of cake. Our garden owners await your visit.

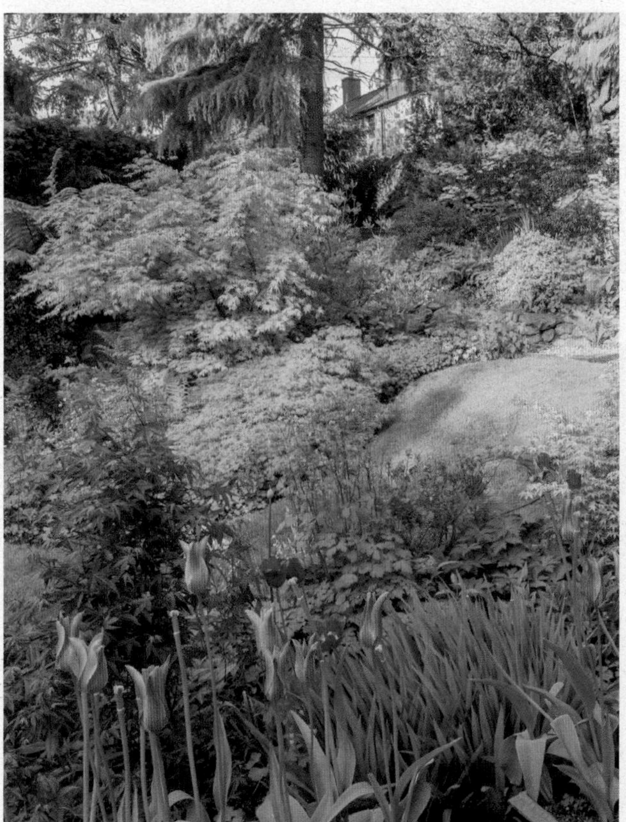

Volunteers

County Organiser
Jane Moore
07769 046317
jane.moore@ngs.org.uk

County Treasurer
Iris Dobbie
01745 886730
iris.dobbie@ngs.org.uk

Publicity
Trish Morris
01745 550121
trishmorris61@yahoo.co.uk

Booklet Co-ordinator
Roy Hambleton
01352 740206
royhambleton@btinternet.com

Assistant County Organisers
Fiona Bell
07813 087797
bell_fab@hotmail.com

Carol Perkins
07808 988556
carolperkins24@yahoo.co.uk

Left: Ty Hwnt Yr Afon

OPENING DATES

All entries subject to change. For latest information check **www.ngs.org.uk**

Map locator numbers are shown to the right of each garden name.

February

Snowdrop Festival

Wednesday 13th
Clwydfryn 9

Thursday 14th
Glog Ddu 16

Sunday 17th
Glog Ddu 16
Hafodunos Hall 19

Thursday 21st
Glog Ddu 16

Wednesday 27th
Aberclwyd Manor 1

March

Wednesday 13th
Aberclwyd Manor 1
Clwydfryn 9

Wednesday 27th
Aberclwyd Manor 1

April

Wednesday 10th
Aberclwyd Manor 1
Clwydfryn 9

Wednesday 24th
Aberclwyd Manor 1

May

Sunday 5th
Ty Hwnt Yr Afon 29

Wednesday 8th
Aberclwyd Manor 1
Clwydfryn 9

Sunday 19th
NEW Erlas Victorian Walled Garden 14

Wednesday 22nd
Aberclwyd Manor 1

Saturday 25th
Hafodunos Hall 19

Monday 27th
Garthewin 15

June

Saturday 1st
Brynkinalt Hall 6

Wednesday 5th
Aberclwyd Manor 1

Wednesday 12th
Clwydfryn 9

Sunday 16th
Scott House 26

Wednesday 19th
Aberclwyd Manor 1

Saturday 22nd
33 Bryn Twr and Lynton 5

Sunday 23rd
33 Bryn Twr and Lynton 5
Gwaenynog 17

Sunday 30th
The Beeches 2
Ruthin Town Gardens 25

July

Wednesday 3rd
Aberclwyd Manor 1

Wednesday 10th
Clwydfryn 9

Saturday 13th
Cilcain Village Gardens 8

Sunday 14th
The Cottage Nursing Home 10
Llandegla Village Gardens 20

Wednesday 17th
Aberclwyd Manor 1

Sunday 28th
Caereuni 7

Wednesday 31st
Aberclwyd Manor 1

August

Sunday 4th
NEW Erddig Allotments 13

Wednesday 14th
Aberclwyd Manor 1

Sunday 25th
Caereuni 7

Monday 26th
Caereuni 7

Wednesday 28th
Aberclwyd Manor 1

Saturday 31st
Brynkinalt Hall 6

September

Wednesday 11th
Aberclwyd Manor 1

Sunday 15th
NEW Erlas Victorian Walled Garden 14

Sunday 29th
Caereuni 7

By Arrangement

Arrange a personalised garden visit with your club, or group of friends, on a date to suit you. See individual garden entries for full details.

Aberclwyd Manor 1
5 Birch Grove 3
Bryn Bellan 4
33 Bryn Twr and Lynton 5
Dolhyfryd 11
Dove Cottage 12
Garthewin 15
Gwel Yr Ynys 18
NEW Neuadd Wen 21
The Old Rectory 22
Pen Y Graig Bach 23
Plas Y Nant 24
Tal-y-Bryn Farm 27
Ty Brombil 28
Ty Hwnt Yr Afon 29
Wylan 30

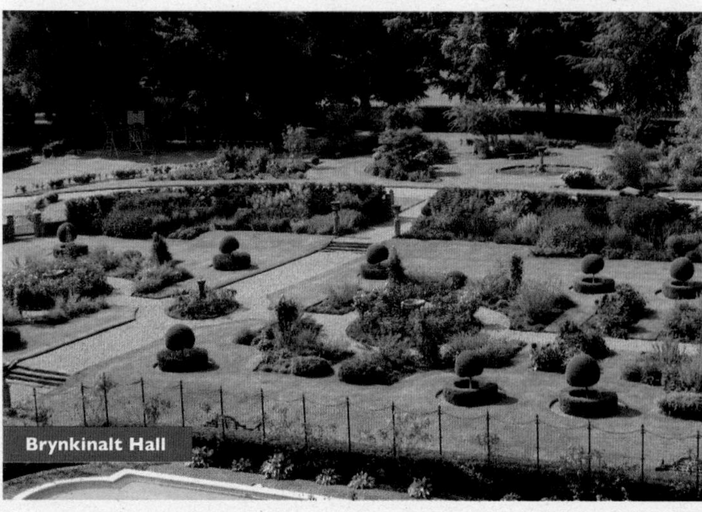
Brynkinalt Hall

THE GARDENS

Tal-y-Bryn Farm

1 ABERCLWYD MANOR

Derwen, Corwen, LL21 9SF. Miss Irene Brown & Mr G Sparvoli, 01824 750431, irene662010@live.com. *7m from Ruthin. Travelling on A494 from Ruthin to Corwen. At Bryn SM Service Station turn R, follow sign to Derwen. Aberclwyd gates on L before Derwen. Do not follow sat nav directions .* **Wed 27 Feb, Wed 13, Wed 27 Mar, Wed 10, Wed 24 Apr, Wed 8, Wed 22 May, Wed 5, Wed 19 June, Wed 3, Wed 17, Wed 31 July, Wed 14, Wed 28 Aug, Wed 11 Sept (11-4). Adm £3.50, chd free. Cream teas. Visits also by arrangement Feb to Dec for groups of 10 to 30.**

4 acre garden on a sloping hillside overlooking the Upper Clwyd Valley. The garden has many mature trees underplanted with snowdrops, fritillaries and cyclamen. An Italianate garden of box hedging lies below the house and shrubs, ponds, perennials, roses and an orchard are also to be enjoyed within this cleverly structured area. Mass of cyclamen in Sept. Abundance of Spring flowers. Cyclamen in August/September. Snowdrops in February. Mostly flat with some steps and slopes.

2 THE BEECHES

Vicarage Lane, Penley, Wrexham, LL13 0NH. Stuart & Sue Hamon. *Western edge of village. From Overton 1st L after 30mph sign towards Adrefelyn. From Whitchurch go along A539 through village & turn R just after church, to Adrefelyn. N.B. SatNavs may show Vicarage Lane as Hollybush Lane.* **Sun 30 June (1-5). Adm £4, chd free. Home-made teas.**

The garden surrounds an 1841 former vicarage and extends to 3½ acres. It has been redesigned to create an attractive open garden laid mainly to lawn with a mixture of mature and younger specimen trees and shrubs. There are shrub, rose and herbaceous beds together with a productive vegetable and fruit area. The walled courtyard has tender plants incl many varieties of agapanthus and hostas. We are delighted to announce that Bernard Porter, The Head Gardener at Bridgemere Nursery in south Cheshire, will be on hand to answer visitors gardening questions. Bernard has over 30yrs professional gardening experience incl running the 6 acre, award winning, garden at Bridgemere. A mostly flat garden with gravelled paths. Grass is usually firm allowing easy access. Courtyard access has three very shallow steps.

3 5 BIRCH GROVE

Woodland Park, Prestatyn, LL19 9RH. Mrs Iris Dobbie, 01745 886730, iris.dobbie@ngs.org.uk. *A547 from Rhuddlan turn up The Avenue, Woodland Park after railway bridge 1st R into Calthorpe Dr, 1st L Birch Gr. 10 mins walk from town centre - at top of high st, turn R and L onto The Avenue.* **Visits by arrangement May to Sept for groups of up to 20. Adm £3, chd free.**

A well established town garden on three sides of this property. The gardens consist of a variety of borders incl woodland, grass, herbaceous, alpine, shrub, drought, tropical and a simulated bog garden with a small pond. The more formal front garden is lawned with borders of mixed colourful planting and box balls. A small greenhouse is fully used for propagation and storing tender plants. Gravel drive, few steps.

4 BRYN BELLAN

Bryn Road, Gwernaffield, CH7 5DE. Gabrielle Armstrong & Trevor Ruddle, 01352 741806, gabrielle@indigoawnings.co.uk. *2m W of Mold. Leave A541 at Mold on Gwernaffield Rd (Dreflan), ½m after Mold derestriction signs turn R to Rhydymwyn & Llynypandy. Bryn Bellan is 300yards along on RHS. Parking is available in courtyard.* **Visits by arrangement Mar to Sept for groups of 5+. Adm £6, chd free. Please discuss refreshments when making arrangements to visit.**

This tranquil, elegant garden is perfect for morning coffee, afternoon tea or evening glass of wine with nibbles. A partly walled upper garden has a circular sunken lawn featuring a Sequoia and white and green themed mixed borders. The lower garden has an ornamental cutting garden, two perennial borders, an orchard and bijou potting shed. Many spring bulbs, iris, peonies, hydrangeas and cyclamen. A very photogenic garden, pre shoot visits and shoots by appointment. Some gravel paths.

5 33 BRYN TWR AND LYNTON

Lynton, Highfield Park, Abergele, LL22 7AU. Mr & Mrs Colin Knowlson and Bryn Roberts & Emma Knowlson-Roberts, 07712 623836, apk@slaters.com. *From A55 heading W take slip rd into Abergele town centre. Turn L at 2nd set of T-lights signed Llanfair TH, 3rd rd on L. For SatNav use LL22 8DD.* **Sat 22, Sun 23 June (1-5). Adm £4, chd free. Home-made teas.** Visits also by arrangement in June.

More changes have been made to the gardens for 2019, mixed herbaceous and shrub borders, some trees plus many unusual plants. Lawn at Lynton replaced with slate chips and more planting. Garage with interesting fire engine; cars and memorabilia; greenhouse over water capture system; surrounding planting coming along nicely, hens now kept at Bryn Twr. Partial wheelchair access.

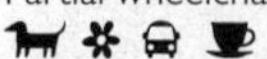

6 BRYNKINALT HALL

Brynkinalt, Chirk, Wrexham, LL14 5NS. Iain & Kate Hill-Trevor, www.brynkinalt.co.uk. *6m N of Oswestry, 10m S of Wrexham. Come off A5/A483 and take B5070 into Chirk village. Turn into Trevor Rd (beside St Mary's Church). Continue past houses on R. Turn R on bend into Estate Gates. N.B. Do not use postcode with SatNav.* **Sat 1 June, Sat 31 Aug (12-4). Adm £5, chd free. Home-made teas.**

5 acre ornamental woodland shrubbery, overgrown until recently, now cleared and replanted, rhododendron walk, historic ponds, well, grottos, ha-ha and battlements, new stumpery, ancient redwoods and yews. Also 2 acre garden beside Grade II* house (see website for opening), with modern rose and formal beds, deep herbaceous borders, pond with shrub/mixed beds, pleached limes and hedge patterns. Home of the first Duke of Wellington's grandmother and Sir John Trevor, Speaker of House of Commons. Stunning Rhododendrons and formal West Garden. Partial wheelchair access. Gravel paths in West Garden and grass paths and slopes in shrubbery.

7 CAEREUNI

Ffordd Ty Cerrig, Godre'r Gaer, Corwen, LL21 9YA. Mr S Williams. *1m N of Corwen. A5 Corwen to Bala rd, turn R at T-lights onto A494 to Chester. 1st R after lay by. House ¼m on L.* **Sun 28 July, Sun 25, Mon 26 Aug, Sun 29 Sept (2-5). Adm £4, chd free.**

A plants man`s garden of rare trees, shrubs, topiary and containers of tender plants set in a quirky themed much loved ⅓ acre garden, incl a Japanese smoke water feature & Italian Tuscany conifers. Also a seaside beach with wild grass sand plumes, a welsh gold mine, old ruin & a Chinese peace garden. There is a Mexican Chapel, 1950's petrol garage, wood mans lodge & a new Harry Potter Tower. No teas at Caeruni but Glyndwr Plant Centre and Coffee Shop LL12 9BU approx 1m from garden.

GROUP OPENING

8 CILCAIN VILLAGE GARDENS

Cilcain, CH7 5PL. *Cilcain is signed from A541 and from the A494 via Tafarn-Y-Gelyn.* **Sat 13 July (11-5). Combined adm £6, chd free. Light refreshments in the Village Hall.**

DELFRYN
Mr & Mrs Phil & Angela Parsons.

6 LÔN CILAN
Valerie & Philip Higgins.

NYTH Y WENNOL
Mr & Mrs Keith & Margaret Humphreys.

NEW **STAC LEE**
Sharon Davies & Ian Gough.

TY MAWR
Mr & Mrs Peter & Susan Richards.

NEW **VILLAGE HALL GARDEN**
Ms Valerie Thompson.

You are invited to enjoy six gardens in the pretty village of Cilcain to raise funds for the NGS and their Village Hall Garden maintenance fund. Some parking is available at the Village Hall and at the bottom of Pentre Hill for Delfryn. Disabled parking on drives at Delfryn and 6 Lôn Cilan. First time opener Stac Lee is a well planned and stocked garden with country views. Rest and admire the views at Nyth y Wennol with its borders and veg plot. Delfryn is a large well planted cottage garden with pond, woodland, large veg plot, roses and seats. Take a walk around Ty Mawr with its flowery meadow and specimen trees and shrubs. The newly constructed Village Hall Garden provides a restful place to sit for a while. At 6 Lôn Cilan you will find well stocked borders and a veg plot. Tickets, maps and good cakes at the Village Hall. The people of Cilcain run their own Village Hall, Show and Community Shop. Wheelchair access is not easy through all the gardens.

9 CLWYDFRYN

Bodfari, LL16 4HU. Keith & Susan Watson. *5m outside Denbigh. ½ way between Bodfari & Llandyrnog on B5429. Yellow signs at bottom of lane.* **Wed 13 Feb, Wed 13 Mar, Wed 10 Apr, Wed 8 May, Wed 12 June, Wed 10 July (11-4). Adm £4, chd free. Home-made teas.**

¾ acre garden, well worth a visit any time of the year. Collection of snowdrops, epimediums, hellebores and daffodils in spring. Recently added a sand plunge alpine/bulb house. Garden undergoing many changes towards lower maintenance and planting of drought tolerant plants. Orchard with various fruit trees now well established. Vegetable and colourful cottage garden planting below the orchard. Garden access to a paved area at back of house for wheelchair users.

10 THE COTTAGE NURSING HOME

54 Hendy Road, Mold, CH7 1QS. Mr. A.G. Lanini. *12m W of Chester. From Mold town centre take A494 towards Ruthin then follow yellow NGS signs.* **Sun 14 July (2-5). Adm £2, chd £0.50. Light refreshments.** Donation to British Heart Foundation.

Beautiful garden set in approx 1 acre. Well-established shrubs, herbaceous plants and abundance of colourful window boxes and

Aberclwyd Manor

© Joe Wainwright

tubs. Recently re-modelled garden we have now added a waterfall feature incl a fish pond and small area to grow vegetables. The central courtyard has two water features. At the bottom of the garden lies a wooden summer house and extended seating.

♿ 🐕 ✽ ☕

11 DOLHYFRYD

Lawnt, Denbigh, LL16 4SU. Captain & Mrs Michael Cunningham, 01745 814805, virginia@dolhyfryd.com. *1m SW of Denbigh. On B4501 to Nantglyn, from Denbigh - 1m from town centre.* **Visits by arrangement Feb to Nov for groups of up to 30. Adm £5, chd £2. Light refreshments.**

Established garden set in small valley of River Ystrad. Acres of crocuses in late Feb/early Mar. Paths through wildflower meadows and woodland of magnificent trees, shade loving plants and azaleas; mixed borders; walled kitchen garden. Many woodland and riverside birds, incl dippers, kingfishers, grey wagtails. Many species of butterfly encouraged by new planting. Much winter interest, exceptional display of crocuses. Gravel paths, some steep slopes.

♿ 🐕 ✽ ☕

12 DOVE COTTAGE

Rhos Road, Penyffordd, Chester, CH4 0JR. Chris & Denise Wallis, 01244 547539, dovecottage@supanet.com. *6m SW of Chester. Leave A55 at J35 take A550 to Wrexham. Drive 2m, turn R onto A5104. From A541 Wrexham/Mold Rd in Pontblyddyn take A5104 to Chester. Garden opp train stn.* **Visits by arrangement June to Aug for groups of 10+. Adm £4, chd free. Home-made teas. Fresh Homemade Cakes.**

Approx 1½ acre garden, shrubs and herbaceous plants set informally around lawns. Established vegetable area, 2 ponds (1 wildlife), summerhouse and woodland planted area. Gravel paths.

♿ ✽ 🚌 🛏 ☕

Your visits help change lives - we are the largest single funder of the Queen's Nursing Institute

13 NEW ERDDIG ALLOTMENTS

Thomas Fields, Erddig Road, Wrexham, LL13 7DT. Wrexham Allotment and Leisure Gardeners Association. *1m S of Wrexham town centre, off the A5152. From J3 on A483 take A5152 to Wrexham, R at mini-r'about into Fairy Rd then 3rd R. From A525 (Bangor-on-Dee) turn L at T-lights onto St Giles' Way, L onto A5152, L at mini-r'about.* **Sun 4 Aug (2-5). Adm £3, chd free. Home-made teas.**

Approximately 150 plots rented from Wrexham CBC, divided into full, half and quarter sizes. Wide range of fruit, vegetables and flowers grown, both traditional and unusual, some plots with greenhouse and/or polytunnel, some with pond and other wildlife features. Site on both sides of gently sloping small valley. Homemade cakes. Entrance area level, main perimeter track double and accessible to vehicles, rough in places. Narrow paths between plots.

♿ ☕

14 NEW ERLAS VICTORIAN WALLED GARDEN

Bryn Estyn Road, Wrexham, LL13 9TY. Ms Kate Harcus, www.erlas.org. *From A483 follow signs for the Wrexham Ind Est. From A5156 follow signs to Wrexham on A534 (Holt Rd). At 2nd roundabout on Holt Rd take 1st L on to Brynestyn Rd, for ½m.* **Sun 19 May, Sun 15 Sept (10.30-3.30). Adm £3.50, chd free. Light refreshments.**

Home of the Erlas Victorian Walled Garden charity, our garden is a place of work, solace & inspiration for adults of all abilities. A garden of 4 parts: The Walled Garden has many delights including a centuries-old Mulberry tree; The West Garden is full of fruit, veg, herbs & our Roundhouse; The Orchard has a mixture of Apple & Pear varieties. Our ecology area provides a haven for flora & fauna. A light lunch and freshly baked cakes will be available. We have wheelchair access throughout the garden, however it is on a slope, but the gradient is not too extreme.

♿ 🐕 ✽ ☕

15 GARTHEWIN

Llanfairtalhaiarn, LL22 8YR. Mr Michael Grime, 01745 720288, michaelgrime12@btinternet.com. *6m S of Abergele & A55. From Abergele take A548 to Llanfair TH & Llanrwst. Entrance to Garthewin 300yds W of Llanfair TH on A548 to Llanrwst. SatNav misleading.* **Mon 27 May (2-6). Adm £5, chd free. Home-made teas.** Visits also by arrangement Apr to Oct for groups of up to 30.

Valley garden with ponds and woodland areas. Much of the 8 acres have been reclaimed and redesigned providing a younger garden with a great variety of azaleas, rhododendrons and young trees, all within a framework of mature shrubs and trees. Teas in old theatre. Chapel open. Some stalls to promote local arts, crafts and foods.

16 GLOG DDU

Llangernyw, Abergele, LL22 8PS. Pamela & Anthony Harris. *Llangernyw is ½ way between Abergele & Llanrwst on A548. SatNav misleading. On Thurs visits turn up Uwch Afon Rd on Llanrwst side of village. At grass triangle follow NGS signs. On Sun park at the Hall, LL22 8TY. Take bus. Then a 250m steep walk down.* **Thur 14 Feb (12-4). Adm £5, chd free. Light refreshments. Sun 17 Feb (11-4). Combined adm with Hafodunos Hall £8, chd free. Thur 21 Feb (12-4). Adm £5, chd free. Light refreshments.**

Approx 2½ acres designed to fit seamlessly into the spectacular landscape. Rare trees and shrubs many grown from seed. Large number of different varieties of snowdrops with many hard-to-find available for sale. On the combined open day see a mass of Galanthus nivalis at the Hall and rare and unusual snowdrops here. Warm up in the new Viking Hut with central log fire or soup in the house. Refreshments at the Hall on the 17th. Soup & roll incl on Thursday openings.

17 GWAENYNOG

Denbigh, LL16 5NU. Major & Mrs Tom Smith. *1m W of Denbigh. On A543, Lodge on L, ¼m drive.* **Sun 23 June (2-5.30). Adm £4, chd free. Cream teas.** Donation to St James Church, Nantglyn.

2 acres incl the restored walled garden where Beatrix Potter wrote and illustrated the Tale of the Flopsy Bunnies. Also a small exhibition of some of her work. C16 house (not open) visited by Dr Samuel Johnson during his Tour of Wales. Herbaceous borders some recently replanted, espalier fruit trees, rose pergola and vegetable area. Grass paths.

18 GWEL YR YNYS

Parc Moel Lus, Penmaenmawr, LL34 6DN. Mr Dafydd Lloyd-Borland, 07968 243119, garden@gwelyrynys.com, www.gwelyrynys.com. *Take J16 from A55. At Mountain View PH take v.sharp L onto Conwy Old Rd. In ½m take sharp R into Graiglwyd Rd. Park at Ysgol Pen Cae, bus to garden. Disabled parking available at garden, please ring.* **Visits by arrangement Mar to Sept for groups of 10 to 30. Please contact us to make your visit personal to your group. Adm £6.50, chd free. Light refreshments.**

A dynamic and exciting ¾ acre hillside garden 650ft above sea level. Imaginative landscaping has been undertaken to complement and blend with the countryside beyond. Natural planting incl a large range of herbaceous plants shrubs and trees. Garden structure benefits from streams, freshwater pond, woodland 'dell' area, bog garden and many ferns and hostas. Excellent views out to sea. Chickens. Refreshment can be made for your individual group requirements. Most areas accessible for wheelchair users.

19 HAFODUNOS HALL

Llangernyw, Abergele, Conwy, LL22 8TY. Dr Richard Wood, www.hafodunoshall.co.uk. *1m W of Llangernyw. ½ way between Abergele & Llanrwst on A548. Signed from opp Old Stag Public House. Parking available on site.* **Sun 17 Feb (11-4). Combined adm with Glog Ddu £8, chd free. Light refreshments. Sat 25 May (12-5). Adm £5, chd free. Cream teas, coffee and cakes in Victorian conservatory.**

Historic garden undergoing restoration after 30yrs of neglect surrounds a Sir G G Scott Grade I Hall derelict after arson attack. Unique setting. ½m treelined drive, formal terraces, woodland walks with ancient redwoods, laurels, yews, lake, streams, waterfalls and a gorge. Mass of snowdrops. Wonderful rhododendrons. Uneven paths and steep steps. Children must have adult supervision at all times. Lunchtime barbecue weather permitting. Most areas around the hall accessible to wheelchairs by gravel pathways. Some gardens are set on slopes.

Ty Brombil

GROUP OPENING

20 LLANDEGLA VILLAGE GARDENS

Llandegla, LL11 3AP. *10m W of Wrexham. Please follow NGS signs for parking in Llandegla village. Minibus available from car park to take visitors to out-lying garden.* **Sun 14 July (1-5). Combined adm £6, chd free. Light refreshments.**

ERW LLAN
Mr & Mrs Keith Jackson.

THE GATE HOUSE, RUTHIN ROAD
Rod & Shelagh Williams.

ISIS
Janet & David Rose.

6 MAES TEG
Martin & Norma Weston.

NEW **MOLECATCHER`S COTTAGE**
Mr Walter Standring.

TY PENDLE
Matt Ellis & Sandra Rogers.

TY SIONED
Marco & Rachael Muia.

Llandegla village lies on the banks of the R Alyn and nestles on the edge of the Clwydian Range, an area of outstanding natural beauty (AONB), in the NE corner of Wales. It offers the visitor a truly old fashioned village welcome in the most picturesque area of the county. Every part of the community appears to enjoy the busy atmosphere of the day when the gardens attract so many visitors to raise funds for the NGS. The garden owners work hard to get their gardens looking their best, the bakers of the village supply tasty cakes for visitors to buy and enjoy in various venues and there are plenty of plants for sale. Not all gardens accessible for wheelchair users due to steps and gravel paths.

Delfryn, Cilcain Village Gardens

21 NEW NEUADD WEN

Llanfihangel Glyn Myfyr, Corwen, LL21 9UH. Miss Susan Hockney, 01490 420431, dottysalmon@aol.com. *When entering the village from Ruthin B5105. Proceed down hill past Crown PH, cross the bridge then take the 1st L hand fork to white house by graveyard.* **Visits by arrangement July & Aug for groups of up to 20. A weeks notice preferable. Adm £2.50, chd free. Light refreshments.**

On the driveway and roadside there is an array of coloured bedding plants and annuals, decorating the area with floral displays in pots and baskets. The slate covered pathway edged with brightly coloured summer blooms leads to the lawn, patio and decking area. The compact patio and seating area is an explosion of summer colour. Garden is wheelchair friendly with easy access to most areas.

22 THE OLD RECTORY

Llanfihangel Glyn Myfyr, Corwen, LL21 9UN. Mr & Mrs E T Hughes, 01490 420568, elwynthomashughes@hotmail.com. *2½m NE of Cerrigydrudion. From Ruthin take B5105 SW for 12m. From Cerrigydrudion take B5105 for 3m.* **Visits by arrangement. Discuss refreshments when booking. Adm £4, chd free. Light refreshments.** Donation to Cancer Research U.K.

This one acre garden is in a beautiful setting along the Afon Alwen valley and has mixed borders; water, bog and gravel gardens; walled garden with old roses, pergola, bower and garden of meditation. In early spring a number of different varieties of snowdrops may be seen together with hellebores, crocus and other spring flowers. Also hardy orchids, gentians, daffodils, rhododendrons and acers. Partial wheelchair access.

23 PEN Y GRAIG BACH

Tremeirchion, St Asaph, LL17 0UR. Roger & Christine Pawling, 07875 642270, christinehoyle@gmail.com. *4m SE of St Asaph. Off A55 take J28/29/30 to Tremeirchion, then B5429 to Bodfari, go 0.7m (wide verge), turn L up hill, L at fork, cont to rd end. From Bodfari take B5429 take 2nd R (after 1¼m).* **Visits by arrangement May to Sept for groups of up to 30. Visitors can book ahead or ring on the day & come if we are in. Adm £4, chd free. Light refreshments. Cake on request.**

2 acre wildlife friendly rural cottage garden. Succession of colour throughout the year. Box hedges and fruit trees enclose 5 plots of herbaceous perennials, unusual climbers, flowering shrubs, soft fruit and vegetables. Over 200 native and ornamental trees. 4 ponds and 3 paddocks which are managed organically for wild flowers and hay. Beehives. At 560ft with stunning views from sea to mountains. Partial wheelchair access, gravel paths between box hedges and grass paths.

24 PLAS Y NANT

Llanbedr Dyffryn Clwyd, Ruthin, LL15 1YF. Lesley, Ian, Dan, Sam & Jamie Callister, 01824 705444, lesleycallister@icloud.com. *From A494 turn onto B5429 Graigfechan,approx 1m,4th turning L private rd. If using Satnav follow postcode LL15 2YA. Proceed through farmyard continue & keep L, uphill to cottage on R, go straight onto forest track. Travel 0.8m on track, drive on R.* **Visits by arrangement Apr to Sept. Adm £4, chd free. Light refreshments. To be discussed when booking.**

Listed Gothic Villa in a serene upland valley (AONB) amid seven acres of gardens, bluebell woods and stream. Rhododendrons, magnolia and specimen trees abound, formal parterre of clipped box and yew. Embryonic Dragon's Head rose garden and trelliage. Procession of seasonal colour led by snowdrops, primroses and daffodils. Other aspects incl water features, loggia, summer and greenhouses, beehives.

GROUP OPENING

25 RUTHIN TOWN GARDENS

Ruthin, LL15 1DP. *Parking available in many car parks in town. No parking at Firgrove.* **Sun 30 June (11-4). Combined adm £7, chd free. Home-made teas at Nantclwyd y Dre & Firgrove.**

BERWYN
Susan Evans.

FIRGROVE
Philip & Anna Meadway, 01824 702677, meadway@firgrovecountryhouse.co.uk, www.firgrovecountryhouse.co.uk.

46 MWROG STREET
Glenna & David Toyne.

NANTCLWYD Y DRE
Denbighshire County Council.

The beautiful medieval town of Ruthin offers 4 contrasting gardens from a colourful little courtyard garden in Upper Clwyd Street to the large restored Lord`s Garden beyond one of the oldest timbered town houses in Wales, Nantclwyd y Dre. Refreshments can be purchased here with proceeds going to the Friends of the property. Plants also for sale. The stunning garden at 46 Mwrog Street has a beautiful beech tree at it`s centre and is surrounded by a great variety of shrubs and herbaceous plants. Very clever design and features. For the second time a bus will be available from the car park by the petrol garage on Park Road to take visitors up to Firgrove, 5 mins away. This plantsmans` garden has a collection of brugmansias, many unusual shrubs, and exotic plantings in containers. Refreshments will also be offered here. This should make a wonderful day enjoying a variety of garden styles and with a little bus trip included. Wheelchair access to most gardens.

26 SCOTT HOUSE

Corwen Road, Ruthin, LL15 2NP. Scott House Residents. *A494 Corwen Road. Disabled parking only at garden. Park in town, then walk from town square onto Castle St, garden 300m beyond Ruthin Castle Hotel, entrance on R.* **Sun 16 June (11-4). Adm £3.50, chd free. Home-made teas.**

Redesigned 2½ acre shared garden surrounding a fine 1930s Arts and Crafts house former nurses home to Ruthin Castle hospital. Breathtaking open views of the Vale of Clwyd. Avenue of Limes and a magnificent Cedar of Lebanon stands sentinel over a newly planted arboretum. Long herbaceous borders planted for summer long interest. New highly scented rose garden and recently constructed vegetable plot. Partial wheelchair access due to steps and terraces.

27 TAL-Y-BRYN FARM

Llannefydd, Denbigh, LL16 5DR. Mr & Mrs Gareth Roberts, 01745 540256, falmai@villagedairy.co.uk, www.villagedairy.co.uk. *3m W of Henllan. From Henllan take rd signed Llannefydd. After 2½m turn R signed Bont Newydd. Garden ½m on L.* **Visits by arrangement Apr to Sept. Adm by donation. Home-made teas.**

Medium sized working farmhouse cottage garden. Ancient farm machinery. Incorporating ancient privy festooned with honeysuckle, clematis and roses. Terraced arches, sunken garden pool and bog garden, fountains and old water pumps. Herb wheels, shrubs and other interesting features. Lovely views of the Clwydian range. Water feature, new rose tunnel, vegetable tunnel and small garden summer house.

28 TY BROMBIL

Broomhill Lane, Denbigh, LL16 3NH. Mr & Mrs Christopher Sanders, 01745 813852, c-sanders@btconnect.com. *Denbigh Town Centre. Closest council car park LL16 3TS. Walk up alley to High St. Garden Gate is next door to Halifax BS. Entry phone button for House.* **Visits by arrangement Apr to Sept for groups of**

up to 20. Adm £3, chd free. Refreshments to be arranged upon booking.
Open the gate to a unique hidden garden below a striking contemporary home. The house and garden are located on a very steep and rocky site. The garden consists of several outdoor 'rooms' at various levels linked by short flights of steps between the buildings. Stone walls, architectural planting, fruit trees, vines and pots make for a rare and very interesting private urban garden. Steep steps could make access difficult for less mobile visitors.

29 TY HWNT YR AFON

Rowen, Conwy, LL32 8YT. Ian & Margaret Trevette, 01492 650871, ian.trevette@btopenworld.com. *Take B5106 from Conwy, R at Groes Inn. Follow signs. Park on rd below Ty Gwyn Hotel, garden 500yds thru village on L fork in rd. Disabled parking on drive.* **Sun 5 May (1-5). Adm £3.50, chd free. Home-made teas.** Visits also by arrangement May to Aug.
¾ acre garden re-landscaped by owners over last 7yrs. With the backdrop of R Ro and preserved woodland beyond have used the gardens natural features of glacial stone, stream and springs to create an amphitheatre of garden shrubs and plants incl spring bulbs, acers, azaleas, camellias, rhododendrons and a multitude of other favourite perennials. Wheelchair access to view most of garden and for home-made teas on the sun terrace provided by Friends of Llandudno Rotary Club. Some steps.

We help ordinary people open the gates to their extraordinary private gardens to raise impressive amounts of money through admissions, teas and slices of cake!

30 WYLAN

Llangynhafal, Ruthin, LL15 1RU. John & Carol Perkins, 07808 988556, carolperkins24@yahoo.co.uk. *3m N of Ruthin. Take A494 from Ruthin to Llanbedr then B5429. After ½m turn R signed Llangynhafal 1½m. Entrance on R by large clump of trees. Yellow NGS sign at end of lane.* **Visits by arrangement May to July for groups of up to 30. Adm £4, chd free. Light refreshments.**
1 acre garden designed by owners for all parts to be easily accessible. Magnificent panoramic views across the Vale of Clwyd with the Clwydian range as a backdrop. Many mature shrubs, mixed borders and assorted water features, with lots of colourful summer planted pots and containers. Winner of Best Kept Country Garden in Ruthin Flower Show 7 times. Gradual grass slope at end of front garden to access back garden.

Garthewin

POWYS

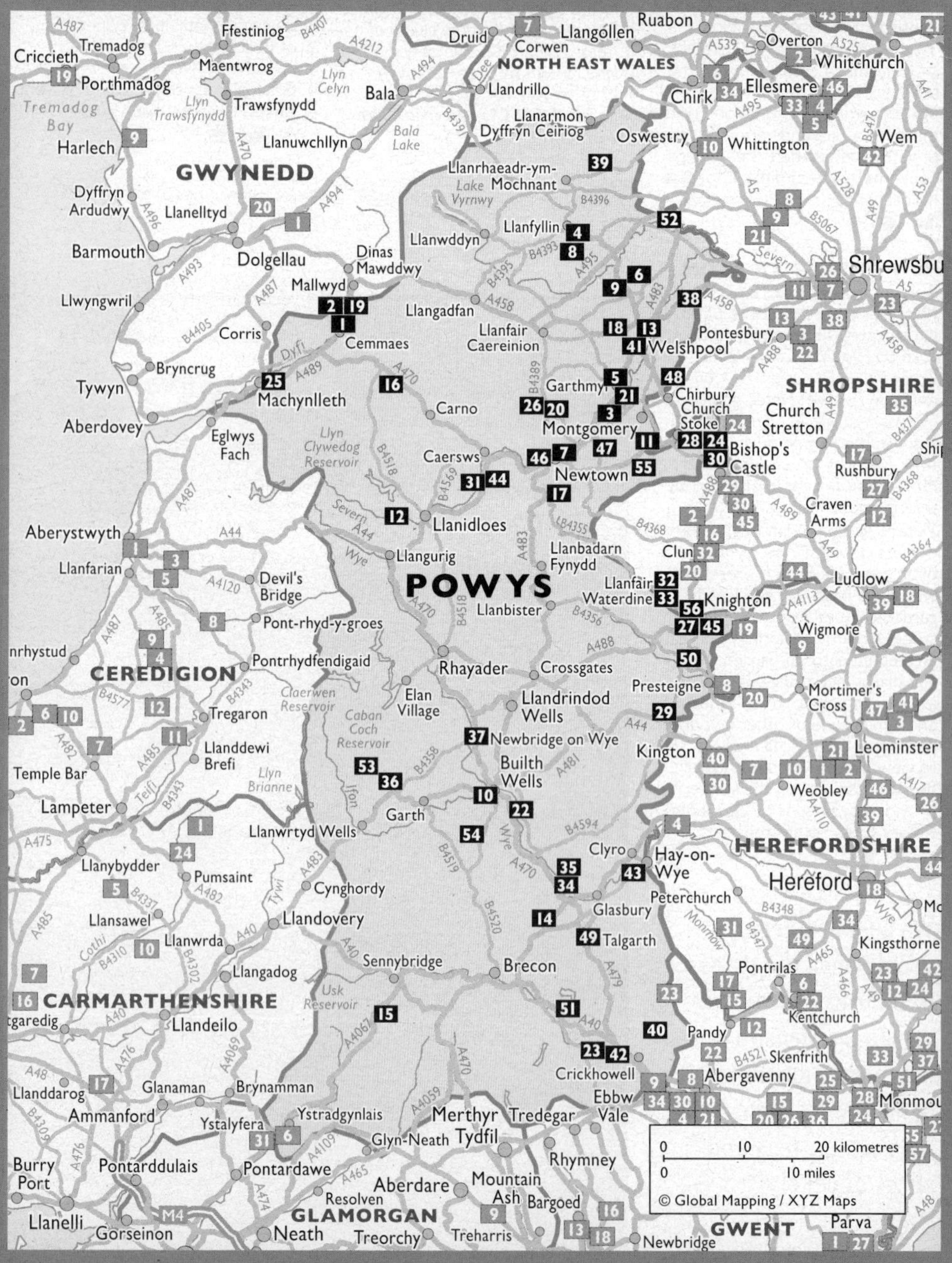
POWYS
GWYNEDD
NORTH EAST WALES
SHROPSHIRE
CEREDIGION
HEREFORDSHIRE
CARMARTHENSHIRE
GLAMORGAN
GWENT
0 10 20 kilometres
0 10 miles
© Global Mapping / XYZ Maps

A three hour drive through Powys takes you through the spectacular and unspoilt landscape of Mid Wales, from the Berwyn Hills in the north to south of the Brecon Beacons.

Through the valleys and over the hills, beside rippling rivers and wooded ravines, you will see a lot of sheep, pretty market towns, half-timbered buildings and houses of stone hewn from the land.

The stunning landscape is home to many of the beautiful NGS gardens of Powys. Gardens nestling in valleys, gardens high in the hills, wild-life gardens, riverside gardens, walled gardens, grand gardens, cottage gardens, gardens in picturesque villages, gardens in towns.... they can all be found in Powys!

Here in Powys all is the spectacular, the unusual, the peaceful and the enchanting all opened by generous and welcoming garden owners.

Below: I The Sign, Berriew Village Gardens

Volunteers

North Powys County Organiser
Susan Paynton
01686 650531
susan.paynton@ngs.org.uk

County Treasurer
Gwyneth Jackson-Jones
01691 648578
gwynethjj@icloud.com

Publicity
Helen Anthony
01686 941795
powys.ngs.publicity@gmail.com

Social Media
Jude Boutle & Sue Cox
powys.socialmedia@ngs.org.uk

Booklet Co-ordinator
Carole Jones
01650 511176
jonesey200@gmail.com

Assistant County Organisers
Simon Cain
07958 915115
simon.cain@westbourneconsulting.com

South Powys County Organiser
Christine Carrow
01591 620461
stevetynycwm@hotmail.co.uk

County Treasurer
Steve Carrow
01591 620461
stevetynycwm@hotmail.co.uk

Assistant County Organisers
Bob & Andrea Deakin
01982 551718
bandeak@googlemail.com

Chris Harris
01982 551418
chris.h48.ch@gmail.com

OPENING DATES

All entries subject to change. For latest information check **www.ngs.org.uk**

Map locator numbers are shown to the right of each garden name.

April

Saturday 13th
Gorsty House 24

Sunday 14th
Gorsty House 24
Maesfron Hall and Gardens 38

Sunday 28th
Fraithwen 20
Llandinam, Little House 31

May

Sunday 5th
Llangoed Hall Hotel 34
Oak Cottage 41

Monday 6th
Oak Cottage 41

Saturday 11th
1 Church Bank 13
◆ Dingle Nurseries & Garden 18
Hyssington Gardens 30

Sunday 12th
1 Church Bank 13
◆ Dingle Nurseries & Garden 18
Hyssington Gardens 30

Saturday 18th
NEW Llanfair Waterdine, Nantiago 32
NEW Llanfair Waterdine, The Coach House 33
Rock Mill 47

Sunday 19th
Gliffaes Country House Hotel 23
◆ Gregynog Hall & Garden 26
NEW Llanfair Waterdine, Nantiago 32
NEW Llanfair Waterdine, The Coach House 33
Penmyarth House 42
Rock Mill 47

Sunday 26th
Glanwye 22
Llwyn Madoc 36

Monday 27th
Llanstephan House 35
Llysdinam 37
Oak Cottage 41

Wednesday 29th
◆ Grandma's Garden 25

June

Saturday 1st
The Hymns 29
NEW Tranquillity Haven 50

Sunday 2nd
Caer Beris Manor Hotel 10
Ceunant 12
The Neuadd 40
NEW Tranquillity Haven 50

Saturday 8th
NEW Bryncelyn 8
NEW Stockton Mill 48

Sunday 9th
NEW Bryncelyn 8
NEW Caebardd 9
Oak Cottage 41
NEW Stockton Mill 48

Saturday 15th
NEW Church House 14
Tremynfa 52

Sunday 16th
NEW Church House 14
NEW Cwm Carnedd Isaf 16
Hurdley Hall 28
Tremynfa 52
Tyn y Cwm 53

Saturday 22nd
Hyssington Gardens 30

Sunday 23rd
Cwm-Weeg 17
Hyssington Gardens 30
Pen-y-Maes 43

Saturday 29th
Bachie Uchaf 4

Sunday 30th
Bachie Uchaf 4
NEW Berriew Village Gardens 5
Esgair Angell 19

July

Saturday 6th
Talgarth Mill 49

Sunday 7th
Ceunant 12
Hurdley Hall 28
Llangoed Hall Hotel 34
Talgarth Mill 49

Monday 8th
Garthmyl Hall 21

Saturday 13th
1 Church Bank 13

Sunday 14th
1 Church Bank 13
Crai Gardens 15
Llandinam, Little House 31
Treberfydd House 51

Sunday 21st
Aberangell, The Old Coach House 1
Aberangell, Pen Pentre 2
Broniarth Hall 6

Saturday 27th
Bryn Teg 7
Ponthafren 46
◆ Welsh Lavender 54

Sunday 28th
Ceunant 12
Fraithwen 20
◆ Welsh Lavender 54

August

Saturday 3rd
NEW Moel-y-Gweltyn-Ucha 39

Sunday 4th
NEW Caebardd 9
Llangoed Hall Hotel 34
NEW Moel-y-Gweltyn-Ucha 39
Tyn y Cwm 53

Saturday 10th
Hebron 27

Sunday 11th
Hebron 27

Saturday 24th
Ponthafren 46

September

Sunday 8th
Llandinam, Little House 31

Saturday 14th
NEW Bryncelyn 8

Sunday 15th
NEW Bryncelyn 8

Sunday 29th
Llangoed Hall Hotel 34

October

Saturday 19th
◆ Dingle Nurseries & Garden 18

Sunday 20th
◆ Dingle Nurseries & Garden 18

By Arrangement

Arrange a personalised garden visit with your club, or group of friends, on a date to suit you. See individual garden entries for full details.

Abernant 3
Broniarth Hall 6
NEW Bryncelyn 8
Castell y Gwynt 11
1 Church Bank 13
Fraithwen 20
Gorsty House 24
Hebron 27
Hurdley Hall 28
The Hymns 29
Llysdinam 37
The Neuadd 40
Plas Dinam 44
Pont Faen House 45
NEW Tranquillity Haven 50
Tyn y Cwm 53
NEW White Hopton Farm 55
1 Ystrad House 56

THE GARDENS

1 ABERANGELL, THE OLD COACH HOUSE

Dolcorsllwyn, Aberangell, Machynlleth, SY20 9AB. Sue McKillop, 01650 511 333, paddy5130@gmail.com, www.theoldcoachhousecottage.co.uk. *On A470 midway beween Dolgellau & Machynlleth. From Mallwyd r'about to Cemmaes Rd, turn R after 3m just after turn for Aberangell village. From Machynlleth, come through Cemmaes and Cwm Llinau. We are 1m on the L.* **Sun 21 July (11-5). Adm £3, chd free. Home-made teas. Also open Aberangell, Pen Pentre. Refreshments also available at Aberangell, Pen Pentre.**

Nestled in heart of Dyfi Valley this small, cottage style garden is haven for birds and pollinating insects. Narrow paths take you around the flower and vegetable beds to a little pond. Planting is informal with mostly perennials and shrubs. Secluded seating areas allow the visitor to relax and enjoy different aspects of the garden with views down to R Dyfi. New hot bed & white border. Home made preserves and conserves for sale. A gravel drive and cobbled area in front of the house leads to a grassy slope into the garden. There are a few low steps within the garden.

2 ABERANGELL, PEN PENTRE

Aberangell, Machynlleth, SY20 9ND. Jacqueline Parsons. *On A470 midway beween Dolgellau & Machynlleth. From A470, follow signs for Aberangell. Past caravan park to Xrds. Turn R, Pen Pentre is 2nd house on R.* **Sun 21 July (11-4.30). Adm £3, chd free. Home-made teas. Also open Aberangell, The Old Coach House. Ice creams for sale.**

The garden at Pen Pentre has been built up around the old Aberangell railway station on banks of R Dovey. Colourful cottage garden borders attracting bees, butterflies and other wildlife. Old railway platform and line are home to soft fruit, herbs and vegetables. The station contains many old artefacts from a bygone era. A new wildflower 'mini meadow' was sown in the autumn of 2018. Apiary. Please note that, due to the various levels and steps, the garden is not suitable for the disabled or less mobile.

3 ABERNANT

Garthmyl, SY15 6RZ. Mrs B M Gleave, 01686 640494, john.gleave@mac.com. *1½m S of Garthmyl. On A483 midway between Welshpool & Newtown (both 8m). Approached over steep humpback bridge with wooden statue of a workman to one side, then straight ahead to the house & parking.* **Visits by arrangement Mar to Aug for groups of 5 to 30. Adm £4, chd free.**

Approx 3 acres incl orchard with stunning display of cherry blossom in April (85 trees). Knot garden, box hedging, roses, rockery, pond, shrubs, ornamental trees, examples of archaic sundials, fossilised wood and stone heads. Additional woodland of 9 acres with borrowed views of the Severn Valley. Formal rose garden recently replanted. Late April 85 cherry trees in blossom. Late June: roses. Picnics welcome from 12pm.

4 BACHIE UCHAF

Bachie Road, Llanfyllin, SY22 5NF. Glyn & Glenys Lloyd. *S of Llanfyllin. Going towards Welshpool on A490 turn R onto Bachie Rd after Llanfyllin primary school. Keep straight for 0.8m. Take drive R uphill at cottage on L.* **Sat 29, Sun 30 June (1.30-5). Adm £4.50, chd free. Home-made teas.**

Inspiring, colourful hillside country garden. Gravel paths meander around extensive planting and over streams cascading down into ponds. Specimen trees, shrubs and vegetable garden. Enjoy the wonderful views from one of the many seats; your senses will be rewarded.

Caebardd

GROUP OPENING

5 NEW BERRIEW VILLAGE GARDENS

Berriew, Welshpool, SY21 8BA. *A483 5m S Welshpool. From Welshpool take A483 S for approx 4m. Turn R onto B4390. Continue through village and turn R to Car Park at school. Map and admission tickets at car park. All within walking distance of car park.* **Sun 30 June (12-5). Combined adm £6, chd free. Home-made teas in the Old School in centre of village.**

NEW CAE BYCHAN
William and Sheila Cooke.

NEW 1 GLAN YR AFON
Ms Lesley Ellis.

NEW THE OLD COURT HOUSE
Michael Davis and Andrew Logan.

NEW 1 THE SIGN
Mrs Irene Breakwell & Mr Tony Ladds.

NEW THE WHITE COTTAGE
Elaine Williams and Ian Hubbuck.

The picturesque village of Berriew is on the Montgomeryshire Canal with the River Rhiew flowing through its heart. Black and white cottages, church, two pubs, shops, William O'Brien artist/blacksmith forge and Andrew Logan Museum of Sculpture. Five very different gardens: The White Cottage traditional cottage garden with lavender, roses, perennials and productive veg plot. 1 Glan yr Afon colourful small garden with bark paths, veg plot and pergola covered with grape vines. 1 The Sign small cottage garden intensively planted and full of quirky features: The Old Court House idyllic situation on banks of R Rhiew terrace with metal staircase by Berriew sculptor/ metalworker William O'Brien, raised beds for soft fruits and vegetables and Cae Bychan on banks of river with traditional planting, roses, prairie border and veg plot. Plants and honey for sale and children's treasure hunt at The White Cottage. Partial wheelchair access.

6 BRONIARTH HALL

Pentrebeirdd, Guilsfield, Welshpool, SY21 9DW. Mrs Janet Powell, 01938 500639, janet09br@hotmail.co.uk. *From Londis petrol station, Guilsfield, take A490 towards Llanfyllin for approx 2m. Turn R towards Sarnau. After 1m turn R for Broniarth Hall.* **Sun 21 July (1.30-5). Adm £4, chd free. Cream teas. Free refills tea, coffee and soft drinks.** Visits also by arrangement first two weeks of July for groups of 10 to 20.

Broniarth Hall is a C17 farm house (not open) with bijou SE facing cottage garden with 2 small ponds, summerhouse, perennial filled beds and aviary. Unique and quirky features and containers. Hanging baskets with summer bedding and foliage plants. A large selection of Heucheras. Stunning views. Lots of plants for sale.

7 BRYN TEG

Bryn Lane, Newtown, SY16 2DP. Novlet Childs. *N side of Newtown. Take Llanfair Caereinion Rd towards Bettws Cedewain and turn L before hospital. Up hill on L.* **Sat 27 July (10-5). Adm £3.50, chd free. Also open Ponthafren. Home-made tea and cakes at Ponthafren.**

An exciting walk through the jungle in Newtown! High above the head are banana leaves and colourful climbers. An exotic Caribbean garden planted to remind me of my childhood in Jamaica. A winding path from the front door around the side of the house to the back door takes you on a journey through another land. A huge number of plants on many levels. All shapes, sizes and colours mixed together as found in tropical jungles, not as in a typical border. Feel transported to another continent. Even in the rain you will get that jungle experience. Manual wheelchair access to most of the garden. Not suitable for mobility scooters.

8 NEW BRYNCELYN

Lluest Lane, Cwmnantymeichaid, Llanfyllin, SY22 5NE. Rosemary Clarke and David Harbinson, 01691 648168, ros11e@btinternet.com. *Going towards Welshpool on A490 turn R onto Bachie Rd after Llanfyllin primary school. Keep straight for 1½m. Turn L at top of rise following yellow NGS signs.* **Sat 8, Sun 9 June, Sat 14, Sun 15 Sept (1-5). Adm £4, chd free. Home-made teas.** Visits also by arrangement June to Sept for individuals/groups of up to 20. Evening visits in June and July.

3 acre country garden and paddocks. Spectacular backdrop of near hills with views to Cefn Coch & Berwyns. Deep beds of perennial planting with mature trees & shrubs chosen to attract birds and insects; circular walk beside the lake and stream. Meet the resident donkeys and peacocks, find a seat and lose yourself in the tranquillity of this special place. Children's play area (supervision required) and children's garden quiz. Partial wheelchair access over gravel area then brick path and grass; excellent views.

9 NEW CAEBARDD

Pentrebeirdd, Guilsfield, Welshpool, SY21 9DJ. Sandy Jones. *From Londis petrol station on A490 nr Guilsfield continue towards Llanfyllin for approx 2m & turn L following NGS signs on single track lane.* **Sun 9 June, Sun 4 Aug (2-5.30). Adm £4, chd free. Home-made teas.**

A meandering garden with established trees and shrubs circling a large pond. Dry stone walls support banks of herbs, wild and herbaceous flowers. Paths lead to hidden Japanese corner with waterfall, bamboos, acers and bridge. A short walk across farmyard takes you to a wild meadow full of wildflowers with paths interlacing to lead onto a raised bed veg plot between orchard and walnut grove. 10 mins hike to top of farm boasts magnificent 100 degree views of Long Mountain, Rodney's Pillar, Shropshire plains around to Berwyns. Cadair Berwen and Allt y Main.There is a seat at the summit for you to sit and catch your breath. Children's Quiz. Most of main garden has wheelchair access but paths in wild meadow are too narrow.

10 CAER BERIS MANOR HOTEL

Builth Wells, LD2 3NP. Mrs Nika Yusifova, 01982 552601, caerberis@btconnect.com, www.caerberis.com. *W edge Builth Wells. From Builth Wells town centre take A483 signed Llandovery. Caer Beris Manor is on L as you leave Builth.* **Sun 2 June (11-4). Adm £4, chd free. Home-made teas.**

An original 1927 NGS pioneer garden. 27 acres of mature parklands, with the River Irfon bordering the property. The grounds were planted early C20 by the Vivien family who were plant hunters. Many varied specimen trees form an Arboretum. Large displays of rhododendrons. An Edwardian Rose archway has been recently replanted with David Austin roses. Lower parkland can be accessed by car or wheelchair.

11 CASTELL Y GWYNT

Llandyssil, Montgomery, SY15 6HR. John & Jacqui Wynn-Jones, 01686 668569, jacquiwj@btinternet.com. *2m out of Montgomery on the Sarn Rd, 1st R, 1st R.* **Visits by arrangement May to July for individuals/ groups of up to 30. Adm £5, chd free. Home-made teas.**

1½ acre garden at 900ft, set within 6 acres of land managed for wildlife. Native woodland corridors with mown rides surround hayfield/ wildflower meadow and pool with turf roofed summerhouse. Enclosed kitchen garden with boxed beds of vegetables, fruit and cutting flowers, greenhouse and orchard. Shrubberies, deep mixed borders and more formal areas close to house. Outstanding views of Welsh mountains. Circular path around the whole property which gives unique views of the house, garden and surrounding countryside. Bring good footwear and enjoy the walk.

12 CEUNANT

Old Hall, Llanidloes, SY18 6PW. Sharon McCready, 01686 412345, sharon.mccready@yahoo.co.uk, www.gardenthesevernway.com. *2m W of Llanidloes. Leave Llanidloes over Shortbridge St, turn L along Pen y Green Rd, approx ½m turn L signposted Llangurig, Glyn Brochan. Follow signs property is on R.* **Sun 2 June, Sun 7, Sun 28 July (1-5). Adm £4, chd free. Home-made teas.**

4 acre riverside garden started in 2013 in a beautiful setting on River Severn just 7m from the source. Wooded wildlife area and wildlife pond, orchard, ornamental garden, herbaceous borders, scented seating areas. Riverside path, meadow and veg plot. A developing garden full of unusual features, new areas being added all of the time. Planting is aimed at pollinators and to encourage wildlife. Sleeping mud maid, clay oven and brook home to Indian Runner ducks, lots of seating areas and recycled features. Accommodation available in shepherd's hut. Some rough terrain and lots of slopes.

13 1 CHURCH BANK

Welshpool, SY21 7DR. Mel & Heather Parkes, 01938 559112, melandheather@live.co.uk. *Centre of Welshpool. Church Bank leads onto Salop Rd from Church St. Follow one way system, use main car park then short walk. Follow yellow NGS signs.* **Sat 11, Sun 12 May, Sat 13, Sun 14 July (12-5). Adm £3.50, chd free. Home-made teas.** Visits also by arrangement May to Sept for groups of 5 to 20.

A jewel in the town. Explore the ground floor of this C17 barrel maker's cottage and walk into a large garden room which also houses a museum of tools from different trades. Mystic pool of smoke and sounds. Outside a Gothic arch and zig zag path lead to a shell grotto and bonsai garden, fernery and many unusual features. Sounds of water fill the air and interesting plants fill the intimate space. Children's garden quiz. Museum of country life. New features for 2019.

14 NEW CHURCH HOUSE

Llandefalle, Brecon, LD3 0ND. Mr & Mrs Chris & Anne Taylor. *Between Brecon and Llyswen, off A470, signposted Llandefalle, then single track lane for ½ mile. Next to Church.* **Sat 15, Sun 16 June (2-5.30). Adm £4, chd free. Home-made teas.**

One acre garden, subdivided into different areas, each with its own character incl orchard. Skilfully landscaped in the 1980s to provide terraces, generous borders and year round interest. New owners have added small pond, herb garden and rill. Tranquil places to sit and enjoy refreshments with fine views to Black Mts. Next to St Matthew's 15th century Church with notable earlier features. Some steps. Wheelchair access to terraces over sloping lawns but only if ground is dry.

GROUP OPENING

15 CRAI GARDENS

Crai, LD3 8YP. *13m SW of Brecon. Turn W off A4067 signed Crai. Village hall is 50yds straight ahead; park here for admission & information about gardens.* **Sun 14 July (2-5). Combined adm £5, chd free. Home-made teas in village hall. There will be gluten free and wheat free cake.**

Set against the backdrop of Fan Gyhirych and Fan Brycheiniog, at 1000ft above sea level the Crai valley is a hidden gem, off the beaten track between Brecon and Swansea. Those in the know have long enjoyed visiting our serene valley, with its easy access to the hills and its fabulous views. In difficult climatic conditions, the Crai Gardens reflect a true passion for gardening. The gardens come in a wide variety of size, purpose and design, and include a range of shrubs, perennials and annuals; organically grown vegetables and fruits; raised beds; polytunnels; water features; prolific hanging baskets, patio containers and window boxes. Not to forget the chickens and ducks. And to complete your Sunday afternoon, come and enjoy the renowned hospitality of the Crai ladies by sampling their delicious home-made cakes in the village hall. Some of the gardens are fully, some partly, accessible by wheelchair. Some have gravel paths or steep grassy banks.

16 NEW CWM CARNEDD ISAF

Dolfach, Llanbrynmair, SY19 7AF. Jenny Hall. *1.75m SE Llanbrynmair. From Llanbrynmair take A470 to Dolfach, then 1st L & follow road up hill passing cemetery & chapel, after ¾m take R fork for house.* **Sun 16 June (1.30-5). Adm £4, chd free. Home-made teas.**

Quiet country garden of approx 1 acre surrounding recently renovated barn. Newly created garden enclosed in stone walls, incl herbaceous and mixed borders, gravel garden with pots, fish pond, raised vegetable beds, soft fruit cage, and paddock with orchard and fernery.

17 CWM-WEEG

Dolfor, Newtown, SY16 4AT. Dr W Schaefer & Mr K D George, 01686 628992, wolfgang@cwmweeg.co.uk, www.cwmweeg.co.uk. *4½m SE of Newtown. Take A489 E from Newtown for 1½m, turn R towards Dolfor. After 2m turn L down asphalted farm track, signed at entrance. Do not rely on SatNav. Also signed from Dolfor village.* **Sun 23 June (2-5). Adm £5, chd free. Home-made teas.**

2½ acre garden set within 24 acres of wildflower meadows and bluebell woodland with stream centred around C15 farmhouse (open by prior arrangement). Formal garden in English landscape tradition with vistas, grottos, sculptures, stumpery, lawns and extensive borders terraced with stone walls. Translates older garden vocabulary into an innovative C21 concept. Under cover area for refreshments if wet. Partial wheelchair access. For further information please see garden website.

18 ◆ DINGLE NURSERIES & GARDEN

Welshpool, SY21 9JD. Mr & Mrs D Hamer, 01938 555145, info@dinglenurseriesandgarden.co.uk, www.dinglenurseries.co.uk. *2m NW of Welshpool. Take A490 towards Llanfyllin & Guilsfield. After 1m turn L at sign for Dingle Nurseries & Garden. Follow signs and enter the Garden from adjacent plant centre.* **For NGS: Sat 11, Sun 12 May, Sat 19, Sun 20 Oct (9-5). Adm £3.50, chd free. Tea and coffee available. For other opening times and information, please phone, email or visit garden website.**

RHS recommended 4½ acre garden on S-facing site, sloping down to lakes surrounded by yr-round interest. Beds mostly colour themed with a huge variety of rare and unusual trees, ornamental shrubs and herbaceous plants. Set in hills of mid Wales this beautiful and well known garden attracts visitors from Britain and abroad. Open all yr except 24 Dec - 2 Jan. Limited access to top areas of garden over gravel path for those with mobility issues.

19 ESGAIR ANGELL

Aberangell, Machynlleth, SY20 9QJ. Carole Jones, 01650 511176, jonesey200@gmail.com, www.upperbarncottage.co.uk. *Midway between Dogellau & Machynlleth. Turn off A470 towards village of Aberangell, then signed.* **Sun 30 June (11-5). Adm £4.50, chd free. Home-made teas.**

2 acre garden plus 23 acres for wildlife bounded by R Angell in Dovey Forest and Snowdonia National Park. Trout lake with abundance of plant and animal life, small wood, aviaries housing our families of rescue owls. Second pond in wildlife meadow with otter holt. Circular walk through fields with spectacular views. New for 2019 greenhouse with herbaceous area, vertical and horizontal log bee hives. Partial wheelchair access, mainly laid to lawn. Access on gravelled area above lake affording excellent views.

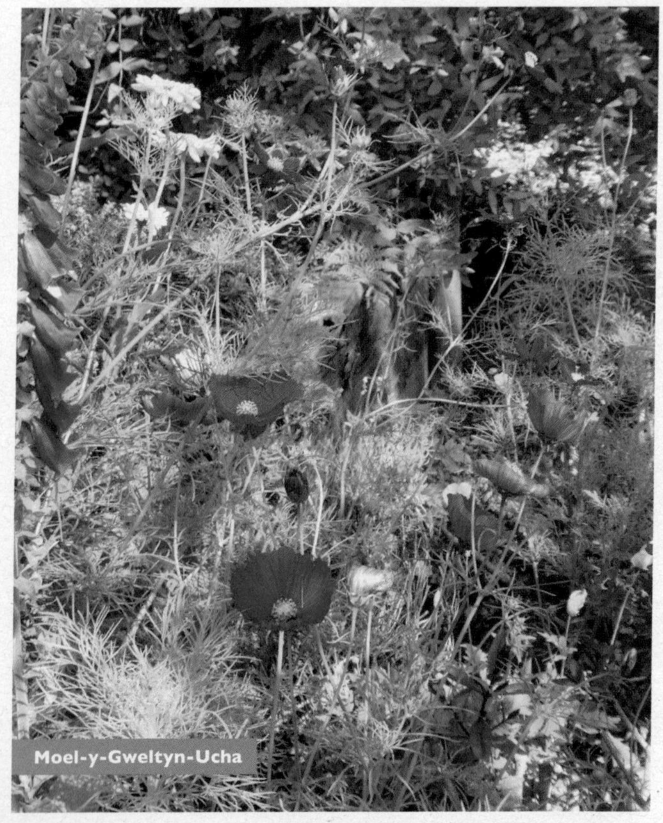

Moel-y-Gweltyn-Ucha

20 FRAITHWEN

Tregynon, SY16 3EW. Sydney Thomas, 01686 650307. *6m N of Newtown. On B4389 midway between villages of Bettws Cedewain & Tregynon.* **Sun 28 Apr, Sun 28 July (2-5). Adm £4, chd free. Home-made teas.** Visits also by arrangement Feb to Oct. Individuals/large groups.

1½ acre plantswoman's garden with herbaceous borders, rockeries and ponds. Planted with rare plants for yr-round interest and for pollinators. Plants in flower every day of the year: spring bulbs, alpines, alstroemeria collection, lilies, vegetable plot and pool. Collection of unusual snowdrops. Beautiful views. New designs for 2019 incl more autumn colour and bog garden. Snowdrops and hellebores in flower February and carpets of cyclamen in September. Partial wheelchair access. Some steps, gravel and slopes.

21 GARTHMYL HALL

Garthmyl, Montgomery, SY15 6RS. Julia Pugh, www.garthmylhall.co.uk. *On A483 midway between Welshpool & Newtown (both 8m). Turn R 200yds S of Nag's Head Pub.* **Mon 8 July (12-5). Adm £4, chd free. Home-made teas.**

Grade II listed Georgian manor house (not open) surrounded by 5 acres of grounds. Long 100 metres herbaceous borders, newly restored 1 acre walled garden with gazebo, circular flowerbeds, lavender beds, two fire pits and gravel paths. Fountain, 3 magnificent Cedar of Lebanon and giant redwood. Partial wheelchair access. Accessible WC.

22 GLANWYE

Builth Wells, LD2 3YP. Mr & Mrs H Kidston. *2m SE Builth Wells. From Builth Wells on A470, after 2m R at Lodge Gate. From Llyswen on A470, after 6m L at Lodge Gate. Will be signposted. Suggest not using SatNav as unreliable.* **Sun 26 May (2-5). Adm £4, chd free. Home-made teas.**

Large Victorian garden, spectacular rhododendrons, azaleas. Herbaceous borders, extensive yew hedges, lawns, long woodland walk with bluebells and other woodland flowers. Magnificent views of upper Wye Valley.

23 GLIFFAES COUNTRY HOUSE HOTEL

Gliffaes Rd, Crickhowell, NP8 1RH. Mrs N Brabner & Mr & Mrs J C Suter, 01874 730371, calls@gliffaeshotel.com, www.gliffaes.com. *3½m W of Crickhowell. From Crickhowell, drive W for 2½ m, L off A40 and continue for 1m.* **Sun 19 May (2-5). Adm £6, chd free. Cream teas. Also open Penmyarth House.**

The Gliffaes gardens and arboretum lie in a dream position on a plateau 120ft above the spectacular River Usk. As well as breath-taking views of the Brecon Beacons and 33 acres of parkland and lawns, there are ancient, rare and ornamental trees, incl giant sequoias, cedars and fine maples. Also many new tree plantings, spring bulbs, rhododendrons, azaleas, shrubs and an ornamental pond. Gliffaes is a country house hotel and is open for lunch, bar snacks, afternoon tea and dinner to non residents and garden visitors. Wheelchair ramp to the west side of the hotel. In dry weather main lawns accessible, but more difficult if wet.

24 GORSTY HOUSE

Hyssington, Montgomery, SY15 6AT. Gary & Annie Frost, 01588 620953, frostiesuk@msn.com. *A488 N from Bishop's Castle. Approx 3½m, turn L signed Hyssington then follow yellow NGS signs. From Churchstoke towards Bishop's Castle 1m then turn L signed Hyssington and follow NGS signs.* **Sat 13, Sun 14 Apr (1-5). Adm £4, chd free. Home-made teas. Opening with Hyssington Gardens on Sat 11, Sun 12 May, Sat 22, Sun 23 June.** Visits also by arrangement Apr to June for groups of 5 to 30. Limited parking at house. No coaches.

A renovation, started late in 2014, of a neglected garden. 2¼ acres, one acre of which is beautiful perennial flowering hay meadow. We are planting to attract wildlife, with wooded and shady areas, herbaceous borders with abundant cottage garden planting, hundreds of bulbs in season, orchard with wildflowers, wildlife pond, and a 'secret garden', planted to encourage pollinators. Beautiful views. A haven for wildlife.

25 ◆ GRANDMA'S GARDEN

Dolguog Estates, Felingerrig, Machynlleth, SY20 8UJ. Richard Rhodes, 01654 702244, info@plasdolguog.co.uk, www.plasdolguog.co.uk/grandmasgarden. *1½m E of Machynlleth. Turn L off A489 Machynlleth to Newtown rd. Follow brown tourist signs to Plas Dolguog Hotel.* **For NGS: Wed 29 May (10.30-4.30). Adm £5, chd free. Cream teas.** For other opening times and information, please phone, email or visit garden website.

Inspiration for the senses, unique, fascinating, educational and fun. Strategic seating, continuous new attractions, wildlife abundant, 9 acres of peace. Sculptures, poetry arboretum. Seven sensory gardens, wildlife pond, riverside boardwalk, stone circle, labyrinth. Azaleas and bluebells in May. Children welcome. Plas Dolguog Hotel open their café in the conservatory - the hotel is the admission point - serving inside and out on patio overlooking gardens.

26 ◆ GREGYNOG HALL & GARDEN

Tregynon, Newtown, SY16 3PL. Gregynog, 01686 650224, enquiries@gregynog.org, www.gregynog.org. *5m N of Newtown. From main A483, take turning for Berriew. In Berriew follow sign for Bettws then for Tregynon (£2.50 car parking charge applies).* **For NGS: Sun 19 May (10-5). Adm £3, chd free. Light refreshments at Courtyard Cafe.** For other opening times and information, please phone, email or visit garden website.

Grade I listed garden set within 750 acres of Gregynog Estate which was designated a National Nature Reserve in 2013. Parkland with fountains, lily lake and water garden. A mass display of rhododendrons and yew hedge create a spectacular backdrop to the sunken lawns. Azaleas and unusual trees. Apiary. Courtyard cafe serving morning coffee, light lunches and Welsh afternoon teas. Some gravel paths.

27 HEBRON
Ludlow Road, Knighton, LD7 1HP. Kevin Collins & Anita Lewis, 01547 529576, kd.collins@hotmail.co.uk. *From Knighton, take A4113 towards Ludlow, house on R opposite playing fields where parking is available.* **Sat 10, Sun 11 Aug (12-6). Adm £3.50, chd free. Home-made teas.** Visits also by arrangement Apr to Nov for groups of up to 20.
½ acre Victorian town garden. Surprises await the visitor: garden is divided into distinct rooms by yew & beech hedges with box topiary and willow arches. Variety of trees incl large silver birches, magnolia, weeping willow and cherry. Many shrubs provide colour throughout the season. Heathers, herbs, vegetables and flower beds. Plenty of seating. Beehives and garden art add an interest. Slate/stone letter carver will be present.

28 HURDLEY HALL
Hurdley, Churchstoke, SY15 6DY. Simon Cain & Simon Quin, 07958915115, simon.cain@westbourneconsulting.com. *2m from Churchstoke. Take turning for Hurdley off A489, 1m E of Churchstoke. Garden is a further 1m up the lane.* **Sun 16 June, Sun 7 July (10.30-5). Adm £5, chd free. Home-made teas.** Visits also by arrangement June & July for groups of 10 to 30.
2 acre garden set around C17 house with additional 18 acres adjoining Roundton Hill National Nature Reserve. Herbaceous & mixed borders, orchard, ponds, topiary & kitchen garden. Mown paths through 5 acre Coronation Meadow lead to newly planted orchard, pastures and new and ancient woodland with brook. Uneven ground and steep slopes give wide ranging views but may restrict access. Stunning views. Live music by Bishops Castle Swing Band on Sun 7 July from 2pm.

29 THE HYMNS
Walton, Presteigne, LD8 2RA. E Passey, 07958 762362, thehymns@hotmail.com, www.thehymns.co.uk. *5m W of Kington. Take A44 W, then 1st R for Kinnerton. After approx 1m, at the top of small hill, turn L (W).* **Sat 1 June (11-5). Adm £4, chd free. Tea.** Visits also by arrangement June & July for groups of 30+.
In a beautiful setting in the heart of the Radnor valley, the garden is part of a restored C16 farmstead, with long views to the hills, and The Radnor Forest. It is a traditional garden reclaimed from the wild, using locally grown plants and seeds, and with a herb patio, wildflower meadows and a short woodland walk. It is designed for all the senses: sight, sound and smell.

GROUP OPENING

30 HYSSINGTON GARDENS
Hyssington, Montgomery, SY15 6AT. *A488 from Bishop's Castle. Approx 3½m, turn L (signed Hyssington), then follow yellow NGS signs. Also signed A489 E from Churchstoke. Park at Village Hall. Shuttle from village to Llanerch Lodge.* **Sat 11, Sun 12 May, Sat 22, Sun 23 June (1.30-5.30). Combined adm £6, chd free. Home-made teas. Refreshments at Llanerch Lodge for May opening, and at Gorsty House in June.**

GORSTY HOUSE
Gary & Annie Frost.
(See separate entry)

LLANERCH LODGE
Martin Bonathan & Sara Metcalf.

Gorsty House is an ongoing renovation of a neglected garden with 2+ acres planted to attract wildlife, incl an acre of beautiful flowering hay meadow, abundant cottage garden planting, hundreds of bulbs in season, orchard with wildflowers, and pond. Beautiful views. Llanerch Lodge is a smallholding in the lee of Roundton Hill, which offers a productive vegetable plot with raised beds, a lovely cottage garden, wildflower meadow, pond, cutting garden and newly planted nuttery and fruit trees, as well as sheep and poultry. Something to interest everyone. Abundant cottage garden planting and wonderful views!

31 LLANDINAM, LITTLE HOUSE
Llandinam, SY17 5BH. Peter & Pat Ashcroft, www.littlehouse1692.uk. *1m from Llandinam Village Hall. Cross river at statue of David Davies on A470 in Llandinam. Follow rd for just under 1m, Little House is black & white cottage on roadside. Limited parking.* **Sun 28 Apr, Sun 14 July, Sun 8 Sept (1-5). Adm £3.50, chd free. Light refreshments.**
⅓ acre plantswoman's garden on a quiet lane surrounded by fields and woodland, bordered by a stream. Slate and bark paths give access to the many features incl fish and wildlife ponds, conifer, azalea, grass and mixed beds, vegetable garden, woodland, mini meadow, sensory garden, grotto water feature, auricula theatre and alpine/cactus house. 500+ different plants, many propagated for sale. Spring; auricula theatre will be at its best with other primulas, winter heathers & hellebores. Summer; the garden in full bloom & the sensory garden alive with colour & wonderful scents. Autumn; cyclamen, grasses, crocosmia, michaelmas daisies & interesting seed heads on show.

32 NEW LLANFAIR WATERDINE, NANTIAGO
Llanfair Waterdine, Knighton, LD7 1TS. Michael Tree. *Approx 3m NW of Knighton on B4355. Turn R at Lloyney & park in field.* **Sat 18, Sun 19 May (2-5). Combined adm with The Coach House £5, chd free. Pimms and nibbles at Nantiago. Home-made teas at The Coach House.**
5 acre garden incl arboretum with monkey puzzle tree, unusual yews and stand of Himalayan Birch. Large pond with magnolias, rhododendrons, azaleas, cornus. Newly planted orchard incl greengage, quince and medlar trees. Turkey, bantams and cockerel. Aviaries with rescued Barn Owls and European Eagle Owl. Collection of 1930's classic cars. Partial wheelchair access.

33 NEW LLANFAIR WATERDINE, THE COACH HOUSE
Llanfair Waterdine, Knighton, LD7 1TS. Audrey Summers. *Approx 3m NW of Knighton on B4355. Turn*

R at Lloyney and park in field. **Sat 18, Sun 19 May (2-5). Combined adm with Llanfair Waterdine, Nantiago £5, chd free. Home-made teas. Pimms and nibbles at Nantiago.**
1 acre magical secret cottage garden with stream planted for wildlife and pollinators. Magnolias, rhododendrons, cowslips, primulas, iris, wildflowers and giant walnut tree. House covered with pyracantha, hydrangea petiolaris, Virginia creeper and lonicera to attract nesting birds. Kitchen garden and bee hives. Teas served from Shepherd's Hut. Gate into adjoining Nantiago.

34 LLANGOED HALL HOTEL

Llangoed Hall Hotel, Llyswen, Brecon, LD3 0YP. Mrs Mandy Hobbs, 01874754525, manager@llangoedhall.com, www.llangoedhall.com. *9m S of Builth Wells. 9m W of Hay-on-Wye. From Brecon and Hay-on-Wye follow signs to Builth Wells. In Llyswen follow A470 N for 1m. Hotel on R.* **Sun 5 May, Sun 7 July, Sun 4 Aug, Sun 29 Sept (2-5). Adm £4, chd free. Home-made teas.**
Large organic garden with encouragement of wildlife surrounding one of the finest hotels in Wales. Shrub and mixed borders, walled area incl formal herb and rose gardens, soft fruit and fruit trees, cutting border and maze. Croquet lawn (learn to play), superb views of the Black Mountains and Upper Wye Valley. plants for sale. Steps down to croquet lawn, some gravel paths.

35 LLANSTEPHAN HOUSE

Llanstephan, nr Llyswen, Powys, LD3 0YR. Lord & Lady Milford. *10m SW of Builth Wells. Leave A470 at Llyswen onto B4350. 1st L after crossing river in Boughrood. From Builth Wells leave A470, Erwood Bridge, 1st L. Follow signs.* **Mon 27 May (1-6). Adm £4, chd free. Home-made teas.**
20 acre garden, first laid out almost 200 years ago and in the present owner's family for more than a century, featuring a Victorian walled kitchen garden and greenhouses, 100 year old wisteria, woodland walks punctuated by azaleas and rhododendrons, specimen trees and immaculate lawns. Beautiful and celebrated views of Wye Valley and Black Mountains.

36 LLWYN MADOC

Beulah, Llanwrtyd Wells, LD5 4TU. Patrick & Miranda Bourdillon, 01591 620564, miranda.bourdillon@gmail.com. *8m W of Builth Wells. On A483 at Beulah take rd towards Abergwesyn for 1m. Drive on Right. Parking on field below drive - follow signs.* **Sun 26 May (2-5.30). Adm £4, chd free. Home-made teas.**
Terraced garden in attractive wooded valley overlooking newly restored lake; yew hedges; rose garden with pergola; kitchen garden and small orchard; azaleas and rhododendrons. As the garden is situated on a slope, it is quite steep in parts.

37 LLYSDINAM

Newbridge-on-Wye, LD1 6NB. Sir John & Lady Venables-Llewelyn & Llysdinam Charitable Trust, 01597 860190, llethr@outlook.com, llysdinamgardens.co.uk. *5m SW of Llandrindod Wells. Turn W off A470 at Newbridge-on-Wye; turn R immed after crossing R Wye; entrance up hill.* **Mon 27 May (2-5). Adm £5, chd free. Cream teas.** Visits also by arrangement.
Llysdinam Gardens are among the loveliest in mid Wales, especially noted for a magnificent display of rhododendrons and azaleas in May. Covering some 6 acres in all, they command sweeping views down the Wye Valley. Successive family members have developed the gardens over the last 150yrs to incl woodland with specimen trees, large herbaceous and shrub borders and a water garden, all of which provide varied and colourful planting throughout the yr. The Victorian walled kitchen garden and extensive greenhouses grow a wide variety of vegetables, hothouse fruit and exotic plants. Gravel paths.

Tranquillity Haven

White Hopton Farm

38 MAESFRON HALL AND GARDENS

Trewern, Welshpool, SY21 8EA. Dr & Mrs TD Owen, www.maesfron.co.uk. *4m E of Welshpool. On N side of A458 Welshpool to Shrewsbury Rd.* **Sun 14 Apr (2-5). Adm £5, chd free. Cream teas. Also speciality sandwiches and cakes.**

Georgian house (partly open) built in Italian villa style set in 4 acres of South-facing gardens on lower slopes of Moel-y-Golfa with panoramic views of The Long Mountain. Terraces, walled kitchen garden, tropical garden, restored Victorian conservatories, tower, shell grotto and hanging gardens below tower. Hundreds of daffodils in spring. Explore the ground floor and outbuildings. Parkland walks with a wide variety of trees. Adjacent 3 acre Equestrian Centre. Afternoon teas served in the dining room or on the terrace. Easter Egg Hunt in the grounds for children. Some gravel, steps and slopes.

39 NEW MOEL-Y-GWELTYN-UCHA

Llansilin, Oswestry, SY10 7QX. Mr Nick & Mrs Sue Roberts. *8m W of Oswestry. Follow yellow NGS signs from St Silin's Church Llansilin. Garden 2.3m W of Llansilin on B4580 towards Llanrhaeadr-ym-Mochnant.* **Sat 3, Sun 4 Aug (1.30-5.30). Adm £4, chd free. Home-made teas. Toilet facilities.**

S facing terraced cottage garden at 900' on steep hillside in stunning location; fabulous views towards Rodney's Pillar & Long Mountain. Colourful, floriferous: roses, shrubs & herbaceous perennials; garden & pond teeming with birds, insects, wildlife. Some steps. Seats enable you to pause, relax & enjoy views. House & garden accessed via 0.4 mile track from parking area. Walking shoes advised.

40 THE NEUADD

Llanbedr, Crickhowell, NP8 1SP. Robin & Philippa Herbert, 01873 812164, philippahherbert@gmail.com. *1m NE of Crickhowell. Leave Crickhowell by Llanbedr Rd. At junction with Great Oak Rd bear L, cont up hill for approx 1m, garden on L. Ample*

parking. **Sun 2 June (2-6). Adm £5, chd free. Home-made teas. Visits also by arrangement June to Sept for groups of up to 10. Homemade teas £3 per head.**
Robin and Philippa Herbert have worked on the restoration of the garden at The Neuadd since 1999 and have planted many unusual trees and shrubs in the dramatic setting of the Brecon Beacons National Park. One of the major features is the walled garden, which has both traditional and decorative planting of fruit, vegetables and flowers. There is also a woodland walk with ponds and streams and a formal garden with flowering terraces. Spectacular views, water feature, rare trees and shrubs, plant stall and teas. The owner uses a wheelchair and most of the garden is accessible, but some steep paths.

41 OAK COTTAGE

23 High Street, Welshpool, SY21 7JP. Tony Harvey. *Entered from back of house via Bowling Green Lane parallel to the High St in centre of Welshpool.* **Sun 5, Mon 6, Mon 27 May, Sun 9 June (2-5). Adm £3.50, chd free. Home-made teas.**
Revamped during the last 3yrs this is a plantsman's small and hidden garden providing an oasis of green in the town centre. Gravel paths and stepping stones meander through a wide variety of plants, incl unusual species. Alpines are still a favourite with more varieties for 2019. Modern representation of a Wardian cabinet, alpine house and collection of insectivorous plants. Gravel paths and steep slope at entrance.

42 PENMYARTH HOUSE

The Glanusk Estate, Crickhowell, NP8 1LP. Mrs Harry Legge-Bourke, 01873 810414, info@glanuskestate.com, www.glanuskestate.com. *2m NW of Crickhowell. Please access the Glanusk Estate via the Main Entrance (NP8 1SH) off A40 and follow signs to car park.* **Sun 19 May (11-4). Adm £7.50, chd free. Light refreshments.**
The garden is adorned with many established plant species such as rhododendrons, azaleas, acers, camelia, magnolia, prunus and dogwood giving a vast array of colour in the spring and summer months. Alongside the Open Garden, we will be holding the annual Estate Fayre, showcasing over 30 artisans with exhibits of works for sale. Penmyarth Church, a short distance from the gardens, will be open. See www.glanuskestate.com, the Glanusk Facebook page and the Glanusk Twitter and Instagram feeds for more information. Home-made cakes, coffee, tea and gourmet catering, licensed bar, 30 artisan stalls. Talks and garden tours. Half of the garden accessible by wheel chair, with views of the other half. We do have a Mule to move people around if they can leave their chair.

43 PEN-Y-MAES

Hay-on-Wye, HR3 5PP. Shân Egerton. *1m SW of Hay-on-Wye. On B4350 towards Hay from Brecon. 2½m from Glasbury.* **Sun 23 June (2-5). Adm £4, chd free. Home-made teas.**
2 acre garden incl mixed and herbaceous borders; orchard, topiary; walled formal kitchen garden; shrub, modern and climbing roses, peony borders, espaliered pears. Fine mulberry. Beautiful dry stone walling and mature trees. Great double view of Black Mountains and the Brecon Beacons. Emphasis on foliage and shape. Artist's garden.

44 PLAS DINAM

Llandinam, SY17 5DQ. Eldrydd Lamp, 07415 503554, eldrydd@plasdinam.co.uk, www.plasdinamcountryhouse.co.uk. *7½m SW Newtown. on A470.* **Visits by arrangement Mar to Nov for groups of 10+. Weekdays only excluding school holidays. Home-made teas.**
12 acres of parkland, gardens, lawns and woodland set at the foot of glorious rolling hills with spectacular views across the Severn Valley. A host of daffodils followed by one of the best wildflower meadows in Montgomeryshire with 36 species of flowers and grasses incl hundreds of wild orchids; Glorious autumn colour with parrotias, liriodendrons, cotinus etc. Millennium wood. From 1884 until recently the home of Lord Davies and his family (house not open).

45 PONT FAEN HOUSE

Farrington Lane, Knighton, LD7 1LA. Mr John & Mrs Brenda Morgan, 01547 520847. *S of Knighton off Ludlow Rd. W from Ludlow on A4113 into Knighton. 1st L after 20mph sign before school.* **Visits by arrangement Mar to Sept. Couples/groups max 50. Adm £4, chd free. Home-made teas with Welsh Cakes.**
Colourful ¾ acre flat garden on edge of town. Paths through arches lead from shady ferny corners to deep borders filled with large range of colourful perennials & annuals. In spring snowdrops everywhere, daffodils & range of spring flowers, rhododendrons & azaleas followed by colourful perennials, shrubs, and 40 varieties roses. Good late summer colour. Enjoy views of hills from the many seats. Yr round colour: daffodils, tulips, clematis, ten varieties alstroemerias, rudbeckias, inulas. Disabled parking in garden.

46 PONTHAFREN

Long Bridge Street, Newtown, SY16 2DY. Janet Rogers (volunteer gardener), www.ponthafren.org.uk. *Park in main car park in town centre, 5 mins walk. Turn L out of car park, turn L over bridge, garden on L. Limited disabled parking, please phone 01686 621586 for details.* **Sat 27 July (10-5), also open Bryn Teg. Sat 24 Aug (10-4). Adm by donation. Home-made teas.**
Ponthafren is a registered charity for people with mental health issues or those that feel lonely or isolated. Open door policy so everyone is welcome. Interesting community garden on banks of R Severn run and maintained totally by volunteers: sensory garden with long grasses, herbs, scented plants and shrubs, quirky objects like Guy the Gorilla. Productive vegetable plot. Lots of plants for sale. Covered seating areas positioned around the garden to enjoy the views. Partial wheelchair access.

47 ROCK MILL

Abermule, Montgomery, SY15 6NN. Rufus & Cherry Fairweather. *1m S of Abermule on B4368 towards Kerry. Best approached from Abermule village as there is an angled entrance into field for parking.* **Sat 18, Sun 19 May (2-5). Adm £5, chd free. Home-made teas.**

2 acre riverside garden on different levels in wooded valley. Colourful borders and shrubberies, specimen trees, terraces, woodland walks, bridges, extensive lawns, fishponds, orchard, herb and vegetable gardens, beehives, dovecote, heather thatched roundhouse and remnants of industrial past (corn mill and railway line). Child friendly activities (supervision required) incl sunken trampoline, croquet and badminton, animal treasure hunt, interactive quiz, wilderness trails. Live music (pianist Dan Lambert) Sensible shoes and a sense of fun/ adventure recommended.

48 NEW STOCKTON MILL

Marton, Welshpool, SY21 8JL. Stephen & Caroline Cox, 01938 561990, carolinecox74@gmail.com, www.stocktonmill.wordpress.com. *6m SE Welshpool. From Welshpool take A483 S. Turn L on A490 for 3.3m (the rd takes L turn 200m after The Cock Inn, Forden) then turn L signed Marton. Continue 1.2 m & turn R before pink building. Park in field.* **Sat 8, Sun 9 June (2-5). Adm £3.50, chd free. Home-made teas.**

Peaceful 3 acre garden by the river Camlad in Vale of Montgomery with lovely views. House next to C19 Grade II listed mill (open). Trees mainly planted 30 yrs ago now matured into striking woodland including Himalayan Birch, Himalayan Cherry, Dogwoods and varieties of unusual conifers. Extensive shrub and herbaceous borders with lovely views. Lawns and walks by the river. Two wildlife ponds. The C19 Old Mill now a holiday let will be open and you can view the original workings.

49 TALGARTH MILL

The Square, Talgarth, Brecon, LD3 0BW. Talgarth Mill, www.talgarthmill.com. *In centre of Talgarth. Park in free car park opp rugby club, turn L out of car park entrance, follow High St to end, cross bridge, the Mill is on your R.* **Sat 6, Sun 7 July (10-4). Adm £3.50, chd free. Refreshments available from The Bakers' Table.**

A pretty riverside garden, maintained by volunteers. Along the riverside there is mixed herbaceous planting, a shady area, and steps up to a productive garden with espalier fruit trees, vegetables, soft fruits and a wildlife area. Places to sit and watch the river and its bird life (dippers, wagtails, kingfishers, herons) and the mill wheel turning. Garden is part of a working water mill that produces high quality flour (Great Taste 1 and 2 star), with our staple bread wheat grown just 7m away. Award winning cafe and bakery which champions local, seasonal produce, gourmet coffee and tea. Garden can be accessed by lift. Wide, flat paths for wheelchair access.

We open the gates to the nation's best gardens, offering a relaxing, memorable and affordable day out. A perfect experience to share with friends and family.

50 NEW TRANQUILLITY HAVEN

7 Lords Land, Whitton, Knighton, LD7 1NJ. Val Brown, 01547 560070, valerie.brown2@btinternet.com. *approx 3m from Knighton and 5m Presteigne. From Knighton take B4355 after approx. 2 m turn R on B4357 to Whitton. Car park on L by yellow NGS signs.* **Sat 1, Sun 2 June (2-5). Adm £4, chd free. Home-made teas.** Visits also by arrangement May to Sept for individuals/groups of up to 20..

Amazing Japanese Stroll Garden with borrowed views to Offa's Dyke. Winding paths pass small pools and lead to Japanese bridges over natural stream with dippers and kingfishers. Sounds of water fill the air. Enjoy peace and tranquillity from one of the seats or the Japanese Tea House. Dense oriental planting with Cornus kousa satomi, acers, azaleas, unusual bamboos and wonderful cloud pruning. Only suitable for the sure footed due to the various levels and steps. Sturdy footwear required.

51 TREBERFYDD HOUSE

Llangasty, Bwlch, Brecon, LD3 7PX. David Raikes & Carla Rapoport, www.treberfydd.com. *6m E of Brecon. From Abergavenny on A40, turn R in Bwlch on B5460. Take 1st turning L towards Pennorth & cont 2m along lane. From Brecon, turn L off A40 towards Pennorth in Llanhamlach.* **Sun 14 July (1-5.30). Adm £5, chd free. Home-made teas.**

Grade I listed Victorian Gothic house with 10 acres of grounds designed by W A Nesfield. Magnificent Cedar of Lebanon, avenue of mature Beech, towering Atlantic Cedars, Victorian rockery, herbaceous border and manicured lawns ideal for a picnic. Wonderful views of the Black Mountains. Plants available from Commercial Nursery in grounds - Walled Garden Treberfydd. House tours every half hour (additional £3), last tour 4pm. Easy wheelchair access to areas around the house, but herbaceous border only accessible via steps.

52 TREMYNFA

Carreghofa Lane, Llanymynech, SY22 6LA. Jon & Gillian Fynes. *Edge of Llanymynech village. From N leave Oswestry on A483 to Welshpool. In Llanymynech turn R at Xrds (car wash on corner). Take 2nd R then follow yellow NGS signs. 300 yds park signed field, limited disabled parking nr garden.* **Sat 15, Sun 16 June (1-5). Adm £4, chd free. Cream teas.**

S-facing 1 acre garden developed over 12yrs. Old railway cottage set in herbaceous and raised borders, patio with many pots of colourful and unusual plants. Garden slopes to productive fruit and vegetable area, ponds, spinney, unusual trees, wild areas and peat bog. Patio and seats to enjoy extensive views incl Llanymynech Rocks. Pet ducks on site, Montgomery canal close by. 100s of home grown plants and home-made jams for sale.

53 TYN Y CWM

Beulah, Llanwrtyd Wells, LD5 4TS. Steve & Christine Carrow, 01591 620461, stevetynycwm@hotmail.co.uk. *10m W of Builth Wells. On A483 at Beulah take rd towards Abergwesyn for 2m. Drive drops down to L.* **Sun 16 June, Sun 4 Aug (2-5.30). Adm £4, chd free. Home-made teas.** Visits also by arrangement June to Aug for groups of up to 30.

Garden mainly started 17yrs ago, lower garden has spring/woodland area, raised beds mixed with vegetables, fruit trees, fruit and flowers. Perennial borders, summer house gravel paths through rose and clematis pergola. Upper garden, partly sloped, incl bog, winter, water gardens and perennial beds with unusual slate steps. Beautiful views. Property bounded by small river. Children's quiz.

54 ◆ WELSH LAVENDER

Cefnperfedd Uchaf, Maesmynis, Builth Wells, LD2 3HU. Nancy Durham & Bill Newton-Smith, 01982 552467, farmers@welshlavender.com, www.welshlavender.com. *Approx 4½m S of Builth Wells & 13m from Brecon Cathedral off B4520 The farm is 1.3m from turn signed Farmers' Welsh Lavender.* **For NGS: Sat 27, Sun 28 July (10-6). Adm £4, chd free. Light refreshments.** For other opening times and information, please phone, email or visit garden website.

Welsh Lavender reopens for the NGS after taking a break in 2017. The team has been replanting the lavender fields and developing the farm's wild meadow banks. Wild swimmers enjoy dips in the pond with spectacular views in all directions. The farm is situated at 1100ft high in the hills of mid Wales where the growing season is short and challenging. Visitors are welcome to roam the lavender fields, learn how the distillation process works, and visit the farm shop to try body creams and balms made with lavender oil distilled on the farm. 10% of sales go to the NGS. Coffee, tea, wine and light refreshments available. Partial wheelchair access. Large paved area adjacent to teas and shop area easy to negotiate.

55 NEW WHITE HOPTON FARM

Wern Lane, Sarn, Newtown, SY16 4EN. Claire Austin, 01686 670 342, enquiries@claireaustin-hardyplants.co.uk. *Please park at The Sarn, Sarn, Nr Newtown, SY16 4EJ and we will greet you.* **Visits by arrangement May to Sept for groups of 15 to 30. Adm £5, chd free. Light lunches available.**

Horticulturist and author Claire Austin's 1½ acre plant collector's garden designed along the lines of a cottage garden with hundreds of different perennials. Front garden mainly full of May blooming perennials, back garden, which is split into various areas, has a June and July garden, a small woodland walk, a Victorian fountain and mixed rose borders. Fabulous views over the Kerry Vale. Wide range of Claire Austin's Hardy Plants for sale at The Sarn.

NPC

56 1 YSTRAD HOUSE

1 Church Road, Knighton, LD7 1EB. John & Margaret Davis, 01547 528154, jamdavis@ystradhouse.plus.com. *At junction of Church Rd & Station Rd. Take the turning opp the Knighton Hotel (A488 Clun) travel 225yds along Station Rd . Yellow House at junction with Church Rd.* **Visits by arrangement June to Sept for groups of up to 30. At least a week's notice for groups. Individuals by arrangement any time. Adm £4, chd free. Home-made teas. incl gluten free cakes.**

A town garden behind a Regency Villa of earlier origins. A narrow entrance door opens revealing unexpected calm and timelessness. A small walled garden and greenhouse lead to broad lawns, wide borders with soft colour schemes and mature trees. More intimate features: pots, urns and pools add interest and surprise. The formal areas merge with wooded glades leading to a riverside walk. Lawns and gravelled paths mostly flat, except access to riverside walk.

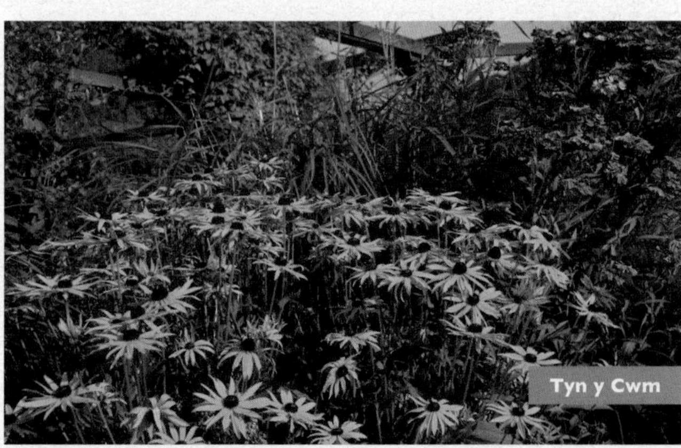
Tyn y Cwm

Early Openings 2020

Plan your garden visiting well ahead – put these dates in your diary!

Gardens across the country open early – before the next year's guide is published – with glorious displays of colour including hellebores, aconites, snowdrops and carpets of spring bulbs.

Cheshire & Wirral

Sat 22, Sun 23 February (1-4)
Briarfield, Burton Village Gardens

Sun 23 February (12.30-4)
Bucklow Farm

By arrangement in February
Rosewood
The Well House

Devon

Fri 7, Fri 14, Sat 22 February (2-5)
Higher Cherubeer

Sun 16 February (2-5)
Bickham House

Gloucestershire

Sun 26 Jan, Sun 9 February (11-3)
Home Farm

Sun 9, Sun 16 February (11-5)
Trench Hill

Hampshire

Sun 16, Mon 17, Sun 23, Mon 24 February (2-4.30)
Little Court

Herefordshire

Thur 6, Thur 13, Thur 20, Thur 27 February (9-4.30)
Ivy Croft

Kent

Sun 26 Jan, Sun 16 February (12-4)
Copton Ash

Sat 8, Sun 9 February (11-3)
Knowle Hill Farm

By arrangement in February
The Old Rectory
Spring Platt

Oxfordshire

Sun 16 February (1.30-4.30)
Hollyhocks

Somerset, Bristol & South Gloucestershire

Suns 2 & 9 February (11-4)
Rock House

Sat 15 February (10-5)
East Lambrook Manor Gardens

Staffordshire, Birmingham & West Midlands

Sun 16 February (11-3)
5 East View Cottages

Sussex

By arrangement in February
Pembury House

Wiltshire

Sat 22 February (10.30-5.30)
Lacock Abbey Gardens

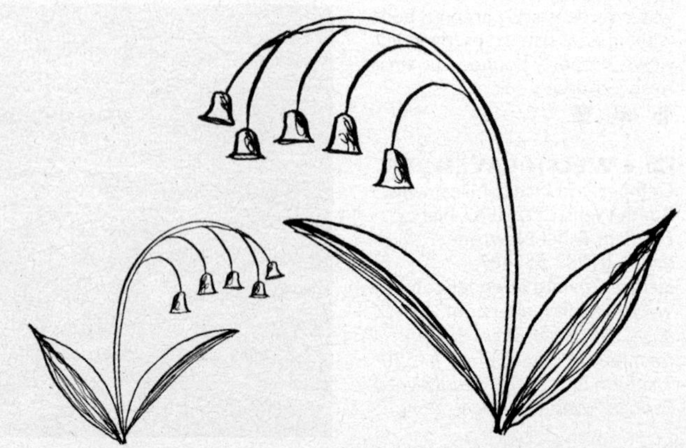

Plant Heritage

National Council for the Conservation of Plants and Gardens

Over 70 gardens that open for the National Garden Scheme are guardians of a Plant Heritage National Plant Collection although this may not always be noted in the garden description. These gardens carry the NPC symbol.

Plant Heritage, 12 Home Farm, Loseley Park, Guildford, Surrey GU3 1HS. 01483 447540 www.plantheritage.com

ACER (EXCL. PALMATUM CVS.)
Blagdon, North East

AGAPANTHUS – FAIRWEATHER NURSERY TRIALS COLLECTION
Fairweather's Nursery, Hampshire

ALNUS
Blagdon, North East
Stone Lane Gardens, Devon

ANEMONE NEMOROSA
Avondale Nursery, Warwickshire

ANEMONE NEMOROSA CVS
Kingston Lacy, Dorset

ARALIACEAE (EXCL. HEDERA)
Meon Orchard, Hampshire

ARUNCUS
Windy Hall, Cumbria

ASPIDISTRA ELATIOR
12 Woods Ley, Kent

ASPLENIUM SCOLOPENDRIUM
Sizergh Castle, Cumbria

ASTER & RELATED GENERA (AUTUMN FLOWERING)
The Picton Garden, Herefordshire

ASTER (SYMPHYOTRICHUM) NOVAE-ANGLIAE
Avondale Nursery, Warwickshire

Brockamin, Worcestershire

ASTILBE
Holehird Gardens, Cumbria
Marwood Hill Garden, Devon

ASTRANTIA
Norwell Nurseries, Norwell Gardens, Nottinghamshire

BETULA
Stone Lane Gardens, Devon

BRUNNERA
Hearns House, Oxfordshire

BUDDLEJA DAVIDII CVS. & HYBRIDS
Shapcott Barton Knowstone Estate, Devon

CAMELLIAS & RHODODENDRONS INTRODUCED TO HELIGAN PRE-1920
The Lost Gardens of Heligan, Cornwall

CARPINUS BETULUS CVS.
West Lodge Park, London

CEANOTHUS
Eccleston Square, London

CERCIDIPHYLLUM
Hodnet Hall Gardens, Shropshire

CHRYSANTHEMUM (HARDY) DISPERSED
Norwell Nurseries, Norwell Gardens, Nottinghamshire
Hill Close Gardens, Warwickshire

CLEMATIS VITICELLA
Longstock Park, Hampshire

CLEMATIS VITICELLA CVS.
Roseland House, Cornwall

CODONOPSIS & RELATED GENERA
Woodlands, Fotherby Gardens, Lincolnshire

COLCHICUM
East Ruston Old Vicarage, Norfolk

CONVALLARIA
Kingston Lacy, Dorset

CORNUS (EXCL. C. FLORIDA CVS.)
Newby Hall & Gardens, Yorkshire

COROKIA
33 Wood Vale, London

CYCLAMEN (EXCL. PERSICUM CVS.)
Higher Cherubeer, Dolton Gardens, Devon

CYDONIA OBLONGA
Norton Priory Museum & Gardens, Cheshire & Wirral

CYSTOPTERIS
Sizergh Castle, Cumbria

DABOECIA
Holehird Gardens, Cumbria

DAHLIA
National Dahlia Collection, Cornwall

DIERAMA SPP.
Yew Tree Cottage, Staffordshire

DIONAEA
Beaufort, Shropshire

DRYOPTERIS
Sizergh Castle, Cumbria

ECHIUM SPP., & CV. FROM MACARONESIAN ISLANDS
The Echium Garden, Nottinghamshire

ERICA & CALLUNA - SUSSEX HEATHER CVS
Nymans, Sussex

ERYTHRONIUM
Greencombe Gardens, Somerset

EUCALYPTUS
Meon Orchard, Hampshire

EUCALYPTUS SPP.
The World Garden at Lullingstone Castle, Kent

EUCRYPHIA
Whitstone Farm, Devon

EUONYMUS (DECIDUOUS)
The Place for Plants, East Bergholt Place Garden, Suffolk

EUPHORBIA (HARDY)
Firvale Allotment Garden, Yorkshire

FRANCOA
30 Compton Way, Hampshire

FUCHSIA HARDY SPP. & CVS.
Croxteth Park Walled Garden, Lancashire

GAULTHERIA (INCL PERNETTYA)
Greencombe Gardens, Somerset

GERANIUM SANGUINEUM, MACRORRHIZUM & X CANTABRIGIENSE
Brockamin, Worcestershire

GERANIUM SYLVATICUM & RENARDII - FORMS, CVS. & HYBRIDS
Wren's Nest, Cheshire & Wirral

HAKONECHLOA MACRA & CVS.
Canterbury Cathedral Gardens, Kent
12 Woods Ley, Kent

HEDERA
Ivybank, Pebworth Gardens, Warwickshire

HELIOTROPIUM
Hampton Court Palace, London

HOHERIA
Abbotsbury Gardens, Dorset

HOSTA (EUROPEAN AND ASIATIC)
Hanging Hosta Garden, Hampshire

IRIS ENSATA
Marwood Hill Garden, Devon

JUGLANS
Upton Wold, Gloucestershire

LAPAGERIA ROSEA (& NAMED CVS)
Roseland House, Cornwall

LEUCANTHEMUM X SUPERBUM (CHRYSANTHEMUM MAXIMUM)
Shapcott Barton Knowstone Estate, Devon

LEWISIA
'John's Garden' at Ashwood Nurseries, Staffordshire

MALUS (CVS. FROM NOTTS & DERBY, LINCS, LEICS & YORKS)
Clumber Park Walled Kitchen Garden, Nottinghamshire

MALUS (ORNAMENTAL)
Barnards Farm, Essex

MECONOPSIS (LARGE PERENNIAL SPP. & HYBRIDS)
Holehird Gardens, Cumbria

MONARDA
Hole's Meadow, Devon

NEPETA
Hole's Meadow, Devon

NERINE HARDY SPP., CVS. & HYBRIDS
Bickham Cottage, Devon

NERINE SARNIENSIS CVS
Bickham Cottage, Devon

OMPHALODES
Hearns House Oxfordshire

OPHIOPOGON JAPONICUS CVS.
12 Woods Ley, Kent

OSMUNDA
Sizergh Castle, Cumbria

PAEONIA (HYBRID HERBACEOUS)
White Hopton Farm, Powys

PELARGONIUM
Ivybank, Pebworth Gardens, Warwickshire

PENNISETUM SPP. & CVS. (HARDY)
Knoll Gardens, Dorset

PENSTEMON
Froggery Cottage, Northamptonshire

PICEA SPP.
The Yorkshire Arboretum, Yorkshire

PINUS (EXCL DWARF CVS.)
The Lovell Quinta Arboretum, Cheshire & Wirral

PODOCARPACEAE
Meon Orchard, Hampshire

POLYSTICHUM
Holehird Gardens, Cumbria
Greencombe Gardens, Somerset

PTEROCARYA
Upton Wold, Gloucestershire

QUERCUS
Chevithrone Barton, Devon

RHEUM (CULINARY CVS.)
Clumber Park Walled Kitchen Garden, Nottinghamshire

RHODODENDRON (GHENT AZALEAS)
Sheffield Park and Garden, Sussex

RHODODENDRON KURUME AZALEA (WILSON 50)
Trewidden Garden, Cornwall

RODGERSIA
The Gate House, Devon

ROSA - HYBRID MUSK INTRO BY PEMBERTON & BENTALL 1912-1939
Dutton Hall, Lancashire

ROSA (RAMBLING)
Moor Wood, Gloucestershire

SANGUISORBA
Avondale Nursery, Warwickshire

SARRACENIA
Beaufort, Shropshire

SAXIFRAGA SECT. LIGULATAE: SPP. & CVS.
Waterperry Gardens, Oxfordshire

SAXIFRAGA SECT. PORPHYRION SUBSECT. POROPHYLLUM
Waterperry Gardens, Oxfordshire

SIBERIAN IRIS CVS: BRITISH, AWARD WINNERS & HISTORICALLY SIGNIFICANT
Aulden Farm, Herefordshire

SORBUS
Ness Botanic Gardens, Cheshire & Wirral

SORBUS (BRITISH ENDEMIC SPP.)
Blagdon, North East

STERN, SIR F (PLANTS SELECTED BY)
Highdown Gardens, Sussex

STEWARTIA - ASIAN SPP.
High Beeches Woodland and Water Garden, Sussex

STYRACACEAE (INCL HALESIA, PTEROSTYRAX, STYRAX, SINOJACKIA)
Holker Hall Gardens, Cumbria

TAXODIUM SPP. & CVS.
West Lodge Park, London

TULBAGHIA SPP. & SUBSP.
Marwood Hill Garden, Devon

VACCINIUM
Greencombe Gardens, Somerset

YUCCA
Renishaw Hall & Gardens, Derbyshire